STEICHEN

Also by Penelope Niven

Carl Sandburg: A Biography

James Earl Jones: Voices and Silences
(with James Earl Jones)

STEICHEN

A Biography

PENELOPE NIVEN

Eastern National
Serving the Visitors to America's
National Parks and Other Public Trusts

Steichen
By Penelope Niven
Copyright ©1997
Reprinted by arrangement with Penelope Niven
and the Barbara Hogenson Agency, Inc.

Published by Eastern National
Fort Washington, Pennsylvania 19034

All rights reserved. Second edition, 2004.

ISBN 1-59091-026-5

*In memory
of
Lucy Kroll,
who opened the doors*

Contents

Preface ix

1. The Land of Freedom (1854-1889) 1
2. Taking the Reins (1889-1895) 17
3. The Toughest Customer (1895-1898) 30
4. Groping for the New (1898-1900) 50
5. Pathfinders (1900) 69
6. Great Men (1901) 93
7. Trusting the Eyes (1901-1902) 111
8. The Modernist Trend (1902) 136
9. True Secessionists (1902-1903) 155
10. Working Out Salvation (1904-1905) 178
11. 291 (1905-1907) 204
12. Young Americans in Paris (1907) 223
13. Color-Mad (1907-1908) 245
14. The Initiator (1908) 265
15. Voulangis (1908-1909) 287
16. The Gospel of New Light (1909) 308
17. Danton (1910) 323
18. Real Friendship, Real Art (1910-1912) 342
19. The Whirlpool of Modern Art (1912-1913) 364

20. Strategic Retreat (1913-1914) 383
21. A Forum for Wisdom and Folly (1914-1915) 408
22. The Death of the Blue Bird (1916) 427
23. The Art of Reading Lines and Shadows (1916-1918)...445
24. Alienating the Affections (1919-1922) 468
25. A Sacrament of Fire (1922-1924) 490
26. The New Pictorial Revolution (1924-1928) 511
27. A New Vision (1929-1934) 534
28. Violating Every Rule (1935-1939) 557
29. A Real Image of War (1939-1943) 581
30. The Universal Language (1943-1946) 605
31. "The Family of Man" (1947-1955) 630
32. The Last Apprenticeship (1955-1959) 652
33. All Giants Being Lonely (1959-1973) 675

Epilogue 701
Guide to Abbreviations and Sources 703
Endnotes 705
Acknowledgments 749
Permissions 753
Index 755

Preface

*When an artist of any kind looks at his subject,
he looks with everything he is.*

–Edward Steichen

Before I discovered Edward Steichen the artist in his photographs and paintings, I encountered Edward Steichen the man in his letters. Until the summer of 1982, I had seen Steichen as a shadow figure in the emerging tapestry of my biography of his brother-in-law, the poet Carl Sandburg. A prodigiously gifted son of immigrants from Luxembourg, Steichen became a controversial, pioneering photographer and modernist—but I first came to know him as the older brother of Lilian Steichen, the remarkable woman who was Sandburg's wife.

At Connemara, the Carl Sandburg Home in Flat Rock, North Carolina, I spent weeks retrieving from under the eaves of the old house bundles of letters and papers Sandburg had left there in musty cardboard boxes. From one of those boxes one summer day, I pulled a letter written on rough-textured paper. The handwriting was at first glance indecipherable—tall letters scrawled on the page, words underlined with a stab of the pen, unorthodox spelling and punctuation spread staccato throughout.

Intrigued, I sat down to read a letter Edward Steichen had written to the Sandburgs, finding myself immediately enthralled with the spirit, the humor, and the mystery of this artist as he revealed himself on paper. Almost at once I knew that I wanted to write about Steichen's extraordinary life and art.

After Sandburg married Steichen's sister in 1908, the two men grew to be intimate lifelong friends—"brothers," they called themselves. Because their personal and artistic lives were interwoven, this trio known to each other as Ed, Paula and Carl shared center stage as I worked on the Sandburg biography. During those years, I was simultaneously coming to know Steichen—turning up his letters all over the globe; poring over his photographs at Connemara, in museums, and in the private family albums; gleaning vital insights about him in the course of nearly three hundred interviews about the Sandburgs.

To Sandburg's three daughters, for instance, Steichen was the beloved Uncle Ed who took their baby pictures, told them wild stories, wrote them tender letters, and shared their illnesses and triumphs. To many women who had known him, he was a dashing, romantic enigma. To others who had worked with him, he was a temperamental taskmaster, even ruthless in his ambitious drive for perfection. To the journalists and cultural figures I interviewed, he was the humanitarian and visionary who, during the Cold War/McCarthy days, created the landmark global photographic exhibition entitled "The Family of Man."

From the moment I discovered that first letter among the Sandburg papers so many years ago, I found Steichen fascinating, complicated, elusive. It became clear to me that although he is a pivotal figure in the art and cultural history of the twentieth century, his enduring contributions have never been fully recognized and appreciated. While there are monographs about his life and studies of his work by art historians, there has never been a biography. The fullest treatment appeared when Steichen was fifty years old, and it was written by his brother-in-law Carl Sandburg to accompany forty-eight photographs published in 1929 in a limited edition entitled *Steichen the Photographer*.

In addition to his pathbreaking achievements as painter, photographer and communicator, Steichen lived a romantic, complicated life in the midst of the turmoil of national and international events. His photographs illuminated the human experience through three wars, the Roaring Twenties, the Depression, and the Cold War. As a young avant-garde artist in Paris early in the twentieth century, he championed the work of such

PREFACE

European artists as Rodin, Matisse, and Picasso, and he introduced them to the American audience at the Little Galleries of the Photo-Secession, which he and Alfred Stieglitz founded in 1905. He also worked selflessly to promote other American painters, including John Marin, Alfred Maurer, Max Weber and Arthur Carles.

Famous on two continents by the time he was twenty-five, Steichen was struggling to rediscover and reinvent himself at thirty. Converting his photographic art into the weapon of military aerial reconnaissance photography during World War I, he was a war hero at forty. As chief of photography for *Vanity Fair* and *Vogue* in the nineteen twenties and thirties, he created enduring images of those two volatile decades of American life. As chief of naval combat photography during World War II at the age of sixty-six, he was a hero again. Afterward, he worked to make the camera a powerful instrument for peace.

Steichen was a scientist as well as an artist. In his garden in Voulangis, France, beginning in 1908, and later in his farm fields in Connecticut, he became a master geneticist, artfully breeding delphiniums, roses, poppies, and other flowers into living poetry. And behind the charismatic, glamorous, often flamboyant public facade, there was a tumultuous private life.

For years I have explored Steichen's revelations of self in his haunting photographic images, and in his own vivid words in letters and manuscripts. With the support of a National Endowment for the Humanities Fellowship, I immersed myself in the study of art history and the history of photography. I searched for Steichen's letters in the United States and in Europe, going beyond the significant collections previously known about at Yale University and the Museum of Modern Art, and in the Carl Sandburg Collection at the University of Illinois in Urbana.

I have had full access, thanks to the generosity of Steichen's granddaughter Francesca Calderone-Steichen, to the papers of Steichen's daughters, Dr. Mary Steichen Calderone and Kate Rodina Steichen. I have also explored, once through Sandburg's perspective and now through Steichen's, the complete range of the Lilian Steichen Sandburg papers, the Margaret Sandburg and Helga Sandburg collections, and the papers of Steichen's parents, John Peter and Mary Steichen. Thanks to a Visiting Fellowship to the Beinecke Rare Book & Manuscript Library at Yale, I was able to study the Clara Smith Steichen letters and manuscripts which are part of the Alfred Stieglitz Archives, Yale Collection of American Literature.

PREFACE

These sensitive and revealing papers, written by Steichen's first wife, had long ago been sealed by Georgia O'Keeffe and were opened to scholars in the summer of 1995, a few weeks before my Yale fellowship began.

After my biography of Carl Sandburg appeared in 1991, Sandburg's daughters, Margaret and Helga, encouraged me to write this life of their uncle. I held back, however, because I have always lived and worked in the worlds of American literary, cultural and social history, not art history. I have no academic credentials to offer as an art historian, no formal training in the history of photography, no skills as a photographer myself. Additional encouragement came from Steichen's elder daughter, Mary Steichen Calderone. She and her sister, Kate Rodina Steichen, daughters of Steichen and his first wife, Clara, had been helpful in my work on Sandburg and the Steichens. Kate was by then deceased, but in November of 1992 I received a letter from Mary thanking me for the "deep and fine portrait" of her uncle Carl Sandburg, and asking why I did not write a portrait of her father. "I would help in any way I could," she wrote.

Mary's namesake, Mary Kemp Steichen, was a woman of generous spirit—a trait that was transmitted to her children, grandchildren, and great-grandchildren. It is not surprising, therefore, that this biography has been greatly enriched by the memories, documents and letters shared by Mary and by her daughter, Francesca, as well as by Steichen's nieces, Margaret, Janet and Helga Sandburg. The Steichen-Sandburg family members gave freely, and expected nothing from me in return except the truth of the story, as best as I could convey it.

As for family photographs and snapshots, it is a gift to this book and, by extension, to interested readers, that Francesca Calderone-Steichen and her husband, Joel Stahmer, and Carl and Lilian "Paula" Sandburg's daughters, Helga Sandburg Crile and the late Margaret Sandburg, generously opened boxes, folders and family picture albums, loaning more than two hundred photographs of Steichen and his family and friends. Many of these are intimate, private glimpses, never before published. For instance, on a visit to Betty Jane Rathbone Turner, a cousin through Steichen's first wife, Clara, Francesca found family photographs that had never been seen before, and that are included here for the first time.

For this new edition of the book, Joanna Taub Steichen, Steichen's third wife and his widow, has generously granted permission to reprint certain family photographs made by Steichen. These photographs illuminate

Preface

Steichen's family life, enabling us to look through the camera's eye at particular moments to see those closest to him as he saw them himself. I gratefully acknowledge Mrs. Steichen's contribution of photographs of family members to this book, for these images will be immensely interesting and helpful to the general reader, as well as to students and interpreters of Steichen's life and work.

For a definitive look at the range of Steichen's extraordinary photographs, readers should visit Joanna Steichen's landmark book, *Steichen's Legacy: Photographs, 1895-1973* (New York: Alfred A. Knopf, 2000). This handsome book contains 288 photographs in duotone and tritone, as well as 32 images in full color—a comprehensive thematic exhibit of Steichen's photographs, exquisitely reproduced. The photographs are accompanied by a candid, revealing memoir written by Mrs. Steichen about her life with the photographer. For an encounter with Steichen's early, formative work as collected by his colleague Alfred Stieglitz, there is Joel Smith's *Edward Steichen: The Early Years* (Princeton: Princeton University Press in Association with the Metropolitan Museum of Art, 1999).

Over many years, photographers, both amateur and professional, caught Steichen's handsome angular face and variable moods. I have searched the world over for these images, as well as for letters written by, to and about Steichen, and essays written by and about Steichen. Gathering vulnerable papers and perishable memories, I have sought to build a solid documentary foundation for this first comprehensive narrative of Steichen's life. Because the celebrity years are more accessible than the seminal years that forged the artist's work, I have given greater emphasis to the young, emerging artist than to the older man, fully formed. I have not offered extended criticism of Steichen's work, however, being the first to recognize that I am not qualified to do so. It is context, not criticism, that this biography provides.

Steichen lived out his life in the heart of the twentieth century, using his camera and his original vision to create unsurpassed artistic portraits, to produce landmark military intelligence, to revolutionize commercial and fashion photography, and to document and celebrate the human spirit. He was a rebel, stubbornly independent and largely self-taught, who believed passionately in the fundamental intersections of art and life, and in the power of art as a universal, civilizing force.

Here is Steichen as others saw and heard him, and as he spoke for himself in his art and in his fluent voice—adamant, exuberant, contentious, ironic. "The artist, in any medium, does not live in a vacuum," he wrote in his autobiography, *A Life in Photography* (1963). "When an artist of any kind looks at his subject, he looks with everything he is." He believed that an artist imbues his work with "everything that he has lived, learned, observed, and experienced...."[1]

This is a portrait of Steichen in his world, living a life, like his art, suffused sometimes with darkness, sometimes with light.

1

THE LAND OF FREEDOM

(1 8 5 4 - 1 8 8 9)

She decided that her boy would grow up in America, which she had heard of and dreamt about as the land of freedom, equality, and unlimited opportunity.[1]

—STEICHEN

SAFE WITHIN THE THICK STONE WALLS of a modest house in the village of Mondercange, in the Grand Duchy of Luxembourg, two small children listened night after night as their grandmother and their great-grandfather told them stories about the past—a rich concoction of memory, myth, and history. Like many Luxembourgers, they grew up hearing vivid stories of haunted castles, of princes who died mysteriously, of abandoned wives of kings, buried alive in dungeons.

Village elders could conjure up sad, thrilling stories of Count Siegfroid of Ardennes, who virtually created Luxembourg in A.D. 963 when he built his splendid fortress over the Roman ruins on a high ridge overlooking the Alzette River. It was the Saxons who had given the beautiful kingdom its name—Lucilinburhuc, "Little Fortress." The word rolled deliciously on the tongue, and modulated, over time, into Luxembourg.

Their homeland was a tiny country only thirty-six miles wide and fifty-one miles long, bordered by France, Belgium, and Germany. Powers as ancient as the Celts and then the Romans had struggled and often died in their greed to rule the sparkling rivers, the twisting valley roads, and the far-reaching hills of Luxembourg, so crucially placed in the center of the maps of Europe that it came to be called "the Gibraltar of the North."

The older of the two children enthralled with their elders' stories was bright-eyed Jean-Pierre Steichen, born December 27, 1854, in Niederpallen, in the township of Redange-sur-Attert. His younger sister, Elisabeth, was born in 1855, crippled by a lame foot. Both children were headstrong: The boy possessed "vanity and passion and a streak of stubbornness," his family remembered, and the little girl's flaming red hair crowned an unhappy face.[2] Orphaned when Jean-Pierre was only five and Elisabeth was four, they were taken in by their grandmother Elisabeth Steichen, who so pitied and indulged them that she affirmed their already-strong tendencies to demand the admiring attention of their elders.

The parents of red-haired, arrogant Elisabeth and headstrong Jean-Pierre were Elisabeth Ehleringer and Jean-Pierre Steichen, who was born January 12, 1830, in Mondercange to a family of landowners and farmers. In the early years of their marriage, Jean-Pierre and Elisabeth Steichen bought a nineteen-hectare farm in Niederpallen and settled down to nurture their two children and to farm. To the casual observer, the fields and meadows of Luxembourg appeared to be fertile and generous, cloaked in sunlight or bathed by the gentle evening mists rising over the river valleys. In reality, however, the parsimonious soil actually made farming grueling work. With enough ingenuity and backbreaking labor, wheat, barley, grain, and root vegetables could be coaxed out of the earth, but it was hard to earn a living. The land gave up iron and metals more readily than food, although the lush vineyards in the Moselle River Valley yielded superior wines.

When Jean-Pierre the elder died suddenly on January 18, 1858, his widow could not keep up the farm alone, and she was forced to sell more than half of their land, keeping only eight hectares for herself and her small children. After her death on February 29, 1860, the rest of the family farm had to be sold, and her grieving children went to live with their grandmother and her father.

At night, under the steep slate roof of the family house, cozy by the fire, the orphaned children listened raptly as their great-grandfather told his own story about being chosen as one of thirty military conscripts from his village in Luxembourg to march with Napoléon to Moscow in 1812, where they watched as the city burned and thousands of men perished from cold and hunger. He was one of only two villagers to survive the campaign and to come wearily back home to Luxembourg. From the time young Jean-Pierre was eight years old, he was his great-grandfather's constant companion, and he remembered that the old man, who lived to be 106, "did nothing—and was lovingly cared for—as a very old fellow full of interesting stories."[3] He became the boy's hero, along with the great Napoléon, whose picture Jean-Pierre would keep nearby until he himself was an old man, telling the story over and over again to his own grandchildren.[4]

Jean-Pierre grew to love the grandmother who reared him, remembering her with admiration as "a real manager, running the farm, always busy."[5] His sister, Elisabeth, called Lizzie, was more aloof, however, and considered herself far superior in social class to the other girls in her village, and even in her convent school in Arlon, Belgium. She especially looked down on her classmate Marie Kemp, and she was no doubt disappointed when, several years later, her brother fell in love with the vibrant Marie, the daughter of a peasant family from Mondercange.

Jean-Pierre was twenty-two then, tall and frail, and neither as capable nor as ambitious as Marie, nearly five months his senior. She was vivacious and striking, with a trim figure, sparkling, intelligent blue eyes, and upswept dark hair. Like her Teutonic peasant ancestors, she possessed remarkable stamina and a capacity for prolonged, patient hard work. By contrast, he was reserved, restless, spoiled by the women in his family, and sometimes temperamental. Marie came to believe early that since he had been a "sickly baby, he'd die early."[6] She would invest her robust good health in caring for him. He was smart and serious. He was handsome. He was a Steichen, the son of landowners, a real catch for a peasant girl.

They were married in the Roman Catholic church in Mondercange on February 26, 1878.[7] At the time of their wedding, Jean-Pierre received a modest inheritance, which he and his bride immediately invested in a small clothing business. Just as quickly, the business failed. From the beginning of their marriage, Marie became the decision maker, so she most likely was responsible for this first crushing loss. Afterward, Jean-Pierre took the only work he could find, as a housekeeping manager for a count on a nearby estate; his chief assignment was to keep the count's alcoholic son from drinking.

With no money left to buy their own house, the young Steichens spent their early domestic life in makeshift circumstances. In fact, sometime in the late 1870s, Jean-Pierre was forced to move with his wife to live with relatives in one of the small houses surrounding his ancestral home in Bivange. There Jean-Pierre and Marie's first child was born on March 27, 1879. Three days later, in the parish church of Bivange, Father Altwies baptized him Eduard Jean Steichen. From the outset, Marie was a passionate mother, completely absorbed in her infant son's care.

Since his orphan boyhood, Marie's husband had longed for a house and some land of his own, for he dearly loved to garden. Now that he had a wife and a child, this longing intensified. At night, as the three of them crowded into the spare room in his cousins' house, Jean-Pierre and Marie worried about their future. Facing the reality that they were unlikely ever to own property in Luxembourg, the young man resolved to join many Europeans in the late nineteenth century who saw emigration to the United States as the only means of securing a better life. And always the dreamer and the risk-taker, his wife not only agreed to this plan, she insisted on it. Marie Kemp Steichen wanted her son to grow up in the United States of America, for this, she had heard, was a country of unlimited freedom, equality, and opportunity.

Consequently, before Eduard Steichen was a year old, Jean-Pierre and Marie Steichen decided it was time to set out for the United States. He would go first and make a place for her and the baby in the New World. The couple packed a dozen trunks with their household possessions, including the Steichen family legacy of heavy woven linen sheets, pillow slips, and other bedding, and sometime in 1880, Jean-Pierre traveled to Le Havre and there boarded ship for steerage passage to New York.

He was part of a large exodus of Luxembourgers displaced in the late nineteenth century by worsening economic conditions. Pampered and shielded by his grandmother, Jean-Pierre took few practical skills with him to the new country, and no training for a trade or profession. Much of the time in steerage was given to talk—alternately hopeful and fearful of the future in the New World. Jean-Pierre's first language was

The Land of Freedom (1854–1889)

Letzeburgesch, or Luxembourgian, a dialect of German studded with French words and phrases, with a grammar so nebulous and complicated that there had been few serious attempts to capture its elusive structure on paper. Like his countrymen, he knew German and French intimately, and those languages no doubt helped him make a few friends in the noisy throng on the steerage deck of his ship.

New York was the city of golden streets, some of them argued; others were bound for Milwaukee, or small towns where relatives had gone before them. There is no record of exactly when or why, but Jean-Pierre Steichen made Chicago his destination. Because Chicago was a smaller city than New York, many immigrants believed that new homes and jobs would be easier to find there. But the city must have been a shock to Jean-Pierre, accustomed as he was to the clean, quiet villages and the pristine walled capital city in Luxembourg.

Nearly a half a million people inhabited this new city, walked its wooden sidewalks, maneuvered its noisy, crowded streets in dust or in mud. Armies of smokestacks emitted waste, as did the trains that pounded into Chicago, hauling grain, hogs and cattle, timber and iron, and wave after wave of immigrants, merchants, hoboes, and tramps. Nine years after the great fire of 1871, Chicago was still reinventing itself, rebuilding pragmatically, unimaginatively, on the shore of Lake Michigan. To the west, in the First Ward or on Halsted Street or South Clark, frame cottages and boardinghouses were quickly cobbled together to house the constant influx of workingmen.

When Jean-Pierre Steichen got off the train, the new Chicago had already spawned the slums and ghettos where the arriving immigrants congregated in enclaves. There, familiar languages and customs helped assuage homesickness and the anxieties of coping with the strange, often daunting new city. If there were jobs, they would be had at the packing plants, the railroad yards, the reaper works, and the sweatshops nearby. But work was sometimes impossible to find, with wages often too paltry to buy food and shoes and to pay rent, even in the cheapest boardinghouses. Immigrant families, many of them displaced farmers, had no choice for housing except the tenements packed into these ethnic ghettos, segregated by the economy and by language and custom from mainstream Chicago, and, thus, from the America they were seeking. This was no utopia; it was, instead, a violent, tumultuous frontier city, already overpopulated, its citizens underemployed, its future in the hands of a few wealthy, powerful men on the one side and the anxious throngs of workingmen, women, and children on the other, hungry for jobs at just wages, and a piece of the American dream.

This was the Chicago that greeted Jean-Pierre Steichen, with his trunks of linen and household goods, his sparse funds, and his hopes for a better life. From the outset, the language and the competition defied his efforts to find work. He found a room in a cheap boardinghouse, and ventured out each day into the crowds of men vying for jobs. But the search seemed futile to him, and Jean-Pierre quickly grew discouraged.

Initially, he wrote letters home to Marie, but as six months went by, his hopes ebbed and his health broke. Ashamed and ill, he fell into a long silence. Alarmed at the lapse in correspondence, Marie waited with mounting anxiety in her in-laws' crowded house. His letters had come steadily for months. When they suddenly ceased, she knew that something was terribly wrong with her husband; otherwise, he would have sent for her by now. She waited an agonizing few weeks and then took matters into her own capable hands. She packed what was left of their belongings, counted her modest funds, dressed her son in "long wool stockings and underslip, a heavy homemade dress and high, soft button shoes, and took the boat train for Le Havre."[8] There, she booked steerage passage for herself and eighteen-month-old Eduard.

More gregarious than her husband, she interrogated her fellow passengers, eager for any scrap of news other Luxembourgers might have had from the United States, especially any news of her husband. The letters he had sent, she kept safely in her purse, especially the last letter she had received, bearing the address of a Chicago boardinghouse. She busied herself during the voyage by caring for Eduard and getting acquainted with the other women in steerage, washing her son's clothes and diapers, hanging them on a makeshift line to dry in the sea air, gossiping, sharing her worries and her determination to find her husband. During the long Atlantic crossing, the young mother held her baby close to her, and in her soft, musical voice, she told him all her fears and her dreams for the life that lay before them.[9]

Weaving her way through the maze at Ellis Island, clinging to her son, Marie Kemp Steichen quickly found people who could communicate with her in German and French as well as in the dialects of Luxem-

THE LAND OF FREEDOM (1854–1889)

bourg and Belgium. Because the last letters from Jean-Pierre had come to her from Chicago, she would begin her search for him there. She would waste no time in New York.[10]

"Chicago. Where is this?" she asked a stranger. From the window of a westbound train, she and baby Eduard watched the country flow by, the strange towns, the varying shapes of the earth and the sky. The countryside of New York and then Pennsylvania, resplendent in late autumn, must have reassured her that this new land had its own beauty. The earth flattened as they neared Chicago. Two hundred miles of open prairie must have seemed strangely barren to Marie, whose personal landscape was one of small farms and thick forests, verdant mountains and rivers enfolding medieval villages.

By contrast, the last hours of Marie's long journey toward Chicago took her through interminable miles of farmland. Here and there, a farmhouse stood stark against the wide prairie sky, dwarfed by a great barn and silo, the house subservient to the farm, the human scale diminished by the amplitude of nature. All of a sudden, the city broke the horizon. After the journey by train through the placid prairie, Chicago was jarring, its sprawling size and its raw energy intimidating.

But Marie had come this far in search of her husband, and she was absolutely determined to find him. The surviving details of her search were etched in family memories: Marie told in later years of stopping strangers in the street, holding Eduard in her arms, asking directions, sometimes in German, sometimes in French, questioning anyone who might help her find the street named in Jean-Pierre's last letter, and then, the right boardinghouse on that street, praying that he would still be there.

Seven or eight months after she bade him good-bye in Bivange, Marie found the shabby boardinghouse, interrogated the landlady, and was finally led to the room where her husband lay, thin, feverish, despondent, nearly penniless.[11] His landlady had been extracting rent for bed and board by claiming, one by one, articles from the carefully packed trunks of family linens, furnishings, and keepsakes.

In a reunion no doubt defined equally by relief, disappointment, and joy, Marie vowed to rectify this unpromising entry to the New World. There was work in the copper mines of Hancock, Michigan, she heard one day. Marie had no idea where that might be, but she had found

New York and then Chicago, and then her husband suffering in his boardinghouse room. She could surely find this Hancock. And so Marie paid the rest of the boardinghouse bill, repacked the diminished stores in their trunks, and took her husband and her son to the far northern edge of Michigan, determined to make a home for them there.

Jean-Pierre, Marie, and young Eduard Steichen traveled for two days by ferry, train, and wagon to reach Hancock, Michigan, a village that still thrives in Keweenaw County, in the heart of copper country.[12] Not many years before the Steichens' arrival, the landscape had been the beautiful, rugged wilderness home of the Chippewa Indians, but that world had been forever transformed by ambitious white men. Along the slopes and tributaries of Lake Superior, the largest body of freshwater on earth, speculators discovered a secret long known to the Indians—the presence of pure native copper. Soon afterward, hastily erected villages, dominated by the intricate, ugly apparatus of the mines, scarred the hills and shoreline. Hancock nestled on the bluffs sloping down to Portage Lake, whose once-quiet waters, interrupted by rapids, now bustled with ships and the businesses that supported the copper-mining industry, including a cooperage to produce barrels, and many acres of docks, shipping platforms, and shipyards.[13]

Marie Steichen had brought her family to the site of one of the richest mining operations in the world. In fact, the first great mining rush in North America came not in the gold mines of California but in these copper mines of northern Michigan. The copper boom inevitably drew capitalists, speculators, adventurers, and a massive immigrant workforce. Hancock was then one of several makeshift towns and villages strewn along the Keweenaw Peninsula of upper Michigan, where thousands of immigrants came from all over the world to labor in the dangerous and lucrative mines embedded with the only pure copper in North America. The Detroit and Lake Superior Copper Company dominated the mining industry in Hancock and owned one of the largest copper-smelting and -refining works in the world, the first in the production of refined copper.[14]

Experts from Cornwall, England, were lured to Michigan to over-

The Land of Freedom (1854–1889)

see the installation and operation of the flourishing mines and the accompanying smelting operations. The mining villages held the Western world in microcosm: German, Prussian, Austrian, Scottish, Welsh, Irish, Italian, French, and Canadian immigrants toiled in the mines side by side with laborers from Michigan, Virginia, Vermont, Wisconsin, Pennsylvania, Massachusetts, Ohio, Indiana, and Connecticut. When the Steichens arrived in 1881, Hancock was a boomtown, with 1,783 people in Hancock City, and another 3,041 in Hancock Township, according to the Houghton County census of 1880. The imperatives of work and survival in the crude copper towns at first ruled out such luxuries as comfortable housing, good public schools, or the cultural amenities of music, books, and art. For ten hours a day, six days a week, men and boys as young as twelve took on the backbreaking, sometimes deadly labor deep in the shafts of the mines. Gangs of young thugs roamed the streets, and at night, boisterous men quenched the dust of the mines in an ever-growing array of saloons.

Hancock was most definitely not a family town, hard as the proper wives and mothers tried to make it so. Children had to be protected from the bullying of teenage ruffians, as well as from the roistering of profane, drunken men and bawdy saloon girls. But the weary Steichens had come too far to consider going anywhere else, and they were determined to make the best of it.

They found two cheap rooms to rent above a store on Quincy Street, and Jean-Pierre quickly hired on at the Hancock mine. Marie found a job at Joseph A. Wertin and Sons, one of the town's seven general merchandise stores; she took Eduard to work with her, or left him with a newfound friend, a neighbor whose children she tended in turn. In later years, residents of Hancock would disagree about the location of the Steichens' first home. It was on the north side of Quincy Street, not far from St. Ann's Catholic Church, some recalled. Others were sure that it was directly across the street from the post office. Someone even offered the apocryphal story that it was over a photography shop, wherein little Eduard Steichen first discovered his destiny.[15]

There were iron mines in Luxembourg, but Jean-Pierre Steichen, no miner in the old country, was unfit in more ways than one for his first job in the New World. He had no skill or training for mining, no desire for it, and little physical endurance to sustain the long hours of unrelenting manual labor. Digging and blasting in the fathoms-deep shafts filled his lungs with debris and smoke, while the air above ground was marred by poisoned discharge from the smelting and refining works. Although he brought home a standard wage for the time, averaging $1.70 per day, his earnings did not justify the jeopardy to his health.[16]

Yet there was no choice but to work long hours, Jean-Pierre in the mines and Marie at the store owned by Austrian immigrant Joseph Wertin. The indignities of the new life seemed to wear Jean-Pierre down more than they did Marie, and at least once, he vented his frustration on her physically. This traumatic event was to be Eduard's earliest memory. He was not more than three years old at the time, but to the end of his life, Eduard would remember that moment when his father struck his mother in anger. The incident shocked and frightened him, and he never knew whether his father had intended the blow for his mother or if she had intercepted a blow meant for her son.[17] Jean-Pierre never did it again, for his wife would not stand for it.[18] Family members recalled, however, that Jean-Pierre kept "a buckled strap hanging on the wall in the kitchen" and occasionally used it to beat Eduard when he was impertinent.[19]

For Jean-Pierre, accustomed to the old European school of child rearing, and his tenderhearted, independent wife, this marked the beginning of a lifelong disagreement about how to discipline their children. In Eduard, it triggered a deep, growing resentment toward his father, as well as a reflexive aversion to conflict and violence. In later years, he remembered or shared little of his childhood in Hancock except that image of his father striking his mother.

On May 1, 1883, a second child was born to the Steichens, a daughter they called Lilian, or Lily. Now with two small children, Marie found it more difficult to leave home every day for her ten-hour stint at the Wertin store. She surveyed the meager services offered to Hancock's citizens and realized that since most businesses catered only to miners, the town badly needed a dressmaker for its growing population of women. Although she had tried her hand at the clothing business in the old country and had failed, and although she had never in her life made a dress, Marie embarked with her customary self-confidence on a new enterprise.[20] She ripped apart one of her own dresses to create a pattern, made

The Land of Freedom (1854–1889)

a new dress, and soon sent out the word that Marie Kemp Steichen, seamstress, was taking orders.

Her first client—a young Italian bride in need of a wedding dress—was so pleased with her gown that she recommended Marie's services to others. Marie quickly began to get other dressmaking work, expanding her circle of friends in the process. Outspoken and vivacious, with an engaging laugh and a quick wit, she was a generous, reliable friend whom women instinctively trusted with their problems and their secrets, as well as with their wardrobes.

Just as her business began to grow, however, Jean-Pierre's health deteriorated alarmingly. More and more frequently, he was falling ill with respiratory problems, strange fevers, and malaise, and Marie was determined to get him out of the mines. She confided her fears to her good friend Mary Dorschey Wertin, the wife of the senior partner in the general store where she had worked. Through the sympathetic Wertins, she was able to arrange a safe job for Jean-Pierre, as a clerk for Joseph A. Wertin and Sons. Thus she managed to rescue him in Hancock, as she had in Chicago.

Marie was far stronger than her husband, physically and intellectually, more driven, better able to cope with the struggles in the New World. She wanted to make a wonderful life for her two children, and she began to see clearly that it would be up to her to secure their future. Marie Steichen was taking the reins in her family life, investing her considerable vision, ingenuity, and physical energy in making their modest fortune. Consequently, as her dressmaking business flourished, Marie decided to turn her attention to another promising new venture—making hats for her customers to wear with their dresses.

In the early eighties, between the panics of 1873 and 1884, there was a window of national economic prosperity, opened in large part by the end of Reconstruction, the expansion of the railroads, and the upsurge in shipbuilding. The citizens of Hancock suddenly enjoyed a little more income, and, consequently, a little more leisure for the cultivation of social life. Churches became the focal point of community activity with their schools, sewing circles, and service guilds, but lodges and benevolent societies also multiplied. Culture came to Hancock in the form of lectures, a random musicale, even a library of three hundred volumes, sponsored by the Emerald Literary Society.[21] While the Mystic Lodge, the Ancient Order of the Shepherds, the Soldiers' and Sailors' Association, and the Robert Emmett Young Men's Benevolent Society were all organizations for men, there were various socials to which the women of the town were invited, and Marie Steichen calculated that these ladies needed new hats to wear.

She found that while she had a knack for making dresses, she made hats with flair, and especially enjoyed designing them. As her skills as a businesswoman grew, her earnings became the mainstay of the family income, and she was soon able to afford an apartment at 321 Quincy Street, in a small two-story wood-frame building that also housed her millinery shop. After Jean-Pierre went off each day to the Wertin store, Marie would care for the children and work in her millinery shop, designing and trimming each hat, keeping the books, and ordering the goods and supplies.[22] She advertised her creations in Hancock's newspaper, the *Northwestern Mining Journal,* as well as in the town clothing and general merchandise stores, and she placed attractively decorated hats in the window of her millinery shop to lure more customers.

Late into the night, while the rest of the family slept, Marie worked on her hats. Then, at six in the morning, she would rise to do the laundry, scrub the Hancock dust and grime from the kitchen floor, tend to the other chores of the household, feed her family, and see Jean-Pierre off to the store. Promptly at eight, she opened her shop for the new day.[23]

A devout Catholic, Marie found renewed strength at Mass when the daily routine sapped her energy or spirits. During the 1880s, Hancock churchgoers could choose from among several congregations—the First Congregational Church, the Methodist Episcopal Church, and two Lutheran churches. However, in 1885, St. Ann's Catholic Church drew so many people from Hancock and surrounding communities that it was by far the largest parish in town. The church gracing the corner of Quincy and Ravine streets, not far from the Steichen apartment, had been organized and built by Father Edward Jacker, a German immigrant whose first American mission had been to serve the Indians of L'Anse in the Portage Lake region of Michigan.[24]

Marie, as her daughter later wrote, came from "plain unlettered peasant stock in medieval priest-ridden Catholic Luxembourg, with its religious processions and pilgrimages and the rest," and she quickly became one of St. Ann's most ardent parishioners.[25] In that church, her bright-eyed little daughter was baptized Lilian Anna Maria Elizabeth Magdalene Steichen.[26] Marie was always the family's spiritual ballast, "a true believer"; she had once taken her younger sister Grete on a pilgrimage from Luxembourg to a shrine in Belgium that boasted a display of the shirt of Christ, in hopes that a miracle would cure Grete's blindness.[27] Even when the miracle did not come to pass, Marie's faith never wavered. After all, she had been taught, faith demanded perseverance and suffering. Jean-Pierre, too, was a Catholic, respectful of rituals but not deeply spiritual.

Now that he was away from the mines, he grew stronger, with time and energy to spare for the work he loved most in the world: tending a garden. There was space behind their apartment building for a little garden, and this was Jean-Pierre's joy. He could be irritable and gruff with his wife and children, moody and arrogant with his neighbors, but the garden on Quincy Street gave him pleasure and serenity, just as his touch brought it to luxuriant life. His flowers grew to be lush and vibrant regardless of soil or weather. His vegetable garden more than fed his family, and from its abundance, he could supplement their income, sending young Eduard out door-to-door to sell the Steichen lettuce, cabbage, carrots, and string beans from large baskets. In fact, the children's happiest times with their father revolved around the garden.[28] While many children would have resisted the hard, dirty work of gardening, tilling and sowing, staking and weeding, Eduard and Lilian saw it as endlessly fascinating play, and an opportunity to enjoy their father's company.

Their mother had the same passion for education that their father had for gardening. She and her husband had learned to read and write English well enough to perform their daily duties, but they found it an awkward, unruly language. Marie was determined that her children would have the best education she could muster for them, but feared that it would not be found in Hancock, Michigan. The Detroit and Lake Superior Copper Company had built a union school in Hancock for the education of all children of the town, whether they were children of union members or not, and the Catholic and the Lutheran churches had started their own schools. Hancock boys could attend school until they were twelve, after which most of them went to work in the mines.

Eduard was an exuberant, inquisitive boy, brimming with energy. A photograph made in 1886, when he was nearly seven, shows him with close-cropped hair, his bright eyes confronting the camera. He wears a tailored suit and a white bow tie. Leaning against him is his sister, not yet three, her dark hair carefully curled. Her white dress fades into the background of the picture, just as she herself often stood in the shadow of her older brother. Close companions from earliest childhood, the brother and sister were both sturdy, athletic, and extraordinarily intelligent. With facial features so similar they could have been twins, the two were kindred spirits, even when Lilian was a tiny child spending her days with her mother in the shop.

Eduard, on the other hand, had the freedom of the rutted Hancock streets, when he was not attending classes at St. Ann's Catholic school, running errands for his mother, working with his father in the garden, or peddling produce around town. He grew up with the children of immigrants as well as of miners born in the United States, discovering early a sturdy self-reliance, and a street wisdom, which gave him independence. He could be a ruffian when he had to, but he knew the meaning of firm discipline at home—his father's strap, his mother's endless, patient lectures. He learned at a very young age that the family had to work hard together and to look constantly for innovative ways to earn money. He also came to expect his father's gloom and petulance, and his mother's unstinting love.

Although he did not always feel comfortable with the rough children who roamed the streets of Hancock, he was feisty and daring, popular enough to lead his compatriots into mischief. One day, Eduard came home from school and barged into his mother's millinery shop, shouting back to someone in the street, "You dirty little kike!"

His mother stopped waiting on her customers and called him to the counter, asking him what he had said. "With innocent frankness, I repeated the insulting remark," he wrote later of the incident. "She requested the customers to excuse her, locked the door of the shop, and took me upstairs to our apartment. There, she talked to me quietly and earnestly for a long, long time, explaining that all people were alike regardless of race, creed, or color. She talked about the evils of bigotry and intolerance. This was possibly the most important single moment in my growth toward manhood."[29]

THE LAND OF FREEDOM (1854–1889)

By 1887, in a gesture of commitment to their new country, Jean-Pierre and Marie Steichen had anglicized their names, as most immigrants did then. The 1887 Hancock city directory listed John P. Steichen, clerk, Jos. Wertin and Sons. There was no mention of the family's principal breadwinner, now called Mary Kemp Steichen.[30] Dissatisfied with their daily life in Hancock, she began to contemplate her children's future. Although Lilian was only four and would not start school for another two years, Eduard was an immediate concern. Wanting to remove him from the crude streets of Hancock and enroll him in school elsewhere, Mary surely would have consulted with Father Jacker about this momentous decision.

After much debate and struggle with her skeptical husband, she decided to send Eduard to Pio Nono College and Catholic Normal School in Saint Francis, a suburb of Milwaukee, Wisconsin. Her boy would have to travel the 275 miles between Hancock and Milwaukee alone by train, a journey of about eight hours, and would board at the school under the care of the priests. She grieved at the thought of sending her son away, but that was the price to be exacted for the kind of education she wanted him to have. Thus it was that one day in 1888, Eduard Steichen bade his family good-bye and boarded the train for Milwaukee, wearing a tag in the lapel of his coat to identify his destination and the name of the priest from Pio Nono school who would meet him.[31]

Surrounded by priests and by older classmates who were preparing for the priesthood, Eduard, for the most part, conformed to the strict regimen at Pio Nono during his years there, so much so that once, out of dread, he cheated on a school assignment. Even as a boy of nine, he was competitive, longing to excel. Assigned to draw a series of tulips in his art class, he felt inadequate to draw them successfully on his own. He decided to get some help, turning first to drawings in a botany book in the school library. Years later, he reconstructed the episode for his friend and brother-in-law Carl Sandburg, who told it this way:

> *He brought in sketches he had made through using transparent paper (which was cheating) and on which he had received help from older persons (which also was cheating). He roughed up*

some of the firm clear lines made through transparent paper (which was not merely cheating, but was cheating "with felonious intent"). Now the priest gave high praise to his sketches. So did others of the elders. His mother declared, "He must be an artist, he shall be a g-r-e-a-t artist!"[32]

Marie—now Mary—was elated when a priest from Pio Nono wrote to praise her son's drawing exercise and to tell her he possessed artistic talent. Now, she decided, Lilian, too, must have the best education, the best environment. Consequently, Mary began to dream about moving her family away from Hancock, perhaps to Milwaukee, where they would be close to Eduard and his excellent new school. There her son could continue to develop the wonderful gift that the Pio Nono priests had discovered. There they would also find good schools for Lilian, when she was old enough, for she already seemed as precocious as her brother.[33] And there they would finally live out their dreams of a better life in a better place.

Resolutely, Mary Steichen held to her killing schedule, so that by 1889, she had saved enough money to finance her new plan. Then, when Eduard was ten and Lilian was six, the family left Hancock for good, to move to Milwaukee. Surely, their mother believed, they would have a better chance there.

2

Taking the Reins

(1 8 8 9 - 1 8 9 5)

Poor father! His children, rebellious, self-willed, with strange incomprehensible (to him) ambitions! His wife always standing by the children—backing them up—finally taking the reins out of his hands so as to help the boy and girl realize their ambitions![1]

—Lilian Steichen to Carl Sandburg

Years later, when Carl Sandburg got to know Mary Kemp Steichen, he called her Whitmanic: "Nothing but the limit, the farthest and highest for her boy and girl," he wrote. "Nothing but the limit for herself, working in the scope of her chances. A rapt enthusiast, giving all, risking all, and no surety of returns."[2] Risk and sacrifice were woven into the fabric of her life, and if giving Eduard and Lilian the best opportunities meant that she had to snatch the reins from her husband's stubborn hands, Mary Steichen was willing to do just that.

She renounced the rough streets of Hancock for the more progressive ones of Milwaukee. If John Peter grumbled about leaving his garden, she could remind him that flowers and vegetables also flourished in Wisconsin soil. Always, their children came first, Mary insisted. Eduard Steichen, in turn, called his mother the "guiding and inspiring influence" in his life, "always an encouraging and a positive force. From my early childhood, she sought to imbue me with her own great strength and fortitude, her deep, warm optimism and human understanding."[3]

The Steichens quickly settled into two floors of a building at the busy corner of North Third and West Walnut streets. This was in the heart of Milwaukee's largest German neighborhood, known in earlier years as Gartenstadt, "Garden City," because of its neat houses with fenced, manicured gardens of vegetables and flowers. To the east and south, closer to Lake Michigan, there were Polish, Irish, and Italian enclaves, but the area from Eleventh Avenue to Western Avenue, intersected by Center, Walnut, and Chestnut streets and Grand Avenue, comprised the equivalent of a German city within the larger circumference of Milwaukee.[4]

Lilian was soon enrolled in first grade in a nearby Catholic school for girls, and Eduard could live with his family and take the streetcar to Pio Nono school to study and to continue his art classes. But now, he did only original work, for he had learned his lesson about copying the work of others. His deception in the art classroom had forced him to work hard, out of embarrassment, pride, and fear of discovery, and, to his surprise and relief, he found he *could* draw very well. Furthermore, he liked doing it. He was also inventive, mechanically adroit, inquisitive, fascinated with science.

With her children happily settled, Mary could concentrate on her own work. As she had done in Hancock, she immediately set up her millinery shop on one floor of their new building, with their household quarters comfortably established upstairs.[5] From the very first week, her shop was bustling with customers, and John Peter easily found a job clerking in a nearby store. The Steichens worked even harder than before, but in far more congenial and rewarding circumstances. In this sophisticated city, with its old-world architecture, food, languages, and culture, they found a community that shared the dreams that had drawn them to the United States in the first place. The sparkling waters of Lake Michigan were a fitting backdrop for a rich and accessible cultural life—symphonies, lectures, and plays, even an art museum. Politicians, led by German and Austrian immigrants, instigated daring, controversial experiments in social democracy. Milwaukeeans demanded equal rights, social services, clean streets and air, good schools, fair courts, law and order.[6]

In leaving Hancock, the Steichens had gone from a village of fewer than 5,000 people to a city with 104,468 inhabitants, according to the census of 1890. Milwaukee had nearly doubled in population since 1880, largely because of the boom in heavy industry. Manufacturing plants, foundries, tanneries, and breweries vied for skilled labor, so that jobs were plentiful. By 1890, the year after the Steichens took up residency there, Milwaukee, with 47 percent of the population foreign-born, was deemed "the most 'foreign' . . . of the twenty-eight largest cities in the United States," with by far the greatest foreign influx and influence coming from Germany.[7] The city was unique among new American cities in its marriage of the American dream of economic opportunity and the old European traditions of community and culture.

You could see Europe in the architecture of Milwaukee, hear it in the streets, taste it in the city's restaurants, beer gardens, and the free-lunch saloons, to which kegs of Milwaukee's finest beer were delivered in beer wagons drawn by handsome matched Belgian horses. Public buildings were designed after classical European buildings, and some wealthy Milwaukeeans emulated the German Renaissance style in their mansions.

Citizens of all economic classes took great pride in the civility of their city, as well as in the rich intellectual and cultural life. Singing societies abounded, and audiences flocked to hear male choruses in community concert halls, symphony orchestras at the Academy of Music, and operas staged at the Grand Opera House. Classical and contemporary plays were produced at several theaters, and family outings could be enjoyed at National Park, which was equipped with a roller coaster, a racetrack, and baseball and cricket fields. The Schlitz Brewing Company built spacious Schlitz Park, boasting its own theater, fountains, and menagerie, as well as outdoor opera performances in the summer.

In the late 1880s, twenty German panorama painters, recruited in Europe, arrived with great fanfare in Milwaukee to work in a huge studio near the corner of Fifth and Wells, where they painted dramatic legendary and historical scenes on immense canvases. Once completed, these spectacular panoramas—of the Crucifixion, perhaps, or momentous events in American history—traveled as lavish entertainments to be shown to audiences gathered in concert halls and auditoriums. One panoramist went on to gain a national reputation as an accomplished painter of scenes from the American West, with some local distinction as a teacher of aspiring artists. He was Richard Lorenz, and, near the turn of the century, he would briefly teach drawing and painting to young Eduard Steichen.

Newspapers were published in every major language spoken in the city, and John Peter and Mary could read the German papers now, in addition to American newspapers written in the English they found so complicated. Mary, more than her husband, avidly followed the political news. Like most American cities, Milwaukee experienced labor strikes, sometimes violent ones, as in the "striking mania" of 1886, when the militia had to be called out to control a mob of strikers meeting at the Milwaukee Garden.[8] That uprising was blamed on the Poles—and the Socialists, a fledgling organization in the United States that was drawing many of its ideals from the German socialism espoused by Karl Marx and Ferdinand Lassalle. Led by German and Austrian immigrants, especially the volatile Austrian Victor Berger, the Milwaukee Socialists aspired to use existing avenues of government to improve the life of working people in the new industrial society.

The Steichens must have welcomed the refreshing conveniences of daily life in Milwaukee. There were modern streetcars; coal-burning hot-air furnaces instead of old woodstoves; and a telephone exchange, although there were only three thousand subscribers by 1896.[9] The city was also fashion-conscious, and, therefore, an ideal place for a good milliner to ply her trade. Consequently, Mary Steichen's business grew quickly, and the family could begin to afford a few luxuries. They acquired an upright piano, which stood in the parlor, covered with a fancy fringed shawl and an array of photographs, including John Peter's prized picture of Napoléon Bonaparte.[10]

Their more affluent life in Milwaukee even afforded the family an exotic pet, a parrot, which resided with them for several years. Eduard taught the parrot to serve as his alarm clock, drilling the bird so that each morning he would screech, "Eddy, get up, it's eight o'clock!"[11] The parrot finally had to be sold after he regularly antagonized friends of the family by answering when no one was home. "Come in, come in!" the raucous bird would shout at the sound of a knock. Perplexed visitors would wait in vain to be greeted, and then depart, offended by the Steichens' seeming rudeness.

Lilian remembered having a doll and doll carriage in Milwaukee, and she loved pushing the carriage in front of the church, where there was one of the few paved sidewalks in the city. A serious, polite little girl, she was chosen by the sisters at the church to present a bouquet of flowers to a visiting bishop. When the momentous day came, however, she was so excited and nervous that she flung the flowers into the bishop's surprised face.[12]

Shrewdly using every possible avenue to promote her millinery business, Mary was not beyond capitalizing on her daughter's charm and good looks. She sewed beautiful dresses for Lilian to wear, did her hair in fancy curls, and made her daughter dress up and show off her latest hat designs.[13] Lilian hated such display; she was so uncomfortable with affectation that the styles she chose for herself later in life were simple, even austere. But the girl with the blue-gray eyes and dimples and the luxuriant dark auburn hair was a lovely model for the hats her mother fashioned for the stylish ladies of Milwaukee.[14]

Often called Lily or Paus'l,* Lilian was a far better, more disciplined student than her brother was. She loved books and music, worked hard at her school studies and her music lessons, and practiced for hours at the upright piano in the front room of their apartment over her mother's shop. Eduard—called Eddy or Gaesjack†—was the articulate extrovert, who increasingly found school inhibiting, often boring. His effervescent personality and indefatigable curiosity did not always mesh well with the strict, rote regimen of the Pio Nono school, although he could be fiercely single-minded when his imagination was engaged.

Something mysterious and untold happened to Eduard at Pio Nono, leaving him with a lifelong distaste for most priests and for organized religion. Family members conjectured that he had overseen a surreptitious sexual advance between two priests, or a priest and a nun, or a priest and one of the boys, but no one fully understood the incident precipitating Eduard's disenchantment with the Pio Nono priests and, consequently, with all clergy.[15] In later years, not even his sister, Lilian, knew

---

* "Paus'l" is an affectionate old-fashioned nickname for girls in Luxembourg, and, according to Margaret Mary Steichen Sandburg, the family's pet name for Lilian.

† "Gaesjack" is pronounced *Gay-shawk*, and it means "Little Jack." In Europe, this was a frequently used nickname for John, especially when a son was named after his father, as Eduard Jean Steichen was named after his father, Jean-Pierre, and his godfather, Jean Steichen.

the source of his disillusionment, just knew it existed, and she accepted her brother's views, whatever their root.

As they grew through childhood, Eduard and Lilian continued to be bound by talent and temperament, sharing a deep understanding and loyalty. "He's a wild boy—*Gaesjack!* I wish he were a little less wild—a little more practical," Lilian wrote of her brother in 1908. "An artistic temperament has its drawbacks!" On second thought, she said, her brother's shortcomings derived not from his artist's temperament but from "plain 'cussedness.' "[16] Her brother had her total love and adulation, however, and she understood his artistic temperament and his "cussedness" because she shared them.

Clearly, it was their mother who ingrained in them a spirited and candid independence and a bold capacity to risk, to experiment, and to explore unconventional pathways. While it was not unheard of for a woman to head a household in the 1890s, Mary Steichen did so with uncommon energy and determination, managing the daily life of the family, shepherding her children, caring for her husband, and single-handedly running her profitable business, although it bore her husband's name in certain city records. Lilian explained in a letter in 1908, "After a while, father quit working (he wasn't earning much and mother's store was paying well) and took charge of the house—cooked and washed and scrubbed—did everything about the house. So mother had that worry off her mind."[17]

But John Peter was a trial to his hardworking wife. He was "always around and interfered in business matters that he didn't understand and couldn't understand—for millinery is a *woman's* business—besides, father was old-fashioned in his business ideas as he is in other things," Lilian wrote. "So there was new worry and anxiety for mother—And every change to a larger store mother made, always met with father's opposition. Father simply represented so much friction to be overcome, in mother's life."[18] In recalling her life at home, Lilian could not remember ever seeing her father show affection toward her mother.[19] Instead, John Peter could be harsh toward Mary, even when she was "sick and exhausted." Lilian believed that her father "would have been happy with a good stupid obedient wife of the old school—a wife who would have accepted a gentle beating from her lord and master every now and then!"

"And," she observed, "he should have had children who feared and obeyed the master of the house...." Instead, he had two rebels, and they had their mother's devotion and unqualified support. "Hard lines," Lilian noted ruefully, "for a man who cherishes the old old German ideal of the father as master of the house and of the wife and of the children."[20]

John Peter Steichen was indeed living a new life in a new world with an unorthodox wife and two extraordinary children, and he simply did not know what to make of his defiant family. More and more, he spent time alone in his new garden, just a little larger than the one in Hancock.[21] Only John Peter's garden submitted to his will.

Mary, the pivot of the family, was the children's mentor, protector, and disciplinarian. Sometimes Eduard and Lilian were a duo in mischief, and so they had to be punished in tandem. Their mother would banish them downstairs to the cellar and lock the door. Secure together, the children made their exile an adventure, talking in whispers so their mother would not hear them and feasting on the stores of the cellar shelves, usually apples and nuts. Once they were sure that school had been let out for the day, they would begin to cry and call out their regret, begging forgiveness and release from the cellar. Their mother would comply, pleased that her punishment had worked. Mary usually relied on serious talks to teach and discipline her children. She would sit down with Eduard face-to-face, analyze his transgression, and "explain and reason, her voice going on and on." Her son would "promise anything to stop the ever-flowing loving counsel."[22]

John Peter could not bear to lay a hand on his beloved daughter, but he still believed that a whipping would make a man of his son. Disapproving as she did of her husband's propensity to use the strap on Eduard, Mary only rarely resorted to corporal punishment. One of these times came on a day when Eduard returned from school to the wonderful aroma of fresh-baked kuchen, intended for his mother's kaffeeklatsch. He asked for some, and Mary refused. He would have his later, she promised. Belligerently, he insisted he wanted it *now*. His mother shouted back that he could be quiet and wait. Hungry and angry, he persisted. His mother took his father's heavy leather strap from the wall, hit Eduard with it, and banished him to the cellar. Once down the steps, he discovered that his head was bleeding. Terrified, he screamed for his mother.

In an instant, she was down the cellar stairs, holding him in her arms, and crying: "I'm a bad mother!"[23]

John Peter and Mary spoke Luxembourgese at home more than English, and they transacted much of their business in Milwaukee in German; their son and daughter, in turn, were multilingual, having grown up speaking German and French, as well. English was for Lilian and Eduard "an acquired tongue," and Lilian, far more sheltered than her older brother, got her English "from books, largely academic books at that." She tended to speak and write a formal English sprinkled with Latinisms, and she found it "up-hill work" to speak idiomatic, Americanized English.[24]

Eduard and Lilian came home after their school classes to a strict routine of chores in their mother's hat shop and their father's garden. Sometime in 1891 or 1892, when he was twelve or thirteen, Mary rewarded her son with a gift of enough money to buy a bicycle. Even then proving to be as imaginative and industrious an entrepreneur as his mother, Eduard used that new bicycle to launch his own business enterprise. Observing one day that Western Union messengers delivered telegraph messages on foot, Eduard rode to the Western Union office to present a novel plan: He could offer improved service and efficiency by delivering telegraph messages all over Milwaukee on his bicycle.

He was hired immediately for fifteen dollars a month, five dollars more than the regular rate, "as the first rubber-tire telegram-delivery service seen in that city." Hearing of his success, Milwaukee's superintendent of Western Union services appreciatively called young Eduard Steichen into his office. "I wanted a look," he said, "at a boy who has new ideas."[25]

Eduard's bold curiosity prompted him to read voraciously about new inventions and scientific discoveries. Machinery intrigued him, and, avid to know how his bicycle worked, he completely disassembled it, then put it back together again. He acquired an old Waterbury pocket watch, took it apart, reassembled it, and discovered that he had two parts left over. Nevertheless, the watch worked perfectly.

In 1892, when he was thirteen, Eduard came across newspaper stories heralding the upcoming World's Columbian Exposition. He read that President Benjamin Harrison had signed an act of Congress in 1890 calling for "an international exhibit of arts, industries, manufactures, and the products of the soil, mine and sea, in the city of Chicago." The world was invited to commemorate Christopher Columbus's discovery of America. Eduard decided to go and see it all for himself.

Excitedly, he began to conserve his earnings from Western Union, stuffing the money into a cigar box, which he hid behind loose plaster in his bedroom wall. With his mother's blessing, he was saving for a journey: He resolved to take himself to Chicago in 1893 to see that city for the first time and to visit the exposition, there to witness for himself the wonders of the world. By late summer of 1893, Eduard's cigar box contained enough money for a week's trip to Chicago. Once there, he "looked, read, listened and rambled among all the marvels of modern mechanics and art, lived on chocolate most of that week...."[26]

Dazzling and audacious in concept and design, the exposition was a pivotal event in the nation's coming of age—an ambitious, self-conscious demonstration of American achievement. Although played out against the grim backdrop of the Panic of 1893 and the resulting worldwide depression, the World's Columbian Exposition of 1893 drew together many of the era's most illustrious figures—scientists, inventors, artists, musicians, politicians, philanthropists, as well as 28 million visitors who wanted to look beyond the threshold of the coming century and see themselves there.

Presidents, princes, princesses, and potentates led the ceremonies surrounding the event: Her Royal Highness, the Infanta Eulalia of Spain attended, as did President Grover Cleveland and the Duke of Veragua, Christopher Columbus's only living descendant. Traveling incognito to the fair was ill-fated Archduke Ferdinand, heir to the throne of the Austro-Hungarian Empire. From art to politics to invention, the celebrated participants in the World's Columbian Exposition had helped to shape their century. Lectures were given by Frederick Douglass, Susan B. Anthony, Elizabeth Cady Stanton, Julia Ward Howe, and Jane Addams. Pianist Ignacy Paderewski and John Philip Sousa performed. The work of James McNeill Whistler could be seen, along with that of Degas, Monet, Millet, John Singer Sargent, and Mary Cassatt, while great murals adorned many of the temporary walls of the exposition.

Hyperbole and effusion defined the exposition, start to finish. "The Largest Photo in the World" was on display, created by photographer Julius Caesar Strauss of St. Louis, who merged nineteen different negatives into one, which he then printed on a continuous sheet of paper, two feet wide and fifteen feet long. If young Eduard Steichen had been inclined then to look at photographs and cameras, he would have had to crisscross the fairgrounds to ramble through several vast buildings, for exhibitions of photographic images and technology were strewn throughout the exposition. Indeed, photography was the orphan child of this world's fair, part science, part technology, part popular culture, part aesthetic medium—a misfit defying classification. The only concentrated display, listed in the program as "Group 151, Photographs and Photographic Apparatus," relegated photography to the official category of precision instruments.

Because the planners of the 1893 exposition emphasized technological, commercial, and industrial innovations, photography was presented primarily as an emerging industry, with intensely competitive tradeshow exhibits staged by Eastman Kodak of Rochester, Blair Camera Company of Boston, Geneva Optical Company of Chicago, and others. The focus was on the tools of the trade, not the photographs being produced; art was an afterthought. The governors of the World's Columbian Exposition could make up their own rules, for only a handful of photographers, including twenty-nine-year-old Alfred Stieglitz of New York, were gearing up then for the prolonged battle over whether photography could indeed become an aesthetic idiom, a legitimate, freestanding art form.

The British exhibition at the fair did show off some fine examples of artistic photography, however, including images by members of the Linked Ring, a rebellious group of British photographers organized in 1892 to protest the conservatism of the Royal Photographic Society.[27] Admiring the aesthetic achievements of the British photographers, Stieglitz had written in 1892 that while American photographers were technically equal to the English, they lacked "taste and sense for composition and for tone, which is essential in producing a photograph of artistic value—in other words, a *picture*."[28] He had been inspired by photographer Peter Henry Emerson, who had written "Pictorial Art is man's expression by means of pictures of that which he considers beautiful in nature," adding that "any Art is a fine Art which can, by pictures, express these beauties."[29] Building on Emerson's ideas, Stieglitz was already articulating the far-reaching concept of pictorial photography—arguing that certain photographs could be *pictures,* just as paintings could, and of equal artistic caliber.

Although the 1893 exposition revealed only a smattering of the photographic experiments undertaken in those days by American pictorial photographers, commercial photography had a heyday. The technological wizardry would have dazzled the inquisitive, untutored eyes of a Milwaukee teenager meandering through the exposition, living on chocolate. You could see the latest in coated glass plates and lantern slides, admire the embryonic techniques in color photography, and marvel at innovations in paper and chemicals.

But Eduard Steichen of Milwaukee was enthralled with motors and machines then, not that "precision instrument," the camera. He wanted to spend as much time as possible in Electricity Hall, with its imposing Corinthian columns soaring forty-two feet into the air. There, he could stand in the crowd to watch awesome demonstrations of the wizardry of electricity. It was the dazzling new innovation of dynamoelectronics that especially intrigued Eduard. Thanks to this brand-new science, motors and machines, powered by electric generators, could accomplish with powerful ease the work arduously done for centuries by man power and horsepower. The evolution of the dynamoelectric generator in the 1880s made possible the conversion of mechanical energy into electrical energy, displacing batteries and for the first time making electric lights practical for general use.

Eduard immediately saw the ramifications of this newly tamed force. Fascinated with the sheer ingenuity of electric power, he foresaw some practical applications, and he invested some of his hard-earned world's fair money in a small electric motor. Back home in Milwaukee, he remembered, "he mastered by himself the leading principles of the science of electrodynamics. He built an electric railway and cars. He tried to hitch the motor to a little red wagon so he would have a horseless vehicle—but it was no go. He decided he would wait before making an automobile."[30]

Years later, Steichen told Carl Sandburg about how he came home from the great world's fair to experiment with the technology he first encountered there; he did not know then that German engineers Karl Benz, in 1885, and Gottlieb Daimler, in 1886, had developed gasoline-fueled internal-combustion engines and were experimenting with engine-powered vehicles. Benz built his first four-wheel car and Henry Ford produced his first motorcar about the same time that fourteen-year-old Eduard tried and failed to make his motor pull the red wagon.

In 1894, now fifteen, Eduard left school after completing eighth grade. Milwaukee students customarily attended school until they finished eighth grade and then made a choice between going on to high school and leaving school to learn a trade, usually through an apprenticeship. For all her open-mindedness about most things, Mary Steichen had old-fashioned practical notions about training her children for the future. High school and college were not even possibilities to consider. Her daughter would apprentice to her in the millinery shop when the time came, and her son would follow the German tradition of apprenticeship to a skilled tradesman. He was an artistic genius, she believed, but she was pragmatic. What could be better than to apprentice him to a Milwaukee lithographic firm for four years? There, he could develop his talent by learning to design posters and advertising copy. Afterward, he would be guaranteed a good steady job.

Consequently, in the fall of 1894, when he was fifteen, Edward's formal education ended and his real education began. He left school to enter a four-year apprenticeship, "in the good old German tradition," to learn to be a designer at the American Fine Art Company, a Milwaukee lithographic firm.[31] He lived at home and worked for nothing the first year as a janitor at the American Fine Art Company, sweeping floors, washing windows, cleaning cuspidors, running errands, and making deliveries. In 1895, his second year, he earned two dollars a week working as a printer's devil, learning the process by which paper was applied to the inked surface of metal plates to produce lithographic prints. His third-year compensation would be three dollars weekly, with a raise the fourth year to four dollars per week. Eventually, he would be allowed to help design posters, show cards, and advertisements. Eduard liked the hard work at the American Fine Art Company. After hours, he continued to draw, and he began to teach himself to paint, often taking his sketchbook out into the countryside.

One day, on a whim, he wandered into a Milwaukee camera shop, where he was quickly captivated by the array of cameras on display. He remembered that the proprietor was willing to answer his endless questions.[32] Eduard began to haunt the shop, hovering over every camera, comparing one with another, and bombarding the patient storekeeper with questions. He would have seen his very first camera when he was photographed with his little sister in Hancock, and he may have looked at the cameras on display at the world's fair, but it was not until 1895, when he was sixteen, that Eduard actually held a camera in his own hands.

The encounter was magnetic. He had discovered a wondrous new tool and he would not rest until he owned one himself. Spilling out his dream to Mary, Eduard gratefully accepted his mother's offer to buy this alluring instrument for him. One day, the dealer pulled out a small secondhand Kodak box camera, offering to sell it cheaply. Eduard could not resist, especially when the dealer told him this was a "detective" camera.[33] He handed over the money his mother had given him, waited as the man went into the darkroom to load the camera with film for him, and listened carefully to the dealer's detailed instructions about exposures. Then Eduard struck out for home, where he eagerly set to work on his first apprenticeship to the camera.

3

THE TOUGHEST CUSTOMER

(1 8 9 5 - 1 8 9 8)

In himself he had the toughest customer of all to satisfy. He felt something desperately experimental and far from finished about every painting or print he completed.[1]

—CARL SANDBURG

WHEN PHOTOGRAPHER ALFRED STIEGLITZ RETURNED TO the United States in 1890 after nine years in Europe, he was twenty-six years old, already obsessed with photography, and therefore dismayed to discover that photography as he had come to understand it in Europe "hardly existed" in the United States. He was even more appalled to learn about the new Kodak camera with its jaunty slogan: "You Press the Button. We Do the Rest."[2]

Kodak had put the camera into the eager hands of millions for the first time, thereby mechanizing and demystifying photography, heretofore such a mysterious process that it had even been called witchery. By 1900, 4 million people in Great Britain alone owned cameras, an estimated one person out of every ten.[3] For better or for worse, the invention of hand cameras in the 1880s had launched a revolution, a turning point in the history of visual reproduction. For forty years previously, cameras had been expensive, large, clumsy, and heavy, making photography a cumbersome as well as an elusive, exclusive process. But these new hand cameras were much smaller in size, and not dependent on the tripod.

The Toughest Customer (1895–1898)

Mass-produced hand cameras like Eduard Steichen's used Kodak were called "detective cameras" because if the photographer chose, he could conceal the fact that he was taking a picture. Already there was a clamor in the press about the possible invasion of privacy inflicted by thousands of amateur photographers lurking about with their hidden cameras.

The most widely known and used hand camera was indeed the Kodak that George Eastman invented and produced in 1888 and that young Eduard Steichen purchased in 1895. This box camera with its fixed-focus lens and quickened shutter speeds further revolutionized photography, expanding the possibilities beyond still life and static portraiture so that photographers could instantly capture subjects and events in action.

Earlier, when Americans in the mid nineteenth century wanted photographs of themselves and their loved ones, they posed for daguerreotype portraits, standing or sitting before a plain background in diffused light from a skylight and, perhaps, from studio windows. It was an expensive proposition, because each exposure could yield only one picture embedded in costly silver plate, unlike the later calotype process, which produced a master negative. This meant that multiple positive prints could be made on relatively cheap paper. Being photographed was still such a novelty, however, that it could be an added, even agonizing challenge to face the bulky daguerreotype camera with a natural expression on your face, then hold completely still for the twenty or thirty seconds of the exposure, eyes unblinking, face unflinching, body stiff. One flicker of movement destroyed the image, forcing photographer and subject to start again. The successful results constituted a photographic legacy of grim-faced ancestors with ramrod-straight posture.

In the early 1880s, by the time Mary Steichen and her friends dressed up for formal photographs, the daguerreotype had been displaced by the more casually posed tintype, using delicately thin but durable iron plates rather than the silver-covered copper of daguerreotype plates. In the mid-1880s, when Mary dressed little Eduard and Lilian in their finery to pose for the photographer in Hancock, he took several ten- to- twelve-second exposures on one negative to produce the wildly popular *carte-de-visite,* a photographic calling card measuring four inches by two and a half. The Victorian family albums on display in most parlors could then be filled with images of family members, friends, and famous or exotic figures printed on *cartes-de-visite* of uniform size worldwide.

By the 1890s, however, the photographer in his studio began losing business to the do-it-yourself craze that equipped the masses with Kodaks and Brownies and other cameras of their own. As Eduard discovered, the new streamlined, speedy, and accessible cameras were within reach of many American families in the 1890s, as exciting a cultural tool as the radio, the television set, and the home computer would become for later generations. Unlike most other cameras, which still required the insertion of plates in a lightproof, built-in chamber called a magazine, Eduard's Eastman Kodak used film in a long roll, containing fifty frames, each two and a half inches in diameter. Another pivotal innovation was Kodak's photofinishing service: Stieglitz had deplored the seductive advertising—"You Press the Button. We Do the Rest."—but it worked.

Eastman offered a responsive public "a photographic notebook ... an enduring record of many things seen only once in a lifetime...." The "fortunate possessor" of the camera could "go back by the light of his own fireside to scenes which would otherwise fade from memory and be lost." The purpose was to bring photography "within reach of every human being who desires to preserve a record of what he sees."[4] These picture records were eventually called "snapshots," after the hunting term that meant shooting a gun from the hip without aiming precisely at a target. Eduard was disappointed, however, that he would have to "snap" fifty pictures before he could see any results, so he quickly photographed his family, the house, the garden, the cat sleeping in the show window of his mother's shop, counting off the exposures until not a one was left. Then he hurried back to the shop with his camera so that the dealer could remove the film and send it off to be developed and printed.

"When the film came back, I had a real shock," he remembered. "Only one picture in the lot had been considered clear enough to print. 'Clear' was the term of approval given to photographs those days. And 'clear' meant that you could see everything that had been photographed. That one good, or clear, picture was the picture of my little sister playing the piano. All the rest were under- or over-exposed."[5]

From his parents, Eduard got characteristic responses to that first experiment in photography. His father complained that it was a waste of time and money to take fifty pictures and get only one clear one. Of course, his mother, to the contrary, told him "the picture was so beautiful" that it justified the forty-nine failures.[6] But Eduard wanted every picture to be beautiful, and he could already see that photography was going to be a baffling, difficult process, requiring patience, skill, and money.

With his love of art and science, he instinctively understood that the camera was a spectacular invention. First, it subtracted the requisite of drawing talent from the act of rendering a picture. The hand that might or might not be skilled in the manipulation of the brush or the pen could experiment with the mechanics of the camera and the chemistry of the darkroom. But second, and more important, photography opened a new dimension of human experience: Heretofore, every means of experiencing images had depended on an intermediary, another eye—the eye of the artist. In photography, the eye of the camera was the witness. Take away photography and its children, motion pictures and television, and you are left with drawing, painting, engraving, etching, and lithography, the art Eduard sought to master at the American Fine Art Company in Milwaukee. In the early 1870s, the lithographic presses had begun to produce chromolithographs, or "chromos," color pictures made possible by the introduction of a series of stones and varying inks to the lithographic process. Distributed by the millions as premiums for newspaper subscriptions and other enterprises, the chromos were "as good as oil paintings," some said.[7] In 1871, one journalist predicted that the chromolithograph meant the end of painting pictures by hand, and that art was "now within the reach of all."[8]

But these prephotographic art forms rendered reality, as well as fantasy, through the subjective filter of another human being's angle of vision and experience. The engraved or lithographic illustrations in books and journals, for instance, brought to the viewer a level of reality—but secondhand, one step removed. Here might be seen the Pyramids, the Great Wall of China, the Tower of London, the king of England, the President of the United States, an Indian chief, yet only as represented and interpreted by the artist. Photography, on the other hand, recorded an intimate yet direct, more objective visual encounter with a subject. The camera could capture immediate, unedited experience, consequently transforming the way the nineteenth-century citizen could view the world.

In the first decades after Louis-Jacques Mandé Daguerre, William

Henry Fox Talbot, and Sir John Herschel unearthed the working ratio of light and dark to chemicals and paper, photography sought to chronicle reality.[9] Even Eduard, a novice with a used box camera in his hands, could see that photography dealt first of all in what he called the inherent "discipline of the literal."[10] For many years, photography had been regarded, Stieglitz wrote in 1899, "as the bastard of science and art, hampered and held back by the one, denied and ridiculed by the other."[11] It was that alchemy—the mysterious amalgam of art, science, and technology—that captivated the imagination of young Eduard Steichen, causing him to make a nuisance of himself in the camera shop in Milwaukee in 1895.

Eduard immediately looked beyond the popular fad of detective cameras and Kodak picture records and saw, as he had seen with the electric motor and his innovative bicycle telegram business, that there were practical applications to be explored. His "first real effort in photography was to make photographs that were useful," he wrote.[12] At the lithographic firm where he worked, the designers copied woodcuts from old illustrated German magazines and books as they created advertisements for Milwaukee brewers, flour millers, and pork packers. But Eduard's initiation to photography convinced him instantly that here was an exciting new way to capture reality. Real Wisconsin pigs differed from the pigs in the old woodcuts, he told the manager of the design department at the American Fine Art Company, and they should be designing realistic advertisements for the pork industry. Painters sometimes worked from photographs of their subjects; likewise, Eduard offered to make photographs that the lithographic designers could use as a basis for commercial drawings.

His boss promised that if Eduard would buy the camera to do the work, he could have time off to do it. Understanding the good business sense of the plan, Mary Steichen agreed to back her son in his latest radical scheme. Consequently, he took his used Kodak back to the photographic shop, explained what he needed, and traded his camera in for a Primo folding view camera, four by five inches, which used plates rather than film. Now Eduard could see the results of his work one photograph at a time, without wasting film. And he decided to learn to develop and print the photographs in his own darkroom, not only to save time and money but also to dive into the technical process of photography.

Like many photographers, he was simultaneously an artist, a scientist, and an engineer: The hands that loved to draw and paint also loved to tinker with the mechanics of things; the mind that appreciated the picture records of photography also craved an understanding of the technology. Consequently, to his mother's dismay, Eduard began to set up his first darkroom in the cellar under the millinery shop and his family home.[13] Mary willingly helped to pay for cameras and developing chemicals, but she balked at first about having the darkroom underfoot. Those were "dangerous, poisonous chemicals" her son was bringing into their home.[14]

Afraid that he would blow up the house—or, at the very least, contaminate the food she stored in the cellar—Mary ordered Lilian and Eduard to remove all the preserves, canned fruits, and vegetables the women had put away in tidy rows on the pantry shelves. Meanwhile, John Peter fumed not only that his son was wasting precious water developing his pictures but that, at last, he had surely gone crazy.[15]

Undeterred, Eduard cut a hole in an interior wall in the cellar and covered it with "several sheets of what was called post-office paper, a brilliant orange-red material." On a shelf outside, he put a candle to serve as his darkroom light. "Shielded behind the post-office paper, which was sufficiently inactinic," he wrote, "I could safely watch the entire process of development."[16] Of course, all he knew about developing then, he had learned from reading the instructions printed on the box of plates. But he would teach himself methodically, by trial and by error, how to control the chemicals, the light, and the plates in his makeshift darkroom.

As an experiment before he tackled the pigs, he photographed a Milwaukee office building. Carefully, he put the first plate in the tray of developer, rocked it vigorously, as instructed, and watched. In a few moments, to his great excitement, an image began to appear and to clarify into the shape of a building. He let out "a terrific war whoop." Fearing that her unpredictable son had been poisoned by his chemicals and was shouting in agony, Mary rushed downstairs, shouting, "Is everything all right?"

"You bet it's all right," he exulted.[17]

Eduard Steichen had developed his first plate. Then, with a relentless, obsessive energy, he repeatedly kept developing that same plate, wanting to be sure he extracted every line and shadow of the photograph. He had followed that approach, too, when he made the exposure, as he wrote in his autobiography:

(I had been told that, in sunlight, with the lens stopped down a little, I should give an exposure of one second. But that was the longest one-second exposure that anybody ever gave, for I just kept holding the shutter open longer and longer.) After a little while in the developing tray, the plate became all black and the image disappeared. However, after fixing, if the negative was held up to a strong light, the image could be seen again. I had my Milwaukee skyscraper. Then I took the plate out to the kitchen sink and washed it and washed it. The instructions were to wash for one hour in running water or in sixteen changes of water. I must have washed that plate for two or three hours.[18]

John Peter had been right after all to complain about wasted water, and, the next day, when the negative was finally dry and Eduard tried to make prints, the negative "was so dense that it took hours in direct sunlight to get a good image on the solio [sic] paper."[19] In his zeal, the young photographer had defeated the purpose of the relatively new gelatin chloride Solio paper, produced by Eastman Kodak in time for the World's Columbian Exposition of 1893 specifically because it could be processed more quickly than traditional albumen paper.* Once again, Eduard trudged to the camera shop to confer with the proprietor, who examined the negative and the proof.

"Overexposed and overdeveloped," he told Eduard, who took his camera home and, undaunted, started all over again.[20]

Sometime during his second year as an apprentice at the American Fine Art Company, Eduard was promoted from typesetter to designer. It happened the day his boss, Mr. von Cotzhausen, the owner of the company, caught him painting a watercolor of bluebirds hovering over buttercups and Queen Anne's lace, a picture that he planned to give to his mother.[21] Never mind that the young man was painting on company time—von Cotzhausen saw immediately that Eduard belonged in the art section,

---

* The earlier albumen prints yielded silver-based photographic images on paper emulsifed with egg white activated in a bath of silver nitrate. The later, much more efficient Solio prints yielded silver-based photographic images on paper emulsified with silver chloride in gelatin.

and he reassigned him to begin training as a designer.[22] Eduard loved the new challenge of honing his drawing skills and learning the art of lettering, yet photography and painting were never far from his mind. He began taking camera portraits of his friends and family, as well as making "phantasy pictures" of the misty landscapes he loved. Habitually, he developed his negatives at home at night, then took them to work with him the next day. "During the lunch hour," he recalled, "I put the printing frame out on the window sill until the print was the proper depth for toning, which I did at home, at night."[23]

While seventeen-year-old Eduard was officially in training to become a lithographic designer, he was simultaneously teaching himself painting and photography in his spare time. On the job at the American Fine Art Company, he designed and printed handsome posters for beer, pork products, and patent medicines "that he was ordered to exploit and sing and make attractive through color and line."[24] After hours, he sketched and painted, often riding the streetcar to the end of the line so he could hike deep into the woods and fields of the countryside, photographing and sketching landscapes.

But most of all, even as a teenager, Eduard was pioneering in the commercial use of photography. He made so many pictures to serve as models for lithographic designs that the musty old books of woodblock prints at the American Fine Art Company were quickly superseded by his growing library of photographs. He roved the countryside with his camera, photographing wheat sheaves and the curling tendrils of the hop vines grown for the breweries. He took sharp, clear pictures of pigs, which were so appreciated by his company's clients in the pork-production industry that they demanded that all future advertising lithographs be sketched from Steichen's actual photographs.[25]

His youthful experiments for the American Fine Art Company established him as one of the first commercial photographers in Milwaukee. Eduard believed from the outset that "usefulness has always been attractive in the art of photography."[26] To his frustration, however, there were no photography classes in the city, no books to be found on photographic technique. His search for them in the Milwaukee Public Library was fruitless, although he did discover and devour some exciting books about painters and painting.

Except for a few magazines on photography that he found in the library, Eduard had little opportunity to learn from others. One pivotal resource for him in those crucial years became *Camera Notes,* the quarterly journal edited by Alfred Stieglitz for the Camera Club of New York from July of 1897 until the July issue of 1902.[27] Nearly a hundred years later, critic Christian A. Peterson noted that *Camera Notes* "ushered in not only a new century, but an entirely different attitude toward photography" touting the medium as a fine art, on a par with painting and sculpture.[28] In addition, Stieglitz's trademark insistence on carefully wrought photogravures provided his readers, including young Eduard Steichen, with the best possible reproduction of photographs. Sometimes the journal, not the camera, was Stieglitz's most potent weapon in his lifelong battle on behalf of photography. From 1893 until 1896, he had edited the *American Amateur Photographer.* Then, with the support of the Camera Club of New York and an annual budget of $250 to publish a thousand copies, Stieglitz launched *Camera Notes* to promote the cause of photography. The journal contained lively articles and fine photogravure reproductions of handpicked photographs.

Eduard probably kept watch over the shelves at the public library, waiting for the arrival of the elegant journal with its customary green Art Nouveau cover. In the inaugural issue of *Camera Notes,* he would have, for the very first time, laid eyes on the work of Alfred Stieglitz, whose *Portrait of Mr. R.* was reproduced as a full-page photogravure, along with a quarter-page halftone of the exquisitely detailed *The Old Mill.* In 1897 and 1898, seminal years for Eduard's own emerging photographic style, he encountered in the pristine pages of *Camera Notes* evocative landscapes such as Hugo Henneberg's *At the Rushy Pool* and Ernest R. Ashton's *Evening Near the Pyramids;* misty seascapes—A. Horsley Hinton's *Requiem* and Robert Demachy's beautifully textured *Rouen;* and F. Holland Day's exotic images, especially *An Ethiopian Chief* and *Ebony and Ivory.* Eduard's eyes could roam the glossy surfaces and artfully caught shadows of Stieglitz's *A Bit of Venice.* He could linger over Rudolf Eickemeyer, Jr.'s luminous portraits, as intimate as the best portrait paintings and as vividly detailed as fine etchings. In the issue of January 1899, Eduard could study the palpable night mist captured in William A. Fraser's *A Wet Night, Columbus Circle, New York.* He was introduced to Gertrude Käsebier's *Portrait Study* in July of 1899, as well as her *Portrait of F. Holland Day.*

Photography as fine art had not yet made its way to Milwaukee, but in the reliable and prophetic pages of *Camera Notes,* Eduard could see a range of photographs executed with verve and skill, reproduced faithfully enough to stimulate his own artistic sense of what his photographs could become.[29] Beginning with the second issue of *Camera Notes* in 1897, hungry as he was for instruction, he could also read articles on aesthetics and on technique. Eduard could follow the vociferous disagreement about the current state of photography as an art medium. British photographer A. Horsley Hinton, for one, admonished the readers of *Camera Notes* that he was "not for a moment prepared to say that photography is accomplishing great art.... It is the artistic *possibilities* and its endeavors that I would be jealous of rather than its present achievements."[30]

As the processes of photography evolved, the debate escalated over the significance of it all. Fred Holland Day of Boston wrote in *Camera Notes* in 1897 that the camera "is just beginning to be taken seriously," but, contemplating the proliferation of the camera in popular culture, he worried that it had "become so common an instrument of torture and pestilence in the hand of a small boy or inquisitive girl, that those who are able to think appear unwilling to consider it worthy of consideration as a real factor in art." However, Day declared, there was no doubt that "the camera, properly guided, is capable of art—real art."[31]

This must have been a catalytic concept for Eduard, who was already earning a good salary in part because he was shrewdly capitalizing on the commercial uses of photography. Day urged that the photographer had to "know good art when he sees it, and then to study it and find out *why* it is good art."[32] Whether it was Day's prompting in *Camera Notes* or Eduard's own instinct that motivated him, he began to read everything he could find about art and artists and to undertake his early tentative crossover experiments, first sketching and photographing a pool in the woods or a meadow at dusk, then painting the same scenes, usually as small watercolors or oils on wood.

He also became a good copyist. He found "a color lithograph of an old man playing a violin," made from a painting by J. G. Brown. When his mother told him the man looked just like her brother, Eduard copied the figure in an oil painting for her Christmas present. Mary was thrilled, and to the end of her life, she was proud of the painting, which hung for generations in a place of honor in the family homes.[33]

"Become a student and lover of art if you would produce it," Fred Holland Day reiterated in his article "Art and the Camera" in 1898. He sent his audience to the masters—Rembrandt, Velázquez, Titian, Rossetti. Furthermore, Day told readers, such as Eduard, who was soaking up every word in Milwaukee, that they should permit themselves to read "absolutely nothing relative to the technical productions of photographs" in order to keep their minds "free from being dogged by the errors of others, and more susceptible to the influence" of their own "errors and achievements, which are of the greatest value and the only means by which any true knowledge may be obtained regarding the possibilities of the camera."[34] Early on, the urge for patient and repetitive risk and experimentation was ingrained in Eduard, and Day's words could only have reinforced this instinct.

However, despite Day's admonition, as Eduard labored to teach himself photography in 1897 and 1898, he scoured the technical articles in *Camera Notes* for practical advice for his incessant experiments in the darkroom. He could pore over practical reports on short- and long-focus lenses and the relative powers of various chemicals used as developers. He could read the lectures delivered to members of the Camera Club of New York, including Professor Dwight L. Elmendorf's assertion that "Given an artistic mind behind the camera, the possibilities of photography are almost infinite."[35]

Alfred Stieglitz, who would for half a century be the most articulate exponent of pictorial photography, was largely mute on the issue in the early years of *Camera Notes*. His articles in the journal at first concentrated on lantern slides, which did not interest Eduard. But he would have found confirmation in Rudolph Eickemeyer, Jr.'s article "How a Picture Was Made" that photographers, like poets, can find subjects near home. Young Eduard must have been heartened also by Eickemeyer's testimony in *Camera Notes* that success rested on a foundation of failures overcome. Experiment, and exercise patience, Eickemeyer urged his readers; use the camera as an instrument for translating artistic sentiment, not just recording lifeless facts.[36]

Eduard would have read in the April 1898 issue of *Camera Notes* about the wonders of the newest Kodak view camera and about how 25,000 people had entered the Kodak photography exhibition held in London. Furthermore, he learned, Alfred Stieglitz himself hung the

The Toughest Customer (1895–1898)

Kodak exhibition when it traveled to New York to the National Academy of Design, and 26,000 people trooped through the show in twelve days. Although photography might have been an obscure enterprise in Milwaukee, Eduard could see that there were thousands of people elsewhere who shared his enthusiasm for the camera.

Meanwhile, Lilian was fascinated with her brother's artwork, and she especially loved to assist him in his makeshift darkroom. She far preferred that to helping her mother make and sell hats.[37] As time passed and there were no chemical explosions, Mary's fears about her son's basement enterprise ebbed. She knew that painting was art: One had only to behold the dark, somber colors and the vivid face of the man in Eduard's handsome oil painting to know that. Photography, on the other hand, could not be art, she felt. Photography was a little machine with buttons to push, and then so much hocus-pocus of light and chemicals; she had to admit it was useful, however, like the scissors and needles that made hats. She clearly saw the practical potential of photography. Her son's enthusiasm, she now decided, was justified so long as he fulfilled his duties at the American Fine Art Company.

Indeed, he was excelling at his new trade. In 1897, he won a prize for an envelope he designed for the National Education Association. He also took up the challenge of designing an advertising campaign for a new medicinal laxative. One of his advertising poster designs for the laxative was so clever that it enjoyed national distribution in newspapers and journals, and even appeared on billboards. He had done the work for Cascarets Candy Cathartic, drawing a beautiful lady, "luxuriant, luring, voluptuous ... representing health, contentment and heart's desire."[38] The lady slept contentedly on a moon-shaped, Art Nouveau capital *C*, the inscription reading, "Cascarets: they work while you sleep."

All this time, Eduard was growing more proficient as a painter, largely self-taught, as he was in photography. He especially loved the "romantic and mysterious quality of moonlight, the lyric aspect of nature." In his free hours after the day's work at the lithographic company, he was either taking pictures or painting watercolors of subjects bathed in twilight or moonlight, and discovering that "painting presented problems of expression similar to those I encountered in photography." Unlike his photographs of the period, which were predominately governed by the need to be realistic, he said that painting afforded him "unlimited opportunities to deviate from the purely naturalistic."[39]

Yet he found himself weaving into his paintings "some of the discipline of the literal that was inherent in photography."[40] This tension animated much of his work over the next few years, as, over and over, he migrated from photography to painting and back again. Often there seemed to be a tug-of-war over whether Steichen the painter or Steichen the photographer would control his seminal work as an artist. Habitually, his subject matter overlapped because the same landscapes inevitably seduced his camera as well as his pencil and his brush. The painter looked over the shoulder of the photographer, while the photographer lurked behind the easel of the painter. Enthralled as he was by the interplay of dark and light in the moonlit scenes he painted and photographed, he kept notes on the actual colors he saw, the subtle increments of gray and black, gold and white, remembering and identifying them by recording the mixture of pigments he would use, and, likewise, methodically recording every stop, setting, and exposure of his camera.

When he was seventeen or eighteen, Eduard rounded up Carl Björncrantz and several other friends who were also fascinated with pictures. Like him, some of them were tradesmen in the graphics occupations of the day. They rented a small room in a Milwaukee office building, paid a model to sit for life drawings, and talked some well-known Milwaukee artists, primarily Robert Schade and Richard Lorenz, into coming to their studio to teach informally and to evaluate their work.[41] Rapidly outgrowing their first room, Eduard and his circle of aspiring artists began meeting in donated space in the basement of a building owned by Milwaukee's Ethical Culture Society. They named themselves the Milwaukee Art Students' League.

Schade, their most frequent instructor, was born in 1861 in New York City, the son of Prussian immigrants. He had studied art with Henry Vianden, a German artist who had been painting and teaching in Milwaukee since 1849. Then Schade had gone on to studies in Munich with Alexander Wagner, who specialized in painting historical subjects. A panorama painter like Richard Lorenz, Schade also earned much of his living as a portrait painter, but, unlike Lorenz, who had no use for the camera, Schade had studied photography.

The German-born Lorenz had trained at the German Royal Academy on a scholarship funded by Franz Liszt. Joining the famous Milwaukee German panoramists in 1886, when he was twenty-eight years old, Lorenz specialized in painting horses for the massive panorama canvases, usually 350 feet long and 25 feet high. While Lorenz concentrated solely on horses, other painters created only human figures and landscapes.[42] The paintings then toured American cities, where enthralled audiences watched the panoramas unfurl on theater stages, an engrossing entertainment, on a par with travelogues illustrated by lantern slides, or, later on, movie newsreels and documentary films.

In 1887, Lorenz discovered the American West and a passion for painting the cowboys and Indians inhabiting that world. His resulting work rivaled that of the premiere Western painter, Frederic Remington. In addition to Steichen and his friends, Lorenz's students included the young Milwaukee socialist Louis Mayer, who went on to study in Germany and then came home to enjoy a career as a regional artist.

While Eduard Steichen was, then and always, essentially a self-taught artist, it was Lorenz, among his occasional teachers, who had the greatest impact. Although Lorenz was not quite forty when he taught Eduard and his friends at the Art Students' League, to them, he was "an old German painter."[43] Lorenz mediated the exuberant, contentious debates over art in the basement headquarters of the Milwaukee Art Students' League. One night, he sat near the door, listening and smoking his pipe as his students argued the merits of one contemporary academic painter.

Finally, he said, "Enough of the 'dummheit' [foolishness]. This talk, talk, talk, talk, talk. You are here to learn how to draw by drawing, not by talking. When you can draw me a shoe that looks like a shoe with a foot in it, then you will have a foundation on which to form opinions. Now you have not."[44]

This was a premise that young Eduard embodied in his own work. He learned to draw by drawing, to take pictures by taking pictures, to paint by painting. As his artistic vision soared, his scientific mind equipped him to experiment incessantly. The discipline of the literal was the key. Lorenz affirmed that principle, but he had little interest in photography, curious when you consider how it could have supported his own passion for the gradually disappearing Native American faces and untouched landscapes of the American West. He told Eduard he was wasting his time with the camera, and the highest praise he ever gave a photograph was to say that it would make a good painting.[45]

In their Milwaukee basement art school, Eduard and his compatriots were battling over the very questions being raised and elucidated at the time by Stieglitz, Day, and others in the front rank of photography in the United States and abroad. The painterly opinion of the medium was that a photograph served to record an object clearly. Beyond that, the photograph could do nothing that could not be done far better in a drawing or painting. Nonsense, champions of photography protested, echoing the landmark defense of photography mounted by Peter H. Emerson in *Naturalistic Photography for Students of the Art,* his classic book, first published in London in 1889. Emerson deplored the "scientific photographer," who looked so microscopically at a butterfly's wing "that he never sees the poetry of the life of the butterfly itself."[46] There were painters, too, who could render the form but never evoke the life of the butterfly.

Eduard believed that the artist, not the physical paraphernalia, shaped an art medium and imbued it with that ineffable essence called art. The gifted artist's duty was to use his vision and his tools, whether camera or canvas, to transmute his subject matter into art. Eduard would soon find welcome affirmation of his evolving theory in critic Charles H. Caffin's book *Photography as a Fine Art: The Achievements and Possibilities of Photographic Art in America.* Caffin set out to validate the movement of advanced photographers who were "striving to secure in their prints the same qualities that contribute to the beauty of a picture in any other medium" and to have their work judged accordingly. "With brush and pigments the painter-artist can accomplish something infinitely superior to the work of the house-decorator," Caffin wrote. "Is he blind to the immeasurably superior results reached by the artist-photographer over him who merely relies upon the mechanical facilities of the camera?"[47]

Yet Eduard never underestimated the fundamental importance of mechanical skill with the camera. Tough customer that he was, always critically examining his own work, holding it up to an exacting standard, Eduard knew he had to master photographic techniques in order to produce clear, sharp pictures. As he progressed, he quickly began earning extra money with his camera. On Sundays and holidays, he wandered through the city parks, photographing laborers at their union picnics or members of the Milwaukee singing societies in concert. For twenty-five to fifty cents a print, he arranged to sell and deliver the snapshots to his willing subjects, many of whom had never before seen pictures of themselves. Discovering that he could take formal portraits and sell them at so much a dozen, he set up a small photographic studio with a friend. He did a "thriving business in the snap-shotting line," Charles Caffin wrote later of Steichen. "No doubt it was an excellent training for eye and nerve."[48]

Eduard's painting, too, provided extra income. He painted busts and heads of beautiful women and made watercolors of Indian heads. Not only did these sell in local department stores, Gimbel's arranged a special window display of them.[49] Clearly, the young man was endowed with his mother's entrepreneurial energy, and through Mary Steichen's example, Eduard was learning to be a hustler and promoter. Once, for instance, he had designed some hats—avant-garde hats, high-fashion hats. Mary made them as he specified, but she predicted they would never sell. "Well, people will see them in the window," Eduard told her, "and then come in the store to see what else there is!"[50] The strategy had worked, and Mary was about to take it a step further.

Seldom able to resist a bargain, she took a gamble one day in 1899, purchasing at a discount a hundred boxes of artificial red roses, so many boxes of roses that they filled an entire room. She would never ever sell them all, her disapproving husband scolded. Determined that she would, and soon, Mary asked Eduard to paint posters of beautiful ladies wearing hats extravagantly trimmed with red roses. Applying the techniques that her son had used to entice customers with his earlier window display, Mary now filled her shop window with Eduard's lavish posters, surrounded by bouquets of the artificial roses. Then she set to work designing a hat with a rose-covered brim.

One Sunday, she coaxed her daughter to wear it to church. Fashion-conscious Milwaukee ladies took note of the milliner's lovely daughter and her hat with the bright red roses. This must be the latest style, they concluded, and in less than a month, the stockpile of roses was gone, and

Mary Steichen's rose-festooned hats were seen all over Milwaukee. Eduard documented the episode of the roses in one of his most memorable early photographs—*My Little Sister with the Rose-covered Hat,* a platinum print made in 1899. Beautiful sixteen-year-old Lilian Steichen is posed out of doors, with the graceful twist of a tree trunk in the background. Her straw hat, slightly askew, is heavy with roses and shadows her pensive eyes.

Like her adored older brother, Lilian was full of dreams in those days. A model student, she wanted to be a poet, and she regularly wrote poems and essays, which her brother read appreciatively and discussed with her. She was a genius, he told her.[51] When she graduated from Milwaukee Public School Number 1, Sixth District, with top honors in her eighth-grade class, her brother gave her a huge bouquet of lilies and a green velvet box. Inside the lid, he had pasted a watercolor of trees and violets beside a pool. "Congratulations and Loving Wishes to Lily, From her big Brother Eddie," he wrote.[52]

Despite Lilian's obvious intellectual gifts and her love for her studies, her parents expected her to learn a trade after she completed her eighth-grade classes. Mary assumed that Lilian would apprentice to her in the millinery shop and that she would one day take over the business, which now employed eight preparers and two trimmer girls.[53] Lilian, however, had other ideas. Determined to continue her studies, she begged her father to allow her to enroll in the public high school nearby. He refused. No daughter of his would go to a public high school; proper Catholic girls did not do that, and he worried that there would be bad influences there. Besides, Lilian had all the education a girl needed, he said.[54]

This time, her mother went along with her father's wishes. Sadly, Lilian took up her apprenticeship at the hat shop, just as her brother's apprenticeship was ending at the American Fine Art Company. When he immediately started working there as a full-time, full-fledged designer, his salary vaulted from nine dollars to twenty-five dollars a week, a high wage for those days, and soon, on the strength of his design work, his salary doubled to the quite magnificent sum of fifty dollars a week.

As he turned eighteen and then nineteen, Eduard was still spending hours with both camera and sketchbook in hand, riding the streetcar as far out of Milwaukee as it went, then striding far into the countryside

The Toughest Customer (1895–1898)

to savor the muted beauty of misty gray days or the waning sun of late-summer afternoons. He loved the luminance of woods and streams in twilight and moonlight, believing that "the woods had moods" that evoked emotions, and longing to capture those lyrical moods in his photographs.[55] His interest in naturalistic, commercial photography was gradually developing into a quest for interpretive photography.

Perpetual experimentation moved him closer to the effect he envisioned, as did serendipitous accidents. When a few raindrops splattered the face of his camera lens one autumn day as he was photographing stark tree trunks in his beloved woods, he discovered that the scene was "transformed by general diffusion."[56] Another day, when he accidentally kicked his tripod during an exposure of several seconds, he discovered that the inadvertent vibration created another kind of diffusion in the picture. These accidents taught him new techniques: He could achieve diffusion at will, and the effect could be artistic. His evocative photographs were beginning to transcend the literal in ways that pleased him.

In his photography and his painting, Eduard constantly experimented, taking the risks and making the mistakes that are essential in the evolution of any original art. In the art books he regularly devoured in the Milwaukee Public Library, he had discovered the work of James Abbott McNeill Whistler and Claude Monet. Eduard was intrigued to learn that instead of painting landscapes in his studio from memory, the French artist went out into the countryside to paint the actual scene before his eyes, imbuing his pictures with shimmering light and air. Sharing Monet's enchantment with light, Eduard believed that the great painter was working on canvas the way he himself wanted to work with the camera.

Still, although later critics called his work Impressionist or Symbolist, Eduard Steichen had no direct knowledge of such formal movements in those Milwaukee days. He simply read what he could find about painters such as Monet, focusing on the individual artist and his work rather than on his affiliation with any school or trend. By osmosis, Eduard absorbed the culture of his times, but he had no backdrops against which to analyze it, and no mentors in Milwaukee to instruct him in a particular style. Only years later would he come to a formal understanding of Impressionism, best explained by Monet himself:

> *A landscape is only an impression, instantaneous, hence the label they've given us—all because of me, for that matter. I'd submitted something done out of my window at Le Havre, sunlight in the mist with a few masts in the foreground jutting up from the ships below. They wanted a title for the catalog; it couldn't really pass as a view of Le Havre, so I answered, "Put down Impression." Out of that they got impressionism, and the jokes proliferated. . . .*[57]

In the spring of 1898, Eduard discovered another artist who would provide him with inspiration. Thanks to a Milwaukee newspaper, he came across a photograph of Rodin's controversial sculpture of Balzac, "called a monstrosity by some and by others a sack of flour with a head stuck on top." To Eduard, however, it was the most wonderful thing he had ever seen—"not just the statue of a man; it was the very embodiment of a tribute to genius," he exulted. "It looked like a mountain come to life."[58] He immediately began to dream about going to France, where such splendid artists lived and did their work. But for now, he had his own work as a professional lithographer, his skill rewarded with a handsome salary. His parents were very proud of him, for they had brought him to the United States in search of just such an opportunity.

In his expansive dreams, however, Eduard coveted much more than this. By trial and error (and mostly error, he wryly observed), he was mastering some of the logistics of photography, recognizing there, as in painting, the fundamental role of composition—learning how to compose on the ground glass before he made an exposure, and how to manipulate the camera and the print to create on paper the effect he could see so vividly in his mind. Enthralled with the process, he worked nonetheless in a vacuum in Milwaukee, with no mentors or peers in photography. Yet instinctively, he made his solitary way from the clear, functional picture as record to the evocative, moody image as art. In the late 1890s, he was pioneering in concept as much as in technique.

At least, thanks to *Camera Notes,* he had made the discovery that there were kindred spirits at work in his medium. Consequently, when he picked up the November 5, 1898, issue of *Harper's Weekly* to read about the serious American and European photographers whose work had been accepted into the first Philadelphia Photographic Salon, he understood the dramatic significance of the event: The oldest art museum in the United States, the Pennsylvania Academy of the Fine Arts, was giving unprecedented recognition to photographs alive with artistic feeling, thereby validating photography as an art medium. He read that the jury included, among others, the great American painter William Merritt Chase and Stieglitz, the photographer who was busily editing the journal that was the lifeline then for Eduard and other amateur photographers around the country. He thought the Philadelphia Photographic Salon was the "most stimulating and exciting thing" he had yet heard of in photography.[59]

When he read the article to his fellow students at the Art Students' League, one young woman suggested that he enter his photographs in the next salon.[60] Some students laughed at the idea, for he had sent some of his paintings to the Chicago Art Institute and had been rejected.[61] However, Eduard resolved on that November evening that if there was another Philadelphia Photographic Salon, he would most assuredly be counted among the photographers submitting their work.

4

GROPING FOR THE NEW

(1 8 9 8 - 1 9 0 0)

Steichen's work refuses to fit itself into any of the various schools at present in vogue. He is groping for the new.[1]

—SIDNEY ALLAN

TWENTY-YEAR-OLD EDUARD STEICHEN COULD USUALLY be seen on Sundays striding through the bustling municipal parks of Milwaukee, his tall, gaunt frame bristling with energy, his dazzling blue-gray eyes and his ever-present camera probing the faces in the crowd. He was there to take more pictures of the working men, women, and children enjoying a few precious free hours on the sunlit shores of Lake Michigan. His wide grin and his disarming friendliness immediately set people at ease. Women and children gravitated to him, and men liked his frank, respectful manner as he solicited their business.

Already the consummate salesman, Eduard offered to take photographs of individuals or a cluster of families and to sell them prints of the best exposures. For many people, young Steichen captured the first and possibly the only photographic record of their faces. Even today, there may be hidden somewhere in the attics, family albums, and archives of Milwaukee those early unsigned pictures, Eduard Steichen's first camera portraits.

He was coming into his own in 1899, working hard at his lucrative job at the American Fine Art Company and carrying on his rigorous experiments as a novice photographer and painter. His sister, on the other hand, was not faring so well. In fact, her life was miserable. She hated the endless humdrum work in her mother's thriving millinery shop. Lilian had been an outstanding student in Catholic school and then in public school. Stubbornly, she held to her resolve to go on to high school, and, just as stubbornly, her father opposed the idea.

Mary Steichen stood in the middle of this long, often-passionate argument between her bullheaded husband and her brilliant daughter, vainly hoping that Lilian would begin to enjoy the work in the millinery shop. For a seemingly interminable year, Lilian endured it, all the while resenting her father's dogmatic stand and her mother's acquiescence to it. Only Eduard, searching for his own new pathways, understood her.

Feeling most alive when reading good literature, Lilian stole scraps of time for this pursuit. Among her favorite writers were Robert Louis Stevenson, Oliver Goldsmith, Robert Browning, and Ralph Waldo Emerson. She could quote Chaucer, and she loved the "pure poetry" of Percy Bysshe Shelley and John Keats.[2] She studied the German poets in German—especially Heinrich Heine. Lilian read Heine's poems in Germanic script from a thick, worn book until she could quote many from memory—"Du Bist Wie Eine Blume," "The Loreley," "Die Schöne Fischermädchen."[3] From the time she was fifteen until she was twenty, she so loved reading poetry that she tried writing what she called her own "apostrophizings (however crude) to the Stars," and she "labored lovingly setting together little word-melodies with nothing to them but the sensuous music of words."[4] She dreamed of becoming a poet.

Eduard encouraged her, just as she applauded his photographic experiments, for the two of them were extraordinarily sympathetic to each other's hopes and dreams. Delighting in the powerful poetry of nature, they "watched storms come up together." Sometimes he woke her early or kept her up late to accompany him on photographic expeditions to his favorite woods on the outskirts of Milwaukee. She remembered nostalgically how they "made pilgrimages together on moonlit nights to birch woods listening in the Silence for the heavy fall of a dewdrop."[5] Their kindred tastes gave each of them a profound, loyal appreciation for the other's work and spirit.

Lilian, the intellectual, also deeply influenced her brother's cultural views, his reading, and his politics. After she introduced Eduard to the plays of Henrik Ibsen, the young Steichens went on to read and discuss the dramas and essays of George Bernard Shaw and the plays and books written by the mystical Belgian Symbolist author Maurice Maeterlinck, never dreaming then that Eduard would go on to photograph and befriend both of these men.[6] Living amid the growing Social Democratic party movement in Milwaukee, Lilian was particularly interested in Shaw's idealistic socialism, articulated by the Fabian Society. Unlike the revolutionary, often radical activism of many international socialist factions, Shaw and the Fabians advocated gradual social reform, the approach Lilian and her mother found attractive.

Eduard, on the other hand, gravitated to Maeterlinck's internationally popular recent books, *The Treasure of the Humble* and *Wisdom and Destiny*.[7] Deeply drawn to Maeterlinck's fatalistic ideas, Eduard had little, if any, knowledge of Maeterlinck's importance as a Symbolist. One of the most opaque yet pervasive aesthetic crusades ever to infiltrate literature, the visual arts, and music, the Symbolist movement was born when the French Romantic poet Baudelaire fell in love with Edgar Allan Poe's writings and his critical theory and brought them to the attention of the French in 1852.

Disciples of the Symbolist movement infused their sensual poetry, plays, paintings, or music with fantasy—superrational, dreamlike images and motifs, embedded with wildly imaginative metaphors and symbols, some so deeply personal as to be enigmatic and often impenetrable. Extolling the realm of imagination and fantasy as it did, the Symbolist movement was a logical nineteenth-century response to the encroaching power of the machine age and the dehumanizing new industrial society. Since this avant-garde vision demanded new vehicles of transcription, traditional forms in music, art, and literature were stretched, if not wrecked or abandoned, by Symbolist artists such as Maeterlinck, the young Irish poet W. B. Yeats, Wagner, and Ibsen.

But in 1899, uninformed about the milieu in which Maeterlinck wrote, Eduard was simply struck by his words in *Wisdom and Destiny*. The wise man suffers, Maeterlinck wrote, "and suffering forms a constituent part of his wisdom. He will suffer, perhaps, more than most men, for that his nature is far more complete.... He will suffer in his flesh, in his heart, in his spirit; for there are sides in all these that no wisdom on earth can dispute against destiny. And so he accepts his suffering, but is not discouraged thereby."[8] According to Maeterlinck's thesis, wisdom could enable the individual to endure his destiny, if not to govern it.

Eduard stood just then on the brink of adulthood, his passage coinciding with the advent of a new century. The *fin-de-siècle* impulses for reflection and prophecy stirred up melancholy as well as anticipation, cynicism as well as hope. Possessing equal capacities for joy and for sorrow, Eduard had inherited conflicting outlooks: his mother's optimism as well as her defensive powers of denial, and his father's gloomy cynicism and sometimes volatile temper. While a contagious joie de vivre usually governed his daily moods, his ebullient nature could be subdued by moody, brooding introspection. Eduard had long ago turned his back on the Catholic church, but not before he had absorbed from his mother a stoicism to which Maeterlinck seemed to be speaking.

He put it his own way in a letter to his friend Carl Björncrantz, telling him that the world was a "great storehouse of pain" that no human being escaped, and that pain should be viewed as a blessing because out of deep suffering and sorrow could come *"great art."*[9] The record is curiously blank on the issue of the particular pain, suffering, and sorrow Eduard had in mind. A virile, adventurous, independent young man of twenty would almost certainly have experimented sexually, if not romantically, by then, would have broken hearts and had his broken, would have endured the tragic disappointments that haunt the young, and would have had his first bitter tastes of failure.

Lilian and Eduard were reading curiously and eclectically at the turn of the century, innocent of any critical assessment or schools of thought, simply responding to ideas on their own personal terms. But it was impossible to live in Milwaukee in those days without an awareness of a burgeoning political movement—socialism—and there is clear evidence that Eduard, Lilian, and Mary Steichen already counted among their close friends some of the leaders of the expanding socialist movement in Milwaukee, including Victor Berger, head of the Social Democratic party of Wisconsin, party secretary Elizabeth Thomas, and Charles B. Whitnall, a wealthy Milwaukee socialist who was particularly fond of young Lilian with her pensive blue eyes, her radiant smile, and her compelling mind.

In fact, despite the reality that he was closer in age to her parents than to Lilian, Whitnall was falling in love with her. She admired the older man, who, after he grew a beard, looked so much like the "old-master pictures of Christ" that Eduard's "greatest aspiration was to paint a Christ" with Whitnall as the model.[10] Eduard never painted Whitnall, whose growing affection for Lilian was a matter of frequent discussion between mother and daughter. Mary was resigning herself to the fact that her two independent children were unlikely to settle down anytime soon to conventional lives.

The Steichens watched Milwaukee socialism close up, in daily action, understanding the movement idealistically as well as practically. Many of the German immigrants inhabiting their Milwaukee neighborhood had left the old country to escape the antisocialist dictums of the Bismarck regime, bringing with them deep-rooted commitments to social justice and parity for working people. The Luxembourg-born, German-speaking elder Steichens themselves were members of the working class, whose faces Eduard photographed on their one day of respite each week. Eduard was one of many Milwaukee apprentices whose work had its root in the proud German tradition of skilled craftsmen, and the Steichens believed that skilled workers deserved strong trade unions to protect and advance their interests. At Social Democratic party headquarters in Milwaukee, Victor Berger and his compatriots worked to calibrate the often-conflicting interests of business owners, trade unions, and workers.

In her mother's hat shop, Lilian understood all too well how unfulfilling work could squelch the worker's spirit. Still, she kept at it, because their mother had taught Eduard and Lilian from childhood the discipline of hard work, along with a deep respect for human dignity and equality. But she had also taught them about dreams and ambition, and the gifted young Steichens, working diligently to produce commercial lithographs and ladies' hats in Milwaukee, were all the while, in Sidney Allan's words, "groping for the new." Lilian had promised herself an education surpassing the norm for young women of her time, while Eduard planned for himself a great career as a painter and photographer. They lacked mentors then, or models to emulate, but they had determination and originality, they had each other, and, most of the time, they had the wholehearted support of their remarkable mother.

They were dreamers, all three of them. Mary's dreams had gotten them to the United States and to their stable, comfortable life in Milwaukee. Eduard's dreams were increasingly visible in his growing portfolio of photographs and paintings, and he had recently resolved that he absolutely had to go to Paris to study art. Another plan was taking shape, perhaps inspired by Rodin's *Balzac,* or by painted portraits by Whistler and other artists he admired, or by such reverential literary studies of great men as Emerson's *Representative Men* (1850)—biographical portraits of Shakespeare, Plato, Goethe, Swedenborg, Napoléon, and Montaigne, with Emerson's reflections on the "uses" of great men.[11]

Eduard may also have known some of Elbert Hubbard's popular *Little Journeys,* 170 booklets written by the flamboyant soap tycoon, popular philosopher, and disciple of William Morris. Hubbard's essays, published by his Roycroft Press in emulation of Morris's Kelmscott Press, were illustrated by lithographs or etchings of such figures as William Morris, Alfred Tennyson, Benjamin Disraeli, and Robert Browning. In any event, artistic homage to great men was in vogue, and Eduard decided that he would apply a new idiom by meeting and photographing great artists—painters, sculptors, writers, and composers. He began to scheme about his journey to Europe and to save every possible dollar to finance it.

Meanwhile, sixteen-year-old Lilian spent her days trimming and selling hats and performing other frustrating duties in her mother's store, all the while dreaming of her own future. Just as art was her brother's passion, education was hers. If public school was out of the question, she would have to find a Catholic school—and one away from home, if possible. Far away. With no one to advise her, she made an arbitrary choice: She knew that the mother of one of her friends had attended the Ursuline Academy, a convent school in Chatham, Ontario. That school was far enough away from Milwaukee and John Peter and Mary. It would do just fine. Getting the address from her friend's mother, Lilian wrote to ask for information.

Then she energetically renewed her campaign to return to school, ultimately persuading her mother to allow her to enroll at Ursuline; together, they chipped away at her father's resistance until he finally relented. In the end, he had to concede that even he could not justify keeping his daughter from a convent, if that was where God had chosen for her to go. So it was that in September of 1899 Lilian left her brother, her parents, and the stultifying millinery shop and matriculated at Ursuline Academy in Canada. There she studied fifteen subjects, including science, mathematics, and languages—German, Latin, and, for three hours daily, French.[12] At first, she was gloriously happy.

Eighteen ninety-nine was a momentous year for the young Steichens. Lilian had her freedom at last, and her chance at further education, and Eduard sent off his first pictures to be juried in a photographic exhibition—the second Philadelphia Photographic Salon, scheduled for October 21 to November 18, 1899. According to the entry materials, only photographs in which there was "distinct evidence of individual artistic feeling and execution" would be accepted.[13]

As Eduard would later learn, he and other photographers could thank Alfred Stieglitz for the landmark existence of the Philadelphia Photographic Salons. Stieglitz had been struggling for years "for the recognition of photography as a new medium of expression, to be respected in its own right, on the same basis as any other art form."[14] He had also fought for an American international photographic salon in the mode of the prestigious European salons, where expert juries chose works to be exhibited and the only prize was the honor of exhibition.[15]

With no patience for mediocrity, Stieglitz always dreamed on a grand scale. His dreams were vindicated when the Philadelphia Photographic Society and the Pennsylvania Academy of the Fine Arts announced that they would jointly sponsor the first annual Philadelphia Photographic Salon in 1898, endowing it with the principles of the London and Paris salons and exhibiting pictures solely because of their artistic merit. Individual artistic feeling and execution were the criteria for choosing the photographs to be displayed. Because the painters appointed to the jury had been too busy to assist with the final judging, the three photographers selected the prints. There had been heated dispute, however, over the very idea of painters judging photographs in the 1898 salon; how would painters feel, some argued, if photographers were invited to determine which paintings were chosen for an exhibition?

As a result, new rules defined the protocol of the second Philadelphia Photographic Salon in 1899. The jury was composed of photographers only—suffragette Frances B. Johnston, whose uncle was President Grover Cleveland; Philadelphian Henry Troth; the wealthy Boston aesthete and dilettante Fred Holland Day; and two newcomers who had dazzled the first salon—Gertrude Käsebier, a forty-seven-year-old mother and former housewife from Iowa, and Clarence White, age twenty-eight, grocery store bookkeeper from Newark, Ohio. Visitors to the prestigious Second Philadelphia Photographic Salon would see the work of the best "pictorialists" in the world.

Eduard Steichen was determined to be included among them. When he had "ordained" himself "a would be exhibitor" at the next Philadelphia Photographic Salon, he wrote in his autobiography, he had to decide strategically which photographs to submit. He opted for "prudence," reasoning, "It seemed unwise to compete with older, more experienced, and better photographers than I."[16] In Milwaukee, where the only photographers Eduard knew took pictures for commerce, not art, he analyzed the photographs that had been accepted by the first Philadelphia Photographic Salon, turning to *Camera Notes* to study the stunning portraits by Käsebier and the exotic studies of faces and scenes by Day. He already admired reproductions of Alfred Stieglitz's masterful work, but he had yet to see White's incandescent landscapes and portraits. All Eduard read told him that the photographs by these four originals had been the highlights of the first Philadelphia Photographic Salon, and he knew right away that the key to any acceptance of his own work for the second salon would be originality, not imitation.

Deliberately and objectively, he scrutinized his photographs in search of prints that differed from those he knew to have been hung in the first salon. He would steer away from the crisp composition of Stieglitz's landscapes, as well as the clear, painterly contours of Käsebier's lyrical portraits. At last, Eduard settled on three prints: a moody, misty landscape; a composition study in which he had used himself as a model; and a portrait of a fellow student from the Milwaukee Art Students' League.[17] In later years, he remembered submitting only the two portraits, but reviews of the exhibition described three Steichen entries. The landscape he chose was one of his series of soft-focus images of the woods near Milwaukee in autumn, most likely the study of leaves drifting on the placid sheen of a lake, later published in *Camera Notes* with another Steichen landscape and the portraits he remembered entering in the salon.

The first, "*Self Portrait. Milwaukee. 1898.*" is intent on design, not self-revelation. Steichen's vague, tall form bleeds into the right margin of the print. The features of his face blur into the shadows. On the wall behind his right shoulder, a small black picture frame echoes the lines of the print itself. Steichen, clad in white shirt and dark slacks, is only a figure in the design, object, not subject. The wall in the background is textured with light, as is the floor in the foreground, where one of his shoes glistens as it reflects the light. His hands are completely invisible. The man in the frame could be anyone; he is inconsequential, except as part of the clean, elegantly simple composition. Yet young Eduard must have relished the image of himself in the shadows, on the brink of emerging, one foot planted firmly forward in the "doorway" of the photograph.

His second portrait entry, *Lady in the Doorway,* had earlier won high praise from his fellow students at the Art Students' League. He had taken that photograph in the summer of 1897 at Gordon Place, the home of a fellow art student. During that summer, the student's mother opened a small house on her handsome estate on the Milwaukee River to the struggling members of the Milwaukee Art Students' League. They had celebrated their good fortune with a housewarming, adorning the cottage with boughs and branches. Eduard arrived early that first day, hurriedly setting up his camera to capture the sunlight spilling in through the cottage door, and when one of the young women walked in, he asked her to pause in the doorway. As he set his camera and checked her image on the ground glass, he experimented, first pulling her in and then out of focus. He liked the feeling of light when the picture was out of focus, and he chose to make it that way.

Like *Self Portrait, Lady in the Doorway* is a composition, not a depiction. The picture plays with light and dark, form and shadow. The anonymous woman framed in the doorway is herself woven of light and dark, pinned to the floor by her shadow, yet formless and free in the vibrant light.

Once he had made these choices, Eduard invested considerable care in preparing the prints. He knew that the pictures accepted in the first salon were much larger than his prints, which he had made on four-by-five-inch plates. However, because he lacked the knowledge and equipment to enlarge his own prints, he asked a young Milwaukee portrait photographer with a professional studio to do the work for him, hovering in his friend's darkroom until the pictures were meticulously printed to his satisfaction on cream-tinted Royal bromide paper, rough in texture. Eduard then framed them simply, with bold black borders edging

Groping for the New (1898–1900)

the two portraits; there was, from the first, an instinctive spare elegance in his presentation. Finally, he carefully wrapped his cache of pictorial photographs and sent them off to Philadelphia.[18]

The distinguished jury for the second salon took its work very seriously, rejecting 780 of the 962 entries, finally settling on 182 photographs that, in their combined estimation, met the highest standards of photographic art in the world. While few European photographers had sent their work over to the first salon in Philadelphia in 1898, word of the successful event drew parcels of entries from across the Atlantic in much greater numbers in 1899. Members of the jury and of the Linked Ring, Britain's distinguished honorary society for progressive photographers, were invited to participate in the 1899 salon without having to subject their work to review. The Linked Ring already boasted a stellar list of photographers: J. Craig Annan, Robert Demachy, Baron Adolf de Meyer, the Austrian Heinrich Kühn, Stieglitz, and Rudolf Eickemeyer, Jr., of the United States.

Almost all of the leading continental pictorial photographers exhibited in Philadelphia in 1899, and Clarence White of the jury contributed multiple photographs, as did Stieglitz, Käsebier, and Day. Käsebier and White had been the outstanding newcomers in the 1898 salon. Following in their footsteps in 1899 was a lanky young nobody from Milwaukee, Wisconsin—Eduard Steichen, a twenty-year-old lithographer, teaching himself photography in his spare time. He must have been jubilant when his letter of acceptance arrived. All three of his prints were chosen to be hung in the company of work by the greatest photographers in the world.

The critics, however, were generally harder on the second salon than the first, and there were mixed reviews for many photographs, including two of the three by Steichen. In his thirty-five-page *Camera Notes* article on the salon, photographer and attorney Joseph T. Keiley singled out Eduard's work, noting that:

> *[Of his] three pictures, two call for remark,* Portrait Study, *No. 273, which was an original and effective treatment of a portrait study . . . and* The Lady in the Doorway, *No. 275, which was also original, if not artistic or serious. I am inclined to think that Mr. Steichen himself rather regarded it as a picture puzzle, for he*

on more than one occasion, I am told, set it on end and asked his friends to guess what it was. There were those who termed it ultra impressionistic; *to me is [sic] seemed ridiculously freakish.*[19]

The Philadelphia Photographic Salon marked the boundary between Eduard's dabbling as a gifted amateur and his future career as an innovative professional. Moreover, he now had his first serious notice as a photographer—of all places, in the wonderful pages of *Camera Notes,* his bible in the Milwaukee Public Library. It surely seemed a miracle that in January of 1900, just five years after he had bought his first camera, and three years after he first discovered Stieglitz's quarterly journal, Eduard was reading about his own work in those authoritative pages. "*Ultra* impressionistic" or "freakish"? Not "serious," not "artistic"? But, at least, "original" and "effective." "The prints were accepted and hung by the jury," he wrote many years later in his autobiography. "I never heard of any bells being rung for them, but I did receive a letter from Clarence White, saying that my two pictures showed originality—'a quality which needs to be encouraged.' "[20]

Eduard and White began to correspond occasionally, and they would find over the years of their friendship that they had much in common, personally and artistically. Eduard came to a genuine admiration of the artistry of Clarence White's photographs, despite the derision expressed by some critics who could not take seriously the work of this man who earned his living as a bookkeeper in a village in Ohio. White lived on so meager a budget then that he had little money to invest in his pictures. Each week, he could set aside only enough to buy two six-and-a-half-by-eight-and-a-half-inch plates. All week long, therefore, as he labored over the accounts for the grocery firm in Newark, White envisioned the two pictures he would capture with that week's precious allotment of plates, planning them meticulously. The discipline enforced by the constraints of time and money yielded luminous images.

"Mr. White is a bookkeeper, but he has a soul which soars far above ledgers and daybooks," his hometown newspaper observed in 1898.[21] There was a fine integrity in White's photographs, a rare sensitivity to the subtleties of nature and the constantly changing interplay of light and shadow, qualities that Eduard strived to capture in his own work. Like

Eduard, White was also completely self-taught, working in the heartland of the country, driven solely by his own passion, talent, and instinct.[22]

Heartened by his first national recognition as a photographer, and an artistic photographer at that, Eduard promised himself that as soon as possible after his twenty-first birthday on March 27, 1900, he would make his temporary departure from the New World and sail for the Old World to study art in Paris. He would look up the great painters and photographers in France and England—men such as the Frenchman Robert Demachy, who was a leader in the battle to establish the artistic integrity of photography. Revealing how even the allies in that fight warred among themselves, English photographer and critic A. Horsley Hinton had just written a barbed attack on Demachy and other photographers who were "devoted to the pictorial application of the process" of "art photography," but who backed down in the "face of intolerant criticism" and "with more show of diplomacy and judgment than of courage" abandoned the term "art photography" to call the new movement the more nebulous "Pictorial Photography."[23]

Whatever the name, Eduard Steichen eagerly embraced the principles of the movement, knowing that at last, he was an official member of the crusade.

Lilian and Eduard celebrated his wonderful achievement in the letters traveling back and forth between Milwaukee and Chatham, Ontario. In the fall and winter of 1899, Lilian was thriving in her convent school, immediately impressing the Ursuline sisters with the energy she lavished on her studies and her religion. She entered the convent school "with a fiery faith," studying the Bible and the *Confessions* of St. Augustine, spending some entire nights prostrate on the cold stone floor in front of the altar with the nuns themselves.[24] A brilliant student, zealously conscientious in her studies and excelling in all disciplines, she brought to her life at the convent school an intensity that touched and sometimes worried her teachers.

Ultimately, however, it was her appetite for reading that brought her face-to-face with a shocking moral dilemma. From a magazine article by Mark Twain she learned about the white slavery that forced women into prostitution. Horrified, she began to question the faith she had inherited from her pious mother and admired in the Ursuline nuns. How could God, as she had been taught to perceive Him, permit such evil? What kind of God was this, what kind of religion? All winter long, Lilian wrestled privately with the terrible questions stabbing her conscience. The rational powers of her remarkable intellect now shook the trusting belief instilled during her sheltered Catholic girlhood. Like her brother, she was endowed with prodigious powers of mind and heart, and this could be a curse as well as a blessing. Already, she had been compelled to choose between her parents' approval and goodwill and her own essential intellectual growth. Later in her life, she would choose to sublimate herself to family, but now she elected the supremacy of her own spirit.

She was torn in 1899 between her new ideas as a budding scientist and socialist, and those instilled by her childhood grounding in her parents' religion. Consequently, before the school term ended, Lilian concluded that she would have to renounce the faith that she felt had betrayed her, just as it had somehow alienated her brother during his days at Pio Nono. While Eduard's brash self-assurance was sometimes taken for arrogance, Lilian exuded a serene, graceful confidence once she had determined a course of action. She wanted to finish the school year; she would bide her time, waiting until she was at home in Milwaukee at the end of the term to share her momentous decision with her mother and father.

Over the years, as Mary's millinery business flourished, the Steichens changed addresses several times in Milwaukee, always moving to larger and better quarters, although staying in the German community in the near north side of the city. At the turn of the century, they were living on Water Street, and Eduard now lived and worked in his own studio nearby at 342½ Seventh Street.[25] There, he could come and go independently, entertain his friends, and devote himself to painting and photography in those hours when he was not working at the lithographic firm. During those precious free hours, Eduard threw himself into further photography experiments, now using a larger camera, in part so that he would not have to depend on another photographer for enlargements.

Informed by articles by Robert Demachy in *Camera Notes* and elsewhere, Eduard was also experimenting with the gum-bichromate process. He was drawn to the economy of it: Rather than using expensive silver or platinum paper for his prints, he could coat inexpensive paper with watercolor and gum arabic and then sensitize it by brushing the paper with bichromate of potash, which dried to become light-sensitive. He could control the brush strokes to achieve a desired result. A thick mixture would yield a granular effect, which set off pictures "representing broad masses of light and dark," while a thinner mixture created a more subtle backdrop for his images.[26] Eduard played imaginatively with the process, making prints in two different tints and even printing a portrait entitled *Polly Horter* on charcoal paper, purposely creating a photograph to resemble a charcoal drawing.

His life was full of unremitting work, but it was work that he loved. He moved from mode to mode producing art lithographs as well as commercial lithographs; pictorial as well as naturalistic photographs; landscape and portrait paintings in oil and in watercolor. In 1900, after he attended a concert given in Milwaukee by the Polish pianist and composer Ignacy Paderewski, Eduard made a lithograph of the event and it was soon exhibited in a window at a Gimbel's store. When Eduard heard that the lithograph had been purchased by Mrs. Arthur Robinson, a neighbor of the Steichens, he called on her to ask her why she liked it.

Because it was very good, she told him, adding that while he might be unknown now, he would not be for long. She asked to see more of his work, and, impressed, she offered to host an exhibit in her Milwaukee parlor. There, Eduard Steichen had his first one-man show, makeshift as it was, with more than fifty sketches, paintings, and photographs propped up on Mrs. Robinson's sofa, chairs, tables, and even on the piano. Friends and neighbors dropped in to see the avant-garde work of John Peter and Mary Steichen's extraordinary son. Some of those staid and proper neighbors must have concluded that while Eduard Steichen might be an artist, at least he was not a shiftless, lazy artist; after all, he had a regular job, a good salary. Even though many of his paintings and photographs were fuzzy and murky, instead of plain and clear, he would probably get better with practice, they thought.

Eduard's photographs quickly received new attention: He could soon say that his work had been shown in Philadelphia, Milwaukee, and Newark, Ohio, for Clarence White had invited Steichen to display his pictures in 1899 in the second Newark Camera Club Exhibition. His recognition spread further after Eduard read about the Chicago Photographic Salon, sponsored by the Chicago Society of Amateur Photographers and the Art Institute of Chicago, to be held at the Art Institute April 3–18, 1900. He eagerly "took the bull by the horns" and entered ten prints, the maximum allowed by the jury.[27] Jury member White was on hand when the prints were unpacked, and he predicted in a letter to Eduard that all ten would be accepted as a block.

Not all jurors agreed, however. Eduard remembered that three of the ten were chosen, but the catalog of the exhibition cites only two, an enigmatic study of a beautiful young woman, entitled *Keats,* and *The Frost-covered Pool,* apparently retitled *The Pool—Evening* after the Chicago show.[28] *Keats* perplexed many who saw it, for the young woman with huge dark eyes holds a book with a " 'soul's awakening' clasp"—her copy of Keats, and hence, the name of the picture, Steichen had to explain.[29]

He made *The Pool—Evening,* a platinum print, in Milwaukee in 1899, photographing a pool at twilight in the woods outside the city. As he described it, this was, "in fact, a picture of just a puddle of water with mud clots protruding."[30] The effect is far more poetic. The slim bare trees in the background are framed against the day's last light and are reflected in the pool glistening in the foreground. There is liquid motion in the pool—visible ripples, the elongating shadows of trees, the clusters of dying leaves swimming toward the viewer. The mood is soft, quiet, evocative of the suspension of daylight and its modulation into night, and of the decline of autumn into winter.

Alfred Stieglitz was represented in the Chicago show by ten photographs, and his compatriot Joseph T. Keiley wrote in the foreword to the exhibition catalog that the Chicago Photographic Salon was designed to "demonstrate the artistic possibilities of photography as a means of giving expression to the individual appreciation of and feeling for that which is pictorially beautiful." He pointed out that Chicago was the second major American city, after Philadelphia, to endorse pictorial photography as an art form by hosting a major salon. Furthermore, he observed, "the art loving public of Chicago" would see "the choicest collection of artistic photographs ever shown in America."[31]

Many of the critics who saw the exhibit attacked Eduard Steichen's *The Frost-Covered Pool* because it was not "properly" focused, but critic Charles Caffin dissented, noting that the photograph "was the work of one who had been deeply moved by the solemn quiet of the scene, and had succeeded in communicating the impression to his print."[32] Indeed, Caffin perceived the young artist's expressed intent: "Emotional reaction to the qualities of places, things, and people," Steichen wrote of those early photographs, "became the principal goal in my photography," adding that he was an Impressionist "without knowing it."[33]

Mary Steichen could not contain her pride in her children; she shared with her neighbors the wondrous news of Eduard's success in the photographic salons and of Lilian's stellar marks at Ursuline Academy. The more reserved John Peter was no doubt relieved that his headstrong, unorthodox son and daughter were finally winning accolades for their work. But his temper was about to be sorely tested, first by Eduard and then by Lilian.

For a year, Eduard had been hoarding the funds to finance his pilgrimage to Paris. In the spring of 1900, soon after his acceptance in the Chicago exhibition and the celebration of his twenty-first birthday, he broke the news to his mother and father that he had decided to resign his good job at the American Fine Art Company and travel to Europe to study art. Carl Björncrantz, his fellow student at the Milwaukee Art Students' League, would accompany him.

John Peter was outraged. Had he not traveled at great cost to this new country in order to make a place here for his family? Had he not toiled in the copper mines until his health was broken? Had he and Eduard's mother not sacrificed to clothe and educate their son? Had he not endured Eduard's wild ideas about painting and photography? How could Eduard give up such a fine, steady job, such a generous salary, such a future? John Peter was shocked into disbelief. He could only conclude once more that Eduard "was crazy."[34]

As her husband stormed on, Mary listened, understood, and enthusiastically affirmed her son's plans. She also offered to augment his savings so as to be sure her boy would have enough money for the year abroad. She then set to work helping him prepare for the journey, even purchasing a large scrapbook to hold all the news clippings she was convinced were to come, so full of faith was she that her son would achieve great fame and success in Europe.

Another steadfast supporter was Clarence White, who had helped to discover Eduard Steichen, becoming his first champion. White continued to send Eduard encouraging letters and also wrote to Stieglitz to praise the young man's work. When Eduard told White that his long-planned journey to France would soon begin, White sent him a letter of introduction, urging him to call on Stieglitz as he passed through New York en route to Paris.

Before he sailed, however, Eduard had to obtain his naturalization papers. In Luxembourg, he had been christened Eduard; his baptismal name was Eduard Jean Steichen, after his father, Jean-Pierre, and his godfather, Jean Steichen. In 1900, he signed the naturalization papers "Edward J. Steichen," although for years he continued to sign his work and his letters with the old spelling.[35] While others sometimes used the English spelling *Edward* during those years, Steichen himself kept to the French *Eduard*, particularly during his sojourn abroad.

A sign of that ambivalence about his name appeared in the text of *Camera Notes* in January of 1901 with the first reproduction of his photographs, thanks most likely to the proofreader's lack of precision. The full-page photogravure of one landscape was credited to Edward J. Steichen of Milwaukee; the self-portrait and another landscape, reproduced as halftones, carried the name Eduard J. Steichen; the halftone print of *Lady in the Doorway* bore the name of E. J. Steichen. Until after World War I, however, he would prefer to spell his name Eduard Steichen.

In late April of 1900, Eduard took an emotional leave of his parents and Milwaukee, traveling to New York by way of Chatham, Ontario, so he could say good-bye to his little sister. Shortly afterward, Lilian packed her books and other belongings and returned to Milwaukee to give up her life as a convent student and as a Catholic. The house and the city must have seemed sadly empty without Eduard, now on his way to Paris, and she must have longed for her brother's support as she confronted John Peter and Mary with her own startling news. She was leaving the convent school and the church, she informed her shocked parents. She was renouncing her faith, and theirs.

Lilian never forgot how her father "in his expansive Luxembourgeois, shouted about the deceit of schooling and what it had done" to his daughter.[36] Had he not opposed this silly, dangerous idea of education for women? Had he not predicted that no good would come of it? For once, even Mary could not support her daughter's action. Weeping and angry, she feared for Lilian's mortal soul, and she forced her reluctant daughter to visit a Jesuit priest to confess her heresy. As the priest interviewed Lilian, he was convinced of her sincerity, and so he could console Mary Steichen: "As long as the child believes that what she does is right, she is still one of us. She has lost faith but it will come back."[37]

With Eduard far away, Lilian faced an unhappy summer alone with her parents' disappointment and anger. No matter what the priest and her mother thought, she had relinquished her faith, but she had not for a moment renounced her dream of a rigorous formal education. Paying no attention to her parents' ongoing complaints, and undaunted by the fact that at the age of seventeen she had dropped out of the Ursuline Academy before completing the high school program, she decided to take the entrance examinations for admission to the University of Illinois. She gathered all the entrance information, found the textbooks for the required high school courses she had not yet taken, and "at home by herself" began to master the necessary work.[38]

During that lonely summer in Milwaukee, Lilian taught herself advanced algebra and geometry, and she studied French and German grammar, reading all the required books for three years' study of German. She compressed into her summer regimen the equivalent of one year's course work in Latin and botany, and she plowed through a year's worth of books for courses in English, American history, and ancient history. All in all, over the space of that summer, Lilian conquered the course work for four years of high school, and by late summer, she deemed herself ready for the entrance tests. On September 1, 1900, she was notified that she had passed the University of Illinois entrance examinations with an average score of 85 percent.[39]

A skeptical Mary had promised her daughter that she could go to the University in Urbana if she passed the tests. Lilian was elated; she loved books and wanted to live surrounded by them, perhaps even to write them. For now, she intended to study library science at the University of Illinois.[40] Even her father could see that this was a practical dream. At summer's end, Lilian bade her parents good-bye once more, leaving Milwaukee to join 289 other women and 680 men to enroll in the university's undergraduate school in Urbana, Illinois.

Never mind the cost, financial or personal. Lilian Steichen was fiercely committed to her dreams of knowledge and independence. Meanwhile, her brother had embarked on his own odyssey. With or without their father's endorsement, Eduard and Lilian Steichen were striding resolutely toward new horizons.

5

PATHFINDERS

(1 9 0 0)

I believe in Steichen's future as a painter, even though I naturally can form no judgment about his color sense until I have seen his pictures in the original.

As a pictorial photographer he already stands at the summit. He is a pathfinder.[1]

—ERNST JUHL

WHEN EDUARD STEICHEN LEFT MILWAUKEE THAT April of 1900, his mother's tearful "Good-bye, Gaesjack" in his ears, he was a completely self-made original.[2] The German critic Ernst Juhl, for one, perceived the young artist's uniqueness, correctly noting that until he went to Paris to study in 1900, "Steichen did not have the opportunity to see art or any pictorial photography. He had no academic schooling in painting, but worked at it alone for two years. That was probably just as well, for he might have been turned aside from his own path if he had followed the example of others."[3]

Critics looking at his work in the early years in Paris pronounced Steichen a Symbolist or an Impressionist, or both. While it may be argued that those motifs emerged consciously or subconsciously in some of his work after 1900, this was not true of his seminal work, as he himself pointed out. Of course, the more art criticism he read in *Camera Notes* and elsewhere, the more he learned about current trends. Reading one critic's attack on his work in the Chicago Photographic Salon, Steichen speculated in 1900 that the man must have learned about Impressionism from a "member of some ladies 'art-club.' "⁴ But movements did not so much shape Steichen as Steichen shaped his own singular way, imbibing what was in the air of the times and, through unrelenting hard work, honoring his own original artistic impulses.

One of those impulses had already inspired him to lead his friends in forming the Milwaukee Art Students' League in hopes of filling a void in their city, and the experiment took hold so vigorously that by 1907 the Art Students' League would become the Wisconsin School of Art, employing a full-time director. By 1962, the seeds young Steichen had planted nearly seventy years earlier had grown into the School of Fine Arts at the University of Wisconsin in Milwaukee.⁵

His characteristic farsighted vision was undergirded by a gift for energetic, practical organization: Once Steichen grabbed hold of a dream, he could figure out how to implement it, charismatically engaging the support of others in the process. Still, by 1900 he had gotten as much out of Milwaukee and the Art Students' League as they had to give him. Consequently, he turned his back on the artistic backwaters of the Midwest and headed to Europe, driven by the restless need for a cultural atmosphere friendlier to innovation, yet steeped in the finest traditions of the past.

Like his doting mother, Steichen was equipped with a bold, adventurous spirit and a rollicking sense of humor.⁶ He had not been in New York since Mary Steichen carried him off the ship in 1881, when he was not yet two years old. Now, to his surprise and pleasure, one of the first sights to greet him on arrival in Manhattan was a huge outdoor advertisement designed after his own Cascarets poster. Covering "the whole side of a warehouse building six stories high and a block long" was the pretty young woman he had painted at the American Fine Art Company back in Milwaukee, sleeping on her C-shaped bed, touting the virtues of Cascarets laxatives.⁷ "I decided then and there," he wrote, "that New York must be the art center of the world."⁸

Steichen had important business to transact in New York before he and Carl Björncrantz boarded their ship for the crossing to Europe and that other art center, Paris. First, he managed to get an appointment to show his paintings to the great American painter William Merritt Chase, who "received him kindly and encouraged him in his resolve."⁹ Then, armed with the letter of introduction from Clarence White and a portfolio of photographs as well as paintings, Steichen went to call on Alfred Stieglitz, whom White had praised as "the leader in the struggle for the recognition of pictorial photography as an art."[10]

Charles Caffin was writing then that Stieglitz was "the incarnation of the movement—artist, prophet, pathfinder."[11] Steichen must have felt that he was going to Mecca when he "strutted" into the Camera Club of New York, his bundle of paintings and photographs under his arm, to call on the brilliant photographer who would ultimately play such a crucial role in his own life in photography.[12]

That spring afternoon, Stieglitz, then thirty-six, and his fellow photographer Joseph Keiley were mounting a show of photographs by members of the Camera Club. The unofficial archivist and historian of Stieglitz's work, Keiley shared a distinction with Clarence White: They were the only two photographers who actually collaborated with Stieglitz to take photographs. Steichen was thrilled to meet Keiley, who had so recently reviewed his own entries in the Philadelphia Photographic Salon in *Camera Notes*.[13] Because Stieglitz and Keiley frequently designed and judged photography exhibitions together, Stieglitz left matters in Keiley's hands that day so he could spend an hour with this intense young stranger from Milwaukee.

Already the dominant figure in the burgeoning photography scene in New York, Stieglitz had been born in Hoboken, New Jersey, in 1864, but had emigrated in 1881 to Germany, his parents' homeland, because his father wanted his children to receive a continental education. Stieglitz's wealthy, cultured parents gave him material and intellectual independence, but only up to a point: Edward Stieglitz decreed that his gifted son Alfred would study mechanical engineering at Berlin Polytechnic.[14] There, Professor Hermann Wilhelm Vogel, chief of the Photo-Mechanical Laboratory, directed young Stieglitz toward a course in theoretical photography. It would, he promised, be practical in the study of engineering.[15]

Perhaps because his domineering father painted and collected paintings, Stieglitz took no interest in that art, but he fell in love instantly with the process of photography. Tall, slim, athletic, with intense dark eyes and thick, unruly hair, he photographed extremely well himself, often exposing his striking profile to the camera's eye. Still, in Berlin in 1883, as a nineteen-year-old engineering student, Stieglitz squandered most of his prodigious energy "playing billiards, chess, and sometimes, cards, at the Cafe Bauer; and playing the piano, seeing something of mixed society, and attending the races, the theaters, the concerts, and the opera."[16] He read avidly, however, particularly the work of the Russians—Pushkin, Turgenev, and Tolstoy. When he discovered the naturalism of Zola, he spent one whole night reading *Madeleine Ferát* aloud to his friends. That capacity for total immersion in a subject defined him.

Fascinated with the magic of the darkroom, Stieglitz bought a small box camera with a single lens in a Berlin camera shop, and he promptly registered to take a course with Professor Vogel at Berlin Polytechnic in photochemistry—the study of chemical changes resulting from radiant energy. Professor Vogel was then hard at work experimenting with "orthochromatic plates," striving to achieve a color photographic process that would rival black and white in balance and clarity. Stieglitz worked with his professor for two years in his painstaking experiments, making photograph after photograph, seeking to render images in authentic colors, probably, he said, becoming in the process "the first amateur to use these 'color sensitive' plates in his own work."[17]

Although Stieglitz's immediate passion for photography quickly dwarfed any remaining impulses toward mechanical engineering, he continued his work with Professor Vogel, whose pragmatic interest in photography, articulated in his *Handbook of the Practice and Art of Photography* (1875), must have led young Stieglitz to perceive a distinct demarcation line between photography as science and photography as art. Vogel promoted photography as a tool used to render exact reproductions of machinery, blueprints and maps for the engineer, and authentic, detailed copies of paintings, sculpture, and architecture. Stieglitz, on the other hand, quickly came to see the camera as an instrument for artistic expression. Consequently, he worked in two laboratories—one, the city, which he began to probe intimately with his camera; the other, the university chemistry classes, which he took solely for what they could teach him about the volatile and elusive process of printing photographs.

Predestined to love the camera, Stieglitz said, he took to it "as a musician takes to the piano or a painter to canvas."[18] He was obsessed with the artistic potential of photography, yet, thanks to Professor Vogel, he comprehended with a keen, informed pragmatism how dependently the art had to lean on the science. Vogel demonstrated that symbiotic relationship with such technical innovations as his method for retouching collodion negatives rather than positives, thereby eliminating the cumbersome handwork of retouching each individual print. Through this labor-saving process, Vogel's name became a household word to grateful portrait photographers around the world. It was fitting that Stieglitz, the father of artistic photography, served his apprenticeship to Vogel, whom he considered the father of scientific photography.[19]

In 1890, Stieglitz returned from Europe to his family's home in New York City a photographer and a visionary, thereafter devoting his life not so much to making photographs, which he did masterfully, but to making photography a respected and legitimate art form. With his firsthand knowledge of the trends and schools of photography in Europe, he advocated the establishment of American salons on the scale of the salons in Paris, Vienna, and London, which displayed the work of talented photographers. He began to champion pictorial photography, quickly becoming one of the foremost American proponents of artistic photography, which transcended the more conventional scientific, technical, or commercial uses of the medium.

His visible, outspoken work as editor of the *American Amateur Photographer* and then of *Camera Notes* quickly launched Stieglitz on a world stage, from which he sustained an immense correspondence, firing off letters to critics such as Sadakichi Hartmann (also known as Sidney Allan) and Charles H. Caffin and to other photographers, such as Fred Holland Day in Boston, Robert Demachy in Paris, and A. Horsley Hinton in London. Fiercely competitive, Stieglitz staked out his territory. Before long, he would consider the uninhibited Day his adversary. Not only did Day's mastery of the camera match, if not surpass, his own, but since Day, too, was bent on organizing exhibitions of photography, the two would thrust and parry for years over the domain they both sought to dominate.[20] Soon Eduard Steichen would find himself unwittingly entangled in the conflict between these two master photographers.

Stieglitz scathingly disapproved of Day's flamboyant experiments, such as his panoramic pageants for the camera, reminiscent of the epics the panorama painters achieved on canvas. In 1898, for instance, Day had set up his camera on a knoll near Boston and staged the Passion of Our Lord, playing the leading role of Christ, surrounded by a throng of extras at the simulated Calvary. To look the part, he had grown a long beard, starved himself to emaciation, designed a crown of thorns, and had himself roped to a cross made with wooden nails carved by a Syrian carpenter. These elaborate logistics yielded his remarkable photographic series *Seven Last Words of Christ*.

Both Day and Stieglitz attracted a growing number of disciples, and Stieglitz usually formed immediate opinionated impressions of the young artists who came to him for advice. He was a busy man, after all, and so got straight to the point with Eduard Steichen. "What have you got under your arm?" Stieglitz inquired, and Eduard pulled out his work—"a portfolio of platinum prints, sketches in oil, lithographs, pen-and-ink, pencil and charcoal drawings."[21] Although Stieglitz had seen Steichen's photographs in the Philadelphia and Chicago salons, he had not seen his paintings before, but he had long believed that the American photographic movement needed the presence of a painter-photographer whose dual expertise would lend further legitimacy to the campaign on behalf of pictorial photography.

Before him now stood a thin, awestruck young artist, fresh off the train from the heartland, his blue eyes flashing out of an angular face, his large hands holding out some beautiful work. Would Stieglitz view young Eduard Steichen as rival or disciple? Fortunately, he liked the young man at once. In fact, Steichen, fifteen years his junior, reminded Stieglitz of himself at age twenty-one—the same European heritage merged with a vibrant American idealism; the same capacity to work arduously, and the same courage to take risks.[22] Stieglitz found the "western youngster" disarming, quickly putting Eduard so completely at ease that he poured out his plans and dreams for the journey to Europe.[23] He had saved enough money to last a year, he thought, and told Stieglitz that he hoped to find commissions for portraits so that he could stay longer.

Young Steichen could see that Stieglitz was especially pleased that he was a painter as well as a photographer, but even while Stieglitz praised Steichen's industry and the wide range of his work, his attention was riveted to the photographs.[24] He studied the lush landscapes captured on "dark grey days" or at twilight, when, Steichen wrote, "things disappear and seem to melt into each other and a great beautiful feeling of peace overshadows all."[25] When Stieglitz asked if any of the pictures were for sale, Steichen confessed that few people in Milwaukee had wanted to buy his paintings, much less these photographs. Besides, he needed to take all of his drawings and paintings to Europe, for with William Merritt Chase's encouragement, Steichen felt he could confidently show the portfolio in Europe as he sought commissions for portraits.[26] An avid collector with an eye for new artists, Stieglitz asked the fee for the photographs, but Eduard had no idea how to price them.

"Well, you don't look any too rich," Stieglitz said. "I'll give you five dollars apiece and rob you at that."[27] He took three prints at what Steichen gratefully considered a princely sum. Most of all, he was honored that the great Stieglitz wanted to reproduce the prints in *Camera Notes*. Stieglitz recalled asking Steichen that day of their first meeting, "Now that you are going to Paris to study art, do you feel that, when you have mastered drawing and painting, you will abandon the camera?"

"Never," Steichen answered instantly. "I shall use the camera as long as I live; for it can say things that cannot be said in any other medium."[28] And as he said good-bye to Stieglitz and strode away, elated by their first encounter, Steichen shouted back over his shoulder, "I will always stick to photography!"[29]

The days were so crowded before his departure for Europe that Steichen did not get to see Stieglitz again, but he did meet the art editors at *Scribner's* and *The Century,* two of the most popular magazines of the day, in hopes of selling some of his photographs. Their response reflected the tenor of the current debate about photography and art in New York: Although they praised his work, they declined to buy it, one of them advising Steichen that while it was all right to photograph, when he got to Paris he should concentrate on *art,* not photography, because a photograph was always *only* a photograph. Later, Steichen described this meeting to Stieglitz in disbelief, finding it difficult, he exclaimed, to fathom such a response from an art editor in 1900.[30]

And Stieglitz, gazing at his newly purchased prints, was convinced he had found a remarkable talent. He had chosen *The Pool—Evening* as one of the first three Steichen prints he added to his private collection. Sometime later, he wrote in pencil on the back of it, "Steichen's first 'masterpiece.' A.S."[31]

Eduard Steichen and Carl Björncrantz had booked steerage passage on a French steamer, the SS *Champagne*. Along with their bicycles, which they had brought from Milwaukee and checked with their baggage, the young men carried ample provisions for the passage. Having heard from their immigrant parents that the food in steerage was revolting, ladled out of buckets into tin plates that passengers themselves had to wash in cold water, they had bought a ham, some cheese, and many loaves of fresh bread for their own private shipboard larder.[32] In the cramped steerage quarters, they slept on straw mattresses in bunks stacked three to a tier, spending as much of each day as possible in the fresh sea air. Mercifully for the crowd of travelers jammed together on the steerage deck, where there was only minimal sanitation, the passage was blessed with pleasant weather, and Steichen and Björncrantz enjoyed good health and good spirits all the way.[33] Thus Eduard Steichen retraced, nineteen years later, the crossing he had made to the New World in his mother's arms in 1881.

During the ocean voyage, he wrote a long, appreciative letter to Stieglitz, pledging with all his power to support the pictorial photography movement and the photographers he had just met who were "hammering hard against severe odds."[34] He hoped he could be of service to Stieglitz in Paris, he said.

A fellow passenger, hearing that Eduard and Carl were artists, gave them the name and address of his sister, who was concierge of an apartment building in Montmartre, the bohemian quarters inhabited by many artists in Paris, and they promised to find her when they arrived. Reaching Le Havre on May eighteenth, Eduard and Carl retrieved their bicycles and pedaled through the verdant French countryside, delighting in the springtime beauty of new landscapes. They meandered along the Seine, photographing and sketching all the way to Paris. There they sought out their shipmate's sister, who rented them a cheap spare room in the attic of her apartment building.

Eduard and Carl immediately "made tracks for the Rodin exhibition just outside the gates to the Paris World's Fair of 1900."[35] Late in the afternoon of their first day in Paris, they reached the Exposition Rodin,

Pavillon de l'Alma, ready and eager to experience the master's work firsthand. Steichen walked into Rodin's exhibition hall that day afire to see for himself the magnificent *Balzac,* which had so captured his imagination in the Milwaukee newspaper.

While he knew something of the 1898 brouhaha over Rodin's *Balzac,* Steichen, like many visitors to the Exposition Universelle of 1900, probably did not know why the great Rodin was displaying his sculpture and drawings in a beautiful building outside the fifteen hundred acres of the official exposition grounds. While Rodin might retrospectively be viewed as the greatest artist in the world in 1900, he was at that moment the object of such irate controversy that a more conventional and therefore acceptable artist overshadowed his reputation. Hence, the "official" sculptor of the Exposition Universelle of 1900 was Jules Dalou, then the most successful and acclaimed sculptor in France.

Rodin's *Balzac,* which had drawn Eduard from Milwaukee to Paris like a magnet, had been vociferously attacked at its unveiling at the Galeries des Machines in the Champs de Mars for the Salon Nationale des Beaux-Arts of 1898. The statue had been commissioned in 1891 by the Société des Gens de Lettres, led by its president, Émile Zola, the novelist and founder of naturalism in fiction. Attributing much of his own naturalist vision to Balzac's prolific realism, Zola saw that Rodin approached clay as he himself did paper—portraying human life objectively, realistically, robustly, stripping away past romanticism, striving for the truth.

"Character is the essential truth of any natural object, whether ugly or beautiful," Rodin believed; "it is the soul, feelings, the ideas expressed by the features of a face, by the gestures and actions of a human being." For the great artist, "everything in nature has character.... And that which is considered ugly in nature often presents more character than that which is termed beautiful."[36] Rodin sculpted Balzac's stocky, ungainly form and his overlarge head, then infused them with the stormy energy of Balzac's spirit. Because Rodin was an unorthodox artist commissioned to sculpt an unorthodox writer, it was no surprise that he created a revolutionary sculpture—not a typical commemorative statue of a public figure, but the body of a man vibrantly alive, his great head thrown back, his fierce eyes seared into plaster, and later, bronze.[37] Rodin explained this radical departure from traditional ceremonial sculpture:

I had to show a Balzac in his study, breathless, hair in disorder, eyes lost in a dream, a genius who in his little room reconstructs piece by piece all of society in order to bring it into tumultuous life before his contemporaries and generations to come; Balzac truly heroic, who does not stop to rest for a moment, who makes night into day, who drives himself in vain to fill the gaps made by his debts, who above all dedicates himself to building an immortal monument, who is transported by passion, whose body is made frenetic and violent, and who does not heed the warnings of his diseased heart, from which he will soon die. . . . In sum, there is nothing more beautiful than the absolute truth of real existence.[38]

In the end, vitriolic controversy drove Rodin and his *Balzac* to retreat; sadly, he called the experience a defeat, returning *Balzac* to his studio, and, for solace, turning his energy to *The Gates of Hell,* another sculpture he had been working on for years. But after a year of self-imposed exile in his studio, the battered sixty-year-old sculptor had recovered enough from the wounds of 1898 to want to share his most significant work with the world.

He had proposed to mount a one-man show at the World's Columbian Exposition in Chicago back in 1893, but he had been rejected. After the *Balzac* fiasco, he was still considered an outcast by many of the powers orchestrating the Exposition Universelle of 1900. Shrewdly and defiantly, Rodin decided that he would build his own exhibition hall to coincide with the exposition in Paris, and he intended to fill the place with his sculpture. Consequently, he had helped to design and finance the Pavillon de l'Alma on the Right Bank of the Seine, choosing a location that was the site of protest exhibitions by other artists years earlier—Courbet in 1851, and Manet and Courbet in 1867.[39] There, in 1900, Rodin and some of his patrons built a graceful, classical one-story hall, lit by tall windows.

Rodin had sculpted the simple, spacious interior of his exposition hall so that some of his work could stand in small chambers set apart by twelve-foot-high partitions, while the larger pieces could be viewed in uncrowded open spaces. Bright yellow interior walls refracted the natural light admitted through the generous windows. There could be seen Rodin's drawings and studies, and the virtuosity of his sculptures—

"dreams in marble," Oscar Wilde called them after Rodin personally showed him *The Burghers of Calais, The Gates of Hell,* and, the centerpiece, *Balzac.*[40]

Eduard had never forgotten his first encounter with Rodin's *Balzac,* reverberating with power even when dimly reproduced in the pages of a Milwaukee newspaper. Now the sculpture actually loomed before him, dominating the center of the exhibit hall, even more magnificent than he had hoped. Suddenly Eduard was diverted by a real-life figure, spying in a darkening gallery alcove "a stocky man with a massive head, almost like a bull's."[41] Instinctively recognizing the artist, Eduard held back, too shy to approach, but he promised himself in that instant of recognition that one day he would surely photograph Auguste Rodin.

Rodin's counterexposition in 1900, although controversial, was still nothing short of a triumph. In fact, for many critics and visitors, Rodin's exhibit was the premier art event of the entire Exposition Universelle in 1900. The sculptor kept his doors open weeks after the exposition officially closed, and he earned enough money from his share of admission fees and the sale of 200,000 francs' worth of sculpture to offset his investment of 160,000 francs. More significant was the redemptive vindication and celebration of his work, including *Balzac,* imbued with so much of his own deep soul.[42]

For Eduard and Carl, their first week in Paris was "overwhelming," with a thrilling new revelation at every turn.[43] Dressed in their American sport coats, knickers, and checkered caps, awkwardly speaking French, exploring the city on their bicycles, they were quite obviously tourists, even in a sea of tourists. Nearly 40 million tickets were sold to the great Exposition Universelle from April until November 1900, and many visitors came during the summer to see the great world bazaar of art, culture, and tawdry exploitation.

Although technology had dominated Eduard's interest at the world's fair in Chicago in 1893, it was art he remembered from the great fair in Paris in 1900, most of all Rodin's sculpture standing beautifully and ironically alone outside the official exposition. Inside, he recalled, Eduard roamed the vast Grand Palais, newly built for the exposition. It was described in a contemporary journal, *Revue des Arts Decoratifs,* as "a sort of railway station where masses of stone have been piled up to support what?—a high, thin roof of glass."[44] He also explored the more graceful Petit Palais, just erected opposite the Grand Palais, "its heavy and awkward brother," for both structures housed the French paintings and sculpture, friezes and monuments chosen or created for official display.[45]

Eduard went, of course, to the Louvre, where he stood transfixed before the permanent treasures there, completely unprepared for the beauty of the old masters. At the Luxembourg Palace museum, he found little of interest until he reached the room displaying the paintings of the Impressionists he had "read and dreamed about. Here were Monet and Degas and Manet," he wrote; "Pissarro and Sisley. The Monets stirred me most. They dealt with something that was still well out of the domain of photography, the magic and color of sunlight."[46] He was beginning to realize that in painting and photography, "the real magician was light itself—mysterious and ever-changing light with its accompanying shadows rich and full of mystery."[47]

By midsummer, however, the city had apparently lost some of its charm, for Paris had grown unbearably hot, dusty, and crowded, and alarmingly expensive for a young man on a fixed budget and with no income. He was having little luck showing his photographs around Paris, and he was further discouraged because Alfred Stieglitz had not replied to his May letter. When the summer heat finally convinced Eduard that he and Carl should leave the city for a while, they set out on a bicycle tour of France, Luxembourg, and Belgium.[48]

By mid-August, Carl had gone on to Sweden, his family's ancestral home, and Eduard traveled to Vienna and then settled down in Luxembourg again for a while, most likely staying with Steichen or Kemp relatives, although he left no record of the details. He was more faithful with camera and palette in recording the dazzling new landscapes he explored that first year in Europe. For instance, *The Judgment of Paris—Landscape Arrangement,* his stark photograph of trees and footprints in an early snow, was reproduced in 1901 in Charles H. Caffin's *Photography as a Fine Art,* along with six other Steichen photographic landscapes and portraits (and nineteen photographs by Gertrude Käsebier, seventeen by Stieglitz, twelve by Clarence White, nine by Joseph Keiley, seven by

Frank Eugene, and one by Fred Holland Day, making it a landmark record of the pictorialist avant-garde).

Unfortunately, only a handful of Steichen's paintings survive from that first year in France—including the watercolors entitled *Street Corner, Havre, France* and *Winding Stream, Rouen*. As was his habit, he often sketched, painted, and photographed the same landscape if it caught his imagination and emotion, sometimes choosing identical perspectives, the same misty lyricism echoing in his paintings and his painterly photographs. The key difference, of course, was color: He painted his small watercolor studies in delicately muted grays and browns, blues and greens, deliberately seeking to evoke mystery, melancholy, and romance.

From the vantage point of his bicycle, weaving his way through the enchanting countryside in France and Luxembourg, Eduard found beautiful scenes to paint and photograph, but his funds were diminishing with distressing speed. Growing economic necessity intensified his early flair for self-promotion; he knew he had no choice but to market his wares. Therefore, in a long, deferential letter, Steichen timorously asked Alfred Stieglitz for some help that summer. Writing from Luxembourg in mid-August, he reported that he would have photographs in shows in London and Vienna and might possibly mount a one-man show in Paris during the coming winter. He very much wanted exposure also in the Philadelphia Photographic Salon of 1900, but he was engaged in significant work that prevented him from sending prints from Paris. Would Stieglitz consider entering on his behalf the prints he was reproducing for *Camera Notes*? Steichen would, of course, pay all expenses incurred.

And, while he was at it, would Stieglitz be so kind as to have the prints framed with a "*very* narrow black line around the mats"? He hoped Stieglitz would forgive a "youngsters [sic] impudence."[49] Thanks to Stieglitz's help, Steichen's work appeared in the third Philadelphia Photographic Salon, held October 22–November 18, 1900.

But in the fall of 1900, after a summer of vagabonding through Europe, Eduard knew it was time to get down to serious work. As his funds eroded, he lived an artist's frugal life in Paris. He rented a cheap room in the bohemian Latin Quarter, walking or bicycling miles on his daily rounds through the city, haunting museums and art galleries, absorbing the art of others while trying to interest salons and galleries in his own work. His spare diet sharpened the bones in his face, and as his tall, lean body grew thinner, he let his dark hair grow longer. Out about the city and in the cheap cafés where other struggling artists gathered, he often wore a cape and a long black tie.[50] Eduard Steichen might look the part of an artist, but he needed concrete recognition in Europe in order to win commissions and income for portraits, whether as a painter or as a photographer.

Sometime in September, he gave up his room in the Latin Quarter and struck out for London, hoping to get some of his photographs into the exhibitions sponsored by the Royal Photographic Society or the Linked Ring.[51] He had met the great Stieglitz in New York; now his hopes led him straight to the other premier American photographer, Fred Holland Day, who had arrived in London in April of 1900, intent on mounting an exhibition that he had christened "The New School of American Photography." Day had brought with him the antagonism of his "arch-rival" Stieglitz, along with a hundred of his own photographic prints, as well as prints by others he intended to exhibit.[52] He also had a list of other photographers—including Eduard Steichen—whose work he wanted to introduce in London.

From youth flamboyant, eccentric, sensual, and apparently bisexual, Day inherited a family fortune, which gave him the leisure to indulge his passions—foremost among them photography and publishing. In Boston, he and his partner, Herbert Copeland, had published a hundred elegant, beautifully crafted editions of poetry and prose, modeling their press on the style of William Morris's Kelmscott Press in England. Day loved Irish and English poets, especially Keats, as well as the controversial voices in the Aesthetic and Decadent movements—Oscar Wilde and Aubrey Beardsley most of all. A mystic, Day explored Eastern religions, theosophy, and Rosicrucianism, and he collected rare books and manuscripts to enrich the library in his elegant home in Norwood, Massachusetts, outside Boston. With his camera, he captured exotic faces and scenes in virtuoso photographs, many of them visually evoking the Symbolist themes expressed in writing by Maeterlinck and others.

By the mid-1890s, Day in Boston and Stieglitz in New York were without peers as the most accomplished American art photographers of the nineteenth century. Possessed by equally passionate visions about the role of photography in the twentieth century, each sought a power base. Using his Boston Camera Club as headquarters, Day wanted to organize an American Association of Pictorial Photographers. He invited Stieglitz to join in, and even to lead the group, but Stieglitz had explicit ideas of his own: *He* was the champion of the new photography, and New York, not Boston, was to be the center. Stieglitz had deemed Day's exhibition at the New York Camera Club in 1898 "the most remarkable one-man-exhibition yet shown" there.[53] He had praised and published Day's photographs in *Camera Notes*. But he was not about to share his podium with Fred Holland Day or anyone else.

Thwarted by Stieglitz in the United States, Day decided to take his vision to Europe, for if he could not introduce the new American pictorial photographers to the world from Boston, he would do so from London and Paris. He conceived an exhibition of about three hundred photographs by other photographers, as well as his own hundred prints. Stieglitz's opposition to Day's project reached London before Day himself did, however, in the form of cables and a warning letter to friends in the Linked Ring that Stieglitz and Keiley refused to have their work included. Undaunted when Stieglitz's allies in the Linked Ring refused to sponsor his exhibit, Day adroitly persuaded their adversaries at the Royal Photographic Society to host "The New School of American Photography" exhibition October 10–November 8, 1900.[54]

Day lived on Mortimer Street in London, not far from his eighteen-year-old cousin and protégé Alvin Langdon Coburn, a prodigy with the camera, who now resided with his possessive mother, Fannie, on Russell Square. Coburn's own gifts as a photographer had been encouraged by Day, who had brought the Coburns with him to London to educate his young cousin in art, photography, literature, and continental culture. Soon after Steichen's arrival in London for his first visit, he met Day, and, through him, the Coburns, and he embraced the company of these other Americans.

Like Steichen, Alvin Langdon Coburn had owned a Kodak for his first camera, but, unlike Steichen, he had a consummate teacher in Day—and a constant shadow in his mother. Stout, protective Fannie Coburn was not only inordinately proud of her son's photographic genius; she was inseparable from him, and, almost on sight, she did not like Steichen, this attractive, brashly independent young man just three years older than her Alvin. She even appeared to some to be jealous of Steichen's talent, fearing, perhaps, that he would be a rival to her son's success.⁵⁵ Nevertheless, the two young photographers became friends and Eduard sketched a portrait of Coburn and gave it to Fannie in 1901.

Immediately fascinated with Day and his work, Eduard was especially intrigued to learn that a special lens had been crafted for Day by the Boston optical firm of Pinkham and Smith. Coburn, too, was thrilled at the effects of diffusion his cousin obtained with the Smith lens, as it came to be called.⁵⁶ It was a "deliberately uncorrected" lens, Steichen noted, achieving an effect much like that he got when he used a wet lens. Day's Smith lens captured a sharp image, unlike the soft-focus lens, yet with a halo encircling the light tones. As Steichen pointed out, almost all prominent American photographers and many Europeans later came to use the Smith lens at one time or another.⁵⁷

Studying the ambitious range of Day's work, Steichen wrote that "Day was an aesthete in everything he did. His manner of mounting and presenting his photographs, using crayons and charcoal and drawing papers in multiple mountings, was certainly of this order, and his photography leaned more to over-refinement than to emotional power."⁵⁸ When Day, in turn, examined Steichen's portfolio, choosing twenty-one of his prints for the London exhibition, Steichen remembered, he officially became "a member of the New School of American Photography!"⁵⁹

He stayed on to help Day hang the American show, a facet of photographic work that Steichen would always enjoy. Day was fastidiously demanding about how each and every photograph should be hung in an exhibition, and Steichen paid avid attention. He also learned from Day the importance of mounting his own photographs himself. "More than half the battle is in the *manner* in which such things are put forth, and my pictures mounted by others would no be longer mine," Day had written to Stieglitz.⁶⁰

In London that September, Eduard finally got the chance to attend his first photographic salons, something he had lacked the opportunity, time, or money to do in the United States. Heretofore, he had seen the work of other photographers only when it was reproduced in journals. Now, thanks to Day's show, he could examine the actual handiwork of the best American photographers of his time, and he could also see the work of international photographers at the Royal Photographic Society Salon, then in progress. He was enthralled with the pictures in Day's exhibition, considering it far superior to the London salon. But there was no work there by Stieglitz, and Eduard could not understand why.

He wrote a long letter to Stieglitz enthusiastically describing Day's kindness to him and the success of the exhibit, lauding its superiority to the "atrocious" and "bizarre" work displayed at both the Royal and London salons. But where were Stieglitz's photographs? Steichen asked him in the letter. Why was he not represented? Käsebier and White were there, but no show could be complete without the presence of Keiley and Stieglitz.[61]

Months sometimes elapsed before Steichen received an answer to his letters in Stieglitz's handsome calligraphy, but Stieglitz wrote back about the salon immediately, "all blushes and compliments" for Steichen's success, happy to have news about the London shows, but not offering his opinion about them, Steichen reported to Day.[62] Young and inexperienced as he was, Steichen was completely naïve then about the politics of photography, unaware of how his letter praising Day must have irritated Stieglitz, who was sulking back in New York. To make matters worse, A. Horsley Hinton had written Stieglitz on October second that he had just met Steichen, that much of his work was commanding a "good deal of attention," and that he was "a close friend of Holland Day's."[63]

Steichen was not yet fully informed about the intricate factions battling for dominance in the world of photography, where the politics of art could be as serious or savage, or as silly, as the politics of any other movement. After the pioneers of pictorial photography had broken away from the scientific and commercial photographers, they split like so many Protestant denominations into various congregations of pictorialists—the New York group led by Stieglitz; the Boston supporters of Day; and the Philadelphia Photographic Society, which divided itself into the Old School, or Rationalists, who wanted to include documentary, scientific, and artistic photography in the Philadelphia Photographic Salon, and the New School of purists devoted exclusively to artistic photography.

Because Stieglitz was a magnet for controversy and dissent, civil war had already broken out within the Camera Club of New York over his dogmatic control of *Camera Notes* as well as photographic exhibitions.

In Great Britain, the Linked Ring battled the Royal Photographic Society Salon, while warring groups splintered into Secessionist coalitions in Munich and Vienna. Paris, on the other hand, suffered from "absolute indifference" to pictorial photography, Robert Demachy wrote to Stieglitz.[64] Unaware of that history, Steichen the political neophyte, badgered Day for an answer about why Stieglitz's work was missing from "The New School of American Photography" exhibition in London.

Stieglitz had been invited to contribute his work, Day explained, but he had refused. Day got in his own jab at Stieglitz, calling *Camera Notes* a "tasteless publication." Later, when Steichen asked Stieglitz directly about the absence of his work in London in 1900, Stieglitz told him the exhibit (which Stieglitz never saw, even in the planning stage) was inadequate, and that the prints (which, likewise, Stieglitz had not seen) were "second- and third-rate" and would not do justice to the photographers involved. "I ultimately became closely acquainted with the work of these photographers," Steichen wrote, "and I never saw better prints from their hands than those exhibited by Day."[65]

"The New American School of Photography" exhibition opened, Steichen wrote, "like a bombshell exploding in the photographic world of London.... It was a red flag waving in the face of the public, and the press had a holiday making fun of it."[66] Although Steichen did not meet him, Whistler had attended the exhibition, especially admiring Clarence White's *Girl with the Pitcher*.[67] Steichen's own work polarized the critics: "For he is to the marrow an artist," wrote Charles Caffin. "One can detect it in all his prints. Some of them we may not care for as pictures—probably they were only experiments, very likely inadequate in expressing what he strove to reach." He praised Steichen's "vividness and power of expression," and he perceived the intersection of Steichen's gifts as painter and photographer.[68] Other critics were repelled, however, and reacted sarcastically:

> *Mr. Steichen, as becomes a leader of the new movement, has a portrait of himself, which he terms "Self Portrait: Composition Study," whatever that may mean. Mr. Steichen represents himself as partially dressed, trousers, shirt, and braces being in position. The print is so trimmed that one side of Mr. Steichen is cut away,*

and had the knife slipped a little there would have been a print without Mr. Steichen.[69]

Bridling at what he termed the abuse of certain British critics, Steichen vigorously defended American photography in "British Photography from an American Point of View," his first published article, which appeared in November of 1900 in the British journal *The Amateur Photographer*. All this led Steichen to discover that it was far better to be controversial than invisible. Now he was launched in London, and while some of the British photographers admiring his work had not yet made up their minds about Steichen the man, he had acquired valuable American friends and colleagues in Coburn and in Day. He particularly appreciated the importance of Day's pioneering achievement as "the first man to assemble a collection consisting exclusively of the work of men and women later recognized as leaders in the most important American movement in pictorial photography."[70]

As the fun and furor of the exhibition subsided, however, Steichen knew he had to return to Paris and get to work. But just before his departure, he got a big commission to photograph the "venerable" painter George Frederick Watts.[71] His splendid, sharply etched pigment print of Watts conjures images of seventeenth-century oil portraits by Rembrandt, but its brilliant contrasts of light and dark, highlighting the white hair and lined eyes of age, suggest that a more recent image may have hovered in Steichen's mind—Rudolf Eickemeyer's magnificent *A Ranchman*, which Steichen had first seen as a photogravure in *Camera Notes* in 1898. He posed Watts in profile in darkness, clad in black, apparently deep in contemplation. The light illumines his white hair, the furrows of his face, and the fingers of his strong hands, set off by white pleated cuffs. His name is etched in block letters at the top of the print, and Steichen signed and dated the photograph in the lower-left corner.

Watts was eighty-three years old when he sat for Steichen, an artist and sculptor whose career had spanned six decades. Steichen wanted to paint and photograph great artists—sculptors, painters, musicians, and writers. This was one principal goal of his trip to Europe, and he saw this photograph of Watts as the beginning of his own portrait series of great men.[72]

With the welcome money from the Watts commission in his pocket, Eduard left London late in October 1900 and quickly found new quarters in Paris—a bright, spacious, second-floor studio on the Rive Gauche at 83 Boulevard du Montparnasse, which he shared with a new angora kitten for company. He soon enrolled to study art at the Académie Julian, the prestigious school founded in Paris by Rodolphe Julian in 1868. Steichen clearly knew what he was doing when he chose to live on the Boulevard du Montparnasse, for while some artists gathered in Montmartre, farther from the heart of the city and therefore even cheaper, Montparnasse was the vital epicenter and haven for foreign artists in Paris in 1900.[73]

The wide gaslit boulevard and the myriad streets twining off it were lined with artists' studios and garrets available at reasonable rents. For the convenience of artists, neighborhood shops stocked art supplies, and artists could wander into the Model Market on the corner of Boulevard du Montparnasse and Boulevard Raspail to choose their subjects for live studies—lithe, muscular young men; beautiful women, some of them prostitutes; people of all ages and backgrounds, sometimes even an entire immigrant family in need of money.

At the center of daily community life stood the cheap cafés, which indulged the artists' voracious hunger for food, wine, and talk. When there were francs to spare, Eduard could join more affluent artists in the elegant Chez Bata or the Café du Dôme, with its zinc bar, marble-topped tables, and black leather banquettes. In the back room were two billiard tables and a smaller table where American artists kept up a perennial raucous poker game. Nearby cabarets pulsed with music, liberated men and women mingled freely, and the air could be wondrously alive with the romance and magic of Paris—or heavy with decadence and distraction. Each artist created his own Paris, and Eduard simultaneously managed to savor the exuberantly free life of Montparnasse and to devote long, uninterrupted hours to work and study.

When he enrolled in the Académie Julian, he chose one of the best-known art schools in Paris, albeit a rather stuffy and rigid one, with branches throughout the city. American artists in particular gravitated to the Académie Julian, whose founder had been classically trained at the Ecole des Beaux-Arts in Paris. Julian and his faculty taught their students the fundamentals of drawing from classical models, believing that only such mastery would lead to artistic freedom. By 1900, five large studios accommodated both classes and student exhibitions.

Steichen actually arrived about a decade too late for his own good, however, stepping into a regimen that was as stifling for him as the Pio Nono classroom had been in Milwaukee. During the 1890s, students and instructors at the school had been embroiled in the lively avant-garde artistic debates and experiments swirling through the Symbolist and Impressionist movements, but by 1900, that had subsided into the more sedate and conservative methods that defined Julian's original purpose.

To transmit to his students the traditional French academic training with an emphasis on drawing and composition, Julian secured the finest teachers, most of them successful artists who had also studied at the Ecole des Beaux-Arts, including artists who been honored by receiving the Prix de Rome. Life models were provided for all the classes, and the comprehensive program offered instruction in sculpture, miniature painting, illustration, and a range of graphic arts. Students came from all over the world, even as far away as Japan, and over the decades, the roster of students included many distinguished artists. Henri Matisse, however, was rejected by the Académie Julian in 1892 because, his teachers predicted, he would never be able to draw.[74]

Steichen was not rejected, but he did not stay long at the Académie Julian. Portfolio in hand, he entered his first class on a Monday morning. His teacher was Jean-Paul Laurens, born in 1838, a well-known painter and one of Rodin's oldest friends. In fact, the two men had posed for each other.[75] Laurens was a "great artist," according to Rodin, who considered the painter's portrait of him masterful.[76] Laurens usually painted grand, often gory romantic history—sweeping dramas of political and religious turmoil, graphic renderings of murders and martyrs.[77] At the Exposition Universelle in 1900, awed visitors had crowded around his huge epic painting *Entry of Pope Urban II into Toulouse*. Along with Claude Monet and his fellow Impressionist painter Albert Besnard, Laurens had contributed a glowing essay of introduction to the official catalog for Rodin's exhibition.

According to Rodin, it was Laurens who obtained the commission for him for *The Burghers of Calais*. Rodin felt he owed Laurens "profound gratitude for having spurred me to the creation of one of my best works."[78] Rodin appreciated the affirmation of Laurens, then far more widely acclaimed as a major artist than Rodin himself. Therefore, when Eduard Steichen was accepted into Laurens's studio at the Académie Julian, he walked into the classroom of a legendary artist.

Laurens's first assignment to his class was a traditional student exercise, a charcoal drawing of a live model—this particular Monday, a tall, sleek Italian athlete. Immediately absorbed in the assignment, Steichen luxuriated in having a whole week to work on one drawing. On Wednesday, Laurens made the rounds of the class to criticize each student's work, severely chastising a Polish student seated near Steichen for the "soft nothingness" of his drawing. As he moved toward Steichen's easel, Laurens grabbed the young Polish artist and forced his attention on Steichen's work.

"This is the way to do it," Laurens told him, praising the "action and vitality" in Steichen's drawing. "And look at the hand," Laurens said. "That's the way Michelangelo drew a hand!"

Eduard was thrilled. "I had gooseflesh all over," he remembered. "My hair commenced to rise. Everybody in the classroom looked round to see who the new Michelangelo was." The young Polish student left class, however, never to return. Afterward, Eduard did not want to touch his wonderful drawing for fear he "would spoil the miraculous thing" he had achieved, so he worked at it tentatively, careful not to disturb the hand. When the day came for Laurens to make his final evaluation of the week's work, he moved to the easel next to Steichen's, volubly admiring a drawing by a French student who had studied at the Académie Julian for quite a long time. Laurens embossed the drawing with his initials, stamped in purple ink, designating it one of the best drawings produced that week.

Then he turned to Steichen's easel, this time as if he had never seen the drawing before, loudly condemning it, deeply embarrassing Steichen in the process. The very same hand Laurens had compared to Michelangelo's work he now pronounced "a block of wood." Crestfallen, confused, and then angry, Steichen nevertheless returned to the Académie the next week to work with oil on canvas, but each time Laurens entered the atelier, Steichen removed his painting and quietly left the room until Laurens departed. Then the young man paying his precious francs for these art lessons returned to his easel and began painting again. But how could he trust criticism—positive or negative—when it was offered so capriciously? He stuck it out that week before deciding not to continue his studies at the Académie Julian, where the standard seemed to him to be "cold, lifeless, slick, smoothly finished academic drawing."[79]

He had come too far and fought too long and hard for his own original style to conform to the unbending protocol of the Académie. Consequently, because Steichen was emphatically not interested in formalized, lifeless art, his professional training came to an abrupt halt in November of 1900. He returned to the familiar atelier of his own experiments and studies, but this time with all the artistic richness of Paris as his laboratory.

When he resumed his photographic work after that brief hiatus, the intersection of painting and photography intensified. While he still enjoyed photographing and also painting studies of the same model or landscape, Steichen was learning in those early days in Paris to empower his images by the judicious choice of medium: Now the alchemy of palette and brush or of camera and chemicals became subservient to the motif he wanted to convey. He began systematically to study individual painters as well as schools of painting at the Louvre, often speculating whether an image rendered in a certain painting could be evoked as well—or even better—in photography. As Charles Caffin noted, in Steichen's hands, photography was not "makeshift, but a separate source of power."[80]

The movement from painting to photography back to painting was becoming a matter of deeply ingrained artistic practice for Steichen, who was beginning to believe that the techniques of painting and photography were in fact complementary. He simply worked in the medium that best suited the images he had to express at the moment, and one art fed the other. As one of the few photographers of his time who simultaneously painted and photographed, Steichen was in a unique position to contrast the two forms and to analyze their relation to each other. He actually began writing about painting and photography in the fall of 1900, and because Stieglitz had invited him to contribute an article to *Camera Notes* anytime he wanted to earn a "few square meals," Steichen offered Stieglitz his article in progress on the "paintre" and the "fotographer," as he spelled the words.[81]

Because Steichen was continually defining and redefining those roles for himself, he wrote and rewrote the essay over the next several years, sometimes ripping it to shreds and starting over again. In the surviving handwritten manuscript, full of the scrawls and scratches of a writer editing himself, Steichen argued with some sophistry that photography was "the art of representation"; that contemporary art reached "its greatest heights" in paintings "actually representing nature"; that those paintings, being representational, were therefore essentially photographic; and that, consequently, although photographers were routinely accused of imitating painting, it was actually painters who had "all the while been making photographs."[82]

In 1900, intoxicated with art and life in Paris, Steichen the painter-photographer embraced the unique powers of his two separate but equal art forms. In a letter to Stieglitz, Steichen reflected that Whistler had created wonderful art in paintings and in etchings. Now Steichen hoped to create wonderful art in painting and in photography, with the camera serving as the tool for his "etchings." He dared to believe, furthermore, that the camera offered exciting possibilities that were "foreign to *any* other medium."[83]

6

GREAT MEN

(1 9 0 1)

My "Great Men" series includes portraits of Rodin, Maeterlinck, George Frederick Watts, the eminent English artist, Zangwell, Lenbach, the great German portrait artist, Besnard, who is perhaps the greatest living exponent of the modern school of art, William M. Chase of New York, Mucha, the painter, and many others. Then, too, I have hosts of pictures of young men, who I expect will be great.[1]

— STEICHEN

IN LEGENDARY PARIS, WHERE "ARTISTS ARE as thick as blackberries in July," people gravitated to Eduard Steichen's airy studio at 83 Boulevard du Montparnasse.[2] Despite his limited means, he was a cordial host who relished the lively companionship and stimulation of avant-garde artists like himself. Handsome, exuberant, almost feverishly charismatic, he attracted friends effortlessly, and age and gender were irrelevant, for Steichen had a gift for friendship that matched his prodigious talent as an artist.

During that winter of 1900–1901, the tight-knit circle of American photographers in Europe led Steichen to a pivotal new friendship with a recently elected member of the Linked Ring, Frank Eugene Smith, who had discarded his last name and was known simply as Frank Eugene.[3] Nearly fifteen years older than Steichen, Eugene was a professional painter who grew up in New York and had been trained at the Bavarian Academy of the Fine Arts in Munich. Like Steichen, he had gotten his first national recognition as a photographer in 1899 at the second Philadelphia Photographic Salon. The marriage of painting and photography inevitably defined Eugene's work, for in the effort to create distinctive artistic photographs, he enhanced his negatives with etched lines, thereby fusing photography and the graphic art of etching. Eugene was both praised and condemned for this intense manipulation of the negative.

Because they were the only two American painter-photographers then seriously engaged in pictorial photography, Eugene was an especially valuable mentor for Steichen. They could share ideas about the relationship between painting and photography, as well as about darkroom theory and practice, speculating together about how far you could go in the manipulation of photographic negatives without prostituting the art of photography. There must have been animated talks late into the night, whether they were together in London or in Steichen's Montparnasse atelier and the cafés in the Latin Quarter, rousing arguments and postulations, especially when Eugene and Steichen got together with Fred Holland Day.

Steichen celebrated his first Christmas in Paris by inviting some friends to a stylish Christmas dinner, most likely his personal version of the traditional lavish and festive Paris banquet.[4] Day was his guest of honor. "No one would expect this brilliant young member of the New American School of Photography to give a dinner in quite the ordinary way, and he didn't," reported the Paris edition of the New York *Herald* December 27, 1900, noting that "the whole of the elegant little function" was worthy of Steichen and the Latin Quarter.[5] Americans in Paris could report their comings and goings to the *Herald*'s Paris bureau, and Day alone was then enough of a personage to warrant some press attention in the social columns. Joining Steichen and Day were Frank Eugene; the American photographer Mary Devens, from Day's Boston circle; and Mrs. William E. Russell and Mrs. Elise Pumpelly Cabot. Steichen decorated his studio with holly, mistletoe, and exotic red silk Japanese lanterns he had acquired from a Japanese government officer at the Exposition Universelle.

The festive party toasted Queen Victoria, the Presidents of France and the United States, and two American photographers who had just been elected to the Linked Ring—Clarence White and Gertrude Käsebier, the first woman accorded that honor. At the end of the exuberant evening, Steichen and his guests sang "a curiously improvised medley of the 'Marseillaise,' 'God Save the Queen' and 'America.'"[6] He had even written out a fittingly photographic menu: "salade *Hollandaise, sauce développement à la glycerine,* marrons glacés *au gum bichromate,* choux de Bruxelles *au carottes des Ecoles Nouveaux,*" and, to toast the "Links," the new American members of the Linked Ring, "vin de Xeres en l'honneur *des nouveaux lincks Americains.*"[7]

As the first year of the new century dawned, Steichen stood exactly where he had hoped to be. His courage, energy, stamina, and determination had gotten him to Paris, where he was just beginning to find himself and to explore the muscular range of his power as painter and photographer. Thanks to his inclusion in the London show and his growing friendship with Day, he had already implanted himself in the center of the American photographic avant-garde in Europe. When he heard from Day that he was preparing to bring "The New American School of Photography" exhibition to Paris in 1901, Steichen immediately invited him to share his Montparnasse studio. Not even a full year in Europe, and now he would play host to one of his country's two greatest photographers! Steichen promptly wrote to tell Stieglitz that when Day came over from London, he would "camp" at Steichen's own studio. As he prepared for the arrival, Steichen cleaned house and hoped his cat would not be too "obnoxious" to his illustrious guest.[8]

Like many bohemians, Day achieved even more striking originality in his personal style than in his art, remarkable as his photographs were. Day was certainly the most exotic, original person Steichen had ever met, sweeping down the streets of London and Paris dramatically dressed in elegant, well-tailored dark suits set off by rich brocaded vests, wearing a pince-nez as a dashing counterpoint to his Vandyke beard, an omnipresent dark cape swirling about him. At home, he dressed with equal flair in various national costumes collected from his world travels, especially fancying Turkish gowns and slippers and the flowing robes of the Orient and Far East. A lifelong bachelor, Day was thought by some to be homosexual or bisexual, and by others, asexual.[9] His reputation as an effete and a dandy had preceded him to England, where Day's friend Oscar Wilde was still an all-too-vivid emblem of debauchery, decadence, and ruin. During the London photography show, one British critic had sternly reprimanded Day for his vivid persona, warning him to "learn at once that the educated British public will not stand for a moment his unblushing effrontery, egotism, and braggadocio, though it will welcome some of his best photographs."[10]

Steichen admired Day's work immensely, but he was equally fascinated with his "braggadocio" and the complicated idiosyncrasy of his personality. On the lookout now for "great men" for his projected series of photographs, Steichen perceived Day not only as a great artist who believed in art for art's sake but as a great man. Furthermore, as Steichen learned from his daily exposure to Day's dramatic stories, the older man not only knew other great men but he counted them as his friends. Through his friendship with Day, Steichen could know at least vicariously some of the most colorful writers and artists of the era, including Oscar Wilde, Aubrey Beardsley, Maxfield Parrish, Stephen Crane, and William Butler Yeats, all of whom had been published by Day and Herbert Copeland, his more conservative partner in his Boston publishing firm Copeland and Day. By the mid-1890s, Day and his partner had come to be known as the most avant-garde American publishers of poetry, bringing out Yeats's *Poems; Sister Songs,* by the mystical English poet and former opium addict Francis Thompson; and Stephen Crane's atheistic volume of poems *The Black Riders and Other Lines,* so controversial that even uninhibited Day had suggested some excisions, which Crane, in turn, refused to make.[11]

In 1896, Day had taken a special interest in "a little Assyrian boy Kahlil G," who had been selling matches on a Boston street corner when social worker Jessie Fremont Beale heard about the thirteen-year-old prodigy and asked Day to become his patron.[12] Day photographed Kahlil Gibran and nurtured his artistic gifts by allowing him to copy his own collection of drawings by Beardsley and William Blake. He also helped young Gibran learn English by introducing him to books, including a volume that profoundly shaped Gibran's mysticism—a translation of Maurice Maeterlinck's *The Treasure of the Humble,* the same book that had captured Steichen's imagination in Milwaukee. Thus it was Day who had planted the seeds for Gibran's *The Prophet,* his hugely popular mystical prose poem first published in 1923.[13]

A gifted raconteur with the personal fortune to subsidize his interests, Day seemed to have lived squarely in the midst of some of the most daring events in the avant-garde artistic and literary worlds of two continents. He was Steichen's link to those dazzling worlds, and the younger man no doubt listened raptly to Day's anecdotes about his circus of a life. It was London bookseller and photographer Frederick Evans who had introduced Day to illustrator Aubrey Beardsley ("all hairs and peacock plumes," Whistler supposedly said of him); in 1900, Day, in turn, introduced Steichen to Evans, whom Steichen photographed in London in the fall of 1900. He posed Evans wearing a top hat, standing with his back to the camera, hands clasped behind him in the folds of his cape, contemplating one of Day's photographs of himself as Christ.

With Day, there was constant drama—sometimes exhaustingly intense and neurotically imaginative. He was gentle and considerate, however, a devoted friend and patron, always ready to offer advice and money, if it was needed. With Day in his Paris studio, Steichen would have no time for discouragement or restlessness. One could no more resist Day's intense enthusiasms than willfully exempt oneself from the aftershocks of an earthquake.

As he grew more aware of the tension between Day and Stieglitz, however, Steichen wrote less to Stieglitz about his friendship with Day, but there were inescapable reverberations. Day stimulated and inspired Steichen, whose bold experiments in photography further intensified while Day was around. Back in the public library in Milwaukee in 1898, Steichen had read Day's articles in *Camera Notes*. Now, in London and Paris, the two men could discuss these ideas at length. Experiment, experiment, experiment, Day taught. Reach, and risk. These principles were to be embraced by Steichen all his life. He had already taken to heart Day's belief that photographers could learn more from the master painters than from other photographers about the composition of landscapes and portraits, and the intricate choreography of light and dark.[14]

Steichen alluded to Day's views when he wrote in his autobiography about composing a self-portrait during Day's residency in his Paris studio. At the Louvre, Steichen had been inexplicably drawn to Titian's *Man with a Glove,* and he set out to interpret it in a pigment print, *Self Portrait with Brush and Palette.* With deliberate irony, he dressed in Day's clothes, literally and symbolically attiring himself as the respected photographer; then he transposed the Titian painting he so admired into a photograph of himself. In that gesture, he appropriated the mantles of

Day and Titian, eliciting from photography and painting what he wanted and needed from each medium. Wearing Day's white scarf and black cape, Steichen took up his own palette and brush and then stood before his camera, he said, to create "photography's answer to 'Man with a Glove.'"[15]

Critic Sadakichi Hartmann, under the pen name Sidney Allan, later accused Steichen of plagiarizing when he based photographs on paintings, deeming such transmutation "undoubtedly imitative."[16] But in these experiments, Steichen was testing his art, wrangling with the connections between painting and photography, jostling one form against the other to see what would happen, what he could *make* happen. All that year in Europe, he prodded the outer limits of painting and photography, as he had done since the beginning, playing with seemingly infinite combinations and permutations of light and dark, tone and texture, an alchemist in the darkroom and at the easel, his imagination brimming with images he simply *had* to get onto paper.

Steichen's most memorable portraits up to 1900 are the self-portraits and his haunting photographs of his beautiful, photogenic sister, Lilian. But because of his growing obsession with the historic theme of portraying great lives, hoping through them to understand the essence of all life, it is significant that Steichen's first two major portraits, prophetic of his emerging style, are of "great men" who personally influenced him: Watts, whom he was commissioned to photograph; and Day, whose artistic affirmation and electric presence so dominated Steichen's life during that first year abroad.

By 1901, after all, Steichen had seen Alfred Stieglitz only once, during that brief but memorable hour in New York en route to Paris. By the time Day moved into Steichen's Paris studio, Steichen had exchanged only a handful of letters with Stieglitz, and because Stieglitz refused to submit his work to Day's exhibition, Steichen had yet to see a Stieglitz print except reproduced in journals. He had seen more than a hundred extraordinary prints by Day, however, had helped him hang the exhibition "The New American School of Photography," had talked with him for hours, and now shared his studio with him. It was Day who gave Steichen his first crucial recognition in Europe, Day whose powerful personal and artistic omnipresence in Steichen's life in Paris carried profound weight in his early work. Contrary to later conclusions, therefore, the first major force in Steichen's life as a photographer was not Alfred Stieglitz, but Fred Holland Day.

Day was the subject in some of Steichen's best work in 1900 and 1901. He painted and photographed Day, making several "very interesting" negatives of him, and then, Steichen wrote Stieglitz, Day, in turn, took a "stunning portrait of me."[17] He persuaded the restless Day to sit for an oil portrait, but not for long; Steichen had to capture his ultimate image of Day in just one two-hour sitting. Steichen also photographed Day in Paris in 1901 in a pose and light evocative of Day's own 1899 portrait of Gertrude Käsebier. In both Day's photography and Steichen's, the subject sits with the left profile turned to the camera. The muted light barely illuminates the face, but it glistens on objects—a pitcher near Käsebier, and her jewelry; a mask mounted on the wall behind Day, a cup he holds, the tip of his cigarette, his well-polished shoe.

In another 1901 photograph, Steichen created the most thoroughly handsome, masculine image of Day in the entire body of photographs of Day by noted photographers, including Coburn and Käsebier. Day wears the famous cape; a slouched hat masks the eyes; one hand almost conceals his bearded chin. That image composed and photographed, the work was just beginning, however; as was becoming his habit, Steichen experimented for almost a year in his studio darkroom with "the original gum-print process, then with other colloids, glues, and gelatins, sometimes in combination, sometimes separately," before he achieved the process and the print that satisfied him.[18]

Steichen would be a lightning rod for attention when Day opened the Paris exhibition of the New American School, featuring thirty-five Steichen prints. Welcoming the upcoming exposure of his work in Paris, Steichen wrote Stieglitz that he hoped the exhibition would help him out financially.[19] He was always short of the money he needed for the expensive supplies his work demanded. From Milwaukee, his mother faithfully sent funds to help Eduard in Paris, as well as to Lilian at the University of Illinois. "I was at school while my brother was studying in Europe—both of us supported by our mother," Lilian wrote in 1908 to correct an impression, left by a *Century Magazine* article about her brother's work, that she herself had helped to pay for Eduard's trip to Paris. "All the credit belongs to her and brother himself. The article does not tell the half of our mother's wonderful goodness."[20]

In the winter of 1901 Eduard was working terribly hard—"hustling," he called it—but not yet achieving the results or the recognition he wanted. He was often tired, and, despite his vibrant new circle of friends, sometimes homesick. He wrote to Carl Björncrantz, who was about to sail home to the United States—"that blessed land"—asking Björncrantz to look in on his parents and to cheer them up if they seemed lonely. He also instructed his friend to tell Mary and John Peter Steichen that their son would come home someday and "bring back the reward."[21] Yet privately, he was beginning to have his doubts.

Soon, however, the leading French pictorialist photographer and critic Robert Demachy would peruse Steichen's photographs in the Paris exhibition and pronounce the twenty-two-year-old painter-photographer the "enfant terrible" of the New American School of photographic art.[22] As Day busied himself with arrangements for the Paris opening of "The New School of American Photography" exhibition, he and Steichen spent a good deal of time with Demachy, the son of a wealthy Paris banker. Like Day, Demachy had inherited enough money to indulge his own eclectic interests. He collected automobiles, for instance, and he delighted Steichen by driving him around Paris.

Unhappily married to a beautiful American woman, Demachy lived with his wife and two small sons in a Paris mansion immense enough to allow them separate lives, she in her own sumptuous apartment on the first floor, and he, by preference, in rooms near the servants' quarters on the top floor of the house that later became the headquarters for designer Christian Dior. Demachy was most at home, however, in the bohemian cafés and ateliers of Paris, with artists such as Day and Steichen. At Demachy's studio under the eaves of his mansion, Steichen reported to Stieglitz, he met "several very charming Parisiannes."[23] That February, Demachy wrote to Stieglitz that Day and Steichen had "stirred me up" and stimulated a "new interest in my old work," adding that he found their photographs "remarkable."[24]

Demachy had waged a frustrating, often solitary campaign as the champion of art photography in Paris, where interest lagged far behind London, Munich, New York, and even Philadelphia. As Joseph T. Keiley observed in *Camera Work*, pictorial photography had struggled for acceptance in France since the 1890s, because the Paris art world had been "narrow and bigoted in its attitude toward pictorial photography . . . and it could not bring itself to believe that with the camera any expression could be given to original pictorial conception."[25]

Demachy had fought long and hard to counteract the French condescension toward pictorial photography. Consequently, he took Day and Steichen to visit the Photo-Club de Paris in February of 1901 in hopes of persuading Day to accept an official invitation to stage his exhibition there rather than at the Paris art gallery that had solicited the show. Parisians were "surfeited" with art exhibits and had little interest in pictorial photography, Demachy told Stieglitz.[26] Day would have no audience at all unless he held his show at the Photo-Club, Demachy contended.[27] To sweeten the invitation, he arranged for the Photo-Club to rig up a system of electric lamps with reflectors to achieve "uniform lighting" that would do justice to the "colour and tone of prints," and to pay for half the cost of printing the catalog.[28]

Consequently, the opening of Day's "The New American School of Photography" exhibition was set for late February at the Photo-Club de Paris, by happenstance coinciding with the advent of a new era, for Queen Victoria died on January 22, 1901. It was an appropriate symbol for the new epoch in photography Demachy hoped to introduce in Paris. As they had in London, Steichen and Alvin Langdon Coburn helped Day hang the exhibit. In Paris, Day omitted some of the London pictures, but he included thirty-five prints by Steichen, fourteen more than in London, and twenty-nine, rather than thirty, by Gertrude Käsebier.[29] Demachy warned Day not to expect the great crowds who flocked to see photographs in Philadelphia or London, for the Paris audience was "hard to move," but he was convinced Day's exhibition would "do worlds of good."[30]

During the exhibition's London showing, British critic Thomas Bedding, editor of the *British Journal of Photography,* had referred to it as the "American Invasion," condemning it as a collection of "deplorable travesties of photographic work which a handful of American photographers, encouraged by the adulatory writings of neurotic 'appreciators,' were deceived into believing were 'artistic' or 'pictorial.' "[31] The French, on the other hand, led by Demachy, were far more sympathetic to the "American Invasion." "The French Public Likes Day!" Demachy reported in *Camera Notes.*[32]

Back in New York, despite his opposition to Day's exhibition and his vigorous behind-the-scenes efforts to abort the show in London, Stieglitz ran Demachy's laudatory review of the exhibition in *Camera Notes* in July 1901, but with a disclaimer, an editorial that, intentionally or otherwise, was an insult to Day and Demachy. Stieglitz attacked publicly and in print the quality of an exhibition he had never seen—at once condemning it, yet, in the process, defending the American photographers against some of their European critics. "It comprises the work of many photographers of all schools," Stieglitz wrote, "and is mainly the result of an exchange of prints at Mr. Day's request with the majority of those represented in the collection. Many of these prints were actually unfinished, or what are termed 'seconds,' that is, prints not up to exhibition finish. Hence, much of the unfavorable criticism."[33] Steichen, however, held to his belief, expressed many years later in *A Life in Photography,* that the prints Day exhibited were as fine as any he had ever seen from the hands of those photographers.[34]

Steichen came away from the Paris exhibition with important new friends and colleagues, a growing visibility as an artist living and working in Paris, a few welcome sales, and a greater sophistication about the political quagmire of pictorial photography. Now alert to the ongoing battles between Stieglitz and Day, in particular, he began to walk a diplomatic tightrope between two strong egos, keenly appreciating each of the masters and wanting to work with them both. And, unlike Stieglitz, Day, and Demachy, Steichen *had* to work for a living, for there was no family fortune to support his passion. Already, he owed a debt he meant to repay to his mother, who from her millinery shop in Milwaukee was sending him money she made from her hats, no doubt over John Peter's irritable protests. Art was Eduard's life, but it also had to be his livelihood. Otherwise, he would have to go home in defeat, and now that he had had a taste of art in Paris, he was not about to give it up.

His best friends in Paris in 1901, after Carl Bjorncrantz had gone home to Milwaukee, were Coburn, Day, and Eugene. Coburn could never get far away from his overbearing mother, but Steichen, Day, and Eugene

GREAT MEN (1901)

made themselves at home in the bohemian life of Paris. Always trailing Day were beautiful women (some of them heiresses to great fortunes) and exciting men. Paris might lag behind London and Munich in its taste for pictorial photography, but the epicurean pleasures of the city were unsurpassed, with its constellation of amusements reaching from posh Maxim's to the rowdy music halls and the glitz of the Folies Bergère. Adulterers of both sexes took advantage of the relaxed sexual mores, which also indulged lusty experiments in free love, and sex was for sale on a spectrum encompassing both prostitutes and the demimonde, the expensive kept women moving with sensuous grace through the rarefied world of the elite. Many artists, writers, and musicians who were engaged in the anarchy of avant-garde art also experimented with love, romance, and sex, a robust sexual energy often being part of the vital life force that drives the creation of art.

Not surprisingly, Eduard Steichen recorded few details of his love life in Paris in 1901. His surviving letters home to family and friends focus on art, as does his correspondence with Alfred Stieglitz. Images of the young, romantic Steichen in Paris float in fragments of memory, family stories half-recalled, enigmatic lines in letters, and in certain portraits evocative of passion and loss. An ever-more-glamorous bachelor, he now enjoyed some recognition as an artist in Paris and in London, and when Robert Demachy photographed Steichen during that time, he portrayed a dandy, elegantly dressed and barbered, holding a dapper cane. According to tales of his romances woven into family lore, passed down decades later from Lilian to her daughters, Steichen enjoyed and appreciated women, and they returned his sentiments.

There were rumors of a tragic affair with a married woman early in his life, but the details are vague. There was also said to be a wealthy young woman from Wisconsin who loved Eduard and was rebuffed because, as an aspiring artist with no income or prospects to offer a bride, he felt he could not marry a wealthy wife. No records confirm her identity, but in family stories, she followed Eduard to Europe to study music in Germany and her name was thought to be Rosa.[35] In words that evoked Maeterlinck's ideas about suffering, Eduard wrote about her in a letter to Carl Björncrantz. He said he was deeply worried then that he had not seen Rosa and had no idea where to find her.[36] There is also speculation, although no documentation, that it is her beautiful, sensual face tilted back into the darkness, eyes nearly closed, cast down, in the rarely reproduced Steichen portrait *The Rose*.[37]

When Rosa could not win a commitment from Steichen, the story goes, she became engaged to her music teacher and traveled to Paris to try to provoke Eduard's jealousy. She wanted to buy one of his paintings for the house she and her fiancé were planning, she said. Furious, he told her the paintings were not for sale. She went back to her room and shot herself. Although details are lost to time, the fact of a shattering suicide haunted Steichen for many years afterward, inevitably shadowing his relationships with the women who later loved him. According to Lilian, "the tragedy struck" her brother's heart.[38]

Steichen's surviving letters from 1901 do not tell of Rosa's tragic death, but the mosaic of events suggests that her suicide probably occurred sometime between April and July of 1901, and not until after his friends Day and Coburn had taken their leave of Steichen and Paris for a photographic jaunt to Algeria in early spring. They were equipped with another newly designed lens to test, a British Dallmeyer lens probably custom-made and adapted for them by Pinkham & Smith of Boston.[39] Day found the lens "a revelation to myself and some half-dozen American photographers who were in Europe at the time."[40] The soft-focus lens had been designed first as a portrait lens, but Frederick Evans used it effectively to photograph the cathedrals of England and France, as well as other architectural wonders. Marveling at the distances it permitted him, Day used it in Algiers for landscapes where he successfully made "what English people told me were the first landscapes attempted with this lens."[41] In later years, Day recalled that both Coburn and Steichen acquired Dallmeyer lenses.[42]

Steichen's studio at 83 Boulevard du Montparnasse was far too quiet and empty once Day departed for Algeria, and Steichen faced loneliness and hard work. He had submitted two paintings to the prestigious Salon des Beaux-Arts of 1901—his *Portrait of F. Holland Day,* an oil, and a large painting, probably a landscape, which he did not expect to be accepted.[43] As his birthday approached in March, he was dejected, writing a glum, homesick letter to his parents.[44] Then, elation: The word came on his birthday that the Day portrait had been accepted by the salon.

Exultantly, he wrote the news to Carl Björncrantz. He had heard that more than three thousand pictures had been submitted; only two hundred were accepted, and very few of those were portraits. Steichen could hardly believe his good fortune: Just a year earlier, he had visited the Grand Palais for the first time, and now one of his own paintings would hang there, he informed his friend.[45]

He had been invited to contribute six photographs of children to an exhibition to be held at the Petit Palais as a sidelight to a retrospective exhibit of great paintings of children, lent from collections around the world. He marveled that his work would now be displayed in both these significant buildings as part of two major events in the Paris art world.[46] He also dashed off the good news on postcards for Stieglitz in New York and the family in Milwaukee, and Mary Steichen proudly shared it with the *Milwaukee Sentinel*. The paper covered the news of Steichen's success in the Sunday edition of April 14, 1901:

AN HONOR TO MILWAUKEE. Striking Success Won Abroad by Edward J Steichen, a Young Local Artist. NOTABLE BIRTHDAY GIFT. Though but Twenty-two Years of Age One of His Pictures Is Accepted by the Salon.

The reporter describing Steichen's honor noted, "The news reached his parents in this city on a postal card phrased in the laconic fashion of youth and it marks another upward step in a career that is attracting wide attention even in the French capital." According to the hometown paper, "It is quite certain that the Milwaukee young man has succeeded in getting himself and his art talked about, which is something that a good many older artists have striven for and failed of doing."

Attention was also given in the article to Mary's daughter, Lilian, who was about to turn eighteen and who was "as clever in her way as the son, for she entered the State University of Illinois after only a year of study at Ursuline convent in Canada...." Furthermore, the newspaper reported, Lilian expected to enter the University of Chicago in the autumn of 1901, and to be graduated in two years, adding, "Some of her brother's cleverest photographs have been studies of his sister, one which shows the two in animated conversation having been one of those that struck the popular fancy at the recent London exhibition."[47] The article also offered the intriguing news that John Peter and Mary Steichen planned to move to Chicago to be near their daughter, an idea that Lilian would surely have discouraged. In fact, the Steichens stayed on in Milwaukee, where John Peter at last joined his wife in taking great pride in the "striking success" of their two children.

And in New York, Stieglitz announced Steichen's success in *Camera Notes,* avowing that his talent must be extraordinary since he had succeeded the first time out in having a painting accepted at the prestigious annual Champs de Mars Salon. Then, taking a stab at critics of Steichen's photography in particular and pictorial photography in general, Stieglitz wrote, "Possibly some of our photographic contemporaries, both here and abroad, who have taken such pleasure in ridiculing his photographic work, will allow that Mr. Steichen is at least a 'real artist' now that he has been publicly acclaimed as such by a jury of his own confrères." Stieglitz was not surprised at Steichen's sudden visibility, congratulating him because "his success in painting means much for pictorial photography." He concluded on a note of mixed propaganda and praise: "Mr. Steichen, although a painter by profession, is also a firm believer in the use of the camera as a means of artistic expression, a means quite as distinctive as the pen and ink, pastel, stylus, water-color, etc. This at all events was the opinion he expressed to us prior to his departure for Paris twelve months ago."[48]

And what a year it had been, culminating in Steichen's extraordinary recognition as a photographer in the London and Paris exhibitions and as a painter in the Champs de Mars Salon. Among painters and photographers in London and in Paris, Eduard Steichen of Milwaukee was already making a name for himself. But the "enfant terrible" could not afford time to rest.

The need to produce images of children for the upcoming exhibition set him off on a search for children to photograph. In the late spring or early summer of 1901, he received tentative approval to photograph the children of the popular Norwegian painter Frits Thaulow, who resided in a lovely house on the Boulevard Malesherbes, having chosen to live and work in Paris after sojourns in London and in Italy.* It is not clear whether mutual friends led Steichen to Thaulow or whether he discovered the attractive family in the 1895 painting by Jacques-Emile Blanche at the Musée d'Orsay. Blanche's painting shows Thaulow at his easel, surrounded by his wife, son, and small daughter. Gregarious, handsome, and independently wealthy, Thaulow was born in Christiania, Norway, in 1847, and for many years he devoted himself to painting Norwegian landscapes and to teaching. According to critics, he was a "full-blooded naturalist with a touch of impressionism" who believed that "the landscape painter should be forbidden to have a studio."[49] A landscape should be "an actual portrait and transcript of nature" painted out-of-doors, he argued.[50] Well-known throughout the Paris art world, Thaulow counted many artists there among his close friends, especially Auguste Rodin.[51]

When Thaulow asked Steichen to join his family for lunch one Saturday so that they could discuss the proposed photographs of the Thaulow children, Steichen strapped his portfolio to his bicycle and rode across the city. Thaulow painted superb snow scenes, Steichen thought; should he show the great artist his own recent watercolor paintings of snow in the Bois de Boulogne? He did so, and later, as Thaulow studied them, the older man said, "It makes me feel my paintings are hard and crude."[52] Immediately impressed with Steichen's paintings and prints, he agreed to let Steichen photograph his children.

Later, Thaulow himself was photographed by Steichen, posing in profile, with soft light sifting through the dominating shadows of the composition. Frank Eugene's influence lurks in the faint etching marks texturing the gum-bichromate print, which a critic in a 1901 issue of *Photography* called an "impertinence" and a "kill-time" triviality because it was not "a portrait in the ordinary sense of the word," but an "irritating trifle that reminds one of Tenniel's illustration of the smile of the Cheshire cat."[53] Thaulow liked it, however, well enough to pay Steichen handsomely for it.

---

*In his letters to Rodin (now at the Musée Rodin), Thaulow spelled his first name Frits. Therefore, I have used that spelling, even though most literature, including Steichen's *A Life in Photography*, refers to him as Fritz Thaulow.

Relaxing in the convivial presence of the painter on that day of their first meeting, Steichen spoke ardently of his admiration for Rodin and his desire to meet him. Because Rodin's Saturday-afternoon open house was a ritual known to his friends and acquaintances, Thaulow immediately proposed that they bicycle out to Meudon so he could introduce Steichen to his old friend Rodin. Thaulow predicted that Rose Beuret, Rodin's common-law wife, would invite them to stay for dinner, but he said they should decline, to spare her the trouble. Steichen, however, "secretly hoped she would be more adamant in her insistence than the Thaulows would be in their refusal."[54]

Excited and apprehensive, Steichen once again secured his portfolio on his bicycle and rode with Thaulow and his wife out to suburban Meudon, where Rodin had his home and his studio on a hill with a breathtaking view of the Seine and Paris in the distance. Rodin, then sixty-one, was gradually building a little kingdom on his hilltop. In 1895, he had bought the steep-roofed, gabled redbrick and stone house called the Villa des Brillants, and most of the surrounding land. There he settled with Rose Beuret, who had lived with him since 1864, when he was an impoverished beginning artist and she was his favorite model. Rodin's hill with its idyllic view was undergoing a transformation that summer of Steichen's first visit, for earlier in 1901, Rodin had bought the land adjoining his property, put it in Rose's name, and begun reconstructing there the pavilion that had housed his 1900 exhibition in the Place de l'Alma, planning to use the building as his atelier. The whole structure had been carefully disassembled and moved from Paris, and the reconstruction was well under way that summer Saturday.

Rodin loved to show the work in progress to guests and no doubt would have given them a tour, but he was in town when Steichen and the Thaulows arrived at Meudon. They were warmly greeted by Rose, the long-suffering, illiterate peasant woman devoted to Rodin and much loved in return by her companion, despite his countless unconcealed love affairs. As his sculptures of her testify, she had been a sensual, beautiful young woman. From the first subservient to Rodin, she cooked and served so diligently that many people assumed she was his servant—as in effect she was. She had also borne Rodin a son, who was sent away to be brought up by Rose's family.

Rose was often ridiculed—snobbish Henry James called her the "never-before-beheld and apparently most sordid and *inavouable* little wife, an incubus proceeding from an antediluvian error, and yet apparently less displeasing to the observer in general than the dreadful great man himself."[55] The poet Rainer Maria Rilke, who became Rodin's private secretary in 1905 and thus came to know Rose well, painted a far more sympathetic word portrait of her with her gray hair and her "dark deep-set eyes," voicing his concern that she was "thin, unkempt, tired, and old, tormented by something."[56] Throughout the years of their stormy liaison, Rodin called Rose Madame Rodin, and Steichen, like many others, certainly assumed that she was Rodin's legal wife.

When Rose greeted Steichen on his first pilgrimage to Meudon, he found her a welcoming hostess. They awaited Rodin in his garden, where he had built a pond now inhabited by swans. A profusion of flowers grew under the trees, and Rodin's dogs sniffed about or slept in the sun. Rodin loved solitary, meditative walks in his garden and the enfolding orchard. He had arranged his own sculptures among the foliage and plants, along with some of his collection of sculpture and other artifacts from antiquity—a young Mithra without a head, sacrificing a sacred bull; an Eros sleeping on a lion skin; small marble altars.[57]

Steichen waited that afternoon in 1901 in Rodin's garden, his impressionable mind and observant blue eyes memorizing every detail. Like Rodin, he would spend an artistic lifetime believing in the perfection of nature and experimenting to capture some of that perfection in art. And he, too, would build a garden that would serve his imagination and spirit as an exquisite and essential refuge.

By the turn of the century, Rodin had become the prototype for the great artist. In *The Ambassadors,* Henry James describes a celebrated sculptor who awed a young visitor "with a personal lustre almost violent," and who "shone in a constellation: all of which was more than enough to crown him ... with the light, with the romance, of glory."[58] That was an apt description of Steichen's emotions as he met Rodin face-to-face in his garden.

"Late in the afternoon," Steichen wrote many years later in his autobiography, "there appeared over the brow of the hill a stocky figure walking rapidly towards the house. I recognized Rodin from the brief glimpse I had had at the exposition."[59] He wore a black hat and a regal beard, and he exuded energy as he walked.

"God! What a photograph that would make!" Steichen exclaimed, and found himself weeping.[60]

"There were the usual formal introductions, and then Rodin and Rose both insisted that we stay for dinner," Steichen remembered. "When Rodin insisted, that's all there was to it. We stayed."[61]

They dined in the garden, as Rodin habitually loved to do. Besides, his house was severely simple, and his garden was a more congenial place to entertain guests than his sparsely furnished dining room. Japanese lanterns were hung in the trees. Rose arranged the table and then went indoors to cook, while Rodin and his guests talked and walked in the garden. Then Rose called them to a wonderful dinner, set off by wines Rodin himself retrieved from his cellar, followed by liqueur and cigars.

Afterward, Frits Thaulow told Steichen to show Rodin his portfolio. Steichen did so with "fear and trembling." He watched as the older man slowly and carefully examined his prints, "giving grunts of approval and, sometimes, words."[62] At one point, Rodin silently took Steichen's hand, his appreciation for the young man's work eloquent in the silence.[63]

When the sculptor laid down the portfolio, Steichen "blurted out" that the great ambition of his life was to make Rodin's portrait. His broad hand on Steichen's shoulder, Rodin said to Thaulow, "You see, Fritz [sic], enthusiasm is not dead yet."[64]

With that, Rodin told Steichen he could photograph him anytime, as often as he wanted to. "Consider my studio yours. Come whenever you like," he said.[65] Saturday afternoons were particularly convenient, since Rodin spent that time with friends and visitors rather than working. So it was that for the next year, usually on Saturday, but sometimes twice weekly, Steichen rode his bicycle out of the city to the serene beauty of Rodin's hilltop garden, and the seeming chaos of this great man's studio.

7

TRUSTING THE EYES

(1 9 0 1 - 1 9 0 2)

The artist ... sees; that is to say, that his eye, grafted on his heart, reads deeply into the bosom of Nature. That is why the artist has only to trust his eyes.[1]

—AUGUSTE RODIN

STEICHEN WAS SOMETHING OF A GYPSY in Paris, moving from one studio to another as his finances dictated. He left 83 Boulevard du Montparnasse for a larger space at 103 Boulevard du Montparnasse in the late summer of 1901. After the exhilarating visit to Rodin at Meudon, Steichen sat down in this studio to compose a letter of thanks, struggling over the written French. Although he had grown up in his parents' multilingual household, the family habitually wrote their letters in German or English, not French. Therefore, he spoke French with more animation and fluency than he could manage when writing the language.[2] Some of his letters to Rodin would be written in clumsy, often inaccurate French, with frank apologies for his limitations. But eager to make the best impression in this first note, Steichen must have called upon a friend for help, as it is composed far more skillfully than his other letters. Later, Steichen routinely wrote to Rodin in English, teasing that it would be easier to translate his English than his French.[3]

"Cher Maître," Steichen began that summer day in 1901, then thanked Rodin for their first visit, and for the sculptor's generous praise of the photographs and paintings Steichen had shown him. He offered to give Rodin some of the photographs, reiterating his sincere hope that "grande maître" would pose for his camera. It would be a great honor, Steichen wrote, barely able to contain his excitement.[4] To photograph this extraordinary artist surrounded by his work at Meudon would be a dream come true, as well as a coveted challenge. Steichen was not shy about accepting Rodin's invitation to visit his studio, and he cycled out to Meudon the very next Saturday.

For twenty-two-year-old Eduard Steichen, the most memorable event in that first exciting year in Paris was the chance to fulfill his dream of knowing the great Rodin. Almost every Saturday for a year, Steichen went to Rodin's studio.[5] During those visits, he observed the sculptor at work and at leisure, studied the masterpieces lining the walls of Rodin's studio, listened to him talk, and watched his supple hands pulling seemingly animate figures from raw marble and clay. Largely self-taught as Steichen was, Rodin told the attentive young man stories about how certain sculptures came to be, and how many of them were born out of long years of struggle, rejection, and hardship. Rodin knew far too well the relentless dedication exacted of most artists—he and Rose had lived and worked in poverty for more than twenty years before he could give up commercial art and decoration to concentrate on sculpture.

There had not even been money to hire models in the earlier days, Rodin recalled, and once in 1863, desperate for a subject, he had drafted Bibi, the janitor who did odd jobs and sometimes cleaned his atelier. Bibi's battered face was hard to look at, so much so, Rodin told Steichen, "At first I could hardly stand it. Then as I worked I found his head really had a wonderful shape. In his own way he was beautiful. That was how I came to model 'L'Homme au Nez Casse' [*The Man with the Broken Nose*]. That man taught me many things."[6] The resulting sculpture determined all his future work, Rodin said, because it launched his habit of sculpting directly from a model, and he considered it "the first good piece of modeling I ever did."[7]

It would be impossible to quantify the influence of such a charismatic master on the seminal work of an ambitious young artist. Long before they met, Rodin had been for Steichen a celebrated, venerated artist and a very public great man. As their private friendship evolved, however, Rodin became Steichen's mentor, a patron, a friend, and an inspiration. From the stimulating dialogue that floated in the air on those Saturday afternoons in the garden at the Villa des Brillants, Steichen absorbed ideas until Rodin's aesthetic philosophy grew to be deeply and permanently ingrained in Steichen's own work. Most of all, Steichen always remembered "how often Rodin had spoken of going to nature for inspiration."[8]

As Rodin expressed it, "When one begins to understand nature, progress goes on unceasingly."[9] But Rodin admonished that "a mediocre man copying nature will never produce a work of art; because he really looks without *seeing,* and though he may have noted each detail minutely, the result will be flat and without character.... The artist, to the contrary, *sees;* that is to say, that his eye, grafted on his heart, reads deeply into the bosom of Nature. That is why the artist has only to trust his eyes."[10]

The young German poet Rainer Maria Rilke, also observed how Rodin drew his "elemental power" from a deep harmony with nature.[11] Already engaged in photographing and painting the woods, fields, and sky that he loved, Steichen would also seek that same harmony throughout his life. In addition, he shared Rodin's conviction that all the arts are connected. As Rodin put it, "Painting, sculpture, literature, music are more closely related than is generally believed. They express all the sentiments of the human soul in the light of Nature." Consequently, artists could step beyond any one medium to learn from artists at work in other forms. It was because he recognized an artistry and vision akin to his own that Rodin read Dante, Balzac, and Baudelaire, just as young Steichen absorbed the writings of Maeterlinck, George Bernard Shaw, and, later on, Carl Sandburg.

In addition, Rodin offered a compelling precept that Steichen sought from the beginning to embody in his own portrait work. "An artist worthy of the name should express all the truth of nature," Rodin argued, "not only the exterior truth, but also, and above all, the inner truth. When a good sculptor models a torso, he not only represents the muscles, but the life which animates them."[12] Rodin had discovered this when he was sculpting Bibi's ravaged face. As Rilke saw, "Again and again in his figures Rodin returned to this bending inward, to this intense listening to one's own depth." At the same instant, Rodin found the inner self of the figure, "bent by its own soul."[13] "I am at the expression of something psychological" in photographic portraits, Steichen said.¹⁴ Penetration of the subject's interior life could be the photographer's purpose just as much as the sculptor's, he perceived, and his ability to tap the core of his subject's character would animate his own best work.

Finally, Steichen saw that Rodin worked intensely hard, to the point of collapse, in order to capture the the inner life. Watching the master at work, Steichen learned anew that prolonged, disciplined labor was essential if the artist hoped to master the fundamental techniques and skills essential to the art. "Craft is only a means," Rodin said. "But the artist who neglects it will never attain his end, which is the interpretation of feelings, of ideas. . . . No sudden inspiration can replace the long toil which is indispensable to give the eyes a true knowledge of form and of proportion and to render the hand obedient to the commands of feeling." Rodin taught that it was necessary to have "consummate technique in order to hide what one knows," for he believed that "the great difficulty and the crown of art is to draw, to paint, to write with ease and simplicity."¹⁵

The result of the artist's long toil is, in Rilke's lovely phrase, "the thought which takes shape in the stone."¹⁶ Much as Steichen had done, Rilke would seek out Rodin in the belief that he was a "supreme" artist because he "was a worker whose only desire was to penetrate with all his forces into the humble and difficult significance of his tools."¹⁷ This masterful union with the tools of his art medium was exactly Steichen's instinctive purpose with the camera and the brush.

In Paris in 1901 and 1902, Steichen did not know whether to call himself a photographer first and then a painter, or the other way around. While the thrilling opportunity to photograph Rodin meant that Steichen was devoting much of his creative energy to photography, he told an American journalist that photography was "only a side issue" with him, and that he was "a painter, first, last, and all the time."¹⁸ No matter how he classified himself, Steichen the painter-photographer was clearly working hard in each idiom then, testing the boundaries between the two forms and writing down his evolving ideas about the connections between painting and photography.

For the time being, however, the techniques of painting seemed to dominate his work: His lyrical soft-focus photographs of that period were distinctive for their deliberate painterly effects, whether he was photographing the same landscape he was painting or catching in his misty-textured photographs the interplay of light and darkness that drew comparisons to Impressionist landscapes. Often, he actually etched lines on the negative itself or hand-painted a print to give it color and depth, or more tone and detail. "We cannot realize that it should seem strange that, if the photographer is desirous also of being an artist, his work shall communicate the spirit of the painter," he wrote in the English journal *Photogram* in 1901.[19]

Despite his expressed first allegiance to painting, however, it was photography that provided most of the modest income Steichen earned then. Even more important to him during his sojourn in Paris, photography offered Steichen his most enthralling subjects, chiefly Fred Holland Day and Rodin, whom he continued to see once or twice a week.[20] Steichen was discovering that he could not photograph more than one subject in a day, however. "It means the complete merging of myself in the personality of my subject, a complete loss of my own identity, and when it is over, I am in a state of collapse, almost," he explained. "The commercial photographer, with his forty sittings a day, cannot of course enter into the individuality of his sitter as I do."[21]

Steichen undertook his first photographic studies of nude models in Paris in 1901, the faces of the model in each case discreetly turned from the camera. He pointed out the reason for this. "For many years everyone had prejudices against posing in the nude and even professional models usually insisted, when they posed for nude pictures, that their faces not be shown."[22] Steichen's nudes are so deftly lit and posed that the resulting photographic images seem textured and three-dimensional, evocative again of the living, breathing contours of Rodin's sculpted figures. Rodin often told his disciples that the human body is the mirror of the soul, and the soul is the true center of beauty: "What we adore in the human body more even than its beautiful form is the inner flame which seems to shine from within and to illumine it."[23] In Steichen's photographs of nudes, there is a diffusion of light and a fluid grace that evokes the "flame" of life and vitality, as if, again, he were sculpting with his camera.

His passionate theme remained the photographic studies of great men, however, and Steichen conceived a motif that would work powerfully in his pictures of Rodin and others. He involved the artist's creations in the picture, using the particular artist's tools in a manner that was not so much consciously Symbolist or contrived as it was a straightforward, eloquent fusion of artist and artifact in his own environment.[24]

He was elated to have the chance to try the technique in a photograph of the shy Belgian writer Maurice Maeterlinck, whose work he had devoured in Milwaukee. The chance came after Steichen received a commission to paint a portrait of Maurice Maeterlinck's flamboyant wife, the actress Georgette Le Blanc, and Le Blanc, in turn, invited him to meet the Symbolist playwright and poet. At their first encounter, Maeterlinck was trying to repair his automobile; the writer was clad in greasy overalls and looking very much, Steichen recalled, like "a husky garage mechanic from Altoona, Pa., rather than a mystic poet."[25] Later, Steichen posed Maeterlinck looking up from his work, pen in hand, a soft light illuminating some of the words on his manuscript.

Steichen applied the same technique in his photograph of Alphonse Mucha, the Czechoslovakian illustrator and painter, asking him to stand before one of his famous Art Nouveau posters of actress Sarah Bernhardt. He posed the French photographer Otto holding an enlarged print in his hand. Another sculptor in Paris, the Frenchman Paul Albert Bartholomé, agreed to go with Steichen and his camera to Père Lachaise Cemetery, where he was posed in profile before his best-known work, *Le Monument aux Morts*. In the finished photograph, the sculptor leans against a colonnade, the handle of one of his tools visible under one arm. Above hovers the sculpted ethereal form of an angel. Steichen achieved a tone, texture, and contour in the picture that is evocative of sculpture itself.

One day in Rodin's studio, Steichen listened as an American woman asked for the sculptor's opinion of the Impressionist painters. Rodin answered, "There . . . are . . . only . . . good . . . painters . . . and . . . bad . . . painters."[26] Trying to discern for himself the difference and to learn from the best painters, Steichen regularly made the rounds of Paris museums, galleries, and exhibitions, but most of what he knew then about painting, he recalled, "was based on Sargent, Whistler and the Impressionists," especially Monet, whose work he had immediately loved.[27] It was an unidentified fellow photographer who radically expanded Steichen's vision of avant-garde painting when he invited Steichen to his studio to see an exhibition he had personally arranged. Steichen stepped into his friend's ten- or twelve-foot-square gallery that day in 1902, the only person on hand to see the walls completely covered with unframed paintings, boldly emotional and dramatic, drastically different from anything he had ever seen. Shocked and even outraged by these disturbing pictures, Steichen wrote later, "If this was great painting, then everything I had conceived and learned was wrong. At the same time, I felt conscious of a curious force and power in these pictures. The contradictory experience was too much for me, and I was actually nauseated."[28] He raced out of the gallery and vomited in the street.[29]

The next day, however, he could not resist going back. Once again, he found himself the only visitor in the room. The paintings, his friend told him, were by Vincent van Gogh, who had committed suicide in a mental hospital in 1890 when he was only thirty-seven. Steichen had never heard of van Gogh, but his second look at the paintings left him, he recalled, "with the strong impression" that they were not so different from what others in the vanguard of modern painting were trying to achieve.[30] Van Gogh's extraordinary Post-Impressionist paintings were for sale in that little room for a thousand francs each—about two hundred dollars in those days—but there were no buyers. Afterward, Steichen was haunted by the brash, sometimes violent colors and forms of van Gogh's paintings, and he was shaken by the artist's uninhibited passion for nature. His own watercolors and oils were muted and constrained by comparison, and not nearly so free and imaginative as his photographs.

During those Paris days, Steichen was learning to trust his own vision, developing a highly original, powerful photographic style that, as far as can be told from the surviving pictures, surpassed his innovations in the portraits, still-life compositions, and landscapes that he was painting at that time. He worked hard at getting exposure in each medium, exhibiting frequently in venues that ranged from the most prestigious salons in Paris to out-of-the-way avant-garde galleries, but his income was disappointing and unpredictable. Caught up in photographing the great men of Europe, he seems to have expanded his plan to include women, as in *Vitality*, his photograph of beautiful Yvette Guilbert, the French chanteuse whose songs chronicled bohemian life in Paris. According to English novelist and playwright Israel Zangwill, whom he also photographed, Steichen's photograph of the English writer Lady Sickert was "a portrait of a great soul."[31] It was his ambition, Steichen said, to create a "photograph gallery of great people," to give the series to a museum, and to publish a book of the portraits.[32]

He lived and worked in Paris with all the panache a poor artist with a growing reputation could muster, savoring the bohemian life of the Left Bank, especially the lively, cheap cafés inhabited by artists and academics. Money was always scarce, sometimes frighteningly so, but Steichen had learned in his Milwaukee boyhood how to be frugal. In Paris, he adopted a jaunty new habit: When he earned a little money from a sale, he would cash some of it into small change and throw it around his studio, like bread crumbs. Then, when he was nearly destitute, he could count on finding some coins strewn about the house, hidden "investments" under the furniture or rugs.

Despite everything, he was "ebullient, energetic, quick-moving," with a flair for the dramatic evident in his flowing capes and fashionable hats, the spare, elegant decoration of his studio, and the ultimate drama of his work. Some friends and critics, including Alfred Stieglitz, even thought "he staged his way through his life."[33]

Many of his friends in those days were artists, and they inevitably brought other artists into his world. In the late summer of 1901, thanks to Day and Coburn, Steichen met the first lady of American photography, Gertrude Käsebier. Just as Rodin was his surrogate father in Europe, during that summer Mrs. Käsebier quickly became the warm, maternal figure of his life in Paris. She had endorsed Steichen's work when she served on the jury of the second Philadelphia Photographic Salon in 1899, and when she arrived in Paris in the summer of 1901 with her daughter Hermine, she immediately looked him up. Their friendship was instantaneous and lasting, with the occasional distance or dispute embedded in it, as in most lifelong relationships, more than offset by an overriding affection and respect.

To Steichen's regimen of hard work and constant worry about

money, Käsebier brought the relief of exuberant company and pleasure that summer of 1901. She was "goodness itself," he wrote to Stieglitz, imbuing him with "new energy and enthusiasm."[34] They saw each other daily, Käsebier reported to Stieglitz in her letters that summer, sharing a "double superlative time in Paris...."[35] She was forty-nine when they met, and Steichen was twenty-two. He sketched her in charcoal, and she photographed him repeatedly. In one of her dusky pictures of him, for instance, he sits on a balustrade, dressed in black, the wide-brimmed black hat overshadowing the profile of his lean face, smoking a long, slender pipe.

Mrs. Käsebier welcomed the handsome young American to her own circle of friends in Europe, which included two beautiful young American sisters she was chaperoning on their first visit to Paris—Clara and Charlotte Smith from the Ozark Mountains of Missouri.[36] Mrs. Käsebier introduced Charlotte, an art student, and Clara, a singer, to Eduard Steichen and other artists, including illustrator Beatrice Baxter (whom Steichen called Beatrix, and whom he photographed in 1901); photographer Alfred Langdon Coburn; artist-illustrator Frances Delehanty; and painter and sculptor Willard "Billy" Paddock, "part of the group of struggling young artists in Paris at the turn of the century."[37] They enjoyed picnics, painting forays into the country, and stimulating talks about art during that idyllic summer. Gertrude Käsebier photographed the young people on one country picnic and took at least two dozen candid photographs of Steichen, later arranging them with his help in an album that by summer's end also held photographs of Steichen by Alvin Langdon Coburn and Beatrix Baxter, as well as other unsigned drawings.[38]

Mrs. Käsebier also fostered romance during the summer of 1901, for Charlotte Smith soon had a suitor in "gentle, modest, idealistic and visionary" Billy Paddock, who had studied painting at the Pratt Institute but was primarily a sculptor, with "wonderful and skillful hands."[39] Steichen, still recovering from the shock of Rosa's death and so perhaps in danger of rebounding, nonetheless turned his pensive eyes toward Clara, the younger of the two Smith sisters, and three years his senior.[40] She was a great beauty, and Eduard Steichen always had an eye for beauty.[41] His early photographs of Clara reveal a sensual, somber young woman who bears a striking resemblance to his mother, Mary, with her regal carriage, her huge expressive eyes, the luxuriant dark hair swept back from her sculpted face.

Whereas Charlotte was warm, serene, and unpretentious, Clara was dramatic and mercurial, with a captivating, sometimes manipulative, somewhat affected charm and grace. Because their father had been a dedicated frontier doctor, often treating patients who could not afford to pay him, he would have little to leave his children "beyond affection and moral principles."[42] The Smith sisters knew that because they lacked dowries and social position, they would have to make their way through life relying on their own industry, with some financial help from more prosperous relatives in St. Louis and Boston. Clara's critical, judgmental mother bitterly looked down on her husband and all others who lacked money and a certain social class, and that attitude, joined to some deep-seated insecurity, impelled Clara to so embroider and exaggerate her family history that fact and fantasy blurred over time into self-serving mythology.

According to Clara, the Smith sisters were descended from Elizabethan courtiers, a Southern slave owner, and an officer in the French and Indian Wars, Col. Nathaniel Gist. When he was captured by Indians after the war, Gist became the consort of an Indian princess who gave birth to a son, Sequoyah. This legendary Indian scholar, artist, and silversmith, presuming Gist to be his father, later took the name George Guess (a phonetic interpretation of the English name) in tribute to Nathaniel Gist. In Clara's account of the family history, the covered wagons carrying the Smith, Havel, and Gist families from Tennessee to the beautiful Ozark wilderness of the Missouri frontier carried priceless treasures: a Dutch Bible, an illustrated edition of *Pilgrim's Progress,* and a well-worn vellum edition of the plays of Shakespeare.[43] To Clara, these possessions testified that despite their upbringing in a log cabin seventy-five miles from civilized Springfield, Missouri, the Smith sisters were cultured and refined.

Charlotte, the elder sister, was a talented musician and seamstress as well as an artist. Clara wrote poetry, studied drama, dabbled at painting, and, because she sang and played the piano beautifully, dreamed of becoming a professional concert singer and soloist. She had been a spirited belle back home in Missouri, so much so that she was once simultaneously engaged to three young men. When one of them sent Clara a handsome little pug dog with a note, a bouquet of flowers, and an engagement ring, Clara kept the flowers but returned the puppy immediately, the rejected engagement ring stuck emphatically on its tail.[44]

After some modest schooling in St. Louis, Charlotte and Clara left Missouri to live in New York so that Charlotte could study art and Clara could pursue her musical interests.[45] Clara remembered that with Charlotte's skillful work as a seamstress as their mainstay, the hardworking Smith sisters managed to support themselves and their studies in New York. Eventually, however, serious Charlotte and restless, ambitious Clara decided to go to Paris to paint and study art and music, most likely turning to one of their more prosperous relatives for a subsidy to help finance their first trip abroad. So it was that during part of their first summer in Paris, they were chaperoned by Gertrude Käsebier.

In the company of these vivacious American women flocking around Mrs. Käsebier, Steichen was relaxed and high-spirited. Because he knew Paris and was known there as a rising young artist accomplished in both painting and photography, he was the ideal host and guide for the admiring young Americans. Completely at home in the bohemian habitat of Montparnasse, Steichen looked very much the dashing avant-garde artist clad in his black turtleneck shirts and an occasional white smock, his dark hair covered by a debonair beret or black fedora. And soon he confessed to being "dotty" over Clara Smith, whom he affectionately christened his "own dear Peety."[46]

He painted a beautiful oil portrait of Clara sometime that summer, posing her in a white satin dress against a white silk background, the green book in her hand the only color in the portrait except for delicate tones of gold in the fabric of her dress. Four decades later, Alfred Stieglitz gossiped that Clara had posed for Steichen's nude photographic studies, that the couple had been intimate, and that Clara had coerced Steichen into marrying her to salvage her reputation.[47] No evidence supports Stieglitz's conjecture, which is strongly countered by Clara's imperious concern for appearances and, more important, by the clear reality in Steichen's letters to her and to others that not only was he in love with this woman but that he, not she, ardently pressed the courtship.

After the tragedy of the enigmatic Rosa's suicide earlier in 1901, Steichen spent the summer working hard in his studio, going out to

Meudon to immerse himself in Rodin's work and his presence, and, in free hours, meandering through the French countryside with Clara, the Käsebiers, and other friends. His life was frenetically, abundantly full, and in the midst of it all, he was falling deeply in love with Clara Smith, and she with him. From the outset, however, theirs was a stormy romance. She could be proud, demanding, difficult, and jealous. He could be infuriatingly absorbed in his work and himself, and, occasionally, in other beautiful women. He apparently confided to her the tragedy of Rosa's suicide, for the event surfaced bitterly in her later letters, as if she was jealous of Rosa, even in death, resentful of the role she had played in Steichen's life before Clara herself ever arrived on the scene.

Charlotte Smith and Billy Paddock, meanwhile, were moving toward what would become a placid and loving marriage, and when they decided to return to the United States and settle down on a farm in Connecticut, Clara returned with them, making her home part of the time with the newlyweds in Still River, Connecticut, and the rest of the time in New York. Although no record remains to explain why, Steichen's letters reveal, in a foreshadowing of events to come, that he and Clara did not part happily.

Returning from a summer bicycle excursion into the French countryside, Steichen found a letter from Rodin inquiring about whether he would make some photographs. Steichen answered that he was invited to spend a few weeks in Munich but that he was at Rodin's disposal until departure. Consequently, Steichen photographed Rodin in the late summer of 1901. He charged ten dollars a print for photographic portraits then, but Rodin paid him at least fifty dollars and sometimes a hundred dollars for his work.[48] The commission would finance his upcoming autumn journey with Gertrude and Hermine Käsebier to Germany and Denmark.[49] In Munich, they went to see the International Art Exhibition, especially the work of the Munich Secessionist painters at the Glaspalast.[50] Steichen was quite taken with the efforts of these Secessionists and intrigued with the bold independence of artists who would defend their avant-garde work by withdrawing from the established group of artists and rallying together to form their own, new alliance.

During that journey, Steichen photographed the German portrait painter Franz von Lenbach, first posing the artist with his tools—the brush and palette—as was now his habit. Next, Steichen decided to emulate one of von Lenbach's self-portraits, in which he usually wore a certain "large, broad-brimmed hat."[51] When von Lenbach could not find his own hat, he borrowed Steichen's, peered enigmatically through his round eyeglasses, and obligingly posed for the portrait that Steichen added to his growing series of images of great men.

For a year, Steichen visited Rodin, pedaling back and forth between his own Montparnasse studio in Paris and Rodin's quarters at Meudon, spending countless quiet hours living with the sculptor's work and giving it long, reflective thought and study. He had made a few straightforward portraits before he finally conceived the image of Rodin he wanted to photograph. Since during this catalytic process he was composing an aesthetic theory as much as a single photograph, Steichen would never again invest so much time and meticulous preparation in the composition of a single photographic portrait. His idea was eloquently simple: He would capture Rodin's spirit through images of the sculptor surrounded by his work.

Sometime in the spring of 1902, he made an appointment to pose Rodin in his crowded studio at Meudon, standing next to his *Victor Hugo* and facing his *Le Penseur* (*The Thinker*). Because Steichen owned only one lens then, "a rapid rectilinear lens of relatively long focus," he said, and not the wide-angle lens needed to embrace the full picture, he had to rely on ingenuity to achieve his vision.[52] First, he photographed Rodin in profile standing before the massive white marble statue of Hugo.[53] He then moved his camera to photograph *Le Penseur* alone, with soft light gleaming on the muscular bronze form. He would merge the two exposures into one picture, he told Rodin confidently, although Steichen had no idea how he was going to do this.

He had set up a basic darkroom in his new studio in the rear of a charming old garden on the Rue Boissonade near the Boulevard du Montparnasse, and there he tinkered with the process of joining the two exposures. "I didn't know enough about the technical problems to solve the job of uniting the two pictures at once," he remembered, "and at first I printed only the negative of Rodin standing near Victor Hugo. Later, I worked out a technique by which I could combine the two negatives and make one print."[54] That accomplished, he set his gifted hands to work pulling from the paper the images he had envisioned when he composed the portraits, working and working over his pigment prints until he was reasonably satisfied with them. As he would always do, he had experimented until he found the technical solution to the picture he had conceived, and the result was *Rodin—Le Penseur,* a stunning pigment print, still considered one of Steichen's finest achievements. Rodin and *The Thinker* face each other, two unforgettable images in profile, the glistening dark bronze of *The Thinker* cast against the brilliant white marble of *Victor Hugo,* all three haunting figures lost in reverie.

Steichen's triumvirate of the artist and his sculptures proclaims not only the character of Rodin but the organic relation of the artist to his art. In the photograph, Rodin is joined to his work so evocatively that it is almost possible to forget that one figure in Steichen's beautiful composition is the living artist and that the two others are his creations, sculpted in marble and bronze, vital manifestations of Rodin himself, exuding energy and life. Steichen's dynamic image of the trinity of the artist and his two figures appears to be a photograph, sculpted, at once depicting as well as containing the contoured dimensions and depths of Rodin's sculpture. And so in the end, the process of this photograph actually involves a quartet—the three figures posed within the picture, and the figure outside—the photographer conceiving and capturing their images. In the act, the camera becomes the chisel, finding the figure in the "stone" of Steichen's imagination.

When the day came to show his work to Rodin, Steichen carefully packed the precious photographs and pedaled nervously back to Meudon, worrying all the way about how Rodin would respond. To his immense relief, Steichen recalled, Rodin "was elated."[55] Rodin's friend and biographer Judith Cladel was at Meudon that day also, and she immediately saw the genius of the photograph. "Ah, it is Rodin. It is you between God and the devil," she said.

"Mais oui," Rodin answered, proud of the print and ready to show it off.[56]

Not surprisingly, Steichen had posed Rodin in the photograph much as Rodin had presented Hugo and Balzac, echoing in his composition the sculptor's own conviction that to capture the power of the mind, it was necessary to emphasize the head as the dominating feature. Steichen gave Rodin other fine portraits of himself that day—a straightforward portrait study with the sculptor facing the camera, his hand raised to his beard; and a soft-focus portrait in which Rodin, eyes downcast, leans on the gentle arc of one of his plaster studies. Steichen's own favorite, he said, was the composite photograph of Rodin, *Hugo,* and *Le Penseur,* because "the silhouette of that massive head" seemed closer to the "Rodin who had created the Balzac than any of the others. It is probably more of a picture *to* Rodin than it is *of* Rodin, because after all, it associates the genius of the man with that expressed by his work."[57]

A drawing based on Steichen's *Rodin—Le Penseur* was used as the frontispiece for a 1902 issue of *Paris World,* and from time to time over the next ten years, Steichen would return to photograph Rodin and his art. There are eighty-one Steichen photographs in the Musée Rodin in Paris—of Rodin himself; of *Balzac* and many other sculptures by Rodin; of his garden, his friends, and his lovers, for Steichen photographed Rose Beuret and, later on, the Franco-American Claire Coudert, Duchesse de Choiseul, Rodin's mistress from about 1907 until about 1912. There are also Steichen's gifts of other prints to Rodin—including *The Pool— Evening* and *Self Portrait with Brush and Palette.*[58] He had first shown the self-portrait to Rodin during dinner one evening at Meudon in 1901, writing afterward with great excitement to tell Stieglitz that Rodin had called it a remarkable photograph and a remarkable work of art—"*a chef d'oeuvre.*" He was not relaying Rodin's remarks out of vanity, Steichen told Stieglitz, but out of "patriotism to photography."[59]

As if to reassure Stieglitz in New York that he was honoring his earlier promise to stick to photography, Steichen added that he wished he could give more time to the camera.[60] Engrossed as he was with painting during 1901 and 1902 in Paris, it was the chance to photograph Rodin that motivated Steichen to commit as much of his time to photography then as he did.

The powerful presence of Rodin in his life was undoubtedly one of the pivotal forces in Steichen's own evolution as an artist. Needless to say, however, Rodin's art meant far more to Steichen than Steichen's art meant to Rodin, for the great sculptor attracted dozens of gifted young artists, men and women, writers as well as visual artists. And countless other photographers had held their cameras up to Rodin's work, and to the vigorous sculptor himself.[61] Unlike some other sculptors who photographed their own work, Rodin did not use a camera to assist in modeling his sculptures or to record them after they were finished, choosing instead to rely on others to take pictures for him. However, of the many photographers who competed to photograph Rodin and his work, including Alvin Langdon Coburn and Gertrude Käsebier, Steichen became the most astute and passionate interpreter of Rodin's sculpture, in part because he wove the artist's work so organically into his photographs either by posing the sculptor with his figures, as in *Rodin—Le Penseur,* or by dramatically eliciting the very breath and spirit of sculptures such as *Balzac.*

Furthermore, unlike many other photographers, when Steichen photographed Rodin's figures, he concentrated on art, not documentation, at once revealing the spirit of Rodin's creation and transmuting it into another work of art—the photograph. Rodin, in turn, recognized and endorsed Steichen's talent, even paying him in advance at times, whereas he subjected most photographers to stringent contracts and controls, requiring approval of all proofs and often editing them or even destroying them if they did not meet his exacting tastes. Steichen he trusted and admired, writing in 1908 that he was "a very great artist and the leading, the greatest photographer of the time."[62]

Steichen could be plagued with doubts, however. One afternoon, he strode about the studio at Meudon, alone with the phantom figures Rodin had immortalized in plaster, bronze, and marble. Suddenly, he felt overwhelmed by the magnitude of Rodin's artistry, and terribly insecure about his own talent. Just then, Rodin entered the studio, to find Steichen weeping. He wanted to know why.

"I've never done anything in my life and I never will," Steichen said despairingly. "Everything is wrong and I'm the wrongest of all." Rodin embraced the young man. "Now I know you are a great artist and have the right stuff in you," he said. "If I didn't still have such moments I would know I was through—finished."[63]

Steichen was twenty-two during that year of landmark professional achievements, alternating as most artists do between abject discouragement and supreme confidence in his work. In the latter frame of mind, he had had the audacity to decline the honor when A. Horsley Hinton notified him from London in 1901 that he had been elected to membership in the already-legendary Linked Ring by the members of that advanced photographic society. The bold decision to turn down that prestigious membership was Steichen's own personal act of secession: He did not want to be formally affiliated with any single body of photographers, he said, "while making the fight for artistic recognition."[64]

He seemed to be winning that fight in 1902. Ever since he had been formally recognized as a painter with the acceptance of his portrait of Day in the Salon Nationale des Beaux-Arts of 1901, Steichen's paintings and photographs had been shown with growing frequency in traditional as well as avant-garde exhibitions and galleries. In 1902, Steichen once again submitted his work to the Salon Nationale, informally called the Salon des Champs de Mars, as well as to the jury from the Société des Artistes Français, sponsors of the elite Salon de Maison des Artistes. To the Salon des Champs de Mars, he sent a few paintings, including the portrait of Clara; several charcoal portraits; and, to test the outer boundaries, at least ten photographs—pigment prints, including his *Self Portrait,* several nudes, and, from his great men series, portraits of Rodin, von Lenbach, Maeterlinck, Thaulow, French painter and etcher Paul Albert Besnard, American painter John White Alexander, who had painted Rodin, German painter and sculptor Franz von Stuck, and others. He was soon invited to exhibit both paintings and photographs at the Salon de Maison des Artistes.

This prestigious Champs de Mars salon had never admitted photographs, but that fact did not deter Steichen, champion of pictorial photography that he had become. Besides, he apparently had the encouragement of that rebel Rodin to submit *Rodin—Le Penseur* as well as the other photographs. The work of established artists such as Rodin and Frits Thaulow was accepted as a matter of course, but admission was a highly competitive honor for newcomers, and photographs had never before been considered. Nonetheless, hoping to "force to an issue the recognition of photography as an artistic medium," Steichen boldly delivered his photographs along with the paintings and drawings and sat back to see what would happen.[65]

He got the results in time for his birthday: the jury for the Salon Nationale des Beaux-Arts reviewed two thousand oil paintings by newcomers, choosing only eighty for admission, including Steichen's painting of Clara, *Portrait en Blanc*.[66] In addition, six of Steichen's large charcoal portraits were accepted.[67] But the stunning news that he immediately wrote to Stieglitz was that for the first time in the history of the Champ de Mars Salon, photographs had been accepted—Steichen's ten pigment prints, chosen on merit alone as *pictures,* regardless of medium. Only painters and sculptors made up the jury, which debated the issue fiercely before coming to a contentious split decision, with some jurors advocating the compromise of classifying the photographs as engravings, "although really they are nothing but remarkable photographs," wrote one of Steichen's defenders.[68] In the end, however, the photographs were accepted, as one critic noted, as "paragons of technique."[69]

Steichen was ecstatic, even though an immediate uproar broke out, with painters and art critics clamoring for the photographs to be banished from the exhibition, if for no other reason than that they felt it was a dangerous precedent and future salons would be deluged with photographic entries.[70] Eventually, however, "jealousies and political intrigue within the Salon itself" kept the photographs from being hung when the show opened April thirtieth for a two-month run.[71] Nevertheless, Steichen and Stieglitz exultantly shared the news, their elation undiluted by the knowledge that the unprecedented decision would be reversed.[72]

In fact, the controversy in this major Paris salon stirred so much publicity that Steichen's new visibility dramatically made the case in Paris that *photography* and *art* might indeed be synonymous terms. As international art critics and editors wrote about the fracas and reproduced Steichen's *Rodin—Le Penseur* in their newspapers, he reveled in the publicity. Some detractors even speculated that Steichen's only reason for submitting the pictures had been to gain notoriety.[73] His fundamental purpose had been to advance the case for pictorial photography, but even so, it was a daring and effective act of self-promotion, quickly landing Steichen on the front pages of *Paris World,* a leading art journal in Paris, and in newspaper stories around the world. From the pages of *Camera Notes* in New York, Stieglitz saluted his most visible and successful young crusader in Europe.

Earning fame by his solid accomplishments in painting and photography, Steichen was fulfilling Stieglitz's prophecy that it would take a successful painter-photographer to win the fight for wider acceptance of pictorial photography. Stieglitz spelled out his praise for Steichen in addresses he delivered to American camera clubs, as well as in the July 1902 issue of *Camera Notes:*

> *Sooner than we had hoped for has come the justification of the high estimate we have always placed upon the possibilities of pictorial photography in the hands of such workers as Eduard J. Steichen. . . . a cable to the New York Herald announced to the public that in spite of a stormy opposition in the ranks of the jury, Mr. Steichen broke down the immemorial barriers of the recognized Salon of the world, the Champs de Mars in Paris, and had been the first photographer whose prints were admitted to an art exhibition of any importance, in which all work had to pass before a strict jury of painters, sculptors, etc., of international repute, in fact one of the highest recognized authorities in the world of art.*[74]

Steichen's achievements drew widespread attention in the American press, as well: "For the first time in the history of Paris art exhibitions," the New York *Herald* reported on March 30, 1902, "photographs have been received as exhibits at the annual salon. The photographs were submitted by Mr. Edward Steichen, a young New Yorker, and are regarded as a great triumph."[75] Not quite two years after arriving in Paris, Eduard Steichen had already won international visibility for upsetting "the traditions of French art."[76]

From New York came further good news: Stieglitz planned to exhibit fourteen of Steichen's photographic prints at the National Arts Club (March 5–22, 1902), in a show entitled "American Pictorial Photography." James Huneker, art critic for the New York *Sun,* pronounced Steichen's work the "star exhibit" and "the highest point to which photographic portraiture has yet been brought."[77] Added to these milestones of Steichen's recognition in Europe and the United States was his successful one-man show of paintings and photographs at La Maison des Artistes on the Rue Royale in Paris (June 3–24, 1902) and an invitation to exhibit in the Salon des Réfuses.[78] So few of Steichen's paintings have survived that there is little visual documentation of his work as a painter in 1901 and 1902, yet he had obviously produced a body of work interesting and ample enough for him to mount a one-man show.[79]

From the earliest days, he gave great care to the framing and mounting of his paintings and photographs, sometimes building the frames himself. This instinct had been enhanced by his work helping Day hang exhibitions, because Day believed so fervently in the "artistic unity of display" that he devoted as much attention to framing and hanging his work, some said, as to its composition.[80] There were forty carefully framed paintings in Steichen's show at La Maison des Artistes, including several portraits: *Head of a Woman, 1901,* a small oil on wood panel; and a haunting portrait of a woman, *Portrait en Gris et Noir,* a larger oil on canvas. There were landscapes echoing the motifs and tones of his landscape photographs: *Moonlit Landscape,* for instance, also oil on wood panel; and two oils on canvas, *Landscape with Avenue of Trees* and *The Garden at Versailles.* The painting attracting the most attention was *Beethoven,* an oil painting that had been rejected by the Salon, along with the paintings Steichen had entitled *Ora Profundis, Russian,* and *A Little Human Being.* (Referring to these paintings, he wrote to Stieglitz, *"Too good that's all."*[81]) All of these works could be seen in his one-man show. Critic Sadakichi Hartmann described *Beethoven* in detail in 1903 just after he saw it for the first time: "It is all black and gray, huge and grim (though no canvas of colossal size) almost Doric in its severity. Everything is sacrificed to the idea, a study of the somber supremacy of genius and the martyrdom of the artist."[82]

Steichen had divided his photographs for the one-man show into two groups, thus documenting his experiments in Paris: "Series A," comprised of straight prints "without any manipulation or retouching"; and "Series B," *"Peinture à la Lumière,"* or "Painting with Light." The prints in this latter series demonstrated a variety of processes that lent themselves to "manipulation in varying degrees."[83] "Steichen, who resembles nobody else, continues to embitter part of the public," wrote his friend Robert Demachy, who had prompted Steichen's interest in the gum-bichromate process.[84] Charles Caffin carefully described that procedure later in a *Century Magazine* article on Steichen's photography, contending that "the process is so elastic that there is virtually no limit, except that of [the photographer's] own skill and feeling, to the changes and effects he can secure. Steichen, for example, with his command of the process, could take another man's negative and produce from it a print that would be characteristically a 'Steichen.'"[85]

This technical virtuosity threw Steichen into the center of still more controversy, but, fortified as he had been by all he had learned from Rodin about "academic misrepresentation and popular indifference," he was aggressively enjoying the fray.[86] Some photographers as well as painters complained that Steichen confused the two forms, allowing his techniques as a painter to seep into the photographic darkroom, cheating with brushwork on his negatives.

Despite the quibbling over Steichen's methods, there was general consensus that his work was extraordinary. He told a journalist in 1902 that he had not discovered anything new in photography, but merely had "a different way of doing things. Photographers have come to do wonderful things with the camera," he continued. "A camera will, you know, do almost anything you ask of it." Through the misty impressionistic qualities of some of his photographs, he was actually seeking fidelity: The sharp contrasts some photographers developed "are not true to nature, not such things as you actually see," Steichen explained. "I work in softer tones, and not only gain in fidelity of reproduction, but get nearer, I think, to the spirit of the subject. Now as to the mechanical process, it is altogether simple. I could give you the formula, but it would be of no particular interest to you, and you really wouldn't be any nearer knowing how than before."[87] He believed that the audience looking at his photographs should not be distracted by questions about the technical processes of photography, any more than their enjoyment of an etching or an oil painting depended on their knowledge of the techniques of etching or of the particular pigments and brushes used in the painting.

To Steichen's pleasure, Maurice Maeterlinck attended his one-man show, taking a particularly keen interest in the photographs, which most visitors passed by in favor of the paintings.[88] Steichen was heartened to hear Maeterlinck's unique and thoughtful reflections on photography, which, at his request, Maeterlinck incorporated into a short essay, later published by Stieglitz. "It is already many years since the sun revealed to us its power to portray objects and beings more quickly and more accurately than can pencil or crayon," Maeterlinck observed. "At first man was restricted to making permanent that which the impersonal and unsympathetic light had registered. He had not yet been permitted to imbue it with thought. But today it seems that thought has found a fissure through which to penetrate the mystery of this anonymous force, invade it, subjugate it, animate it, and compel it to say such things as have not yet been said in all the realm of chiaroscuro, of grace, of beauty and of truth."[89]

The May 1, 1902, issue of the British photographic art journal *Amateur Photographer* reproduced several Steichen portraits, landscapes, and figure studies from the ten photographic prints, six large charcoal drawings, and one large canvas accepted by the Champs de Mars Salon, hailing him as a foremost representative of the American School, which Steichen himself had defended in his 1901 article in the journal. His portraits were "eccentric in the extreme," wrote H. Vivian Yeo that May, concluding that Steichen was "nothing if not an impressionist."[90] Sadakichi Hartmann and *Paris World* critic Katherine Knode, on the other hand, were calling him a Symbolist.

Yet Steichen, savoring his triumphs in Paris, was essentially, defiantly, independently himself, assimilating only what he liked and needed from the work of others and putting his indelible stamp on the original result. It was a mark of his stunning overnight success that in 1902, when he was twenty-three, he had the ardent defense of many of the significant art critics and journals of his day, from the German art critic Ernst Juhl in the official journal of the photographic societies of Germany and Austria, *Die Photographische Rundschau,* to Stieglitz in *Camera Notes,* to Robert Demachy in the *Bulletin du Photo-Club de Paris.* His hometown newspaper took proud note of his "world-wide reputation" as a "master innovator in photography" and his "high place" in the art world.[91]

But the sheer intensity of his work had taken its toll, and after the controversy of the Champs de Mars affair and the exhausting labor of assembling the one-man show, Steichen was mentally and physically exhausted, at the verge of a breakdown. Furthermore, he was broke. Good luck seemed to find him, he had written Stieglitz back in March, "but hang it all—money doesn't."[92] Even the little treasury in the dark corners of his studio was exhausted. He could not bring himself to make yet another appeal to his sympathetic mother. Once when he had done so, she had mailed him all the money she had saved to pay rent on her millinery shop. (God had provided, she later reassured him, by sending a drenching Sunday rain, which ruined so many good hats that ladies rushed to her store to order new ones on Monday.)[93]

Finally, to make matters worse, Steichen and Clara Smith broke off their romance. His surviving letters tantalize with their allusions to the rift, without divulging the details, but when he remembered the time of their estrangement later, he told her apologetically, it made his heart grow cold.[94]

Women in Paris often fell in love with Steichen at first sight, charmed by his lean good looks and his bohemian glamour. Even in Montparnasse, he cut a figure, with his long, wavy hair, his wide-brimmed black hat and black cape, and a vest made of antique brocade, probably inspired by or even inherited from Fred Holland Day.

During the winter and spring of 1902, he frequently ate lunch and dinner alone in a cheap café near his studio. Kathleen Bruce, a beautiful young English sculptress, spied him there, and was immediately infatuated. "I knew his work," she remembered. "It was well known. It was good."[95] For several months, she remembered, they exchanged glances and smiles across the café, but did not speak.

Then, to her dismay, she heard that Steichen planned to return to New York. The night before his departure, as she sat reading Maeterlinck, Steichen finally spoke to her. She recounted the incident in detail in her autobiography years later:

"You know, Esmeralda, that I'm going home tomorrow?"
Esmeralda—why Esmeralda? I never knew.
"I know," I said, without turning my head.[96]

Steichen offered to give her a copy of his photograph of Maeterlinck, promising to bring it to her apartment nearby. True to his word, he delivered the photograph and, according to Bruce, told her he regretted that he had not found her sooner. Then he kissed her, leaving her, she wrote, "drunk" with joy, and although their paths did not immediately cross again, Kathleen Bruce idolized Steichen. "For four stormy years," she recalled, "I was faithful to that hour."[97]

Steichen's one-man show closed near the end of June. Worn and ill, depleted of energy and spirit, he decided that after two wonderful, turbulent years abroad, it was time to go home. Longing to see his sister and his parents, he told them he was coming for a vacation, but Steichen was a visible figure in art circles now, prey to gossip as well as news, and a London newspaper attributed his departure to "continued ill-health, caused we believe by overwork...."[98] In late July, he packed his negatives and paintings, closed his studio, bade his friends good-bye, and attended a farewell luncheon that Rodin and Rose gave in his honor at Meudon.

Then he left Paris for Rome. On earlier brief visits, he had fallen in love with that city, returning whenever he could eke out the means to do so. As he walked the grounds of the Villa de Medici, he was struck by the sight of great old trees still brimming with sap and new shoots, so much so that their trunks were banded in iron to keep them from bursting. He had described them to Gertrude Käsebier in a letter from Rome, telling her he felt that way himself.[99] He rested in Rome briefly to gather his strength before traveling on to Hamburg, Germany, to board ship for his return to the United States.

By August 1902, Steichen was sailing homeward aboard the *Pennsylvania*. As he looked back on his two-year sojourn in Europe, according to an article in a Milwaukee newspaper, he supposed he had achieved more success as a photographer than as a painter, but he pointed out that he had been painting "in a serious vein" for only two years, whereas he had been "puttering with the camera" for nearly eight years.[100] In reality, Steichen had gone to Paris an unknown artist, searching for style and subject. He was returning home in poverty and surrounded by controversy, it was true, but he was a star, with a name and a body of work recognized in Europe and in New York.

He had made one more interesting sale before his departure, which probably helped finance his trip: After several of his photographs were exhibited in the Brussels Photographic Salon, the Belgium government purchased *The Black Vase* for the permanent collection of the National Gallery of Brussels—the first photograph ever accorded such an honor in Belgium.[101] Consequently, Steichen left Europe amid another furor, this time from painters protesting the addition to their national museum of his enigmatic photograph of a young woman holding a black vase almost lost in the shadows. "'The Black Vase' is one of those queer things that are nothing and mean nothing, but to which it is, nevertheless, impossible to deny a large measure of artistic feeling," a critic had written in 1901 in the London journal *Photography*.[102] It pleased Steichen no end that during this landmark year of his artistic triumph in Europe, a Belgian critic pronounced him "the Rodin of photography."[103]

8

THE MODERNIST TREND

(1 9 0 2)

He was back in New York in 1902—a stripling of 23 years—alive with unrest, seething with plans for work—established in a little room at 291 Fifth Avenue, which later became the headquarters of the Photo-Secession movement. Growing to include painters and sculptors of the modernist trend, the movement was designated as 291.[1]

—CARL SANDBURG

MARY KEMP STEICHEN, ALWAYS HER SON'S best promoter, saw to it that his return to the United States was properly noted by Milwaukee journalists, then proudly pasted their newspaper stories about her boy in her ever-expanding scrapbook. "Edward J. Steichen of Milwaukee and New York, portrait painter and photographer, arrived on the *Pennsylvania* from Hamburg," one journalist reported August 7, 1902.[2] Another newspaperman provided this information: "Full of enthusiasm, and in a naïve and delightful state of satisfaction with the world and his art, Edward J. Steichen has returned to Milwaukee for a brief sojourn before he opens his studio in New York."[3]

The reunion in the Steichen house at 423 Fifteenth Street in Milwaukee in August of 1902 was joyful. Lilian was home from her studies at the University of Chicago, where she had enrolled in the fall of 1901. The prospect of studying library science had lured her to the University of Illinois in Urbana, but after discovering that a bachelor's degree was essential before she could enter the library school there, she decided to complete her undergraduate studies in Chicago. Her parents were happy when she moved closer to Milwaukee, and now with Eduard's homecoming after two years and four months, the family would be complete again.

He came home thin and haggard, and Mary and Lilian were distressed to see his bone-weariness. Lilian remembered that her mother "cooked everything she could think of, from crusty apple pies to stuffed glazed chickens," while interrogating her son in the familiar, musical Luxembourgeois.[4] Glad as he was to see Eduard, John Peter Steichen probably looked askance at his son's long, unkempt hair and his bohemian clothes—the cape, the black scarf, the gray linen shirt with its loose kimonolike sleeves. Yes, Eduard Steichen certainly *looked* like an artist, according to the *Milwaukee Sentinel* reporter called out to interview him by his best press agent, his mother.

Asked his plans, Steichen responded that he would first rest at home for a while with his family and then he would give New York City a try. The *Sentinel* pronounced him surely among "the foremost of Milwaukee boys to reach high place [sic] in the world without," where he had "made the acquaintance of and photographed nearly all the personages known to Paris."[5]

The journalist found Steichen personable, "delightful," "simple and frank" in his talk. It was to this admiring reporter that Steichen disclosed his goals: "I am going to open a studio in New York, but I mean to keep in touch with the art work of Europe, because I believe that art is cosmopolitan, and that one should touch it at all points. I hate specialism. That is the ruin of art. I don't believe in art schools. I believe in working in every branch of art. That's what Michael Angelo [sic] did. He was painter, sculptor and architect and supreme in all. No man will ever be great who specializes."[6]

Exhausted and ill, Steichen settled down to rest and recuperate. He had barely unpacked his bags at his parents' house in Milwaukee, while still awaiting the arrival of the crates of paintings and photographs he had shipped from Paris, when word came that he had unwittingly stirred up a hornet's nest in German art circles. German critic Ernst Juhl, art editor of *Die Photographische Rundschau* (*The Photographic Review*), had praised and featured Steichen's work in the July 1902 issue, choosing eleven Steichen photographs for reproduction in a portfolio in the journal, including the self-portrait and portraits of Frits Thaulow, William Merrit Chase, Rodin, von Lenbach, Day, and Mucha. As he introduced the twenty-three-year-old American to the German audience, Juhl placed Steichen's work not only in the forefront of the "wholly new style of photography" called the American School but at the very summit of pictorial photography.[7] The conservative German audience responded with "a storm of indignation," threatening to abandon the journal over what they saw as intemperate, uninformed remarks about photography and art, illustrated by Steichen's strange and baffling pictures.[8]

The ensuing uproar forced the editor of the journal to act swiftly: "In order not to endanger the continuation of the *Rundschau* after it has flourished for so many years," he announced, "Herr Juhl has resigned his position as of August 1."[9] Steichen was resting at home with his family in Milwaukee when he heard of the fiasco. He wrote to tell Stieglitz that he wanted to help Juhl "if it costs me my eye teeth."[10]

There, in microcosm, could be seen the international controversy that erupted wherever photography was offered as art, as it had been by photographer Peter Henry Emerson, who had galvanized the debate in the first place in "Photography as a Pictorial Art," the landmark speech he delivered to the Camera Club in London on March 11, 1886. Emerson, a former medical student and Ralph Waldo Emerson's fourth cousin, had followed that widely quoted and reprinted address with his book, *Naturalistic Photography for Students of the Art* (1889), amplifying his belief that a work of art is "an expression by means of pictures of what is beautiful, and the points to gauge in a picture are to notice what a man wishes to express, and how well he has expressed it." He contended that the "photographic artist" and the painter worked for the same ends and that photography was superior to etching, woodcutting, and charcoal drawing because, he explained, "The drawing of the lens is not to be equalled by any man; the tones of a correctly and suitably printed picture far surpass those of any other black and white process."

In the words that Alfred Stieglitz had embraced, Emerson concluded that "in capable hands, a finished photograph is a work of Art."[11] The skilled photographer was limited by the camera in only two ways: the ability to yield color and to render relative values, although, Emerson felt, the latter problem could be offset by the tone of each photograph.

Later events triggered a crucial shift in his viewpoint, however, as further dialogue with painters shook his conviction that photographers could render the beauties of nature with more artistic effect than painters. Finally, when scientists convinced him that it was impossible to control tones in the development process, Emerson abandoned altogether his view that photography could be a fine-art form, publicly reversing his far-reaching opinion in 1891.

Nevertheless, Emerson's 1886 definition of art—and hence of photography as art—constantly resurfaced in the arguments mounted by later champions of pictorial photography. While Emerson might have changed his mind, many of his disciples had not. Therefore, his radical view still reverberated in the aesthetic theory as well as in the photographs of many others, including Stieglitz. Nonetheless, turn-of-the-century art critics, American and European, continued to hurl their scorn at pictorial photography—the "bastard of science and art," as Stieglitz had defensively called it.[12]

It was fortuitous that Steichen returned from Europe just at that crucial instant when Stieglitz, the acknowledged leader of American pictorial photographers, was recruiting allies to further the cause. By the time Steichen reached New York in 1902, pugnacious Stieglitz was orchestrating a far-reaching revolt, and he wanted Steichen to participate. After months of acrimonious conflict with members of the Camera Club of New York over the course Stieglitz was steering in *Camera Notes* and in photographic exhibitions, he had dramatically announced his resignation as editor of the club's official journal, effective with the July 1902 issue of *Camera Notes*.

Close on the heels of his resignation letter on February 24, 1902, had come the "American Pictorial Photography" exhibition Stieglitz had engineered at the National Arts Club at 37 West Thirty-fourth Street in New York. There, beginning on March fifth, he had shown the work of thirty-two American photographers, including his own prints, along with those by Steichen, Clarence White, Frank Eugene, Joseph Keiley, and Gertrude Käsebier. (Stieglitz had further antagonized Fred Holland Day by inserting two of his photographs in the show, despite Day's decision not to participate.) Frustrated and hamstrung by the traditionalists at the Camera Club of New York, Stieglitz had independently produced the exhibition, attributing its sponsorship to "the Photo-Secession." Not even a March blizzard deterred an enthusiastic crowd from attending the opening and hearing Stieglitz lecture on "Pictorial Photography and What It Means."

Like Steichen, Stieglitz had followed the progress of the European artists and their dissident groups—the Munich Secessionists—German artists who had broken away from the German academic traditions in painting in 1892—as well as the Viennese artists who had seceded in 1897 and the avant-garde artists in Berlin who had followed suit in 1898. Stieglitz had taken admiring note of the German Secessionists in his 1899 article in *Scribner's Magazine* entitled "Pictorial Photography," describing them as "a body of artists comprising the most advanced and gifted men of their times, who (as the name indicates they have broken away from the narrow rules of custom and tradition) have admitted the claims of the pictorial photograph to be judged on its merits as a work of art independently, and without considering the fact that it has been produced through the medium of the camera."[13] Stieglitz was determined to put a stop once and for all to the tired notion that photographs could not be works of art.

The American etcher and Whistler apostle Joseph Pennell, for one, had long been a particularly venomous critic of photography, charging in 1897, "To fake up photographic prints so that they shall look like drawings or paintings is a sham which one would think any person who pretended to call himself an artist would be ashamed to descend to." Pennell was adamant that photography would *never* be considered a fine art, and he and others worried that such a notion was a symptom of the encroaching menace of the machine age, for as surely as there were mass-produced, machine-made (and thus inferior) carpets and shirts, there were going to be mass-produced, machine-made (and thus inferior) pictures.

The artistic debate over mechanical pictures, mass-produced by cheap cameras in the hands of the "great, ignorant, artless public," as Pennell called them, revealed an ongoing tension between the artistic elite and the general society.[14] Further, it echoed the alarm over the "dangers" of mass production in clothing and other goods, the fears that the machine would render the worker, the craftsman, and the artisan obsolete.

Steichen, Stieglitz, and other photographers had no iconoclastic desire or intention to destroy art through photography; to the contrary, they were working passionately to free and expand the very concept and parameters of art. Not only had Steichen and others written to Stieglitz from Europe about their firsthand observations of the vital secessionist movements but Steichen had also written appreciatively of the Munich Secessionists in 1901 in his outspoken *Photogram* article on the American School of photography, which Stieglitz reprinted in his final issue of *Camera Notes* in July 1902. Steichen observed:

> *The secessionists of Munich—in fact, all secessions, and it is to a secession better than anything else that the new movement in photography can be likened—gave, as the reason of their movement, the fact that they could no longer tolerate the set convictions of the body from which they detached themselves, a body which exists on conventions and stereotyped formulae, that checked all spirits of originality instead of encouraging them, that refused its ear to any new doctrine—such groups gave birth to secession.*

Steichen sent an urgent message to critics debating the artistic impact of photography: "Let it not be the medium we question, but the man. Our consideration of lithography was a lowly* one 'till Whistler made it art.' " He argued in the *Photogram* essay that there would be finer photographers, if photographers would "concern themselves more with art and less with photography." In the final analysis, "Results alone are arguments," said Steichen. Did not "wise men (sages)," on first seeing the work of the French Impressionists, " 'hee and haw' amongst themselves until they came to the verdict of insanity"?

He believed that "the greatest lesson the average photographer has to learn is to *unlearn,* and one of his first lessons would be to overcome the idea of a 'sharp, brilliant' photogram being a good one." There is "no absolute black and no absolute white to be seen in nature," he pointed out. Steichen noted that he and other photographers felt that "lower tones have more of a tendency to make things beautiful than tones more brilliant, and hence the repeated use of them. One strives for harmony—

---

* Note that in the *Photogram* essay, the word *lowly* was used; in *Camera Notes,* it became *hourly.*

harmony in color, in values and in arrangement." In summation, he returned to the artist himself: "If there are limitations to any of the arts they are technical; but of the *motif* to be chosen the limitations are dependent on the man—if he is a master he will give us great art and ever exalt himself."[15]

The debate over Steichen's work encapsulated the whole controversy over photography as art. Critic Charles Caffin noted retrospectively in *The Century Magazine* in 1908 that painters and photographers agreed on one point: "The prints did not really represent photography. They charged that Steichen, because he practised painting as well as photography, confused the two forms."[16]

The attention to Steichen's work testified that at least he was being taken seriously. Already he had fulfilled Stieglitz's prophecy that only a good painter could ultimately help win respect for photography as an art medium. Observers who wrote about Steichen in 1902 sought to define him: He was influenced by Stuck, by Whistler, by Rembrandt, the Impressionists, the Symbolists.[17] He was a painter who had "taken up artistic photography as another painter might take up lithography or etching," one critic contended.[18] To the contrary, others argued, he was a photographer who happened to paint, and he was better known for his photographs than for his paintings.[19] Chameleonlike, Steichen eluded them all.

It was a *Milwaukee Journal* reporter, no doubt summoned by Mary Steichen, who probably came closest to the truth about Steichen in 1902, emphasizing that he was self-taught, a "master innovator" in photography and a noted painter. Steichen told this reporter that he had no use for art schools. Recalling his miserable weeks of formal study in Paris in 1900, he complained that the Académie Julian had "killed more artists than one can number."[20] Art critic Katherine Knode, writing in the *Paris World,* was also struck by Steichen's "peculiar and justifiable pleasure in the fact that he is practically self-taught."[21] He did, however, credit the "instruction and encouragement" of Robert Schade at the Milwaukee Art Students' League with starting him on his way.[22] But since then, Steichen acknowledged, he had been deeply influenced by his encounters with greater artists, especially Rodin.

Now, gathering his strength in Milwaukee, he stood on the threshold of an exciting new era. Returning to the United States just as the

The Modernist Trend (1902)

American Photo-Secession was born out of a strange marriage of conflict and innovation, Steichen arrived in time to work side by side with Stieglitz to breathe vigorous life into the movement. One project in particular intrigued Steichen: Inevitably, Stieglitz's new endeavor would involve the production of a journal, and Stieglitz asked Steichen to design a striking cover for it. Consequently, during those depressing, restless days in Milwaukee, as he struggled to regain his energy, Steichen found welcome diversion "fussing around" with the cover design for the new journal Stieglitz had already christened *Camera Work*.[23]

As much as he wanted to get back to New York, however, Steichen was still recuperating in Milwaukee in September, striving to recover his physical strength and his financial footing. He was painting again, and he wrote to Stieglitz that he was trying to deal with a swamp of letters requesting reproductions and articles, although he did not spell out the details. (Many of them were generated, no doubt, by the controversy over the article by Juhl and over the Belgian purchase of Steichen's photography.) Mainly, Steichen was anxious and unhappy, in large part because he was very worried about money—broke, heavily in debt, and not sure what lay ahead, he wrote Stieglitz that fall. He worried that he had wasted his time on photography. Meantime he was sick of resting, Steichen complained. He needed to get back to work.[24]

His beautiful sister, Lilian, was a godsend as Steichen recuperated on Fifteenth Street in Milwaukee, chafing at his dependence after the freewheeling days in Paris. At nineteen, Lilian was now a stellar student at the University of Chicago, on fire with excitement about her own new life. Unlike her brother, who had no use for formal schooling, Lilian embraced the demands imposed by her professors—especially English professor Oscar Lovell Triggs and economics professor Thorstein Veblen. She had also flung her considerable energy into the socialist movement in Chicago, joining the organization that gathered dozens of factions into a national Socialist party in January of 1901. Lilian had earlier converted her mother to the cause in Milwaukee, of course, and now resolved to do her best to recruit her brother.[25]

Blue eyes ablaze with idealism, Lilian felt herself called by "a Voice from the World of Action." Her political conversion prompted her, she said, to turn away from such "aesthetic enjoyment" as reading the classical poets and writing her own "little word-melodies," for she now believed most classical and contemporary literature, music, and visual art to be "by and for the privileged minority—it is a thing of Snobbery—a diversion of the leisure class." She wanted something "more inclusive, more universal! Something that is for the Masses!"[26] She was planting in her brother's creative imagination an idea that would grow there for decades, until he expressed it in the culminating work of his life, the 1955 photographic exhibition entitled "The Family of Man."

Over the years, Lilian also argued eloquently for a realism in art that not only reflected the actual lives of working people but was within their reach to enjoy. She was, in fact, an advocate of what Walt Whitman and the German socialists called democratic art. Most poets bored her, she wrote, because they gave "pictures of life which were less wonderful, less poignant than the picture I made for myself out of the stuff of experience and study—study of twentieth century social science for instance. In their day these poets' pictures were more wonderful than the ones that people could make for themselves—for these poets saw all that the contemporary scientists saw, and saw it transmuted, emotionalized, humanized moreover. But the world moves on," she reflected. "It has moved very rapidly in the last fifty years—most rapidly in the last ten years. The old science—the old Weltanschauung is outdated: so too the old poetry." So, too, she and her brother agreed, was the old visual art.

She praised modernism in literature: "Now modernism stands for succinctness—Ibsen, Shaw in drama—Jack London in fiction."[27] Lilian also passionately admired "the divine madness of poesy"—or art—when it was wed to "the diviner madness of revolutionary agitation."[28] She had become a cynic about art for art's sake only, and a champion for art with a purpose, preferably a message. That summer, at home with her brother, she "jeered at him so much that he lost faith—or nearly lost faith in art too." When Eduard agreed to give a talk on art to the Milwaukee Camera Club, she noted, he attacked "art and artists both mercilessly, indiscriminately!"[29]

As Steichen discovered when he returned to the United States in 1902, the country was far more obsessed than Europe with modern technology, to the detriment of the arts. To the cadences of the cakewalk and ragtime jazz, Americans marveled at the first flight of the zeppelin and at the advent of motor-driven bicycles and the motorcar. They listened with wonder to tenor Enrico Caruso's voice on the first phonograph recording, and they heard that human speech had actually been transmitted by way of radio waves. More and more American homes boasted telephones, and Marconi had transmitted telegraphic radio messages from Cornwall, England, all the way to Newfoundland. Clearly, it was time for innovation in art as well as in technology.

The lively and contentious debates over photography as fine art reflected the profound changes marking the turn of the century, especially the contemporary self-consciousness and anxiety about the new science and technology. The camera was just one machine among many "impossibilities," as Henry Adams labeled them, in a burgeoning industrial technology that was rapidly transforming modern life. The "Century of Steam," as the nineteenth century was often called, was being superseded by the new "Century of Electricity." Just as the telephone, the telegraph, the automobile, the zeppelin, and the prospect of other airships connected people and places in unprecedented ways, the camera empowered them to stamp themselves and their experiences on paper as static images caught in moments of time, while unprecedented change washed over them.

The controversy over photography as fine art clearly mirrored a pervasive national worry over the power of science and its new machines to disrupt and even destroy the familiar patterns of life. The camera was an emblem for these changes, thanks to George Eastman's innovations, which had instantly transformed photography into an accessible, democratic medium, unlike traditional art forms. Now millions of people could make snapshots, while few could paint pictures; one person or one museum could own a painting, whereas countless people could own prints of a single photograph. (Walt Whitman had posed the same subversive threat to conventional forms of poetry, for if his radical free verse could be read and comprehended by citizens comprising the democratic average, just about anybody might take to *writing* poetry as a result.)

Art was a luxury unavailable to many Americans, however, for the country was still climbing out of the economic depression of the 1890s, and rampant labor unrest fed the socialist movement. Americans also wrestled then with their national and cultural identity in the new industrial age, led now by the vigorous young President, Teddy Roosevelt, who had succeeded William McKinley after a madman assassinated the President at the Pan-American Exposition in Buffalo, New York, in September of 1901. President McKinley had led the nation into and out of the Spanish-American War in 1898, and thus toward its first self-conscious experience of world power. Roosevelt would expand and solidify that power, in the process shoring up a bold new sense of American culture, evident in the groundbreaking work of modern inventors, entrepreneurs, writers, painters, and photographers.

Americans stepping into the twentieth century encountered intellectual upheaval at every turn. In the light of the work of Charles Darwin and Karl Marx, of William James (*The Principles of Psychology,* 1890), John Dewey (*The School and Society,* 1899), and others, modern men and women were examining their own lives through a radically shifting modern "lens."[30] Americans were reading Rudyard Kipling's *Kim* and Frank Norris's *The Octopus,* but they were paying little attention to a new, posthumous edition of Whitman's *Leaves of Grass* or to *Sister Carrie,* a radical new novel by the Indiana journalist Theodore Dreiser. American art, literature, and music were, for the most part, still derivative, if not out-and-out imitative of work produced in Europe, but boundaries were stretching, thanks to innovators such as Dreiser and Stieglitz.

During that late-summer reunion in Milwaukee, Eduard and Lilian Steichen found themselves facing the new century with excitement—two pioneers confronting uncharted territory, both driven toward modernism by a kindred energy and spirit. Steichen came home to the great New World that the old poet Walt Whitman had hopefully foreseen in 1892—the vibrant, amorphous, experimental American republic. And as the republic was experimental, Whitman had observed, so should its art be. He had contradicted gloomy critical views that science and the machine age would obliterate poetry and the arts, confidently predicting that "new and evolutionary facts, meanings, purposes" would inevitably produce "new poetic messages, new forms and expressions."[31] Furthermore, Whitman preached, poetry (and by extension, all arts) must embody "absolute faith and equality for the use of the democratic masses."[32] And the new century needed poems—art—"of realities and science and of the democratic average and basic equality...."[33]

As Steichen, Stieglitz, and others effectively transmuted photography into an art form, they brought it very close to the threshold of democratic art Whitman had imagined.[34] For many Americans, however, the national ideal of the "democratic average and basic equality" threatened dangerous change and loss—a treacherous miscegenation of art and culture. Traditional structures seemed vulnerable to rampant free forms—free verse, naturalism in drama and fiction, a vibrant Post-Impressionism and naturalism in painting and sculpture, and that insistent new graphic art form, photography. The worry over lack of purity in photography vaguely echoed the more serious ongoing debates about eugenics. Straight, documentary photography was one thing—pure, utilitarian, valuable in its place. But the attempt to mate the photograph to the painting was quite another matter. Superimposing artistic values and painterly techniques on photographs, and the resulting "manipulation" of photos, corrupted art, hybridized it, yielding "bastard productions."[35]

In the midst of the furor, critic J. C. Warburg observed sensibly, "Photography means, it is well to remember, *drawing by light*. The word is there for everybody's use, and to try and limit it to a particular narrow meaning is very like the owner of an estate trying to block up a 'right of way' over his property.... We live in a free country, and it seems very undesirable that a man should have his works sneered at as illegitimate when he happens to be a little less dogmatic in his ideas of what constitutes photography than someone else."[36] Indeed, changing times demanded that dogma be banished so nothing stood between the artist and the public, and the modernist trends that would define their new century.

Steichen arrived in Manhattan in the autumn of 1902, somewhat restored to health and bridling to get back to work, but to his great disappointment, he immediately found New York quite different in every regard from Paris. After his exhilarating exposure to great art and great men in Europe, he told art critic Charles H. Caffin later, his "own ideas had been broadened and deepened, his faculties enlarged, and his technical equipment fortified. More than that, he had enjoyed the sympathy of others in his own artistic strivings and everywhere an atmosphere charged with artistic enthusiasms." As Caffin noted, in contrast to his often controversial visibility in Paris art circles, Steichen now found himself "an unknown man, newly launched into the maelstrom of New York, interested in something which the majority of people cared nothing about."[37] He might have returned immediately to Europe had it not been for Alfred Stieglitz.

Right away, Stieglitz took the young man to meet the members of the Camera Club of New York and to show him the club's fine darkroom facilities, the best Steichen had ever seen.[38] He joined the Camera Club on the spot in order to work in that state-of-the-art darkroom.[39] (Later on, even after his very public dispute with the Camera Club, Stieglitz still retained his own club membership so that he, too, could continue using the superb facilities there.[40])

Deciding to look for cheap quarters near the Camera Club, Steichen quickly surveyed the neighborhood. "Around the corner, between Thirtieth and Thirty-first streets, was a block of brownstone fronts, old residences then occupied by small shops and offices," he remembered. "On the top floor of one of these, at 291 Fifth Avenue, I found a small room that was reasonable enough in rent for me to take it over. I had a small, street-level showcase made and hung out my shingle as a professional portrait photographer."[41] There were other photographers and artists along that popular stretch of Fifth Avenue, which was studded with galleries, cafés, and restaurants, as well as with other businesses that were gradually taking over the comfortable residences lining the avenue and the more intimate side streets. Just a block away from Steichen, at 273 Fifth Avenue, Gertrude Käsebier had her simply furnished studio in a town house between Twenty-ninth and Thirtieth streets, clearly marked by a sidewalk showcase displaying her current work. He could enjoy her company and advice, and he was frequently invited to have dinner with Stieglitz and his wife, Emmeline, nicknamed Emmy, at their apartment at 1111 Madison Avenue.

"At Stieglitz's home," Steichen recalled, "I was able for the first time to see some of his world-famous photographs."[42] *The Net Mender* could be seen there, a woman tending her nets on a quiet shore in a photograph as exquisitely detailed as a fine etching. Nearby hung *The Letter Box,* the image of two barefooted German girls in front of a mailbox. After studying the photographs in Stieglitz's private gallery, Steichen decided on two favorites—the first, *The Hand of Man,* a geometrical study of modern life, with a steam locomotive poised on an arc of tracks, its

The Modernist Trend (1902)

black smoke smudging the mist, with smokestacks and telephone poles jutting through the hazy background.[43]

The second, *Winter—Fifth Avenue,* struck Steichen as "entirely different" from any photograph he had seen in Europe or elsewhere.[44] Stieglitz had taken the photograph during a blizzard on February 22, 1893, testing himself and his first-ever hand camera to discover if what he saw in the drama of a horse-drawn bus struggling through darkening wind and "blinding snow" could be "put down with the slow plates and lenses available."[45] Other photographers laughed at the result, but the picture was a "new vision" for Stieglitz, capturing just exactly the effect he sought, and marking "the beginning of a new era."[46] Steichen immediately perceived the brilliance of the photograph, and he told Stieglitz so. He definitely admired Stieglitz's photographs far more than his taste in paintings, however, finding a certain grotesquerie, for instance, in two large reproductions of the work of the German Secessionist painter Franz von Stuck hanging in one room of Stieglitz's home.

With Stieglitz's encouraging, stimulating presence in his daily life, Steichen soon found New York taking on a more congenial face. No doubt subsidized at first by his mother, he was soon settled into his own quarters, and customers quickly began to wander into his studio, referred by Stieglitz and others, or attracted to the neat, elegant shingle advertising his presence at 291 Fifth Avenue and to his showcase of photographs (he had, after all, learned how a clever display could lure customers to his mother's millinery shop back in Milwaukee). The Stieglitz network alone brought him many patrons and commissions for paintings as well as photographs, and he hoped that soon he would be earning enough to support himself. Inevitably, the portrait work Steichen produced for satisfied clients drew even more customers. He produced his prints in the photographic laboratory at the Camera Club, just minutes away, where he could also talk shop and exchange gossip with Stieglitz and his Camera Club cronies, who stood then in the very center of the American photography world.

Ever since its birth in July of 1897, Stieglitz and his colleagues had used *Camera Notes* as their platform to promote the visibility and growth of their medium. Ostensibly the official organ of the Camera Club of New York, *Camera Notes* inevitably functioned as Stieglitz's own powerful voice, for he had exercised full editorial control from the inception of the journal, including in each issue at least two photogravures "chosen from the best material the world affords."[47]

By 1900, in part because of Stieglitz's meticulous attention to hand-printing the carefully prepared copper plates in ink on fine paper, the photogravure had itself come to be admired as a fine graphic art form akin to lithographs or etchings, so much so that by midcentury, copies of *Camera Notes* and *Camera Work* were often found stripped of their beautiful photogravures. Stieglitz himself had learned this expensive and time-consuming photomechanical process in the 1890s when he worked as part owner, thanks to his father, of the Photochrome Engraving Company in New York, from which he "retired" in 1895. As an editor, Stieglitz usually entrusted the photogravure work only to skilled printers in Europe, often hand-tipping the plates into the five hundred to one thousand copies of the journal himself rather than having them directly bound in. His rich sensibility led him to prefer heavy white stock with a beveled edge for the gravures, although he sometimes turned instead to parchment or the fragile Japan tissue he and his circle found so delicately responsive to the nuances of their photographs.

Published quarterly from July 1897 until July 1902, *Camera Notes* was for most of its tenure the most visible and vocal advocate of photography as a legitimate fine art in the United States and abroad. Stieglitz astutely chose to publish the photographs of international as well as American photographers, and he gathered about him an able team of writers, often reprinting reviews and technical articles from around the world. Among frequent contributors were the English photographer and prolific critic A. Horsley Hinton; critic Charles H. Caffin; the artist and teacher Arthur Wesley Dow; Dallett Fuguet, the photographer and poet whose creative output was subordinated to his work as reviewer and editor; amateur photographer John Francis Strauss; Stieglitz's staunch friend and supporter, the lawyer, photographer, and critic Joseph Keiley; and, of course, Stieglitz himself.

Perhaps the best and certainly the most outspoken critic among the regulars was eccentric, exotic Sadakichi Hartmann, who was himself highly photogenic with his high cheekbones and dark features, emphasized by his habitual black cloak and signature pince-nez. Born to a Japanese mother and a German father in Nagasaki, Japan, in 1867, Hart-

The Modernist Trend (1902)

mann was educated in Germany before being sent by his father to live with relatives in the United States about 1882, when he was a precocious and defiant fifteen-year-old. He studied art in Philadelphia, read voraciously, and discovered the poetry of Walt Whitman, then living as an invalid in his brother's home in nearby Camden, New Jersey. In 1884, Hartmann, seventeen, managed to meet Whitman, who was then sixty-five. That began a seven-year-long friendship between the handsome teenager, then aspiring to become an actor, and the poet, "sick and grown old," beset by "ungracious glooms, aches, lethargy, constipation, whimpering *ennui*."[48]

As a teenager in Philadelphia, Hartmann worked at odd jobs as a printer's devil, a lithographic stippler, and a negative retoucher, in addition to selling tombstones and perfume. His father's brother in Germany had ignited his love for the visual arts, and Whitman was undoubtedly the catalyst for Hartmann's interest in writing poetry, fiction, and drama. Whitman left an indelible imprint on the young man's emerging aesthetic views, especially his opinions about the place of art in American life.[49]

Hartmann, Keiley, and others in the pages of *Camera Notes* mounted a consistent and vigorous defense of photography as fine art. Keiley, for instance, attacked the "art-snobbery" and the "narrow snubbery" of those who argued that photography was "purely mechanical and hence entirely devoid of any direct artistic value." However, he did acknowledge the problems created by provincial photographic societies with low standards, the "Art-babbling Plate-spoiling" camera clubs who produced "badly fogged pictures" and called them "impressionistic studies." Keiley conceded that this trend did "incalculable mischief" to serious art photography.[50] "New ideas are always antagonized," pioneering Gertrude Käsebier was reassuring her colleagues then. "Do not mind that. If a thing is good it will survive."[51]

Stieglitz and others acknowledged that part of photography's problem was also its strength—its "democratic strength," in Sadakichi Hartmann's words. Because the camera was within hand's reach of millions, there were millions of photographs, and, according to Stieglitz in 1899, there were as a consequence three classes of photographers: "the ignorant, the purely technical, and the artistic."[52]

In the midst of all this hubbub of debate, Steichen settled down to work, concentrating for the moment on commercial photography so that he could earn his living and repay his mother, as well as take care of debts he had left behind in Paris for supplies and other expenses. It was Steichen the artist, not Steichen the businessman, however, who welcomed Sadakichi Hartmann to his studio at 291 Fifth Avenue in December 1902 to give an interview for Hartmann's series of articles on American artists. Believing that the only way to grasp an artist's individuality was to meet him in his workplace, Hartmann had over the years visited 450 or more American artists in their studios.

After he spent that "dark, chilly December afternoon" with Steichen, he wrote a detailed narrative of the encounter, which was later published in Stieglitz's new journal, *Camera Work*. Hartmann climbed the "slippery iron stairs of a humble and reticent office building," he wrote, and, with the help of the porter, took the rickety elevator to the top floor to Steichen's small, plain studio, bare of furniture, and artistically decorated in tones of gray and terra-cotta, accented by a few treasures—a Japanese lantern, a large brass bowl, a fragment of a statue by Rodin. Hartmann looked past a "sort of orderly disorder" and a "gypsy fashion" to assess the artist: a tall, pallid young man with square shoulders, an angular face, steady eyes, "dark, disheveled hair," looking like "some old statue carved of wood," and, at times, like "a modern citizen of Calais" or "some gallant figure of Sir Reynolds's time."

To the sound of rain drumming on the window glass, he perused Steichen's paintings, sketches, and photographs, especially admiring his painting of Beethoven and the landscapes, in which, he said, Steichen had "created a world of his own, but one based on actual things, translated into dreams." He was struck by the preponderance of lines, "surprisingly eloquent and rhythmical," in Steichen's work: "Nobody has carried the composition of lines further than Mr. Steichen. All his pictures are composed in vertical, diagonal, and outer-twisting line-work," which served as "accentuation," each line being endowed with "a mystic quality, and they run like some strange rune through his tonal composition." Color was subordinated to tonal value in the paintings, Hartmann wrote. He decided that Steichen was "a poet of rare depth and significance, who expresses his dreams, as does Maeterlinck, by surface decoration, and with the simplest of images—for instance, a vague vista of some nocturnal landscape seen through various clusters of branches, or a group of beech and birch trees, whose bark forms a quaint mosaic of horizontal color suggestions—can add something to our consciousness of life."[53]

He caught what Steichen was striving for in the landscapes he painted and photographed. "We occasionally find ourselves in darker parts of the world, and as a rule, feel more easy there," Steichen had written in 1901. "What a beautiful hour of the day is that of twilight when things disappear and seem to melt into each other, and a great beautiful feeling of peace overshadows all. Why not, if we feel this, have this feeling reflect itself in our work?"[54]

Writing evocatively about Steichen's paintings, Hartmann rendered an important visual inventory of the body of work that existed in 1902: a "violent color-study of a sailor, reclining, with a red bowl in his hand; the heads of four Parisian types; an old man, an artist with his model," crossing a bridge over the Seine; the portraits of Day and Käsebier; portraits of women and of a young girl. Hartmann particularly noted Steichen's clever, symbolic use of flowers "to tell the characters of his sitters," revealing "how deeply he can read in the human soul."

He moved from the paintings to scrutinize the photographs, finding them equally powerful: "It proved to me once more that in art the method of expression matters naught, that every effort, no matter in what medium, may become a work of art provided it manifests with utmost sincerity and intensity the emotions of a man face to face with nature and life." He was moved by Steichen's skill in grasping the personality of his subjects—especially Rodin, the "masterpiece" of Steichen's collection of photographs. They turned last to Steichen's photographic studies of nudes.

"These nudes nobody seems to understand," Steichen said. "Do they mean anything to you?"

Hartmann smiled in reply. "He does not know that my whole life has been a fight for the nude," he wrote later, "for liberty of thought in literature and art, and how I silently rejoice when I meet a man with convictions similar to mine." Hartmann found Steichen's nudes "a strange procession of female forms, naïve, non-moral, almost sexless, with shy, furtive movements, groping with their arms mysteriously into the air or assuming attitudes commonplace enough, but imbued with some mystic meaning, with the light concentrated upon their thighs, their arms, or the back, while the rest of the body drowned in darkness." Yet he considered the nudes inferior to Steichen's other work, and he believed that those photographs would be "absolutely incomprehensible to the crowd."

The photograph *Rodin—Le Penseur* overshadowed all, however, "a whole man's life condensed into a simple silhouette," a picture so splendid and powerful that it should "once and for all, end all dispute whether artistic photography is a process indicative of decadence." Hartmann took his praise a step further: "A medium, so rich and so complete, one in which such a masterpiece can be achieved, the world can no longer ignore. The battle is won!"

After that December afternoon in Steichen's studio, Hartmann wrote, "The 'artistic photograph' answers better than any other graphic art to the special necessities of a democratic and leveling age like ours," here evoking Whitman's words. Hartmann went on to pronounce this drive toward democratic art "the principal reason why Steichen has chosen [photography] as one of his mediums of expression."[55] As a consequence of that first visit, Hartmann perceptively articulated a basic truth about Steichen's motive, long before Steichen fully realized it himself.

9

True Secessionists

(1 9 0 2 - 1 9 0 3)

With every human being a new world is born which did not exist before he saw it, which will never exist again when death closes his eyes. To represent the world, which is nothing but life as seen by the individual, is the aim of the artist. They are the story-tellers of some foreign land which they alone have seen and which they alone can depict for the benefit of others. To listen to the inner voice, to be true to themselves, to obey nobody, that is their law ... they alone are true Secessionists.[1]

—Sadakichi Hartmann

In his Paris days, Steichen and other young American artists had "lived on Painting, Painters," his friend the illustrator Beatrice Baxter remembered in later years.[2] In New York at first, however, Steichen lived on photography and photographers. In Paris and London, Fred Holland Day and Auguste Rodin had been the dominant shadows in Steichen's emerging work. Now in New York, he was drawn into the center of the circle of American photographers governed by Alfred Stieglitz, whom Sadakichi Hartmann had ordained the first and foremost "champion of artistic photography in America."[3] Stieglitz was about to become for Steichen the idealized master artist he had first encountered in Europe in Day, the photographer, and Rodin, the sculptor.

Once he could see for himself the "sharp, irreconcilable antagonism" between Stieglitz and Day, Stieglitz's chief rival, however, Steichen knew not to sing Day's praises or compare his work to Stieglitz's.[4]

For years, Day and Stieglitz had been jockeying for leadership of the new movement in American photography, but by 1902, Stieglitz had firmly taken the reins for two important reasons: First, he had stayed at home in New York while Day roamed Europe and Africa. Then he had succeeded in building a conspicuous power base through his control of *Camera Notes* and of photographic exhibitions such as the American section of the Glasgow International Arts and Industrial Exposition in 1901, where he showed the work of thirty American photographers, featuring his favorites—Frank Eugene, Joseph Keiley, Gertrude Käsebier, Clarence White, Eduard Steichen, and, of course, himself. This was followed by his March 1902 success at the National Arts Club in New York with the "Exhibition of American Photography," arranged, as Stieglitz put it, by the Photo-Secession.

Far more politically adroit than Day, Stieglitz had worked for years to establish an American enclave of photographers who could work freely, originally, experimentally, unencumbered by the disapproving restraints that had constantly threatened his work at the Camera Club of New York. Prickly and cantankerous when he was challenged, Stieglitz had mounted a boycott of the prestigious Philadelphia Photographic Salon in 1901 over their decision to include scientific and documentary photographs, and Steichen and many others joined in, with Day in the end being the only American pictorial photographer to enter work. Stieglitz was also infuriated by the ongoing practice of giving to painters—and sometimes poor painters, at that—the right to jury photographs for contests and salons.[5] This confluence of antagonisms ultimately led Stieglitz to contemplate rebellion—secession—and thus to connect a resonant and prophetic name to the 1902 National Arts Club exhibit of the work of American photographers.

The exhibit had garnered mixed reviews, although largely favorable, and Steichen himself had won high praise. But, still working in Paris when the show opened, Steichen did not actually see the photographs that comprised the exhibit until he was living in New York late in 1902. In Paris, he had seen only photographs of the exhibit's installation, and his "over-all impression was rather helter-skelter," he remembered. "At the time, I thought it looked more like a junk shop than an art exhibition."[6] Steichen had learned from Stieglitz's rival Day how to

True Secessionists (1902–1903)

frame and mount an exhibition artistically, and he would do his best to improve Stieglitz's presentations later on. But Steichen admired the beautiful quality of many of the pictures Stieglitz had displayed in the National Arts Club exhibition, and once he was back in New York, he eagerly joined other photographers who had been represented in the show in pressing Stieglitz to formalize this Photo-Secession he had created in name and spirit to sponsor the exhibition.

When in 1902 Stieglitz "suddenly saw himself surrounded by a lot of men and women who professed to be artists in their life as well as in their work," Hartmann wrote, the Photo-Secession was launched—the inevitable result of Stieglitz's long struggle for the acceptance of pictorial photography and for the freedom of photographers to work in the medium as they chose.[7] The Photo-Secession was born out of a progression of conflicts, for no man as adamantly opinionated as Stieglitz steered clear of controversy for long; moreover, Stieglitz actually seemed to thrive on crisis. In particular, he collided over and over again with his staid fellow members at the Camera Club of New York, until, inevitably, the growing tension between Stieglitz and his *Camera Notes* compatriots in one camp and conservative members of the Camera Club in another led Stieglitz to give up his office as vice president and—conspicuously and dramatically—to resign from the club and from *Camera Notes*.

He had given his dramatic "Valedictory" as editor of *Camera Notes* in July of 1902, on the grounds that recent events within the Camera Club of New York made it "incompatible with the ideas and principles for which we have striven."[8] Stieglitz reported with satisfaction that he and his staff had published 21 issues, or 21,000 copies, of *Camera Notes,* at a total cost of $18,000 only $850 of which the Camera Club had contributed.[9] But now he and his colleagues would step aside so that the club would have "a free hand to inaugurate and shape its own policy, unhampered by the convictions to which we are so uncompromisingly pledged."[10] The "Valedictory" was signed by Stieglitz and his associate editors Joseph Keiley, Dallett Fuguet, John Francis Strauss, and Juan C. Abel.

Afterward, Stieglitz gave himself up to a state of exhaustion and collapse, which some members of his large family diagnosed as "mental breakdown"—although a Stieglitz breakdown, according to his niece

Sue Davidson Lowe, became "an affliction borne with extravagant endurance by those members of the family whose 'nerves' and 'sensitivity' marked them for special suffering."[11] Thanks to a complete rest at the Stieglitz family compound at Lake George, New York, Stieglitz recovered quickly and exuberantly from his collapse and threw himself immediately into his bold new experiment in photography, laying out plans for his new journal, *Camera Work,* which would provide a far more independent platform for his cause.

"In fact," Steichen remembered, "no one but Stieglitz seemed to know just what 'Photo-Secession' meant."[12] And Stieglitz himself acknowledged that the name could be ambiguous: "The idea of 'Secession' is hateful to the Americans—they'll be thinking of the Civil War. I am not. *Photo-Secession* actually means a seceding from the accepted idea of what constitutes a photograph; besides which, in Europe, in Germany and in Austria, there've been splits in the arts circles and the moderns call themselves Secessionists, so *Photo-Secession* really hitches up with the art world." Then, interestingly enough, considering the reverence with which today's scholars hold the early days of photography, Stieglitz added that there was a sense of humor in the name.[13]

Thus, long before it had a framework or an official membership list or a home, Stieglitz's daring, defiant movement had a name, a sense of humor, and a voice—the new journal *Camera Work.* Consequently, from the outset the movement could chronicle and celebrate itself, and its most articulate prophet, Sadakichi Hartmann, correctly predicted that if Stieglitz and his colleagues persisted in their work, the Photo-Secession would begin "a great movement that will have a permanent value in the annals of American Art."[14]

Stieglitz was busily engaged in this movement when Steichen came to town, even to Stieglitz's eyes the bohemian avant-garde artiste, "a very different Steichen, long-haired, cloaked, full of gestures."[15] On Steichen's arrival in New York, he also had a grand reunion with Gertrude Käsebier, herself just home from Europe. Together, they spent time with Stieglitz, who was bursting with ideas for his new journal. He told Steichen he had promised to devote the first issue of the journal to Käsebier's work; the second would focus on Steichen.[16] Steichen was pleased to be featured, although disappointed not to be first. Stieglitz, Steichen, and

TRUE SECESSIONISTS (1902–1903)

Mrs. Käsebier were traveling by train back into Manhattan from an excursion to the country when Steichen nearly alienated both of his elders over the matter. Thinking that Mrs. Käsebier, almost deaf, could not hear him, Steichen allegedly begged Stieglitz to feature his work, not hers, in the first issue of *Camera Work*.[17] He was young and, despite his success in showing his work in Europe, he was poor, he argued. Far more than Käsebier, he needed the attention and the money.

Käsebier was "the pioneer," Stieglitz told Steichen reprovingly; besides, he had already promised her the inaugural issue.[18] Käsebier apparently overheard the whole discussion and, for a time, Steichen felt the chill of her disappointment in him. Their friendship withstood the incident, but according to Stieglitz, Mrs. Käsebier later "called Steichen an ingrate and warned Stieglitz that Steichen would do the same to him."[19]

Steichen further pressed the matter of that first issue of *Camera Work* in a letter to Stieglitz, pleading his case to be the first featured photographer for aesthetic as well as financial reasons. By the late summer of 1902, he and Stieglitz apparently had already decided on the block of Steichen photographs to be featured in the second issue of *Camera Work* in the spring of 1903, to be accompanied, Steichen hoped, by the vivid description of photography that Maurice Maeterlinck had given him in Paris and promised to transcribe for him for just such an endorsement. Steichen was receiving other requests to publish his photographs in 1902; he complained to Stieglitz that certain unspecified photographic people wanted to exploit him and that, while he was accustomed to being used, he needed something in return—income and exposure.[20]

That aside, however, he did not want to allow reproduction of his photographs elsewhere first, thus compromising the "freshness" of his pictures scheduled for *Camera Work*. But timing was critical for him while he tried to build a business in New York, and he felt hamstrung. While he did not want to allow other journals to publish the photographs he and Stieglitz had earmarked for *Camera Work,* they were his best work, and if he permitted his lesser work to be published, his reputation and therefore his business might be diminished. He would probably have to wait six or eight long months for the appearance of the second issue of *Camera Work* to publish his photographs for the American public. Always the promoter and hustler, Steichen urged Stieglitz to reproduce his pictures in an issue of the journal coinciding with his move to New York.[21]

Implicit in his message was the fact that Mrs. Käsebier in her bustling Fifth Avenue studio was already one of the best-known portrait photographers in New York. Although she was earning her own way with her beautiful camera work, she also had a safety net—the forbearance and financial cushion of a wealthy husband. Steichen, the poor young upstart genius, believed that he clearly needed the exposure more than Mrs. Käsebier. But Stieglitz had made his decision and his promise, and he would not deviate from either, much as he admired Steichen's work and welcomed him back to the United States. Promising to be a "good boy," Steichen acknowledged in his letter to Stieglitz that he should stop pestering him, since Stieglitz had troubles enough of his own, and he pledged his wholehearted support to Stieglitz, whatever he decided to do.[22]

By December of 1902, however, feeling "restive and a little belligerent about the vagueness of the Photo-Secession," Steichen urged Stieglitz to call a meeting to create an organization to support formally the intriguing, enigmatic title and the handsome new journal that was nearly ready to be mailed to its first six hundred subscribers, and Stieglitz did so on December twenty-second.[23] As he recalled events in later years, Stieglitz had known from their very first meeting in 1900 that Steichen would become his "co-worker," and when he revealed his plans for the Photo-Secession in 1902, Steichen argued against including "inferior workers" in the movement. According to Stieglitz, Steichen contended that only he, Stieglitz, Day, Käsebier, and Clarence White should belong to the inner circle, but Stieglitz strongly disagreed, telling Steichen he "would not let his helpers down like that."[24] Stieglitz envisioned a council of founding fellows to include himself, Steichen, Day, Käsebier, and White, as well as Frank Eugene, Joseph Keiley, photographer William B. Dyer of Chicago, Stieglitz's *Camera Notes* colleagues Dallett Fuguet and John Francis Strauss, and photographers Eva Watson-Schütze, John Bullock, Robert Redfield, and Edmund Stirling.

At the December meeting, Stieglitz's colleagues wanted to make him president of the new enterprise, but he refused the "too ostentatious" title, opting instead to be called the director of the Photo-Secession.[25] Befitting the nature of the group, the members decided not to bind the organization to a constitution or bylaws. Of the seventeen fellows elected, twelve were named founders and council members, including Steichen and his friends Frank Eugene, Käsebier, and White.[26] Twenty-eight associates were elected to membership on December 22, 1902, and at a subsequent meeting on February 13, 1903, including all the American members of the Linked Ring, which Stieglitz hoped ultimately the Photo-Secession would surpass as the most prestigious honorary society for photographers in the world.

"Now the Photo-Secession was a fact," Steichen wrote sixty years later, "based on a carefully outlined plan."[27] The stated goals of the Photo-Secession were "To advance photography as applied to pictorial expression; To draw together those Americans practicing or otherwise interested in the art, and To hold from time to time, at varying places, exhibitions not necessarily limited to the productions of the Photo-Secession or to American work."[28] Reflecting on the "bitter strife" out of which art photography was born, Stieglitz wrote that the American Photo-Secession aimed to "compel" recognition, "not as the handmaiden of art, but as a distinctive medium of individual expression."[29]

Stieglitz was a gifted editor, as he had demonstrated time and again in *Camera Notes,* and it was inevitable that the Photo-Secession would declaim its continually evolving, often contradictory ideals in the journal—"the mouthpiece of the Photo-Secession."[30] Now unfettered by any organization, Stieglitz and his associates designed an elegant, beautiful, totally independent new journal that could be valued "for its pictures alone," as well as for its articles about modern photography.[31] Stieglitz had decided to name it *Camera Work* to ratify, both literally and symbolically, his "growing belief that any faithful rendering of deepest experience, in whatever medium—expressed with a sense of wonder and sacredness—might properly be termed *camera work.*"[32] He produced the journal over the years with the assistance of associate editors Joseph Keiley, Dallett Fuguet, and John Francis Strauss, who had ably and patiently helped him publish *Camera Notes.*

Steichen, whom Stieglitz chose as his graphic designer, had shown him several tentative designs for the inaugural cover before they settled on clean, elegant simplicity—handsome lettering encased in slender borders, suggestive of an understated Art Nouveau style, with the issue's number and date given in Roman numerals. Steichen also designed a striking Eastman Kodak advertisement for the back cover of the journal's first issue, making sure it harmonized with the front. In the early years, Steichen also helped Stieglitz choose paper, typography, and colors for the whole publication, while Stieglitz himself meticulously oversaw the reproductions of photographs—especially the photogravures, which he regarded as the next best thing to the original prints.

Stieglitz and Steichen insisted on only the best material and process to ensure exquisite reproductions, so that the reproductions at times "surpassed the originals in richness of tonality."[33] A perfectionist, Stieglitz retouched any flaws by hand if necessary, often personally tipping in the photogravures and even wrapping the journals for mailing, as he had done for *Camera Notes*.

The first issue of *Camera Work*, dated January 1903, was in the mail by mid-December 1902, and there were 647 subscribers.[34] Advancing and containing art as it did, it was itself a work of art throughout the fourteen years of its existence. As Stieglitz's later colleague Paul Rosenfeld wrote, "the lover's touch" had been "lavished on every aspect of its form and content. Spacing, printing, and quality of the paper, the format of the pages, the format of the advertisements, even, are simple and magnificent."[35]

From the outset, Stieglitz filled the pages of *Camera Work* with essays and reviews by flamboyant Sadakichi Hartmann and other respected critics—Charles Caffin, Joseph Keiley, A. Horsley Hinton, and J. B. Kerfoot in particular. George Bernard Shaw contributed occasionally, as did H. G. Wells, Steichen's sister, Lilian, and his friend Maurice Maeterlinck. Later on, in August of 1912, *Camera Work* would be the first American journal to publish the writing of Gertrude Stein.

The members of the Photo-Secession often gathered for leisurely, animated talks at dinner in a private dining room adorned with smilax vines, upstairs at Mouquin's, a French restaurant in Manhattan. There they discussed photography as a fine art, argued the relative merits of various photographs, and tossed about ideas for upcoming issues of the new journal. Beautifully designed, smartly written and edited, and extravagantly illustrated, *Camera Work* captured the spirit and vision of

True Secessionists (1902–1903)

Stieglitz and his compatriots.* As art historian William Innes Homer later pointed out, *Camera Work* was, for much of its fourteen-year tenure, the "most advanced American periodical devoted to the arts."[36]

Never close to his own father, young Eduard Steichen easily turned to surrogate fathers—older men who were kindred spirits, Rodin foremost among them. Fifteen years Steichen's senior, Alfred Stieglitz was very much at home as teacher and mentor to younger disciples, but he was not for a moment inclined to be a father figure to a handsome younger man, nor did Steichen seek that emotional connection. Instead, he found his idealized father in New York in 1902 in Stieglitz's father, Edward. Born in Saxony in 1833, the elder Stieglitz was a German immigrant who had arrived in the United States as a lad of sixteen and quickly worked his way to financial success as a dry-goods merchant in the new country. After service in the American Civil War, Edward Stieglitz married Hedwig Werner, an immigrant from Offenbach, Germany, eleven years his junior, and they settled in Hoboken, New Jersey. He resumed his profitable work as partner in a dry-goods company in lower Manhattan, across the Hudson River, and indulged his passions for an eclectic range of activities, from drawing and painting to horse racing.

By 1881, when his oldest son, Alfred, was seventeen, Edward had made his fortune, retiring at the age of forty-eight to enjoy life, work seriously at his painting, and take his family back to Europe to educate his six children there. Tall, erect, imposing, he was a formidable figure to many people, including rebellious Alfred, who criticized his father much as Eduard Steichen found fault with John Peter Steichen. Alfred called his father high-strung, autocratic, "vain, impatient and impossible to speak to," but he admired him nonetheless.[37] Steichen and the elder Stieglitz, however, quickly developed "a very particular and close friend-

---

* To the disappointment of collectors, complete runs of *Camera Work* are rare, in part because Stieglitz destroyed many copies in later years. In 1973, Aperture published *Camera Work: A Critical Anthology*, edited by Jonathan Green; this book contains selected articles and reproductions of photographs from the journal.

ship and mutual affection," and Steichen became part of the extended Stieglitz family, welcome and at ease in the homes of various Stieglitzes in New York and at the family compound at Lake George. Dr. Leopold Stieglitz, Alfred's brother, became Steichen's physician, and Alfred's wife, Emmy, was especially cordial to young Steichen, inviting him back again and again for dinner at their Madison Avenue apartment, where Steichen enjoyed playing with Alfred and Emmy's dark-haired four-year-old daughter Katherine, called Kitty.[38]

Steichen was not privy then to the tensions in Alfred and Emmy's marriage, which had been arranged for them by their families. Emmy Obermeyer Stieglitz was the younger sister of Joseph Obermeyer, Stieglitz's friend and business partner. She has often been written off as a spoiled, silly, unintelligent, selfish woman, incapable of understanding Stieglitz, and the architect of such a miserably unhappy home life and marriage that poor Stieglitz was rescued in later years, not a moment too soon, by Georgia O'Keeffe. While Emmy was no intellectual or artistic mate for Stieglitz, she genuinely loved her irascible husband, was devoted to their daughter and their home life, and could offer him what he had to have to do art for art's sake—space and privacy, and a lot of money.

When the two young people married in 1893, Emmy's fortune, combined with a modest annual trust from the Stieglitz family, ensured that Alfred Stieglitz could have the luxury of doing what he wanted to do, and he did. He and conventional, proper Emmy lived largely separate lives, she caring for Kitty, shopping, socializing, overseeing their New York apartment, and traveling to fashionable spas and resorts in season, and he totally absorbed in his photography and his Photo-Secession work, then collapsing in the summers at Lake George. Their resulting marriage was agonizing at many times, in many ways—but agony in marriage is usually a two-way street. It was every bit as difficult for Emmy, who suffered her husband's long absences from home, his often condescending, sometimes verbally abusive lectures, and his total absorption in photography, while she longed for affection and companionship. She was wiser than many realized, poignantly putting her finger on the inescapable chasm between them as she contemplated their life together: Her husband was always absorbed in "semi-abstract things," she wrote to him, "while the small but real things of life" mattered to her.[39]

True Secessionists (1902–1903)

When Steichen dined with Alfred and Emmy and admired the photographs on their walls, he at first saw only the comfortable tableau of fashionable, cordial wife, accomplished husband, and beautiful child. He also became a regular among the "guests, forever guests" who filled the Edward Stieglitz household, "but mainly musicians, artists and literary folk, rather than business people," Stieglitz remembered.[40] A competent amateur painter, Edward Stieglitz collected art on a modest scale, usually buying from artists he had met. The German artist Fedor Encke had actually lived with the Stieglitz family for an extended time in their house, which was equipped with such modern conveniences as "gas chandeliers, steam heat, fireplaces and even special taps for iced as well as hot water."[41]

Encke had been commissioned to paint an official portrait of financier J. Pierpont Morgan, who had avowed, "No price is too great for a work of unquestioned beauty and known authenticity."[42] Frustrated by Morgan's frenetic schedule and his inability to sit still, Encke sought a photographer to assist him so that he could secure images of Morgan with the camera and then paint him at his leisure. Encke naturally turned to Stieglitz for a suggestion, and Stieglitz recommended Steichen. There would be good money for the job, with the possibility of other orders from Morgan and those close to him.

Morgan agreed to be photographed in Steichen's studio, but he decreed that he would sit for only two minutes. Steichen had to photograph him first, of course, in the pose Encke had chosen for the portrait. If there was time, he could shoot another pose. The appointment was set for January 8, 1903, and Steichen set to work early that morning with the help of the patient janitor in his building, posing the man in a chair to duplicate the setting of Encke's painting in advance of Morgan's arrival.

Escorted by Encke, Morgan strode into the studio, took off his hat, set down his foot-long cigar, and posed for Steichen exactly as he had for Encke. Without wasting an instant, Steichen completed the two- to three-second exposure. As quickly, he asked Morgan to assume a different pose. "Just swing your head around and we'll have it," Steichen directed his impatient subject. "Just swing your head around!"[43]

The pose was uncomfortable, Morgan complained, and Steichen told him to move to a more natural position. "He moved his head several times," Steichen remembered, "and ended exactly where it had been 'uncomfortable' before, except that this time he took the pose of his own volition. But his expression had sharpened and his body posture became tense, possibly a reflex of his irritation at the suggestion I had made. I saw that a dynamic self-assertion had taken place, whatever its cause, and I quickly made the second exposure, saying 'Thank you, Mr. Morgan,' as I took the plate holder out of the camera."[44]

Three minutes had elapsed between Morgan's arrival and his departure. The financier was impressed. "I like you, young man. I think we'll get along first-rate together," he told Steichen. At the elevator, Morgan pulled out five one-hundred dollar bills, handed them to Encke, and sent him back to Steichen's studio. "Give this to the young man," he ordered.[45]

It was a fortune, and Steichen put the bills carefully away in his studio, quickly packed his equipment, and found a cab to take him to his second assignment that day—to photograph the beautiful Italian actress Eleonora Duse at the Savoy Hotel. Unlike Morgan, Duse was completely unself-conscious before the camera, the most natural subject Steichen had ever photographed. He brought along a bouquet of roses for her to hold in her hands. When she "bowed her head, smelled the flowers, and lifted her head," he was "spellbound," even though her movements spoiled five plates. (Later, learning of the bad plates, she offered to go to Steichen's studio to sit for him again. "I don't feel a bit like having my picture taken," she told him that day. "Let's chat." She sat on a packing case in Steichen's Spartan studio, oblivious to her secretary's impatience, and talked with Steichen about "people and faces and art."[46])

That single day's work—the sharp, angular brilliance of the Morgan photograph and the incandescence of the Duse—aptly illustrates the range of Steichen's power as a portrait photographer. Morgan's head dominates his portrait, massive and heavy as Rodin's *Balzac,* and there is something both menacing and guarded in his eyes. The light catches his gold chain and watch, the white sheen of his hair and his starched collar, and the gloss of the arm of the chair, looking for all the world like a knife poised in his hand for attack. That was pure accident, not intention, Steichen claimed afterward of the stunning illusion of the tycoon armed with the deadly knife.

There is diametric contrast in the lovely dark image of Duse, a gentle swath of light haunting her face and her solemn eyes. Whereas Morgan's character is starkly revealed in his portrait, that of the actress is masked, concealed, only the enigmatic eyes hinting at deep emotions close to the surface. In that one remarkable day's work, Steichen demonstrated how intimately he knew his art; he was learning to read his subjects astutely, to divine the essence of the person, and to discern adroitly the exact instant when camera and character should connect. He had articulated his evolving strategy in his article "The American School," published in *The Photogram* in 1901:

> *People before a camera are apt to assume an unreal, stony expression, and that especially when they realise that it is all to happen in one second or a fraction thereof, but to hold this look for any length of time is impossible, and in the space of a minute a series of expressions are apt to give something of a "composite" such as a painter would strive for. This for character; then to make the result more than just the mere portrait, one arranges the masses and lines so as to form an interesting and artistic composition, and very often this, it may be seen, is achieved by the use of accessories, in the way of objects, or the placing of lines and masses in the background.*[47]

Morgan's aggravation about posing had revealed the "composite" of his character; the "accessory" of the roses had helped Steichen capture Duse's "Mystical, exalted, delicate, tragic" aura.[48]

The Morgan sitting also crystallized for Steichen one of the most useful lessons he ever learned as a portrait photographer. When Morgan sat in the customary pose, as if for the painter's portrait, all Steichen saw was "the map of his face, blank and lifeless. But when he was irritated, even by a trifle, something touched the quick of his personality and he reacted swiftly and decisively. The lesson was that a portrait must get beyond the almost universal self-consciousness that people have before the camera. If some moment of reality in the personality of the sitter did not happen, you had to provoke it in order to produce a portrait that had an identity with the person. The essential thing was to awaken a genuine response."[49] From that point on, Steichen usually found the way to provoke the "moment of reality," the "genuine response." The striking clarity of character now emerging in his pictures marked a dramatic shift from his early, idealized photographic portraits.

Steichen went back again and again to the darkroom at the Camera Club to work on the Morgan prints. Only when he developed the negatives did he become conscious of Morgan's nose, disfigured over the years by acne rosacea, a chronic skin disorder.[50] "In the studio, it was his eyes that were the point of focus," Steichen recalled. "But in the photographs, his huge, more or less deformed, sick, bulbous nose seemed now to rivet the attention, and I did not know what to do. What kind of man was Mr. Morgan in this respect? If I should retouch the nose, he might be angry about it." Steichen knew that in the only photograph he had seen of Morgan, he wore a "beautiful, neat Roman nose." He retouched Morgan's nose in the photograph he made for Encke, but on his own negative, he retouched only "to make the nose a little more vague and remove spots that were repulsive." Predictably, Morgan liked the totally retouched photograph and ordered a dozen for himself. He examined the other print, thought it was awful, and ripped it to pieces. "This act of tearing up something that did not belong to him riled my blood," Steichen remembered. "I was not angry because he did not like the picture but because he tore it up. That stung very deep."[51]

Steichen continued to experiment with that negative until he achieved a print that satisfied him; he later exhibited the photograph in Germany and in France, as well as in Washington, Philadelphia, Buffalo, and Pittsburgh. When he exhibited it in New York, Morgan's librarian, Belle Greene, called it the finest portrait of Morgan in any genre. She borrowed it to show it to Morgan, who swore he had never seen it; he asked to buy the print, which belonged to Stieglitz. He was willing to pay five thousand dollars, but Stieglitz refused. Morgan then sent Belle Greene to Steichen to order some prints for him.

"Well, when I get around to it, I'll make some prints for him," Steichen told her.[52] For the next two years, Steichen ignored the cablegrams and letters about when the prints would be ready. This was, he recalled, his "rather childish" revenge for Morgan's hurtful act in destroying the first proof.[53] Finally, Steichen figured he had kept the impatient tycoon waiting long enough, and he got around to making the prints Morgan had ordered.

TRUE SECESSIONISTS (1902–1903)

True to his word, Alfred Stieglitz featured the work of Gertrude Käsebier in the first issue of *Camera Work*. Steichen had to be content to contribute a short article entitled "Ye Fakers," in which he commented sarcastically on the controversy over "manipulation" in photography. "In fact, every photograph is a fake from start to finish, a purely impersonal, unmanipulated photograph being practically impossible," he chided critics who could not comprehend the intricate dynamics of the photographer, the camera, and the "personal intervention between the action of the light and the print itself."[54]

In April of 1903 in the second issue of *Camera Work*, however, reproductions of Steichen's work stood in the spotlight. Mingled with articles on a wide range of topics by J. B. Kerfoot, Dallett Fuguet, and others were Sadakichi Hartmann's account of his visit to Steichen's studio and critic Charles H. Caffin's "Appreciation" of Steichen's work. The issue also contained Maeterlinck's "Je Crois," his testament to photography as art, with special praise for Steichen's pictures. To Steichen's particular delight, Stieglitz included "Of Art in Relation to Life," a short essay by Lilian Steichen (misspelled Lillian in the journal, probably because of Steichen's carelessness in such matters).

Steichen had discussed the emerging Photo-Secession and its new journal at some length with his sister, who was in her final year of study at the University of Chicago. Because he had always encouraged her writing, she sent him some poems and offered to send him a "camera article." He wrote to her frankly that he had "little hopes" to get the poems published, for they were too "lovely" and too "subtle." He was interested in her essay, however, whether or not it coincided with the principles of the new Photo-Secession, so long as it was worth publishing on its own. He asked his sister to send him a rough draft so that he could give her technical information as needed.

The intensity of his own often disheartening struggle for recognition permeated his advice to his sister: He urged her to send him anything she wrote, but he warned that it could be "devilishly hard" to get published. While he had total faith in her talent, the key to artistic success, he told Lilian, was to work incessantly and to fight aggressively, knowing that the artist would always face conflict and struggle—and the battle only became harder as the artist grew better.[55]

Lilian's short essay on art and life was written in a stilted rhetoric that grew out of the socialist rather than the poet in her. (A chastened Lilian would later observe ruefully that "the socialists having a sense for art, that I have met, have been half-baked in their science; and the scientific constructive sane socialists have been not even so much as half-baked in their ideas on art."[56]) In her article, there were echoes of William Morris's premise that the foundation of art is reverence for "the life of man past and present and to come," and that art could not be "merely a handmaid to the luxury of rich and idle people."[57] She explained art "as the self-realization of personalities whose experiences are of such surpassing nature that they can not be expressed adequately by the ordinary ways of social intercourse and utilitarian production. A subtler medium is required to transmit the thoughts and feelings of the artist-soul in their intense individuality. . . ."[58]

Mary Steichen was overjoyed to see her daughter's words and her son's photographs published in the handsome journal that reached her by mail in Milwaukee in the spring of 1903. Steichen's images—seven photogravures and four halftones—were beautifully reproduced, including three nude figures, two landscapes, and the portraits of Rodin, French sculptor Paul Albert Bartholomé; German painter Franz von Lenbach; Rodin's great friend, the French painter Albert Besnard, regally draped in a floor-length fur coat; an unnamed woman in *Portrait;* and Steichen himself in *Self Portrait.*

As he had known it would, the reproduction of his pictures in *Camera Work* in April immediately enhanced his visibility as a photographer in New York. When six of his paintings won accolades that same month in an exhibition at the Colonial Club at Broadway and Seventy-second Street in New York, Steichen the painter also made his presence emphatically known in Manhattan. Nineteen young American painters were featured in the Colonial Club show "on the theory that the unknown men of to-day sometimes make the leaders of tomorrow," and it was noted that not even half a dozen of the painters were known to the art world.[59] Steichen's paintings were singled out for praise in one New York newspaper: "Six pictures by Eduard J. Steichen, including a portrait of Beethoven and landscapes with figures, are as impressive as anything here. The painter capable of composing the night scene of animated figures moving among trees before a wall, entitled 'The Crinoline Party,' is worth watching."[60]

Readers who wanted to know what Steichen looked like, wrote the critic, could see William Merritt Chase's portrait of Steichen currently on exhibit by the Society of American Artists. Steichen's friend Willard Paddock also had paintings in the Colonial Club show, "a pleasant introduction," this critic observed, although "Paddock's name conveys nothing to the present writer."[61]

Steichen's name, however, appeared more and more frequently in New York newspapers, and 1903 proved to be a remarkably productive year for both Steichen the photographer and Steichen the painter. Along with the bonanza from the Morgan sitting, he added proceeds from the sale of two oil paintings to art patrons Kate and John Woodruff Simpson of New York, who would become his longtime friends. A wealthy corporate lawyer and Rodin's generous patron, Simpson had in 1901 commissioned a Rodin sculpture of his beautiful wife, the daughter of banker and Metropolitan Museum of Art benefactor George Seney. As Steichen's own network of patrons and friends expanded to include the Simpsons and others, his New York studio was visited by more clients in search of distinctive photographic portraits.

Steichen also took his camera out of the studio, roving the city, capturing a nocturnal view of the Brooklyn Bridge, for instance, and other cityscapes. He photographed landscapes at Lake George and on Long Island Sound, and he went to Boston to photograph the eighty-one-year-old writer and clergyman Edward Everett Hale, author of *The Man Without a Country*. During a visit to Lake George in May, distracted by the "godly" beauty of the mountains, the apple blossoms and the moonlight, he wrote to tell Stieglitz that save for the finishing touches—adding some flesh tones—he had completed a photographic portrait of Kitty Stieglitz.[62]

It was also a year of awards. His photograph of Bartholomé earned the President's Cup of the Camera Club of New York, the highest recognition for a newcomer to the club. He won a top award in the Eastman Kodak Competition, special recognition in the Wiesbaden Awards in Germany, and first prize in the portrait category in the Bausch & Lomb Quarter-Century Competition. His fortunes were definitely turning for the better in the "maelstrom of New York."[63] Perhaps he could finally support himself and, he began to think, a wife.

Not long after he had settled into his life at 291 Fifth Avenue, Steichen had resumed his relationship with beautiful, baffling Clara Smith, who sometimes stayed with friends not far away at 226 Fifth Avenue. Surviving letters and family memories do not render the details of Clara's life in New York in 1902 and 1903. Charlotte, her sister and longtime companion, lived in Connecticut now that she and Willard "Billy" Paddock were married, and it is logical to surmise that Clara spent time with them but worked and probably studied music in New York, where she most likely settled in order to be near Eduard Steichen. Unlike Emmy Stieglitz, who seemed constitutionally incapable of sharing her husband's passion for art and ideas, Clara was keenly interested in Steichen's work. With her love of music, art, and theater, she was enough of an artist herself to understand something of his temperament. She was also realistic about her own limitations: During their courtship, at least, she seemed to understand that her artistic talent was modest by comparison to his.

Clara was a strong, opinionated woman, but Steichen felt at home with such women, admiring as he did the strength his beloved mother and sister possessed. Nonetheless, Clara's strength sometimes turned to stubbornness and she could be unreasonably difficult, Steichen learned early in their courtship. Fully aware of her physical beauty, she was accustomed to being admired, and she took pride in her upbringing: "In my young life I heard no slang, or oath of malediction, seldom a cross word," she wrote in a memoir. "I have long since sought for myself such peace and unity." She had been taught that "everything had a right and a wrong to it," she remembered. She may have grown up in a frontier cabin in the Ozarks, but "true dignity presided" in the Smith home. "Small fry were for ever being reminded that we were a cut above those we met from time to time." Her parents sometimes challenged the choices their children made: "Now what do you want to go with him, or her, for? They are nobodies!"[64]

Clara Smith wanted to command her own destiny, even to reinvent her history if it suited her purposes. She came from a well-to-do southern family, she would tell her friend the journalist Agnes Ernst in 1909 in a private conversation. The story grew even more dramatic: Clara said that when she was twenty, her mother tried to force her to marry a man she hated. When she refused, her mother told her she never wanted to see her again, then left her stranded at the pier in New York with fifty cents in her pocket.[65] In New York, she lived with Charlotte, who was also estranged from their mother, according to Clara. To support herself, Clara worked as a housekeeper in her sister's apartment building. Overcome with sympathy for Clara, Agnes Ernst found her "embittered, but on the whole very sane and very loveable."[66]

As an independent woman in her mid-twenties, Clara had held off many suitors, but Eduard Steichen was different from all the others. He fascinated her with his powerful artistic energy and his early fame—not to mention his charismatic smile, his brooding intensity, his tall, lithe body, and the handsome face with the radiant gray-blue eyes. Was he better than she, or was she a cut above him? She hadn't decided. Leftover feelings of childhood insecurity haunted her. She had been "nervously ill in examinations at school," never doing herself justice, often freezing when the teachers asked her questions, standing "rigid" and with "sealed lips," despite the fact that she knew the answers perfectly. Even when it was not her fault, she felt "deeply chagrined" if she gave an inferior performance at the piano, or elsewhere.[67]

Steichen and Clara's two-year courtship was passionate, by turns stormy and sunny, and always vulnerable to geographical distance, poverty, her insecure nature, their mutual stubbornness, his intense absorption in his work, and his affinity for women. He had more of a gift for friendship than Clara, and men and women flocked to be with him in New York as they had in Paris. Clara was jealous early on, and Steichen apparently gave her reason to be. Yet despite their continual problems, sometime in the spring or summer of 1903, they began to talk about marriage. He did not see at first what difference a wedding would make, but he eventually relented. The decision made him happy, Steichen wrote to Stieglitz from Milwaukee during a visit with his parents.[68]

In September 1903, he had taken the train out to Milwaukee, where once again he basked in his mother's loving hospitality. Until her death in 1933, he would make this sort of pilgrimage to Mary every year to replenish his health and spirit. Her brisk understanding, her unswerving faith in him, and her lavish affection nourished him as nothing else could. He had more patience now for his gruff father, and he kept him silent company in his flourishing garden. The work in the garden was soothing, the feel of the sunlit earth in his hands full of promise and life. Steichen slept and read, talked to his mother, enjoyed Lilian's company when she visited from Chicago, and wrote to Clara, who was waiting for him on the East Coast.

Lilian later described Clara as "a strong woman, vivacious and energetic," who wrote "very good poetry."[69] Yet although he told his family about his love for Clara and they were happy at the news of his impending marriage, Steichen did not introduce his future bride to his parents and sister before their wedding, most likely because of the time and expense of the train trip from New York to Milwaukee. Besides, Clara and Mary would have agreed, it would not have been proper for an unmarried young man and woman to travel such a distance without a chaperon. When he visited Milwaukee alone just weeks before his October wedding, however, the family could see how happy he was, how much in love, and he kept "singing" Clara's praises "from morn till night."[70]

He had not realized that their wedding would make so much difference to him, he told Clara in a letter that September, but now he could hardly wait to be married, and he was nearly overwhelmed with happiness. He was obsessively worried and superstitious that something would happen to her, however, now that everything seemed "so beautiful," and he even had nightmares in which Clara was in great danger. Nervously urging her to "be so careful," he telegraphed her to stay in Connecticut with Charlotte and Billy Paddock until he returned to New York, and he wrote directly to Charlotte, asking her to keep Clara there. He would love her always, he promised, and sent love as well from his family in Milwaukee.[71]

Eduard and Clara had set a wedding date for October 3, 1903, and from Milwaukee, just three weeks before their marriage, he wrote her a long confessional of love and regret. Steichen acknowledged that he had hurt Clara badly, but someone—most likely Clara herself—blotted out the incriminating explanatory words from the page of the letter. The surviving lines suggest a pact between them: He had wounded her, he knew, and he sought her forgiveness for an infidelity, pleading that in spite of that, he had always been faithful to her in his "heart & soul." They were going to wait until their honeymoon for physical intimacy, all the while being "sweet," "clean," and "true" each to the other, and he pledged never to hurt her again.[72] Nothing survives to reveal her response to his penitent letter, or to his promises—except that they went forward with their wedding plans.

Friends looking back on the match offered varying impressions of the couple: Agnes Ernst, who frequently visited the Steichens in the early years of their marriage, thought Clara was a wonderful woman, adored by Steichen.[73] To the contrary, "Clara was a terror," Stieglitz said of her years later when he was also spreading his opinion that Clara had coerced Steichen into marriage to salvage her reputation. Furthermore, Stieglitz conjectured thirty years later, Clara's family objected to her marriage to "an impecunious artist," although, or perhaps *because,* their daughter Charlotte had married another one in Billy Paddock.[74] If the devoutly Catholic Steichens had any religious objection to their son's marriage outside the faith, there is no record of it.

Despite such later speculation, however, there is the ineludible fact that during their courtship, Steichen's love letters to Clara verged on reverence: She was holy, sweet, pure, "sacred" to him, and he was "jubilant" in heart and soul.[75] They were married in historic Trinity Church in New York City on Saturday, October 3, 1903, in a small, quiet wedding in the presence of the Paddocks and a few friends, including Stieglitz, who looked so exhausted that Steichen worried about him afterward.[76] Engraved cards announced the wedding of Mr. Eduard Steichen and Miss Clara E. Smith and informed their relatives and friends that they would be at home Saturdays beginning November first at 291 Fifth Avenue, New York City.[77]

Thanks to the generosity of the Stieglitz family, Clara and Eduard set off for a honeymoon trip to Oaklawn, the Edward Stieglitz house at Lake George. Even their ride up on the train was idyllic, Steichen wrote to Stieglitz afterward, telling his friend that he would not have felt properly married without Stieglitz's presence at the wedding, then adding that he and Clara wished that his mother, Mary, and Stieglitz could be with them at Lake George to enjoy the solitude.[78]

At Lake George, Steichen photographed his beautiful, somber bride in her simple white wedding dress, its bodice delicately shirred and trimmed with fine lace. (There is no record of the seamstress, but one wonders if Charlotte and Clara designed and made the gown while Clara waited for Steichen in Connecticut.) One evening at dusk, Steichen photographed the two of them together. He is dressed in black. He looks at his camera from under a lock of dark hair, the long hair gone now, the hint of a smile in his eyes and on his lips. Clara stands touching him, her head tilted away. Her beautiful face, so eerily like Mary Steichen's, is inscrutable.

Steichen left his record of their honeymoon in these photographs and in paintings, and in at least two letters to Stieglitz from Lake George. He began the first with a drawing of two bees flying toward a great flowerlike sun, and he told how he and Clara reveled in the beautiful, luxurious solitude. Not even a cold rain dispelled the glory of the place or their joy in each other. But most days, according to Steichen's ecstatic descriptions, the sun bathed the landscape in wondrous light, the hours transforming the sky from pristine blue to the splendid purple of evening, pierced by a large luminous golden moon unlike any he had ever seen before. He and Clara "floated" into the night "deliciously—languidly," in the spirit of the wild ducks winging their way south for the winter.[79]

Steichen responded intensely to the extravagant beauty and peace of the setting, telling Stieglitz how wonderful it was to be momentarily free of cares, worries, duties, and to think only of themselves. "Everything is ablaze," he exulted, with "light colour—love.—"[80]

His euphoria gave way to practical matters in a second letter to Stieglitz that blissful October, for he had misplaced a twenty-dollar bill and had to ask for a temporary loan. In a burst of energy, he was trying to paint the beauty of Lake George, he wrote, no doubt hoping to infuse his paintings with the emotions of the honeymoon. He described and diagrammed for Stieglitz three paintings of Lake George landscapes: a "violent" scene of birches in brilliant color with the mountains in the distance; "Hunters Moon," with one huge tree drenched in the afterglow of dusk, cattails jutting through the water in the foreground, wild ducks soaring through the sky, vivid moon hanging over all; and a third painting, still taking shape in his mind, which would seek to capture the clouds and the wind.

Intriguingly, his rhetoric was muted in this second letter, as if the newlyweds' passion had begun to pale or there were early harbingers of disenchantment: The glory of autumn was "wearing off," he wrote to Stieglitz, although the diminishing colors were "dignified and noble."[81]

TRUE SECESSIONISTS (1902–1903)

Steichen and Clara conceived their first child on their honeymoon, a fact Stieglitz delighted in sharing at Oaklawn with friends and strangers alike whenever young Mary Steichen visited in later years. He would put his arm around the girl and interrupt all conversation to announce, "You see how everything comes full circle? This girl was *conceived* at Oaklawn."[82]

In late October of 1903, Eduard and Clara Steichen reluctantly took leave of their paradise at Lake George and traveled on to Newark, Ohio, to visit Clarence and Jane White. There Steichen photographed White, who had helped to launch his career, and White photographed the newlyweds. Soon afterward, the young Steichens were back in New York, at home at 291 Fifth Avenue.

10

WORKING OUT SALVATION

(1904-1905)

> *This protest, this secession from the spirit of the doctrinaire, of the compromiser, at length found its expression in the foundation of the Photo-Secession.... The Secessionist lays no claim to infallibility, nor does he pin his faith to any creed, but he demands the right to work out his own photographic salvation.*[1]
>
> —ALFRED STIEGLITZ

"PHOTO-SECESSION!" SADAKICHI HARTMANN WROTE IN 1904. "People wonder what the Secessionists really want, and yet their aim is such a simple one. They want to be artistic, that is all.... Their first and last aim is to do artistic work."[2]

At least one Photo-Secessionist, Eduard Steichen, had two aims: to do his artistic work in his own way and to enjoy the kind of warm, supportive family life with Clara that he had known with Mary and Lilian. His sister had received her bachelor's degree in philosophy from the University of Chicago on December 22, 1903—the very day of the first formal organizational meeting of the Photo-Secession in New York—and, much as he wanted to be with Lilian in Chicago to celebrate, Steichen could not be away from New York then, even if he could have afforded a train ticket to Chicago. Earning honors in English and election to Phi Beta Kappa, Lilian Steichen won more awards at commencement than any other student in her graduating class, and Eduard arranged for a great bouquet of lilies, her namesake flower, to be delivered to her in his absence.

WORKING OUT SALVATION (1904–1905)

Before his marriage to Clara, what Steichen knew of domestic life with women was the unconditional love and encouragement of his mother and sister. In particular, his mother's devotion to her children translated into generous self-sacrifice. John Peter may have expressed his disapproval and doubts about the enterprises his unorthodox son and daughter undertook with such enthusiasm, but not Mary. She, Eduard, and Lilian remained loving compatriots in an unrelenting drive toward self-expression. Steichen soon discovered that this would not always be the case with Clara.

The bridal apartment-studio at 291 Fifth Avenue seemed too cramped from the beginning, long before the baby's expected arrival in the summer of 1904. Steichen needed long periods of quiet and solitude to do his work, and his wife needed his companionship, as well as a real home of her own, not an artist-husband's studio. Stieglitz recalled that Clara began "upbraiding" Steichen, complaining that the only reason he could paint was that she did all the chores—scrubbing, cleaning, cooking, washing dishes.[3] With no money for hired help and a husband too absorbed in his work to share the domestic chores his mother and sister had always seen to in his youth, Clara began to feel that Steichen was holding her back from her own creative expression. She was not happy to be left alone, either, so soon after their honeymoon, especially when morning sickness took hold and her pregnancy became more troublesome.

They were hardly settled in New York before Steichen was immediately caught up with preparations for a series of major Photo-Secession photography exhibitions, working side by side with Stieglitz and Keiley on all the arrangements as both the Capitol Camera Club of Washington and the Camera Club of Pittsburgh invited Stieglitz to mount exhibits in the name of his new organization. Stieglitz decided to schedule them in sequence as touring shows, to be held at the Corcoran Gallery of Art in Washington in January 1904, and then to open in Pittsburgh at the Carnegie Institute Art Galleries in February. Steichen designed a stark, handsome cover for the deluxe edition of the exhibition's catalog. Only the words "PHOTO-SECESSION" appeared boldly on the cover, in the same typography Stieglitz and Steichen used in *Camera Work*. Inside ran the title, "A Collection of American Pictorial Photographs," with photogravures of seven images. With Alvin Langdon Coburn, who had returned from London in 1902 to take his own studio at 384 Fifth Avenue, Steichen and Stieglitz went to Washington to hang the 159 prints in the show in the Corcoran's hemicycle. Steichen was determined to avoid the hodgepodge effect of the first Photo-Secession exhibition at the National Arts Club in New York by relying on his own elegant taste, augmented by all he and Coburn had learned from Fred Holland Day in London and Paris about how the setting could dramatically enhance the power of photographs.

The Washington show was a resounding success, with an opening-night crowd "so large as to be almost a crush and to render any adequate viewing of the pictures a matter of difficulty," according to the *Washington Post*.[4] The exhibit ran for twelve days before moving on to Pittsburgh, where Stieglitz included 128 additional prints. Four thousand people attended the Corcoran exhibition; eleven thousand people saw the show in Pittsburgh, where the tasteful installation and the handsome catalog were much admired, along with the photographs. All in all, the two exhibitions gave Stieglitz and his Photo-Secession stunning exposure.

Home from Pittsburgh and the "belching & bellying roar" of its steel industry, Steichen told his family that the exhibition had been very hard work, but he said he doubted that the Photo-Secession's effort and purpose would be fully recognized or appreciated. For the most part, the collection was splendid, he thought, full of fascinating expressions of individuality, despite the use of that common "mechanical medium," the camera.[5]

In *Camera Work*, Sadakichi Hartmann hailed the Pittsburgh event as "indisputably the most important and complete pictorial photographic exhibition ever held in this country."[6] Of course, Stieglitz had commissioned the article, humorously noting the momentous nature of the event by telegraphing Hartmann from Pittsburgh: "The Shrine will be opened tomorrow. Take the next train and join us. Money enclosed. We can not do without you. We need somebody to write us up."[7]

Hartmann disliked the dilapidated red background of the walls at the Carnegie Institute Art Galleries—"a state of affairs over which the Secession had, unfortunately, no control"—but he applauded "the arrangement, the lighting of the galleries, which concentrated the light upon the pictures and left all else in semi-darkness." He thought the show was hung with "exquisite taste" and praised Steichen's catalog cover design. He pronounced Steichen's prints the best work in the exhibit, and "the best which the Secession has produced." "None can deny his power," he wrote of Steichen:

> *He stands in a class by himself. That which he shows us is not always photography, but invariably belongs to the domain of art. ... Like a highwayman he lies in wait for beauty, seizes her, and drags her away as she passes. ... To him life is a sojourn in darkness, illuminated by innumerable streaks of lightning. These he tries to grasp.*

As for the other photographers, he thought Stieglitz held his own, but he preferred Stieglitz's earlier work to his more recent images. He welcomed the newcomer Coburn, and he admired Clarence White's "rare refinement" although he saw him as a photographic illustrator more than an artistic photographer. Frank Eugene had "nothing new to show," Hartmann wrote; furthermore, he did "slovenly work." The "strongest woman photographer" at present was Mary Devens, he thought, not Gertrude Käsebier, whose new work lacked "spontaneity and virility." He cautioned that the Photo-Secession must protect itself against "routine, imitation, and mannerism," which would lead to "the decline of art." While Hartmann was convinced that the better photographers sought to be artistic, whether or not they belonged to the Photo-Secession, he speculated that the real fight was not so much about aesthetics as about independence.[8]

Later in February, costumed in the guise of one of his pseudonyms, Klingsor the Magician, Hartmann delivered a rousing speech at a dinner for Photo-Secession members at their favorite French restaurant, Mouquin's. He christened them "those valiant knights of Daguerre," embarking "fully armed with kodaks and cameras" on a "perilous journey."[9] Stieglitz reprinted Hartmann's ebullient remarks in *Camera Work* in April 1904, and he also published Hartmann's mischievous "Monologue," a parody of Shakespeare's *Hamlet*, transposed to Manhattan, between Thirtieth and Thirty-first streets, the site of 291 Fifth Avenue, and starring "Hamlet-Steichen, wearing a Japanese obi as a necktie."

To paint or photograph—that is the question:
Whether 'tis more to my advantage to color
Photographic accidents and call them paintings,
Or squeeze the bulb against a sea of critics
And by exposure kill them? To paint—to 'snap':—
Perchance to tell the truth:—aye! there's the rub.
... Paintographs or photopaints; a sad plight,
Which makes me rather bear (at times) the painter's ills
Than turn entirely secessionist....[10]

There is no record of Steichen's reaction to Hartmann's wicked assault on his " 'fakey' " talents.[11] The parody foreshadowed a more serious critical attack on Steichen and other photographers, however, for even before his laudatory articles and his satirical "Monologue" appeared in *Camera Work* in April, Hartmann published a quite different perspective in the March 1904 issue of *American Amateur Photographer*, offering "A Plea for Straight Photography." The Photo-Secession exhibition at the Carnegie Institute still won his praise, but now Hartmann challenged the techniques employed by certain photographers. In particular, he charged that Steichen, in such prints as *Moonrise* and *The Portrait of a Young Man*, and Frank Eugene, in his *Song of the Lily*, had overstepped "all legitimate boundaries" by deliberately mingling "photography with the technical devices of painting and the graphic arts." They were guilty, according to Hartmann, of painting "more than once, entire backgrounds into their pictures."[12]

In the face of similar criticism three years earlier, Steichen had written that artistic photographers were "more concerned with art than with dark room textbooks."[13] The pictorial photographer's purpose was artistic creation, and the means to that end were secondary, he thought. While Eugene often painted or etched extensive backdrops in his photographs, most of Steichen's early background effects were achieved not because he was a fine painter but because he was by now a master printer, thanks to years of experimentation in the darkroom and, in large part, to that early apprenticeship at the Milwaukee lithographic firm. As art historian Joan Harrison later pointed out, "Jealous detractors accused him of fakery but Steichen was less interested in fooling anyone than in exploring every avenue of creative printmaking."[14]

WORKING OUT SALVATION (1904–1905)

He experimented boldly to achieve his innovative work in the darkroom—coating his platinum prints with gum bichromate, for instance, and then using a multiple gum process to overprint the same image in a different pigment. In his 1904 portrait of a woman, entitled *Experiment in Multiple Gum,* he made a first printing of solid lamp black, a second printing of flat terre verte, and a third printing of pale sepia and black, developing the three printings by floating the paper in cold water or printing on dyed paper without any "local manipulation," he noted on the mount of the picture.[15] In a letter to Stieglitz, Steichen described the intricate process for his platinum and ferroprussiate (blue) print *Moonrise. Mamaroneck, New York, 1904:* For the initial printing, he used a gray-black platinum, followed in the second stage by a plain blue print he called "secret," and, finally, by greenish gum.[16] It was this virtuoso fusion of materials and methods, achieved through countless patient, ingenious hours in the darkroom, that yielded the consummate Steichen prints.

Hartmann, however, like many other critics, failed to understand and appreciate the subtle complexities of the photographic process, dismissing the artistic effects of various photographers as "the trickeries of elimination, generalization, accentuation, or augmentation." Disapprovingly, he singled out Steichen, Eugene, Käsebier, and Coburn for wasting their talents on wizardry with filters, papers, pigments, pens, and brushes—methods that, in his dogmatic opinion, did not belong in photography and possessed "no justification to exist" and "no permanent value and no future."

Only Stieglitz remained in all his work a straight photographer, according to Hartmann, who wanted photographers to be "legitimately" artistic—no "scrawling, scratching, and scribbling on the plate." Only through the practice of straight photography could pictorial photography be recognized as a fine art, he believed. All the photographer had to do, Hartmann suggested, was to compose a picture "so well that the negative will be absolutely perfect and in need of no or but slight manipulation." He contended that photography had to be "absolutely independent and rely on its own strength" in order to live up to the claims the Secessionists made for their medium.[17] In rebuttal, Stieglitz, Steichen's champion in 1904, offered a graphic demonstration of Photo-Secession straight photography in the January 1905 issue of *Camera Work,* featuring five photographs by Clarence White, along with Steichen's portrait of White, all reproduced directly from the original negatives. Stieglitz wrote, "We have six examples of the 'straightest' kind of 'straight' photography reproduced in these plates of Messrs. White and Steichen."[18]

Sensitive to a fault, Hartmann wallowed in the politics of photography, playing all sides against the middle most of the time—Stieglitz against Day; the "pictorial extremists," as he called Stieglitz and the Photo-Secessionists, against the more conservative American photographers such as Curtis Bell, another professional portrait photographer doing business on Fifth Avenue, and the driving force in the emerging Salon Club of America, as well as the Metropolitan Camera Club, and the American Federation of Photographic Societies. Ferociously protective of his own territory, Hartmann began to consider Steichen an interloper who had come home from Europe like some prodigal son, displacing him and others who had been close to Stieglitz. He came to feel that Stieglitz had treated him "shabbily," had snubbed him in favor of Steichen.

Hartmann and Stieglitz kept up a sporadic and contentious correspondence for almost forty years, with Hartmann usually complaining, carping at Stieglitz and others, or seeking to borrow money, and Stieglitz alternately soothing, lecturing, and sending money to Hartmann—or sternly turning him down. In the summer of 1904, when Hartmann wrote a furious letter listing his current grievances against Stieglitz, most of them had to do with Steichen. It made his blood boil, Hartmann fumed, that Stieglitz invited him to lunch only to pay more attention to Steichen, and to side with Steichen on certain issues even though, Hartmann insisted, "I was indisputably in the right."[19] By late 1904, tiring of what he termed Stieglitz's dictatorship, Hartmann had moved openly and bitterly into the enemy camp, aligning himself with Stieglitz's latest rival, Curtis Bell, whose twenty-member Salon Club of America ("more normal and liberal" than the Secessionists, Hartmann sniped) was planning to sponsor an ambitious American Photographic Salon in December of 1904, open to photographers around the world.[20]

As for Steichen, he had scant time at first for politics or critics, for he was barely earning enough to meet his growing financial obligations. Because his mother was in poor health in Milwaukee, he was sending his parents money, although his first concern had to be Clara, who was growing ever more petulant and dissatisfied as her pregnancy wore on.

He scrambled for commissions, desperate to support his wife and parents and to prepare for the baby's needs. He hoped for a daughter, and he told Stieglitz he would be happy when the baby arrived. He got a "queer lump" in his throat whenever he thought of being a father, and found it a "wonderful feeling" to be expecting a child.[21]

Still, he was deeply conscious of the responsibilities he carried, and when Lilian reluctantly turned to him for a loan, he somehow managed to send her the five dollars she needed, telling his "sweet sister" not to worry about repaying the money anytime soon, saying that when she had funds to spare, she should give them to their parents. Lovingly, he tried to cheer her up, promising that "everything lies before us.—We'll do it sure."[22]

Twenty-one-year-old Lilian was having a difficult time getting settled after her graduation. With her startling blue eyes and vibrant energy, she caught the attention of men, but she seemed disinterested, even oblivious, and had no interest in marriage. An independent, stubbornly self-sufficient woman for her time, she dressed plainly, heedless of fashion. An active socialist, she attended party meetings and translated socialist tracts from German into English, and, to her parents' dismay, she became an adamant vegetarian as well as an avowed atheist. Her quiet, graceful manner belied the intensity of her beliefs, however. Like her brother, she was irrevocably and sincerely a nonconformist, not out of defiance or pretense, but out of a deep and serene conviction.

Throughout January and February of 1904, she worked at various jobs in Chicago, principally as a translator, rendering platitudes from Latin or German into English for a new book of quotations that was intended to rival Bartlett's. When the project was abandoned, she went back to Wisconsin to live with her parents and to search for a teaching position.[23] She arrived home to find her mother so worn down by her work in the millinery shop that Mary had at last begun to acquiesce to her husband's lifelong dream of owning a farm.

After years of supporting her children, Mary turned to her son for help, and he managed to augment her savings by five hundred dollars so that she and John Peter could buy a small two-story white frame house and four acres of farmland near Menomonee Falls, Wisconsin, about fifteen miles outside Milwaukee. She would pay him back as soon as she sold the millinery shop, she promised.[24] He was glad to take a turn at helping his mother, after all her financial support over the years, but it was a grave measure of her flagging health and energy that she would accept a loan, even from Eduard, and then allow her daughter and husband to take charge of the move from Milwaukee to the country during the late winter of 1904.

Away from the city, John Peter was soon deeply happy, a farmer at home at last on his own land, where he could raise corn, potatoes, and other produce, gather apples from his orchard, grapes from his arbor, firewood from his own small woods. Mary, however, was lonely—and relieved that Lilian would stay at home with her for a while.

Searching for her own future course, Lilian wrote to her brother that winter about her plans to find a teaching position for the fall of 1904. He was pleased, he wrote back. She had been doing hack work in Chicago, he felt, although he acknowledged that a certain amount of mundane work was essential to move them closer to their ultimate goals. She had always urged him to aim high, he reminded her, now returning her own advice. She could do some good, of course, in the publishing job, but he knew she was destined for much greater achievement. She needed to be independent in order to do her best work, freely choosing her own life, her own "where" and "when." But, perhaps with Clara's discontent echoing in his ears, he cautioned that if Lilian chose to be a wife and mother, she would gradually have to relinquish this freedom, for her wifely and motherly instincts would eventually take over. While he was not discouraging marriage, he told Lilian that she would serve as a "greater factor," if she could be a mother intellectually, to "modern humankind." She would be "great" and "glorious" no matter the direction she chose, he concluded, if she would always be true to her best, deepest self.[25]

Lilian stayed at her parents' new farm through the spring and summer, sending off letters of inquiry about jobs, helping her mother organize the house, and assisting her father in the garden and the overgrown orchard. As the summer of 1904 began, Lilian accepted an appointment to teach Latin and serve as librarian for the Valley City State Normal School in far-off Valley City, North Dakota, and began to plan for an August departure.

From this time onward, Steichen offered a cheerful, generous response anytime the family in Wisconsin needed money, at times sending them funds he could not really spare, scrounging for extra money to do so, and often incurring Clara's wrath in the process. With a wife to support and a child on the way, it was difficult to get ahead, much less to save money for the baby's hospital expenses and her care afterward. Fortunately, in the spring, Clara's pregnancy advanced without serious problems, and they both looked forward to parenthood.

It was also fortuitous that Steichen was discovering a growing demand for his photographic portraits in 1904, in part because of the new visibility gained from publication and exhibitions. The July 1904 issue of *Camera Work* contained *The Critic,* his photograph of Sadakichi Hartmann, whom Steichen had painted, as well. (After his 1902 visit to Steichen's studio, Hartmann urged Stieglitz to "invite Mr. Steichen and me to luncheon *very soon*" so that Steichen could "study" Hartmann's face in preparation for painting his portrait.[26]) Steichen continued to exhibit work abroad—in Vienna, Dresden, Paris, London, and the Netherlands in that year alone, thanks to the Photo-Secession exhibitions that Stieglitz sent to Europe, and his photograph of Rodin won the Best Picture award at the International Exhibition in the Hague.

In addition to his portrait work, Steichen turned his camera toward the city around him, photographing Trinity Church, perhaps for Clara as a memento of their first wedding anniversary. Then, like Stieglitz, Coburn, and other photographers, he was drawn to the beautiful triangular form of the recently completed, gracefully designed Flatiron Building a few blocks down Fifth Avenue from his studio, an architectural feat so much admired that Hartmann wrote "An Esthetical Dissertation" about it for *Camera Work* in October 1903, when Stieglitz's own Flatiron photograph was reproduced in the journal. Steichen photographed the Flatiron from several angles, then experimented in the darkroom with various prints of it—from brown pigment gum-bichromate on what appeared to be gelatine silver; to gelatine silver touched with yellow, green, and black; to the well-known blue-green pigment gum-bichromate over platinum that was widely reproduced from 1909 onward.[27] As enchanted with color as he was with light, Steichen stretched to their outer limits the rather primitive resources then available for printing with color.

From Robert Demachy, who had first mastered the technique in France, Steichen had learned that with the gum process, he could choose and mix pigments and "by changing their relative proportions" achieve "an infinity of different shades of colour."[28] His technical skill as a printer and his passion for color as a painter combined to make his superb experiments with gum bichromate prints surpass anything achieved by other photographers of the period. Steichen's "gums" were "of the very first order and quite personal" as was characteristic of his work, Demachy told Stieglitz.[29]

New York scenes and friends populated Steichen's photographs during his first two years as a resident of the city, but he was primarily absorbed then in studio portraits, and his prices escalated as his business grew. Occasionally, he photographed friends gratis, out of affection. He and Clara were enjoying a lively circle of interesting people in New York, among them the beautiful singer and pianist Mercedes de Cordoba, who first posed for Steichen in 1904 in a striking profile. A photogenic model, she appeared also in photographs by Joseph Keiley, and she posed for Steichen's *The Brass Bowl* that year, her long, graceful fingers resting on the great brass bowl that was one of the few ornaments in Steichen's studio.[30] The Steichens innocently played matchmaker for the eligible Miss Cordoba, most likely with some help from Clara's brother-in-law, Billy Paddock, who introduced them to a fellow Pennsylvania Academy of the Fine Arts graduate, Arthur B. Carles. The handsome, gifted young painter from Philadelphia was a prize pupil of William Merritt Chase, and Steichen and Carles liked each other at once, embarking on an enduring friendship. Sometime in 1904, thanks to the Steichens, Carles met Mercedes de Cordoba and was immediately infatuated with her. Nothing came of his desire for romance in New York that year, but long after he left the city, Carles could not forget her.

Steichen was working hard as both photographer and painter in 1904, as Sadakichi Hartmann's ironic poem confirmed: "Paintographs or photopaints; a sad plight \ Which makes me rather bear (at times) the painter's ills \ Than turn entirely secessionist...." Hartmann had stabbed closer to the truth than he realized when he played with those words, for the photographer and the painter in Steichen often wrestled for dominance. He was earning a more steady income from the portrait photography, but the commercialism of it began to trouble him, as much as he and Clara needed the money. He was painting prolifically, chiefly landscapes, often treating one subject on film and then on canvas. Lake

George, when they were lucky enough to spend time there, was a favorite motif for photographs and paintings, for instance.

In late spring of 1904, his mind brimming with images he wanted to paint, Steichen took his wife back to Lake George, hoping that Clara, now nearly eight months pregnant, would enjoy a rest from the city and that he could spend some uninterrupted time at his easel. He painted at least two large oils during that stay: *Spring—Cherry Bloom* and *Lake George,* a nocturne with a great evergreen tree looming in the foreground of the moonlit lake.[31] Even then he did not put aside his camera: he experimented with color filters, producing his first color photographs using a repeating-back camera and three-color separations. To achieve these prototypes of later autochrome pictures, Steichen first made three individual black-and-white negatives, shooting through red, blue, and green filters, and then printed them with red, blue, and green bichromate.[32] He told Stieglitz he was working hard on the "color biz" with "remarkable" results, despite the "crudities of working material," and planned to send some of the prints to the 1904 London photographic salon.[33]

Shortly before their departure for Lake George, the Steichens had seen Alfred, Emmy, and Kitty Stieglitz off to Europe, an affectionate leave-taking, full of mutual concern for the Stieglitzes' safe voyage and for the healthy arrival of the Steichens' baby in July. Steichen took several compelling pictures of the Stieglitz family in 1904, apparently aboard ship prior to their departure, photographing plump, pensive Emmy and solemn little Kitty, and then Stieglitz with Kitty, arm in arm, the child facing the camera square on, the father turned slightly away from her, their eyes on the verge of smiling. In another image, Kitty stands poignantly alone in the center of the composition, gazing directly into the camera, while Stieglitz, dark-haired and handsome, stands in profile two or three feet to her left. (Did Steichen pose them, or did they arrange themselves in that tableau that foreshadowed the distances that would separate husband and wife, parents and child?)

Stieglitz intended to carry on his fight for photography that summer in Europe, having arranged a strenuous schedule to see photographers as well as exhibitions, all that superimposed on the family vacation itinerary. But soon after the family arrived in Germany, Stieglitz collapsed and had to be hospitalized—"imprisoned," he told Steichen—for a total rest cure in a private clinic in Berlin, where he would remain for several weeks.[34]

It is not clear whether sheer exhaustion, some physical malady, a classic nervous breakdown, or a combination of these put Stieglitz into the serene confines of the Berlin clinic run by a Dr. Boas. Some biographers have suggested that this dramatic collapse, like others in his life, stemmed from Stieglitz's hypochondria as well as from his inveterate need to escape from Emmy.[35] He held court in letters from the comfortable isolation of his clinic, rejoining his family a month later when he felt rested and somewhat stronger. While Stieglitz traveled alone to London to make his photographic rounds, Emmy went about her business, having the family's clothes and household goods custom-made in Europe. That summer, she busied herself being fitted for gowns and choosing new linens for their New York apartment, ordering tablecloths in Stuttgart that were simple and plain "without any pattern," an idea she borrowed from the Steichens because she thought it was "very refined and pretty."[36]

In New York, deeply worried over Stieglitz's health, Steichen wrote letters to cheer him and keep him informed about ongoing Photo-Secession activities in New York. With Stieglitz in Europe and everybody else who could afford a vacation absent from the hot city, there were "No scraps—no arguments '—nothindoin,'" Steichen reported at first. Still, he passed along petty snippets of gossip—Gertrude Käsebier had allegedly tried to purchase prints from *Camera Work* photogravure plates to sell; Horsley Hinton was being an "ass" by writing carping criticism of Steichen and others.[37] But in the domain of photography, the big news of the summer had to do with Curtis Bell, who was pushing aggressively to organize his society of American photographers formally in order to sponsor an international exhibition of photographs in December of 1904 that would be more open, less elitist, and more democratic than the Philadelphia Photographic Salons and the exhibitions organized by Stieglitz.

Steichen urged Stieglitz to consider a formal announcement of the incorporation of the Photo-Secession, for which legal documents had fortunately been drawn up just that May.[38] Eagerly, Steichen pushed for a published statement about the Photo-Secession and its hopes to mount an international exhibition, thinking this would preempt any declaration of Bell's new coalition. Sadakichi Hartmann would trumpet Bell's plans in the July 1904 issue of the *American Amateur Photographer,* thereby moving irrevocably into the enemy camp, but hiding behind another pseudonym—"The Chief"—and prostituting himself in the process, Steichen thought.[39] Steichen said he would await Stieglitz's approval, of course, for any formal statement about the plans for the Photo-Secession, but he chafed at the endless foolish quarrels over photographic techniques and territory.[40]

If anything, the threat from Bell and the enemy camp rallied Stieglitz's spirits, for he zestfully welcomed the challenge of battle. In later years, his memories of that 1904 collision with Curtis Bell were actually expressed in images of warfare: He was fighting for his own life as well as the "lives of all true workers, whether American or any other," he recalled. "Photography was being made safe for Democracy as early as 1902. I was considered a tyrant, un-American and heaven knows what. While I was in Europe, Mr. Curtis Bell, who was a photographer, and steward of the *Lotus Club* [sic],* became imbued with the idea that it was time to save photography from Stieglitz and what Stieglitz represented. As I had said, it was time for him to milk the cow and castrate the bull."[41]

According to Stieglitz, Bell was determined to create an organization "with the purpose of holding a photographic exhibition as a challenge to all I had stood for and worked for in my country."[42] To make matters worse, in Stieglitz's eyes, Bell solicited the support of wealthy patrons—such as the Morgans and the Goulds—and would choose painters rather than photographers to jury his exhibition, thus pandering, in Stieglitz's scornful view, to traditional artists in hopes of gaining their approval and thus legitimizing photography. "I let it be known," Stieglitz recalled, "that neither I nor any of the Photo-Secession could in any way be identified with this noisy project for popularizing the 'art' side of photography, under the auspices of the so-called professional art patrons and the professional artists."[43]

So the battle lines were drawn, and as soon as he was able, Stieglitz lobbied in Europe on behalf of his Photo-Secession and against Bell's up-

---

* The Lotos Club was founded in 1870 as an elite club dedicated to the arts.

start First American Photographic Salon, calling on key photographers to boycott it. In August, he sent out a letter to fellow Secessionists on behalf of the Council of the Photo-Secession, urging them not to take part in Bell's salon and signing the letter "Alfred Stieglitz, Director."[44] He also sent an impassioned letter to the London *Times* and various photographic journals.

Steichen, meanwhile, fueled Stieglitz's anger with speculation that Sadakichi Hartmann had been a Judas, suggesting that after overhearing their earlier conversations about the aims and organization of the new Photo-Secession, Hartmann had reported to Bell, thus setting Bell's plans in motion.[45] Furthermore, Steichen urged Stieglitz to make it clear to photographers in Europe that Bell's salon was going to be shoddy. Stieglitz held off on his formal announcement of the incorporation of the Photo-Secession, however, reassured by Secessionist photographer A. K. Boursault that while other photographic groups were "slumbering" all summer, he, Steichen, and the other Photo-Secessionists in New York stayed "wide awake upon what is going on around us."[46]

As the summer advanced, Steichen's personal life overshadowed politics, however, and he wrote to the Stieglitzes about Clara's ongoing good health as the time for their baby's birth drew near. She was in high spirits until hot weather settled like a smothering cloak over the city, causing her to suffer physically and emotionally. They experienced several anxious "false alarms" in June, he wrote in separate notes to Stieglitz in the hospital and Emmy at the Hotel Kaiserhof in Berlin, but they were still counting the days until their child arrived.[47]

On July 1, 1904, Clara Smith Steichen gave birth to their first daughter, Mary, named for her father's mother and her mother's aunt. Receiving Steichen's telegram with the good news, Emmy wrote to her husband, who had gone, against his doctor's orders, to Dresden to see the Photo-Secession photographs included in the International Art Exhibition, Europe's most prestigious show. She told Stieglitz wistfully, "Steichen had his wish fulfilled. Wish we had another ... Do you!"[48]

Delighting in the beautiful dark-haired baby, Steichen immediately began to document her growth in pictures. In the family albums, Clara is lovely in flowing gowns, holding Mary up to the light. They were "doing *splendidly*," Steichen exulted, hardly able to contain his joy. It was *"great great"* to be a father.[49] Back at the Little Farm in Wisconsin, Mary and

John Peter Steichen were proud grandparents, eager to see their first grandchild, and Eduard and Lilian affectionately rechristened them, in the German way, Oma (Grandmother) and Opa (Grandfather).[50]

Suddenly, however, their fortunes turned. Clara's recovery was slow, in part because the postdelivery routine in those days kept mothers in bed for three weeks. Steichen's letters during that summer also suggest that she probably suffered some degree of postpartum depression. While they were still in the hospital, Mary caught a cold and then broke out in severe prickly heat, "all a fire" and crying "pitifully."[51] It broke Steichen's heart to see the baby suffer.

Their studio-apartment on the top floor of the Fifth Avenue brownstone was unbearably hot in the summer, and he worried about how they would manage when he brought his family home from the hospital. From the very first year of their marriage, the Steichens became regular summer houseguests of first one friend and then another. Their budget allowed them no vacations except those offered through the hospitality or charity of friends, and far in advance, they would start planning how to escape the steamy city—cheaply—in July and August.

In 1904, Steichen hoped that Edward and Hedwig Stieglitz would fulfill a promise to invite him and Clara to bring the baby to Lake George for the summer, but when no invitation came, he conjectured that he had somehow offended Mr. Stieglitz. There was no money to move the family out to Long Island or up to the Adirondacks into rented summer quarters to escape the city heat, for his mother's store still had not been sold, and on top of the five-hundred-dollar loan, he was sending money to Wisconsin for his parents' living expenses. There were also the expenses of helping Lilian get settled in her new teaching post in North Dakota. He had pinned his financial hopes that summer to a commissioned oil painting of the young daughter of a New York family, but the father, while "delighted" with the finished portrait, was very slow to pay him, and he desperately needed the funds.[52]

To his great relief, Charles and Caroline Caffin, hearing of the Steichens' problems, invited them to come up to Mamaroneck to stay with them during August, once Mary and Clara were released from the hospital. The Caffins' generous invitation was a godsend.

Mary Steichen's attention during the summer of 1904 was split three ways—toward her husband, who was lavishing his energy on the garden and orchards of their farm and needed her help; toward her son, far away in New York, where Clara and the wondrous new baby, her namesake, were beset with problems; and toward Lilian, who was excited to be going off alone on the train to teach school in Valley City, North Dakota, on the remote edge of civilization, it must have seemed to Mary. The State Normal School in Valley City had just opened a new library in their brand-new building, and Lilian would be in charge of the "beautifully decorated and well lighted" room with its three thousand books "classified, catalogued, and indexed according to a model system, by an expert in that work."[53]

Just three decades before Lilian arrived there, dust-covered from her long trip by train, Chippewa Indians and French trappers and fur traders had constituted the majority of the area's population, later supplanted by God-fearing, hardworking pioneers and "vagrant cowboys, renegade Indians, vicious killers, money grabbers, and women of questionable business and character."[54] Farming and milling formed the sturdy economic backbone of the town, and immigrants from Norway, Sweden, and Germany began to arrive in Valley City by 1882, seven years before statehood split the Dakota Territory in half in 1889.

The Valley City State Normal School was founded in 1890, housed in a handsome new building whose clock tower could be seen all over town. By the time Lilian arrived, Valley City, population about three thousand, boasted such amenities as a telephone exchange, several churches, a grand ball and other social occasions, a pretty city park by the river, at least two newspapers, and an opera house that apparently never actually housed an opera, although the dance hall on its third floor enjoyed lively use.

Lilian's picture appeared in the 1904 *Quarterly Bulletin of the State Normal School* with a brief article describing her credentials, depicting her as "the daughter of a prominent German family in Milwaukee" who spoke German and French fluently, noting her Phi Beta Kappa membership and other scholastic honors, and calling her "a writer and critic of no mean ability, some of her articles appearing in the leading magazines of the country." (Actually, her *Camera Work* essay was the only one on record.) Furthermore, she was said to be "young, vigorous, and enthusiastic and withal a woman of unquestionable talent and leadership."[55] Assigned to teach Latin and run the library, Lilian soon took on additional duties teaching German and geography and directing plays. A born teacher, she would work in North Dakota for two years. Popular with her students and colleagues alike, she relished the adventurous independence her new life gave her.

In New York in August of 1904, Eduard Steichen's euphoria after his daughter's birth soon gave way to a nightmare. Worrying constantly over Clara and Mary—and money—Steichen was driving himself dangerously hard that summer, not only at his own painting and photography but also at the task of jurying the American Photo-Secession entries for the Linked Ring's Photographic Salon, which was scheduled to open in London on September sixteenth. Because Stieglitz, Steichen, and others had boycotted the 1903 salon, they were invited to make their own selection of entries by American "Links" and then to transmit them as a group for automatic inclusion in the exhibition. Steichen, Joseph Keiley, and photographer C. Yarnall Abbott made up the jury, with Abbott being the toughest judge, Steichen thought, while he himself was the least severe, because he wanted to include many exhibitors, not just an elite few. Afterward, Steichen would oversee the painstaking work of having prints mounted and framed, than packed and shipped.

He was disappointed in the dull, "pathetic" prints submitted by Gertrude Käsebier and the poor composition of some of Coburn's new work, but the jury admitted them anyway.[56] The salon imposed a limit of ten prints from any one photographer, and Steichen himself offered nineteen photographs for Abbott and Keiley to review.[57] Surprised and excited when they insisted on sending twelve Steichen prints, he was just egotistical enough to agree, he told Stieglitz, zestfully envisioning the uproar there would be in London because he had exceeded the limit.[58] He believed he was entitled to break the rules and show twelve prints because he had not recently exhibited in London and furthermore, he thought, the British members of the Linked Ring deserved some cheeky defiance from the American Secessionists.[59] One "whopper" of a print, his own favorite of the lot, was *The Big Cloud,* a sixteen-by-twenty-inch photograph of Lake George, with a luminous white cloud shimmering over the stark black mountain, the image intensified by paper dyed a vivid yellow-green.[60]

That big job done, he was worn out. Moreover, he was constantly provoked that summer, infuriated at every turn by the antics of some faction of photographers, or firing off angry letters to critics, such as Hartmann, who had attacked his work. To further exacerbate matters, Steichen picked up an issue of *Photo-Era* in August and discovered two of his own prints reproduced there. His angry investigation revealed that Sadakichi Hartmann was the culprit, having sold them straight out of *Camera Work*, claiming he had Steichen's approval.[61] Always needing money, Hartmann presumed for years on Stieglitz's goodwill, asking for advances and loans, but this reckless purveying of Steichen's work defied explanation, even that given to Steichen by Thomas Cummings, editor of *Photo-Era*, who explained that he had "erred unwittingly" and expressed his deep regret. He had purchased the pictures "in good faith," he wrote, to illustrate Hartmann's article, believing Hartmann when he claimed that he had his friend Steichen's "consent to sell and permission to publish."[62] That fiasco terminated all relations between Steichen and Hartmann.

To climax this summer of his disillusionment with such infighting, deceit, and exploitation, Steichen found his photograph of Rodin reproduced as the frontispiece of an English edition of a book on the sculptor. He was given no credit and the print was copyrighted in someone else's name. He despaired that he was being cheated out of the rights to his own work. All the more reason, he believed, to support Stieglitz in his aims to create an international society of photographers. Perhaps a coherent union would promote certain standards of collegiality and courtesy. He pledged his wholehearted support to Stieglitz in his ongoing crusade in Europe and the United States, more convinced than ever that Stieglitz was the heart and soul of the movement in the United States and abroad.[63]

But fed up for now, Steichen decided that his best strategy was to excuse himself from the fray and to do his own work. He missed Stieglitz terribly, realizing in his absence how he had come to depend on the older man for encouragement, criticism, companionship. Steichen developed his prints and arranged his group of entries for the London show with Stieglitz's opinion in mind, as his approval mattered above all.[64]

Now Steichen also hoped that Stieglitz would approve of his new aspiration—to work with three-color photography. Longing for one of the early German Perchromo color cameras, equipped with special filters and screens, he wrote to Stieglitz in Europe, seeking a subsidy for his dream. For fifty or sixty dollars, Stieglitz could buy the equipment for him in Munich. He would repay the loan over the winter, giving Stieglitz his choice of the best print he made in the first year. If his color experiments failed—and he was sure they would not—Stieglitz could choose a black gum print.[65] He hoped to have the camera in time to photograph the brilliant autumn foliage at Lake George.

It is not clear whether Stieglitz fulfilled Steichen's request, but camera work was immediately forgotten when Mary grew miserably sick with colic and eczema soon after Steichen took the baby and Clara to Mamaroneck. Clara, still weak, and in pain from a chronic retroversion of the uterus, was overwhelmed by this latest setback, and both Steichens were distraught at their daughter's suffering, blaming her problems on poor care during the hospital stay.[66] Once again, Dr. Lee Stieglitz came to the rescue, treating Mary and soothing Clara's nerves, and the Steichens settled briefly into a comfortable routine in the Caffin household.

Mary weighed nine pounds at the age of five weeks, and grew "more lovable and enchanting" each day, Steichen wrote to Stieglitz.[67] He tramped the beaches and marshes of Mamaroneck in search of scenes to paint, but he found them uninspiring, full as his mind was of images of Lake George. Although Clara and Mary seemed to be mending at last that August, Steichen could not shake his own exhaustion or the vague feelings of illness he attributed to overwork and the tension of the long summer. One evening, after a cocktail, he developed chills and a high fever. Alarmed, Clara called the local doctor, who downplayed Steichen's symptoms and tried to break the fever. When it continued to climb, Clara telephoned Lee Stieglitz in Manhattan, who ordered her to bring Steichen into the city immediately for examination. Appalled by Steichen's appearance and his high fever, Lee diagnosed typhoid and immediately hospitalized him. Clara "almost went wild," Steichen wrote to Stieglitz—first Mary, then Eduard, and she herself barely back to full strength—but with Caroline Caffin's calm help, she entrusted Steichen's care to Dr. Stieglitz and the staff at Presbyterian Hospital in New York and devoted herself to nursing and caring for Mary.[68]

Steichen lay in the hospital for three weeks, too ill to lift his head from the pillow. For the first week, he was a "mystery case" as doctors disagreed over Lee's diagnosis, but in the end, typhoid was confirmed.[69] By the third week of his hospitalization, a haggard Steichen was able to sit up in bed long enough to write to Stieglitz in London about his illness, and two weeks later, he was well enough to rejoin his family and friends in Mamaroneck. He told Stieglitz that the Caffins had provided a home and their gracious practical help to the Steichens for much longer than they could have imagined.[70] Kate and John Simpson, hearing of their plight, offered unlimited financial assistance, even directing their broker in New York to authorize Clara to draw directly on their account as she wished.[71]

The Stieglitz family also rallied around the Steichens, and Edward wrote to tell them that when they were able to travel, he wanted them to spend much of the autumn at Lake George. That bright prospect cheered Steichen enormously, for he yearned to paint the lake and hills he had come to love so dearly.[72] Those hopes were soon crushed, however, when Edward notified Steichen that he himself was going to Oaklawn in October, and since there was only one heated room, which he would have to use, it would be best for the Steichens not to come. Determined to get to Lake George somehow that fall, Steichen then decided to rent a room for his family at an inn, joking in a letter to Stieglitz that he would not dare take the chance of living at the Stieglitz farm with Papa Stieglitz *and* baby Mary, for he was sure "we would *all* die—!!!"[73]

By mid-September, Steichen was strong enough to turn his thoughts to Stieglitz's stay in London and Paris, encouraging him to call on Rodin. He could report that he was gaining energy and that Clara had rallied to do a wonderful job of mothering little Mary. Their traumatic summer seemed to strengthen the bond between the Steichens, teaching them both how precious life is, especially family life. He had new admiration for his wife, for her strength and patience in the face of their ordeal, and for her willingness to sacrifice herself for Mary and for his work. He had always loved her as a "sweetheart," he wrote to Stieglitz, but now that they had been tested in fire, he loved her equally "as a woman." He also shared with Stieglitz his determination to merge work and family into a *"vital force"* in his development.⁷⁴ A family should not be a detriment to an artist, but a power for the good, and he, for one, swore not to subordinate his personal life to art.

He looked forward to Stieglitz's return from Europe, for the turbulent months of their separation had burdened them both with illness, family stress, and front-line combat in the world of photography. On a personal note, Steichen said he felt he got nowhere in his vision of the future without Stieglitz's advice.⁷⁵ By October, when Stieglitz and his family had returned to New York from Europe, the Steichens were in residence at Lake George, replenishing their energy after the summer illnesses. Happy at last, Steichen was preparing for a landmark one-man show of his paintings to be held in a few months' time at the prestigious Eugene Glaenzer and Company Galleries on Fifth Avenue in New York. All told, with the new pictures taking shape that autumn at Lake George, and those already in his studio, he would have twenty-nine paintings ready for the Glaenzer exhibit, set to open February 25, 1905.

Back in New York after the invigorating respite at Lake George, Steichen was too busy with his preparations for the Glaezner show and his studio portrait work to be of much help to Stieglitz—and Stieglitz, freshly home from Europe and far behind in his work, badly needed help, especially with the October issue of *Camera Work*, which had been seriously delayed by his absence. But Stieglitz's huge concern was the reality that by the time he returned to the United States in the fall of 1904, Curtis Bell had succeeded in organizing his First American Photographic Salon, where he would exhibit four hundred international photographs in New York, beginning in December.

Charging that Stieglitz and his Secessionist colleagues were elitist, Bell advertised his Salon Club of America to "hold out a hand to everyone who is *trying* to follow an idea."⁷⁶ When he invited entries, ten thousand photographs arrived. As he had promised, Bell organized a jury of twenty-one painters to pass judgment on the photographs, foremost among them William Merritt Chase, Childe Hassam, and John La Farge. Stieglitz and his allies saw to it that none of the Photo-Secessionists participated in Curtis's exhibit. Nevertheless, another impresario had now staged a landmark show in Stieglitz's territory. He had always wanted to sponsor his own international exhibition, and to facilitate an international organization of pictorial photographers. He had broached his ideas to photographers in Europe during the summer, but it was difficult to orchestrate so many strong egos, much less to find a suitable space for the show he envisioned. And he did not want to appear now to mimic Curtis Bell.

Stieglitz, Steichen, and their fellow Secessionists were somewhat mollified to discover that Bell's much-heralded salon exhibition, opening December fifth, would be held at the Clausen Galleries, a relatively small space on the upper floor of a brownstone at 381 Fifth Avenue, and not in a prestigious gallery. Furthermore, the jury of painters had allegedly reviewed those ten thousand photographs in less than sixteen hours before choosing 369 that Stieglitz, Steichen, and others deemed average to poor in quality. Of the major photographers of the time, only Fred Holland Day participated, all others having heeded Stieglitz's boycott. There was a pall over Day's collection, however, because all of his extraordinary negatives had just been lost in a fire that ravaged his studio in November.

Bell may have produced his exhibit, but Stieglitz had been a powerful jury of one to prevent most serious pictorial photographers from taking part in it. With the aggressive support of Steichen, Boursault, Keiley, and kindred "workers" around the world, Stieglitz had thereby asserted the power and vitality of the Photo-Secession in the contentious dominion of international photography.

In that belated October 1904 edition of *Camera Work*, J. B. Kerfoot, literary critic for *Life* and soon to become Stieglitz's associate editor, had some fun creating ink-blot silhouettes of certain leaders of the Photo-Secession, sketching pithy word portraits to accompany them. Coburn was Parsifal, "Pouting because the Grail eludes him"; Mrs. Käsebier was "The Madonna of the Lens"; Stieglitz, his hair "a little rumply," was Alfred the Great and Daniel in the lion's den. Steichen was "one of the lions," Kerfoot wrote. "See how meek he looks? Would you take him for the king of the beasts? Ah, Steichen! With that recumbent mane, that forelock softly drooping, who would guess the fiery eye, the tossing of the mane, the ROAR—?"[77]

Early in 1905, Steichen was totally absorbed in his own work, and the effort paid off handsomely. Among certain circles in New York, it became the thing to do to travel down to the once-fashionable brownstone at 291 Fifth Avenue, climb the iron stairs of the stoop, ride to the top floor on the faltering elevator, and step into Steichen's studio for an innovative photographic portrait. Often the photographer's beautiful wife was on hand, carrying a pretty gray-eyed baby. Among the cultural figures who sat for Steichen in 1904 was the composer Richard Strauss, in a portrait too cleverly symbolic, too forced, to suit Linked Ring fellow Frederick H. Evans, the London bookseller and critic who practiced pure, straight photography in his celebrated pictures of French and English cathedrals. Reviewing the London Salon of 1904, Evans wrote that he much preferred Steichen's portraits of von Lenbach, Chase, and Rodin to the one of Strauss, calling the first three "superb and unquestionable masterpieces!"[78]

But Steichen's style perfectly suited wealthy socialite Rita de Acosta Lydig, who, among other notorious extravagances, supposedly spent a thousand dollars each month on white flowers to adorn her New York town house and tipped her maid with emeralds. Steichen photographed her with the white cyclamen she loved, and the resulting photograph, *Cyclamen—Mrs. Philip Lydig. New York*, enhanced Steichen's growing success and recognition as a fashionable portrait photographer skilled in posing celebrities. His earnest European series of great men was being superseded in New York by his lucrative portraits of the rich and trendy—not because of a callous opportunism, however, but because of the financial urgency of his family obligations, for four people depended on his financial support then—his parents as well as his wife and child.

Steichen's career as a painter flourished as well because of the hugely successful one-man show at Glaezner and Company, February 25–March 10, 1905. The sales and the reviews of his paintings surpassed his hopes. The April 1905 edition of *The Critic* praised his "warm, sober landscapes and figure paintings," his "extraordinarily luminous" scenes, and his "grip on the real qualities of nature." Paintings singled out for comment were *The Road to the Lake—Moonlight, The Moonlight Promenade—the Sea,* and a nude study, *A Spring Song.*[79] His private clientele of loyal patrons also grew, and, to his gratitude, it seemed that the "entire Stieglitz clan" purchased his paintings over the years.[80]

Stieglitz invited Charles FitzGerald, one of the art critics from the New York *Sun,* to write about Steichen the painter and photographer for the April 1905 issue of *Camera Work*. FitzGerald was a proponent of straight photography and a savvy, influential observer of trends in modern painting. For years, he and Stieglitz would disagree robustly and publicly about painting and photography. Professing his ignorance as to whether Steichen was more painter or photographer, FitzGerald wrote that although the painter was accomplished and ingenious, his paintings were trite, artificial, superficial, and deliberately sentimental. Steichen observed "a nice ingenuity in the use of color, a definite sense of harmony, though employed generally without reference to the perceptive faculties and making for a sensuous effect habitually premeditated, and adapted, as it were, in each case to the subject in hand." However, FitzGerald detected in Steichen's work no trace of deep feeling, or "mystic apprehension of nature."

The much-admired *Beethoven* was, in FitzGerald's opinion, "turgid, mock-profound." The *Nocturne of the Black Women* demonstrated a "symbolistic dressing and portentous air of tragedy," yet its mystery "appeared to come from without, not from within." The "spirit of artifice" predominated the exhibition; the atmosphere was "oppressive and stuffy as that of a hothouse."

FitzGerald's summation was a slam at Stieglitz's whole crusade: "Here is a 'master of photography,'" he concluded, "with the painter's means of expression all at his command. Supposing him to possess the rare qualities with which he is credited by his fellows, there is, I maintain, no technical cause or just impediment why they should not be declared in his paintings. The result of the practical test is discouraging, and considering this as an indirect demonstration of the qualities and conditions that make for mastery of the camera, I, for one, can see no reason for revisiting my previous estimate of the limitations of photography."[81]

As Steichen's friend Charles Caffin later observed, however, the prestigious Glaenzer exhibition "proved an artistic success" and brought Steichen to the attention of "a very discerning class of picture-lovers."[82] The exhibition nearly sold out, and it was so financially profitable that Steichen decided he could afford to move his studio and his family into larger quarters.

Some years before, the walls between 291 and 293 Fifth Avenue had been removed so that one elevator could serve both buildings, effectively converting them into one structure. Consequently, when the young Steichens took the creaking elevator upstairs to their studio at 291, they actually shared a landing and hallway with the inhabitants of 293. Therefore, they heard the news right away when their neighbor across the landing decided to vacate a more spacious apartment, which was graced with a large skylight. Steichen and Clara immediately relinquished crowded 291 and moved into the larger quarters just across the hall at 293 Fifth Avenue.

The young Steichens spent part of the summer of 1905 in Huntington, Long Island, at Rosemary Cottage, the Lloyd Harbor home of Roland and Mary MacFadden Conklin, wealthy art patrons who had bought Steichen's paintings and would commission a family portrait of Mrs. Conklin and their daughter Rosemary.[83] Clara is beautiful, even jubilant, in the family photographs Steichen made then. Baby Mary, despite some dietary problems, is blooming and smiling in her mother's arms. Papa, behind the camera, is reaping a harvest of photographic honors. He had just won two first prizes in the Eastman Kodak Competition, and a first prize in the Goerz Competition.

Steichen's photographs in the London Photographic Salon that fall received high praise from critic A. C. R. Carter. He was tired, he complained, of "that addled question in the short catechism of the camera, 'Is photography an art?' with all its bungling answers in extenso," asserting emphatically, "Let the answer be: 'Yes: It is Steichen.' "[84]

11

291

(1 9 0 5 - 1 9 0 7)

On November 25, 1905 . . . the members of the Photo-Secession and their friends went on to 291 Fifth Avenue to witness the fact that the Secession now had a home of its own. . . .[1]

—STEICHEN

ONE EVENING IN 1905, STEICHEN AND Stieglitz stood deep in conversation on the corner of Fifth Avenue and Thirty-first Street, two gifted, charismatic men. At forty-one, inveterately idealistic and opinionated, Stieglitz exuded vitality. Steichen at twenty-six was handsomer and more self-assured than ever. While their "joint faith and belief in photography" was their paramount interest, Steichen remembered many years later, they had grown very close both professionally and personally after Steichen's return from Europe, becoming not so much mentor and disciple as colleagues who shared a "deep, warm friendship."[2] With their similar names and their mutual passion for photography, Eduard Steichen and Alfred Stieglitz were sometimes even mistaken for each other.

Their family lives were also comfortably intertwined by this time: Steichen remained a particular favorite of Alfred's parents, Edward and Hedwig Stieglitz; Clara and Emmy Stieglitz had become good friends, and the Stieglitzes doted on Mary, just as Clara and Steichen befriended young Kitty Stieglitz. Emmy's brother Joe Obermeyer was part of the circle, along with Alfred's brother Lee, who as a physician had expertly guided the Steichens through the ordeals of typhoid and childbirth. He also treated little Mary's frequent bouts of colic and eczema, charging only modest fees, if any at all.

The two friends stood in the lamplight that pivotal night in 1905, lost in talk about the Photo-Secession, discouraged by their failure to organize international photographers into one association, and still mulling over the best rejoinder to Curtis Bell's photographic exhibit of the past December. In later years, at one time or another, Steichen and Stieglitz would offer differing accounts of when, how, and why they actually settled on the momentous plan they set in motion that night on the street corner, but one clear thread of memory wove consistently through their stories: They were both determined to exhibit the best work created by Photo-Secession photographers.

They considered their options, and it was Steichen who resolutely said at last, "Something must be done to give New York at least a chance to see what we have been doing all these years."[3] Stieglitz reminded him that it was difficult to locate and pay for exhibition rooms, but Steichen suddenly realized he knew just the place for their own gallery. He told Stieglitz that 291 Fifth Avenue had stood empty since his move across the hall, and the two adjoining rooms had just been vacated by two women artists. With contagious exuberance, he began dreaming out loud. Why not turn that space into galleries to hold Photo-Secession exhibitions?[4]

Stieglitz was skeptical at first, doubting that there was enough good photography to support continuous exhibitions. "That's not my idea," Steichen replied. "We'll bring the enemy into our camp."[5] They had long agreed that all artists, regardless of medium, worked for a common purpose—true expression. So why not bring the work of painters as well as photographers into the gallery? His mind racing, Steichen promised Stieglitz he could surely get the drawings of Rodin for an exhibition, and he suggested that they create a Salon des Réfuses in the United States, modeled after those in France. (Later, Steichen ruefully remembered, they found out that little good work was being rejected from exhibitions because so little good work was being submitted in the first place.[6])

In the end, Stieglitz embraced the idea. He wanted New York to see the work of the Photo-Secession, as well as outstanding photographs from other countries, "hung in the proper way and in the proper surroundings." He knew, he said, that he could count on Steichen's enthusiasm, and "above all, on his ability."[7] Therefore, Stieglitz negotiated arrangements with the agent for the landlord (at that time, Marshall Field of Chicago), signing a one-year lease for all three rooms at fifty dollars a month, and budgeted an additional three hundred dollars to install electric fixtures and remodel the rooms to serve as galleries. Steichen himself offered to see to the renovation and decoration.

With Clara's help, Steichen immediately set to work designing and decorating the three rooms across the hall at 291. His vision sprang from his dramatic flair for showmanship as well as from his original, elegant sense of design, already heightened by his exposure to art and its presentation in Europe. As he conceived the look and feel of the Little Galleries of the Photo-Secession, he acknowledged a special debt to the great Austrian architect and designer Josef Hoffmann, a founder of the Vienna Secession movement, who believed in the English Arts and Crafts movement concept of the total work of art. According to that view, a space, whether a private residence or an exhibition gallery, should be designed in harmony with all of its contents so that they functioned beautifully and practically as an entity.[8] Borrowing several specific ideas from Hoffmann, who had designed some of the exhibitions he had visited in Vienna, Steichen created a simple, austere background, painting the walls with muted colors deliberately chosen to complement and enhance the photographs that would be hung there. Then, still emulating Hoffmann, he chose fabric with interesting textures for draperies and wall coverings, and installed subtle lighting, carefully placed to highlight each wall where pictures would be hung.[9]

The larger, fifteen-by-eighteen-foot studio space at 291 was painted dull olive, with deeper, darker tones in the same general color range accenting the woodwork, moldings, and trim. The ceiling and canopy were painted a "very deep creamy gray," and Clara stitched curtains of olive-sepia sateen while Steichen covered some of the walls with warm olive gray burlap. He planned to use one of the small rooms to show prints on light mounts or in white frames, and so he covered those walls with bleached natural burlap, painting the woodwork and molding pure white. Clara finished that room with curtains of dull ecru. The walls of the other small room were then washed in soft hues of "gray-blue, dull salmon, and olive gray." For optimum lighting of the shows, Steichen oversaw the strategic installation of electric lights, skylights, and a carefully designed dropped ceiling, masked by translucent cloth.[10]

He and Stieglitz, both sticklers for aesthetic details, were very pleased with the results. Stieglitz announced their innovative plans in *Camera Work* in October 1905, at one swoop saving face in the matter of the international exhibition that had been preempted by Bell's show and heralding the advent of his own ambitious permanent gallery space:

> *It had been planned by the Photo-Secession to hold in New York, early next spring, an exhibition, consisting of the very best that has been accomplished in pictorial photography, from the time of [pioneering Scottish photographer David Octavius] Hill up to date, in the various countries. Many of the prints have been selected for the purpose, but, owing to the impossibility of securing at any price adequate gallery accommodations during the desirable New York season, the exhibition is held in abeyance.*
>
> *The Photo-Secession, for the present thus unable to hold the proposed big exhibition, has determined to present in detail some of the work which had already been selected and which would have been embraced therein, and for that purpose has leased rooms at 291 Fifth Avenue, New York City, where will be shown continuous fortnightly exhibitions of from thirty to forty prints each. These small but very select shows will consist not only of American pictures never before publicly shown in any city in this country, but also of Austrian, German, British, and French photographs, as well as such other art-productions, other than photographic, as the Council of the Photo-Secession will from time to time secure.*[11]

Steichen personally put up the inaugural exhibit of one hundred photographs by Photo-Secessionists, hanging each print judiciously away from its neighbors in its own domain of space. Japanese vases sat in elegant counterpoint to the prints, and Steichen's great brass bowl, which became an emblem of the Photo-Secession, stood on a pedestal in the center of the large gallery that opening night, overflowing with autumn leaves. By November twenty-fourth, the galleries were ready and the first show completely installed. The next evening, Photo-Secessionists and their family and friends celebrated at a festive dinner at Mouquin's and then walked over to claim their own headquarters at 291 Fifth Avenue.

During that first season, according to Stieglitz, more than fifteen thousand people came to the Little Galleries at 291, but the success sprang from more than numbers. The galleries embodied a movement, a vision, and spirit. "I sewed and hemmed and hung the first curtains for '291,'" Clara Steichen wrote years later in *Camera Work*. "Since then others have hemmed and hawed and hung there; but never with more appreciation than I, for so large a spirit in so small a space."[12]

In New York, Steichen and Clara lived literally in the middle of the Photo-Secession's inaugural visibility and success. The Steichens agreed to keep a key to the thriving avant-garde gallery so they could unlock the door for visiting hours. From the first, however, Stieglitz so loved the place that he himself held court there almost every hour the galleries were officially open—from ten until noon, and then from two until six, six days a week. Not only did he have his own headquarters, at last, but he had the ideal venue for escaping Emmy. But for Eduard and Clara, now only Sundays were completely private and quiet.

From March 16 to 31, 1906, the Photo-Secession walls were filled with Steichen's own photographs, including his recent experiments with three-color photography. To his surprise, before the one-man show was over, visitors had purchased more than half of his prints.[13] His commercial portrait business grew as well, so much so that he began testing the demand for his portraits by asking exorbitant prices—only to have them willingly paid. Yet soon, despite this new financial stability, Steichen felt himself growing restive and dissatisfied, and he was doing so well commercially that he started to worry about what it meant.

"As a matter of fact," he remembered, "I began to be troubled when I heard that being photographed by Steichen was considered quite the thing to do. More important, I was dissatisfied with most of the work I was doing, for it had become rather routine. And I found I was getting orders for prints, not from the photographs that I thought were the best, but from the more static, conventional ones. I made up my mind to get away from the lucrative but stultifying professional portrait business...."[14] He and Clara even began to talk of moving back to Paris.

Continual growth and challenge would always be as essential to Steichen as breathing—and as reflexive—and, after nearly four years in New York, he felt that he had been forced into a certain mold there, compelled to stamp out photographs and paintings on demand. "It became the proper thing to have a Steichen photograph," he recalled. "I found that I was unconsciously making the kind of pictures they wanted. So, I thought it was time to give myself a good kick in the pants and get out."[15] Ironically, then, it was commercial success rather than failure that drove Steichen to consider giving up his business in New York in 1906 and moving back to France.

All his life he would migrate from medium to medium, risk to risk, never settling permanently into one regimen or enterprise. Despite his irrepressible entrepreneurial spirit, he was passionately artistic, yet innately, objectively self-critical (equally strong left-brain and right-brain zones, modern jargon would suggest). The scientist and engineer in him compelled him to experiment, hypothesize, analyze, and synthesize, while the artist in him drove a deeply original visual imagination. For a photographer, that was a useful marriage of technical acumen and lyrical vision. Still in his twenties and now enjoying extraordinary international recognition, Steichen's lucid intellect could govern the passion of artistic expression, sometimes to its detriment, however. Critic Charles FitzGerald had intimated this, and Lilian thought so: "Ed has a big heart himself," she would write in 1908, "but he doesn't let it speak enough as yet in his work—tho he is planning work for the future that will be Heart as well as Art!"[16]

Dissatisfied as he was in 1906, Steichen instinctively turned toward Paris and its liberating creative ferment. It is uncertain whether Clara fully supported the decision to move, especially with a child to consider, but she must at least have felt some ambivalence about the prospect. Perhaps she thought that their money would go further there, and that she might enjoy a more conventional home and the opportunity to express her own interests in music, but it could not have been easy to consider transplanting Mary, especially given her health problems. Yet at least the Steichens shared a history of rich experiences in Paris—and romantic memories.

Eduard, of course, had business to complete before they could take any drastic action. In April 1906, he worked with Stieglitz and Joseph Keiley to arrange a major Photo-Secession traveling exhibition, which would be hung at the Pennsylvania Academy of the Fine Arts. The three men traveled to Philadelphia to install the show, 132 prints by American and foreign photographers, "the best show of pictorial photographs ever made," according to the minutes of the Academy.[17] The exhibition ran from April thirtieth to May twenty-seventh, but before it came down, Steichen, Clara, and Mary, not quite two years old, were on their way to Wisconsin to spend the summer with his parents and sister.[18]

Lilian was then facing her own uprooting from the North Dakota school district where she had taught and directed the library for two years.[19] She may have agitated too aggressively to improve the library, as well as to obtain a raise for herself in 1906, for her contract was not renewed. "Miss Lilian Steichen is a young woman of superior ability and pleasing personality," her employers wrote in the spring of 1906, explaining that while she was an excellent teacher and that they would like to keep her on the staff, the raise she sought was not forthcoming. "It is to be regretted that lack of funds compel the board to make her present salary a maximum one."[20]

Lilian finished her term in Valley City in June of 1906 and returned to the Little Farm at Menomonee Falls to join in the family visit with Eduard, Clara, and Mary before they moved to Paris. It is not clear whether this was little Mary's introduction to her aunt and her grandparents; there are indications that Steichen had taken Clara to Wisconsin for Christmas in 1904 and that his mother may have traveled to New York for a visit, but the elder Steichens' first glimpse of their first grandchild is not recorded. In any case, the frail child had come to the farm suffering from rickets that summer, but she was a "brick" through it all, growing stronger in the Wisconsin countryside and endearing herself to all the adults hovering around her.[21] Still learning to talk, Mary called her doting grandparents "Oma" and "Opa," as they wished, but she had trouble with Lilian's nickname—"Paus'l." Aunt Paula was as close as she could come, and so she gave her aunt a name that would stick.[22]

All in all, it was a pleasant, indolent summer, the first real vacation Steichen had ever allowed himself, and a welcome rest, because he and Clara had come to the farm exhausted. For once, Steichen had absolutely no desire to work, hardly touching his camera or his paints in Wisconsin. Instead, it was a time to "play and think," he said.[23] Revived by the tranquil days in the country, he began to plan for an adventure that had long been a dream of his. Leaving Clara and Mary with his family in the latter part of June, Steichen struck out alone for three weeks to explore the American West.

He had never seen that vast territory, and he tried to no avail to persuade Stieglitz to join him. Everybody else was laughing at his determination to travel to Colorado and the Rocky Mountains, failing to understand his need to see the majestic landscapes of his own country before embarking again for Europe.[24] It was an arduous trip, but a wonderful one, thanks in part to the hospitality of members of the Denver Camera Club who helped him travel all over Colorado by automobile and horseback "for free," he wrote Stieglitz appreciatively.[25] In addition, he spent eight days and four nights traveling by train through Nebraska, Colorado, and New Mexico, photographing unforgettable views, such as one vista in Colorado called "Garden of the Gods." Later, haunted by the lonely splendor of it all, he painted several dramatic western landscapes.

He spent several blessedly quiet days in the pure mountain air at a ranch in the Rocky Mountains, traveling for hours by horseback to ever-higher altitudes, until, he joked, he could see all the way to the Flatiron Building in New York.[26] The spacious prairie and the soaring mountains formed a "boundless whole," so magnificent that he almost regretted his decision to go back to Europe.[27] At home again in Menomonee Falls with his family, Steichen wrote elatedly to Stieglitz that the journey had been one of his greatest experiences ever, not from his viewpoint as an artist, but from the larger viewpoint of life. He also returned from the western odyssey, he said, hungry to get back to work and awestruck not only by the immense spaces but by the pioneering men and women who had first traversed and claimed them.[28] In a way, Steichen and Clara were now embarking on that same kind of expedition as they uprooted themselves and the baby and turned toward a new life abroad.

John Peter Steichen was no doubt mystified by his son's latest scheme. There Eduard went again, relinquishing a perfectly good business in New York, and now with a wife and child to worry about. For what? What was there to pull him once more toward Europe, to the world John Peter himself had turned his back on a quarter of a century earlier? Mary most likely understood, or tried to, and no doubt she wept, wondering when she would see him, Clara, and her only grandchild again.

Back in New York for a month before the planned October departure, Steichen apparently sent Clara and little Mary up to Connecticut for a visit with the Paddocks, then threw himself into more work.[29] Stieglitz was arranging a special deluxe Steichen Supplement to *Camera Work* and Steichen was intimately involved with the design as well as the choice and presentation of the prints. Maurice Maeterlinck's short essay "I Believe" would be used to introduce the volume of twenty-nine Steichen plates, his words echoing Steichen's sense of wonder at the alchemy of light and darkness. Later that year, when he saw the edition, Maeterlinck wrote to congratulate Steichen on his ability to discipline the rays of the sun "as a painter disciplines his brushes."[30]

By early October, Steichen had reorganized his business affairs, closed his studio, deposited his funds in a bank account that Stieglitz could oversee for him, and made the final arrangements for the voyage to Europe. Before he left New York, however, Steichen wanted to enjoy one last exuberant Photo-Secession luncheon with Stieglitz and their compatriots. Steichen had become the older man's most energetic ally, and sometimes he felt that he and Stieglitz carried the entire pictorial photography movement on their shoulders; he confided in Stieglitz that he feared no one else even comprehended what they were striving to achieve.[31] He thought that perhaps he could broaden their visibility in Europe and win allies to their cause. He was sad to leave his parents and sister, the Stieglitz family, and New York itself, but Steichen turned his eyes toward Paris, knowing that it would do him good and that he could do good there for his family, for himself, and, he promised Stieglitz, for the Photo-Secession.

Steichen had traveled back from Europe in 1902 in steerage, but through the generosity of an unidentified patron or friend, he, Clara, and Mary were booked into a comfortable first-class stateroom aboard the S.S. *Zeeland,* bound for Antwerp, Belgium. The crossing was "hideous," however, Steichen wrote to Stieglitz. The ship was battered by a brutal daylong storm, followed by three days of extremely rough water. Two-year-old Mary was terribly seasick, then developed a cold and severe croup, and finally she refused to eat and grew "hysterical." Clara panicked and "lost her head once or twice," Steichen wrote dejectedly, suggesting that Stieglitz would understand about hysterical wives and children from his own experience.[32] They could not have managed without the stateroom and the good service, and Steichen arranged for his family to recuperate for a few days in Antwerp before taking the train to Paris.

By late October, he had moved Clara and Mary to Paris, but their initial search for an apartment was discouraging. A husband and father now, Steichen discovered that settling into life in Paris with a wife and child was a far more complicated proposition than roughing it as an art student. The typical cheap studios for artists were not at all suitable for "delicate little baby girls," he wrote to Stieglitz.[33] To make matters worse, he found to his dismay that prices in Paris had almost doubled in the years he had been away. In the end, he had to pay far more than he had planned (three thousand francs a month, plus five hundred francs more for taxes and other expenses), but he and Clara finally rented a wonderful apartment in his old building at 103 Boulevard du Montparnasse, in the very heart of the ever-growing international colony of bohemian artists in Paris.[34]

Across the wide boulevard, near the intersection of the Boulevard Raspail, the Café du Dôme was still bright and bustling day and night, overflowing with artists from every country of Europe, but getting a run for its money from the newer Café de la Rotonde, which had opened in 1903 in the handsome building next door to Steichen and Clara. By 1906, these two rival cafés standing face-to-face on either side of the street had become the daily headquarters—"home," many called them—for throngs of artists and writers. Almost around the clock, you could stroll into either of these bistros and find good food and drink, lively conversation, wicked gossip, and willing companions in a variety of amusements, from poker to billiards to romance.

But the Steichens had little time or inclination then for the exuberant, sometimes raucous café life at their doorstep. The first tenants in their spacious new apartment, they set to work decorating it. The rooms they rented on the top floor at 103 Boulevard du Montparnasse included a studio thirty-five feet long, sixteen feet wide, and eighteen feet high—so large, Steichen wrote Lilian, that their parents' farmhouse could almost fit into it. Best of all, it was lined with windows. In addition, they had a modern kitchen, a dining room, and two bedrooms. Sunlight and fresh air flooded the rooms, and there were other modern conveniences—an elevator, electric lights, and, as a "real tour de force," a bathroom.[35] To Clara's dismay, Steichen viewed a bathroom as the ideal darkroom.

Along with personal items and Steichen's professional paraphernalia, they had brought with them a few furnishings from New York, including a handsome fumed oak Stickley chair that Emmy Stieglitz's brother Joe had given them for a wedding present. It was Steichen's favorite chair, both for his own comfort and for posing his subjects. With his cleverness for design and Clara's skill as a seamstress, they quickly turned the apartment into an attractive backdrop for their home life as well as for his work. He clearly intended to use his studio for exhibiting as well as for taking photographs, and he painted the walls a "brilliant" gold and trimmed the woodwork in a "very deep greyish cream."[36] Graceful gold draperies and wall hangings set off the windows and cleverly concealed storage cabinets made out of some of the packing cases that had transported their belongings from New York. Other packing cases were converted into chiffoniers, handsomely painted olive gray, along with the studio doors and wainscoting. He was replicating the style of the galleries he had designed at 291 Fifth Avenue, and he wrote to tell Stieglitz so, sending along snapshots to demonstrate.[37]

Over the studio skylight, Steichen rigged two sets of curtains—one thick and dark, the other lightweight and translucent—so that he could pull them up or down to achieve the lighting effects he wanted for his photographs—and to set off the paintings he displayed on easels and tables around the spacious gallery. The photographs Steichen sent to Stieglitz showed that he had even devised a fabric lamp shade to conceal the bald electric lightbulb dangling from the ceiling.[38]

Compared with their cramped quarters in New York, the Steichens were living in luxury in Paris, and Clara engaged a maid to help her with the apartment and the baby. To their relief, little Mary bounced back quickly from the harrowing journey, and she actually began to thrive in Paris, growing "brighter and stronger everyday," Steichen wrote his sister. In fact, her proud father noted, she was growing faster mentally than her parents could follow, and she quickly began chattering in French phrases. She was a happy child, he reported, with red cheeks, glowing eyes, and a "husky" appetite.[39] She had recovered from her illness at sea and from the summer bout with rickets, but to prevent a relapse as well as to treat her lingering digestive problems, they kept her on a careful diet—no meat, a little fish and an egg twice weekly, and vegetables and pap the rest of the time.

Back in New York, Stieglitz missed Steichen keenly. "Thank God, he's going," Emmy Stieglitz had exclaimed when her husband had told her that Steichen planned to return to Paris. "Now we two can travel and you can give up all that nonsense, for without Steichen you can't go ahead."[40] Irked at the suggestion that his success at 291 depended on Steichen (and dismayed at the prospect of spending more time traveling with Emmy), Stieglitz immediately decided to lease 291 for an additional two years. "You can thank yourself," he told Emmy, who wept as he told her about the new lease he had just signed. "I had no idea of doing this until you spoke as you did."[41]

Of course he could run the Photo-Secession and its official gallery without Steichen's help, but he missed him keenly nonetheless. Steichen was "a tremendous help, spiritually as well as practically," Stieglitz wrote to Austrian photographer Heinrich Kühn in November of 1906. He added that Steichen was writing letters from Paris "quite gaily."[42] Steichen was indeed wholeheartedly glad to be back in Paris, where he soaked up the city's energy and sought out the artists who were his friends there. And now that he was away from it, he realized how much he truly disliked the often petty politics of the circle of Photo-Secession photographers in New York.

With his family comfortably settled, Steichen temporarily took a brief detour into politics of another kind. Lilian had so stimulated his interest in socialism that one night not long after his return to Paris, he went out in a driving rain to hear a speech by the socialist leader Jean-Joseph-Marie-Auguste Jaurès. He could get no closer than two blocks away from the auditorium because there was such a crowd waiting in line to listen to Jaurès, the most articulate of the French socialists. A deputy—a member of the French parliament—from 1885 to 1889, from 1893 to 1898, and again from 1902 until 1914, Jaurès was a leader of the Parti Socialiste, a pivotal figure in the 1906 Parti Socialiste Congrès, and a major figure in the international socialist movement. In 1904, he had founded *L'Humanité,* the most influential socialist journal in France, which he edited until his death in 1914.

Disappointed that the throng of fans kept him from seeing Jaurès that rainy night, Steichen nevertheless wrote to tell Lilian about the crowd standing in the storm, celebrating that there was such a turnout.[43] He promised his sister that he would persist until he met both Jaurès and the French novelist and critic Anatole France—actually Jacques-Anatole-François Thibault—who wrote passionately about social justice. Steichen also reported that after the charismatic Jaurès spoke to his audience forthrightly that night about the financial difficulties confronting *L'Humanité,* three thousand new subscribers signed up within two weeks. Lilian was thrilled that her brother was on the scene to witness the very events she was reading about in newspapers in Princeton, Illinois, where she had taken work as a high school English and Latin teacher.

Steichen must have been relieved that Lilian could live independently again, for he was still supporting Oma and Opa in Wisconsin. Not long after her children had left the Little Farm, Oma began having eye trouble, and when she wrote to Steichen about her worries, he sent additional money to pay for an eye specialist. The funds further drained the financial reserves he had built in New York from the profitable sales of his photographs and paintings there. He had sold seventeen of twenty-two paintings on display at the Glaezner Gallery, as well as more than half the photographic prints in his Photo-Secession show, which commanded handsome prices, fifty to one hundred dollars each—according to Charles Caffin, "the largest amount yet paid for photographic pictures." Caffin observed that people had begun to look at photographic prints "in the spirit of the connoisseur, estimating them on their own merits, according to their technical qualities and capacity to satisfy the esthetic sense. They had got away from the idea of photographs that are turned out mechanically by the dozen, and had learned to scrutinize the individual print as they would an individual print in etching or engraving, and to discover that it possessed certain qualities that gave it uniqueness." This trend, Caffin predicted, could only be good for pictorial photography and such masterful "artist-photographers" as Steichen.

Caffin also understood Steichen's reluctance to settle into any limiting pattern of work, admiring his "constant freshness of invention, backed by incessant experiments with the various mediums."[44] Risk and experimentation, Steichen instinctively knew, were crucial to his continued growth. Despite his success, he had infinitely more to learn, and what he needed then, he could find only in Paris. He eagerly rediscovered the enchanting city, seeing the Louvre as if for the first time, mingling with other painters and photographers in the cafés and small galleries, and visiting the Salon d'Automne, which he found terribly disappointing.

He sought out old friends in Paris, and when Alvin Langdon Coburn and his mother came over from London, Eduard and Clara had dinner with ambitious young Coburn, who sported a new red beard, and Mrs. Coburn, the consummate stage mother. The Steichens found Fannie Coburn more overbearing than ever, for she bragged about her son's growing fame in London and fancied herself a photographer, too. Steichen did not fully trust Coburn, recognizing that he could be duplicitous if it served his own career, but he wrote to Stieglitz about his sincere admiration for Coburn's newest work.[45]

Although Steichen missed his almost-daily discourse with Stieglitz, he was not a regular correspondent, unlike Stieglitz, who sometimes answered twenty or more letters a day. Due to procrastination—or an aversion to writing letters (he dealt in images more than words, after all)—Steichen sometimes saved up European news and gossip for Stieglitz for weeks, then feverishly covered eight, ten, or even twenty thin pages with news scrawled in his muscular, elongated, often illegible handwriting.

His occasional letters from Paris in 1906 recorded the growing worry the two men shared that conservatives were taking control of the Linked Ring in London. Therefore, when Stieglitz learned that one ally, the British photographer Frederick Evans, would not be serving on the jury for the Linked Ring's 1906 salon, he decreed that members of the Photo-Secession should not submit their work, fearing that it would be ignored. Steichen, Clarence White, and most of the other members obliged, but twelve defiant Secessionists entered their pictures anyway, including Gertrude Käsebier and Coburn, who now lived permanently in London with his mother. Nevertheless, Stieglitz's boycott was effective, for only 1,039 prints were submitted to the jury, the smallest number of entries ever for this salon.[46] Coburn, further ignoring Stieglitz's disapproval, took on the job of hanging the show.

On an impulse, Steichen traveled over to London to see the exhibition, leaving Paris at noon one day in late October and arriving in London in time for dinner at seven with photographers George Davison, J. Craig Annan, Coburn, and a few others.[47] The American presence was sorely missed in the salon, Steichen reported to Stieglitz with relish; furthermore, Linked Ring politics were as messy as they had imagined them. He tried to avoid even speaking to A. Horsley Hinton, who had often criticized his work and who thought Steichen's manners caddish. Steichen, in turn, dismissed Hinton as a "slimy snake."[48] Personalities aside, Steichen was not alone in his appraisal of the salon; Scottish photographer J. Craig Annan wrote to tell Stieglitz that he had enjoyed a few hours with Steichen, and he said that while the salon was "fairly good," it "suffered very much" from the absence of photographs by Steichen and Clarence White.[49]

The hit of the salon was Coburn's *Penseur*—a startling and soon notorious photograph of George Bernard Shaw posing nude as *The Thinker*. Shaw himself, fifty and famous, had proposed this parody of Rodin's *Le Penseur,* and although Steichen believed the photograph to be mediocre, he considered it a "master stroke of advertising."[50] Except for a few beautiful photographs by Gertrude Käsebier, Steichen found the exhibition thin and disappointing on the whole. Steichen reported that, true to his promise to Stieglitz, in his meetings with British photographers he had defended the Photo-Secession, roundly condemning the Linked Ring jury system and proposing that for the 1907 salon, Stieglitz and his colleagues in New York should jury the American photographs themselves and submit the chosen ones as a group.

Back in Paris, Steichen tried to get down to serious work. Because he and Clara were already living far beyond their means, he grew terribly worried about money. His studio was organized so he could paint as well as photograph and exhibit, and thus advertise all of his work, but he would have to struggle for commissions in either medium in Paris. He had known it would take time to build a business there, but he had not anticipated that his funds would diminish so quickly. As hard as times had been before that autumn of 1906, he had never in his life felt so glum and "completely down and out."⁵¹

Steichen had not yet gone to see Rodin, and he was eager to tell the sculptor about the new Photo-Secession galleries at 291. Venturing out to Meudon that autumn, Steichen found Rodin's studio throbbing with energy and activity, despite the fact that the master had been ill for much of 1906. Because Steichen's promise of a Rodin exhibition had been one reason for Stieglitz's decision to establish the Photo-Secession galleries in the first place, Steichen hoped Rodin would immediately agree to let him arrange an exhibition of his drawings.

The old sculptor was overwhelmed in 1906 with endless business matters, for great success can in its own way be as oppressive and exhausting as failure or anonymity. The young German poet Rainer Maria Rilke had hovered about earlier that year to help the master with his work and his public engagements. Like Steichen, Rilke was both enamored of the great artist and in awe of the force of his genius. Rilke had hoped he could help Rodin make order out of the chaos of his obligations, in order to free him for his creative work.

Also like Steichen, Rilke was struck by the continuing evolution of Rodin's little kingdom at Meudon. Since Steichen had last visited there, Rodin had built several small houses that spilled down the garden slope. From September 1905 until May of 1906, Rilke had lived comfortably in one of Rodin's pavilions, with a spectacular view of the Sèvres valley. Abruptly in mid-May, however, Rodin fired Rilke, supposedly for corresponding too personally with Rodin's friends.⁵² Prone as he was to lavish his fatherly affection and counsel on gifted young men, Rodin had treated Rilke like a son—only to be greatly disappointed in him. When soon afterward Steichen reappeared at Meudon, Rodin must have been glad to be reunited with another surrogate son. One left in disgrace, and one came back full of news about his successes in the United States and about the exciting gallery in New York where he and Alfred Stieglitz now wanted to display Rodin's drawings.

However, Rodin had had a short and unhappy experience with a New York exhibition in 1903, when the American actress and dancer Loïe Fuller had persuaded him to let her present a small number of his sculptures in his first one-man show in the United States. Fuller was an entertainer, however, not a patron of the fine arts. Her show business career actually began in Chicago, where, as a child, she was a sensation as a temperance lecturer. Her original Art Nouveau dances had made her notorious in France, where she gave six hundred flamboyant performances at the Folies Bergère, dancing her provocative Flame Dance and Serpentine Dance swathed in colored electric lights and billowing silk scarves. It was a mark of her stardom that she was the only woman to have had her own theater at the Exposition Universelle in Paris in 1900.

Fuller had charmed and wheedled Rodin until he gave her permission to arrange the Rodin show held at the National Arts Club in New York in September of 1903. Exhibited along with about nineteen of Rodin's bronzes and plasters was Steichen's photograph of Rodin with his *Victor Hugo* and *The Thinker*.[53] The exhibition had lasted a week, and Steichen, of course, had made a point to see it, writing afterward to tell Rodin that he would be surprised at how much his work was appreciated in the United States. Furthermore, Steichen said, he hoped that American art patrons, especially J. P. Morgan, would buy Rodin's work and provide large commissions for Rodin's new sculpture museum, but he noted ruefully that the people with the most money usually possessed the least understanding of art.[54] After the show closed, and apparently without consulting Rodin, Loïe Fuller had tried to sell some of his pieces to the Metropolitan Museum of Art, planning to take a commission for herself. When the museum made an offer, Rodin grew suspicious of her motives, demanding that Fuller return all his work immediately.

He could not trust Loïe Fuller, but he knew he could trust young Steichen with his work. Hearing him out, Rodin was "immensely pleased" at the prospect of a show of his drawings in New York, and he told Steichen to go ahead and choose the pieces he wanted.[55]

For Christmas of 1906, the Steichens gave their little girl a rocking horse and a doll with a wardrobe of dresses sewn by Clara, but it was a sad holiday, full of discouraging letters from home. Kitty Stieglitz was sick. Charlotte and Billy Paddock, longing to have a baby, had been elated when Lee Stieglitz told them Charlotte was pregnant, and they had immediately written to share the news with the Steichens. Later, when the Paddocks and Dr. Stieglitz had a "row" over "something or other," Steichen wrote to Alfred Stieglitz, they went to another doctor, who told them Lee's diagnosis had been wrong.[56] Steichen and Clara wept when the Paddocks' sad news reached them in Paris during the Christmas holidays. Worst of all, Oma Steichen was suffering with her eyes so much that Steichen feared his mother would live the last years of her life in "pain and sorrow."[57]

In the midst of these worries, Steichen went ahead with his promised efforts to arrange the Rodin exhibition for 291, in the belief that he and Stieglitz had definitely agreed that Rodin's drawings, never before seen in the United States, would be the inaugural exhibition at 291 of works of art other than photography. Consequently, Steichen was shocked to find in his mail in January of 1907 an announcement that the Photo-Secession galleries would host a one-woman show of watercolor drawings by the painter and illustrator Pamela Colman Smith. Angry and disappointed, Steichen rushed to the nearest telegraph office. Forced to be extremely frugal by that time, he counted out his words and his francs. He would have to pay twenty-five cents per word for the address as well as for the text of the telegram, so he stripped the message of every extraneous syllable. That thrift would haunt him in later years, when he tried to clarify his role in launching the exhibitions of modern art at 291.

"DO YOU STILL WANT RODIN DRAWINGS?" Steichen wrote at first. Then, frugally editing his text, he scratched out the word *still*. Consequently, Steichen's transmitted telegram read, "DO YOU WANT RODIN DRAWINGS?"[58] Some later readers mistakenly concluded, therefore, that Stieglitz's exhibition of the Pamela Colman Smith drawings had actually inspired Steichen to send the work of Rodin and other European artists to 291. This misinterpretation meant that Steichen would seldom get the credit he deserved for his pivotal and prophetic role in bringing avant-garde art to 291, to New York, and to the country as a whole.

Unfortunately, Stieglitz himself perpetuated that false notion years later, recalling in 1942 that by 1907 he had grown "sick and tired of the arrogance of the photographers who had banded about" him.[59] Unexpectedly, Pamela Colman Smith appeared at the gallery one day to show him a portfolio of her drawings, he said, introducing herself to Stieglitz as a close friend of the actress Ellen Terry and Gordon Craig, Terry's illegitimate son, a well-known actor, director, and stage designer. She dropped other names—those of the poets W. B. Yeats and Arthur Symons—telling Stieglitz she wanted to exhibit her work at 291 because she needed the money, but most of all because she wanted to promote beauty in all the arts. Stieglitz could seldom resist an attractive woman on an artistic mission, and when his eyes fell on Smith's illustration *Death in the House,* he immediately decided to exhibit her work. He said he made that decision because this single image—the profile of a skeleton dominating the foreground of a room—"really illustrated my feeling at the time."[60]

Actually, the Pamela Colman Smith exhibition was quite a hit, in part because of a favorable review in the New York *Sun*. More than 2,200 people came to see Smith's seventy-two drawings and paintings during those bitter winter days, so many that the show, originally scheduled to run January 5–15, 1907, had to be held over for an extra eight days.

Of course, Stieglitz still wanted the Rodin drawings for his next exhibition at 291, and Steichen went ahead with the plans despite his deep disappointment. But the incident marked the first fissure in Steichen's esteem for his trusted friend and colleague, for Steichen could not help but believe that Stieglitz had gone back on his word.

12

YOUNG AMERICANS IN PARIS

(1 9 0 7)

From the very beginning of my second sojourn in France, I had started to make plans for continuing the exhibitions of modern artists at 291. Like most young Americans in Paris, I had made the acquaintance of the Steins, Gertrude and Leo, as well as the Michael Stein family. At Leo and Gertrude Stein's we could see all types of modern paintings, from Cézanne and Renoir to Matisse and Picasso.[1]

— STEICHEN

NOT LONG AFTER THEIR ARRIVAL IN Paris, Eduard and Clara Steichen met some wonderfully eccentric Americans who not only enlivened their social circle but demonstrated a prophetic understanding of modern art. They were a family, two brothers and a sister—Michael, Leo, and Gertrude Stein. The first family member to settle in Paris was tall, erudite Leo, an incurable dilettante who, among other idiosyncrasies, had the disarming habit of "turning handsprings for relaxation"—a stunt that occasionally backfired and left him nursing a sprained ankle or other injuries.[2] Irrepressible Leo had first settled in Paris in 1903, when he was thirty-one, and the rest of his remarkable family followed soon thereafter.

An art lover since childhood, Leo Stein had moved to Europe at the turn of the century to study Italian Renaissance art and write a book about it, but he eventually grew tired, he said, of "slowly blazing" his way through the "aesthetic wilderness."³ Besides, he had always wanted to paint. One catalytic evening soon after his arrival in Paris, Leo sat talking and drinking in a café with the still-unknown young cellist Pablo Casals, then earning his living as an accompanist. Inspired by their conversation, Leo immediately decided to abandon his myriad scholarly pursuits and become an artist. He felt that he could not write authentically about art and artists without testing his own idealism and talent on canvas. Besides, he confessed, he yearned for the emotional "unburdening" that might come from producing art rather than analyzing it.⁴

That very night, after his dinner with Casals, Leo Stein sequestered himself in his hotel room, shed his clothes, posed himself before a mirror, and commenced to draw nude life studies. A few days later, he moved on to more conventional exercises, drawing sculptured figures at the Louvre and studying briefly at the Académie Julian, as Eduard Steichen and other American artists in Paris had done. Although he passionately loved painting—avidly taking to the brush, as he described it—his true gifts would ultimately lie in recognizing, collecting, and interpreting art, not in creating it.⁵

Soon after Leo's brilliant younger sister, Gertrude, arrived in Paris in 1903, the two Steins set up housekeeping comfortably together in a small but charming two-story apartment at 27 Rue de Fleurus in the sixth arrondissement, just off the Boulevard Raspail, not far from Eduard and Clara Steichen's more spacious studio and apartment. The Steins also rented a sort of annex, an atelier in their apartment courtyard, unconnected to their living quarters. Leo kept on painting and Gertrude began writing a transparently autobiographical novel, unpublished in her lifetime, about a heroine caught up in a passionate lesbian relationship.⁶ Soon Gertrude and Leo were holding court for a stream of visitors from nine until eleven each Saturday evening in their atelier.

Meantime Michael, the eldest Stein, settled with his wife, Sarah, and their eight-year-old son, Allan, two blocks away at 58 Rue Madame. Because Sarah Stein also possessed a passion for art and collected paintings with intelligent foresight, she and Michael began holding their own weekly open house for friends as well as strangers who wanted to see their flourishing art collection. Gertrude had once told her sister-in-law that she was a consummate hostess—a "salon-lady"—a role both women, in fact, played brilliantly in those Paris years.⁷ The younger Steins attracted the more bohemian young avant-garde, while over at Michael and Sarah Stein's, the guests tended to be older and slightly more orthodox, the evenings more sedate, the talk more refined.

Both Stein salons quickly became magnets in Paris for Americans abroad, as well as for artists, writers, musicians, philosophers, bohemians, and assorted avant-garde adventurers from around the world. Many people came each Saturday night mainly to visit the Steins, of course, and to partake of the wine and the lively conversation, or just to see and be seen. Others, however, gravitated to the controversial paintings on the walls. It was soon impossible to predict who might appear at these salons on any given night; indeed, it might be said that everybody interesting, famous or not, came to visit the Steins on Saturdays. Over the years, the American art critics Bernard Berenson and Henry McBride came, and British critic Roger Fry. Pablo Casals attended, as did dramatist and poet Jean Cocteau and dancer Isadora Duncan and her brother Raymond Duncan, a neighbor in Leo and Gertrude's building. As the family art collections grew, the artists themselves would flock to the Stein salons in growing numbers—Henri Rousseau, Georges Braque, Francis Picabia, Marcel Duchamp, and the awkward, gifted American Alfred Maurer, among many others.

Eduard Steichen, then twenty-eight, would have been introduced to the Steins as the successful young American painter and famous art photographer, newly returned to Paris from New York with his striking wife, who dabbled in music and sometimes modeled for her husband. In Gertrude and Leo's atelier, Steichen and Clara soon met Pablo Picasso, who was twenty-six years old in 1907, as was his beautiful mistress, Fernande, usually decked out in one of her extravagant hats. Picasso, whose Blue and Rose periods were already behind him, had recently completed portraits of Leo, Gertrude, and young Allan Stein.

But Steichen much preferred the innovative brilliance of Henri Matisse's paintings to what he saw of Picasso's work at the Steins', so much so that even before he met Matisse and began to visit his studio, he longed to show the artist's remarkable watercolor paintings and drawings at the Little Galleries of the Photo-Secession in New York. Because of the limited space at 291, no large paintings could be displayed, so the show would have to be limited to small drawings and watercolors, and Steichen soon enlisted Sarah Stein's help to persuade the artist to consider such an exhibition. "She began working on Matisse," Steichen remembered, "and after I met him he promised full cooperation."[8]

It was at Michael and Sarah's apartment that the Steichens were actually introduced to Henri Matisse, then thirty-eight and still relatively unappreciated in France. Clara especially enjoyed Mrs. Matisse, who, like Clara herself, felt more at ease on the sidelines, listening to the others talk. Everyone admired Matisse the man as well as the artist, whom Leo described appreciatively: He was "bearded, but with propriety; spectacled neatly; intelligent; freely spoken, but a little shy—[painting] in an immaculate room, a place for everything and everything it its place, both within his head and without."[9] Gertrude wrote her own characteristically convoluted portrait of Matisse, embedding in her dense syntax an understanding of his ongoing evolution as an artist.[10]

Many years later, Gertrude Stein sketched a word portrait of Eduard Steichen: "In those early days a photographer came to Paris and knew us all. He was Steichen. He had been one of Stieglitz' [sic] men and came over very excited about photography. Pretty soon he decided that ordinary painting did not interest him, one could do all that with photography, that is to say that the photographs of pictures looked just like the photographs of real landscapes or of still lives if they were good pictures, and so there must be something else and so he became very interested in modern painting and was one of those who told Stieglitz and the rest of them all about it."[11]

Steichen could thank the four Steins for his catalytic introduction to modern painting, because in their homes, where he was a frequent guest, they were providing the best showcases of modern art in Paris in those days. When Eduard and Clara stepped into Leo and Gertrude's studio at 27 Rue de Fleurus for their first visit, for instance, they saw hanging on the whitewashed walls Picasso's *Young Girl with a Basket of Flowers* and *Head of a Boy;* Cézanne's *Portrait of Mme Cézanne,* his *Bathers,* and his study for *The Smoker;* Daumier's *Head of an Old Woman;* Renoir's *Two Women;* Matisse's *Woman with the Hat;* and Toulouse-Lautrec's *The Sofa.* Leo Stein's portraits of his brother Michael shared space on the walls with paintings by Manguin, Delacroix, Bonnard, and Denis.

Steichen already knew the work of some of these artists—Daumier, Toulouse-Lautrec, and, of course, Cézanne and Renoir. But others were unknown to him, as they were to most Americans and many Europeans at that time. He longed to buy a painting by Cézanne, who had died in 1906, but his budget was too badly stretched to allow it. The Steins certainly did not have a great fortune to invest in art, but they happened to be in the right place at the right time, equipped with some money and their discerning, adventurous appetites for fine art. During those years in Paris, from 1903 until World War I, the Steins each received about $150 monthly from a family trust fund—enough in those days to live comfortably in Paris, entertain, travel, and collect the pictures that they were buying relatively cheaply from artists whose careers were just beginning. The paintings of Matisse, Picasso, Braque, and other gifted artists were there to be appreciated, but until they were "discovered," they were for sale at bargain prices. Fortunately for the Steins, they found themselves, as Gertrude wrote, "in the heart of an art movement of which the outside world at that time knew nothing."[12]

It was Bernard Berenson who had first encouraged Leo to begin collecting the work of contemporary painters in Paris. Because Berenson sent him to Vollard's gallery for his introductory glimpse of the paintings of Cézanne, Leo had managed to buy Cézanne's *Landscape with Spring House* in 1904. An instinctive collector, as the books, Japanese prints, and Italian furnishings he was storing and hauling around Europe confirmed, Leo was soon avidly buying contemporary paintings—at first work by Renoir, Cézanne, and Gauguin, and later, by Picasso, Braque, Matisse, and others. He first purchased work by Toulouse-Lautrec in 1904, and in the spring of 1905, he bought paintings by van Gogh, who had died fifteen years earlier. Leo's epiphany came in the autumn of 1905, when in the scant space of a month he discovered the paintings of both Matisse and Picasso. Matisse was enjoying some growing recognition by then, but volatile young Picasso stood just on the brink of notoriety. Leo Stein perceived their power at once, and he claimed long afterward to have been "alone in recognizing these two as the important men."[13] He reported to friends in the United States that he was deliberately building a collection of "L'Art Moderne."[14]

Leo, Gertrude, and Sarah Stein had bold, daring tastes, and they eagerly purchased and exhibited on their atelier walls works by some of the artists who had most offended and scandalized viewers at the Salon d'Automne of 1905, held in October at the Grand Palais. The paintings were aberrations, the critics scoffed—"unspeakable fantasies," barbaric and naïve.[15] One critic at the Salon d'Automne had looked at the riotous, voluptuous colors and forms created by Matisse, Derain, Manguin, Dufy, and others, then glanced at the classical bust by Donatello that permanently graced the staid gallery. At that moment, he ruefully christened a movement: *"Donatello chez les fauves,"* meaning "Donatello among the wild beasts."[16] Thus, the name Fauves was first officially used to designate this art movement at the Salon d'Automne of 1906.[17]

The momentous Salon d'Automne of 1905, Leo wrote to a friend, had "left two pictures stranded in our atelier. All our recent accessions are unfortunately by people you never heard of, so theres [sic] no use trying to describe them, except that one of those out of the salon made everybody laugh except a few who got mad about it, and two other pictures are by a young Spaniard named Picasso whom I consider a genius of very considerable magnitude and one of the most notable draughtsmen living."[18]

Steichen and the others would listen, fascinated, as bearded, bespectacled Leo stood before his pictures on those Saturday nights in Paris, brilliantly expostulating on art and interpreting the paintings for his guests. While Leo paced and talked, Gertrude (who was thirty-three in 1907) sat in a high-backed Italian Renaissance chair so large that she had to "peacefully let her legs hang" over the edge of the seat, only occasionally rising to talk to her visitors.[19] Short and stout, with long dark hair casually upswept over an animated face, she had shrewd brown eyes that seemed at once elusive and direct. She enjoyed singing, smoking cigarettes, and listening to the endless talk that filled her atelier. Her growing circle of friends and admirers found Gertrude's personality magnetic and her laugh robust and infectious, although a few of them considered her something of a bully.[20]

Michael's warm, gracious wife, Sarah (or Sally, as some called her), mothered the young Steins as well as many of their friends. She also took a practical as well as an aesthetic interest in the artists they collected. From the first, she was such a sensitive patron of Henri Matisse's art that he sought her criticism of his work in progress, and he came to believe she knew more about his paintings than he himself did. Sarah remembered that at the 1905 Salon d'Automne, she had been so profoundly affected by Matisse's controversial *Woman with the Hat,* which somehow reminded her of her mother, that she immediately decided that her family should buy the painting. To the contrary, Gertrude recollected, *she* was the one who had engineered the purchase of *Woman with the Hat,* which had been roundly ridiculed by some critics at the 1905 Salon d'Automne. "People were roaring with laughter at the picture and scratching at it," she recalled in *The Autobiography of Alice B. Toklas.*[21]

Leo, of course, told a third story about the painting's acquisition. He thought it was a "brilliant and powerful" portrait, but the "nastiest smear of paint" he had ever seen.[22] Using his wife as his model, Matisse had painted a stunning woman with red, violet, and green hair; he outlined her features in bright green; then painted her sumptuous hat purple, orange, green, and yellow, against a wash of softer green, lavender, pink, peach, and lemon. Leo remembered that he went home for a couple of days to absorb "the unpleasantness of the putting on of the paint," and then *he*—not Sarah or Gertrude—instigated the family's offer on *Woman with the Hat.*[23] All of the opinionated, territorial Steins agreed on one point, however: By way of the salon's secretary, they had offered Matisse four hundred francs (one hundred francs equaled about twenty dollars then), but he had declined to sell.

Immediately, the Steins agreed to pay him his asking price of five hundred francs, thus purchasing their first Matisse.[24] The artist himself called Sarah Stein "the really intelligently sensitive member of the family," and Matisse believed that it was indeed Sarah who had initiated the purchase of his *Woman with the Hat.*[25] Of the four Steins, Sarah from the outset not only had the strongest affinity for Matisse's work but, in the autumn of 1907, helped to organize Matisse's highly regarded art school in Paris, even studying there herself. Soon many of his paintings graced the walls at Sarah and Michael's apartment, among them *Madame Matisse (The Green Line),* a portrait in a simpler, starker style than *Woman with the Hat.*

Although closer in age to Leo and Gertrude, Eduard and Clara found Michael and Sarah more comfortable and congenial companions. Their apartment walls at 58 Rue Madame were laden with paintings by Cézanne, Renoir, Picasso, and, of course, Sarah's favorite, Matisse. Soon after Eduard and Clara met Henri and Amélie Matisse at the Steins', the two couples began to see each other socially at the Steichens' apartment or at the Matisses' small apartment in the Rue de Sèvres, just steps off the Boulevard du Montparnasse. Amélie's gentle kindness set Clara completely at ease, while Steichen was deeply impressed by Matisse's formidable artistic gifts and his courageous integrity in the face of prolonged rejection and criticism.

Like Rodin, Matisse had waged a long struggle for recognition, enduring such severe poverty that sometimes he could not even afford to buy paints. In fact, Matisse and his wife lived far more modestly in Paris in 1907 than Steichen and Clara did, and, faced with his own escalating worries about money, Steichen no doubt took heart from the Matisses' disciplined use of every moment and every franc. He must surely have noticed the coincidence that Matisse's wife, like his own mother, supported the family during difficult times by establishing her own millinery shop. Talks about art with Matisse stimulated Steichen intellectually as well as aesthetically, and the two men shared an ardent appreciation of Rodin's sculpture and of Cézanne's mastery of color and light. Steichen quickly came to feel that Matisse had mastered figure paintings as eloquently as Cézanne had mastered the landscape, and he concluded that Matisse himself was the "most modern of the moderns."[26]

Until they found these new friendships, the Steichens had been surprisingly lonely in Paris. At first, they had been preoccupied with family illnesses and with settling into their apartment. Some of Steichen's old friends from his earlier sojourn in Paris no longer lived in the city. Furthermore, the camaraderie that Steichen the bachelor had enjoyed in the bohemian circle of young artists in Paris from 1900 until 1902 was certainly not comfortable for Steichen the husband and father in 1906, especially because Clara was becoming an ever more jealous and possessive wife. She had even begun to look suspiciously at women Steichen had known in Europe long before they had met, and to resent his devotion to his own mother. He tried to include Clara in social gatherings with his business associates in Paris, but most of the photographers he knew in Europe lived in London then, and Clara could not leave Mary to travel freely with him on his frequent visits there.

During Steichen's trip to London in the fall of 1906, Alvin Langdon Coburn had introduced him to Baron Adolf de Meyer, a bon vivant and an accomplished photographer then in his late thirties. In London and Paris, society gossips enjoyed dissecting what little they knew of the history of glittering, glamorous de Meyer and his beautiful wife, Olga, the socially prominent daughter of a Polish prince. De Meyer was a decadent snob, some said, and not a baron at all; most people believed him to be homosexual, and her to be the illegitimate daughter of Edward, the Prince of Wales, ostensibly her godfather. For thirty-five years, until Olga's death, the dazzling de Meyers stayed married—apparently congenially so. The enigmatic baron was widely known for his elegant manners, his theatrical taste in clothing, and his sophisticated, ultrafashionable lifestyle.

Long before he met de Meyer, Steichen had drawn his own supercilious impression of the baron from a portrait Gertrude Käsebier had made of him in 1903 in his rented palazzo on the Grand Canal in Venice: In the photograph, clad entirely in white, de Meyer leans diffidently against a garden wall, behind a cluster of wildflowers. In Käsebier's portrait, de Meyer's tall, slender frame and his elegant, angular profile actually bear a startling resemblance to Steichen himself, yet Steichen drew from the image the impression of an effete playboy. After the two men met, Steichen decided that while de Meyer made a better impression in person than he did in Käsebier's picture, he was still without doubt a "pimp of a man."[27]

De Meyer's image aside, his photographs spoke exquisitely for themselves, and Steichen admired his work profusely, finding it extraordinarily original. While de Meyer was already widely known for his beautifully executed portraits of society figures and his fluid studies of dancers in Sergei Diaghilev's Ballets Russes, Steichen particularly appreciated a "stunning" still life of a handful of violets drooping over the rim of a sunlit glass vase.[28] He would soon grow to like de Meyer, whom he found "just aching all over" to join the Photo-Secessionists, especially to be exhibited at 291 and published in *Camera Work*.[29]

Steichen's friendship with Coburn in those days was continually strained by an aggressive territorial rivalry, usually instigated by Coburn, who often imitated Steichen as if he were a slightly older brother (Steichen was three years Coburn's senior). When Steichen photographed Rodin and George Bernard Shaw, for instance, Coburn quickly followed suit; when Steichen mastered a photographic process, Coburn often sought him out as a teacher and then strove to surpass him. Steichen bridled at Coburn's inordinate, self-absorbed ambition, manifested in sometimes flagrant self-promotion, as well as his incessant attempts to arrange photographic exhibitions—all tendencies he himself possessed. But in

Steichen's opinion, Coburn's bungling efforts to gather photographs from others for exhibitions in London ignored and undermined the hard work he and Stieglitz had undertaken on behalf of the Photo-Secession.

The two men could be petty toward each other: Steichen believed that Coburn deliberately hid his latest work whenever Steichen visited his studio in London. Consequently, in advance of Coburn's visit to Paris late in 1906, Steichen cleared his studio of all prints Coburn could possibly emulate. Others who knew the two men believed that Coburn behaved arrogantly toward Steichen because he clearly envied Steichen's achievements. "What a man Steichen is," photographer Child Bayley wrote to Stieglitz. He believed both Coburn and his mother were "frantically jealous" of Steichen.[30]

Both Coburn and de Meyer made Steichen angry that winter with their hurried attempts to arrange a European photography exhibition in 1906, further convincing Steichen that he and Stieglitz had to move forward aggressively with their dream of making the Photo-Secession international so that they could exert control over such efforts. In fact, Steichen reported to Stieglitz, he gave Coburn and his ever-present mother such an angry lecture on the qualities of a "real *Photo secessionist*" that they both turned pale.[31]

Hearing from Coburn about Steichen's fury over their plans for the show, Baron de Meyer called on Steichen "all ablaze with apologies."[32] Steichen then patiently explained to him how the Photo-Secession actually worked—which was exactly however Alfred Stieglitz wanted it to work. He urged de Meyer not to use Coburn as an emissary, but to communicate directly with Stieglitz himself from that time on about any European exhibitions involving American photographers. De Meyer did so, and Stieglitz recognized not only the beauty of his work but the potential value of his social connections in Europe. Although the two men did not meet face-to-face until Steichen introduced them in 1909, they were great friends from that time on.[33]

From his vantage point in Europe, Steichen could see far more clearly than Stieglitz that it was time to transform the Photo-Secession into an international force.[34] Each time he traveled to London on photography business, Steichen returned to Paris more convinced than ever that the Linked Ring was ineffective, no longer of any use to the Photo-Secession, and that the United States, not England, had become the vital center of modern photography. Furthermore, Steichen argued that they should handpick the membership of the international Photo-Secession and confine it to professionals, not to hobbyists or amateurs—a point of perennial disagreement between Steichen, who had to earn a living, and Stieglitz, who possessed the financially secure man's disdain for "commercial" art.[35]

In New York, Steichen had lived professionally and socially in the center of Stieglitz's circle of photographers, but now in Paris, most of his friends were painters and other artists he met through the Steins. Once the Steichens had become regulars at the Stein salons, Eduard and Clara discovered an ever-expanding circle of lively new acquaintances. A few of those friendships—with Matisse and later the painters Alfred Maurer and Marsden Hartley—moved quickly beyond the occasional Saturday-evening encounter to have a catalytic effect on Steichen's own artistic life. More personally, Gertrude Stein gave Clara a surrogate mother and Mary a surrogate grandmother when she introduced them to one of her closest lifelong friends, the Boston critic and journalist Mildred Aldrich, then in her early fifties, whom Gertrude described as "a stout vigorous woman with a George Washington face, white hair and admirably clean fresh clothes and gloves."[36]

At that time, Aldrich lived frugally in a small top-floor apartment nearby, with a cageful of canaries for company. Clara soon began to confide in the older woman, seeking her advice on everything from Mary's health and education to Steichen's moods, never mind that Mildred herself had never had a child or a husband. But then, everyone loved and trusted Mildred, including Picasso, who thought she epitomized the best of America.

Picasso was two years younger than Steichen, and although they both had spent time in Paris in 1901, they did not know each other then. After both young men returned to Paris, Gertrude Stein brought them together. But Picasso and Fernande were among the few people Gertrude and Leo regularly invited to dinner before the nine o'clock open house each Saturday night, while Steichen and Clara were invited to dine only once in a while.

Steichen was not included in the Steins' inner circle as an artist, either. As far as is known, he never photographed the Steins, and the Steins never bought a Steichen painting or photograph. They not only collected

Picasso's early work but also had engaged him to paint the family portraits, although neither Picasso nor Stein could remember later how or when they had decided to begin her portrait in 1905, the first time since he was sixteen that Picasso had asked anyone to pose for him, Stein claimed.[37] Before they had finished, Gertrude posed for Picasso eighty or ninety times in his disheveled studio on the Rue Ravignan, sitting in a large, decrepit armchair while he sat nearby on a small kitchen chair, surrounded by his harlequin studies and canvases.[38]

After Picasso finished Gertrude's portrait, he told her correctly, when she protested that it did not look like her, that one day it would. In turn, Gertrude composed a word portrait of Picasso: "Something had been coming out of him, certainly it had been coming out of him, certainly it was something, certainly it had been coming out of him and it had meaning, a charming meaning, a solid meaning, a struggling meaning, a clear meaning."[39] While Gertrude believed that Picasso's work surpassed Matisse's, Leo, to the contrary, did not think that Picasso would last, predicting that future studies of classic painting would be entitled "Histories of Painting from the Beginning to Renoir, or perhaps, Matisse."[40]

Just as Sarah, of all the Steins, had established the closest personal friendship with Matisse, Gertrude formed an intimate bond with mercurial, arrogant, prodigiously gifted Picasso. A rebel herself, she recognized and embraced another maverick when she saw one. Leo drew an interesting parallel between his sister and her dear friend: "Picasso was for essentials a feeble, not a powerful artist. He tried to circumvent this by novel inventions of form. Gertrude couldn't make ordinary syntax and words in their meanings have any punch, and like Picasso she wanted Cézanne's power without Cézanne's gift. So she perverted the syntax."[41] To the end of his life, he believed that his sister's "critical interest in art and literature was awakened by her personal problems in writing," adding, "The Cézanne, Matisse, Picasso pictures that I bought were of great importance to her in respect to her work and then became an interest independent of that and in time this interest in pictures came to be only second to her writing."[42] Furthermore, Leo also contended that his sister and Picasso shared an unrealistic passion to create "great and original" forms in art, and, in the process, turned out "the most Godalmighty rubbish that is to be found."[43]

Although Steichen shared Leo Stein's estimations of both Matisse and Picasso, he was deeply affected by the paintings he saw at the Steins'. He wanted to introduce this electrifying modern art to the American audience who visited the galleries at 291 Fifth Avenue. To learn more about it all, he himself began to haunt the Paris galleries and studios where the Steins had found many of their treasures. Moreover, with Sarah already working enthusiastically as his advocate with Matisse, Steichen began to think next about a Picasso show, turning to Gertrude for help in "softening" Picasso.[44] The Matisse exhibit would take place in 1908, but the Picasso exhibit would take longer, and the collection of drawings and watercolors finally shown at 291 in 1911 marked Picasso's first exhibition in the United States.[45]

In later years, Alfred Stieglitz often was credited with first bringing the work of Matisse and Picasso to the American audience. In reality, Steichen did that, thanks to his own spacious vision and his vital friendship with the Steins, who found the work and bought it, then shared it generously with Steichen and Clara and the multitude of others who came to call on those Saturday nights in Paris.

When Steichen had first arrived in Paris at the age of twenty-one, he had been quickly established as the American boy wonder with camera and brush, the "enfant terrible," Robert Demachy had christened him. But Demachy had worried when Steichen returned to the United States in 1902 that he had left Paris too soon, for Demachy believed that no other environment was as congenial or catalytic for artists. Not only did artists judge their own work "much more severely" in relation to the work of others, Demachy mused in a letter to Stieglitz, but there was an artistic "phenomenon akin to the induction coil in physics" that could only be found in the rich "milieu" of Paris.[46]

Demachy had long admired Steichen's work as a photographer, but in 1907 he was more impressed by Steichen's progress as a painter. He had admired Steichen's early paintings for their "absolutely original" conceptions, the skillful drawing, and the "powerful sense of colour."[47] While he had known about Steichen's recent success as a photographer, he marveled now at his development as a painter. Like other Parisians, he saw Steichen's *Little White Cottage, Lake George* on display in the 1907 spring salon.[48]

However, the Paris that had welcomed Steichen in 1900 with accolades for his paintings and photographs seemed to confront him with one obstacle after another in 1906 and 1907. He had fled New York for Paris once he began to fear the intrusive power of commercial motivation in his art, but perhaps he had waited too long and thus ensnared himself in an endless circle. His earlier success as an artist in Paris and New York had, of course, prompted the growing popular demand for his work and the concomitant high prices for Steichen portraits in New York—and he and Clara had quickly become dependent on the financial fruits of that commercial success. Now in Paris, Steichen found to his dismay that there was a dearth of commissions and income, and a resulting paucity of time or energy for his experiments with painting and photography. Disillusioned, he must have wondered if his success had come too soon, only to vanish like fool's gold.

To save money, Steichen considered relinquishing the expensive apartment at 103 Boulevard du Montparnasse, but he quickly realized that the cost of moving and finding other quarters would be a false economy. Besides, he and Clara had invested so much time and money to make a comfortable family home and an attractive place of business that they wanted to keep it at all costs. Steichen firmly believed that you had to present a certain image, because people respected your work more if they thought you had enough money.[49]

During the winter of 1906–1907, just in time, Steichen found a buyer for his painting *Hunter's Moon* and he discovered a market for prints of his photographs of Rodin and of actress Eleonora Duse, offering them for sale in Paris galleries for twenty to thirty dollars each.[50] Also during this period, Steichen and Clara had a visit from gallery owner Eugene Glaenzer, who had sponsored Steichen's successful 1905 one-man show in New York. After viewing Steichen's paintings spread about on easels in his beautifully decorated studio, Glaenzer "snapped" up one painting for 2,500 francs—about five hundred dollars in those days. It is hard to be sure which painting Glaenzer purchased, for Steichen recorded only that it was one he had completed the preceding summer, probably in Wisconsin, and promptly forgotten about. One day in Paris, looking for work to sell, he pulled the canvas and framed it. Then, stunned by the effect, he decided that it was the best painting he had done so far, especially in regard to color.[51]

Glaenzer also bought an unspecified Steichen photograph for 250 francs, or fifty dollars.[52] (Afterward, Steichen wrote Stieglitz in awe that Glaenzer had just sold New York industrialist and art collector Henry Clay Frick a painting by the nineteenth-century French painter Jean-François Millet for $100,000.[53]) Glaenzer's purchase immediately relieved Steichen's short-term financial problems, and he felt vindicated in hanging on to the new apartment, feeling that the "swell looking place" had greatly helped his sales not only because he at least *appeared* to be prospering but also because his fine studio gave him the courage to ask an exorbitant price.[54] Steichen kept Stieglitz informed of the oscillation of his finances because he relied on Stieglitz to be his banker in New York. Stieglitz dispensed funds as needed from Steichen's Knickerbocker Trust account. In turn, Steichen sold subscriptions to *Camera Work*, to be paid directly to Stieglitz—including 250 francs for the special, deluxe Steichen number of *Camera Work* that had appeared in April of 1906.

Steichen and Clara spent the Glaenzer money as fast as they got it. The carefree, adventurous bohemian artist had been forever displaced by the husband and father coping with family responsibilities, crushing expenses, higher prices, and no steady market for his work. With the residue of his savings being eaten up by daily expenses and family medical emergencies, Steichen worked overtime trying to sell photographs and paintings, with disappointing results. He walked a daily tightrope between the driving urge to create art for art's sake and the practical need to sell his art for his family's sake.

He longed for time to explore his range as a painter and a photographer, to experiment, to pour his energy into the art and see where it would lead him. Instead, there was rent to pay, the grocery and medical bills, the maid's salary. Clara was a devoted wife and mother, but a demanding one, and he did not expect her to go out to work, as Amélie Matisse had done for years. He was determined to provide a comfortable life for Clara and Mary, and he did not for a moment begrudge the funds he sent back to Wisconsin to his parents, although Clara quickly grew to resent that steady drain on their reserves, confirmation in her mind that

Steichen loved his mother more than he loved her. To no avail, Steichen would tell her that while indeed he did love his mother more than all other women, he loved his wife dearly in a different way.[55]

All in all, Eduard and Clara's new life in Paris was proving a bitter disappointment to both of them, putting an increasing strain on their marriage. The futility of it frustrated Steichen beyond words, and the stress further eroded his relationship with Clara, now thirty-one, who coveted much more for herself. She most assuredly did not want her own life to be a sad reprise of her mother's life, lived out in sacrifice because a talented husband failed as a businessman.

By the spring of 1907, the Steichens were so nearly broke that Steichen felt once again like the impoverished, struggling artist he had been when he had left Paris in 1902. Recognition, honors, and fame did not pay the bills. In 1907, having had little luck selling his old paintings or securing commissions for new ones in that city of thousands of painters, he fell back on the very strategy that he had repudiated when he left the United States in 1906: He tried to attract an affluent clientele for the fashionable photographic portraits that had been his economic mainstay in New York. Failing even at this, he began to travel in search of commissions. Petulantly, Clara resented her husband's seeming freedom to travel while she was pinned at home, busy with young Mary. While Eduard painted and worked at his photography, Clara chafed at her ongoing domestic duties, yearning for her own career as a singer or writer. She also wanted more leisure and money to travel than their new life in Paris afforded, and she envied the pretty clothes and jewelry other women wore. Probably from Gertrude and Sarah Stein, who loved and collected antique jewelry, Clara got the idea of scouring secondhand shops and bins at the market for cast-aside trinkets or rosary beads. She began to fashion unusual jewelry from her secondhand treasures, so skillfully that wherever she wore the necklaces, they were admired; sometimes she even earned pocket money by selling the pieces to friends.[56]

One evening during those Paris years, Steichen and Clara were invited to dine with Gertrude and Leo Stein. It was Clara's tall, handsome husband, with the charismatic blue-gray eyes and the irresistible laugh, who usually charmed any gathering. Clara's beauty was admired, but she seemed cold in contrast to her ebullient spouse—stern, judgmental, even imperious. Some of those traits were ingrained in her, but her demeanor also masked shyness and a sense of inferiority. She held her own that particular night with the Steins, however.

Gertrude was wearing one of the striking necklaces she herself had made of old rosary beads bought cheaply in a Paris market stall. Her guests admired it, and when someone asked where she had found the necklace, she speculated in a convoluted monologue about whether a rosary bead could in reality be converted into an ordinary bead, or whether some lingering mystery forever infused the rosary bead, or if it was vanquished when the bead was turned to a secular use.

Others joined in the discussion. Finally, Clara, in her composed, musical voice, had the last words.

"Bead is a bead is a bead is a bead," she said.[57]

Steichen's anxiety about providing for his wife and child and advancing his creative work soon pushed him far past exhaustion, until he worried that it was difficult to think clearly.[58] To make matters worse, Mary had been chronically ill with bronchitis, and Clara was sick much of the time with recurring back problems and other unspecified ailments. The prolonged illnesses jeopardized Clara's fragile emotional stability, and there are hints that she suffered from bouts of depression. Soon Steichen himself looked so haggard and run-down that friends and colleagues worried about his health, as well. Demachy wrote to Stieglitz in alarm about Steichen's obvious exhaustion from overwork, reporting that he was "so fagged and tired out" that he could not work, and was "really looking ill and over strung."[59]

As doctor bills and other expenses mounted and Steichen plunged into serious financial difficulty, he reluctantly took a part-time job working for the Paris photographer Otto, who specialized in making photographic prints from enlarged negatives. Wanting to learn Steichen's secrets so that he could produce prints of fine Steichen-like caliber, Otto paid Steichen twenty dollars a day at least two days weekly to teach him and to do other work in his studio at 3 Place de la Madeleine. Steichen felt like a "day laborer," he wrote to Stieglitz.[60] It was unpleasant, but he was forced to do something, even though the wages were not enough to solve his problems.

In desperation, Steichen asked Stieglitz to transmit to him five hundred dollars out of his dwindling account in New York's Knickerbocker Trust Bank. If he failed to make a go of it in Paris, he told Stieglitz, he would just return to New York to concentrate on portrait photography, and say "to h——l" with art.[61] For that contingency, he had left just enough money in his Knickerbocker Trust account to move his family back to New York, or even to Wisconsin if worse came to worst. By October of 1907, that withdrawal would, in hindsight, prove a fortuitous decision, for in the Panic of 1907, a devastating run on the Knickerbocker Trust Bank left Alfred and Emmy Stieglitz, Gertrude Käsebier, Alvin Langdon Coburn, and many other friends and acquaintances with huge financial losses.

As he had done so often in the past, Steichen dealt with hard times by losing himself in new work. Back in the United States, two of his paintings had been exhibited at the Carnegie Institute Annual Exhibition in Pittsburgh, held April 11–June 13, 1907: *Moonlight Promenade, Coopers Bluff* (later entitled *Cooper's Bluff—Moonlight Strollers*), an oil on twenty-one-by-twenty-five-inch canvas, painted in 1905, and *Nocturne of the Black Women: Screeching Birds*. Because Eugene Glaenzer had urged Steichen to devote himself to many experimental studies for new paintings, he began to contemplate painting some nudes, but he concentrated instead on a few "rather interesting" French landscapes. Yet even in Paris, his "favorite motif" was still Lake George, he affirmed in a letter to Edward Stieglitz.[62]

He ventured beyond those familiar landscapes to work on a large Colorado landscape of moonlit mountains, with snow glinting on one mountaintop under a dark sky brimming with stars.[63] Hoping that Edward Stieglitz—whom he affectionately called "Rex"—would purchase the new painting, Steichen sketched it in a letter, at the same time confessing his loneliness and his constant worries about money. Because he was getting financial "cold feet," Steichen teased, he was not painting with "warm colors."[64]

At the same time, experimenting restlessly with photography, Steichen decided that since there was little portrait business to keep him in the studio, he would explore Paris for new subjects. Because he did not own the hand camera he needed for such roving photography, he borrowed a Goerzanschutz Klapp camera, a German hand camera, and set out to try his first "serious documentary reportage."[65] He went to the festive Steeplechase Day at the Longchamps races, excited by the prospect of taking pictures spontaneously and capturing the immediate moment rather than composing a contrived image. Steichen was snapping photographs of the fashionably dressed crowd at the racetrack when suddenly a carriage drove up to transport a group of smartly dressed women, while nearby, a drably dressed flower girl tried to peddle her vivid bouquets.[66] Perhaps his own hard times riveted his attention to that instantaneous image of wealth and poverty—the flower girl and her lush flowers subjugated—like his art—to the pressing reality of economic survival. Steichen deliberately captured that juxtaposition of wealth and poverty in his photograph—the fashionable women at the center, heedless of the flower girl, who is pushed aside into the shadows. The resulting photograph, placid and beautiful on the surface, contained a reverberating subtext of social commentary that was later lost when others reproduced it with the focus on the white-clad ladies of leisure stepping into their carriage, relegating the flower girl to the dark margins of the picture.

Steichen cited that picture as the beginning of his interest in documentary and news photography.[67] At that moment, in a Whitmanic sense, the axis of his work rotated toward realism. Walt Whitman had contended that "the true use for the imaginative faculty of modern times is to give ultimate vivification to facts, to science and to common lives, endowing them with the glows and glories and final illustriousness which belong to every real thing, and to real things only."[68] This quest for "real things only" then permeated the American impulse toward modernism in the visual arts, in music, and in literature, where the documentary mode was superseding the romantic.

Lilian had often talked to her brother about Whitman and about the socialists, who advocated the marriage of art (the imaginative faculty) to "facts, to science and to common lives." His early response may have been the little flower girl in the shadows failing to sell her wares to the grandly dressed women at Steeplechase Day in Paris. Intentionally or not, Steichen had captured in that single burnished image one example of the "democratic average" that Whitman and such socialists as Lilian Steichen envisioned.

Alfred, Emmy, and Kitty Stieglitz, accompanied by Kitty's faithful governess, embarked for Europe aboard the opulent new *Kaiser Wilhelm II* at the beginning of June 1907. The journey came during a time of particularly intense personal and professional crisis for Stieglitz: Disheartened by the diminishing fortunes of *Camera Work* and the Photo-Secession movement, and by chronic troubles in his marriage, he had confided to his father his growing sense of failure. Edward Stieglitz tried to console his son: Not only had he excelled in his profession; he had become the leader of an important new movement.[69] Unconvinced, Stieglitz set off abjectly to Europe with his wife and child at the beginning of June. At least there would be a reunion with Steichen in Paris.

Eager to see his old friend, Steichen offered to help Stieglitz make arrangements for his schedule and his family's lodging in Paris, suggesting that the Stieglitz family lease a small furnished apartment in his building at 103 Boulevard du Montparnasse. Clara would help Emmy engage a maid and a cook—they could be as comfortable as if they were in their apartment in New York—and the women and children could enjoy daily outings in the Luxembourg Gardens nearby. Emmy, however, preferred more luxurious quarters in a Paris hotel on the Right Bank, just as she had insisted on booking expensive passage on the luxurious new *Kaiser Wilhelm*. After all, she was paying most of the bills.

Stieglitz recalled that he hated the "atmosphere of first class on that ship, especially since it was impossible to escape the *nouveaux riches*."[70] The third day at sea, Stieglitz strode to the end of the forward deck and suddenly looked down, "spellbound," into the contrasting world of steerage, fascinated by the shapes and colors he saw there—"simple people; the feeling of ship, ocean, sky; a sense of release that I was away from the mob called 'rich.'"[71] He rushed back to his stateroom to retrieve his Gravlex camera, loaded with "only one plate holder with one unexposed plate," and ran back to photograph *The Steerage,* a picture, he recalled, "based on related shapes and deepest human feeling—a step in my own evolution, a spontaneous discovery."[72] Like Steichen that year, Stieglitz had taken a crucial step toward documentary photography, and when he first saw *The Steerage* published, he announced, "If all my photographs were lost and I were represented only by *The Steerage,* that would be quite all right."[73]

The Steichens and Stieglitzes enjoyed a happy reunion in Paris, but their visit suddenly had to be curtailed when Stieglitz fell ill. As a result, Stieglitz was forced to forgo a momentous event at the Photo-Club de Paris, the launching of a revolution in photography—the debut of the Lumière Company's long-anticipated, exciting new autochrome plates. The pioneering Lumière brothers, Auguste and Louis, had patented their Cinématographe in 1895, thereby effectively giving the world the first moving pictures. Now, after working for fourteen years to achieve true color photography, they finally announced with great fanfare that they would unveil the landmark Lumière autochrome plate at the Paris Photo-Club in June of 1907.

After prolonged experiments, they had devised an innovative plate whose surface, before being emulsified, was evenly covered with a careful blend of minuscule grains of starch, one-third of which had been dyed green, another third orange, and the final third violet. The image to be photographed was exposed through the back of the grainy plate, and then a transparency was made by developing a negative, which was converted to a positive by means of the reversal process. The transparency, held up to light, reproduced colors vividly, with unprecedented beauty and fidelity.

Steichen was a particularly excited onlooker at the Photo-Club that day, having experimented for years with color photography. Stieglitz, on the other hand, had to wait impatiently in bed in his hotel room for Steichen's report on the historic demonstration. The sample photographs the Lumières displayed were "pretty good only," Steichen reported to Stieglitz afterward.[74] The process appeared to be so "fascinatingly simple," however, that Steichen immediately set to work trying out the plates he had purchased for himself.[75]

His first two pictures were disappointing—"comparative failures," Stieglitz called them.[76] Nevertheless, Steichen and Stieglitz were convinced that color photography had finally arrived, and by the end of a week of experiments, Steichen had achieved captivating results that far surpassed anything the Lumières had gotten from their own process.[77] The Lumière breakthrough, Stieglitz predicted with great excitement, would permit "every photographer to obtain color photographs with an ordinary camera and with the greatest ease and quickness."[78]

For Steichen, the arrival of the Lumière autochrome plates in Paris turned out to be the "great photographic event of 1907."[79]

13

COLOR-MAD

(1 9 0 7 - 1 9 0 8)

All are amazed at the remarkably truthful color rendering; the wonderful luminosity of the shadows, that bugbear of the photographer in monochrome; the endless range of grays; the richness of the deep colors. In short, soon the world will be color-mad, and Lumière will be responsible.[1]

—ALFRED STIEGLITZ

ONCE AGAIN, STEICHEN AND STIEGLITZ WERE obsessed with photography, their disenchantment vanquished, their doldrums and headaches forgotten, their wives and daughters ignored that summer in Europe while the two men lost themselves in pioneering experiments with color. They had long ago mastered the black-and-white print, and between them had tested almost all of the earlier color processes and found them wanting. Now they celebrated the exciting reality that the commercial Lumière autochrome plates, although expensive at twenty-five francs each, marked a major breakthrough in color photography—the first "practical, direct color photographic process to become available," Steichen noted.[2] Stieglitz predicted that "what the Daguerreotype has been to modern monochrome photography, the Autochromotype will be to the future of color photography."[3] He quickly threw aside other travel plans in Europe that summer to experiment with the new autochrome process, calling the technical challenges of color photography even more exciting than horse racing.[4]

Both of them scientists as well as great artists, Steichen and Stieglitz immediately understood the sheer technical ingenuity of the Lumière process and sought to take it further than the Lumière brothers themselves had imagined. Steichen not only quickly achieved beautiful transparencies; he also overcame the biggest drawback of the Lumière plates when he devised a "simple" and effective technique for printing the photographs so that the brilliance and fidelity of the color was not diminished on paper.[5] He immediately set to work on an article about the procedure, based on a three- or four-color principle, but the idea was so logical that he was terribly afraid someone else would discover it before he and Stieglitz could present the technique in *Camera Work*.[6]

Enthralled with the "fine, irregular grain" of the plates, which lent a "beautiful, vibrant quality to the light," Steichen withdrew money from his carefully hoarded funds to buy more Lumière autochrome plates to add to the three dozen the Lumière brothers had given him for his first experiments. Soon he was producing colors more vividly realistic than those any other photographer had achieved with the process.[7] In early July, he kissed Clara and Mary good-bye in Paris and took some of the plates over to London to shoot his first color portraits, hoping to capitalize on this stunning new technology by simultaneously experimenting *and* making money.

He was sorely disappointed, however. First of all, he found his colleagues in London woefully ignorant of color photography—and therefore highly skeptical. Moreover, the British press was scoffing at the Lumières' invention, having seen only some mediocre autochromes made from their plates that Lumière's rival Kodak had allegedly circulated to downplay the process.[8] Finally he got a commission for twenty-five dollars to photograph a woman who, as it happened, knew George Bernard Shaw and agreed to transmit a letter to Shaw from Steichen. He had always wanted to photograph the great playwright and Fabian socialist; besides, Shaw, a talented amateur photographer, would surely be intrigued by these new color plates, he felt. Furthermore, Steichen thought, Shaw's "rosy complexion" and "luminous blond-red hair and beard" made him "a natural target for color photography."[9]

On July twelfth Steichen took his camera to Shaw's London home, where the legendary author sat for Steichen's first autochrome portraits.[10] The two men spent an affable time getting acquainted before Steichen was ready to shoot. Steichen immediately liked the convivial playwright, finding him gracious and almost playful but with an intriguing cynical edge to his personality as well as to his conversation.[11] Shaw showed Steichen his own excellent photographic portraits of Alvin Langdon Coburn and Frederick Evans, and to Steichen's amusement, predicted that Coburn would be upset to learn that he had sat for a Steichen photograph.[12]

Steichen later called Shaw his best model, although the day after their meeting, Steichen wrote to Stieglitz that he felt Shaw was almost impossible to photograph. While the camera could record his lean, tall frame, there was something "airy"—almost ethereal—about his eyes and his coloring, even the white now dominating his red hair and beard.[13] Still uncertain about working with the Lumière plates, however, Steichen worried about whether he could convey a worthy image of the living Shaw.[14]

For an instant during their session, Steichen caught Shaw looking at his hand, as if reading his palm, and he quickly made a picture.[15] According to Steichen's letter to Stieglitz, Shaw compared the pose to *The Hand of God,* Rodin's exquisite study of an immense, graceful hand holding a miniature human form emerging from rough stone. Eventually, Steichen told Shaw wryly, they would photograph him posed as each of Rodin's sculptures.[16]

Well, he had "seen" and "done" Shaw—"(photographically of course)," Steichen wrote to Stieglitz the day after their photo session.[17] Stieglitz later showed Steichen's color transparencies to a German photographer whom Stieglitz called "one of the greatest of all color experimenters," and the man responded that "in color photography he had seen nothing quite so true and beautifully rendered as Shaw's hands and wrists." Furthermore, Stieglitz himself observed, "Probably nothing in painting has been rendered more subtly, more lovingly, than has been by the camera in this instance."[18]

Through these dazzling new color photographs and his irresistible enthusiasm, Steichen spread the gospel of the Lumière plates in London, whetting Shaw's interest, generously sharing his work with Coburn and Davison, and quickly converting influential photographer Child Bayley, who went "daffy" over Steichen's work and immediately lauded the plates in *Photography,* the journal he edited in London.[19] "*Photography* came out at once with a blare of trumpets about the wonderful invention," Stieglitz exulted.[20] Captivated, Bayley, Davison, Coburn, and other photographers in London immediately undertook their own color experiments. "Things are going excellently over here," Bayley wrote to Stieglitz that summer, adding his thanks "for how much I owe Steichen & yourself."[21]

Demand so quickly exceeded supply in Europe that by late July it was impossible to buy Lumière plates. Fortunately, Steichen still had a few on hand in London, enough to fulfill an unexpected order to photograph Lady Hamilton, wife of the renowned British military officer Sir Ian Standish Monteith Hamilton. At least he would earn enough to pay for the trip that way before moving on to Venice to take some pictures, and then to Munich to join Stieglitz, Frank Eugene, and Heinrich Kühn in some intensive color experiments.[22] Before he left London, Steichen made another particularly successful autochrome—of four guests on George Davison's houseboat. Later in the year, he took individual color portraits of Alfred, Emmy, and Kitty Stieglitz, of Mrs. Condé Nast, wife of the publisher, and of photographers Clarence White and Gertrude Käsebier.

To their displeasure, Clara Steichen and Emmy Stieglitz found themselves once again taking second place to photography as their husbands played jubilantly with this new toy. In late July, however, Steichen dashed back to Paris for a quick reunion with Clara and Mary before going on to Munich to meet Stieglitz, Eugene, and Kühn. Eager to escape Clara's moodiness, as well as to join his friends, Steichen soon bade Clara and Mary good-bye again in Paris and rushed to the quaint little village of Tutzing, Germany, where Stieglitz and their colleagues were already working with the Lumière plates. There, Steichen and his fellow photographers enjoyed an uproarious good time playing with the autochrome process, convinced that it opened new doors for artistic expression.

Deeply impressed by Steichen's results, Stieglitz immediately asked to print his superb color photographs of Shaw and Lady Hamilton in *Camera Work*, and he began planning a London exhibition of his own prints as well as those by Steichen and Eugene. Stieglitz confidently predicted that the remarkable clarity and richness of color would soon make the world "color-mad."[23] Certainly the photographers in Steichen and Stieglitz's circle were color-mad that summer, finding this new technical advance endlessly fascinating and invigorating. Coburn went over to Paris from London in September of 1907 to observe in the darkroom as Steichen developed each three-color transparency as easily as if it were an ordinary negative.[24] Then, after Coburn had eagerly appropriated Steichen's methods with the Lumière plates, he went back to London and deviously gave the impression to the British press that he was the chief proponent of this latest advance in photography. Steichen told Stieglitz with disgust that Coburn was promoting himself "to beat the band" as the expert in Europe, and Steichen predicted he would do the same thing soon in New York.[25]

For the British journal *The Studio,* Coburn set out to prepare an entire special issue devoted to color photography, hounding Steichen for months for permission to reprint his autochromes.[26] Finally, in April of 1908, Steichen wrote what Coburn called "a perfectly splendid letter" declining, for reasons neither man made clear.[27] Steichen was most likely either too preoccupied with work and family pressures or too resentful of Coburn's self-serving intrusion in his territory to comply, and the issue eventually appeared in the summer of 1908 with Steichen's color photographs conspicuously absent.

In August of 1907, Steichen temporarily suspended his color experiments, taking his camera to the International Socialist Convention in Stuttgart, Germany, where a thousand official delegates from thirty countries were joined by an audience of more than fifty thousand. Back in Wisconsin with their parents for the summer, Lilian Steichen was eager for firsthand news of the event. She had hoped for a long time that Eduard would "help the movement with his art."[28] In Stuttgart, he did so in a way, setting up a makeshift studio in the congress hall to earn some money photographing the major figures in the European socialist movement—Jaurès; the German Social Democrat August Bebel; the French socialist Jules Guesde; the American socialist and sociologist Robert Hunter, whom Steichen had come to know well in Paris; and the English Marxist socialist Henry Mayers Hyndman.

Steichen advertised his services that week—and his stature as no ordinary commercial photographer—by displaying copies of *Camera*

Work that Stieglitz sent him from Munich. Some of the portraits he made at the congress, along with one of his photographs of Shaw, would be used to illustrate *Socialists at Work,* a book of biographical sketches by Robert Hunter, published by Macmillan in 1908.[29] Steichen had a "great" time at the gathering, where he found the French socialists "raising merry h—l," and he left Stuttgart impressed by "such force and power of men."[30]

Throughout the summer of 1907, while Steichen had enjoyed his working jaunts to London, Venice, Munich, and now Stuttgart, Clara cared for precocious three-year-old Mary. Clara was suffering from the chronic back pain that created misery for her and others around her.[31] Only strong painkillers gave her relief from the undiagnosed condition that she called vaguely over the years the "weakness in her spine," or her "spinal infection." Whether real or psychosomatic, the pain was physically and emotionally debilitating, and it intensified that summer during a bout of what her French physician termed *colique nephritis,* a painful kidney infection, accompanied by a mystifying facial palsy, which fortunately disappeared as quickly as it had come.[32] Added to Clara's woes were Mary's chronic health problems—respiratory and digestive illnesses that a modern physician would almost certainly have treated as allergies. During these sieges, mother and child inevitably wound up emotionally distraught, so it was difficult to keep a maid even when the budget allowed funds for one.

Clara spent most of the summer ill, exhausted, and in constant crisis, convinced that Steichen was neglecting her and dallying with other women. When she saw Steichen's autochromes of the house party on George Davison's boat, she exploded, sure that Steichen had deliberately left her behind so that he could have an affair with one of Davison's young guests. While there was no proof of this, Clara drew Stieglitz, Mercedes de Cordoba, and other friends into the quarrel. In particular, she poured out her anger to Stieglitz—in person and in notes that were at times incoherent and illegible, as if her rage had constricted her handwriting. She hurled furious charges at Steichen: He ignored her, she claimed; he forced her to borrow money from strangers; he did not give a damn about her or Mary.[33] Dreading her outbursts, Steichen would work hard, then hurry home to Paris, hoping to appease her. Clara would be temporarily calm and peaceful until he left, and then her doubts tormented her once again.

"The happy things go slipping past & no one plans for me & I can't grasp them," Clara lamented. She longed to get to the seashore for a rest but doubted that would be possible. "Feel done—tired—sore—and ragged," she complained in a letter to Stieglitz. It was "so trying to talk to people," she wrote. "The pressure has been steady & strong & I'm going under sure as Fate."[34]

Steichen and Stieglitz had hoped that their wives would enjoy some summer leisure together while they were engrossed in photography, but Clara was as bored and unhappy without Eduard as Emmy Stieglitz was without Alfred, who was similarly wrapped up in his camera and his friends. When Emmy was in Paris, the two women amused themselves sightseeing, shopping, and going out to lunch and tea, but Emmy's obsession with having expensive, fashionable dresses made in Paris "sickened" Clara, she complained to Stieglitz.[35] One summer night when Steichen popped back into the city between destinations, he took Clara and Emmy to the theater, and kindhearted Emmy arranged a tea at the Steichens' apartment the next day for some of her wealthy American friends, in hopes that they would commission Steichen photographs.[36]

Clara needed more than Emmy's company, however, and she spent much of her time in bed, depressed, "too tired to wriggle into clothes."[37] Engrossed as he was with color photography, Steichen saw far more of Stieglitz than of his own family. Steichen had given her the impression that he and Stieglitz planned to spend much of the summer together, Clara wrote to Stieglitz, but since her own poor health, her lack of money, and her inclination barred her from being Emmy's constant companion, she wondered if perhaps she had ruined their plans. "I'm in the way again," she concluded morosely, hoping for Stieglitz's sympathy and reassurance.[38] Instead (his own marital problems much on his mind), he urged her to trust and love her husband, to maintain a tranquil, pleasant home, and to consider how her behavior affected Steichen's morale and his work.[39] "You can trust me—I'll smile," Clara replied sarcastically, but she apologized for the quarrels he had witnessed, and professed her love for her husband. "Don't for dare to say I don't understand him—" she wrote; "I do & I love him—& that you can't deny."[40]

Steichen and Stieglitz commiserated in letters and in person about married life—Alfred and Emmy's chronic incompatibility and unhappiness and Eduard and Clara's growing bitter discord. The difference was that Alfred no longer loved Emmy, but he was largely dependent on her ample income, while Eduard still loved Clara, who was totally dependent on his inadequate one. But the Steichens quarreled more and more frequently and publicly, and, to Steichen's deep embarrassment, there were more "rotten rows" during the summer of 1907, marring the time the Steichens and Stieglitzes had hoped to enjoy together.[41] Clara was pathologically jealous of Steichen, convincing herself that he was having "experiences" with other women, and, despite her resolve, accusing him as soon as he set foot in the door from a trip away from Paris.[42] He had a volatile temper, too, and the airy studio atop 103 Boulevard du Montparnasse reverberated that summer with loud, wounding quarrels. Afterward, Eduard and Clara tried desperately to make amends to each other.

Sometime in August, in the aftermath of such a battle, Eduard and Clara conceived a child. Clara soon grew violently ill with morning sickness, sometimes frightening little Mary, who would see her mother during her bouts of nausea. There seem to have been painful conversations between Eduard and Clara about whether to have the child, no doubt because of their worsening marital and financial problems and Clara's and Mary's constant illnesses.[43] According to Steichen, Clara even took "heroic measures" to try to abort the pregnancy, but she failed, apparently suffering intensely as a result.[44] For the time being, they kept their news a secret, even from the Stieglitzes, attributing Clara's continued illness to her back problems.

On September twenty-sixth, barely off the ship and back at 291 in New York, Stieglitz summoned the press for a dramatic announcement. "Color photography is an accomplished fact," his press release read. "Mr. Alfred Stieglitz, having just returned from Europe, has brought with him a selection of color photographs made by Eduard J. Steichen, Frank Eugene and himself.... These pictures are the first of the kind to be shown in America. You are invited to attend the exhibition."[45] On September 27, 1907, at 291 Fifth Avenue, he unveiled the autochromes to members of the press and other curious viewers crowded into the Photo-Secession galleries. Stieglitz had now officially "set loose upon America" the wonders of color photography.[46]

The October 1907 issue of *Camera Work* launched a yearlong Photo-Secession emphasis on color photographs, carrying three Steichen autochromes—of Lady Hamilton, Shaw, and the group on the houseboat—and a rhapsodic article on color photography by Stieglitz. Steichen, however, was disappointed in the quality of the reproductions, finding them a "long long way" from doing justice to the original prints, which in turn were never as vivid as the transparencies. The likeness of Lady Hamilton was so distorted, in fact, that he asked Stieglitz to entitle it *Portrait of Lady H.* because it would be a "sin" to suggest the reproduction actually looked like her.[47]

At 291, Stieglitz continued his focus on the novel autochromes by mounting a special Photo-Secession show of his own color pictures, along with work by Steichen, Eugene, and Clarence White. Another special "Color Number" of *Camera Work* appeared in January 1908, but without an article on color photography that Steichen had been promising Stieglitz for several months. When Steichen's handwritten manuscript, thirty-seven legal-sized pages long, finally reached New York, Stieglitz rushed it off to the typist, having made only minor editorial corrections, for inclusion in the April 1908 issue of *Camera Work*.

This lucid account of the evolution of the Lumière plates contained one of the most detailed explications of his work habits that Steichen would ever write—and simultaneously it revealed his knowledge of the history of color photography and his grasp of the intricate science supporting the Lumières' innovation. Moreover, Steichen took other photographers step by step through his own adaptations of the Lumière process so precisely that he considered publishing a cheap popular handbook on how to use the autochrome plates for distribution in England, Germany, and France. He asked Stieglitz's advice, hoping that he would see to publication in the United States, and predicting it would be lucrative. "I have *got* to make money," he wrote urgently.[48]

Steichen brought the painter's exquisite sense of the nuances of color to his technical mastery of this new photographic process. Consequently, he was uniquely prepared to extract the finest results from the Lumière plates.

His detailed article painted a revealing self-portrait of an artist deeply absorbed in his work, at the same time offering a master class in Steichen's painstaking photographic techniques. The essay revealed the methodical scientist manipulating filters, lights, chemicals, and dyes, delicately calibrating exposures for summer light and autumn light, choreographing minutes and seconds to achieve the luminous colors only a keenly sensitive eye could find in nature. He also charted his experiments with artificial light, getting results, he said, akin to the colors some painters achieved by lamplight. On a practical note, Steichen wished that someone would market an emulsion the photographer could use to coat the glass of the hundreds of used plates left after his experiments, thus recycling them. "Personally I have no medium that can give me color of such wonderful luminosity as the Autochrome plate," Steichen concluded. "One must go to stained glass for such color resonance, as the palette and canvas are a dull and lifeless medium in comparison." Still, he cautioned that much of the wondrous clarity of the color was inevitably lost between the plate and the paper on which the image was printed. Until the color printing process caught pace with the plates themselves, color photography would be at best "a compromise—an experiment."[49]

The Lumière plates had their detractors and skeptics, of course, but *Camera Work* was not alone in its praise of the process. Critic J. Nilsen Laurvik wrote about the new color photography for *The Century Magazine* in January of 1908, calling pictorial photography "the most modern of arts in that it is most truly of our own time," in part because it kept in touch with "the newest developments in all fields of science."

Now Steichen, Stieglitz, and other photographers, like the Impressionist painters, sought to master the complicated chemistry of light and color to produce beautiful images. "In a word," Laurvik continued, "color-photography ushers in a new era in the study of color, that promises to revolutionize color-printing, and that will surely exert a most important influence on the art of painting, establishing as it does the soundness of the much-abused theories of the Impressionists."[50] Best of all for Steichen, *Century* paid three hundred dollars for reproduction rights to two of his autochromes to illustrate Laurvik's article.[51]

As he rapidly became known as the master of this new form, Steichen was convinced that he could make a great deal of money producing color images. More important, however, the advent of color reinvigorated photography for Stieglitz and Steichen just at the moment when each man was moving toward a new realism in subject matter. Previously, some of the manipulations they had practiced with black-and-white photographs had been motivated by the desire to give their pictures the dimension of color. But now color could be achieved by an efficient mechanical process, and, Stieglitz cautioned in *Camera Work*, "Handwork of any kind will show on the plates—that is one of the blessings of the process—and faking is out of the question."[52]

When Steichen and Mary got sick with colds in the fall of 1907, the three Steichens left Paris to recuperate at the home of some generous friends in the country. They had hoped that they would all grow stronger during a week away from money woes, surrounded by the tranquil beauty of nature, but instead they only grew worse.[53] Steichen halfheartedly began several paintings and took a few pictures, but he was "too d—n blue" to work for long or to write letters. "Still feel like h—l," he wrote to Stieglitz after they returned to Paris.[54]

Despite his personal problems, he soon turned his attention to the long-promised exhibition of drawings by Auguste Rodin. Sometimes alone, sometimes with Clara, he made several trips out to see Meudon to visit Rodin, who had once again strayed from the faithful Rose. This time, he had not only upset Rose but had alienated most of his friends by falling flagrantly in love with a vivacious, ambitious married American woman—forty-year-old Claire Coudert, Duchesse de Choiseul. Fourteen years earlier, her family had arranged her marriage to a Frenchman, bartering their wealth for his title. When the errant duchess fell madly in love with Rodin, she demanded a conspicuous role in his life, and she got it. She had even gotten Rodin to dress up in silk knee britches and attend a court ball in London during the summer of 1907.

With the distractions of his work and the unhappy, warring women in his life, Rodin was enormously preoccupied during 1907, but Steichen had kept cajoling him to loan his work for the exhibit at 291. Time and again, the sculptor would summon Steichen to Meudon to make his own free choice of drawings, only to waver in his permission. To make matters worse, Steichen heard that the Salon d'Automne had announced an exhibition of Rodin drawings and had prepared a catalog for it. But in the end, to Steichen's vast relief, Rodin did not allow his work to be shown in the salon. Finally, he let Steichen select the wash drawings he wanted to take to Stieglitz at 291, but just when Steichen thought the matter was settled, Rodin vacillated once more, refusing to relinquish the work.[55] Steichen began to wonder if the duchess could be sabotaging his efforts to take Rodin's work to the United States.

Once more, toward year's end, however, Rodin invited him to Meudon, this time ready at last to entrust the drawings to Steichen and the Photo-Secession galleries. Rodin himself had ranked them in three groups—A, B, and C—according to his estimation of their quality, and he gave Steichen one of the best of them to keep. Steichen told Stieglitz that he hid it in a drawer in his studio, for fear that a potential client would be so shocked by it that he would lose a commission.[56]

In the end, Steichen selected fifty-eight of Rodin's recent drawings, all of them startlingly erotic depictions of female nudes. Since boyhood, Rodin had loved to draw, studying at the Ecole Impériale Spéciale de Dessin et de Mathématiques—or "Petite Ecole"—with Horace Lecoq de Boisbaudran, a great teacher who taught his students to observe keenly and then draw from memory, and to draw human figures that were freely, spontaneously engaged, not classically posed. Obsessed with the beauty of the human figure, Rodin created thousands of drawings over many years, with a freedom no doubt far surpassing his teacher's intentions. For a time, his drawings primarily served his sculpture as detailed studies of various dimensions and angles. During the 1890s, however, Rodin seemed to fall in love with drawing all over again, for its own sake, creating over the next decade at least five thousand images of the female body—images that to some people were appalling perversions and to others beautiful celebrations of female sexuality.[57]

A woman's body was almost a landscape, Rodin thought, and his provocative drawings tenderly, audaciously explored its every nuance, contour, and sensual gesture.[58] Their inhibitions seemingly flung aside with their clothes, a host of voluptuous young models posed for Rodin in his studio, singly or in groups, lying or standing, arranging limbs and shoulders as the artist commanded, sometimes masturbating, sometimes appearing to make love to one another. In his sixties and seventies, Rodin was said to have seduced his models as well as other women with these virile drawings, and Steichen knew they would cause a major shock of disbelief in New York. He relished the prospect. At last, Steichen had the coveted drawings in hand. "They *are howlers,*" Steichen reported to Stieglitz.[59]

It was a great event for 291, and, more so, for American art. It was also a coup for Steichen, who, unlike many American immigrants, had returned to the Old World to embrace European art and culture, deliberately assimilating it into his own life and work. Thanks to his intimate exposure to the work of Matisse, Picasso, and Rodin, Steichen's own artistic vision was expanding, not only to shape and stretch his work as a painter but to awaken his eye to colors and forms that he wanted the American audience to see. He resolved to take back to 291 not only Rodin's shocking sketches but some of these new paintings and drawings by others, which, in all their controversial modernity, would shape the art of the future. Thus the gifted son of European immigrants began to build a significant cultural bridge between the Old World and the New World by launching a series of remarkably foresighted American encounters with the modernist figures in European art. While the Steins bought modern art for their own pleasure and shared it with their friends, Steichen wanted to share it with a much wider audience, and Stieglitz and the Little Galleries of the Photo-Secession in New York would be the conduit. Steichen set to work single-handedly to transmit to Stieglitz in New York the freshest, most exciting, most controversial art he was discovering in Paris—the glorious new shapes, styles, and colors of art in Europe. These paintings and drawings defied tradition, shocked the senses, and thereby challenged the mind and its creative vision.

Back in Paris, Steichen carefully packed the precious Rodin drawings and entrusted them to a Miss Vosburg to deliver to Stieglitz.[60] He hated to let go of them, he said, because they were so wonderful to study. Yes, when Stieglitz mounted this exhibit of Rodin's work at 291, it would rock New York. Steichen was sure of that, and he longed to be on hand to see it for himself.

Worn down with family and business problems in the fall of 1907, Steichen could not muster the energy or enthusiasm to do any serious work.

Moreover, he was thoroughly disgusted with the ugly politics of the Linked Ring in London, where personal ambitions dominated any serious efforts to exhibit and thereby sell good photographs. Steichen could be as cantankerous with photographers in London and Paris as Stieglitz was with those in New York, Philadelphia, and Boston. Furthermore, both men were appalled by the poor quality of photographic work being done in Paris, where even color photography was being trivialized into a fad.

The French photographers had gone crazy over the plates and special color lenses, Steichen told Stieglitz in disgust. When Demachy photographed Steichen, he was so absorbed in measuring distances and exposures that he appeared to forget about his subject, and Steichen had to pose himself. During that photo session, he tried to talk to Demachy about his perennial financial troubles, but he expected and in the end received little advice from him. After all, Demachy, who had inherited a fortune, had no real interest in business. Plagued as he was by his chronic financial worries, Steichen, the inveterate self-promoter, suddenly found he had no stomach for taking his work to the public as Coburn was doing, and performing like "any other old clown," he told Stieglitz.[61]

Along with the rest of the world, he was also disillusioned with Wall Street and the fallout from the Panic of 1907. Financier J. P. Morgan, whom he had photographed years earlier, stopped the panic by importing $100,000,000 in gold from European banks, but individuals and corporations were still reeling from the collapse of so many banks. The Stieglitz family had been hard hit, but Steichen's losses were modest by comparison with most of his friends. Still, he joked sadly, if things got any worse, he might just move to Russia and "join the blooming reds."[62]

The Lumière brothers talked to Steichen during that time about a deal to demonstrate their plates, but when they offered him "small potatoes," Steichen told them to "go to H—l," as it would be more profitable for him to buy their plates at twenty-five francs each than to accept their offer.[63] But providentially, when Steichen sold a painting late in 1907 and obtained several unexpected commissions for photographic portraits, the financial outlook turned reasonably "cheerful" for a change. The Salon d'Automne was far better than usual, and four Steichen paintings, to his pleasure, were displayed prominently, including one—a new still life of roses painted in the country—that was a "swell hit." His energy and his hopes thereby restored, he was soon painting and photographing *"hard."*[64]

As 1907 ended, however, Steichen faced the future deeply unhappy in his marriage and frustrated in his business, with every problem now exacerbated by the prospect of the new baby. Sometime in January, he confided his troubles to Stieglitz, who apparently understood how Steichen felt about having more children. At least Clara was feeling better, Steichen reported, and although he had not wanted this child, and could hardly believe it had happened, he was getting used to the idea. He truly hoped that it would turn out well in the end.[65] He asked Stieglitz not to mention the matter, and while Stieglitz may have honored that request, he ignored Steichen's urgent plea that he destroy this letter as soon as he read it.[66]

Money had been much harder to come by in Paris, where the good times were better and the bad times worse than anywhere else in the world, Steichen thought. Still, the exhilarating milieu was all he had anticipated, and despite everything, he felt himself growing as a painter and a photographer, especially through the pioneering experiments in color photography. He began to believe he could earn more money if he spent a few weeks of the winter in New York showing and selling his art and gathering new commissions, but it would be too expensive for the whole family to travel, even if Clara had been well enough.

Learning that her sister and brother-in-law, Charlotte and Billy Paddock, were coming over to Paris early in 1908, Steichen saw the perfect solution. The Paddocks could stay with Clara and Mary while he traveled to New York. Consequently, he quickly began to make plans, but even so, Rodin's exhibition would open in New York at the Little Galleries of the Photo-Secession on January 2, 1908, nearly two months before Steichen could make the Atlantic crossing.

By Christmastime, Clara and Eduard were healthier, but Mary was desperately ill again with chronic bronchitis. Somehow, perhaps making frames in his studio, Steichen cut his left hand so severely that he could not work for a week. Absorbed in their family problems, he and Clara decided to send autochrome prints to friends and family for Christmas gifts, and Steichen asked Stieglitz to withdraw twenty-five dollars from his bank account and send it as his gift to Oma in Wisconsin.[67]

On New Year's Day, the Steichens left Paris by train in the midst of a gentle snowfall to have lunch with Rodin and Rose at Meudon, taking along a recent autochrome print as a holiday gift. Rodin, in turn, gave each of the Steichens a beautiful drawing, then overwhelmed Steichen to the brink of tears by handing him a check for a thousand francs. After lunch, as they walked in Rodin's peaceful garden, surrounded by snow-covered hills, Steichen and Clara listened to Rodin expound vigorously on a number of subjects—from art, to love, to politics, to the meaning of life itself.[68] Believing that Rodin's brilliant command of words equaled his domination of the clay he worked so beautifully, Steichen went back to Paris that New Year's Day inspired by the visit.

Just as Steichen and Stieglitz had hoped, the Rodin show was a seismic event in the New York art world. Critic J. N. Laurvik, writing in the *New York Times,* virtually guaranteed a capacity audience when he wrote about "these amazing records of unabashed observations of an artist who is also a man." One could wonder, he suggested, that "this little gallery has not long since been raided by the blind folly that guards our morals." He believed that Rodin's drawings had something in common with Whitman's poetry—"all natural acts are to him clean and beautiful"; the art possessed "a modesty that defies prudishness"; Rodin, like Whitman, did not look "askance at life." He urged everyone interested in the development of "the modern spirit in art" to see Rodin's drawings at 291.[69]

They came in droves. New York art patrons and critics alike were entranced—aghast or enthralled, depending on the viewer. Arthur Symons wrote in the catalog text that Rodin's drawings revealed woman as both animal and idol, "Every movement of her body, violently agitated by the remembrance, or the expectation, or the act of desire. . . ."[70]

Lured by newspaper coverage of Rodin's shocking art, people eagerly packed the galleries at 291 Fifth Avenue for the three-week run of the show to see for themselves. In the crowd one snowy day was an intense young art student named Georgia O'Keeffe, sent there by her teacher from the Art Students League to see the great sculptor's drawings. One of her teachers had suggested that Rodin or Stieglitz, or both, might be trying to fool the American public by showing such a "ridiculous group of drawings," and she was curious.[71]

The first time Georgia O'Keeffe saw Alfred Stieglitz, he strode into the small gallery carrying some photographic gear, and brusquely directed her and her classmates to the Rodin drawings. She remembered that they were "curved lines and scratches with a few watercolor washes and didn't look like anything I had been taught about drawing."[72] Afterward, far more than the drawings, O'Keeffe remembered Stieglitz, his dark eyes glaring through his pince-nez, defending Rodin's work with "fantastic violence" when her classmates began to challenge him.[73] O'Keeffe slipped away to the far end of the adjoining small gallery, waiting for the fury to subside.[74] She had never heard anything like that argument, she recalled, and she did not see Stieglitz again until several years later.

Artist Marius de Zayas also attended the controversial Rodin show at 291, later deeming it the most important American art event before 1913 and the Armory Show. And Steichen saw just "the elements needed to stir up things in New York," de Zayas said with approval.[75] But Steichen had only just begun to stir things up. He wrote to Stieglitz from Paris in late January that he had another "cracker-jack" show that would be every bit as significant as the Rodin exhibition. He wanted to present drawings and paintings by Henri Matisse, whom Steichen had already christened the "most modern of the moderns." He assured Stieglitz that Matisse's work was "*abstract* to the limit."[76] As his plans for the trip to New York crystallized for late February 1908, Steichen planned to transport the Matisse drawings and paintings personally, in hopes that they could be exhibited at 291 in the spring.[77]

The Steichens' circle of friends in Paris encompassed many artists by this time, including the young American painter Arthur Carles, who had arrived in Paris in June of 1907. At first, Carles lived in a room in Gertrude and Leo Stein's apartment building, but he later moved to a room in the Steichens' building at 103 Boulevard du Montparnasse, where Steichen often loaned him studio space. Carles had come to Europe on a traveling fellowship from the Pennsylvania Academy of the Fine Arts and a commission from Saint Paul's Episcopal Church in Philadelphia to travel to the Vatican and replicate Raphael's *Transfiguration* for an altarpiece. The Steichens had known Carles, of course, since their New York days; now in Paris, Steichen at twenty-eight and Carles at twenty-six quickly became best friends, both of them strikingly handsome, dashing, affable, charming—and fervent about their work.

Carles was a painter with a vigorous, rapidly emerging style and a dynamic sense of color. His work was transformed by his encounter with modern French painting at the 1907 Salon d'Automne, as well as at the Steins', although he did not fully understand Matisse and Picasso at the beginning. His paintings were exhibited in the 1908 Salon d'Automne, side by side with the works of Kandinsky and Matisse. Of all the European artists, Carles came to prefer Cézanne and Matisse for their virtuosity with color, and with his infectious excitement, Carles soon intensified Steichen's interest in his own painting.[78]

Carles also took a lively interest in festivities at the two Stein salons on Saturday evenings, especially when the Steichens' attractive friend Mercedes de Cordoba attended. She was living in Paris then, working as a fashion illustrator, and Carles immediately began courting the beautiful young artist and musician, frequently painting her. In fact, her sensual, exotic beauty, half French, half Spanish, made her a popular model for others, including Steichen. Because Clara, Steichen, Mercedes, and Carles were soon spending much of their time together, Steichen introduced Carles to Rodin, and Carles, in turn, introduced Steichen to the painter John Marin. Steichen, Carles, and their circle frequented the Café du Dôme in Montparnasse, where talk of art was exuberant and endless.

One night, Steichen held forth on his conviction that the exhibitions sponsored by the conservative, cliquish Society of American Painters in Paris were confined to the work of artists who had not developed beyond early Impressionism. Furthermore, the Society of American Painters "rigorously excluded all the younger and bolder painters from their exhibitions," Steichen observed.[79] He wanted to rescue American painters in Paris from stifling orthodoxy, and so he proposed another secessionist group.

On February 25, 1908, just days before his departure for New York, Steichen convened a lively gathering of young painters at his studio at 103 Boulevard du Montparnasse for a serious meeting. They were all working artists in Paris then. The aristocratic Virginian Patrick Henry Bruce came that night. He had met Matisse at the Steins', studied with him, and begun painting beautiful landscapes and still lifes inspired by Matisse's own work.

Shy Alfred Maurer also came to the Steichens' that night. The son of a German immigrant, "Alfy" Maurer was born in New York in 1868. His father, a lithographer who had won fame as an artist for Currier and Ives, always dominated and intimidated his talented son, who finally

COLOR-MAD (1907–1908)

won a measure of affirmation and financial independence in 1901 with the Carnegie Medal and its generous award of fifteen hundred dollars. Gertrude Stein affectionately described him as "a little dark dapper man with hair, eyes, face, hands and feet all very much alive."[80] He was a favorite of the Steins, "an old habitué of the house," who, Gertrude noted poignantly, "had followed, followed, followed, always humbly always sincerely. . . ."[81] Also coming to know Picasso and Matisse through the Steins, Maurer was deeply influenced by Matisse's work.

Jo Davidson, the sculptor, was there, and Russian-born Max Weber, who was ten when he and his mother had settled in Brooklyn in 1891. From 1898 to 1900, he had studied with Arthur Wesley Dow at the Pratt Institute, and he had lived in Paris since 1905. There, he had studied for two years at the Académie Julian and other schools before he discovered Cézanne's work at the Salon d'Automne of 1906 and 1907. Like Bruce, he studied with Matisse in 1908. Weber, too, savored the evenings at the Steins', where he befriended Henri Rousseau and Picasso, and kept his intelligent eyes fixed on the kaleidoscope of images animating the work of Matisse, Cézanne, and Picasso, investing his own painting with their energy, as well as with ideas he drew from African art.

Brilliant John Marin was also there. When his mother died just nine days after his birth in New Jersey in 1870, his father had given him to his grandparents and two aunts to be reared. As a small boy, he loved to draw, but he was given no formal training. After making mediocre grades at Stevens Institute of Technology in Hoboken, New Jersey, he was told to withdraw. He eventually worked for several years as an architectural draftsman, then tried his hand at his own free-lance architectural business, but all he really wanted to do was to paint. Like Steichen, Marin taught himself, roaming about the country and experimenting with landscape painting. Finally despairing that he would ever amount to anything, his aunts permitted him to take up studies in 1899 at the Pennsylvania Academy of the Fine Arts. There, Marin had met Arthur Carles, before going on to study at the Art Students League in New York.

Marin relied mainly on his own experiments in drawing, painting, and etching, and he arrived in Paris in 1905, supporting himself as an etcher. Carles had taken Steichen to the Paris exhibition where he first saw Marin's work, and, greatly excited by the luminous watercolors, Steichen immediately asked for an introduction. He found Marin to be as "interesting and fine a person" as he was an artist.[82] Although he would send Marin's paintings over to Stieglitz in New York early in 1909, it would be the summer of that year before Steichen would have his first opportunity to introduce the two men in Paris, further expanding that fraternity of American artists standing on the cultural bridge between Europe and the United States, between modernism and tradition.

Marin earned Steichen's immense respect: "I don't know any other painter," he wrote more than half a century later, "who was so little influenced by the work of anyone else. Certainly none of the Post-Impressionists, Fauves, Cubists, or Cézanne, had any effect on Marin. They simply did not interest him. Everything came out of John Marin himself."[83]

On that momentous February night in 1908, after much wine and lively debate, Steichen and his friends organized the Society of Younger American Painters in Paris, a secessionist group of young avant-garde artists who rejected the values and politics of the conservative "petrified body" of the Society of American Artists in Paris.[84] Over the next few months, they made big, bold plans: They hoped to win recognition at international exhibitions; they wanted to stage their own exhibit in the spring of 1908; and they vowed to recruit and welcome new members who shared their enlightened views. Charter members included Steichen and Carles, of course, and Davidson, Marin, Bruce, and Richard Duffy. Painter D. Putnam Brinley, another of Steichen's close friends, would serve on the advisory board with Steichen, Maurer, the etcher Donald Shaw MacLaughlan, and Max Weber.[85]

"After several more meetings," Steichen remembered, "we announced in the Paris edition of the New York *Herald,* and cabled to the New York edition, that the Society of Younger American Painters in Paris had formed."[86] Steichen the painter, like Steichen the photographer, would soon be "color-mad."

Edward Steichen's mother, Mary Kemp Steichen. Hancock, Michigan, ca. 1885.
Carte de Visite, Hancock, Michigan. Francesca Calderone-Steichen Collection.

The guiding and inspiring influence in my life, she was always an encouraging and a positive force. From my early childhood, she sought to imbue me with her own great strength and fortitude, her deep, warm optimism and human understanding.

— Edward Steichen, A Life in Photography, *1963*

Edward Jean Steichen, about eighteen months old.
Carte de Visite, Luxembourg. Helga Sandburg Collection.

Brother and Sister—Edward and Lilian Steichen, 1886.
Helga Sandburg Collection.

My Little Sister, Milwaukee, 1895. This is the first "good, or clear" picture that Steichen made, using a secondhand Kodak box camera. See page 32.
Photograph by Edward Steichen. Reprinted with permission of Joanna T. Steichen.

Brother and Sister—Edward and Lilian Steichen, Milwaukee, 1900.
Photograph by Edward Steichen. Reprinted with permission of Joanna T. Steichen.

Edward and Clara Steichen on their Honeymoon, Lake George, New York, 1903.
Photograph by Edward Steichen. Reprinted with permission of Joanna T. Steichen. Francesca Calderone-Steichen Collection.

Clara and Mary in Sloane Hospital, New York, July 15, 1904.
Photograph by Edward Steichen. Reprinted with permission of Joanna T. Steichen. The Carl Sandburg Home NHS Collection, Flat Rock, North Carolina.

Edward Steichen and baby Mary, 1904.
Francesca Calderone-Steichen Collection.

Father and daughter. Steichen holding Mary, 1905.
Helga Sandburg Collection.

Clara Smith Steichen.
Copy print of oil portrait by Marion Beckett, 1915.
Collection of American Literature, The Beinecke Rare
Book and Manuscript Library, Yale University, New
Haven, Connecticut.

Edward Steichen with Flower.
Copy print of oil portrait by Marion Beckett, 1915.
Collection of American Literature, The Beinecke Rare
Book and Manuscript Library, Yale University, New
Haven, Connecticut.

Lilac Buds–Clara, Long Island, New York, 1906.
Photograph by Edward Steichen. Reprinted with permission of Joanna T. Steichen. Francesca Calderone-Steichen Collection.

Kate and her father working in the garden at Voulangis, ca. 1909.
Francesca Calderone-Steichen Collection.

Mary and her father with Petit Frére, the donkey, in the garden at Voulangis, summer 1909.
Francesca Calderone-Steichen Collection.

Mary and Kate in Their French Peasant Dresses, Voulangis, France, ca. 1913.
Photograph by Edward Steichen. Reprinted with permission of Joanna T. Steichen. Francesca Calderone-Steichen Collection.

Left to right: Steichen's brother-in-law, William Dryden Paddock, husband of Clara's sister Charlotte; Mary Steichen, standing behind sled; family friend on the sled; and Steichen, Christmas Day, 1914 in Connecticut.
Elizabeth (Betty) Jane Rathbone Turner Collection.

Captain Edward Steichen and camera, serving with the American Expeditionary Force in France in 1918.
Helga Sandburg Collection.

Yes, write it down if you wish. The United States government has one of the great creative artists of the world now training young men to go over the top with cameras instead of guns.

—*Mary Kemp Steichen to newspaper reporter, 1917*

14

THE INITIATOR

(1 9 0 8)

He certainly has important and remarkable accomplishments, and one of them (which I have never seen mentioned) is the fact that he was the initiator of the introduction of modern art in America.[1]

—MARIUS DE ZAYAS

EDUARD STEICHEN SAILED FOR NEW YORK on the *Provence* on or about February 29, 1908, carrying valuable cargo—paintings, drawings, and lithographs by Henri Matisse, along with his own new photographs and paintings, enough for a long-promised one-man show of photographs at 291 as well as a solo exhibition of paintings. Although he had been working very hard, the quantity of his own paintings and photographs fell far short of his hopes. He had been spending most of his time in the darkroom that winter, sometimes working feverishly all night, turning out autochromes "hard and fast."[2] He was particularly excited about his results with artificial light, having gotten almost perfect results working with a color screen and a flashlight. Of course, he confessed in a letter to Stieglitz, he had nearly bankrupted himself buying the plates to feed his ongoing obsession with color.[3]

This obsession seemed to infuse all of his work, spilling over onto canvas as well, for the paintings carefully wrapped and packed in his trunks for the journey to New York also revealed new experiments with color. Steichen the painter seemed to be emerging from night into daylight, relinquishing some of the dark, subtle shades of his earlier nocturnes for the rich, sun-dusted arcs of the Rocky Mountains, as in *Across the Crest of the Great Divide,* or vibrant still lifes such as *Vase of Flowers.* Even his more recent nocturnes of Lake George landscapes shimmered with brighter moonlight that illuminated his compositions with new depth and color, as in the figures of a woman and a dog in *Balcony, Nocturne, Lake George,* for instance, and in the soaring clouds in *Shrouded Figure in Moonlight.*

He had not been back to New York since he, Clara, and Mary made that stormy crossing in 1906, and his February 1908 voyage launched a series of solitary annual pilgrimages from Paris to New York for Steichen. He would return to New York every year from 1908 until the onset of World War I to promote and sell his own work and to serve as a self-appointed envoy representing contemporary artists on both sides of the Atlantic. Caught up as he was in the excitement of arranging exhibits for 291 in those early years, Steichen would later come to believe that his own contributions to the Photo-Secession were underestimated or misunderstood, as well as his pivotal role in the "introduction of modern art in the United States."[4]

There were many reasons that this was so, having to do in part with the capriciousness of human memory, the multitude of later books devoted to Alfred Stieglitz and Georgia O'Keeffe, and the personal politics behind the pages of later books on the history of photography. However, the documents of the time reveal that beginning in 1908, out of a generous commitment to Stieglitz and other artists—and to art itself—Steichen became a courier, annually crisscrossing the ocean, intellectually and physically importing and exporting modern painting and photography. He sought simultaneously to introduce certain European and American painters to the American audience, and specific American painters and photographers to the European audience. Undergirding this zealous mission was his conviction that the artist had to fight for freedom of expression, for continual growth, for proper recognition through thoughtfully arranged exhibitions, and for spiritual as well as economic survival.

For years after that initial winter journey from Paris to New York in 1908, usually at the expense of his own financial resources and artistic energy, Steichen championed the work of Cézanne, Rodin, Matisse, Picasso, and many other Europeans, as well as that of John Marin, Alfred Maurer, Stieglitz, White, Coburn, and a host of other Americans. He personally scouted for exhibition material and often single-handedly carried out the exhausting chores of gathering, framing, packing, shipping, unpacking, mounting, and promoting shows of the work of other artists. His brilliant bifocal vision as painter and photographer, as American and European, equipped him uniquely to be the lookout on two continents for the extraordinary new painters and photographers of his time. He wanted to show and sell his own work, of course, but he was crusading for all good artists, hoping that at 291 Fifth Avenue, he and Stieglitz could provide a welcoming, if temporary, home to their work.

By early March, Steichen was in New York, preparing his one-man show of forty-seven photographs and fifteen autochromes at the Little Galleries of the Photo-Secession, to run March 12–April 2, 1908. At the same time, there would be an exhibition of his paintings and photographs at the National Arts Club in New York, followed by an exhibit of paintings at the Pratt Institute April 15–22, 1908. How he hoped that his sales at the two shows would "replenish the coffer."[5] He was, after all, the financial mainstay for his family in Paris and his parents at the Little Farm in Wisconsin. He longed to see his mother and sister, and he promised to take the train to Milwaukee as soon as he could leave New York.

Meanwhile, it was wonderful to be reunited with Stieglitz at 291. The two men now shared not only the exhilarating bonds of their work but also the most intimate secrets of the chaos in their respective private lives. Steichen had confided the news by letter when he and Clara had had a "h—l of a row again."[6] He had been disappointed in his hope that the explosion would ultimately clear the air and help Clara to get hold of herself. Unfortunately, a pattern was emerging in Clara's behavior: seething unhappiness, paranoid distrust, outburst, confrontation, appeasement, relative peace; then the cycle began again.

But as battered as Steichen felt from the ongoing stress of his work and marriage, he was also deeply worried about Stieglitz that March of 1908, finding him exhausted, terribly nervous, and short-tempered with himself and everyone else.[7] Stieglitz faced a host of problems, first the prospect of losing 291, for it was time to renew the lease and his landlord wanted a contract for four years at double the rent. Stieglitz had been subsidizing 291 and *Camera Work* himself in the face of declining support from the contentious Photo-Secessionists, some of whom objected obstreperously to his new interest in painters and sculptors. He could not go on without moral and financial support. This crisis was compounded by the financial losses his family suffered during the Panic of 1907, not to mention his chronic miseries with Emmy.

Stieglitz was especially despondent about the prospect of losing 291, but at first, Steichen thought it might be a good thing for Stieglitz to give up the Photo-Secession galleries and simply get away from New York. Perhaps if he and Emmy could just manage to get along well enough, the answer to all their problems might be a year's rest living abroad. For his own survival, Steichen warned, Stieglitz had to have some respite from all the pressures of his life.[8] Not that Paris was the answer, for he knew Stieglitz much preferred other European cities. For his part, however, Steichen now felt himself intimately connected to Paris, believing that the city he loved had more to offer than any other place in the world—despite "its natives."[9]

Stieglitz apparently began to mull over the idea of living in Europe again, but meanwhile, Steichen's energetic presence in New York definitely lifted his spirits. In fact, Steichen seemed to be his only trustworthy Photo-Secessionist ally; furthermore, he had arrived bubbling with new ideas for Photo-Secession exhibitions, such as the drawings and paintings by Henri Matisse. Although Stieglitz knew little of Matisse before Steichen wrote about him, he was immediately fascinated with the collection Steichen had assembled to reveal the evolution of the painter's work. Next time he visited Paris, Steichen urged, Stieglitz must meet Matisse and the Steins—elegant, gracious Sarah and Michael; intellectual Leo, as opinionated and loquacious as Stieglitz himself; and Gertrude, with her omniscient eyes and her robust, contagious laughter. Why, sometimes when he was blue, he went to the Steins' home just to hear her laugh, he remembered later.[10] But Steichen thought Leo was actually the extraordinary Stein, recalling that most people who cared about painting were "much more interested in Leo than in Gertrude."[11]

He no doubt tried to elucidate for Stieglitz the impact these modern paintings were having on his own work—photography as well as painting. Those by Matisse and the Fauves in particular transfixed his attention because, he believed, they were "anti-photographic."[12] These modern pictures, unlike many conventional paintings, were totally unlike photography, and this realization jolted Steichen into an entirely new way of working. Heretofore, he had incorporated many painterly effects into his photographs, even intentionally making photographs that looked like paintings. But now, thanks to the impact of these new paintings by Matisse and others, Steichen resolved to choose his medium more deliberately, and to subordinate it to his purpose. If he wanted to create a literal image of a place or a person, the camera would be his tool, and an even more effective one now that it could embody color. Otherwise, he would turn to the antiphotographic art of painting.

That March, Steichen also installed his own photographic exhibit at 291, featuring the autochromes—"remarkable achievements," according to a rave review in the *New York Globe*. Steichen was a "master of composition" in color and in his monochrome photographs, the critic continued, singling out for special praise his portraits of Rodin and the painter Charles Cottel—*The Man that Resembles Erasmus*—and *After the Grand Prix-Paris,* his study of women at the races. Steichen's *Moonlight Impression from the Orangerie,* one of his Versailles series (most likely *Nocturne—Orangerie Staircase, Versailles*), was "a genuine work of art any way it is looked at," according to the reviewer, who hailed Steichen as an unusually artistic man, "who is not to be ignored for a moment, and who in his way is making art history."[13]

Steichen would take his clippings home to his mother, who pasted them into her ever-growing scrapbook. He had been featured in *The Century Magazine* in February of 1908, in the lead article by Charles H. Caffin, entitled "Progress in Photography with Special Reference to the Work of Eduard J. Steichen." Caffin lauded the "brilliant" career of Steichen the "artist-photographer," devoting seven pages of double-columned text to an account of his work and his life and illustrating the piece with six Steichen photographs, for which the magazine paid Steichen a then-generous fee of fifty dollars each for reproduction rights.[14]

Caffin was part of the Photo-Secession inner circle, and so he could give Steichen and Stieglitz invaluable press exposure, but they gained a new press agent the day that a young reporter climbed the steps and took the creaky elevator to the attic at 291 Fifth Avenue to interview

Alfred Stieglitz. She was Agnes Ernst, a beautiful, intelligent, highly self-sufficient young working woman, the first female reporter ever for the New York *Sun*. Because her father was deeply in debt, Agnes had to find a job to support herself, but her parents had in mind something more genteel than journalism; when she announced her plans to become a reporter, her mother wept and her father told her he would rather see her dead.[15]

She had already visited Stieglitz at 291, where photography was considered art, "a revolutionary thought in those days," she noted, and now she wanted to write a story about the founders of the gallery.[16] There, she met a "slightly built man, with beetled eyebrows, named Stieglitz," and he introduced her to "another young chap named Steichen." They talked for six hours about the "future of photography versus painting." Agnes Ernst immediately loved the spirit of rebellion so apparent in these two friends, and she wanted to champion the "battle that Steichen and Stieglitz had begun to wage against the academic smugness then prevalent in the American world of art." She delighted in their bravado, their "gusto for life and beauty," their "flouting of accepted traditions," their genuine convictions as "independent thinkers."[17]

Stieglitz and Steichen, in turn, profoundly admired beautiful women of intelligence, wit, and spirit, and they were instantly charmed by Agnes Ernst. "Her arrival was an event," Steichen said, "for she was not only by far the loveliest girl who had ever been in the gallery, but she was also, in the collective opinion of the Photo-Secessionists, a girl with a mind."[18] Steichen and Stieglitz both took credit for christening Agnes Ernst the "Girl from the Sun," and while she and Stieglitz would disagree and grow apart in later years, Agnes and Steichen remained friends for the rest of their lives. Her 1908 article for the *Sun* articulated Stieglitz's philosophy—and, by extension, the views of the struggling Photo-Secession—in language evocative of some of the socialist themes in the air in those days: "We are striving for freedom of experience and justice in the fullest sense of the word.... We believe that if only people are taught to appreciate the beautiful side of their daily existence, to be aware of all the beauty which constantly surrounds them, they must gradually approach this ideal...."[19]

The Initiator (1908)

"I have some faint hope that my brother will come over to America this spring," Lilian Steichen had written in February of 1908 to a new suitor.[20] She and her mother longed to have Eduard at home to celebrate his twenty-ninth birthday on March twenty-seventh, and he was doing his best to oblige them.

He wrote a hasty note to Lilian, "short—brisk—full of the rush of work," she said in a letter. "When you've read the note you've gotten a vivid impression of the rush, rush, rush—of getting up an exhibition in very short time. But you haven't any facts—practical points like dates. He's a wild boy—*Gaesjack!*" She wished that her brother were "a little less wild—a little more practical!" She decided, on reflection, however, that she did her brother an injustice when she attributed any of his "shortcomings" to his artist's temperament. "I'll take that back—say his shortcomings are due to plain '*cussedness.*' That sounds lots better—Edward [*sic*] would like it better too. And it's much nearer the truth. For Edward hasn't any nonsense about him."[21]

She was writing about Steichen to a thirty-year-old Illinois political organizer, soapbox orator, and would-be poet whom she had met at Social Democratic party headquarters in Milwaukee in December of 1907. The son of Swedish immigrants, he was tall, thin, shabbily dressed, and possessed of a fiery intensity. He introduced himself as Charles Sandburg, having revised his Swedish name Carl to something sounding to him far more American. Twenty-four-year-old Lilian was wearing her "long black hair in a simple Gretchen braid around her head" that day, Sandburg remembered, and as they talked of the work he would be doing for social democracy, "her blue eyes were alight with enthusiasm." He immediately asked her out to dinner, but she declined because, as she said, "In those days no really nice girl would have had dinner with someone she had just met." She did, however, give him the address of her boarding house in Princeton, Illinois, for she was on her way back to her job teaching "literature and expression" at the high school there.[22]

Lilian still frequently translated socialist literature and propaganda for the flourishing Social Democratic party. In Milwaukee, she and her mother were actively involved in party politics, had many longtime friends who were socialists, and passionately supported the socialistic ideals of equality, humane living conditions, and economic parity. They were especially concerned about the plight of working women and children, and they believed indignantly that women should be allowed to vote. John Peter Steichen had no real interest in politics, but Lilian described her mother as "a party member and a private Agitator!—And such a Heart!"[23] And as far as Lilian was concerned, her brother was a "scientific sane constructive" socialist, despite the fact that he had no party affiliation.[24]

In the conservative little town of Princeton, Illinois, where in addition to teaching English, Latin, and public speaking, she directed plays, Lilian was a maverick. But "Princeton doesn't mind," she said; "—they accept me as I am. Put me down as 'peculiar' of course but don't molest me. I walk the streets hatless most of the time—a thing I couldn't do in Milwaukee without attracting attention. Here it's hardly noticed. I don't go to church Sundays—that isn't noticed either. I talk socialism, and radicalism generally, whenever I get the chance—that doesn't disturb Princeton either." She believed that people in Princeton simply did not see her nonconformity as "part and parcel of a large, really formidable movement—a movement that threatens to overturn their institutions. If they scented the danger, they would cease to be tolerant."[25]

There were leaders among the Milwaukee Social Democrats who admired Lilian for more than her intellectual acumen and her political fervor. She was strikingly beautiful, with luminous blue-gray eyes, high cheekbones, and sensuous lips. Unlike most young women of her age, she believed in strenuous outdoor exercise, and her long, solitary walks left her windblown and disheveled—and brimming with good health and vitality. "I think for myself," she wrote in 1908. "I dare to have natural feelings. And I'm not afraid to speak my thoughts and feelings. I give Nature a fair chance to work in me. No artificialities for me! No corsets, no French heels, no patent medicines! No formal receptions! No mad chase after the very latest styles in dress!"[26]

Simple clothes (usually made by her mother) set off her petite figure, and her musical voice charmed others in conversation. But absorbed as she was in ideas and books, Lilian was completely unaware of the effect she had on men. One officer in the Social Democratic party of Wisconsin, an older, married man, loved her devotedly and quietly. Brilliant and wealthy, he was apparently willing to leave his marriage for her, if she would agree to have him.[27] Another admirer, Victor Berger, the head of the party, and also married, was unabashedly attracted to Lilian Steichen. He asked her, in the interest—or guise—of varietism and eugenics, to mate with him and bear his child. He wanted, he said, to perpetuate his blood by breeding selectively, with a superior female, thus improving the race.

Enlightened and liberated as she was, Lilian was appalled.[28] Besides, a virtual old maid at twenty-four, she still clung to a romantic, idealistic faith in lifelong mating—"two people matching each other in mind & heart & body, the mates believing that they will continue till death perfect mates," sharing the "belief that the present identity of mind & heart will continue always."[29]

When Lilian and Charles Sandburg began corresponding in January 1908, she had no idea that he might be that lifelong mate, but by early spring, the letters were flying between them, sometimes two or three daily. She wrote after her classes in Princeton, and he answered from a stream of towns in Wisconsin, where he was working factories and street corners, soliciting new members for the Social Democratic party. He sent her poems and political tracts he had written. She sent him long letters and copies of her famous brother's pictures and clippings. "I'm glad you are interested in photography as an art—a distinctively modern art. And that you appreciate my brother's work," she wrote February twenty-fifth, the day, coincidentally, that her brother, still in France, was convening his artist friends to form the Society of Younger American Painters in Paris.[30]

She wrote to Sandburg about democratic art, passionately advocating "pictures of life" that were "realistic" rather than "romantic rot," poems that were "direct and simple," striking at the heart of the universal human experience—a conception that would reverberate throughout Steichen's lifelong work, and Sandburg's.[31] Through his deep studies of Whitman and Shaw, Sandburg had come to his own ideas about art for the general audience, not just the elite, with the realities of the human condition as subject.[32] In fact, he told her, he had been lecturing on Whitman and Shaw for several years in small prairie towns, city lecture halls, and even at Elbert Hubbard's Roycroft community in East Aurora, New York.

While Charles Sandburg had fallen in love instantly with Lilian Steichen, she was not at all attracted to him at first. Two months into their correspondence, however, she had changed her mind, living for the letters that arrived from Oshkosh, Manitowoc, Sheboygan Falls—and for the pithy columns Sandburg wrote for the *Social-Democratic Herald,* the *Manitowoc Daily Tribune,* or other Wisconsin newspapers. At the end of February, she invited Sandburg to her parents' farm for a visit during her March vacation from school, using her brother as the reason, still hoping that Steichen could come to the farm for his birthday.

"I should so much like to have him meet you," Lilian wrote to Sandburg; "—he would appreciate your poems and love you as an S.D.P. organizer!" She wanted to show Sandburg *Camera Work* so that he could see "the really good reproductions" of her brother's work, as well as the actual prints of her brother's photographs, which were "immeasureably [*sic*] beyond these."[33]

When a note from Steichen confirmed that he would indeed be home by March twenty-seventh, Lilian eagerly shared the news with Sandburg. They would celebrate her brother's birthday all together, Lilian told Sandburg, "a great event in the family!"[34] By mid-March, Lilian and Sandburg were writing less about politics and democratic art and more about wonder, hope, and love. "So glad am I that on the great wide way we have met," he wrote.[35] He had been writing poems to her. "And I have really some part in the making of your warm human poems!" she exclaimed in a letter to him March sixteenth. "Really? this thought is what fills me with such sweet wonder and hope—"[36]

Steichen, meanwhile, was still in New York, with his nose "to the grindstone," he wrote his parents and sister.[37] "It's surely work—work—work—with him these days," Lilian reported to Sandburg shortly before their rendezvous at the farm.[38] Steichen was in fact tremendously busy in New York, coordinating the sale of some of the Rodin drawings and making arrangements for the upcoming exhibition of drawings, lithographs, etchings, and watercolors by Matisse. But once his own exhibitions were launched and every detail of the Matisse show was in place, an exhausted Steichen boarded the train and headed west.

He made it to Wisconsin in time for his birthday and a grand reunion and celebration—embraces and tears from his mother and sister, a warm handclasp with his father. His mother immediately subjected him to her usual intense scrutiny: He was too thin—was he sick? Had he been working too hard? How were Clara and Mary? Was Clara faring well in her pregnancy? Should he have left her alone so far away? Was he happy?

His sister, on the other hand, radiant and distracted, announced to her curious brother that a young man would be arriving for a visit, that he was a poet, and that "she was interested in him."[39] His mother was in "a real dither," Steichen remembered. "Nothing like that had ever occurred to her. Lillian [sic] was still her little girl. This was serious."[40] There was a long deliberation about what to cook for dinner. Mary wanted to prepare a feast, and she decided to cook a turkey, on the theory that "poets when they did eat wanted something substantial and a lot of it...."[41]

"Now she had told us that he was a poet," Steichen wrote. "That's about all anybody knew about him at the time, that he had said he was a poet. This was almost a decade before *Chicago Poems* [1916] was published."[42] Steichen was curious, Mary was excited, and John Peter was gloomy. Watching his father step to the window and look out over the fields of his little farm, Steichen "could hear him think, 'My god, another longhair. He'll never be able to be any help on this farm.'"[43]

When it was time for Lilian to drive six miles to Brookfield station to meet Charles Sandburg's train, her father hitched the horse to the buggy and insisted that he should drive because the darkening skies threatened a spring storm. Determined to make the drive alone, Lilian refused her father's offer, however. She had seen her poet only once, but when Sandburg stepped off the train, she was struck by how old and tired he looked. Pity filled her. She could only imagine how hard he must have been working, for how long, to look so worn.[44]

Her father had been right about the storm, but at least Lilian and her weary poet were in the buggy turning back toward the farm when the strong winds hit and lightning sheared the black sky. "Such a night as it was, slashing rain & a wind [that] took the carriage off its braces," Sandburg remembered, and "our hands talking louder than the howling gale." If they had not recognized their love before, the storm made it clear: "It all seemed as tho it had to be—all imperially natural—We—Two out of a world-stress like that surging between sky & land—finding ourselves—not each other, but our-*selves*—"[45] They called it the "baptismal rain."

Back at the farm, Steichen and his parents watched the storm subside, the travelers arrive at last, and the tall stranger lift Lilian down from the buggy. Mary welcomed Sandburg with enthusiasm, but John Peter was formal and reserved in the presence of this young man who had his daughter's rapt attention. Steichen's birthday properly celebrated, the turkey devoured, Lilian and Sandburg spent several "strange, halcyon days calm with the gestation of new life-forces."[46]

Steichen took his first photographs of Sandburg during that week, as well as photographs of his mother and sister. "Edward Steichen is an artist," Sandburg said when he saw the proofs. "We all know our best selves, the selves we love. And he caught a self I pray to be all the time! By what wizardry of sight and penetration, he came to get that phase of me in so little a time, I don't know. It took more than eyes—it took heart & soul back of the eyes."[47]

Much as she adored her brother and craved his company, Lilian was swept up in the new love for her poet, and they kept to themselves for hours, walking, talking, deciding to be married as soon as possible, apparently finding enough solitude somewhere for lovemaking—not so surprising for young socialists enamored of free love, but a major breach of puritanical early-twentieth-century decorum and morality.

Sandburg wanted to get to know the whole family, especially Lilian's glamorous, famous artist brother. The two men took long walks through the countryside. Sandburg was tall, thin, and dark-haired, a year older than Steichen, who just surpassed him in height, if not intensity. They talked of art and socialism, of Whitman and Shaw. Sandburg must have been fascinated to hear Steichen's personal impressions of Shaw and Robert Hunter and the other socialists he had met and photographed in Europe. They shared a sympathetic view of the plight of working people, with Steichen describing to Sandburg the dangers to workmen who built modern skyscrapers such as the Flatiron Building in New York, which he had photographed.[48]

From the farm, Sandburg wrote to Philip Green Wright, his favorite college professor, who still lived and taught in Sandburg's hometown, Galesburg, Illinois: "After strenuous weeks northward, have been spending a few days, living the Muldoon life on the Steichen farm, with the folks of Edward Steichen, the painter and art photographer. The March Century has its leading article about him but does not mention the fact that he is a warm socialist."⁴⁹ But Sandburg did not even mention to his professor that he was courting Steichen's beautiful, headstrong sister. For Steichen and Sandburg, a lifelong friendship began that week. "My sister acquired a husband," Steichen wrote years afterward; "I acquired a brother."⁵⁰

Steichen's visit to the farm was brief, and back in New York, he and Stieglitz prepared the press announcement about the Matisse exhibition, to be released April first: "Matisse is the leading spirit of a modern group of French artists dubbed 'Les Fauves,'" they wrote. "It is the good fortune of the Photo-Secession to have the honor of thus introducing Matisse to the American public and to the American art-critics."⁵¹

Together the two friends carefully mounted the work of this "very anarchist ... in art," as Stieglitz called Matisse.⁵² Steichen had brought some of his watercolors; some striking lithographs from Matisse's 1906 series; and a large number of figure drawings, including female nudes.⁵³ They prepared no catalog for the exhibition, however, deliberately leaving viewers to their own interpretations. The show opened April sixth and ran until April twenty-fifth at the Little Galleries of the Photo-Secession. This was Matisse's first exhibition in the United States, and the ensuing controversy excited Steichen and Stieglitz no end. "The New York 'art-world' was sorely in need of an irritant and Matisse certainly proved a timely one," Stieglitz wrote in *Camera Work*.⁵⁴

Some of the nude female figures were "of an ugliness that is most appalling and haunting, and that seems to condemn this man's brain to the limbo of artistic degeneration," J. Edgar Chamberlain commented in the New York *Evening Mail*. He predicted that Matisse's pictures would likely "go quite over the head of the ordinary observer—or under his feet."⁵⁵ James Huneker at the New York *Sun,* however, recognized and applauded the "agility" and "velocity" of Matisse's drawing and painting, and he urged New Yorkers to see the show at 291:

> *Take the smallest elevator in town and enjoy the solitude of these tiny rooms crowded with the phantoms of Stieglitz and Steichen. No one will be there to greet you, for Stieglitz has a habit of leav-*

ing his doors unlocked for the whole world to flock in at will. And it is in just such unconventional surroundings that the work of Matisse is best exhibited. The brown bit of paper that does duty as a preface tells us that this fierce rebel is a leading spirit of a modern group of French artists dubbed "Les Fauves."

Huneker had seen Rodin's nudes: They were "academic" and "meticulous" compared with Matisse's "memoranda of the gutter and brothel." He perceived Matisse's work to be the sketches of "a brilliant, cruel temperament," with "the coldness of the moral vivisector."[56] Many members of the Photo-Secession were skeptical about what Stieglitz and Steichen were trying to do at 291, but Steichen's passion for Matisse's avant-garde paintings and drawings rekindled Stieglitz's own excitement about revolutionary art. Given the miserable months he had spent fretting over the future of 291, Stieglitz was thrilled by the uproar over Rodin and now Matisse. His excitement was only heightened by the fact that he and Steichen were almost alone among Photo-Secessionists in their enthusiasm for Rodin and Matisse, and for exhibiting drawings and paintings at 291 along with photography.

Aside from a vacation at Lake George, nothing refreshed Stieglitz more deeply than vigorous controversy. He was in his element, and later he observed, "The Photo-Secession's presentation of the [Matisse] collection in April, 1908, together with the January show of Rodin's drawings, marked the true public introduction of modern art in the United States."[57]

"This was my initiation of modern art in America," Steichen reflected years later. "Stieglitz showed it and stood in the gallery and fought for it; and I traveled back and forth between Paris and New York all this while."[58]

Years later, Carl Sandburg described Steichen as "one of the steady uncompromising young strugglers in the movement that brought what is known in America as modernist art." He went on to call the "291 Fifth Avenue attic" a "rallying point" where Stieglitz, Steichen, and their colleagues "toiled, made mistakes, had their fling of follies and vanities," all the while creating and promoting significant art. They also "evolved theories and originated viewpoints that were to become operative twenty years later when 'modernist art,' the touch of the cubist, the post-impressionist, the abstractionist, were to be seen in multiple forms in millions of homes...."⁵⁹

Afterward, however, few people remembered that it was Steichen who had brought Americans their first glimpse of the drawings of Rodin and Matisse, and that he did so in 1908, under attack, five years before the landmark Armory Show of 1913, which is usually credited with the introduction of modern art in the United States.

As always, Mary Steichen was sick and depressed after her children left the farm. "The short visit from Ed upset her," Lilian reported to Sandburg, "and she is worried about his health and his happiness—and the new baby. It's no use. I tell mother to let us children bear the burden of our own cares—but she's gotten so used to shouldering responsibilities that she can't help it. So she worries on Ed's account."⁶⁰ Because he usually confided in his mother, he almost certainly shared with her his growing unhappiness in his marriage and his bewilderment at Clara's temperamental, erratic behavior. His and Clara's courtship had been so stormy and difficult that even in the early days of their passion for each other, they had not been so mutually transfixed as his sister and Sandburg were at the Little Farm that week. It was probably difficult to watch the passionate attraction between the two and to sense their affinity of spirit, without feeling even more acutely disappointed in his own marriage.

Eduard left his mother worried about his well-being, and knowing she might not see him again for another year. Back in New York, he sent her the favorable notices of his paintings that had appeared in the *New York Times* and the *Evening Mail*. A few of Steichen's paintings on display at the Glaezner Gallery possessed "marked individuality and beauty," the *Times* critic wrote, especially admiring Steichen's *Canon de Los Animas Perditas, Colorado,* "an impressive and poetic interpretation of an extraordinarily rewarding subject." This painting and another of a Colorado night scene were apparently based on photographs Steichen had made during his 1906 western journey. Despite his new experiments with color, he was still at his best painting nocturnes, the *Times* critic believed, finding his paintings in sunlight static and expressionless. Steichen so effectively evoked "the tenderness and mystery of the twilight," the reviewer concluded, "that he has taught his public to expect distinction in his achievement and to resent anything but the best from his brush."[61]

Steichen could also send home to his mother a copy of the April edition of *Camera Work*, containing his three color gravures and his article "Color Photography."[62] The May 1908 issue of *The Craftsman* gave his photographs, including his autochromes, a fine review: "With just the same command over the camera as a painter has over his brush or a sculptor over his chisel, Mr. Steichen produces work of real and lasting artistic value, and the results are as truly his own as in his paintings...."[63] Heartened by that response, as well as by the excellent sales of his prints at 291, he told an interviewer, "I shall use the camera as long as I live, for it can say things that cannot be said with any other medium."[64] His exhibitions had been successful critically and commercially, far surpassing his hopes.

Lilian wrote from Illinois in mid-April to tell Steichen that she and Sandburg planned to be married, and to discuss their parents' finances. She had managed to save four hundred dollars, and she told him she could give their parents three hundred to run the farm for a year.[65] The rest would be her nest egg for the marriage. Steichen wanted his sister to keep all her savings, however, knowing the unexpected demands a couple could encounter in married life. To his great relief, his paintings had sold "like hotcakes."[66] The photographs had also sold well, with Stieglitz himself buying several for his private collection. (Steichen remembered with gratitude the earlier times when his only income from photography had come from purchases by Stieglitz.[67])

Already delighted—and vastly relieved—that the trip had been such a financial success, Steichen took it as a welcome bonus when he got a lucrative commission from popular *Everybody's Magazine* to make photographic portraits of President Theodore Roosevelt; the Republican presidential candidate in the 1908 election, Roosevelt's secretary of war, William Howard Taft; and Robert La Follette, the progressive U.S. senator from Wisconsin. Steichen would be paid an unprecedented five hundred dollars per portrait for the photographs, which would illustrate

The Initiator (1908)

Lincoln Steffen's article "Roosevelt—Taft—La Follette on What the Matter Is in America and What to Do About It," in the June 18, 1908, issue of *Everybody's Magazine*.

The coffers thus handsomely replenished, Steichen planned to sail for Paris sometime in early May. Thus, he would have to miss his sister's wedding, and in the hectic days before he left New York, he found no time to answer her letter about the wedding. Temporarily energized by Steichen's presence, Stieglitz now had to face the fact that Steichen was headed back to Paris. He told his friend he had decided at last to give up the Little Galleries of the Photo-Secession, forced to it by fatigue and finances. Sadly, therefore, in the wake of the hugely successful Matisse exhibit, Steichen helped Stieglitz close 291, taking down the drapes Clara had sewn for the galleries years earlier, packing up equipment and photographs, withdrawing every sign of the momentous exhibits that had electrified the little rooms for the estimated fifty thousand people who had visited there.

Then, magically, a new patron came to the rescue—wealthy, aristocratic young Paul Haviland, of the Haviland China dynasty, whose father directed that business in France and the United States, and whose mother was the daughter of art critic Philippe Burty. Endowed with a keen artistic sense, Haviland had discovered Stieglitz and 291 when he and his brother Frank Burty Haviland attended the Rodin exhibition in January and purchased several drawings each. By the time Paul Haviland learned of the possible demise of the Photo-Secession galleries, the rooms at 291 had already been leased to a Fifth Avenue clothier who had been working in part of Steichen's former studio at 293 Fifth Avenue, by then split and leased as two separate apartments. But the tailor's rooms were still available, and Haviland straightaway leased those rooms for three years at a rent of five hundred dollars annually, which he personally guaranteed.

Only then did he announce his plan to Stieglitz, who found multiple reasons to resist—pride, first of all, and exhaustion, and the reality that the new space at 293, only fifteen feet square, was smaller than the familiar old one at 291. But Steichen urged him to accept the offer, greatly admiring and trusting Haviland for his exceptionally "fine clean clear headedness."[68] From London, Coburn joined in, passing along

George Bernard Shaw's advice to keep the gallery open. It was foolish, Shaw believed, to "destroy an existing organization" until there was "something better to take its place."[69]

Playing the role Steichen had assumed when the original galleries opened, Haviland promised Stieglitz that he personally would see to cleaning, painting, and furnishing the new gallery. All Stieglitz had to do was say yes and move in, Haviland coaxed.[70] At last, Stieglitz accepted the "miracle" of Haviland's generosity, although he decided at once to solicit other patrons to join in contributing funds for the new lease as well as for utilities, printing, and other costs. And despite the change of address, Stieglitz officially christened his new gallery 291 because it was "more euphonious than 293."[71] Besides, Steichen, Stieglitz, and many other regulars at the Little Galleries of the Photo-Secession had long referred to the place affectionately simply as 291. Pleased that the decision was made, Steichen urged Stieglitz to get settled in the new rooms, free at last of financial worries about the Photo-Secession, and then to get some rest.[72]

Lilian had almost given up on hearing from her brother about their wedding plans, she told Sandburg. "I don't even know whether he's still in N.Y. or whether he has sailed! Maybe my letter didn't reach him in N.Y. and so was forwarded to Paris.... Maybe he got my letter, was busy, and is putting off answering—as usual! I've told you about his cussedness about writing letters!"[73]

Finally, aboard ship just before the *Kaiser Wilhelm II* left harbor, Steichen scrawled an answer to his sister. She was obviously so in love that she was in a "bad way," he teased her, adding seriously that she should absolutely follow her heart if her "good sense" would allow her to. He reassured her that his trip had been such a financial success that he could support their parents for the coming year. He wanted her to be responsible only for herself. Besides, knowing as he did the intimate details of their parents' financial situation, Eduard scolded his sister for her "impracticalness," chiding that Mary and John Peter had never managed on as little as three hundred dollars annually. He had wanted to bring Lilian and their mother to Paris for a visit that summer, but her wedding plans canceled that idea. He was happy for her, he concluded, loved her dearly, and hoped "oh so hard" for her happiness.[74]

Then he handed his letter to a steward so it could go ashore with the pilot boat guiding his ocean liner through the Hudson River toward the open sea.

He returned to an unhappy wife, nervous and uncomfortable in her last month of pregnancy and fatigued from two months of coping alone with Mary's exuberance and her strong will. His triumphs in New York faded in the face of the family's emotional needs, but he was still glad to be back in Paris. He called on Rodin to tell him about the great success of his 291 show, and he found him delighted about the national attention as well as with the sales at 291—a record for sales of Rodin's drawings.[75] Matisse also was "jubilant" about the response to his first American show, including the income it generated, and he showed Steichen some "stunning" new paintings.[76] Steichen wrote to Stieglitz that giving such affirmation to other artists was part of the "beauty" of their mission at 291.[77]

Steichen's return lifted Clara's spirits, as did the wonderful news of their replenished bank account. He already knew exactly how to spend part of their money: The serene days on his parents' farm had whetted his appetite for peace, for the quiet of the country, for some land and some privacy. Deep down, he simply shared his father's hunger for a garden. As much as he loved Paris, Steichen now longed for the country, especially as summer approached. Perhaps Clara would feel better there, and Mary and the new child would surely have more room to grow and play. Therefore, sometime during that spring of 1908, he went out to explore the countryside in search of a new home for his family.

Almost nineteen miles outside Paris, in Voulangis, near Crécy-en-Brie, he found the perfect house and quickly dug into his newly replenished funds to pay for the lease—only twelve dollars a month, including all furnishings and a beautiful garden, already planted and blooming. Three stories tall, counting the attic, it was one of the largest houses in the tiny village of Voulangis. Its white shutters, ivy-covered plaster walls, and enchanting garden could close out the world; the high stone garden walls enfolded an oasis for a young family and a working artist. He and

Clara would keep their apartment-studio in Paris, but would move out of the city for the summer.

Eduard and Clara immediately loved the charming house with its tiled roof, its high ceilings and fireplaces, the parlor and sunny, spacious kitchen downstairs, the upstairs bedrooms, ensuring privacy for parents, children, and even a guest or two, all furnished "to perfection."[78] But even more, Steichen loved the flower garden, already blooming with the roses, iris, larkspur, and other blossoms planted there by the owner and his gardener. The flowering cherry trees would yield two and a half bushels of fruit that first summer, and the vegetable garden served up peas, new potatoes, beans, and lettuce, promising a later rich harvest of cauliflower, cabbage, eggplant, and beets. He thought they had found a paradise.[79]

That May in the flower garden at Voulangis, not long before the baby was born, Steichen painted Clara posing gracefully behind some tall iris.[80] The move to the country had indeed made her healthier and more relaxed, and so they were getting along more peacefully together. The initial reluctance about the new child apparently forgotten, they were now hoping for a son, whom they planned to name Auguste, for Rodin. Instead, their second little girl was born on May 27, 1908.

Excited and proud nonetheless, Steichen cabled the good news home to his family in Wisconsin and to Stieglitz in New York, who had promised to spread the word among their mutual friends. From Trinity Lodge Hospital at 4 Rue Père Nicole in Paris, Steichen also sent a note to the Rodins at Meudon that a beautiful little girl had arrived and that mother and child were doing well.[81] He then wrote to tell Clara's aunt Mary in the United States that the "petit frère" had turned out to be a little girl. Clara had had a relatively easy, normal delivery, he reported, and the doctor assured them she would recover quickly. She looked like a flower, younger and "more girlish" than ever. The baby was beautiful, he wrote, and already seemed to be much stronger and healthier than Mary had been as an infant.[82]

Back in Princeton, Illinois, Lilian quickly sent a note to tell Sandburg that the "May-baby" who was supposed to be a little brother had turned out instead to be a little sister. Since he was to be called Auguste, Lilian wondered if she would now be called Augusta.[83] Actually, Clara and Steichen thought they would name her Kate Rodina, until the local Catholic priest insisted that the child be given a saint's name. Consequently, the Steichens settled on Charlotte Kate Rodina, after Rodin, and Clara's sister and their friend Charlotte "Kate" Simpson, still Rodin's primary patron in the United States.[84] The families had grown close because the Steichens regularly extended their hospitality to the Simpsons during their annual trips to Europe, reciprocating for their pleasant days at the Simpsons' country estate.

Steichen nicknamed the baby Mike, but they usually called her Kate Rodina, or simply Kate. Little Mary, not quite four, did not at first know what to make of the small stranger in her mother's arms. Extraordinarily intelligent, Mary was a headstrong, sometimes difficult child, remarkably curious and opinionated for one so small. She could quickly drive her mother to exasperation. But after a week of having the new baby at home, Steichen noted, Mary seemed to be "simply crazy" about her.[85]

The peace of the country enfolded their beautiful house at Voulangis that summer, blessing the Steichens with a new tranquillity.[86] Little Mary danced like a butterfly in the garden, where she could run safely and freely and play in the sun without wearing any clothes at all. The bright-eyed, active baby was growing plump, but Clara was still weak, not improving nearly as fast as Steichen had hoped, and, quite possibly, suffering from postpartum depression. He worried about her, but at least they were more comfortable than in Paris. He had indeed found a paradise in this beautiful countryside. Voulangis would be good for them, and for his work, and he was eager to turn his full attention to painting for a while.

Their new home needed a name, he decided—and soon he found it in the work of his friend Maurice Maeterlinck, the Belgian writer. In 1905, Maeterlinck had begun working on perhaps his most famous and enduring play, *L'Oiseau bleu,* a dramatic fairy tale in which two children, Tyltyl and Mytyl, search for the magic blue bird of happiness, based in part on J. M. Barrie's *Peter Pan.*

Ever since the Milwaukee days, Maeterlinck had been the writer who most profoundly touched Steichen's imagination and his soul. Now he wanted to embrace in his own daily life the optimistic spirit and themes of Maeterlinck's play—the transcendent joys of simplicity, home, family; the tantalizing quest to conquer nature, unravel the mysteries of life, and truly live happily ever after.

In the end, unfortunately, Maeterlinck's children do not find the blue bird, having failed to recognize it when it was right before their eyes. Given the fragile truce between Eduard and Clara that summer, this choice of a name for their new home resonated with hope and irony. Was there also, in Steichen's love for Maeterlinck's play, an undercurrent of optimism—or cynicism? A looming doubt—or some persistent faith? Time would tell. But in the summer of 1908, Steichen knew what he and Clara must name their house in Voulangis. They called it Villa L'Oiseau bleu.

15

VOULANGIS

(1 9 0 8 - 1 9 0 9)

I had this little house in Voulangis.[1]

—STEICHEN

IN MID-JULY OF 1908, STEICHEN wrote to Stieglitz that the four Steichens were comfortably settled in their "simply ideal" country house and spacious garden at Voulangis.[2] Baby Kate and Mary were thriving, Clara was growing stronger, and Steichen, at last, was beginning to paint again. They could live more cheaply away from the city, afford domestic help, imbibe the sun, the good air, the serenity. Their bountiful vegetable garden fed the Steichens and the throng of friends who often came out on the train from Paris, thirty kilometers away. With the help of their Breton maid, Francine, Clara prepared beautiful meals from the garden's summer yield. While Steichen painted or developed photographs in his studio in a corner of the garden, Mary played in the open air, with baby Kate happily looking on.

Soon Steichen began digging in his new garden with the same zest his father invested in the little farm in Wisconsin, coming away from the labor deeply refreshed—and increasingly fascinated with the mysteries of the genetics, germination, and growth of plants. He especially loved the flowers in his garden. (Once, during his first years in Paris, he had taken the train out to Giverny, hoping to meet Monet and to photograph him in his garden. But he got only as far as Monet's gate before losing the "courage to pull the cord and go in—I just felt that I would be a gross intruder," and so he never saw that garden immortalized in Monet's paintings.[3])

From the beginning at Voulangis, in his own garden, he wanted to paint and to photograph flowers, but before long, he was also deeply absorbed in planting and breeding them. Over time, his hybrids surpassed their "parents": He created new varieties of Oriental poppies, distilled a pure blue petunia from the adroit crossing of seeds, and bred bright, perennially sturdy delphiniums, or larkspur. His flower beds were designed as purposefully and adventurously as a palette—white lilacs, red peonies, white phlox, a rainbow of nasturtiums. Rambler roses, iris, and begonias flourished under his hands, blooming into rich fullness and color. Steichen's garden soon became much more than a pleasant setting for the painter's easel; it was both backdrop and central subject in his paintings, such as *The Voulangis Doorway* (1909), in which the graceful curve of a pathway leads to the door, banked with flowers.

The Steichen children grew up at Voulangis surrounded not only by flowers but also by stimulating conversation and beautiful music. There was a piano in the parlor for Clara to play, and she often accompanied herself as she sang. When Mercedes de Cordoba was visiting, she gave intimate concerts for Arthur Carles, to whom she was now engaged, as well as for the Steichens and other friends. Carles painted such a moment in *Interior with Woman at Piano* (1912), an oil in which Mercedes plays the piano for friends in the Steichen living room.

As always, Steichen was the magnet for any gathering of friends, attracting his fellow artists to the little house and garden. Some, like Carles and John Marin, moved to an inn in Voulangis for extended periods of time so they could paint with Steichen. When he first invited Marin out for a summer visit, the artist brought his familiar watercolors, mainly "the ochres, Paines Gray, neutral gray, lamp black, the brown umbers, and Van Dyke browns," Steichen remembered. He himself used to favor these subtle tones, but now Steichen's own watercolor box held "all the permanent prismatic colors, *vert émeraude,* rose madder, vermilion, the cadmiums, cobalt, and cerulean blue, and none of the neutral colors." When Steichen finally coaxed Marin to try his box, the artist began a new painting of Steichen's garden, voluptuous with flowers—and "at the first crack a new Marin came out with lovely, vibrant sunlight and color."[4] From that day on, Marin's palette included these more vivid colors, and although some later critics attributed that new use of color to the influence of Matisse, John Marin discovered color in Steichen's beautiful garden at Voulangis.

Both Marin and Carles painted memorable scenes at Villa L'Oiseau bleu. Carles's lavish oil entitled *Landscape—Garden in France* captured the brilliant profusion of flowers in Steichen's garden, with the purple steeple of the village church jutting through the background. The men often rambled beyond the garden to the village and the beautiful Morin Valley countryside to paint. Carles especially loved to sketch and paint the small, elegantly simple Romanesque chapel in Voulangis, and *L'Eglise,* his large oil painting of the place, was exhibited in the Armory Show in 1913.

Critic Charles Caffin came over from New York to visit that summer, and Steichen introduced him to the art scene in Paris, entertained him in the country, and talked over his current ideas about new 291 exhibits and the "unlimited" good material available from artists in Europe.[5] He had already written to Stieglitz to propose lithographs by Charles Shannon, drawings by Gordon Craig, and, for the "red rag" to stir things up as he had done with the Rodin and Matisse exhibits, drawings and paintings by that "crazy galloot [sic]" Picasso, if he could be persuaded to set aside his reluctance to exhibit.[6] Stieglitz had sent Steichen photographs of the new gallery he and Haviland had set up at 291, and, demonstrating his usual meticulous interest in every detail, Steichen suggested lowering by about six or eight inches a shelf that surrounded the room, in order to give some "breathing space" to larger prints and paintings.[7]

He urged Stieglitz above all to get some rest at Lake George, and to hold exhibitions to a minimum during the coming season in order to protect his health and energy. At the same time, to counter the mounting criticism by many Photo-Secessionists about the attention to nonphotographic work, Steichen advocated establishing a clear new policy for 291 exhibitions to account for the interest in "stuff outside photography."[8]

It was a nearly idyllic summer at Voulangis, and the Steichens postponed their move back into the city as long as possible, savoring the exhilarating autumn weather. By the time they headed to Paris sometime in October, they had already decided to lease Villa L'Oiseau bleu again for the summer of 1909.

In October of 1908, Rodin invited Steichen to come to Meudon to photograph his magnificent *Balzac*. From that moment in Milwaukee when Steichen had first read newspaper accounts of the controversy over the *Balzac,* he had, of course, been a self-appointed champion of Rodin and his work, but Steichen was not the first photographer Rodin summoned to Meudon to photograph his famous sculpture. The French photographer J. E. Bulloz took some cloudy, static daylight views of the *Balzac,* which Rodin had ordered moved out of the constricting space of his studio and placed on a special revolving platform built in his garden. He wanted pictures of the statue standing free in the open air, but the Bulloz pictures lacked depth and life, serving a practical, documentary purpose, perhaps, but lacking any artistic value. Rodin wanted photographs that did justice to his art, and so he asked Steichen to come.

In the garden at Meudon, after studying the *Balzac* from every angle in the sun, Steichen noted the harsh chalky texture of the white plaster cast, and he decided he wanted to photograph it by moonlight. Rodin heartily agreed, for just a night or two before, he had contemplated the *Balzac* at night, illumined by the October moon. It was "particularly wonderful," he told Steichen.[9] The sight only confirmed Rodin's long-standing theory, expressed before he had completed the statue in 1898, that "the natural principles of sculpture made to be seen in the open air" embodied "the search for contour and for what the painters call *value.*" To understand this idea, one had to "think about what one sees of a person stood up against the light of the twilight sky: a very precise silhouette, filled by a dark coloration, with indistinct details."[10]

Both Rodin and Steichen had long experimented with nocturnal light—Steichen in his photographs and paintings and Rodin in sculpture, posing figures against strong backlighting in his studio and studying them by candlelight to see if they came to life.[11] Yes, Steichen should photograph the statue by moonlight, Rodin agreed. Most of Steichen's own nocturnes were made at dusk, when there was still light to be gleaned from the atmosphere; it would be a new challenge to rely on the moon. He would have to estimate the exposures and discover the timing by trial and error.

For two nights, beginning at sunset and working until sunrise, Steichen photographed the *Balzac,* an incandescent giant in the moonlight, its profile etched against the surrounding night sky and the gentle Meudon hills and valleys. He remembered it as one of the "most wonderful experiences" of his life, working under the waning moon, hearing the "swish of the frost" as he walked to and fro in Rodin's quiet garden.[12] Using the moon as his only source of light, he tried various settings, from fifteen minutes to an hour. Carefully, he noted the time of each exposure, making them almost hourly—at midnight, one, two, three, and four o'clock in the morning, and another just before dawn. Finally, near sunrise after the second night, Steichen got the last exposure.

Then, too weary even to close up his shutter, he went into a small shed nearby, where Rose had made up a cot for him. There, he slept until about eleven o'clock in the morning. In the garden, Rose greeted him with coffee and a good breakfast, and when he lifted his napkin, he found two thousand-franc notes tucked underneath, the equivalent of four hundred dollars—"a fabulous present" for his work, he wrote years later, and a typically generous act for Rodin.[13]

Back in his darkroom in Paris, Steichen set to work immediately to produce fine pigment prints to show Rodin, bypassing proofs completely. "The prints seemed to give him more pleasure than anything I had ever done," Steichen remembered.[14] In the Musée Rodin one can see the *Balzac* series that Steichen prepared for Rodin, bearing his handwritten notes and the title designations: *The Silhouette 4 a.m., Towards the Light— Midnight, Midnight, The Open Sky, 11 p.m., Cinquantenaire de Balzac,* and so on.

"You will make the world understand my Balzac through these pictures," Rodin told Steichen. "They are like Christ walking in the desert."[15] Several days later, Rodin sent Steichen a bronze statue, *L'Homme Qui Marche (The Walking Man),* his symbol, he said, for what he hoped Steichen's entire life would be—"a continuous marching onward."[16]

Steichen shared his excitement about the experience with Stieglitz in a letter, hoping that Stieglitz would approve and would show the

Balzac series at 291.[17] They were the only photographs he had made in months that truly excited him, and everyone who saw them was dazzled by them.[18] Stieglitz was no exception, later purchasing a set of the prints and arranging to exhibit the series at 291 for three weeks, beginning on April 21, 1909.[19] In addition, Stieglitz called the remarkable photographs to the attention of his readers in the October 1909 issue of *Camera Work*, publishing an article by Charles H. Caffin.[20] And Rodin himself paid warm tribute to Steichen in an interview with George Besson, published in *Camera Work* in October 1908:

> *I believe that photography can create works of art, but hitherto it has been extraordinarily bourgeois and babbling. No one ever suspected what could be gotten out of it; one doesn't even know today what one can expect from a process which permits of such profound sentiment, and such thorough interpretation of the model, as has been realized in the hands of Steichen. I consider Steichen a very great artist and the leading, the greatest photographer of the time. Before him nothing conclusive had been achieved. It is a matter of absolute indifference to me whether the photographer does, or does not, intervene. I do not know to what degree Steichen interprets, and I do not see any harm whatever, or of what importance it is, what means he uses to achieve his results. I care only for the result, which, however, must remain always clearly a photograph. It will always be interesting when it be the work of an artist.*[21]

As first Rodin and then Stieglitz praised the *Balzac* series, Steichen had the applause of two of the men who mattered most to him. He especially appreciated the fact that Stieglitz "seemed more impressed than with any other prints I had ever shown him."[22]

It is a sign of his dual commitment to painting and photography that Steichen was painting as well as photographing Rodin's *Balzac* in 1909. There is no surviving painting of the *Balzac*, although there are other Steichen paintings of that period: *Nocturne from Rodin's Garden—The Viaduct* and *Nocturne of the City of Paris—From Rodin's Studio.* When he first pulled the pigment prints in his darkroom, however, Steichen must have seen that he could not create a painting—or perhaps even other photographs—to surpass these images of Rodin's *Balzac*. Only a decade had passed since Steichen's first recognition as a photographer in 1899 at the second Philadelphia Photographic Salon. Those ten years of intense experiments and struggles had ultimately yielded some beautiful, highly original landscapes and portraits. Now these haunting photographs *of* Rodin's work of art turned out themselves to *be* Steichen's work of art. In many ways, these extraordinary pictures mark the culmination of his work as a pictorial photographer, and his photography was about to be superseded for a time by his painting.

Along with the *Balzac* series, Steichen sent Stieglitz another possible exhibition for 291—a group of watercolors by one of the young American artists in Paris whom he championed. These were the "real article," he promised Stieglitz as he dispatched a package of watercolors by John Marin, hoping Stieglitz would give Marin a show in New York.[23] Steichen considered Marin the best watercolorist he had ever seen, and with the twenty-four Marin watercolors, he included fifteen small oil paintings by Alfred Maurer—also "howlers as *color*."[24] Marin's work was akin to Whistler's, Steichen believed, while Maurer was at least on the surface influenced by Matisse. Both men needed money badly, and Steichen hoped Stieglitz could sell their work at 291—pricing the Marins at twenty-five to thirty-five dollars each, the Maurers at thirty dollars, with a 20 percent commission to go to 291.[25] Steichen was so avidly concerned about his protégés that he even drew a sketch to show Stieglitz how he thought their debut show should be hung.

Stieglitz had never before been attracted to watercolors, but Marin's immediately caught his attention. "From the moment I first saw Marin's work I felt, 'Here is something full of delight,'" Stieglitz remembered.[26] He heartily agreed with Steichen that Marin and Maurer deserved to be introduced to the American art public, and so Stieglitz and Steichen arranged their first American exhibition at 291 in April of 1909.

The Maurer-Marin show was "overrun with people," Stieglitz reported. "Maurer was the excitement, Marin the loved one. Marin's watercolors sang their quiet song while the Maurers seemed like instruments of music run riot."[27] Maurer had succumbed to the radical, too-modern influence of Matisse, while Marin failed to be modern at all, critics decided, but Stieglitz defended both men, especially Marin. His work was timeless, full of life. He was an *American* painter, "a natural singer," Stieglitz insisted, echoing Whitman's thesis about the truly American artist.[28]

Steichen had given 291 another landmark show, and when Stieglitz traveled to Paris in the summer of 1909, Steichen introduced him to Marin, who became Stieglitz's lifelong friend. The fact that theirs was an extraordinarily harmonious relationship is a credit to the maturity, tact, and patience of John Marin, for Stieglitz could be hard on friends. The two men never "had a word of difference," Stieglitz recalled many years later. "Each has remained free, true to himself and so true to the other."[29]

Their foray into country living had been so successful that Steichen and Clara looked forward throughout the fall and winter of 1908–1909 to a return to Villa L'Oiseau bleu. Steichen worked hard all the while on various projects, in particular preparing thirty prints for the "International Group" being coordinated by Heinrich Kühn, with Stieglitz's support, at the mammoth Dresden Photographic Exhibition (the Photographische Ausstellung), to be held from May to November 1909.[30] At the same time, he sustained his constant efforts on behalf of the 291 exhibitions, shouldering the responsibility of scouting and choosing shows of the work of European artists, even recruiting articles for *Camera Work* from European critics.

In late February, Steichen had a visit from one artist whose work he was aggressively recruiting—Gordon Craig, the flamboyant stage designer, actor, and director. He was the illegitimate son of the great actress Ellen Terry, who doted on him and encouraged his work in the theater.[31] Tall, gifted, handsome, and chronically restless, Craig had by the age of thirty-four fathered eight children by two wives and two mistresses—most recently the dancer Isadora Duncan, from whom he was now estranged. When Craig called on Steichen, he was in Paris, en route to Florence, where he had founded a school of acting, and he would soon be off to Russia to see Maeterlinck's *L'Oiseau bleu,* for which he had designed the stage sets.

Photogenic Craig, usually dramatically costumed, was also an ideal subject for photography, as Steichen's portraits of him demonstrated. Craig's skillful, highly imaginative sketches for stage settings call to mind the Art Nouveau drawings of Mucha and Klimt. In keeping with his vision of presenting all the arts at 291, Steichen persuaded Craig to leave some drawings with him for possible exhibition in New York.

More and more frequently, artists and art lovers arriving in Paris sought out Steichen for his growing reputation as a cordial American who knew the complicated terrain of the Paris art world and would generously help others navigate it. When Agnes Ernst, the high-spirited, beautiful "Girl from the Sun," bustled into Paris in the fall of 1908 to begin postgraduate studies at the Sorbonne, Steichen immediately agreed to introduce her to the artists he knew in France, for she wanted to subsidize her studies by writing articles about European art and great artists. To finance her year abroad, she had borrowed five hundred dollars from a friend, which she hoped to repay by selling her articles to the New York *Sun* and other publications. (She was also "trying desperately and consciously to escape" her own "unruly disposition and father complex," she wrote years later.[32])

Agnes kept such a meticulously detailed record of her busy life in Paris that one wonders how she could have found the energy to live it so richly—and, simultaneously, to write about it so prolifically. Most of the diary was recorded in love letters addressed enigmatically to a young man she seemed to adore—curious, since she gave him graphic accounts of her flirtations and dalliances with several other men, including the one who later became her husband.

In late October of 1908, Agnes Ernst had spent a day at the Salon d'Automne at the Grand Palais, mightily impressed by the paintings, as well as the jewelry, pottery, bookbinding, and other crafts. She had been pleased to see that her friend Eduard J. Steichen's work was exhibited—"two color arrangements" and "a moody, dreamy thing called 'Le Cheval Blanc,'" but while she found Steichen's paintings interesting, she felt they were unremarkable compared to others in the salon.[33]

On March 3, 1909, Agnes Ernst called on Eduard and Clara Steichen in their apartment in Paris, hoping to persuade Steichen to make photographic portraits of her and her friend and suitor, the enormously wealthy American financier Eugene Meyer, then visiting from the United States. Meyer would pay Steichen handsomely to do the work because he especially wanted portraits of Agnes, who enjoyed imagining that there would be gossip as a result: New York would "talk its head off," she wrote.[34]

Steichen, of course, was happy to have the commissions. He was also ready to introduce Agnes to the great Rodin, but it was Eugene Meyer who actually arranged the meeting between the great sculptor and the "Girl from the Sun." Meyer already enjoyed the exciting hunt and chase of collecting art, shrewdly considering it an investment as well as a pleasure. Therefore, he had arrived in Paris with a letter of introduction to Rodin from a mutual friend, the American sculptor Gutzon Borglum, and on March first, he rented an automobile—a driving "machine," as Agnes called it—to drive out alone to Meudon for his first encounter with the legendary artist.[35] Steichen heartily supported Meyer's wish to own sculpture by Rodin, in particular urging him to purchase a casting of *Paolo and Francesca,* Rodin's haunting study of Dante's tragic illicit lovers, because he wanted to see it go to the United States.[36] Accordingly, Meyer decided to buy that work, along with a copy of Rodin's *Sphinx,* a nude female figure on her knees, her arms and breasts thrust upward in the pose that had so shocked officials at the World's Columbian Exposition in Chicago in 1893 that the sculpture was banned from public exhibition and shown only to visitors who obtained special permits.

Three days after his introduction to Rodin, Meyer took Agnes to meet the sculptor in his Meudon studio. Afterward, Agnes and Meyer spent two and a half hours at Steichen's studio, posing for the black-and-white portraits Meyer had commissioned. It was a profitable afternoon for Steichen, as Meyer also bought two large prints of his photographs of Rodin.[37] They had a "delightful time," Agnes reported in her diary that evening, with Steichen encouraging her to come back for help with her own photography.[38] Because he also proposed to photograph her in color, she returned on March twenty-fourth to pose all afternoon in her gray suit and hat, her riding habit, and her favorite green dress.[39] That day, Steichen gave her the prints he had made earlier of Eugene Meyer, which she found wonderful, and although she loved the color portraits he had made of her, the autochromes so disappointed Steichen that he wanted to do them over again, perhaps later at Voulangis.

True to his promise to introduce her to the modern European art world, Steichen began to show Agnes examples of work by a variety of artists he found compelling. He wanted her to know European photographers as well, especially his old friend Robert Demachy, and so he invited her to a soiree on March tenth at the Photo-Club de Paris, where the best photographers of France were displaying their work. Viewing that exhibit, she immediately realized that Steichen could surpass them all.[40]

Afterward, Steichen took Clara and Agnes to a party at the Taverna Royal with the painter Lawrence Fellows and his wife and other artists and photographers, who delighted Agnes with their "exceptional intelligence."[41] Ever the observer, Agnes sat back and watched Clara Steichen that evening. She was growing fond of her, but she saw with concern that Clara was not always prudent in her behavior toward Steichen. Although Clara appeared to "jar" Steichen at times, he was the "soul of devotion and leniency."[42] Still, Agnes liked Clara more each time she saw her, finding her a "wonderful" woman, despite her "very normal" intelligence.[43] Agnes relished her regular visits to the Steichens' attractive apartment at 103 Boulevard du Montparnasse, where the three Americans talked for hours, sometimes with four-year-old Mary and ten-month-old Kate "climbing all over their mother and amusing us very much."[44]

During one long afternoon while Agnes was posing for photographs in Steichen's studio, Clara poured out her life story, dramatically embellishing the hardships of growing up on the frontier and fending for herself in New York. That night, Agnes wrote in her diary that she liked Clara and Steichen immensely, and found them sincere, entirely self-made, and so unpretentious that they hated "anything which suggests sham."[45]

When Steichen learned that Agnes was going to cover the international congress of suffragettes in April of 1909, he voiced his own strong opinions on the subject—influenced, no doubt, by his outspoken mother, sister, and wife. He was vehement about the "woman question," convinced that women could attain their rights only when they could vote. He was outraged over the economic inequities women suffered, wanting for women the same economic independence that empowered men. Agnes thought Steichen was unusually enlightened in his opinions about women's rights.

As her admiration for him grew, however, doubts began to creep in about Clara. At first, Agnes had felt that Clara possessed "the comfortable undisturbed temperament which genius needs" and so was the ideal wife for Steichen, but she was soon seeing unmistakable signs of what she considered unfounded jealousy and possessiveness.[46] When the three of them shared a cab, for instance, Clara would rush to sit between Steichen and Agnes, telling them that if she did not sit "in the middle, you won't talk to me at all."[47] On one occasion, just as Agnes and Steichen were leaving the Steichens' apartment to visit Rodin at his Paris studio, Clara took Agnes aside. Wasn't she "generous" to allow "such good-looking people as you [and] Steichen to go out together?" she asked a surprised Agnes.[48] Agnes realized that Clara was trying to make a joke of it, but she did not miss the veiled subtext of insecurity and jealousy. She resolved then and there to cultivate Clara's friendship but to spend as little time alone with Steichen as possible, innocent as their friendship was.

Agnes, Steichen, and Rodin had spent an hour one day in March looking at Rodin's erotic drawings, and then discussing prices.[49] On the way home, Steichen promised Agnes that he would talk Rodin into *giving* her another drawing. The two of them had talked animatedly that day about art and artists. Agnes felt that Steichen treated her as a fellow artist, not a woman, and she liked that, writing in her diary that she and Steichen were building a close friendship, feeling as if they had known each other for years."[50]

Art-loving Americans in Paris stepped into a tightly intertwined circle in those days, with the Steins and Rodin as major pivots. Steichen and Clara seemed to live in the center of the more respectable bohemian circle of painters, musicians, and writers in Paris, yet even so, the lifestyle was free, often epicurean, and largely uninhibited. Indeed, their community of friends and acquaintances sometimes seemed connected as intimately and even incestuously as families in a backwater hamlet.[51] Because everyone knew everyone else, gossip flew from mouth to mouth. In that heady milieu, both Steichen and Clara took an interest in protecting and even chaperoning beautiful, single, twenty-two-year-old Agnes. Consequently, when she dropped into Steichen's studio one April afternoon to show him a letter from Rodin inviting her to visit his studio, he was immediately worried on her behalf, for Steichen fully understood the whole Rodin, not just the artist.

"Well, it's one of two things," Steichen told Agnes. "He wants to sell you drawings or he wants to make love to you." Agnes could already sense that with women, Rodin was promiscuous. She had heard that few women could resist Rodin's advances.[52] Even Clara no doubt agreed that it would be a good idea for Steichen to accompany Agnes to Rodin's studio in Paris to finish negotiating some purchases she was making for Eugene Meyer.

The inevitable day came, however, when Agnes went to visit Rodin alone at Meudon, bearing in mind the Steichens' firm warnings about what to expect from this old man who adored all women, especially beautiful young women. And as predicted, he tried to seduce her, holding her hand and kissing it "voluptuously," she reported with satisfaction in her diary. He then took her arm "bruskly [sic], impetuously" with a "wonderfully caressing touch...."[53] Rodin wanted her to pose for him in the nude, but she declined—out of vanity more than principle—confessing to her diary that she would not "hesitate for a moment" if she had "a beautiful body."[54] Deflecting Rodin's sexual advances by asking him disarming questions about his work, Agnes soon turned from ingenue into a serious student of his art.

Steichen was angry at Rodin when Agnes confided in him the details of her first solitary visit to Meudon, but she defended the lusty old sculptor, forty-seven years her senior, telling Steichen that Rodin could not have done his magnificent work were he not "made that way."[55] Besides, Agnes was already adroit at provoking the interest of men and then rebuffing their advances with such charm that they remained her devoted friends. She deliberately calibrated her relationship with Rodin, as she did with many other men, transmuting it into a tantalizing but platonic flirtation, seducing him, but only at arm's length. Soon Rodin was giving her private lectures on sculpture, illustrating them with drawings and demonstrations in his studio. She was especially sensitive to Rodin's advancing age, for he was sixty-nine in 1909. Young as she was, Agnes understood that loneliness was a condition of greatness, especially as a great artist aged. Greatness exacted a dear price, particularly when the world lost sight of "the man in the artist."[56]

During their frequent long talks about art, Steichen told Agnes emphatically that Rodin and Matisse were without question the two most important men in the Paris art world. They decided that spring to collaborate on studies of each artist, with Agnes writing long pieces about Rodin and Matisse, and Steichen providing photographs to illustrate the two articles. To expedite that project, Steichen and Clara took Agnes to the Michael Steins' so that she could see their collection of Matisse's paintings and drawings.

While she could forthrightly interview Matisse, Steichen cautioned Agnes that they should not at first discuss with Rodin her intentions to write an article about him, because when he knew that he was being written about or photographed, he became "a poseur."[57] Steichen was also worried about jeopardizing his own friendship with Rodin, who was magnanimous about sharing art but decidedly territorial about sharing his friendships with women.

One April day in 1909, the Steichens invited Agnes to accompany them to the opening of the Salon Nationale des Beaux-Arts, but when Clara became ill that spring afternoon, Steichen and Agnes set out alone. If they saw Rodin at the exhibition, Steichen warned Agnes, they should dodge him, for he would be jealous if he saw the two of them together without Clara.[58]

If she had any doubts about Steichen's opinions of modern French art, they were banished that day by what they found at the exhibition. It was mediocre, Agnes wrote in her diary. Furthermore, Steichen was elated that the work was unimpressive. Rodin had contributed a single bust to the salon, and Steichen and Agnes saw him standing near it, holding court, surrounded by admirers, but they did not approach him. He was so formally dressed, Agnes wrote, that she almost failed to recognize the artist who usually wore a simple peasant's blouse and his favorite slouch hat.[59]

After they left the salon, Steichen took Agnes to a nearby café for tea, where they lingered for a long talk. She had always felt more at home with men and their ways than with women, and she prized this solitary afternoon with Steichen, even though they were both conscious of Clara, waiting at home. Agnes regretfully saw the Steichens leave for Voulangis in mid-April, but they had invited her to visit them in the country and to bring her camera along so that Steichen could begin her photography lessons. He promised to take her out into the countryside to make photographs, which they would then immediately develop and print in his darkroom at Villa L'Oiseau bleu.[60]

When she went out to Voulangis in early June, however, something happened to change the comfortable character of her friendship with Steichen. Agnes kept such a faithfully detailed record of daily events during her sojourn in Paris that she almost certainly painted a clear picture in her diary of what transpired that June day—but the pages that would have spelled out the story have disappeared from the record. There remains a cryptic diary entry noting that Clara had invited her to return to Villa L'Oiseau bleu; "but," Agnes wrote, "I cannot possibly do it after my scene with Steichen."[61] There is another fleeting reference to the incident in her diary for August 9, 1909, when she reflected that she could not have the "good talks with men" in Europe that she was accustomed to having with men in the United States. Sexual issues seemed to complicate genuine friendship between women and men—especially single women and married men, Agnes thought. She wrote in her diary that she was resigned to this reality "because I cannot forget the Steichen affair."[62]

Perhaps the conflict between Steichen and Agnes was simply a fierce artistic disagreement, or some misunderstanding involving Rodin or Clara. But the few surviving clues in Agnes Ernst's diary insinuate that she believed Steichen was romantically attracted to her and that he must have told her so and wanted to make love to her. While the intimation remains along with the mystery, the verifiable ensuing facts are that Eduard Steichen and Agnes Ernst transcended the incident to remain steadfast friends for a lifetime, and after she married Eugene Meyer in 1910, he, too, became one of Steichen's closest friends, as well as his financial adviser.

"My friendship with Steichen has ripened over the years as few early friendships do," Agnes Ernst Meyer wrote in her autobiography in 1953. "My children have loved this warm, great-hearted man since earliest infancy. He has become a part of our family history which he has recorded over the years in a superb series of photographs."[63]

When news reached Voulangis that Alfred Stieglitz's father, Edward, had died in New York on May 24, 1909, Steichen felt as if he had lost his own father. He called the elder Stieglitz "my dear old Rex," and he had enjoyed a warm, affectionate relationship with him entirely apart from Alfred. Edward's death was an "awful shock" to Steichen, and he worried about how Alfred's mother, Hedwig, would get along without her husband.[64] His own mother was scheduled to sail May twenty-fifth for Europe and the long-deferred visit to Voulangis.

She longed to see Eduard and his family, but during the winter she had suffered a variety of ailments, including insomnia, and did not know if she could withstand such a long journey.[65] Promising to take care of John Peter, Lilian had urged her mother to make the trip, hoping that "the week crossing the ocean will do her good—the salt air, the change of scene and everything"—especially the reunion with her beloved Ed.[66] When two of her close friends from Milwaukee told her they were planning to go to Europe in late May and would travel with her, Mary had given in to her son's persistent invitations to come, and he made the arrangements for her to sail on the *Kaiser Wilhelm der Grosse* on May 25, 1909.

"I onely hope that my good Son dont leave his hearth [heart] run away with his heath [head] and that he can aford this trip for me, whithout crippling his finances," she wrote in a note to Alfred Stieglitz.[67] The Steichens had, in fact, been "dead broke" and "swamped with bills" in 1909, until Paul Haviland's uncle bought one of the paintings Steichen had left with Stieglitz in New York. All of a sudden, they were solvent again and Steichen at last had enough money to bring his mother to France for the summer.[68] She would help celebrate little Mary's fifth birthday and see baby Kate Rodina for the first time, as well as the wonderful new house and garden. Then, in early August, she would go on to visit her brother and her old home in Mondercange, Luxembourg. Eduard and Clara were alarmed to see her extremely "exhausted & worn" on arrival in Paris in June, but after a few days of sleep and rest at Voulangis, she seemed restored to health. "The best doctor in the world is happiness, is it not so?" wrote Clara, relieved at her mother-in-law's recovery.[69]

Paris was "Beautiful Wunderfull," Mary wrote to Mary Sandburg, sending back to the United States a picture of herself with Mary and baby Kate and their new donkey, and providing a vivid written portrait of life at Voulangis, as well: "You see what a nice little girl Mary is, and Baby Kate is so sweedt and big and strong and the Baby Donkee arrived just a few days after me so Mary is under the impression that I had something to do with his arrival. The mama Donkee is a fine animal, she can run as fast as a horse with all of us on the Basquet Cart. All people here who got littl Cildern keep Donkees ensteadt of horses because the ar not afraid of everething as horses, and so is more save for the Children." Mary loved Villa L'Oiseau bleu with its six-foot walls "all around, and so manny fruit trees of all kind, and flowers roses all colors, in fact everebody here has so manny roses Frances is a big rose garden."[70]

She missed her husband and Lilian and Carl; the newlyweds were traveling so continually for the Social Democratic party in Wisconsin that Mary christened them her two gypsies. Still, she was deeply contented at Voulangis, where her grandchildren wanted to spend every moment with her. With her grandmother—her Oma—Mary was sweet and well-behaved, feeling the same warm love her father gave her. Oma had worried so over little Mary's health problems that she was relieved to find year-old Kate "big and strong."[71]

Like its name, Villa L'Oiseau bleu, the house and garden in Voulangis seemed the setting for a fairy-tale childhood. "Until I was 9, I lived with my mother and father in a sort of magic, enchanted garden in France," Mary Steichen wrote years later, "a walled garden which my father has made famous in some paintings and photographs. It was a very free existence. He believed that nude bodies were beautiful for children. Nudity wasn't practiced so much by adults in those days. But I have a lovely photograph of him holding my sister's hand, my hand, one on each side of him, and our little nude bodies are prancing along with him in the garden."[72]

The Steichens lived in "an atmosphere of passionate appreciation of beauty and a passionate disregard for forms and formality," which deeply influenced their children. Mary was willful and "highly emotional," keenly responsive to "the gifts of life, of feeling, of beauty, and of song." She felt that was her father's legacy to her, born out of his own joyous vision of life. "He saw beauty and instantly drew it out," Mary said.[73]

"Until I was ten, we were a family growing up together," Mary also wrote poignantly in later years. Her father imbued her "with the love of the beautiful in concrete things—animals, flowers, the human body. His gift for looking at people as people was such that I am not aware of his ever having made me feel a child. I just felt like *me,* with him, that is."[74] From the beginning of her life, she knew her father loved her unconditionally, as he had been taught by his mother to love.[75]

It was quite different with her mother, however, and Clara and Mary had "many conflicts," Mary remembered.[76] "My mother had a bad influence on me," she wrote in later years. "She was a sad, very unhappy woman. She was compulsive. She was angry. She was hostile."[77] Mary was haunted for years by her mother's punishments. When the child was four or five, Clara found her masturbating, and, horrified, she punished her verbally as well as physically. Mary was traumatized.[78] She reflected many years later, after a prolonged study of human sexuality, that a child's natural pleasure in her own body was "either acknowledged by punishment, which produces fear and guilt, or it's never acknowledged at all, which to the child means that it is considered not to exist. But the child *knows very well that it does exist.* So it's like punishing him because he's lefthanded, and the child finds himself condemned to a kind of existential nightmare."[79]

Nevertheless, she regretted that she "was a very difficult child," Mary acknowledged candidly in retrospect; "and it scared my mother to death."[80] All her life, Mary adored her father and felt his deep influence. "He was very bright intellectually," she wrote in later years, "and so was I. He must have had a very high IQ. And I know I have a high IQ—not genius range, but high. And I was intellectually minded. I loved learning. I read enormously.... And he encouraged this. He encouraged anything I wanted to do. There was never a word said that might imply, Well, you'll never be able to do this because you're a female."[81] Just as his mother had done for him, Steichen brought Mary up with the idea that she could achieve anything she set out to do.

———

All of the Steichens, including Oma, were relieved to learn that despite Edward Stieglitz's death, Alfred, Emmy, and Kitty were going to go ahead with their long-planned summer excursion to Europe. After Steichen met their ship on June twenty-first, he and Clara entertained them in Paris and in Voulangis. Right away, Steichen wanted to introduce Stieglitz to all of the Steins, as well as to Rodin and to such gifted young artists as John Marin. They found Marin in his studio, "standing at his press in shirtsleeves, printing etchings." Stieglitz was instantly drawn to the "free, bold and distinctly Marin" style evident in the young artist's latest paintings, and he immediately bought a watercolor for 125 francs. Later, when he, Marin, and Steichen were relaxing in a nearby café, Stieglitz handed Marin 250 francs more, explaining that he could not in good conscience take the beautiful watercolor for any less.[82]

When Steichen took Stieglitz to meet Sarah and Michael Stein, Stieglitz was as bowled over by their Matisses as Steichen had hoped, finding, he said, many paintings that were "new and all exceptionally wonderful to me."[83] That introduction successfully accomplished, it was time to take Stieglitz to meet Leo Stein. At 27 Rue de Fleurus, Steichen and Stieglitz found Leo and Gertrude Stein alone in their atelier. Stieglitz's probing eyes took in the paintings covering the walls from ceiling to floor; the books, papers, and statuary everywhere; and a "bald man with eyeglasses and whiskers" and a "dark and bulksome" woman half-reclining on a chaise longue.[84] She did not speak a word, but she seemed to Stieglitz to understand everything that was transpiring. The room was so chilly that Stieglitz kept on his cape, forgetting his discomfort as soon as he heard Leo Stein begin to speak.

"I quickly realized I had never heard more beautiful English nor anything clearer," Stieglitz remembered. Uncharacteristically quiet, he listened mesmerized for an hour and a half while Leo "held forth on art." Stieglitz was persuaded by Leo's criticism, although Steichen "blanched" when Leo labeled Rodin and Whistler as second- or third-class artists and proclaimed Matisse a better sculptor than Rodin.[85]

"Mr. Stein, why not write down all you have said," Stieglitz invited. "It is the most wonderful thing, in a way, I have ever heard about art." He offered to publish "anything and everything" Stein might send to *Camera Work*.[86] Leo declined, however, explaining that he was still trying to evolve his philosophy of art and could not write about it until it was complete.

According to Stieglitz, a dejected Steichen poured out his worries on the way home from that encounter. "I had better stop painting. If Rodin and Whistler amount to nothing, where do I come in? I would rather have you and Stein approve of my work than any other people in the world. In Stein's eyes I must be out of the picture."[87]

"Do you paint for yourself or to please others?" Stieglitz asked. "What has Stein, or what have I, to do with your paintings?"[88] He did not record Steichen's answer, but it was a question very much on Steichen's mind in 1909, and afterward.

The Steichens entertained a procession of visitors that summer at Voulangis: Alfred, Emmy, and Kitty; Arthur Carles and Mercedes de Cordoba; the beautiful American artist Katharine Rhoades, Agnes Ernst's good friend; Stieglitz's cousin Flora Small and her husband; and Dr. Lee Stieglitz, who was providentially on hand one summer night when little Mary complained of stomach pains. He immediately diagnosed appendicitis and arranged for Mary to be rushed to the American Hospital in Paris for surgery.

Mary herself was a "little wonder" about it all, her father reported, taking the news calmly when the doctors and her parents explained what was about to happen.[89] Steichen and Clara were distraught, however, and Oma, caring for Kate and waiting anxiously at Voulangis, was almost sick with grief.[90] They had had "nothing but worry," Steichen wrote to Rodin in July of 1909 from the hospital. Although she was recovering, Steichen said, he had been too upset about Mary's health to work.[91] For days afterward, he was a "wreck, mentally and physically," and it was a great comfort to all of them to have Oma on hand when Mary returned to Voulangis.[92]

Leaving his family at Villa L'Oiseau bleu, Steichen went back into Paris to witness the marriage of Arthur Carles and Mercedes de Cordoba on July 22, 1909. They were "terribly in love," Clara wrote to Stieglitz's mother, and they planned to honeymoon at the little inn in Voulangis—although, Clara mused, no place could be "so beautiful & perfect for a honeymoon as Lake George."[93] The bride's mother also stood with the couple as a witness, her heart full of grave misgivings about her daughter's marriage to this handsome artist. She could not imagine that his bohemian lifestyle could support her daughter and a stable family life, and she would eventually turn out to be right.

VOULANGIS (1908-1909)

Such was the perennial economic struggle of artists, including Steichen, but he was fortunate enough to possess two gifts to exploit—painting and photography. He also knew that artists could face long financial uncertainty, regardless of the magnitude of their talent. Even the great Rodin had achieved his wealth late in life. Matisse and Picasso were still poor, Picasso living in rooms that verged on squalor, and Matisse managing, through great discipline and the devotion of his wife, a stable family life.

Steichen, like Matisse, was absolutely devoted to his children. But unfortunately, Steichen and Clara had not built the strong, equal partnership that undergirded Matisse's work and the Matisse family life. Accustomed to acceptance and tolerance from his mother and sister, as well as their unconditional love, Steichen never quite knew what to expect from Clara or how to respond to her mercurial moods and demands.

Yet there were good, peaceful times within the family, especially during Oma's long visit that summer. And Steichen's daughter Mary came to this conclusion: "In the years at Voulangis the lovely garden created by my father came to mean much the same to him as did the garden at Giverny to Monet—a bottomless well for creativity, peace, challenge, joy, inspiration, surcease, renewal—and sheer sensual pleasure. What a marvelous time he had hybridizing and growing flowers larger and more exquisite than anyone could have imagined, and how triumphantly he adored them."[94]

16

THE GOSPEL OF NEW LIGHT

(1 9 0 9)

Steichen (in deep meditation): "Ah, to know that one's work is the perfection of art! To have invented the Steichen type. I do not photograph. I raise my camera in defiance. I chant the gospel of new light ... which dazzled Commander Stieglitz and his triumphant march to Dresden." [1]

—SADAKICHI HARTMANN

ALVIN LANGDON COBURN CALLED IT A "Grand PowWow" when he heard that Steichen, Stieglitz, Frank Eugene, and Heinrich Kühn had spent several days together in Munich in late July of 1909 conducting further experiments with Lumière autochrome plates and generally enjoying one another's company. From Munich, the quartet traveled together to Baden-Baden, where Steichen introduced Stieglitz to Baron Adolf de Meyer, launching their long, congenial friendship. Coburn predicted that Stieglitz would like de Meyer because he was "Secession to the *backbone!*"[2]

Steichen, Stieglitz, Eugene, Kühn, and de Meyer then proceeded to Dresden to visit the international photographic exhibition, where, thanks to Kühn, their own work was on prominent display.[3] Soon after the show, Sadakichi Hartmann wrote a mischievous attack on the key Photo-Secessionists in an unpublished "Mystery Play in Two Exposures Dedicated to the Photo-Secession"—a mock "court-martial" to ferret out photographers guilty of faking their prints by adding highlights, painting in color, or etching in backgrounds.[4]

Although Hartmann also spoofed Stieglitz, Coburn, Clarence White, Gertrude Käsebier, Frank Eugene, and other Photo-Secessionists in his drama, Steichen—his character as well as his art—bore the brunt of the satirical assault. Dubbing Steichen "the modern Daguerre," Hartmann painted him as arrogant, self-important, a prima donna:

"Who is he with the swelled head roaming in thought?" the judge asks. Steichen replies:

> "Who am I. Futile question. I am the whole thing. I am Steichen. I am a friend of Stieglitz. I am from Milwaukee. I know a thing or two when I see them. Even in my infancy I sought the ideal."

Charged with "appropriating" highlights and imposing them on his photographs, Steichen answers that light gives to "every picture the significance, the depth, the spiritual gravity. The high lights lead me on, they shaped my destiny, and made me, ah, so great—I sometimes weep over my own greatness."

"You are a clever chap, I dare say," the judge concludes, "only the size of your head seems to be abnormal."[5]

What seemed to Hartmann to be cocky self-assurance could also be explained as Steichen's supreme confidence in himself as a photographer. But in 1909, despite a respectable commercial success selling paintings, he was still struggling with his identity as a painter, working very hard at it that fall, although unsure of the quality of the results. Perhaps he could "tell better" when he showed them to Stieglitz in New York, he wrote, for he had come to value his friend's opinions about his paintings as well as his photographs.[6] Stieglitz had been "very enthusiastic over Steichen's work" that summer, Clara had written to Hedwig Stieglitz. "He feels Steichen is feeling more & more clearly his way & is having courage to express himself as well . . . & he says he can see & feel the peace & quiet here & more than that he sees the results in E's work!"[7]

Preparing for another winter's journey back to the United States to exhibit and sell his photographs and paintings, Steichen painted at Voulangis well into October of 1909. Once again, he and Clara were reluctant to leave the beautiful house and garden in the country. They promised each other and the children that they would spend the next summer as well at Villa L'Oiseau bleu, a routine they would follow until 1914.

Eager to please his wife, Steichen had hoped that the summers in Voulangis would give Clara more of the comfort and security she needed, but even with the help of the maid, Clara often felt overwhelmed by her domestic responsibilities. "I find I tire easily," she complained in a letter to Stieglitz's mother. "I am always fagged. I think the responsibility of the children weighs on me." After five years of motherhood, she feared she was growing "one sided—and I long to be free just for 24 hours but that will never be I guess."[8]

Unfortunately, the peace Stieglitz and others initially felt at Voulangis came from the beautiful place itself, not from its inhabitants. Clara's moods fluctuated so wildly, even with Mary and Kate, that Steichen doubted he could ever make her happy. He hated conflict, and they argued too often, too bitterly—usually over his friends. Steichen was always inviting their friends to Voulangis, and while Clara sometimes enjoyed their company, often it became just so much work. Their garden was a gathering place, and she wanted to be hospitable, but even with Francine's help, it was too much for her sometimes. Yet if she complained too persistently, Steichen just left her at Voulangis and went into Paris to work in his studio there. He could go off that way on a moment's notice, but she could not, with the two little girls needing her. "I never leave home for the night," she wrote, but that seemed to be her own choice.[9] She complained to others—with no apparent justification—that Steichen sometimes left her alone at Voulangis without enough money, and without even saying where she could find him. Years later, that recollection, whether real or imagined, could still bring her to fury and tears.

Clara had expected so much more for herself, for she had, after all, been the belle of the town; she could have married anyone she chose. Like Eduard, Clara had grown up in a household of strong women. Just as Mary and Lilian Steichen had compensated for the weaknesses they perceived in John Peter Steichen, the women in Clara's family had tried to counteract the failures of their men, including Clara's own gentle, compassionate physician father, who had selflessly practiced medicine and yet hopelessly failed to make money at it. As a girl, Clara had known how it felt to endure a father's preoccupied absence and to do without the luxuries other girls had.

Now she found herself living in France with a husband who was more and more absent, absorbed in his work, and unable, for all the energy he exerted and the attention he won, to provide the luxuries she wanted for her children and herself, luxuries she saw other women enjoy. And it did not help to know that her husband was still supporting his parents back in Wisconsin and would most likely have to do so for the rest of their lives.

Even the magical garden at Voulangis could not vanquish the troubles that tore at Clara and Steichen. More and more often, he commuted to Paris, turning his back on his tearful, angry wife and leaving her with the children in Voulangis, first as his work demanded, and, later, as time wore on and their unhappiness became habitual, to escape to some temporary freedom from Clara. Sometimes work compelled him to be away, but there were selfish absences—such as the pleasure trip to Baden-Baden with Stieglitz and the others—which gave him respite and diversion but left her seething with anger, feeling neglected and suspicious. As gloomy and contentious as she could be when her husband was at home, Clara grew dismally unhappy when Steichen was away from her for long, but when he came home again, she interrogated him in detail about his activities, suspecting that there were love affairs.

Madly in love with him herself, she saw how other women of all ages fell in love with her husband. He was attracted to beautiful women, and Clara knew it. Knowing Paris and their avant-garde circle of friends, she did not trust them or her husband. Perhaps even more than physical infidelity, Clara deeply feared the bonds of affection that Steichen forged with women such as Agnes Ernst, and she felt intensely threatened by her husband's propensity to turn to other bright, gifted women for alliances of spirit and mind.

Often while Steichen was away from home, Clara vented her frustrations on her older child. Mary was so like her father that her mother often made her a scapegoat. "She took it out on me by being destructive and hostile and jealous and cutting me down all the time, with truly destructive phrases which I prefer not to repeat," Mary remembered years later.[10] Kate, a gentler child with a sweeter nature, was her mother's favorite, as Mary seemed to be her father's, and Clara treated Kate quite differently, lavishing on her all the affection she withheld from Mary and Steichen.

Her father had "a really inexhaustible supply of love," Mary wrote in later years.[11] As she grew older, Mary also came to understand that her mother was lonely—and very jealous of her father, who, she wrote cryptically in later years, "was a womanizer in a very sensitive and wonderful way."[12] It is not clear whether Mary was suggesting that her father entered into close relationships with other women that were not sexually consummated, or that he routinely indulged himself in affairs. Whatever the explanation, for Clara there could have been nothing "sensitive" or "wonderful" in her husband's associations with other women, only the deep pain of betrayal. She was jealous of almost every woman who crossed Steichen's path.

Among their friends in New York, London, and Paris, there were many rumors about Steichen, extending to the possibility of an illegitimate son, but the gossip was rooted in conjecture rather than in documented fact. Agnes Ernst's diary, with its mysterious missing pages, left enough evidence to suggest a romantic, if not sexual, overture from Steichen. More seriously, Clara herself alleged that at least two women were sexually involved with Steichen during those years from 1908 to 1911. He was immensely discreet about his extramarital love life, if any, but his later letters to Clara seem to echo the highly unconventional opinions his sister had expressed in 1908.[13]

Not long before her marriage, for example, Lilian had written to Sandburg:

> *I believe our love will outlive the stars—as you do. But neither of us believes in trying to chain love with promises of eternal fidelity. We don't believe in any promises. And we know that no promises of eternal love can make love last forever. Love is free: you can't chain it—it comes and goes freely—when it wants to go it shakes off easily all the chains that may have been put upon it and that seemed to hold it prisoner while it stayed in reality of its own free will.*[14]

For her brother in 1909, however, every verifiable fact suggests that, whether out of his "own free will" or from a deeply felt sense of obligation, or both, Steichen's love for his wife and children and his loyalty to his family responsibilities were never in question. Nevertheless, no matter what the truth was, all four Steichens had to live with what Clara *believed* to be true, and with her anguish about it.

Both the women she saw then as seductresses and rivals were artists. She herself could have been an artist, Clara still believed, had Steichen not deprived her of the time and energy to develop her music and writing. Years earlier, sensitive to the costly personal sacrifices women traditionally made to husbands and children, Steichen had cautioned his own sister that once she married, she would be gradually compelled to subordinate or even relinquish her own talents and ambitions because the instincts of motherhood would inevitably govern her heart and mind.[15]

In reality, Clara's talents were modest, yet Steichen always encouraged her to express them and worked terribly hard so that she would not have to earn money. But Clara's pain and anger twisted around her paranoid conviction that she would lose him to other women who had been fortunate enough to express themselves artistically.

The first alleged other woman was the sculptor Kathleen Bruce, the lovestruck young woman who had gazed longingly at Steichen across the tables of the cheap café in Paris in 1902. A regular at Gertrude and Leo Stein's salon when she was in Paris, Bruce made her way into *The Autobiography of Alice B. Toklas* as "a very beautiful, very athletic English girl, a kind of sculptress."[16] (Actually, Kathleen Bruce was Scottish, the eleventh child of the Canon of York, and orphaned when she was sixteen.)

An art student in Paris from about 1899, when she was twenty-one, to 1906, Bruce had studied with Rodin, who had introduced her to the charismatic young dancer Isadora Duncan in 1903. Soon Kathleen was traveling with Isadora as she danced on tour in Europe, and in the fall of 1903, she joined Duncan and her brother Raymond Duncan on their long-anticipated first journey to Greece. There, not far from Athens, Isadora bought a hill called Kopanos, and set out to build her own Greek temple. They often camped out on the slopes of Mt. Hymettus, Kathleen remembered, sleeping on rugs on the hillside, with a stick and a gasoline can for an alarm against intruders, whether curious people or stray animals.

Bruce was goodness itself to her friends, dropping everything in her own life if she felt she was needed. She was the one Isadora had turned to when she was hiding away in a small Dutch village on the North Sea, awaiting the birth of her first child, fathered by Gordon Craig during their adulterous affair. The two single women lived "on a lonely foreign beach" while the world-famous dancer, who had scandalized thousands with her barefooted dances and her free lifestyle, now stitched baby clothes and wrestled with her fears, doubts, and loneliness.[17] At one point, Kathleen had even saved a despondent Isadora from drowning herself in the sea, and she cared for her friend during the agonizing delivery of her daughter, Deirdre, born September 24, 1906.

By Kathleen Bruce's own account, she was innately prudish and a virgin when, in 1908, she married explorer and hero Robert Falcon Scott, the doomed leader of the British quest to be first to reach the South Pole.[18] Their son was born in 1909, but they spent most of their married life apart because of Scott's Antarctic exploration, launched in 1910. He died a hero in the Antarctic in 1912, defeated by starvation, frigid cold, and his Norwegian rival, Roald Amundsen, who had been second to reach the North Pole, after Robert E. Peary.

Robert Falcon Scott's tragic death was not confirmed until February of 1913, and when her husband was posthumously knighted, Kathleen Bruce Scott was quickly named Lady Scott, thereafter becoming a very visible widow in Great Britain.

In her autobiography, Bruce remembered that it was during the clandestine interval in Holland during Isadora Duncan's pregnancy that she first confessed to Isadora her infatuation with Eduard Steichen. Duncan immediately decided to summon Steichen to Holland to take her portrait so that Kathleen could be reunited with this man she had loved from afar. Steichen was a married man now, Bruce protested, and she had not seen him or heard from him since he kissed her on his last night in Paris in 1902. Nevertheless, Duncan was determined to bring the two together. Humiliated, Bruce fled to London, she recalled, only to receive an urgent telegram from Duncan begging her to return because she was terribly ill. Bruce immediately headed back to Holland, where to her astonishment, she wrote, Steichen himself met her train.

Duncan the matchmaker urged Bruce to love Steichen "good" and to "stop being so English." And if Bruce did not want Steichen, she told her friend, "I'll have him myself. He's lovely."[19] Promising herself not to get involved with a married man, Bruce was nevertheless aflutter, she remembered, when Steichen made her feel that she was the only woman he had ever cared for. The two of them traveled back to England, where, according to Bruce, they spent an idyllic and platonic week together.[20]

Bruce's romantic story, if true, played out at a different time, however, for Steichen was not in Europe during the months of Duncan's pregnancy in 1906. He, Clara, and Mary were still in the United States preparing to move to Paris. Steichen reported to Stieglitz in an undated letter, written sometime in 1907 or 1908, that he had seen Bruce in London, and that she had persuaded him to let her sculpt his portrait. He had actually gone to London on that trip to photograph Isadora Duncan after photographing Gordon Craig in Holland, he wrote to Stieglitz, but because Duncan was ill for several days he had been forced to postpone making her portrait.[21] Steichen was so pleased, however, with Bruce's "fine portrait" of him that he planned to have a bronze of it made for Mary.[22]

Later, when Clara heard about it, she confronted Steichen furiously, sure that he was in love with Kathleen Bruce. No, he absolutely was not, he insisted, to no avail. According to Bruce's memoir, however, Steichen had spoken thoughtlessly to Clara about how Kathleen's eyes looked in the sunshine, how her hair looked covered with raindrops.[23]

During one of their arguments over Bruce, Clara grew so distraught that she swallowed the contents of a vial of harmless crystals that a horrified Steichen took to be poison. She was rushed to the hospital to have her stomach pumped.

Waiting helplessly while doctors and nurses treated his wife, Steichen telegraphed Bruce that Clara had swallowed poison. She wired him to meet her at the steps of the Madeleine, away from her own *quartier*, so she would not be recognized if, as she feared, Clara died and there had to be an inquest. Bruce wrote that Steichen begged her to visit Clara, believing that if his wife could see that she was "just beautiful and innocent and young and not some terrible creature," it would "dispel the dreads and horrors from her mind."[24]

According to Bruce, she agreed to this implausible plan, went to call on the Steichens under the pretense of delivering a book, and so assuaged Clara that she invited her to stay for supper.[25] When Steichen escorted

Kathleen to her train afterward, she bade him good-bye, she wrote, and said, "Never ask me to do a mean thing like that again."[26]

The bitter arguments over Kathleen Bruce continued for years. One day at Voulangis, Clara's fury drove Steichen to such despair that he fled the house and jumped into a shallow cistern, with Clara trailing behind.[27]

These frightening quarrels must have wounded the children as much as the two combatants, if not more so, but Steichen seemed as helpless to anticipate or prevent them as Clara was to control the overwhelming force of her jealousy.

Clara also claimed that her husband had had an affair with Isadora Duncan.[28] The history of how and when Isadora and Steichen first met is murky, but there was an abundance of rumor about them. Clara and Steichen saw Duncan dance in Paris in 1909, and afterward Clara wrote to tell Hedwig Stieglitz her impressions: "I enjoyed so much the Duncan dances. She herself is so cheap—so vulgar—I really wish I'd never met so foolish & stupid a creature. How on earth a person can execute—can daily *live* such beautiful things as her dances & still have such a common *low* view of life of language of people of herself as that woman does is beyond me."[29] About that same time, Steichen also introduced his wife to Duncan's paramour, Gordon Craig, whom Clara found "interesting, intelligent & very wonderful to look at."[30]

Clara knew a good deal about Isadora's reputation for promiscuity, the source of much gossip after 1900 and the onset of her great notoriety, and she almost certainly knew about Duncan and Craig's little daughter, Deirdre. But she did not know all of Duncan's history. Like Steichen, Isadora Duncan had first seen Paris at the turn of the century, and she had stood mesmerized by Rodin's art in the Pavillon de l'Alma at the Exhibition Universelle of 1900. Later, still haunted by the power of Rodin's work, Isadora had made her own pilgrimage to Rodin's Paris studio, finding him "short, square, powerful, with close-cropped head and plentiful beard."[31]

Duncan had watched fascinated that day as Rodin showed her his statues and "ran his hands over them and caressed them." She also stood by as he worked with clay, forming a woman's breast, which seemed to palpitate beneath his fingers. Then he asked to go with her to her own studio so she could dance for him. There, she changed into her tunic and performed an interpretative dance based on an idyll of Theocritus, while Rodin watched "with lowered lids, his eyes blazing. . . ." When she stopped, she remembered, he approached and

> ran his hands over my neck, breast, stroked my arms and ran his hands over my hips, my bare legs and feet. He began to knead my whole body as if it were clay, while from him emanated heat that scorched and melted me. My whole desire was to yield to him my entire being, and, indeed, I would have done so if it had not been that my absurd up-bringing caused me to become frightened and I withdrew, threw my dress over my tunic and sent him away bewildered. What a pity![32]

All her life, she regretted "this childish miscomprehension which lost to me the divine chance of giving my virginity to the Great God Pan himself, to the Mighty Rodin. Surely Art and all Life would have been richer thereby!"[33]

Isadora did not see Rodin again until 1903, the year she danced for him at Vélizy. It is not clear whether Steichen met Isadora through Rodin, through the Steins, or through Gordon Craig, the love of Isadora's passionate life. But Craig's innate restlessness and the conflicting demands of their careers—their art—had stanched the fires of their relationship by late 1908, although Isadora claimed she never stopped loving him.

By early January 1909, Isadora was in Paris to dance at the Trocadéro, and her performance was the talk of the city. Only five feet six inches tall, she appeared much taller on stage. She wore her dark hair short, usually parted in the middle and pulled gracefully back to the nape of her neck. She was not thin, as some dancers were, but voluptuous, and her paradox of innocence and sexuality was unforgettably captivating to audiences, even though she shocked them.

It was coincidental that Duncan and Craig, then estranged, were both in Paris early in 1909, around the time that Craig and Steichen spent time together. Steichen photographed Craig posed in profile, wearing a white shirt, open at the collar. He looks toward a window, holding in his hands a folio, pens, and brushes—the usual Steichen composition of the artist with his tools. Craig and Steichen were so similar in profile that some have mistaken this portrait of Craig for a Steichen self-portrait.

Duncan is said to have danced in the garden at Voulangis. In Steichen's 1909 oil painting *Moonlight Dance, Voulangis,* the tiny figure of a graceful dancer swathed in white light, dancing before an audience of dark figures, is almost certainly Isadora. Her arms are uplifted in what Steichen later called Isadora's "most beautiful single gesture, the slow raising of her arms until they seemed to encompass the whole sky."[34]

Clara repeatedly accused her husband of having an affair with Duncan, and, just as incessantly, he denied it. He infuriated Clara once, however, by telling her that Duncan was "a splendid woman, a fine woman, a fine mother, and a potential figure in the art world." "Everybody's fine except myself and everybody's children are fine except mine," Clara snapped back.[35]

In one of Steichen's provocative photographs of Isadora, made sometime in 1909 or 1910—after a rendezvous, Clara must have believed—she is lying on her abdomen on a bed or a couch, bare arms stretched forward, hands clasped, her dark hair loose about her uplifted face and shoulders, her languid body covered by a flowered robe or blanket. It is an intimate portrait of a beautiful, private woman—not the great Isadora in performance, as in Steichen's later pictures of her. But if Duncan and Steichen had consummated an affair in 1909, it would have been a fleeting one, for Isadora had her hands full then with a triangle of forceful men, cunningly playing them one against the other.

Isadora Duncan had a way of seducing attractive men to assuage any unhappiness or turmoil in her personal life, and Steichen was often alone in Paris, in search of his own solace and diversion. But despite Steichen's denials that he and Isadora were lovers during the years the Steichens leased Villa L'Oiseau bleu, Clara herself adamantly insisted that it was so, then and later. She wrote angry letters about it to Stieglitz in 1916 and to her own daughter Mary as late as 1941.[36]

Steichen had, of course, hurt Clara badly with an infidelity before they were married, and he almost certainly transgressed during their marriage, although, it would appear, not with the women who bore the brunt of Clara's fiercest accusations. Whether prompted by her husband's actions or not, she lashed back with a jealousy that fomented until it became abnormal. Modern psychiatry would most likely account for

The Gospel of New Light (1909)

Clara's pathological jealousy as part of either a paranoid or a histrionic personality disorder.[37] Later in her life, Clara wrote a poignant and revealing self-portrait: "Directly candid myself, I am slow to suspect betrayal or unkindness by others, but once decided, being from Missouri, I furiously demand that I be shown, then make my own decisions as to what is to be done, bearing the hurt therefrom as best I know." She also reflected, looking back on her frontier ancestors, that "the feudin' and fightin' kept every one on the *qui vive*. Forgiveness was unthinkable and considered a waste of time...."[38]

During the fall of 1909 Steichen was "working like mad" to assemble some dazzling new exhibitions for Stieglitz and 291.[39] Determined that 291 should have an international mixture of shows, he was becoming quite an impresario. He had already completed arrangements for the exhibition of Gordon Craig's drawings and etchings and was negotiating for bronzes by Rodin, more drawings by Matisse, some woodcuts by a Finnish artist, and drawings by the Polish-born artist Elie Nadelman. Then, to fulfill his dream of showing the work of the Society of Younger American Painters in Paris, he was gathering paintings by Arthur Carles, Alfred Maurer, and other members of the group he had organized in in 1908. All the while, he worked fervently on his own paintings and photographs.

Steichen's strenuous work on behalf of other artists was all the more remarkable because he neither sought nor derived personal recognition or financial benefit from it. Always in his own painting and photography, of course, there was a driving commercial purpose—not that he sought wealth, but he was financially responsible for his wife, his children, and his parents. Rodin, his master, believed that if art required the artist to neglect his family's well-being and to live on the edge of destitution, so be it. Rodin had always honored art over everything else in his life, convinced that the true artist had to work tirelessly and stubbornly, engaging "all his forces to the service of his art," and, ironically, strengthening and invigorating his gifts through that very process of renunciation.[40]

For Steichen this was not an option, however. Just after Mary's birth in 1904, he had idealistically resolved to contravene the traditional notion that family life was a hindrance for an artist.[41] He had been determined to fuse his family life harmoniously with his life as an artist, he had written to Stieglitz, expressing the conviction that with Clara's help, his family would become an inherent part of his art as well as his soul.

Yet over the years, despite his best intentions and often because of financial anxiety, Steichen had given precedence to his work, and Clara had grown to resent and often exaggerate the sacrifices she felt she had made for her husband's career. Finally, they found themselves entrapped in a destructive cycle: The occasional tentative peace that Steichen needed for productive times with his family, his work, and his garden was inevitably ruptured by venomous rows over his independence and his alleged sexual encounters with other women. Then, once more, he and Clara would come to another uneasy truce before the next inescapable uproar. Steichen may have shared the romantic and sexual mores of other avant-garde artists in Paris and elsewhere, but he was nonetheless a traditionalist when it came to supporting his family. The one lingering bond he and Clara still had deeply in common was their commitment to their children.

Steichen also felt an enduring obligation to other artists, Rodin and Stieglitz foremost. He threw himself into the highly ambitious, farsighted enterprise of introducing modern art to American viewers, gathering paintings, prints, and sculpture all on his own to ship to Stieglitz for unveiling at 291. They made a strong team: In Paris, Steichen handled temperamental artists such as Matisse and Rodin, while in New York, Stieglitz dealt with irascible, mercurial artists and critics such as Max Weber and Sadakichi Hartmann. Despite the headaches, Steichen and Stieglitz lavished precious energy and time on the Photo-Secession projects, often at the expense of their own work, their family lives, their financial well-being, and their health. In fact, as his financial and marital pressures mounted, Steichen developed a nagging ulcer, which jeopardized his generally robust physical stamina.

Nonetheless, keenly attuned as he was to trends and innovations in modern art, Steichen generously promoted the work of other artists by introducing and transmitting it to American audiences at 291. Busy as he was producing and planning to show his own paintings and photographs at 291 and elsewhere, he frequently reassured Stieglitz that his work arranging Photo-Secession exhibitions by others came first. Because

THE GOSPEL OF NEW LIGHT (1909)

transoceanic communication could be frustratingly slow and expensive, it was quite a logistical feat to pull these exhibits together, and Steichen and Stieglitz exchanged long letters about them, as well as terse, economically worded cables—"OK" or "DON'T"—in answer to questions.

They were two equally stubborn perfectionists, and when necessary, they gave each other forthright advice, criticism, even reprimands. Steichen fired off an angry letter to Stieglitz when he discovered that his friend had spoken importunely to John Marin's father about the difficulties of making a successful living as a painter. As a result, the elder Marin had written a doubting letter to his son, causing him such misery that John Marin could hardly work, until Steichen sympathetically intervened.[42] He championed other artists and their freedom to do their work, in part because Steichen himself had to struggle for every hard-won hour in the studio or darkroom, had to summon immense powers of concentration to achieve the serenity and solitude crucial to the creative process.

Steichen was fighting to make a living and to improve his own work, all the while cobbling together his exhibitions of modern art—four years before the landmark Armory Show in New York, and a year before the first Post-Impressionist show in London.

During those years in Paris, there was a winter ritual: Just after Christmas, Mary and Kate would watch their father carefully pack his photographic prints and negatives and his paintings in great straw hampers. Then he would pack his trunk, kiss the family good-bye, and, carefully tending all that baggage, depart to board the steamer that would take him to New York. There, he would show and peddle his wares, hoping to make enough money to support his wife, children, and parents for another year.

Because of limited available sailing dates for the United States that December of 1909, Steichen feared he would have to spend Christmas at sea—a great disappointment, he worried in a letter to Stieglitz, because he was "old fashioned" about Christmas, which meant to him his children "and home."[43] In the end, however, he was able to book passage on December twenty-ninth. Even though by then he had already shipped the work by Marin, Craig, and Nadelman to Stieglitz, Steichen's hampers were nearly bursting with art. When he sailed for New York, he would take with him some new Rodin drawings, along with more drawings by Matisse—even though he fretted that they were not compelling enough for an exhibit.[44] He would also take a collection of his own best work because he had scheduled a one-man show of his photographs and paintings, to be held January 17–29, 1910, at the prestigious Montross Gallery at 372 Fifth Avenue, not far from 291. In the gallery at 291, Stieglitz would be exhibiting Steichen's photographs from January twenty-first until February fifth.

For the two shows and the sales he hoped they would generate, Steichen had printed limited editions of six copies each of his photographs, including the *Balzac* series, *The Flatiron,* the western series, and portraits of Anatole France, Duse, Shaw, Taft, Roosevelt, Watts, Strauss, and others. There were twenty-seven photographs in all, as well as thirty-one paintings. New paintings far exceeded new photographs in his exhibition, and they were far more personal: The enigmatic *Moonlight Dance—Voulangis* was there, surrounded by landscapes of Paris, as well as by scenes of the Morin Valley, nine in all. He also offered five vivid paintings in a series called *In Our Garden at Voulangis—White Phlox, White Lilac, Red Peonies, Nasturtiums,* and *Baby Mary.*[45]

The prospect of a reunion with Stieglitz in New York offered Steichen the "best consolation" for having to leave his family behind in Paris. Each time he looked at his two beautiful little daughters—especially Mary—he got a lump in his throat, he said. Perhaps, he teased only three months short of his thirtieth birthday, this nostalgia simply meant that he was just growing old.[46]

17

DANTON

(1 9 1 0)

... The almost brutal strength of [the photography of] Steichen with its highlight accentuation carried the mind directly to the dominating personality of Steichen himself—big, rugged, full of activity, emotional—a veritable Danton among pictorialists, a mind whose mental horizon is very broad and whose convictions are very strong and eager to force themselves on others—a man certain to make staunch friends and bitter enemies, and with all, a good fighter and one free from petty jealousies.[1]

—JOSEPH T. KEILEY

SKILLED AS HE WAS AS A painter by the time he was thirty years old, Eduard Steichen was a far more powerful photographer—"a veritable Danton among pictorialists," according to his longtime friend Joseph Keiley, the Secessionist critic, photographer, and lawyer. Georges-Jacques Danton, the eighteenth-century French revolutionary, had ultimately modulated his radical views to a more moderate philosophy, yet he was done in at the last by Robespierre during the Reign of Terror and guillotined. Those unfortunate facts aside, Keiley's curious analogy applied: Steichen was indeed "big, rugged, full of activity, emotional"—a rebel with an expansive mind, possessed of strong, aggressive, often defiant convictions about art.

For a decade, he had been pioneering with Stieglitz to establish photography once and for all as a legitimate art medium, and they had made such great strides that Stieglitz was regarded as the international leader of the modern photography movement. Steichen was hailed as a revolutionary photographer, a master of the art. He stood alone in photographic achievement in the estimation of many of his peers, and with the superb photographs of Rodin's *Balzac* he had made in 1908, he had seemed to reach the zenith of his work as a pictorial photographer. Gratifying as that was, he still wanted to become a great painter, yet by his own estimation and to his profound disappointment, he believed he had failed. His paintings were skillful, sometimes quite good, often applauded—and so commercially successful that in 1910 he was earning his living by painting more than by photography. Yet he knew, long before others, that his range was limited, and he feared that it would remain so, even if he apprenticed himself exclusively to painting.

Still, Steichen kept on painting with deep commitment in those years in Paris and Voulangis, in part because he was surrounded not by photographers but by painters and sculptors—many of whom he was also serving as American agent and advocate. Instinctively embracing the modernist spirit, he passionately appreciated and promoted the paintings of his colleagues, yet Steichen's own surviving paintings from the years in France, when painters and painting dominated his life, seem for the most part conventional, even contrived, as if he could not create on canvas the vital resonance of his photographs.

He had a fine eye for the emerging work of the pioneering modernists, especially Matisse, Marin, and Picasso. Later, he would take it upon himself to arrange groundbreaking American exhibitions of work by such giants as Cézanne and Constantin Brancusi. The bold, pioneering risk-taker in photography could immediately discern, often long before others, the originality and force of the work of other painters. But because Steichen seemed unable to express those same qualities dynamically in his own painting, there was a significant contrast between the far-reaching innovations of his photography and the inhibition of most of his paintings.

This reality, coupled with the catalytic ideas of some of his associates, had him thinking deeply about the functions of photography and painting during that time. The ongoing debate in the Steichen-Stieglitz circle about the relation of the two forms was reflected in Sadakichi Hartmann's provocative unsigned essay in *Camera Work* in October 1909, which suggested that over the years photographers and painters had imitated one another. As photographers "strenuously strove to become 'pictorial,'" painters sought "the accuracy of the camera plus a technique that was novel—and unphotographic."[2]

Steichen had recently concluded that photography should render human beings, creatures of nature, or nature itself with the exactitude made uniquely possible by the camera. He reiterated that he was drawn to Matisse and the Fauves principally because they were antiphotographic: Not only were their paintings unlike photography; these artists were doing work in painting that could *not* be done *better* in photography.[3] Despite his earlier convictions to the contrary, Steichen had concluded by 1910 that photography should not be painterly; likewise painting, he now believed, should be antiphotographic, producing original images, forms, and emotions without necessarily adhering to literal, pictorial representation. Furthermore, Steichen's long admiration of Paul Cézanne finally brought him to the view that Cézanne was the painter "who consciously took the first great step toward the complete elimination of the literal representation of objects in modern art...."[4]

For years, Steichen had merged the values and motifs of the two arts, often blurring their boundaries in the process, but now he wanted to treat them as two distinctive genres, allocating to each one the motives and subjects it could best express. Steichen had already talked with the Steins and others about these ideas, especially about the antiphotographic painting of Matisse and other modernists, and he no doubt had interesting discussions with the sculptor Elie Nadelman, whose work had excited a good deal of attention in Paris in 1909 and whose drawings Steichen had already shipped to 291. Nadelman was one of several sculptors—including Rodin, Matisse, and, later on, Brancusi—whose aesthetic principles greatly interested Steichen the photographer as well as Steichen the painter during the first two decades of his career.

Unfortunately, Nadelman's show had to be returned to Europe for an exhibition before Stieglitz could find a place for it in the crowded 291 schedule, but the essay Nadelman had written for the exhibition catalog of his drawings appeared in *Camera Work* in October of 1910. In the journal, Nadelman condemned artists who were "ignorant of *the true forms of art*," who simply copied or imitated nature and thus created only "*photographic reproductions,* not works of art." He wrote, "It is form in itself, not resemblance to nature, which gives us pleasure." Nadelman also insisted that the "true form of art" was "significant and abstract, i.e., composed of geometrical elements." While Picasso and his friend and colleague Georges Braque were at that time a little more than two years into their brilliant experiments in Cubism, they seemed to begin painting from the outside of the subject and then to work inward, dismantling the subject and in so doing creating a new spatial reality. Nadelman, to the contrary, suggested working from the inside of the subject outward: The "life of the work should come from within itself," he wrote.[5]

Steichen the photographer had long ago established his own distinctive style, but Steichen the painter was still struggling against the barriers of the traditional motifs that had always governed his work on canvas. Like Picasso and Braque, he seemed to be working from the outside inward, but without achieving their originality and power. Still, there is no doubt that Steichen was a masterful emissary for the modernist work of other painters, as the January 1910 issue of *Camera Work* revealed with the announcement of the sparkling series of exhibitions he had arranged for that year at 291.

Steichen had acquiesced to Stieglitz's request for an exhibit of his color photographs at 291 to coincide with his one-man show of paintings and photographs at the prestigious Montross Gallery. In February of 1910, the 291 gallery would display John Marin's first one-man show, including watercolors, pastels, and etchings, among them ten etchings from Voulangis. Henri Matisse's color-wash drawings, a sequel to his 1908 exhibition, as well as black-and-white photographs of a few of his paintings could be seen from February twenty-seventh until March twentieth. March would also bring the long-awaited exhibition of paintings by the group Steichen had organized, the Society of Younger American Painters in Paris: Alfred Maurer, John Marin, Steichen, Lawrence Fellows, Arthur Carles, Max Weber, and D. Putnam Brinley. Stieglitz added to the show paintings by Marsden Hartley and Arthur Dove, who was making his debut at 291. From March thirty-first until April eighteenth, viewers could see more of Rodin's provocative watercolors and drawings, forty-one in all; and December tenth would mark the opening of the exhibit of Gordon Craig's drawings and etchings.

In addition, the 1910 season would offer American art lovers their first show of lithographs by Toulouse-Lautrec, Cézanne, Renoir, and

Manet, many of which Stieglitz had first seen in the Paris galleries he had visited with Steichen the previous summer. Steichen almost single-handedly brought off this glittering parade of exhibitions, thereby staging in the ambitious little rooms at 291 Fifth Avenue a major preview of the art of the future.

He spent much of February in New York poring over every detail for the upcoming 291 season, scribbling notes for the announcements, sketching plans for mounting the pictures, taking meticulous care with the work of others as if it were his own. There were exuberant good times with the 291 crowd—Stieglitz at the center, surrounded by Steichen, the painters Marin, Hartley, Weber, and sometimes Dove, or the brilliant caricaturist Marius de Zayas and cantankerous Sadakichi Hartmann, as well as Charles Caffin and Joseph Keiley. When Steichen arrived that winter of 1910, Weber was actually living temporarily at 291, having come to Stieglitz so broke that he was homeless. Stieglitz had arranged for him to stay for a few months in a room adjoining the 291 gallery—the studio of interior decorator Stephen Lawrence, who spent long periods of time out of town. Hospitable Lawrence also let Stieglitz convert his bathroom into a darkroom, and he indulged any number of loquacious Photo-Secessionists who fled 291 on cold winter days to warm themselves at his stove. Most days, Stieglitz and his entourage would troop over to nearby Holland House or Mouquin's for lunch and more boisterous talk. The fellowship did Steichen good.

At the same time, he was putting the final touches on his one-man show at the Montross Galleries—and his work paid off handsomely, attracting most of the art critics in New York, as well as large numbers of curious viewers, and several collectors who bought paintings. Steichen was a painter of such visibility that his New York show was an event, especially with its novel juxtaposition of paintings and photographs. He was better known in Paris then, but even so, by 1910 he was one of the best-known young American painters in New York.

His work was controversial, however—but that, he found, was very good for attendance as well as for sales. Some critics deemed his paintings fresh, original, and vivacious, although others saw them as superficial and contrived. Charles Caffin linked Steichen to Cézanne, while others compared his work favorably or unfavorably to that of Whistler or Matisse or the Impressionists. Elizabeth Luther Cary of the *New York*

Times was sure that his painting was shaped by Matisse, even though Steichen "does not himself admit his discipleship to Matisse or anyone else." She found his work "highly individual," his use of color "sumptuous and barbaric." However, she thought the paintings lacked "the sense of form that penetrates the most mysterious veils of color in the work of the great masters."[6]

Photographer and critic Royal Cortissoz, writing in the *New York Tribune,* found the exhibition esoteric and disappointing. Steichen "does with the brush precisely what he does with the camera—save that he does not do it quite so well," Cortissoz wrote. "His work ... though immensely clever, seems done wholly from the outside."[7] But Steichen's show was not to be missed, according to Arthur Hoeber of the *New York Globe,* who could be searingly critical of painters. He gave this exhibit a favorable review, however, writing that he had always found Steichen "original, novel—we might say poetically socialistic!"

Hoeber and others especially praised Steichen's powerful, majestic *Across the Great Divide,* a landscape photographed and then painted after his odyssey to the southwestern United States.[8] Also popular were the nocturnes Steichen had painted in and around Paris and Voulangis, and a still life of poppies so vibrant, Hoeber wrote, that "a more brilliant result with pigment on canvas we have yet to see. It fairly radiates light and glows in its luminosity...."[9]

Offering a less enthusiastic review of Steichen's exhibition was James Huneker, then one of the most sophisticated and respected art critics in the country. While some critics thought Steichen was a painter first and then a photographer, Huneker noted in the New York *Sun* that Steichen was "better known as photographer than as painter" and had been "much of late in France." He thought that Steichen's paintings were "at their best transcripts of moods of mystic rapture in the presence of a moonlit garden or aroused by the sweep of the Garden of the Gods." But although Huneker detected some advance in Steichen's art since his 1909 exhibition, overall he considered the work too "ethereal, too impalpable," and too limited in range.[10]

Steichen's one-man Montross exhibition would be remounted December 11–31, 1910, at the Worcester Art Museum in Worcester, Massachusetts.[11] In New York, his paintings sold well and sometimes lucratively, but Steichen was always keenly aware of his limitations, and his proximity then to other serious painters only emphasized his shortcomings. Once, when he had visited Matisse in his studio in the Hôtel Biron at the corner of the Boulevard des Invalides and the Rue de Varenne in Paris, he found Matisse painting a still life of a geranium. One bloom on the plant, said Steichen, was "the most screaming, screeching, aniline-pink you could imagine. That flower's color not only actually dominated the whole studio, I thought, but should have dominated the painting...." Yet Matisse had painted the flower a "dull, drab, pinkish gray." When Steichen asked Matisse about the difference, and how and why he had chosen the color in the painting, Matisse answered simply, "I couldn't do it any other way."

In that moment, Steichen realized, "I would never have that kind of control as a painter over my materials. I would have got as near that pink as I could and *that* would have dominated my painting."[12] Control was key for him: While he could manipulate, dominate, and govern the camera, his paintings, to the contrary, defied him. There were enigmatic portraits; beautiful landscapes and still lifes, often vibrant with mood and color; an occasional abstract experiment. But surrounded as he was by the vigorous experimentation of Carles and Marin, exposed to the revolutionary new work by Matisse and Picasso, deeply influenced by the legacy of Cézanne, Steichen was fighting a losing battle to find his own vision and style.

Still, he certainly held his own among other young American painters of the day, as demonstrated by the response to his work during the 291 exhibition of the Society of Younger American Painters in Paris. These "Younger American Painters" made their collective debut at 291 on March 21, 1910, in the first display in the United States of paintings by American artists who had been clearly influenced by the European modernist painters. Stieglitz had shrewdly timed the event to open before the April 1–27, 1910, Independent Artists Exhibition—a show of the work of 103 contemporary painters and sculptors being orchestrated by artists Robert Henri and John Sloan, among others. And in part because Stieglitz deliberately jumped the gun on that rival show, the 291 exhibition garnered much attention for these new artists.

The critics chose their favorites among the 291 "Futurists," as James Huneker of the *Sun* christened them—Weber, Maurer, and Hartley for Huneker; Steichen for Stephenson of the *Post;* Weber and Steichen for

Elizabeth Carey at the *Times,* who this time liked Steichen's "barbaric force"; Marin, Maurer, and Steichen for James B. Townsend of *American Art News.* Steichen's paintings stood, by consensus, in the forefront of that controversial show. Critic B. P. Stephenson reported in the New York *Evening Post* that some of the Steichen pictures on display had not been included in his recent Montross show because Mr. Montross feared they might frighten away customers.[13]

Townsend urged art lovers "who wish to keep abreast with the spirit of the times and to know what are the new movements in art, to visit this little display by these young experimenters, these birdlings, who are trying their wings, which will be found weirdly interesting." While some of the artists, in his opinion, were the "vivisectionists of modern art," working in a "pathological art laboratory," not all the paintings were "productions of the criminal [sic] insane." He found the works of Maurer, Marin, and Steichen not only "sane" but delightful in their "richness and riot of color and sunlight" and their "delicacy of tone."[14] Sadakichi Hartmann commended the American painters as a group, noted the influences of Cézanne and Matisse, and concluded that the dominant trait of this new school was their passion for color.[15]

Steichen's paintings appeared in another group exhibition later that spring of 1910 when Montross exhibited the work of fourteen painters in April—including Steichen, Kenyon Cox, W. L. Lathrop, Childe Hassam, Elliott Daingerfield, and Arthur Wesley Dow. The "most startling" painting in the exhibit, according to James Huneker of the *Sun,* was Steichen's enigmatic *Nocturne After the Storm—Three Women.* He described it for his readers:

> *Three gaunt creatures, one nude, the others clothed in conventual [sic] robes—one may wear widow's weeds—are grouped on the edge of the world, or eternity, it doesn't matter which; a sense of illimitable space is suggested. The palette is daring. Profound blue of ultramarine, a wonderful band of green with the acid blacks and rose tint, comprise the dissonal scheme. . . . Through sheer emotion the artist has harmonized what would be in other hands harsh and unlovely hues. The symbol, what is it? An agonized soul stares through the eyes of the nude woman. We recall a similar design by the Norwegian painter Edvard Munch; a group of*

three, widow, wife and maid, but there is little of the unearthly in his picture. Whatever Mr. Steichen intends, he has made a striking, indeed poignant composition, one in which the eternal feminine is shown in a strange light.

Huneker also praised Steichen's portrait of Clara, "en plein air" in the garden at Voulangis—"a triumph of outdoor lighting. The happy, handsome lady is bathed in sunshine as she stands in her garden at Voulangis." He liked " 'The Lotus Screen,' that attractive decorative canvas," which had appeared earlier at 291, and which, riotous with purple, orange, and green, immediately evoked images of paintings by Matisse. It was set off to greater advantage in the larger Montross Gallery, however. "The woman of exotic beauty [S.S.S.—Stieglitz's sister Selma Stieglitz Schubart] still gazes at one across as she lounges in a chair. She has disquieting eyes. . . . Mr. Steichen is to be congratulated."[16] Huneker had suggested earlier that there were "potentialities as yet only hinted at in the art of Steichen."[17]

Steichen was heartened by the critical response to his work in New York that spring, and his wife would be pleased with his earnings, for he sold several thousand dollars' worth of paintings and photographs. While records do not yield the exact amount, gossip and rumor prompted speculation that Steichen realized as much as eight thousand dollars that winter and spring from the sales of his work in New York—a substantial amount of money in a time when the average American workingman earned $1.44 a day.[18]

Steichen went to Wisconsin in late March of 1910 to celebrate his success as well as his thirty-first birthday. At the Little Farm in Wisconsin, he enjoyed a reunion with Oma, Opa, and Lilian. Steichen still called his sister the Belgian nickname "Paus'l," the word his daughter Mary had earlier converted into Paula. Charmed when he heard about the child's mispronunciation, Carl Sandburg followed little Mary's lead and affectionately renamed his wife Paula, so that most people from that time on knew Lilian Steichen as Paula Sandburg. Likewise, she had renamed her husband, insisting that he reclaim his given name, Carl—much more befitting a poet, she thought, than Charles, as well as an affirmation of his Swedish roots.

Sandburg was not able to leave his work on the Social Democratic campaign in Milwaukee to join the family reunion in Menomonee Falls, however. He was using every strategy he knew as a muckraking journalist and an ardent soapbox orator to help the Wisconsin Social Democrats take over city hall in Milwaukee in the election set for April 5, 1910. Meanwhile, Paula was enjoying her own political involvement as a suffragette and precinct worker, at the same time keeping house and, to augment their austere budget, raising three hundred Plymouth Rock and Buff Orphington chickens in the yard of their little rented house on Hawley Road, on the outskirts of Milwaukee. Farming was in the Steichen blood, and Lilian had pushed hard for "three acres and liberty," until Sandburg had given in to her plan to rent a house with a yard and buy an incubator and six hundred eggs.[19]

When Sandburg and his colleagues won the hard-fought election, their victory made Emil Seidel the first socialist mayor in the United States. Hearing from his parents that Seidel had rewarded Sandburg's support by appointing him his secretary, Steichen wrote to his sister that he did not know what deserved more congratulations—the election or the chickens—and he joked that he assumed that all the chickens were socialists. He thought it was wonderful that the Social Democrats had won the election, he also wrote, especially since only a few years earlier socialists were regarded as "common & base," even "half criminal." Steichen took the socialist victory in Milwaukee as a sign that the world was, after all, a "great place."[20]

During his visit, Steichen had also heard from Lilian about the radical new poetry Sandburg was writing in the hours left over from politicking. Unlike Steichen, who already enjoyed recognition for his art on two continents, Sandburg was unknown and undiscovered as a poet, except for the publication of a handful of poems in minor journals. Intrigued by Lilian's description, Steichen urged his sister to send him some of Sandburg's new manuscripts. While he did not pretend to know anything about literature, Steichen reminded Lilian, he did have very definite opinions about what he liked, and he anticipated correctly that he would like his brother-in-law's work.

By mid-April, his business accomplished, Steichen was ready to go home to Clara and the children, and to his garden at Voulangis. "My son will sail tomorrow," Mary Steichen wrote to Clara Sandburg, Carl's mother, sadly on April 13, 1910. Once again, she had counted the days until his arrival, had cherished every moment with him during his short stay at the farm, and had wept at his leaving her for another year. Nevertheless, she was "happy to think he will be with his dear ones soon, who need him more than wee [*sic*] do."[21]

His coat pockets stuffed with presents and his bank account handsomely replenished, Steichen got an exuberant welcome home in the spring of 1910. As soon as they could get away from Paris, the four Steichens settled into their rented house at Voulangis, where, that summer more than ever before, the garden became both a paradise and a laboratory for Steichen and his children.

His curiosity about the dynamics of heredity had led him to begin crossbreeding flowers diligently during the summer of 1909.[22] Steichen began experimenting with delphiniums first because he considered them the most beautiful of all perennial garden flowers. Choosing one delphinium with a fine architecture but a pallid color, and another with poor form but brilliant color, he decided to mate the two, then eagerly waited to see what would happen. To his delight, they yielded beautifully shaped flowers colored a startling blue. He was enchanted by these initial results, so much so that from the summer of 1910 onward, Steichen was obsessively absorbed in genetics, at first hybridizing gorgeous delphiniums in his garden, then crossbreeding poppies because he wanted to transcend their already-flamboyant colors. He kept his gardener busy with those experiments, as well as with the routine work of pruning cherry trees and cultivating the plump vegetables that fed the Steichens and their friends from spring well into the fall.

Events at home inevitably jarred his peace that summer. If he and Clara were not at odds over her jealous outbursts, they were arguing about the children or almost any other matter. One day, in one awful instant, however, their arguments were dwarfed by a terrible accident. Their gardener climbed a fruit tree, as he had a hundred times before, suddenly lost his balance, and plummeted to his death. The Steichens were horrified, as well as overwhelmed by grief for the man and his family. In fact, the emotional toll of the accident left Steichen too distraught to work for months.[23] He made what financial restitution he could to the gardener's widow and children. Costly as it was, he wanted to do it, but only a technicality spared him the obligation of paying the family 40 percent of the gardener's salary for life.

For many weeks after the tragedy, unable to recapture the energy to paint or photograph, Steichen simply gave himself up instead to the healing work in his garden.

While adult problems swirled around them, Kate and Mary escaped into their delightful playground in the walled garden at Voulangis. As they grew, both little girls became ever more enchanted with music, poetry, art, and dance. In fact, when Isadora Duncan had come to visit sometime in 1909, she saw Mary's grace and beauty and immediately wanted to take her into her dance troupe. Harboring her own bitter feelings toward Duncan, Clara firmly declined the invitation, and that was the end of that.

From the age of six, Kate, like her mother and sister, wrote poetry. She also possessed a beautiful soprano voice, and she would turn out to be the musician, inheriting her mother's love for music, but with a greater talent for performance.[24] Because the Steichens chose to educate Mary and Kate at home in their earliest years, precocious Mary would be nine and Kate nearly seven before they started going to the local Catholic school, but they were continually exposed to their parents' rich cultural and artistic world, and they grew up speaking French with as much ease as English. Clara saw to it that her daughters wrote letters, diaries, and poems in both languages, and she oversaw their music lessons, while Steichen encouraged them to draw and paint with him in his studio.

The most enduring lessons their parents taught Mary and Kate no doubt came from the open dissension in their marriage. In later years, Mary had a sharp memory of Clara in the living room at Voulangis, playing the piano, weeping, and singing "My Old Kentucky Home." She was just a young wife and mother then, Mary later realized, transplanted from Missouri to France, married to Steichen, "a tremendous man, passionate, marvelous, gifted and a great womanizer."[25] As much as Mary adored and defended her father, however, she was very like her mother in temperament as well as appearance, and while the two often seemed locked in contention, Mary secretly longed to please her mother. Once, when Clara found it necessary to paddle her but did not strike her hard enough to cause pain, Mary even pretended to cry so as not to hurt her mother's feelings.[26]

"You carry your parents around with you to the day you die," Mary wrote; "you internalize a parent figure who may not be exactly like your parents but who is probably based on them, who says you should or you shouldn't. I had carried my mother around with me, then 'buried' her because she had been so damaging to me—hostile about this thing [sexuality] that was so much a part of me."[27]

Her father, on the other hand, lavished on her his love, acceptance, and companionship. "In a tree-screened corner of the garden in Voulangis," Mary wrote many years later, "he erected what must surely have been one of the world's earliest pre-fabs—a skylighted north-facing studio where oil paints held sway. I loved it and its smell of turpentine and the peace that would descend on my father as he stood in front of his easel balancing his palette and whistling his tuneless but musical little whistle under his breath."[28]

Because of the internationally visible success of the year's 291 exhibitions, Steichen suddenly found himself being "pestered to death" by artists who wanted to be included in the Secessionist shows, he wrote to Stieglitz in the autumn of 1910. They would have to take precautions not to become a "charity bazaar," however, holding out instead for the *"real real real"* in contemporary painting and photography.[29] Meanwhile, in New York, Stieglitz was getting more than his own share of pestering on the eve of a landmark Photo-Secession exhibition set to open at the Albright Art Gallery in Buffalo, New York. Because Stieglitz and Steichen had staged only one photographic exhibition at 291 in 1910—Steichen's one-man show of color transparencies—there was speculation that Stieglitz and his cohorts were losing interest in photography and moving into other venues. But in reality, Stieglitz was planning this huge international photography exhibition, at once a retrospective of the achievements of photography and an affirmation of the secure future of photography as a fine art.

The exhibit had been set in motion in 1908 when the Photo-Secessionists had been approached by Dr. Charles M. Kurtz, director of the Albright Art Gallery, about a major international show of pictorial photography. After Kurtz's death in 1909, the project was turned over entirely to Stieglitz and the Photo-Secessionists, who decided to organize both invitational and open, juried divisions for Americans and foreigners. Photographers not invited to participate could submit their work to a jury composed of Stieglitz, photographer Clarence White, critic Charles Caffin, and painter Max Weber.

As usual, controversy flared over whether Stieglitz and his Photo-Secessionist camp could choose a representative group of photographs, and many photographers threatened to boycott in protest of Stieglitz's leadership. In spite of that, almost six hundred photographs were ultimately included in the exhibition. Accompanying Stieglitz to Buffalo to hang the show were two current favorites from his inner circle, Paul Haviland and Max Weber, along with his old friend Clarence White. Steichen, of course, regretted that his return to France kept him from going to Buffalo for the exhibition, but he was very tired of the politics surrounding the event—all the "haranguing" and "theorizing" which consumed so much energy in Stieglitz's circle in New York. Still, he was confident, he told Stieglitz, that the Buffalo show would be a great success for the Photo-Secession and for Stieglitz.[30]

Indeed, more than fifteen thousand people attended the Buffalo exhibition from November third to December first in the cavernous Albright Art Gallery, which Stieglitz, Haviland, Weber, and White had imaginatively transformed into the more intimate setting the photographs needed. Although Weber had masterfully arranged the show, he was so jealous of Steichen's place in Stieglitz's affections and so scornfully critical of Steichen's art that he refused to lay a hand on Steichen's pictures and would have no part in hanging them. Stieglitz and Haviland had taken over that job, artfully arranging Steichen's photographs on a screen in the museum's largest gallery, visible from the nearby sculpture court. Visitors and critics alike naturally gravitated to them, admiring Steichen's "incomparable technique and the broad simplicity of his efforts."[31]

Of the 600 photographs on display, 250 were for sale and 65 were purchased, with the Albright Gallery buying 13 prints for its permanent collection—the first American museum ever to ratify pictorial photography in that way. Among the Albright purchases were Steichen's *Moonlight Impression from the Orangerie, Versailles Series,* a gum-bichromate print made in 1908, and Stieglitz's *The Street, Fifth Avenue,* a photogravure made in 1896. Stieglitz wrote to his old friend Ernst Juhl that with the success of the exhibit and the Albright Gallery purchase of pictures for a permanent gallery of photographs, his long-held dream had come true—"the complete acknowledgment of photography by an important institution."[32]

Sadakichi Hartmann viewed the exhibition as "a conquest," "a triumph," unexcelled "in clarity and precision of presentation."[33] He especially praised the work of Käsebier, White, Stieglitz, and de Meyer, and he put Steichen in the company of the Viennese "trifolium," the Austrian photographers Hugo Henneberg, Heinrich Kühn, and Hans Watzek, who had advanced pictorial photography in Austria and Germany.[34] Using one of his pseudonyms—Sidney Allan—Hartmann also covered the exhibit for the New York *Evening Post.* There, however, he described Steichen as a painter-photographer who manipulated his prints, a process Allan decried, since he himself was "a champion of straight photography." He did concede, however, that Steichen had achieved "great triumphs" with the gum-bichromate process.[35]

The International Exhibition of Pictorial Photography at Buffalo marked the dramatic climax of the long battle to establish photography as a respected art idiom. Stieglitz's longtime colleague Joseph Keiley, one of the ablest commentators on the history of the Photo-Secession, analyzed the significance of the Buffalo event: It had in reality been a quarter of a century in the making, he thought, and "every step of the way has been fought."[36] He praised the leadership of Stieglitz, convinced that his achievements as the champion of pictorial photography would reverberate through the history of modern art.

Keiley revisited the Buffalo exhibition on a stormy winter day when very few people ventured out. In the quiet gallery, he thought about the "vitally palpitating life" and the "creative forces" flowing from these remarkable photographs. There was the work of Clarence White, who had first seen Eduard Steichen's promise; now they were compatriots in the Buffalo show, where visitors could see Steichen's photographs, with their "almost brutal strength" and "highlight accentuation," hanging near White's prints, with their "delicate poetic charm" and musical line and light. Steichen's old friend Frank Eugene also had work in the Buffalo show. Eugene's photographs reflected his skills as painter as well as photographer, Keiley thought, and he admired the "beautiful, jovial, healthy, full-blooded life" of the man and his prints.

Alfred Langdon Coburn's prints, hanging nearby, revealed his constant experimentation with composition and design. On the other hand, there was Gertrude Käsebier; if Stieglitz was the patriarch of modern photography, she was the matriarch, and far too independent in personality and art to do anything but antagonize Stieglitz. By extension, Keiley, Stieglitz's close ally, was disapproving of Käsebier's "artistic irresponsibility and indifference to mere technique," her "curious impulsiveness" and "inner blind groping to express the protean self within." Annie W. Brigman, to the contrary, was a woman photographer who seemed "to have sought to grasp the very soul of nature," and her personality, Keiley allowed, was lost "in the poetry and charm of the themes portrayed."

Different as they were, all of these photographers, he felt, owed a debt to Stieglitz—the "central, observing, guiding mind that appeared to see and understand the evolving minds about him, and to be endeavoring to evoke from each that which was the finest and best...."[37]

From his modest base at 291, Stieglitz had indeed made an extraordinary, far-reaching contribution to modern art. He was the general, largely bound to 291 headquarters on lower Fifth Avenue in New York, relying far more than most people knew, then or later, on Steichen—Danton—who was scouting in the field, looking for the future in art, finding it, and bringing it home from Europe to 291.

Steichen and Clara were struggling so in their marriage throughout 1910 that his work showed increasing signs of the strain. Usually, his professional life afforded some respite from the turbulence of his private life, but he was so weary of their marital problems by then that flaring tempers at home inevitably spilled over into his relationships with colleagues. Generously, Stieglitz had wanted to feature Steichen's Lumière autochromes in a 1910 issue of *Camera Work*, yet Steichen was so uncharacteristically truculent about providing the negatives and guide prints that the photographs did not appear until July of 1911. On these and other matters, Steichen tested Stieglitz's patience and, it was suggested, retaliated for the fact that Stieglitz put together a 291 exhibition of the work of Dove and Hartley without consulting him.[38] But others more accurately attributed Steichen's distracted testiness to his bitter problems with Clara.

He must have recognized that two of the anchoring relationships of his life were changing dramatically and simultaneously during that time. Coincidentally, just as Steichen and Clara were growing perceptibly farther apart, Stieglitz was beginning to depend less on Steichen and to rely more and more often on others for artistic advice. It was primarily a simple matter of proximity: Steichen knew the European artists, but he was an expatriate. He and Stieglitz saw each other only twice a year, during Steichen's winter treks to New York and Stieglitz's summer journeys to Europe. But Max Weber, Paul Haviland, and others knew the European art world almost as well as Steichen did, and they were coming to New York for longer sojourns. Steichen had introduced Weber to Stieglitz in the first place, of course, and had been the first to urge Stieglitz to give Weber's work a chance at 291. Now, Weber in particular was usurping some of Steichen's authority as the expert on European modern art, bending Stieglitz's ear about the future of 291. Indeed, for a time, until the two volatile men could no longer stand each other's company, Weber urged Stieglitz toward some of the avant-garde painters beyond Steichen's circle or appreciation—chiefly Henri Rousseau, whom Weber had known during the last years of Rousseau's life, before his death in September of 1910.

Manfully, Stieglitz did try to include the feisty Weber in his world in New York, but Weber was prickly, competitive, and aggressive in his self-assurance, and easily offended. Weber alternately appreciated and resented Stieglitz's patronage, but only Steichen's steadfast insistence that Weber warranted a one-man show at 291 had guaranteed that the pugnacious artist would have such an honor in the first place. Steichen wrote that Weber was a "little fighting cock," whose beliefs were "sacred to him"—and Weber fought Stieglitz "tooth and nail."[39] Yet Stieglitz and Steichen believed in the work no matter how much the man irritated them, and they continued to promote Weber's art. Agnes and Eugene

Meyer, loyal patrons of 291, soon began to purchase Weber's paintings, paying five hundred dollars for a Weber painting in 1911.

Nevertheless, Weber had taken a keen dislike to Steichen as well as to Stieglitz. Terribly jealous of Steichen and his success as both painter and photographer, he saw him as a rival and an opportunist who exploited his own art and the art of others for commercial reasons. His vituperative charges that Steichen had sold out his art for greed foreshadowed criticism that would swirl about Steichen for the rest of his life. Weber seems to have transmitted his views to the writer Temple Scott (pen name for T. H. Isaacs), who had contributed an article to *Camera Work* in January 1910 and therefore was in touch with ongoing events at 291.[40] About that same time, Scott sketched a character based on Steichen in his thinly veiled roman à clef, *The Silver Age and Other Dramatic Memories,* a story based on Weber's life:

> *Stecker [Steichen] had succeeded in hitting the town at the Montrose Gallery, because Stecker knew the ropes. Stecker was a better business man than he was an artist. He had gone back to Paris now, to his little cottage embowered in roses, where his wife had been waiting for him during the three months of his stay in New York, and had taken with him eight thousand American dollars!**
> *No, he did not envy him. Stecker was a fine fellow and meant well. He deserved his success. Still, he was not the big man Finch [Stieglitz] thought him. He was in the swim, with the rest. . . . He was shrewd, very clever and facile as a colorist; a hard worker, and an excellent talker; but an artist! Weaver [Weber] shrugged his shoulders. He knew how to advertise. If the critics of the newspapers had sneered, they had not ignored him. And to be talked about in any way, means publicity, and publicity may become a road to success. . . .*[41]

Stieglitz tried to commiserate with Steichen about Weber's attacks, but Steichen, who frequently exercised a gift for diplomacy, shrugged off the criticism. He was not going to allow Weber's "idiosyncrasy" to trou-

---

* As earlier noted, this was most likely hearsay. Steichen's earnings for that year have not been documented, but even half this amount would have been a large sum at that time.

ble him, Steichen wrote in a long letter to Stieglitz. Actually, he did not care about Weber's opinion of him or his work, Steichen insisted. Only Stieglitz's judgment mattered to him—and Stieglitz understood his work in spirit as well as in technique. Besides, Steichen told Stieglitz, Weber was perfectly entitled to criticize his work; such criticism was "legitimate" as well as quite in keeping with the essential spirit of the Photo-Secession.[42] He did, however, regret Weber's hypocrisy in praising him to his face and attacking him behind his back, especially after Steichen had been such an aggressive advocate for Weber's talent and had encouraged Stieglitz to exhibit his work at 291.

Weber was certainly correct in observing that Steichen was a skillful businessman with a flair for advertising himself and his work. With growing expertise, born of constant necessity, Steichen aggressively promoted himself as well as others. For years, he had switched from one medium to another, sometimes painting and photographing the same subject matter with much the same results, so many variations on a theme. Many times, however, he had simply chosen the medium that was more expedient financially, and he now feared that both his painting and his photography had suffered as a result.

As is often true, Steichen sometimes underestimated the importance of what he did best—photography—and worked compulsively at what gave him more difficulty—painting. In 1910, his paintings were again accepted at the Salon d'Automne, but he disparaged the honor: His work had received good reviews, but it was meaningless, he wrote to Stieglitz, just so much puffery, and the salon itself he found appallingly mediocre.[43]

Later, he told Carl Sandburg about the ongoing daily struggle that had taken place between painter and photographer during those years in his studio and garden at Voulangis, indicating that by late 1910, the painter had taken the upper hand. "The camera is a neglected instrument," Sandburg wrote; "on tripods in a garrett [*sic*] the long-legged spiders climb. The seeker is painting—landscapes, portraits, flowers, panels, mural decorations. He is still 'finding himself.' "[44]

18

REAL FRIENDSHIP, REAL ART

(1 9 1 0 - 1 9 1 2)

Real friendship is rarer than real art—That is, heavens knows, rare enough these days.[1]

—STIEGLITZ TO STEICHEN

STEICHEN GAVE HIS OLD FRIEND AND mentor Stieglitz a special Christmas gift in 1910—a drawing Rodin had given Steichen in appreciation for his help in arranging the show at 291. This exquisite figure on horseback should really go to Stieglitz at 291, Steichen wrote, but he asked Stieglitz not to mention the gift to Rodin, for fear he would be displeased that it had been given away.[2] Stieglitz and Emmy sent their customary Christmas check to the Steichens in Paris, where Oma had joined the family for a long visit through the holiday season.

Despite the geographical distances and Stieglitz's new reliance on Haviland and Weber in New York, the personal lives of the Steichens in France and the Stieglitzes in the United States were still as interwoven as if they were family. Eduard and Clara and Alfred and Emmy were especially close, despite their infrequent times together and their parallel sagas of marital discord. Over the years, the Steichens helped the Stieglitzes with arrangements for their pilgrimages to Europe, entertained them in Paris and Voulangis, introduced them to friends, and looked their after baggage and mail.

REAL FRIENDSHIP, REAL ART (1910–1912)

Steichen tried to persuade Alfred and Emmy to rent a comfortable house in Voulangis for the summer of 1911, and he even promised to help find a cook. Kitty Stieglitz, although six years older than Mary, was a favorite playmate of the Steichen children whenever she came to France, and Steichen thought the countryside and the companionship of his lively daughters would be especially good for Kitty. However, Emmy still preferred luxurious hotels, and Kitty loved going with her governess, Clara, for long, relaxed visits to Clara's home in the German village of Gifstein. "I really think Clara's home is much nicer than Mrs. Steichen's," Kitty had written to her parents one summer.[3]

For Steichen, feeling increasingly expatriated, and always hungry for news from New York, Stieglitz's letters were the vital channel for information and gossip.[4] Stieglitz likewise depended on Steichen's vivid accounts of artistic events in Europe, and he sternly reprimanded Steichen when he let too long a time elapse between letters. He was sending Stieglitz a continual stream of ideas for more new exhibits at 291, still pressing for a show of Picasso's drawings and paintings because he knew it would stir up the sort of controversy he and Stieglitz loved to generate in New York.[5] Steichen also proposed an exhibit of Cézanne watercolors, a collection of fourteenth- and fifteenth-century Persian paintings, and a show of Steuben glass.[6] He promised he could provide anything else Stieglitz might want.

For several months, they carried on their transoceanic debate about the upcoming season at 291. By year's end, Steichen had changed his mind about the Picasso show, however, perhaps fearing that because Picasso suddenly was highly visible in Europe, he would not be such a novelty after all. More likely, however, it was because Steichen, like many others, was mystified by the new paintings being created by Picasso and his friend Georges Braque.[7]

These were the days before Picasso's great acclaim, when he was constantly experimenting in his studio in Paris; in fact, when he and Braque began their experiments in Cubism in Paris in 1907, neither artist was as well known there as Steichen. By some accounts, it may have been Henri Matisse who christened their radical new approach to painting, evident in the six abstract landscapes Braque had submitted to the Salon d'Automne in 1908. Matisse, serving on the jury that emphatically rejected all six, reportedly exclaimed that Braque was just "making little cubes." Later, when Braque succeeded in showing his work in a Paris gallery, critic Louis Vauxcelles had noted that he had reduced "everything, places and figures and houses, to geometric schemes, to cubes," and he soon referred to Braque's style as Cubist, which had become a standard term by 1909.[8]

By 1910, Picasso was painting Cubist portraits as well as Cubist still lifes, revealing, as critic Leon Werth wrote, "their structure, substructure, and superstructure."[9] The paintings were attracting excited attention in Paris, Budapest, Düsseldorf, Munich, Berlin, and London. There had been so much exposure of Picasso's work that Steichen suggested they wait a year before showing it at 291, but Stieglitz wanted to go ahead with the exhibition.[10]

Consequently, Steichen helped Picasso and artist Frank Burty Haviland (Paul Haviland's brother) make the final selections so they could demonstrate the evolution of Picasso's work—from the earliest to the latest examples. Steichen had admired Picasso's nudes and his harlequin studies, but he frankly did not like the new Cubist style. Steichen himself had experimented with Matisse's Fauvist use of color and form, and had listened to his statement that "there is an inherent truth which must be disengaged from the outward appearance of the object to be represented. This is the only truth that matters."[11] In essence, Picasso and Braque were striving for that "only truth that matters" in their fracturing of literal reality, just as Matisse himself was challenging conventional concepts of color. Yet neither Steichen nor Matisse, whom Picasso was beginning to regard as a rival, could grasp the new forms coming from Picasso's fervent brush.

In his own painting, Steichen seemed more at home with surfaces than with depths, yet he aspired to render light and color as he believed only Cézanne had been able to evoke it on canvas, and to achieve contour and form as Rodin felt it in his palm and kneading fingers. From the first moment in Rodin's studio ten years earlier, Steichen had grasped the sculptor's perspective—his opulent, passionate realism, his hands evoking breath from stone. But Picasso's Cubism baffled him, Steichen confided to Stieglitz in a long letter. Unlike the earlier work, which he had admired, he found the new paintings all inscrutable "angles" and "lines" and the "wildest" work he had ever seen.[12]

At the Steins' salons, Steichen saw the young Spaniard frequently and studied his evolving art in the Steins' collection. He knew Gertrude's great affection for the man as well as her passion for his paintings. Still, Steichen confessed to Stieglitz that while he found Picasso an "extraordinary chap," he absolutely could not fathom these new paintings.[13] He deplored Picasso's limited use of color and the growing abstraction in his recent work—especially a Cubist charcoal entitled *Nude Woman*, drawn in Cadqués in the summer of 1910.[14] Steichen supposed he was just too "sensitive to flesh" to comprehend that study, he remarked in his letter to Stieglitz, but he had included it in the Picasso exhibition, and when Stieglitz saw it in New York, it so intrigued him that he bought it for his own collection.[15]

Steichen asked Stieglitz not to share his opinions about Picasso's work with anyone else in the Photo-Secession circle, for he did not want to prejudice them in any way. Rather, he wanted them to see the radical work of this still relatively unknown twenty-nine-year-old painter and to judge it for themselves.

Conscientiously, meticulously, as was his habit with all the artwork he gathered for 291, Steichen oversaw in Paris all the arrangements for Pablo Picasso's first exhibition in the United States, arguably his first major one-man show anywhere.[16] Scheduled to open at 291 on March 28, 1911, it included eighty-three watercolors and drawings. Perhaps Picasso was becoming a great artist, Steichen told Stieglitz before the exhibition, but he confessed that he could not honestly say he saw it yet.[17]

When Steichen traveled to New York on his annual winter business trips, he stayed with various members of the Stieglitz clan in New York. At times, he was the houseguest of Stieglitz's wealthy brother-in-law Joe Obermeyer. He teased Lilian Steichen Sandburg about having a valet to care for him at the Obermeyer home, promising his socialist sister that he did not abuse the privilege and saying that if anything, Middleton, the valet, was his superior.[18]

Frequently over the years, he stayed with Agnes and Eugene Meyer when he was in New York. While he continued to enjoy a warm friendship with Agnes, he was growing even closer to her husband. Twelve years older and slightly shorter than his beautiful wife, Eugene Meyer was, at thirty-five, a self-made millionaire. Steichen and others had thought at first that this was an incongruous match in many ways. Eugene's parents were Jewish immigrants, while Agnes's grandfather and two uncles were German Lutheran clergymen, although her father was the "black sheep in his clerical family."[19] The wealthy, influential Meyers might have expected a better match for Eugene than this outspoken young woman, daughter of a man who was flagrantly and chronically in debt.

Some people speculated that ambitious Agnes had married Meyer for his money. But from the moment Meyer had first laid his appreciative eyes on Agnes Ernst in 1908 at the America Art Galleries on Twenty-third Street in New York, he knew she was the woman he wanted to marry. He relished her feisty intelligence as well as her beauty, and he shared her informed passion for art, so much so that both of them considered it perfectly fitting that they had met in an art gallery. From the first, he had courted her shrewdly, becoming a welcome and generous member of her avant-garde circle in Paris during her months as a student. There, he was the charming host for restaurant dinners and excursions to the theater, which had been great luxuries for Agnes and her bohemian friends, including Eduard and Clara Steichen.

The Meyers had turned to their friend Steichen for Agnes's wedding pictures, and he gladly obliged. She was twenty-three when she married Eugene Meyer on February 12, 1910, two years to the day after they first saw each other. Immediately after their wedding, Eugene had paid off all of his new father-in-law's sizable debts. After a week at Meyer's farm at Mount Kisco, New York, accompanied by a valet and a maid, the couple set off on an extravagant round-the-world honeymoon, embarking in a fancy private railroad car for the Grand Canyon, Los Angeles, and San Francisco. From there, they embarked on a prolonged cruise to Japan, Korea, China, Java, and India. They would then go on to Europe.

While his wife looked at works of art, Meyer did business in every port. Since he held large investments in copper stock, he was, he said, "hell-bent on fixing up the copper business," which was in trouble then.[20] They traveled on the Trans-Siberian Railroad to southern Manchuria and on to Moscow by private car. By the time they reached Berlin and Paris in June of 1910, Agnes was suffering morning sickness. They re-

Real Friendship, Real Art (1910–1912)

turned to the United States in August of 1910, and their first child, Florence, was born in 1911. Because Meyer had begun financing Agnes's love of art even before their marriage, she quickly made herself at home with her husband's huge fortune. They soon became the first significant patrons of the artists of 291.

The Meyers traveled to Europe in the winter of 1911 to buy furniture and art for the new house they had bought at Park Avenue and Seventieth Street in New York. They asked Steichen to join them in London to counsel them about art purchases as they began to build a superb, eclectic collection. They absolutely trusted Steichen's advice and instincts about what they should buy; furthermore, they commissioned him to create murals to decorate the foyer of their new town house. The project would engage much of his energy as a painter for the next three years. He no doubt talked it over with Matisse, knowing that his friend had received a lucrative commission in 1909 to create *Dance* and *Music,* two large murals for a Russian patron. Matisse had advanced the art of decorative painting, and had also discovered that working on the spacious canvases of the murals enlarged the scope and vision of his other paintings.

In January of 1911, Steichen and Stieglitz were finishing plans for Cézanne's first one-man show in the United States, to open at 291 in March. While they had included some of Cézanne's lithographs in a group exhibition at 291 in the late winter of 1910, along with lithographs by Manet, Renoir, and Toulouse-Lautrec, the all-Cézanne exhibit to be held March 3–25, 1911, would introduce his beautiful watercolors to an American audience.

Several years earlier, not long after Cézanne's death in 1906, the Steichens and the Stieglitzes had ventured out in a thunderstorm to see an exhibit of Cézanne's watercolors at the Bernheim-Jeune Gallery in Paris. Stieglitz later described the experience in the storm-darkened gallery: As he stood before such landscapes as *Mont Ste-Victoire, 1904–06,* he saw "what appeared to be hundreds of pieces of blank paper with scattered blotches of color on them." Steichen persuaded Stieglitz to inquire about the prices.

"A thousand francs?" Stieglitz asked incredulously when he heard the answer. "You must mean a dozen. There is nothing there but empty paper with a few splashes of color." Elsewhere in the gallery, Steichen,

Clara, and Emmy laughed at Stieglitz. "I knew I had been absurdly stupid," he remembered. "To be truthful, my remarks resulted from my having been flabbergasted by the pictures."

Later, in a nearby café, Steichen proposed that they play a joke on the critics in New York. "I can make a hundred watercolors like those at Bernheim's in a day," Steichen told Stieglitz. "They were not signed. I needn't sign mine. You can announce, 'Exhibition of Watercolors by Cézanne.'"

"It's a go," Stieglitz agreed, laughing at the prospect. "Anything to try out the critics. Once they have written, I shall tell the public the practical joke we have played." But Steichen suddenly turned serious and withdrew his offer. "I guess I had better not," he said, and, for the time being, they dropped the idea.[21]

While the Stieglitzes were in Paris during the summer of 1909, Steichen and Alfred had attended another Cézanne show at the Bernheim-Jeune Gallery. They "laughed like country yokels" as they foresaw "what a red rag this would be in New York."[22] Afterward, Steichen had worked doggedly for months on the arrangements to bring Cézanne's work to 291 for his debut in the United States, finally telegraphing Stieglitz on January 24, 1911, that he had just shipped twenty Cézanne watercolors on the *Savoie*.[23] They were a "fine lot," he reported, and he planned to ship the Picasso show on the next boat.[24]

"Art is the taking of the essence of an object or experience and giving it a new form so that it has an existence of its own and an essence of its own," Steichen later told Carl Sandburg.[25] While he did not fully appreciate the radical new forms expressed in Picasso's Cubism, Steichen had immediately comprehended the essence of Cézanne's work—his superb use of color, light, and form to reveal the complicated contours of the world, its mysterious depths and ragged edges as well as its smooth skin.

Steeped in Cézanne's work, Steichen longed to own one of his paintings, but lacking the funds to buy one, he urged Eugene Meyer to buy a Cézanne still life, thrilled to think that if he did so, the United States would have a Cézanne.[26] "Eugene cabled Steichen to buy the still life yesterday," Agnes wrote to Stieglitz. She thought it was "marvellous."[27]

His own marriage in a constant state of uproar, Steichen thought that the Meyers were a "great team."[28] He was glad for the time with them in London, for as he accompanied them to choose English furniture, he gained a much clearer sense of their tastes and, therefore, of the kind of murals he should design for their new house in New York. In fact, after the trip, he discarded some preliminary plans for the decorations and started anew. He also used the time with the Meyers to urge Eugene to become an "active member" of the Photo-Secession and to provide some financial support, especially for worthy painters such as John Marin, whose work Steichen encouraged the Meyers to purchase next.[29]

Despite his avowed weariness with the politics of photography, Steichen took a great interest in advising the newly formed London Secession that winter, especially after spending time in London in February of 1911 with portly Child Bayley and "charming" George Davison, the gifted photographer who had served as his host on previous trips to London, and who had made a fortune as a founding director and investor in England's Eastman Photographic Materials Company.[30] English photographer Malcolm Arbuthnot had written to Stieglitz in 1910, seeking his help in countering the fractious politics of the Linked Ring by forming an international society of photographers. As matters stood, Arbuthnot reported, a "small band of British workers" remained "homeless" and needed an organization and a purpose. He sought Stieglitz's advice as to their "best course."[31]

On the scene in 1911, Steichen no doubt spoke for Stieglitz when he talked the group out of trying to establish a permanent photographic gallery immediately, encouraging them instead to proceed slowly as he and Stieglitz had done with the Little Galleries of the Photo-Secession. After listening to Steichen, the London photographers decided to exhibit about forty-five prints in a small gallery in May, work by the London Secessionists: J. Craig Annan; the American Alfred Langdon Coburn, then living permanently in London; Arbuthnot and Davison; Baron Adolf de Meyer, and others. The "camera workers" in other countries invited to submit three prints each included Clarence White, Frank Eugene, Annie W. Brigman, Gertrude Käsebier, Fred Holland Day, Heinrich Kühn, George Seeley, Stieglitz, and Steichen. For once Stieglitz, who rarely exhibited his work, agreed to send prints to the London Secession show.[32]

Steichen had promised his "best assurance of the acceptance of these invitations," Arbuthnot wrote in his announcement of the exhibition, which was held at the Newman Art Gallery in London May 10–June 3, 1911, and then moved on to Liverpool.[33] Steichen helped the London group mount and frame the photographs, for he wanted them to emulate the tasteful, uncluttered style of 291 exhibits. The London Secessionists would not prompt a serious revival of pictorial photography in England, Steichen told Stieglitz, but he thought it prudent to help sustain a "nice little fire" in the event that Stieglitz ever needed a base for a foreign show of Photo-Secession photographs. Most of all, Steichen wanted to see the Photo-Secession at last become international in its visibility and scope.[34]

As it happened, the international influence of 291 in New York reached a controversial climax when the Cézanne show—twenty watercolors—opened at 291 on March 1, 1911. People "laughed their heads off," Steichen remembered.[35] Despite Stieglitz's first reaction to Cézanne's work in Paris, Steichen and Weber had both praised Cézanne's art so long and so fervently that when Stieglitz unpacked the watercolors for the March show, he took another, more careful look. To his surprise, he found the paintings "no more nor less realistic than a photograph." Moreover, Stieglitz thought them "as beautiful a lot" as he had ever known, and he predicted that Cézanne's pictures would become immensely fashionable and very expensive.[36]

The English critic Clive Bell had already hailed Cézanne as the "Christopher Columbus of a new continent of form," but it was a mark of the cultural lag between continents that when the Cézanne exhibition opened, New York was not impressed.[37] After all, until Steichen sent the Cézanne paintings to 291, the only Americans who had actually seen the artist's work were those people fortunate enough to get to Europe, where Cézanne, just five years after his death, was still controversial and too unorthodox even for the far more sophisticated European audiences. "Of all the exhibitions we had at 291, this one was probably the most sensational and the most outrightly condemned," Steichen wrote later. "Of course, appreciators of avant-garde art thought it was the best we had ever had."[38]

Steichen and Stieglitz played a mischievous joke on the curious and unsuspecting art patrons who came to see the exhibit that March. For some time, Steichen had "been haunted" by their earlier idea of testing the critics and the 291 audience by painting a fake Cézanne. Just before the show, for the fun of it, he created a painting that was not a copy of a particular picture, but a landscape "in the style of the Cézanne watercolors," as abstract as anything Steichen had seen in Paris.[39] As bemused visitors flocked to 291 for Cézanne's show, they paid particular attention to Steichen's pseudo-Cézanne, hanging innocently among the authentic paintings. Agnes Meyer remembered that "it was the most popular picture in the exhibition."[40] There were even several interested buyers, but Steichen quickly told them that this painting was on loan, not for sale.

Not since he was a small boy copying a tulip in his art class had he created a fraud, and now, as then, he found it very disturbing. "I was petrified by the whole experience," he remembered. "I burned the fake as soon as I could get my hands on it, and only then did I breathe freely again." He was ashamed of himself for perpetrating such a prank, and disappointed that there were so many people who fell for his hoax. For him, it was not his own skill as a painter that had brought off the deception, but the gullibility of art patrons who "pretended to appreciate things they didn't really understand."[41]

The fuss over the highly publicized Cézanne show was quickly followed by an uproar—"a frenzy and a fury," Steichen called it—over Picasso's eighty-three drawings and watercolors.[42] In the *New York Globe*, outspoken Arthur Hoeber expressed the majority opinion of the Picasso exhibit:

The display is the most extraordinary combination of extravagance and absurdity that New York has yet been afflicted with, and goodness knows it has had many these two seasons past. Any sane criticism is entirely out of the question; any serious analysis would be in vain. The results suggest the most violent wards of an asylum for maniacs, the craziest emanations of a disordered mind, the gibberings of a lunatic![43]

Picasso's first American exhibition was a dismal failure, critically and financially. Because Steichen and Stieglitz were always intent on revealing the evolution of the work of any artist they exhibited, Steichen, Haviland, and de Zayas had carefully chosen Picasso's eighty-three drawings, watercolors, and etchings to illustrate his journey from the beginning to his current absorption in Cubism. But despite the huge, curious crowd attending the show, only two of the pieces sold. A pencil drawing done by Picasso when he was only twelve was purchased for twelve dollars, and Stieglitz, now a convert, paid sixty-five dollars for Picasso's Cubist drawing entitled *Nude*.

Stieglitz remembered years later that he had urged an official at the Metropolitan Museum of Art to buy the entire collection of Picasso's work displayed at 291, especially since it so vividly depicted Picasso's growth as an artist. But the man replied that "he saw nothing in Picasso and vouched that such mad pictures would never mean anything to America." It was a decision Stieglitz deeply regretted, believing that "at the time the collection could have been had for $2,000."[44] He would press the cause of modern art further in 1911 by urging the Metropolitan to sponsor an exhibition of Cézanne's work, saying, "Without the understanding of Cézanne—and this one can get only through seeing his paintings, and the best of them—it is impossible for anyone to grasp, even faintly, much that is going on in the art world today."[45] But no one listened to him that time, either.

The crowds kept coming to 291, even if they did not like everything they found there. They came in such numbers that Steichen and Stieglitz wondered in 1911 whether they should try to hang on to the now-legendary galleries, since they were rapidly outgrowing the space. Bursting with ideas for new exhibitions—including a show of Arthur Carles's paintings—Steichen turned his own energies once again to both photography and painting.

Immersed in studies for the Meyer murals, he took on another new challenge when Lucien Vogel, publisher of the chic French journals *Jardin des Modes* and *La Gazette du Bon Ton,* dared him to use his camera to promote fashion as a fine art.[46] Steichen experimented with photographs of gowns designed by the great Paris couturier Paul Poiret, and the pictures were published in the April 1911 edition of *Art et Décoration,* to illustrate an article entitled "L'Art de la Robe," written by Paul Cornu. Steichen's dark soft-focus photographs of posed models highlighted the textures of the fabrics and hinted at the design of the dresses they wore. He was intrigued with this evocative as well as practical dimension of photography. Back in Milwaukee fifteen years earlier, he had transformed the advertising graphics in his lithographic firm by photographing real pigs rather than relying on the customary woodblock illustrations. Now he enjoyed this striking new use of his camera, supplanting conventional fashion sketches with stylish photographs. He was too engaged in painting to take the fashion photography experiment further in 1911, but he would return to it later on, with results he could not have foreseen.

Checks from the Meyers for his ongoing work on the murals now provided the Steichens with their primary source of income. Steichen was no stranger to murals, for in addition to Matisse's work, he had been exposed to that of the old German panorama painters in Milwaukee. In addition, he had loved the innovative work of the Viennese decorative artists—especially the Austrian painter Gustav Klimt, who had founded the Vienna Secession school of painting, and he knew about Klimt's erotic, allegorical turn-of-the-century murals, which had been banned by the University of Vienna. At the Salon d'Automne of 1910, which included two of Steichen's own paintings, the exhibition of paintings was overshadowed by the sumptuous decorative arts section, featuring the work of Munich artists. Although they were good, Steichen had reported to Stieglitz at the time, they did not come near the work of the Viennese decorative artists Josef Hoffmann and Klimt.[47]

The elaborate art of decorative murals engaged Steichen's rapt attention because, in addition to the Meyer project, he had recently been commissioned by the French government to paint a mural interpreting the American spirit through vignettes of New York.[48] But his head was full of visions for the Meyer murals, and he was driving himself hard to execute them. These were dear friends as well as patrons, after all, and if necessary, he would let photography and all other matters go, putting the Meyer murals first.

As always, he set his work aside when Stieglitz was in France, and in May of 1911, Stieglitz, Emmy, and Kitty arrived, planning to stay in Europe until October. For once, Stieglitz would be in Paris at a time when he could see for himself the exhibitions—the Champs de Mars Salon, the Salon des Indépendants, the Salon d'Automne—that for so long Steichen had urged him to see. In the autumn of 1911, Stieglitz spent three extraordinary weeks in Paris, visiting Picasso, Matisse, Rodin,

Gordon Craig, and others, escorted by de Zayas or Steichen, or both.⁴⁹ Steichen took Stieglitz to see Matisse (who looked more like a mathematics professor than an artist, Stieglitz thought) in his austerely furnished Paris studio. That day, Stieglitz tried to purchase a "magnificent flower piece" for five thousand francs, only to learn that Matisse had already sold it, for far less, to a Russian collector.⁵⁰ He declined Matisse's offer to paint another one for him.

In Matisse's dining room, Stieglitz was surprised to find a row of twelve exquisite Cézanne watercolors. Matisse explained that while he ate his breakfast, he was "constantly contemplating these watercolors." Matisse told Steichen and Stieglitz, "They are my teachers for the present."⁵¹

Stieglitz left Steichen and Paris convinced anew of the landmark importance of the 291 shows, he told Sadakichi Hartmann. He thought Steichen was "growing fast" in his work. As for himself, Stieglitz believed he had experienced one long "crescendo" of a year—the Buffalo show, all the exhilarating shows at 291, and the three glorious weeks in Paris—undoubtedly "the most remarkable year" in his career.⁵²

Stieglitz went home, however, deeply worried about Steichen and Clara. The tension between them was palpable. Clara needed constant reassurance of her husband's love and loyalty, and she continually tested him, making barbed comments, demeaning and criticizing him, trying to provoke quarrels with him in the presence of their friends. And Steichen, plagued by the need to support his family in France and in Wisconsin, desperately craved rest, peace, uninterrupted hours alone in his work so he could gain control of the "chaos of ideas" in his mind—but that was not to be.⁵³

Yet he tried to put the best face on his situation. Clara was nervous and not "up to scratch physically," he wrote to Stieglitz near the end of 1911, but he assured him that otherwise all was well and that his garden at Voulangis was richly abloom with chrysanthemums.⁵⁴ Deny and divert—those seemed to be his tactics, not only in his letters but also in his daily life. Deny the seriousness of the domestic problems. Divert attention elsewhere—to his garden, to his art, to the art of others.

Real Friendship, Real Art (1910–1912)

Arthur Carles, Steichen's closest friend in France, got his exhibition at 291 in January of 1912, thanks to Steichen. The show of this American artist was followed by an exhibit of recent paintings and drawings by Marsden Hartley and then paintings and pastels by Arthur G. Dove, his debut one-man show. Then, in March of 1912, Henri Matisse was in the spotlight at 291 for the third time. "His bronzes and drawings are hitting people hard," Stieglitz wrote to Alvin Langdon Coburn, but most American critics were not impressed.[55] "Matisse is here at the Photo-Secession Galleries to indicate to the public his independence of his followers," wrote Elizabeth Carey in the *New York Times*. "A gothic fondness for the hideous is one of his links with mediaevalism."[56]

Stieglitz was counting his successes that spring, a "continuous series of triumphs," he wrote to Child Bayley. During the past seven years, he estimated, 160,000 people had visited the gallery, to encounter not only the newest, most radical European and American artworks but something more—an idea and a spirit. He was excited by advances in painting and sculpture, but photography was a different case. While he found that the old photographs of Steichen, White, Eugene, Coburn, Demachy, and a handful of others gave him even more pleasure in 1912 than they had in earlier years, Stieglitz did not see any growth in pictorial photography. Gertrude Käsebier, he carped, had "degenerated into a regular commercial factory." Clarence White, busy teaching to earn a living, had failed to develop intellectually. Frank Eugene was a great success in Munich, but he devoted too much of his time to painting and teaching, Stieglitz felt. And Stieglitz thought Steichen was not paying attention to photography.[57] Even worse, in Stieglitz's view, Steichen was working on the Meyer murals, doing decorations for money, not art for art's sake.[58]

The most frequent visitors to the Steichens' house and garden at Voulangis were Arthur and Mercedes Carles and Agnes Ernst Meyer, who brought into the intimate Steichen circle two artist friends, Katharine Rhoades and Marion Beckett. As Agnes herself described them, they were "two of the most beautiful young women that ever walked this earth."[59] The three of them made such a striking trio—classically beautiful, fashionably dressed, brimming with charm, energy, and talent—that they were christened the "Three Graces." Tall, elegant Katharine, the daughter of a wealthy New York family, had studied at the Brearley School in New York. After her father's sudden death, she had traveled in Europe in 1909 with two classmates, sculptor Malvina Hoffman and painter Marion Beckett, a gentle, lovely young woman from a distinguished family in New York. Despite her instinctive possessiveness and jealousy, Clara seemed to like and trust Katharine and Marion, at least at the outset, and she formed a particularly close friendship with Marion. In fact, she soon came to consider "the girls," as she called them, her best friends.

From 1910 until 1914, almost any summer day at the Steichens' Villa L'Oiseau bleu in Voulangis would have looked idyllic to one who did not know the subtexts and undercurrents playing out in the languid air. The garden was filled with beautiful women, handsome men, lively talk, a drift of piano music from the house, the fragrant opulence of Steichen's flowers, the exuberance of his daughters. Arthur and Mercedes Carles often were there, both of them talented and dramatic, although their gifts were already being dissipated by his drinking and womanizing. Katharine Rhoades also visited, always painting, writing poetry, and searching for her true self. Her quiet, more serious friend Marion Beckett painted there, and gently befriended Steichen's wife and children. Agnes Meyer would breeze in, at first with Eugene, but then alone on her self-indulgent jaunts to Europe, leaving her husband and their growing brood of children to be cared for by servants in New York. Marsden Hartley came, as did John Marin and other artists, as well as various members of the large Stieglitz clan, passing through for a day or two. Clara still perennially complained that she ran a pension for their friends—and she was beginning to think that most of them were her husband's friends, not hers.

Beginning in 1910, in those innocent summers before World War I, the garden at Voulangis was the scene of happy annual reunions, of leisurely luncheons amid Steichen's flowers, of starlit summer evenings of talk, music, and laughter. Over time, Steichen, Carles, Marion, and Katharine drew, painted, and photographed one another.

For Katharine, Steichen's garden in Voulangis was one of the happiest places on earth. Agnes Meyer, like all of the Steichens' many friends, found tranquillity and warm hospitality in the Steichens' "peasant house and lovely garden."[60] But it was not an Eden. Rumors floated about in the Stieglitz circle in later years that Steichen had been attracted to Katharine Rhoades, although there is no surviving evidence to confirm a romance.[61] But from the moment they were thrown together in 1910, he was clearly fond of Marion Beckett, the more reserved of the trio of "Graces." So was Clara, however, and at least for a time, she felt secure enough in Marion's friendship not to see her as a threat. In fact, the most pleasant hours Steichen and Clara spent together then usually came in the company of congenial friends. When there were no guests at Villa L'Oiseau bleu to buffer him from his wife, Steichen came and went frenetically, and when he did stay at home, he lost himself in work or in play with his daughters.

In later years, Mary Steichen came to believe that her father was, "like many artists, a living contradiction in terms: the hardnosed realist he insisted on becoming in photography seemed the direct opposite of the romanticist whose heart melted, eyes misted, and voice caught whenever he thought, spoke of or dealt in any way with painting, children, dogs or cats, beauty in any form...."[62] He loved his children and his flowers passionately—and his cats, horses, dogs. He would write to Stieglitz at one point that the whole family was doing fine, except for the dog—and that upset him, he said, "more than is good for any of us."[63]

At Voulangis, he always threw himself headlong into the redeeming work of cultivating and breeding his flowers. He was also photographing plant forms and painting flowers. With his garden blooming profusely under his tender, skillful hands, he had intensified his serious study of the literature of plant breeding, seeking out every new publication on the subject. In the summer of 1909 Steichen had bought a dozen varieties of delphinium from Victor Lemoine, who had originated them, and he purchased seeds for another dozen varieties produced by James Kelway & Sons in England. In 1912, Steichen acquired seeds directly from horticulturist Luther Burbank, who was then carrying on his experiments with vegetables, fruits, and flowers in California.

Believing he must specialize in his genetic experiments, Steichen decided to concentrate on his three favorite flowers—the delphinium first, because he thought it the most beautiful of all perennials. He could already see from his experiments that there were unlimited possibilities for future hybrids. He chose poppies not only because of their vivid beauty but because Burbank believed they afforded new ways of breeding a perennial to an annual species.[64] During those years, Steichen meticulously re-created certain mutations that Dutch botanist and geneticist Hugo de Vries (1848–1935) had achieved with poppies.[65] But he especially loved petunias, his favorite annual, the "most generous of blooming plants," and excellent material for testing Mendel's theories about improving and fixing seed strains.[66]

Steichen's passion for art and for flowers was everywhere evident at Voulangis. His spacious prefabricated studio, screened by trees in a corner of his garden, provided the privacy and room needed for his larger paintings. In fact, he liked it so well that he had recommended it to Matisse, who built a similar one. When she was not playing with Kate, Mary loved painting with her father in that garden studio. Steichen gave Mary her very own watercolor kit, equipped, as she remembered it, with "little solid cubes of wonderful colors with the same glorious names as the ones on his palette: Prussian, Ultramarine or Cobalt blue, Gamboge . . . Malachite green, Brunt [sic] Sienna, Raw Umber, Yellow Umber, and of course the reds." Content in her father's studio, Mary would sit "transfixed" before her treasure box of colors, rolling "those strange and magical names" over her tongue, choosing which ones to rub on her own wet brush.[67]

Mary was the beneficiary of her father's fascination with color. In his early days as a painter, Steichen had been more at home with a subdued palette of browns and grays, in part because he had been influenced by and had written about the French painter and lithographer Eugène Carrière and his misty renditions of nudes, of mothers and their children, and of such great men as Rodin.[68] Those quieter hues were also, of course, the only photographic colors until the Lumière plates afforded the photographer the range of the rainbow.

Time, technology, and the example of painters such as Cézanne and Matisse had liberated Steichen to embrace vibrant color, and so had his garden at Voulangis, just as it had freed Marin, Carles, and other visiting painters to abandon their drabber early work for the brilliance of sunlight and flowers. Increasingly, Steichen's garden became a source of artistic and personal fulfillment, a sanctuary from all pressing demands

REAL FRIENDSHIP, REAL ART (1910–1912)

of life. There he could carry out his ongoing experiments in form, color, and value in three media—his paintings, his photographs, and his plants. As he continued to grapple with new forms in painting and photography, however, his frustration mounted, for he was splitting his creative energy, allocating part of it to a new reality in his photographs, part to a quest for abstraction in his paintings, and part—the compelling, commercially driven part—to working on the decorative panels for Agnes and Eugene Meyer.

As his domestic life and his art—especially his painting—confronted him with more intense challenges, Steichen kept on searching obsessively for control, for order, for harmony. He would conceive a new painting, only to have its execution defy and disappoint him. Even if he succeeded, who would buy it in the end? he wondered. Like the old days in New York, when customers asked him repeatedly for photographs in the Steichen style, gallery owners and others who bought his paintings now wanted only his familiar romantic landscapes or still lifes.

Worse than the professional frustrations, the wife he loved had somehow been transformed into an unpredictable stranger. He hardly knew what to expect from Clara anymore, and he dreaded the capricious, violent outbursts that kept him and the children constantly on guard. Only his photography and his flowers seemed safe haven, usually responding to the touch of his hand as he dreamed they would. With hard work, he could transform and transmute nature itself in his flower garden. With his camera, he could record the fruits of his work. Nature, he realized more than ever, was the key to creativity. From the aging master Rodin, he took a defining principle: "All art not based on nature is tommyrot, bluff, blague."[69] Steichen held fast to that certainty.

During that "Flower Year," flowers inevitably became a unifying motif in the ambitious and lucrative project he had undertaken for Eugene and Agnes Meyer. As he worked for months to create the mural for their Park Avenue foyer with its spiral stairs, he found his ultimate theme and design in his garden. He would paint women and flowers—beautiful women embodying the flowers, the flowers, in turn, symbolizing life and beauty. Eagerly he set to work on *In Exaltation of Flowers,* choosing the friends and the flowers in his Voulangis garden as models. The project would take years to finish, but Agnes Meyer, Marion Beckett, and Katharine Rhoades gladly posed for him. It is not clear whether Clara modeled for the mural at the beginning, or if she refused, but he surely would have asked her.

Katharine and Marion spent part of the summer of 1912 in Voulangis, staying at the village inn near the Steichens' home, where Mercedes and Arthur Carles also were staying. In fun, high-spirited Carles and Katharine Rhoades had organized a geranium club in the Steichens' garden, later filling their letters with whimsical names—Mr. Geranium-Man, Geraniumette. Marion Beckett called herself "Petunia." These names were literal references to Steichen's murals, for he painted Katharine in the panel called *Rose Geranium*. Clara's sharp eyes did not miss the best panel of the seven-part mural, *Petunia-Caladium-Budleya*. To model for the panel depicting his favorite flower, Steichen had chosen Marion. Suddenly, jealousy took hold, swiftly transforming Clara's relationship with Marion Beckett.

During all those years of exciting, unorthodox art exhibitions at 291, Stieglitz and Steichen had thoroughly enjoyed shocking and educating the American public. It was Stieglitz who turned adventurously in 1912 from visual to verbal challenge by publishing an essay by Gertrude Stein. He had long sought to publish articles by Leo Stein, whose theories he greatly admired, but Leo was a perfectionist, intent on fully refining and testing his views before he would share them on paper. Gertrude, on the other hand, was ready and eager to be published in the United States.

Gertrude Stein's first published piece in any periodical appeared in a special issue of *Camera Work* in 1912.[70] Her essays on Picasso and Matisse stunned readers who had never experienced anything like Stein's maddening serpentine prose. Of Matisse, she wrote, "Some said of him, when anybody believed in him they did not then believe in any other one. Certainly some said this of him. . . . Very many did come to know it of him that he was clearly expressing what he was expressing. . . ."[71] Of Picasso, she said, "This one was one having always something being coming out of him, something having completely a real meaning. This one was one whom some were following. . . ."[72]

Stieglitz later told Carl Van Vechten that when he first read Stein's essays on her good friends Matisse and Picasso, he decided to publish them primarily because he did not immediately understand them.[73] He was not alone. "Just when you think Alfred Stieglitz has exhausted his bag of startling, novel, appalling tricks," warned Arthur Hoeber of the *New York Globe,* "—he comes forward with something so startling, novel, appalling that you ask for mercy." For Hoeber, Stieglitz and *Camera Work* had finally reached the "high water mark of incoherency and craziness." Hoeber contended that Gertrude Stein had produced "superb nonsense" and "imbecile nothings," but Stieglitz defended her essays.[74] They were, he contended, analogous to the work of the painters she described.

When that special August 1912 issue of *Camera Work* reached Steichen in France, he was disappointed that a Matisse-Picasso number should have come out before a Cézanne number. He thought Stieglitz had put the cart before the horse. But when he read Gertrude Stein's essays, he knew that her text was Stieglitz's main motive for publishing the issue. The first time Steichen read the Stein pieces, he laughed. The second time, he was interested. The third time, he said, he finally understood it—but he had no desire ever to read it again.[75]

Stein herself indicated that one reason she was alone at the first in understanding Picasso's Cubism was that she was "expressing the same thing in literature."[76] Biographers and other scholars would later analyze the "literary cubism" of her work.[77] But Steichen looked up from his first encounter with Stein's essays in *Camera Work* and detected another influence—the work of French writer Charles Péguy (1873–1914), a socialist, founder of a journal called *Cahiers de la Quinzaine,* and the author of poems and meditations, as well as works on Joan of Arc, Victor Hugo, and Péguy's own mentor, the philosopher and, later, Nobel Laureate Henri-Louis Bergson.

Steichen wrote to tell Stieglitz that for several years a Frenchman had been writing in a style similar to Gertrude's, and he promised to send Stieglitz a copy of Péguy's work. He noted ruefully that it would probably not be as effective in French because that language could be convoluted anyway. Soon afterward, as promised, Steichen mailed Stieglitz the book by Péguy that he believed to be an influence on Stein's unique essays, noting that Péguy's book was written in 1908 and published in 1909. He marked several passages that struck him as forerunners of Stein's style but said he thought that, by comparison, Péguy's book was not "worth a dam." If Gertrude Stein's style had actually been influenced by Péguy's, Steichen said, Stein wrote with less poetry but far more power.[78]

The Steichens' American friends had gone home by the autumn of 1912, and as winter closed in, Steichen retreated into solitude, even losing interest in the art world. He was disgusted with the Salon d'Automne, he wrote in a rambling letter to Stieglitz. Braque and other Cubists—not including Picasso—had set off a storm with what Steichen viewed as their mediocre, even foolish paintings. He found some sardonic amusement in the ironic fact that the Fauves appeared to "devour" one another. Maybe he was just growing old, Steichen reflected a few months before he turned thirty-four, or maybe he was just weary. Whatever the explanation, he was sick of all " 'art' twaddle."[79]

He retreated into his painting, seeing no artists but Marsden Hartley, who spent Thanksgiving with the Steichens at Voulangis. Steichen respected Hartley's need to search for his own style; after all, he himself was caught up in that quest.[80] He saw Rodin only occasionally—chiefly when the older man wanted prints or something else from him, but he was relieved to learn that Rodin and the duchess had ended their stormy relationship. He had not seen Matisse in ages, and he suspected Matisse was miffed that his sculptures had not sold at 291. But Steichen heard that Matisse was getting rich selling his work in Europe, with orders for sculpture editions lined up for the next three or four years.

When Stieglitz asked if he could show some of Steichen's older photographic prints at 291 that winter, Steichen readily gave him permission. He offered to supply a list of prints and people who owned them, since many people believed that Stieglitz was the only person ever to purchase Steichen's prints.[81] Stieglitz was delighted to hear that Steichen had bought a new camera and wanted to order a Smith lens for it so that he could make photographs that winter between periods of paintings. At least Steichen had not lost interest in photography, and he told Stieglitz he hoped to have enough new photographs for a show in 1913.[82]

Near the end of 1912, Steichen and Clara struggled through another "rumpus spell" that left him feeling empty, lifeless.[83] The climax of one furious argument drove Steichen to such desperation that he slashed and destroyed one of his carefully wrought murals. Was it one that Clara may have modeled for? Or did she provoke him, out of her new suspicions about his feelings for Marion Beckett, to destroy an image of Marion? Those details are not known, but to people who were there soon afterward, Steichen explained that he had simply gotten tired of that decorative panel.[84] Only to Stieglitz, then deeply mired in his own marital problems, did Steichen confide the truth behind its ruin.

Once again, however, the therapy of working with his flowers saved him, the prospect of their beauty and harmony renewing him mentally and spiritually. The next season's intricate breeding plans demanded his full attention, and escaping into their endlessly absorbing details, he emerged soothed and refreshed. Soon the work on several ten-foot canvases for the Meyer murals was progressing nicely once more, and he was refining his overall design by constructing models scaled to one-third the size of the ten-foot panels that would actually be installed. Once the models were finished and evaluated, he could choose the most beautiful panels from the group he had painted and situate those in the final mural.[85] He was pleased with the way the decorations were evolving, and he told a curious Stieglitz that without seeing them, he could not possibly have the faintest notion of what the murals were becoming.[86]

As usual, by the time Christmas of 1912 drew closer, Steichen was plying ideas for new shows at 291. Marion Beckett, who had returned home to the United States, was much on his mind those days. Steichen missed her quiet, cheerful presence, her sweet stability, and her lucid intellect. He also admired her painting, telling Stieglitz that Marion had achieved the finest progress of any painter whose work he had been following that year.[87] Steichen thought Marion Beckett and Katharine Rhoades deserved their own exhibition at 291.

19

THE WHIRLPOOL OF MODERN ART

(1 9 1 2 - 1 9 1 3)

You people in New York will soon be in the whirlpool of modern art. I, on the other hand, am out of it. The present enthusiasm is for cubism of one species or another and I think cubism whether in paint or ink is tommyrot.[1]

—LEO STEIN

IN PARIS AS WELL AS NEW YORK, the air bristled with exciting change, and Steichen could taste it and feel it, although he could not yet fully define it.[2] Not all of it was to his liking, however, for in 1913, for the first time ever at 291, Stieglitz mounted a series of exhibitions that were not in their majority suggested, conceived, gathered, and designed by Eduard Steichen. The 291 shows that season emphasized painting and drawing—caricatures by Alfred J. Frueh and Marius de Zayas; drawings and watercolors by Abraham Walkowitz in his first one-man show; twenty-eight watercolors by John Marin with American themes; abstract New York studies by the charming playboy Francis Picabia; and a second show by Walkowitz.

In this changing of the guard, Stieglitz was once again relying less on Steichen's advice and ideas transmitted from Paris, and more on the energy and taste of his newer 291 colleagues on the scene in New York. He was leaning especially on two lively members of the current 291 circle—handsome, aristocratic Paul Haviland and the brilliant Mexican caricaturist Marius de Zayas, whom Stieglitz had discovered not long after he arrived in New York in 1907 as a political refugee. The son of a controversial Mexican poet laureate and journalist, de Zayas had come to New York when he was twenty-seven, after his family had been forced out of their native country by the dictator Porfirio Díaz.

De Zayas was soon contributing his urbane, witty, sometimes wicked caricatures to the *New York World,* and his art so impressed Stieglitz that he had given de Zayas his first one-man show at 291—his first exhibition anywhere—in January of 1909. This gifted young artist and critic had thereafter made himself at home at 291 until he left New York in 1910 to study art in Paris, where he was soon enjoying long talks about art with Eduard Steichen. After one visit, de Zayas wrote to Stieglitz from Paris in his idiosyncratic English, "He is too big to many a brain to understand."[3]

The two men had shared forays into French galleries and art shows, where de Zayas, with Steichen's exuberant help, began his own catalytic discovery of European modernist art—prowling the salons and exhibitions to study abstract painting. At the same time, he was reading Darwin and Freud in an effort to comprehend the evolution of art and the workings of the artistic mind and impulse. In 1910 and 1911, when Steichen and de Zayas had also spent time together in Paris scouting for art for 291, de Zayas began courting the Cubist painter Georges Braque in hopes of arranging an exhibition of his work. Like Pablo Picasso, de Zayas collected African sculpture and therefore immediately understood that African art was a shaping force in the art of the "revolutionists" in Paris.[4] Dilettante that he was, de Zayas crafted his sophisticated caricatures, expanded his interests to embrace musicology and cinema, and wrote prolifically on matters of art, culture, and taste.

"Art is dead," he proclaimed dramatically in an article in *Camera Work* in July of 1912, aligning himself with Stieglitz's pessimism rather than Steichen's optimism.[5] Even so, his essay was a winner, Steichen wrote to Stieglitz, probably because he and de Zayas had already talked over so many of the ideas.[6] Still, the article depressed Steichen because he feared it was all too true that, as de Zayas argued, current movements in art, including Cubism, were not so much "indications of vitality" as "the mechanical reflex action of a corpse subjected to a galvanic force."[7]

Unlike many of their contemporaries in this first modernist generation, Steichen and de Zayas saw Picasso, Braque, and other Cubists as reactionaries who were destroying conventional art forms, rather than revolutionaries who were creating new ones. As de Zayas described current art movements, "the so-called 'Too-advanced-for-their-epoch' geniuses" were "rummaging about in ancient cemeteries, looking for the artistic truth," and when they thought they had found it, they altered it "to the point of exaggeration and ridicule," instead of reproducing it, in the process deforming "the anatomy of the human body and all forms in nature to suit the arbitrary and incomprehensible whims of symbolism."[8]

Steichen and de Zayas shared another fundamentally unorthodox perspective on contemporary art: While many visual artists among the modernists (Picasso, Braque, Marcel Duchamp, for instance) tended to detach themselves from politics to concentrate on the expression of the inner life, Steichen and de Zayas believed it impossible for an artist to live in isolation from the world. In this, they were more akin to Rodin, and to writers such as Ibsen, Yeats, and later Carl Sandburg, with whom Steichen had long talks about art and its pivotal role in national and international life. Steichen, his immigrant mother, and his sister and brother-in-law embraced the ideals of socialism and carried the profound conviction that no one should be blind to the social reverberations of the times. That was a view de Zayas and his expatriate poet father also shared fervently, for their very freedom of expression had been thwarted when the dictator Díaz drove them out of Mexico because the senior de Zayas had used his newspaper and his poetry for social protest. Their own lives had demonstrated to Steichen and to de Zayas that they were inextricably bound to the times in which they lived, that all people necessarily inhaled the political air of their era.

"If it be true to say that every people gets the government it deserves, then it is also true to say that every epoch develops its own particular Art," de Zayas wrote.[9] Furthermore, he contended, every individual artist is inherently connected to his or her epoch: No person can "live outside of humanity, for no matter how great his power of abstraction or how complete his isolation, the idea he conceives is inalienably related to the [human] race, the time and the place."[10] He indicted Matisse as well as Picasso and other Cubists as "pretended discoverers of artistic truth, moved by egotism," who imposed themselves as apostles "of a new art, so new that they claim to be of the future." Instead of this rampant egocentric individualism—this anarchism—de Zayas advocated the "synthesis of the collective idea." He wrote, "These collective ideas, condensed and synthesized by the individual genius, are precisely those which are expressed in the masterpieces of Art."[11]

Like many of the modernists, Steichen cared deeply about art as a means of individual expression. He went further than that, however, believing art to be a crucial force with the power to connect the individual outwardly to his society as well as inwardly to his own soul.[12]

In Paris, Rodin had dreamed up a new project, and he needed advice from Steichen and Stieglitz. He wanted the two men to help him publish a book of his drawings, a prospect that Steichen found exciting, for he knew that together he, Stieglitz, and Rodin could design a "real rip snorter" of a volume.[13] Problems arose immediately, however, when Rodin decided that the drawings could not be reproduced unless Steichen photographed them. To no avail, Steichen tried to explain that a good engraver could reproduce them without the intervention of photography. Rodin only grew "peevish" and accused Steichen of trying to shirk his responsibility to help with the project.[14]

Then the sculptor came up with another idea, which Steichen thought to be more feasible, he told Stieglitz—a "de luxe" limited edition of the love sonnets written by the great painter and sculptor Michelangelo, to be illustrated by ten Rodin drawings. Steichen suggested that Stieglitz publish an edition of a thousand copies, half of them in French, the other half in English. Steichen would choose the paper and ink and design the cover.[15] They decided in April of 1913 to go ahead with plans for the book, although they would abandon the project before year's end because of the chronic uncertainties and difficulties of working with Rodin.

During that time, Rodin, then seventy-three, was in anguish over the collapse of his long love affair with Claire de Choiseul, whom many of his close friends, including Steichen, had often called "that Damn Duchesse." For several years, she had virtually taken over Rodin's life—arranging exhibitions for him, selling his work for much higher prices than he had commanded before, monitoring his meals and his friendships, traveling with him, entertaining for him, and running an ever-more-complicated household for him in Paris. From the beginning of their affair, the duchess came obstinately between the love-blind Rodin and many of his oldest friends, even virtually displacing poor Rose, who was now alone most of the time in Meudon.

From their first meeting at Meudon back in 1901, the great Rodin had generously befriended Steichen, treating the then-unknown young American artist like a son. Over the years, their friendship had always yielded reciprocal benefits; Steichen not only was Rodin's photographer of choice, for instance, but when he had introduced Rodin's drawings to the United States, he had generated welcome income for the sculptor in the process. Yet by late 1912, their warm relationship had been strained for more than a year because of Claire de Choiseul, who surely saw Steichen as a rival each time he arranged a successful exhibition for Rodin or answered Rodin's summons to discuss other enterprises, such as the book that never came to pass. Prompted by his mistress, Rodin had begun to look at everyone suspiciously, even his most trusted old friends and colleagues, and Steichen—dynamic, charming, and especially loved and trusted by Rodin—was no exception. He had long blamed Rodin's growing petulance squarely on the duchess, who never seemed to leave Rodin's side.[16]

While the old man still shared his ongoing work with Steichen, especially his exquisite new drawings, Steichen felt he had to treat his volatile friend gingerly. Customarily after they had exhibited Rodin's work at 291, Stieglitz would keep his drawings on hand for a time to expedite sales for Rodin. But after Rodin's last exhibition at 291, Steichen had written several anxious letters to Stieglitz, urging him to return all Rodin's drawings immediately, along with an explicit accounting of each one sold.

As Rodin's love affair disintegrated, Steichen wrote Stieglitz cryptically that his position in the matter was "delicate."[17] Steichen and Clara had enduring affection and respect for Rose, and, like Rodin's other friends, they greeted the news of the duchess's departure with great relief. Rodin's breakup with the "well-known Franco-American Duchess" had made the front page of the *New York Times* September 16, 1912. The reasons for their final quarrel were murky, having to do with some missing Rodin prints and allegations by his friends that Claire de Choiseul had exploited him, perhaps even defrauded him.[18] Whatever the cause of the rift, Steichen, Clara, and other friends shared Kate Simpson's opinion, expressed in a letter to Rodin, that he was better off because he needed, as an artist, to be a world unto himself.[19]

But long after he had banished the duchess, Rodin bitterly mourned her absence, retreating into the sanctuary of his work, as Steichen, his disciple, had learned to do and more and more often now had to do. Other lessons from Rodin informed Steichen's work, as well. Rodin admonished that "nature exceeds—and greatly—human genius; she is superior in everything; to believe that you can equal her, to believe that you can create outside her is as stupid as wanting to measure the stars with our hands...."[20] Perhaps this was an admonition to the young modernists who had turned their prodigious talents toward dissecting and reconfiguring nature—the eternal "juggling" of colors, light, shapes, structures, as Steichen himself described modern art.[21] Perhaps it was in part because Rodin's ideas were by then so deeply imprinted in Steichen's psyche that he could not embrace Picasso and Braque's Cubism and other radical experiments in abstraction, nor effectively incorporate these ideas into his own work.

When he had organized the Society of Younger American Painters in Paris that February night in 1908, Steichen had assumed his role as the convener, the leader, and the champion of American modernist painters in France. Nonetheless, his friend de Zayas had detected no significant modernist influences in Steichen's painting when he first saw it in 1910, and little had changed by 1912. Quite clearly, Steichen was a far more conservative painter than many of his friends and colleagues. But whether or not his own work reflected it then, Steichen keenly understood that all of the arts were changing because the fundamental, traditional perspectives of the universe were being dramatically transformed in science, in philosophy and psychology, and in politics. Inevitably, that change spilled over into the arts: Gertrude Stein was painting abstract portraits in words; composers such as Arnold Schoenberg, with his tone poems, and Alexander Scriabin, with his dissonance, were reordering traditional tonal structures and creating a kind of cubist music fraught with strange new sounds.

The modern vocabulary of science, psychology, and philosophy found its way into Steichen's own discourse about art, as well as into discussions in salons and journals such as *Camera Work*, where Freud's work prompted critic Benjamin de Casseres to write about the unconscious in art, while Darwin's theories stimulated de Zayas and others to explore the evolution of art and the artistic mind. With Paul Haviland, de Zayas wrote *A Study of the Modern Evolution of Plastic Expression,* published in 1913, using the work of Freud and Darwin to explain the dynamics of the unconscious in artistic expression. At 291, Steichen and his peers also argued the ideas that French philosopher Henri Bergson articulated in his best-selling book, *Creative Evolution* (1907). Stieglitz had twice reprinted excerpts from Bergson's writings in *Camera Work.* It was direct intuition, not analysis, Bergson wrote, that led to knowledge and truth—and, by extension, many artists felt, to art.

Back at work on the flower panels in his studios in Voulangis and in Paris in 1912, Steichen had little time to speculate on theories of aesthetics, however, or to work intuitively or otherwise on his photography and his own experiments in abstract painting. He had a commission to honor, and that meant working full-time on the mural for Agnes and Eugene Meyer. In fact, he was so completely absorbed in the work that he fell uncharacteristically out of touch with events in Paris as well as New York—until tantalizing rumors suddenly began reaching his ears about a big international art exhibition to be held in New York. Something significant was brewing, and he begged Stieglitz for details. Everybody was asking him about it, from Rodin to French journalists, Steichen said, but he was completely in the dark.[22]

He had heard from friends in Paris that Marsden Hartley was working on a large modernist exhibition in New York, but Hartley had not said a word to Steichen about it, not even during their Thanksgiving holiday together.[23] There had already been two major Post-Impressionist exhibitions in England, he knew. The first of these Post-Impressionist shows, held in 1910, provided 25,000 people with an introduction to the work of Cézanne, Gauguin, van Gogh, and the younger French painters. This was followed in 1912 by the second Post-Impressionist show, which was more comprehensive and even more contemporary. The critics Roger Fry and Clive Bell seized the opportunity these shows provided to advocate the "doctrine" of modernism, with the dual tenets of "pure form and aesthetic emotion."[24] No more of John Ruskin's fealty to nature, they declared; the artist had entered the realm of fealty to himself and his own struggle with the canvas—or the camera.

The Whirlpool of Modern Art (1912–1913)

By breaking free of conventional forms, the artist could exert unprecedented new creative control; by repudiating known patterns, he could create previously unknown and unknowable forms and universes.

Of course, Steichen had worked for years to the point of exhaustion and bankruptcy to export the new art to New York for the 291 shows, and now he wanted to know what on earth was about to happen. It appeared that he would just have to find out for himself when he arrived for his customary winter sojourn in February of 1913. There, Steichen soon learned from Stieglitz and other friends the details of the huge international art exhibition organized by the recently formed Association of American Painters and Sculptors, spearheaded by painter Walt Kuhn, critic and painter Walter Pach, and Arthur B. Davies, an illustrator and painter of the Ash Can school.

Kuhn and Davies had started out a couple of years earlier to organize a large exhibition of American art, which was to include a limited number of radical modernist paintings by European artists. Along the way, however, finances and other expediencies forced a change in plans, so that the show was transformed into a major exposition of European art—the first of its kind on such an immense scale in the United States. In the fall of 1912, Kuhn, Davies, and Pach had made the rounds of Paris galleries and salons, including, of course, the Stein apartments, to gather progressive art for the show. Meanwhile, under the supervision of artist William Glackens, invitations had gone out in the United States to American artists to submit their work for consideration. Stieglitz reportedly objected to the "undiscriminating vastness" of these invitations—yet apparently Steichen was not even on the list.[25]

Steichen must have been immensely disappointed, for this was an enterprise after his own heart. This was the work he and Stieglitz had been doing for years at 291, except magnified now, and there was no doubt that their bold, pioneering shows at 291 had helped pave the way for an international exhibition on this massive scale. Steichen must have been hurt, too, that some of his longtime friends and colleagues had helped to plan the exhibit without sharing the news with him—especially Marsden Hartley, his Thanksgiving houseguest, who had been evasive about the show, although for months he had been advising two of the prime movers behind the exhibition, Davies and Kuhn. In fact, Davies had helped raise money in 1912 to finance Hartley's first trip to Europe.[26]

Steichen's friends Alfie Maurer and Jo Davidson had also helped Kuhn when he came to Paris to seek out art and artists, and Arthur Carles had two paintings accepted for the show, including *Interior with Woman at Piano,* which had been painted in Steichen's own parlor at Voulangis.

Even Stieglitz knew far more about the upcoming event than he had shared with Steichen. Along with Claude Monet, Odilon Redon, Augustus John, and Auguste Renoir, Stieglitz lent his name as an honorary vice president for the International Exhibition of Modern Art, which was scheduled to open at the Sixty-ninth Regiment Armory on Lexington Avenue at Twenty-fifth Street on February 17, 1913. This exhibition would be known ever after as the Armory Show. But Stieglitz played no active role in the enterprise, although, as part of the advance publicity, he gave an interview to the *New York American,* where he was quoted as lauding the exhibition for its "battle cry of freedom."[27]

Steichen saw the show for himself on February seventeenth, when he and the bon vivant and artist Francis Picabia joined the throng at the festive opening ceremonies. Although Picabia's work was included in the show and won even more attention than Picasso's, the two men were "mutually depressed" by most of what they saw as they surveyed paintings and sculpture in the vast hall.[28] Picabia vowed that it made him decide to become a chauffeur, while Steichen said he was going to be a potato farmer. (Steichen joked later that although Picabia did not keep his word, he did—proudly winning the prize for the outstanding potato crop in the entire department of Seine-et-Marne for 1913.[29])

Of course, there were other painters in the 291 circle whose work was not included, either—chiefly Arthur Dove and Max Weber. Weber had petulantly declined to show anything at all when only two of his paintings were chosen for the show. Yet in addition to Carles, Maurer, and Hartley, John Marin was represented there (by fourteen paintings), as were Abraham Walkowitz, Patrick Henry Bruce, Katharine Rhoades, and Marion Beckett—the latter with two paintings, one of them a portrait of Steichen. All but the women had already had at least one show at 291. (Despite Steichen's continual lobbying, Beckett and Rhoades would not have their own exhibition there until 1915, and that would be their first and only show at 291.)

Except for the 291 group show of the Society of Younger American Painters in Paris in 1910, Steichen himself had never exhibited his own paintings at 291, although Stieglitz had asked him to leave some there for possible sale. The paintings he packed in his hampers for the annual winter odysseys to New York were bound for Knoedler or Montross—the visible, commercial, prestigious Manhattan art galleries where his work could be seen and bought.

In trying to understand his disappointing exclusion from the Armory Show, Steichen perhaps wondered whether his body of work was too thin, or if the work itself was deemed inferior. Was his reputation among the committee insufficient to warrant an invitation? Was he too conventional, not modern enough? Was he overlooked, or dismissed, or, worse, ignored or forgotten? Perhaps he was taken less seriously as a painter by early 1913 because he had put aside most of his ongoing experiments to concentrate on his decorations, the Meyer murals.

Steichen and Picabia roamed the vast hall in the armory, drinking in the display of European art that ran a dazzling gamut from realism to Impressionism to Post-Impressionism, from Fauvism to Cubism, from classicism to romanticism. Under the immense Armory roof was gathered an unprecedented collection of works by established and emerging European and American artists—Cézanne, Gauguin, van Gogh, Rodin, Matisse, Picasso, Braque, Whistler, Hassam, Brancusi, Marin, members of the Ash Can School, better known as "The Eight," whose huge paintings of American realism had not been exhibited at 291, Steichen remembered, because they were simply too large for the small spaces of the gallery.[30] The scandal of the show, everyone agreed, was Marcel Duchamp's *Nude Descending a Staircase, No. 2*. The painting was later acquired by art patrons Louise and Walter Arensberg, who founded their own important salon in New York.

Stieglitz, like Steichen, may also have felt like an outsider looking in on the Armory Show, for he busily occupied himself elsewhere. From February fourteenth until March fifteenth, in his quiet oasis at 291, Stieglitz exhibited his own photographs, the only one-man show of his work ever to hang there. As for Steichen, he still believed that Stieglitz more than anyone else, including the masterminds of the Armory Show, was leading one of the most significant art and cultural movements ever in the "evolution of America."[31]

In late March, Steichen returned to France aboard the Cunard line's RMS *Mauretania,* eager to get back to his garden at Voulangis and to his daughters—"Mickey" and "Bubbles," he called the little girls—vivacious, opinionated Mary, already a beauty at the age of eight, and sweet, effervescent Kate, nearly five. And always, after his months in the United States, he turned toward home with the hope that he and Clara might somehow find a new peace in their marriage.

The homeward voyage gave him time to think about the exciting weeks in New York, and the leisure to write a long, reflective letter to Stieglitz, spilling out his own ideas on modern art. In this letter, he said it had been good to reconnect with his circle in New York but, as usual, he wished that there had been more private time with Stieglitz. As he looked back at the time spent at 291, he told Stieglitz he found it part "inspiration" and part "country circus."[32] He worried in his letter about the current trends in art and science, unable to accept fully such experimental movements as Cubism—even Marsden Hartley's "intuitive abstraction," his "subliminal or cosmic cubism," as Hartley himself described the paintings that sprang from his "spiritual illuminations."[33] Steichen had even more trouble with Synchromism (literally meaning to synchronize color), a style of color painting launched by American painters Stanton Macdonald-Wright and Morgan Russell after their exposure to modern art in Europe, especially the work of the Fauves. These two painters advocated the use of color as an element that operated freely in a painting, emancipated from all its previous objective, realistic uses. Because they contended that color should be perceived and used as pure form, most Synchromists created paintings that actually resembled brilliantly colored kaleidoscopic patterns.

Far too much of modern art, Steichen feared, was being influenced by science—and art could never become a science, nor should it, he argued. There was great danger in test tube art, he wrote, because the evolution of art was essentially an inner, subjective, even spiritual process, not an external, scientific dynamic.[34] As his ship churned across the Atlantic in late March of 1913, Steichen wrote that he was keenly aware of a strange "world hunger," partly social, partly economic, but clearly universal. The art world, like the larger world around them, was volatile, even chaotic, he thought, with artists searching incessantly—even recklessly—for form and meaning.[35]

For himself, for Stieglitz, and for all artists, Steichen believed, the quest was for truth and understanding, without which no artist, no matter how great, could create anything genuine. He had left New York dazzled, intimidated, and not a little perplexed by much of the art he had seen at the Armory Show. Now the bracing sea air seemed to clarify his vision and to ground him again in the reality of his own instincts and intuitions as an artist.[36] In every arena of life, old ideas were being abandoned, new ones born. He wrote to Stieglitz during that voyage that even traditional concepts of marriage were being transformed, with the physical drives being transcended by a greater spiritual love. In fact, he ventured to say, he could imagine practicing abstract or spiritual love more readily than he could see himself as an abstract painter.[37]

Some of this new art would last and shape the future, he knew, but some forms of it would disappear, like so many abandoned toys. He had no idea whether his own future work would resemble Picasso's or any other artist's, and furthermore, he did not care. In the aftermath of the Armory Show, Steichen declared his independence of movements. As had always been true in his life as an artist, he would be guided by his own star, listen to his own heart and soul, teach himself by trial and error and constant experiment what he had to learn. Some mystical force had always driven his best work, he felt, and without that drive, he could do nothing.[38]

Meanwhile, he was glad to see that, as always, Stieglitz was doing great work. Steichen hoped, furthermore, that someday someone would write the true history of 291, for there had never before been anything to resemble its work or spirit, and he was convinced that there never would be again. He was always enthralled by the debates that heated up the gallery, and he had listened more than he had talked during his recent visits to 291, amused and sometimes baffled, finding in no other place in the world such exuberant argument or such divergence of belief—from "deathly" ignorance to stunning wisdom.[39]

The heart of it all, Steichen wrote with sincere appreciation in that shipboard letter, was Stieglitz himself, creator and leader of one of the most important movements in American cultural history.[40] Many years later, he carried in his memory a montage of images of Stieglitz at 291, his brow furrowed as he scrutinized photographs and paintings to hang on the walls or figured out ways to help his artists, arranging income for

Weber, Marin, Hartley, Dove—and Steichen himself at crucial times. "During those winters in New York, I was able to observe the prodigious amount of work that Stieglitz did," Steichen wrote in his autobiography years later.

> *His patience was unbelievable. With only a brief interruption for lunch, he stood on the floor of the Galleries from ten o'clock in the morning until six or seven o'clock at night. He was always there, talking, talking, talking; talking in parables, arguing, explaining. He was a philosopher, a preacher, a teacher, and a father-confessor. There wasn't anything that wasn't discussed openly and continuously in the Galleries at 291. If the exhibitions at 291 had been shown in any other art gallery, they would never have made an iota of the impact they did at 291. The difference was Stieglitz.*[41]

As Steichen drew closer to home, he grew more and more eager to get back to his family and his garden. While he had come to a general grasp of evolution from his reading of Darwin, he had actually begun to understand genetics by experimenting with his flowers, acting as a surrogate creator as he forced or altered the colors and shapes of delphiniums, poppies, roses, and petunias. As a bonus, he enjoyed watching his flowers bloom with even greater beauty because of his own handiwork.[42]

Yes, he was hungry for his garden and all it could teach him, and he also needed to immerse himself once more in work on the seven canvas panels he was painting for the Meyers.

As he painted that spring, his scale model of the Meyers' foyer still stood in his studio for reference. Some of the actual panels measured 119 and 5/8 inches by 99 and 1/12 inches, while others were the same height but 55 inches wide. He adorned the huge canvases with paintings of his flowers and the figures of Agnes Meyer and their mutual friends Katharine Rhoades and Marion Beckett, wearing gracefully draped robes.[43] One panel, *Petunia—Begonia Rex—The Freer Bronze,* depicted Agnes Meyer's friendship with art patron Charles Freer by setting one of his rare Oriental bronzes from the ninth century B.C. in the foreground of a wonderfully angular bower of petunias and begonias. (Steichen had bred and probably named this begonia for Stieglitz's father, whom he had affectionately nicknamed Rex.)

These quite remarkable mural designs were painted in oil in bold, radiant colors. The stark black figures and planes of the composition were caressed with vibrant gold leaf, a material the Viennese artist Gustav Klimt had habitually used and that Steichen had experimented with as early as 1907 in a striking modernist still life entitled *Vase of Flowers*.[44] The panels were suffused with the richly varied influences in his work—Klimt, of course, and also the Art Nouveau posters of his old friend Alphonse Mucha, then living and working in Paris in the Rue du Val-de-Grâce, not far from Steichen's apartment on the Boulevard du Montparnasse. There are also hints in Steichen's murals of the highly stylized stage drawings of Gordon Craig—not only in their geometry but also in their evocation of stage settings, for in Steichen's stylized figures and design for the panels, there was something theatrical. There were also vivid warm colors suggestive of Matisse and Cézanne—yet these were also the colors Steichen's garden gave him.

The seven panels were named for the flowers they contained: the graceful figure of a nude woman (Isadora Duncan, perhaps?) discreetly intertwines with the flowers in *Gloxinia—Delphinium;* the panel named *Clivia—Fuschia—Hilium—Henryi* [sic] most likely portrayed Agnes Meyer—the "Girl from the Sun"—for the regal woman in this panel stands before a sunlike disk. In a letter to her husband, Mercedes Carles documented Steichen's deliberate portrayals of Katharine in *Rose Geranium* and Marion in *Petunia—Caladium—Budleya,* which was by many accounts the handsomest of the panels.[45] Here, Steichen painted a beautiful woman, her elegant head turned in profile as she gazes at a sumptuous blue iris. Her quiet robe is set off by a brilliantly colored shawl flocked with abstract flowers that also seem to be bright eyes openly facing the world—direct, unafraid, perceptive, welcoming.

In the background of this panel, there stands the enigmatic figure of a woman, her vulnerable nude body white as plaster, her head swathed in a white robe, her uplifted hand poised in the act of covering or uncovering her eyes, one cannot be sure which. Is this provocative image a sculpture—or a woman of stone, unseeing, her face, her eyes, her soul deliberately masked?

This single panel may have been Steichen's only transcription of an ongoing dilemma of the heart—his conflicting loyalty to Clara and his growing love for Marion Beckett. Marion stands vibrantly in the foreground of his work, surrounded by his beautiful flowers, herself alive with color and grace, all-seeing. In the shadows of the background, clinging to seemingly lifeless branches of a tree, there is a shrouded figure who could be Clara, her face cloaked and concealed, as if by choice, as cold as stone. If so, this panel would be one of the most autobiographically revealing images Steichen ever created, a confession in paint, auguring greater heartache to come.

Steichen's plan then was to finish as much of the mural work as possible in Paris and Voulangis during the remainder of 1913 and then to roll and pack the canvas panels of *In Exaltation of Flowers* for his journey to New York in the winter of 1914, when he would set up his canvases in the squash court at the Meyers' country estate in Mount Kisco, New York, finish them there, and prepare to install them in the house on Park Avenue. By the time they were completed in 1914, he would have invested more than three years of his creative energy and a significant chunk of his artistic reputation in the project, and although the Meyers would pay him the handsome sum of fifteen thousand dollars, it had to occur to him from time to time that that was not compensation enough.

During the spring and summer of 1913 in France, however, Steichen gave himself some necessary distance from the murals, taking photographs and experimenting with his Graflex camera, now outfitted with a new small Smith lens.[46] Eagerly, he embarked on a series of photographs of flowers, insects, and plant forms. The photography and the mural work so absorbed his energy and interest, in fact, that he did not devote as much time to his garden that spring as he had thought he would. Still, thanks to the skill and attention of a new gardener, his flowers were beautiful, and his experiments were thriving. Although Steichen did not expect to get the same results without doing the work himself, the spring and summer of 1913 taught him that with others working under his careful direction, the flowers could still grow "finer every year."[47] When a few acres of land just across the winding road from the Voulangis house became available, he arranged to lease and then to buy them, planting them with seeds from his most successful crosses. The next season, with the help of four gardeners, Steichen was tending nearly eight acres of brilliantly colored, architecturally splendid delphiniums, poppies, and petunias.

His garden had a dramatic new centerpiece in 1913—a fine Brancusi sculpture of a gracefully elongated bronze bird. The minute he saw the piece, Steichen knew that somehow he had to own it.[48] His quest for the bird began a "warm" lifelong friendship with Romanian-born sculptor Constantin Brancusi, whom Steichen had first met in his early years at Rodin's studio.[49] He had seen Brancusi there often, he said, finding the man himself even more fascinating than his work, but somehow he lost track of Brancusi, despite the fact that from 1908 until 1914, their studios were just a few blocks apart in Paris. They moved in different circles, however, and Brancusi did most of his work alone, removed from movements and cliques of artists.[50]

Born to peasant parents in 1876, Brancusi had studied art in Bucharest, then actually walked from there to Munich and from Munich on to Paris, where he studied at the Ecole des Beaux-Arts. He was often too poor to eat. By 1906, Brancusi had met Rodin and, on the strength of his art, had been invited to work in Rodin's studio. He stayed only a short time, however, fearing that Rodin's overwhelming presence would stifle his own original work.

Years later, at the Salon des Indépendants in 1913, Steichen discovered Brancusi's "beautifully, highly polished, golden bird"—the bird in flight, one of several sculptures first named *L'Oiseau d'Or* and then renamed *Maiastra*.[51] It was "the most wonderful concept and execution I had seen by any sculptor with the exception of Rodin," Steichen recalled.[52] He thought of urging Eugene Meyer to buy it in marble, but he decided to purchase the cheaper bronze casting for himself. He could not afford such a work of art, he was sure, but he inquired about the cost anyway. "One thousand francs [two hundred dollars]," he was told.[53] Even though that amount of money was out of the question, Steichen asked for Brancusi's address and then went home to pore over his budget. By some "squeezing and cutting"—even paring back the family food allowance—he thought he could afford five hundred francs.[54] He set out to present the offer to Brancusi himself.

When Steichen reached the courtyard of Brancusi's studio, the concierge shouted for the sculptor, who leaned his shaggy head out of the window and recognized Steichen from their encounters at Rodin's. "We greeted each other almost like old friends," Steichen remembered, and he did indeed persuade Brancusi to let him buy *L'Oiseau d'Or* for five hundred francs if it did not sell during the exhibition.[55] To Steichen's immense relief, the sculpture did not sell for the asking price, and so he went to Brancusi's studio, counted out the hard-won five hundred francs, and took the bird home to Voulangis.

He decided to keep it in the garden, an idea that so intrigued Brancusi, the sculptor went out to Voulangis to see for himself how it looked. Delighted with the setting, he not only approved of this new home for his bird in flight, he offered to design a special base to hold it. He and Steichen set off for the nearest lumberyard, where Brancusi chose a large piece of wood, from which he crafted a pedestal that "harmonized with the short stone pillar on which the bird rested." Afterward, the bird in flight "reigned over" Steichen's lush flower beds.[56]

Steichen stepped out into his garden one day to find Mary in a heated debate with Brancusi about *L'Oiseau d'Or*. Little Kate had an imaginary playmate named Lidi, but Mary was a realist. "No bird could sing with its head like that," Mary insisted to Brancusi, pointing to the tilt of the bird's head.[57] She argued that birds sang with their heads held skyward. Patiently, Brancusi told Mary the legend of Maiastra, the mythological bird who was speaking, not singing, guiding a Romanian prince through life. Not for one moment satisfied with legend, young Mary held out for the literal, declaring that it made no difference whether the bird was talking or singing—he would have to point his beak up to the sky. She even drew her own rendition of the bird to prove her point.

In subsequent renditions, Steichen noticed, Brancusi gradually "raised the head of that bird—straightened it out until it went straight up."[58] He never asked Brancusi if little Mary had transformed his vision of the bird, yet in the final version, *Bird in Space,* created in 1935, "not only was the movement sharply upward, but the abstract suggestion of an open mouth was also made by an abrupt, bias-cut angle at the top."[59]

Steichen wrote to Stieglitz, offering some lively opinions about the paintings he saw that spring of 1913 at the Salon des Indépendants in Paris. Cubism was in, he thought, and Picabia was already out. Matisse, preparing for a one-man show, was not represented at all, and Brancusi had entered such wonderful work that Steichen urged Stieglitz to invest two hundred dollars in one *"beautiful bronze"* that Brancusi had patinated so that it looked almost like the original marble.[60] Sure enough, Stieglitz ordered a Brancusi sculpture, leaving the selection to Steichen, who arranged with Brancusi for two beautiful pieces to be sent out to Voulangis so that Emmy Stieglitz could make the final choice during her forthcoming trip to Europe.

Year by year, the tension between Alfred and Emmy chipped away at their marriage. By 1913, Emmy was so estranged from her husband's domineering family that she was no longer welcome at the family compound at Lake George, but most of the problems in the marriage were rooted in irreconcilable differences between Alfred and Emmy themselves. It seemed by then that the only threads still stitching their marriage together were their love for their daughter Kitty, and Alfred's reluctant dependence on Emmy's money. After Emmy, Alfred, and Kitty vacationed together for a few weeks at the New Jersey shore, father and daughter settled in for two months of vacation with the Stieglitz clan at Lake George in August of 1913 while Emmy traveled in Europe with only her young niece for company.

Emmy spent a few days with the Steichens at Voulangis in September and had a "wonderfully refreshing cheerful" time of it, she wrote to her husband. Her letters paint a bright portrait of what would be the Steichens' last summer in France. Emmy found Steichen's garden especially beautiful, with Brancusi's "wonderful shining eagle" reigning over the flowers. Steichen had promised to introduce her to Brancusi, Emmy told Stieglitz, although he had warned her that the sculptor was "dreadfully moody." Steichen and Clara took Emmy for walks and carriage drives through the countryside, and Clara sang for them with "fine feeling." Emmy admired Mary's beauty and her paintings, and found Kate "cunning though not pretty." All of them were excited at the prospect of a visit from Marion Beckett and Katharine Rhoades.

In copious detail, Emmy relayed the news of their circle to her husband: Mercedes and Arthur Carles were going to have a baby, and Emmy promised to crochet a coverlet for them when she got home. She had looked at the Meyer canvases and did not know what to make of them. They did not appeal to her as they now stood, she said tactfully, but she knew that they would be very different by the time Steichen completed the project. Emmy told Stieglitz that one figure looked so exactly like Marion Beckett that Steichen planned to change it. As for Steichen, Emmy worried, he looked terrible. She doctored him herself with calomel and magnesia, and was pleased when he seemed to feel better.[61]

She fretted at length over the decision on the Brancusi bronze, welcoming Steichen's advice but reflexively worrying that she might displease her husband with the wrong choice.[62] Good-hearted Emmy also worried about the tension between Steichen and Clara, evident to her even in the midst of the social whirl that marked her own visit to Paris. She shared almost daily teas and dinners with Marion, Katharine, and the Steichens, and a highlight of the stay for Emmy was the Saturday when ruggedly handsome Constantin Brancusi joined them all for a trip to the Louvre, the Muséo des Arts Décoratifs, and the Trocadéro. They finished that exciting day with dinner and an excursion to a delightfully raucous public fair in the Quartier Montparnasse. Brancusi was charming, and Katharine and Marion were lovely girls, Emmy thought. She just wanted everyone to be happy.

While Emmy seldom probed beneath the surface of life, even she perceived that Steichen seemed ill and tense, and Marion looked not only unwell but much older. Clara was struggling that summer—simultaneously loving Marion as a friend and fearing her, as she feared many other women, as a rival for her husband's love and attention. Nervously, Clara redoubled her vigilance when Marion and Katharine were visiting Voulangis and Paris, and it was a great relief to her when everyone departed and left them to themselves.

Steichen missed them, however; having Katharine and Marion at Voulangis was like a blood transfusion for him, he wrote to Stieglitz after they had gone. He urged Stieglitz to look after them in New York.[63]

20

STRATEGIC RETREAT

(1 9 1 3 - 1 9 1 4)

It was so difficult to know the situation that I finally sent a cautious cable to Eugene Meyer in New York: "What do you advise?"

A prompt reply came back: "Advise strategic retreat."[1]

— STEICHEN

FOR MANY MONTHS, STIEGLITZ HAD BEEN working hard in New York on an April–July double number of *Camera Work*, which would finally be published in November of 1913. Because it featured Steichen's photographs and color reproductions of his paintings, the two men consulted frequently on the proofs. This special issue testified eloquently to Stieglitz's regard for Steichen's work, as did a letter he wrote in September while working on advertisements for the journal.

Stieglitz composed this blustery letter to the Bausch & Lomb Optical Company, longtime patrons of the journal, chastising them because they had declined to renew their contract for space in *Camera Work*. He informed them he had been working for four years on the Steichen number now going to press, saying that it was perhaps the "most important number that has yet been published." Finally, Stieglitz lavished praise on Steichen, calling him "without a doubt the greatest photographer living; in fact the greatest that ever lived. He is an American."[2]

Having converted his letter of protest into one of his most passionate defenses of the journal, and of Steichen's work, Stieglitz dispatched it to Bausch & Lomb. The firm immediately renewed their advertising contract.

The culmination of Steichen's prewar evolution as a painter and photographer was documented in that long-awaited double issue of *Camera Work,* and he was deeply moved when it finally reached him in Paris. As he turned the pages of the journal, Steichen hoped that his work was worthy of Stieglitz's faith in him, he wrote to his old friend, adding that he was at all times keenly aware of his faults.[3] The issue contained admiring words from Steichen's friend Marius de Zayas: "The work of Steichen brought to its highest expression the aim of the realistic painting of Form. In his photographs he has succeeded in expressing the perfect fusion of the subject and the object."[4]

Even though Stieglitz had been planning this issue since long before the Armory Show, there seemed to be special affirmation in his inclusion of reproductions of Steichen's paintings along with his photographs. "In this Number of CAMERA WORK we introduce to our readers, for the first time, Steichen the painter," Stieglitz wrote. He went on to explain that because it took a long time to achieve art reproductions of high quality, the "latest phase of Steichen's evolution as a painter" did not appear in the issue. Then Stieglitz offered a tribute to his friend and longtime ally:

> *We take this opportunity again to put on record, inasmuch as we believe that CAMERA WORK is making history, our indebtedness to Steichen. The work of "291" could not have been achieved so completely without his active sympathy and constructive cooperation, rendered always in the most unselfish way. It was he who originally brought "291" into touch with Rodin, the recognized master, and with Matisse, at the time that he was regarded as "The Wildman." It has been Steichen also who, living in Paris, has constantly been on the watch for talent among young Americans there, and, as for example, in the case of Marin, has introduced them to the spirit of "291."*
>
> *He has embodied that spirit in the most vital and constructive form.*[5]

Strategic Retreat (1913–1914)

In addition to this gratifying praise, superb reproductions of fourteen Steichen photographs and three of his paintings graced the pages of this issue. Stieglitz and Steichen had chosen to include several photographic portraits of beautiful women—dancer Isadora Duncan, chanteuse Yvette Guilbert, socialite Mrs. Philip Lydig—along with photographic images of Matisse, Anatole France, William Howard Taft, Gordon Craig, and George Bernard Shaw. Years earlier, Sadakichi Hartmann had written an interesting commentary on some of these pictures, and it still held true: "There is something so intellectually vivacious about Steichen's portraits . . . that a man with pictorial instincts must take a liking to them. But Steichen always wants to assert himself. He gives us a commentary on the sitter. He is not satisfied with showing us how a person looks, but how he thinks the person should look."[6]

One page especially stood out for the Steichens, for Stieglitz surprised them by publishing a poem Mary had written when she was not quite nine. She had said in part,

Oh, the skylark, the skylark,
The beautiful skylark
I heard in the month of June,
It was nothing but a dark, dark
Speck. And nothing but a tune.[7]

Stieglitz had inscribed the Steichen number for his friend, writing from 291 on November 26, 1913, "Dear Steichen, This is the first copy of the 'Steichen Number.' . . . Nothing I have ever done has given me quite as much satisfaction as finally sending this Number out into the world." Stieglitz concluded his inscription with the words Steichen would always treasure: "Real friendship is rarer than real art—That is, heavens knows, rare enough these days."[8]

During 1913, Steichen had supported his family on his commission from the Meyer murals and with the profits from selling his prizewinning potatoes and their seeds. Now a professional farmer as well as an artist, he still faithfully sent money back to Wisconsin for his parents, supporting "Oma and Opa always, including buying their houses," a family member recalled.[9] In Voulangis in those days, Steichen was better known as a good farmer than as a famous artist, and when vast, angry distances loomed between him and Clara, he could continually lose himself in hard toil in his garden, where the sweet earth welcomed his touch. The garden was a realm he could trust, no matter that he still could not paint as he wanted to paint, much less abort the growing misery of his marriage or alter the swift-changing currents in the world of modern art.

In the winter of 1914, Steichen set off on his annual journey to the United States, most likely carrying with him in the carefully packed hampers of paintings some of the completed mural decorations for the Meyers. The trip was, he said afterward, a nightmare.[10] He was ill much of the time, as well as haggard from the worry and stress at home. He had been treated for an ulcer before he left France, and he now feared that it was flaring up, or, worse, that he might have an even more serious stomach disorder.

When Steichen arrived in New York that winter, he found Stieglitz despondent as well, for his old collaborator Joseph Keiley had died of Bright's disease on January 21, 1914, after lying for ten days in a coma.

Of course, there were pleasant times during Steichen's visit to New York. Soon after his arrival in January, he went with Eugene Meyer to pay a visit to Detroit industrialist Charles Freer, who had amassed his fortune as the creator of the American Car and Foundry Company. His passion for art had earlier led Freer to a long, close friendship with Whistler. An avid collector with exquisite taste, Freer had the money to indulge his passion for Whistler's work as well as for Chinese and Japanese art. As a great art patron, Freer would later give the nation his vast collections and the money to build the Freer Gallery of Art as part of the Smithsonian Institution in Washington, D.C.

After Freer had met Agnes Meyer by chance at an exhibition of Chinese paintings at a gallery in New York in 1913, he quickly befriended her and her husband. Although Freer never married, he always loved to flatter and indulge beautiful women. For example, when the Meyers first visited Freer in his mansion in Detroit, Agnes found a delicate pink rose floating in her freshly drawn bath. Because Agnes herself was an incorrigible flirt who assumed that most men were intent on seducing her, she decided that she needed a chaperon when she set out alone on another occasion to visit Freer for a few days at his home. Therefore, "out of consideration of Eugene's sense of propriety—and Mr. Freer's sense of the aesthetic," she took Marion Beckett with her, since Beckett possessed "such beauty as to challenge the Greek goddesses."[11] On a subsequent visit, Agnes was accompanied by Katharine Rhoades, who made such an impression on Freer that she later became his companion and assistant. According to Agnes, it was Freer who named the trio of friends the "Three Graces," and they in turn called him "the General," after Whistler's "General Utility." (Flirtatious Agnes sometimes addressed him as "My dear and very wicked General."[12]) None of them knew at the beginning of their friendship that Freer had chosen not to marry because of a family history of congenital syphilis.[13]

Agnes quickly joined Freer in collecting Oriental art, often splitting with him unique collections of Chinese art chosen and shipped by Freer's agents directly from China. In fact, under Freer's tutelage, Agnes and then Katharine would become expert students of Oriental art. Agnes was so fascinated that she even studied Chinese for two years at Columbia University, setting to work there on research that would culminate in a book on Chinese painting.[14]

Steichen, too, was impressed with Freer and his expertise, and no doubt he invited him to the exhibit of his paintings held at the National Art Club from February second until March seventh. Steichen had little new work to show there, however, because he had invested most of his energy in the Meyer murals. Rather than take the long train trip west that winter, he arranged for a ticket so his mother could travel to New York to visit him and see the show. Glad as he was for the reunion with Oma, Steichen was quickly worn out from the need to look after her and, simultaneously, to try to transact his business.

Still, in many ways it was easier to visit with her in New York than in France, for Clara had come both to love and resent her mother-in-law, and her irrational jealousy of Mary Steichen intensified as the years went by. In his handsome photographs of them, Steichen's wife and his mother look strikingly alike, but these two strong, willful, beautiful women had quite different outlooks. Mary Steichen had loved and nurtured her son unconditionally, and she was fiercely proud of him, while Clara placed conditions on love. From her earliest experience, love was entangled with possession, achievement, and approval.

Like her peasant mother-in-law, Clara was a pioneer, yet she fancied herself the disadvantaged child of the American aristocracy. She took pride in her family tree, keeping an ornately printed copy of it among her papers and sharing copies with her daughters. Over the years, she grew to consider herself superior to all of the Steichens, including her own much-loved daughters, and to attribute all faults she perceived in her children to their "peasant" Steichen genes and influences.[15]

Yet, in the early years, she had loved having Oma visit them in France, and she had appreciated the older woman's sympathy as well as her help with the children. Clara told friends over the years that she, too, enjoyed having a grandmother about. "We've needed one a long while & its [sic] nice to at last have such a real one," she had written to Stieglitz's mother. She felt great empathy for what she perceived as her mother-in-law's loneliness and unhappiness at home. Oma had a "starved heart," she thought, and Clara knew how that felt.[16]

Oma always reveled in her time with Mary and Kate, tending them, cooking for them, telling them stories, and watching them play in the garden or ride their donkey, Petit Frère. Mary received from her grandmother the same love and warmth that enfolded her when she was with her father, and she came to believe that he had gotten his ebullient "freedom of spirit" from his mother. After all, Oma herself had that spirit and naturally infused her son and daughter with it.[17] "I believe," Mary said many years later, "that my father was early set free to discover the secret that there is no such thing as too much love and that you never take away love from one person by also loving another."[18]

Tenderhearted Oma was terribly worried about Lilian and Sandburg during her visit to Steichen in New York, she told him, for his sister and brother-in-law were going through a bleak time in Chicago. Their first child, Margaret, was now nearly three years old, but they had recently lost a baby, Madeline, who had been stillborn, almost certainly because of a doctor's mistake. To make matters even darker, Sandburg was out of work, and he was mightily discouraged by his efforts to place the unorthodox, sometimes radical poetry he was writing.

Worried about the burdens his friends and family were carrying then and worn down by his own cares, Steichen felt so ill and distressed that he was not himself, even with his old friends at 291. Privately, he shared with Stieglitz his despair over the ongoing bouts with Clara, and Stieglitz, beset with his own headaches with Emmy, surely commiserated.

However, there was one celebration—Mercedes Carles gave a surprise party for Steichen in March to celebrate his thirty-fifth birthday. Because his Voulangis garden was the theme, Katharine Rhoades appeared in a geranium costume and Marion Beckett came dressed as a petunia. The table was decorated with a miniature garden, a replica of the one in Voulangis, right down to Brancusi's bird.

Soon afterward, Steichen sailed for France, worried about being an ocean away from his family now that there were rumblings over problems between the Triple Alliance of Germany, Italy, and Austria-Hungary and the Triple Entente of France, Great Britain, and Russia.[19] During the past year, the Balkan Wars had jolted Europe, until treaties between Greece and Turkey and Serbia and Turkey had delineated an uneasy peace. But perhaps, Steichen hoped, all these rumors were unfounded, only politics as usual.

In Paris, Mary and Kate had discovered a colorful surrogate grandmother in Mildred Aldrich, the cigarette-smoking, bighearted American journalist who was an intimate member of the Stein circle, as well as a character in her own right. Mildred's friends were legion—the actress Ellen Terry, Gordon Craig and his wife and children, Isadora Duncan, Mabel Dodge, Constantin Brancusi, Leo and Gertrude Stein, Alice B. Toklas, art critic Henry McBride, and many others. Shrewdly perceptive about people, Mildred was also unflinchingly forthright with them. Lacking children of her own, she lavished love on the children of others, especially Kate and Mary Steichen. While her goddaughter Kate was a particular favorite, both girls called her Aunty Milly, and Clara leaned on her as a surrogate mother as well as a surrogate grandmother.

The Steichens, in turn, were as much of a family as Mildred had in France. Therefore, they celebrated when, in early June of 1914, Mildred moved into a rented "peasant's hut" on a hilltop at Huiry, overlooking the Marne, just a few miles from Voulangis. She was nearing sixty-one when she settled alone into her rustic house in the country in search of cheaper quarters, and "perfect peace."[20] For a couple of years, she had been suffering from respiratory and heart disease and "an unquiet spirit."[21] Her doctor had long urged her to get out into the country air, and, like the Steichens, she found the peaceful countryside a tonic after Paris. She soon found a loyal friend and helper in Amélie, a housekeeper with a "checkered career," although now a married woman who lived within minutes of her house.[22]

Soon the Steichens and Mildred Aldrich were exchanging almost daily visits, with Clara and the children often riding over in a cart pulled by one of their donkeys, and Steichen overseeing the work of expanding Mildred's flower garden. Six-year-old Kate especially loved to spend time with Mildred, feeling somehow closer to women than to men. After all, "Mary was always Daddy's girl," Kate remembered, "and I was always Mommy's. It was a split family."[23]

They were still together as a family, however, for the first seven months of 1914, their last year in what they called "the enchanted garden" at Voulangis. The walled garden was now surrounded by the additional acres of Steichen's delphiniums, poppies, petunias, and roses. In June of 1914, he was awarded a gold medal by the Meaux Horticulture Society for excellence in breeding delphiniums. People often came to Voulangis looking for "Steichen, the gardener, the plant breeder," seeking to buy the new varieties of Oriental poppies he had created or wanting to purchase seeds from his pure blue petunias or delphiniums, or to see his lavish begonias, iris, and rambler roses.[24]

Steichen spent part of each day walking attentively over his acres of plants, his eyes expertly scanning them, his hands deftly examining shoots and blooms. He was an instinctive scientist, always experimenting—testing, for instance, Wisemann's theory that acquired characteristics are not transmissible. To do so, he told Sandburg, he mutilated nearly a thousand young poppy plants, stripping off their buds so that they grew up "deformed, some of them throwing up aborted flowers in all kinds of curious shapes and twisted stems," until there was nothing "normal" about them. Then he would gather and sow the seeds of the aborted flowers and cultivate them carefully. Some of those plants grew up "aborted flowers, whereas seeds gathered from a normal, untouched row of poppies" all produced perfect flowers.[25]

STRATEGIC RETREAT (1913–1914)

During the summer of 1914, his flower gardens were near bursting with the blooms of the third or fourth generations of his careful experiments, and he was eagerly mapping out plans for the coming year's plantings. To his pleasure, old friends who were artists came to help him enjoy the sight, and they spent days at a time in the garden, painting and talking. Occasionally, they ventured away from Voulangis on outings into the countryside.

During a summer expedition to the resort town of Talloires on Lac d'Annecy, near the Swiss border, Steichen, Arthur Carles, and Katharine Rhoades were caught without coats or umbrellas in a sudden powerful storm. Instead of taking cover in the hotel nearby where Clara, Marion Beckett, and Mercedes Carles waited, they raced up the mountain to watch the storm up close. The men had to pull an exhausted Katharine up the final ascent of the steep, narrow trail, but at last, in the wind, under the black sky, they stood together on a great rocky ledge overlooking the lake far below. Despite the high winds and drenching rain, the three friends waited in the "terrible wonder" of the storm until, Katharine said, they became a part of it, finding it "magnificent" and "stupendous."[26] Steichen wished *Götterdämmerung* would happen in that instant, in that very place.

As suddenly as it had come, the storm was gone. Then, in the clearing skies, another mountain appeared out of the clouds across the lake, etching such an indelible image in Katharine's mind that she painted the scene later on. After the sodden trio raced down the mountains to rejoin Clara, Mercedes Carles, and the rest of their party, someone, probably Clara, chided them: They shouldn't have done it. It was foolish. They'd be sick.

It was a telling moment, encapsulating the tension between the artists and the others, especially the artists and their mates. Carles and Steichen were always racing up metaphorical mountains after storms in those days, leaving their wives behind to be practical and dutiful, whether they wanted to be or not. At twenty-eight, high-spirited Katharine Rhoades, single and herself an artist, was free as a skylark, as was Marion Beckett. They were exuberant companions for the men in their circle of artists.

Inevitably, there was gossip in Paris and New York about Carles and Steichen and the two beautiful women. When some of it drifted to her ears, Katharine was alternately hurt, amused, and annoyed. She defended the "very fine friendship" that she enjoyed with Steichen. She thought of him as one of her best friends, she told Agnes Meyer, and held him in "enormous" affection and respect.[27] She believed that platonic friendship between men and women was entirely possible, contrary to the shortsighted view that men and women could be only spouses or lovers. Theirs was a rare friendship, and she was not about to relinquish it because narrow-minded people disapproved.

Steichen's friendship with Marion Beckett was more complicated, however. He may have had fleeting affairs with more worldly women, but Marion was different. Even the people who knew them best during those years disagreed about the nature of their relationship, but one thing was clear to most of them: Marion was not the kind of woman to enter heedlessly into an affair with a married man, particularly when that man's wife was her good friend. Yet the existing eyewitness accounts vary as to whether Steichen and Marion were lovers, verifying only that they were part of a tight-knit circle of friends during their reunions in New York or Paris and Voulangis.

Carles, who had a very attentive eye for beautiful women, was at least briefly infatuated with statuesque Katharine Rhoades, but she was carrying on a private, increasingly intimate correspondence with another man, who came to love her very much and wooed her as energetically as his circumstances allowed. He was married, twenty-two years her senior, and her mentor and friend. He was Alfred Stieglitz.

By 1914, Stieglitz, the father confessor, hopelessly mismated with sweet, self-indulgent, well-meaning Emmy, had carried on throughout the twenty-one years of their unhappy marriage with a number of flirtations with beautiful women, in person and in letters. It was Katharine Rhoades who monopolized his romantic imagination throughout 1914 and 1915. Apparently, she was more than his latest fantasy. She was for him that exotic, irresistible, and prophetic combination of struggling artist and beautiful, vibrant, intelligent woman. His love for Katharine left such a stamp on Stieglitz that he confessed in old age that if he had been a "real man" with "strength and sinew," he would have transported her to "some mountaintop, built a little house for her, given her children and let her paint."[28]

STRATEGIC RETREAT (1913–1914)

In the spring of 1914, Agnes Meyer set off alone to Europe, feeling "rebellious" over what she viewed as "the crushing" of her personality.[29] Her patient husband, deeply worried about business and the talk of war, stayed behind in New York with their two young children. He sent Agnes off with his blessings, although he quickly became irritated by her provocative letters about her adventures, including visits to old boyfriends. During her "wonderful" and "illuminating" journey, she spent several weeks in Paris looking at public and private collections of Asian and European art, and buying a Picasso still life.[30] She was hoping to persuade Eugene to buy another "glorious" Cézanne, and when Steichen came into town from Voulangis, he and Agnes went to a Toulouse-Lautrec show that made them wish for his company, she wrote to Stieglitz.[31]

She also told Stieglitz that Steichen had assured her he was nearing the end of the work on the remaining mural canvases. She predicted that once Steichen had installed the murals, he would move away from the 291 sphere to stand alone "for the first time."[32]

Actually, the murals would never be hung in the Meyers' foyer. Agnes returned to the United States later that summer, where she found out that she and her husband faced crushing financial difficulties. In New York that fall, Steichen walked all over Manhattan with a troubled Eugene Meyer for most of one night while Meyer poured out his worries. Republican that he was, Meyer had feared that business in general would decline under the new Democratic President, Woodrow Wilson. Indeed, Meyer had suffered such huge losses in a weakening stock market and had so overextended his cash reserves that he and Agnes faced what they felt to be severe cutbacks. The major casualty would be the Park Avenue town house, for before the end of the year, Meyer would be forced to sell it. Although Steichen's carefully wrought canvases would later be exhibited, they would never be installed, and many years later, when the panels were found rolled up, stored away, and forgotten, the children of Agnes and Eugene Meyer gave them to the Museum of Modern Art in New York. Agnes and Eugene were forced to cut back their expenses in other ways that autumn of 1914, and Steichen must have listened ruefully to their idea of economy: They took quarters in the posh St. Regis Hotel after their town house was sold, but they held on to their farm in Mount Kisco. Agnes had to give up her personal maid and hire a woman who could double as a maid and a nurse for the children.[33]

Later, shrewdly capitalizing on the wartime economy, Meyer took stock of the materials needed to sustain a military effort—copper wire and other copper products, as well as chemicals for the blue dye used in U. S. Navy uniforms, for instance—and helped to launch highly lucrative businesses to supply the Allies. By 1915, he had built up his fortune again—by some accounts to about $60 million.

Steichen was so haggard and ill again during the summer of 1914 that he had to be hospitalized for a recurrence of stomach pains. After a week's worth of testing, the doctors could find no physical problems. What's more, his ulcer had healed. His friends then attributed his suffering to nervousness and stress. When Agnes joined the Steichens at Voulangis in July, she was happy to find Steichen better, less worried about himself and "determined to get well."[34] He was photographing his flowers, and one memorable and portentous image survives: *Heavy Roses. Voulangis, France. 1914,* a lush still life of roses, with one ripe flower dominating the rest—some of them in partial bloom, some budding, others bent, sagging, and dying.

Near the end of July, there was a gathering of old friends in the Steichens' garden at Voulangis, where the delphiniums were particularly beautiful that summer. Agnes was still there; Katharine and Marion were there painting, and amusing Clara and the children; de Zayas and Brancusi were frequent guests. No doubt there was much talk about a recent circular letter from Stieglitz asking all the "fellows" to write about what 291 meant to them, for a special segment of *Camera Work.*

Stieglitz had turned fifty in January of 1914, just as his journal, which had originated in 1903, was entering its second decade. A master of introspection, he was in a mood for retrospection that year, as he admitted in the issue of *Camera Work* dated July 1914 but actually published in January of 1915. His theme: What is 291? Unsure of the answer himself, he decided to poll the others who had lived through the movement with him and produce an issue of *Camera Work* devoted to myriad answers to the question. There would be no pictures, only words, limited to fifteen hundred from each respondent. "And I would ask them to eliminate, if possible, any reference to myself," he wrote.[35] Eventually, he received sixty-eight responses, and he published every one of them.

Eduard and Clara Steichen and some others in the 291 circle would not be able to answer Stieglitz's July letter promptly, however. Their summer had been pleasant and leisurely, although short on rain, which made Steichen's garden work more demanding. Early in July, an ominous tornadolike wind had howled through the valley, bringing thunder and lightning but not a drop of rain. Otherwise, July was placid and beautiful.

In Paris that summer, Gertrude Stein was refurbishing her apartment at 27 Rue de Fleurus with part of the money—four thousand dollars—she had made from selling three Picasso paintings. Her brother Leo had moved to Settignano, Italy, and she and her companion, Alice B. Toklas, had traveled to London to confer with publisher John Lane about an edition of Stein's *Three Lives*. Gertrude tried her best to "look like a genius," she wrote to Mildred Aldrich and other friends, promising to visit Mildred soon in the peaceful countryside.[36]

Ironically, Mildred's "perfect peace" was about to be destroyed, for the Great War was moving inexorably closer to the beautiful valleys surrounding her house on the crest of the hill, and the valley Steichen had roamed and painted, the valley where his children played and his beautiful flowers grew.

On June 28, 1914, in Sarajevo, Serbian nationalists had assassinated Archduke Francis Ferdinand, heir to the throne of Austria, and his wife. Long a fragile house of cards, the European alliances began to topple, and a month later to the day, Kaiser Wilhelm declared war on Serbia. Agnes Meyer remembered that she and her friends were spending a carefree week in late July with the Steichens at Voulangis then: "Mercifully unaware of impending doom, we enjoyed each other and the lovely French countryside whose tranquillity was so soon to be shattered."[37] By July thirtieth, as the Steichens and their friends enjoyed a summer lunch in the walled garden at Voulangis, Austria and Russia had mobilized their forces. On July thirty-first, as she had promised her husband she would, Agnes sailed for the United States on a Dutch steamer, one of the last ships to leave Europe before the onset of war.[38] Katharine Rhoades departed, too, but Marion Beckett stayed on with the Steichens for a few more days—until the life they all had loved in Voulangis was changed forever by the unprecedented events of early August.

They could hardly believe the news they were hearing. Chaos followed a massive and deadly chain reaction of events: On August first, Germany declared war on Russia; on August third, Germany declared war on France, and on August fourth, sent troops into Belgium, supposedly a neutral haven. Then the Germans quickly invaded pacific Luxembourg, Steichen's birthplace, and France and Britain declared war on Germany.

"Everyone's life changed within twenty-four hours," Steichen later said.[39] As the village *garde champêtre* walked through Voulangis on August third, beating his drum and issuing official government orders, a worried Steichen scrawled a hasty note to Stieglitz with the news that war was "inevitable now."[40] The French militia controlled the railroads, and Steichen thought that a carefully organized "tremendous war machine" had spread through France, touching every town and village, including his own. Voulangis stood about 120 miles from the western frontier of the war, the border of France and Belgium—a distance the well-trained German army could march in eight days, fighting all the way.[41] All around them, men were departing for the war with dignity, determination, and calm. With the town bakery closed down, the women of Voulangis began baking all their own bread and enough more to share with others. Villagers of all ages, from old men and women to young children, were trying to harvest the crops. All this was directed from Paris, Steichen told Stieglitz, and working "like a clock." He thought he and Clara had ample stores of food, especially with their "fat" vegetable garden, and enough cash on hand to sustain them for a while.[42]

On the theory that in case of imminent danger, Uncle Sam could rescue them, Steichen quickly took steps to register their names and addresses with the American embassy in Paris, as well as with the Paris office of the New York *Herald*.[43] At the moment, however, all civilian travel was impossible. Marion Beckett was still with them, and they were wild with worry about her parents, who had been traveling in Russia. Already, Steichen wrote Stieglitz, he could see that war was hell. Nevertheless, they were determined to be prepared for any eventuality.[44]

STRATEGIC RETREAT (1913-1914)

Clara immediately set out for Huiry, about six miles away, to urge Mildred Aldrich to return with her to Voulangis, thinking they would all be safer in a group. To the contrary, she would stay right where she was, Mildred insisted, although touched by Clara's concern. Then what did she propose to do if the army came retreating across her garden? Clara wanted to know. Mildred laughed. It seemed impossible that the Germans would pass the French frontier. "She had come over feeling pretty glum—my dear neighbor from Voulangis," Mildred wrote. "She went away laughing. At the gate she said, 'It looks less gloomy to me than it did when I came. I felt such a brave thing driving over here through a country preparing for war. I expected you to put a statue up in your garden 'To a Brave Lady.' "[45]

In the midst of those harrowing days, as if it were not calamity enough to have an enemy army advancing relentlessly toward them, Clara and Steichen had a heart-wrenching quarrel. Only Clara's version of what she saw, or thought she saw, has survived. Returning from an errand—her drive over to Mildred's, perhaps—she walked into her house at Voulangis, then went upstairs to her daughter Mary's room, where she found Marion Beckett lying on Mary's bed, with Steichen standing there beside her. Had Marion suddenly become faint or ill, in need of a place to lie down? She had a room in a nearby inn, after all, and spent only her days with the Steichens. Was Steichen comforting her because she was overcome by fear for her parents and for all of them?

These were plausible explanations, but Clara was convinced she had interrupted an intimacy between Steichen and a mistress. Would he have been so crude and foolish as to risk a tryst in his own child's bedroom? The scene was totally innocent and misconstrued, insisted Steichen—as did others who heard the story repeatedly in the long aftermath of Clara's fury. But Clara was adamant. They had betrayed her, she wailed. Betrayed her—her husband and her best friend, in her own child's bed.[46] She vowed never to forget that moment, or to let anyone else forget it. Consequently, for Eduard, Clara, Mary, and Kate Steichen, their last weeks together at Voulangis were a personal nightmare, with the family struggles playing out now against the terrible new reality of war.

In his vivid letters to Stieglitz that summer, however, Steichen spoke only of the war, writing that Germany had dealt France a "hellish card," which he feared could "only be fatal"—unless some miracle intervened. This war had barely begun, and already they were surrounded by suffering.⁴⁷ The escalating strain and tension were "terrific," Steichen wrote to Eugene Meyer.⁴⁸ All communications had been cut by the War Bureau. Bucolic Voulangis, like Huiry, was nestled in a district "between Paris and Meaux little known to the ordinary traveler," Mildred Aldrich had written, but Voulangis was even farther off the beaten track than Mildred's hamlet.⁴⁹ Now the railroad, that vital artery, was pumping only soldiers and supplies between Paris and the frontier. The Steichens were isolated, although probably safer in the country, at least for the moment. So far, there were adequate provisions. Their horses were requisitioned by the French army, and they gladly gave them up to the cause; after all, France had been their home for eight years.

Foreigners were forbidden to travel beyond their towns and villages without permission, however, and suddenly, the Steichens had to answer for their name. Were they German—and therefore the enemy? Were they spies? There were many Germans living in the towns and villages near the frontier, and three Germans had tried to dynamite a railroad bridge between Huiry and Meaux. Already, Germans who could not prove French citizenship were being confined in a concentration camp. Luckily, the Steichens had passports that legally confirmed their nationality, so he felt that they would be safe on that score.⁵⁰

There were sporadic bright moments—the news of England's entry into the war "filled the cup" with faith that the Allies would ultimately win, Steichen wrote Eugene Meyer. He was stirred by the daily sight of men from his village walking resolutely off to the train station, just as if they were headed out to work in the fields, bearing themselves with simple dignity, without "flaggy patriotism."⁵¹

Steichen was very proud of France but terribly worried about what to do for his family's ultimate safety. Because reliable news was difficult to come by in Voulangis, he wanted to cable Meyer for advice about whether they should leave France. Finding it impossible to get through, he had to write a letter instead, with no idea of whether it would ever reach the United States. He was caught in a painful dilemma: Was it safe to stay, or time to go? France was home, after all, and how would he house and support his family once they returned to the United States? Once there, should they stay in New York, or go to Wisconsin or Connecticut, where they had family? He hoped Meyer could help him settle the quandary, and he urged him to cable his answer.[52]

Meanwhile, despite her emotional turmoil—anger, pain, fear for the future—Clara rose to the challenge of caring for her household, helping out in the village, and seeing about Mildred Aldrich, who was alone at Huiry except for Amélie. She was living there in an "awful silence, Mildred wrote."[53] Yet she was still determined to remain in her house, and she thought she had all the provisions she needed. The only hardship so far seemed to be getting cash, but Clara brought her a hundred francs, enough to sustain her for a while. Mildred found it comforting that in the Steichens she had "a family of friends" close by.[54]

Near as they were to the frontier, the war news arrived late and incomplete. The New York *Herald* European edition was reaching them two days late, heavily censored, Steichen wrote Meyer. He hoped that the American people would give France their sympathy and support. And he asked a special favor of Meyer: If anything happened to him and his family and news of this reached Eugene Meyer, would he assume the task of informing Mary Steichen at the Little Farm in Wisconsin?[55]

At the beginning, for thousands of people, World War I was gripping, fascinating, even stimulating. They knew they were in the midst of one of the "world's great upheavals," Steichen wrote to Stieglitz.[56] The two old friends were not alone in their forecasts that the war would be brief and replete with massive devastation and death, but that it would ultimately bring about regeneration. Steichen wrote to Meyer that August about his hopes that the war would finally prove to be a "great thing for humanity," predicting that a new order would emerge from the wreckage and great opportunities for rebuilding society would follow.[57]

Over on her hilltop at Huiry, however, Mildred Aldrich, who could remember the American Civil War, saw the future much more realistically. The war would be "the bloodiest affair the world has ever seen—a war in the air, a war under the sea as well as on it, and carried out with the most effective manslaughtering machines ever used in battle."[58]

By early September, as the Steichens and their friends still waited anxiously at Voulangis, the German army bludgeoned Belgium and then, penetrating the French border, bombarded a series of quaint, vulnerable French towns—Barcy, Monthyon, Penchard, Neufmontiers. Suddenly, the Steichens and their friends understood all too clearly what the war meant. Throughout the day, the skies vibrated with the engines of planes ferrying men and supplies between Paris and the frontier. Mildred Aldrich sat in her hilltop garden, watching those "cars in the air," such a new invention, about to transform the technology of war. The trains heaved through the valley, jammed with French soldiers—"no uniforms," Mildred could see, "just a crowd of men—men in blouses, men in patched jackets, well-dressed men—no distinction of class."[59]

From their garden, the Steichens could see the somber convoy of ambulances en route to the front to gather up the wounded. Eager to help victims of this unprecedented carnage, Clara began talking about taking the children to a pension near the American Hospital in Paris so that she could work there as a nurse. Steichen himself was looking for some way to be useful in the cause, and in the meantime, he hoped that the United States would not, because of its neutrality, withhold money for the urgent work of the American Hospital.[60] In that spirit, he and Clara gave the hospital a donation of a hundred francs, money they really could not spare.

Steichen was outraged over the murderous invasion of France—the rattling of guns, the whir of bullets, the thousands of bodies falling to the rich earth just miles from his house. Because of national "egoism," the world was "committing suicide," he wrote to Stieglitz, and the United States had chosen simply to sit by and watch. The seeming insanity of the German onslaught horrified and repulsed him—the sheer "banging away of might might might." He thought that German brutality—especially against the valiant Belgians—reeked of the Stone Age. Germany was guilty of a heinous crime against humanity, he charged, but he kept faith that ultimately humanity would win out. Steichen shared with Stieglitz his fervent hope that the "genius" of the human soul would not be destroyed by the bloodletting but would, in the end, prevail.[61]

Barely a month into the war, however, life as they knew it in France had so drastically changed that Steichen gravely feared it would, after all, become a long ordeal. Cut off as they were from news, it was difficult to decide what to do. At last, he got a wire from Eugene Meyer: "Advise strategic retreat," he reportedly said.[62] Unsure if this meant that he should leave France at once, Steichen managed to get a cable out to Meyer on August twenty-second, asking him to confer with Stieglitz and

Simpson and then to advise him further about exactly what to do. In Voulangis, he and his family had a house and food. He knew they would only be able to take hand baggage with them if they had to leave Voulangis, assuming they could leave at all. Was ship passage to the States even a possibility? What would they do if they could get there? Within days, these were moot questions.

With the German army drawing inevitably closer to Voulangis and surrounding villages, many people were fleeing, although an intrepid few seemed determined to stay in their homes. Most of her neighbors were gone, Mildred Aldrich reported to Gertrude Stein. She was staying, however, and doing "as well as such anxious nights and days will allow."[63] But soon, new and alarming rumors convinced Clara and Steichen that they had to get their children to safety, and a second cable from Eugene Meyer sealed their decision: "Suggest immediate orderly retreat."[64] Steichen and Clara hurriedly packed their bags and his cameras; arranged with a gardener and Francine, their maid, to check on their house; made arrangements for the family pets—the donkey, the dog, the rabbits—whom Mary and Kate could hardly bear to leave; and then said their good-byes. The treasures of their entire life together were there in the house and studio, and in the garden—paintings and glass negatives; some carefully gathered artworks and antique furnishings; Steichen's favorite chair and Clara's piano; the children's toys; and Steichen's flowers.

Almost all of his paintings had to stay behind, and all of the negatives and photographs. Just before he left, Steichen apparently hid Brancusi's bronze bird in the cellar, then took the treasured Rodin bronzes, wrapped them carefully, and buried them deep in his garden. Then he walked one last time through the sturdy bright rows of his flowers, especially the delphiniums. Would he be back to them by winter, by spring? On an impulse, he gathered some seeds to take with him. There was room, at least, for those.

On the night of September second, Steichen, Clara, Mary, and Kate boarded a cattle train in Paris, packed with refugees bound for Marseilles, for Steichen had been able to secure passage for New York on September tenth. He was determined to get Clara, Mary, and Kate safely aboard ship, but he had some doubt about himself, since all physically able men of any age were being mobilized as the enemy neared Paris.[65] While some of the citizens of Paris were "weak & panicky," Steichen wrote to Stieglitz, the bombs from airplanes had so far not generated any widespread fear. As their departure approached, he and Clara and the children were calmer than they had been in days, even "cheerful & hopeful."⁶⁶ Marion Beckett had apparently traveled with them as far as Paris; then she went on alone to London to return separately to the United States.

They had gotten out of their beloved Villa L'Oiseau bleu just two days before a German patrol reached Voulangis, and when the Germans marched toward Paris in September, the Steichens' garden lay directly in their path.⁶⁷ German cavalry scouts trampled the poppies in his fields, and later, French and British soldiers pitched their tents where Steichen's delphiniums and petunias had flourished. Over time, what the hooves of enemy horses did not destroy in Steichen's garden, neglect and winter finished.

Later, little Kate wrote a poem about it all: "Beautiful world. Beautiful world. How can you stand the war."⁶⁸

Waiting at the pier as the Steichens' ship docked in New York in late September were Charlotte and Billy Paddock, Agnes and Eugene Meyer, and Katharine Rhoades. Afterward, their friends were haunted by the arrival scene: First Clara walked down the long gangplank alone, holding on to the rail, tears in her eyes, a "strange expression of despair" on her face, Katharine told Stieglitz. Clara greeted them all as if she scarcely knew them, or was "too dazed to respond." Katharine and the Meyers looked for Steichen, then finally saw him standing at the top of the gangplank, "hopelessly weary," Katharine said, and "full of a strained sorrow—weighing down all about him."⁶⁹ On either side of him, clasping his hands, stood his daughters—Mary, now ten, who had not returned to the United States since they moved to Paris when she was two, and Kate, six, who had been born in France, had known no other country and no home but the apartment in Paris and the house in Voulangis.

That forlorn, disturbing tableau troubled the Steichens' friends for weeks afterward. "I wish one could take the burden of sorrow bodily out of a person's life—& hold it for them until they have strength enough to encompass it & look at it more clearly," Katharine wrote Stieglitz.⁷⁰ She wanted to take them to her house in Massachusetts to rest, and the Paddocks wanted to take them to Connecticut, but the Meyers insisted that Eduard, Clara, and the children should go with them to Seven Springs, their spacious farm in Mount Kisco. Katharine was glad, for she knew "*so* much more can be done for them all. I love them all so much."[71]

Their friends worried about these expatriates who had come to New York with the clothes on their backs and a few possessions thrown into the bags they could carry. Mary and Kate now spoke French far more fluently than English, and the English they spoke was marked with a French accent. France was home for them, and they were terribly homesick. With more than the war taxing them, both Steichen and Clara seemed dazed and exhausted for most of the month they spent resting at Mount Kisco, soothed by the Meyers' abundant hospitality.

Agnes Meyer wrote to Charles Freer in early October to tell him that the Steichens had arrived safely. She reported also that they had heard from their Voulangis gardener that the Germans had not damaged their home or any other houses in the village, although neighboring villages had been "terribly treated."[72] Mildred Aldrich for one had watched aghast from her nearby hilltop as a battle raged for eight hours on the plain below. She wrote to Gertrude Stein and Alice B. Toklas that the heavy artillery and shelling left "all the towns and villages in sight—Dammartin, Neufmontiers, Penchard, Chocanin—in flames, and four thousand unburied Germans on the field."[73] Dauntless Mildred immediately joined her neighbors and "helped clean up" the English troops after the battles of Mons, Cambrai, Saint-Quentin, and La Fère. They offered supplies, food, and medical care to the English as they retreated, and they heard the repercussions as British soldiers blew up all the bridges on the Marne to halt the German advance.

Mildred worried about the Steichens' house, for each time she looked out at the vistas she had loved, she saw the smoke of cannon and watched her peaceful valley being transformed first into a battleground, then a burial ground. By November, she wrote, the plain where so many Frenchmen had died in battle was covered with flowers and flags after thousands of people in black decorated the "lines and lines of graves with their crosses with soldiers' hats hanging on them."[74]

In the United States, meanwhile, many friends rallied around the weary Steichens. Mercedes Carles visited them in Mount Kisco and found Clara looking better than she had expected, and Steichen worse, although both of them seemed terribly sad. It was sometime in mid-October when, feeling much better but still resting in Mount Kisco, Steichen set up the ill-fated Meyer murals in the improvised studio in the squash court at Seven Springs Farm, determined to finish them even though the Meyers had been forced to give up their town house.

By late October, he felt ready to go into New York for a reunion with Stieglitz and 291. But before he left, he wanted to plant the delphinium seeds he had carried over from Voulangis. With the Meyers' blessing, he spent some time digging in their garden, pouring his seeds into American soil. He would not be able to tend them as he would have in Voulangis, or to carry out further experiments and crossings, but they took root and grew so hardily that thirty years later, during another war, Steichen could look at the beautiful delphiniums in Agnes Meyer's Seven Springs garden and see evidence of the original progeny he had developed in France before August of 1914.[75]

By now, Eduard and Clara were talking seriously about what to do and where to live, for Mary and Kate needed to be enrolled in school and Steichen had to earn money. As comfortable as the Meyers had made them at Seven Springs, they needed to be in their own home. Someone—either Katharine or the Paddocks—helped them find a summer cottage in Sharon, Connecticut, where they could live rent-free for a time. Beyond the war weariness, Steichen and Clara needed some privacy to try to tend to their marriage.

Agnes Meyer, Katharine Rhoades, and Marion Beckett had a happy reunion in the fall of 1914, then set out together on October 16, 1914, to visit Charles Freer in Detroit. Before she left, Katharine learned that Steichen planned to visit Stieglitz in New York, and she was worried. Stieglitz wrote his long, secret letters to her from 291 rather than from home, where Emmy might find out, and Katharine feared that somehow Steichen would discover that there was something unusual going on between them. "The letters must stop," she warned Stieglitz.[76] She did not want Steichen to change his feelings toward Stieglitz on her account.

Strategic Retreat (1913–1914)

The two men would find their friendship changing dramatically that fall, but not because of their respective interests in Beckett and Rhoades. One unfortunate casualty of the Great War was the old harmony and trust between Steichen and Stieglitz. One has only to look at their letters to others during the first months of the war to know how their arguments must have gone when they stood face-to-face at 291. Steichen, passionately pro-France, had left virtually everything he owned in Voulangis, his home vulnerable to the encroaching German army, and had seen lives, including his own, torn apart by the war. Stieglitz, on the other hand, purporting to be an isolationist and a pacifist, still leaned toward support of Germany. Safe at home and as self-absorbed as ever, he was fretting over the fact that the whole block of Fifth Avenue from Thirty to Thirty-first streets was scheduled to be demolished the following May. Nevertheless, he foresaw a "great season" ahead for 291. He would continue the work "in the little garrett [sic] just as if it were to stand for ever," he pledged.[77]

The war was "having a very depressing effect on the people about New York," Stieglitz reported to Annie Brigman. Everyone could hear hard times "knocking loudly at the door," but at least, for once, Americans were confronted with "a *real* thing. . . . Thank heaven there is at least something real and live, even if it takes the form of death. To me the War, terrible as it may seem to others, is a most wonderful thing. It was inevitable. There is no one to blame for it, and it is stupid to lay the blame to anyone."[78]

Then Stieglitz articulated the view that appalled almost everyone close to him, including Emmy and Annie Brigman, to whom he wrote that if he had to give his sympathy to a nation, it might go to Germany, which had been "more constructive, more farsighted as a nation than any other people. Militarism or no militarism. Killing in war, to me, is not quite as rotten as killing by inches, and unseen, in times of what people call 'Peace.' And see what 'Peace' can bring and what civilization really means."[79]

Then Stieglitz, embroiled in his ongoing strife with Emmy, offered a revealing analogy: "What are nations but a series of families. And what does one find in families. Is there not this constant war: this desire to destroy: brother and brother, father and son, husband and wife, etc. etc.

And so this gasing about ideals, about what nations ought to do, makes me sick. Let people start with themselves. And if they would war will become unthinkable."[80]

At the outset of that autumn of 1914, however, Steichen and Stieglitz were very glad to see each other, although Steichen was terribly disappointed to find 291 itself "in the doldrums." The now-grimy burlap walls were symptomatic, he thought, of a "dust-covered atmosphere about the whole place."[81] What's more, the gallery was empty except for a few 291 regulars, including Agnes Meyer and Marius de Zayas, who had recently returned from a summer in Paris, where he tried unsuccessfully to join the French general staff. The purpose of his trip had been to gather artwork for a series of 291 exhibitions, and when he returned to New York in mid-September, he had succeeded—war or no war—in bringing enough art for three shows. First would be an exhibit of West African sculpture, introduced to him by Picasso; then paintings and drawings by Picasso and Braque, loaned by Francis Picabia (who was stuck in Paris because he had been drafted into the French army); and an exhibition of abstract paintings by Picabia himself, each canvas large enough to fill a whole wall at 291.

Stieglitz had welcomed de Zayas back as "one of the few really loyal friends of '291' and at the same time a constructive helper," and the two men had mounted the exhibition of African sculpture and carvings before Steichen first arrived at the gallery in early November.[82] Taking one disapproving look at the installation, however, Steichen immediately persuaded Stieglitz to let him spruce it up, just as in the old days.

With suddenly renewed energy, Steichen took the sculptures down, then bought reams of black, yellow, and orange paper, which he used to splash the drab burlap walls with bright abstract geometrical shapes, "like a background of jungle drums."[83] When he mounted the sculptures against this vivid new background, the whole room suddenly sprang to life. The show stayed up until December eighth, then was followed by the exhibition of charcoal drawings and oils by Braque and Picasso from the Picabias' collection, as well as some pre-Columbian pottery and carvings.

Steichen took credit for persuading Stieglitz to show the Braque and Picasso works and for designing the background for the show. This time, he bought cheap cheesecloth to cover the walls, and he dug out from storage some old denim curtains to be dyed black. Juxtaposed to the cheesecloth and newly dyed denim, the pictures, intermingled with some African sculptures, transformed the 291 galleries so that they were "clean, fresh, and alive again"—although something was still missing. Then Stieglitz's loyal, eccentric assistant Emil Zoler, who was helping Steichen, offered a big wasp's nest as the "real object" that Steichen sought as a centerpiece. From the very first exhibition at 291, Steichen had habitually juxtaposed some element from nature to the artworks on display—dried flowers or leaves in a simple brass bowl, for instance. This delicately contrived wasp's nest, full of angles, arcs, and cones, was nature's own artful sculpture, as intricate as the most convoluted Cubist drawing or painting. "A wasp's nest was perfect, especially in relationship to the Cubism we had on the wall," Steichen remembered.[84]

"Well, what are you going to do after this?" Stieglitz asked Steichen.[85] Steichen had no idea. The best he could do for the moment was to settle his wife and children in Sharon, Connecticut, in the borrowed summer cottage, and then try to find work in New York. Shaken by his own intimate encounter with the war, Steichen now urged Stieglitz and their colleagues to broaden their work at 291 "into something that could lead to our becoming a civilizing force in the world."[86] He wanted the 291 circle to expand now to encompass music and poetry and all the other arts in a new global arts organization.

As it stood, Steichen believed, the Photo-Secession, as they had known it, was dead.

21

A Forum for Wisdom and Folly

(1 9 1 4 - 1 9 1 5)

An oasis of real freedom . . .
A Negation of Preconceptions
A Forum for Wisdom and for Folly . . .[1]

—EUGENE MEYER

DESPITE THE HEATED DEBATES AT 291 about the war, Alfred Stieglitz seemed engrossed in his own endeavors, busily preparing his special "What Is 291?" edition of *Camera Work,* as if the world around him were not convulsed with change. Steichen called Stieglitz's preoccupation with the issue a trivial, meaningless "project of self-adulation."[2] Nevertheless, at Stieglitz's stubborn insistence, he finally sat down to write the answer to the question Stieglitz had first posed that summer of 1914, before the world went mad.

Most of the sixty-eight people who answered Stieglitz's call sent virtually unqualified praise for 291, responses that would be printed in the *Camera Work* issue dated July 1914. In contrast to the general outpouring of praise stood Steichen's essay—an aggressive criticism of 291. Most of his compatriots had reflected on what 291 *was,* and what it had been, with the consensus being that 291 was essentially Alfred Stieglitz. That was true, Steichen agreed, but with his own head full of dreams of what the Photo-Secession could yet *become,* he wrote what even he himself called "the only sharp minority opinion."[3]

A Forum for Wisdom and Folly (1914–1915)

He had never really known what 291 was, Steichen reflected, and he thought this inquiry into its meaning was "impertinent, egoistic and previous [sic]," sounding too much like an obituary or an inquest. He believed 291 owed its success to its openness to "the great unforeseen" and its progress to "sudden and brusque changes caused largely by an eager receptivity to the unforeseen." Still, Steichen paid heartfelt tribute to Stieglitz's "broad generous understanding and support" to the individuals who formed "the aggregate '291,' " noting that to many of them, Stieglitz had "been of greater importance in our personal development than it would ordinarily seem any single unrelated individual could possibly be."

Although Steichen observed that 291 had paved the way for the success of the Armory Show, he charged that since then, 291 had been marking time—perhaps because of complacency, or the "discouragement that follows achievement," or "inertia caused by the absence of new or vital creative forces." Then came the words that stung: 291 was no longer a "living issue," and the publication of this edition of *Camera Work* may have been "simply the result of 291's finding itself with nothing better to do."

With the war, they were confronted by another great "unforeseen," Steichen argued, then proceeded to the crux of his protest: "If ever there came, within our time, a psychological element of universal consequence that could rouse individuals out of themselves as individuals and grip humanity at its very entrails, surely it was this one." Instead, 291 simply kept on producing *Camera Work*—"a book about itself"—and kept on marking time. Steichen saw this as a fatal failure, just as every other "human institution failed, demoralized by the immensity of the event and blinded by the immediate discussion of it, instead of instantly grasping the significance of the great responsibility that was suddenly ours. It failed to grasp the necessity of making of itself a vast force instead of a local one."[4]

Steichen's negative words made inescapably clear the growing strain now testing his long friendship with Stieglitz. They found themselves differing openly—not only about the fundamental philosophy of 291 but also about the direction of art and its very function in contemporary society. Furthermore, they also disagreed emphatically about the war—a war in theory to Stieglitz, cloistered at 291; a war in grim fact to Steichen, bereft of his home and his livelihood.

To make personal relations between the two men even more awkward, Clara was bombarding Stieglitz and Emmy and others in their ingrown circle of friends with anguished letters and calls about her marital troubles. Steichen was both humiliated and frustrated by Clara's behavior, for he was still clinging to the hope that they could work out their problems in private. But despite Steichen's passionate denials, Clara was convinced she was the wronged woman, betrayed by Steichen and Marion Beckett, and she wanted everyone else to know about her pain. Consequently, much genuine concern—as well as lively gossip and speculation—circulated in the private talks and letters their friends shared in New York and elsewhere. Even in the middle of the war zone in France, Mildred Aldrich, one of Clara's favorite confidantes, wrote about the latest events in the Steichens' marital saga in her letters to Gertrude Stein and Alice B. Toklas.

Unhappily aware of this interest in his problems, Steichen kept his own counsel—except for occasional talks with Stieglitz, who in turn was giving Steichen as well as Clara his fatherly, superior, often judgmental advice. Stieglitz knew far more about Steichen's intimate battles with Clara than Steichen knew of Stieglitz's current situation, however. Although Steichen was aware that Stieglitz and Emmy were still driving each other to distraction with their endless, hopeless disagreements about everything under the sun, he did not know that Alfred was at that very same moment clandestinely writing his love letters to Katharine Rhoades, all the while flirting on paper and in person at 291 with his lovely young secretary, Marie Rapp.

Longingly, Emmy admired men who put their families first, whose eyes glowed with pride when they talked about their children, who were proud of their wives and spent time with them. All Alfred did was ignore or criticize, she fumed. The "advancement of art" should not come at the expense of family life, Emmy complained. She did expect Stieglitz to understand, however, for he was not "that sort of man!" She understood more about their marriage than Alfred may have realized. "Even with money you and I would not suit," she wrote sadly.[5]

Stieglitz seems to have been a verbally abusive husband, writing Emmy scathing, scolding letters, as if he were criticizing a child, and apparently speaking "roughly" and sternly to her when they were together.[6] He was engaged in matters of universal importance, he believed, while

A FORUM FOR WISDOM AND FOLLY (1914–1915)

Emmy could not seem to think past her next new dress, picture show, golf game, or dinner. She realized clearly, however, that he was always involved with abstractions, while the "real" things of life meant most to her. She was also sad to hear him praise the war, she told him, for no matter what cleansing process he foresaw, so much death and misery were too terrible to justify it. Sometimes she thought Alfred was made of "stone," and his words made her "shudder."[7]

These parallel domestic wars wore down Stieglitz and Emmy as they did Steichen and Clara, and it was now an added stress for both men that they were for the first time at serious odds with each other over the universal issues of art and politics. Displaced by the war, Steichen found himself uprooted and adrift in his career as well as in his marriage, and he needed the familiar old anchorage of his work with Stieglitz on behalf of 291. But it seemed that not even that little sanctuary was immune to the upheaval of the times.

———

"At the outbreak of the First World War we fled France and spent a dreary winter in a summer cottage in Connecticut which had been loaned to us," Mary remembered. "I went to school there, and with my French accent and independent ways my schoolmates regarded me as a very strange child."[8] Her mother and father were preoccupied with their own worries, however, and Mary and Kate had to cope as best they could. All winter, Clara was "terribly sad," friends observed.[9] At least she had friends and family nearby, for Katharine Rhoades would spend part of the winter with relatives in Sharon primarily to be close to the Steichens, and Clara's sister and brother-in-law lived not far away.

During the late fall of 1914, Paula Sandburg traveled for two days by train from Chicago with three-year-old Margaret for a reunion and a long visit with her brother and sister-in-law. Steichen met them in New York, then took them on the commuter train to Sharon, where Paula found Eduard and Clara's house cold and drafty, although surrounded by beautiful countryside. "Sunday we had a long walk Ed—Clara & I over the hills—hills all about—and brooks," Paula wrote to Sandburg back in Chicago.[10] She wished he could see Mary and Kate's "stunning" paintings and hear them sing. "Kate's voice is marvelous," Paula wrote,

"—so pure and like a bell—I've never heard a youngster of her age sing anything like she does." They were a "pair of wonderful girls."[11]

Steichen wanted all the news about his brother-in-law, who was now working in Chicago as a reporter for *The Day Book*, an unorthodox Scripps tabloid newspaper. But thirty-six-year-old Sandburg was more than a journalist now; he was at last gaining some recognition as a poet, thanks to his recent publication in Harriet Monroe's innovative *Poetry: A Magazine of Verse*. Paula had never relinquished her faith in her husband's future as a poet, and she had carefully typed the manuscript they submitted to Monroe, expertly compensating for a broken typewriter key that they were too poor to have repaired.

Harriet Monroe was the Stieglitz of poetry and Chicago, serving as the champion and patron of such struggling artists as William Carlos Williams, James Joyce, Robert Frost, and Vachel Lindsay—and now Carl Sandburg, whom she had introduced to the great Irish poet William Butler Yeats at a banquet in March of 1914, just before she gave Sandburg's radical poems their first significant publication.

Coincidentally, the Sandburgs were wrestling with their own marital troubles just then, for the tall, handsome Swede had his head turned by the sudden adulation of "all these women in and out of the *Poetry* office," as Paula recalled it.[12] Forthright as she was, she had confronted her husband with her worries; reminding him that they had built their marriage on a "pact" of freedom and trust, she asked if he wanted a divorce.[13] Seriously shaken, Sandburg had reaffirmed his love for his wife, and then, as was his way, he joked that he was not about to put himself through all that courting again.[14]

Before Paula left Sharon to go home to Chicago, Steichen shared with her a special souvenir, and afterward she exulted to Sandburg, "I have seeds from Voulangis for vines & trailing things, scarlet morning Glory & verbenas and more than I can tell!"[15] Except for a mention of their walk, however, Paula's letters were strangely void of any reference to Clara.

Calmed and heartened by this visit with his sister, Steichen seemed himself again, "in fine spirits—outwardly at least," Katharine Rhoades reported to Stieglitz.[16] Katharine was adroitly juggling friends and relationships in their tight-knit group: Stieglitz was still inundating her with letters, while Katharine was simultaneously carrying on a correspondence with both Stieglitz and Emmy. Katharine saw Steichen and Clara regularly, further endearing herself to both by her solicitous attention to their needs as they got settled. All the while, she maintained her frequent correspondence and occasional visits with her best friend, Marion Beckett, with whom Steichen now apparently had no communication at all.

Eager to protect herself and Stieglitz from discovery and disapproval, Katharine had begged him, albeit to no avail, to curtail his steady stream of letters to her. In the autumn of 1914, she began urging Stieglitz to stop writing to her for his own sake, feeling that the letters absorbed too much of his energy. Besides, the more she learned about the Steichens' problems, the more she worried about causing Emmy unhappiness. Katharine and Marion surely talked about Stieglitz and Steichen, for after a visit with Marion, Katharine told Stieglitz, "One causes despair in another—the other produces tragedy—a third is numbed.—Life stops.... The letters—We have discussed how they might be misunderstood...." She had not thought before then, she told him, of the "terrible unhappiness they would cause."[17]

Yet Stieglitz kept on courting Katharine in his seductive letters, and she kept filling page after page with her feathery script and her ideas on love. "The only two terms apparently applied as a relationship between Man & woman not married to each other—are—friendship—and love affair," Katharine wrote Stieglitz that November.[18] Neither seemed to describe their relationship, she thought, believing instead that they were, as Walt Whitman would say, comrades—intimate companions of the soul. But fifty-year-old Stieglitz, married though he was, wanted far more than that from beautiful young Katharine Rhoades; he wanted marriage, but he lacked the courage to break free from Emmy. As if he enjoyed the suffering, and the hopeless romantic drama of it, Stieglitz continued to open his heart to Katharine for months. "I can't give what you want therefore I'm not quite the person we feel that I am," she told him. "I wish you could find that person."[19]

When an unsuspecting Emmy poured out her woes to Katharine over the telephone, sadly telling her that she knew that she herself could never be anything to her husband, Katharine anxiously reported to Stieglitz: "She said she was in a terrible condition mentally—I felt it in the sound of her voice."[20]

Back in Huiry in the autumn of 1914, as Mildred Aldrich held out on her hilltop, she wrote such vivid letters about what was happening in front of her eyes that her friends in the United States collected them for a book. The letters would be serialized in the *Atlantic Monthly,* then published in a best-selling book entitled *A Hilltop on the Marne: Being Letters Written June 3–September 8, 1914.* The dull boom of cannon decimated the peace in her valley, Mildred had written, and she could not get her mind off the terrible suffering that would be caused by a frigid winter. She had made it into Paris to get money and provisions and to see Gertrude Stein and Alice B. Toklas. Back home, she wrote to Alice that she worried constantly about the soldiers "out there in the north."[21]

In Connecticut, Steichen and Clara were riveted to every detail of news from the war zone. Knowing that it would be a meager Christmas there, they decided to take matters into their own hands. Steichen solicited cash contributions from their friends in the United States, especially those who had spent time at Villa L'Oiseau bleu, and he wrote to Matisse and other friends in Europe, asking them to help provide a Christmas fund for the children of Voulangis. Then he and Clara added what money they could and subsequently sent a bank draft for five hundred francs to town officials so that the children of their beloved village would have some sort of Christmas despite the misery of that first wartime winter.

Clara set her daughters to work making Christmas gifts for Mildred Aldrich and others close to them. Mary and Kate especially relished packing a Christmas box full of practical things for their aunty Milly, adding pictures they had painted for her, along with poems they had written. As they sent the box off to France, their parents tried to prepare them for the fact that it might not get through. Separately, in her own private letters to Mildred, Clara sent war clippings from the New York papers and other news from the States, as well as more intimate details of her growing rift with Steichen.

On December 26, 1914, the Steichens and the Paddocks joined Katharine Rhoades and her family for a sledding party. The weather was bitterly cold—ten below zero that morning—yet it was a "glorious" day for coasting down the snowy Connecticut hills.[22] The Steichen children had a wonderful time, unaware of the fact that it would be their last Christmas together as a family. Steichen and Clara had quarreled for years, patching up their differences time and again, but this time there would be no truce.

Mildred had suspected this from Clara's sad letters, and she alluded to it in a letter of thanks she sent to Connecticut when the surprise Christmas box miraculously found its way to Huiry.[23] Concerned about Clara's unhappiness, Mildred took time out from her intense correspondence about troop movement and wartime tragedy to ask Kate to hug and kiss her mother and "whisper in her ear—'That is from aunty Milly' and then ask her to hug back and say 'So is that.' "[24]

What Mildred did not tell the Steichens that New Year's Eve when she wrote to Kate was that she could see French troops crisscrossing the valley, more than a hundred wagons of ammunition with "aeroplane floats, and a big escort camped along the hill from Couilly to Meaux."[25] Huge searchlights probed the skies on the lookout for German planes, and newspapers and rumors reported a massive movement of German troops. Two hundred soldiers from Mildred's commune had marched away to battle, and thirty-one of them were dead by New Year's Day. That toll could be multiplied by every town and village in France. Now each time Mildred saw a person climbing over the hill on foot or in a donkey cart, she knew that someone else had set out to search for a hospital or a wounded soldier, or for some final word of a loved one's fate.

With his wife and daughters settled into some semblance of a routine in Connecticut, Steichen spent much of his time in New York during the winter of 1915, staying with Emmy's brother Joe Obermeyer and preparing for his exhibition at M. Knoedler & Company in New York. The show was scheduled to open January twenty-fifth and run for two weeks. It included twenty-one paintings, plus the seven canvases listed in the catalog as "Mural Decorations Painted for Mr. and Mrs. Eugene Meyer, Jr. Motive:—In Exaltation of Flowers."[26] After the show closed February sixth, it would be shipped on to Chicago.

Disappointed as Agnes and Eugene Meyer had been to lose their town house and, with it, the opportunity to install the long-awaited murals, Agnes was excited about having the murals on display in New York. The younger viewers at the exhibition praised Steichen's murals, but the older viewers, painters as well as critics, condemned them, she wrote to Charles Freer. She found it "discouraging" to hear such criticism, but none of it shook her faith in Steichen's work, she told Freer.[27]

Steichen also showed a representative collection of small pictures—the work he had been able to take out of France, as well as paintings already in the United States because they were owned by his friends and patrons. Agnes thought it interesting that the public, which called Steichen's paintings "extreme" five years earlier, now embraced that earlier work and disliked his "new manner!"[28] Freer visited the show with Agnes one day and predicted that "Steichens [sic] art will have the high appreciation it deserves."[29]

After one of his exhibitions, most likely this one, Marion Beckett wrote to Steichen about his paintings. She was "deeply impressed," but she hoped he would honor his own style, and not be caught up in fads, trends, and movements, telling him emphatically that he would "not go too quietly into that 'Painting of the Future'!"[30]

Two days after Steichen's show was unveiled at Knoedler, Stieglitz opened an exhibition of paintings by Marion Beckett and Katharine Rhoades—their first and only show at 291. Katharine's work on display included a self-portrait, a brilliantly colored Voulangis landscape, and a portrait of Mary Steichen. Marion's portraits included one of Emmy Stieglitz, one of her father, one of herself, and one of Katharine Rhoades. She also showed her portrait of Eduard Steichen—"carrying a stalk of hollyhock over his shoulder," the New York *Herald* critic wrote, "reminding one of the flower pictures by this artist shown at the Knoedler galleries."[31]

The critics objected that the traditional and not particularly distinguished paintings by Rhoades and Beckett seemed a serious departure from the abstract art they expected to see at 291, but Agnes Meyer, devoted to her friends, thought that their exhibition made a "very pleasant and very dignified impression." Besides, Agnes wrote, the experience would be good for them, as would any criticism that came their way.[32]

Stieglitz's love for Rhoades may have clouded his appraisal of her art in this case, but he did for her in January of 1915 what he would do before very long for another young artist—Georgia O'Keeffe—that time, with powerful repercussions in the American art world.

Finally, at her insistence, Stieglitz agreed to stop writing intimate letters to Katharine, but even though he told her to burn his letters, she kept them carefully packed away, apparently destroying them only many years later.[33] Stieglitz, however, would hold on to Katharine's letters until he died.[34]

"All the fellows wish to be remembered," Stieglitz wrote from 291 to photographer Annie Brigman in February of 1915: "Steichen, De Zayas, Marin and Haviland. They are all growing wonderfully, but the times are trying for them all."[35] Another constant presence at 291 then was Agnes Meyer, who was hell-bent on saving 291 from what she saw as its imminent demise. Although Stieglitz had expressed his intentions to keep *Camera Work* going, the "What Is 291?" issue, published in January 1915, would not be followed by another edition until October of 1916; eight months later, in June of 1917, Stieglitz would put the final issue of *Camera Work* to bed. The journal—and an era—were coming to a close, in large part because energy and money were ebbing away as the war wore on.

Agnes Meyer, along with Paul Haviland and Marius de Zayas, had an inspiration, however, and Agnes wrote to tell Charles Freer that she and others at 291 wanted to broadcast their views on art and life and many other compelling subjects.[36] She, de Zayas, and Haviland wanted to publish a monthly magazine dedicated to "the most modern art and satire."[37] They asked Stieglitz to help found and publish it at 291; furthermore, they wanted it to be called *291*. Stieglitz not only agreed; he joined Haviland and Agnes Meyer in funding the magazine. To her satisfaction, Agnes was chosen to write one of the first long articles, a challenge that kept her busy, since she had to maintain her roles as a "mama, a farmer and the wife of a busy husband."[38]

The first issue of the ambitious, expensive, short-lived journal appeared in March 1915. Steichen contributed a satirical drawing, *What Is Rotten in the State of Denmark*, to the first issue of *291* and another, *Le*

Coq Gaulois, to the May issue, but his entries were halfhearted at best, for he had his doubts about where all this was headed. Charles Caffin, who, like Steichen, was one of Stieglitz's oldest, most trusted colleagues, was also candidly skeptical about the magazine, calling it in an article in the *New York American* "uncouth ... devoid of mental nutriment" as well as "human feeling," and "sterile."[39]

Meanwhile, in Sharon, Connecticut, Clara had been lonely and housebound for most of the winter of 1915 because Steichen was always in New York, and both her children suffered from long bouts of influenza. From her sickbed, Mary wrote to her aunty Milly, who answered, "Lots of the children at Crécy have had grippe, and tonsillitis and scarlet fever, so it is a good thing that you are not there, isn't it?" She urged Mary and Kate not to forget their French, and she told them she was going to Voulangis soon to kiss Tommy, the horse, and to "see if the posies are doing their duty and getting all their prettiest clothes on to be ready for you when you and Kate come back hand in hand, and I hope it will be soon. . . ."[40]

Without giving details, Stieglitz told Annie Brigman in April that times were "most difficult" for many of the closer associates of 291: "Tragedies are happening, or about to happen, unpreventable ones, even attempts at suicide; and possible suicide a fact."[41] Was he referring to Clara Steichen? She was growing more desperately jealous and unhappy by the week. In later letters to Stieglitz, pouring out her confusion and pain, she would allege that Steichen had married her only because he had still been in shock over Rosa's suicide. In 1915, she herself was not sure she wanted to go on living.

For twelve years, Steichen and Clara had been around and around the painful orbit of their conflicts. He could be maddeningly cold to her, and she could be so verbally violent that it shook him for days afterward. He thought that her ferocious words were, at bottom, the "true picture" of her inner feelings. Her unpredictable moods and those volatile scenes stood out "indelibly" in his mind, he told her, for they had happened as long as they had known each other. Clara poured this out to Stieglitz in a series of painfully personal letters over the next two years, sometimes copying lines and whole passages of letters Steichen wrote to her and rebutting them point by point. If her venomous outpourings were not so devastating, Steichen suggested to Clara, they might even be called high art. Although she had "unbounded faith" in Steichen the artist, why did she demonstrate no faith whatsoever in him as a man and a spouse? her husband asked her.[42] Because she could not trust him, she shouted back. She wanted to possess him completely, he countered, and he would not be possessed.

He was ashamed of her, she protested. She expected him to be the Father, the Son, and the Holy Ghost, he charged. He could not be perfect. He was human. She expected too much, he said. Yes, she replied, because he did not give her enough of himself and his love.

The accusations flew back and forth: She was quarrelsome and unreasonable. He was dictatorial and domineering. He didn't really love her, she cried. Oh, but he did, he declared; furthermore, his present love for her had survived despite the "damnable" obstacles she herself had thrown in their way.[43]

Clara seemed to thrive on their quarrels; at least his full attention was riveted on her then, until he stalked away. He hated conflict, however, and thought it was "utterly sordid." They knew each time they started an argument exactly how it would transpire, he told her. It was scripted by years of practice, and it always degenerated into "trench warfare."[44]

And what about Marion Beckett? she wanted to know. Insistently, she begged him to explain to her what she had seen that fateful day in Mary's room in the little house in Voulangis.

He was adamant: She had seen nothing. Nothing had happened. There was nothing to explain.

She didn't believe him.

With this venom between them, Steichen spent much of his time working in New York that spring, staying with Joe Obermeyer at 57 West Fifty-eighth Street. He was desperate to earn money, and his work, he felt, provided a welcome and legitimate excuse to stay away from Clara. She decided in turn that she had to get away, and because she wanted her children to know her family, she took her daughters on a trip to Missouri to visit her elderly parents. Kate Steichen loved her "ancient, white-bearded grandfather," but she remembered her grandmother as "a devil as my mother was a devil."[45]

One day, Clara and her relatives took Mary and Kate out to the site of the family homestead in the Ozarks to see the original log cabin and a house built later on land once called Keetsville, Missouri, because of Clara's grandmother Keet. Kate fondly remembered that day with her grandfather, the "horse-and-buggy doctor," when she was "a little girl fresh over from France."[46] Always enchanted with nature, she set out running through the field, failing to see a barbed-wire fence until she had collided with it. The barbed wire cut into her throat and trapped her.

"Take me to the child," said Clara's physician father, who was almost blind.[47] Kate remembered looking up into his face, feeling his skilled hands, and knowing he would save her. It was, after the retreat from the war, one of the most traumatic experiences of her young life.

All too soon, there was another. It had been a spring of bitter argument for Clara and Eduard, a passionate reprise of the years of discord between them. They stood then at an impasse, one that Clara sought to end dramatically. Despite the vigorous protests of her husband, her family, and her friends, Clara threatened to take her daughters and make the risky ocean voyage abroad in order to move back to their house in Voulangis. She would live there, in her own home, Steichen and the Great War be damned. She would not be deterred, even by the news that on May seventh, the Germans sank the *Lusitania*.

Still officially neutral and isolated from the war, the United States was thrown into uproar over the tragedy, which cost 128 innocent American lives. The *Lusitania* tragedy brought Steichen and Stieglitz to the "climax" of their disputes over the war, Steichen remembered.[48] "It served them right," Stieglitz argued in defense of the Germans. "They were warned in advance that the ship would be sunk."[49] Steichen was appalled at the intimation that innocent people deserved to die, and Stieglitz's remarks hardened his resolve to make a significant contribution to the war effort on behalf of the Allies.

"Much of the enthusiasm that had existed at 291 gradually disappeared because of the war," Stieglitz reflected defensively in later years. "Close friends seemed to fall by the wayside. I could not turn 291 into a political institution, nor could I see Germany as all wrong and the Allies as all right.... Colleagues tried to prove to me that Beethoven was no German, that all the cruelty in the world came from Germany and that every Frenchman and Englishman was a saint. I was truly sick at heart."[50]

Steichen had more heartbreak to bear that bitter spring than his conflict with Stieglitz, however. Bent on vengeful punishment because she still believed that her husband was embroiled in an affair with Marion Beckett and that all their friends and family were in collusion to protect Steichen, Clara began to make plans to take her children and go home to Voulangis. Unfortunately, few documents have survived from that fateful May of 1915 to clarify the sequence of events. There were acrimonious arguments between the Steichens over Clara's threat to leave, and over the fate of their daughters. Steichen may even have offered her an uncontested divorce if that was what she wanted. But his wife appeared to be hell-bent on going back to France, and while Steichen could not stop her, he vowed to do his best to keep his daughters safe with him in the United States. He knew he might have to put them in boarding school while he worked in New York to support the family. Clara was not about to leave her children, however, imagining that Steichen would immediately turn to Marion Beckett for help in caring for them.[51]

There must have been furious confrontations between the couple, no doubt overheard by the children, and there were intercessions by alarmed and disbelieving friends and relatives in New York and Connecticut before a compromise was negotiated. Clara would take Kate with her to France; Mary would stay with her father in the United States, but she would live with Lee and Lizzie Stieglitz during the school year, beginning in the fall of 1915, when she would be enrolled at the prestigious Brearley School in Manhattan.

During those last miserable days in May, as Clara frantically packed for her foolhardy voyage, Mary came down with chicken pox and was turned over to Lee and Lizzie Stieglitz so that Lee could see to her recovery. In Manhattan just before sailing, Clara went to the Stieglitzes to say good-bye to Mary. As Clara recalled that sad farewell twenty years later, she said that Steichen had cautioned her beforehand that there should not be "any tears" or dramatic scenes. This admonition proved that her husband was cold and heartless, she believed, and she ascribed it to his

"Prussian mind." Furthermore, according to Clara's account years later, Mary looked up at her that day from her sickbed in the home of Dr. Lee Stieglitz, her face covered with chicken pox, her blue eyes wide, and begged to go home with her mother.[52]

"It seems Steichen decided I was ruining Mary's life, so I gave her up, damn him," Clara told Stieglitz.[53] But in giving up Mary, Clara attached herself obsessively to Kate. As Mary herself put it, her mother "fastened onto" Kate and "lived her life vicariously through her. And manipulated and controlled her. I was fortunate to be separated from my mother by the time I was 10."[54]

Four lives changed forever that day in late May of 1915 when in a desperate and reckless act Clara took Kate and stormed back to France. Nothing Steichen or anyone else had done, said, or promised had dissuaded her, yet she would later blame her husband bitterly for making her risk her life, having convinced herself irrationally that he had forced her to go back into the war zone.

"Mrs. Steichen arrived at Bordeaux a week ago last Saturday," Mildred Aldrich told Gertrude Stein on June 9, 1915. She immediately went over to Voulangis to welcome Clara and Kate, where she learned from Clara that Steichen had stayed in New York and "she left Mary with him at school."[55]

Worried as she was about the Steichens, Mildred was glad to have Kate and Clara back, and she soon heard in even more vivid detail about Steichen, Marion Beckett, and the miserable winter. Clara often rode over to Huiry at six in the morning, hitched her horse to a tree, and joined Mildred for coffee in the orchard on the hilltop. Sometimes, Clara and Kate drove over in the wagon to take Mildred to Voulangis to visit. It was a safe-enough journey when there were Allied soldiers protecting the area. "We are still surrounded with soldiers," Mildred wrote Gertrude. "We have cavalry here and there is artillery all along the road between my house and hers. . . . All day yesterday we heard the cannon again."[56]

Clara was dramatically living out her revenge on Steichen by fleeing with Kate to France and the war zone. Their friends and relatives in the United States were shocked and appalled. Oma and Opa, the Sandburgs, the Paddocks, and others were particularly heartsick over the danger to Clara and Kate, as well as over the bitter breach in the family. During the early part of that summer of 1915, Steichen and Mary stayed on in the borrowed cottage in Connecticut, where Steichen wore himself out with physical labor around the place, even going over for several days in a row to the large house nearby where Katharine Rhoades was living with her mother, in order to mow their lawn and garden. Meanwhile, he struggled to get back to his painting and photography.

By mid-June, Clara and Kate were settled enough at Villa L'Oiseau bleu so that Clara had time to write letters to many friends back in the United States. During the months after her self-imposed exile to France, Steichen was too strapped financially to maintain a permanent residence for Mary and himself. The George Pratts helped to send Mary to Camp Kehonka on Lake Winnipesaukee for most of the summer, and she was joined there by Carolyn Pratt and Kitty Stieglitz. Otherwise, Steichen and Mary were roving houseguests in New York and New England, spending time with the Rhoadeses, the Paddocks, the Obermeyers, the Pratts, the Meyers, and various members of the Stieglitz family. Several wealthy friends helped Steichen raise the tuition fee for Mary's school, and he would pay a modest amount to the Stieglitzes for her board. He planned to stay nearby at Joe Obermeyer's when he was in New York. This way, he could see Mary regularly, but it was Lizzie Stieglitz who would look after his daughter on a daily basis.

Emmy Stieglitz, still ostracized from Lake George, went to New Hampshire in July to visit seventeen-year-old Kitty and eleven-year-old Mary at camp, where they were spending their summer swimming, boating, and playing tennis, a temporary respite from the turmoil their parents were living through. From 1913 to 1915, Kitty had spent each August at Lake George with her father and without her mother. During one of those summers, Emmy had written wistfully to Alfred, "I wish you had married someone else who would fit into your family better and who would have found everything they did just right and smiled at everything.... I miss Kitty dreadfully and only hope no one is speaking ill of me to her."[57] Clara Steichen had chosen her exile, but Emmy's had been imposed upon her, and their daughters played together that summer under the brilliant New Hampshire sky while family life as each of them knew it—dysfunctional though it was—changed forever.

Clara and Kate were now living in a very different Voulangis from the one they had left so traumatically nearly ten months before. They lived surrounded by soldiers, and all civilians were under strict police surveillance. Throughout most of September, Clara was stranded at home after suffering a badly sprained ankle, and as winter set in, daily life grew even more difficult.[58] Once her ankle healed, Clara did almost all of her own housework, as well as all of the mending and gardening. She also sewed for the soldiers, and she spent one day a week cutting flowers in the garden and then packing them for ambulances to take to soldiers in the hospitals. For relaxation, she practiced the piano a couple of hours daily, and she gave Kate piano and singing lessons. She also began teaching Kate to ride so she could do so as fearlessly as Mary, and found a teacher to give Kate daily school lessons. Clara helped to harvest vegetables from the garden, "wheelbarrowing" her winter potatoes in, she told Stieglitz, and tying up "five wheelbarrows [full] of beans on the stalk."[59] Amid the nerve-racking daily changes of troop movements, she found the garden work calming.

Everyone in the village had war stories to tell of French soldiers spending weeks in the trenches, fighting valiantly, hand to hand if need be. Clara was haunted by the specter of thousands of wounded being transported to hospitals in Paris, but she tried to conceal her anxiety from Kate.[60] They slept together every night, and often, curled up in bed, Kate created poems that Clara would write down for her, a child's view of the Great War. One of the child's poems read, "All our minds like flames were on the World. / All our bombs were on the world instead of having peace...."[61]

Steichen wrote several letters to Clara in the fall of 1915, pleading for her to return home, but she ignored them. Nevertheless, she was devastated when she did not hear from him on their wedding anniversary in October. "There will never be another October for me. And never another plea from me to him," she swore in a letter to Stieglitz.[62] Yet she wrote a plaintive note asking Steichen to come to Voulangis for Christmas and New Year's Day—an impossibility, under the circumstances. Even if he could have afforded the journey, his travel would have been restricted. Just before Christmas, the French government ordered all foreigners in France to stay in their communes, and Mildred complained that she could not even leave her house to mail some Christmas packages, including a book for Gertrude and red stockings for Alice. Worst of all, she could not travel the handful of miles to Voulangis to spend Christmas with Clara and little Kate, who provided the only inspiration she could see for even observing Christmas in wartime. "We are only seven miles apart—we might as well have the ocean between us," Mildred wrote to Gertrude and Alice on Christmas Day.[63]

Mildred received at least one Christmas present, however—the news that her book was a best-seller in the United States, where citizens were hungry for just such a personal chronicle of the war. All told, *A Hilltop on the Marne* would go through seventeen printings. For their part, Clara and Kate shared some music, some poems, and some homemade gifts at Villa L'Oiseau bleu, but it was a very lonely, depressing day, with Kate weeping that it could not be Christmas without her sister there.[64]

The day was a little happier back in the United States, where Steichen and Mary went to spend Christmas with Oma and Opa at the Little Farm at Menomonee Falls, Wisconsin. Steichen's mother, like his friends back east, grew alarmed when she saw how thin and despondent he was, however. The vibrant life had drained from his eyes, and he seemed burdened with the weight of the world. Mary, on the other hand, seemed to be thriving, and she enjoyed the warmth and excitement, the presents from her grandparents and the Sandburgs, and Oma's wonderful cooking, especially her succulent Christmas cake, a family tradition. To her delight, Mary also received Christmas letters from her mother and sister, but when Steichen learned that there was not even a word to him, he grew even more melancholy.

Despite all their problems, he still loved his wife, felt compassion and loyalty for her, and wanted desperately to hold on to their marriage.

He wrote to her after Christmas that the unique love between husband and wife, forged by the birth and care of their children, was too "vital" and "fine a thing to endanger."[65] He urged her to help him keep that love alive. "Dear crazy Steichen.—Trying to be a family-man & an artist all at once!" Clara had told Stieglitz bitterly.[66]

Steichen had called Stieglitz a father confessor because he habitually played that role for dozens of people. Throughout 1916, he played it, willingly or not, for Clara Steichen. During that horrendous winter of war in France, Clara lost the remainder of her fragile equilibrium. Confined to her house and garden and the village, cut off from Mildred Aldrich, whose wisdom and strength might have helped her, she sent a flood of chilling letters to Stieglitz about Steichen, her writing suffused with pathological anger and jealousy.

She even threatened to kill herself and Kate: "Let him take his life and his fine friends, But this particular one let me tell you has me to settle with, I'll hold on here as well as I can but if I decide the game isn't worthwhile I'll quietly get out of it and take this baby with me." She had put aside enough money to bury them decently, she wrote. "I despise this man, I despise his name I bear, I loathe every cent he gives me."[67]

One can only imagine what life was like for Kate.

22

THE DEATH OF THE BLUE BIRD

(1 9 1 6)

Your singing heart is laid away
Beneath the gold of autumn sun....[1]

—CLARA STEICHEN

STEICHEN SEEMED TO GO ON HIATUS in 1915, producing little significant work from then until late in 1919. It is tempting to blame World War I for disrupting his development as an artist, laying waste to his career in New York and Paris, aborting the paintings and photographs that might have been created, and ultimately channeling his work in new directions. While an exploration of his life during these war years yields few artifacts in the way of pictures, there is much evidence of how both global and personal tragedy sapped his creative energy and made it impossible for him to carry on with his work as he had done it before.

While Steichen the avant-garde artist and photographer had enjoyed a bohemian lifestyle, especially before his marriage, he was also an innately conscientious man with a deeply ingrained work ethic, implanted from earliest boyhood by his immigrant parents, who had given him his first job when they sent him out to peddle vegetables in Hancock, Michigan. His sense of responsibility had been intensified by his Catholic upbringing, and, like his parents but unlike his far more liberal sister, he respected the Catholic views of marriage and family life. Over the years of his marriage to Clara, there had been other artists in Steichen's circle of friends who were cavalier in their treatment of wives and children, but Steichen had early in his career deliberately set himself the goal of merging art and family into a positive, united force, thereby enriching and empowering both his work as an artist and his life as husband and father.

His commitment to support Clara and their family had, in fact, been the driving force most of his professional life, and, consequently, it had profoundly shaped his evolution as an artist, even arguably holding him back because so much energy was defused in the chronic fights with Clara, so much money was demanded to support their spacious apartment in Paris and their leased house and acres at Voulangis, and so little peace was to be found to allow the artist in him to experiment and grow. Now here they stood after twelve years of marriage, their family split in half, both Eduard and Clara wildly unhappy, the ocean between them a melancholy metaphor for their tragedy.

Steichen could not understand his wife, and he was distraught. The misery Clara inflicted on herself and on the people she loved most could not be simply written off as malevolence. He carried the guilt of past indiscretions, casual incidents in his own mind, although shattering to Clara. But Steichen adamantly maintained that he and Marion Beckett were innocent of Clara's charges against them, and by every other testimony, no one but Clara actually believed then or later that Steichen had been unfaithful to her by having an affair with Marion.

Why, then, would she persist in her belief at the risk of destroying her marriage and her family and jeopardizing the safety and well-being of her children? There was passionate warmth and goodness in Clara Steichen—and passionate fury, pain, and jealousy—so much of the latter that even a layperson sees glaring evidence of mental illness manifested in Clara's agony.

Modern psychiatry identifies a set of paranoid disorders: "persistent persecutory delusions or delusional jealousy, not due to any other mental disorder, such as Schizophrenic, Schizophreniform, Affective, or Organic Mental Disorder." The paranoid disorder gives rise to simple or elaborate "persecutory delusions" that may revolve around a "single theme or series of connected themes, such as being conspired against, cheated, spied upon, followed, poisoned or drugged, maliciously maligned, harassed, or obstructed in the pursuit of long-term goals."[2]

Furthermore, the disorder may be manifested only in "delusional jealousy ('conjugal paranoia'), in which an individual may become convinced without due cause, that his or her mate is unfaithful. Small bits of 'evidence,' such as disarrayed clothing or spots on the sheet, may be collected and used to justify the delusion." The individual afflicted with this disorder may demonstrate anger and resentment, as well as a tendency toward "social isolation, seclusiveness, or eccentricities of behavior. Suspiciousness, either generalized or focused on certain individuals, is common. There is a sense of grandiosity and superiority. Letter writing, complaining about various injustices, and instigation of legal action are frequent."[3]

Interestingly, unlike many disorders that manifest in youth, the paranoid disorders normally begin in middle or late adult life and are chronic, with few if any periods of remission. Furthermore, there is rarely any serious impairment in daily functioning, and "intellectual and occupational functioning are usually preserved, even when the disorder is chronic. Social and marital functioning, on the other hand, are often severely impaired."[4] Certain severely stressful life events may trigger the disorder, especially in individuals—like Clara Steichen—who may have already demonstrated symptoms of a paranoid personality disorder. These events include drastic changes in a familiar environment— brought on by immigration and emigration, for instance. Often, then, acute paranoid disorders may be seen in immigrants, emigrants, refugees, persons newly inducted into military service, or prisoners of war.

This could be a profile of Clara Steichen. Her conviction that her husband had betrayed her drove her paranoia, and Clara's delusional jealousy manifested itself early in her marriage, with or without cause. Steichen himself clearly contributed to her unhappiness through his errant behavior during their courtship and in the early years in France, but she was also openly jealous of his mother, and of any woman whom her husband worked with or befriended. There had been perennial skirmishes over other women during their marriage, but the catalyst for this full-blown delusion must have been that moment in Mary's bedroom at Villa L'Oiseau bleu when she came upon her husband and her friend— an innocent scene by all accounts, but for Clara, "evidence" that justified the delusion.

The flight to France bears out certain associated features of the paranoid disorder—dramatic social isolation in Clara's case, relative seclusion with Kate behind the walls of the Voulangis house, rampant suspicions directed at Steichen, Beckett, all of their friends, and even her own family. And there was the letter writing: Beginning in 1915, Clara narrated her agony (and her delusions) in countless lengthy letters, especially to Alfred Stieglitz—letters so painful to read that his executors sealed them for a half century after his death. True to the profile of this disorder, Clara reiterated for thirty years afterward her complaints about a series of imagined injustices done to her by Steichen, Beckett, her children, her friends, her family. She often threatened and tried to initiate litigation, and she finally would do so, for all the world to see.

To confound matters further, "the essential feature" of this kind of paranoid jealousy is "the insidious development of a Paranoid Disorder with a permanent and unshakable delusional system accompanied by preservation of clear and orderly thinking."[5] True to this syndrome, despite her suffering and the concrete daily fact of a war in progress all around her, Clara managed to run her house at Voulangis, to take reasonable care of her daughter's physical, if not her emotional, needs, and to help her neighbors and the war effort.

She also possessed some of the classic "predisposing factors" for the disorder. Her childhood insecurities intensified when she and her sister Charlotte were forced by limited family resources to fend for themselves, depending on the charity of relatives and on their own hard work for their education, their art and music lessons, their first journey abroad—the amenities that many young women received as a matter of course. Moreover, from the time she married Steichen, Clara was in a very real sense both émigré and immigrant, moving as his world dictated from New York to Paris, living alone in France with her children for months at a time while he commuted to New York.

Then came almost simultaneously the "discovery" of Steichen and Beckett in her own house in Voulangis, the sudden forced abandonment of that house and all it meant to her, and the migration back to New York. Less than a year later, Clara crossed the ocean again to punish Steichen—and, by extension, Mary and Kate—for a crime he did not commit.

Clara spent much of the wartime winter of 1916 writing her tormented letters, as well as composing poems brimming with her problems. She also set Kate to work making up poems, then transcribed them for her daughter as quickly as Kate uttered them. Somehow, Clara procured an old typewriter, and on it she pounded out the letters and the poems and sent them to Stieglitz in New York. She asked if he could get some of the poems published for her, and he promised to try. He would certainly publish some of them in *Camera Work,* he told her, if he was ever able to get out another edition.

He and Clara's sister Charlotte, both terribly worried about her, leafed through the poems together and sent a few of them out unsuccessfully to *Century* and *Atlantic Monthly.* There were more than fifty of them in all, agonizing vignettes of what she was suffering then: the helpless citizen vulnerable to the terrors of war, but most of all, the wronged woman spinning variations on the theme of heartbreak. Clara was forty, worried about menopause, overweight and depressed about relinquishing her physical beauty, and sure she had lost her husband to a younger, more beautiful woman. "I shall be beautiful when I in death / Lie in white loveliness, soft as a dream, / Safe from the mock of your critical glances— / Deaf to the anger of quickening lips . . ." she wrote in a poem called "Peace."[6]

In addition to writing her poems, Clara continued to type long, vituperative, pathologically jealous letters attacking Steichen and Marion Beckett. In what may have been a deliberate attempt to humiliate Steichen further, she wrote most of them to Stieglitz rather than to Steichen himself. From across an ocean, Stieglitz gave advice, but he surely did not comprehend how gravely ill Clara was, how much in need of help. Besides, unknown to Clara, Stieglitz was coming to the end of his pursuit of Katharine Rhoades, Marion Beckett's best friend. Moreover, he was just months away from the beginning of his long, life-transforming love affair with Georgia O'Keeffe. As Emmy Stieglitz and Georgia O'Keeffe both could later have testified, Stieglitz was not the best adviser for a woman who felt betrayed by her husband.

She should get ahold of herself, Stieglitz told Clara sternly. She herself admitted that she possessed a "very jealous disposition." Jealousy was always "destructive," wrecking lives, especially one's own, Stieglitz wrote to Clara. He hoped she would realize that the chaos of her life was rooted as much in her own "irrepressible jealousy" as in what she called Steichen's "utter selfishness."

Stieglitz urged Clara to allow Steichen peace to work so that he could provide for her and the children. He scolded that it was "diabolical" of her to charge that Steichen had forced her to go, and typical of her unstable behavior since he had known her. Steichen would never change his nature, Stieglitz continued, any more than Clara would. Besides, in Stieglitz's opinion, it was no crime to admire good-looking women, and it was not "entirely" Steichen's fault if women were fond of him. He had never seen a "finer relationship" than that between Marion Beckett and the entire Steichen family, and Clara "did a terrific wrong" by behaving as she did, *"no matter what thing you may have seen. No matter what you may have thought."*[7]

Needless to say, Alfred's letters to Clara renewed her fury and drove her to tears, but she kept on writing to him, and he kept on answering. After all, the only three people she trusted, she told him, were Stieglitz himself, his mother, and Mildred Aldrich. In a long poem to Mildred, Clara praised her strength and friendship, which helped Clara to keep "clear of falser things" when her soul was "afire with bitterness," her life "shattered." Clara wrote, "My hurting self is all astray / And I am lost unless someone / Comes more than half the way to me."[8]

At the same time that she was inundating Stieglitz with mail, she and Steichen fired away at each other in letters that were destroyed or otherwise lost to history. However, in two particularly venomous letters Clara wrote to Stieglitz, she quoted Steichen's intimate letters to her, bitterly annotating them point by point.

While he appreciated the fact that it had been a "calamity" for her to be married to an artist, Steichen had written in one of these letters, such a marriage provided benefits she would not have enjoyed had she been married to a shoemaker. He then explained what it meant to him to be an artist, standing essentially alone in his struggle, constantly "seeking and searching into life and humanity," and trying to find his place in relation to the whole of life. His job was not necessarily painting, he told Clara, and no matter what work he chose to do in the future, he would always be the "same seeker."[9]

Her husband had indeed been "seeking and searching"—with other women, ever since their marriage, Clara wrote cynically to Stieglitz—"and it was only with [Isadora] Duncan and [Kathleen] Bruce that I'd ever objected"—until Marion Beckett came along.[10] The longer

The Death of the Blue Bird (1916)

Clara remained in Voulangis, the sound of cannon in her ears and the daily deprivations of wartime staring her in the face, the more furiously convinced she became that Marion had stolen her husband and defiled her home.

Despite protests and disclaimers from Steichen and others, Clara was still positive that he was in love with Marion Beckett, who was with her family and friends in the United States then, trying to reorganize her own life. It drove Clara wild to know that Steichen and Beckett, although not necessarily together, still moved at will in the lively circle of friends she had left behind, for there were regular exchanges of visits at 291 in New York, at Lake George, at the Meyers' estate in Mount Kisco, and at Katharine's family home in Connecticut.

But there was no romance, Steichen and others maintained. Furthermore, he wrote to Clara during their ongoing transatlantic quarrel by mail, while he was not about to fall in love, Clara would know if he ever did, because he had enough "sporting blood" in him to run away with the new love. She was the one who had thrown their relationship into the "hellfire" of jealousy and mistrust, he told her, adding soberly that the love still existing between them could not be destroyed by anyone but themselves. Besides, he teased Clara, he was no polygamist, for he obviously could not even manage one woman.[11]

He urged her to trust him, and, if she did not, to share his letter with Mildred Aldrich, hoping that with her good common sense, Mildred could help Clara understand and accept what he was trying to communicate to her. He pleaded for her understanding that he was living his life "towards an achievement." He was deeply committed to a heartfelt "moral responsibility" to Clara, to Mary and Kate, as well as to himself. He had always tried his best to shoulder his responsibilities to them—but his best was a man's best, and not "an angels [sic]."[12]

Steichen's distress intensified when he discovered that Clara had in effect broadcast to their friends his most intimate expressions of his "inner self."[13] The revelation left him feeling victimized, but his sadness and concern for Clara prevented him from being angry. Clara, however, was furious, and the intemperate letters she wrote to Agnes Meyer, Katharine Rhoades, Emmy Stieglitz, and other friends now charged Steichen with neglect as well as infidelity. Most of their friends supported Steichen but pitied Clara. Emmy told Stieglitz during the summer of

1916 that she had received a photograph of Clara and Kate made in Voulangis, adding that Clara looked "so worried and sad, I feel so badly for her."[14]

Yet the brunt of Clara's desperately unhappy letters hit Stieglitz, who was still beset with his own domestic problems. He wrote long, heated letters in response, analyzing Clara's behavior as well as Steichen's. She had sought to "possess" Steichen, "body and soul," Stieglitz told Clara disapprovingly, and that was as "impossible" as it was inconceivable. She had worked herself into a state, he wrote, deluding herself that she was poor and abandoned. One could torment oneself to the brink of insanity, he warned, in the process destroying oneself and everyone else.

Even Charlotte wrote to her sister defending Steichen, but Stieglitz proved to be his most articulate champion. Steichen might be "careless" and thoughtless, Stieglitz observed, but he truly loved Clara and was working very hard to provide for her and the children, and only for them. Stieglitz scolded Clara that it was not possible for Steichen to work well and productively if he had to live in a continual state of anxiety. Surely Clara, above all others, should understand how easily Steichen was given to despair and discouragement, yet how persistently he tried to do everything possible for her and the children, despite every obstacle. How, Stieglitz wanted to know, could Clara expect more "of any human being?"[15]

But Clara was beyond reach. She saw herself as "a fat frump of a wife," penniless, persecuted, discarded by her husband for a younger, more beautiful woman—"the only kind of woman Steichen is capable of giving one damn about." No logic or reassurance could change her views. "Goodbye Stieglitz," she wrote. "I'm not going to bother anybody again—One gets to be as big a bore as life itsself [sic]."[16]

Nevertheless, despite her "goodbye," Clara's deluge of letters and poems continued throughout the spring and summer of 1916. Stieglitz reminded her that Steichen was "no different today than he was the day he married you, and you know it. You wanted him and you took him with his faults as well as his virtues. And you know as well as I do that he has plenty of the latter."[17]

By summer of 1916, Clara was writing bitterly that she no longer cared whether Steichen and Beckett "did or didn't," or whether she herself "won" or not, as long as she could have what another woman could not—Mary and Kate. She would despise Steichen to his dying day, she swore. She would also hate his mother "as long as I've breath to, for creating the impression that I'm extravagant," she wrote to Stieglitz. She had convinced herself, furthermore, that Oma had supported Steichen's "affair" with Marion because she had always wished that Marion were her daughter-in-law, not Clara.[18] And she began to think about suing Marion Beckett.

Meanwhile, an ocean away, distraught about his marriage and the wartime dangers surrounding Clara and Kate, Steichen was working and worrying himself nearly to death. But he could not persuade Clara to come home, nor could he afford to go to Voulangis after her, only to turn around and bring Kate and Clara back to the United States. He knew he could not hope to earn a living in France as a foreigner during wartime, for it was hard enough in New York. And although the wartime economy offered few profits for artists, Steichen kept on doing the only work he knew how to do—painting and photography—struggling frantically to raise the money he needed to support Clara and Kate in France and Mary in New York.

He appreciated the unorthodox but effective arrangements worked out for his daughter. Mary was settled into a room in the Manhattan home of Lee and Lizzie Stieglitz while she attended the Brearley School in New York. Uncle Lee, as she called Dr. Stieglitz, taught her mathematical games and encouraged her interest in math and science. He also took her along in the buggy when he made house calls on patients, giving her experiences that led to her interest in practicing medicine later on. Although Mary's love for painting was stifled by her art class at Brearley, so much so that she stopped painting and drawing, she fell in love with science during her first biology class. Like her mother, Mary played the piano with deep emotion "that swept everybody off his feet," but she confessed that she was "awful technically" because she would not practice.[19] She loved poetry, especially Vachel Lindsay's, and while she liked her uncle Carl Sandburg's poems, too, she confessed that she did not understand them.

During the early war years, Mary loved visiting Aunt Charlotte and Uncle Billy Paddock in Connecticut, picking and eating white peaches from their orchard, helping her aunt broil a steak in the fireplace, or watching her uncle, still a working artist, "peeling his fruit with his beautiful sculptor hands, handling his knife as though it was the finest little tool."[20]

She often traveled with her gypsy father to spend time with the Meyers, Katharine Rhoades and her family, and other friends, and they usually spent Christmases with Oma and Opa Steichen at the Little Farm in Wisconsin. Remembering those holidays years later, Mary wrote, " 'Oma' was positive that her Ed was the most wonderful boy in the world. She also made me feel that she was positive that I was wonderful too. I was not yet in my teens, but we three would laugh and chatter together, discussing everything under the sun; I don't believe we were conscious of the differences in our ages at all."[21]

Mary and her father drew closer during those years while the other half of their family lived in France. But Mary carried scars from her childhood, often feeling lonely and abandoned. "I always was dissatisfied with the way I was," she remembered. "I knew that I was very selfish, very hardheaded, very stubborn. I wasn't loved very much by my peers. In school I was admired a lot, maybe envied, but I wasn't loved, and I wanted to be somebody other people would love."[22]

In the meantime, from Voulangis, Clara charged in her angry, rambling letters to relatives and friends in the United States that Steichen failed to support her and Kate, that they could hardly eat or pay their expenses. She had warned Steichen that "if ever he left me here again penniless facing all the damnable mess of these authorities I'd see to it that his name and this woman's was strung to the corners of the earth."[23] Yet the records show that in 1916 alone, Steichen managed to send Clara 20,128 francs, or $3,825, a sum far surpassing his earnings, much of it money borrowed from friends.[24] This gave Clara a monthly income of $318, exceeding, by comparison, the monthly stipend of $150 each that Gertrude Stein and Leo Stein drew from their trust funds to support a reasonably affluent lifestyle in Paris, as well as their investments in art. Even with escalating wartime prices in Voulangis, Clara could hardly have been considered destitute in 1916.

Friends who saw Steichen during that time of their separation were alarmed at his depression. He struggled to do his work, relying more and more frequently and reluctantly on the largesse of friends for shelter and meals for Mary and himself, so he could send every available dollar to Clara and Kate. Steichen's anxiety about Kate extended to the smallest detail of her daily life. She was a "growing proposition," he had told Clara, and he wanted her to have plenty of milk, butter, eggs, and meat, no matter how much they cost. Clara had retorted that the first three could hardly be had "for love or money."[25]

Clara might be trumpeting their struggles to the world, but Steichen had not even confessed to the Sandburgs and Oma the complete details of his ongoing ordeal. Yet back in Wisconsin, Oma, always a world-champion worrier, grieved over what she did know of the plight of her son and his family, and she and Paula sent Steichen loving letters of support and concern. He in turn was very interested in his brother-in-law's work, since Henry Holt and Company would soon publish Sandburg's first major book of poetry, *Chicago Poems*.

When Steichen offered to help with the book, the Sandburgs immediately asked him to create the cover for it.[26] Befitting the radical power of *Chicago Poems*, Steichen designed a stark, elegantly simple cover, deliberately counteracting the fussy glitter of the Art Nouveau covers of some contemporary books.

More important, he wanted to demonstrate his conviction that artists in every field should work together. He expounded on that idea in a long letter to his sister—an impromptu treatise that expanded his argument in the 291 essay and offered a powerful revelation of how the war had already transformed his vision of the art of the future. Steichen's message was twofold: The art world had to be organized like an army to fulfill a definite mission; and that mission was for art to become the redeeming, unifying, civilizing "master force" of life. A work of art could no longer simply be the "exquisite expression" of just one self-serving individual artist. All of mankind was hungry for art that spoke universally to life itself.

Studding his letter with military imagery and wartime jargon, Steichen advocated mobilizing art so that it could serve as a powerful force for preparedness for life in a world gone "mad." The time had come for society to discover that art goes to the essence of life, and to the "heart" of humanity. Poets, painters, photographers, sculptors, musicians, and novelists should all join together to create new, unified forms of artistic expression.

The urgent task of reconstruction after the war would belong to artists, not to military and political leaders, Steichen wrote to his sister. He grieved that in this massive war, brought on, he felt, by the moral bankruptcy of modern society, a few enemy bombs could obliterate the art of all foregoing centuries. The "ghastly months" of the war already had convinced him that artists themselves must see to it that in the future, the world prepared itself for life, not for death.[27]

Not surprisingly, given the prolonged stress of his life, Steichen's health broke down in May 1916, so seriously that he had to undergo surgery. The problem was most likely either an ulcer or his gallbladder, or another of the apparently congenital gastrointestinal problems that he and his mother and sister suffered from all their lives. Katharine Rhoades telegraphed Stieglitz on May thirtieth to ask him to wire her the results of Steichen's operation.[28] Stieglitz quickly complied, following his wire with a letter to say that he had visited Steichen in the hospital, where he was "fairly comfortable" after "suffering quite a little pain," which had been relieved by medication. The surgery had been successful, however, and Steichen was in every way "progressing normally," Stieglitz reported.[29]

But Steichen's long recuperation set him even further behind financially. In New York, his paintings and photographs had earned barely enough to support one household, much less two, even though sympathetic patrons had bought his work and helped him in more personal ways. Two mainstays during this time were his longtime friends Kate Simpson and Helen Sherman Pratt, the wife of George DuPont Pratt and daughter-in-law of Pratt Institute founder Charles Pratt, a partner with John D. Rockefeller in the Standard Oil Company. Helen Pratt took a special motherly interest in young Mary, not only contributing to her school tuition and camp fees but even paying for her piano lessons.

While Mary was at camp in New Hampshire that summer, Steichen spent some of the time recuperating in Mount Kisco and making photographs of flowers in the Meyers' summer gardens—such as his beautifully composed gelatin silver print *Lotus, Mount Kisco, New York*. By September, he was painting with renewed zeal at Bouquet Lodge, an inn in the tiny hamlet of Willsboro, New York, on Lake Champlain, less than fifty miles from the border of Canada. He told Stieglitz in a letter that he was trying, as always, to "get control" of his work.[30] He was also swimming and playing tennis, hoping to rebuild his strength, but it was slow going. After he and Mary shared a trip to Montreal in October, he asked Stieglitz if he might borrow plate holders for his camera so he could make a series of autochromes of Mary. Already, at twelve, she was statuesque, growing more beautiful day by day, and doing fine emotionally, he thought, despite the rupture in their family life.

That brief interlude of rest and work was suddenly shattered by an "irruption of the usual muss," however.[31] At Villa l'Oiseau bleu in wartorn Voulangis, Clara was off on another rampage at her typewriter. By autumn of 1916, Clara's sad, bitter letters, compulsively reciting her litany of Steichen's offenses, had alienated almost all of her circle in the United States—Kate Simpson, Agnes Meyer, even patient Katharine Rhoades, and Clara's own sister, Charlotte. Only Mercedes ("Mercy") Carles held to their friendship.

The final straw in Eduard and Clara's long-distance battle came sometime during the final months of 1916, when Clara wrote to Stieglitz and to other friends and family members to charge—falsely—that Steichen refused to send money to support her and Kate. At last, she drove Steichen to resort to her own tactics: He prepared his own letter to disseminate to the people who had received her false allegations of financial neglect. He abhorred the act of writing such a letter, but he felt she had left him no choice. Over and again he wrote and rewrote the draft, measuring and then tempering the words. He also evidently sought Stieglitz's counsel about it, writing it with Stieglitz's encouragement, and the practical support of Stieglitz's secretary, who typed the letter for Steichen to mail.

He carefully laid out the dates and receipts for the 20,128 francs he had sent to Clara over the past year. He had no idea of what her expenses were, he told her, and he asked her, in fairness, to send him her budget so he could be sure to cover it. He told her that he had already sent her a sum far in excess of what he had earned that year, saying he had been able to do so only because he and Mary had "accepted the proffered kindness and generosity of friends."[32]

Clara had bought a Victrola that year, and the tone of Steichen's letter triggered more paranoia, convincing her that someone in the village had spied on her and reported the acquisition to Steichen. Furthermore, she wrote to Stieglitz that she and Kate were being hounded by villagers because Steichen was not with them; why, their neighbors called them names, she complained, and even spat at them as they rode their horses or walked through Voulangis.[33]

Clara worried constantly over her "scattered flock," especially Mary, who she feared was already lost to her and firmly bonded to Steichen in the United States.[34] Now Kate became her whole life, an immense burden for a little girl to shoulder. The child stayed on the alert, keenly sensitive to her mother's tormented moods. Clara took immense pleasure in Kate's growth, and she tried to share it with Stieglitz: "She is full of beauties—If she can find the mode of giving them up to day-light, and not choking her own soul to death with them you'll see things." Clara predicted that Mary, on the other hand, was "so clever she stands in her own light—so selfishly disposed so DEMANDING—Life will be hard with her."[35]

There were times when Clara's letters were quieter, replete with her longing for peace and tranquillity. When Stieglitz wrote to ask her whether the convent bell still pealed across the lake at Voulangis, she answered wistfully, "To be like the Lake—quietly ourselves even after our storms—to rest within our rim and listen to any bells or music floating out across us and to us. Thats [sic] the peace we all of us who feel or seek or hope—*finally realize is the best of all.*"[36]

During those war days, Clara and the other citizens of Voulangis could not even travel the few miles to Crécy without a government permit, which took up to two weeks' time to process, but somehow she and Kate managed to get to Paris in late summer and then out to Meudon to call on the Rodins. Clara typed a single-spaced four-page account of her visit, entitled "A Tribute," contrasting the happy journeys of earlier years with this solitary wartime "pilgrimage." Women wore black dresses now, she observed, instead of the bright frocks of prewar days. With most men at the front, the transportation system now employed "an army of young French women." Even the cobblestone streets she and Kate walked to reach Meudon seemed subdued by war, but Paris, in the distance, appeared reassuringly to belong "still to her splendid self."[37]

Clara thought Rose had changed little in the years since their last visit, but Rodin himself was older, wearier, unwell, she perceived, as she found him swathed in a great brown robe, sitting in his dusky salon, his massive, "splendid head" and the "great bulk" of his figure outlined by the sun at the window.[38] A progression of strokes had quelled the great mind and spirit. For a few moments, she sat beside Rodin in silence as he held her hand. When she rose to go, he took her arm, put on his wide-brimmed faded gray hat, and walked with her to garden, Rose leading the way.

There, amid a "tangle of weed and grass and vine ramble," *The Gates of Hell* stood still unfinished, since 1880 a magnificent work in progress.[39] Clara embraced Rodin and Rose Beuret, and, weeping, bade them good-bye for the last time. As she and Kate walked down the hill to catch their train, Clara turned back, to see Rose adjusting Rodin's hat to protect him from the sun.

At home in Voulangis, she sketched the scene on her typewriter, painting Rose as Clara had hoped to live out her own life:

She was content. And he, he at peace with the rare realization of a great creative work accomplished.

To have done one's best with one's life is indeed great. He is content.

To have served one's best in one's Life is even greater. She is content.[40]

Later, Clara wrote to tell Rose she would always remember her advice that with an artist, you had to be patient. Rose boosted her own courage, Clara wrote, and, believing herself to be the tolerant, long-suffering wife, sent her homage from one "patient" woman to another.[41]

But if she harbored some hope that she and Steichen might salvage their marriage, her poems betrayed her conviction that they were finished.

The strain of wartime was telling on her, Clara wrote nervously to Stieglitz in December 1916. The situation grew ever more dangerous, and only when she occasionally housed a French or British officer did she feel completely safe. Their second wartime Christmas in Voulangis was a quiet one. Kate composed a poem for her mother, and Mildred Aldrich got permission to spend a few days with them, a welcome presence in an otherwise cheerless house.

Christmas also brought a check from Stieglitz, along with a severe reprimand: Clara's vociferous and "promiscuous" charges against Steichen and Marion Beckett had at least "borne fruit," causing a "complete severance" between the Beckett family and Steichen.[42] The daughter of New York solicitor Charles H. Beckett, Marion had grown up in a cultured home with devoted parents and every privilege that wealth could offer. As Clara's letters and charges multiplied, the Becketts must have been deeply offended and embarrassed. While they had known the Steichens through their long friendship with Marion, the elder Becketts no doubt advised their daughter that for her protection, the whole family should break off any communication with Steichen, and they did so.

Stieglitz was appalled, and he chastised Clara accordingly. She had deliberately stirred up trouble with her letters, and she obviously had no idea how serious her charges were, he contended. What would she do if she were required to offer "positive proof" and "actual evidence" to support her claims that Marion Beckett was Steichen's mistress? He gravely doubted that she could do that, and he could not imagine that Clara understood the harm her reckless charges caused others—or herself. It was one thing, he fumed, to accuse her husband in private, but quite another to broadcast her accusations to the world. Stieglitz hoped fervently that 1917 would not only mark the close of the Great War, but, more personally, the end of "hostilities" between husbands and wives who purported to care for each other.[43]

Eight years earlier, Clara and Steichen had named their home for Maeterlinck's *The Blue Bird*. Now she sent Stieglitz a poem, hoping he would find a publisher for it. "Death of the Blue Bird," she called it. It ended:

THE DEATH OF THE BLUE BIRD (1916)

Your singing heart is laid away...
Where hidden crags' indifference
Shall guard the blue beat of your wing
Until your echoed song shall cease.[44]

Like most Americans, Alfred Stieglitz struggled to carry on life as usual during the war. To his relief, the buildings on his block of Fifth Avenue had not been razed yet after all, for the war deferred many business endeavors. Although the old brownstone housing 291 might be standing, the spirit of the place was dying before his eyes. His year at 291 had been "most unpleasant," he wrote to Annie Brigman in 1916. He had "managed to 'lose'" almost all the friends who came regularly to 291. The whole painful experience seemed, he said sadly, to mirror the "world in miniature."[45]

Stieglitz may have lost many of his old friends, but one of the most important friendships of his life remained intact. Much has been made over the years of a permanent rift between Steichen and Stieglitz caused by their differences over World War I. Their letters reveal a different story, however. The two old friends did indeed disagree profoundly about the war, about art and certain artists, about commercial art, and about many other matters. Stieglitz had surely been hurt by Steichen's stinging review of 291 in *Camera Work*. Endowed as each man was with immense talent, driving ambition, and powerful ego, rivalry was inevitable, yet each of them had traditionally spoken and written with genuine admiration for the other's work. Furthermore, competition and disagreement seemed to enhance rather than diminish their personal regard for each other in those years, and they loved and respected each other as longtime friends, professional differences aside.[46]

Their correspondence confirms that Stieglitz's friendship was especially important to both Steichen and Clara from 1915 through most of 1917, as he served them both as mentor, father confessor and the elder dispensing advice and, when needed, practical, material aid. In addition, the Stieglitz family had so incorporated Steichen and Mary into their circle that Mary continued to live with Lee and Lizzie when she was not staying with her father.

From time to time during this period, Stieglitz apparently grumbled his criticism of Steichen to his family, friends, and colleagues, but on Steichen's side, there is no evidence of anything other than his enduring affection and esteem for Stieglitz. Moreover, during and just after the war, their long friendship was marked by such intimacy that Stieglitz was the only person on earth other than Eduard and Clara who knew the depths of their misery. And although Clara was pelting their friends with letters about their troubles, Stieglitz remained Steichen's only confidant during the long, sad disintegration of his marriage.

23

THE ART OF READING LINES AND SHADOWS

(1 9 1 6 - 1 9 1 8)

As the war rumbled on, Steichen ... developed the art of reading lines, shadows, blurs, camouflage. ...[1]

—CARL SANDBURG

WHILE STEICHEN AND CLARA BATTLED OVER the remnants of their marriage, Alfred Stieglitz struggled to maintain order in his own life. First there was an ongoing revolt among the ranks of his colleagues. Not satisfied with publishing the new journal *291,* Agnes Meyer, Marius de Zayas, and Francis Picabia pressured Stieglitz to open a new gallery wherein the work of modern artists would not only be tastefully exhibited but also aggressively promoted and sold, as was true in almost every art gallery in New York except 291. There Stieglitz held to his traditional, somewhat condescending view that to actively advertise and sell art was somehow to prostitute the art and the artist. Although, in fact, Stieglitz often sold the work of painters he exhibited at 291 and arranged financial support for Marin and a few others, these were usually private transactions, behind the scenes, with the buyer, not the seller, almost always initiating the purchase.

His friends saw matters differently, with a far more practical understanding of the typical artist's financial predicament. Agnes Meyer had already warned Stieglitz in a letter that unless they looked toward the future, they would fall into a "deep gulf of inactivity and aimlessness," and 291 would surely die an "involuntary" and "nasty" death.[2] But according to Stieglitz, he decided on his own that he should close 291 "principally because of the war," at the very same moment that de Zayas, Picabia, and Meyer chose to open The Modern Gallery.[3] He wanted to help his friends with the new gallery as well as the new magazine, and so lent his physical presence as well as three of his prints to one of the shows there.

All in all, The Modern Gallery at 500 Fifth Avenue held twenty-nine exhibitions from its opening in October 1915 until it closed its doors in 1918, and during that time, Stieglitz was lonely at 291, which was suddenly no longer the hub of activity. For the first time in years, however, he felt there was opportunity to do his own photographic work.[4] He had been spending three days weekly at the Modern Gallery, but by January of 1916, amid growing contention with Agnes and de Zayas over how things should be done, Stieglitz cut his connections there, in effect also terminating these close friendships.

Steichen, meanwhile, was painting and photographing "in a half-hearted way," he recalled, deeply preoccupied with his crumbling personal life.[5] He spent time at 291 only occasionally in those days, but he no longer helped Stieglitz with 291 exhibits. Their friend Paul Haviland, always a steadying influence at 291, had gone back to France to help his family with the war effort. Stieglitz himself was trapped in his own lonely, stultifying marriage, helplessly watching the old days and the old guard being eaten up by time and the war. These were dark days for Steichen and for Stieglitz—except for two bright new artists whose providential arrival at 291 offset the casualties in Stieglitz's world.

The first was a New Yorker, the handsome young photographer Paul Strand, whose experiments in photography had been shaped at New York's Ethical Culture School, where he took classes taught by Charles Caffin and documentary photographer Lewis Hine. Like Steichen, Strand had been deeply influenced by the pictorial work done in earlier years by Gertrude Käsebier, Clarence White, and Stieglitz himself.

The other artist was Georgia O'Keeffe, a young woman whose austere beauty and voluptuous paintings overwhelmed Stieglitz and transformed his life. At 291, from April 3 to May 14, 1917, he gave her her first

The Art of Reading Lines and Shadows (1916–1918)

solo exhibition. Stieglitz had first seen O'Keeffe's work on New Year's Day of 1916, his fifty-second birthday, when her friend Anita Pollitzer came to 291 and rather timidly asked him to look over some drawings. O'Keeffe, then twenty-eight, was teaching art classes in Columbia, South Carolina, at Columbia College, a small Methodist liberal arts school for young women. Her friend had asked her not to share her drawings with anyone, Pollitzer told Stieglitz, but these had just arrived and she could not resist seeking his opinion. He thought they were extraordinary—evidence at last of "a woman on paper."[6]

Stieglitz surely did not realize when he saw O'Keeffe's remarkable drawings that the young artist herself had actually visited 291 in the past, nor was there any particular reason for him to remember her. O'Keeffe had been so impressed with the art Stieglitz displayed at 291 that she became "more interested" in what Stieglitz would think of her work, she said, "than in what anyone else would think."[7] When she had visited 291 to see an exhibition of Marin's watercolors, she listened to Stieglitz's account of Marin's hard struggle. O'Keeffe stared at one abstract blue crayon sketch and began to think, "If Marin can live by making drawings like this—maybe I can get along with the odd drawings I have been making."[8]

Without O'Keeffe's permission, Stieglitz had included her sensuous abstract charcoal drawings in a group show at 291 in May of 1916. He did not even get her name right, however, attributing the work to Virginia O'Keeffe. The drawings "created a sensation," Stieglitz recalled, although there were conflicting opinions: Some viewers were "deeply moved, as though before a revelation," while others were "horrified" that Stieglitz would exhibit such work on the very same walls that had held the art of Matisse, Picasso, Cézanne, Hartley, Dove, and Marin.[9]

When O'Keeffe got word that drawings by someone named Virginia O'Keeffe were stirring up a small commotion at 291, she strode over to the gallery to take a look. The drawings were hers all right, and she did not hesitate to tell Stieglitz to take her work off his walls immediately. He remembered being confronted by a thin girl with a Mona Lisa smile, dressed in a "simple black dress with a little white collar."[10] They argued about her drawings in the gallery, then continued the disagreement over lunch. In the end, she left her work on display at 291. O'Keeffe and Stieglitz continued their electric encounter in letters that summer while Georgia dealt with family affairs before moving on to begin the school year teaching in Canyon, Texas.

It was during that 1916 exhibition at 291 that Steichen had had his first look at O'Keeffe's drawings. Steichen remembered that he and Stieglitz were "dumbfounded. In these abstract drawings was a woman who spoke with amazing psychological frankness of herself as a woman."[11] Ironically, O'Keeffe's stunning show was the last exhibition ever to be mounted at 291. Finances and wartime wore him out, and Stieglitz would close the historic little gallery for good on July 1, 1917, though still keeping a small office at 291–293 Fifth Avenue in the familiar old building, now haunted by so many ghosts.

"Yes, write it down if you wish," Oma Steichen told a Chicago journalist in Maywood, Illinois, in the summer of 1917: "The United States government has one of the great creative artists of the world now training young men to go over the top with cameras instead of guns."[12] Vowing to help make the world safe for democracy, Woodrow Wilson and the United States had declared war on Germany on April 6, 1917. Steichen volunteered for military service that summer, hoping to join the Signal Corps, which had charge of military photography. "I wanted to be a photographic reporter, as Mathew Brady had been in the Civil War," he remembered, "and I went off to Washington to offer my services."[13] Moreover, Clara and Kate were still in Voulangis, and duty in France would enable him to see his wife and daughter. He also dreamed of going back to Europe to help defend the country he loved, and to call on Rodin in military uniform, "as a symbol of America coming over to help France."[14]

At thirty-eight, Steichen was eight years over the age limit set by the Air Corps, but he was absolutely determined to serve, and so he quickly filled out the paperwork and gladly submitted to a battery of tests. Serious as he was about this mission, however, after a long day of examinations he could not resist playing a joke on the army medical staff members testing him for color blindness. Handing him a multicolored mass of wool skeins, they ordered Steichen to locate the red ones. Dramatically, Steichen walked around the table, studying the matter, then finally declaring that he did not see a single red strand. Before they could flunk him, however, Steichen announced, "That's Rose Madder and that's Crimson Lake and this one's Chinese Vermilion and this one's Magenta.... There isn't a single *true* red among 'em!"[15] The army accepted him anyway, commissioning him a first lieutenant in 1917.

Not long afterward, Steichen traveled to Illinois to visit his sister and brother-in-law and his parents, whom he and Paula had settled just blocks from the Sandburgs in a modest house at 1005 Ninth Avenue in Maywood, a Chicago suburb. A Chicago newspaper carried an anonymous news account of his homecoming that could well have been written by his brother-in-law, for it included one sentence, more poetic than reportorial, that foreshadowed a later Sandburg description of Steichen: He was, the article said, a "creator of nocturnes, delicate studies of moonlight and evening haze and all the half-world lights that fascinate an Impressionist."[16] Three years later, Sandburg would call Steichen a "painter of nocturnes and faces, camera engraver of glints and moments, listener to blue evening winds and new yellow roses...."[17]

On August 2, 1917, the War Department created a Signal Corps Photographic Division, with Maj. James Barnes commanding Lieutenant Steichen and three other officers. The division was ordered to "take charge of all matters of photography pertaining to the Signal Corps, in connection with both aviation and the general photography of military operations."[18] At the outset of United States involvement in the war, in fact, the U.S. Army Signal Corps oversaw all photographers in the American Expeditionary Force (AEF). Although Major Barnes knew nothing about photography except for "whatever he had learned on a hunting safari when he made a motion picture of wild animals," Steichen remembered, Barnes immediately grasped the importance of aerial photographic military observation, and he set out to study all the pertinent literature he could find, including British intelligence reports and French aviation photographs.[19]

Of the four men on Major Barnes's original staff, three had some prior knowledge of photography. The exception was Capt. Charles F. Betz, a career soldier just promoted from sergeant to captain, who knew nothing about cameras but everything about army procedures. Albert K. Dawson and Edwin F. Weigle, both first lieutenants, had already photographed the war at the front in Europe as neutral observers, before the

United States joined the battle. But the expert on photography was Steichen—"an artist and art photographer," Major Barnes wrote later, who was "in the first rank of his profession in America and Europe." Without Steichen's "aid and advice," Barnes reflected, "the Photographic Division might, at any time, have gone on the rocks."[20]

To Major Barnes, Lieutenant Steichen, and their colleagues fell the crucial task of conceiving and then organizing the first aerial photographic reconnaissance operation in United States military history. Worrying that his government seemed to think they could create this unprecedented program "by the wave of a wand," Barnes quickly took advantage of the aerial-reconnaissance expertise of the English and French officers who had been sent over to the United States to assist their new allies.[21] Because first and foremost they needed men with any kind of photographic training, Barnes saw to it that newspapers and magazines throughout the United States carried official military advertisements pleading for qualified photographers to join the AEF. At the same time, Barnes and Steichen combed through membership lists of American amateur and professional photographic groups in search of recruits. Soon they had gathered a staff of "sixteen office men and a dozen technical aides," who worked around the clock in their temporary Washington headquarters.[22]

"My boy is in Washington now," Oma Steichen proudly told a reporter. "He works all day and then goes back to his desk and works all night.... I cannot tell you all. I am telling you this only because I want you to know the American soldier has the best and the most practical art photographer in the world now at work on helping organize the bureau that will photograph the war."[23]

It was daunting work—establishing military training camps for detachments of photographers; building photographic laboratories; requisitioning supplies and equipment; designing a curriculum and finding instructors to teach the highly specialized skills needed for aerial military photography. For the first few months, Major Barnes and his staff had to oversee the more conventional military ground and news photography operations (after all, the Civil War and the Spanish-American War had been covered by still photographers). Almost as an afterthought, they were also responsible for orchestrating the unprecedented new aviation photography operation. Their most urgent job became to persuade the

The Art of Reading Lines and Shadows (1916–1918)

"burdened" general staff that not only was aerial photographic reconnaissance important but that "nearly nine-tenths of the information for the offensive or defensive" in the war was being produced by "the work of cameras under trained direction in the air."[24] Once the cameras had recorded the "lines, shadows, blurs and camouflage" of enemy movements, skilled men in portable field laboratories immediately had to process the pictures "accurately and scientifically" and move them quickly to headquarters and to commanding officers on the front lines.[25]

It was an awesome job, and Barnes, Steichen, and their colleagues knew they were going to have to improvise as they went along. But seized with the life-and-death urgency of their mission, Steichen shed the weariness and despondency of the past three years. For the first time since he had been forced to leave Villa L'Oiseau bleu in 1914, he embraced the challenge of exciting new work.

Not only would he have to expand his mastery of the camera to work with precision at high altitudes and great speeds, he would also need a working knowledge of wartime aviation. At the outset of the war, there had been only a few thousand total Allied and enemy aircraft, but by war's end, that number had multiplied to more than 105,000 planes. The proliferation of planes was accompanied by astonishing advances in speed and climbing capacity as well as in the accuracy of antiaircraft guns. By the time Major Barnes and Lieutenant Steichen reported for duty, successful aerial reconnaissance, "photographic and otherwise," was executed at unprecedented heights of twelve to fifteen thousand feet, and even more.[26]

As World War I wore on and the flying machines became critical military weapons, the airplane industry continually responded with dramatic technical innovations. The clumsy, scantily armed planes used at the war's outset had been quickly replaced in 1915 by the faster, lighter, more deadly German monoplanes, the Fokker Eindeckers, whose forward-firing machine guns had raked the landscapes of France's Western Front the summer that Clara Steichen went home to Voulangis. Britain's prompt answer to the Fokkers, which weighed a mere fourteen hundred pounds, including pilot and equipment, was the even lighter, faster, more deadly Sopwith Camel.

The newborn aeronautical industry was waging its own furiously competitive war, from the farsighted engineers who instantly redesigned and improved fighter planes to the assembly-line workers who built the new planes in unprecedented numbers and at record speed. By the end of the war in 1918, more-powerful engines would mean that flying speed had escalated from 82 miles per hour to 150 miles per hour, and highly skilled pilots and gunnery mates deployed more sophisticated machine guns in the air.

Because Barnes and Steichen knew that they had to study the photographic reconnaissance techniques already employed by the flying Allied photographers, the major wrestled with the wartime bureaucracy until he finally got War Department approval to borrow an experienced British aerial photographer to help them. He was Major C.D.M. Campbell, head of the British Photographic Division, "the one man responsible, more than any other, for the organization and early working of the Field Air Forces."[27] Short and wiry, with a heavy Cockney accent, Campbell trained his men to operate machine guns and cameras with equal precision. Otherwise, the vulnerable little planes would not be fully manned.

Barnes and Steichen had to battle the American general staff, which had so far demonstrated no commitment to the importance of aerial-reconnaissance photography, nor any real appreciation of the camera as a "weapon of war," as Major Barnes called it.[28] Now with Campbell as an ally, Barnes and Steichen were able to convince the chief of staff of the army and other key leaders of the artillery, the infantry, the intelligence division, and the aviation division that in this war, for the first time in history, aerial-reconnaissance photography could produce stunning offensive and defensive intelligence information in the field, on the spot—often delivering a photograph to a general on the ground barely fifteen minutes after it was made in the air, instantly yielding unprecedented knowledge of enemy strategy.

Back in Wisconsin, Oma Steichen's talk with the newspaper clearly reflected Steichen's excitement about the dynamics of military photography: "Hundreds of young men, drilling with cameras instead of guns—that must be something worth looking at," Oma told the reporter. "I hope some time men will fight with cameras instead of guns."[29]

By September, Barnes had sent two detachments of American news and publicity photographers overseas—about fourteen in all. He and his staff had also established programs for the production of still and moving pictures. Their training centers showed movies and lantern slides of German lines and other war areas, and gave soldiers hands-on training in a mock field laboratory and an old Standard training plane mounted with an English camera in its suspension. The military assumed control of some photographic schools in the United States, and laboratories finally "went up like magic," Barnes recalled, but supplies and equipment were still desperately hard to come by. Steichen was "invaluable" to Barnes in his successful efforts to procure cameras, fast-speed lenses, and chemical supplies. They were caught up in the "nearly impossible task of making something out of nothing," Barnes realized.[30] But Steichen took to the job with zeal, as excited as he had been in the old days when he was a boy with his first camera.

In the fall of 1917, Clara shut up the house in Voulangis once again and returned to the United States because her father was dying. Hurrying to reach his bedside, Clara did not even stop in New York to see Mary en route to Missouri. The stress of being torn from her home once more left nine-year-old Kate very ill with a severe case of shingles. Clara had only a beautiful color photograph to give her a glimpse of Mary, now thirteen, and still living with Lee and Lizzie Stieglitz in New York because the school term was under way. By now, Clara was sure, Mary had been hopelessly "soiled" by Steichen's influence.[31]

Longing to see Kate, Steichen sent her an AEF service pin from Washington, but the child refused to wear it. "It will never be possible to re-create or revive in any way in her her love for her Father," Clara wrote to Stieglitz with satisfaction. "She's been thru too much."[32]

Clara stood beside her own father's coffin at his funeral that autumn of 1917, her mind full of the images of death that had surrounded her for the "weary months" of the war. "Death does not matter," Clara wrote in the midst of her own difficult life; "it is but a passing moment into an eternity in which I believe." She revered her father's kindness, his service to others, his sense of duty. "It is a very great deal to have been the daughter of such a man," she wrote in later years. "It is the only inheritance I ever received." But her father had foreseen and forewarned that Clara would live a difficult, unhappy life, she remembered, often cautioning her gently that her own strong, often-rigid nature would lead her to that fate.[33]

After her father's death, Clara apparently decided to remain in the United States for the duration of the war. The last months in Voulangis had been unbearably tense and difficult, and Kate remembered that she and her mother often went hungry. After they returned to the United States, Kate became a "pillar to post child," she said, spending time with relatives and friends, uprooted time and again, never attending the same school or living in the same house for more than a year, if that long.[34] Because of the warmth and stability Clara's sister offered, Kate grew to love her leisurely summer visits in Connecticut with Aunt Charlotte and Uncle Billy Paddock on their farm.

In the autumn of 1917, having just completed a dangerous ocean voyage and having just buried her father, Clara was angrier at her husband than ever. Believing that Steichen had heartlessly taken Mary away from her, Clara retaliated in kind, doing her best to keep him away from Kate.

In October of 1917, Major Barnes and Steichen, newly promoted to captain, got their orders to go overseas immediately.[35] Steichen made financial arrangements for his family—a portion of his salary to be sent to Clara, still in Springfield, Missouri; part to be sent to Lee and Lizzie for Mary's care; and a part, as always, to go to Oma and Opa. What should she and Kate do if she needed a doctor while he was overseas? Clara wanted to know. Lee could care for Mary in New York, but what was she supposed to do in Springfield? When Steichen directed her to the charity doctors all army dependents had to use then, Clara's charges of neglect resumed.

Unfortunately, he could do nothing about Clara, but he could throw himself into the war work. For nearly twenty years, he had devoted his photography to gentle landscapes and probing portraits, helping to lift photography to a superbly expressive fine art by his visionary skill. Now in a swift transformation of purpose, Steichen had converted his camera into a weapon, the deadlier for his consummate ingenuity and expertise.

He and Major Barnes sailed for Brest on November first on the *America,* a confiscated German steamer, in convoy with four other confiscated German ships. For Steichen, the voyage was "impressive and thrilling," simultaneously a leave-taking and a homecoming, as well as a journey into the dangerous unknown.[36] Every day of the passage brought harrowing rumors of "narrow escapes from submarine attacks," Barnes wrote, especially because Brig. Gen. B. D. Foulois and his personal staff were aboard.[37] Foulois had just been appointed general commander of all AEF Air Service activities because he was the most experienced aviator in the entire American military. Orville and Wilbur Wright had taught Foulois to fly in 1911, and he had served with distinction with Gen. John Joseph "Black Jack" Pershing in Mexico in 1916, commanding the First AeroSquadron. Their convoy crossed the Atlantic uneventfully that November, two weeks later reaching a country, Barnes observed, "desperately hard pushed to maintain the drain upon its own resources from all sides."[38]

For months, Steichen had dreamed about his reunion with Rodin, but his emotional return to France after three years came just days too late. Grief-stricken, Steichen learned that Rodin, then seventy-seven, had died shortly before his arrival. Steichen immediately tried to arrange to attend the funeral as the official representative of the U.S. Army. There was no time to go through protocol, but Major Barnes gave Steichen permission: "Sure, you go and say that you represent the American Army and General Pershing."[39] And the Society of Younger American Painters in Paris, Steichen thought.

To pause at just the right instant in some fragile historic film footage of Rodin's funeral is to catch a glimpse of the face of Eduard Steichen, who was standing in a throng of mourners in the garden where he had photographed Rodin's *Balzac* so long ago.[40] The urgency of the war prohibited a national funeral with appropriate honors, but government officials gathered at Meudon along with academicians, politicians, artists, musicians, and friends. Steichen saw many of his own old friends and acquaintances in the crowd, including Judith Cladel, who told him that on January 29, 1917, just two weeks before her death, Rodin had married faithful Rose Beuret. Then old age, illness, and the war had finally killed her: She and Rodin, like many of their countrymen, had endured the frigid winter weather without fuel. Rose had contracted bronchitis in their bitterly cold villa, and pneumonia inevitably followed.

Cladel told Steichen that Rodin's last days were "one of the most ghastly experiences anybody could have gone through" because of the "schemers around him representing the state, and individuals conspiring to get control of his work through various wills."[41] Once ignored and then maligned by his countrymen, Rodin had ultimately been hailed as a great artist; as death approached, many greedy factions clamored for a stake in the wealth his work would surely generate far into the future. But Steichen had long known and loved Rodin, for himself alone, and he had witnessed Rodin's toil and had tried to emulate him as an artist.

He had also listened over the years to Rodin's teachings, learning from him the essence of the art of portraiture: to "pierce without pity the innermost crannies" of the soul of the subjects, "to strip them of disguise," to "drop the veil."[42] Most of all, Steichen had learned from Rodin that "nature is the infinite and variable model that contains all styles."[43] Steichen had endeavored for years to embody that principle within his photographs and paintings.

Standing in Rodin's familiar garden that cold November day, his heart heavy with memories and gratitude, Steichen was disappointed to hear the "stuffed-shirt talks about 'La Gloire de l'Art Français.' "[44] He learned that Georges Clemenceau, just named premier of France, had ordered an honor guard back from the front to attend Rodin's funeral. He could see a contingent of French fighter planes keeping a vigil in the sky above. After all the official speeches, the feminist author Caroline Rémy Séverine "rose unannounced," Steichen recalled, "and made a wonderful, fervid speech about Rodin as an artist and as one who understood humanity and womankind particularly. It was a startling deviation from the official ceremony, the only human note, the only thing honestly said about the man and the artist Rodin."[45] And when Rodin was buried beside Rose in the Meudon garden at the feet of *Le Penseur*, Steichen dropped a handful of earth into the grave, and for the last time, he left the garden and studio where so much of his own art had been born.

The Art of Reading Lines and Shadows (1916–1918)

Back in the United States, meanwhile, sitting on the sidelines for the first time in his life, Stieglitz was writing to other friends that it had been a nightmare to have to give up 291. He wrote Annie Brigman that he had wanted to close the gallery in *"Glory"* despite the "treachery" and "cruelty" he felt he had suffered in the past few years. He could report that the small gallery space had never seemed more wonderful to him than during the days when it held its last exhibition, the paintings of Georgia O'Keeffe, a "Woman on Paper—" he exulted. "Fearless. Pure Self Expression."[46]

He also wrote wistfully about other lives—Steichen and other members of the old 291 circle serving with distinction in France. Stieglitz despised the idea of war, he told Annie Brigman, but he would surely be there himself, if only he were a younger man.[47]

Steichen had first been assigned to the Army Signal Corps, which until January of 1918 was responsible for all American war photography, but a trip to Saint-Omer to observe British aerial photography operations led him to request and receive a transfer to the new AEF Air Service after aerial photography was reassigned to that agency. Major Barnes was still his superior officer, and as they settled into makeshift headquarters in Paris, the two men were at first hopelessly overwhelmed by logistics. Understaffed, lacking the most rudimentary equipment, they tried to remember that "the whole photographic situation for the overseas Air Service" was an entirely new problem.[48]

Steichen wrote to Stieglitz with as many details as he was free to offer, saying that he was working hard and in many ways reliving the experience of trying to put 291 "on the map," embroiled once again in battles and politics as a champion of photography, except that this time human lives were at stake. He described his new life, sleeping amid the "rumble" and "whizz bang" of enemy planes and bombs, mingling with and greatly admiring the courage of men who had survived in the war zone for three years. He also told Stieglitz that he had made a brief stop in Voulangis en route to another destination, and so had gotten a nostalgic glimpse of the past.[49] During this visit or perhaps a later one, his daughter Mary remembered, her father had a reunion with Francine, their Breton maid, and "they kissed and cried together."[50]

Global and personal events since 1914 could have made a cynic of

Steichen, however. The battlefields of France and England, as well as the great cities of Europe, provided the laboratory for experiments with new technology—the aeroplane, the tank, the armored car, the camera, the cable (by war's end, all Allied reconnaissance aircraft were fitted with wireless equipment), the new wireless telephone, the submarine, the kite balloon, nerve gas and other deadly chemicals. In the horrible confusion of wartime, surrounded by troops marching into battle—and back again, if they were lucky—life appeared to be a chilling game, with individual lives seeming to count for little, Steichen wrote to Stieglitz.[51] Still, Steichen somehow found the experience resonant with meaning and purpose, all the while deploring the fundamental "imbecility" of war.[52]

Like many soldiers, Steichen had gone to war in part to escape problems in his own life, but his energies were quickly riveted to the challenge of covering the Great War with a camera. By 1917, when Steichen began to design the strategy for AEF airborne photographic reconnaissance, more-powerful airplane engines meant that battles could be waged at altitudes of eighteen and twenty thousand feet. The startling advances in aviation required concomitant changes in the cameras planes took aloft. This unforeseen application of photography required larger cameras, with bigger plate surfaces and larger focal-length lenses. Barnes recalled that only two manufacturers in the world produced the "heavy crown Barium glass necessary in the building of these high speed, high power lenses for aviation purposes—Carl Zeiss of Jena [for the Germans], and the Parra-Mantois factory in France [for the Allies]."[53] By late summer of 1917, thanks to the new automated De Ram camera, military photographers no longer had to drop their exposed plates into a daylight developing tank aboard the plane while they were still airborne, or drop exposed film or plates by parachute to couriers waiting on the ground. Instead, this innovative camera relieved the photographer of the fundamental chores of setting exposures and handling plates or film. He could now substitute as a gunnery mate and lookout, attacking the enemy with machine gun as well as camera. In the usual two-man observation plane, this assistance could be critical to the very survival of photographer and pilot.

Major Barnes relied on Captain Steichen's ties in France, as well as his language facility, for help in procuring the meager supplies they could assemble. During the winter of 1918, they were moved from Paris to Chaumont to Tours, still making do without American planes, cameras, and lenses. It was March before the United States military command sent them personnel, and mid-June of 1918 before they received "photographic material of any consequence" from the United States.[54] Of the thirty men assigned to their unit, only ten possessed even modest experience with photography. The others had only pretended to be photographers in order to go overseas. "Luckily, both Steichen and I possessed a sense of humor," Barnes wrote. "We fell into one another's arms and laughed until we cried."[55]

As impoverished as they were for men and supplies, Steichen and Barnes triggered an important reform in Allied military photography. Working closely with British and French aerial photographers under the direction of the Allied Technical Division in Paris, they suggested that there should be a uniform plate size for all cameras used by Allied military forces. Previously, because the French and British photographers had used differing sizes, French intelligence photographs had to be reduced or British prints enlarged if the pictures were to be used interchangeably. Now, thanks to Steichen and Barnes, the Allies began using an eighteen-by-twenty-four-centimeter plate and a fifty-centimeter lens, as well as French lenses and French heavy crown barium glass.

The two men also studied the methods of the French and British aerial photographers, incorporating into their own training programs the best of each for the unpredictable day when they would finally have fully equipped training centers and American planes. For the moment, contrary to American propaganda stories, there were only eleven American planes in France—the clumsy de Havilland Fours that were so "nose-heavy," they had to be weighed down with bags of sand so they would not tip up—"flaming coffins," pilots called them, because they inevitably burst into flames if their landings went even slightly askew.[56]

Late in February of 1918, Steichen and Barnes visited French troops at the front above Chalons-sur-Marne, about ninety miles from Paris. This journey gave Steichen another intimate look at the countryside he had enjoyed in better times. But when an air raid had savaged the town just the night before, not even the American Red Cross supply station had escaped German bombs, and trees were eerily draped in bandages. Returning to their quarters one night, Steichen and Barnes heard strains of an organ and men's voices singing a hymn. Following the music to a thirteenth-century cathedral, they entered, to see the priest praying over rows of kneeling men, an entire French regiment gathered in the wan light of a single candle. Outside in the frigid night, the men took up their rifles and lined up in their companies as their officers whispered commands. At daybreak, they were going to the battlefront, or "over the top."[57]

By late spring of 1918, despite the odds, Major Barnes felt that the entire American Photographic Division was functioning professionally. He and Steichen had adapted the best methods of the French and British photographers. They had culled personnel lists to assemble the best possible technical staff. Photographic laboratories had been set up and supplied, and two well-equipped photographic supply depots had finally been put into place. Steichen later told Sandburg how he had "studied over the best lenses for use in the cameras that clicked off exposures from underneath biplanes traveling a hundred miles an hour, 15,000 to 20,000 feet above enemy territory they were photographing" and how he "sympathized with the sturdy lads who almost suffocated in the little pup-tent darkrooms, cellars and dugouts used in field service" while they "developed the art of reading lines, shadows, blurs, camouflage in the finished prints of the day's duty."[58]

After all the "trials and tribulations" of organizing their mission, Steichen was promoted to major and given orders to report to Col. R. O. van Horn, chief of the AEF Advance Section at the Chaumont headquarters of AEF chief of staff, General Pershing.[59] From then on, Pershing and his staff depended on Steichen for guidance on "everything photographic."[60] Major Barnes called Steichen his "mainstay, guide, counsellor and friend," and he missed his daily presence once Steichen was reassigned to Pershing's staff. On June 1, 1918, however, Barnes himself was reassigned to the United States, where he would head the School of Aerial Photography in Rochester, New York. Now Major Steichen would run the Photographic Division in France, overseeing a staff of about twenty officers. Steichen wrote to congratulate Barnes on June first, thanking him for his strategic leadership and for being a "fine, steadying influence" on all his men.[61] Barnes left France confident that Steichen would run the Photographic Division brilliantly.[62]

Over time, Steichen's staff grew to a total of about fifty-five officers and a thousand enlisted men who performed the endless complex tasks of their photographic operation—manning and servicing planes, cameras, field darkrooms, photographic laboratories, and supply depots, as well as preparing and delivering critical intelligence reports based on photographic reconnaissance. Sandburg recalled Steichen's stories of working incessantly during the war, sometimes grabbing part of a night's sleep on the seat of a car and, even in his dreams, figuring "how to spot the enemy's positions, how to knock hell out of the opposition and tear the living guts out of him." Forgotten were "Monet, Cézanne, Kadinsky, even the Vorticists, every white hope and red flame of art."[63]

From the beginning of their mission, both Steichen and Major Barnes had relied heavily on the skill and experience of Major Campbell, head of the British Photographic Division. Sadly, they watched him struggle to keep working despite the fact that he was dying of consumption. Finally Campbell was ordered to go home to England, where he died before summer's end. More than anyone else, Major Campbell had taught Steichen and his colleagues the dynamics of aerial photography: how to capture the crucial images while riding cramped in flimsy planes at high altitudes; how to process reconnaissance pictures in makeshift field darkrooms or, in some instances, aboard the plane itself; and how to decipher the images. Major Barnes wrote:

> *The reading and interpretation of airplane photographs demands a peculiar mind, the type of mind that would work out chess problems or, nowadays, cross-word puzzles, perhaps. To the uninitiated a photograph of a line of entrenchments and myriad shell holes might mean very little, but to the puzzle solver, working over a clear photograph, with a magnifying glass, those shadows and lines and suggested slopes and rises mean much. They tell a story. . . . Those funny, little dots are iron fence posts with strong wires strung along them. The men who went to that big shell hole left no trace of a path, for they reached their hidden machine gun implacement [sic] by walking along the lower wire as a sailor would use the foot rope on the yard of a sailing vessel. . . . The battle between the camera and camouflage was on. It was like a poker game with aces up the sleeve.*[64]

By virtue of their decision to use filters on their cameras, the Germans were first to master the game. As a result, they could discern "where artificial leaves and paint took the place of the natural foliage.... Then the deception crept in. Great, false ammunition dumps were erected or dug and they were camouflaged as a lure. The real dump might be in the connecting cellars of a ruined and demolished village, or in the excavated embankment of an abandoned railway. It was an interesting game," Barnes wrote.[65]

And a deadly one. By the last months of the Great War, aerial-reconnaissance photography had "grown from an experiment to an exact science," wrote one Royal Air Force major. The fledgling airplane industry had so transformed itself during the war that a new industry was born. But before the output and efficiency of aircraft had been improved, "strategical reconnaissance was only possible under conditions of high risk and at great expense in casualties," the RAF officer reported in 1919. "It is one thing to fly a hundred miles behind the enemy lines on an aeroplane with all the appearance and many of the attributes of a Christmas tree and fitted with an engine on which but little reliance could be placed but there is greater joy and more profit in making the same journey in machines possessing both speed and reliability and equipped in such a manner as to make aerial fighting less one-sided in its results."[66] Still, it was insanity to climb the skies in these vulnerable airships, so many matchsticks bound together by so much net, nothing between the pilots, gunners, and cameramen and enemy fire but air and wind, and a kind of mad daring.

When Steichen was assigned to orchestrate the massive photographic preparations for covering the Second Battle of the Marne, he spent a week billeted in his own house in Voulangis. In the few moments he could grab for himself, he rummaged through his studio and home, with their surfeit of memories, and explored the shambles of his garden, bereft of flowers and of Brancusi's bird, which he had safely stored in the house. The outlying fields where his delphiniums and poppies had grown had long since succumbed to war and neglect, but within the walls of his original garden, he found about a dozen "survivors" of his delphiniums.[67] Eagerly, he explored the sheltered gardens of neighbors to whom he had given cuttings, there to discover other plants that had been grown from his seed. With loss all around him, without and within, he took immense pleasure in the survival of this handful of flowers.

Steichen the warrior was both artist and engineer, fusing his innate artistic and scientific skills to the newest technology. During the Second Battle of the Marne, he met Gen. Billy Mitchell, who wanted to know when his planes would be equipped with ninety-centimeter cameras for high-altitude photography.

"Sir, we have six already," Major Steichen was able to report.[68] Why were they not in use? General Mitchell inquired. Steichen explained that pilots in the aerial observation squadrons complained that the cameras took up so much room that gunners could not operate freely, and he reminded the general that on many aircraft, photographers had to do double duty as cameramen and gunners.

General Mitchell told Steichen he wanted to take a camera up in an airplane himself—if Steichen could supply the camera, which he did that very day. Impressed with Steichen's grasp of this new weapon of reconnaissance photography, Mitchell cut orders for Steichen to be attached to his staff during all subsequent military operations. The two men met again at Colombey-les-Belles, in the Advance Zone for the Battle of Meuse-Argonne, where, within twelve hours, Steichen's staff set up a complete field darkroom in an old brewery building, hooked up water and electricity from a truck generator, and worked around the clock to print fifty pictures from each of thousands of reconnaissance negatives, for distribution to headquarters as well as to front-line commanders.

"When will we have some prints?" Mitchell asked Steichen early that first day. "We delivered the first five thousand this morning," Steichen answered.[69] He knew by the grateful response that he and his staff of photographers and technicians had made an enduring friend in General Mitchell.

Steichen wrote to his parents in November of 1918 that he had been at the front for more than a month in support of the Allied effort to put a "stranglehold" on that *"vital part"* of the front line.[70] Predicting wearily that they would succeed, that the war would soon end in victory for the Allies, that in the end there would be peace, he mourned the many brave people who had died in this cataclysmic war—six million dead by the time it was over, more millions wounded, and many more millions of lives forever transformed in the process.

For Steichen the man, the war triggered a deep depression. For Steichen the photographer, the experience galvanized a dramatic change in direction. In his autobiography, he wrote, "The wartime problem of making sharp, clear pictures from a vibrating, speeding airplane ten to twenty thousand feet in the air had brought me a new kind of technical interest in photography completely different from the pictorial interest I had had as a boy in Milwaukee and as a young man in Photo-Secession days. Now I wanted to know all that could be expected from photography."[71]

Steichen's friends and family had thrown themselves into the war effort in a number of ways. Mildred Aldrich waited it out in her little house on the hilltop near Voulangis, when she was not doing volunteer work in army hospitals. She also wrote three books that were sequels to *A Hilltop on the Marne.*[72]

Having quickly made a fortune from his wartime enterprises, chiefly Anacondia Copper and Fisher Body, Eugene Meyer moved to Washington in 1917 to begin his long-planned public service, first as head of the nonferrous metals division of the War Industries Board, and then, for a salary of a dollar a year, as director of the War Finance Corporation. Leaving their four children (ages six and under) in New York in the care of their governess and a staff of servants that included a German cook, Agnes went with her husband to establish herself as one of the most glamorous hostesses in wartime Washington. At the Philadelphia Navy Yard, Arthur Carles and other Philadelphia artists directed the painting operation to camouflage battleships, and Carles, his wife, and others who had lived in France worked on behalf of French war refugees.

Marion Beckett left the United States on September 15, 1917, to serve as an army nurse in France, but she hurriedly returned in November of 1917 (about the time that Steichen arrived in France) because of her father's terminal illness, arriving just hours before he died. "Marion is very well—deeply interested in her work," Katharine Rhoades wrote to Stieglitz soon after Charles Beckett's funeral.[73] She finally returned to

France sometime in February of 1918. Rhoades thought her friend looked "very well" and knew she would do a "heap of good—'somewhere in France,'" she wrote to Stieglitz afterward.[74] Apparently, Beckett's path crossed Steichen's only once during the war—a chance encounter at a Red Cross refreshment tent behind a battle line.

Carl Sandburg, meanwhile, was writing fervent war and antiwar poetry and covering the outposts for the Newspaper Enterprise Association in Stockholm, Sweden. There, he got himself into trouble with the State Department by associating with and accepting incriminating material from the Russian spy Michael Borodin—including propaganda films and documents that Sandburg intended to use as background for his stories on the war. In Maywood, Paula Sandburg and Oma and Opa Steichen avidly followed the war news, watched the mails for letters from Carl and Ed. Paula was pregnant with her third child when Sandburg sailed for Scandinavia in the autumn of 1918, and in November, a little sister, Helga, had joined seven-year-old Margaret and two-year-old Janet.

Stieglitz, "the warhorse," as Steichen and others called him, had set off a raging battle on his own personal home front. In 1917, falling madly in love with Georgia O'Keeffe, he had begun to photograph her, first her graceful hands and her angular, inscrutable face and then her voluptuous body. O'Keeffe later diffidently described this powerfully erotic series of nude studies: "There were nudes that might have been of several different people—sitting—standing—even standing upon the radiator against the window...."[75]

By July of 1918, Stieglitz had abandoned Emmy and Kitty, who was about to enter the sophomore class at Smith College, and had moved into his niece's East Fifty-ninth Street studio in New York to live with Georgia O'Keeffe. Shocked and enraged, Emmy locked her husband out of their apartment.

Of all of them, however, Clara Steichen, for once in her life, was having a wonderful time—working as a volunteer to speak and lead the singing at rallies for the Liberty Loan effort in towns and villages throughout the American Southwest. Mildred Aldrich wrote to Gertrude Stein in 1918 to tell her about Clara's "tremendous success" out on the road, "stumping" for the Liberty Loan. Some days, Clara spoke to two or three different audiences of two hundred to three thousand people, "creating wild enthusiasm." Aldrich sent Stein clippings about Clara's work, observing that Clara possessed a "great big voice for it & she can lead the singing."[76]

In France at war's end, Steichen was a hero, honored for his innovations, bravery, and service. No honors, however, could redeem or obliterate the personal depression that descended after the armistice of November 11, 1918.

"The wholesale murdering was over," Steichen remembered, "and wild celebrations began that night: cheering, yelling, screaming, booze, noise." He went to his barracks room and collapsed into bed. "The whole monstrous horror of the war seemed to fall down on me and smother me," he wrote.

> *I smelled the rotting carcasses of dead horses, saw the three white faces of the first American dead that I had seen. I could hear the rat-a-tat-tat of machine-gun fire as one lay flat on one's belly trying to dig into the earth to escape it, and the ping-ping-ping of the bullets coming through the leaves overhead. I saw the dried blood around the bullet hole in a young soldier's head. And he was only one of hundreds of thousands. How could men and nations have been so stupid? What was life for if it had to end like this? What was the use of living?*[77]

He had never had to face an enemy in hand-to-hand combat or shoot to kill, yet, through the power of photography, Steichen had played a palpable role in the fates of multitudes—enemy and ally, soldier and civilian. He had transformed his art into a weapon of unprecedented magnitude, arguably saving many lives, although inevitably causing the death of many others. On that despairing night when others around him celebrated the armistice, Steichen suddenly realized that through the whole of the war he had "never been conscious of anything" but the job he and his colleagues had to do, grappling all the way with overwhelming logistical and technical obstacles—constantly improvising and, somehow, expertly executing the ghastly mission given him to do.[78]

The Art of Reading Lines and Shadows (1916–1918)

For days, he went through the motions of his postwar duties, lost in a depression that started to ebb only as he began to think that through art he could make "an affirmative contribution to life." That growing resolve "restored some sanity and hope, and the desire to live took hold again."[79]

Now he desperately needed home, family, flowers. He traveled to Voulangis once more to see how his neighbors and his house and garden had fared, only to hear story after heartrending story—the individual sagas of human suffering composing the epic tragedy of the Great War. His sturdy house was intact, for the most part, and he resurrected the Rodin bronzes from their hiding places. In the wreckage of his garden, a few defiant roots and stems survived. In his studio, canvases lay rotting. The worst casualty? Most of his glass negatives were indelibly pocked with mildew and mold, or shattered beyond use, these ephemeral images of the first half of his life now lying in ruins in the abandoned studio in his garden at Voulangis.

24

ALIENATING THE AFFECTIONS

(1 9 1 9 - 1 9 2 2)

Miss Marion H. Beckett, daughter of the late Surrogate Charles H. Beckett and one of the legatees under his will, filed an answer in the Supreme Court yesterday to a suit by Mrs. Clara S. Steichen for damages for alienating the affections of Edward J. Steichen, an artist.[1]

—NEW YORK TIMES

"WE HAVE A HUNCH THAT ED will be here on his birthday, March 27th," Paula Sandburg wrote jubilantly to her husband in 1919.[2] Sandburg had returned from Stockholm by way of Christiana, Norway, after his months as a war correspondent, only to be detained in New York by American and British intelligence officers and other officials on suspicion that he had violated the Trading with the Enemy Act by bringing ten thousand dollars into the country for the Finnish Information Bureau of the United States. He was also investigated for bringing back a trunk full of Swedish and Norwegian socialist papers and Russian books, newspapers, and pamphlets to use in postwar coverage for his work as a journalist with the Newspaper Enterprise Association. The War Department and the Bureau of Investigation confiscated most of this material, along with the money, but they released Sandburg on January 28, 1919, without bringing charges against him.

Paula urged her husband to come home to Illinois by late March. She knew that if it was "humanly possible," Steichen would "eat his Birthday dinner at Oma's," Paula told Sandburg. "It's going to be *al*mighty interesting—You & Ed here at once."³ Later, from Chicago, Sandburg wrote to a friend, "I have been having a big powwow with Maj. Edouard Steichen, who is not only the world's greatest art photographer and impressionist painter, but was Chief of the Photographic Section of our air forces."⁴

It was interesting that Sandburg spelled Steichen's first name as he did, for Steichen himself had made a practical revision during the war, relinquishing the European Eduard (or Edouard) for the English spelling Edward.* While that spelling may have been proscribed by AEF clerks, it was also a significant affirmation of Steichen's American military service and his naturalized American citizenship.

He had stayed in France after the armistice to supervise his staff as they completed a photographic record of all battlegrounds and encampments where the AEF had fought major battles. That mission finished, Steichen was stationed in Washington, D. C., throughout most of 1919 to help establish a permanent division of Aviation Photography. On a trip to New York during this time, he was overjoyed to see Mary again, but it appears that Clara again refused to allow him to see eleven-year-old Kate.

After Clara had finished her Liberty Loan adventure, she and Kate had moved back to New York, where they had been living at 42 East Seventy-eighth Street since 1918. Clara had found a part-time job and had enrolled Kate in school, but she soon decided to send her away to boarding school. "I am not going to the same school next year," Kate wrote Mildred Aldrich in 1919, "because they will not take girls as small as I in boarding and I have to be a boarder, because Mother of course still works, and she could not, or at least she could, but does not want to leave me in an apartment house alone.... We are both very homesick for France."⁵ Until she was eighteen years old, Kate's father would be a virtual stranger to her.

Despite Clara's culpability in the matter, she felt it was a bitterly sad state of affairs that her family was split apart—Steichen in Washington and Mary in her third year at Brearley, still living with Lee and Lizzie Stieglitz. Their house on Sixty-fifth Street was her winter home, just as

---

* For this reason, from this point on in the text, the new spelling will supersede the former European spelling.

her aunt Charlotte's Connecticut farm was her summer refuge. Although Clara planned to work throughout the summer of 1919, she arranged for Kate to spend June with a family friend in rural New Jersey. Either Steichen or Nell Pratt paid the fee so that Kate could spend July and August at camp; then she would join her mother at Aunt Charlotte's in September until school started. Kate and Clara were very happy when Mary agreed to vacation with them there.

Meanwhile, Steichen would see to it that Mary escaped New York for the summer months by going to camp before returning to Connecticut, while he himself worked in Washington. When he finally retired from military service on October 31, 1919, he was Lt. Col. Edward Steichen, much-decorated hero of the Great War, ready to make his own peace through his art and, if possible, with Clara.

This was not to be, however. For five years, war or no war, Clara had been threatening to string a Steichen-Beckett banner to the ends of the earth if she had to, and in 1919, she finally did so—with dramatic vengeance. Steichen was stunned at the news that Clara had filed a lawsuit against Marion Beckett in New York Supreme Court, and he was appalled to read the details in the *New York Times* on July 5, 1919. ARTIST'S WIFE SUES FOR LOSS OF HIS LOVE ran the headline of the article. "Mrs. Edouard Steichen Says Marion Beckett Alienated Her Husband's Affections. Asks for $200,000 Damages. Declares Other Woman Followed the Painter to Paris, Where He Was Honored by France."[6]

In her "alienation of affections" suit, Clara charged that Marion had posed as her husband's model, had opened a Paris studio in order to be near him, had followed Steichen from Paris to New York, had received Steichen in her hotel suite in Voulangis, had accompanied him on trips to New York and to Vermont, and had disrupted the peace of Clara's household in France. Furthermore, she alleged that Steichen had sought military duty solely and purposely in order to be with Marion Beckett in France "without molestation from his wife."[7] She also charged that he had neglected to send Christmas greetings to his family from France in 1918. According to Clara, she had confronted Marion Beckett more than once, urging her to stay away from her husband, her children, and her home. "I made every concession possible for a wife to make," Clara stated, "but failed against the wiles of this defendant."[8]

Clara's bizarre and apparently unfounded interpretation of events must have caused grave distress to retiring Marion Beckett and her family in New York. Several weeks elapsed before she filed a devastating answer to Clara's suit, announced in a brief notice in the *New York Times* on August 28, 1919: "Steichen was estranged from his wife because of 'her own disagreeable conduct,' " Beckett countercharged; furthermore, "any affection which the plaintiff's husband had for the defendant was wholly voluntary and was in no way encouraged or induced by the defendant."[9]

Deeply pained and embarrassed for everyone concerned, Steichen wrote to Stieglitz from Washington about the "beautiful story" the newspapers were carrying, confident that his old friend could surely imagine how the scandal made him feel. With apologies, he asked for Stieglitz's help; his lawyer was planning his defense strategy and was "very anxious" to talk with Stieglitz, he said. Steichen hated "like hell" to be forced to impose on Stieglitz and other close friends in such a sordid matter, but was grateful that their offers of support had already reached him.[10] When Stieglitz answered immediately that he was indeed willing to help, Steichen wrote back to thank him for his "bully letter," promising to wire Stieglitz when a court date was set. He reported that Arthur Carles would also be speaking in his and Marion's defense.[11]

Of their friends who took sides, almost all allied themselves with Steichen, with Selma Stieglitz Schubart, Lizzie Stieglitz, Kate Simpson, and others offering to testify on his behalf. Unfortunately, as Clara had surely foreseen, the suit quickly became a very public case: Steichen was famous enough and Beckett's family prominent enough so that the scandal of this lawsuit was tantalizing fodder for the national press.[12]

"Dear Ed," Sandburg wrote to his brother-in-law when the news reached him and Paula in Illinois.

> *What can we say more than that we are all tied up closer to you and with you than ever before . . . and as fate deals the cards sometimes there is reason to say, "This the worst of all possible worlds." . . . If luck can come from wishing, daytime and night-time wishing, you will have it from us out here.*[13]

Trying to cope with his own postwar disillusionments, Sandburg had been fired by NEA and was covering race conflicts—part of the violent aftermath of World War I—for the Chicago *Daily News* that summer of 1919. As he finished a powerful, often embittered collection of poetry called *Smoke and Steel,* which would be published in 1920, he decided to dedicate it to his brother-in-law.[14] Surprised and deeply touched when the news reached him, Steichen stayed up all night rereading Sandburg's *Chicago Poems* aloud from cover to cover.

He joked with Sandburg about just how many copies of the new book he would have to buy to demonstrate his gratitude.[15] Just before *Smoke and Steel* went to press, Steichen asked Sandburg to be sure his name was spelled correctly, because every time he achieved "something first class," someone misspelled his name—"Stickmen or Strecher," for instance. He gave Sandburg emphatic instructions that his name should be written "EDWARD J. STEICHEN. Please."[16]

In New York, Stieglitz was willing to come to Steichen's defense in the Beckett court matter, not only out of loyalty and his conviction of the innocence of Steichen and Marion Beckett, but also because he and Emmy were then embroiled in their own strife over another woman. Of course, Emmy's complaints against her husband were offered in private, despite the fact that his liaison with Georgia O'Keeffe was being lived out quite openly in New York. Still, Emmy and her protective brother Joe Obermeyer did hold the financial leverage, and Stieglitz was feeling persecuted because Emmy's income was no longer his to use freely as in the past.

When the inveterate sponger Sadakichi Hartmann wrote to Stieglitz in 1919 to ask for a loan of ten dollars, Stieglitz answered with a vivid description of his own straitened circumstances—a fifty-five-year-old man trying to live on love with his thirty-one-year-old mistress: He could buy enough food for twenty days with ten dollars, Stieglitz protested. He was struggling along with only meager funds, feeling isolated and alone. There was a major compensation, however: Stieglitz was working with the camera again simply to fulfill his own vision and to satisfy himself. Everyone who had seen his new work pronounced it a "revelation." The photographs, Stieglitz wrote, were "straight," achieved without "tricks of any kind.—No humbug.—No sentimentalism." He was photographing O'Keeffe incessantly, he said, and he was still, as in the old days, doing battle on behalf of photography.[17]

Their lives intimately connected for nearly two decades, Steichen and Stieglitz now found that circumstances had forced them onto parallel paths toward new achievements in photography. With his stunning erotic serial images of O'Keeffe, Stieglitz was becoming a unique portrait photographer, finding all the subject he wanted or needed in this one woman he loved, and therefore concentrating even more closely on the particular.[18] Steichen, meantime, was turning his camera to encompass the general in a wide spectrum of images, moving in the process toward his own "revelation" in straight photography—no "tricks," no "humbug," no "sentimentality." Just as love for O'Keeffe motivated Stieglitz, hatred for war drove Steichen. Behind the camera, meanwhile, both men confronted the messy business of transforming their personal lives.

Estranged from Emmy, who was crushed and mortified that he had taken a young mistress, Alfred nevertheless tried to help his wife with her financial affairs as well as her emotional crisis, writing to her in 1919 that he had nothing but goodwill toward her, as did Georgia O'Keeffe. He professed his "intense desire to minimize [sic]" Emmy's suffering, as well as "Kitty's & mine—And also Miss O'Keeffe's."[19] Yet he could be so blatantly insensitive as to propose in a letter to Kitty that it might do Emmy good to have dinner with him and O'Keeffe—that if his wife and his mistress only got to know each other, O'Keeffe would be every bit "as kind to [Emmy] as I am." He just wished that Emmy would demonstrate "greater elasticity."[20]

Rancorous years would go by before Stieglitz and Emmy were finally divorced in 1924, six years after Stieglitz had left Emmy to live with O'Keeffe. But image-conscious Emmy had no desire to string out banners bearing her husband's name with that of his mistress. And during those years, a vulnerable Kitty, hopelessly and unfairly thrust into the middle of her parents' battles, wrote letters to her father demonstrating far more wisdom and good sense than any of the three adults in the destructive triangle. Her letters reveal a mature, even astute understanding of the conflicts between her parents. She wanted happiness for them both, recognized the flaws in their marriage, was willing to meet O'Keeffe—but not at Lake George, where her father wanted to vacation with his mistress and his daughter. Kitty drew the line there. That would wound her mother deeply. How would he feel, she asked her father, if the situation were reversed and her mother wanted her "to live under the self same roof" with a man who had "taken *your* place?"[21] What her father did was his own business, but she herself would not inflict further pain on her mother.

Notoriously hard on his friends, Stieglitz inflicted even greater harm on the women who loved him, as Georgia's and Kitty's eventual breakdowns would testify. And during this difficult time, his own marriage coming asunder, his wife and daughter in crisis, Stieglitz the father confessor was not the best source of marital advice for Clara and Steichen, or anyone else. Yet from 1917 until 1921, he would keep dispensing it, apparently unconscious of any hypocrisy in the act.

Steichen had hoped to have some time off in 1919 to take Kate, eleven, and Mary, fifteen, to Illinois for a visit with his mother and father and the Sandburgs. Instead, he had spent a "trying hot summer" in Washington, caught between his military work and the humiliating legal battle with Clara. He could only hope he was contributing enough to justify his monthly military salary.[22] During the war years, all art suspended, Steichen had no other income.

Sometime during this period, Steichen's longtime friend and patron Nell Pratt apparently tried to intervene in hopes of settling the Steichens' legal battles out of court. According to Clara, Mrs. Pratt offered her "years of education for the girls" and "a home in Paris" if she would return to Steichen. It was the "temptation of her life," Clara told Stieglitz years later, yet she refused.[23]

She had other plans on her mind. Apparently leaving Kate in the care of Charlotte Paddock, Clara traveled alone to Paris in September of 1919, then out to Voulangis for what would be her last journey to Villa L'Oiseau bleu. On September eighth, before she left the house where she had known so much joy and so much pain, she arranged to ship a number of items back to New York—antiques, including an exquisite French table; a marble sculpture of a woman's torso by Auguste Rodin and other Rodin sculptures and drawings; an Egyptian bas-relief; other household furnishings and some porcelain pieces; and some of her husband's paintings, including an unfinished landscape of the beautiful countryside surrounding Voulangis. Then she turned her back on the beloved house, the garden, and the village, and returned to New York.

On October 31, 1919, his military mission complete, Lt. Col. Edward J. Steichen retired from the army much-decorated: He had received the Croix de Guerre Belgique with two stars, and the Croix de Guerre de France, as well as the chevalier de la Légion d'honneur (he would wear that red ribbon with pride almost continuously for years afterward) and the Médaille d'honneur des Affaires étrangères, along with a Distinguished Service Citation presented by General Pershing. Steichen packed up his gear in Washington and wearily went to New York to deal with the court case, take stock of his life, and make some plans for his future. He was, his brother-in-law wrote, "a perplexed artist."[24]

Rootless, virtually homeless, finding few possibilities for work in New York, Steichen looked at the wreckage of his life and longed to go back to Voulangis. When an unidentified patron or patrons commissioned him to paint two portraits for five thousand dollars each, he used the money to set aside necessary funds for his wife and daughters and then to stake his return alone to France.

Steichen found conditions heartbreaking in Paris and Voulangis. To make matters worse, he returned to Villa L'Oiseau bleu, only then to discover that Clara herself had virtually cleaned it out, taking almost everything of value, including most of the antiques and works of art he had collected over the years. She had also absconded with some of Steichen's paintings. His greatest loss was that of the soon-to-be-priceless Rodin bronzes, which had survived the war but not, apparently, the marriage. Of all Steichen's cherished gifts from Rodin, Clara had left behind only one Rodin plaster.

Her confounding behavior left him deeply saddened, but not angry. His chief anxiety, he wrote to Stieglitz, was that Clara would sell these treasures imprudently and hastily in order to pay her legal bills—and, as a consequence, would cheat their daughters out of that part of their inheritance. Then he ruefully quoted Isadora Duncan's famous observation that there was nothing on earth as "terrible or as immoral as a virtuous *woman.*"[25]

During the winter of 1920, Steichen found in postwar Paris the very same melancholy, "funereal" atmosphere that then pervaded New York, he wrote to Stieglitz, for the two friends agreed sadly that art was an inevitable casualty of the Great War.[26] In Paris soon after his return, Steichen attended an art exhibition by two modern Italian painters and wrote to tell Stieglitz that their work could be dismissed as failed attempts to achieve what O'Keeffe had so beautifully mastered nearly a decade earlier. He also said he found the state of photography deplorable, and he thought it a fitting requiem that there were plans to create a museum of photography in Paris.[27]

As he had in the prewar days, Steichen sent Stieglitz news of other artists in Europe: More than a decade earlier, Matisse had been jubilant at the few modest purchases made by patrons at his first 291 show. Now he was doing some beautiful new work and selling it for huge prices even before the canvases were dry. Brancusi was the same fine person, a "regular Diogenes," working so independently that he seemed not to need any other audience than his own taste and standards, Steichen told Stieglitz. Steichen relished the atmosphere of Brancusi's studio, where his work seemed to be alive and growing as if part of a thriving "forest" of sculpture. He was fascinated to watch Brancusi wrestling with figures he had shown years earlier at 291, working and reworking the same material as if it were entirely new, still trying to achieve the ideal. And the sculptor had created a wonderful new version of his bird, Steichen reported.[28]

He found Picasso experimenting with an array of new ideas—some wonderful, some "childishly stupid," but all extraordinarily successful. In fact, Steichen predicted, Picasso would soon be a millionaire.[29] Picabia, however, had become one of the chief priests of the newest cult—Dadaism—and was publishing trendy *391*, an avant-garde journal founded in 1917 by Picabia, his wife, and other artists and expatriots living in Barcelona during the war. Steichen wrote bitterly about Dadaism, calling it "cheap perfume" applied in the futile effort to overpower the "stench" of the 7 million corpses given up to the war.[30] He was appalled at the specter of postwar Paris, where money seemed to rule everything, where passion was supplanted by sheer lust, where the tango was a sordid substitute for love, where no one seemed to fathom the truths to be learned from the tragedy of war.[31]

He could see everywhere he went in France that the long struggle to survive had worn the country out and that peace presented its own rough challenges. Amazed at what people would cling to as home, he would almost weep at the hopeful sight of tiny new gardens planted amid the rubble of a house or an entire village. Yet in spite of all he had lost, Steichen exulted at Voulangis in 1920 in the most beautiful spring he had ever enjoyed there. Trenches and shell holes were being obliterated with fresh soil as farmers plowed fields that had so recently been overrun with destruction and death. Here in work and in nature's powers of rebirth lay true peace and healing.[32] Serenity and security waited in the dark layers of the sacred earth. His marriage, like the world, was in chaos, but he could at least make the world of his flowers beautiful and whole again.

Steichen immersed himself more deeply than ever in the study of genetics and began formulating an ambitious plan for breeding his flowers. Soon the magic garden at Voulangis began to thrive once more. He had returned home to Voulangis to try to cleanse his mind and spirit of all conflict, so that once again he could work. "When I finally returned to my house and garden at Voulangis," Steichen remembered, "I entered a time of deep, earnest soul-searching that led to three of the most productive years of my life."[33]

First he spent what he described as a "monastic" year, painting and taking pictures, "wrestling" with light.[34] Endowed with immense talents both as an artist and a scientist, he had previously subordinated science to art. Now at Voulangis, according to Sandburg, Steichen "locked himself up and did nothing but experiment for a year. It was like the tale of [the composer Niccolò] Paganini spending a year in a mountain cave perfecting his technique with finger exercises."[35]

Steichen's AEF experience had demanded logic, analysis, and research, and as a result, the scientist in him now seemed to be unleashed to dominate his work. Because the AEF photographic work had infused him with a new passion for "sharp, clear pictures," and a new "technical interest in photography," he tackled the camera now as if he were using it for the first time.[36] Just as his flowers had flourished and surpassed themselves only when he cut the stalks back to the root, he now repeatedly forced himself back to the rudiments of photography. He spent many months of "reapprehension," incessantly photographing a cup and saucer set against a backdrop that modulated from white, to ever-darkening grays, to black velvet.[37] By his own reckoning, he photographed that white cup and saucer a thousand times, making notes on each exposure, studying the outcome, then trying again.

Like Sandburg, Steichen compared this discipline to the finger exercises exacted of a good pianist, having far more to do with skillful technical execution than artistic conception. He was "trying to learn what photography could and could not do," Steichen said. "When you make a photograph you have to learn to look at the subject as it is going to appear in the finished print and you can only do it if you understand everything thoroughly and that's the reason I kept on with that damned cup and saucer. It became part of my breathing and my bloodstream."[38]

Eager to know more about physics, mathematics, and botany, he turned to his garden to study the ratios of plant growth and structure. Captivated by the spiral form, he began to examine it as a fundamental of nature, and his attention to his plants in turn kindled new experiments with the camera. The confluence of his studies with his renewed interest in realistic photography prompted him to compose innovative pictures probing the spiral as subject-motif. *Pear on a Plate. France. c. 1920,* for instance, is a starkly beautiful close-up study of a single pear poised on a white plate whose smooth surface encases a spiral of light and shadow. In the famous *Wheelbarrow with Flower Pots. France. 1920,* Steichen captured an abstract arrangement of spiraling circles—dozens of empty flowerpots of all sizes thrust inside one another and then stacked horizontally in a worn wooden wheelbarrow. Other well-known studies from this series include *Harmonica Riddle. France. c. 1921, "Triumph of the Egg." France. c. 1921,* and the exquisitely simple, much-reproduced *Spiral. France. c. 1921,* the image of a snail's shell.

Now fascinated with geometrical forms in nature, Steichen also started exploring the golden measure, or the golden section—the division of a geometrical figure or a line so that the ratio of the lesser to the greater part is equal to the ratio of the greater part to the whole. Soon these forays into geometry were undergirding Steichen's growing quest to capture the truest possible volume, plane, depth, and contour in his photographs.

Deeply engrossed in this new apprenticeship, Steichen eventually wore himself to "a frazzle."[39] In August of 1920, therefore, he decided to go to Venice to spend a week or ten days just floating flat on his back in a gondola on the Grand Canal. En route to his hotel on his first night in

Venice, he heard some exuberant voices in the distance, and he recognized one of them as the melodic voice of Isadora Duncan. She and her current lover, a much younger man—her "Archangel," as she called the gifted pianist Walter Rummel—were in Venice with the Isadorables, her dance pupils and surrogate daughters. (Her own two young children, one sired by Gordon Craig and one by Paris Singer, had drowned in a tragic automobile accident in April 1913.)

Isadora and company were headed for Greece, where she had a house at Kopanos, and, ever the seductress, Isadora lured Steichen to Athens. She firmly believed that "a woman who has known but one man is like a person who has heard only one composer."[40] An expert at playing one man against another in the effort to anchor a certain man's love, she was probably trying to arouse Rummel's jealousy, for she feared that he was attracted to her adopted daughter Anna, one of the young Isadorables. Rummel, the grandson of Samuel F. B. Morse, was thirty-three, tall and sensitive, possessed of a gentle charm and a prodigious talent. "He was like a dancing saint on a brazier of live coals," Isadora wrote in her autobiography, *My Life*. "To love such a man is as dangerous as difficult."[41]

Her protégée Anna, the woman she feared to be her rival, was then as young and gloriously beautiful as Isadora herself had once been. Although Isadora was still vibrant and lovely at forty-three, she was now the voluptuous matron more than the svelte maiden. At forty-one, Steichen was a mature, handsome, virile man, and Isadora surely believed that his presence would jar Rummel back to his senses. The bait for Steichen was photography. They would borrow a motion-picture camera when they got to Athens, she cajoled, and Steichen could make motion pictures of the great Isadora dancing at the Acropolis. The next morning, he was on the steamer *Canonia* with Isadora, headed for Greece and his first encounter with that country.

When he arrived in Athens, Steichen was enthralled by the "most kind sunlight and the smells of the hot, baking land...."[42] The capricious Isadora quickly changed her mind about the motion pictures, however, claiming that she preferred, after all, to have her legendary dancing preserved in memory, not on film. But she would, as a consolation, permit her old friend Steichen to take some still photographs. He had left Voulangis in search of total rest and so, unarmed, he had to borrow

Brownie cameras from the hotel's headwaiter and from Irma Duncan, another of Isadora's beautiful pupils. Yet each time they climbed the Acropolis to the Parthenon, Duncan reneged. The camera was intruding, she protested, when actually, the emotional crisis with Rummel had taken all the joy of the dance out of her.

At last, Steichen managed to coax Isadora to stand just in front of the portal to the Parthenon, setting up his camera far enough away to encompass the whole wall. "The idea was that she was to do her most beautiful single gesture," he remembered, "the slow raising of her arms until they seemed to encompass the whole sky. She stood there for perhaps fifteen minutes, saying, 'Edward, I can't. I can't do it. I can't do it here.' But finally, after several tries, I saw the arms going up."[43] That image secure, he posed Duncan in her Greek tunic before the columns of the Parthenon—the only photographs ever made of Duncan in the place that had so enkindled her art. "Her whole art of dancing was inspired by the Greek architectural friezes and the drawings on Greek vases," Steichen wrote. "She was a part of Greece, and she took Greece as a part of herself."[44]

On August 30 at the temple and theater of Dionysus, Steichen used Irma Duncan's camera to photograph the Isadorables, especially Thèrése Duncan, another adopted daughter, and the most talented, in his opinion. There were rumors of a brief affair between the beautiful young dancer and the handsome, strangely sad photographer. If so, it must have especially wounded Isadora then, just two years Steichen's senior, but ten years older than Rummel. The journey had already become "Love's Calvary" for her.

Yet each morning, she taught her pupils, including Anna, with Steichen hovering about, photographing freely. When they finally traveled on to her house at Kopanos, unattended since before the war, they found it in ruins, now a ramshackle home to shepherds and their herds of mountain goats. Isadora decided she would rebuild, and she had a "dancing carpet" and a grand piano installed in a sheltered part of the house so that each afternoon they could watch the sun set behind the Acropolis while Rummel played Bach, Beethoven, Wagner, and Liszt. After one of those sunset rhapsodies, Isadora saw Rummel look up and lock Anna's eyes in a meeting "flaming with equal ardour in the scarlet sundown."[45] Enraged, Isadora spent the night wandering the hills near Hymettus. Afterward, she asked Steichen and a few of her pupils to accompany her to the "golden sands" of Chalcis, by way of ancient Thebes.

Nothing could console Isadora during that sojourn in Greece, however—not the sacred landscapes, nor the ebullient Greek wines, nor the sympathetic company of an attractive old friend. These undercurrents flowed through the striking photographic images Steichen gathered during his unexpected vacation in Greece.

Unlike Isadora, Thèrése Duncan was happy to be photographed. She was, Steichen thought, "a living reincarnation of a Greek nymph."[46] Absorbed in photographing the architectural wonder of the Parthenon one day, Steichen momentarily lost his view of Thèrése, but he could hear her. When he called out to her, she raised her arms to answer. "I swung the camera around and photographed her arms against the background of the Erechtheum," he wrote.[47] The result was *Thèrése Duncan: Reaching Arms. The Parthenon,* an image with the dancer's graceful, evocative arms in the foreground, timeless statues frozen in the background. Next, he said, they "went out to a part of the Acropolis behind the Parthenon, and she posed on a rock, against the sky with her Greek garments. The wind pressed the garments tight to her body, and the ends were left flapping and fluttering. They actually crackled. This gave the effect of fire," and it yielded the haunting photograph Steichen called *Wind Fire.*[48]

One day as Steichen, Isadora, Rummel, and the Isadorables climbed to the Parthenon, they stopped at an abutment from which Pericles was supposed to have spoken to a crowd below. Impulsively, Steichen strode out onto the platform and recited the poem "To a Contemporary Bunkshooter"—Sandburg's assault on the flamboyant evangelist Billy Sunday.

"That's wonderful," Isadora Duncan told Steichen at the end of his dramatic performance, "but is it poetry?"[49]

In September of 1920, young Mary Steichen skipped her senior year at Brearley to begin premedical studies at Vassar, with much encouragement from her father and Lee Stieglitz. Soon after Mary moved out of the quarters where she had lived while boarding at the home of Lee and

Lizzie Stieglitz at 60 East Sixty-fifth Street in Manhattan, Lee offered them to his brother Alfred and Georgia O'Keeffe. They moved there in December of 1920, to remain until 1924.

Once again, Nell Pratt acted as a surrogate mother to Mary, helping Steichen pay for her tuition and her clothes, while Lee Stieglitz continued to offer academic and career advice as Mary worked hard in her premed courses. At Vassar, Mary recalled, she was "the glamorous young woman who spoke French perfectly" and "who could ride horses better than anybody else."[50] Underneath, however, she was very lonely, but in those years, she did not let anyone but her father and Oma get very close to her.

Steichen returned to the United States late in 1920 to face hearings on Clara's lawsuit, for Clara was implacable in her determination to take her suit to trial. Just a month before pretrial testimony was scheduled to be heard in early December of 1920 in the case of *Clara Steichen* v. *Marion Beckett*, Steichen sued Clara in an effort to recover the property that she had removed from Villa L'Oiseau bleu. Once again the Steichens' legal squabbles made the *New York Times:* "E. J. Steichen, Artist, Now Sues His Wife, Asks Return of Antiques Following her Alienation Action Against Miss Beckett."[51] Steichen charged that Clara had removed art objects and antiques, for a total loss to him of $35,000 in personal property.

As the state supreme court held the pretrial hearing on Clara's suit, the Steichens' friends in the United States and in Europe renewed their worry (and their gossip), with most of them still giving their sympathies to Marion and Steichen. Clara usually wrote the details of the proceedings to Mildred Aldrich at Huiry, and Mildred passed the news along to Gertrude Stein, Alice B. Toklas, and others. After Mildred read the newspaper reports on the Steichens, she wrote to Gertrude Stein in December of 1920, predicting that the case would be dismissed. She wondered what Kathleen Bruce, Lady Scott, would do, however, when she heard that Clara was introducing her name as "evidence" of Steichen's penchant for infidelity. Clara would actually be guilty of libel, Mildred worried, for she really had "no case at all" against Bruce or Marion Beckett. In fact, what Clara had "considered proof," her own lawyers "luckily" did not permit her to introduce in court.[52]

But Clara's allegations were already smeared over the columns of various newspapers. She had attempted suicide, she stated during the hearing, because of her husband's involvement with a woman (Kathleen Bruce) who belonged to the bohemian artists' colony in Paris. She had so trusted Marion Beckett that she had allowed her to become virtually a member of her household in Voulangis.[53]

The Steichen-Beckett trial itself took place in March of 1921, with Clara testifying on March first about the wrongs she believed she had suffered because of Marion Beckett. She then underwent cross-examination by Beckett's attorney on March second. But Katharine Rhoades, Lizzie Stieglitz, Mercedes Carles, and other witnesses called by the defense told quite a different story, echoing Marion's mother's assertion that "there was nothing improper about the conduct of either my daughter or Colonel Steichen during the long course of our acquaintance."[54] Lizzie Stieglitz also testified that Clara had told her she had brought the suit because she needed the money. ("That suit—so justifiable—undertaken to try to get money to make a home for the children just as I told Lizzie," Clara wrote to Stieglitz in 1935, still reliving the event. "And she testifying that I just needed money—and not giving my reason.... I meant to give one third to Mary—equal to Kate and provide for some old people with the remaining."[55])

Marion herself was a dignified and effective witness, testifying with quiet composure that there had never been any impropriety in her relationship with Steichen, that despite Clara's insinuations, she had always been properly clothed when she posed for Steichen and she had never entered a darkroom with him except briefly to develop photographs, and that after she recognized Clara's extreme jealousy, she saw Steichen only three times. One of those times, she said, had been only a few moments in a crowd in France during the war, when she was doing Red Cross work and Steichen came through the sector where she was serving refreshments from a makeshift hut near the front. She could only conclude, Marion observed, that Clara's obsessive jealousy was a sign of illness.

The entire Beckett defense was built on the premise that Clara Steichen had always been openly jealous of any woman who was both an artist and a friend or colleague of her husband, and the most damning testimony against Clara came from her own words and letters. On cross-examination of Clara, for example, Marion's attorney introduced the matter of her prior jealousy of Isadora Duncan by reading Clara's letters to Marion expressing her fears that Steichen and Duncan were having an affair—a charge Clara had also made to other friends. Under oath, however, Clara expressed her conviction that there had never been a romance between Duncan and her husband. And how did she know that? the attorney inquired. Because, she said, her husband had told her so.

The final day of the trial brought Clara her most bitter blow: Weeping at times through his testimony, Steichen himself took the stand to speak on behalf of Marion Beckett. Clara was abnormally jealous and possessive, he testified sadly, even jealous of his mother. From the earliest days of their marriage, they had been tested by her jealousy and her occasional threats of suicide. She had driven him to such depths that he, too, had attempted suicide. He was often afraid to go home on the weekends, he stated, because one week Clara would believe him to be in love with Isadora Duncan, and the next time, she would fixate on Marion Beckett or someone else. In fact, he asserted, it was Clara herself who had first invited Marion to visit them at Voulangis. "Mrs. Steichen became attached to Miss Beckett," Steichen testified, "and it pleased me because it gave my wife a better hold on herself. Miss Beckett tried to get me into a less irritable state and said I ought to be lenient with Mrs. Steichen because she was ill."[56]

The case went to the jury on March third. After just fifteen minutes of deliberation, the verdict came back in favor of the defendant, vindicating Marion Beckett and leaving Clara more distraught than ever. "I hear that Steichen wept in court," Mildred Aldrich wrote to Gertrude Stein soon afterward. "Well that's over, thank God. It has worried me. I'll tell you how she took the case when I see you."[57]

In truth, however, it was far from over for Clara—or for Steichen, despite the exoneration implicit in the verdict. In reality, he found the experience a devastating invasion of the privacy of his troubled marriage, of his family life, and of his friendship with Marion Beckett. And once again, conflict with Clara had shattered his hard-won sense of peace, left him despondent, and destroyed his will and energy to work.

After the Paris edition of the New York *Herald* reported that Clara had lost her case, Mildred gossiped in more detail with Gertrude and Alice about Clara's downfall: Her "foolish habit" of writing damaging words in letters to friends proved to be incriminating, for Marion Beckett's lawyer introduced into evidence letters Clara had written when she

ALIENATING THE AFFECTIONS (1919–1922)

was "mad with jealousy" over Isadora Duncan. Steichen testified in court that Clara's habitual jealousy was her "only fault," making their married life "impossible," Mildred wrote, adding that the Supreme Court had completely exonerated Marion Beckett. "Voilà," Mildred concluded. "I *knew* it would end that way."[58]

Clara was now a virtual outcast in the Steichens' old circle, but friends and family continued to rally around Steichen during the miserable months after the court case. Stieglitz invited Steichen to Lake George for a visit with him and O'Keeffe, but Steichen declined, knowing that since 1919, when the family had sold Oaklawn, the main house, the remaining farmhouse was much too crowded most of the time with family and friends.[59]

Moreover, with his monthly financial obligations to Clara and his daughters, and the burden of debt he had incurred to keep them going through all the turmoil of the war and then the separation and the trial, Steichen had no time to vacation. The absolute necessity to earn money quickly jolted him out of his malaise, and he spent the summer of 1921 in New York, working hard at some commissions that yielded enough money for him to pay off about half of his debts and save enough to live on for six months in Voulangis.[60]

In the fall of 1921, Steichen traveled to Elmhurst, Illinois, the Chicago suburb that was now home to his parents and the Sandburgs. There he found Oma getting along about as well as one could expect "under the circumstances."[61] She was terribly anxious about her children and grandchildren, for Paula and little Margaret had been gravely ill, and Edward and Clara had been fighting in court for all the world to see. No matter how she may have felt about Clara by then, Oma was a devout Catholic, and the prospect of a divorce broke her heart. And there were her beloved granddaughters Kate and Mary, for so long separated from each other, little gypsies, almost homeless. Edward was a constant worry to her, as he had been all his life. He worked too hard, rested too little, carried too much worry around inside him.

Oma and Opa now lived in a small house just blocks away from the Sandburgs, who were "buried with troublesome and painful illness,"

Steichen reported to Stieglitz. His sister, in great pain with gallstones, was overwhelmed at the same time with anxiety over ten-year-old Margaret's baffling illness. Margaret had developed epilepsy, for which there was no effective treatment at the time. Meanwhile, in the midst of it all, Steichen said, his brother-in-law sailed along calmly, endowed as he was with an "iron" constitution and nerves.[62]

Sandburg and Oma cared for Janet and Helga while Paula took Margaret to Battle Creek, Michigan, for an experimental epilepsy treatment, based on severe fasting. Steichen wrote to cheer his sister when he heard that Margaret was improving, congratulating Paula on her patience and little Margaret on her *"HEROIC COURAGE."* He would have to wait until he got rich again to give her a big present, he said, but until then, he wanted Margaret to wear his Legion of Honor cross, and he sent it along so that she could pin it proudly on her pajamas.[63]

That autumn, Mary returned to Vassar and Kate enrolled in the Model School of Hunter College in New York.[64] Clara was apparently working part-time in a Manhattan office, although Steichen still provided most of her income. With these complicated family arrangements in place, Steichen longed to go home again to the peace and privacy of Voulangis. Sometime during that fall of 1921, he sailed for France aboard the SS *Olympic,* traveling this time, he wrote to Stieglitz, like a millionaire in a suite with a private bath, thanks to a discount arranged by a friend who knew someone in the shipping company. Nostalgically, he remembered his ocean crossing in steerage in 1900, when he was twenty-one, full of hope and unencumbered by obligations.[65]

Since July of 1921, Arthur and Mercedes Carles and their eight-year-old daughter had been living in Steichen's house at Voulangis, and it was good to return home and find the place full of life, a child at play in the garden, the studio filled with vibrant paintings—in this case, Carles's. (Back in New York, Clara wept when she heard the news that another family had moved into Villa L'Oiseau bleu.) Carles commemorated that stay with richly varied abstract paintings, as well as a beautiful oil on canvas entitled *Steichen's Garden.*

Back in the now-tranquil house and gardens at Voulangis, Steichen had time to reflect on the traumatic events of the past year. He had been vindicated in regard to Clara's spiteful suit and to the countersuit he had stubbornly filed to recover the antiques, paintings, and sculptures she had taken from Voulangis, but it seemed that no amount of negotiation or compromise could possibly repair the harm done. Clara had refused to see him when he tried to meet with her in New York before his departure, and he almost certainly returned to France already determined to initiate divorce proceedings.

He did so in the French civil court at Meaux on November 5, 1921, arranging, with his French attorney's advice, to have Clara served in New York with a formal request to restore conjugal cohabitation—the first step toward filing for divorce on grounds of abandonment. He also charged her with cruelty, harshness, and serious insults—also grounds for divorce in France. A writ of summons, issued on January 6, 1922, by Sheriff Soyez of Crécy-en-Brie, ordered Clara to appear in the French court on February 8, 1922.

Mildred Aldrich's housekeeper, Amélie, heard about Steichen's divorce suit on the train, and she rushed home to tell Mildred. "Poor Clara!!" Mildred immediately wrote to Gertrude Stein. "She has fixed her affair." Because Marion had been found innocent in the New York trial, Clara could not file a countersuit, Mildred said. She speculated that Steichen would sue Clara for divorce on grounds of desertion.[66]

When Clara did not travel to France to appear in the Meaux court, she was ruled in default and judged the guilty party. Enraged, she hired her own French lawyer and answered with a writ of her own on June 16, 1922. Steichen countered with charges of abandonment and refusal to restore cohabitation. Each of them wanted custody of Mary, about to turn eighteen, and Kate, fourteen. Clara also wanted a hundred dollars a month in alimony, to be reduced by half when Mary turned twenty-one in 1925.

A preliminary hearing was called for July 7, 1922, "Between Edward Steichen, painter, decorated with the Legion of Honor, residing at Voulangis, plaintiff" and Mrs. Clara Smith Steichen, whose legal residence was listed as Voulangis. She was actually residing then at 23–25 West Eighty-third Street in New York, "without authority from her husband or court," the writ of summons read.[67]

Despite the long and tragic erosion of their marriage, Edward and Clara had loved each other passionately in the early days. He had elevated his love for her to religious heights in the letters he wrote before they married: She was holy, pure, and sacred; he loved her with his soul as well as his heart.[68] Now, not quite twenty years later, the history of their marriage was condensed to cold, spare details in a legal document: Married October 3, 1903, in New York . . . two daughters . . . moved to Voulangis in 1908 . . . serious misunderstandings began prior to the war . . . Mrs. Steichen quarreled frequently with her husband, during which quarrels she "used to abuse him" . . . In September 1914 as the enemy approached, they left for America, where they lived together during a certain time. . . . Mrs. Steichen stayed in America after the war. . . . Mr. Steichen "had been decorated with the Legion of Honor for his splendid conduct, and earned the rank of colonel." . . . He "requested his wife to return to him and he went to America to fetch her. . . . However, upon his locating her, Mrs. Steichen refused steadfastly to receive him at her residence." . . . She refused to resume cohabitation. . . . He returned to Voulangis.[69]

He never wanted to hurt her again, he had told her on the eve of their wedding in 1903, begging forgiveness for an infidelity during their courtship.[70] Over their years together, however, there had been prolonged and bitter reciprocal pain. Too many times, his thoughtless actions were to blame for her outbursts, and as the years wore on, her apparent personality disorder was manifested in more frequent and sustained irrational episodes. They were a volatile combination, these two, and, in the end, they nearly destroyed each other, and their children along with them.

On July 17, 1922, Steichen got his divorce in France, but Clara was granted custody of the children and a hundred dollars a month in alimony, to be reduced by half when Mary came of age. On July 27, 1922, a clerk officially registered the French divorce decree, granted at the civil court of Meaux, Seine-et-Marne, severing the marriage between Edward Steichen and Clara Smith Steichen. But Clara wanted the last word, and she quickly filed her own divorce suit in the United States, in the state of New York. Through that court, on September 22, 1922, the Steichens entered into an agreement of separation stipulating that she would not oppose the French divorce action, that he would pay the alimony of one hundred dollars monthly to her lawyer in New York, and that he would pay her that sum for life.[71] She saw to it that both daughters heard all the sordid details of her suit charging their father with adultery, neglect, and abandonment, and then she demanded, despite the custody order, that the girls be compelled to state which parent they preferred to live with. Not surprisingly, Kate chose her mother and Mary chose her father.[72]

For all four Steichens, the bitter divorce proceedings brought only nominal, legal closure to years of turmoil and pain.

25

A Sacrament of Fire

(1 9 2 2 - 1 9 2 4)

It was a sacrament of fire at high noon.[1]

—CARL SANDBURG

DURING THE FOUR YEARS AFTER WORLD War I, when he was fighting his legal battles with Clara and struggling to refind himself in his work, Steichen spent his happiest, most peaceful hours back in his garden and studio at Voulangis. "Steichen is painting flowers near Paris," Sandburg had written to a friend, "and says if he keeps on some day he may do something worth looking at."[2]

Art and nature, the two constants in his life, would prove to be his most dependable companions as he lived and worked in solitude in France. There, Steichen continued his experiments in photography, while at the same time intensifying the search for his own distinctive style and subject matter in painting.[3] In the chaos of the postwar days, his desire for control of his art drove him squarely back to the fundamentals of technique in each medium.[4] As he considered "the whole Post-impressionist movement in painting," he was deeply troubled by the absence of a "basic discipline as its general point of departure."[5]

As had been his way since the early days in Milwaukee, he had thrown himself into yet another apprenticeship, perpetually experimenting with the technical applications of his art. More profoundly, he began to reconsider the purpose and potential power of both photography and painting, searching for a new realism, new methods for "representing volume, scale, and a sense of weight," new techniques for replicating three-dimensional images.[6]

Rodin's words echoed through Steichen's probing studies at Voulangis and his ever-evolving aesthetic theory: "When one begins to understand nature, progress goes on unceasingly."[7] As a botanist and gardener, Steichen was brilliantly equipped to embody the principles of nature in his art, and he set out on further investigations of the ratio of plant growth and structure, using his own garden as a laboratory. There, watching the continual migrations of even the tiniest snails, each carrying "a house constructed in the perfect geometric form of a spiral," he fell more deeply in love with that graceful and utilitarian form. The motif was repeated everywhere in his flowers and in his "most succulent" plants.[8] Many times he put his camera to the face of sunflowers, whose seedpods were strung on a spiral. Seeking a link between the omnipresent spiral forms in nature and Plato's section, he discovered that Leonardo da Vinci had possessed a similar interest in the Golden Section, and that Goethe, too, was fascinated with the spiral.

Steichen's purpose, as Sandburg recorded it, was to "find a series of equations and ratios that hold throughout the living forms of the natural world, hoping to formulate a set of figures that would balance and guide him" in drawing and painting, as well as in making photographs. "He went to plants, trees, flowers, seed pods," Sandburg observed, "—and came with such frequency on certain proportions and ratios of growth that he worked out a system of equations and adopted it."[9] As Steichen lost himself in these studies, the natural world that he had always loved and cultivated—as well as photographed and painted—suddenly seemed more intensely alive to him than ever before.[10] His serial photographs of shells and plants, such as *Sunflower in Seed, Aging Sunflower, A Bee on a Sunflower, Backbone and Ribs of a Sunflower, Foxgloves,* offer sequential studies of objects in evolution. His camera explored every curve and angle of the sunflower in various instants of growth. These photographs also radiate a voluptuous sexual imagery and energy, vibrant with the universal life forces Steichen was then exploring as naturalist and artist.

His formal education had ended with the eighth grade in Milwaukee, but now, in his early forties, Steichen had to teach himself plane and solid geometry, even the knack of the slide rule, so that he could calculate for himself the dimensions and correlations of the forms that so intrigued him. He pored over Ouspensky's *Tertium Organum,* especially the concept of dynamic symmetry. He was elated to discover Theodore Andrea Cooke's *The Curves of Life, Being an Account of Spiral Formations and Their Application to Growth in Nature,* published in 1914—with Rodin's philosophy of nature printed as an epigraph. In those pages, Steichen found elucidation and confirmation of his theories—the spiral forms imprinted in shells and plants; the architectural functions of the spiral; Leonardo's discoveries connecting the "growth of the spiral to the proportions of the human body"; and, demonstrated in astronomical photographs, "the spiral nebulae in the heavens." One day, Steichen was convinced, scientists would determine that the entire universe was built on the logarithmic spiral.[11]

His gifts as scientist as well as artist converged in his ongoing efforts to capture photographic images that realistically reflected volume, weight, and depth. Through his experiments photographing apples and pears from the trees in his garden, he discovered that diffused light could realistically illuminate volume as well as form.[12]

He was quickly engrossed in this new dimension of photography, imaginatively juxtaposing the real and the abstract, the literal and the symbolic. His experience with the lucid demands of military photography underpinned these calculated photographic experiments in his Voulangis studio. He came out of his "laboratory" empowered to achieve impeccably clear images of realistic objects, resonating with symbolic meaning. These discoveries yielded enduring and beautiful still-life images, such as *Three Pears and an Apple. France. c. 1921* and *An Apple, a Boulder, a Mountain. France. c. 1921.*

His abstract arrangements of apparently dissimilar objects—a harmonica juxtaposed to a glass bell used to protect plants from frost, for instance—resulted in interesting compositions, but these images left his friends baffled and perplexed because they had no idea how to interpret the intended symbolism of the objects he had so carefully arranged. This trial-and-error process gave Steichen a lasting insight, one that would be invaluable later in such epic projects as "The Family of Man": Symbols communicated significant meaning only if they were intelligible and universal.[13]

Steichen's postwar obsession to conquer form and technique in photography was matched for a time in those years at Voulangis by his determination to master the art and science of drawing, thereby to enrich his painting. Arthur Carles had taken a great interest in Steichen's experiments in geometry while they were together at Voulangis, and afterward Carles sent him several copies of a journal from Yale University, Jay Hambidge's *The Diagonal.* Doing his own experiments with the section, Hambidge had conceived of a square composed of a series of rectangles. He isolated the rectangle in the proportion of root 5 as "the most important and beautiful form," the geometric basis, he thought, of Greek vases and of the Parthenon itself.[14] Steichen noted that George Bellows and other painters had incorporated into their paintings Hambidge's system of the diagonal, but he dismissed it himself as a two-dimensional symmetry that could not be applied to realistic three-dimensional paintings. Yet he continued to play with Hambidge's ideas, cutting a rectangle of paper into three triangles, each in extreme and mean ratio, the golden mean.

Soon these "curious shapes" that Steichen now distilled from the rectangle kindled the idea for a children's book, and he eagerly shared the concept with Paula and Sandburg.[15] He did not know for sure, he said, whether it was a book for "kids"—or for "grown up kids"—but he thought it would be fun to create his own fanciful universe inhabited with creatures inspired by the triangles.[16] Steichen hoped Sandburg might work with him on the text, for his brother-in-law was even then enjoying the success of his own new book for children, *The Rootabaga Stories;* originally written for his own daughters, it was published in 1922.

Sandburg, like Steichen, was still reeling from the disillusionment of the war and the thorny problems of the postwar era. For the past twenty years, Sandburg had been an investigative journalist, a social reformer, and a radical poet experimenting with realistic images and themes, but now, just as the aftermath of the war propelled Steichen toward a new realism, it turned Sandburg in the opposite direction, from realism to romanticism and myth. Consequently, Sandburg's immediate response to what he had called the "imbecility of a frightened world" had been to invent some of the first thoroughly American fairy tales for children.[17] Although *The Rootabaga Stories* were on the surface created for his own small daughters, they were infused with parody and satire of the corrupt world that grown-ups had invented.

Steichen had followed the evolution of Sandburg's stories, which were set in an imaginary kingdom and undergirded with social commentary. Their talks most likely helped to trigger Steichen's desire to create this series of abstract geometrical designs for a children's book, conceived and executed, he said—in a revelation of his own new purpose as an artist—with "rigidly disciplined control" in composition of form and color.[18] He wrote to the Sandburgs from Voulangis that because he had relinquished all hope that adults could understand art in "its real creative sense," he was going to "begin with the Kids." Therefore, he set out to create his own picture book for children about some "thingamabobs" who were vividly alive, although they had never actually lived anywhere in the known universe.[19] He named his characters the Oochens, designed each one out of three triangles, and created an imaginary republic for them to inhabit. In that magical domain, the Oochens were protected by a decent and orderly government led by a president named Khor. His fellow citizens were "dignified and beautifully old, yet fresh as a red autumn dawn with green ducks across the sky," Sandburg wrote appreciatively.[20]

Key Oochens included the Peeping Gagaboo, Thinkrates the Philosopher, a Pink Faced Politician who wept constantly because "the world was going to the dogs," the Cinnamon Bun B'ar, and a Lyric Poet called Mushton-Slushley. Khor's messenger, who could instantly transport his thoughts to the far and near reaches of the republic, was the Radio Gull, a "lovely creature" composed of three white triangles on a blue background."[21] Sandburg thought Steichen's Oochens were "as tender as Hans Christian Andersen and as precise and thoroughly reasoned as Albert Einstein."[22]

Although Steichen never finished the book, many of the bright, angular Oochens he painted over the years would later be exhibited among his paintings. "In the small tempera paintings I made of the Oochens," Steichen wrote in his autobiography, "I experienced a sense of freedom I had never experienced before in painting. I believe it came from the knowledge that I was doing something based on nature's laws. The inexorable discipline gave me a new kind of freedom."[23]

A Sacrament of Fire (1922–1924)

The Oochen studies and other pictures taking shape on the canvases in his Voulangis studio were remarkably different from the flower murals he had painted for Agnes and Eugene Meyer. Arthur Carles had displayed two of the mural panels in 1921 in the Exhibition of Paintings and Drawings Showing the Later Tendencies in Art, an American modernist show he had organized, with the help of Alfred Stieglitz, at the Pennsylvania Academy of the Fine Arts in Philadelphia. Steichen's work had been widely condemned, Stieglitz reported afterward, noting ruefully that the "intolerance of the half-baked is something awful" and speculating that Steichen felt "keenly the slams" directed toward his murals.[24] But it was Steichen's absorption in his new, self-imposed apprenticeship, not his reaction to criticism, that inspired the transformation of his painting.

For example, his studies of the golden mean generated a remarkable abstract painting entitled *Le Tournesol*—or *The Sunflower*. Steichen had long been studying and photographing his sunflowers, but now he painted them in tempera and oil on canvas, starkly framing the pink, golden, and green spirals of the flower against bold black, white, russet, and ocher triangles, the forms that dominated his imagination then. The painting, chosen for the Salon d'Automne in Paris in 1922, was a harbinger of the new directions he was setting for himself as a painter, armed with his discovery of the paradoxical freedom that sprang from unremitting discipline.[25]

But slowly and surely, the camera, not the palette, became the magnet for his energy and excitement. Perhaps, he began to think, he should give up painting altogether in order to concentrate on photography.

Sometime during 1921, on a visit to the New York School of Photography, Steichen had met an extraordinary young woman, "beautiful, fashionable, auburn-haired, creamy-skinned" Dana Desboro Glover, an aspiring photographer and a working actress.[26] She was born Dana Glover in Greeley, Kansas, in 1894, but her parents soon joined in the land rush to Oklahoma, where Dana, grew up, one of five sweet, sunny-haired sisters whose childhood clothes were often made out of flour sacks. The violent prairie weather left her with a lifelong terror of storms. Little is known of her father, but Dana's mother was a strong midwestern pioneer woman who loved to sing folk songs and who had ridden wild horses, staked her claim in Oklahoma, and farmed corn, alfalfa, and soybeans.[27]

At sixteen, to help support the family, Dana started acting with a small traveling tent-show company in the Midwest and West, using the stage name Dana Desboro. By the time she was nineteen, she had become the leading lady of the popular Princess Stock Company, hailed by critics for her "wisdom, resourcefulness and keen intelligence" and her "graceful and spirited interpretation of roles that required the technique of the true artist."[28] She had "rare talent," maybe even genius, one critic declared.[29] At twenty, Dana had graduated to the Washington Square Players, and after a performance in Philadelphia, the critics praised her for casting her "spell on the audience in no uncertain fashion."[30] She appeared with Billie Burke in *The Rescuing Angel* in 1917, and with George M. Cohan in *The Tavern* in 1920.

Steichen was about forty-two when he met Dana, then about twenty-seven. She was a vibrant, beautiful woman, with gentle grace, a dazzling smile, a mischievous sense of humor, and, most important, a serene, steady spirit. She was thrilled to meet Steichen the famous photographer and war hero—and he, in turn, found Dana quite simply unforgettable. But Steichen was still married then and too painfully embroiled in his problems with Clara and the humiliating court case to risk exposure by any semblance of involvement with another woman. Heaven help the woman as well as Steichen if Clara and her lawyer even suspected an extramarital romance during the litigation.

Still, fortuitously, their paths had crossed, and sometime in 1922 after the trial was over, Steichen saw Dana again in New York. This time, he photographed her in the evocative two-color portrait *Dana and the Apple. New York. 1922*. The camera hides nothing of their mutual attraction—evident in the way the camera caresses her face, in the way her eyes flirt and tempt the photographer. Dressed in a navy-and-orange knit dress, hair slightly disheveled, she sits with her arms folded, her shining gray eyes smiling seductively, a partially eaten red apple resting on a Chinese pillow in the foreground.

A Sacrament of Fire (1922–1924)

By the early winter of 1923, Steichen was ready to call a halt to his apprenticeship at Voulangis, and sometime toward the end of that solitary sojourn, he had an epiphany. The story was told and retold in many versions over the remaining years of his life, the details, apocryphal or literal, varying with the teller of the tale. Even Steichen himself changed his account over time, but in 1928, only a few years after the actual event, he told Sandburg the story, and his brother-in-law told it this way:

> *Steichen is now about ready to quit painting, to swear off brushing oils and pigments on canvas. One morning his gardener places before him on the breakfast table a painting, a copy of a Steichen picture. "Where did that come from?" Steichen asks François, a Breton peasant in wooden shoes, an ox of a man raised on potatoes and cabbage. "I did it," replies François. "You painted that picture?" "Yes." "Why," shouts Steichen, "it is better than mine!"*
>
> *He buys the painting from François. He keeps it. Years pass and many throwouts go to the trash cans. But the François painting is kept as a treasure, a mascot, a signpost, a guidon, a talisman. "It was the one thing needed to finally convince me that so far as I was concerned painting was the bunk," says Steichen.*[31]

Sharing a lifelong dialogue with Steichen about the artistic process, Sandburg intimated that part of Steichen's motivation to abandon painting sprang from his weariness with the fakery and snobbery in "the world of painters and critics who devote their days to Blah."[32] Over the years, Sandburg enjoyed repeating the story Steichen had told him about a prank played by several artists who dipped a mule's tail in paints of various hues, then held a canvas up to the mule's twitching "paint brush" until a vivid "abstract" design filled the canvas. The identity of the "artist" concealed, the mule's painting was mounted in an exhibition, where it "amused, mystified, and pleased" a number of people.[33] For Steichen, this prank, like the imitation Cézanne he had earlier painted as a hoax at 291, underlined the unpredictable subjectivity of artistic standards. Ultimately, it seemed to be "anybody's guess what is a work of art."[34]

Deciding in 1923 that his long, deliberate apprenticeship was over, Steichen traveled back to New York, planning to stay for a while this time. As he told Sandburg, he had a living to make.[35] The war and divorce had further impoverished him. He was forty-four, heavily in debt, and tired of worrying about money and imposing on the charity of friends.[36] His wealthy friends were still subsidizing music lessons and helping to pay tuition for Mary and Kate. He had alimony to pay, and daughters to clothe, support, and educate. Steichen had concluded that photography would be the surest way of earning the income he needed, and he briefly toyed with the idea of making motion pictures before deciding to stay with still photography. New York would surely offer more opportunity for him than postwar Paris. If not, he told Sandburg, he might try selling his "line of goods" in Chicago.[37]

On arrival in New York, he happened to thumb through a recent copy of the elegant and fashionable monthly *Vanity Fair*, where he discovered a page of portraits of ten "Master American Portrait Photographers," accompanied by a short essay of appreciation written by Frank Crowninshield, editor of the magazine. "It is undeniable that America now leads the world in photography, a profession especially exacting when it concerns itself with portraiture," the text read. "Here are ten masters in New York who have never regarded their profession as a business, but always as an art." There, Steichen found one of his own self-portraits; underneath it, the caption read, "An unrivalled master." He was in the company of Stieglitz, "the doyen and all-around master," who practiced photography "when the mood prompts"; Francis Bruguiere, "the upholder of taste and creator of painters' backgrounds"; and Edward Thayer Monroe, Alfred Cheney Johnston, Pirie MacDonald, Nikolas Muray, James E. Abbe, Maurice Goldberg, and Arnold Genthe. Crowninshield praised Steichen as "the greatest of living portrait photographers," and he observed that, unfortunately, Steichen had "abandoned the camera for the palette."[38]

This being the diametric opposite of the truth, Steichen wrote to thank Crowninshield and to set him straight. In turn, Crowninshield immediately invited Steichen to join him for lunch with Condé Nast, owner and publisher of *Vanity Fair* and *Vogue*. With his trademark pince-nez, Condé Nast did not look like a former poor boy from St. Louis, son of a ne'er-do-well father and a Catholic mother, who engraved in him the work ethic that led to his great success. From the moment Nast had bought *Vogue* in 1909 and *Vanity Fair* in 1913, he ran both magazines with domineering passion, quickly turning Condé Nast Publications into a lucrative dynasty.

Nast already knew Steichen's work in a very personal way, for Steichen had photographed the first Mrs. Condé Nast about 1907. The commission to photograph Clarisse Nast had come indirectly from Rodin, by then already infatuated with Mrs. Nast's sister, Claire Coudert, the notorious Duchesse de Choiseul. Steichen's painting *The Apple Bloom* had apparently been used as a cover for *Vogue* sometime between 1906 and 1908.[39] And later, probably in 1917, Steichen had photographed Mrs. Nast again, as well as her young daughter Natica. When his *Portrait of a Child* was reproduced in the August 1917 issue of *Vanity Fair,* Steichen was described as "our ablest and best known photographer," who had "deserted the dark-room in order to become a modernist painter of high distinction."[40]

Steichen had also been featured in *Vanity Fair*'s "Hall of Fame" in January of 1918, along with art critic Frank Jewett Mather, Jr.; scholar Geoffrey G. Butler, head of the British mission to the United States during World War I; and architect Thomas Hastings. Steichen was recognized, the text read, "Because he made a great and well-deserved reputation as a photographer. Because he was the center of a storm that raged about the famous Photo Secession Galleries over the question of 'art and photography,' in which many angry critics participated. Because, not being satisfied with what he had done with the camera, he took to painting and made a success in that medium, too. And, finally, because, when the war broke out, he obtained a commission in the United States Signal Corps as captain and is now on active service under Major James Barnes."[41] A couple of facts came out slightly askew, but this recognition in the "dignified authentic journal of society, fashion, and the ceremonial side of life," as *Vanity Fair* described itself on its masthead, testified to Steichen's stature.[42] The exposure in *Vanity Fair* meant that, in the eyes of cosmopolitan Americans, he was an artist and a citizen who had arrived.

Both the 1918 and the 1923 tributes ran Steichen's striking self-portrait, taken just before he entered the war—handsome and dapper in a bow tie, his camera visible, no animation around the sad, sensual mouth, just the unflinching gaze of his eyes. The photograph was run correctly, although without a credit, in the 1918 issue of *Vanity Fair.* In the 1923 issue, it was acknowledged as a self-portrait, but the image was reversed and the camera was cropped out of the picture. Steichen, somber and brooding, looked uncannily like a beardless young Abraham Lincoln.

To his surprise, during that luncheon in 1923, Nast and Frank Crowninshield offered Steichen a job as chief photographer for Condé Nast Publications, publishers of *Vogue, Vanity Fair, House & Garden,* and *Jardins des Modes,* popular magazines for and about the wealthy, stylish, sophisticated, and celebrated. Steichen's charge would be to make portraits of prominent people for *Vanity Fair* and, anonymously if he wished, to take fashion photographs for *Vogue,* which had just lost its famous fashion photographer, Steichen's old friend Baron Adolf de Meyer.

In 1914, Condé Nast had hired de Meyer to be *Vogue*'s first full-time official photographer, signing him to an exclusive contract for a hundred dollars weekly to take pictures for *Vanity Fair* as well as for *Vogue.* For his misty, elegant photographs, de Meyer posed his subjects against a signature dark background, encasing them in flattering light and shadow, and creating sumptuous images of wealth and glamour. But in 1922, Nast's archrival, William Randolph Hearst, wooed de Meyer with a much higher salary to work for him at *Harper's Bazar.* Condé Nast hated to lose to Hearst an any score, but he had already tired of the repetition of de Meyer's melodramatic style. Now Nast jumped at the opportunity to recruit the great, original Steichen, who would surely bring a more contemporary look to portrait and fashion photography. He sensed that Steichen could lead his magazines visually out of the immediate postwar days into the experimental, innovative, triumphant twenties.

Steichen immediately reached for the challenge. Thinking out loud after Nast and Crowninshield stunned him with the offer of a job, Steichen replied that he had already taken "probably the first serious fashion photographs ever made"—for *Art et Décoration* in Paris in 1911.[43] As to the question of anonymous photographs, if he published a photograph, he would certainly sign his name and stand by it. Otherwise, he would not allow it to be published in the first place.

Delighted, Nast confirmed the offer, and a few days later, he called Steichen in to confer about salary. Steichen proposed a figure that made even Nast blink—$35,000, a huge sum then, when the average yearly salary in the United States was less than $1,500.00.[44] Condé Nast had never paid a photographer so much, he said skeptically. Disarmingly, Steichen reminded Crowninshield and Nast that they themselves had proclaimed him the greatest of living portrait photographers.

"Nast gave in," Steichen told the Sandburgs.[45] While no contract was signed, Steichen got the salary he wanted, and he embarked on what would be a fifteen-year-long tenure at Condé Nast Publications, producing, Sandburg wrote, "a fascinating parade of actors, singers, playwrights, authors, dancers, vaudevillians, prize fighters, performers of stunts and creative artists" and thus reaching a huge audience.[46] From the outset, Steichen gave Condé Nast what he wanted—beautiful, elegant photographs that clearly presented the fashions being featured in *Vogue* and the faces being celebrated in *Vanity Fair.*

He also played a role in helping the Nast magazines reach their glory years. In 1923, when Steichen was hired, Condé Nast Publications earned $241,410 after taxes; by 1928, that figure had ballooned to $1,425,076.[47] By 1928, the circulation of *Vogue* had grown to nearly 139,000 readers, up from nearly 17,000 in 1909, while *Vanity Fair* had nearly 85,000, a jump from nearly 13,000 in 1913.

In April of 1923, Steichen wrote jubilantly to Agnes Meyer that he had taken the job as photographer for *Vanity Fair* and *Vogue,* with a "fine studio" in the Beaux Arts Studios on Fortieth Street, where he was working "night and day."[48] He had stored some of his paintings and other belongings in the Meyers' garage on Amsterdam Avenue, and he wanted to claim them, for Steichen was planning to settle down once again to live and work in New York.

From his brother Lee's house on East Sixty-fifth Street where he and O'Keeffe were still living in 1923, Stieglitz viewed Steichen's new job with rapt disapproval, over the years roundly condemning Steichen for his great commercial success, while at the same time claiming credit for recommending him to Crowninshield in the first place. He wrote to photographer Child Bayley with the news, and Bayley responded, "With you, I wonder if the old Steichen will reappear." He wondered, Bayley said, what motivated Steichen to make such a change.[49]

A host of reasons prompted Steichen's turn toward lucrative commercial photography, not the least of them the unexpected chance, after years of financial struggle, to make some money at last and free himself of burdensome debt. And if by "the old Steichen" Bayley and Stieglitz meant the bold, highly original pioneer, they would not be disappointed in what lay ahead.

• ———

Later in 1923, enthralled with his new role at Condé Nast Publications, Steichen was dispatched to Paris for an assignment for *Vogue,* traveling luxuriously, as most high-level Nast employees did—in contrast to the logistics a frugal self-employed artist habitually faced. Afire with a new sense of purpose, Steichen stole a few days from his work to go out to Voulangis. Ever since the war had ended, throughout all the months of experimentation there in the beloved garden and studio, he had been working doggedly to become a better artist. Now the path was absolutely clear to him: He would renounce painting once and for all and give all his creative force to photography.

He summoned François, his loyal Breton gardener, to Villa L'Oiseau bleu and gave him some shocking orders: He was to help pull every single one of Steichen's paintings off the studio walls and out of storage on shelves or in cupboards; then he was to start a bonfire, Steichen commanded. They were going to burn every scrap of canvas they could get their hands on.

"I was through with painting," Steichen remembered when he was eighty-four.

> *Painting meant putting everything I felt or knew into a picture that would be sold in a gold frame and end up as wallpaper. The statement I had made so spontaneously to Stieglitz in 1900, "I will always stick to photography!" rang in my ears. It was true. Photography would be my medium. I wanted to reach into the world, to participate and communicate, and I felt I would be able to do this best through photography. I decided on another apprenticeship. I would learn to make photographs that could go on the printed page, for now I was determined to reach a large audience instead of the few people I could reach as a painter.*[50]

After his stunned gardener recovered from the surprise, the two men "had a heyday" pulling out into the garden painting after painting,

A Sacrament of Fire (1922–1924)

the work of two decades, paintings that Steichen estimated he could have sold for about fifty thousand dollars.[51] They lit a bonfire, fed it with Steichen's canvases, and then danced around it wildly. "It was a sacrament of fire at high noon," Sandburg reported. "At first Steichen came near crying as the flames licked up the oils and canvas. Then he sang the song he and Billy Mitchell gave in duo during the war:

"Where will we all be one hundred years from now?
Pushing up the daisies, pushing up the daisies,
That's where we'll all be, one hundred years from now!" [52]

Other accounts of Steichen's sacramental fire were gradually transformed into legend. As years passed, his own periodic narratives of the event focused on different details. In 1958, for instance, thirty-five years after the episode, Steichen told photographer and art historian Beaumont Newhall that while the encounter with the gardener's primitive painting usually got the attention, it was World War I that had actually propelled him to destroy his paintings, awakening him to the humanistic possibilities of photography.[53] Through his photographs, Steichen believed, he could truly reach out to the world he inhabited, and more closely connect to life.[54]

A year later, in 1959, when he turned eighty, Steichen wrote that he was "producing pictures surrounded with a gold frame that reached a small audience while the photographic image had unexplored areas which, on the printed page, would reach vast audiences. I therefore spent two years of isolation, experimentation and research—a second technical apprenticeship preparing for my newfound conception of the medium as a means of communication."[55]

By the time Steichen wrote the story in 1963 in his autobiography, *A Life in Photography,* memory had fused different time periods, so that, contrary to his own account to Sandburg in 1928, he recalled burning the paintings on the very day he discovered François's primitive painting—still safely preserved in the Steichen Archive at the Museum of Modern Art in New York. Although his account of the sequence and the details of this pivotal event may have varied through the years, decades afterward, Steichen offered the truest interpretation of its meaning: "The bonfire, I see now, was not ever a symbol, really; it was a culminating gesture."[56]

That sacramental fire brought not only the culmination of the first half of Steichen's life work but also catharsis, new commitment, and powers of communication that not even Steichen, the consummate seeker and dreamer, could have fully imagined on that fateful day as the ashes of his paintings smoldered in the earth at Voulangis.

Steichen told Sandburg that when he got back to his quarters in the Beaux Arts Studios in New York after the bonfire at Voulangis, he "cut into shreds a remaining twenty odd paintings in oil and called for the janitor to remove them from the rubbish. The frames went to the Whitney Studio Club for distribution among hopeful students."[57]

Steichen was now driven more than ever before by the need for total control in his work, wresting from his art the order he had been denied by the war and the disintegration of his home life. Years earlier, when George Bernard Shaw had told Steichen that he had wanted to be a painter but could not draw well enough to satisfy himself, Steichen confided that he had the same problem.[58] Nevertheless, by 1923, he had been painting for more than a quarter of a century, and had achieved recognition and commercial success beyond that enjoyed by many American painters of his generation.

Steichen possessed a strong ego. (Otherwise, how could he have achieved his work? How could he have persisted, endured, survived?) Yet he was ruthlessly self-critical. The scientist and realist in him counterbalanced the artist and romantic. Therefore, he could see himself for what he was, and, more important, for what he could and could not become. The last self-directed apprenticeship in painting at Voulangis, rich as it was with experiments in drawing, had convinced him that he was nearing the limits of his talent as a painter. At the same time, he was just beginning to comprehend his power and potential as a photographer.

Man Ray later tried to sum up Steichen's career as an artist: He was "a painter to begin with—well, a decorative painter. He wanted to be a society painter, as I did, too."[59] In reality, it was precisely because Steichen did *not* want to be known only as a decorative painter or a society painter that he abandoned painting and turned his full, forceful energy to photography.

A SACRAMENT OF FIRE (1922-1924)

Clara Steichen, looking on from a distance, thought Steichen deceived himself and others over the years in his explanations of why he stopped painting. Quite simply, she thought, he had failed. She wrote to Stieglitz in later years, "In his heart he is self-disappointed—he wanted to be a painter."[60]

What he wanted even more was to be an artist who spoke *to* and *about* the world he inhabited. The message was beginning to override the art medium. In the early years, his sister had worried that despite his great success, Steichen painted and photographed with his mind and talent but not with his heart. Now the war had changed him forever, and so had the tragedy of his marriage to Clara. He was moving closer to his ultimate philosophy of art:

When an artist of any kind looks at his subject, he looks with everything he is. Everything that he has lived, learned, observed, and experienced combines to enable him to identify himself with the subject and look with insight, perception, imagination, and understanding. The technical process simply serves as a vehicle of transcription and not as the art.[61]

He had always switched from painting to photography, from one technical process, one vehicle of transcription, to another. But he had always been better at photography than at painting, and so he had exerted a powerful influence on modern photography. To the contrary, his influence in modern painting had little to do with his own work and everything to do with his unselfish, discerning appreciation for the work of other painters.

From the earliest days, before he knew it himself, Stieglitz and Fred Holland Day had understood that Steichen was a photographer first and a painter second. With his genius for camera and darkroom technique, Steichen had taken standard technical processes such as the gum-bichromate process and achieved results that far surpassed the work of others.[62] Immediately grasping the potential of the autochrome process and the Lumière plates, he had pioneered in early color photography. His recent success with military reconnaissance photography was just one more instance of Steichen's pathbreaking technical achievement. By 1923, he possessed a mastery of the art and science of photography on a par with Rodin's mastery of sculpture. Now in the twenties, as he realized that he could come closer to fulfilling his own demanding artistic vision through photography, he became obsessed with photography's *applications*—its theme, purpose, and potential.

On March 5, 1923, Steichen clearly announced this turning point in his work and his career in a prophetic speech at an exhibition and meeting of the Pictorial Photographers of America, foretelling his bold new commitment to "the meticulous accuracy of the camera." There had been no real progress in photography since the daguerreotype, Steichen reportedly asserted, thereby seeming to repudiate all the work he and Stieglitz had achieved since 1900. The soft-focus lens, for years his own tool of choice, he now called the "most pernicious influence in the pictorial world," and he stated that he deplored the trend toward "fuzziness" demonstrated in the work of contemporary "artistic" photographers.[63]

Photography should be an "objective art," the great pioneering pictorialist now contended. The photographer should take "things as they are, without injecting his personality into the picture." The *New York Times* noted that Steichen "urged a return to sharp pictures," and the paper quoted him as saying that he did not care about "making photography an art." Instead, he simply wanted to make good photographs. "Take things as they are," he urged his listeners; "take good photographs and the art will take care of itself."[64]

From now on, Steichen would specialize in this one art form, boldly roaming the vast frontier of modern photography, and venturing far past its apparent limits.

Free of Clara, free of painting, Steichen poured his energy night and day into the new job at Condé Nast Publications. He was also caught up in a passionate romance with Dana Desboro Glover. From the beginning of his new life in New York, Steichen and Dana were together as much as possible, soon living together, and, in every real sense, married from 1923 onward. They were a glamorous couple in a city and a decade defined by glamour. She already shared his passion for photography, and he took pride in her theater career. As Steichen joyously tackled his exciting, lucrative job at *Vanity Fair* and *Vogue* with resurging energy, Dana starred

A Sacrament of Fire (1922–1924)

in productions mounted at the Harlem Opera House by the Jessie Bonstelle Stock Company, which produced such stars as Katharine Cornell.

Although Steichen reported that he and Dana were married in 1923, at least one person later doubted that there had ever been a legal ceremony. Others contended, however, that Steichen and Dana had been married on Steichen's forty-fourth birthday in March of 1923 in Blairstown, New Jersey, where Dana's family owned a farm. Efforts in later years to locate a marriage certificate in Blairstown and in Warren County, New Jersey, were thwarted by the fact that all marriage records prior to July 8, 1937, had been destroyed in a fire.[65]

As everyone who knew Steichen and Dana would testify, however, theirs was a true marriage. Steichen's niece Helga Sandburg remembered that Dana was "always wildly in love with him" and that she gave Steichen the harmony, companionship, and devotion he had craved for years.[66] He, in turn, quickly began to trust her as his collaborator as well as lover. During their first years together, even as Dana continued her stage work, she always subordinated it to Steichen's needs. It was clear from the outset of their relationship that he and his work came first. They shared private interests as well, for, like Steichen, Dana loved books and music, and she quickly fell in love with his flowers. The couple also shared at least one vice—chain-smoking—but then, for a glamorous actress and a handsome photographer in the sensual, defiant twenties, cigarettes were almost part of the wardrobe.

Not long after Steichen and Condé Nast had come to terms on his salary, Steichen traveled out to Elmhurst, Illinois, to see his parents and the Sandburgs and to share the news about the wonderful job in New York. He also showed the family his photographs of Dana. As soon as he introduced her to Oma and Opa and the rest of the Sandburgs, they, like Ed and Carl, immediately loved the beautiful young woman with the "low laugh" and "musical voice," who, every year possible from 1923 on, came with Steichen to join in the family Christmas celebration, and who wrote them lively, affectionate letters between visits.[67]

A poignant vignette played out on a Manhattan street in late summer of 1923. In the city on business with her aunt and her mother, Marion Beckett passed Clara Steichen on the sidewalk. Clara "stared hard & passed almost touching me," Marion told Stieglitz, but because she was "dreaming (as usual)," Marion did not even see Clara. She knew that must have been upsetting.[68]

A woman ahead of her times, Marion had adopted an infant son in January of 1923. There were, of course, ensuing rumors that she had borne Steichen a son, but that did not appear to be the case. Actually, she had the courage and the family resources to become a single mother, and she reveled in the beautiful child she adopted. Katharine Rhoades, the boy's surrogate aunt, helped Marion find a studio in Washington, D.C., where the two women would share an apartment and the care of the little boy. Two years later, Marion adopted an infant girl so her son would have a sister. She brought up her adopted son and daughter, continued to paint, and kept Stieglitz aware of her activities through occasional letters. Writing him from Washington in the autumn of 1924, she reported that Katharine Rhoades had seen Steichen in New York and found him "looking well—& working hard."[69] She exhibited her paintings at the Montross Gallery in New York in 1925. After years spent living in Washington and vacationing in Vermont, Marion moved with her children to upstate New York.

Clara Steichen, meanwhile, was trying to build a new life for herself in New York and Connecticut. Clinging to her animosity for Steichen, she lived vicariously through Kate and Mary, who was a brilliant student at Vassar. By her junior year, boredom and restlessness prompted Mary to give up her premed program, even though she had finished all the requirements, and to begin a study of English, music, and drama. Soon gorgeous, statuesque Mary Steichen, not quite twenty, had decided to become an actress.

In the meantime, fifteen-year-old Kate had enrolled at Kendall Hall, a boarding school on the North Shore, near Beverly, Massachusetts. Her best friend there was Mildred Hayes, nicknamed "Mid," who found Kate "very dramatic, very realistic. If she saw a sun spot, she'd sit on the floor in the middle of the sunlight, put her hair down, and let the sun shine on it. She was lots of fun—and still a serious person." Mid admired Kate's "magnificent voice," and she listened to her friend's dreams of being a concert singer, "which never evolved, and which broke her heart."[70] Unlike her mother and older sister, Kate was blessed with a sturdy, resilient, even optimistic spirit, evident in her music and poetry.

In the summer of 1924, when Kate had just turned sixteen and Mary was about to turn twenty, Clara lived near her sister Charlotte in South Kent, Connecticut, in a small cottage that she had made charming and inviting on very little money. She had a "play garden with flowers abloom and a tiny terrace," she told Stieglitz. Inside, near the fireplace, stood Kate's piano. On the wall, there was Steichen's portrait of Clara as "a funny wondering girl in Paris" many years earlier, and another Steichen painting, a still life of geraniums. "What an innocent thing I was," she wrote to Stieglitz, "and as Kate says, 'Still are.' "[71]

When she was not away at school, Kate was living with her mother in Connecticut, buried "deep in her music," Clara wrote Stieglitz. Clara described her daughter as "the lovliest [sic] thing I know." Kate was tall and "curiously fair and dark at the same time" with "liquid" gray eyes, a "delicious" wit, and a "knowledge of affection for human beings and beasts that almost makes her Hindoo [sic]. Wild things come to her—her walks mean she comes home trailing strange beetles, frogs who stay put on command, baby rabbits who thrive on her bottle feedings and make wonderful models as she photographs 'em." Kate was studying piano and voice, and her voice had "such dramatic beauty and maturity" that her teachers predicted a singing career for her.[72]

In 1924, Mary, who was about to begin her senior year at Vassar, went to visit her mother and sister briefly before going to study acting in a summer program, sailing through, Clara said, "en route to Gloucester dramatic school. She is beautiful, restless, brilliant, strangely affectionate and indifferent which seems familiar."[73] In other words, Clara suggested, Mary was her father's daughter. Underneath the veneer, Mary was actually quite lonely, however. Close as she had been to her father, she began to feel as if he abandoned her in later years as he lost himself in work. Before Vassar, she had lived with Lee and Lizzie Stieglitz as a surrogate daughter, for the Stieglitzes embraced with "a very strong feeling" people who were not members of their family. She was grateful to them: "It was really very wonderful," she remembered, "but it doesn't take the place of a mother and father. I was lonely. I had to visit around in the summer because I didn't have a permanent home and family. Sometimes

I stayed with my Aunt Charlotte and Uncle Billy in Connecticut on their farm. She was my mother's sister and, after my father, the strongest influence in my life. She taught me to love hard work, no matter what it was."[74]

Clara was glad to live close to her sister again, and she felt happier and more at peace in the mid-twenties, despite her constant worries about her health, for she had had two serious operations and "an almost fatal attack of ptomaine."[75] Steichen still sent her the monthly check, and her alimony equaled the national average yearly wage, but she told Stieglitz that she felt she had to dig her living "out of the ground almost and the only sign of rage for months is when I find the pesky rabbits, half tame through Kates [sic] pettings have beat me to my darling salads."[76]

Clara wanted to give Kate a special sixteenth birthday gift in May of 1924—Steichen's painting of the doorway at Villa L'Oiseau bleu, a work that now belonged to Stieglitz. Nonplussed, Clara wrote to ask him for it, offering to trade him a Steichen still life. She wanted more than anything to give it to Kate, she told Stieglitz, for Kate dreamed of going back to Voulangis, walking through the door, and finding "some of the old happiness that was there."[77]

"Think over the picture and try to persuade yourself that what my old heart is set on, can be done," Clara wrote to Stieglitz.[78] When she had not heard from him ten days later, she lashed out at him in an angry letter, so furious that her handwriting was barely legible.[79] Stieglitz wrote back in early July to say that he wanted to make a birthday present of the painting. Generously, he gave Kate *The Voulangis Doorway,* the beautiful oil on canvas her father had painted in 1909, in the happier times, retrievable now only in memory.

The Blue Sky—Dana, 1923. Dana Desboro Glover, Steichen's second wife.

Photograph by Edward Steichen. Reprinted with permission of Joanna T. Steichen. The Carl Sandburg Home NHS Collection.

Mr. And Mrs.—Carl and Lilian Sandburg, 1923.
Photograph by Edward Steichen. Reprinted with permission of Joanna T. Steichen. The Carl Sandburg Home NHS Collection.

Helga Sandburg, Steichen, Bosco the dog, Carl Sandburg, and Janet Sandburg on the dunes of Lake Michigan about 1927.
Photograph by Lilian "Paula" Steichen Sandburg. The Carl Sandburg Home NHS Collection.

Steichen with Fingal, one of his first Irish Wolfhounds, Connecticut, 1920s.
Francesca Calderone-Steichen Collection.

Four generations of the Steichen family, about 1929: Front row: Kate Steichen, Oma Steichen holding Mary's daughters—baby Linda and Nell Martin; and Steichen, the proud grandfather. Back row: Opa Steichen, standing, and Mary Steichen Martin, kneeling.
Sandburg Family Collection. The Carl Sandburg Home NHS Collection.

Navy Commander
Edward J. Steichen
photographing the
action on the USS
Lexington, 1943.
Photograph by Victor Jorgenson.
United States Navy, National
Archives.

Captain Edward Steichen
with Chamorro children on
Guam, 1945.
Photograph by Charles Kerlee. United
States Navy, National Archives.

Steichen with His Family, 1945: Dana, Kate, Mary (now Dr. Mary Steichen Calderone), Steichen's granddaughter Francesca, Steichen, and Dr. Frank Calderone, 1945.
Francesca Calderone-Steichen Collection.

Steichen Between His Daughters Kate and Mary, 1945.
Francesca Calderone-Steichen Collection.

Steichen and Sandburg watching Francesca dance, Umpawaug Farm, 1949.
Francesca Calderone-Steichen Collection.

Steichen swinging his granddaughter Francesca in the wood basket, Umpawaug, Connecticut. Brancusi's sculpture, *Bird in Space,* is in the background.
Photograph by Mary Steichen Calderone. Francesca Calderone-Steichen Collection.

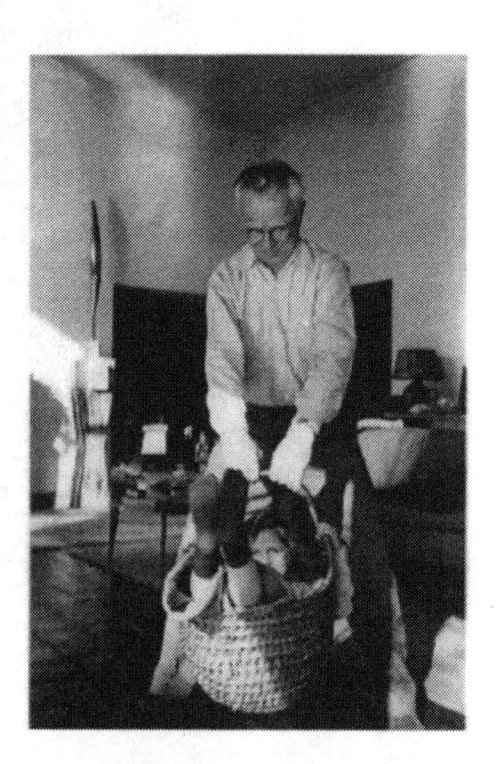

Dana Steichen at Umpawaug in 1952.
Photograph by Dorothea Lange. Copyright the Dorothea Lange Collection, Oakland Museum of California, City of Oakland. Gift of Paul S. Taylor. Francesca Calderone-Steichen Collection.

Steichen and Joanna on July 20, 1959, at the American Airlines press luncheon for Carl Sandburg at "21" in New York, just before Steichen and Sandburg departed for Russia.
Helga Sandburg Collection.

Joanna, Umpawaug Farm, 1959. Photograph by
Edward Steichen of Joanna Taub Steichen, his third
wife.
Reprinted with permission of Joanna T. Steichen.

Edward Steichen at ninety.
Photograph by Joseph Consentino. Reprinted with permission of Joseph Consentino. Francesca Calderone-Steichen Collection.

He will die telling God that if he could live a few years longer he might be the photographer he wanted to be.

—*Carl Sandburg,* Steichen the Photographer, *1929*

26

THE NEW PICTORIAL REVOLUTION

(1 9 2 4 - 1 9 2 8)

The power of his work made the public in general conscious of the new pictorial revolution brought by photography.[1]

—ALEXANDER LIBERMAN

FROM THE OUTSET OF HIS BRILLIANT career at Condé Nast Publications, Steichen was zestfully pioneering again, this time in pictorial journalism. He had used his camera for art, for war, and for science. Now he would use it for fashion, for advertising, and for celebrity portraits published for the mass market. He had gone unabashedly commercial.

In the 1920s, as his *Vanity Fair* fame grew, Steichen was beleaguered by people who now wanted to be captured in a Steichen photograph. Finally, unable to meet the demand, he announced his fee as a thousand dollars a sitting for portraits, figuring that would curb the requests. Instead, as had been true in the early days in New York, he found that orders for his work shot up in proportion to his prices.

Soon he was beset by the old, instinctive fear that his work would grow stale, static, and mechanical, but there were great practical benefits to holding a lucrative job and at the same time doing all the freelance work he chose to do. He could set up his own ideal studio and laboratory in the quarters Condé Nast provided for him in the Beaux Arts Studios at 80 West Fortieth Street in New York. He could finally, to his vast relief, pull himself entirely out of debt. And he could lead another revolution in photography.

Steichen had always possessed a remarkable gift for being in the right place at the right time—or ingeniously converting his particular circumstances to the right place and time. Now he foresaw a new age in photography, replete with exciting documentary, journalistic, and commercial potential. He stood in just the right spot, at just the right instant, with just the right alchemy of skill and experience to produce photographs to be reprinted for mass circulation. The old lithographing skills also equipped him to understand the intersection of the work of the photographer with that of "the caption writer, layout man, engraver, printer, pressman," Sandburg observed. "When a photograph is planned for halftone reproduction, to be located in the midst of type letters and impressions of black ink," Sandburg continued, "the making of the photograph is then a special piece of work. The feeling that governs the craftsman in such work is different from that in making a print to be hung on a wall, kept in a portfolio or otherwise have its life alone and away from printer's ink. The handling of light and shadow in a photograph for a magazine page, reading section or advertising required a new technique."[2]

In 1959, Alexander Liberman, longtime art director of *Vogue,* retrospectively assessed Steichen's work at Condé Nast Publications, writing that "many of Steichen's greatest photographs were published" in the pages of *Vogue* and *Vanity Fair.* "His portraits of the important people of his day were made at the turning point of pictorial journalism; the technical progress of engraving and speed printing needed photography," Liberman observed. "Steichen's work dramatized the welding of pictorial journalism with the new means of communication."[3] As had always been his propensity, Steichen understood how new advances in technology, converging as they did with new appetites for mass communication, could transform the modern purpose and power of photography. At *Vanity Fair* and *Vogue,* as he had at 291 in the old days, he was soon leading a "new pictorial revolution."

The editors of *Vanity Fair* chose the celebrities Steichen would photograph for the slick pages of the magazine. Because his subjects were "in the public eye at the moment," Steichen felt that he was practicing photojournalism—in the mode that writer Pierre Mac Orlan would later de-

The New Pictorial Revolution (1924–1928)

scribe as the photographic "observation of contemporary life apprehended at the right moment by an artist capable of seizing it."[4] Steichen also believed that there were only two problems in photography: how to conquer "that charlatan, light," and how to capture a moment of reality with just the flicker of the camera's eye.[5] The challenge was heightened in portrait photography because the photographer had to provoke an emotional response in the subject in order to "spark him into life."[6] Usually, Steichen's first glimpse of his *Vanity Fair* subjects came on the day when they arrived to be photographed. He relied on years of experience to read these faces instantly and to penetrate the masks.

Steichen's assistant during his fifteen years at Condé Nast was James McKeon—"Mac"—a short, curly-haired Irishman inherited from Steichen's predecessor, Baron de Meyer. The first day they worked together, Steichen remembered, Mac arrived with a "staggering array of flood-lights, reflectors, and other fancy equipment."[7] Steichen had never worked with artificial light, but he was not about to confess that he had no idea what to do with the complicated paraphernalia Mac had lugged into the studio.

Improvising instead, he authoritatively barked orders at Mac: "Put the big one over here, and the other ones behind it.... And now bring me a large sheet."[8] Steichen took the sheets from the mystified assistant, carefully folded them, and draped them over some chairs lined up in front of Mac's lights, concealing the lights so they did not interfere with the model. Mac looked at his new boss with great respect. This was clearly a novel technique. Baron de Meyer had never asked for a sheet. In Mac's opinion, this fellow Steichen was certainly living up to his reputation as a great, innovative photographer.

He still used natural daylight, but Steichen discovered that these dazzling electric lights could serve as his "greatest ally" in achieving variety of tone and depth in fashion photography. Over the years, he added more and more lights, until, he said, in the last years of his tenure at *Vanity Fair* and *Vogue,* he had "lights going all over the place."[9] He also experimented with a dramatic and elegant new background of white, gray, and black vertical panels. Other fashion photographers, of course, were quick to try to copy Steichen, and although these pseudo-Steichen photographs did not trouble Steichen himself, the protective Mac fumed about them. Looking at the panels set up for a photo shoot one day, he said glumly, "Well, boss, I suppose we use the same new background this time?" Steichen replied, "Mac, if I were any good I could take pictures in front of the same background for fifty years. But, if you like, we'll change it a little." In fun, he and Mac flipped the familiar panels into a horizontal arrangement and, Steichen remembered, *Vogue* was still hot from the press when other magazines began to imitate that improvisation and pose their own models in front of horizontal panels.[10]

Over the next fifteen years, he captured lively portraits of everybody who was anybody, or about to become somebody. He especially wanted to photograph the truth behind the illusion in theater and motion pictures, and by so doing, he usually caught the essence of private character in the public faces he photographed in the twenties and thirties: John Barrymore, Lillian Gish, Charlie Chaplin, Katharine Cornell, Gloria Swanson, Greta Garbo, Marlene Dietrich, Mary Pickford, Martha Graham, Katharine Hepburn, Paul Robeson, Joan Crawford, Fred Astaire, Lynn Fontanne, Fredric March, W. C. Fields, George Gershwin, playwrights Eugene O'Neill and Noël Coward, and many more.

Steichen also produced vivid still photographs of scenes and improvisations from plays and motion pictures. Most of the celebrity portraits were photographed in Steichen's New York studio, but he made an annual pilgrimage to Hollywood to take pictures of actors and actresses in the midst of their work—such as elusive Greta Garbo on the movie set where she was starring in *A Woman of Affairs* in 1928.

This ninety-minute silent film was based on Michael Arlen's play *The Green Hat,* produced on Broadway in 1925 and then starring Katharine Cornell. (No doubt because Steichen had photographed Cornell in costume for the play for the November 1, 1925, issue of *Vogue,* he mistakenly called Garbo's movie *The Green Hat* in his autobiography.[11]) *A Woman of Affairs* cast Garbo, the new young star, with romantic leading men John Gilbert and Douglas Fairbanks, Jr., in a melodramatic story of doomed lovers.

Carl Sandburg had been writing movie reviews for the Chicago *Daily News* since 1920, and the brothers-in-law sometimes covered the same film stars, Steichen in pictures, Sandburg in words. In Garbo's sizzling 1927 film *Flesh and the Devil,* costarring screen idol John Gilbert, Sandburg found Garbo "lovely, pitiful," and wanton and predicted that she would thereafter be "a star to be reckoned with."[12] Steichen was equally enchanted when he squinted through a crack in the wall of the set to watch Garbo at work on the movie set of *A Woman of Affairs*.

Granted just five minutes to photograph her that day during a break in shooting, he made several quick exposures. When he stopped and complained about her fluffy movie hairdo, Garbo swept her hair back from her beautiful face and Steichen asked her to repeat the gesture. The haunting picture that emerged from that revealing instant is one of Steichen's best-known images, as well as the single picture by which many movie fans came to remember Greta Garbo.[13]

Steichen and Sandburg shared a boyish fascination with other movie stars—especially Charlie Chaplin, whom they considered the ultimate film artist. In fact, they had seen *The Gold Rush* three times, finding it "immense" as a "piece of story telling" and saluting Chaplin for being a highly original, "independent artist."[14] When Chaplin rushed into Steichen's New York studio for one twenty-minute photo session he had begrudgingly scheduled, Steichen put the actor so at ease with his genuine praise for *The Gold Rush* that he got some vivid pictures—and the two men talked until four the next morning.

As always, Steichen found that his portrait work demanded total concentration, not only from him but also from his staff and his subjects, whom he sought to infuse with his own intense energy in order to make the pictures come to life. He had to be "the clown, the enthusiast, the flatterer," he recalled, all the while "building up" the picture—"its lights, shadows and lines, its essential fashion photograph requirements—distinction, elegance, and chic."[15] He was so engrossed in working with a model one day that when Condé Nast strode through the door to watch the session, Steichen could not think who he was. "On my soul I couldn't remember his name," Steichen said, "although I knew him as well as I know my secretary." Steichen "mumbled some sort of an introduction," and only after Nast's departure did the name come back to him.[16]

Steichen told journalist Robert Marks that artists risked failure when they ceased to observe "the commonplace man," an idea he shared with his sister and brother-in-law.[17] Steichen made most of his generous income at first, of course, by photographing extraordinary people for Condé Nast, but he would soon turn to commercial advertising, choosing "the commonplace" man and woman for subject matter as well as audience. By 1924, his position at *Vanity Fair* and *Vogue* clearly established,

Steichen had signed a lucrative contract to work for the J. Walter Thompson Advertising Agency.

Mass advertising was a relatively new force in American life in the twenties. Historian Samuel Eliot Morison has described the advertising revolution caused by the advent of the automobile and the motor age, and the new "prestigious urges to spend and buy:—a bigger car than your neighbor's; a luxury cruise, an all-electric kitchen, mink coat and diamonds for Mother."[18] The flourishing advertising industry, empowered by the modern technology of radio, as well as by new ways of producing photographs in newspapers and magazines, was transmitting a bold, brand-new message to the American masses: Make more and more money, and buy more and more things. This, in the decade of the twenties, seemed to define the new American dream. In particular, the women of America were ready for change after the prolonged Great War. Lobbying for Prohibition, emancipation, the vote, they embraced new freedoms of style as well as substance. Braids, buns, and corsets were out; short hair and short skirts were in.

At *Vanity Fair* and *Vogue,* Steichen stood in the prestigious center of this new world. Equipped with his camera and his own innate elegant sense of style, he enthusiastically embraced the task of shooting the latest fashions and fads for these two magazines. In the process, he singlehandedly offered the American public some of their most alluring, captivating, definitive images of the Roaring Twenties.

And he did it with panache. Before joining Condé Nast, he had always dismissed the "layout and presentation of *Vogue* and *Vanity Fair* as namby-pamby, meaningless, and conventional," he recalled.[19] Compared to the formal, soft-focus, sometimes overly fussy fashion photographs of Baron de Meyer, Steichen's clean, cutting-edge modern images both liberated and celebrated women. According to Steichen, a friend wrote to Condé Nast during those years that while Baron de Meyer "made every woman look like a cutie," Steichen could make "even a cutie look like a woman."[20] (As Nast's biographer Caroline Seebohm recounted the story, Condé Nast himself once told Steichen, "Every woman de Meyer photographs looks like a model. You make every model look like a woman."[21]) The salient point is that Steichen honored the *woman* in each photograph he took. Rather than subjugating the model to the gown or the composition, he made personal portraits with the woman, not the dress, as centerpiece.

As a result, as Condé Nast editorial director Alexander Liberman later put it, Steichen's breakthrough photographs captured vibrant, "immensely seductive" images of women. Unlike other fashion photographs, Liberman said, Steichen did not "concentrate on the dress and throw away the woman." He dignified woman's image. He could make every model who sat or stood for a portrait look unique, beautiful, self-possessed. He also made it fun, putting his models completely at ease, Georgia Carroll Kaiser recalled. When she posed for Steichen at *Vogue*, she was only eighteen, and she thought he was an old man until she met him and witnessed his contagious joy in life and in his work. Steichen was no "morose artist," she was glad to see, and she was "not in the least nervous" before Steichen's camera. For all his sophistication, she found a refreshing, boyish innocence in him.[22]

Steichen acknowledged that because he had little interest in fashion per se, he relied heavily on Carmel Snow, the bright and energetic editor who began working at Condé Nast Publications in 1921 and became fashion editor of *Vogue* in 1926. Steichen appreciated Snow's policy of providing photographers whatever they needed and wanted for a photo shoot, without question, and they were a highly effective team from the beginning, believing as both of them did that the editorial eyes, the fashion eyes, and the camera eyes had to collaborate.

Because Steichen found the layout of *Vogue* and *Vanity Fair* too dull and conventional for his taste, he was pleased when in 1928 Condé Nast hired a new art director, Turkish-born Dr. Mehemed Fehmy Agha. Nearly twenty years Steichen's junior, Agha had worked for *Vogue* in Berlin before his appointment as art director for *Vogue, Vanity Fair,* and *House & Garden*. For all three magazines, Agha stringently implemented significant design changes, some of which Nast had conceived earlier with layout designer Eduardo Benito. Steichen heartily approved of the innovations—the elimination of italic typefaces, the asymmetrical configuration of photographs on the magazine pages, a dramatic use of white space, to name a few. Agha, in turn, admired what he called Steichen's "masterly simplicity."[23]

Steichen also skillfully employed that clean simplicity of style in the innovative advertising photographs he took for the J. Walter Thompson Agency. For years, he had deplored the inferior photography used in most advertisements, and now he saw his work for J. Walter Thompson as an opportunity to enhance the quality of commercial photography by introducing the element of naturalism. He would realistically photograph ordinary household goods, using the typical housewife as his model. His first client was Jergens, and to advertise their lotion, he decided to photograph the hands of a woman peeling potatoes. Ironically, he photographed the hands of Mrs. Stanley Resor, wife of J. Walter Thompson's president, at first glance hardly the typical housewife. But her hands, with their short nails and strong fingers, seemed at home with the work. "I could tell by the way she cut the potatoes that this wasn't the first time she had done it," Steichen recalled.[24]

When he had arrived in New York back in 1900 as a novice from Milwaukee, he had found his Cascarets advertisement splashed across a Manhattan billboard. Now, in national magazines, his handsome pictures sold Kodak film, Jergens lotion, Pond's cold cream, Pond's skin freshener and tonic, and Lux soap, as well as shoes, hats, toothpaste, and other products, and he was proud of the work. "Practically all artists who do commercial work do it with their noses turned up," Steichen told Sandburg during those years. "They want to earn enough money to get out of commercial art so as to take up pure art for art's sake. That viewpoint doesn't interest me; I know what there is to know about it—and I'm through with it. I welcome the chance to work in commercial art. If I can't express the best that's in me through such advertising photographs as 'Hands Kneading Dough,' then I'm no good."[25]

He defended his position in an interview, explaining that he intended to create advertising photographs that could stand as museum pieces.[26] In most of his fashion and advertising photography, he did indeed achieve an unprecedented clarity of tone and of focus on object or product, without sacrificing the artistic quality of his work. Many of the resulting images, detached from their literal text, can stand alone as artistic photographs. For instance, *Summer Sportswear,* appearing in the July 15, 1928, issue of *Vogue,* highlights the latest casual, high-fashion style of the late twenties—short skirts, jaunty blazers, bold costume jewelry, the cloche hat. But there is artistry in the composition as three beautiful women and a young girl pose in profile, their eyes fixed on a far horizon;

The New Pictorial Revolution (1924–1928)

the camera lavishly transmits every graceful curve of hand and face, every texture and fold of fabric.

One of Steichen's most frequently reproduced high-fashion portraits captures the sheen and glamour of a black-and-gold evening ensemble by the designer Cheruit, featuring Marion Morehouse, Steichen's favorite *Vogue* model. (She later became the wife of poet e.e. cummings, who was then writing for *Vanity Fair*.) In this portrait, which first appeared in *Vogue* in the May 1, 1927, issue, Steichen not only recorded a fashion design reflecting the extravagant glitter of an era; he also portrayed a vibrant, beautiful woman in the celebratory manner of his earlier portraits of women such as Mrs. Condé Nast and Yvette Guilbert. In that same issue appeared his totally different image of Morehouse, outfitted in a mackintosh and riding clothes. A crop in her hand, she stands somberly before the dark wooden door of a stable. As the eye admires the elegant images of Morehouse, the imagination is drawn to these photographs because they are rich in subtext; stories seem to lurk in the shadows. A nude torso illustrating a *Vogue* article entitled "Beauty Primer" is as evocatively languid and graceful as Steichen's nude studies taken twenty-five years earlier.

Throughout the decade of the twenties, Steichen was having fun with photography again, toying with its potential, exuberant as a child at play. But he was also pushing himself hard to keep up with the demands of work at Condé Nast Publications and to take maximum advantage of his fruitful contract with J. Walter Thompson, where he was at the outset guaranteed twenty thousand dollars a year in assignments.[27] That combined with his $35,000 yearly salary at Condé Nast and other occasional lucrative freelance assignments gave him his first taste of financial security. By the mid-twenties, love and money had worked a happy transformation in Steichen's life. Now free of debt, he could support his daughters and easily make his alimony payments to Clara. Furthermore, he could do his work with unprecedented support and encouragement from a generous employer who valued his talents and subsidized any equipment or staff Steichen needed to make his stunning pictures. Best of all, he now had the devotion of a serene, stable wife whose joy in life matched his.

Friends and family noted the physical transformation: The tense, haggard artist who had struggled through the decade from 1913 to 1923, overwhelmed by the protracted trauma of war and divorce, was now transformed into a handsome, robust, confident man. He exuded good health and vitality, along with an electric sense of self and purpose. But there was also a new wariness, a tensile armor of reserve. His experiences with Clara and with war had eroded his trust in others. For all the warmth and poise of his public persona, he grew more inwardly private.

"He has had defeats and bitter disappointments," Sandburg reflected, "enough to kill off any army mule; and is a classical instance of a man stubbornly controlling the design of his life to a far degree." Moreover, Sandburg believed, Steichen had "had to pay the penalty of too early success, has eaten ashes—and gone on."[28]

Sandburg believed that although Steichen was "essentially melancholy and brooding," his healthy sense of humor enabled him to keep events in perspective. Sandburg called him "a measurably silent man whose words count when spoken," and he thought Steichen looked like a priest in those days—"solemn, with grave spiritual quality," an artist whose work was governed by a "passionate and grave sincerity."[29]

Alfred Stieglitz, long a marriage counselor to Edward and Clara Steichen, never could seem to resolve his own domestic problems. Finally, in September of 1924, after six contentious years, Alfred and Emmy Stieglitz were divorced. During all that time, Stieglitz had lived openly with O'Keeffe, with Emmy at first clinging to the hope that he would come back to her, and then holding to a proud refusal to give Alfred the divorce he wanted. Their daughter, Kitty, meanwhile, was trapped in the center of the triangle composed of her passionate father, her desperate mother, and the aloof, inscrutable Miss O'Keeffe.

Nevertheless, the gallant young woman earned her degree with honors at Smith College in 1921, and in 1922, the year that Stieglitz's mother, Hedwig, died, Kitty married Milton Sprague Stearns. She gave birth to their son in 1923, only to suffer a postpartum depression that apparently triggered the onset of schizophrenia. Kitty had to be hospitalized, and her doctors, including her uncle Lee, concluded that her volatile relationship with her father was so entangled with her illness that they forbade him to see her. Stieglitz had lost his mother and then his daughter, and he agonized over his failure as a father. Soon he had slipped into a deep depression, as well. Work had pulled him out of it by the autumn of 1923, as had the support of O'Keeffe and his family, as well as friends such as Paul Strand's wife, Rebecca, and loyal Katharine Rhoades, whose spirit he captured in a vivid series of photographs of trees and sky.

After the divorce, Stieglitz pressed a reluctant O'Keeffe to marry him, but she refused. Often she felt smothered by him, and she found it difficult to concentrate on her art in the midst of his frenetic lifestyle, surrounded by the throng of people who populated his world in New York and at Lake George. She also disliked his continual flirtations with other women—including Rebecca Strand and even her own sister Ida. In the end, it was Kitty's terrible illness that brought O'Keeffe to the altar with Stieglitz. Lee and the other doctors advised Stieglitz that only his marriage to O'Keeffe would vanquish once and for all Kitty's futile hopes that her parents would reconcile someday. At the civil ceremony on a gloomy December day in New Jersey (for Stieglitz was forbidden by his New York divorce decree to remarry in that state), Stieglitz and O'Keeffe were married. Artist John Marin and Stieglitz's brother-in-law, lawyer George Engelhard, were the only witnesses to the ceremony, where Georgia O'Keeffe firmly declined to utter the customary promise to honor and obey.

In the end, her father's remarriage apparently made little difference to Kitty Stieglitz Stearns, who never recovered from her illness and lived out her life in private institutions. She died in 1971 at the Westchester branch of New York Hospital in White Plains, New York. Stieglitz was never permitted to see his daughter again, although he sent her gifts—including a copy of Sandburg's *Rootabaga Stories,* which he and O'Keeffe had enjoyed. He also mailed her checks and short letters, which she sometimes answered briefly in a handwriting that regressed over the years to the childlike script and syntax of her happier letters from long-ago summers in Europe or in camp in New Hampshire. And Emmeline Obermeyer Stieglitz rose magnificently to the challenge of adjusting to divorce and caring for her daughter. Until her death in 1953, she visited Kitty weekly, wrote gracious notes to Alfred about matters concerning their daughter, and took great pride and interest in her son-in-law and grandson, Milton Junior.

Stieglitz was hard on the women who loved him. O'Keeffe wrote in later years:

There was such a power when he spoke—people seemed to believe what he said, even when they knew it wasn't their truth. He molded his hearer. They were often speechless. If they crossed him in any way, his power to destroy was as destructive as his power to build—the extremes went together. I have experienced both and survived....[30]

When Kate Rodina Steichen was about seventeen, she left boarding school to study music privately in New York. Clara moved into Manhattan from Connecticut to provide a home for her in a cheap apartment on Bank Street in Greenwich Village. When Kate's school friend Mid Hayes came to visit, she was alarmed to see evidence of rats and roaches in the flat, but Kate and Clara seemed happy enough there, Mid thought, and were taking it all in stride. Sometime in the mid-twenties, Mid decided to join Kate in New York, where they both studied music. By the time Mid went to live with Kate and Clara that winter, they had moved to a more comfortable apartment on Fifty-seventh Street.

From this home base, Mid and Kate ventured out to take their private music lessons, enjoy the city, and attend every symphony concert and opera they could drum up tickets for. Wagner was their favorite. During the winter that she lived with Kate and Clara, Mid did not once hear Clara sing, and so did not know until many years later of Clara's interest in music. Clara cooked and cleaned for them, but she never accompanied the girls to musical events, and as far as Mid could tell, she did not have an outside job. She grew very fond of Clara, whom she called Mama Steich (pronounced *Steisch*), and thought her a handsome woman whose beauty was being eroded by time and bitterness.

"She had a chip on her shoulder because her life had gone down hill so badly, compared to the wonderful life she had been living," Mid remembered. "She was practically destitute."[31] Clara frequently complained to Kate and Mid that she thought Steichen was getting five hundred dollars a print, a lot of money in those days, "but he was stingy enough to give her only $125 a month to live on, and that was not enough."[32] Of course, Mid had no way of knowing that Clara's divorce settlement mandated a monthly payment of a hundred dollars for life, which Steichen was paying, or that in addition he now paid for tuition, music lessons, clothing, travel, medical bills, and other expenses for his daughters. Mid also assumed that Steichen could have gotten his daughter any kind of a job if she wanted one, even as a professional singer, but Kate refused to ask. "If I can't make it on my own, I don't want help," she said emphatically.[33]

With the old bitterness intact, Clara told Mid that Steichen used to "disappear for two or three days at a time and never said when he'd be home, and she would be left without money and food." Mid listened to the older woman's stories about her husband cutting a glamorous figure in the early days in Paris with his long hair, his cape, and his walking stick, looking like the "true artist." Mid also got to know Charlotte and Billy Paddock on visits with Kate to their "dilapidated old country farmhouse" in Connecticut, where, Kate recalled, Charlotte roasted ham or chicken on a spit in the kitchen fireplace, her "brilliant silver-gold" hair gleaming in the firelight.[34]

Sometime between 1916 and 1920, according to Mary, she and Kate had posed for several of their uncle's sculptures. Mary described Paddock as a "gentle, modest, idealistic and visionary man, really not of the Twentieth Century but one who belonged in the late Nineteenth Century in the Burne-Jones and Rosetti era." Mary remembered watching her uncle "handle his tools and his materials (plasticine) with appreciation and fascination. He made all of his own tools from wood from around the hilltop farm."[35]

"He did a head of each of us," she recalled, "but except for these we modeled for various nude figures for his fountains, flower arrangements, etc."[36] Mary and Kate each kept small plasters and many photographs of those works.

According to Clara, Billy Paddock made inappropriate overtures to Kate during one of her sojourns at the Paddock farm during the twenties; Clara thus decided to relinquish the cottage she loved in Connecticut. "Kate's foolish vanity at the farm—led me to take her away—twas the only way," Clara wrote years later to Stieglitz. "My Sister will never know why that was—twas a terrible situation—it broke me flat—to leave the little cottage where I made flowers bloom—and [had] grown to love and could have lived in peace of mind."³⁷ Clara told Stieglitz that her efforts to protect Charlotte from knowing about the matter estranged her not only from her sister but from their wealthy aunt in Boston, who had been giving Clara a stipend of three thousand dollars a year for three years.

Clara feared that she was losing Kate to her sister and Mary to her former husband, for Steichen took Mary on a grand tour of Europe for two months in 1925 to celebrate her graduation from Vassar. Mildred Aldrich reported to Gertrude Stein in August that Mary had "covered herself with glory" at Vassar, and now she planned to become an actress. Mildred said that Steichen agreed with her when she told him the theater was a "dirty business," but he added that he did not foist opinions or advice on anyone. When she inquired about his work in New York, Steichen told Mildred that business was "too good," overwhelming him with more work than he could handle. And, Mildred gossiped, Steichen reflected that while the money was "agreeable," every time he came back to France, he wondered why he even "bothered" with New York.³⁸

He and Dana spent part of each summer in Voulangis, and in 1926, Steichen treated Kate to her first trip to Europe since she and Clara had returned to France during the war. A frightened child when she last saw Voulangis in 1917, Kate was about to turn eighteen when her glamorous father took her to France on the SS *Paris* to celebrate that significant birthday. She recorded the wonderful details in a leather diary entitled *My Trip Abroad,* saving with other keepsakes of the trip the printed menu of her nine-course birthday dinner May twenty-seventh, celebrated aboard ship. Steichen had spent little time with his daughter during the years of Clara's custody, and they delighted in each other's company during their weeks abroad. For Kate, a highlight of the journey was a reunion with Mildred Aldrich at Voulangis. Knowing his daughter's love of music, Steichen took her to the opera and the ballet in Paris. They also saw La Revue de Paris, lunched in fashionable restaurants, dined with Brancusi and other friends, and spent nostalgic summer days at Voulangis.

When Kate visited some of Clara's relatives in England, they went to the Brighton Hippodrome, the Sussex County Cricket Club, and a benefit theatrical garden party in Chelsea. Thrilled to be with her father

The New Pictorial Revolution (1924–1928)

again, Kate kept notes and snapshots in her diary, along with several carefully pressed poppies from the garden at Voulangis. By the time father and daughter sailed for home on June 30, 1926, aboard the SS *Olympus,* they no longer felt like strangers to each other.

It was a momentous year for Mary, as well. She had fallen in love with a young actor, W. Lon Martin, whom she called "a very beautiful young man."[39] At twenty-two, Mary looked strikingly like her mother had looked in Steichen's first portraits of Clara back in the days of their romance. Many remembered that she was "very romantic . . . one man in the world for me and all that," and she and Lon were married after a brief, intense romance.[40] She apparently was pregnant at the time of her wedding, for Clara gave the couple an antique cradle for a wedding present; a daughter, Nell, was born to the young Martins that same year.[41]

After years as an expatriate, Steichen found a special bonus in living in the United States—for now he could spend more time with his daughters and his new granddaughter, as well as with his parents and the Sandburgs in Elmhurst. His nieces, Margaret, Janet, and Helga Sandburg, adored their uncle Ed, who played with them as if he, too, were a child. Helga remembered the enchantment of Steichen's visits: "Our uncle and father clowned for us; we roared with laughter, helpless; weak, we flung ourselves on the rug at their feet. There was no one so funny as those two. And arm in arm they would sing in maundering tones, 'Where is My Wandering Boy Tonight?' and 'A Boy's Best Friend is His Mother.' "[42] She and her sisters especially relished Steichen's playacting, and his dramatic recitation of "The Wreck of the Hesperus" usually brought the enraptured children to tears, as it had Mary and Kate before them.[43]

With Steichen now living and working in New York and Sandburg frequently there to work with his editor and publisher, Alfred Harcourt, the two men increasingly shared creative ventures and mutual friends. Occasionally, Steichen and Sandburg would round up Stieglitz and O'Keeffe to go out for Chinese food in New York. Judging Sandburg to be a fellow fighter and dreamer, Stieglitz confided in him that he no longer had money, nor, he said, had he had even a fraction of the money he was reputed to have. The two men liked and trusted each other, and their friendship soon existed independent of Steichen. For his part, Steichen genuinely appreciated O'Keeffe's paintings and Stieglitz's new work, although he saw less and less of the couple, submerged as he was in his own work.

When he could get away, Steichen traveled to Illinois, where he and Sandburg enjoyed talking about art, politics, baseball, and movies on vigorous walking expeditions into the countryside. They would occasionally stop at a local tavern for popcorn and beer, then walk for miles more. The two of them spent "long intense talking hours," Helga recalled, sometimes over Paula's pancakes or corn fritters smothered in syrup, or hot home-fried doughnuts.[44] The Sandburg children saw their uncle and their father somber and brooding, as well as laughing and joking.

Sandburg was then engrossed in work on the two volumes of *Abraham Lincoln: The Prairie Years,* and Steichen was proving to be an invaluable adviser, helping him choose historic photographs to illustrate the biography. Once when someone showed Helga, Margaret, and Janet a picture of Abraham Lincoln and asked them to identify it, they answered unanimously that it was their uncle Ed. Mary, too, thought that when her father's "dark forelock fell over his forehead" he was a "dead-ringer for Abraham Lincoln."[45]

And also like Lincoln, when he was caught up in work, Steichen could deny himself sleep, food, and comfort, driving himself to exhaustion. In 1926, art director Ruzzie Green of the Stehli Silk Corporation asked Steichen if he would make a series of photographs to be converted into designs for bolts of silk for dresses, scarves, and other decorative uses. Indeed he would, Steichen responded—so long as he was not required to photograph "flowers and garlands."[46] Green urged him to photograph anything he chose. Steichen relished the assignment, but it was a challenge to complete in addition to all his other work commitments. He was extremely interested in the chance to create novel designs, and he set his imagination free to roam over the homeliest objects—matches, matchboxes, sugar lumps, nails, tacks, mothballs, beans, rice, coffee, eyeglasses, thread.

Marvelous abstract photographs emerged, so cleverly composed that the eye chases curves and angles, seeks out the shapes hiding in shadows, and only then begins to recognize that the forms dancing in the light are mundane artifacts: *Matches and Match Boxes, Spectacles,* the luminous *Spectacle Butterfly,* the wonderfully spiraling *Wandering Thread.* Stehli Silks transformed these innovative photographic designs into beautiful silk fabrics, which quickly sold out. They were, Sandburg wrote admiringly, "justifications of the Machine Age."[47]

By fall of 1926, however, overloaded with work, Steichen had pushed himself to physical and nervous collapse. Sandburg described Steichen at work during that time, circling his camera and his subjects in his studio, wearing a "blue or gray negligee shirt" and the omnipresent quarter-inch crimson silk ribbon of the Legion of Honor. Steichen ate rapidly, finishing his meals before the others at the table; slept in the nude, when he slept at all; and drove himself, Sandburg believed, until "overwork and overeagerness about work brought him down."[48]

"He used to work all day and most of the night till in the winter of 1926 he found he had lost the habit of sleeping at all," Sandburg noted. "Old Mother Nature was handing him revenge and pay; he was sent to Asheville, North Carolina [a popular refuge for someone suffering what was known in those days as a nervous breakdown] to stay in bed a month and sleep. Since then he has reorganized his habits and learned to forget his work more, get outdoors more and sleep more."[49]

"Feeling like hell," Steichen checked himself in for a total rest in the rough-hewn luxury of the Grove Park Inn in Asheville, then boldly advertised as the finest resort hotel in the world.[50] Dana kept vigil while he rested for four weeks in the stone-clad inn on a hilltop, where, later, Scott Fitzgerald would stay on his visits to his wife Zelda, hospitalized on an opposite hill at Highland Hospital, a haven for wealthy psychiatric patients. (With its incredibly pure air, Asheville was also a center for tuberculosis patients, and novelist Thomas Wolfe's mother kept a boardinghouse not far from the grandeur of the Grove Park Inn.) While he recuperated from his "bad collapse [of] nerves," Steichen read Sandburg's Lincoln biography, calling it a "grand grand job" and writing to tell his brother-in-law that he was doing nothing but reading, sleeping, and breathing the fresh air.[51]

Back home in New York, chastened by the lesson that his breakdown had taught him, Steichen calibrated his life more thoughtfully from that time on. Ordered by his doctor to work only part-time for a while, he delegated some of his assignments to photographer Charles Sheeler, whom he had hired to work with him at Condé Nast. During the first half of the decade of the twenties, Steichen was still straddling two continents, still leasing the house and gardens at Voulangis. After his collapse, however, he and Dana began to make different plans, regretfully deciding in 1927 to relinquish their summer journeys to Voulangis.

Sometime during that last summer in France, he and Dana attended a party in Paris, where they encountered Isadora Duncan, probably more than a little drunk. "Steichen, let's sing all the American songs we know," she begged. They sang for hours—"Swanee," "Old Black Joe," "The Sidewalks of New York," "Molly and I and the Baby," singing until they cried. A few months later, Duncan was dead, strangled in a freak accident when the signature flowing scarf around her neck caught in the wheel of a sports car. "She was one honest-to-God American," Steichen told Sandburg later.[52]

Steichen enjoyed an annual reunion with sculptor Constantin Brancusi each summer in France, and he had completed arrangements to purchase another Brancusi bird in 1926. He had fallen in love with it in Brancusi's Paris studio during the summer of 1924 when the sculptor had shown him a rough bronze cast, just back from the foundry—the unfinished bird already coming alive in angles that enchanted Steichen. When he saw it again in Brancusi's studio in 1926, he bought it for six hundred dollars.

Steichen, Dana, and Brancusi had sailed for New York together in the fall of 1926 because Brancusi wanted to be in New York for the opening of an exhibition of his work, organized by Marcel Duchamp, at the Brummer Gallery in November. Brancusi was photographed aboard ship in the company of Steichen's dog.[53] The Brummer exhibition featured the series *Oiseaux dans l'espace,* from 1923, 1925, and 1926, as well as *Colonne sans fin*—his *Endless Column.* In 1920, Brancusi had carved a version of his *Endless Column* among the trees of Steichen's garden at Voulangis.[54] Surely in those days in Steichen's garden, one carving, one painting and photographing, there was a mutual understanding, if not an actual dialogue, about the shaping principle by which the two men were working then. Steichen's fascination with the triangle may even have prompted the striking interplay of pyramids and rhomboids in *Colonne sans fin,* Brancusi's abstract geometrical experiment.

Both Brancusi and Steichen were probing for the essence of things,

THE NEW PICTORIAL REVOLUTION (1924–1928)

deftly exploring nature as object, subject, and theme. Hovering in the background of their work was the master Rodin, even though both Brancusi and Steichen had always groped stubbornly and independently toward a personal aesthetic theory. Brancusi, after all, had studied only briefly in Rodin's studio, so convinced was he that "under a great tree nothing grows."[55]

When Brancusi's *Bird in Space* was finished and ready to be moved to the United States in 1927, Steichen declared the value of the sculpture and arranged its shipment. As a work of art, the piece should have cleared United States customs duty-free, but when Steichen called for it in New York, the customs officer saw nothing artistic in it, classified Brancusi's soaring bird as a kitchen utensil, and assessed duty on six hundred dollars. Steichen was forced to pay two hundred dollars or abandon his bird.

At a dinner party sometime later, he told the story to Alice Whitney (Mrs. Harry Payne Whitney, later a founder of the Whitney Museum of American Art). As a patron of art, she was appalled at the implications of such an arbitrary decision, and she offered to finance a lawsuit in defense of art in general and Brancusi's bird in particular. Soon the case of *Brancusi v. the United States* was on the court docket, the catalyst for a lively public debate over the very definition of art.

IF IT'S A BIRD, SHOOT IT, read the headline in the *New York Mirror* on October 22, 1927, after Steichen, the lawyers, and the bird wound up one gray day in court. The judges heard a deposition from Brancusi himself, as well as Steichen's testimony. Sculptor Jacob Epstein, art critics, and museum directors supported Steichen's contention that the bird was art, but the best evidence was the bird itself, gleaming in the dreary courtroom. Defending the notion that art had to depict an object in nature realistically, in its true proportion and dimensions, the attorney general asked Steichen if this was the kind of bird he would shoot at if he saw it in the woods.

Steichen testified persuasively about how Michelangelo and other great sculptors were not literally true to nature. Besides, he said, there was no such thing as true proportion in a work of art. Only a cast could capture exact proportion—a chiropodist's cast, for instance, exactly renders the feet, corn, bunions, and all—but its literal depiction is hardly a work of art. The judges ruled in Steichen's favor, he got his money back from the government, and a new legal standard was set for the definition of works of art: United States customs officials could no longer impose their own criteria of what constituted a work of art; they would have to abide by the opinions of qualified, recognized art experts.[56]

Because Brancusi called the case "the Brouhaha," Steichen used that name when he photographed the *Bird in Space* later in a stark series of thirty to forty images. And he remembered the trial with zest: "The Bird was his own best witness. It was the only clean thing in the courtroom. It shone like a jewel. Brancusi was vindicated. It proved that he was an artist, not a plumber."[57]

Late in 1927, Steichen and Dana began to scour the New York and Connecticut countryside in search of some land. Steichen wanted to escape the city. He wanted the peace he found only in nature, flowers, a garden. He wanted a farm. In 1928, they found it near West Redding, Connecticut, 240 acres that they called, for business purposes, the Umpawaug Plant Breeding Farm. From then on, no matter how much time they spent in New York or in travel, Umpawaug was home for the Steichens.

Sandburg was one of their first visitors there, accompanying Steichen, Dana, and Fingal, their Irish wolfhound, on an inaugural tour of the property. They showed him where the first two acres of flowers would be planted and explained their plans to dam the lake. Steichen was reclaiming the dream of breeding flowers on a large scale. Helga Sandburg remembered that once he settled in to the work at Umpawaug, her uncle's fingernails, like her mother's, were usually "rimmed with soil."[58]

The need for land and space stirred in the Steichen blood: In Michigan, Paula and Carl Sandburg were accumulating acreage and designing the house they built on a Lake Michigan bluff. They called their farm the Paw Paw Patch, and Dana and Steichen went there for rest whenever they could. Paula held the camera up to family faces in those days—photographing her poet husband, her photographer brother, her beautiful sister-in-law, and her own three children in various exuberant poses on the dunes.[59]

At Umpawaug, Steichen and Dana began to design a house to supplant the cottage where they were living temporarily, and they immediately started expanding their gardens until, at the height of the Umpawaug Plant Breeding Farm operation, they cultivated up to 100,000 delphinium plants annually—masses of beautiful blooms spanning the spectrum of blue to violet, lavender to purple, pink to mauve, along with the constant white. They lived in Manhattan most of the week, then hurried to the country on weekends to lose themselves in work on the farm. Their beautiful flowers computed to so many numbers in the ledgers Steichen kept as he meticulously recorded crosses, colors, architectures, yields. Umpawaug grounded him again in nature, providing an essential refuge from the city and a necessary relief and counterbalance to the heady, harrying demands of his work for Condé Nast. Without Umpawaug, Steichen reflected in later years, he would not have sustained that work as long as he did.[60]

In 1928, Lon and Mary Steichen Martin's second child, Linda, was born during what Mary remembered as "a messy period" in her life.[61] The marriage had been wrong from the outset, and Mary knew that it did her handsome young husband "as much harm as it did me."[62] Steichen and Dana adored his two little granddaughters, and he worried about Mary's impending divorce, which occurred before Linda was two years old. Discouraged in her acting career, Mary now found herself "casting around" for a way to support her daughters.[63] She was twenty-six then, but even with her Vassar degree, she found few productive outlets for her energy and ambition. Her father hired her to be his secretary for a time, and she underwent two years of Freudian psychoanalysis, hoping, she recalled, to become "someone I liked."[64]

The specter of Clara haunted her, the unhappy woman traumatizing the unhappy child, squelching her spirit, her creativity, her sexuality. Clara's efforts to stop Mary from masturbating as a child had affected Mary's early marital life "quite severely," she remembered.[65] Years of therapy and work would lead not only to resolution but, ultimately, to her international success as head of the Sex Information and Education Consortium of the United States (SIECUS). But by the early thirties, the need to survive independently would override everything, and Mary would take what work she could find in New York, living with her children in Brooklyn and clerking in a department store.

Mary hated the job, but she loved being a mother, and she poured her energy into caring for her daughters. Looking about for books to interest them, she discovered the dearth of picture books for small children, so she decided to create one herself. Her idea was to show children realistic photographs of objects that were part of their daily lives—shoes and socks, toys, toothbrushes, and such. She enlisted her enthusiastic father to take the photographs for the project that culminated in *The First Picture Book—Everyday Things for Babies,* published in 1930 by Harcourt, Brace and Company. The innovative book was so successful that a sequel, *The Second Picture Book,* appeared in 1931.

During this time, eager to establish a career, Mary took some aptitude tests that pointed her back toward her original interest in science. Because she had taken a premed course at Vassar, she decided now to become a nutritionist. Sharing her plans with friends, Dr. Florence Clothier and her husband, Harvard Medical School dean Dr. George Wislocki, Mary got strong advice to go to medical school instead and become a doctor. With children to support, it would take years, but in 1939, by the time she was thirty-five, Mary had earned her M.D. at the University of Rochester, ranking thirteenth in a class of forty-five.

It has been said that over his years as a plant breeder, Steichen achieved with delphiniums the supreme mastery of nature that horticulturist Luther Burbank had accomplished with potatoes, poppies, lilies, tomatoes, corn, and Shasta daisies. (He had, after all, purchased delphinium seeds from Burbank in 1912, and written about Burbank's theories.) Steichen has, in fact, been called both the Burbank of modern plant breeding and the Rembrandt of modern photography. Throughout the 1920s, he was aggressively experimenting with straight photography and lifting it to a new level by affirming the scientific integrity of the art. Furthermore, his successful work on the Stehli Silk project had left him with a keen interest in design. When the Hardman Piano Company commissioned him to design some modernistic pianos in 1928, it was a mark of

The New Pictorial Revolution (1924–1928)

his value to both organizations that he negotiated agreements with Condé Nast and with the J. Walter Thompson Agency to reduce his responsibilities and at the same time increase his pay. Afraid that Steichen would give up his advertising work, J. Walter Thompson actually doubled his annual guarantee from twenty thousand to forty thousand dollars.[66]

Just seventeen days before Black Tuesday and the shocking collapse of the stock market, the October 12, 1929, issue of *Vogue* appeared, its glitzy pages brimming with fashion photographs and smart articles on style. There was also an article by Steichen, recapitulating his conviction that photography had the edge over painting because of "the supreme ability of the lens to record a given instant." He contended, furthermore, that a fashion photograph was even more complex than a landscape photograph because the fashion image was "the picture of an instant made to order." The lens of the camera, Steichen pointed out, "functions without opinion, prejudice or partiality. The intelligent use of this instant lens function constitutes good photography."[67] And good photography, he believed, could be simultaneously beautiful, artistic, useful—and profitable.

This was an opinion he shared with his sister and brother-in-law. Throughout the late twenties, Steichen and Sandburg had long talks about the emerging new modern art forms, especially the motion picture and the radio, with their potential for artistic expression as well as mass entertainment. As they contemplated the role of art and the artist in modern life, they heartily agreed that art should be a civilizing force in the world. The artist had a duty to speak to the times, to live in the world, not apart from it, and to reach out to average citizens. Art should be accessible and comprehensible to the masses. They scorned the ivory-tower critics who intimated that any art that the public could understand and enjoy must somehow be inferior.

They saw no reason, furthermore, why an artist should not earn what Sandburg termed a decent bricklayer income. But these opinions were about to get Steichen and Sandburg into trouble.

27

A NEW VISION

(1 9 2 9 - 1 9 3 4)

Going along a railroad one day I see a thing I have seen many times. But this day I suddenly see. 'Tisn't that you see new *but things have prepared you for* a new vision.[1]

—SANDBURG QUOTING STEICHEN

BY 1929, STEICHEN, FIFTY, AND SANDBURG, fifty-one, had achieved national fame—Steichen through *Vanity Fair* and *Vogue,* and Sandburg through his best-selling biography *Abraham Lincoln: The Prairie Years.* Steichen was being wooed by almost every major advertising agency in the country, while Sandburg was negotiating with D. W. Griffith to write an epic Hollywood film about Lincoln. Steichen's contract with J. Walter Thompson gave him the latitude to take on contracts with rival agencies, and when Griffith and Sandburg failed to come to terms on a movie contract, Sandburg turned to other projects. But the two men barely had time to enjoy their hard-won prosperity and applause before they were buffeted by the criticism of artists, writers, and critics who believed that such conspicuous commercial success implied prostitution of the talent and integrity of the artist.

In 1929, these two mavericks found themselves in the center of a storm of criticism. The lightning rod was a book instigated by some of Steichen's wealthy friends, including Helen Resor, wife of the head of the J. Walter Thompson Agency. Entitled *Steichen the Photographer,* this was a handsome limited edition of reproductions of forty-nine of Steichen's photographs, accompanied by a memoir written by Sandburg in 1928; the book was published in 1929 by Harcourt Brace.

After Sandburg and Steichen combed over the manuscript line by line, Sandburg annotated the final revised draft: "Manuscript of *Steichen the Photographer* done in the summer of 1928 and given to the typist after being gone over by Steichen and me."[2] The subsequent critical uproar over the book centered on Steichen's assertions about the historical importance of commercial art. The repercussions would linger for decades afterward in judgments rendered by critics about Steichen's photography, as well as Sandburg's poetry.

Steichen ranked "close to Ben Franklin and Leonardo da Vinci when it comes to versatility," Sandburg proclaimed effusively in his preface to the book. He confessed his bias at the outset—"the author may be allowed prejudices in writing about his wife's brother"—and warned that it was "not at all a statement of the life, career and works of Edward Steichen." Rather, it was "a little record and memoir of data, opinion and whim, as between friends."[3] Only 925 copies of the expensive book were published—the twenty-five-dollar cost mandated by the superb reproductions of the forty-nine Steichen photographs—but hostile critics immediately pounced on its controversial text.

"Except for experiments and diversions, Steichen's work is now entirely in the commercial field," Sandburg wrote in *Steichen the Photographer*. Furthermore, he reported, Steichen called all his work commercial, "with neither apology nor pride." Steichen declared, moreover, that there had never been a time when the best artistic work was not commercial art. Sandburg, who shared Steichen's opinions on the matter, expounded on the theme:

> *He [Steichen] points to Michael Angelo selling his life work to a church of vast power, receiving generous sums of money from ecclesiastical patrons who approved the designs before they were executed. Lorenzo the Magnificent and similar plutocrats influencing the folk-ways of their time (as the millionaires of our own day affect the crowd mind) granted commissions to Raphael, Titian, Botticelli, Leonardo da Vinci, who gave their most creative life moments to pictures that pleased their patrons.*[4]

According to Sandburg, Steichen believed that throughout history the artist had often been "what we might call a glorified press agent," and that most art "was used to sell religion to the people, or, to use their own language, to create good will and bring about good works in the cause of the Church."[5] In addition, there was utilitarian art such as, Steichen suggested, the priceless Greek vases gracing museum collections in the twentieth century—essentially common household appliances in their time, produced in affordable quantity for consumers. He told Sandburg that in the modern era, art for art's sake was dead, if such a concept had ever existed, and that they now lived in a commercial age. Furthermore, it was simply not true, as many artists and critics contended, that commercialism destroys art. "As a matter of fact," Sandburg wrote in the text, "the great art in any period was produced in collaboration with the particular commercialism of that period—or by revolutionists who stood far and clean outside of that commercialism and fought it tooth and nail and worked for its destruction."[6]

Sandburg then attributed to Steichen ideas and language that strongly echoed some of his own earlier socialist tracts:

> *The organic economic structure of any society in human history, the character of its materialism, the technic of its material nourishment—the way by which it emerged from the wilderness, came out of the primitive and survived—has been the dominant and controlling fact in its art. . . . It seems to be Steichen's theory that the technic and the creative imagination of a man can work as surely in commercial art as in "art for art's sake." He believes his Vanity Fair portraits of Charlie Chaplin, of H.L. Mencken and of Evelyn Brent, as offhand instances, are as good as his best portraits in the non-commercial field. He sees as many aesthetic values in certain shoe photographs for Vogue as in photographs of roses and foxglove to which he gave the limit of his toil and creative pressure.*[7]

Steichen told Sandburg that if his "technic, imagination and vision" were any good, he should be able to apply the "best values" of his "non-commercial and experimental photographs into a pair of shoes, a tube of tooth paste, a jar of face cream, a mattress, or any object" that he wanted to "light up and make humanly interesting in an advertising photograph." Steichen was finished with art for art's sake, Sandburg announced, convinced that if he could not express the best that was in him in his advertising photographs, he was no good anyway.[8]

Steichen argued further that, "with rare exceptions," artists who did not have to worry about earning money had historically been "poor producers." Denied the luxury of working only when inspired, the commercial artist had to "get himself in a lather of emotion at a given time—say two-thirty in the afternoon. Any afternoon." Steichen reflected that commercial pressure could be "an amazing, productive force," and he had come to believe that few painters or photographers "would create any living art if they didn't have pressure blowing down on the backs of their necks."[9]

The critics had a field day with the iconoclastic argument. Critic Mike Gold, writing in *The New Masses,* blamed Sandburg rather than Steichen for glorifying commercial art in an "amazing and shameless essay" that advised young people "to sell their talents to Big Business."[10] In the January 22, 1930, issue of *The New Republic,* Stieglitz's old friend and colleague Paul Rosenfeld, the novelist and music critic, attacked the book for making it appear that the great artists were motivated by the "main enemy of art, modern mercantile advertisement." Furthermore, he charged, it was an "atrocity" that the book failed to do justice to the "spirit" and "purity" of the Photo-Secession. Rosenfeld then devoted the bulk of his article to a discussion of the Photo-Secession, lavishing praise on Stieglitz's "spiritual force" and his "miraculous" work, believing it to be superior to Steichen's "tendency toward the showy and inflated."[11]

Ironically, Steichen's defense of commercial art had actually been composed the year before the crash of the national economy in 1929, but in the ensuing national turmoil, the stance taken by Steichen and Sandburg would be viewed by some as cynical, shallow, or crassly self-serving. And with the limited circulation of the book, far more readers were exposed to the critical attacks than to the primary source itself, and so they formed their opinions secondhand. But the impression stayed that Steichen and Sandburg had sold out, exploiting the mass audience for profit.

As for the two collaborators, they soon found that commercial art was as vulnerable as any other enterprise to the turbulence of the national economy. Soon after the stock market crash of Black Tuesday, October

29, 1929, when the value of Condé Nast Publications stock collapsed from $93.00 to $4.50 per share, Steichen joined his colleagues straightaway in taking a 10 percent salary cut. Nast's fortune was lost in an instant, and he had to take out an immediate loan of $2 million to keep his magazines in print.

Sandburg soon would see his own salary at the Chicago *Daily News* cut in half, and he quickly set to work on *The People, Yes,* a long epic poem about the Depression.[12]

During the years of her former husband's great success, Clara Smith Steichen lived her life as something of a gypsy, moving from country to country, from borrowed house to cheap apartment, bitterly reliving all the wrongs, real and imagined, she believed Steichen, Mary, and now Kate had inflicted on her. At sporadic intervals, she still wrote rambling letters to Stieglitz, going over and over the pain of her life. She would drop out of sight for long periods of time, to resurface in times of crisis, when her unhappiness erupted anew and even intensified.

Events in 1928 had triggered particular despair and depression for her. First came the news of Mildred Aldrich's death, a grievous loss for Clara, who counted her one of the few enduring, trustworthy friends in her life. Then she heard from Kate that Steichen and Dana had purchased Umpawaug. She was enraged. "I remembered that Steichen had bought three homes for his mother and paid the mortgage off on the last one while Lee kept Mary and Gene my cousin here fostered Kate," she wrote to Stieglitz, "and I remembered he had intended buying Oiseau Blue [*sic*]...."[13] She felt homeless and destitute, having moved from various apartments in New York to the small cottage on the Paddock farm in Connecticut. In the late twenties, she had lived for a time in Springfield, Missouri, all the while yearning to move back to France. It was unfair, she felt, that Steichen had bought such a large estate for his young wife.

And the more she thought about Steichen's Connecticut farm, the more Clara believed that he ought to give her more money. In 1928, therefore, she tried to get her attorney in New York to reopen the divorce settlement and sue for more alimony. He replied that he was sorry to note her "very strong tinge of despondency," but he told her that the "constant harboring" and "nursing" of her "grievance" would ultimately prove to be a great detriment to her best interests.[14]

She worried constantly through the years that Steichen would stop paying alimony, but, as her lawyer pointed out, Steichen reliably sent her a monthly check. He faithfully abided by the civil agreement worked out in New York State in 1922. During the Depression, Steichen's lucrative salary and commissions were reduced as hard times worsened; all the while he continued to support himself, Dana, Oma and Opa, and, for a time, Mary and her two children, as well as subsidizing some of Kate's expenses. Beginning in 1931, when it was discovered that Oma had cancer, he paid for the best available medical care for his mother. In addition, he was building a house at Umpawaug and pouring money into his plant-breeding operation there. Steichen's lifestyle, his family obligations, and his ambitious plant-breeding program at Umpawaug required a large sum of money. While Clara and some of her friends thought Steichen owed her greater financial support, her own lawyer declined to press for it, and Steichen did not offer it.

Clara never remarried, worked at part-time jobs now and then, and, with the help of bequests from a wealthy aunt, managed to travel regularly: In the early thirties, she would spend three months in New Mexico, and in 1931 and 1932, she would live for a time in Huiry, France, where Mildred Aldrich had lived until her death. She may even have resided for a time in Mildred's old peasant cottage, then owned by Alice B. Toklas. As she lived unhappily in the past, however, Clara's chronic resentments festered and ate away at her. Over the years, she expressed growing contempt for her former mother-in-law and others she considered enemies. As Clara knew, Alfred Stieglitz had always respected and loved Oma Steichen, yet in her letters to Stieglitz she contemptuously described Oma as boastful, deceitful, and ignorant.[15]

Mary Kemp Steichen had lived for and through her children for fifty-four years. For the last three decades of her life, she hovered over her five granddaughters when they were near her and wrote them long letters when they were away. After she and Opa began living near the Sandburgs, in the houses Steichen bought for them in Maywood and then in Elmhurst, Oma took a daily hand in the children's care. Her prolonged anxiety about Clara and Edward's problems eventually took a physical toll. Oma had been a good Catholic, but sometime during the last years of her life, she had a falling-out with the church, and she stopped going to Mass and Confession. Her dispute with the priest may have stemmed from the church's position on divorce, for Oma could clearly see now that divorce was the inevitable recourse for her son.

Her kitchen was still the heart of family celebrations at Christmas and birthdays, and for generations afterward, Steichen family members would bake Oma's cookies and try to replicate her succulent Christmas cake, bursting with fruit, nuts, and spices. Steichen would devour the cake, announcing, "Now a cake like that has an existence of its own; a personal essence is created around it. I call such a cake a Work of Art."[16]

Oma passed down to her daughter and granddaughters her recipe for wine, with instructions in her phonetic spelling to "keep this in verry save place as it is verry good resepie." Once the grapes were crushed and fermented, and the sugar added (two pounds of sugar per gallon of juice), Oma told her family to let the wine ferment again "till it stops sissling, then close it up and let it lay for one year or longer the longer the better."[17]

For years, the Sandburgs lived only steps away from the elder Steichens, and after the Sandburgs moved to Michigan in 1928, Oma missed them terribly, she wrote in a letter, for "Opa dont [sic] talk, is outside or in the basement or sits by the Radio." Opa was always working in his garden or cleaning around the house, Oma said. He could never sit still, she wrote Margaret Sandburg, "but that is why he feels so good nothing like work he say, to keep you well and in good spirits." As the years passed, unfortunately, Oma's eyes and heart began to fail, and illness progressively sapped her energy until, she wrote, "I just sit or walk around, got not much to do, if I could see I would have enof to mend and fix up, and can not read much either."[18]

Sadly, Christmas of 1932 was not the same for Oma and her family. For the first time in her life, she was too ill for the usual festivities, and so she spent the holiday quietly at home in Elmhurst with Opa, Edward, Dana, and the Sandburgs, who left their daughters in Harbert, Michigan, with the housekeeper. "I am sorry that you all can not come with Mama and Daddie to us, but I would get to escited with so many you understandt dont [sic] you?" she wrote to twenty-one-year-old Margaret.

"And you will see Unkel Ed and Dana, as they will come all togethre [*sic*] to Harbert, and then you will have your real Christmas."[19]

Steichen visited as often as he could during the months afterward, and he asked Paula to make arrangements for "any thing and everything" their parents needed and to send the bills to him.[20] Meanwhile, it was a consolation that Paula could be with their parents often. She was a "grand" person when there were hard times, he reminded Oma and Opa, as well as when everything was "peaches and cream."[21]

As the country plunged deeper into the Depression in the early thirties, Steichen began to capitalize on his commercial exposure to use his camera as a vehicle for social commentary. In 1931, for instance, he was engaged by J. Walter Thompson to make public-service photographs to publicize the Manhattan Eye, Ear and Throat Hospital, which not only served clients who could pay but also offered pro bono services to charity patients, whose numbers grew during the Depression. When Steichen arrived at the hospital to shoot the pictures, he found his subjects—actual patients at the hospital's clinic—seated in a waiting room. Some of them were blind, or nearly so.

In love with light himself, Steichen knew immediately how he wanted to photograph them when he saw the sun rays streaming through the skylight at the top of the steps. He and Mac hauled every light they had up the stairs and arranged them under the skylight. Steichen then asked his subjects to climb the stairs. He chose a mother carrying an infant to stand in the center of the picture; otherwise, he left the patients as they had arranged themselves. He told them all to look upward, then gave Mac the signal to turn on the flood of lights.

Steichen's photograph, *The Clinic,* or *On the Clinic Stairs,* depicted thirty human beings on a symbolic pilgrimage through the hunger, despair, and fear of the times. Faces uplifted, eyes captivated by the surge of light, they pause on the triangle of stairways, waiting hopefully in line for medical care. The compelling image moves beyond effective advertising into the realm of powerful social commentary. Steichen was probing the documentary power of the camera, producing his own social commentary on a conspicuous podium with unprecedented outreach. Sandburg had earlier commented on the wide range of Steichen's visibility:

> *On the one hand, through the Condé Nast magazines known as "the quality group," he reaches a maximum of the select and aristocratic audiences of America. On the other hand, through the J. Walter Thompson advertising photographs in the big-circulation magazines, a single photograph running in several magazines the same week or month, he reaches almost the total literate population of the country.*[22]

The J. Walter Thompson Agency engaged Steichen to shoot a number of additional public-service promotions, and in many of them, his camera revealed the heartbreak of people displaced, perhaps forever, by the social and economic catastrophe of the Depression. For the Travelers Aid Society in 1932, he photographed *Homeless Women: the Depression*. Harried faces blaze out of the darkness—women of all ages, proud touches betraying their previous circumstances—a choker of pearls, a silk scarf, a necklace, a mottled fur collar, each one primping a little for the camera, then forgetting it, each lost again in the private misery exacted by the collective national tragedy. One sad little girl has her arms fastened around her mother's neck. "Where to? What next?" Sandburg was writing in his Depression epic, *The People, Yes*. Those questions hover in the anxious eyes of the women in Steichen's photographs.

In a sense, on the pages of the nation's magazines and journals, Steichen now mounted weekly or monthly photographic exhibitions that reached vast audiences in far greater numbers than the "wallpaper" of his paintings ever had. And here in his gifted hands lay the power to mass-produce message as well as art. As he had done in New York and in Paris as a young man, he was photographing celebrities, yet he also photographed the faceless, anonymous, Everyman and Everywoman, just as he had done as a teenager roaming the lakeshore of Milwaukee, taking pictures of working people on holidays.

World War I had left Steichen disillusioned, yet determined that art could serve as a civilizing force in the world. He had produced some of the most vivid and visible pictures of the Roaring Twenties, had done as much as any single photographer to chronicle that decade and to inundate the American consciousness with its first fashion-fad, celebrity-culture images. Now the Depression gave him sober subject matter, prompting the conscientious drive to harness his photographs once and for all to that civilizing force.

In a sense, his professional life had run parallel to the national experience, and, like the country, he himself was being jolted into maturity by the catalytic events that were shaping the national destiny. The war and then the Depression had forced the people of the United States to grow up at last, to relinquish the relative innocence of the nineteenth century; the cocky self-assurance of the first decade of the twentieth century; the smug isolation of the second decade, shattered by the war; and the flamboyant self-indulgence of the twenties. And it seemed to Steichen that everywhere he turned during those dark years, he saw a new maturity, born out of desperation and survival, reflected in the strength and inherent kindness of the American people, the same qualities he had first learned from his mother.

Much of Steichen's photographic work during the thirties was a testament to his belief that the camera could be as powerful a communicator as language itself. The visual image reverberated with meaning and subtext, its message all the more intensely personal because words were unnecessary, and traditional language did not intervene between the human being and the photograph. Having shared his photographs with the mass audience through the vast outreach of magazines and newspapers, Steichen now began to consider enlarging his photographic images and projecting them on bigger and bigger "screens."

He had painted murals in the past. Imprinted somewhere in his artistic consciousness were the old lessons from the Milwaukee panorama painters, whose epic paintings evoked battles, annunciations, extraordinary human achievements. Now Steichen wanted to create photographic murals or panoramas—"pageants," he called them. He had his first chance when the new Museum of Modern Art in New York sponsored an invitational competition in 1932, asking sixty-five American artists, including Steichen and Georgia O'Keeffe, to enter mural designs illustrating some facet of the postwar world. Steichen's study of the George

Washington Bridge was chosen to be exhibited at the museum in May in the show "Murals by American Painters and Photographers." The competition was hastily arranged, with the organizers fully aware of the exciting work going on at that very moment at the new Rockefeller Center, then under construction.

There, the industrial designer Donald Deskey was overseeing the ambitious project to adorn the new Art Deco Radio City Music Hall with work by the best modern artists. Forced by his tight budget to offer each artist a flat, democratic honorarium of fifteen hundred dollars, Deskey sought to fill Radio City Music Hall with stellar American art. In 1932, Steichen was commissioned to create one of the many decorations for the new Radio City Music Hall—a photo mural for the Center Theater. Another artist who accepted a commission was Georgia O'Keeffe—without telling her husband, who sought to govern her career and her artistic choices. Worse yet, in Stieglitz's opinion, she had agreed to decorate the second-floor ladies' powder room with a mural.

Steichen's photographic mural for the twenty-five-by-five-foot walls of the Radio City Center Theater depicted great scientific achievements, from railroads and skyscrapers, to aviation, starting with the Wright brothers' first biplane. Over some of the forty-foot enlargements, he superimposed captions, maps, and diagrams, whetting visual interest while at the same time advancing the photographic narrative. One observer noted, "When he makes a photo-montage he includes negatives as well as positives, lettering, maps, blueprints, in short any sign or symbol to make the meaning of the picture clear."[23]

One beautiful autumn weekend in 1932, Steichen, Dana, Kate, and one of Steichen's assistants set out on an automobile trip to the Adirondack Mountains, photographing beautiful scenery en route for Steichen to weave into another mural he had been commissioned to create, this time for the New York State Building at the upcoming 1933 world's fair in Chicago. Because Steichen considered Lake George to be one of the loveliest places in the state, he and his party stopped there on a Friday afternoon to photograph the scenery. More than that, Steichen and Dana hoped to see Stieglitz and O'Keeffe. They received a cordial welcome from Stieglitz's niece Georgia Englehard, but they were disappointed to hear that Stieglitz and O'Keeffe were away. Steichen sat down in the Stieglitz farmhouse, swamped with memories, and wrote an affectionate

A New Vision (1929–1934)

note to Stieglitz. The lake was beautiful as always, he said, but it was his old friend Stieglitz he had really wanted to see.[24]

Normally, Stieglitz and O'Keeffe could be found at Lake George in September and October, but they had returned to New York on September twenty-fourth so that O'Keeffe could work on plans for the photomurals she had been commissioned to install at Radio City Music Hall. She would soon withdraw from the project, ostensibly because of construction delays, but actually because of her own fragile mental and physical health—she was exhausted not only by her husband's stubborn anger about the murals but by the constant stress of her life with him. It is not clear whether Steichen had any idea of the chaos in Stieglitz's personal life then. Having worked intimately with Stieglitz for years, he surely knew how Stieglitz had alternately nurtured and dictated O'Keeffe's development as an artist, until, in 1929, she had in effect declared her personal and artistic independence in Taos, New Mexico.

In 1925, Stieglitz had founded the Intimate Gallery in a space on the top floor of the Anderson Galleries on Park Avenue. From December 1925 until its closing in May 1929, the Intimate Gallery housed exhibits by O'Keeffe, Marin, Arthur Dove, Marsden Hartley, Stieglitz, and a few others. After the smaller Intimate Gallery closed its doors, Stieglitz opened An American Place, a new gallery on the seventeenth floor of a brand-new office building at 509 Madison Avenue. There, in addition to other exhibits, he showed John Marin's watercolors and O'Keeffe's startling new paintings of New Mexican scenes. His indispensable right hand by this time was twenty-four-year-old Dorothy Norman, the wife of Edward Norman, a Sears, Roebuck heir, and the mother of a two-year-old daughter. Delicate, sensitive, and highly intelligent, Dorothy Norman had fallen in love with Stieglitz soon after she had met him in 1927, never mind that he was forty-one years older than she.

At first, she had volunteered to perform even the most mundane chores to help him in his important work. By 1930, she was handling many of his business affairs, managing the gallery, buffering him from many distractions so he could work, nurturing his ego—serving, in effect, as the "good" wife he had always felt he deserved, while his real wife concentrated on her own art, or tried to. In one of the most affirming gestures Stieglitz had ever received, Dorothy also saw to it that for the first time in his life he had a well-equipped darkroom so that he could do justice to his prints. (He and Steichen had for many years commandeered the family bathrooms for darkrooms, to the dismay of the women in each family.)

Inevitably, along the way, Stieglitz and Dorothy became lovers, and they carried on an intimate, almost-daily correspondence when they were apart. Having abandoned Emmy and Kitty for Georgia, Stieglitz now, at least emotionally, had abandoned Georgia for Dorothy, a woman nearly twenty years younger than his wife, and seven years younger than his own daughter. By the time of Steichen's impromptu visit to Lake George in 1932, Stieglitz had been embroiled in the Georgia-Dorothy dilemma for almost as long as he had sustained the Emmy-Georgia quandary, once again seeming to thrive on the romance and excitement he apparently gleaned from such hurtful domestic chaos.

This time, however, there were unmistakable signs of stress and age, for Stieglitz had suffered a terrible attack of angina in 1928, the first in a series of problems with his heart. O'Keeffe and her sister Ida had nursed him through that attack, and O'Keeffe had suffered her own health problems. For Stieglitz and O'Keeffe, the personal problems were always intensified by financial tension, for the Depression was having its inevitable fallout in the art world, and despite O'Keeffe's ascendant visibility, she had not yet made the great fortune that would come in time. In fact, as O'Keeffe and Stieglitz biographer Benita Eisler revealed in 1991, the widely published reports in 1928 that O'Keeffe's calla lily paintings had been purchased for $25,000 by a French collector actually grew out of a hoax—a publicity stunt orchestrated by Stieglitz to draw attention to O'Keeffe and escalate the prices of her work.[25] Stieglitz had actually written a letter to the editor of *Art News* to report the nonexistent sale: "She is receiving—don't faint— $25,000 for them," he exulted; "I can hardly grasp it all."[26]

Anderson Galleries owner Mitchell Kennerly was supposedly a party to the misrepresentation, although he had hoped in vain that his wealthy mistress would buy the paintings for a generous price. Although Kennerly apparently eventually returned the paintings to O'Keeffe, who still held an IOU for them in 1931, she allowed herself to be interviewed more than once about the astonishing price supposedly paid for her paintings.

These events take on a particular irony in the face of Stieglitz's

A New Vision (1929–1934)

long, imperious, and, as it turns out, hypocritical attitude toward Steichen's financial success. Publicly and privately in the late twenties and thirties, Stieglitz roundly condemned Steichen for his commercial motivation. And once again, as had been true in his marriage to Emmy, Stieglitz was living almost entirely on his wife's money, albeit a different wife. Even during the Depression years, O'Keeffe's work sold steadily and profitably enough so that she could support them both. All the while, Stieglitz was promoting and even exploiting his wife's unprecedented commercial success—surreptitiously, even disingenuously, if need be.

Steichen, on the other hand, did his work and stated his purpose for all the world to see. "I was never ashamed of using my talents to make money," Steichen observed matter-of-factly, not defensively. "I feel that all art is commercial—no one creates anything just to put it away and forget it."[27] Stieglitz, who had always maintained an opposite viewpoint, was hypocritically holding court at An American Place on Madison Avenue, condemning Steichen and others who made money from art.

Stieglitz told a new young friend, photographer Ansel Adams, that the "racketeering" in the "so-called" art world grew "more & more brazen & engulfing."[28] Yet he extended a measure of understanding to Adams that he seemed to deny Steichen. Adams had family responsibilities, Stieglitz acknowledged in a letter, and the obligation to support his family brought on the "clash" between the "ideal" and the "commercial." He told Adams sympathetically that he could not "escape" the commercial imperative unless he was prepared to "starve" and to "have your family starve."[29]

And Stieglitz could give scathing rebukes to patrons of An American Place who queried him about an artist's commercial success. "Do his pictures sell well?" one woman asked innocently as she viewed paintings by Arthur Dove. "What does that have to do with Art?" Stieglitz shot back. "The number of pictures liked or sold tells one nothing about the stature of an artist."[30]

Mary Kemp Steichen gave her son a young Douglas fir to plant at Umpawaug in the early 1930s, a small but symbolic part of the rich legacy this mother handed to her children. To the grief of her family,

Oma was pronounced terminally ill with cervical cancer in the late spring of 1933. When the news reached him, Steichen was preparing to go to Washington to photograph President Roosevelt and his cabinet, but he told Paula he would drop those plans and travel directly to Illinois to be with Oma and Opa. She apparently reassured him that there was no need to cancel his plans, but the two of them agreed that it was best for Oma to be told the reality of her condition, knowing that she would want the truth, and suspecting she probably knew it anyway. Steichen was distraught about his mother's illness, hoping that Oma would not suffer great pain. While he tried to accept the reality of it, he wrote to Paula, "it hurts & hurts...."[31]

He wrote to assure his mother that he could fly to her on a moment's notice; he, Opa, and Paula would love her "back to health," he promised, signing his letter in the old way—"your Gaesjack."[32] She was the "grandest sweetest" mother in the world, Dana wrote to Oma in June. She and Ed were "perfectly sure" that Oma would get well.[33]

They hoped at first that surgery might help, but the doctors recommended instead a series of radium treatments. After his assignment in Washington, Steichen went to spend some time with Oma and Opa, hovering over his mother as she struggled with the first treatments. *"We are winning,"* he encouraged her, although he knew the treatments were causing her great pain.[34] By some terrible mistake, Oma was given excessive doses of radium, which made her terribly ill.[35] Afterward, she failed rapidly.

Paula wrote to Steichen and Dana that she was "taking less and less nourishment . . . tense day & night, waking & sleeping—her voice high-pitched, unnatural—until yesterday afternoon when she could utter only husky whispers." One midnight, she cried out in the old language, "Go away all of you. Leave me. Can't you see I am dead." She slipped into silence for a few hours, then opened her eyes and recognized Opa and Paula. "Opa, Opa, Opa," she whispered. "Lily, Lily, Lily. Bleiv bei mer [Stay with me]."[36]

Later when she slipped into a relaxed, natural sleep, Paula and Opa hoped that she might have made a miraculous turn for the better, but the doctor foresaw that Oma would not survive the week. It was a "terrifying time for Opa, Mother, and Uncle Ed," Helga recalled.[37] They clung together, the four of them, as in the old days in Hancock and Milwaukee.

A NEW VISION (1929–1934)

Although her husband, son, and daughter kept watch at Oma's bedside as she died, nothing prepared them for the immense grief of losing this extraordinary woman, the anchor of their family, the heart.

Margaret, wanting to remember only her grandmother's warmth and vitality, refused to look at her body in its casket. Fury overwhelmed grief when Opa learned that the Catholic priest in Elmhurst refused to conduct Oma's funeral service because she had not attended church in a long time. Her simple funeral took place at a local funeral parlor instead, and afterward, Paula carried out Oma's wishes for cremation. Ever since she had read the stories of Edgar Allan Poe, Oma had been afraid she might be buried alive.

She was nearly eighty when she died. Possessed of a powerful optimism, Mary Kemp Steichen had sustained an abundant faith in the goodness of people. She had courageously carried her son to the New World, had rescued her husband from the Chicago boardinghouse, had made a home and a livelihood for her family, had recognized the great gifts within her children, and had invested all her own hope, money, and pride in their dreams. She had been a fortress for her family all their lives. The lilt of her voice and laughter had so imprinted itself that there was a distinctive musical intonation in the voices of her children and their children, even in Paula's granddaughter Paula and Edward's granddaughter Francesca, who were born long after Oma died.

The Steichens and Sandburgs were devastated to lose her, taciturn Opa most of all. He refused to leave their little house in Elmhurst, even though Steichen wanted to buy him a new one near the Sandburgs in Michigan. This house was home, every corner holding memories of Oma. Outside lay his garden. There would be solace in the earth. He would stay, he insisted, until he died, and then they could bury him wherever they wanted, so long as they buried Oma's ashes beside him.[38]

"Whatever I am comes from my mother," Steichen often said. "I don't know what she had. But I wish I possessed a fraction of it."[39]

Kate Steichen was twenty-five in 1933, living and working in New York as a professional singer with WPA opera and concert groups. She had studied voice seriously for years, since the days when her mother and aunt Charlotte would drive her in Charlotte's Model T Ford to her voice lessons three days weekly.[40] Seeking extra income in the early thirties, Kate joined the choir at the Church of the Incarnation in New York, where she met Carol Silverberg, a young journalist and amateur singer who sang alto in the choir. Soon afterward, Carol and Kate took an apartment together; they lived together until Carol's death in 1979.

Kate and Carol could be seen flying up and down the winding Connecticut roads in Kate's 1930 Model A Ford roadster, a gift from her father. She had named the car "Lidi" after the imaginary companion of her childhood days. Steichen and Kate supported each other fully in their relationships. Kate thought Dana, her young stepmother (almost fourteen years her senior), was the most beautiful redhead she had ever seen, and as dear to her as a sister. She believed her father and Dana had a perfect marriage.[41] To Paula, Steichen had confided his initial worries about Kate's lesbian relationship with Carol, but his sister encouraged his acceptance of Kate's choice, and Dana saw to it that Carol became a member of the family.[42]

Clara, on the other hand, was appalled. From her infancy, Kate had been her favorite, her pet, her bedmate during the frightening self-imposed exile to Voulangis during the war, her hope for the future. Because Clara had always believed that Steichen never really wanted Kate, she compensated accordingly, lavishing on her younger daughter, who was so like Steichen, the warmth and affection she sternly denied Mary, who was so like herself.

Clara had always heaped criticism on Mary, to the point of verbal abuse. Now Kate got her turn as the object of Clara's fury as she moved openly and exuberantly into her lifelong partnership with Carol Silverberg. Clara alleged that Kate was sexually depraved and irresponsible—like her father. She felt Kate had ruined her life and her art. She was a heedless, ungrateful daughter, Clara claimed. As was her habit, Clara poured out the details in letters to Stieglitz: "No, I can never forgive the unnecessary injustice done me—or the (apparently [sic]) deliberate changing of Kate—She is so coarse—so imitative of her Father its [sic] sad—All his cheaper qualities and poses and to recall her fragile wistful lovliness [sic]—and beauty of mind its [sic] sickening. She [sic] so busy being his offspring she lost sight of her own precious outlook. Maybe she'll fare better—I doubt it. Mary is at least HONEST."[43]

A New Vision (1929–1934)

Deeply hurt by her mother's response to her choice of lovers, Kate simply withdrew from Clara's life. "I am through," Clara told Stieglitz. "She defends herself—ONLY—it disgusts me. I am no strict moralist—nor do I try to pump such into others—but Stieglitz—loyalty—unselfish devotion for years through poverty—of work in sizzling summers—in bitter winters—what of those, Stieglitz?"[44]

Clara perceived that Kate was "glad to be free to go her own ways," she told Stieglitz.[45] But she grieved bitterly about Kate's life. "No," she wrote to Stieglitz in 1932, "you do not know and never will alas, know the lovely child that Kate was—with her strangely balanced mind straight from another world almost, and of beautiful chrystaline [sic] beauty. Thats [sic] all over—she fell for the hard-boiled things New York does to people of her kind. But, she deliberately chose it ... and I long ago learned not to interfere with others, so be it."[46]

———

In 1934, Dorothy Norman led Stieglitz's friends and admirers in the production of *America and Alfred Stieglitz,* an ambitious book paying tribute to Stieglitz on his seventieth birthday. Still the source of ongoing painful conflict between Stieglitz and O'Keeffe, Norman was the chief editor of this *Collective Portrait,* along with novelist and critic Waldo Frank, critic Lewis Mumford, novelist and critic Paul Rosenfeld, and Columbia University professor Harold Rugg. The roster of contributors to the book Norman engineered was impressive—including, among others, the poet William Carlos Williams; photographers Child Bayley and Paul Strand—the old and the new guard; painters Marin, Hartley, Dove, and Demuth; dramatist Harold Clurman; writers Sherwood Anderson, Jean Toomer, and Gertrude Stein. There were no words in the book by O'Keeffe, although photographs of twelve of her paintings appeared, along with one of Stieglitz's photographs of her. All of the writers celebrated Stieglitz, and many of them set the man and the work in interesting cultural context.

Steichen, however, was very much in the shadows—a few mentions, a few photographs reproduced. This was, after all, Stieglitz's book, yet by overlooking Steichen's pivotal role in the history of 291, the book contributed to the subsequent neglect of Steichen's landmark contributions. Stieglitz sent an autographed copy of *America and Alfred Stieglitz* to Clara Steichen in Majorca. She especially relished the articles on 291. "The book is a real treasure," she wrote to Stieglitz. "Very fair very fine. Cant [sic] think how it could have presented the growth of it all better... and the brass bowl—the curtains—I can still see that little place—and hear the fire engines dashing across the avenue at 30th street and hear nice Lawrence come into his place—it has not receded far—it all—could—never be beyond tears in my eyes if I dwell upon it... I almost believe that you did what you wanted to do with your life—I hope so."[47]

In 1934, Steichen, reputedly the most famous and most expensive photographer in the world, had his own photographic laboratory, as well as a studio—whose simple interior included a few movable panels for background and a variety of lights and lamps. He abhorred painted scenery or cast-shadow backgrounds, and he was an innovator in the on-location shot, taking his subjects to "mansions, apartments, ships, night clubs, theaters, ballrooms, flying fields, offices, gardens, churches," and other appropriate settings.[48]

His habitual flair for the dramatic joined with his no-nonsense practicality in solving the parking problem on narrow Manhattan streets. In 1938, one amazed witness described watching Steichen drive up to his building on East Sixty-ninth Street, open an immense door that doubled as a reception-room wall, and steer his roadster over the red-tiled floor, past his secretary's desk, and straight into "a vaulted studio the size of an old-fashioned stable."[49] As Matthew Josephson reported in *The New Yorker* in 1944, Steichen had "an oversize elevator, with huge doors, installed" in the building on East Sixty-third Street where he had a third-floor studio. "Visitors in the reception room of his studio would see the door of the elevator open suddenly, and Steichen would come driving out in a Ford roadster and park it near his reception desk." It was, Josephson wrote, "like a sequence in a Keystone Comedy."[50]

Steichen and Dana drove to Connecticut to spend long weekends, holidays, and most of each summer at Umpawaug. There they happily tended the flowers growing on the acres of undulating land that had been home to the Algonquin Indians before the seventeenth century.[51] Over time, Steichen and Dana designed and built their own house at Umpawaug, all angles and glass, framing the sweeping outdoor views. By the mid-thirties, Steichen had begun working a four-day week in New York so that he and Dana could spend the other three days with their flowers in the country. Dana gradually began to spend more of her time in Connecticut than in New York as the plant operations grew more demanding.

Until they were in their eighties, Steichen and his sister shared a passion for genetics—he in his flowers, luminous in the Connecticut sun, and she in finely bred silky-coated goats who produced record quantities of milk and even more finely bred offspring. Opa Steichen was no doubt the progenitor of their expertise. In their childhood years, they had happily followed their father around his own garden, inheriting from him a respectful knowledge of the rhythms of nature.

Steichen and Paula had become "sharks at genetics," Sandburg said of his brother-in-law and his wife.[52] Steichen was obsessed with breeding flowers in Connecticut, while out on the dunes of Lake Michigan, where the Sandburgs now lived year round, his sister was on the threshold of her own exhaustive, almost-compulsive experiments in heredity, breeding champion dairy goats. She had come to her interest in goats by happenstance. When their young daughter Helga had wanted a cow to raise in Michigan, the Sandburgs persuaded her that a goat would be less expensive and more portable. With her congenital stomach problems, Paula found it a happy bonus that goat's milk was far easier to digest than cow's milk, and she was soon making cheese and ice cream from the milk her goats produced in ever-growing abundance as her breeding expertise grew.

The Steichens and the Sandburgs enjoyed the story of a man in Goshen, Indiana, who bred gladioli until he produced a strain with ruffled petals, and who got kicked out of the Baptist church for "trying to improve on God's handiwork."[53] That, in essence, was the challenge that Steichen and his sister had embraced. They shared the belief that as evolutionary theory revealed more about elemental life, it inevitably illuminated and clarified some of the mystery of human life. "Flowers are just as gullible as human beings," Steichen said. "They respond to the same stimuli. I've learned more about people from flowers than from people."[54] For instance, Steichen and Paula believed that all growing creatures—people, animals, flowers, trees—responded to the same environmental stimuli: light, dark; heat, cold; water, drought; nurture, deprivation. If a carefully controlled optimal environment yielded healthy, strong, beautiful plants and animals, would not the same be true for human beings? If only you could breed the fear and destruction and sheer foolishness out of people! Steichen saw "no real hope" for improving the human race "until we start breeding them properly," he told a journalist in 1938. "But the tragedy is, nobody knows how to go about it, for nobody knows what to breed for—what to aim at."[55]

Disenchanted and disillusioned by human behavior—politics, war, unruly affairs of the heart—Steichen welcomed the retreat into life with his flowers. He was seldom happier than when he put on his worn khaki suit from Sears, Roebuck and a tattered hat and set out to spend the entire day in the fields. There he could obliterate imperfection and work patiently, peacefully, and single-mindedly toward the ideal, exerting his innate need for control. It was an impulse Paula shared. She had lost one child at birth, and, until she died at the age of ninety-four, would nurture two daughters who were disabled. Revealed in her passion for breeding animals was her desire to understand the choreography of heredity and environment, pattern and chance, to create perfection where she could.

After the long hiatus from plant breeding at Voulangis, Steichen had eagerly taken up the intricate work of breeding his flowers at Umpawaug. As was his way, he immersed himself in studies of heredity, reading every new and standard work on genetics and designing a master plan for growing delphiniums. When he and Dana said the last goodbye to Voulangis, he had carried back carefully selected seeds from his best plants. He then cultivated them in beds at Dana's family farm in New Jersey. One disastrous spring day, just as the seeds were sprouting, a hen and several chicks wandered out of their pen, pillaged the garden full of delphinium seedlings, and destroyed most of the plants. Steichen salvaged the rest, and he arranged for his old gardener François to ship more seeds from Voulangis. These Steichen planted in the Umpawaug gardens, adjacent to ten thousand plants grown from seeds he had purchased from delphinium specialists around the world.

Kate and many others knew his drive for perfection. "He ruthlessly goes among selected rows and aborts their growth," Sandburg wrote;

"yet even this he does seeking for the 'sports,' the individuals out of which may be created superior species."[56]

As the Steichens' delphinium operation became a major business, he began scavenging the catalogs of world flower markets, importing new seeds from wild delphinium species to cross with the plants he had developed in his gardens. The work was painstaking, slow, and discouraging, he told a journalist, full of dead ends and expensive defeats.[57] But Steichen was good at the work; under his skillful hands, new races of delphiniums were born, their soaring stalks and spires infused with vivid new colors.

Steichen could see clearly the "blue print of the ideal." He believed that with carefully designed and extravagantly implemented plans, he could create ever more beautiful flowers, surpassing the breed.[58] He was caught up in more than science and commerce, however. Ever since the early days at Voulangis, he had believed that breeding flowers was a "creative art" that used "living materials," eons in the making, to create poetry. He realized when he sifted the pollen grains of one flower onto the pistil of another, he was creating "new races of flowers," enthralled that "in a few hours, mutations of plant material were produced that might not occur in nature for a thousand years."[59] Still the difficult work of that creation was "microscopic," he believed, when compared to the effort it took for an artist to create in any other medium, including photography.[60]

Steichen thought of himself as an artist-breeder applying marvelous genetic discoveries to the "palette" of his garden. X rays and drugs such as colchicine could dramatically accelerate the evolution of chromosome structure, mutating plants in hours rather than eons. In the early thirties, Steichen began experimenting with colchicine at Umpawaug soon after botanists discovered that it could double plant chromosome counts. (As it happened, he had been prescribed colchicine, the then-standard treatment for gout.) One day, he confidently expected to produce a delphinium plant whose brilliant color and soaring height would live up to the blueprint he carried in his head. He was also committed to a second important goal: He would create a sturdy facsimile of that prototype delphinium so that it could be sold at any Woolworth store anywhere in the country for a dime a plant and could be easily grown by any home gardener. He had succeeded in mass-producing photography as art. Now he was plowing much of his income from photography into the black soil of Connecticut, stubbornly determined to mass-produce his flowers so that anybody could enjoy these living poems.

At Voulangis, the younger Steichen had played with flowers, achieving results by spontaneous luck as much as scientific experiment. At Umpawaug, he became an expert naturalist and scientist, happily absorbed in both the sheer physical labor of gardening and the intellectual excitement of contriving and experimenting to transcend the handiwork of nature. When his mother was dying, he had promised her that eventually he would enrich the world by creating the most beautiful delphiniums ever seen and making them available to everyone.[61] He invested huge sums of money in the endeavor, as well as infinite patience.[62] Other men indulged themselves with sailboats, motorboats, and cars, he noted.

Whether he was working as a photographer or a plant breeder, Steichen frequently said, he had learned to be "as determined as the tides of the sea and as patient as the Roman Catholic Church."[63]

28

VIOLATING EVERY RULE

(1 9 3 5 - 1 9 3 9)

In general... I've undertaken breeding delphiniums very much as I went about the study of photography years ago. I bought a camera textbook. Systematically, I violated every rule.[1]

—STEICHEN

IN 1935, STORIES OF ADOLF HITLER's treatment of the Jews in Germany begin to filter into the American national consciousness. "We were getting the news of Hitler's early humiliation of the Jews," Steichen remembered; "they were made to wear arm bands, their stores were labeled, their windows were smashed. I wanted one picture as a sort of answer to this."[2] At the time, Steichen was making several photographs for a fund-raising booklet for the Federation of Jewish Philanthropies. He saw this as a chance for the camera to be a mighty pen, transcribing photographically his ideals of social justice.

He wanted to counter the anti-Semitism of Hitler's Germany with a powerful image of the enduring strength of humanity, reverberating wih "a certain majesty."[3] Perhaps his own mother was the symbol for the photograph that resulted. "I asked for a white-haired, strongly built woman and a huge Bible," Steichen recalled. "She was brought to the studio dressed just as I photographed her in 'The Matriarch.' She couldn't understand my language, and I couldn't understand hers, so my communication with her was all in sign language; but she seemed to grasp it."[4] The final, widely reproduced image depicted a proud old woman stalwartly facing whatever future there might be, her hands, swollen with age and arthritis, resting on the gilt-edged pages of the Scriptures.

Steichen derived far more satisfaction from this kind of photographic work in the mid-thirties than from his fashion and celebrity photography. He was fifty-six years old in 1935, and the dean of Condé Nast photographers—a talented staff who could be flamboyant, egotistical, and demanding, as could their leader, Steichen himself. ("Some of the young men who have worked as his assistants in his studio half-reverently call him 'Goddo,'" a journalist reported.[5]) Other staff photographers included Charles Sheeler, with Steichen since the twenties; photographer and painter Man Ray; British photographer and designer Cecil Beaton; and Horst Bohrmann of Germany, who later changed his name to Horst P. Horst. In 1935, Horst was assigned to photograph the latest Paris designer fashions for the pages of *Vogue* in the United States.

Condé Nast and his editor in chief Edna Chase apparently were aware of Steichen's growing restlessness ("Always the same old line, the same old slogans," he began telling Dana after a time), yet they did not want him to feel at all displaced by Horst's growing visibility at *Vogue*.[6] "I have a feeling that we are often pressing you into sittings which do not really interest you," Mrs. Chase wrote sympathetically as well as diplomatically in 1935 after Horst was transferred to *Vogue* in New York. She conjectured that Steichen carried out many assignments "because you know our needs—and not because you find them stimulating or exciting. Also, because we have had so much space to cover and because of the exigencies of our budget, we have often asked you to take more things at a sitting than you have wanted to do. With Horst here, I think we could eliminate some of this kind of work, make the actual sittings easier, and get more exciting and distinguished ideas for your assignments."[7]

Steichen's reputation was embedded in the granite of public legend by then, and he had stayed with Condé Nast Publications longer than he had held to any one project or organization in the past, making a great deal of money in the process. If his workload grew easier because Horst was there from 1935 onward, all the better for the other projects that caught his fancy. He still enjoyed the challenge of photographing interesting people: Publisher Henry R. Luce; actor Charles Laughton; the far-sighted chairman of the New York State Council of Parks (1924–1962) Robert Moses; and playwright Luigi Pirandello were among the luminaries who sat for him in 1935.

All the while, Steichen was vigorously photographing nature—especially the "gaunt skeletons of chestnut trees" devastated by disease in the woodlands near Umpawaug.[8] His concern for the environment led him and Dana to make frequent journeys to Thoreau's Walden Pond over two years to photograph that setting in all four seasons. The photographs were used to illustrate a 1936 Limited Editions Book Club version of Henry David Thoreau's *Walden, or Life in the Woods* (1854). Without these outlets, Steichen knew, he could never have sustained his work at Condé Nast for all those years.

Kate Steichen visited her mother in 1935 at her cottage at "Casa Bleu & Blanc" in Puerto Pollensa, Majorca, and then met Carol Silverberg in Le Havre, en route to a vacation in Paris.[9] Clara was not in good health, suffering from the cold even when temperatures were mild, because surgery had left her with poor circulation in both legs, and her heart had "gone to smash."[10] And she was still outspoken in her disapproval of Kate's relationship with Carol.[11] She sat alone in her cottage in Majorca full of self-pity because it was a "bitter, stormy place," she could only afford fifteen dollars a month for rent, and she wanted to be in France. Nevertheless, she had decorated her rooms attractively in flowered yellow calico and native rush and straw furniture, covered the black-and-white-tiled floor with cheap old Majorcan goatskin rugs, and splashed big bowls of red geraniums against the high whitewashed walls.

Clara still longed for the old days in Voulangis. One by one, to raise money, she had sold the art treasures she had kept from her marriage—some of them hers with Steichen's blessing, and some taken from the house at Voulangis and never returned to him even after his successful court suit. She had already sold the Marin painting that used to hang above the bed she shared with Steichen, as well as a lovely watercolor and an oil by Matisse and a Rodin drawing. She had given Kate and Mary each a Brancusi sculpture and a Rodin bronze. Once when she ran out of funds, Clara had written to ask Kate to sell her Brancusi and send her the money.

"Reliable purchaser found for Brancusi," Kate had wired back immediately. "Will you accept three hundred dollars. Answer paid."[12]

Clara considered the offer, and she decided that Kate was trying to buy the statue herself with money she had inherited from Nell Pratt. Knowing that Kate had always loved the bird and that her birthday was approaching, Clara decided to let Kate buy the statue herself for her own birthday present.

"Yes," Clara wired. When the check came to Clara, it was from Steichen. "She had got him to pay that for her," Clara wrote to Stieglitz furiously. "She could have hung out for a little more."[13] But Steichen was in effect buying back his own possession, then giving it to his daughter.

In the mid-thirties, according to Clara, some of her French friends wanted to nominate her to receive the Legion of Honor, although it never came to pass. "I would have reverenced it—twas the sole honor I ever craved," she told Stieglitz. "I could see myself having it over my peace-at-last-head and tired old heart—and giving the decoration itself to my hometown." Having no idea about the technicalities of the award, and "ashamed," she said, "to ask how much it would cost to even keep in countenance with the Legion," she decided to seek the advice of Gertrude Stein, who had led the successful effort to have the Legion of Honor granted to Mildred Aldrich.[14] In Paris on a short visit, Clara called on "Stein, the Great in more ways than name."[15]

When the conversation inevitably turned around to Steichen, Stein held forth on how, in her judgment, Steichen was not really an artist. Yet when Clara passed on the rumor that he was earning a hundred thousand dollars a year, Stein seemed to change her opinion. In her view, Picasso, Matisse, or anyone else who earned a huge sum of money for his art had definitely proven his worth as an artist.

By 1935, Clara had come full circle in her attitude toward her two daughters. "I have great respect for Mary—none whatsoever for Kate or her Father—yet Kate is little short of a tragedy. Born a genius—she lacked the 'guts'—the WILL to suffer to live it and give it birth." She had grown to be "a small edition of her Father." He had contaminated Kate with his genes, his example, his money, even his family: "Got her

Violating Every Rule (1935–1939)

started on Sandburg junk—he who knew—much less felt—nothing of music. A mere poseur."[16]

Clara had been happy when she learned that Mary had divorced Lon Martin. From a distance, she adored her granddaughters, Nell and Linda. In New York and Connecticut, Steichen and Dana frequently saw the grandchildren, and Steichen doted on this new generation of girls in his family. In 1934, while thirty-year-old Mary took classes at Columbia University Medical School, she had decided because of her long hours away from them to put Nell and Linda in boarding school in Massachusetts, almost certainly with her father's financial help. Nell, the older child, was very much like Mary: "She looked like me and had a powerful personality," Mary remembered.[17] She missed Nell and Linda terribly, but she consoled herself with the thought that this temporary separation was necessary to secure their future.

In May of 1935, however, nine-year-old Nell had to be rushed to the hospital, where within just a few agonizing days she died of pneumonia. It was the one "crucifying death" in Mary's life.[18] Her grief was "unspeakable," Mary said. "I knew I had to live through that; get on top of it. But I was in the egotistical framework of 'Why did this happen to me?' 'Why this child?' This just fed into my sorrow and my bitterness and my anger that it should have happened."[19]

Steichen and Dana were distraught over the loss of his granddaughter. "She was a genius—if there ever was one," he said of Nell. "And, of course, a genius is somewhat of a problem child. But her mother was just getting everything worked out for her when the child contracted pneumonia, and—and went away from us. I learned another lesson in human endurance from that child. The doctors gave her up three times. And three times she rallied. She fought for her life superbly. But..."[20]

Just days after she buried her daughter, and still numb with shock, Mary had to take her exams at Columbia. A week later, she had to undergo gynecological surgery. Near physical and emotional collapse, she took Linda and went to stay with Dana and Steichen at Umpawaug. Mary spent the summer hating the world for taking her daughter. "Then one morning," she remembered, "I suddenly woke up and realized that my hands were reaching out to many, many mothers before me and after me; that I was just one in a long, long chain of mothers who had lost or who would lose their loved children. This put the whole thing in perspective for me. The reality of that began to help me find my balance."[21]

She resumed her medical studies, completing her degree at the University of Rochester Medical School in 1939, and then went on to further study on a Public Health fellowship. During that time, she met Dr. Frank Calderone, a "very brilliant and interesting person" a few years her senior.[22] He was "a health officer at the Lower East Side Health Center," she said, "and at the beginning of a distinguished medical career" that was to include the New York City Health Department, the World Health Organization, and the United Nations Secretariat Health Services.[23] They would marry in 1941, and later have two daughters, Francesca and Maria.

Clara was wild with grief when the cable arrived that May night in 1935 in Majorca to notify her of Nell's death. "The cable Sat-night brought a new sort of heartache to me—God—I thought I knew them all," she wrote to Stieglitz. "That precious little life—my poor Mary—so passionately adoring of her children. I can hardly say I knew the darling Nell—I can always say I tried so hard to. I sent gifts sometimes—and only this last Xmas were they acknowledged—a letter from Nell herself—my only one.... Sometimes I recall how that little line in '291' looked—'Clara Steichen-Mother-Voulangis.' "[24] She immediately wrote to Kate to urge Mary and Linda to come and stay with her while they recovered. Now Clara grieved intensely for the daughter she never saw, as well as the granddaughter she hardly knew. Later, she wrote to Mary that she had learned that only "time the kindest friend one can ever have would assuage your wound."[25]

Clara had only the old bitterness for Steichen, and now she took a macabre satisfaction in imagining his grief over Nell's death: "I feel today Steichen would give all his bestial enjoyments of his women—bring back to life his suicide—seek on his stubborn knees forgiveness of so many of us he has wronged ... if only he could bring back that sweet little soul ... he is helpless—and so be it, say I."[26]

In later years, Clara designed a memorial to Nell and had it installed in a church in Springfield, Missouri, the town she considered her permanent family home. She sketched the monument herself, with an angel encircled by a wreath at the top, just under the cross. She also composed the text: "In Memory of a Lovely Child . . . in the sweet belief that I shall be priviledged [sic] to know her in the presence of Him who called the children unto Him and blest them. . . ."²⁷

Throughout the thirties, Clara and Stieglitz continued to exchange occasional letters; Clara's long ones to him were full of the past, retreading the same old, embittering memories of life with Steichen, part rancor, part deep regret. She was troubled by news Stieglitz had written her of Georgia O'Keeffe's illness in the mid-thirties, and she hoped that O'Keeffe was still painting. She wrote to Stieglitz that at least O'Keeffe "hasnt [sic] failed you or herself—and you certainly never failed her. . . . I always loved her own way of weaving colors—flowing them—never torturing them—I at the same time always loathed that 'sex' stuff she labored like a woman in childbirth to put on canvas."²⁸

Art was important, of course, but for all women, Clara wistfully wrote, a home was "the finest monument of human endeavor."²⁹

After Nell's death, Steichen plunged back into work, always for him the most reliable solace. Businessman Tom Maloney, head of his own advertising agency, approached Steichen that year with the dream of founding and editing a journal to be called *U.S. Camera,* a photo annual similar to *Deutche Lichtbuilt* in Germany, and *Photographie* in France, handsome annual anthologies of the best photographs produced in each country during the current year. Maloney, also from Milwaukee, had created a dummy of the journal and arranged to take it to Steichen, "the most noted photographer in America."³⁰ He watched apprehensively as Steichen spent about fifteen minutes looking over the proposal.

Steichen liked the idea as well as this energetic young man from Milwaukee, and he agreed to help, so long as the project did not consume too much of his time. He even suggested a committee to select pictures for *U.S. Camera:* Dr. Agha from Condé Nast and photographers Charles Sheeler, Arnold Genthe, Anton Bruehl, Paul Outerbridge, and Larry Hiller. He himself would serve as chairman. The first hardcover issue of *U.S. Camera Annual* was a best-seller in 1935, favorably compared to the German and French annuals that had inspired it. For twenty-five years,

Maloney would edit the *U.S. Camera Annual,* as well as its offspring, the *U.S. Camera Magazine,* crediting Steichen's strong leadership and support for much of his success.

Steichen had his first one-man show at the Museum of Modern Art in 1936, exhibiting in an unorthodox medium: flowers. In the mid-thirties, he had served the American Delphinium Society as president and won international recognition for his splendid perennial delphiniums. Although he and Dana had experimented with poppies, lilies, and hemerocallis over the years at Umpawaug, delphiniums remained their passion and their greatest success.

They were hands-on farmers, working long hours in their fields, especially during flowering season. They now had the help of three full-time employees, year-round, with as many as four or five seasonal employees each summer. Because so much of his land was rocky, Steichen cherished the usable soil. He had achieved particular success with the flower beds he planted in a peat field, once a cranberry bog. He dynamited huge ditches around the perimeter to drain the field, which was flat as a pancake, and then dug out the swamp maples and underbrush, prepared the rich soil, and laid in his seed, which grew beautifully in that special bed. By contrast, he and his assistants had to pulverize the rocky soil in his conventional fields down to eight or ten inches, using a power tiller. It was impractical to go much deeper. Keeping meticulous records, Steichen fed and irrigated the plants, believing that water was probably more important than plant food in average soil.[31] His plants were vulnerable to the bitter winters, but he preferred to risk loss to freezing than to incur greater loss from covering his plants and having them rot.

Steichen and Dana worked in the fields together, labored together over their plant-breeding records, and endlessly discussed the intricate decisions to be made, season after season. They believed it was within their grasp to achieve a rainbow's gamut of colors for their lavish delphiniums—red, salmon, pink, orange, yellow, copper, tan, even more vivid blues. They relished the beauty of the tall, graceful spears and luxuriant blooms, but they made dispassionate, scientific decisions about which would survive to parent the next generation of seedlings. About one plant in a thousand passed muster. They knew their flowers so well, their idiosyncrasies, their history, their potential, that Steichen compared himself to the old woman who lived in the shoe—except that he had fifty thousand "children."[32]

He told an interviewer that he had undertaken breeding delphiniums about the same way that he had taken up the study of photography—reading the appropriate textbook and then deliberately breaking the rules.[33] He likened his experiment photographing the cup and saucer a thousand times to his decision to grow delphiniums by the thousands, not the hundreds.

When *Better Homes & Gardens* published a feature on his delphiniums in 1938, Steichen contributed a color photograph for the cover and he and Dana posed in the fields with their glorious delphiniums, some of them soaring seven feet tall.[34] The article recounted details of the 1936 exhibit at the Museum of Modern Art (MoMA)—the "floral bombshell" that drew crowds of horticulturists, art patrons, and folks just curious to see what all the fuss was about.[35] Once more, Steichen was stretching the boundaries of artistic expression during a period when there was intense debate about the essential character and boundaries of modern art. The Steichens' 1936 delphinium show marked the first time that living material had ever been exhibited as art at MoMA, or perhaps in any other American art museum.

Steichen's Delphinium in 1936 had "Hollywood adjectives hanging on the ropes," one journalist wrote. "Seven-foot spikes with five feet in flower; magnificent pure blue selfs [meaning a flower of a single color], purples, whites, exquisite clear hues; individual florets measuring three inches or more...; strong, wiry spikes and laterals... you never saw such healthy flowers in your life."[36] The show lasted for eight days at the Museum of Modern Art in late June of 1936. As the week wore on, the stunning display of flowers was freshened and updated with more exquisite delphiniums newly plucked from the gardens and trucked in from Umpawaug. Steichen estimated that during that week he showed five hundred to a thousand delphinium spears of various colors in three small galleries on the ground floor of the Rockefeller House at 11 West Fifty-third Street, the museum's first home, before the present building was erected on the same site. The show revealed the artful beauty of the flowers, first of all, and then a fascinating dimension of Steichen the artist, not to mention the adventurous, if controversial, spirit of the Museum of Modern Art.

Art or not, it was a gorgeous spectacle, even to the eye untrained in horticulture. Steichen was pleased that some viewers wept, and that more than forty newspapers in seventeen states paid attention to the show. That, in his view, implied that flower breeding had been officially recognized as one of the arts. A Chicago critic suggested that if "sticks and stones, bits of newspapers and other objects suggested by the 'cult of the ugly' can be pasted on the canvases of Picasso, Braque, Duchamp and Picabia and called 'art,'" then so could beautiful flowers.[37] The flowers themselves got rave reviews from horticulturists and novices alike. The garden editor of the New York *Herald Tribune* called it "the most amazing exhibit of delphinium we have ever seen in this country by one man or by all men and women put together. Here one man has proven again that with nature, almost anything is possible."[38]

One of those beautiful hybrids had been named Carl Sandburg, and Steichen photographed his brother-in-law with the elegant tall spires of his namesake. In a playful barter, Steichen named other hybrids, his living poems, after poets—Archibald MacLeish, Paul Claudel, and William Carlos Williams. In exchange, they wrote poems about delphiniums. In fact, Sandburg actually wrote more than one poem about flowers, Steichen's and Paula's, leaving among his papers at his death a suite of ten short unfinished poems entitled "Experiments Toward a Poem on Delphiniums."[39]

At the time of his exhibition, Steichen was serving on the MoMA Advisory Committee on Photography, so he knew something about the programs and the budget at the fledgling institution, founded in 1929.[40] He paid for the exhibition himself—a total of $203.45—relished its success, and realized, too late, that it had cost him his anonymity as a plant breeder. For years, he had worked in seclusion, protecting his plants and his privacy at Umpawaug. Now in the aftermath of the exhibition, Steichen was so distracted by outside demands for his flowers that his work at Umpawaug suffered dramatically that summer and fall. From then on, he was deluged with requests for seedlings and advice, and he felt compelled to run a public statement in the trade journal *Delphinium:* "To obviate unnecessary correspondence, please note that STEICHEN DELPHINIUMS are still in the process of development. They will not be released until the standard that has been set for them in a definite breeding program has been achieved to the satisfaction of their author."[41]

In the mid-thirties, Steichen and Sandburg still encountered criticism for their 1929 discussion of the merits of commercial photography. They had coined their own gleeful names for their critics; the "art for art's sake boys in the trade," Steichen named them.[42] Sardonically elongating every syllable, Sandburg called them the "Abracadabra Boys." The two men were then elbow-deep in their crusade to advance the concept of democratic art. If they made money in the process, that was all right, too, because for more than half their lives, poverty was a condition they had known all too well. Now in the 1930s, Sandburg was widely hailed as the poet of the people, his name a household word. And thanks to the vast circulation of the Condé Nast magazines, Steichen was the photographer of both the elite and of the masses.

Some of his pictures had already become cultural icons, especially his portraits of such famous actors as Greta Garbo, John Barrymore, Gary Cooper, and Lillian Gish, and world leaders such as Winston Churchill and Franklin Roosevelt. Moreover, his fellow photographers abroad still considered him an artist of the first rank, for he had been elected an Honorary Fellow of the Royal Photographic Society of Great Britain in 1931.

Steichen's work reached people in ways he could not have imagined. A young black porter on the 400, the fast train between Chicago and Minneapolis, found that one benefit of the job was getting to read the magazines his passengers left on the train. He had played basketball on a black semipro team, but he had big dreams of becoming a photographer, and he had recently acquired his first Kodak camera. Admiring the work of Steichen and other photographers, he imagined seeing his own pictures in magazines.[43] This young man was Gordon Parks, and later on, when others closed doors in his face because he was black, Roy Stryker, for whom he had worked at the Farm Security Administration, sent him to Steichen. He found Steichen one day "wolfing down a huge corned beef sandwich," but Steichen was willing to listen to Parks's plight.

"The son of a bitch," Steichen roared after Parks told him how the art director at one magazine had shunned him because of his race.[44] Steichen immediately sent him to Alexander Liberman, who had joined the staff of *Vogue* in 1941 and became its art director in 1943. Liberman hired Parks to work at *Glamour,* the new Condé Nast journal designed to interpret "fashion, beauty, and charm in terms of the average woman's daily needs" and to "do for Hollywood what *Vogue* has done so magnificently for Paris and New York."[45]

By the late thirties, Steichen had become an institution at Condé Nast Publications, known for his virtuoso camera work, his demanding insistence on perfection, even his trademark wide-brimmed black Stetson hat. He had been around so long that some of the deliverymen who worked for Condé Nast Publications had actually taken to calling him "Old Man Vogue Himself."[46] But by 1937, the "Old Man" was deeply restless, searching for new challenges. As had been true for him in 1906 and again in the late 1920s, he worried that his clients now expected him to replicate time and again the same old Steichen style. He realized that he was churning out portraits that were becoming mechanical, and subsequently he feared that a "certain kind of dishonesty" was seeping into his work.[47] In essence, he felt smothered by his own great success.

Whenever possible, he had converted his studio into the stage on which his subjects could perform—Martha Graham pantomiming dance poses, because the camera was too slow to record her in motion; Paul Robeson, or Katharine Cornell, or Gloria Swanson, or W. C. Fields improvising; Lillian Gish moving magically before the camera, as if it were an admiring audience. Clare Boothe Brokaw had written in *Vanity Fair* in 1932 that Steichen "often appears to—and probably does—fall in love with his sitters, but the moment the last plate is exposed his ardour abruptly cools."[48] But now, Steichen seldom felt that ardor, even temporarily.

And he was finding his advertising assignments even more stultifying than the portrait work. Because his agreements with Condé Nast and J. Walter Thompson had left him entirely free to work for anyone except Hearst, Steichen had over the years taken on contracts with other major advertising agencies, including N. W. Ayer & Son, Lennen & Mitchell, and Geyer, Cornell & Newell. At *Vogue* all these years, he had worked with some of the highest-paid, most visible fashion models of the day, but for J. Walter Thompson and the other ad agencies, he still chose un-

Violating Every Rule (1935–1939)

known models with ordinary lives—the office worker, for instance, whom he hired as a hand model for Jergens lotion. Sometimes he photographed the products only: Sandburg reported that Steichen could devote a whole afternoon to posing a container of Pond's skin freshener and tonic against a background of mirrors and white jonquils, or photographing oblong white flakes of Lux soap.

He had enjoyed his lucrative fifteen-year-long association with Condé Nast and with J. Walter Thompson and his other agency clients, and he and Dana were grateful for it, but Steichen was tired now of working for other people. He had begun to resent the unending technical and production labor essential to carry his workload and sustain his success. A key ingredient of a masterful Steichen photograph had always been his genius in the darkroom, and even an uninformed eye can perceive the difference between the prints Steichen made and reproductions of his photographs by others. An inventory of the way he spent his time in 1937 revealed that he was giving 80 percent of his working hours to the production details required for photo sessions and only 20 percent to taking and processing pictures.

He was hungry for more time with the camera, and for further refinement of his skills, and that took concentration and experimentation. In 1937, nearly sixty, his head was as full as ever of dreams, projects, and potential photographic experiments. He was too young, he felt, to retire, but he wanted to leave Condé Nast and the advertising accounts and move on to something entirely new. The financial future seemed manageable, if not secure, for the Depression had treated Steichen more kindly than it had many other Americans, and his old friend Eugene Meyer—a financial wizard long before his Depression years' service as governor of the Federal Reserve—had skillfully guided Steichen's investments. He was free to choose his future, and he and Dana ultimately decided that he would close his New York studio on January 1, 1938, in effect marking the end of his work with fashion and advertising photography, and almost all other commercial work.

In recent years, he had grown especially weary of the machinations of advertising photography, finding the emerging sexist content especially distasteful—as if a woman could not win or keep a man's love without using certain products. "Among these were the sex appeal approaches designed to sell lotions or cosmetics or hair preparations by implying that a girl stood no chance of finding a mate unless she used these products," Steichen complained.[49] The very issue of *Vogue* that announced his retirement in January of 1938 carried some of the advertising themes he found offensive: "Keeping the vibrant beauty in your face, may well mean keeping the happiness in your life," ran the text for an advertisement for Marie Earle creams and emulsions.[50] In that same issue, women were offered "Nine Beauty Resolutions for the New Year" by Helena Rubinstein Cosmetics, to save them from wrinkles, aging eyes, "crepey, lined necks," old-looking hands, dull, lifeless skin, the tired, drawn look—so that they could stay young, smooth, graceful, soft, beautiful, glowing, radiant, and alluring in perpetuity.[51]

None of the advertising photographs in that January 1938 issue of *Vogue* was taken by Steichen, but he must surely have been unhappy with the use made of his lovely photograph of a model in a chiffon Marganza dress. His photograph accompanied an article called "Models Made to Order," which revealed how the Models Preferred Agency could take "nice-looking girls and women ... good working material" and in just six weeks enable them to "emerge, poised, groomed, moving with assurance and grace, their figures remodeled, their faces revamped. And, in the interim, they are trained like race-horses."[52] Steichen had always recoiled at the idea of photographing women as objects, especially "remodeled" or "revamped" or "trained" objects. Yes, it was clearly time to move on.

The advertising industry recognized the body of Steichen's achievements as a commercial photographer when he was honored with the 1938 Silver Medal at the national Advertising & Selling Awards, formerly the Harvard Advertising Awards, for raising the artistic quality of advertising, "both through his productions and his influence," and for setting new standards of art in the ad campaigns he mounted for Cannon Mills, Steinway pianos, Woodbury soap, Eastman Kodak, and Community Plate. "In each case," the citation read, "his pictures evoke strong emotional suggestion, artfully adapted to the subject."[53] Both the Woodbury and the Cannon Mills campaigns featured graceful photographs of the same nude model, her face bathed in light, her body framed from the waist up, her breasts demurely concealed—a nude study in the soft, lyrical, artistic style of his earliest nude photographs in Paris thirty-five years previously—yet these were risqúe photographs for an advertising campaign in the 1930s.

Now Steichen was free to embark on one more apprenticeship, this time with color photography. Ever since his experiments with the Lumière plates in 1907, he had found color tantalizing, and the available color processes disappointing. In 1932, Condé Nast had engaged German-born photographer Anton Bruehl and color technician Fernand Bourges to collaborate on producing excellent color plates for *Vogue,* bestowing on Steichen the chance to create the first color photograph ever for a *Vogue* cover. His landmark picture had appeared in July 1932—a gorgeous study of a model clad in a vivid red bathing suit, holding a beach ball up to a sparkling blue sky. Despite this success, and the debut of Eastman Kodak's Kodachrome color film in 1935, Steichen was still positive that better color processes could be devised. He dismissed contemporary color photographs on the grounds that they were just a step past hand-tinted prints; he planned to experiment in the late 1930s, as he had just after the turn of the century, in hopes of extending the range and fidelity of color.

In 1938, *Popular Photography* pronounced Edward Steichen a living legend—and an "out-and-out crusty" one who disdained to talk to reporters. He was the best-known photographer in the United States, and probably the best-known delphinium breeder in the world. When he lectured to the New York Horticultural Society in 1937, there was such a clamor for tickets that organizers moved the usually modest event to the Park Central Hotel ballroom, which still could not accommodate everyone who wanted to hear Steichen.

In his late fifties, he was "a thin, tall man with lively, greying hair and a reticence of speech and manner which melted into quick laughter that creased his face with a hundred tiny smiles, and stayed in his eyes long after he had stopped smiling," *Vogue* journalist Margaret Case Harriman told readers of the magazine in 1938. "He never talked very much, but, when he did, he spoke decisively in an accent that was pure American."[54] When the editor of *Popular Photography* assigned journalist Rosa Reilly to interview Steichen, she searched for some background on the famous photographer. She had heard people call him a genius, and some thought that, like most geniuses, he could be temperamental and brusque. Reilly read what she could find about Steichen, including Sandburg's *Steichen the Photographer,* and concluded, with relief, that Steichen was human, "not the crabbed, barbed-wire crank he is represented to be."[55]

When she met Steichen in his studio, she found him "more violently alive than any personality" she had ever encountered. He had gray hair, "brittle blue" eyes shining with humor, or with "heat lightning," and a mouth etched with "hunger, misunderstanding, hopelessness, dissatisfaction with his work, his world, himself." As he had done for decades with other people, he talked to her about his obsession with " 'that old charlatan' light."[56] And why was he closing up his studio? she asked before she left. Because, he said, he was tired of taking orders.

"A scientist and a speculative philosopher stands back of Steichen's best pictures," Sandburg wrote.[57] Some later critics suggested that there was too much science and glossy technique and not enough heart in Steichen's photographs. In the late thirties, he himself knew that his skilled hands rather than his deep heart had been propelling much of his recent work. That is why he chose to go in a different direction after 1938, deciding as he had done before to give himself a "kick in the pants" before someone else did.[58]

But first he needed a long rest, and he and Dana wanted to travel. The Carl Zeiss Company helped equip Steichen with a sleek, lightweight 35-mm Contax camera. He stocked up on the new Kodachrome film, and he and Dana set out on an idyllic, two-month-long expedition to Mexico, feeling like honeymooners. There were enthralling new vistas to photograph under the startlingly bright Mexican sun. Steichen, this "legend in the photographic world," was not really retiring, Rosa Reilly wrote. He was merely "transplanting himself" to Yucatán, "where, under warm and luminous tropical skies, he will study the ancient Maya civilization and continue the pursuit of his lifelong mistress—*light.*"[59]

He had told Sandburg in 1929 that he was only beginning as a photographer, that he was still in his apprenticeship, that he did not expect to be any good until he was sixty-five or seventy.[60] He was only fifty-nine in 1938, not retiring, he insisted, but seeking once again to give himself a "revitalizing change," and to "move into new areas."[61] And he was not about to be written off as a legend, flattering as that might be to other artists. Steichen took such adoring talk impatiently: "What do you think

VIOLATING EVERY RULE (1935–1939)

I am—some god sitting up on Olympian heights talking down to people?" he protested to one journalist who too effusively admired his work. "I'm not. I'm just a plain photographer—like the rest—still trying to learn. I've been trying to learn for forty years."[62]

Steichen's retirement was international news, with a *Time* magazine writer noting, "If Chrysler Corp. were to retire from the automobile industry or Metro-Goldwyn-Mayer from the cinema, the event would be more surprising but no more interesting to either business than Steichen's retirement was to his." Furthermore, according to the *Time* report, when Steichen told Alfred Stieglitz that he was leaving commercial photography, "the impresario of 'An American Place' was so pleased he could scarcely speak."[63]

The *Time* reporter who interviewed Steichen saw a "bubbling, generous, rather boyish man" with long gray hair and spectacles who had long ago become the highest-paid photographer in the United States. But, the journalist suggested, a younger generation of photographers—such as Berenice Abbott, Edward Weston, Paul Strand, Ralph Steiner, Walker Evans—now found Steichen's photographs dated—too painterly and unrealistic, his "love of lighting effects and studio magic" somewhat "stagy."[64]

Steichen was embarking on new adventures, however. With his newly unfettered life, his new featherweight portable camera, and his alluring Kodachrome film, he set out early in 1938 to explore Mexico, excited as a boy. He was enchanted by the statuesque Tehuana women of the Isthmus of Tehuantepec. In the Yucatán, he photographed the gentle, animated faces of the Mayan Indians, living replicas of the faces he saw carved in their ancient frescoes. For two months, he and Dana tramped through ruins, bombarding archaeologists with questions. They came away refreshed and invigorated by a journey into new landscapes and ancient history.

The Mexican odyssey deepened Steichen's knowledge and understanding of a particular culture and its past, and, consequently, of the universal impulses most cultures share—for discovery and invention, for science, for survival, for community, for art, for love. As part of the celebration of his fifty-ninth birthday, spent in Mexico, Steichen stopped smoking, but unfortunately, Dana continued the habit. They went home to Connecticut trim and tan and deeply refreshed, ready to savor the lessons learned in the exotic landscapes of Mexico.

In February, Carl Sandburg's face had appeared on the cover of Henry Luce's *Life* with the caption "Sandburg Sings American."[65] As Steichen closed out the fifteen-year-long chapter of his career as a commercial photographer, Sandburg neared the end of thirteen years of work on his four-volume epic, *Abraham Lincoln: The War Years*. The brothers-in-law were each figuratively "singing American" at the end of the thirties, sharing visions of how to chronicle the American dream, which had originally led their parents to the United States, with all its promise, illusion, and hope.

Helga Sandburg believed that her uncle and her father, two "blood brothers," came to share a deep awareness of their mortality in the late thirties. With that came the strong desire to "finish their work while holding on to their health...."[66] Steichen especially admired Sandburg's "Americanization work," as Sandburg called his driving mission in the twenties and thirties. His book-length poem, *The People, Yes,* was a vast American mural in words, almost photographic in its sometimes bitterly realistic images of Americans during the Depression. In his poetry and prose, as well as in *The American Songbag* (1927), Sandburg had collected American voices in slang and song, and American history in the Lincoln work. Now Steichen wanted to have his own say about the American experience—using the language of photography.

That close-knit trio, Edward, Carl, and Paula, believed more than ever in the power of democratic art to transform life, and in the responsibility of the artist to address the issues of the times. Paula told Steichen and Dana that Sandburg was moved to tears, day and night, by "all the trouble of the World."[67] And as the nation moved inexorably closer to war, Sandburg wrote that Steichen himself embodied the American dream. "Property is nothing. Toils, hardships, and dangers are little or nothing to him alongside the American Dream. He is no particular hand at patriotic speeches, but he has some mystic concept of this country and its flag."[68]

Yet other, younger photographers led the way at the end of the thir-

VIOLATING EVERY RULE (1935-1939)

ties in turning the camera to the American condition. As Beaumont Newhall noted in *The History of Photography,* the Depression provoked a new realism in photography and in motion pictures. Both still and movie cameras recorded haunting images of Americans swept under by the great tidal wave of the Depression. This movement in photography was launched in part when President Roosevelt founded the Resettlement Administration in 1935 to help Dust Bowl farmers and other agricultural workers displaced by natural disaster or by new agricultural machinery. Undersecretary of Agriculture Rexford G. Tugwell was put in charge of the RA, and he chose his former student, Roy E. Stryker, to serve as chief of the Historical Section of the agency. Just as government historians made meticulous photographic records of military operations, Stryker was directed to compile a detailed photographic document of the problems of American farm life, as well as of the efforts of the Resettlement Administration to improve the lot of American farm workers and their families. The organization was absorbed into the Department of Agriculture in 1937 and renamed the Farm Security Administration, or the FSA, "one of the so-called alphabet departments of the U.S.A.," Steichen teased.[69]

The FSA photographers compiled an unprecedented photographic mural of America, massive in scale as well as in fidelity to the infinite homely details of human misery. Dorothea Lange, Walker Evans, Ben Shahn, John Vachon, Arthur Rothstein, Marion Post Wolcott, Carl Mydans, and others collaborated in a stunning composite of American life in the thirties. Stryker, not a photographer himself, oversaw his staff with keen sensitivity for their craft and for the process they were, in a sense, inventing as they went along. He looked at documentary photography as "an approach, not a technique," whose purpose was "to speak, as eloquently as possible, of the things to be said in the language of pictures."[70]

Steichen was one of thousands to visit the International Photographic Exposition in New York's Grand Central Station in 1938 to look at more than three thousand pictures, the largest collection of photographs ever assembled in one exhibition in New York. More than any other part of the show, the gripping, even agonizing pictures by the FSA photographers stirred emotion and controversy, and Steichen was deeply moved by what he saw. On display were unforgettable images of the times: Walker Evans's haunting picture of the empty plates held in the waiting hands of flood refugees; Dorothea Lange's *Sharecroppers,* an image of three figures toiling in an Alabama farm field.

Steichen called the FSA photographs "a series of the most remarkable human documents that were ever rendered in pictures." They were "charged with human dynamite," telling stories with such power, Steichen observed, that technical questions about lenses, film, and exposures were irrelevant. The unforgettable was contained in the indelible "weird, hungry, dirty, lovable, heartbreaking" images. These FSA photographers had so vividly captured living experience on film that Steichen praised their collective work as a "unique and outstanding achievement."[71]

As soon as possible, he devoted most of an issue of *U.S. Camera Annual* to a cross section of the images, accompanied by his own informal history of events leading up to the FSA photographs. Writing somewhat defensively of the "glibness" of writers who dissected and analyzed various stages and types of photography, Steichen arrived at the conclusion that the "beginning of photography and the end of photography is documentation, and that's that." He gave his full endorsement to the power and beauty of the FSA photographs exhibited in New York, however. He also noted with some satisfaction that the " 'art for art's sake' boys in the trade were upset, for these documents told stories and told them with such simple and blunt directness that they made many a citizen wince."[72]

As he contemplated the FSA pictures in those turbulent prewar days, Steichen ruminated on the possibility of another new "apprenticeship." He was analyzing the potential of documentary photography: It could simply report an objective, realistic story—or it could be selectively, deliberately, editorially utilized as propaganda—for positive as well as negative purposes. "Pictures in themselves are very rarely propaganda," he pointed out. "It is the use that is made of pictures that makes them propaganda."[73] During the coming decades, Steichen would use his camera masterfully to document and to report. He would also do more than any other single photographer to turn the art of photography into a powerful instrument of forceful, positive propaganda.

The young Steichen had labored over his artful pictures of particular landscapes, single faces, still-life objects. The mature Steichen, approaching his sixties, was now eager to compose on a grander, epic scale. In the late thirties, he began to dream of creating a huge photographic

VIOLATING EVERY RULE (1935-1939)

exhibition devoted to the spirit and face of America. He wanted to hold it at Grand Central Station. He would cover those cavernous walls with images of America.[74] He would express America to itself.

———

There were some idyllic days for Steichen and Dana before war changed the world again. At Umpawaug, they decided to build their dream house. Soon after they bought the land, Steichen and Dana had erected a prefabricated house at Umpawaug and it had served them well enough during the years when they migrated from Manhattan to Connecticut and back to the city. But, once Steichen "retired" and Umpawaug became their permanent home, they began to design and build a larger house. It was going to function first as a studio and then as a house to live in, Steichen often said.[75] One of the last visitors to their prefab cottage was Sandburg, hiding away to correct page proofs for the mammoth Lincoln biography.

When Sandburg came to breakfast the morning after he had corrected the last page proof, he looked "serene and relaxed," as if the years had fallen away. Steichen was by then something of an expert on Civil War photography, having advised Sandburg and accompanied him on some of his searches into such important Lincoln collections as the one gathered by Frederick Hill Meserve. As he looked at his brother-in-law that morning, he was reminded of Gardner's rare photograph of the relieved, smiling Lincoln on the day after the surrender at Appomattox. Sandburg's expression evoked Lincoln's smile of "infinite warmth and tenderness" in the Gardner image.[76]

Steichen got his camera and caught Sandburg in several moods that September morning, each so striking that he wove them into a montage of six exposures, which became the most celebrated photographic image ever made of Sandburg. It was a miniature "mural" of the multiple facets of Sandburg's work and character: He was the conspicuous poet of the people; the biographer of Lincoln and others, including Steichen; the folk musician and folklorist; the writer of fiction for children; the nationally known journalist, whose newspaper columns and radio broadcasts served as his podium on national and international issues; the father and husband, and Steichen's "blood brother." The photograph was reproduced in *Vanity Fair* and elsewhere many times over the years, and when Sandburg was asked to supply a picture of himself, his favorite choice was always Steichen's *Montage*. (He also favored some tender photographs that Dana made, for she had continued to refine her own skill as a talented photographer over the years.)

By January of 1939, Steichen reported to the Sandburgs that he and Dana hoped to break ground on the new house by the first of February.[77] After they had conceived the basic plan, Steichen hired the architectural firm of Evans, Moore and Woodbridge of New York to execute the design. The Steichens had long admired the stark planes and angles of houses designed by Frank Lloyd Wright, and he and Dana wanted comparable spacious expanses of glass to set off the Umpawaug vistas of woods, hills, and water. They wanted flowing, open spaces within the house. One of the architects reported that Steichen would have built the house as one single large room had that been feasible.[78]

At the heart of the house was a large living room with floor-to-ceiling windows, fourteen-foot-high ceilings, and alcoves set under lower ceilings for dining or working. One corner of the living room opened as a porch, thanks to movable accordion steel wall sections. The exterior of the house was constructed of glass and gray-stained cypress. Inside, there were white plaster walls interspersed with walls paneled in California pine and Duali plywood, with the same woods used for built-in cabinets and furniture. Steichen and Dana's bedroom was set apart by a configuration of hallway, bathroom, and closet. There was a thirteen-by-nineteen-foot studio for Steichen, with its own balcony, and the adjoining garage could be converted into additional studio space if he needed it.[79] On the ground floor of the house were two bedrooms and two baths. Their home overlooked the sparkling pond Steichen had christened Jergens, after the hand lotion that had paid for its creation.

Sandburg described the finished structure, surrounded by woods and hills and "tens of thousands of delphinium plants": It was a "house of glass walls overlooking pond lilies where giant frogs croak in August midnights, its waterfalls leaping tall boulders, and one skyline where every spring the mystic white shadblow says greeting to hard-rock palisades...."[80]

It was striking and modern, an artist's house, simultaneously beautiful and functional. The house was featured in the February 1944 issue of Condé Nast's magazine *House & Garden,* in an issue forecasting the future of American homes. The magazine's cover contained a line from Abraham Lincoln: "I like to see a man proud of the place in which he lives. I like to see a man live so that his place will be proud of him."[81]

The Umpawaug guest quarters were frequently occupied by Mary, Linda, Kate, and Carol. When energetic Paula Sandburg broke away from her burgeoning goat farm to take a rare vacation, she visited her brother and Dana, and Sandburg was often in residence. Steichen and Dana enjoyed having the house full, and it was by all accounts a happy home, usually filled with music. Dana had a passion for Beethoven, studied his life as avidly as she listened to his music, collected copies of letters, musical scores, books, and other documents pertaining to his life. She hoped someday to write a book about the composer.

Like many American families, the Steichens gathered around the radio every Sunday afternoon to listen to the NBC Symphony Orchestra, conducted by the great Arturo Toscanini. Steichen, however, elevated listening to a science and an art form, even building an innovative radio and phonograph system for his house. With that project, he achieved such remarkable fidelity that vocalists, hearing their own records on Steichen's invention, told him that he made their voices sound better than they actually were. He was a "musical purist," Carol Silverberg remembered, who would not "permit acoustical interference of any kind to interfere with his reception of that exquisite music."[82] Ten minutes before the broadcast began, Steichen and Dana turned off every noise-making appliance in the house—the furnace, the water pump, even the refrigerator. The telephone was taken off its hook. Steichen demanded total silence for the duration of the concert, even if food spoiled a little and people had to shiver as the house grew cold.

The Steichens and the Sandburgs shared a lifelong delight in holidays, especially Christmas and Thanksgiving. When the two families could not celebrate Christmas in the same place, they sent gifts and letters. Paula now made Oma's traditional Christmas cake, wrapped it carefully, and shipped it to her brother shortly before Christmas. He teased in a letter of thanks that after he had eaten a generous slice of her cake, downed with some brandy, he could perform any feat her rambunctious goats could perform—"except give milk."[83] Another Christmas, when Paula sent plum pudding, it was pronounced the greatest plum pudding in history, while the fruitcake had managed to surpass all previous magnificent fruitcakes, becoming the finest fruitcake in the stratosphere.

Dana and Steichen loved having Mary, Linda-Joan (as Steichen called his granddaughter), and Kate and Carol home for holidays. They dined at a long table set near the tall windows in the living room, looking out over the trees and the pond, where wood ducks and mallards lived year-round. Once the Thanksgiving turkey ceremoniously arrived at the table, Steichen played the Don Cossack Chorus's recording of the Lord's Prayer, sung in Russian. Then he walked to the end of the table, kissed Dana, and, with a flourish, began to carve the turkey. After dinner, to cheers and applause, Steichen entertained with his standard rendition of "The Wreck of the Hesperus," accompanied, friends remembered, by the elocution gestures he had learned as a Milwaukee schoolboy.

And there were the luxurious private hours, sitting in the sunlit living room listening to music, watching the light glisten on the smooth face of the pond, or walking together over the quiet acres of their farm, surrounded by flowers. In Dana and Umpawaug, Steichen found peace, found home.

29

A REAL IMAGE OF WAR

(1 9 3 9 - 1 9 4 3)

My own feelings of revulsion toward war had not diminished since 1917. But, in the intervening years, I had gradually come to believe that, if a real image of war could be photographed and presented to the world, it might make a contribution toward ending the specter of war.[1]

—STEICHEN

LIKE MILLIONS OF CONCERNED AMERICANS, ED and Dana Steichen turned on their radio on September 3, 1939, to hear President Franklin Delano Roosevelt's Fireside Chat. His reassuring words reverberated from radio sets and consoles all across the country. In Harbert, Michigan, on the shores of Lake Michigan, the Sandburgs tuned in, and Opa Steichen, six years a widower, listened as he smoked his pipe in his quiet, empty house in Elmhurst, Illinois. One listener in Bennington, Vermont, was Clara Smith Steichen, a war refugee for the second time in her life, having been forced, like other Americans living abroad, to return to the United States. She had apparently chosen Bennington because she had hospitable friends there. ("Stieglitz—could I ever be lucky enough to again possess a copy of the Steichen number of Camera Work?" she wrote that fall to the old friend whom she had visited on her way through New York. "I havent [sic] even a photo of myself—or the children as children—nothing to show but memories, for all the years...."[2])

Just as radio had been the national lifeline for coverage of the Depression, it was the international link for ongoing news of the war in Europe. Their sophisticated radio set in Connecticut connected the Steichens to a global community, albeit a conflicted one, and on the September broadcast they heard the President reiterate his hope that the United States could stay out of the war in Europe. Still he warned that "the peace of all countries everywhere is in danger" and that "every word that comes through the air, every ship that sails the sea, every battle that is fought, does affect the American future."[3]

Within months, however, Mussolini had declared war on Britain and France, and the Germans invaded Denmark and Norway, as well as the vulnerable little countries of Holland and Belgium—and Steichen's own Luxembourg. The proliferating chaos in Europe spurred aggressive preparedness efforts in the United States: In 1940 Roosevelt pressed for an unprecedented $1.8 billion defense budget, established the Office of Emergency Management, and began to organize a peacetime army. When Congress passed the Selective Training and Service Act in 1940, more than 16 million American men received registration notices for the first peacetime draft in American history.

That fall, gravely concerned about world events—and far too old for the draft at age sixty-one—Steichen nevertheless decided to try to reactivate his World War I status as a reserve officer. He was "eager to participate in creating a photographic record of World War II," he wrote, and he turned to his old friend Eugene Meyer, hoping he might pull some strings in Washington.[4] In the wake of the stock market crash of 1929, President Hoover had persuaded Meyer to join the Federal Reserve Board, and then to serve as its chairman. In 1931, Meyer had conceived the Reconstruction Finance Corporation to help stabilize the world economy, and for a time he chaired both the RFC and the Federal Reserve Board. In 1933, he had offered newly elected President Roosevelt his resignation as Federal Reserve governor, and he was generally praised for his effective work stemming the tide of the Depression.

After President Roosevelt accepted his resignation, Meyer had briefly and unhappily retired, nearly driving his wife, Agnes, crazy with his unchanneled energy—until he succeeded in buying the *Washington Post* that same year. It was to Meyer, the publisher of the *Washington Post*, then, that Steichen turned for help getting into military service. Meyer had not only overseen Steichen's investments for many years but he also advised him on other business matters. In 1937, he had tried to arrange for an agent to represent the sale of Steichen's photographs because he thought Steichen was "not a business getter; he is an artist."[5] Meyer also routinely advised Steichen on complicated government regulations pertaining to the importation of rare and unusual plants from Europe, and Steichen sometimes called on Meyer to have someone at the *Post* do research for him—on the treatment of seeds and plants with colchicine to produce changes in chromosomes, for instance.[6]

In turn, Steichen advised the Meyers on art matters and took family photographs, and when Meyer bought the *Washington Post,* he sought Steichen's technical advice about how to achieve the best newspaper halftones. In the late thirties, as the war accelerated, Steichen had urged Meyer and his newspaper to employ "inspirational slogans" as the "quickest way to start the spiritual as well as the practical activities we need to set going now."[7]

When Steichen asked Meyer to sponsor his efforts to reenter military service, Meyer quickly obliged, conferring with an Air Corps major to obtain the essential forms for Steichen to complete. Then he told Steichen to come to Washington and "work on it yourself. I cannot do it for you."[8] He took his efforts one step further, however, writing to Donald M. Nelson of the National Defense Council on October twenty-sixth about Steichen's distinguished background as a photographer as well as a military officer with the American Expeditionary Force. Meyer noted that Steichen had orchestrated the Inter-Allied Aerial Photographic Council for "standardization of air photography," and had been awarded the Legion of Honor.[9]

Not even Meyer, however, could persuade military authorities to reinstate a sixty-one-year-old man, no matter if he was the legendary Steichen. Immensely disappointed, Steichen looked for ways to work as a civilian to take photographs on behalf of the war effort. The powerful FSA photographs stayed in his mind, and he was now even more determined to create his own photographic mural. All these forces ultimately coalesced into his landmark photographic exhibit, "Road to Victory."

Eighty million Americans listened to a two-hour-long election-eve radio broadcast November 4, 1940, in support of Roosevelt's candidacy for a third term as President. The last speech of the marathon was given by politically independent Carl Sandburg, Roosevelt's staunch friend. Sandburg, who had won the Pulitzer Prize in history for his hugely successful four volumes on Lincoln and the war years, now urged his fellow Americans to vote for FDR instead of Wendell Willkie because he believed that Roosevelt, like Lincoln, possessed the wisdom to carry out "the good sense of the nation."[10]

Reelected by a total of 27 million votes to Willkie's 22 million, the President went on the radio in December, expressing "the plain truth" about the escalating gravity of the war. "Let us no longer blind ourselves to the undeniable fact that the evil forces which have crushed and undermined and corrupted so many others are already within our own gates," he warned. The United States Navy fleet was patrolling the Pacific Ocean, and the President wanted to provide the friendly countries of Europe "the implements of war, the planes, the tanks, the guns, the freighters which will enable them to fight for their liberty and for our security . . . so that we and our children will be saved the agony and suffering of war which others have had to endure." He was mobilizing the nation so that "every machine, every arsenal, every factory," every needed worker could be committed to producing needed war materials "swiftly and without stint." Under his command, the United States would serve as "the great arsenal of democracy."[11]

Steichen and Sandburg immediately saw that the American people needed words and pictures to unite them. During a decade of rising interest in documentary photography, photographers and writers had already begun to collaborate on books that married words and photographic images to record contemporary life. Erskine Caldwell and Margaret Bourke-White joined forces to create *You Have Seen Their Faces,* their 1937 study of the South. The poet Archibald MacLeish wrote a poem text to accompany a collection of FSA photographs in the book *Land of the Free* in 1938. Dorothea Lange and Paul S. Taylor worked together on *An American Exodus* in 1939. In 1941, James Agee and Walker Evans produced the unforgettable *Let Us Now Praise Famous Men.* That same year, Steichen and Sandburg joined the procession, beginning their

A Real Image of War (1939–1943)

collaboration on a patriotic photographic mural constructed by Steichen, with text by Sandburg.

And Steichen tried one more time to get back into military service. He went to Washington, hoping that a personal interview would persuade the military establishment to let him in the door. A polite officer interviewed Steichen, making notes on a form, "but when he came to the year of my birth, 1879," Steichen remembered, "he put down his pen with an air of finality and told me he was sorry, but I was beyond the age limit for induction into active service."[12] The message was clear: This was a young man's war and Steichen was entirely too old to be accepted for active duty.[13]

In June of 1941, Steichen wrote an article for *Vogue* entitled "The Fighting Photo-Secession," in which he praised Alfred Stieglitz for his historic work on behalf of pictorial photography. Dispirited and lonely, Stieglitz was deeply touched. In addition to his anxiety about the war, his health was gradually failing as his heart grew weaker, and Georgia O'Keeffe was spending more and more time in New Mexico engrossed in her work, rather than in his needs at Lake George or in New York. He was "virtually—literally—alone . . ." he had written in 1940 to his old friend Annie Brigman. His heart was not strong enough for "demands it should be able to meet."[14]

He wrote with gratitude to Steichen for the *Vogue* article in June of 1941. He had read the "gloriously generous" essay on the fighting Photo-Secession over and over again, Stieglitz told his old friend, and was simply "bowled over" by it. The article—the gesture—both were "Real Steichen," Stieglitz wrote, and he was deeply moved, almost beyond words. Steichen had cheered him and many others with the tribute.[15]

While Stieglitz by many accounts fell out with Steichen—over art, over war, over commercialism—Steichen had never wavered in his affection and respect for Stieglitz. After all, there was Stieglitz's notorious and temperamental propensity to exile almost everyone, at one time or another, to some remote realm of disapproval or inattention. But that June of 1941, once and for all, Stieglitz cordially summed up his sense of their long friendship: All these years later, they were both continuing the old fight on behalf of photography as a medium of expression. He sent Steichen his enduring appreciation and his love, signing himself, "Ever your old Stieglitz."[16]

In September of 1941, David H. McAlpin, a trustee of the Museum of Modern Art, proposed that the museum sponsor a major photographic exhibition on national defense. A grand-nephew in the Rockefeller family, McAlpin used his inherited wealth to indulge his love of painting and photography. He was an early, anonymous benefactor of photography and photographic exhibitions at MoMA, which Nelson Rockefeller served as president from 1939 to 1940 (and later on, in 1946).

In 1937, with McAlpin's anonymous financial support, young Harvard graduate and MoMA librarian Beaumont Newhall had curated the first exhibition of photography at the museum. Newhall himself was an amateur photographer, as well as a budding photographic historian. The ambitious exhibit he called "Photography 1839–1937" encompassed the history of photography, and it included 841 photographs, among them works by Steichen, Paul Strand, Berenice Abbott, Ansel Adams, Margaret Bourke-White, Henri Cartier-Bresson, Edward Weston, Man Ray, Charles Sheeler, and Walker Evans. Harboring his old prejudices against institutions and exhibits he himself had not organized, Stieglitz declined to participate or to serve on the advisory committee on photography for the exhibition, but Steichen later enthusiastically agreed to help Newhall in that way.

The success of the exhibit added momentum to a drive to establish a permanent department of photography at MoMA, championed by McAlpin, who persuaded Nelson Rockefeller and the museum board of trustees to act favorably on the proposal submitted by Beaumont Newhall and his wife and colleague, Nancy.[17] Consequently, the department of photography was officially created in September of 1940, with Newhall appointed curator and McAlpin named chairman of the Photography Committee. At McAlpin's insistence, photographer Ansel Adams became vice chairman.

A REAL IMAGE OF WAR (1939–1943)

In 1941, Ansel Adams organized "Images of Freedom," a novel exhibition of photographs of America and the American people during the early war years. That fall, McAlpin approached Steichen with the idea of mounting a huge MoMA exhibition featuring national defense as the theme. Newhall and Adams were already working on a mammoth retrospective, "Photographs of the Civil War and the American Frontier." McAlpin wanted an additional exhibit to salute the American men and women "behind the man with the gun" in Europe.[18]

Given his visibility and experience, Steichen was the ideal choice to be a prominent guest curator. McAlpin would oversee the funding effort, and he and Monroe Wheeler, then director of exhibitions at MoMA, persuaded Steichen to take on the project, promising him all possible support from MoMA and giving him carte blanche in the conception and design of the exhibition. Steichen gladly relinquished his comfortable routine at Umpawaug in October of 1941 to pour his energy into the effort, working without pay. He asked Sandburg to join him to write the text. He considered calling it "Panorama of Defense," but instead he took his working title from Roosevelt—"The Arsenal of Democracy."

Here, finally, was Steichen's chance to create "a contemporary portrait of America," a photographic mural of the American people defending their children, their heritage, their freedom.[19] He set out to find the best still photographs in the country, more than 100,000 prints from around the nation, from which he chose nearly 50 images. A third of those came from the FSA archives. Roy Stryker himself showed Steichen the FSA collection and explained its organizational scheme—a model that would soon serve Steichen well.

Then, in a cataclysmic instant, Pearl Harbor demolished what remained of normal life in the United States. Japanese planes had dealt death from the sky over Pearl Harbor, Sandburg wrote in his syndicated news column, "in a savage and undeclared war killing American sailors and soldiers by thousands."[20] On that December 7, 1941, Steichen and Dana were spending the weekend at Kings Point, Long Island, with Tom Maloney. They were just finishing a meal when the terrible news came over the radio. "Then, more than ever, I felt my disappointment at not having been readmitted to the Air Force," Steichen said.[21] He told Dana and Maloney, "I wish I could get into this one, but I'm too old."[22]

Helga Sandburg remembered that her uncle telephoned the War Department to ask again if they would accept him as an adviser or a specialist on photography, and once again, he was turned down.[23]

According to one account, Steichen approached the undersecretary for the air in the Navy Department, Artemus Gates, explaining how he might "lead, direct and recruit talented photographers" to make a historical record of the war.[24] Gates, in turn, relayed Steichen's ideas to Capt. Arthur Radford, head of the Training Division of the Bureau of Aeronautics.[25] But all attention was, for the moment, directed toward the "Day of Infamy."

On December 9, 1941, President Roosevelt broadcast a grim litany of the invasions and attacks leading up to Pearl Harbor. "We are now in this war," he told the nation, his voice stern and heavy. "We are all in it—all the way. Every single man, woman, and child is a partner in the most tremendous undertaking of our American history." The United States would accept no outcome other than "victory, final, complete." A "terrible lesson" had been learned and must never be forgotten: "There is no such thing as security for any nation—or any individual—in a world ruled by the principles of gangsterism." Americans, FDR said, were builders, not destroyers. They were going to win the war, and win the peace to follow. They were going to ensure a world "in which this nation, and all that this nation represents, will be safe for our children."[26]

"In their journey of destiny the American people on December 7 came to a Great Divide," Sandburg wrote in his nationally syndicated news column on December 28, 1941. "And they crossed over. Millions of plans and projects canceled themselves like writing on sand after a storm wave."[27] One project was transformed: The vast mural of pictures and words that Steichen and Sandburg were shaping for the Museum of Modern Art changed overnight. Immediately, Sandburg reported, "the aim and the main idea of the exhibit was to make a portrait of the American people at war."[28]

Yet Steichen still felt deeply disappointed not to be an official part of the war effort. He strongly believed that as a citizen with a specialized skill to contribute, he had no choice but to serve. Unbeknownst to Steichen, help came from a former colleague, Samuel W. Meek, who had been vice president of J. Walter Thompson. A decorated marine in World War I, Meek was serving as an aviation consultant to the Navy

Department in the early months of World War II. When he learned of Steichen's efforts to join the navy, and his dejection at being turned down, Meek used his influence to bring Steichen's ambition to the attention of navy brass in Washington.[29]

There appear to have been several forces at work simultaneously to aid Steichen's cause. Art historian Christopher Phillips has recorded the account of John Archer Morton, a navy yeoman assigned to review applications of aspiring officers and cadets. According to Morton, he came across Steichen's application, supported by his impressive World War I service credentials, and urged his commanding officer to sign up the famous photographer before the navy lost him to another branch of the military.[30] Consequently, by this account, Steichen's papers were immediately flown to Capt. Arthur Radford in Washington, then in charge of training naval aviators.

The precise history of Steichen's invitation to assume active duty is clouded by time, but the result is clear: To his elation, Steichen was summoned to the telephone one winter day, to hear a Navy Department official inquire if he would be interested in taking photographs for the navy. "I almost crawled through the telephone wire with eagerness," Steichen recalled.[31]

He took a train for Washington that very night, arriving at Naval Headquarters early the next morning to meet with Captain (soon to be Admiral) Radford and Comdr. W. W. Doyle.[32] Steichen turned on the charm, quickly recounting his World War I experiences, his collaboration with Gen. Billy Mitchell, his innovations in aerial photography. Radford was impressed. When Steichen assured him he could tell the complete wartime story of naval aviation through photographs but that he would have to create a small unit of six crack photographers to accomplish this, Radford immediately agreed. He directed Steichen to organize his men as a special photographic unit in the Training Literature division of Naval Aviation. Under those auspices, they would document the Naval Aviation story and in the process generate images that could be useful in recruiting up to thirty thousand new navy pilots a year—a taxing challenge for Radford and his staff, since they had to compete with the Army Air Corps for pilots.[33] Steichen got his wish, and his orders, and he jubilantly telephoned the news to Dana and to the Sandburgs in Michigan.

"The delphinium experiments are put on hold," Helga wrote in her journal. " 'The Glass House' he and Dana have just moved in to overlooking the new lake (and the Irish wolfhounds) are to go into a caretaker's hands. He's going to war. Dana is finding an apartment in Washington. Uncle Ed is on fire."[34]

Steichen had begun cutting back on the Umpawaug delphinium production as soon as he realized that United States participation in the war was inevitable, and now the tractors plowed under the rest of his flowers. For the future, he and Dana saved a few hundred plants that promised to be excellent breeding stock. His affairs were in order. He could go on active duty immediately. Without giving Steichen's name, Sandburg wrote about his brother-in-law in one of his national news columns in March of 1942:

The war came, and he plowed under one of the nicest plant-breeding fields worth looking at in the United States of America. . . . Now at sixty-two he is wearing the uniform of a lieutenant commander in the navy. Now his experience on the battle lines in France in 1918 comes into use. . . . Now the navy will send this man of service, one of the supreme technicians, where he seems most needed. He wants to give the one best thing he has to give to America's war effort.[35]

In January 1942, cleared by a special medical waiver because he was over-age, former U.S. Army Col. Edward Steichen was effectively "demoted" to the rank of lieutenant commander in the United States Naval Reserves and ordered to active duty. Rank was unimportant to him; all that mattered was that he had made it into active military service. Before reporting to his assigned Washington headquarters, however, Steichen was deployed by the navy on special assignment to finish assembling and overseeing production of the revised exhibition at the Museum of Modern Art. Now retitled "Road to Victory," the show gave Steichen his podium for the photographic pageant he had long envisioned.

In those early months, as American troops marched to war and Americans at home mobilized with zeal to fight on the home front, the

A Real Image of War (1939–1943)

exhibit would also become a riveting instrument of propaganda. Steichen threw himself headlong into the mission of choosing the images for "Road to Victory," searching in government and business archives as well as in museum and newspaper files to assemble "a procession of photographs of the nation at war."[36] By April of 1942, he had come to a final decision on 150 compelling photographs—not all of them technically outstanding, but each one, according to the MoMA *Bulletin,* a "thrilling, visual" image of "our nation in this critical day and age."[37] He did not include any of his own pictures.

With Dana's patient assistance, Steichen arranged the 150 eight-by-ten-inch prints on the floor of the house at Umpawaug. Soon, Sandburg arrived to work hard on the text for nearly two weeks. First, Steichen showed him each photograph and described how the print would look when enlarged to an eight-by-ten-foot or sixteen-by-twenty-foot mural. Sandburg labored over a text that was sometimes sentimental, sometimes strident, but heartfelt throughout. He discovered that his brother-in-law was "no slouch of an editor" of verbal as well as visual texts. In fact, Sandburg said, Steichen "wangled, joked and threatened better texts" out of him than he himself believed possible.[38]

Meanwhile, installation designer Herbert Bayer and MoMA staff members constructed a model of the entire second floor of the museum so that Steichen could indicate exactly where each photograph was to be installed. Bayer, born in Austria, was a painter, photographer, and designer who had studied at the Bauhaus. He left Germany in 1937, then returned to do the dangerous work of collecting materials for a Bauhaus exhibition he had been commissioned to install at MoMA in 1938. After that successful show, he stayed in the United States, working as a freelance designer.

He and Steichen got along "extremely well," Bayer recalled.[39] Steichen constantly sought Bayer's opinion, and as they studied photographs spread all over the floor, Steichen often grew emotional "about American things."[40] Bayer and Steichen wanted to enfold viewers physically and psychologically in the world of the exhibition, so dramatically that they would feel themselves a part of it. Therefore, Bayer extended the viewers' field of vision by constructing raised ramps overlooking the floor, walls, and ceiling. He used minimal structural elements, mounting photographs on panels just off the walls, so they seemed to be floating. Walls, ceiling, and floors were painted white, and all photographs were black and white.

The scale of the exhibit was staggering: Murals ranged from three by four feet to ten by forty feet. Sandburg introduced it grandly: "Here a procession of photographs marches, makes its report to the nations on the American people, their home front and fighting fronts, our wartime America. It carries faith and expectancy that the modern genius of man can go far and is beyond defeat and conquest, in line with the ancient proverb 'The fireborn are at home in fire.' "[41]

Steichen wrote to tell his sister that the show felt full of promise as it went up, that Carl had composed some "grand captions," and that he and the museum staff were "fiercely proud of them."[42] Each room of the exhibition was a chapter, Sandburg observed, and "each photograph a sentence." He described Steichen's expansive vision of the exhibit: "His faith in his America runs deep. The photographs he chose present a people and a country who have strengths, lights, and faiths to wrestle with any dark destinies ahead." The exhibition was, Sandburg believed, "a massive portrait and an epic poem of the United States of America at war and on its road to victory."[43]

Visitors who wound through the rooms and up and down the ramps of the massive exhibit actually stepped inside the experience, surrounded by faces, landscapes, and vignettes of people at work and at war. In one chilling juxtaposition of images, a bomb exploded a battleship at Pearl Harbor; underneath that mural, as if looking up at the holocaust, Japanese ambassador Nomura and Japanese peace envoy Kurusu sat in comfort, laughing. In the facing mural, Dorothea Lange's image of a lone, stubborn farmer stood over its caption: "War—they asked for it—now, by the living God, they'll get it."

Steichen and Sandburg hoped that the bitter lessons of wartime would carry over into peacetime.[44] They had jointly chosen as the opening text lines from Roosevelt's message to Congress, delivered on January 6, 1941, proclaiming the famous Four Freedoms: freedom of speech and expression, freedom of worship, freedom from want, and freedom from fear.

"America, thy seeds of fate have borne fruit of many breeds, many pages of hard work, sorrow and suffering," Sandburg's text concluded; "... tomorrow belongs to the children."[45]

A REAL IMAGE OF WAR (1939–1943)

A week before "Road to Victory" opened with fanfare in May 1942, Steichen, the high school and art school dropout, was awarded an honorary master of arts degree from Wesleyan University in Middletown, Connecticut. He could not quite believe it, he wrote to his sister; he wished he could have shared it with his mother.[46] Then he and Dana were off to New York for the show, which would attract more than eighty thousand mesmerized visitors during its six-month run at the Museum of Modern Art.

After its smashing success in New York, "Road to Victory" traveled, drawing banner crowds in Cleveland, Chicago, St. Louis, San Francisco, Portland, Oregon, and other, smaller cities. A replica of the show was carefully packed and shipped to England, only to be sunk en route by an enemy submarine. A second replica made it safely through dangerous seas to London, and other circulating shows traveled to Honolulu, to Australia, and to other Pacific ports. The show also traveled through South America, under the auspices of Nelson Rockefeller and the Office of Inter-American Affairs.

The United States Army mounted "Road to Victory" at one embarkation port so that troops waiting to go overseas could see it, and a pocket-sized edition of pictures and text from the show was published for wide distribution among the armed services.[47] This especially pleased the two men. Steichen wrote gleefully to tell Paula that they were "breaking into print," and that he looked forward to years of "teamwork" with Sandburg.[48]

As photographic historian Christopher Phillips has noted, "Road to Victory" was "a new kind of photographic exhibition, in which Steichen orchestrated the work of many photographers around a single theme, attaining a level of visual complexity and emotional power seldom before encountered."[49] Most critics were effusive in their praise for the exhibition. It was "overwhelming," wrote Henry McBride in the New York *Sun,* with its drama and its enormous photographs of war efforts.[50] Edward Alden Jewell, writing in the *New York Times* June 7, 1942, deemed it MoMA's most valuable service to the public to date, a magnificent achievement, as well as a supreme contribution to the war effort—and the art season's "most moving experience."[51]

Looking back on it two years later, Steichen said that "Road to Victory" was essentially another type of one-man show, a pageant fusing images by numerous photographers to explore a theme. Furthermore, it was for him an exercise in preparation for his larger purpose—to create through photographs an "epic" portrait of the United States.[52]

———

Before he left for active duty in the army, Beaumont Newhall assisted with some of the complicated details of "Road to Victory," including keeping records of the thousands of pictures submitted and photographing the installation, while Ansel Adams popped in and out to watch the hubbub. By then the earnest self-appointed advocate of the young guard of photographers, Newhall wooed the legendary Alfred Stieglitz to be his mentor. He had mixed feelings about Steichen, however, who was now invading his own territory. Far more conservative and esoteric than Steichen, Newhall had not been happy about Steichen's splashy show, which went against the grain of his own more elitist philosophy of museum work—and which had garnered crowds and critical attention far surpassing Newhall's own exhibitions at MoMA.

In his wartime absence, Newhall's wife, Nancy, was holding down his job at MoMA by the summer of 1942, at a paltry salary. During this period, Nancy Newhall was interviewing Stieglitz with the intention of writing his biography (a project she never finished). She visited Stieglitz two or three times weekly, listening carefully during their interviews but not transcribing their conversations until "immediately afterward," when she was alone. Her notes, therefore, as she herself acknowledged, were "filtered through two memories, his and mine."[53]

Many of her notes offered garbled, distorted, or downright inaccurate "information"—either because of Stieglitz's inadvertent errors of memory, or his misrepresentation, or her own lapses in recalling his words. Consequently, it is difficult to reconstruct the context or to verify the reliability of words she attributed to Stieglitz, including the frequently quoted passage in which he labeled Steichen a "turncoat" who sold out to commercial photography, and reported—mistakenly—that Steichen did not come to see him "for more than twenty years." When Mrs. Newhall asked Stieglitz why this was so, she wrote, "Stieglitz

A Real Image of War (1939–1943)

thought a moment, and then said, 'If you will remember Steichen was born a peasant and wanted to be an actor, perhaps it will be clear to you.'"[54] Steichen was indeed "born a peasant"; no surviving evidence even hints that he ever wanted to be an actor. And although Nancy Newhall wrote further that she thought Stieglitz's remark was "snide, even envious, and unworthy of Stieglitz," she herself echoed it in her own letter to Stieglitz in 1942, and it was often repeated elsewhere.[55]

She attributed another curious reflection to the old photographer: "Stieglitz thought of his fight for the young Steichen years earlier. Now he himself was down and out. What would Steichen do for him?"[56] Was she—was Stieglitz—suggesting that Steichen should provide financial assistance?

Nancy Newhall's view of Edward Steichen was inevitably shaped by opinions held by her husband and by Stieglitz. She certainly shared her husband's distaste for Steichen, and she was appalled at the work that fell into her lap in the aftermath of "Road to Victory." She wrote furiously to tell Stieglitz all about it, knowing he would take some vindictive pleasure in her complaint. Indeed, she wrote, Stieglitz was right; Steichen was "essentially a peasant." The office where he had worked on "Road to Victory" was a "pig sty," overrun with prints, negatives, and papers. Steichen had left the room in such chaos, Newhall complained, that she had no idea where many of the photographs came from and therefore could not return them. His demands had worn out the museum staff, she wrote. Furthermore, as she looked through the mass of photographs that had been reviewed for inclusion in the exhibition, Newhall told Stieglitz that Steichen had consistently selected images that were "coarse," "earthy," and "piglike."[57]

Caught up in the territorial politics of the photography world of her time, Nancy Newhall still spoke for an articulate minority, led by her husband and Ansel Adams, when she suggested that Steichen's "Road to Victory" was sentimental.[58] But the overpowering consensus in those shattering months after Pearl Harbor was that this landmark exhibition was unabashedly patriotic, affirming the national spirit and resolve. It was also robust propaganda, in its root meaning—propagating the country's faith in itself and its new cause.

Decades later, in hindsight, such an event might be judged sentimental or overblown, but what matters about "Road to Victory" is what the unprecedented exhibit itself said, in its own moment in history, to and about the people for whom it was created, and how they themselves perceived it.

Still, there is no doubt that between the two of them, Steichen and Sandburg could make quite a mess of an office. "Creative clutter," Sandburg would call it in his own workroom at home. Nancy Newhall was understandably piqued to have to clean up after them. But in fairness, Lieutenant Commander Steichen had, in fact, been promised full support by MoMA, and he had been ordered back to Naval headquarters in Washington immediately after the opening of "Road to Victory."

He spent much of the summer of 1942 on official tours of naval air stations, photographing navy personnel at work. From Washington in October, he was expanding the "Road to Victory" traveling show to include material from the U.S. Merchant Marines and the U.S. Marines Corps, thus overcoming two "bad gaps" in the exhibition, he told Sandburg.[59] The Office of War Information had decided to ship the exhibition first to Honolulu, to open on December seventh, the anniversary of Pearl Harbor. Steichen wrote Sandburg to tell him this news, adding, "Hot diggity. Pass the ammunition."[60]

The war spared no one the usual domestic cares. Living alone in the house in Elmhurst, Illinois, for the nearly ten years since Oma's death, Opa Steichen was growing feeble from frequent bouts of illness. In 1941, he had to undergo radium treatments for cancer, with more success than had been the case for Oma. After the Sandburgs' youngest daughter, Helga, had eloped with young Joe Thoman in Michigan, Carl and Paula had built a small cottage for them in the orchard at Chikaming Farm, their land on the Michigan dunes. Helga and Joe's son, the Sandburgs' first grandchild, was born just days before Pearl Harbor. (As soon as they could, Paula and Helga had taken the baby to Opa, so he could hold his great-grandson in his arms. Paula wrote to Opa, "Helga wants to show you what a fine great-grandson you have."[61])

After Helga and Joe had settled on a farm in Illinois, Paula tried to persuade her eighty-eight-year-old father to come to live in Michigan in the little orchard cottage. "It would seem perfectly ideal as Opa would be

A Real Image of War (1939–1943)

by himself, and yet we could see him a dozen times a day, and we could take care of him if he should become ill," she wrote to her brother.[62] Opa was stubborn, but she thought they could convince him if they could just get him to Michigan for a visit to see for himself.

"We tried all last year to get him to come," Paula wrote, "but it seems to be next to impossible to drag him away even for a short visit. He is so interested in every shrub and flower, and keeps busy transplanting and making plans for next year's garden. I sometimes think he is the most contented man on earth."[63] "Dear Children," he had written one autumn. "I cant [sic] come to Harbert now because here is the time to transplant the perennial flowers and Bulbs. That will keep me busy the rest of the month to prepare the ground and transplant them." He lived for the blossoming of his flowers each spring: "The snowdrops are about 3 inches high with big white buds and the blue Scillas are one inch out of the ground," he wrote. "They are very late this year."[64] At last, however, his failing health brought him around to their point of view. Steichen put Opa's house on the market, and Paula and her daughters settled Opa into the orchard cottage, where they lavished attention on him.

There were other family problems: When Dana's mother, Maggie, died in October of 1942, Dana was "completely crushed," Steichen told Sandburg.[65] Uprooted from Umpawaug and cast into the Washington whirlwind, Dana was "unhappy and lost."[66] Oma's death still seemed unreal to her, after many years, Paula told her sister-in-law sympathetically. Dana felt that same sense of disbelief, along with guilt and regret because there were "so many things I should have done."[67] She longed to talk things over with her sister-in-law, but wartime and geography made that impossible. In the end, her husband told her that those who loved her could help her only so much with her grief and regrets. Unfortunately, she—and she alone—would have to resolve any feelings of guilt or remorse, he said, and deep sorrow ebbed away only as time passed. This he knew from his own encounters with death and other losses—from Rosa, to Clara, to Oma.

They were living in those days for Steichen's job, Dana told Paula, rising at 6:30 each morning in their rented Georgetown quarters so that Steichen could work a twelve-hour day, then falling into bed at 9:30 each night so he could start over again the next day.[68] Steichen was bursting with renewed energy and vigor, alive with the new challenge. "War. War again," he remembered. "Hitler moving into Poland—I knew that I couldn't keep away from it. I had a feeling, a hangover from the last war, that if we could really photograph war as it was, if war could be photographed in all its monstrous activity, that that would be a great deterrent."[69]

Steichen's subject was war, but his purpose was peace. Bent on capturing the "real image of war," his first task in Washington was to choose his team of photographers.[70] They would have to come on board as officers, he insisted to navy brass, so that they could work with as much flexibility and authority as possible. Wayne Miller, a young navy ensign and aspiring photographer, heard from Radford about the great Steichen and the new photographic unit he was putting together.

"We have a photographer coming in," Radford told Miller, "name of Steichen or Stuchen, something like that. Maybe there's a place for you in what he's putting together."[71] He told Miller at the time that Steichen was working on the exhibition at MoMA. Nervously, Miller had arranged to meet with Steichen in New York and show him his photographs. Miller was the first man Steichen chose, and the least experienced. Many years later, when he asked Steichen what had impressed him about his pictures, Steichen told Miller the truth, with a smile: "Your photographs were terrible; what I liked was your youth and enthusiasm."[72]

Another of Steichen's photographic recruits was Victor Jorgensen, a photographer and reporter for the Portland *Oregonian*. He knew about the legendary Steichen and so "was prepared for the white hair that seemed to snap in the wind like a hoist of signal flags," but he was not prepared for the almost-palpable energy emitting from the man.[73]

Wayne Miller remembered riding to Florida on the train with Steichen and peering over the edge of the upper berth, to see Steichen "groping along the bedroom wall in search of his glasses. He had been a Lt. Colonel in WWI with General Billy Mitchell," Miller wrote. "Why was this old man here in another war? How long would he last?"[74] Forever, it seemed to his men as they got to know him.

Jorgensen was dispatched to Florida to join Steichen's elite photographic unit, already at work there. "I had a split second for the reflection that if anyone were to characterize this man he would have to start with energy—unbounded and seemingly limitless," Jorgensen recalled.

A REAL IMAGE OF WAR (1939–1943)

"The subsequent weeks convinced me. We ran up and down the broad expanses of the Naval air stations all over Florida and when we weren't running, we were charging, and when not charging, dashing. A sort of galloping trot seemed to be Steichen's slowest speed."[75]

Steichen chose experienced *Life* photojournalist Horace Bristol to join his crew, along with flamboyant Charles Fenno Jacobs, who had worked for *Life* and *Fortune*. Tom Maloney had referred talented commercial illustrator Charles Kerlee to Steichen, and he selected motion-picture photographer Dwight Long to round out the original unit. His hopes of adding the gifted *Life* photographer W. Eugene Smith were dashed when Smith, whose eyes had been injured in a dynamite explosion, failed the vision test. Smith recalled that after Steichen appealed unsuccessfully on his behalf, Steichen arranged a job for him at Ziff-Davis publications as a war correspondent.[76] In addition, Steichen had recruited Arthur Rothstein of *Look*, who also failed the requisite navy physical examination.

Except for the novice Miller, the men needed little training, and Steichen saw to it from the first that they had as much autonomy as possible. Remembering the excruciating logistical problems of processing film footage during World War I, Steichen insisted on establishing his own exclusive photographic laboratory. Leo Pavelle, head of one of the finest commercial labs in New York, rounded up technicians to do the work in the state-of-the-art darkrooms set up in the Fisheries Building on Independence Avenue in Washington, D.C. Nearby, in a temporary navy office building on Constitution Avenue, Steichen put Wayne Miller in charge of organizing their unit offices. Steichen and his men also needed innovative equipment, not the navy's camera of choice, the relatively slow Speed-Graphic, and somehow Radford obligingly helped him circumvent the usual cumbersome channels for purchase orders.

Steichen's original mission, officially defined and actually rather limited, was to tell the story of Naval Aviation through photographs and to contribute pictures that could be used for promotion, for recruiting, and even for propaganda. From the outset, Steichen gave unorthodox orders to his unorthodox crew: "Be sure to bring back some photographs that will satisfy the Navy brass, but spend most of your time making those photographs which you feel should be made."[77] Steichen was all for it when Horace Bristol was invited to sail on the USS *Santee* in late October 1942 to photograph Operation Torch, the Allied entry into North Africa. Bristol sent back pictures of the carriers at sea, and Allied men landing in Morocco with Old Glory flying overhead. His stirring images caught the imagination of Americans back home, as well as the admiration of the Navy Department in Washington.

Consequently, another carrier commander invited Steichen to send a photographer with him to New Caledonia. Charles Kerlee executed that assignment so successfully that he was promptly assigned to the staff of the newly launched USS *Yorktown,* headed for the Pacific theater. When Dwight Long was detached to film motion pictures of *Yorktown* maneuvers, Steichen knew that his Naval Aviation unit was making a name for itself.

He was still outrunning the men on his crew, most of them half his age, "carrying three cameras which he poked into every nook and cranny," Jorgensen remembered.[78] "The Old Man" never seemed fazed by the pace or the demands. The navy routinely notified Steichen in March of 1943, near the time of his sixty-fourth birthday, that he would have to retire from active duty. Oh, no, he wouldn't, Steichen vowed. He quickly and successfully communicated his case to the soon-to-be secretary of the navy, James Forrestal. Steichen not only remained in the navy, he was promoted to commander.

He ventured out from Washington to photograph various navy installations that year, including the strategic submarine station at Groton–New London, Connecticut, where the sleek technology was secondary, in the eye of his camera, to the men and women doing the work.[79] Then he was forced to take time out for surgery on his shoulder; afterward, an excruciating attack of bursitis put him in the navy hospital in Bethesda, Maryland, for treatment and recuperation. But in the fall of 1943, hale and hearty again, Steichen finally got the assignment he had been longing for.

"Get the gear together, and be sure to take enough," he ordered Victor Jorgensen.[80] They were reporting for duty on the USS *Lexington*—"The Blue Ghost," as the Japanese would call her after her forays in the Marshall Islands and the Gilbert Islands. Jorgensen immediately put together a list of cameras, film, and other equipment he thought they would need for the voyage and then showed it to Steichen.

"Double it," Steichen ordered.[81] When they flew out on a Pan Am

A REAL IMAGE OF WAR (1939–1943)

Clipper, they were accompanied by nine hundred pounds of gear. After his tearful leave-taking from Dana, Steichen traveled to the Midwest for a "sweet interlude" with Opa and the Sandburgs.[82] Afterward, he and Jorgensen flew first to Honolulu, where, according to Jorgensen, "the Old Man" was treated like the celebrity he was by some of the fleet admirals, who insisted on having Steichen take their pictures. After Steichen and Jorgensen took a launch to Ford Island, they set up a makeshift portrait studio, and Steichen obliged the admirals. Then they joined the USS *Lexington,* where they waited several days before learning of their ultimate destination—landings on Tarawa and Makin—Operation Galvanic.

Aboard the *Lexington* on November 10, 1943, a few hours before their departure, Steichen wrote to tell the Sandburgs that he was enthralled with the immense carriers, called "flattops" by the men who inhabited these "floating air bases."[83] His officer's quarters aboard ship were luxurious, surpassing the best accommodations on commercial ships, he told his family. He would write as often as he could; meanwhile, worried about his wife at Umpawaug, awaiting his return, he asked the Sandburgs to give her some extra "love and cheering up" in his absence.[84]

The *Lexington*'s executive officer, Bennett W. Wright, was assigned to welcome Steichen aboard and facilitate his work. Letters from Washington directed that Steichen and his crew should have the run of the ship, and Wright escorted them around the massive carrier, alerting them to dangerous areas. Steichen made one request, however, that safety concerns forced Wright to deny: He wanted to stand on the carrier's flight deck to photograph planes taking off and landing. Undaunted by the warning to stay clear of that dangerous vantage point, Steichen stretched out in the safety net extending from the flight deck—the sky above him, nothing but ocean beneath him. From that adventurous angle, he could capture the planes coming in and going out, as well as the landing signal officers (LSOs) launching these perilous missions and then guiding the men home again.

Steichen was up before general quarters each morning, and still up and snapping pictures after midnight, keeping a log of the operation that would later be published by Harcourt, Brace and Company as *The Blue Ghost* (1947). Others recalled watching in amazement as Steichen roamed the ship, turning up everywhere with his Medalist and Ikonata cameras "clanking together around his neck," as Jorgensen put it.[85] One morning, Steichen stood on the aft flight deck, totally absorbed in photographing the landing signal officers who were guiding incoming planes from the dawn patrol. Impervious to the planes landing behind him, Steichen concentrated on the LSOs on their tiny platform, signal paddles in hand, choreographing the planes.

Suddenly, a Hellcat fighter headed for the ship, much too low and much too slowly. Despite a last-minute spurt of power, the plane slid to the edge of the carrier deck, skidded past the signal platform, and fell into the sea. When the signal officers saw the plane out of control, racing toward them, they jumped from their platform into the safety net below—landing on a surprised Steichen, who was still shooting away. Victor Jorgensen raced down to the deck, fearing he would find Steichen prostrate—injured or dead. Two officers, one an ex–football player weighing 210 pounds, disengaged themselves from the tangle of limbs and netting. Then Steichen, grinning, loped toward Jorgensen.

"I think I got it! . . . The picture, right when the thing was over head."[86] This photograph joined his others taken aboard the *Lexington* as one of the best and most widely known of Steichen's personal photographs of World War II.

On the bright moonlit night of December 4, 1943, Adm. Charles A. Pownall dispatched fighter planes from the *Lexington,* the *Yorktown,* and the *Cowpens,* the other carriers in the convoy, to attack Japanese airfields on Kwajalein, an island in the chain of the Marshalls. A key part of their mission was to obtain reconnaissance photographs. As the flying squadrons returned to the *Lexington* from those first attacks on the Japanese airfield at Mili Atoll, Steichen hurried around the flight deck, photographing the planes.

"That's a hell of a place for the Old Boy to be," a signalman warned Jorgensen. Before he could explain why, Jorgensen saw one incoming plane collide with a wire, accidentally triggering its weapon, and then he heard the "chilling sputter of a heavy machine gun firing." Jorgensen watched helplessly as "the tracers seemed to float slowly down the middle of the deck, pass over Steichen's head and arc gracefully on ahead. At the first stutter every man on the flight deck was flat on his face except Steichen. He calmly swung from side to side with his Medalist up to his eye, shooting the sprawled out sailors at his feet. The signalman leaned over the rail and yelled, 'Get the hell out of there, ya crazy bastard!' " As furious as the signalman was, he had to admit that Steichen was "a right lively old coot."[87]

As carefully planned as these attacks had been, everything seemed to go wrong. Hours later, four Japanese torpedo bombers took aim at the *Lexington*. Three were intercepted by the carrier's gunners, but the fourth launched a torpedo that missed the ship by a hair's breadth.

As the second wave of Japanese planes swept toward the *Yorktown* a scant half hour later, Steichen climbed aboard deck on the *Lexington*, equipped with his aerial camera, and Kerlee and Long joined him, carrying the movie camera. This is what they had come to do. The brutal attack wore on into the night, a life-or-death contest of thrust and parry, circle and evade, under the relentless exposure of a full moon.

Around midnight, a Japanese acoustic torpedo jolted the *Lexington* into a locked turn, forcing the ship to travel in circles, and setting it up as a clear and easy target for Japanese bombers and torpedo planes. Crew members wrestled for a half hour (it seemed like an eternity, Jorgensen remembered) before they were able to right the ship. But the attack had rendered the rudder useless, so the ship would have to be steered back to safe harbor by propeller alone. Steichen was convinced the crippled *Lexington* was about to sink. He and Jorgensen had devised an emergency procedure to protect at least one camera and a supply of film in just such a calamity. If the ship was about to go down, they would thrust a dry camera and film into an aerograph balloon so the protected gear would float and stay dry until they could retrieve it.

When they had practiced the drill together, it worked like a charm. For one photographer alone on a limping ship, it proved to be impossible, however. Gripping the camera in his teeth, Steichen grappled in vain to stretch the opening of the balloon wide enough to insert the photographic gear. Along came Captain Stump, commander of the ship, mystified to see the famous photographer with a camera in his mouth. Steichen extricated the camera long enough to explain that he was protecting it so it would stay dry when they abandoned ship. The *Lexington* was in no danger of sinking, Stump assured Steichen, and the captain and his men got their first laugh of the long, harrowing day.

The danger had seemed endless that moonlit December night in the Marshall Islands as forty to fifty Japanese torpedo bombers attacked in unremitting waves. Dancing through the paths of the tracer shells emitting from the giant carrier *Lexington,* some of the enemy planes had eluded the fire, but others exploded in the air or vanished in the dark ocean. After it was over, Steichen said, homesickness swept over him, the yearning for peace. For the first time since he had deliberately plowed his flowers into the earth before leaving Umpawaug for war, Steichen felt a "real delphinium heartache."[88]

30

THE UNIVERSAL LANGUAGE

(1 9 4 3 - 1 9 4 6)

Photography is a universal language. It doesn't require any translation.[1]

—STEICHEN

As THE SHIP'S CAPTAIN HAD PROMISED Steichen, the carrier *Lexington* made it safely back to Pearl Harbor, and Steichen boarded a plane bound for California, determined to get home to Dana in time for Christmas at Umpawaug. He stopped in Michigan for a brief visit with the Sandburgs, and Helga remembered that her uncle talked animatedly late into the night about his adventures, the most exciting of his life. "Our family has a hero," Helga wrote in *". . . Where Love Begins,"* a 1989 memoir based on her detailed journals. "He is towering and his blue eyes direct. When he arrived wearing an overcoat with twelve gold buttons and with eagles on his cap and stripes on his shoulders and sleeves, everyone cheered."[2]

He told them about the night on the USS *Lexington,* when the moon's "blaze of brightness" summoned memories of other moonlit nights—those he painted and photographed in nocturnes as a youth, when for him "the moonlit scene" was "nature's supreme evocation of beauty." Then he talked wistfully of the moonlight bathing the hills and meadows surrounding Dana and the house in Connecticut. He remembered the hell of the Japanese attack on the *Lexington* when the moon, like a ghostly spotlight, exposed American ships to enemy planes. "I would have reached up," he swore, "and plucked that moon from the sky with my fingers if I could have!"[3] In *The Blue Ghost,* Steichen again recalled the betrayal of the moon. "All hell is let loose around us," he had scrawled in his log. "How I now hate that smooth bland moon, want to scratch it out, blast it to smithereens."[4]

He also recounted other stories of close calls during the mission. "Perhaps I told you of Steichen on the Lexington," Sandburg wrote to a friend later. "A disabled plane hit the flight deck with its engine slewing off to kill two men and cripple five others, its whirling propeller knocking off Steichen's cap! So when we meet I call him The Phantom."[5]

In *Steichen at War,* his comprehensive study of Steichen's work and leadership during World War II, photographic historian Christopher Phillips described Steichen's meticulous attention to detail once his men had secured their photographic images: "He was an uncompromising perfectionist," Phillips wrote of Steichen.

> *He insisted that the photographers under his command return their exposed film to Washington rather than attempt to process it in the field.... From the negatives, contact sheets were prepared and sent directly to Steichen's office; there, he and his assistants scrupulously inspected them all.... Wielding an editor's blue grease pencil, he indicated not only which images were to be enlarged, but how they should be cropped and printed. The print quality he demanded from the laboratory was notoriously high. Work that failed to meet his standards went back to be repeated, often accompanied by the instructions that the lab printers learned to chant in unison: "Deeper, darker, DOWN!"*[6]

Now under Steichen's direction, Dwight Long was shooting a motion picture to be called *The Fighting Lady.* Part navy, part Hollywood, the film set out to depict the war through the eyes of the ordinary sailor, and it dazzled audiences with its air-combat scenes filmed in color, with camera angles replicating the pilot's view—cameras attached to the wings of the planes as well as to the guns. Produced by Twentieth Century–Fox, the film opened in special showings for navy personnel in Washington, personally introduced by Steichen, who spoke enthusiastically about the gun-camera color pictures of air combat—"one of the greatest miracles of photography."[7]

Audiences could see and hear the war close up, with their own eyes and ears—even the crash and disintegration of a Hellcat on a carrier deck, with the pilot miraculously stepping out of the wreckage. Said Steichen, it was the "most dramatic crack-up you will ever see."[8] The movie drew large crowds and the income it produced went into the Navy Relief Fund.

From the Navy Department of Aeronautics in Washington, Steichen wrote to tell his sister that his work was growing ever "more arduous," now that the secretary of the navy had asked him to expand his photographic work beyond Naval Aviation to encompass all areas of the navy. He told Paula about ongoing work on *The Fighting Lady,* as well as on preparation of "Power in the Pacific," an exhibition of still photographs of the war to be shown at the Museum of Modern Art. After he wrapped up these projects, he hoped to return to the Pacific theater himself. He had never felt better in his life, he promised her, so she was not to worry about him.[9]

Meanwhile, Sandburg had taken on a Hollywood venture of his own when MGM paid him $125,000 to write an epic wartime American novel to be made into a motion picture. The novel was entitled *Remembrance Rock,* although the film was never made. Steichen was happy to hear that Sandburg was working on a novel, believing that no matter "how good or how badly" Hollywood might have treated it, the book needed to be written.[10]

When Steichen celebrated his sixty-fifth birthday in March of 1944, Dana baked an orange birthday cake, and Steichen blew out all the candles after singing a lusty happy birthday to himself. "E.J. is well," Dana wrote to the Sandburgs. "Same old merry go round..."[11] His photographs from the South Pacific were great, she told them, promising that they would see the pictures. Steichen would work as long and hard in 1944 as he ever had in his life. He told Paula that he had no choice. It was his mission.[12]

Clara Steichen was living in New Orleans and in Springfield, Missouri, during the forties, still estranged from her daughters, and writing occasional letters to Stieglitz that dredged up the old anger toward Steichen.[13] Mary had been married to Dr. Frank Calderone since 1941, the year she had completed her master's degree in public health at Columbia University, and she was now working as a school physician on Long Island, where she and Frank and her daughter Linda were living.

Kate, meanwhile, continued singing in churches and choral groups in New York, where she had been a member of the WPA Opera during the 1930s. She became an active member of the Wilton, Connecticut, Choral Club after she and Carol Silverberg bought a rustic ten-by-twelve-foot weekend cabin in the woods nearby. Kate and Carol still shared an apartment in New York, where Kate worked as a floral designer and as an office assistant in an architectural firm. But no matter how happy Kate seemed to be in her relationship with Carol, Clara disapproved, blaming Steichen for Kate's homosexuality.

Steichen was still sending Clara's lawyer her monthly checks, and she had apparently inherited some Smith family money, but she pled poverty to old family friends, accusing Steichen of giving her nothing. Hearing that, Mary wrote angrily to tell Clara that if she continued to portray herself to friends as destitute, "I shall be extremely resentful of such a gross untruth." Mary also urged her mother to let go of the past, telling her that for her own part, "There is no room in my life for any bitterness or looking backwards."[15] Unfortunately, after nearly thirty years of estrangement from Steichen, and now living through a second world war, Clara still clung to the old anger and bitterness, unable to make peace with the past, or her children, or herself.

Sometime during the fall of 1944, Steichen paid a final visit to his father at the Sandburgs' Chikaming Farm. He spent a few days enjoying quiet hours with Opa, animated talks with Carl and Paula, and romps with Helga's children—Joe Carl, now nearly three, and year-old Karlen Paula. When her husband went overseas, Helga and her children had moved back to live in the orchard cottage, and because Opa was growing more frail, Paula had moved him into the big house so she could be near

The Universal Language (1943–1946)

him in the night. The household had two new members, both of Japanese-American ancestry—a secretary and a farm helper hired by the Sandburgs in protest of the internment of Japanese-Americans. Janet and Helga also worked with Paula and some hired hands to care for the thriving herd of goats.

Opa had enjoyed his life with the Sandburgs on the wild dunes of Lake Michigan more than he had expected.[16] For some time now, however, he had suffered progressive memory loss and disorientation from hardening of the arteries; his body was simply wearing out, his life ebbing away. Not long after Steichen's departure, Opa's health took a dramatic turn for the worse, and he died peacefully on the night of December 9, 1944, just three weeks short of his ninetieth birthday.

Before her death, Oma had written all the letters to the family, signing them "With udels [sic] of love, Oma and Opa," or "With love and kisses to you all, Oma and Opa." After her death, to the family's surprise, usually taciturn Opa had taken up the job of writing to his children. The Sandburg granddaughters saved his letters, written in a script very like his son's, most of them spelling out details of the weather and the flowers in his garden. He seemed to measure his years after Oma's death by how much sun and rain there was, how much snow, how many roses, hollyhocks, daisies, larkspur, petunias, snowdrops. And, like his son, he grew delphiniums, tall and lustrous blue.[17] Undemonstrative for most of his life, he began expressing his affection in the later years, faithfully signing his letters just as Oma had: "With love and kisses to you all."

As they had promised they would, the Sandburgs placed the urn with Oma's ashes in Opa's casket because "it was his wish they could share together the same oblong corner of earth."[18] Sandburg, the son of Swedish immigrants, honored the old Scandinavian custom of breaking evergreen branches to place on the coffin at funerals. He saw to it that there were pine sprigs for each member of the family to throw on Opa's coffin as it was buried in Riverdale Cemetery, near Harbert in Chikaming Township, Berrien County, Michigan.[19] It was a gesture Steichen would emulate at other funerals for years afterward. Sandburg gave his father-in-law's eulogy:

> *He had a quiet passion for the earth where flowers and plants can take root and grow and rise to face the sun. Whatever lessons of*

comfort and strength may be found, in the never ending changes and resurrections of the earth, his hands and his eyes knew those lessons. His dust goes back now to the earth from which it came. He is no stranger to this nourishing soil....[20]

Later, Paula herself planted arborvitae around her parents' tombstone, which read simply:

STEICHEN.
MARY 1854–1933
JOHN PETER 1854–1944.

In 1945, Steichen was sixty-six and a hero. Audiences were still marveling at *The Fighting Lady,* the lush, dramatic color film that "The March of Time" creator Louis de Rochemont had produced and William Wyler directed, using sixty thousand feet of raw 16-mm navy film footage, with Steichen looking on to be sure that it was "military & not Hollywood."[21] American viewers were mesmerized and critics were impressed by the unprecedented "virtual reality" of the planes landing and taking off, the guns firing in the air.

Wayne Miller gave cinematographer Dwight Long much of the credit for the special effects. When Long went to sea aboard the carrier *Yorktown,* Miller remembered, "On his own he talked the aircraft mechanics into changing the positions of the gun cameras in the wings." Until then, the cameras were mounted flat in the wings in order to fit the space. As a result, Miller explained, "when the film was developed, you had to twist and turn your head in order to see what was happening. Dwight got them to change the position of the cameras so that they would be upright. He also arranged that they have an overrun capability so that the cameras could continue filming the deadly effects of the pilot's attack. By chance his roommate on this carrier was a pilot that Dwight had photographed extensively. Later, in some spectacular movie footage, he was shown being shot down. When Steichen learned of this, *The Fighting Lady* came into being."[22]

Audiences were enthralled by the footage of Japanese bombers erupting into flames, exploding before their eyes, then falling into the sea. A thunderous sound track rendered the ear-shattering noise of war, as well as capturing the eerie, intimidating silences. The film was unsparing with its graphic scenes of injured pilots and other casualties—even showing caskets, bedecked in flags, ready to be buried in the sea. *The Fighting Lady* won the Academy Award for Best Documentary Feature in 1944 and the Art Directors Club Award in 1945, as well as other honors.

At the Museum of Modern Art in New York, from January 23 until March 20, 1945, enthusiastic patrons trooped through "Power in the Pacific," the second joint navy and MoMA exhibition organized by Steichen. His own pictures were unimportant to him. He wanted to create a photographic mosaic of World War II naval aviation, using the images created by his navy photographers. He took immense pride in the work they had achieved; he was simply their director, he thought, pointing them toward the fulfillment of their own potential. He prized first and foremost their individual interpretations of the war, believing that together they were breaking new ground in photography.

As the war continued and their work received wider attention, Steichen and his gritty unit, which was beginning to be known as "Steichen's Boys," won the respect of their colleagues. They enjoyed great visibility and success, while also causing occasional controversy. At the urging of Admiral Radford and other officers, Adm. Chester Nimitz, the chief of naval operations, gave Steichen standing, open orders authorizing him and his men to go anywhere they wished to go, to board any ship to take photographs, to fly military priority on any plane, to travel essentially at will. Some onlookers conjectured that Steichen and his men were informants secretly dispatched by the Navy Department to evaluate their efficiency and effectiveness.

Gradually, Steichen added other crack photographers to his elite crew: Charles Steinheimer, John Swope, Thomas Binford, Barrett Gallagher. Before it all ended, his small coterie of photographers had traversed the world with their cameras, compiling an unprecedented chronicle of the world at war. In 1945, Secretary of the Navy James Forrestal ordered Steichen to assume command of all navy combat photography and appointed him director of the newly established U.S. Navy Photographic Institute. Overnight, his command exploded from ten photographers to four thousand men—photographers, technicians, and other staff support personnel—and he was soon promoted to captain. His new mission was twofold, and an extension of the goals he had set for himself with his original Naval Aviation group: to chronicle the history of the war—for the official record—and to communicate events and themes—for public information and understanding.

Whether Steichen was at his desk in Washington or on the prow of a ship in the Pacific, his men knew that they had his ardent support. His photographers had only one continuing gripe, and try as he would, Steichen could not alleviate it. They wanted byline credit for their dangerous and compelling photographic work when their prints ran in newspapers and magazines around the world. That was against military policy, however, and not even Steichen, with all his clout, could change that.

In Steichen's war, the camera served not as a weapon or a tool, as in World War I, but as a witness. He gave himself orders to go back to the Pacific in 1945 to cover the action at Iwo Jima and on Guam, making plans to fly to Guam to inspect personally the photographic offices and laboratories at the new navy command station there. In the meantime, in his official capacity, he was privy to plans for the impending invasion of Iwo Jima. He wanted to cover it himself, and he asked his old friend Tom Maloney, now a war correspondent, to accompany him. But before he left for Guam and Iwo Jima in March of 1945, Steichen took Dana to Michigan to spend some time with the Sandburgs in their big white house on the crest of the Lake Michigan dunes.

It would be their last time together there, for the Sandburgs were looking for a more spacious farm, in a more temperate climate. Paula wanted to expand her goat breeding and dairy operation and was worn out by this last brutal Michigan winter, when the goats had to be barn-fed for months. Besides, the family needed more space and more privacy, for Sandburg was such a popular national figure that increasing numbers of strangers wandered up to the door in hopes of talking to the poet, or getting an autograph or a lock of his famous white hair. Remembering the glorious Carolina mountains from their 1926 retreat there, Dana and Steichen encouraged the Sandburgs to look at land in western North Carolina. There, a thermal belt enfolded several pleasant mountain towns—including Asheville, Hendersonville, and Flat Rock.[23]

There was much talk during that visit about the Sandburgs' plans, as well as Steichen's wartime adventures. Helga was still living in the orchard cottage with John Carl and Karlen Paula. Scholarly Margaret Sandburg and her shy, gentle sister Janet watched in amusement as Uncle Ed played with Helga's children, frolicking on the floor on his hands and knees, pretending to be a dog, growling, barking, doing tricks. Paula recorded these special days in family snapshots. On the sunny steps of the house she had designed, Paula posed her brother, sixty-six and still cutting an elegant figure in his uniform, with her grandson in his sailor suit. Both of them saluted smartly for the camera.

There were walks and talks, and sumptuous meals—roast beef and Yorkshire pudding, a Lord Baltimore cake laden with macaroons, pecans, almonds, and cherries, plenty of goat's milk to drink, and wine, made from Oma's old recipe, to toast Steichen's upcoming birthday, as well as the liberation of Luxembourg, the homeland. Helga was "surprised and also enchanted," she wrote, when her uncle kissed her that night—not as a niece, but as a desirable woman. "Honored and curious. It is, as he says, Biblical."[24] She wrote about it in her journal that night, and years later wove the memory into "*. . . Where Love Begins.*" Her uncle walked her home at the end of the evening to the Orchard Cottage where she lived with her children, took her in his arms, and kissed her passionately. "There is forty years difference in our ages. This has nothing to do with incest. This is tribute. I am not about to reject this man I adore. And also I may learn something. As time goes on and the war reaches an end and 'the boys' come home, Helga hopes to garner more kisses, more honors."[25]

She wondered, in that wartime, on the advent of his return to the Pacific, if he carried with him some sense of "his fragility, his mortality."[26]

After he flew back into the heart of the war zone, Dana felt as if Steichen had been away a "hundred years already and should be coming home" instead of traveling to the "other end" of the universe.[27] He spent his birthday with Admiral Nimitz on Guam, then headed for Iwo Jima, a little scrap of land in the Pacific strand of islands—the Bonin, the Volcano, and the Marianas. The brutal struggle over the island was testimony to its strategic value as a landing field for the Pacific air fleet. When

Steichen and Maloney finally went ashore once Iwo Jima had been secured, they saw a charred, "bitter, desolate, godforsaken" island, Maloney remembered. Steichen and his men photographed it all—"the havoc, the soldiers, the invasion, and its results."[28]

That night, Japanese soldiers who had been hiding underground slipped into American encampments and tossed hand grenades into the tents where navy pilots were sleeping. It was a horrible finale for Steichen's close-up of war. The carnage haunted him, further hardening his resolve to turn images of war into instruments for peace. Among the pictures Steichen took on Iwo Jima are two unforgettable images. In *After the Taking of Iwo Jima Island,* four fingers of a hand jut through rocky debris, the dying gesture of a Japanese soldier trapped in the bomb blast. To take the other picture, Steichen knelt to photograph one crushed flower blooming upward through the rubble of rocks and tree limbs.

Steichen wanted to be the Mathew Brady of World War II, Wayne Miller remembered, to photograph war as it had never been photographed before, not for the sake of the war but for the sake of an enduring peace. Steichen continually encouraged Miller and the other combat photographers to focus on the fighting men themselves, rather than on machines and weapons, to go forward in "a warmer and more human direction."[29] The technology of war was inevitably rendered obsolete, he observed; the human factor in war was the constant.

When Steichen had entered World War I after years as a champion of photography as an art form, he had undergone a profound transformation of viewpoint, coming out with a keen, almost reverent sense of the realistic, naturalistic possibilities of photography. Now Steichen's post as chief of all navy combat photography in World War II stretched his already-expansive vision of the medium's documentary potential. Ironically, the experience in his second war also brought Steichen back to his original excitement about photography as fine art. After four years devoted to making his camera testament of World War II, Steichen said he came to a "deeply revitalized passion" for the unlimited possibilities of photography as an art form.[30] He would spend the rest of his life fostering and promoting the artistic work of other photographers, just as he had facilitated the work of photographers as well as painters and sculptors at 291 during the old Photo-Secession days.[31]

Thus, these two world wars, as much as any other pivotal episodes in his life, forced Steichen to an ultimate synthesis: No matter the instrument or the medium, art and reality were equivalents. The camera could fuse truth and art; a photograph could tell the truth artistically *and* realistically at once, and one mode did not preclude the other.

Furthermore, prodded by the war, by his own continually evolving aesthetics, and by the passionate convictions he and his sister and brother-in-law held about social justice, Steichen now wanted to use his art to address head-on "the living issues" of his times.[32] Having seen enough conflict and discord to last a lifetime, he still held stubbornly to the belief that for all their contentious struggles, people were more alike than they were different. Perhaps the camera could probe the universal essences of life, could explain men and women to themselves, could even help them aspire to harmony and unity, rather than capitulate to chaos and conflict.

During one of their wartime talks, Sandburg reminded Steichen of how often Lincoln had spoken during the Civil War of the family of man, a resonant, biblical phrase that Sandburg had woven into his own poetry and prose. Steichen, too, appreciated the phrase and the concept, now more than ever. He began to think in new ways about the exhibition he had dreamed of since the FSA photographs had first stirred his imagination during the Depression. Nations had been horrifically ravaged in the Second World War. Countless individual lives had been destroyed in the maelstrom; in some countries, a whole generation of men and women had been wasted.

The catastrophic tragedy underscored the simple truth Sandburg had written in *The People, Yes*. Like it or not, every man, woman, and child on the planet was irrevocably a member of "the little Family of Man / hugging the little ball of Earth."[33]

Back in the United States in early April 1945, for a few days' leave at Umpawaug, Steichen was taking an official tour of a nearby navy shipyard when he heard the news of President Roosevelt's death. Immediately he called his Washington office to dispatch his men to photograph the American people mourning their commander in chief. Wayne Miller and Fenno Jacobs were already gearing up to take their cameras into the streets of Washington, D.C. As the news sped through the nation's capital, and on April fifteenth, the day of the national funeral, the photographers chronicled a profoundly moving pageant of grief and respect. Miller made the sad journey to Hyde Park to record pictures of Roosevelt's final homecoming and his burial. Afterward, a bereaved nation had to pick up the reins of war again.

It finally ended in Europe May 7, 1945. After the cataclysm of the first atomic bombs at Hiroshima and Nagasaki, the war was officially over in the Pacific on September second. Steichen was removed from active-duty status October 22, 1945, but he worked on his last project for the navy until January 1946—a book commissioned by James Forrestal soon after he put Steichen in charge of all naval photography. Forrestal wanted a book of navy photographs that covered all navy actions, and he wanted it edited, designed, and published immediately. Every navy man and woman would receive a copy. When *U.S. Navy War Photographs: Pearl Harbor to Tokyo Bay* appeared in 1946, it sold at a rate of a million copies a month.

Other branches of the military service had excellent photography units, of course, but Steichen's navy combat photography unit won special recognition for its masterful technical work in World War II. "The primary reason for the consistent high quality of the navy pictures," wrote photojournalist Susan D. Moeller, "was that Edward Steichen... headed the naval aviation's photographic unit.... The images that came out of this unit were frequently technical masterpieces—a tribute to their leader's emphasis on the craft of photography. But the best of the navy photography is notable not for its artistry but for its depiction of the 'essence' of war."[34]

In all the wars before, there had never been anything like the photographic record his navy photographers had made of this war, Steichen told a reporter.[35] But the war had worn him out—the inhuman, insane misery of it, the wanton suffering and destruction. After the photographic laboratory in Washington had been dismantled, the navy photographers honored at an awards ceremony, and the book put to bed, Captain Steichen—officially discharged and decorated with the Distinguished Service Medal—went home to Dana and Umpawaug. He was nearly sixty-seven, and he was exhausted—not so much physically as emotionally. Kate, waiting in Connecticut to give him a laurel wreath and a victory celebration, could read his depression in his face and in the sagging of his usually erect shoulders. He had his own wounds from this war, Kate could see. She disposed of the laurel wreath. Her father would, over time, have to find a way to heal himself.[36]

The Christmas of 1945 was a good one, despite everything. Steichen and Dana spent four days on Long Island with Mary and Frank Calderone and Mary's nineteen-year-old daughter, Linda Martin. Dana wrote to Paula Sandburg on New Year's Day that it was wonderful to be civilians again.[37] They were inundated with snow, and Umpawaug had never looked more beautiful. Steichen needed the refuge of home, and of his own safe land, where new flowers could grow from the old seed.

People who knew him well often reflected that to understand Steichen, you had to look at his flowers as intently as you looked at his photographs. Plant breeding prompted Steichen to express some of his "best" and "most strongly intellectual" attributes, Matthew Josephson had written to him as he worked on a *New Yorker* profile of Steichen in 1944. Josephson could see that this work was not a hobby for Steichen but a "search" for "life, nature, beauty, color. . . ."[38] As always, Steichen's flowers meant escape into a beautiful, orderly world that yielded to his control. They obeyed him, but they also invigorated, refreshed, consoled, and delighted. He could lose himself in his garden and, shedding the old skin, find himself anew.

Meanwhile, the Sandburgs were uprooting themselves from Michigan that winter and moving to Connemara, a beautiful 245-acre pre–Civil War estate in hilly Flat Rock, North Carolina. Dana had helped her sister-in-law find this ideal place. "The health of the Missus, the ancient desire of Helga for a farm and horses, the plight of barn-fed goats who want pasture, these sent us to N.C. I told'em I'd go any place they picked," Sandburg wrote to a friend.[39] Paula orchestrated the job of transporting 42,000 pounds of books, papers, furnishings, and other belongings, as well as three daughters, two grandchildren, and more than thirty prize dairy goats. Daughters Margaret and Janet would live at home with their parents all their lives. After Helga and Joe Thoman were divorced on July 31, 1945, Helga and her two children became members of the household. All the Sandburgs hoped that Dana and Steichen would travel to Connemara for a long visit by springtime.

Steichen told his sister immediately after the war he was just another GI feeling "lost and bewildered," and trying to catch up on his sleep.[40] Several interesting jobs were staring him in the face, he reported. Of course, he said, he could just as well take it easy or get into another plant-breeding mood. But he had been asked to become the consulting picture editor of a new illustrated magazine to be published by *The Saturday Evening Post* group. He had an offer to direct television programs. Tom Maloney wanted him to take an active role in his photographic publications. And he had been approached about heading up the department of photography at the Museum of Modern Art. He would not pursue the new magazine or television work, but one idea proposed by Maloney intrigued him.

His World War II experience, Steichen recalled, convinced him of the immense power and potential of photography as simultaneously a "means of documentation" and "an art form."[41] It was this duality he sought to explore in his work after the war. Knowing this, Tom Maloney thought of the Museum of Modern Art as the ideal arena for Steichen's future life in photography. Maloney helped to persuade Henry Moe, Stephen Clark, and MoMA director Alfred Barr to create the new position of director of the Department of Photography, thereby giving photography parity with painting, sculpture, and other arts at MoMA. And he lobbied to give the job to Steichen.

In the meantime, at home contemplating his future, Steichen and Dana worked hard getting Umpawaug organized again. They cleaned house thoroughly, hired a new gardener, and started the spring planting, thrilled to be ordering seeds and working in the delphinium fields once more. But in New York, a political storm was brewing over Steichen's possible appointment as director of photography at the Museum of Modern Art.

As Maloney explained the sequence of events, Steichen had struck up a friendship with Henry Moe, director of the Guggenheim Foundation and an influential board member at the Museum of Modern Art. One day at lunch, Moe asked Maloney for a recommendation for the new post of director of photography at MoMA. "What about Captain Steichen?" Maloney asked.

THE UNIVERSAL LANGUAGE (1943-1946)

"I hoped that would be your answer," Moe said to Maloney. "Will you ask him?"⁴²

Maloney agreed to put the question to Steichen when he dined with him and Eugene Meyer to celebrate Meyer's seventieth birthday.⁴³

"E.J., Henry Moe has asked me to ask you something," Maloney told Steichen. "Would you accept the position of director of photography at the Museum of Modern Art? Henry wants that."⁴⁴

"Yes. You bet your life I will," Steichen answered, with an enthusiasm almost equivalent to his description of crawling through the telephone wire to accept the chance for active duty with the navy. For Steichen, it was déjà vu: "Here I was back again with the old platform for the Photo Secession, still believing that the best way to further the recognition for photography was to place it alongside the other art forms."⁴⁵

The backstage political maneuvering had apparently begun at MoMA at least a year earlier, however, and Stieglitz, Ansel Adams, and Beaumont Newhall believed that Steichen was behind it. There is no evidence, however, of any prior discussions between Steichen and Maloney about the job. Beaumont and Nancy Newhall definitely expected that Beaumont would receive the appointment. He had done well in his own military career as a photo-intelligence officer in the army, and he had, after all, set up the department of photography at MoMA before the war. Yet as early as October 1944—at least fifteen months before Steichen's papers made any reference to the idea—the Newhalls were writing to each other about their fears of Steichen's encroachment in their territory. Nancy Newhall, for example, had worried in a letter written to her husband on October 29, 1944, that Steichen might want the job, and that he had clout with the trustees who could help him get it.⁴⁶

Newhall then wrote back quickly in alarm that it had never occurred to him that he might not get the appointment as director. He would be greatly disappointed; furthermore, he and Nancy would have no choice but to leave the museum. Newhall told his wife that it would be impossible for them to work for Steichen because his perspective on photography was so "utterly different" from theirs, and Steichen himself was "so self-centered and difficult" with an aggressive "megalomania." Furthermore, Newhall believed, he and his wife could not work under anyone; to do so, he wrote to her, "would be to yield prestige to someone who knows less than we do—for we are better equipped for the job than anybody else (with the obvious exception of Stieglitz)."[47]

Over the next few months, Newhall worried continually about his apparent failure to win the directorship at MoMA. He thought about Steichen's spectacular "Road to Victory" exhibit, which had "eclipsed all the little shows" preceding it. Newhall believed that he had always put on "small, quiet, unobtrusive" tasteful shows.[48] He saw that Steichen, on the other hand, was interested in "the illustrative use of photography, particularly in swaying large masses of people."[49]

Ansel Adams had written to Newhall in 1945 appraising Steichen's "Power in the Pacific," finding it almost exactly the opposite of what he believed the Museum of Modern Art should strive for. Adams called the show "slick, mechanically excellent, superficially moving by virtue of the tremendous scale and impact of the subject." In his opinion, however, the exhibition struck no spiritual note, expressed no reasons for the war, revealed nothing about what the photographers thought or felt. Still, Adams recognized that for every one person exposed to what he and the Newhalls were trying to do in photography, "there are literally thousands who are exposed to Steichen, *U.S. Camera, Popular Photography,* and advertising expressions.... The enormous and conscience-less ballyhoo and presentation simply hypnotize the mass of spectators."[50]

As early as October 1944, a year before Maloney said that he first presented the possibility to Steichen, MoMA staff members had been spreading rumors about Steichen's possible appointment. In the fall of 1945, Nancy Newhall told her husband that Stieglitz had warned her that they should look out for Steichen because he "wants your department at the Museum." Without giving any reason or background for his caution, Stieglitz said, "Never underestimate Steichen. He's always doing something; he's a power. Watch out." Nancy Newhall suggested that Stieglitz believed Steichen wanted to use MoMA "as a great stage from which to direct further vast exhibitions of photography as communication and exhortation, not as an art."[51] So ran the merry-go-round of gossip in the small world of MoMA-connected photographers.

On December 10, 1945, Tom Maloney sent MoMA trustees a three-page draft proposal recommending that Steichen be appointed director of the museum's Department of Photography, and that he choose his own staff and focus. Newhall spent part of Christmas Day of 1945 writing to

Ansel Adams about "the threat to the Department brought about by Steichen and Maloney."⁵² He told Adams that Steichen's vision of photography veered so dramatically from their own that even if he stayed at the museum, he could never implement his own ideas. Newhall was sure that Steichen would "run into the ground" all they had achieved as well as "create such turmoil and make such demands that things would be in an awful mess."⁵³ While he had respected Steichen's early photography, Newhall said, he believed that Steichen no longer cared about art and beauty, but now saw photography "only as documentation of the social scene, or as a journalistic medium used for propaganda."⁵⁴

Without informing Newhall, the board of trustees of the Museum of Modern Art accepted Maloney's proposal and offered Steichen the directorship of the Department of Photography early in February of 1946. Shocked by the official news that Steichen had been appointed, Newhall resigned as curator of photography on March 7, 1946. Furthermore, according to Newhall, several photographers—including Harry Callahan, Helen Levitt, Brett Weston, Willard Van Dyke, and Edward Weston—wrote letters to the MoMA board to protest Steichen's appointment. The most outspoken Steichen opponent, however, was Ansel Adams, who suggested that with Steichen, the museum was turning its back on creative photography, opting for photography as illustration rather than expression.

Adams had been deeply annoyed in 1941 when Tom Maloney's *U.S. Camera* had criticized "Sixty Photographs," the MoMA exhibition Newhall had curated, with Adams's considerable help. The unsigned article, which Adams attributed to Maloney and Steichen, complained that inadequate attention and space had been given to the images in the exhibit, in comparison to much larger simultaneous exhibitions of Frank Lloyd Wright's architecture, D. W. Griffith's films, and Thérèse Bonney's photographs of Finland in war.⁵⁵ Adams himself had planned the presentation of the exhibit down to its finest detail, he complained to Stieglitz in 1941. He suggested that negative criticism from Maloney and Steichen was incomprehensible, and prejudiced. He did not blame Maloney personally, Adams told Stieglitz, but he charged that Steichen was guilty of "conduct unbecoming an artist, or an intelligent human being."⁵⁶

Like Newhall, Adams was furious that he had not been consulted before the Steichen appointment in 1946. Also, like Newhall, his animosity toward Steichen had at least a five-year history. Adams charged that to pass over Beaumont Newhall in favor of Steichen, with his propensity for the "spectacular and 'popular,' " was a "body blow to the progress of creative photography." Adams contended that photography demanded more "penetrating evaluations" than any art form, yet was especially vulnerable to "superficial and glamorous showmanship. . . ." He believed that with the Steichen appointment, the MoMA board was "trading gold for brass." Further, he wrote, while the great shows of war photography were important, they were "objective and illustrative—not creative or contemplative." They drew crowds and public attention to MoMA, but in Adams's opinion, they were more suitable for Grand Central Station (often a site for grand photographic displays) than for the Museum of Modern Art.[57]

On March 15, 1946, Adams wrote to Stieglitz that it was a good thing he was not in New York; if so, he would probably indulge in a "window breaking spree" at MoMA. The officials who made the Steichen appointment were "stupid fools," he added, symptomatic of the times with its "glorification of the *empty*."[58]

Newhall departed bitterly in the spring of 1946, and in May, according to Nancy Newhall, the thirty members of the MoMA Advisory Committee on Photography resigned as a group because of unhappiness over the general development of the museum, including "the whole photography mess."[59] The Newhalls and Adams clearly believed that Steichen had executed a calculated coup of the Department of Photography.[60] Newhall described in his journal an impromptu meeting with Steichen on May 9, 1946, when he stopped by to do some errands at MoMA. "I barged right in, and was warmly greeted by Steichen," he wrote.[61]

According to Newhall, Steichen then told him that he had made a great contribution to American photography. He was hurt, Steichen said, when he "found out through the photographic grapevine" that Newhall was "hostile." Steichen was "emotionally shaken," Newhall thought, appearing to be on the verge of tears.[62] But Newhall believed Steichen was "turning on that powerful emotional quality of his," although "a little too late."

He told Steichen he wanted to help if he could, and Steichen in turn promised his help to Newhall. He was moved, Newhall recalled, but "I

THE UNIVERSAL LANGUAGE (1943–1946)

was brought back to my senses by Ferd Reyher, with whom I had dinner. He said the only thing to do . . . was to look Steichen straight in the eye and say shit and walk out."[63]

In the MoMA struggle over power, territory, and politics, there were echoes of a familiar refrain: First, there was the chronic disagreement over fundamental purpose in art, and especially in photography. Steichen had already been fighting that battle on the front lines in Europe back in 1902, the year Ansel Adams was born, and in 1908, the year Beaumont Newhall was born. Steichen had metamorphosed through several evolutions as an artist by 1941, when, at age sixty-two, he provoked the wrath of Adams, thirty-nine, and Newhall, thirty-three. Throughout his career, he had apprenticed himself over and over again, seeking new possibilities in photography, his artistic medium of choice. There was a timeless reprise in the brouhaha at MoMA over whether photography, or any art form, could be art if it also *communicated*—and, worse, effectively communicated to the *mass of common people*. Steichen had heard this debate many times before, especially in 1923 when he had turned deliberately to commercial photography at *Vanity Fair* and *Vogue,* and in 1929, when he and Sandburg had started a firestorm among certain critics—the most vocal of them allies of Stieglitz—with their joint testimony in *Steichen the Photographer*.

Adams and Newhall had aligned themselves with Stieglitz, the impresario of modern photography, sharing his passionate convictions about the purpose and purity of photography as art. They were the classic "art for art's sake boys" who had nipped at Steichen's heels for nearly three decades, and although Steichen respected their talents and their tenets, he went on his own stubborn, independent way, as he had been doing since Adams and Newhall were in diapers, as he had always done.

Adams was a great photographer, as obstinately original and independent as Steichen himself; Newhall was primarily a critic and historian who occasionally practiced photography. The two men shared a strong philosophy about the very purpose of the Museum of Modern Art, particularly the mission of the Department of Photography, a second major point of conflict in the territorial struggle over the directorship. Young Beaumont Newhall, who after leaving Harvard became the MoMA librarian, took a curatorial, archival approach to photography. His own work in photo intelligence in World War II had been limited and secretive by its very nature, and this seemed emblematic of his vision of modern photography. He collected a fine body of photographs for the museum's new permanent collection, seeking within the academy of the museum to collect, preserve, and protect photography as art. It was a conservative, even elitist strategy, having more to do with the welfare of certain exclusive images than with the interests of the art-loving public.

As a navy photographer, Steichen had worked on a broader human canvas, more and more deliberately using his camera to document and to communicate. Roaming the world for nearly half a century, he had indeed become a populist, as fervent in the forties and fifties as his sister and brother-in-law had always been. He was in tune with the photography of the present and the future, having come to believe that photography's most important function was to communicate. In his mind, this heightened rather than diminished the importance of the photographer as an artist. Besides, he cautioned, "One is forced to recognize that photography, considered purely as an art form, faces the fierce competition of the other older media. In direct and certainly in mass communication by images, photography is without a peer."[64]

No doubt Steichen was at least momentarily shaken by the criticism he heard, secondhand, about his MoMA appointment. Still, he was a veteran, in more arenas than war, and he had work to do. Apolitical though he was in many ways, he could be an astute politician when he had to, and he had a knack for making friends in high places.

Steichen left little private indication of how he felt about the controversy over his appointment, although his public version of events coincided with Tom Maloney's account. But since Photo-Secession days, Steichen had never liked the babble of politics, and by now he had honed to a fine art the ability to lose himself in his work. At home at Umpawaug, he helped his new gardener get organized for spring planting, and he bided his time until the MoMA leadership had all the logistics in place for his new job. Then he threw himself eagerly into the process of getting organized at MoMA. "I could not have dreamed up a more ideal proposition," he wrote years later.[65]

"E.J. is excited about his jobs," Dana wrote to Paula. He was bursting with "plans—ideas and work."[66] Indeed, Steichen found himself working harder than ever before, he wrote to his sister, telling her that the Department of Photography at MoMA was now on his shoulders and that he would be organizing the department "from the ground up." He reassured her that she was not to worry about him, however, for he had learned not to let his work wear him out as in past years. Once again, Steichen and Dana reorganized their lives, preparing now to spend much of their time in New York. Dana worked on her typing skills so she could help him with his voluminous personal correspondence, and they both rejoiced that the new job would provide a "real stenog" to handle the official correspondence.[67] Dana also planned to find a cook, so that she could help Steichen with other museum work, and she hoped that both of them would have some free time left over for their own photography.

However, Steichen's first major decision after accepting the MoMA appointment was to give up being a photographer. He would have to be entirely objective in evaluating the work of other photographers, he knew; he would need to focus on the creation of exhibitions of photographs by others. Consequently, for the time being, at least, he put his cameras away.

Steichen got the news on July 10, 1946, that Alfred Stieglitz had suffered a severe attack of angina on July sixth at An American Place, his beloved gallery at 509 Madison Avenue in New York. The Newhalls had found him there and helped him home to his apartment at 59 East Fifty-fourth Street. He was an old man, failing, closer to death than anyone liked to think. He lived alone during the time his wife worked at Ghost Ranch in Abiquiu, New Mexico, where she felt most truly alive and free to paint. He was with her wherever she was, Stieglitz had written to her on June third. "And you are ever with me I know."[68]

He wrote to tell his wife about the attack, reassuring her by saying, "Nearly all right. Nothing for you to worry about."[69] But three days after the angina attack, Stieglitz suffered a massive stroke and had to be hospitalized.

Dressed in a comfortable red cotton dress and her everyday work shoes, Georgia O'Keeffe was driving from her isolated ranch to a country store in the nearby village of Española when the boy dispatched to bring her a telegram waved her down on the highway. The wire contained the news of her husband's grave illness, so alarming O'Keeffe that, without turning back to her ranch to pack, she drove immediately to the airport to fly back to New York. Not even she could rouse Stieglitz from his coma, however, and he died in Doctors Hospital shortly after midnight on Saturday, July thirteenth.

Steichen had long ago befriended Stieglitz's first wife, Emmy, and his second wife, Georgia, as well as Stieglitz's "other women"—Katharine Rhoades and Dorothy Norman, both of whom had remained Stieglitz's loyal friends even after romance had ebbed away. Not only had Stieglitz been his mentor and colleague, Stieglitz and his family had opened their homes to Steichen and his family over the years. He owed Stieglitz an immense debt, and now that he himself was sixty-seven, he better understood the magnitude of this.

The flood of memory swept Steichen back to 1900 and his exultation when the great Stieglitz saw and understood his work, affirmed it, even bought a few prints. There was the exhilaration of the 291 experiments, and the joy of sharing Paris with Stieglitz, of taking him to galleries, to the studios of Rodin and Matisse, to the salons of Leo, Gertrude, Michael, and Sarah Stein. There, Stieglitz had been able to peruse their extraordinary art collections and intimately discover the work of Cézanne, Renoir, Rodin, and Whistler.

Steichen worried in retrospect that he and Clara had strained matters for the Stieglitz family during all the years of turmoil in their marriage. He saw more clearly over time how they may have thoughtlessly imposed on a friendship—with his own moodiness and distractions and Clara's histrionics.[70] It would have been understandable if the Stieglitzes had come to resent him and Clara.

Stubborn and egocentric himself, Steichen recognized another obstinate old goat when he encountered one, and Stieglitz had matched and even surpassed Steichen in exerting his will. He came to feel that Stieglitz "only tolerated people close to him when they completely agreed with him and were of service." Yet he kept unwavering admiration for the "prodigious amount of work" that Stieglitz accomplished, his "almost unbelievable" patience. He remembered how Stieglitz had talked incessantly, often in parables, teaching, explaining, debating, how he had served countless artists, patrons, and friends as "a philosopher, a preacher, a teacher, and a father-confessor."[71]

The Universal Language (1943-1946)

Now that inimitable voice was gone. They had quarreled bitterly twice, once over 291, once over World War I. Stieglitz had severely disapproved when Steichen took up his career with Condé Nast and J. Walter Thompson, and Steichen knew it, knew how committed Stieglitz was to the "purity" of art. Aside from his own conviction that what he was doing *was* art, with a wide democratic outreach, Steichen resented Stieglitz's criticism on different grounds. It was one thing, he felt, to advocate purity when you had the material resources of your family to rely on. It was quite another when you were poor and completely self-supporting, trying to commit to your art and to keep yourself and your family alive.

World War I had tested their friendship. France was another mother country to Steichen; he had made his home there for years, had grown flowers in the earth there, had found himself as an artist there. Stieglitz had spent his seminal years in Germany, had long admired German art, culture, and technology, had discovered photography and himself as a photographer in that country. In artistic theory and practice, they had crossed a continental divide in their relationship during the early twenties. Although Steichen accepted that as a matter of free choice for them both, Stieglitz condemned Steichen the commercial artist to friends and strangers alike.

Unlike the authoritarian Stieglitz, Steichen listened more than he talked, welcomed dialogue, did not require total agreement from his friends. Always in his relationship with Stieglitz, there had been the prevailing undertow of affection, gratitude, respect. And, between the two men, there was in later years more communication, even consensus, than many believed. In the collective portrait *America and Alfred Stieglitz,* which spoke for and about Stieglitz, Paul Rosenfeld had articulated a view of democratic art that exactly matched Steichen's own vision: "Thus, American Photography is an instrument and an incentive toward 'the humanization of society, the furtherance of the cause of social justice, the creation of a democracy of the spirit.' "[72]

Steichen was glad he had paid his own public tribute to Stieglitz and the old Photo-Secession in June of 1941 in *Vogue*. He had written then in the essay he called "The Fighting Photo-Secession" that "the heritage stemming from this Photo-Secession movement stands out in bold relief, as a great tree against the sky, and the trunk of that tree is Alfred

Stieglitz."⁷³ Stieglitz may have been right when he told Dorothy Norman that when he died, Steichen would be his greatest mourner.⁷⁴

According to the obituary in the *New York Times,* the family did not plan a funeral service, yet Steichen and Dana, the last to arrive, joined about twenty other friends and family members in the silence of the Frank E. Campbell Funeral Home on Madison Avenue. Stieglitz had wanted "no ceremony, no eulogy, no music," his niece Sue Davidson Lowe remembered, and his wishes were honored.⁷⁵ Georgia O'Keeffe was "strained but under control," Nancy Newhall thought, while Sue Davidson Lowe recalled her unforgettable "majesty."⁷⁶ Dorothy Norman, his devoted friend, was "utterly shattered, weeping, even on Steichen's shoulder."⁷⁷ Before they departed, Stieglitz's widow and his friends and family walked quietly by the casket.

Steichen had long ago embraced Sandburg's Scandinavian custom of laying an evergreen bough on a coffin, liking the symbolism of it, the gesture toward ongoing life.⁷⁸ He brought with him from the country a pine bough from a tree he had planted years earlier at Umpawaug and called "Alfred's tree."⁷⁹ When it was Steichen's turn to pass the coffin of his friend and mentor, he laid the fragrant pine branch on the black muslin. Unaware of the meaning this custom held for Steichen, a few onlookers thought he was being theatrical, maudlin, even insincere.⁸⁰ To the contrary, the evergreen bough was his customary token of homage to a deceased friend or relative, a heartfelt, instinctive gesture. As he walked away, Steichen found himself weeping.

Given the personal politics often following death, some of Stieglitz's friends were offended when Georgia O'Keeffe turned to Steichen for immediate help in the days after Stieglitz died. She wanted no part of Stieglitz's colleague and surrogate wife, Dorothy Norman, or the Newhalls, for instance. She and Steichen were mavericks, like Stieglitz, secure in their own prodigious gifts, grounded in a strong sense of self—outsiders in a very real way, and, for all the adulation, consummate loners. She and Steichen had known Stieglitz as few others ever had, and they had loved him, not just for his magnificent, infuriating genius but also for the profound goodness in him.

Stieglitz had told Nancy Newhall and others how years ago Steichen had wept when he first saw Stieglitz's photographs of O'Keeffe. He believed that "Steichen at his best, when he is true to himself, is as sensitive as a fine woman, and he *sees.*"[81] But in the end, it was O'Keeffe who saw Stieglitz most clearly, and she articulated his essence, years after his death, in her introduction to *Georgia O'Keeffe: A Portrait by Alfred Stieglitz*. "For me he was much more wonderful in his work than as a human being," she remembered. "I believe it was the work that kept me with him—though I loved him as a human being. I could see his strengths and weaknesses. I put up with what seemed to me a good deal of contradictory nonsense because of what seemed clear and bright and wonderful." She never knew Stieglitz to travel anywhere to photograph, she recalled. "His eye was in him, and he used it on anything that was nearby. Maybe that way he was always photographing himself."[82]

31

"The Family of Man"

(1 9 4 7 - 1 9 5 5)

A camera testament, a drama of the grand canyon of humanity, an epic woven of fun, mystery and holiness—here is the Family of Man![1]

—CARL SANDBURG

"STEICHEN HAS IN HIS LIFETIME BEEN many things," according to a *Life* magazine recapitulation of his career at midcentury. "His paintings hang in the Metropolitan and Luxembourg Museums. His research into plant genetics has produced new types of delphiniums. But mostly he has spent his life in the pursuit of 'that charlatan, Light,' as he calls the art of photography. Today, at 71, he is the dean of American photography and director of photography at New York's Museum of Modern Art."[2]

With Stieglitz's death, Steichen indeed became the elder statesman of American photography. Stieglitz and "the Fighting Photo-Secession" must have been very much on his mind as he began his work at the Museum of Modern Art. He took up the reins later than expected, apparently because of the familiar old dynamics—politics in photography and museum circles and problems in fund-raising. Indeed, little had changed since Photo-Secession days, and that fact depressed him. Steichen wrote to tell Wayne and Joan Miller that life could be "vague and unsettled" even for "young fellers" such as himself. He observed that millionaires and "big 'bizness' " were demonstrating their usual conservatism about

"The Family of Man" (1947–1955)

funding a new project—adding that the new project in this instance "is me." He was ready to forget the whole idea—to say to hell with it—when matters were resolved, and Steichen's appointment was made official.³

"It is very gratifying to the Trustees of the Museum and to me personally to have Mr. Steichen's acceptance of the Directorship of the Museum's Department of Photography," MoMA president Nelson A. Rockefeller said in his press announcement in July of 1947.

> *Without question he is today American's foremost figure in the field of photography.... There is something peculiarly fitting in this affiliation of Steichen with the Museum of Modern Art. In the early part of this century it was he who suggested to Stieglitz the original idea for the Photo Secession Gallery, later to become the famous "291," cradle of modern art in America.*⁴

As was his habit, Steichen was dreaming on a grand scale—and now, with the support of MoMA and the photographic industry, which had endorsed his appointment, the chances were high that his dreams could be realized. He wanted to compose a "picture of America," he said, "the warm sweetness of its homes, the greatness of its industries, the productivity of its farms, the sweep of its landscape, its big cities, its small towns and above all—the faces of the people."⁵ He was enthralled with the great democracy of photography, supposedly practiced now by 20 million people in the United States, he pointed out. Here was democratic art as he and the Sandburgs had long conceived and embraced it. Photography, Steichen told Maloney at *U.S. Camera* in Lincolnesque words, was an art form "capable of giving us a creative record of the people made by the people. The sensitivity of photography as a medium, together with its almost universal use, makes it an instrument that responds readily to the fertilizing influence of ideas."⁶

With the collaboration of his navy photographers, who had learned how to photograph "with the mind and the heart," Steichen had compiled "an epic pictorial record of humanity at war."⁷ Now he wanted to create another vast mural or montage, a panorama, an epic pictorial record of humanity at peace. Steichen was on fire again with the new potential of photography, perceiving it more than ever before as "an art, as a vital modern means of giving form to ideas."[8] And the territory of ideas was unlimited, awaiting exploration by a new generation of artists with cameras.

For his debut show as director, he turned to "what seemed to me the most promising and most vital area of photography, the field of documentary photo-journalism."[9] He featured the work of three photographers: Wayne Miller's chronicle of the birth of his son; Homer Page's photo narrative of an American Legion convention; and Leonard McCombe's photo essay on Berlin war refugees.

From the outset, many of his critics overlooked Steichen's stated conviction that the dual purpose of the museum exhibitions was simultaneously to make visible "works of art that might only be understood at the time by a handful of people as well as such forms of modern art that had large audiences."[10] He was seeking to open new horizons both for the informed elite and the uninformed mass audience. "Anybody that came with any kind of a new idea—I put my arms around them," he said. "Photography has too much of a tendency to remain static, and there is a new growth." He was convinced that the future of photography lay in "going out to get life."[11]

During his more than fifteen years as director of the Department of Photography, Steichen organized forty-four exhibitions, running an international gamut from the earliest photographers to the newest and most modern, and highlighting landmark innovations in photography, past, present, and future. Steichen often praised Beaumont Newhall's work in founding the museum's permanent collection of photographs, an archive of images from "earliest times to the present," from "every school, every direction, every tendency, and all photographic processes."[12] He wanted to expand and show that collection as well as to bring the contemporary world of photography to the walls of the museum, reaching beyond the relatively small audience of the artistically literate to the vast general audience. (Harvard graduate Newhall ruefully recalled that MoMA director John "Dick" Abbott had compared Steichen's vision of the museum's photography department to Harvard football, at the same time telling Newhall his own ideas could "be compared in popularity to crew on the Charles River."[13])

In 1950, while the MoMA galleries held a typically eclectic parade of photographs—by Robert Capa, Eugène Atget, Alfred Stieglitz, Lewis

"THE FAMILY OF MAN" (1947–1955)

Carroll, and many others—Steichen stepped briefly back into navy uniform when his old friend Admiral Radford, now commander in chief of the Pacific fleet, summoned him to serve as an official adviser on navy photography during the Korean conflict. Steichen directed an exhibition of contemporary war images, many of them photographs by David Douglas Duncan, whose book *This Is War* Steichen called "the most forceful indictment of the subject ever put forth by photography."[14] He saw with great disappointment, however, that while viewers momentarily found the pictures "wonderful, tragic, and some of them, ghastly," they quickly forgot them.[15]

They would tell him the exhibit was remarkable, Steichen complained, "and then they go out and have some drinks." For him, the 1951 exhibition was clearly a failure. He and so many others had photographed "the horrible monstrosity we call 'war,'" the "butcher shop" that set civilization back "to the animal stage," he told Wayne Miller.[16] "Although I had presented war in all its grimness in three exhibitions, I had failed to accomplish my mission. I had not incited people into taking open and united action against war itself."[17]

Then he had an epiphany: If the negative images would not stimulate positive action, perhaps the *positive* would yield results. He would have to create "a positive statement on what a wonderful thing life was, how marvelous people were, and, above all, how alike people were in all parts of the world."[18] Immediately, Steichen knew what to do with his longtime dream of an epic exhibition about Americans and American life. He would transform it from an American to a global, universal pageant, with the human condition as the theme.

Casting about for ideas, he turned, as he did again and again throughout the years, to his brother-in-law's books. As he leafed through Sandburg's Lincoln biography, three familiar words jumped out of the text of a speech by Lincoln: *family of man*. It was a resonant phrase that Sandburg had woven into his poetry, most recently *The People, Yes* (1936). There, once and for all, was "the all-embracing theme for the exhibition," Steichen wrote.[19] He scrawled a quick synopsis of his new vision, gave it to the stenographer to type, and then presented it to René d'Harnoncourt, the director of MoMA, and to the MoMA trustees. They approved Steichen's idea despite the knowledge that it would be a costly, time-consuming project. There were vocal dissenters, of course, especially those who did not want to see so much money and time invested in photography at the expense of the other arts. But when Nelson Rockefeller pledged the additional financial resources this ambitious project would require, "The Family of Man" was born.

To trace the conception of "The Family of Man" is to begin in Hancock, Michigan, in the 1880s, where, as Steichen often acknowledged, the seeds were sown in his boyhood, in every lesson his mother taught him about compassion and tolerance. The embryo of the idea grew during World War I and matured during the Depression, with the FSA photographs as catalysts. The shape expanded during and just after World War II, then was further defined during the Korean War. And although the exhibit would not be launched until 1955, for more than half a century afterward it could still be seen in one world venue or another. Steichen would call "The Family of Man" the "most important undertaking" of his long career.[20]

As he set out to create this mammoth show, Steichen's philosophy of exhibitions began to crystallize: This was to be an unprecedented theme exhibit designed so that a series of photographs could "collectively communicate a significant human experience." The process was more akin to producing a play or writing a novel or philosophical essay than to displaying the work of individual artists, he thought. The show not only had to be organized around an "intrinsic aim that gives it an element of the universal and an over-all unity"; it had to become an artistic entity itself, with an existence and character all its own, like "any other work of art."[21] The successful exhibition, in other words, must not only *present* works of art effectively but must itself *become* a work of art.

Steichen observed that while the director determines the pace when images are revealed in movies or on television, in the museum gallery, to the contrary, it is the individual visitor who chooses the pace and even the sequence of images. Steichen had sometimes single-handedly mounted early Photo-Secession exhibits and so knew instinctively the intricate interactions of background, angles of vision, textures, contours, the nuances of emotional impact. Over a lifetime, he had become a master of exhibition design, but despite his years of experience at 291 and elsewhere, he now listened respectfully to Herbert Bayer, George Kidder Smith, and others who had installed earlier MoMA exhibitions, learning from each of them. By the time he had finished his work on this radical new production, "The Family of Man" would become virtuoso performance art, its millions of viewers themselves intrinsic actors on the global stage Steichen created.

The dean had to take time out occasionally to accept the accolades and awards a lifetime of achievement afforded. He had received the *U.S. Camera* Achievement Award in 1949 as the individual who had rendered the most outstanding contributions to photography. In May of 1950, the American Institute of Architects sponsored a retrospective Steichen exhibition in Washington, D.C., awarded him its Fine Arts Medal, and named him a "Master of Photography." The May 15, 1950, issue of *Life* carried "A Portfolio of Photographs by Edward Steichen." In 1952, he was given the *Popular Photography Magazine* Award for his leadership of photography in America, and for his role in facilitating the progress of photography as an art, a science, and an industry.

By then, he was obsessed with his latest project, deeply absorbed in the specific plans for "The Family of Man." In 1952, with the Swiss émigré photographer Robert Frank serving as his translator when his own French and limited knowledge of German would not suffice, Steichen set out on a photographic quest to twenty-nine cities in eleven European countries, intent on gathering pictures from all over the world. On his way from Paris to Rome and Geneva, he wrote to tell Helga and her family that he was working "harder than ever before," and having a great deal of fun.[22] As Wayne Miller said, "The Family of Man" was an "impossible idea but it was Steichen-size and he pulled it off."[23]

On October 16, 1952, Clara Smith Steichen died in the American Hospital in Paris. The newspaper gave no cause of death, and family papers contain few details other than that she was seventy-seven years old and had had a long history of health problems. Clara had written Mary a bitter note in 1939, but she kept it, adding a sad coda in 1941, and sometime, somehow, the letter eventually made it into Mary's hands. Alluding to her disapproval of Kate's lesbianism, she still held faith, Clara wrote in those pages, that Kate would "liberate herself someday. If not I shall love her the more, for all she may never believe that." Clara also wrote to Mary that she had grieved more for the loss of Nell than for any of her other great losses.[24]

Clara had been bright and beautiful, and for years much loved by her husband, her children, and her friends. Tragically, she herself had done more than anyone to destroy that love. Later clinicians would most likely have diagnosed a paranoid personality disorder, or perhaps an even more severe mental illness as the years wore on. Perhaps modern therapy and treatment could have assuaged the tumultuous suffering that produced her suffocating loneliness and the angry attacks on those closest to her.

Steichen's early love letters testify that for a long time he had truly loved this woman. Once he had betrayed her trust, however, she aggressively, self-protectively distrusted his every move and word. Ruthless years of strife and unhappiness finally led to divorce. Nevertheless, it appears that Steichen did not speak unkindly of Clara during all the years of her fierce verbal assaults in letters to him and to others, as well as in conversation.

Beyond the wounds the couple had inflicted on each other, however, the Steichens' daughters carried deep scars from their childhood. Years after Clara's death, Mary was still groping for some resolution of her unhappy history with her mother. The precocious child whose hands were restrained so she could not masturbate grew up to become Dr. Mary Steichen Calderone, an internationally known expert on human sexuality and planned parenthood, a cofounder of the Sex Information and Education Consortium of the United States (SIECUS).

Kate Rodina Steichen, the loving songbird, had been forced by her frantic mother into wartime exile in France. From the time she was seven, Kate listened as Clara tried to teach her to hate and distrust all men, especially her father. Ironically, in her near half-century partnership with Carol Silverberg, Kate, of all of the family, sustained the longest happy human companionship. This was probably true in part because Kate had a resilient capacity to forgive, love, and accept, while Mary was very much like her mother in her reserve, her fear of rejection, and her self-absorption. Like Clara, she could appear cold, aloof, imperious, and judgmental. It was not until 1978, long after her mother's death, that Mary, then nearly seventy-four, finally made peace with Clara.

"I had carried my mother around with me, then 'buried' her because she had been so damaging to me," Mary wrote. Mary recalled awaking one morning with the vivid memory of Clara sitting at the piano in the house in Voulangis, weeping and singing "My Old Kentucky Home." Distraught, Mary telephoned her own daughter Linda, Nell's younger sister, by now a skilled therapist in Chicago. Linda sensitively guided her mother through the "incredible therapeutic experience" of forgiving Clara, until finally, Mary remembered, she was relieved "of a terrible incubus I'd been carrying around all those seventy-three years."[25]

Clara Smith Steichen had exposed her deep, unhappy heart in the poems she had entrusted to Alfred Stieglitz during World War I. Her last letter to Alfred Stieglitz was dated July 11, 1944, written from Springfield, Missouri, during her long refuge from the war in Europe. She was still hunting a copy of the Steichen Supplement to *Camera Work*, yet still scornfully attacking her former husband. Having just read "Commander with a Camera," Matthew Josephson's two-part *New Yorker* profile of Steichen (June 3 and June 10, 1944), she took it apart. Steichen's true allegiance was German, not French, she argued illogically. She blamed the Germans—and by extension, Steichen—for depriving her of her peaceful cottage in "lovely lost Mallorca." It was always a German, she wrote, who robbed her "of what should be mine rightfully."[26]

Her letter to Stieglitz contained a laundry list of old grievances: She resurrected her charges against Marion Beckett; complained that Steichen would not give her money and would not help Kate financially; and denigrated her daughters for the lives they had chosen to live. As for herself, Clara maintained, she would take her "bare bald poverty dammit—and I'll live it and hug it close."[27]

"Byebye old dear," she ended this last letter to Stieglitz. "One thing cocksure—You never sold yourself down any river—But many were those who pulled themselves up by your coattails. As tho' you didn't know it—by now."[28] Inexplicably, she signed the letter Claire Steichen.

Sadly, Clara herself had long scripted and lived out the dominant themes of her life—the abandoned wife and mother, the outsider, the war refugee, the exile. From war-ravaged Voulangis back in 1916, she had written a wistful poem called "Peace" and mailed it to Stieglitz in New York, softer words, perhaps her own elegy:

*I shall be beautiful when I in death
Lie in white loveliness, soft as a dream. . . .
Wrapped in the light of the ages I'll lie
Loving the peace of my own quiet soul—
Face to Eternity—I shall sleep well,
Dreaming of beauty denied me in life—
I shall be beautiful then.*²⁹

After the war, Steichen and Dana regularly shared their growing excitement about "The Family of Man" with Wayne and Joan Miller in California, filling their letters with details about the emerging plans for the new exhibition. As Miller recalled,

> *Dorothea Lange was in touch with Steichen, and she suggested we get together a group of photographers from the [San Francisco] Bay area and talk to them about the exhibition and encourage their participation in supplying photographs for the show. That was done, and Steichen came out around the time of his birthday in March of 1953, met about seventy active photographers from the area, and shared with them his dream. He was still exploring the concept, so he was bouncing ideas off these photographers, and I remember how so many of them didn't understand his vision, and didn't see how it could relate to their work. Some of them thought he was kind of goofy, really, full of pie-in-the-sky ideas. Dorothea Lange was gung ho because she understood and shared his dreams and ideas. But he had trouble with some in this audience. They heard him but shook their heads a little bit and walked off. This was the beginning of what we often ran into as we worked on "The Family of Man."*³⁰

Photographer Fred Lyon not only was invited, but he photographed the crowd as they stood on the deck of Miller's house listening to Steichen's eloquent words, a preview of the printed circular he would send out to photographers all over the world. (Later, Steichen used that text as the basis for his prologue to the exhibition, and the book that fol-

"THE FAMILY OF MAN" (1947–1955)

lowed.) They heard Steichen explain that "The Family of Man" exhibition would demonstrate once and for all "that the art of photography is a dynamic process of giving form to ideas and of explaining man to man. It was conceived as a mirror of the universal elements and emotions in the everydayness of life—as a mirror of the essential oneness of mankind throughout the world."[31]

Steichen was seeking photographs of lovers and families and children, he said that March day. He wanted images of home and the environment and the richness of the earth; of "the religious rather than religions," and of "basic human consciousness rather than social consciousness." He hoped for photographs that would reveal "dreams and aspirations" and "the flaming creative forces of love and truth and the corrosive evil inherent in the lie."[32] He knew he was going to need a remarkable full-time assistant to make these dreams come true—someone who profoundly understood photography as well as Steichen's own personal vision of the work to be done.

Wayne Miller, of course, was the perfect man. After his service on Steichen's unit in the war, he not only knew photography but he understood Steichen himself—his multiple strengths; his mercurial temperament when he was deeply absorbed in his work; his relentless, sometimes unreasonable demands for perfection; the paradox of his vacillation from vulnerable self-doubt to supreme self-confidence. Professionally and personally, Miller knew and loved this complex man, and when Steichen offered him the job, "it was easy to say 'yes,'" Miller recalled.[33]

During those years, Steichen's Department of Photography inaugurated a series of exhibitions called "Diogenes with a Camera" to show how various photographers interpreted the truth. He himself was Diogenes during the search for images for "The Family of Man," and his alter ego and collaborator was Wayne Miller. Once the arrangements were made at the Museum of Modern Art for his appointment, Wayne and Joan Miller packed up their four children and moved to New York, where they quickly settled into a strenuous routine. Steichen began spending Monday through Thursday nights with the Millers in their New York apartment, and on weekends Steichen and the six Millers headed to Umpawaug. There, Dana waited for them, having spent her week working long days, sometimes into the night, on her own obsession, writing a romantic biography of Beethoven.

Dana's intense and informed love of music had always given her much pleasure, and because Beethoven had become her special passion, she read every available biography and study of the composer's work. Especially intrigued by the mystery surrounding Beethoven's love life, Dana had begun to investigate the identity of "Beethoven's beloved," the enigmatic woman who supposedly inspired some of his finest work. Because she had decided to write a book about her theories, Dana stayed in Connecticut while Steichen was immersed in "The Family of Man" in New York. Like her sister-in-law, Paula Sandburg, she needed work of her own, and during these years she was investing twelve to fourteen hours daily in her project, even translating Beethoven's letters herself with the help of a German-English dictionary. She was, her proud husband said later, exploring Beethoven's "sublime and exalted compulsions"—and she no doubt understood them better for understanding Steichen.[34]

The Umpawaug weekends were spent relaxing and working, with the Millers and their children enjoying the privacy of the guest quarters. The children loved roaming the Umpawaug acres and swimming with Steichen. "He had the uncanny ability to talk and play with children on their own terms," Miller recalled. "He liked their genuineness. He detested the 'phonies' of the world." Miller photographed Steichen at play, just one of the kids, splashing in the water, tossing leaves into the air, kneeling to investigate an anthill. Steichen made his own pictures of the Millers, as well. "Our children were his friends and he treated them as equals," Miller remembered. "But, I believe, mostly they were seeds of hope and promises of accomplishments to come."[35]

All art begins with the blank wall, the blank page, the clean film, the virgin marble. Steichen told Miller that the "blank wall is an appalling thing to look at . . . when you start out to do something, that vague thing called creation." Even now, in his seventies, he was still awestruck at the mystery of it. His theme for "The Family of Man" was deceptively simple: He wanted to illustrate the oneness of human life—the likenesses, the similarities, the simple connections. He wanted the "element of love" to dominate the entire exhibition. And he wanted the show to radiate a

"THE FAMILY OF MAN" (1947–1955)

sense of optimism. "We have survived everything and we have only survived it on our optimism," he told Miller. "And optimism means faith in ourselves, faith in the *everydayness* of our lives."[36]

Miller said, "The whole show is a reflection of his whole life. The show's success, its failure depends on the man's own philosophy of life. It's just Steichen himself."[37] His life had given him the theme and vision for his exhibition, and all he needed to do now was to choose the images and the Spartan text to accompany them. He set Miller to work helping him with the first and fundamental task, and later he persuaded Dorothy Norman and Carl Sandburg to help him with the second. Then he would "amalgamate" all the images and words into a unified whole.[38]

Once the official call for entries for the show went out, Steichen and Miller were inundated with pictures of all sizes and styles from around the world—"finely mounted prints from students," Miller reported, along with snapshots torn from family albums, and tear sheets and portfolios from professional photographers.[39] The work would bring them to physical and emotional exhaustion time and again over the three years they poured themselves into organizing "The Family of Man."

Meanwhile, Steichen's other duties were not suspended during that time: He sustained a busy public schedule, oversaw the other demanding exhibition and administrative work at MoMA, and gave occasional lectures. When in 1953 Sandburg published the first volume of his autobiography, *Always the Young Strangers,* Steichen installed an exhibition at MoMA by the same name, depicting the immigrant experience. He chose the American section for an exhibition of contemporary American and Japanese photography for the National Museum of Modern Art in Tokyo, and he supervised an exhibition of postwar European photography at MoMA.

He told a journalist during this time that he considered photography more than a medium: It was a "force."[40] He also acknowledged his debts to Stieglitz and reported that, in memory of Stieglitz's early generosity to him, he saw ten or twelve young photographers each week. If he liked their work, he bought a print or two for the MoMA collection—a nonexistent study collection, he confided to Miller.[41] As a gesture of tribute to Stieglitz, Steichen would usually pull out his wallet and pay for the prints himself—five dollars per print, the exact sum Stieglitz had paid the young Steichen for his first prints. His relationship with Miller had by then developed into something that closely resembled the one that Steichen had forged with Stieglitz, at once mentor and disciple, close friends, and amiable colleagues. "When we rarely locked horns," Miller said, "he would become impatient and annoyed with the young disrespectful son he never had."[42]

For two years, Steichen and Miller sorted through millions of photographs, seven days a week, around the clock, Miller said.[43] From northern China came pictures of bemedaled farmworkers: from Russia, salon prints of Russian industrial accomplishments; from Kansas, "artsy oversized prints of thinly clad sylvan dancers."[44] Steichen had been seventy-three when he and Robert Frank toured Europe on the first leg of "The Family of Man" expedition. He would be just two months short of seventy-six when the show finally opened at MoMA. During those years, he pushed his staff incessantly but still, according to Miller, demanded far more of himself than he did of the others.

They worked in a Fifty-second Street loft MoMA leased for them at a cheap rent because the building was scheduled for demolition. The landlord tore down some walls for them so they could create a large working space. One small back room held an army cot so that Steichen could take naps or sleep overnight if he wanted to—a challenge, however, because a striptease joint downstairs flooded them with bump-and-grind melodies all night long, night after night. Consequently, Steichen preferred to go to the Millers' quiet apartment to rest. Besides, he loved their company.

As the work wore on, Wayne and Joan would fall into bed exhausted at night, only to hear Steichen in his room, still awake, still working, pacing the floor while he tangled with ideas and problems left over from the day. Joan Miller remembered asking, "My God, won't he ever quit?"[45]

"He went through Hell," Wayne Miller said, recalling how Steichen was constantly "pushing, pushing, pushing, trying to understand better that dream he had, how to give it shape, how to choose photographs to illustrate these concepts."[46] First of all, there was the backbreaking labor—the myriad number of photographs to be solicited and examined. Miller spent months searching through trunks and files of photographs belonging to professional photographers and methodically surveying such massive archives as the Time-Life photographic files, which housed 3 million images. He also scrutinized the photographs held by countless domestic and foreign picture agencies, government agencies, private corporations, newspapers, and magazines. At day's end, he would pack up the boxes of photographs he wanted Steichen to review and haul them back to the museum.

Next day, together, they would sort the images into three categories—"no good," "maybe," and "save." Miller then carefully returned the rejected pictures, and the other two groups were transported to their makeshift studio, where they were meticulously logged in by two or three staff assistants and stamped with an identifying number. Steichen and Miller consulted the numbers only; they did not know until later the identity of the photographers whose work they had chosen.

Through this painstaking process, millions of pictures were eventually reduced to about ten thousand, which were then sorted into thematic groups. Steichen and Miller next began to grapple with the amorphous shape of the exhibit, working seven-day stretches at times, rising at six, going to bed at midnight, if they were lucky. They had aching eyes, aching backs, and aching knees from crawling over the studio floor, peering at image after image. Miller remembered five-minute catnaps on the floor, with the striptease music throbbing in the background, doses of sleeping pills, countless mugs of strong black coffee.

For the duration of their work, Steichen constantly questioned himself, his purpose, his strategy, scrutinizing, testing, and retesting his method and his message. He had always worked that way, whether with photographs or with plants, the scientist interrogating the artist. Steichen subjected himself to a "continuous inward searching and questioning," tormented with doubts that "perhaps he was wrong."[47] He also consulted experts because "he hungered for the counsel and wisdom of the best minds he could entice to our work space," Miller recalled.[48] Photographers came to examine the pictures, along with editors, writers, publishers, social scientists, businesspeople, family, and friends.

This was a bold, courageous exhibition in postwar America during an era defined by regional, national, and global divisiveness; the ever-hardening factions of the Cold War; the volatile responses to the Supreme Court rulings on racial segregation in the United States; and the proliferating power of McCarthyism, which, as CBS executive Frank Stanton noted, was "riding roughshod" over a nation whose leadership was "cowering, in a sense, before McCarthy."[49] Over the globe hung the appalling specter of the new hydrogen bomb, even surpassing the atom bomb in its awesome power to control and terrify.

It was also a time, as Steichen observed, when "the subject of human rights was becoming an international political football."[50] His plea for abiding peace, for global unity, for international brotherhood and sisterhood was uttered against this backdrop of unprecedented internal and external mistrust. Sometimes, Steichen wondered if there ever had existed in any age a family of man, if Lincoln in his own fractious time had been deluded, if he himself were foolish to try to articulate such a hope.

"His only tools were the photographs," Miller said. "And his belief in man's inherent goodness. He had no weapons other than a single-minded courage to state truth as he understood it."[51] From the beginning of the long process to the very end, Steichen was plagued with doubts. Miller, who heard them all, remembered the recurring anxieties: "What will people think of it? Will they identify with these simple and yet complex themes? Will it reach some and not others? Have we gone too far ... or done too little? Can it be successful?"[52] Steichen and the Millers, Joan said, "had hopes that people wouldn't think that this was a naïve, heart-on-the-sleeve sort of thing. We had hopes that the values we were dealing with would be recognized and honored by others. Steichen knew when to turn back before it got corny ... and he knew when things were getting overdone.... The closer you can get to the edge without falling off, the better it's going to be. Steichen pushed to the edge, and because of that, he knew how vulnerable he was."[53]

There were tough decisions about photographs they knew were controversial—a lynching, the atom bomb, a picture of physicist Robert Oppenheimer that might provoke the McCarthyites to destroy the show. As they made their choices, art and communication often collided with the prospect of censorship—and censorship lost. "The Hell with them," Steichen finally told Miller. "The pictures are important statements and they are good photographs. How can we see the good unless we see the bad? Keep them in."[54]

Steichen was "sick at heart" in those days, Miller said, over the "continuous public pounding by the hate and fear-mongers." He and Steichen believed adamantly that if they could illustrate their conviction

"THE FAMILY OF MAN" (1947–1955)

that there was "more love than hate in the world, photography would be making a timely contribution."[55] As pictures poured in, the richness and variety far surpassed even the expectations of the optimistic Steichen. Paring their ten thousand prints down to five thousand was relatively easy, but cutting five thousand to one thousand was "a real struggle and was often heartbreaking," Steichen remembered.[56] But once they had settled on the final thousand photographs, they planned to condense those to four hundred, establish the major thematic groups, and construct a sequence. In the end, the exhibition included 503 photographs from sixty-eight countries.

Infused as "The Family of Man" was with Steichen's optimistic faith in humanity—or his sentimental humanism, as some viewed it—it was also grounded in a powerful admonition against the war of the future. In Operation Ivy in 1954, the Atomic Energy Commission arranged the largest thermonuclear explosion in history, deliberately testing a hydrogen bomb and, in the act, devastating Bikini Atoll in the Pacific and accidentally wounding nearly three hundred Americans and Japanese. In April of 1954, those Americans who had television sets could see Operation Ivy for themselves, and the government had to carry out a delicate propaganda mission—to reassure the people of the nation and their allies that the United States possessed both the deadly technology to obliterate the known world in an instant, and the will and wisdom not to do so unless forced to such extreme action by its enemy, the Soviet Union.

Appalled by the terrifying magnitude of these unprecedented weapons, and noting that many Americans seemed numb or oblivious to the danger, Steichen and Sandburg articulated their concerns in the vocabulary each knew best—photographic images for Steichen, poetry for Sandburg.[57]

Miller remembered that he and Steichen spent many months on the war panel for "The Family of Man" before Steichen decided they would focus on future wars rather than past ones. Thus they created one of the most dramatic stations in the exhibition—a darkened room surrounding a massive color photograph of an exploding atom bomb, the eerily beautiful mushroom cloud, the deadly emblem of the times, an image already stamped in the minds of the children of that generation. (To grow up in the supposedly idyllic early fifties was to confront the dragons of polio, civil-defense drills, and bomb shelters, haunted by the fear that if you were somehow lucky enough to escape unscathed by polio, you risked instant obliteration from a trigger-happy Communist who could detonate the bomb.)

"The darkened room with the atom bomb shot," Miller reflected—"it took Steichen's sort of courage to do."[58] In an age when razor-sharp lines were drawn between nation and nation, race and race, ideology and ideology, Secretary of State Dulles was cautioning that the United States would "never have a secure peace or a happy world so long as Soviet communism dominates one-third of all the peoples that there are."[59] President Dwight D. Eisenhower was calling for peaceful coexistence, christening the bombs "atoms for peace" and expressing the hope that nations would not actually bomb one another out of existence. As he put it, people had to find ways of living together.[60] That was exactly Steichen's point, although he was deliberately, almost indifferently apolitical, steering clear of the politics of the day but driving straight to the heart with an instinctive humanism, a universal ethic prizing love, birth, and celebration, abhorring hatred, violence, and killing.

Underneath it all lay the bedrock of Mary Kemp Steichen's plain decency and common sense: Before he was ten years old, she had ingrained in her son's conscience her own conviction of the dignity and the "essential oneness" of people everywhere.[61]

After the MoMA staff suggested several architects to design the "The Family of Man" installation, Steichen immediately gravitated to one of them, Yale University School of Architecture's Paul Rudolph, whom he knew to possess "imagination and understanding" and, "above all," a "superb sense of design."[62] But because Rudolph did not immediately respond to Steichen's vision, the two men spent weeks discussing the installation before Rudolph built a scale model.

With photo selection and installation well under way, Steichen was ready to turn to his wordsmiths, Carl Sandburg and Dorothy Norman. One of the most frequent occupants of the loft over the striptease joint, Sandburg hammered out the the text on an old typewriter set up so that he could keep his eyes on the pictures as he worked. Back on Christmas Day in 1952, Sandburg had actually finished composing a poem he thought they might weave into his prologue. He had been working on it for years, drawing its shape and themes from the ancient Welsh poet Taliesin and from the Cheyenne Indian chief Hiamovi—just the kind of universal sources Steichen was after in the pictures.

"Dear Ed and Dana," Sandburg had written from Flat Rock just before his seventy-fifth birthday in 1953. "Nearest I have come so far to a poem on The Family of Man is this enclosure.... It is so damned simple and childish that I expect some people to say it runs over into the silly...."[63] The last few lines of the poem would be used to conclude Sandburg's prologue to "The Family of Man":

There is only one man in the world and his name is All Men.
There is only one woman in the world and her name is All Women.
There is only one child in the world and the child's name is
All Children.[64]

Steichen entrusted to poet, essayist, and publisher Dorothy Norman the job of choosing captions for the exhibition pictures, drawing from the great literature of the world. Aside from the fact that he respected her eclectic knowledge of literature and her exquisite taste, she almost certainly symbolized for him a link to Alfred Stieglitz. Steichen understood the significant role she had played in the work of Stieglitz's last years, especially as O'Keeffe had spent more and more time away. He knew that with her sensibility and experience, Norman could produce just the texts his pictures needed, but because she was so busy with her own writing and publishing, Norman almost declined to help him.

As he began to see actual images juxtaposed to one another, Steichen worried that the show was lifeless, and he became more convinced that only Norman could create the lively text essential to illuminate the pictures and weave them together. His excitement was so contagious that she relented.

At MoMA, Steichen showed Norman copy prints, one by one, pouring out his interpretation of each picture. Sometimes words came immediately to Norman's mind—excerpts from the Bible, from Joyce's *Ulysses,* from Greek tragedy, the Bhagavad-Gita, and American Indian writings. Otherwise, she roamed through her large library for pithy lines to juxtapose to the photographs, eventually preparing one thousand three-by-five cards, each containing a quotation. Steichen rejected her offerings outright only once—when she gave him the cards for the segment on childbirth. Steichen had once told Oma that the greatest regret in his life came from knowing that he could not bear a child. After Norman, the mother of two children, handed him her captions on childbirth and left the studio, Steichen tossed the cards on the floor in disgust. "She's forgotten what it's like to have a baby!" he fumed.[65]

Until the end of their extremely demanding work on the show, Steichen kept control of decisions that articulated the great themes of "The Family of Man." He had deputized Wayne Miller to make the final choices on pictures depicting work, however, and had entrusted to Joan Miller the task of choosing the final images of women and children. As a unifying image for the show, Steichen chose Eugene Harris's whimsical picture of a young Peruvian playing the flute, and Dorothy Norman attached Plato's words: "Music and rhythm find their way into the secret places of the soul." Wayne Miller experimented with various sizes and positions before setting prints of the Harris picture throughout the exhibition, like touchstones marking the journey.

As Steichen and Miller moved closer to choosing the final batch of photographs for the exhibit, photographer Homer Page set to work supervising the production of prints at Compo-Photocolor in New York. Steichen, a master printmaker, set impeccably high standards, of course, for the quality of the exhibition prints, all the while keenly aware of the technical challenge of achieving uniform results from such disparate prints or negatives, especially in the enlargements. Page regularly delivered the prints to Steichen for his appraisal, and Miller recalled the ensuing scenes: "This one's a humdinger," Steichen would say, or "Oh, oh, this isn't sharp," or "it's too contrasty," or "Too flat" or "too light," or "Too dark, do it again."[66]

"These rejected prints would go back to the laboratory, where the technicians would again wrestle with ten-foot sections of forty-inch paper," Miller remembered. "Steichen, together with Homer, would sometimes go to the lab and critique the wet prints. He was a perfectionist. It wasn't easy."[67] Even so, despite their efforts, some of the most con-

"THE FAMILY OF MAN" (1947–1955)

sistent criticism later leveled at "The Family of Man" attacked the quality of the prints.

Steichen and Monroe Wheeler, MoMA's director of exhibitions and publications, saw early on that "The Family of Man" warranted a catalog or, better yet, a book. Steichen envisioned an inexpensive edition of the book, accessible to all, and a limited deluxe edition, offering the finest reproductions and printing available. To Steichen's disappointment, however, several publishers came to the cluttered loft and went away uninterested in the project because color reproductions would be too expensive and a book of black-and-white photographs, they believed, simply would not sell in the mass market. Then one fortunate day, an acquaintance approached Steichen on the commuter train to tell him he had heard about "The Family of Man." He was Jerry Mason, a young publisher just beginning his career. Steichen should indeed do a book on the exhibit, Mason told him, and he wanted to publish it himself.

Steichen told Mason candidly about the rejections from other publishers, warned him of the implicit risks, and generally tried to talk him out of the idea. But Mason persisted and secured the rights to go forward. His Maco Magazine Corporation would print the cheaper edition, and he convinced Simon and Schuster to buy the rights to do the deluxe edition. For the general edition, Mason planned a first printing of 135,000 copies, which he intended to sell for a dollar a copy.

"Jerry, you're crazy," Steichen told him in alarm. "We can't let you do that. You'll lose your shirt."[68] But Mason foresaw better than anyone else the long future of "The Family of Man." More than 5 million copies of the book were eventually sold.

At last, on January 25, 1955, a gala preview heralded the arrival of "The Family of Man." "Steichen and Dana, Paula and Carl, and Joan and I had dinner," Wayne Miller remembered, but they were so nervous about the show and its reception that "it wasn't really a joyous occasion because we were going to the formal opening. Nelson Rockefeller was going to speak, and Carl, and all the biggies in New York City were there."[69]

Steichen watched the faces of guests as they experienced the show—and he was not disappointed. Those attending the preview were visibly moved by the exhibit. The next day, long before the Museum of Modern Art opened, a crowd began waiting in line, soon flooding the long crosstown block in front of the building. People came and kept on coming in record-breaking numbers. People saw the show, remembered it, and came back again.

When Steichen wrote in his introduction to "The Family of Man" that it was "the most ambitious and challenging project photography has ever attempted," the statement could also be translated to read "the most ambitious and challenging project Steichen ever attempted."[70] Over the years others, including his sister, had accused Steichen of working with his mind more than his heart, but his heart was everywhere in this project, exposed for all to see. As he himself wrote, "The Family of Man has been created in a passionate spirit of devoted love and faith in man."[71]

Steichen had included in the exhibition a few very personal family pictures—for instance, the one of Oma, smiling on her front porch, a loaf of freshly baked bread held in her hands. The image is superimposed on a flourishing sunlit wheat field, juxtaposed to a Russian proverb: "Eat Bread and Salt and Speak the Truth." This was one of only three Steichen photographs chosen for "The Family of Man," joining his 1913 picture of Mary and Kate with a playmate in the garden in Voulangis and his recent photograph of one of the Millers' exuberant young daughters diving bare-skinned into the pond at Umpawaug. Steichen had also included Wayne Miller's photographs of Joan giving birth to their son David, with Wayne's physician father presiding at the delivery.

After the Millers returned to California, Steichen kept them informed of the outpouring of interest generated by the MoMA exhibition, reporting that he was turning into a "radio, television and interviewee ham." He was also trying to organize his work at the museum so he would be completely free to undertake new projects now that, to his great satisfaction, "The Family of Man" seemed to be around "to stay."[72]

When Miller once asked Steichen in an interview if he was satisfied with the work he accomplished during World War II, Steichen snapped back, "Wayne, I don't know what satisfied is. How can anybody be satisfied?"[73] Still, he was elated over the success and the enduring impact of "The Family of Man," for it far surpassed his dreams and expectations. He would never be content for long with any of his work, but "The Family of Man" came close to meeting his vision of what an exhibition should be. A triumphant "article of faith," it was his most ambitious portrait and his subject was the entire human race.[74]

Steichen was already dreaming about his next show, however. "Each time in his life he grabbed hold of something bigger than anything he'd ever done before," Miller reflected. "And the show was hardly hanging on the walls and opened before he was saying, 'Now the next show I'd like to do would be a big show about women—and one on hunger and poor people—and one about blacks.' Steichen was just champing at the bit to go on and do something even bigger."[75]

It would be difficult to surpass this exhibition, however. As Eric Sandeen discussed at length in *Picturing an Exhibition: The Family of Man and 1950s America,* this was "not so much a successful photographic exhibit as a widely publicized and enthusiastically attended event in the popular culture of the day."[76] "There are photographs that talk to people," Steichen reflected. "There is no esoteric appeal there—just man explaining man to man."[77] And part of that universal message ought to be love, he believed: "Unless we have the element of love dominating this entire exhibition—and our lives—we better take it down before we put it up."[78]

32

THE LAST APPRENTICESHIP

(1 9 5 5 - 1 9 5 9)

During the last five or six years of my work at the Museum, the itch to photograph again became so strong that I decided I would have to do something about it. I assigned myself a disciplined third apprenticeship.[1]

—STEICHEN

LATE ON THE NIGHT WHEN THE last detail of "The Family of Man" had finally been set in place, Edward Steichen, nearly seventy-six, danced an impromptu jig on the sidewalk in front of his loft studio and the striptease club on Fifty-second Street. Wayne Miller, who was with him, predicted that Steichen would soon pick up his cameras, start taking pictures again, and "find out who he is. I'll be amazed," Miller added, "if he doesn't soon start his best work."[2] There were critics who contended for many years afterward that "The Family of Man" *was* Steichen's best work, and Dana called it "E.J.'s masterpiece."[3] She more than anyone knew how wholeheartedly he had poured himself into the creation of it, and believed that "if only one tenth part comes through," all the work would be justified.[4] It was without doubt the culmination of Steichen's career, as well as a landmark event in the history of American photography.

Record-breaking multitudes of people lined up to see the show in the United States as well as in major cities and frontier outposts

The Last Apprenticeship (1955–1959)

around the world. Jerry Mason's print edition of "The Family of Man" brought the exhibit to the eyes of millions more.

In intriguing ways, "The Family of Man" became a work in progress as time moved along, its success grew, and circumstances prompted Steichen to do some editing. He eliminated a horrifying picture of a lynched black man, for instance, because of its ambiguous notoriety. Steichen feared "that this violent picture might become a focal point," Miller explained, "so that people would focus on that and that would be used in press stories about the show and people would miss the point, the theme of the show being interrupted by this individual photograph."[5] And the pivotal photograph of the exploding atom bomb was not published in the book because, Miller said later, it required color reproduction for maximum effect, and that was prohibitively expensive.[6]

The book's omission of that riveting image opened the way for critics decades later to charge that Steichen in 1955 had been both callous and mawkish, that he had pandered to middle-class sentimentality while ignoring or muting the dangers of nuclear annihilation. But Steichen's creation of this photographic pageant cannot be accurately assessed in hindsight, stripped out of its social context, any more than Carl Sandburg's poetry and his Lincoln biography can be clearly appraised removed from the era in which—and about which—he was writing. These men and their work were in fact bound inextricably to the era and the global circumstances in which they existed. And out of their passionate commitment to address the times in which they found themselves, they consciously absorbed the risk of eventually becoming dated and irrelevant. Cultural historian Eric Sandeen has written perceptively about this:

> *Steichen responded directly to the most important threat to humankind—nuclear weapons—in a truly global theater. To criticize the exhibition from the perspective of the 1990s, with all that we have come to know about the ambiguity of photographs and the power of technology to subjugate cultures around the world, is too easy. We need to be able to account for the legitimate seriousness with which the exhibition approached its task and for its impact in 1950s culture.*[7]

That impact was global. By the spring of 1955, not long after the exhibit opened at MoMA, Steichen was already hard at work orchestrating the prolonged world tour of "The Family of Man." He worried now about whether the exhibition would do as well in Asia as he felt it would in Europe, but, as it turned out, according to Steichen, the show actually "made its greatest impact" in Asia.[8] He traveled with the exhibition to Tokyo, Paris, Berlin, Amsterdam, Munich, and London, eagerly watching and photographing the faces of the enthusiastic international audience who thronged to see "The Family of Man."

By 1963, when Steichen was eighty-four years old, more than 9 million people in sixty-nine countries had seen the exhibition in one of the six circulating editions of the show sponsored by the United States Information Agency. The Museum of Modern Art also sent the original exhibition and a scaled-down edition on tour through the United States. An estimated one million people saw "The Family of Man" in Japan when four editions of the exhibit were replicated in differing sizes there to travel throughout that country, including a microcosm of the show for display in villages. Another million and a half people visited the show in India. Some critics of "The Family of Man" believed that the show was a propaganda tool of the USIA, perhaps in collusion with MoMA and the museum's longtime patron Nelson Rockefeller, who had overseen USIA programs in Latin America. Supporters of the exhibition perceived its stunning worldwide success as affirmation of its universal themes, not its politics, if any. Steichen and Miller had worked in their Manhattan loft with their eyes on people, not politics and propaganda. There was no doubt that "The Family of Man" was message-driven, but the message grew out of Steichen's conscience and vision, not out of any bureaucratic purpose.

The faces in the exhibition belonged to "Mr. Everyman—you, me, somebody from Tibet," Miller said.[9] A judiciously placed mirror surprised viewers by weaving their own living images into the tapestry of the photographs. The people of every country, "the illiterate as well as the intelligentsia," Steichen realized, "looked at the pictures, and the people in the pictures looked back at them. They recognized each other."[10]

The circulating editions of the show were in such demand that they were quickly booked two years into the future, and newspapers around the world covered the progress of the exhibition, noting the record crowds drawn to the compelling, universal message. Steichen was personally touched by the response in Paris, where newspapers, from the conservative *Le Temps* and *Le Figaro* to the leftist *L'Humanité,* carried feature stories on "The Family of Man," illustrated by double-page picture spreads. Steichen was also moved to hear that on the last day of the showing in Guatemala, several thousand Indians traveled out of the hills on foot or on mules to see the exhibition. It had struck an international chord that reverberated far beyond Steichen's wildest hopes, and, as a bonus, awards poured into the Museum of Modern Art for this greatest of all photography exhibitions, as the Kappa Alpha Mu Award described "The Family of Man."

Perhaps more revealing than the press coverage were the opinions of other photographers. *Aperture* magazine, the relatively new but highly regarded photographic journal of the decade, devoted an entire segment to the show. Entitled "The Controversial Family of Man," the issue cited and quoted twenty-three reviews of the exhibit.[11] One of the most thoughtful treatments was written by Dorothy Norman, who had of course been significantly involved in creating the exhibition's text. She contrasted the show to the private work achieved by Stieglitz, with his focus on the individual artist and viewer, communicating with and through the intimate one-person show or the small group exhibition. Steichen, on the other hand, worked on an immense public scale, drawing the mass audience to the spacious message-driven panorama of his collective photographic exhibitions. Norman believed that both postures were legitimate and essential, and she wisely observed that "The Family of Man" should never be judged for what it was not and did not aspire to be, but, instead, for what it was.[12]

Photographer and critic Minor White noted that while the show was dominated by "very straight forward semiphotojournalistic documentation," some of it was still "really magnificent aesthetically."[13] He had helped to mount "The Family of Man" at the George Eastman House, the International Museum of Photography founded in Rochester, New York, in 1949 and headed, at the suggestion of Steichen and others, by Beaumont Newhall. When Steichen traveled to Rochester to see the exhibit, he called it the best installation that had yet been done outside of MoMA.

More than twenty years later, White was asked if, like many of his contemporaries, he felt that the exhibition "put back the art of photography many years." "It may have put the aesthetic thing back a little bit, but that didn't hurt," White answered. "It was good to have that setback." White clearly understood that the exhibition was designed "not for the aesthetes in photography, but for people."[14]

Herbert Bayer, who had designed "Road to Victory," believed, no doubt correctly, that his work had influenced the eventual shape of the installation of "The Family of Man." Yet when he saw the show, he found it retrogressive, sentimental, and "a little pompous, too," he said, adding, "But this was Steichen's outlook."[15] However, Bayer joined critic Hilton Kramer; Steichen's perennial critic Ansel Adams; Phoebe Lou Adams (in the *Atlantic Monthly*); and cultural critic and historian Jacques Barzun (in his 1959 book *The House of Intellect*) as part of the small minority of critics to find serious fault with "The Family of Man" in its own time.

Kramer attacked both Steichen and his exhibition in a scathing review in the October 1955 issue of *Commentary,* observing that Steichen's whole "versatile career" comprised "a historical prologue relevant to the exhibition's cultural significance" and functioned as a "brief history in the diffusion of photography in our culture." Kramer claimed that "in the process, the *art* of photography was bound to get away, lost in a jungle of science and journalism." He charged, furthermore, that Steichen had "abandoned himself to the journalistic solution of his problematic role in the Museum," contending that "as so often happens in our culture when art abandons itself to journalism, its mode of articulation has a distinct ideological cast—in this instance, a cast which embodies all that is most facile, abstract, sentimental, and rhetorical in liberal ideology."[16] This was a serious charge in a country that had in the previous presidential election liked Ike enough to give him a landslide victory over the liberal "egghead" Adlai Stevenson.

Kramer further wrote that Steichen's compatriot Sandburg had become a foolish parody of himself, writing a giddy prologue to the book of exhibition pictures that read "like nothing so much as a school boy imitating a young American poet of forty years ago named Carl Sandburg." He found Steichen's choice of images and Sandburg's choice of words forced and simplistic. Steichen was guilty of "wholesale abandonment of

The Last Apprenticeship (1955-1959)

artistic principles," Kramer continued. He accused Steichen of "obscuring the urgency of real problems under a blanket of ideology which takes for granted the essential goodness, innocence, and moral superiority of the international 'little man,' 'the man in the street,' the abstract, disembodied hero of a world-view which regards itself as superior to mere politics." Moreover, Kramer argued, Steichen's exhibit was already obsolete—"a reassertion in visual terms of all that has been discredited in progressive ideology."[17]

As for Barzun, he objected to, among other things, Wynn Bullock's photograph of a "rather tendentious female nude, prone amid the ferns of a forest glade." Barzun noted that "this is followed by episodes of kissing and caresses in public places.... The theme of copulation is frequently repeated notably as a restorative after the half-dozen pages devoted to schoolwork."[18]

Steichen's responses, if any, to these critical appraisals have not survived, but mischievous Carl Sandburg jumped to his brother-in-law's defense when he read Barzun's comments. "Jacques Barzun," he later wrote to journalist Harry Golden, "must be one of the first products of artificial insemination."[19]

All in all, the writer André Maurois probably spoke most eloquently for the critical majority in his summary of the power of "The Family of Man":

When photography reaches the quality of these pictures and when the selection of photographs hung here is directed by such an ideal of conception, it becomes an art. It delights with its beauty and awakens true and noble emotions which will contribute to the strengthening of the bonds between the human family.[20]

Those glory days of the exhibit's great success found Steichen in his prime, inordinately vigorous and hardy for a man of seventy-six. He was brimming with the vitality and joy that spring from creative fulfillment, and with the constant flow of new ideas generated in the active, creative mind. At the same time, his wife shared his euphoria, for Dana's manuscript was growing toward completion, and she had entitled the biography *Beethoven's Beloved.*

During the years of his absorption in "The Family of Man," Steichen stayed so obsessed with his work that he seemed to take Dana for granted, relying on her steady, self-effacing presence but giving her little affirmation in return. Dana remained at Umpawaug, deeply immersed in her writing and research. When Steichen joined her on weekends, Dana often sat at her piano as sun splashed in through the tall windows, and they read, walked, and busied themselves with the delphiniums. Both avid bird-watchers, they observed the wood ducks and black ducks mating, and they welcomed the red-winged blackbird home to his annual nesting site. Sometimes wild pheasants preened themselves in the sun near the house. The delphinium fields were flourishing, studded at peak season with tall, voluptuous spears of blossoms, brilliant in the sun. Visitors to Umpawaug were greeted by the vista of a sea of blue delphiniums surrounded by golden sunflowers.

One spring morning, Steichen looked out his bedroom window and suddenly was struck by the beauty of a small shadblow tree, bursting into its first full bloom. He had planted the tree himself two decades or more earlier, when it was a seedling only a foot tall. If the shadblow had blossomed this beautifully before, he had never noticed it, and now the tree stirred the old, latent instincts, "the itch to photograph."[21] Immediately, he resolved to pick up the camera again, but this time to limit himself to only what could be seen from the windows of his home at Umpawaug. This was another cup-and-saucer exercise in the fashion of the long-ago second "disciplined apprenticeship" he had undergone alone at Voulangis, except now he had chosen a living subject. As he undertook this new, tightly focused experiment in photography, Dana encouraged him, as she had in so many previous projects.

Weaving in and out of her flowers and her house at Umpawaug Dana always wore Chinese gowns in a rainbow of colors, Joan Miller remembered, and a Chinese hat. "That was her costume, her uniform. She didn't have to worry about what she was going to put on. She always looked just beautiful, and I found her a very lovely person. I remember Mary [Steichen Calderone] saying what a self-effacing person she was, but I found her quite open."[22] It was to Joan, in fact, that Dana confided that she had suffered "from deep depression after her mother died, and some of that was because Steichen was so focused on his work."²³ Dana also told Joan that she felt she had given up a great deal to marry Steichen: "She had been a successful actress. After marrying Steichen, she felt it was no longer appropriate for her to pursue this career."²⁴ As she realized that her husband was always going to be fully engrossed in his work, Dana joined in as much of it as possible, and she filled long periods of time alone with her writing, her music, and the ongoing supervision of the house and the delphinium operation.

The Millers, like the Sandburgs, appreciated Dana's grace and serenity, her loyal patience with Steichen, and her capacity for fun. "When she came into the city, she always had a good time," Joan recalled. "She would sit next to Steichen and have a ball. Certainly, the marriage was very successful."²⁵

During the spring and summer of 1956, Dana was exhausted, and she and Steichen assumed it was from overwork on her book. Yet the ominous fatigue persisted, and worsened—a foreboding shadow in an otherwise bright time. Those who saw Dana then were more worried about her than they would admit. Perhaps it was the inordinate stress of completing the book, they thought.

Dana had smoked all her adult life, trying now and then to stop, to no avail. She did try to cut back that summer, on the theory that some of her shortness of breath and fatigue might stem from too many cigarettes smoked automatically as she pored over her manuscript. And perhaps, she and her husband decided, a change of scenery, away from the omnipresent typewriter and research notes, would yield more rest. Consequently, the Steichens traveled to Connemara for a reunion with the Sandburgs, as they had done so many happy times before. "CAKES BAKED OUR FACES CLEAN STOP WHEN DO YOU ARRIVE SANDBURGS," the Sandburgs telegraphed the Steichens in Connecticut.²⁶ "FABULOUS APPETITE PANTS PRESSED ARRIVE USUAL TRAIN SATURDAY MORNING STEICHENS," Dana telegraphed in return.²⁷

During their 1956 visit, Paula worried that Dana seemed tired, lacking her usual vivacious energy. She did not join in the customary walks with the family up and down the Connemara trails latticing Little Glassy Mountain. Dana had written after one Connemara vacation. "Such food—such ecstatic madness—such poetry." The Sandburgs would "live forever," and she planned to live forever with them.²⁸

Helga's daughter, Paula Steichen,* wrote about her great-uncle Ed's visits to Connemara, recalling the wonderful stories he and Sandburg would tell "with widened eyes and dramatic motions of the arms," shouting and shaking their fists "with imaginary fury until the family was sliding off their chairs in laughter." Steichen called the little girl "Princess Paula" or "Paus'l the Second," and she in turn loved his smile and "the sight of his shining blue eyes." As he had played with Mary and Kate in the fragrant garden at Voulangis, Steichen played with young Paula and John Carl at Connemara. "On the front lawn," young Paula remembered, "he would swing me round and round by his arms until the two towering pink dogwood trees above us were a dream of spinning blossoms and the dogs were barking wildly at our side."[29]

One balmy summer night, she and John Carl were permitted to stay up late because Steichen was giving a party. On a spacious lap of mountain rock behind the old house at Connemara, a fire was lit, an abundant picnic set out—potato salad and fresh vegetables from the garden, meats to be grilled on the campfire, crocks of goat's milk and goat's milk ice cream. Young Paula remembered sitting in the darkness as Steichen and the rest of the adults in the family sang "with surety and a passionate sweetness" songs from their days together in Michigan and Illinois. The party ended, as all Connemara parties did, with "Tipperary," "Bye Bye Blackbird," "There's a Long Long Trail A-Winding," and, for the finale, "Good Night, Ladies."[30]

Back at Umpawaug in August of 1956, near the time of her sixty-second birthday, Dana's growing worry about her health caused her to go to her doctor for tests. The results were devastating. Dana and Steichen heard the words in shock. Follicular lymphoblastoma—leukemia. The prognosis was bleak.

Heartbroken, Steichen now wanted to devote himself to his wife. Dana became all that mattered to him, and he took a leave of absence from the museum to spend every moment caring for her. At first, she did

---

* Several years after Helga Sandburg divorced her first husband, the father of her children John Carl and Karlen Paula, she remarried, and her children used her second husband's last name. When that marriage ended in divorce, the children, then teenagers, wanted to choose their surnames, and both chose Steichen, their grandmother Paula's maiden name, becoming John Carl and Paula Steichen. The family often used the nickname "Young Paula" to differentiate between grandmother and granddaughter.

The Last Apprenticeship (1955–1959)

not want to tell the Sandburgs she was sick, and she turned to the work on her book "with a new and feverish intensity," Steichen said later.[31] "She worked hard on it," Paula Sandburg told Helga, "would go until noon, then tear herself away, go to the icebox, walk around the house once and back to work. She was obsessed with getting it done."[32]

Dana finished the last pages of *Beethoven's Beloved* in the winter of 1957. By now desperately ill, she had to be hospitalized at the Roosevelt Hospital Private Pavilion in New York for futile treatments, but Steichen saw to it that his wife was granted her wish to spend her last days at Umpawaug. There in the glass house overlooking the brittle winter landscape (the shadblow tree dormant in the icy wind), Dana Desboro Glover Steichen died on February 20, 1957.

"He called us immediately when Dana died. I left immediately to be with him," Miller remembered.[33] At Steichen's request, Miller photographed Dana in the coffin placed in the living room, her thin face lovely and serene in the light from the great windows they had designed to frame the Umpawaug vistas. Miller photographed Steichen weeping in a doorway. Something in Steichen died when Dana died, some vital, irretrievable part of himself. And, his niece Helga thought, Steichen even felt betrayed by Dana's death, for she was so much younger than he and by all rights should have outlived him and cared "always for him."[34]

Dana was cremated February twenty-third. Kate and Mary and the rest of the family gathered at Umpawaug, and Miller stayed with Steichen as long as he could. But Steichen was "devastated," Paula later told Helga.[35] He vowed to see to the last details of Dana's book, to see it through publication, and he did so, with Kate's help, for she was by then an assistant to editor Ken McCormick at Doubleday, Dana's publisher.

"The death of this beautiful, gracious and talented woman ... was a traumatic loss to all of us," Carol Silverberg remembered. "I owed her a special debt, for it was she who drew me into the Steichen family fold, and she who contributed warmth and goodwill to all our gatherings."[36] But Steichen's profound grief surprised even his sister. "When she died, my brother simply went to pieces," Paula said. "All of his will left him and he became so lethargic that he could not lift a hand."[37] Deeply depressed, Steichen turned to his surrogate family, the Millers, and headed for their home in California to be with Wayne, Joan, and the children.

The Millers gave him companionship or solitude, as his needs dictated. Hoping to pull him out of his depression, at least temporarily, they took Steichen on a trip to see the magnificent giant and coast redwood trees. "The experience of seeing the tallest trees in the world seemed to reawaken in Steichen that old sense of the power of nature, of forces bigger than mankind. He reacted to it profoundly," Miller remembered.[38] A few days later, Steichen sat down with oils and masonite board and painted what he saw—the old instinct to paint revived by this new encounter with the enduring forces of nature.

Miller photographed Steichen sitting in the sun at work at a makeshift easel. "I'd say it took Steichen a couple of days to complete the painting," Miller recalled.[39] He gave it to the Millers, and after his return to Umpawaug, he experimented "in new directions as a painter" over the next two years with a series of abstract paintings grounded in the Chinese cosmological tenets of yin and yang, the duality that yields all that comes into being.[40] Perhaps he was exploring on canvas the depths of his relationship with Dana, trying to paint his way to some acceptance. He had shared with her the most intimate, most sustained companionship of his lifetime—thirty-four years in all. He could not imagine going on without her.

Fortuitously, getting her book to press offered him one reason to keep going, somehow connecting his days without her to all the years they had shared. As he guided his wife's manuscript into print, he wrote about her work for inclusion on the book jacket, praising her extraordinary "determination" and devotion. He spoke of her "deeply discerning revelation" of Beethoven's romance as well as "his miseries" and his "sublime and exalted compulsions."[41] Dana was a wise, gentle, and intuitive woman, the great love of Edward Steichen's life. No doubt her loving perception of the complexity of her husband's genius equipped her with special insights into Beethoven, whose music and image had so haunted the young Steichen that he had painted the composer in 1902.

Dana had spent years exploring Beethoven's love for a mysterious woman, and the powerful repercussions when love and work converge. There was no mystery or dispute about Dana Steichen's loving, steady hand in her husband's great work, however, and the years of their mar-

The Last Apprenticeship (1955–1959)

riage define the beginning and the end of a significant era in Steichen's creative life. With Dana at his side—or waiting patiently at home—he enjoyed accelerating fame and prosperity through three major careers—as a fashion and commercial photographer, as a military photographer, and as director of the Department of Photography at the Museum of Modern Art, where "The Family of Man" crowned his achievements.

Dana's death killed some essential fire in Steichen, however, and although more projects and great honors and acclaim lay ahead, he would never work again with the same intensity and passion. And then as if her death were not enough, his own robust health betrayed him: He suffered his first stroke in 1957, then set out afterward on a lonely, futile struggle to recapture his old powers.

How could he fill the days and nights after Dana died? Numb, he felt he had to go on with a lecture on experimental color photography at the Museum of Modern Art, long scheduled for March 2, 1957. He told his attentive audience that the creative photographer always experiments, that every single photograph is an experiment, that an artist could not be an artist on some days and not on others. You could not turn the artistic sense on and off at will. But he did not share with the audience his private grief, or his discouraging inability to take up the camera or any other interest again. He worked halfheartedly throughout 1957 on a retrospective exhibition of the best photographs in the history of photography, growing snappish when anyone challenged his credentials to select the pictures. "I think I've seen enough of photography, of art, of photographers and of artists in my life to have some authority to make the selection," he announced peevishly.[42]

Steichen accepted several awards after Dana died in 1957, including an honorary doctorate of fine arts from the University of Wisconsin and the Japanese photographic organization Nippon Kogaku K.K.'s first annual outstanding achievement award for using photography to foster international understanding, an honor conferred in voting by international photographers, editors, and photography organizations. At the commencement exercises in Wisconsin, his boyhood home state, Steichen looked "grim . . . his hands at an awkward angle, the gold ring for Dana on the finger," Helga remembered.⁴³ He told others how he wished that Oma could have been there. Photographs show him wearing a beard later on in 1957, a consequence of the stroke, which made it difficult for him to shave unassisted. "He is a handsome man and I do not like the beard at all!" his sister told her family.⁴⁴

For a long time after Dana died, Steichen could not bear to stay at Umpawaug. Sometime during that difficult year, a fire in his laboratory destroyed many of his negatives, except for those stored in the house in Connecticut or at MoMA.⁴⁵ For the first time in his life, he felt helpless, as if he lived at the mercy of capricious enemies—age, death, fate.

Work offered some consolation, especially the ongoing "third apprenticeship" photographing the shadblow tree. He took still pictures of the little tree in every season and every light, then began photographing it in color and, in 1959, with a motion-picture camera. "Here was something in nature which repeated everything that happened in life, even to human relationships," he told a journalist in 1959.

> *For a full three years I photographed the little tree throughout all seasons and at all hours of the day, in all kinds of weather. The trees around it even began to play a role. There's a group of birches behind the bush. One of them began to lean forward. Deeper and deeper he bowed until, in the pictures, he and the shad began to look almost as mingled as lovers. And, as in life, he leaned over too far and broke his neck.*⁴⁶

The tree became Steichen's emblem for the inevitable passages of human life as mirrored in nature—the cycles of love, life and death, rebirth, and death again. His obsession with the tree brought him resignation, then acquiescence to the inescapable power and mystery of life.

He was eighty years old in 1959—at times still surprisingly vigorous and vital, despite his stroke, and still uncommonly dapper and handsome with his white hair and his now-dramatic beard. Visiting the Millers that year in California, he went ice-skating with the children, fell on the ice, and deeply bruised his arm. He had to wear it in a sling for weeks afterward, and most people assumed the octogenarian had had another stroke. No, he loved to tell them, he just overshot the mark while he was ice-skating with the young folks.

The Last Apprenticeship (1955–1959)

He had developed cataracts in both eyes, and he wondered how he would survive if he should go blind. One eye could be treated surgically, his doctors reassured him, but they were uncertain about the other. "I'll never be totally dark," he told a journalist. "That's fortunate; I'm an image-monger and I'm sure most of my perception leading to understanding is visual."[47]

Steichen was a celebrity in 1959, when he turned eighty, and major newspapers and magazines took note of that milestone in his life with admiring profiles. Gilbert Millstein writing in *The New York Times Magazine* in 1959 named Steichen the "combined Lorenzo de'Medici and [Sol] Hurok" of photography—"that is, the chief spiritual patron and most powerful salesman of the medium as art." Looking back at Steichen's career at the Museum of Modern Art, he observed that Steichen's assumption of the directorship there "was much the same as though Picasso had consented to become curator of painting at the Louvre and his effect on the medium as impresario is probably incalculable."[48]

Steichen at eighty was a wise man with "large, steady, unflinching eyes" and a "soft, husky voice," according to his old Condé Nast friend, Alexander Liberman, who christened him the greatest living photographer in a 1959 article in *Vogue*. He saw Steichen then as "a man of enormous enthusiasms," emitting a "magnetic, inspired force."[49] But Steichen confessed to Gilbert Millstein that he was "angry," and he did not know "just why. I think it's more myself than anything else." As he looked back at his life, Steichen mused that he had spent "six years in uniform, fifteen in journalism and advertising," and now "almost twelve years at the Museum trying to pass on to a younger generation what I've learned and fighting to keep photography from being channeled. But there's so much undone, so much I can think of doing, enough to fill the lifetime of six other people."[50]

He spoke for himself in more detail in "My Life in Photography," the lead article in *The Saturday Review* of March 28, 1959, a week after he turned eighty. He was still painting, he confessed in his essay, but he promised this would not "make me a renegade to photography," pledging to remain "true to what I said to Alfred Stieglitz in 1900 that 'I will always stick to photography.' "[51]

Saturday Review readers who remembered the Homer Page photograph of a youthful, ebullient Steichen on the magazine's cover on June

15, 1955, must have been shocked to see the Leo Stashin photograph of the old, bearded, fading Steichen on the 1959 cover. Dana's death and his own decline were written all over his face.

Steichen and Sandburg were embarking on a great adventure in 1959, preparing to accompany "The Family of Man" to the Soviet Union. Sandburg would go as an American specialist under a grant from the International Exchange Service of the Department of State. Steichen was offered that same official sponsorship, but he declined it so he could be as free as possible to explore Moscow and its environs and to talk with Soviet artists and citizens.[52] In essence, the two octogenarians would serve as ambassadors on a cultural exchange program to Stockholm, Paris, London, and Moscow.

"Carol and I spent a wonderful afternoon with Daddy at Umpawaug Saturday," Kate wrote to the Sandburgs in June of 1959. "First let me say that I got in my bid to go to Moscow (Bid No. 50 I believe!) and was quite sensibly turned down by Steichen. In my small way I am enough like him to understand that this is something that he must do alone."[53]

In Moscow, Steichen and Sandburg would officially help to open the American National Exhibition on August twenty-fifth. "The Family of Man" would be on display at the American Pavilion, sponsored by the United States Information Agency.[54] The American embassies in Paris and Stockholm had requested appearances by both men.

This would be a pilgrimage home for them both—Sandburg to Sweden, his parents' homeland, and Steichen to France. First John Peter Steichen and then Mary Kemp Steichen (with the child Eduard in tow) had traveled in steerage to the United States almost a century earlier, as had Clara Andersson and August Sandburg, with a few pennies and great dreams. Now their sons would fly first class by jet to one great European city after another, staying in deluxe hotels, their expenses paid by the United States government, their work honored and celebrated around the world. In every city, they would be asked to speak about "The Family of Man." Alexander Liberman wrote in *Vogue* August 1, 1959, that the exhibition was "more than an art show. Steichen used photogra-

The Last Apprenticeship (1955–1959)

phy here for a moral purpose as all great art has been through the centuries. The pictures shown were good pictures but they were also symbols."[55] Millions of people worldwide had already testified that those photographs were universal symbols, and Steichen and Sandburg now had the opportunity to take them behind the Iron Curtain.

Before their departure, however, they had to say good-bye to an old friend, Eugene Meyer, who had years earlier chosen his son-in-law Phil Graham, husband of Agnes and Eugene's daughter Kay, to succeed him as publisher of the *Washington Post*. By 1959 Meyer, now nearly eighty-four, found himself frequently hospitalized, fighting cancer and heart disease, often venting his frustrations on Agnes, who kept Steichen informed about her husband's health problems. Wanting to pay their respects one last time before leaving the country that summer, Steichen and Sandburg visited Meyer in Washington, where he was hospitalized and near death. They arrived on July sixteenth for State Department briefings on their jaunt to Moscow, then went immediately to be with Meyer, who had already slipped into a coma.[56] "I was at his bedside almost as a member of the family," Steichen remembered.[57] Meyer died July 17, 1959, and after a private family service and a public memorial service, he was buried in the family mausoleum in Kensico Cemetery, near his farm in Mount Kisco.

Until Agnes's death in 1970, she and Steichen and their children and grandchildren would share a circle of friendship. From New York, where she was now medical director of the Planned Parenthood Federation of America, Mary kept up her own correspondence with Agnes, one that ranged from politics and social issues to personal family news. In the autumn of 1958, she had sent Agnes "a press clipping montage" about the adventures she and her husband, Frank Calderone, had shared flying his hydrofoil. "Frank is the very first person in the world to take one out into the open ocean," Mary enthused. "What we have been doing is very similar to what Lindbergh did to popularize the airplane in his barnstorming days."[58]

Steichen paid tribute to Agnes and Eugene Meyer as "exceptionally gifted and intelligent citizens, endowed with sharp social consciences." He also believed that they had built "the healthiest and soundest marriage I ever knew."[59]

The State Department had orchestrated such a tight schedule for Steichen and Sandburg that they were unable to attend the Meyer memorial service. Their journey to Moscow would officially begin with their flight to Paris, scheduled for 7:00 P.M. on July twentieth. Sandburg was represented then by the dynamic literary and theatrical agent Lucy Kroll, who was highly skilled at getting and keeping him organized, right down to putting a bowl over his shaggy head and giving him a haircut when he needed one. Steichen's capable assistant and right arm at MoMA then was Grace Mayer. Paula helped as much as she could from Connemara with last-minute details, and, of course, the State Department staff had worked out every step of the journey.

The son of an immigrant railroad worker, Sandburg loved to fly, and he had been a guest of honor on the first cross-continental jet flight. He had been working that summer on an advertising campaign for American Airlines, coordinated by Joanna Taub, a talented young copywriter for the Young and Rubicam Agency in New York. Because she loved airplanes and poetry, she had the idea of engaging Sandburg to record some of his poems on flying and aviation. She proposed to use them as commercials on the radio program called "Music Till Dawn."

Knowing Sandburg's poetry well, Joanna Taub created a sample script and sent it to Lucy Kroll, who, in turn, got Sandburg's approval, despite the fact that he rarely lent his words to any commercial endorsement. Hearing of the impending trip to Moscow, Taub and her agency persuaded Sandburg to tape the commercials before his departure, and she traveled to Chicago to work with the old poet while he transacted some other business there. Sandburg found her enchanting. Like Steichen, he appreciated strong, beautiful, intelligent women, and his age had not for an instant impeded his impulse to flirt and flatter. Indeed, he was so taken with twenty-five-year-old Joanna Taub that he wanted to introduce her to Steichen.

He did so during that trip to New York on the eve of their departure for Moscow. Sandburg arrived in Manhattan in his usual whirlwind July seventeenth, and he settled into his own personal guest quarters at the home of artist and classical guitarist Gregory d'Alessio and his wife, the cartoonist Hilda Terry. Joanna Taub was on Sandburg's mind: She was young, clever, attractive. She enjoyed his poetry and knew it well.

THE LAST APPRENTICESHIP (1955–1959)

She loved music, and she wanted to learn to play the guitar, his instrument of choice. He had promised to give her a rare lute-shaped guitar, and he was ready to deliver on that promise. He called to invite Joanna to a guitar party to be held at the d'Alessios' home on July nineteenth, the night before he and Steichen were to leave for Moscow.

She accepted, and when she arrived, Steichen was there, his arm in the sling, still disabled from the skating accident at the Millers'. He liked Joanna Taub from the first moment. Steichen appeared to some that night to be weary and withdrawn from the celebration going on around him. Still, host Gregory d'Alessio remembered Steichen on that occasion as "charming and hearty, tall and straight, jolly and animated—his eye as keen for a pretty girl as his brother's-in-law."[60] Steichen left the party early, while Sandburg, the ham and the center of attention, strummed the guitar and sang and talked far into the night.[61]

For the next day, July twentieth—the day of Steichen and Sandburg's night flight to Paris and then to Moscow—Joanna had arranged a press luncheon at the popular restaurant "21," to launch the American Airlines advertising campaign featuring Sandburg reading his poetry in his mellifluous baritone voice. Steichen was invited, and Joanna, intrigued and curious, arranged to be seated next to the great photographer. While Sandburg at eighty-one was a cheerful, benevolent grandfatherly figure, Steichen at eighty was, by the testimony of many women who knew him then, still a remarkably vital, charismatic, sexy man. When Wayne Miller, out in California, later saw a photograph taken at the luncheon at "21," he remembered, "there stood Sandburg and Steichen, with his arm in the sling, shaking hands with Joanna Taub. Steichen's eyes were bugging out of his head."[62] She was "slim, black-haired, lovely, long-limbed," Helga Sandburg recalled; "Her face is slim, a wistful mouth with a scar to its right.... There are a few gray hairs in the glossy long black locks."[63]

Later that afternoon, when Joanna accompanied Sandburg to MoMA, Steichen gave her a print of his montage of Sandburg, signed by the two of them. Then Steichen flew off to Moscow with her image on his mind, and when Joanna sent them a bon voyage telegram, addressed to Carl Sandburg, Steichen kept it for himself.[64]

For Steichen, the two-week-long sojourn in the Soviet Union was "the high spot" of the entire "Family of Man" project.⁶⁵ At the official opening of the American National Exhibition in Sokolniki Park, Steichen and Sandburg were seated on the ceremonial platform with Premier Nikita Khrushchev. Steichen held a small Minox camera in his one good hand, aiming it every now and then at the throng of photographers and movie and television cameramen who were covering the event. Vice President Richard Nixon attended, with other officials from both countries, and Nixon and Khrushchev would enjoy their obstreperous "kitchen debate" later that week.

Millions of Soviet citizens came curiously to witness the latest wonders of American art, science, and technology and to parade through "The Family of Man" installation, one of the most popular components of the American exhibit. As he had done in other cities of the world, Steichen stood unobtrusively to watch the people—more than seventy thousand in one day—streaming through the exhibit. He photographed them as they got caught up in the show, watching as he had in other countries as people paused before the pictures, touched, often transfixed.⁶⁶

Because Steichen had declined the official State Department credentials prepared for Sandburg, he was permitted to travel more freely and independently in and around Moscow.⁶⁷ He was allowed to meet with Russian professional photographers for a freewheeling question-and-answer session. Steichen also sought out Russian painters during that fortnight in Moscow, sympathizing with their isolation, not only from the world but within their own country, where they had no venues to exhibit their work. He accompanied Sandburg to meet Russian writers, including the poet Yevgeny Yevtushenko, whom Steichen called the most important figure he met in the Soviet Union.⁶⁸ (Later, Yevtushenko dedicated a book to Steichen as a gesture of appreciation for what their visit meant to him.) While Yevtushenko was a loyal Soviet citizen, protective of Soviet artists, Steichen found him open-minded and delightfully opinionated. But Steichen and Sandburg discovered that when their conversation with others of the Russian literary establishment began to move too freely, "it would end with a change of subject as abrupt as a curtain being pulled down."⁶⁹

Steichen eagerly accepted the invitation of a group of young artists to go to their homes and studios and see their paintings. "We are not per-

The Last Apprenticeship (1955–1959)

mitted to show these in public," they confided, displaying to Steichen some surprisingly contemporary abstract work. Their unorthodox paintings would be confiscated if they were discovered, Steichen was told. One artist begged Steichen to accept his abstract painting. "Take this with you," he urged Steichen. "You can bring it home and your people will see what we are trying to do here!"[70] Steichen surreptitiously brought the painting home, as well as a small sculpture given to him by another Soviet artist—"independent workmen," he called them.[71] He would take the painting to the Museum of Modern Art as an example of contemporary Russian art.

Steichen's experience in the Soviet Union further deepened his commitment to the premise of the "The Family of Man." In fact, he decided, the Russian people "were more like Americans than the people of any other country I have visited."[72] But after two weeks, he was happy to be headed for Stockholm, and then for Paris, London, and home. Landing in Stockholm on August fifth, Steichen remembered, "I suddenly became conscious that, for the first time in two weeks, I was breathing freely again. Freedom is something that is in the air of a country."[73]

In Sweden, the press photographed the illustrious brothers-in-law—Steichen handsome and dapper in a summer suit, Sandburg beaming and rumpled in comfortable pants and coat, a polka-dot bow tie, the same shirt he had worn for several days in a row, and a fedora hat. Steichen photographed Sandburg posing before a massive bronze statue of King Carl XII of Sweden, for whom Sandburg had been named, and when he later sent Sandburg and Paula a print of it, he inscribed it affectionately "King Carl & Fool Carl."[74] The old poet was showered with honors from his parents' homeland—an honorary degree at the University of Uppsala, and a gold medal from the hands of King Gustav VI.

From Stockholm, the two men flew to Paris on August fifteenth, an emotional homecoming for Steichen. Between ceremonial public lectures and receptions, he took Sandburg to the Musée Rodin and to pay his respects at Rodin's tomb. The brothers-in-law lingered there for a long time while Steichen reminisced about Rodin, telling Sandburg how Rodin's art and friendship had transfigured his own life and work. "We went to Rodin's tomb and museum Sunday," Sandburg wrote to his wife back at Connemara, "& Ed was marvelous in commentary & illumination. Soon now to London & New York & talks with you. Your Carlo."[75]

These two weary but triumphant cultural ambassadors had barely landed in New York on August twenty-sixth when they were asked to appear on Lawrence E. Spivak's *Meet the Press* on NBC. With his customary exuberant hyperbole, Sandburg had called "The Family of Man" the greatest epic poem in history. He expounded during the broadcast: the Russian people came in throngs, despite the relative silence of the press, and they acted "as though they were seeing people rather than pictures of people."[76]

Was there censorship? the panel wanted to know. Steichen had modified the exhibition elsewhere—in Japan in 1956, for instance, in an act of artistic diplomacy, he had withdrawn five photographs connected to the atom bomb and had added sixty images provided by Japanese photographers.[77] But on that September day in 1959, *Meet the Press* journalist Bob Considine asked Steichen to explain why, in Moscow, "this particularly poignant photograph—of George Silks . . . which symbolizes the hunger of the world, was given the bum's rush, let's say, out of the exhibit."[78]

He had not wanted to remove Silks's photograph of a Chinese child begging with an empty rice bowl, Steichen reported, but the Soviets had insisted that the image of hunger in China verged on anti-Communist propaganda. He also pointed out that the Soviet government censors had had no such objection to a photograph of famine in India. Later, he heard that a Nigerian activist had ripped several pictures out of the Moscow "Family of Man" display, incensed because "Americans [*sic*] and West Indian Negroes, Africans and Asiatics" were presented as "comparatively social inferiors—sick, raggerty [*sic*], destitute and physically maladjusted. African men and women were portrayed either half clothed or naked." The dissenter, Theophilus Neokonkwo, found that choice of photographs "insulting, undignified and tendentious."[79] This was criticism that pained Steichen, going as it did against the grain of his intentions.

Asked if he could tell from his trip to Russia if people were happy there, Steichen replied, "Happiness, real happiness is an inner thing. It's a very difficult thing to see."[80] Toward the end of their *Meet the Press* interview, Lawrence Spivak asked if there were any surprises in their visit, any revelations. Steichen answered in the affirmative: "There were a lot of things we didn't know. I've often said Carl was an old man because he was 81 and I'm only 80, and he says that I've got a heck of a lot to learn, therefore. I went out to learn."[81]

Home again, Steichen returned to the Museum of Modern Art in 1959 to oversee preparations for other exhibits and to serve as chairman of a multiracial National Urban League project called "America's Many Faces." He was given the New York Botanical Society's Distinguished Service Award that year for his lifetime of work and leadership as a plant breeder. And with Kate's help at Doubleday, he attended to the last details of the publication of Dana's book, *Beethoven's Beloved*. His wife had written a painstaking book, laying out her purpose in an introduction entitled "Overture": She had traced "through an intensive reading of Beethoven's letters and through a fresh look at some of the materials brought together by earlier biographers, the course of the composer's lifelong love for Countess [Anna Maria] Erdody, the woman of whom we believe he was thinking when he wrote: 'I found only one. . . .' "[82]

In her thirteen-hundred-page manuscript, she had offered her own original "musical corroboration" for the choice of Countess Erdody as Beethoven's "Immortal Beloved." In the published book, however, this part of her work was discussed in an appendix. The question of *how* Beethoven wrote his music, Dana made clear, "belongs to the musicologists." Living as she had for thirty-four years with an artist whom she deeply loved, Dana had worked with "the utmost patience and responsiveness" to penetrate the mystery of Beethoven's creative powers, and, by extension, the mystery of art itself.[83]

As she was finishing her manuscript in 1956, Dana was racing against the looming reality of her own death. The final moving passages of "Miserere," the chapter on Beethoven's death March 26, 1827 (so near Steichen's birthday), had been written as she herself was dying. And in the haunting "Coda" on the death of the countess in 1837, Dana wrote words that ironically foreshadowed the years her husband would have to spend without her: "It seems likely that her courage gave way when Beethoven died," she said of the enigmatic countess. "We trust it was so; it would hardly be bearable to know that added to his own great sufferings had been the agony of watching the slow disintegration of his Beloved, unable to share with her his own unconquerable courage that had seen him through every cruel hurt meted out to him."[84]

The "Coda" ends with words that Beethoven had written to his countess, and that Dana surely meant as well as a blessing for her own husband: "Whatever her frailties, Beethoven loved her until there was 'not a heartbeat more.' 'Also when you do not see me ... believe ... always ... I am ... around you ...'

forever thine
   forever mine
      forever us.' "[85]

33

ALL GIANTS BEING LONELY

(1 9 5 9 - 1 9 7 3)

Sometimes old men sitting near the exits of life, say, "There were giants in those days." They wanted stones to sit on, stones to throw at each other, great stones for companions, for loneliness, all giants being lonely.[1]

—CARL SANDBURG

IN HIS POEM "TOPSTONE," CARL SANDBURG sketched a portrait of old men—lonely giants—"sitting near the exits of life." He did not publish it in his lifetime, but when his daughter Margaret found the manuscript among his papers long after his death, she knew that he was writing about himself and her uncle Ed, and she published the poem in 1978 in *Breathing Tokens,* a volume of her father's previously uncollected poetry.

"Topstone is the name of the great rock across the lake from Edward Steichen's home, which is called Umpawaug," Margaret wrote in her notes to the book. "The 'old men' of course are Sandburg and Steichen, both of whom liked the idea of great stones as companions, and 'stones to throw at each other' is an allusion to the continual jibing that went on between the two."[4] These two men of great achievement displayed no rivalry toward each other, however, only understanding, encouragement, and friendship.[3]

For more than half a century, they had buffered each other from the loneliness and isolation that can often confront the artist, but now

Sandburg was worried that Steichen's prolonged mourning for Dana had left him almost reclusive. ("Grief is one of the great known etchers," Sandburg had written in another poem. "Sorrow is a writer on faces. / Study the wilderness under your own hat / And say little or nothing of how / You are not unaccustomed to thorns."[4])

Steichen needed a new companion, Sandburg decided—and he knew just the woman. He himself found young Joanna Taub delightful company and his brother-in-law was very much at loose ends two years after Dana's death. No matter that Ed was eighty and Joanna was in her twenties. Sandburg thought he might as well throw them together to see what would happen. In New York on business, he told Joanna that he was headed to Umpawaug on the train to spend the weekend with Steichen. He accepted her offer to drive him up to Connecticut, where the threesome spent a comfortable evening in Steichen's beautiful house. Joanna returned to Umpawaug with Sandburg the following weekend, and from then on she and Steichen began spending time together.

Early on, she started referring to him as "the Captain." A graduate of St. Agnes School for Girls and Smith College, Joanna enjoyed riding horseback, and she had earned money during her college days teaching riding classes to children and acting in summer stock. By her mid-twenties, she had worked her way up to become the top radio and television writer for a major advertising agency, in part because her knowledge of aviation equipped her to create the unique advertising campaign for American Airlines. She had a passion for flying, and she took her first flying lesson in a Piper Cub on Bastille Day in 1957. Before she met Steichen and Sandburg, she had bought a used two-seat, single-engine plane.

Sandburg had predicted that Joanna would be good for Steichen, and, sure enough, he fell in love with her charm and beauty, as well as her attentive companionship. She, in turn, was drawn to his genius, his "confident spirit, his talent, his apparent wisdom, his ageless, radiant vitality."[5] The Sandburgs approved, especially after Joanna came to the rescue when Steichen, alone in his apartment in New York, suffered a second stroke in November of 1959. By sheer willpower, he struggled to reach the telephone to call Joanna. All he could manage to say was, "Come."[6]

Joanna got him to the hospital, visited and tended him there, brought her guitar to play for him as he recuperated. Afflicting the right side of his body as it did, the stroke left him limping and unable to write legibly or to speak clearly. "It was too bad he had that stroke which so affected his voice," Margaret Sandburg remembered. "He used to be able to roar out in a way that would amuse Dad, but after the stroke he could just barely get words out. It was as if something was in the way. He knew what he wanted to say, but he just couldn't speak in the same old way. I felt very sorry for him. He couldn't have liked it that way."[7]

He worked relentlessly at the therapy to restore the lost skills, until, after a time, only a slight limp remained. After he was released from the hospital, Joanna spent weekends with him at Umpawaug and Steichen came to depend on her mightily for companionship and practical attention. Paula called her "the angel," believing that Joanna had come to her brother's rescue. Yet, terribly worried about Steichen's prolonged "slump" after the stroke, Paula traveled to Umpawaug to spend time with him that fall.[8]

Meanwhile, Steichen wrote to try to reassure Mary's daughter Francesca that he was doing fine. It was only a "slight" stroke, he told his granddaughter, and the impairment was temporary. He promised her that by the time he saw her at Thanksgiving, they would enjoy a waltz together. His granddaughters Linda Joan, Francesca, and Maria affectionately called him "Bumpa." Because Francesca had just written an article about him for her school paper, he wrote to let her know that he was moved, and proud of his "beautiful granddaughter." But he signed his letter Bumpa in a quavering, almost illegible handwriting that was poignantly different from the bold Steichen scrawl of healthier days.[9]

Joanna Taub was Steichen's mainstay through his long convalescence, although some people looked skeptically at her evolving relationship with a man who was older than her parents.[10] But she was an independent career woman, unaffected by what others might think of her choices. On March 19, 1960, when Steichen was eight days shy of eighty-one and Joanna was twenty-six, they were married. "Mother reports that her brother married the 'angel' on the nineteenth of March and that it is 'confidential' although she surely doesn't see why," Helga Sandburg remembered.[11] And Kate's good friend Mid Cain née Hayes recalled that Kate telephoned to tell her about Steichen's marriage, reporting that "it was a great romance, because it was an exchange of glances across a crowded room, and it was love at first sight. I thought it was ridiculous," Mid continued, "because no young woman was going to fall in love with a man in his eighties.... I thought it was a figment of Kate's imagination."[12]

As his slow rehabilitation continued, Steichen was at first unable to carry on his projects at MoMA. As a result, Joanna took on much of the hard work of culling thirty thousand of his prints to make choices for "Steichen the Photographer," the retrospective exhibition to be mounted at MoMA in 1961 in honor of his eighty-second birthday. In September of 1960, Paula, Margaret, and Helga Sandburg visited Steichen and Joanna at Umpawaug for a few days before they all joined Sandburg in New York for the opening of *The World of Carl Sandburg* on Broadway. (The show, written and produced by Norman Corwin, starred Bette Davis and her husband, Gary Merrill, during its Off-Broadway run, with Lief Erickson replacing Merrill on Broadway after Davis and Merrill separated.) Steichen himself drove to meet his sister and nieces at the train in Ridgefield, Connecticut, looking very much the distinguished, if eccentric, artist with his high boots, jaunty dark blue beret, and flowing beard.

"My romantic uncle was always a poseur," Helga wrote, remembering the stories of his return from Europe in 1902, with long hair and a swirling black cape. "And now the beard and the young wife. The costume. The flair," Helga mused. But this time, there was no posing; he could not conceal his fragility from his sister and the nieces who adored him. They saw "his hurt dazed eyes," his tremors, his pale face. He was clearly ill, and, long afterward, Helga remembered "those ravaged eyes." At the train station, he embraced "His adored 'Little Sister,'" kissing Paula over and over again "before all the curious people and passengers." "Mother, female, is strong," Helga wrote. "He is not. They both feel it."[13]

Watching Joanna's careful, firm ministrations to Steichen, Helga, too, thought they were good for each other. "He spoils her, wanting to know her each wish and repeating her beauty to her continually," Helga wrote, but she observed that "Joanna's mother is not yet used to the situation." Helga remembered that Mrs. Taub said to someone then, "Help me to get back my little girl."[14]

Watching him struggle through the simplest physical activities during their visit, Paula urged her brother to consult another doctor for a second opinion, just to be sure all factors of his illness were being addressed. She always did that with her goats, she teased.

"I've always thought myself indestructible," Steichen conceded sadly, "and now I'm not sure."[15]

He was determined, however, to be on hand for Sandburg's opening night September 14, 1960, at the Henry Miller Theater on Broadway, even driving his wife, his sister, and his nieces into Manhattan himself in his Lark convertible, his old wide-brimmed black hat from the Voulangis days protecting him from the wind. Although most of the New York critics gave *The World of Carl Sandburg* good reviews, it closed after only a month on Broadway, but Steichen was there on opening night to salute his brother-in-law in one more adventurous project.[16] Steichen was "wobbly," Helga wrote in her journal that night, but Joanna was "stunning" before the flashing of press cameras.[17]

Steichen and Sandburg were then moving inexorably and simultaneously toward the realm of physical infirmity and, eventually, senile dementia. Joanna suspected that with Sandburg, who had not suffered two strokes, as Steichen had, there was some degree of laziness when his memory failed. When Sandburg occasionally called her Dana, for instance, she would respond pointedly by calling him Robert Frost. That barb usually jolted Sandburg temporarily back into clarity.[18]

As Steichen struggled to come back from the stroke and endured prostate surgery and another long bout of illness in 1960, his robust energy ebbed, to his immense frustration. But his health seemed to improve a little whenever he got out of the city into the sweet, clean air at Umpawaug. There he could be tempted to overexert, however, especially with five thousand delphinium seedlings thriving under the gardener's care. Steichen and Joanna moved a photographic technician into the small house at Umpawaug so that he could help them sort through several thousand containers of negatives and choose the final images for the upcoming MoMA exhibit. Alarmed when she saw the scope of the work, Paula worried that her brother would have another stroke. No, he was being the *"soul of caution,"* he promised the Sandburgs.[19]

"It's damn sweet news that you are up and around and working to the good, according to Paula," Sandburg wrote to Steichen. "Love to you and to the extraordinary and beautiful Joanna."[20] She was always at Steichen's side in the early years of their marriage, whether they were traveling or whether he was ill. They were a "wonderful team," Sandburg thought.[21] Steichen would never have gotten ready for the big 1961 MoMA retrospective exhibition without Joanna and his photographic assistant constantly helping him at home, and his invaluable assistant Grace Mayer overseeing matters at the museum, where he still officially served as director of the Department of Photography.

"Steichen the Photographer" opened at the Museum of Modern Art on March 27, 1961, Steichen's eighty-second birthday. A feast of three hundred images harvested from the more than thirty thousand surviving photographs, it represented his life's work. The handsome catalog for the exhibition included essays by Alexander Liberman of *Vogue,* MoMA director René d'Harnoncourt, Carl Sandburg, and Steichen himself, with a detailed chronology compiled by Grace Mayer. The dazzling exhibit commemorated Steichen's long career as well as his lofty international stature in the art and photography worlds, and it went on to tour in nearly forty cities in fourteen countries from 1963 through 1970.[22]

The Museum of Modern Art seized the moment to announce plans to open the Edward Steichen Photography Center in the new MoMA building then under way.[23] It pleased him that MoMA had established a center for the study of the history of photography in his honor. There scholars and researchers could work in the library and examine original prints by Steichen, Stieglitz, Gertrude Käsebier, Ansel Adams, and many other luminaries in photography. In 1968, under the direction of Grace Mayer, MoMA would initiate the Steichen Archive, beginning to collect books, periodicals, documents, papers, and memorabilia that, in conjunction with MoMA's collection of Steichen photographs, would illuminate his life and work.[24]

It was a mark of Steichen's international fame that MoMA was not the only institution to honor him, for accolades poured in from around the world. He had received the German Prize for Cultural Achievement in Photography in 1960, awarded by the Photographic Society of Germany, which also established the Edward Steichen Prize for Cultural Achievement in Photography, recognition treasured by the old man who sixty years earlier had scrimped for francs to travel from his studio in Paris to Berlin and Munich and other great cities of Europe to see for himself the work of the great turn-of-the-century pictorial photographers.

In 1961, soon after the MoMA retrospective, the Royal Photographic Society of Great Britain gave Steichen their Premier Award, and he became the first foreigner to be honored by the Photographic Society of Japan. There were honors at home, too: Steichen was awarded the 1962 *Art in America* Award, and later that year, he received special homage from Agnes Meyer, the long-ago "Girl from the Sun," his patron since the early days. Now missing Eugene, and struggling with her own infirmities, Agnes gave MoMA ten thousand dollars in Steichen's honor to support the Department of Photography.[25]

Steichen and his artistry had achieved "almost legendary dimensions," according to Dimitrie G. Popescue in a Romanian broadcast on the *Voice of America* in 1962, sharing with his listeners the fact that Steichen's exhibition at MoMA had opened with eight studies of Romanian-born Constantin Brancusi's *Bird in Space*. "Steichen's work, indeed, reflects existence itself," Popescue said, "with its daily improvisations as well as its eternal aspects. His artistic vision encloses in an instant of time an entire universe of the deepest human significance."[26]

The Sandburgs could not be with Steichen to celebrate his birthday and the opening of the MoMA exhibition. Indefatigable Carl Sandburg was in Hollywood working with George Stevens on *The Greatest Story Ever Told,* and Paula was not well. "I'm glad you call it an ailment and not a disease," Sandburg wrote to his wife during he Christmas holidays in 1960, after she let him know she was sick. "All along the Steichens always have had ailments and not diseases with the single exception of Oma at her end." He pointed out "how tough and nice" Steichen had "been coming through his late ailments." Sandburg reminisced about earlier, brighter Christmases "when Ed would come on from New York and you and Oma were lighted like Christmas trees about his coming, the rushing around and the hullabaloo nearly got you down."[27]

All would be well, Sandburg hoped, for robust good health was imprinted in the Steichen genes. He urged his wife, "Remember your great grandfather who went through all of the hunger and cold and deep snow out of Moscow with Napoleon" and lived to be past 106. And soon, he promised, he would be at home with her at Connemara, where they could take long walks "holding hands" and he could once more admire her beautiful Nubian goats "as creations of yours, creations as definitely as either photographs or delphiniums created by Ed plus God."[28]

Steichen took Joanna to Connemara in 1961 so that she could see the place he loved best after Umpawaug. From California, Sandburg wrote emotionally to Steichen about the "knowledge, wisdom, training, guidance, that I have had from you." As he worked in Hollywood—his office used to be Marilyn Monroe's dressing room and they had become great friends—Sandburg predicted that Steichen had "some of his greatest work just ahead."[29]

Part of that work had to do with Steichen's experiments photographing his shadblow tree. Using 35-mm color film, he had taken several hundred slides of the tree. Now he planned to arrange a progressive sequence of the still images on slides so as to "weave them into a consecutive series, thinking of it as a concerto, with the little tree the solo instrument and the neighboring trees and pond the members of the orchestra."[30] Clicking one slide after another on the screen, however, he was disappointed that these ragged interruptions destroyed any mood he had hoped to create with the images.

When Steichen shared the slide show one night with documentary filmmaker Pare Lorentz and his wife, Elizabeth Meyer, the daughter of Agnes and Eugene Meyer, Lorentz suggested that Steichen transfer the slides onto movie film so that the images could dissolve and flow into one another. Excited, Steichen took the suggestion a step further, setting to work with an Ariflex movie camera to capture his "photographic concerto" on motion-picture film. "Why not start the series over again as a motion picture," he thought, "and take advantage of the wind and the rain and the movements of the water . . . the noises of wind and of rain splashing on the water and the sounds of birds, frogs, and insects."[31]

Back at work at MoMA, meanwhile, knowing as he did the historical amnesia that afflicted many Americans, Steichen invested his energy in exhibits to commemorate events that he felt should reverberate forever in the national consciousness: the excruciating madness of war; the high cost exacted when individuals are denied their rights and dignity; the "endurance and fortitude that made the emergence from the Great Depression one of America's victorious hours."[32] His shows had encompassed that spectrum—the wartime exhibits, "Road to Victory," "Power in the Pacific," and "Korea"; the epic plea for unity in "The Family of Man." In 1962, he addressed the Depression in "The Bitter Years," a retrospective of the images made by the Farm Security Administration, led by Roy Stryker. This was Steichen's way of paying homage to the "peerless" FSA photographs that had influenced his major thematic exhibitions at MoMA.[33]

He believed, furthermore, that a new and rather self-absorbed generation of Americans, with "problems of its own," needed to look back into the national memory for inspiration. "We were living now with the continuing Cold War between East and West," Steichen reflected, as well as with the "almost daily threat" of the annihilation of the entire human race "through the nuclear bomb." It seemed to him a horrible kind of mass suicide. And the nation had "recently seen near-panic over a stock market that dropped swiftly from a dizzy altitude and made too many citizens feel discouraged and sorry for themselves." He thought that the powerful images of "stamina presented by our people during the 'bitter years' of another critical period might perform a revitalizing function."[34]

He also hoped that someday there might be a national photographic organization to document the United States and its people in all seasons and endeavors—a chronicle, like his record of the shadblow tree—but on a human scale. Perhaps that dream of his could be achieved by the "free-spirited, independently thinking young photographers" of the new generation—"seekers, probers, and explorers of new horizons."[35]

He himself had been seeking, probing, and exploring new horizons all his life, but now health and old age were wearing him out. In July 1962, Steichen officially retired as director of the Department of Photography at the Museum of Modern Art. He and Grace Mayer would see "The Bitter Years" through conception to installation, but that exhibition was his swan song. Grace Mayer would serve for years afterward as curator of photography, under the able direction of Steichen's successor, John Szarkowski.

Steichen went home to Umpawaug, where he could now devote endless hours to his delphiniums and his shadblow tree. His brilliant mind, with its prodigious scientific and artistic powers, still seemed vigorous enough, brimming with ideas and projects. He had much more work to do, but his aging body and flagging physical energy began to stand in the way of it. He despised these limitations, this ultimate loss of control. For the first time in his life, Steichen was beginning to feel useless, and frustration, anger, and irritation erupted as his physical energy diminished. Family and friends worried over the changes in him, and Agnes Meyer, the oldest friend he had, apart from his sister, took Steichen and Joanna to Martinique for a vacation, hoping the rest and sun would rejuvenate him.

Agnes also generously oversaw Steichen's financial well-being, taking over, with her attorney's help, the role that Eugene Meyer had performed before his death, advising Steichen as needed about his investments and financial concerns. Appreciating that, Mary wrote to Agnes Meyer in 1963:

> *Joanna told me that if they continue at their present scale of living, they will have exhausted their capital resources in six years. For this reason Frank and I were relieved to know that Daddy has reconsidered and is not planning to will his fine works of art away from the estate. He is conscious that there will be need to provide not only for Joanna, who by the time it is necessary may have well passed the age when she can easily get a job, particularly in view of her lack of training and interim experience, but is also aware that he must think about my sister Kate.*[36]

Mary even suggested that her father take advantage of tax laws to give Joanna a nontaxable gift of sixty thousand dollars to reduce potential inheritance taxes.[37] When Agnes discovered in 1964 that Steichen was getting ready to dip into his capital to pay living expenses, she decided to make annual gifts of three thousand dollars each to Steichen and Joanna, the maximum sum then allowed for gifts without taxation.[38]

With Joanna's help, Steichen published *A Life in Photography* in 1963, advertised as "the dramatic summation of 69 years of photography by Edward Steichen."[39] He wrote his autobiography to accompany 234 photographs chosen from his thirty thousand negatives—essentially the replication of images selected for "Steichen the Photographer" in 1961. The book was dedicated to his mother "with homage, gratitude, respect, admiration, and love," and he wrote at the outset about her childhood lecture on "the evils of bigotry and intolerance"—the "day the seed was sown that, sixty-six years later, grew into an exhibition called 'The Family of Man.' "[40] *Look* magazine published an excerpt of text and photographs on November 5, 1963, so sure that most of its 7,400,000 readers would know Steichen and his pictures that the excerpt ran as the lead article, with no editorial comment or background.

That same year, Sandburg published *Honey and Salt,* his last collection of poetry—and then, for both men—diminuendo. Other giants had gone one by one: Rodin, Matisse, Fred Holland Day, and Stieglitz, all so many years ago. In 1957, Brancusi had died, "a great artist," Steichen said, "a great human being and a very dear and much lamented lost friend."[41] Eugene Meyer was gone. Down at Connemara, Sandburg lived in growing senescence, alternately benign and cantankerous, often shouting out his frustration as age and illness imprisoned him in a body he no longer recognized. Only Paula could soothe and settle him.

For Steichen, ever more vulnerable to a growing haze of forgetfulness and confusion, life began to be so much ceremony, a ritualistic going through the motions. In 1963, President John F. Kennedy decided to replace the Medal of Freedom, first given in 1945 for meritorious acts on behalf of the security of the United States, with the Presidential Medal of Freedom, the nation's highest peacetime honor, to be given in recognition of significant contributions to the quality of American life. On July 4, 1963, the President announced a prestigious honors list of thirty-one individuals, including Edward Steichen. Plans were under way for a White House ceremony to honor the thirty-one medalists when the tragedy of the President's assassination shattered the nation.

"Daddy took it very hard as did I," Mary wrote to Agnes Meyer, "and of course the impending Freedom Medal ceremony is going to exert great strain on him. Joanna and I are somewhat worried because he simply keeled over from the strain of last week end. He has been put on a tranquilizer...."[42] But in December of 1963, Steichen traveled to Washington to accept the Presidential Medal of Freedom from Lyndon Johnson. "Photographer and collector," his citation read, "he has made the camera the instrument of aesthetic perception and thereby transformed a science into an art."[43] Other recipients that day included, among others, Marian Anderson, Pablo Casals (in absentia), Felix Frankfurter, Rudolf Serkin, E. B. White, Thornton Wilder, Edmund Wilson, Andrew

Wyeth, Pope John XXIII (posthumously), and, in special tribute, the late President.

When President Johnson bestowed the same honor on Sandburg in 1964, the Steichens joined Carl and Paula at the White House for Sandburg's ceremony. The brothers-in-law accepted an award in tandem when the National Council of the Arts and Government honored both Steichen and Sandburg in October of 1965 in a ceremony featuring tributes by Senators Jacob Javits and Claiborne Pell, pianist Van Cliburn, and dancer José Limón, with Agnes Meyer serving as honorary chairman.

In the weeks before he turned eighty-five in March of 1964, Steichen conserved his energy for the gala black-tie birthday dinner Agnes Meyer was planning for him in Washington. On Thursday, April 9, 1964, guests stepped out from every chapter of Steichen's long life. Sandburg and Paula were among the eighty people invited to the Meyer mansion for the celebration, as were Wayne and Joan Miller; Joanna and her parents, Dr. and Mrs. W. James Taub of Hopewell Junction, New York; Mary and her family; Kate and Carol; Helga and her husband, Dr. George "Barney" Crile of Cleveland, Ohio; René d'Harnoncourt, Monroe Wheeler, Grace Mayer, and John Szarkowski of MoMA; Tom Maloney; Chief Justice and Mrs. Earl Warren; the ambassador of Luxembourg, Georges Heisbourg, and his wife; and Admiral Felix Stump.

Steichen, still with a thick, long beard, wore his Presidential Medal of Freedom, and he got a bear hug from Sandburg, kisses from Paul, and embraces from the eighty close friends invited to celebrate with him.[44] It was a "shining occasion," Grace Mayer wrote to Agnes afterward. She paid tribute to Steichen as one of the people "I most respect, most admire and most love."[45]

For Steichen, however, travel even over short distances grew more and more taxing, and he usually returned from trips exhausted. But in 1966, he and Joanna managed to travel to Europe, where they visited Pablo Casals and Picasso and attended the exhibition of "The Family of Man" at a castle in Clervaux in Luxembourg. An American magazine reportedly offered him as much as fifty thousand dollars to photograph Picasso, but Steichen declined emphatically. He was just going to see his old friend, and he would not take his camera along to intrude on that private visit. He introduced Joanna to Picasso, who introduced them to his wife,

All Giants Being Lonely (1959–1973)

Jacqueline Roque. The old men sat with their beautiful young wives in the sun at Notre Dame de Vie, Picasso's villa in the hills overlooking Cannes. They reminisced about the old days when they were both struggling young artists in Paris, mavericks stubbornly determined to work in their own original, independent ways.

"Edward," Picasso teased that day, "do you remember when I gave you my first batch of paintings to take back to America and sell?"

"I certainly do," Steichen answered.

"Yes," Picasso replied, "but you didn't sell any."

"Pablo, you're wrong. I sold three of them. The first three ever sold in America." He knew, Picasso said, laughing; he was just testing Steichen's memory.[46]

When photographer Paul Strand had photographed Picasso in 1956, when the painter was seventy-five, Picasso asked if Strand knew Steichen and Stieglitz. Indeed, Strand replied, he knew them very well. "You know, they were the first ones to bring my work to America," Picasso told Strand. "I noted he said Steichen *first*, not Stieglitz," Strand remembered. "Steichen was very important. He was a photographer who made contributions in other ways besides photography. The whole cultural life, as far as painting was concerned, was changed by his bringing modern art to America."[47]

During that last journey to Europe, Steichen made one final pilgrimage to Luxembourg, to see "The Family of Man" in Clervaux and to be honored by his homeland. He had offered permanent custody of one of the traveling editions of the show to the government of Luxembourg as a lasting gesture of remembrance.[48] For photographer Marcel Schroeder, Steichen posed in front of his mother's birthplace in Mondercange, erect and elegant, a walking stick in his hand, the beard neatly groomed, looking for all the world like Opa. He had most likely surpassed the hopes that burned in Marie Kemp Steichen's heart as she transported her son to the new country in 1881. But he himself had not finished dreaming. At Umpawaug, he had turned his skillful hands to the work of breeding a new Oriental poppy, telling visitors that he imagined that giving birth to a new plant yielded emotions akin to what "a woman gets when she bears a child."[49]

Until the end of his life, there were flashes of his characteristic wit and brilliance. In 1969, for instance, celebrating his ninetieth birthday at a fête at the Plaza Hotel in New York, Steichen made a brief, feisty, much-quoted speech:

> *When I first became interested in photography, I thought it was the whole cheese. My idea was to have it recognized as one of the fine arts. Today I don't give a hoot in hell about that. The mission of photography is to explain man to man and each man to himself.*[50]

Some of his perpetual critics, particularly Beaumont and Nancy Newhall, interpreted the "hoot in hell" remark to mean that Steichen had never been seriously committed to photography as art, thus confirming their belief that he was a hypocrite and dissembler. But to misread that quotation was to misread Steichen: In reality, he was recapitulating, distilling in a phrase the hard-won revelations of a lifetime of passion and discipline in art. Photography was fine art and far, far more, he was saying one more time. Photography more than any other visual art medium had the transforming power to communicate, to chronicle, to clarify, even to unify.

He would live four more years, working in the energetic moments his body dealt out to him with increasing parsimony. Steichen served perfunctorily as the editor for a collection of photographs entitled *Sandburg: Photographers View Carl Sandburg*, published by Harcourt, Brace & World in 1966. Otherwise, he was spending all of his time at Umpawaug, except for a day a week at MoMA, where he enjoyed his role as director emeritus of the Department of Photography. But life became essentially a series of losses—his vision impaired despite the cataract surgery; his body refusing to support the work he wanted to do; his mind betraying him, spurting to full life and cognizance sometimes, deserting him otherwise, leaving him frightened and perplexed, sometimes incoherent, and more and more isolated within himself.

Then, on July 22, 1967, Carl Sandburg died. At the local funeral home in Hendersonville, North Carolina, Steichen stood for a long while, supported by his cane, looking for the last time into Sandburg's face. Bereft as they felt with one of their tight-knit threesome gone, Paula and Steichen agreed this was not a time to mourn, but to rejoice in Sandburg's long, exuberant life. At lunch before the memorial service, Steichen and journalist Harry Golden toasted Sandburg with glasses of goat's milk from Paula's champion herd, and afterward, smoking cigars, the two men read aloud from Sandburg's *Complete Poems.*

Steichen and Joanna joined the family and a few chosen friends for the private memorial service near Connemara at Saint John-in-the-Wilderness Church in Flat Rock, North Carolina. He wanted his sister to lean on him, and she did, serene and at peace with her husband's death, celebrating their long life together. As the family left the old house on the hill to descend to the church, Steichen broke a bough from one of the white pines overhanging the drive at Connemara. In the cool sanctuary of the little chapel, Steichen tenderly arranged the evergreens on Sandburg's coffin, as Sandburg surely would have done for him.

Helga remembered watching the television film of the funeral afterward, with "Mother and Uncle Ed going up the stairs, he sort of blindly forging forward and holding her hand in a fierce way, she luminous."[51] When he went back to Connecticut, Steichen took with him "onionlike stalks" that he had purloined from Paula's Connemara garden. "Piracy on the high seas!" he teased, knowing his sister would gladly let him take the white and crimson lilies home to transplant at Umpawaug.[52]

Oma, Opa, Nell, and Dana had gone, and now Carl. This fifth great bereavement crystallized the loneliness Sandburg had articulated after one of their rambles at Umpawaug. He had put in his poem the image of the two of them sitting and contemplating the rocky cliffs, just two old seekers and dreamers approaching the end of life, two lonely giants reaching out to each other and to nature for companionship.

Sandburg was eighty-nine when he died, and Steichen made it to ninety and somehow kept on going. But he told people gathered at the Plaza Hotel to celebrate his ninetieth birthday in 1969 that he did not see how his sister could endure life without Sandburg. "I can hardly stand it myself," Steichen mused. "I didn't see him too often in the last years, but there was always the telephone and we talked. I miss him terribly."[53] And, considering his brother-in-law's life and work, Steichen had written in the introduction to *Sandburg: Photographers View Carl Sandburg,* "All the important matters of his heart and mind stand revealed in his writings."[54]

Steichen's memory lapses accelerated rapidly in the late sixties, and his loneliness increased proportionately. Deeply concerned, Agnes Meyer continued her financial assistance to Steichen at least through 1970, and she frequently provided vacations for Steichen and Joanna.[55] Joanna watched over Steichen, helping him with his projects and providing his daily care with the help of Serge and Helen Milaschewitsch, a local couple who had been devoted to Steichen and Dana and who had now worked for Steichen for almost fifteen years. But the Steichens' marital relationship apparently grew strained during the late sixties as his increasing age and infirmity converged with Joanna's growing anxiety about money and her need to create an independent life of her own. As Mary had foreseen, Joanna needed to train for a career, for by 1966, she was in her early thirties and her husband was eighty-seven. She enrolled in classes at the Columbia University School of General Studies in 1966, spending more and more of her time in their apartment at New York, while Steichen remained at Umpawaug with Serge and Helen.

As time passed, the relationship between Steichen and his third wife appeared to some to become adversarial. He had been hard on his wives. Steichen had never been an easy man to live with, especially in the last years, when his energy was depleted, the world he had seen with unrelenting clarity was shrouded in an ever-growing haze of confusion and disorientation, and his great mind was wearing out before his strong body completely failed him. By her mid-thirties, Joanna had spent a decade being Mrs. Edward Steichen, wife, assistant, companion, and nurse. She may have felt a growing urgency to prepare herself for the time when she would be Mrs. Edward Steichen, widow—or Joanna Taub Steichen, person in her own right.

When Steichen drew up his will in 1964, he had named Mary's husband, Dr. Frank Calderone, as one of the three executors of his estate, along with Joanna and psychiatrist Eugene "Bill" Meyer III, the son of Eugene and Agnes Meyer. By 1969, Frank Calderone had stepped into the often-thankless role of informal go-between for family members, meeting privately with Kate, with Mary, with Steichen, and with Joanna to discuss concerns about Steichen's medical care and his other needs; Joanna's financial future; the implications of Steichen's will; the complicated family schedules; and the conflicting opinions about what was best for Steichen's health. The issue of Steichen's clarity of mind would become critical in his last years as his family wrestled with questions about his health care and his estate. But in 1969, when he was ninety years old, Steichen told Frank Calderone at Umpawaug that "it was his intention to live as long as he could and ... he would live in his own home on his property there. He had no intention of dying."[56]

Steichen and Joanna seemed to enter a new phase of life in 1970 as she spent more and more time in New York as a graduate student at the Columbia University School of Social Work. To care for Steichen at Umpawaug, Joanna hired a companion to augment the services of Helen and Serge Milaschewitsch. Frank Calderone clipped and filed among his papers an advertisement from a Connecticut newspaper:

> COMPANION *for frail, sometimes temperamental old man. Live in full time job, could be shared by 2 people, splitting the week. Man or strong woman (might consider retired couple, if one has secretarial and bookeeping [sic] skills). Must be intelligent, responsible and completely dependable. Write sending brief resume and list of references.* ...[57]

The position was filled by a capable, kindly woman named Elisabeth King, who came to live at Umpawaug and care for Steichen as his nurse-companion.

As his daughter and as a physician, Mary took an aggressive, opinionated interest in her father's health and well-being. She had been in her mid-fifties when Steichen married Joanna Taub. It was, no doubt, difficult for her to witness her father's seeming obsession with a third wife, one who was nearly thirty years younger than she. Mary and Kate, who had in many ways felt abandoned since their parents' bitter separation in 1915, had been comfortable in the warm family circle woven by Dana during their father's second marriage. Now her father's attachment to Joanna may have seemed to Mary a kind of rejection.

For whatever reason, Mary's love for her father in those last years was interlaced with intermittent anger toward him, and toward his wife, and there were periods of estrangement between father and daughter. All her life, however, Mary had loved Steichen fiercely, choosing him over her mother, and defending him against Clara. Now as she watched her seemingly invincible father age and suffer, she stepped into that same protective posture, trying to ensure that "our father's health and welfare should in no way be jeopardized by radical changes in his environment, and that he was entitled to everything that money could buy to make it possible for him to enjoy the remaining time in his life."[58]

Mary worried not only about her father's welfare but about Kate's financial future. With her own career and the support of her husband, Mary was provided for, but Kate had worked for a modest salary as assistant to editor Ken McCormick at Doubleday, with no adequate pension to fall back on. Aware of that, Steichen had willed nothing to Mary and part of his estate to Kate, with the bulk of the estate designated for Joanna. But Kate did not know the terms of the will, and, always the family peacemaker, she wanted no conflict over money and possessions. Such stress had to trigger painful memories of her parents' long, excruciating struggle over such matters. Kate therefore begged Mary not to cause any problems for her sake. And she expressed great surprise when Frank Calderone told her in 1970 about Steichen's will.

"When Daddy gave me the Brancusi I was led to believe that was my entire inheritance," Kate told her brother-in-law. She did not want to "get involved in any legal situation.... All I want is that my father should end up his last days in peace."[59]

In those days of his growing infirmity and senescence, Steichen sat alone by his overgrown pond at Umpawaug and worried about the ultimate disposition of his paintings and photographs. At one point, he asked Mary to donate his 1920 oil painting *Scarlet Poppy* to the Museum of Modern Art, but Mary refused. It was the one of all his paintings that held greatest meaning for her, for her father had given it to her during her first year at the University of Rochester School of Medicine. "He, who never went beyond the eighth grade, came himself to hang it over the mantel in my living room, which instantly became no longer bare," Mary remembered. "We looked at it silently for a long moment, then he turned to me and, using my baby name, remarked, 'You know, Mickey, I think that's the best damn painting I ever did.' "[60]

All Giants Being Lonely (1959–1973)

With increasing frequency during the last years of Steichen's life, Frank Calderone found himself standing awkwardly between Mary, his wife and Steichen's protective daughter, and Joanna, his young mother-in-law and coexecutor. In 1971, according to a story in the *Washington Post*, Joanna was studying for her master's degree in psychiatric social work and living in New York, spending weekends at Umpawaug.[61] She was approaching forty, compelled to look ahead, for Steichen would not live forever. While she worked on her degree at Columbia, Elisabeth King continued to live in the house at Umpawaug and care for "the Captain," as she, too, called Steichen. His other constant companion was a three-legged beagle named Tripod, a dog who had actually adopted him, Steichen said, when he limped up to the house at Umpawaug one day.[62]

During those days, Steichen smoked a stream of cigarettes and cigars, drank strong coffee, enjoyed wine with his dinner, ate ice cream, despised growing older. At five each evening, he tuned in British journalist David Frost's television show. He and his gardener continued to experiment with the new Oriental poppy in the Umpawaug fields. Between visits, Elisabeth kept Mary and Kate informed about their father's daily life, writing to Mary in December of 1969 that there were accelerating signs of senile dementia now, but otherwise he seemed to stay reasonably well, even taking his morning walks despite "snow, and cold weather." She read to him after his afternoon nap, often rereading articles about Mary because he forgot that he had heard them before. Elisabeth congratulated Mary when she was named one of the fifty most famous women in the world, telling her, "The Captain thought it was wonderful."[63]

Because of financial worries, Steichen had informed the town officers of Redding in 1969 that he would consider selling up to 412 acres of his Umpawaug land for community recreation and conservation use. The transaction had been set in motion by early February 1970, and on January 30, 1971, in a hard-fought referendum, Redding voters approved the huge expenditure of $682,000 to buy 270 acres of Steichen's estate on Topstone Road, including woodlands, fields, the 650-foot-tall Topstone Mountain, and the 17-acre man-made lake. Steichen sold an additional 117 acres of land to Redding Open Lands, Incorporated, or ROLI, the nonprofit organization founded by citizens of Redding to protect the area against development and subdivision. Steichen's forty-three-acre Huckleberry Swamp was deeded by ROLI to the Connecticut Audubon Society, and he told Frank Calderone that he was happy that "bulldozers would never be on my land."[64] But events during the time of the referendum deeply upset Steichen, because by 1971 he did not fully understand or remember what had transpired with his land, or why it was being sold.

"I put in a call to Joanna Steichen at Mt. Sinai Hospital where she is now working," Calderone wrote on February 8, 1971, indicating that he wanted to congratulate her on the sale of the land. Now she would not have to worry about money, he said, "because with interest and capital she should be able to take care of the Captain for quite a number of years."[65]

The promise of financial security did not seem to reduce tensions, however, and Elisabeth King observed that Steichen "was very upset on Monday and wouldn't sleep alone and wanted her to stay upstairs with him and to leave the lights on. She said this always happened after Joanna left."[66] Steichen wanted lights burning all night in case the doctor had to come, Elisabeth said, but most of all, he was afraid that he might die alone in the dark.[67]

As he approached his ninety-second birthday, Steichen sank further into senility, although he and Joanna and their attorneys did join local dignitaries for a ceremony in the Redding Town Office Building in early March. There, according to the local newspaper, "Capt. Edward J. Steichen" received a check for $675,000 from the town of Redding for their purchase of 270 Umpawaug acres, and another check for $290,000 from Redding Open Lands, Incorporated (ROLI).[68] The sale of his Umpawaug acres had alleviated all financial worries once and for all.

Steichen's earnings as a photographer had for many years subsidized Steichen the farmer, paying for the acquisition of the vast acreage he had needed for the Umpawaug plant-breeding operation. Now Steichen the farmer had come to the rescue of Steichen the artist, as he harvested nearly a million dollars from the sale of his delphinium fields. The funds could ensure the peace Kate wanted for her father, the comfort and safety Mary sought for him, and the space and independence Joanna wanted for herself.

As Joanna returned to her life in New York, Elisabeth King stayed

All Giants Being Lonely (1959–1973)

on with Steichen at Umpawaug, cooking and nursing, reading to him, finding a local man to come in weekly to bathe him and trim his beard. When he seemed "depressed," she knew that reading to him about Mary always lifted his spirits, she wrote. He spoke of his daughters proudly, Elisabeth told Mary. Doing so always took "him out of his loneliness."[69]

In 1984, a little more than a decade after Steichen's death, his widow Joanna would publish a book entitled *Marrying Up: An American Dream & Reality: Why Some Make It Into the Inner Circle and Others Never Will,* the outgrowth of "How to Marry Money," a popular course she taught at the Network for Learning in New York. Clara Smith Steichen had always believed that when she married Steichen, she had married down. Joanna Taub Steichen, it would appear to some, believed that she had married up.

She wrote in her book that she had married a man who was acclaimed for his extraordinary achievement as an artist. While Steichen's financial success by no means approached the magnitude of that earned by Picasso or a handful of other artists, he had still attained artistic stature that served as an equivalent of wealth. With Steichen, she told her readers, she had stepped into a "world of movers and shakers, wealth and achievement," noting that she had sat at the President's table in the White House in the Kennedy and Johnson administrations; had been a guest of Pablo Casals as well as Pablo Picasso; had seen her own homes featured in *Vogue;* and had been named by *Women's Wear Daily* on a list of women distinguished for the "ladylike look," along with Audrey Hepburn, Babe Paley, and others.[70]

Steichen was, Joanna wrote, the "best man" she had met who left it unmistakably evident that he was truly interested in her. But theirs was not an "easy" marriage, she noted, and, as is true of all choices, it eliminated certain options at the same time that it opened others. Still, she wrote, she was positive that she "would not have done anything better" with her life "at that time."[71]

Mary Steichen Calderone wrote to her cousin Helga Sandburg Crile in November of 1972 warning that "Uncle Ed is weakening day by day."[72] He was ninety-three, dependent on a pacemaker, and losing his battle against senile dementia. His body was frail as paper, the skin slack and white, the great, once-gifted hands laced with blue veins. Muscles softened and withered, no longer fed by vigorous walks and hard work, and his wondrous mind shut down at last, as if from a surfeit of life itself. He now slept much of the time.

"He is physically quite weak although able to get around," Mary told Helga, "and of course his mental powers have failed greatly in the past year. He has great difficulty remembering even from minute to minute, although of course he will have moments when his memory particularly for very long past events is surprisingly good."[73] Did images of other giants march before him then—Oma and Opa, his sister, Lilian, the masters Rodin, Day, Stieglitz, Matisse, Brancusi, Sandburg? Were there the softer images of Clara and the little girls in the garden at Voulangis in the good days, Dana's frank smile and knowing eyes, and Joanna's vivid face?

Was he aware of the battle lines being drawn around him as his life ebbed away? Mary stood resolutely on one side, loving him as fiercely as she had in the old days when they were alone, the two of them against the world; Joanna stood adamantly on the other, torn by the duty to her old, dying husband and the duty to herself. Kate, as always, tried to play the mitigator, craving for her father serenity and peace. And had Steichen made his own peace with life, and so with death?

In North Carolina, his little sister had by now given up her own memory to time, stricken as her husband and now her brother had been by senility—another lustrous mind stripped of its richness, left with the debris of dying cells, strokes, great age. After Sandburg's death, Lilian Paula Steichen Sandburg had sold Connemara to the Department of the Interior so that the beautiful old mountain estate could become a national park. She had then sold her famous goat herd, bought a spacious house in nearby Asheville, settled her daughters Margaret and Janet there with her, and begun to let go of her own life.

Mary wrote to Helga, "I don't know what the situation is with your mother but I think all of you ought to be prepared for his slipping away at sometime in the not too far distant future." Sadly, Mary mused that she and her aunt Paula, Steichen's sister, were "the two people now left in the world who have known him the longest."[74] Mary gave the Museum of Modern Art thirty of her father's prints that year, ranging from a photograph of her parents on their honeymoon at Lake George in 1903, to her own baby pictures, to photographs of her daughters, including Nell.

As the winter of 1973 began, Steichen was clearly dying. In March, a wire broke in his pacemaker, and Joanna, with the agreement of Mary and Steichen's doctor, made the decision not to replace it and not to rely on any artificial life support. By March eighteenth, he was settled in a hospital bed at Umpawaug, growing more frail hour by hour. Joanna was in New York most of the time, working to complete requirements for her master's degree from the Columbia University School of Social Work, with graduation scheduled for May sixteenth. By now, Steichen was attended by a night nurse and a new nurse-companion, this time a man. Joanna believed that Steichen understood that he was dying, and even welcomed the impending release.[75]

During his final months, beavers were damming the pond near Steichen's Huckleberry Swamp, felling black cherry trees to build a lodge on the banks on the south side of the wetland. When their engineering feats caused flooding on nearby Chestnut Woods Road, Steichen's helpers and neighbors worried that the beavers would harm Steichen's shadblow tree. He had come to feel that the beautiful little tree "became almost the essential part of my life experience and gradually I took this material and wove it into something like a poem or a piece of music, with soft, quiet movements and turbulent ones, with love, hate, anger and tragedy."[76] But he had long ago set his cameras aside, and the tree now bloomed, rested, then bloomed again, with no camera record, no witness.

Meanwhile, in New York, waiting for the end, Joanna wrote to Steichen's family to discuss his memorial service. The Captain never cared for rituals or ministers, she said, and she proposed a dignified memorial service at the Museum of Modern Art instead of a funeral—perhaps with Beethoven's Quartet no. 16 as music, and maybe an arrangement of his delphiniums. She suggested that a day or so before or after the memorial service, members of the family could receive special guests at Umpawaug.[77] Wayne Miller flew to the East Coast from California as soon as he received Joanna's letter of March eighteenth about Steichen's decline. He and Joanna were at the bedside at 11:30 on Sunday morning, March 25, 1973, when Steichen died at Umpawaug, just two days before his ninety-fourth birthday.

Loving light as he always had, at least he did not die alone in the dark.

After his death, Steichen's neighbors merged Huckleberry Swamp with nearby land to create the Edward Steichen Memorial Wildlife Preserve.[78] Birds and wild animals could roam that habitat in peace, foraging in Red Maple Swamp and Huckleberry Swamp, which were verdant with the wildflowers rooted there since Indian days—jack-in-the-pulpit, enchanter's nightshade, pokeweed, interrupted fern, silvery spleenwort, bishop's cap. Still blooming in the fields closest to the Umpawaug house where he had lived for more than thirty years could be seen the progeny of the delphinium seeds Steichen had brought from Voulangis and mingled with fine seeds gleaned from gardens around the world.

For years after Steichen's death and Sandburg's, and Paula's in 1977, Sandburg's "Experiments Toward a Poem on Delphiniums" lay unfinished on the pages he had left behind at Connemara. He had written there of

> *two delphiniums with seeds lighted in soil*
> *with stalks prepared in loam*
> *toward the upheave of insurrection*
> *into the bloom of resurrection. . . .*[79]

Steichen had been a rebel, a pioneer, a master of insurrection. His persistent and daring acts of rebellion created art out of life itself. His luminous work fed on his passion for light, and for life, each of his thousands of photographic images a kind of resurrection. But he summed himself up simply in 1959, looking back: "I think I did whatever I was doing as well as I could—at the time—and under the conditions."[80]

All Giants Being Lonely (1959–1973)

What eulogy for a giant? Photographer and colleague Charles Sheeler, his neighbor for a time in Connecticut, had called Steichen "a great hearth around which we all gathered for warmth."[81] Wayne Miller, his surrogate son, said "Steichen was a warm, emotional, hungry man. He was in love with: Children, Women, Fertility, the Creation of life."[82]

Sandburg, too, had alluded to the hunger back in 1929, in *Steichen the Photographer:*

> *He will die telling God that if he could live a few years longer he might be the photographer he wanted to be. His mother once said at the yearly Christmas dinner, "I suppose you want a camera in the coffin with you when you are buried." He answered, "Yes— and over the grave put my radio set." He will die a seeker and a listener.*[83]

Critic Robert Hughes in *Time* magazine named him the patriarch of the Family of Man, noting that "Much of his art lay in his impeccable and patient sense of selection...."[84] Steichen's death was reported on the front page of the *New York Times* and in the pages of journals and newspapers, large and small, around the world. The *New York Times* obituary by Alden Whitman began on page one and spilled over an entire additional page, with five photographs—Steichen's portraits of J. P. Morgan, Greta Garbo, and Carl Sandburg, and pictures of Steichen by Wayne and Joan Miller. He was, Whitman wrote, "the country's most celebrated and highest-priced photographer," a "craftsman of genius who transformed his medium into an art," a "humanist" who "gave his century a new vision."[85]

His niece Helga, getting the news by cable in Spain, wrote a poem to her uncle on a night train en route from San Sebastián to Barcelona:

> *... We spoke of love and your Family of Man.*
> *We mentioned how your life was fields and flowers,*
> *Complex cameras or simple pigment, paint,*
> *Women, two wars, strong heart for certain men;*
> *We saluted your humility, arrogance; we named you*
> *   sinner, saint.*[86]

Steichen was cremated as spring returned to Umpaw[...] shadblow promised new blooms. He had asked that some o[...] strewn by the Topstone boulder, where he and Sandburg [...] the sun.⁸⁷ In the swamp, the green heron and the black ducks were nesting. The full-throated birds came back, the blackpoll warblers, the redstarts, the sparrows, the eastern bluebirds. Before long, there would be spires of delphiniums reaching toward the light.

Sandburg had sketched their predecessors in his unfinished poem:

Leaves of cups and bells nod in the
sun laugh in the fine dust of the
wind over one newborn delphinium
laughing at the long scroll of
marriages whereby she is the lat-
est child bringing to the bright
air her shape to the dark earth
*her shadow.*⁸⁸

Edward Steichen left his enduring shape and shadow in the bright air, in the dark earth, in his flowers, his photographs, his paintings, his friends, his family, his century.

Said Mary, "My father never followed any star but his own."⁸⁹

Epilogue

In 1966, Mary Kemp and John Peter Steichen's son, Edward, had returned to their homeland to be honored by the Grand Duchy of Luxembourg as a Commandeur de l'Ordre de Mérite. That same year, in tribute to Steichen, and in accord with his wishes, the United States government presented to his native country a traveling edition of "The Family of Man." So it was that his two countries ensured that Steichen's legacy would live on within the ancient stone walls of Clervaux Castle in Luxembourg.

On June 3, 1994, Luxembourg's prime minister and minister of Cultural Affairs, J. Jacques Santer, presided at the inauguration of this painstakingly restored permanent installation of "The Family of Man" in the beautiful castle, now a museum and a national historic site. "Luxembourg has not always been the well-to-do country we know today," Prime Minister Santer observed at the opening ceremony. "Towards the end of the nineteenth century, roughly 120 years ago, thousands of Luxembourgers emigrated to the United States to find better working and living conditions."[1]

Among them had been Jean-Pierre Steichen, nearly defeated by the old land and the new, and stalwart, irrepressible Marie Kemp Steichen, a bright-eyed little boy in her arms. Their vision and experience infused every carefully chosen photograph in "The Family of Man."

On that June day 113 years after Marie Steichen had set out to rescue her husband and nurture her son in the New World, Luxembourg's prime minister praised Edward Steichen for remembering his roots. "Before settling down here in the old Castle of Clervaux," Santer continued, "the restored exhibition was shown in Toulouse, Tokyo and Hiroshima." "The Family of Man" is timeless, he asserted, and universal. He expressed his thanks to "all those who helped us to restore it in a way that people could rediscover the exhibition—and themselves!"[2]

Steichen's friend and colleague Wayne Miller spoke to the international audience gathered that day about the exhibition's long odyssey through the minds and hearts of millions of people:

> *[Steichen] would be thrilled to learn that a copy of the birth photograph from this exhibition is on each of two Voyager spacecraft—that were designed, according to Carl Sagan, "as emissaries of Earth to the realm of the stars."*[3]

In Luxembourg, as in nations throughout the world, people have found themselves and their own lives mirrored in the images Steichen chose for "The Family of Man," his testament to the universal necessity of dreams, hope, love, and peace. Edward Steichen's worldview transcended time, place, and politics, as deceptively simple and as profoundly complex as the Sioux Indian saying to be found in the text of "The Family of Man":

> *With all beings and all things*
> *we shall be as relatives.*[4]

Guide to Abbreviations and Sources

EXCEPT FOR THE RARE CORRECTION OF an obvious typographical error, letters and manuscripts have been transcribed in the text exactly as written, in the belief that I should not alter another's work, and that, in any case, idiosyncrasies of spelling, grammar, and punctuation reflect the individuality of the writer and the flavor of the correspondence.

Titles and sources of Edward Steichen's writings are cited in full as they appear in the notes. Because space prohibits a separate bibliography, the notes can be consulted for titles and sources of works quoted or cited.

Whenever possible, I have relied on their own signatures and correspondence for the spelling of the names of Steichen's associates. Therefore, while some print sources use Adolph de Meyer, for example, rather than Adolf, or Heinrich Kuehn, rather than Kühn, I have spelled the names as given in primary documents.

Because Edward and Lilian Steichen habitually failed to date their letters, I have enclosed in parentheses exact dates when verifiable, and approximate dates when context suggests them. While in every possible instance I have worked from original manuscripts and letters, or from photocopies thereof, I have also cited print sources when they exist, as in Lilian Steichen's letters to and from Carl Sandburg in *The Poet and the*

Dream Girl: The Love Letters of Lilian Steichen & Carl Sandburg, for example.

Steichen's photographs may be seen in William A. Ewing, ed., *Edward Steichen* (Paris: Photo Poche/Centre National de la Photographie, 1993); Ronald J. Gedrim, ed., *Edward Steichen: Selected Texts and Bibliography* (Oxford, England: Clio Press, World Photographers Reference Series, 1996); Ruth Kelton, ed., *Edward Steichen* (New York: Aperture, 1978); Dennis Longwell, *Steichen: The Master Prints 1895–1914: The Symbolist Period* (New York: Museum of Modern Art, 1978); Edward Steichen, *A Life in Photography* (Garden City, New York: Doubleday & Company, in collaboration with the Museum of Modern Art, 1963).

KEY TO ABBREVIATIONS IN THE ENDNOTES

AAA: Archives of American Art, Smithsonian Institution, Washington, D.C.

AEMC LC: Agnes Ernst Meyer Collection, Library of Congress, Washington, D.C.

ALP: Edward Steichen, *A Life in Photography* (Garden City, New York: Doubleday & Company, in collaboration with the Museum of Modern Art, 1963)

ASA Yale: Alfred Stieglitz Archive, Beinecke Rare Book and Manuscript Library, Yale University, New Haven, Connecticut

CSC UI: Carl Sandburg Collection, University of Illinois Library, Urbana, Illinois

EMC LC: Eugene Meyer Collection, Library of Congress, Washington, D.C.

ESA MoMA: Edward Steichen Archive, Museum of Modern Art, New York

FCSC: Francesca Calderone Steichen Collection

GSC Yale: Gertrude Stein Collection, Beinecke Rare Book and Manuscript Library, Yale University, New Haven, Connecticut

HSC: Helga Sandburg Collection

KRSC: Kate Rodina Steichen Collection

MSC: Margaret Sandburg Collection

MSCC: Mary Steichen Calderone Collection

PEN: Penelope Ellen Niven

WMC: Wayne Miller Collection

Endnotes

Preface

1. Edward Steichen, *A Life in Photography* (Garden City, New York: Doubleday & Company, in collaboration with the Museum of Modern Art, 1963) (no pagination), page following plate 164; hereafter: *ALP.*

1. The Land of Freedom (1854–1889)

1. Edward Steichen, *ALP,* page preceding plate one.
2. Helga Sandburg, *A Great and Glorious Romance: The Story of Carl Sandburg and Lilian Steichen* (New York: Harcourt Brace Jovanovich, 1978), 24. Background and details on the Steichen family are based on "Chronological Findings and Personal Memories Concerning the Luxembourg Origin of Families Carrying the Name 'Steychen = Steichen,'" prepared by Joseph Steichen of Luxembourg, November 1959, unpublished typescript, loaned by Helga Sandburg and Mary Steichen Calderone; "Steichen Family History," prepared by Helga Mary Steichen Sandburg Crile, unpublished typescript, loaned by Helga Sandburg; "The Luxembourg Genealogy of Mr. Edward Steichen, Director of the Department of Photography in the Museum of Modern Art in New York," prepared by Joseph Steichen, May 1957, unpublished typescript, Edward Steichen Archive, Museum of Modern Art, hereafter: ESA MoMA. See also family interpretations in Helga Sandburg, *A Great and Glorious Romance;* Paula Steichen, *My Connemara* (New York: Harcourt, Brace & World, Inc., 1969); Margaret Sandburg, ed., *The Poet and the Dream Girl: The Love Letters of Carl Sandburg & Lilian Steichen* (Urbana: University of Illinois Press, 1987); Carl Sandburg, *Steichen the Photographer* (New York: Harcourt, Brace and Company, 1929).
3. Lilian Steichen Sandburg to Edward Steichen, August 25, 1957, ESA MoMA.
4. Margaret Sandburg interview with Penelope Ellen Niven (hereafter: PEN). Helga Sandburg, *A Great and Glorious Romance,* 27. After receiving a copy of the Steichen genealogy from Joseph Steichen in Luxembourg, Edward Steichen wrote to Lilian Paula Sandburg, August 20, 1957, that the only interesting facet of the story for him was the account of the great-grandfather who went with Napoléon to Moscow, "as it was told to us" by their father; Margaret Sandburg Collection, hereafter: MSC.
5. Lilian Steichen Sandburg to Edward Steichen, August 25, 1957, ESA MoMA.
6. Helga Sandburg, *A Great and Glorious Romance,* 27.
7. Steichen gives the date as 1876, *ALP;* the Steichen family history, based on documentary records, says 1878. Some years after Jean-Pierre Steichen married Marie Kemp, Elisabeth Steichen, who had looked down on the Kemps since childhood, married Marie's brother Jean Kemp, a cabinetmaker from Mondercange. Sometime in the 1880s, Jean and Elisabeth Steichen Kemp emigrated to Buenos Aires, Argentina. Knowing as they did only the diminutive Grand Duchy of Luxembourg, they did not realize until it was too late that North and South America were so very different or so very far apart. Nevertheless, they remained there and lived a long and prosperous life in Argentina.
8. Helga Sandburg, *A Great and Glorious Romance,* 25.
9. Margaret Sandburg interview with PEN; Helga Sandburg, *A Great and Glorious Romance,* 25.
10. Helga Sandburg, ibid.
11. Margaret Sandburg interview with PEN; Helga Sandburg, *A Great and Glorious Romance,* 25.
12. Various sources, noted previously, say EJS was eighteen months old when he and his mother came to this country. Given his March 27, 1879, birth date, this would place him and his mother in New York sometime in mid to late October 1880 (allowing time for the passage). The standard date for arrival in Hancock is 1881, with no month given. We can surmise that, given some recovery time in Chicago, the family reached Hancock in the winter of 1881.
13. Tom Sieg interview with PEN. Journalist Tom Sieg grew up in Hancock, Michigan.
14. *History of the Upper Peninsula of Michigan Containing a Full Account of Early Settlement; Its Growth, Development and Resources; An Extended Description of Its Iron and Copper Mines* (Chicago: Western Historical Company, A. T. Andreas, proprietor, 1883), 288. Background and details on Hancock and copper mining are also drawn from David J. Krause, *The Making of a Mining District: Keweenaw Native Copper, 1500–1870* (Detroit: Wayne State University Press, 1992), and Henry Rowe Schoolcraft (Mentor L. Williams, ed.), *Narrative Journal of Travels Through the Northwestern Regions of the United States Extending from Detroit through the Great Chain of American Lakes to the Sources of the Mississippi River in the Year 1820* (East Lansing: Michigan State University Press, 1953), 302.
15. "Salient Features of Ed Steichen's Hancock Life Difficult to Obtain," *Hancock Daily Mining Gazette,* undated, courtesy of the Houghton County Historical Society, Houghton, Michigan.
16. *History of the Upper Peninsula of Michigan,* 289.
17. Lilian Steichen to Carl Sandburg (April 12, 1908), Carl Sandburg Collection, University of Illinois Library, Urbana, Illinois, hereafter: CSC UI; Helga Sandburg, *A Great and Glorious Romance,* 27. See also Margaret Sandburg, ed., *The Poet and the Dream Girl,* 86. Throughout the narrative, I will cite both the original letter from which I quote and the published source in which that letter may be consulted.
18. Lilian Steichen to Carl Sandburg (April 12, 1908), CSC UI; Margaret Sandburg, ed., *The Poet and the Dream Girl,* 86. Helga Sandburg, *A Great and Glorious Romance,* 27.
19. Helga Sandburg, *A Great and Glorious Romance,* 27.
20. Ibid.
21. *History of the Upper Peninsula of Michigan,* 291.
22. Lilian Steichen to Carl Sandburg (April 12, 1908), CSC UI; Margaret Sandburg, ed. *The Poet and the Dream Girl,* 84.
23. Lilian Steichen to Carl Sandburg (April 12, 1908), CSC UI; Margaret Sandburg, ed., *The Poet and the Dream Girl,* 82.

24. Biographical details on Father Edward Jacker may be found in *History of the Upper Peninsula of Michigan*, 294.
25. Lilian Steichen to Carl Sandburg, March 18, 1908, CSC UI; Margaret Sandburg, ed., *The Poet and the Dream Girl*, 39; Helga Sandburg, *A Great and Glorious Romance*, 28–29; Margaret Sandburg interview with PEN.
26. Lilian Steichen, unpublished manuscript (chronology), MSC.
27. Helga Sandburg, *A Great and Glorious Romance*, 29.
28. Carl Sandburg, *Steichen the Photographer*, 9.
29. Edward Steichen, *ALP*, page facing plate one.
30. A. H. Holland, *1887–8 Hand-Book and Guide to Hancock, Michigan* (Marquette, Michigan: Mining Journal Book and Job Print, 1887), 99.
31. Carl Sandburg, *Steichen the Photographer*, 10.
32. Ibid.
33. Steichen family background was provided in numerous Margaret Sandburg and Helga Sandburg interviews with PEN.

2. TAKING THE REINS (1889–1895)

1. Lilian Steichen to Carl Sandburg (April 12, 1908), CSC; Margaret Sandburg, ed., *The Poet and the Dream Girl: The Love Letters of Carl Sandburg & Lilian Steichen* (Urbana: University of Illinois Press, 1987), 85.
2. Carl Sandburg quoted in Paula Steichen, *My Connemara* (New York: Harcourt, Brace & World, Inc., 1969), 129.
3. Edward Steichen, *ALP*, page facing plate one.
4. Roger D. Simon, "The City-Building Process: Housing and Services in New Milwaukee Neighborhoods, 1880–1910," *Transactions of the American Philosophical Society*, vol. 68, part 5 (July 1978): 10–12.
5. Details of life in Milwaukee are based on the following sources: Margaret Sandburg interviews with PEN and Helga Sandburg interviews with PEN. See also Helga Sandburg, *A Great and Glorious Romance; The Story of Carl Sandburg and Lilian Steichen* (New York: Harcourt Brace Jovanovich, 1978), 42–43; Paula Steichen, *My Connemara*, 123–128; Faith B. Miracle, "Carl Sandburg and the Steichens, The Wisconsin Years," *Wisconsin Academy Review*, vol. 34, no. 3 (June 1988): 4–10; Margaret Sandburg, "The Wisconsin Years," unpublished manuscript, MSC.
6. Background on Milwaukee is drawn from the following sources: Meta Berger, unpublished autobiography, Manuscript Collection, Wisconsin State Historical Society, Madison; Margaret Sandburg, "The Wisconsin Years"; Emil Seidel, unpublished autobiography, Manuscript Collection, Wisconsin State Historical Society, Madison; Bayrd Still, *Milwaukee: The History of a City* (Madison: State Historical Society of Wisconsin, 1948).
7. Still, *Milwaukee*, 258.
8. *Milwaukee Sentinel*, May 6, 1886.
9. *Milwaukee Sentinel*, July 14, 1937.
10. Edward Steichen to Paula Steichen, inscription in Carl Sandburg's *Steichen the Photographer*, September 7, 1946, Paula Steichen Collection; see Paula Steichen, *My Connemara*, 124.
11. Paula Steichen, *My Connemara*, 126.
12. Ibid., 125.
13. Ibid., 124.
14. Margaret Sandburg interview with PEN.
15. Helga Sandburg interview with PEN; Helga Sandburg, *A Great and Glorious Romance*, 42.
16. Lilian Steichen to Carl Sandburg, March 15, 1908, CSC UI; Margaret Sandburg, ed., *The Poet and the Dream Girl*, 34.
17. Lilian Steichen to Carl Sandburg (April 12, 1908); Margaret Sandburg, ed., *The Poet and the Dream Girl*, 84.
18. Ibid.
19. Lilian Steichen Sandburg's daughters, Margaret, Janet, and Helga Sandburg, knew their grandfather Opa Steichen to be loving and playful. Margaret, in particular, always took issue with her mother's characterization of John Peter as the stern, forbidding, recalcitrant father.
20. Lilian Steichen to Carl Sandburg (April 12, 1908), CSC UI; Margaret Sandburg, ed., *The Poet and the Dream Girl*, 84–85.
21. Margaret Sandburg interview with PEN.
22. Helga Sandburg, *A Great and Glorious Romance*, 29.
23. Ibid.
24. Lilian Steichen to Carl Sandburg, March 12, 1908, CSC UI; Margaret Sandburg, ed., *The Poet and the Dream Girl*, 32.
25. Carl Sandburg, *Steichen the Photographer* (New York: Harcourt, Brace and Company, 1929), 11.
26. Ibid.
27. In November of 1893, the Linked Ring sponsored the first international salon of pictorial photography.
28. Alfred Stieglitz, "A Plea for Art Photography in America," *Photographic Mosaics*, 1892, 135–137.
29. Peter Henry Emerson, "Photography, A Pictorial Art," *The Amateur Photographer*, vol. 3 (March 19, 1886): 138–139.
30. Carl Sandburg, *Steichen the Photographer*, 11. Sandburg was writing whimsically here about Steichen building an automobile, but it is interesting to note that Steichen was experimenting with the technology at this time. Henry Ford founded the Ford Motor Company in the United States in 1903.
31. Edward Steichen, *ALP*, page following plate two.
32. Ibid.
33. Ibid.

3. THE TOUGHEST CUSTOMER (1895–1898)

1. Carl Sandburg, *Steichen the Photographer* (New York: Harcourt, Brace and Company, 1929), 15.
2. Alfred Stieglitz quoted in Dorothy Norman, "From the Writings and Conversations of Alfred Stieglitz," *Twice a Year*, no. 1 (Fall–Winter 1938): 95.
3. Helmut and Alison Gernsheim, *The History of Photography from the Camera Obscura to the Beginning of the Modern Era* (New York: McGraw-Hill, 1969), 425.
4. George Eastman to John M. Manley, December 15, 1906; quoted in C. W. Ackerman, *George Eastman* (Boston: Houghton Mifflin, 1930), 76.
5. Edward Steichen, *ALP*, page following plate two.
6. Ibid.
7. Elbert Hubbard discusses the chromos in *Little Journeys to the Homes of the Great* (New York: Wm. H. Wise & Co., 1928, memorial edition), 33.
8. Ibid.
9. Of the many volumes written on the history of pho-

tography, the following have been the most helpful: R. Child Bayley, "Photography Before Stieglitz, 1839–1900," in Waldo Frank et al., *America & Alfred Stieglitz* (New York: Literary Guild, 1934); Cecil Beaton and Gail Buckland, *The Magic Image: The Genius of Photography from 1839 to the Present Day* (Boston: Little, Brown and Company, 1975); Peter C. Bunnell, *Degrees of Guidance: Essays on Twentieth-Century American Photography* (Cambridge and New York: Cambridge University Press, 1993); Charles H. Caffin, *Photography as a Fine Art: The Achievement and Possibilities of Photographic Art in America* (originally published 1901; reprinted, with an introduction by Thomas F. Barrow, Dobbs Ferry, New York: Morgan & Morgan, 1971); William Crawford, *The Keepers of Light: A History & Working Guide to Early Photographic Processes* (Dobbs Ferry, New York: Morgan & Morgan, 1979); Peter Galassi, *Before Photography: Painting and the Invention of Photography* (New York: Museum of Modern Art, 1981); Helmut Gernsheim, *The Origins of Photography*, vol. 1 (New York: Thames and Hudson, 1982); Sarah Greenough et al. *On the Art of Fixing a Shadow* (Boston, London, and Toronto: National Gallery of Art and Art Institute of Chicago, with Bulfinch Press/Little, Brown and Company, 1989); Eaton S. Lothrop, Jr., *A Century of Cameras from the Collection of the International Museum of Photography at George Eastman House* (Dobbs Ferry, New York: Morgan & Morgan, 1973); Beaumont Newhall, *The History of Photography from 1839 to the Present* (New York: Museum of Modern Art, distributed by New York Graphic Society Books/Little, Brown and Company, Boston, 1988); Naomi Rosenblum, *A World History of Photography* (New York: Abbeville Press, 1984); John Szarkowski, *Photography Until Now* (New York: Museum of Modern Art, 1989); Robert Taft, *Photography and the American Scene: A Social History 1839–1889* (New York: Dover Publications, 1964); William Welling, *Photography in America: The Formative Years, 1839–1900* (New York: Thomas Y. Crowell Company, 1978).

10. Edward Steichen, *ALP*, second page following plate two.

11. Alfred Stieglitz, "Pictorial Photography," *Scribner's Magazine*, vol. 26 (November 1899): 528.

12. Edward Steichen, *ALP*, second page following plate two.

13. Family memories conform to the account given by Steichen in his autobiography: He told the story to his brother-in-law Carl Sandburg, who related it in *Steichen the Photographer* in 1929. In later years, his Sandburg nieces heard the story from him and from their mother, Lilian Steichen; Margaret Sandburg interview with PEN.

14. Edward Steichen, *ALP*, page following plate two.

15. Helga Sandburg interview with PEN; see also Helga Sandburg, *A Great and Glorious Romance: The Story of Carl Sandburg and Lilian Steichen* (New York: Harcourt Brace Jovanovich, 1978), 43, and Paula Steichen, *My Connemara* (New York: Harcourt Brace & World, Inc., 1969), 126.

16. Edward Steichen, *ALP*, page following plate two.

17. Ibid., second page following plate two.

18. Ibid.

19. Ibid.

20. Ibid.

21. Helga Sandburg (*A Great and Glorious Romance*, 43) says that the painting was to be a gift for Mary Steichen's fortieth birthday. Paula Steichen (*My Connemara*, 126) suggests that it was to be a Christmas gift. Margaret Sandburg, in an interview with PEN, said she believed that it was a Christmas gift.

22. Helga Sandburg, *A Great and Glorious Romance*, 43.

23. Edward Steichen, *ALP*, second page following plate two.

24. Carl Sandburg, *Steichen the Photographer*, 13.

25. Edward Steichen, *ALP*, second page following plate two.

26. Ibid.

27. While Steichen wrote in *ALP* in 1963 that he read *Camera Notes* when Stieglitz sent it to him after he went to Europe, he told Carl Sandburg during their interviews for *Steichen the Photographer*, published in 1929, that he eagerly read every issue of *Camera Notes*. See *Steichen the Photographer*, 16.

28. Christian A. Peterson, *Alfred Stieglitz's Camera Notes* (New York: Minneapolis Institute of Arts in association with W. W. Norton & Company, Inc., 1993), 9.

29. Peter Galassi notes that Steichen also read *The American Annual of Photography*, whose "photomechanical reproductions, including thirteen illustrations to a single article by Stieglitz" introduced "an elite international movement to Steichen, then a young lithographer's apprentice in Milwaukee Wisconsin...." See Peter Galassi, *American Photography 1890–1965* (New York: Museum of Modern Art, Harry N. Abrams, Inc., distributors, 1995), 14.

30. A. Horsley Hinton, "Both Sides," *Camera Notes*, vol. 2, no. 3 (January 1899): 79–80.

31. Fred Holland Day, "Art and the Camera," *Camera Notes*, vol. 1, no. 2 (October 1897): 27–28.

32. Ibid.

33. Mary Steichen eventually gave the treasured painting to her daughter, Lilian, who gave it in turn to her daughter Margaret Sandburg.

34. Fred Holland Day, "Art and the Camera," *Camera Notes*, vol. 2, no. 1 (July 1898): 5.

35. Dwight L. Elmendorf, "Choice of Subject and Exposure," *Camera Notes*, vol. 1, no. 4 (April 1898): 116.

36. Rudolph Eickemeyer, Jr., "How a Picture Was Made," *Camera Notes*, vol. 1, no. 3 (January 1898): 64.

37. Margaret Sandburg interview with PEN.

38. Carl Sandburg, *Steichen the Photographer*, 13–14.

39. Edward Steichen, *ALP*, second page following plate two.

40. Ibid.

41. Steichen either anglicized or misspelled Richard Lorenz's name in *A Life in Photography*, giving it as Lorence. He also usually gave Lilian's name incorrectly as Lillian.

42. For background on panorama painting in Milwaukee, see Porter Butts, *Art in Wisconsin: The Art Experience of the Middle West Frontier* (Madison, Wisconsin: Madison Art Association, 1933), and Bayrd Still, *Milwaukee: The History of a City* (Madison: State Historical Society of Wisconsin, 1948), 409–412.

43. Edward Steichen, *ALP*, third page following plate two.

44. Ibid.

45. Ibid.

46. Peter H. Emerson, "Science and Art," in *Naturalis-*

tic Photography for Students of the Art, 3d ed. (New York: Scoville & Adams, 1899), Appendix A, 68.

47. Charles H. Caffin, Photography as a Fine Art: The Achievements and Possibilities of Photographic Art in America (New York: Doubleday, Page & Company, 1901), vii.

48. Charles H. Caffin, "Progress in Photography with Special Reference to the Work of Eduard J. Steichen," The Century Magazine, vol. 85, 4 (February 1908): 484.

49. Carl Sandburg, Steichen the Photographer, 12.

50. Ibid., 13.

51. Lilian Steichen to Carl Sandburg, February 25, 1908, CSC UI; Margaret Sandburg, ed., The Poet and the Dream Girl: The Love Letters of Carl Sandburg & Lilian Steichen (Urbana: University of Illinois Press, 1987), 19.

52. Helga Sandburg, A Great and Glorious Romance, 45.

53. Paula Steichen, My Connemara, 127. Margaret Sandburg interview with PEN. See also Helga Sandburg, A Great and Glorious Romance, 45.

54. Lilian Steichen, unpublished manuscript (chronology), MSC.

55. Edward Steichen, ALP, third page following plate two.

56. Ibid.

57. Maurice Guillemot, "Claude Monet," La Revue Illustrée, March 15, 1898; reprinted in Charles F. Stuckey, ed. Monet: A Retrospective (New York: Park Lane, 1985), 196.

58. Edward Steichen, ALP, page following plate twelve.

59. Ibid., fourth page following plate two.

60. Ibid.

61. Carl Sandburg, Steichen the Photographer, 16.

4. GROPING FOR THE NEW (1898–1900)

1. Sidney Allan [Sadakichi Hartmann], "Eduard J. Steichen, Painter-Photographer," Camera Notes, vol. 6, no. 1 (July 1902): 15.

2. Lilian Steichen to Carl Sandburg, February 15, 1908, and February 24, 1908, CSC UI; Margaret Sandburg, ed., The Poet and the Dream Girl: The Love Letters of Carl Sandburg & Lilian Steichen (Urbana: University of Illinois Press, 1987), 10, 15–16.

3. Ibid.; information on Heine, Margaret Sandburg interview with PEN; see also Margaret Sandburg, ed., The Poet and the Dream Girl, note, 46–47.

4. Lilian Steichen to Carl Sandburg, February 15, 1908, CSC UI; Margaret Sandburg, ed., The Poet and the Dream Girl, 10.

5. Lilian Steichen to Carl Sandburg, February 25, 1908, CSC UI; Margaret Sandburg, ed., The Poet and the Dream Girl, 19.

6. Carl Sandburg, Steichen the Photographer (New York: Harcourt, Brace and Company, 1929), 16; Edward Steichen, ALP, fifth page following plate twelve.

7. See W. D. Halls, Maurice Maeterlinck: A Study of His Life and Thought (Oxford: Clarendon Press, 1960).

8. Maurice Maeterlinck, Wisdom and Destiny, trans. Alfred Sutro (London: George Allen & Unwin, Ltd., 1898), 97–105.

9. Edward Steichen to Carl Björncrantz (ca. 1901), Edward Björncrantz collection.

10. Lilian Steichen to Carl Sandburg, April 6, 1908,

CSC UI; Margaret Sandburg, ed., The Poet and the Dream Girl, 53.

11. Emerson's Representative Men was inspired by Thomas Carlyle's On Heroes, Hero-Worship, and the Heroic in History (1841).

12. Lilian Steichen, unpublished manuscript (chronology), MSC.

13. Announcement quoted in Camera Notes, vol. 2, no. 3 (January 1900): 135.

14. Alfred Stieglitz quoted in Dorothy Norman, Alfred Stieglitz: The Aperture History of Photography Series (New York: Aperture, Inc., 1976), 6.

15. See Alfred Stieglitz, "A Plea for a Photographic Art Exhibition," American Annual of Photography and Photographic Times Almanac, 1895, for example.

16. Edward Steichen, ALP, fourth page following plate two.

17. Steichen wrote in ALP that he submitted two prints, the self-portrait and Lady in the Doorway. Joseph T. Keiley's review in Camera Notes, however, refers to three pictures by Steichen, commenting on the two portraits, but not identifying the third photograph. See Joseph T. Keiley, "The Salon: Its Purpose, Character and Lesson," Camera Notes, vol. 3, no. 3 (January 1900): 145.

18. Edward Steichen, ALP, fifth page following plate two.

19. J. Keiley, "The Salon," 145.

20. Edward Steichen, ALP, fifth page following plate two.

21. Newark Advocate, Newark, Ohio, November 19, 1898.

22. Clarence H. White, "The Progress of Pictorial Photography," Annual Report of the Pictorial Photographers of America (New York: 1918), 14; quoted in Maynard P. White, Clarence H. White (New York: Aperture, 1979), 6.

23. A. Horsley Hinton, "Some Distinctions," Camera Notes, vol. 3, no. 3 (January 1900): 92.

24. Helga Sandburg, A Great and Glorious Romance: The Story of Carl Sandburg and Lilian Steichen (New York Harcourt Brace Jovanovich, 1978), 46–47; Margaret Sandburg interviews with PEN.

25. The Seventh Street address appears in the catalog of the Chicago Photographic Salon of 1900, archives, Art Institute of Chicago.

26. Edward Steichen, ALP, fifth page following plate two.

27. Ibid.

28. Catalog of the exhibition, the Chicago Photographic Salon, April 3–18, 1900, archives, Art Institute of Chicago. Steichen occasionally renamed prints: Woods in Rain. Milwaukee. (1898), for instance, was also called Woods Interior. Self-Portrait with Brush and Palette. Paris. was also called Self-Portrait.

29. "View Pictures by Amateurs," news clipping, no other identifying data, ESA MoMA.

30. Edward Steichen, ALP, fourth page following plate two.

31. Joseph T. Keiley, foreword to the catalog of the exhibition.

32. Charles Caffin, "Progress in Photography with Special Reference to the Work of Eduard J. Steichen," The Century Magazine, vol. 85, no. 4 (February 1908): 486.

33. Edward Steichen, ALP, third and fourth pages following plate two.

34. Ibid., fifth page following plate 2.
35. Margaret Sandburg interview with PEN.
36. Helga Sandburg, *A Great and Glorious Romance,* 47.
37. Ibid.
38. Lilian Steichen, unpublished manuscript (chronology), MSC.
39. Ibid.
40. Ibid.

5. PATHFINDERS (1900)

1. Ernst Juhl, "Eduard J. Steichen," *Die Photographische Rundschau,* July 1902, 129.
2. Carl Sandburg, *Steichen the Photographer* (New York: Harcourt, Brace and Company, 1929), 17.
3. Juhl, "Eduard J. Steichen," 127–129; translated in Beaumont Newhall, ed., *Photography: Essays & Images* (New York: Museum of Modern Art, 1980), 173–176.
4. Edward Steichen to Alfred Stieglitz, May 17, 1900, Alfred Stieglitz Archive, Beinecke Library, Yale University, hereafter: ASA Yale.
5. Kent Anderson, *Steichen/109* (Milwaukee: University of Wisconsin–Milwaukee Art Museum, 1988, 3). A 1906 publication by the Milwaukee Art Students' League stated its mission to "maintain a regular, practical School of Art for the State of Wisconsin . . . offering every facility for a thorough art education in the lowest rates possible"; see Henry Stoerzer and Max L. Roeck, *An Offer to Students of the Art Students League,* 1906.
6. Paula Steichen, *My Connemara* (New York: Harcourt, Brace & World, Inc., 1969), 125.
7. Edward Steichen, *ALP,* page facing plate three.
8. Ibid.
9. Charles Caffin, "Progress in Photography with Special Reference to the Work of Eduard J. Steichen," *The Century Magazine,* vol. 85, no. 4 (February 1908): 419. Steichen had also shown his paintings to painter John W. Alexander, who likewise encouraged him, according to what he told Caffin.
10. Edward Steichen, *ALP,* page facing plate three.
11. Charles H. Caffin, *Photography as a Fine Art: The Achievements and Possibilities of Photographic Art in America* (New York: Doubleday, Page & Company, 1901), 24.
12. Edward Steichen to Alfred Stieglitz, October 19, 1900, ASA Yale.
13. According to the Milwaukee Public Library Reference Index, February 1994, the library began subscribing to *Camera Notes* with the very first issue in 1897.
14. Paul Rosenfeld, "The Boy in the Dark Room," in Waldo Frank et al., eds., *America & Alfred Stieglitz* (New York: Literary Guild, 1934), 65; see also 59–88 for biographical portrait of Stieglitz.
15. Caffin, *Photography as a Fine Art,* 24.
16. Rosenfeld, "The Boy in the Dark Room," 66.
17. Caffin, *Photography as a Fine Art,* 24–26.
18. Alfred Stieglitz quoted in Thomas Craven, "Stieglitz—Old Master of the Camera," *The Saturday Evening Post,* January 8, 1944, 14.
19. Dorothy Norman, "From the Writings and Conversations of Alfred Stieglitz," *Twice a Year.* no. 1 (Fall–Winter 1938): 94.
20. See, for example, Alfred Stieglitz to Fred Holland Day, March 4, 1899, Fred Holland Day Collection, Norwood [Massachusetts] Historical Society; Day to Stieglitz, April 17, 1906, ASA Yale; Stieglitz to Day, May 21, 1910, Fred Holland Day Collection, Norwood Historical Society.
21. Caffin, "Progress in Photography," 486; Carl Sandburg, *Steichen the Photographer,* 17.
22. Caffin, "Progress in Photography," 483–498; Sue Davidson Lowe, *Stieglitz: A Memoir/Biography* (New York: Farrar Straus Giroux, 1983), 114. Other interesting accounts of the first meeting include Steichen's own in *ALP,* page facing plate three; Carl Sandburg, *Steichen the Photographer,* 17–18; Helga Sandburg, *A Great and Glorious Romance: The Story of Carl Sandburg and Lilian Steichen* (New York: Harcourt Brace Jovanovich, 1978), 46.
23. Edward Steichen to Alfred Stieglitz, October 19, 1900, ASA Yale.
24. Edward Steichen, *ALP,* page facing plate three.
25. Eduard J. Steichen, "The American School," *The Photogram,* vol. 8, no. 85 (January 1901): 6.
26. Caffin, "Progress in Photography," 491.
27. Carl Sandburg, *Steichen the Photographer,* 18.
28. Caffin, "Progress in Photography," 491. Caffin had interviewed Stieglitz as well as Steichen about this episode. Lilian Steichen considered this article a reliable account of her brother's life and work. See Lilian Steichen to Carl Sandburg, February 15, 1908, CSC UI; Margaret Sandburg, ed., *The Poet and the Dream Girl: The Love Letters of Carl Sandburg & Lilian Steichen* (Urbana: University of Illinois Press, 1987), 12.
29. Edward Steichen, *ALP,* page facing plate three.
30. Edward Steichen to Alfred Stieglitz, May 17, 1900, ASA Yale.
31. *The Pool–Evening, 1899,* Art Institute of Chicago.
32. Edward Steichen, *ALP,* page following plate twelve.
33. Edward Steichen to Alfred Stieglitz, May 17, 1900, ASA Yale.
34. Ibid.
35. Edward Steichen *ALP,* page following plate twelve.
36. Albert E. Elsen, *In Rodin's Studio: A Photographic Record of Sculpture in the Making* (Ithaca, New York: Cornell University Press, 1980), 171.
37. For detailed background on Rodin's *Balzac* and on the construction of the Place de l'Alma, see Ruth Butler, *Rodin: The Shape of Genius* (New Haven: Yale University Press, 1993). Photographs reveal that *Balzac,* like many other Rodin sculptures, was exhibited in plaster at the Exposition Universelle in 1900. See, for example, *Actualité francaise,* February 21, 1901; reprinted in Butler, *Rodin,* 357. See also Elsen, *In Rodin's Studio.*
38. Elsen, *In Rodin's Studio,* 183.
39. For a full account of this Rodin exposition, see Butler, *Rodin.*
40. Oscar Wilde to Robert Ross, July 7, 1900, quoted in Rupert Hart-Davis, ed., *The Letters of Oscar Wilde* (New York: Harcourt, Brace and World, 1962), 831.
41. Edward Steichen, *ALP,* page following plate twelve.
42. Butler, *Rodin,* 358.
43. Edward Steichen, *ALP,* page following plate twelve.
44. Philippe Julian, *The Triumph of Art Nouveau: Paris Exhibition 1900* (New York: Larousse & Company, 1974), 43.
45. Ibid.

46. Edward Steichen, *ALP*, page following plate twelve.
47. Ibid., third page following plate twelve.
48. Edward Steichen to Alfred Stieglitz, August 12, 1900, ASA Yale.
49. Ibid.
50. Aylesa Forsee, *Famous Photographers* (Philadelphia: Macrae Smith Company, 1968), 18.
51. Edward Steichen, *ALP*, page following plate twelve.
52. Lowe (*Stieglitz*, 185) writes, "Steichen insisted from the start on preserving a degree of independence that was sometimes an affront to Alfred. Even after 1900, he exhibited works, and cultivated a friendship, with Alfred's arch-rival, the photographic entrepreneur F. Holland Day."
53. Alfred Stieglitz, "Exhibition of F. H. Day's Work," *Camera Notes*, vol. 1, no. 4 (April 1898): 119.
54. For background on "The New School of American Photography" exhibition, see "The English Exhibitions and the 'American Invasion' " (unsigned article), *Camera Notes*, vol. 4, no. 3 (January 1901): 166–167; R. Child Bayley, "American Pictures at the London Salon," *Camera Notes*, vol. 4, no. 3 (January 1901): 171–175; Thomas Bedding, "American Pictures at the London Salon," *Camera Notes*, vol. 4, no. 3 (January 1901): 162–164; A. Horsley Hinton, "American Pictures at the London Salon," *Camera Notes*, vol. 4, no. 3 (January 1901): 169–170; E. J. Wall, "American Pictures at the London Salon," *Camera Notes*, vol. 4, no. 3 (January 1901): 164–166, 169. See also William Innes Homer, *Alfred Stieglitz and the Photo-Secession* (Boston: Little, Brown and Company, 1983), 34–42.
55. See, for example, Mike Weaver, *Alvin Langdon Coburn: Symbolist Photographer* (New York: Aperture, 1986), 6.
56. In fact, in 1908, Coburn wrote the text for an advertising brochure ("The Question of Diffusion," *Semi-Achromatic Lenses*, Pinkham & Smith brochure, ca. 1908) for the Smith lens, saying in part, "When the history of Artistic Photography comes to be written, the question of diffusion will assume its real importance, and the Smith Lens will receive the recognition it so fully deserves. . . . You have no more of what Bernard Shaw calls one of the 'infuriating academicisms of photography,' one plane of the picture sharp and all the others woolly and unnatural, a thing that no self-respecting human eye would ever see."
57. Edward Steichen, *ALP*, second page following plate twelve.
58. Ibid.
59. Ibid.
60. Fred Holland Day to Alfred Stieglitz (1898), ASA Yale.
61. Edward Steichen to Alfred Stieglitz, October 19, 1900, ASA Yale.
62. Edward Steichen to Fred Holland Day (ca. 1900), Fred Holland Day Archive, Norwood Historical Society.
63. A. Horsley Hinton to Alfred Stieglitz, October 2, 1900, ASA Yale.
64. Robert Demachy to Alfred Stieglitz, February 6 (1901), ASA Yale.
65. All quotations in this paragraph are from Edward Steichen, *ALP*, second page following plate twelve.
66. Ibid.

67. Fred Holland Day, "The New School of American Photography," *British Journal of Photography*, November 20, 1900, 760.
68. Caffin, *Photography as a Fine Art*, 155–156.
69. Unidentified news clipping, ESA MoMA.
70. Edward Steichen, *ALP*, second page following plate twelve. Steichen's article "British Photography from an American Point of View" was reprinted in *Camera Notes*, vol. 4, no. 3 (January 1901): 175–181.
71. Edward Steichen, *ALP*, second page following plate twelve.
72. Ibid.
73. For background, see F. Berkeley Smith, *The Real Latin Quarter* (New York: Funk & Wagnall, 1901); Billy Klüver and Julie Martin, *Kiki's Paris: Artists and Lovers 1900–1930* (Harry N. Abrams, Inc., 1989); Roger Shattuck, *The Banquet Years: The Origins of the Avant-Garde in France, 1885 to World War I* (New York: Vintage Books, 1968); and Robert M. Crunden, *American Salons: Encounters with European Modernism 1885–1915* (New York and Oxford: Oxford University Press, 1993).
74. Catherine Fehrer, "New Light on the Julian Académie and Its Founder" (Rodolphe Julian), *Gazette des Beaux-Arts*, May, June 1984, 214.
75. Paul Gsell, *Rodin on Art*, trans. Romilly Fedden (New York: Horizon Press, 1971), 144.
76. Gaston Schefer, *Galerie contemporaine*, Winter 1883–1884.
77. Gsell, *Rodin on Art*, 144.
78. Ibid.
79. All quotations relating to the Laurens incident are from Edward Steichen, *ALP*, second and third pages following plate twelve.
80. Caffin, *Photography as a Fine Art*, 156.
81. Edward Steichen to Alfred Stieglitz, October 19, 1900, ASA Yale.
82. Edward Steichen, "Painting and Photography," *Camera Work*, no. 23 (July 1908): 3–5. Steichen's handwritten draft of this essay has survived among Alfred Stieglitz's papers at the Beinecke Library, Yale University, and provides useful documentation of how Steichen wrote articles out in longhand, liberally revised them, and then sent them to Stieglitz, who usually did very little editing.
83. Edward Steichen to Alfred Stieglitz (1901), ASA Yale.

6. GREAT MEN (1901)

1. Unidentified newspaper clipping (August 30, 1902), Maternal Scrapbook, ESA MoMA. Grace Mayer of MoMA, in consultation with the Milwaukee Public Library staff, was unable to locate the source for this clipping, contained in full in Mary Steichen's scrapbook.
2. *Milwaukee Sentinel*, April 14, 1901.
3. Frank Eugene Smith should not be confused with the American photographer W. Eugene Smith, whom Steichen would come to know years later.
4. For a discussion of the vivid social history of the Paris banquet, see Roger Shattuck, *The Banquet Years: The Origins of the Avant-Garde in France, 1885 to World War I* (New York: Vintage Books, 1968).
5. "Banquet D'Atelier," *New York Herald*, Paris edition, December 27, 1900.
6. Ibid.

7. Ibid.
8. Edward Steichen to Alfred Stieglitz, (ca. early 1901), ASA Yale.
9. For the fullest study of Day, see Estelle Jussim, *Slave to Beauty: The Eccentric Life and Controversial Career of F. Holland Day, Photographer, Publisher, Aesthete* (Boston: David R. Godine, 1981). See also Verna Posever Curtis and Jane Van Nimmen, eds., *F. Holland Day: Selected Texts and Bibliography* (New York: G. K. Hall & Co., 1995), and Henry G. Fairbanks, *Louise Imogen Guiney* (New York: Twayne, 1973). See Mike Weaver, *Alvin Langdon Coburn: Symbolist Photographer 1882–1966* (New York: Aperture, 1986) for speculation on whether Day's homoeroticism affected the work of his cousin Alvin Langdon Coburn.
10. Argus, "Mr. H. Day's Cryptograms," *British Journal of Photography,* December 7, 1900, 772.
11. Fresh from his fame for *Maggie: A Girl of the Streets* (1893) and *The Red Badge of Courage* (1895), Crane was not about to let Day and Copeland cut any of his atheistic free verse, although even adventurous Day had suggested some excisions. In 1895, Day published Crane's book of poetry intact.
12. Estelle Jussim, *Slave to Beauty,* 114.
13. Ibid., 114–116.
14. F. Holland Day, "Art and the Camera," *Camera Notes,* vol. 2, no. 1 (July 1898): 5.
15. Edward Steichen, *ALP,* fourth page following plate twelve.
16. Sidney Allan [Sadakichi Hartmann], "Eduard J. Steichen, Painter-Photographer," *Camera Notes,* vol. 6, no. 1 (July 1902): 15.
17. Edward Steichen to Alfred Stieglitz (ca. early 1901), ASA Yale.
18. Edward Steichen, *ALP,* fourth page following plate twelve.
19. Edward Steichen to Alfred Stieglitz (ca. early 1901), ASA Yale.
20. Lilian Steichen to Carl Sandburg, February 15, 1908, CSC UI; Margaret Sandburg, ed., *The Poet and the Dream Girl: The Love Letters of Carl Sandburg & Lilian Steichen* (Urbana: University of Illinois Press, 1987), 12. The article in question: Charles H. Caffin, "Progress in Photography with Special Reference to the Work of Eduard J. Steichen," *The Century Magazine,* vol. 85, no. 4 (February 1908): 483–498.
21. Edward Steichen to Carl Björncrantz (ca. 1901), Edward Björncrantz collection.
22. Edward Steichen, *ALP,* fourth page following plate twelve.
23. Edward Steichen to Alfred Stieglitz (ca. early 1901), ASA Yale.
24. Robert Demachy to Alfred Stieglitz, February 6 (1901), ASA Yale.
25. Joseph T. Keiley, "Robert Demachy," *Camera Work,* no. 5 (January 1904): 17.
26. Robert Demachy to Alfred Stieglitz, February 6 (1901), ASA Yale.
27. Ibid.
28. Ibid.
29. *An Exhibition of Prints by the New School of American Photography Supplemented by an Additional Collection of One Hundred Examples of the Work of F. Holland Day of Boston* (London: Royal Photographic Society, 1900); *Catalogue des Oeuvres de F. Holland Day et de la Nouvelle Ecole Americaine, Exposees au Photo-club de Paris* (Paris: Photo-Club de Paris, 1901).
30. Robert Demachy to Alfred Stieglitz, February 6 (1901), ASA Yale.
31. Thomas Bedding, "The English Exhibitions and the 'American Invasion,' " *Camera Notes,* vol. 4, no. 3 (January 1901): 163.
32. Robert Demachy, "The American New School of Photography in Paris," *Camera Notes,* vol. 5, no. 1 (July 1901): 33–36; 39–42.
33. "Editorial" [Alfred Stieglitz], *Camera Notes,* vol. 5, no. 1 (July 1901): 33.
34. Edward Steichen, *ALP,* second page following plate twelve.
35. Helga Sandburg, *A Great and Glorious Romance: The Story of Carl Sandburg and Lilian Steichen* (New York: Harcourt Brace Jovanovich, 1978), 53. There is also a fragmentary reference to a Rosa among Steichen's papers in ESA, MoMA (March 18, 1901), but it reveals no firm identity or details.
36. Edward Steichen to Carl Björncrantz (ca. 1901), Edward Björncrantz collection.
37. See *The Rose,* Charles H. Caffin, *Photography as a Fine Art: The Achievements and Possibilities of Photographic Art in America* (Doubleday, Page & Company, 1901), 145.
38. Related in Margaret Sandburg and Helga Sandburg interviews with PEN; Helga Sandburg, *A Great and Glorious Romance,* 53–54. See also Clara Steichen to Alfred Stieglitz (February 1916), ASA Yale, and Clara Steichen to Alfred Stieglitz, May 27, 1935, ASA Yale.
39. Mike Weaver, *Alvin Langdon Coburn,* 29.
40. Fred Holland Day to unnamed correspondent, July 8, 1921, Norwood [Massachusetts] Historical Society.
41. Ibid. Frederick Evans spoke of the technical virtuosity of the lens in "Pure Photography," an address delivered to the Royal Photographic Society, April 25, 1900; reprinted in *The Photographic Journal,* April 30, 1900, 241.
42. Fred Holland Day to unnamed correspondent, July 8, 1921, Norwood Historical Society. Steichen would have owned this lens sometime after 1901, for he did not have it at the time he first photographed Rodin in 1901.
43. Edward Steichen to Carl Björncrantz (March 27, 1901), Edward Björncrantz collection.
44. Ibid.
45. Ibid.
46. Ibid.
47. "An Honor to Milwaukee," *Milwaukee Sentinel,* April 14, 1901.
48. [Alfred Stieglitz], "Eduard J. Steichen's Success in Paris," *Camera Notes,* vol. 5, no. 1 (July 1901): 57.
49. Carl Laurin, Emil Hannover, and Jens Thiis, *Scandinavian Art* (New York and London: Benjamin Blom, 1968), 507.
50. Ibid.
51. Thaulow died in Holland in 1906. His *Evening in Pittsburgh* became part of the permanent collection of the White House.
52. Edward Steichen to Alfred Stieglitz (summer or fall 1901), ASA Yale.
53. Quoted in Beaumont Newhall, ed., *Photography: Essays & Images* (New York: Museum of Modern Art, 1980), 175.
54. Edward Steichen, *ALP,* fourth page following plate twelve.

55. Henry James to Edith Wharton, October 20, 1914; Lyall H. Powers, ed., *Henry James and Edith Wharton, Letters: 1900–1915* (New York: Charles Scribner's Sons, 1990), 313.

56. Rainer Maria Rilke quoted in Ruth Butler, *Rodin: The Shape of Genius* (New Haven: Yale University Press, 1993), 368.

57. Paul Gsell, *Rodin on Art,* trans. Romilly Fedden (New York: Horizon Press, 1971), 10.

58. Henry James, *The Ambassadors* (Oxford and New York: Oxford University Press, 1985), 137.

59. Edward Steichen, *ALP,* fourth page following plate twelve.

60. Carl Sandburg, *Steichen the Photographer* (New York: Harcourt, Brace and Company, 1929), 23.

61. Edward Steichen, *ALP,* fourth page following plate twelve.

62. Ibid.

63. Edward Steichen to Alfred Stieglitz (ca. 1900), ASA Yale.

64. Edward Steichen, *ALP,* fourth page following plate twelve.

65. Carl Sandburg, *Steichen the Photographer,* 24.

7. Trusting the Eyes (1901–1902)

1. Paul Gsell, *Rodin on Art,* trans. Romilly Fedden (New York: Horizon Press, 1971), 33–34.

2. For example, Lilian Steichen wrote to Carl Sandburg, "Mother wrote in German as she usually does." Lilian Steichen to Carl Sandburg (April 1908), CSC UI; Margaret Sandburg, ed., *The Poet and the Dream Girl: The Love Letters of Carl Sandburg & Lilian Steichen* (Urbana: University of Illinois Press, 1987), 86. Most of Mary Kemp Steichen's letters to Alfred Stieglitz and his family were written in German. On the rare occasions when she wrote to Rodin, she did so in French, and her letters to her children and grandchildren were written in English most of the time.

3. Edward J. Steichen to Auguste Rodin (no date, written from 103 Boulevard du Montparnasse), Musée Rodin, Paris.

4. Ibid.

5. Edward Steichen, *ALP,* fourth page following plate twelve.

6. Carl Sandburg, *Steichen the Photographer* (New York: Harcourt, Brace and Company, 1929), 26.

7. Rodin quoted in Albert E. Elsen, *Rodin* (New York: Doubleday & Co., Inc./Museum of Modern Art, 1963), 112.

8. Edward Steichen, *ALP,* fourth page following plate sixty-two.

9. Auguste Rodin, *Camera Work,* Special Steichen Supplement, April 1906.

10. Gsell, *Rodin on Art,* 33–34.

11. Rainer Maria Rilke, *Rodin,* trans. Jessie Lemont and Hans Trausil (London: Grey Walls Press, Ltd., 1946), 8.

12. Gsell, *Rodin on Art,* 178.

13. Rilke, *Rodin,* 23.

14. "Tells About His Work," unidentified news clipping (1902), Maternal Scrapbook, ESA, MoMA.

15. Gsell, *Rodin on Art,* 99–101.

16. Rilke, *Rodin,* 35.

17. Rainer Maria Rilke, "Auguste Rodin," in Albert Elsen, ed., *Auguste Rodin: Readings on His Life and Work* (Englewood Cliffs, New Jersey: Prentice-Hall, Inc., 1965), 144.

18. Unidentified Milwaukee newspaper (August 30, 1902), Maternal Scrapbook, ESA MoMA.

19. Edward J. Steichen, "The American School," *The Photogram,* vol. 8 (January 1901): 2.

20. Steichen writes a few details in his letters to Rodin, unfortunately undated, but, from context, clearly written in 1901; Edward Steichen to Auguste Rodin (written from 83 Boulevard du Montparnasse); Edward Steichen to Auguste Rodin (written from 15 Rue Boissonade), Musée Rodin, Paris.

21. Unidentified Milwaukee newspaper (August 30, 1902), Maternal Scrapbook, ESA MoMA.

22. Edward Steichen, *ALP,* fifth page following plate twelve.

23. Gsell, *Rodin on Art,* 117–118.

24. For a Symbolist interpretation of Steichen's photographs, see Dennis Longwell, *Steichen: The Master Prints 1895–1914: The Symbolist Period* (New York and Boston: New York Graphic Society/Museum of Modern Art, 1978), 11–21.

25. Sandburg, *Steichen the Photographer,* 27.

26. Ibid., 26.

27. Gilbert Millstein, " 'De Lawd' of Modern Photography," *The New York Times Magazine,* March 22, 1959, 34.

28. Edward Steichen, *ALP,* fifth page following plate twelve.

29. Millstein, " 'De Lawd' of Modern Photography," 34.

30. Ibid., 34.

31. "Tells About His Work: Edward J. Steichen Speaks of Some of His Ideas About Art in Photography," unidentified news clipping (August 30, 1902), Maternal Scrapbook, ESA MoMA.

32. Ibid.; quoted also in Helga Sandburg, *A Great and Glorious Romance: The Story of Carl Sandburg and Lilian Steichen* (New York: Harcourt Brace Jovanovich, 1978), 54.

33. Helga Sandburg, *A Great and Glorious Romance,* 53.

34. Edward Steichen to Alfred Stieglitz (summer 1901), ASA Yale.

35. Gertrude Käsebier to Alfred Stieglitz, August 21, 1901, ASA Yale.

36. Kate Rodina Steichen interview, September 1987, Wilton Library, Wilton, Connecticut.

37. Mary Steichen Calderone to Donelson F. Hoopes, April 17, 1967, Mary Steichen Calderone Collection.

38. The album may be seen in the Gertrude Käsebier Collection at the Museum of Modern Art, New York. See also Barbara Michaels, *Gertrude Käsebier: The Photographer and Her Photographs* (New York: Harry N. Abrams, Inc., 1992), 172, n. 49.

39. Mary Steichen Calderone to Donelson F. Hoopes, April 17, 1967, MSCC.

40. Clara Smith Steichen's age is based on the divorce decree entered July 22, 1922, Meaux Court of Writs and Judgments, Voulangis Seine et Marne.

41. Kate Rodina Steichen interview. Kate said, "My father always had an eye for beauty; in fact, he was a very sexy guy."

42. Clara Smith, "An Ozark Childhood," unpublished manuscript, MSCC.
43. Ibid.
44. Kate Rodina Steichen interview. According to Kate Steichen, her mother told her that she and her sister had attended balls at West Point when their brother Erneste Smith was a cadet there. Furthermore, Clara claimed to have been the color girl at her brother's graduation, an honor given to a beautiful girl, who then presented the flags to the senior class. A search of the United States Military Academy Special Collections records, however, reveals that Erneste V. Smith, born in Springfield, Missouri in 1864, was a graduate of the class of 1886 at West Point. If Clara was born in 1876, as she indicated, she would have been only ten years old at the time of her brother's graduation, and six at the time of his matriculation–far too young to go to balls at West Point. The 1886 graduation program and records make no mention of the color girl. In the Steichen Family collection of photographs, there is a picture of Clara taken at West Point in 1894. Erneste V. Smith was a career military officer, retiring as a colonel in 1928. He died in San Francisco, California, in 1940 at the age of seventy-five. I gratefully acknowledge the research assistance of Deborah McKeon-Pogue, USMA Library, Special Collections Division.
45. Ibid.
46. Edward Steichen to Clara Smith (postmarked September 17, 1903), ESA MoMA. No reason can be ascertained for the choice of this nickname.
47. Nancy Newhall, "Alfred Stieglitz: Notes for a Biography," in *From Adams to Stieglitz: Pioneers of Modern Photography* (New York: Aperture, 1989), 120–121.
48. Edward Steichen to Alfred Stieglitz (ca. 1901), ASA Yale.
49. Edward J. Steichen to Auguste Rodin (1991), Musée Rodin, Paris.
50. See Michaels, *Gertrude Käsebier*, 172, n. 54.
51. Edward Steichen, *ALP*, fifth page following plate twelve.
52. Edward Steichen, *ALP*, fourth page following plate twelve.
53. Elsen, *Rodin* (192) documents that it was the marble *Victor Hugo* that Steichen photographed, rather than a plaster study.
54. Edward Steichen, *ALP*, fourth and fifth pages following plate twelve.
55. Ibid., fifth page following plate twelve.
56. Ibid.
57. Ibid.
58. Index to Steichen prints at the Musée Rodin, Paris, prepared by Dr. Laura Dubus, by commission of Penelope Niven.
59. Edward Steichen to Alfred Stieglitz (ca. 1901), ASA Yale.
60. Ibid.
61. See, for example, Kirk Varnedoe, "Rodin and Photography," in *Rodin Rediscovered* (Washington, D.C.: National Gallery of Art, 1981), for a discussion of the photographs of Marconi, Eadweard Muybridge, Eugène Druèt, Haweis and Coles, and others. See also Helene Pinet, "Rodin et les photographes americains," in the exhibition catalogue for "Le Salon de Photographie" (Paris: Musée Rodin, 1993), for a discussion of photographs by Steichen, Adolf de Meyer, and Alvin Langdon Coburn.

62. Auguste Rodin, "Pictorial Photography—A Series of Interviews," *Camera Work*, no. 24 (October 1908): 13–22.
63. Carl Sandburg, *Steichen the Photographer*, 25–26.
64. "Milwaukee Boy Honored: Paris Salon Admits Ten of Steichen's Photographs," unidentified news clipping, Maternal Scrapbook, ESA MoMA.
65. Charles Caffin, "Progress in Photography with Special Reference to the Work of Eduard J. Steichen," *The Century Magazine*, vol. 85, no. 4 (February 1908): 494.
66. *Catalogue, Salon Nationale des Beaux-Arts, 1902*, Musée Rodin, Paris.
67. Ibid.
68. "Photographs in the Salon, Innovation to Be Introduced for First Time in Paris Art Exhibition Saturday," New York *Herald*, March 30, 1902.
69. Katherine Knode, *Paris World;* quoted in "Milwaukee Boy Famed in Paris: Eduard J. Steichen at the Age of 23 Upsets Traditions of French Art," unidentified news clipping; Maternal Scrapbook, ESA MoMA.
70. Edward Steichen to Alfred Stieglitz, March 27, 1902, ASA Yale.
71. Alfred Stieglitz, *Camera Notes*, vol. 6, no. 1 (July 1902): 50.
72. Edward Steichen to Alfred Stieglitz, March 27, 1902, ASA Yale.
73. Caffin, "Progress in Photography," 494.
74. Alfred Stieglitz, "The 'Champs de Mars' Salon and Photography," *Camera Notes*, vol. 6, no. 1 (July 1902): 50.
75. "Photographs in the Salon."
76. "Milwaukee Boy Famed in Paris."
77. New York *Sun*, March 12, 1902.
78. Edward Steichen to Alfred Stieglitz, March 27, 1902, ASA Yale.
79. See the catalog of Steichen's exposition at the Maison des Artistes, June 3–24, 1902, ESA MoMA.
80. *Camera Notes*, vol. 1, no. 4 (April 1898): 119.
81. Edward Steichen to Alfred Stieglitz, March 27, 1902, ASA Yale.
82. Sidney Allan [Sadakichi Hartmann], "A Visit to Steichen's Studio," *Camera Work*, no. 2 (April 1903): 26.
83. Edward Steichen, *ALP*, fifth page following plate twelve.
84. Robert Demachy, *Bulletin du Photo-Club de Paris*, May 1902.
85. Caffin, "Progress in Photography," 493.
86. Ibid.
87. "A Master of Photography," *Milwaukee Journal*, August 29, 1902.
88. Edward Steichen, *ALP*, fifth page following plate twelve.
89. Maurice Maeterlinck, "I Believe," *Camera Work*, Special Steichen Supplement, April 1906, 1.
90. H. Vivian Yeo, "The American School and Mr. Steichen's Pictures," *Amateur Photographer*, May 1, 1902 (no page numbers visible, clipping drawn from Maternal Scrapbook, ESA MoMA).
91. "A Master of Photography."
92. Edward Steichen to Alfred Stieglitz, March 27, 1902, ASA Yale.
93. Carl Sandburg, *Steichen the Photographer*, 31.
94. Edward Steichen to Clara Smith (postmarked September 17, 1903), ESA, MoMA.
95. Kathleen Bruce Young Scott, Lady Kennet, *Self-*

Portrait of an Artist: From the Diaries and Memoirs of Lady Kennet (London: John Murray, 1949), 27–30.

96. Ibid.

97. Ibid.

98. Unidentified news clipping, Maternal Scrapbook, ESA MoMA.

99. Edward Steichen to Gertrude Käsebier (1901), ASA Yale.

100. Unidentified news clipping, Maternal Scrapbook, ESA MoMA.

101. A print of this photograph may be seen at the Metropolitan Museum of Art.

102. Quoted in Beaumont Newhall, ed., *Photography: Essays & Images* (New York: Museum of Modern Art, 1980), 174.

103. "Milwaukee Boy Honored."

8. THE MODERNIST TREND (1902)

1. Carl Sandburg, *Steichen the Photographer* (New York: Harcourt, Brace and Company, 1929), 29.

2. Unidentified news clipping, August 7, 1902, Maternal Scrapbook, ESA, MoMA.

3. "Tells About His Work," unidentified news clipping, August 30, 1902, Maternal Scrapbook, ESA MoMA. Although Steichen was still spelling his name Eduard, the Milwaukee newspapers, for the most part, anglicized his name.

4. Helga Sandburg, *A Great and Glorious Romance: The Story of Carl Sandburg and Lilian Steichen* (New York: Harcourt Brace Jovanovich, 1978), 80.

5. *Milwaukee Sentinel,* (August 1902), Maternal Scrapbook, ESA MoMA.

6. Ibid.

7. Ernst Juhl, *Die Photographische Rundschau,* vol. 16 (July 1902): 127–129.

8. Beaumont Newhall, ed., *Photography: Essays & Images* (New York: Museum of Modern Art, 1980), 173.

9. Quoted in ibid., 173.

10. Edward Steichen to Alfred Stieglitz (1902), ASA Yale.

11. Peter Henry Emerson, "Photography as a Pictorial Art," *The Amateur Photographer,* vol. 3 (March 19, 1886): 138–139.

12. Alfred Stieglitz, "Pictorial Photography," *Scribner's Magazine,* vol. 26, no. 5 (November 1899): 528.

13. Ibid., reprinted in Newhall, *Photography,* 163–166.

14. Joseph Pennell, "Is Photography Among the Fine Arts?" *The Contemporary Review,* vol. 72 (December 1897): 824–836.

15. Edward Steichen, "The American School," *The Photogram,* vol. 8 (January 1901): 3–9; reprinted in *Camera Notes,* vol. 6, no. 1 (July 1902): 22–24. For the suggestion that Steichen's emphasis on the word *secession* (see extract on page 141) may have influenced Stieglitz's choice of name for his new movement, see William Innes Homer, *Alfred Stieglitz and the Photo-Secession* (Boston: Little, Brown and Company, 1983), 52.

16. Charles H. Caffin, "Progress in Photography with Special Reference to the Work of Eduard J. Steichen," *The Century Magazine,* vol. 85, no. 4 (February 1908): 493.

17. Sidney Allan [Sadakichi Hartmann], "Eduard J. Steichen, Painter-Photographer," *Camera Notes,* vol. 6, no. 1 (July 1902): 15–16.

18. Ibid., 15.

19. "Milwaukee Boy Honored: Paris Salon Admits Ten of Steichen's Photographs," unidentified newspaper clipping, Maternal Scrapbook, ESA MoMA.

20. "A Master of Photography," *Milwaukee Journal,* August 29, 1902.

21. Katherine Knode, *Paris World;* quoted in "Milwaukee Boy Famed in Paris: Eduard J. Steichen at the Age of 23 Upsets Tradition of French Art," unidentified newspaper clipping, Maternal Scrapbook ESA MoMA.

22. Ibid.

23. Edward Steichen to Alfred Stieglitz (1902), ASA, Yale.

24. Ibid.

25. Lilian Steichen to Carl Sandburg, February 15, 1908, CSC UI; Margaret Sandburg, ed., *The Poet and the Dream Girl: The Love Letters of Carl Sandburg & Lilian Steichen* (Urbana: University of Illinois Press, 1987), 10–12. Since the last long period of time the sister and brother shared was the summer of 1902 in Milwaukee, when Steichen returned from the first trip to Paris, this must be the time Lilian Steichen is describing in this letter and in her letter to Carl Sandburg of February 29, 1908.

26. Ibid.

27. Lilian Steichen to Carl Sandburg, February 24, 1908, CSC UI; Margaret Sandburg, ed., *The Poet and the Dream Girl,* 15–16.

28. Lilian Steichen to Carl Sandburg, February 29, 1908, CSC UI; Margaret Sandburg, ed., *The Poet and the Dream Girl,* 20–21.

29. Ibid.

30. It was still too early, in 1902, for Americans to be widely aware of Sigmund Freud's *The Interpretation of Dreams,* published in Germany in 1900.

31. Walt Whitman, "A Backward Glance O'er Travel'd Roads," *Leaves of Grass with Autobiography* (Philadelphia: David McKay, 1900), 548.

32. Ibid., 549.

33. Ibid., 552.

34. Whitman also loved photographs, was often photographed, and wrote poetry and prose studded with visual allusions. In 1880, Whitman first published the poem "My Picture-Gallery," writing, in part:

In a little house keep I pictures suspended....
Here the tableaus of life, and here the groupings of death;
Here, do you know this? this is Cicerone himself,
With finger rais'd he points to the prodigal pictures.

35. J. C. Warburg, "Pure Photography," *The Amateur Photographer,* September 6, 1901, 182–183, used the phrase "bastard productions."

36. Ibid., 183.

37. Caffin, "Progress in Photography," 494. Steichen told Lilian Steichen that this article was accurate, and the Steichens shared it freely with friends and family.

38. Edward Steichen, *ALP,* second page following plate twenty-eight.

39. Ibid., page following plate twenty-eight.

40. Christian A. Peterson, *Alfred Stieglitz's Camera Notes* (New York: Minneapolis Institute of Arts in association with W.W. Norton & Company, Inc., 1993), 60.

41. Edward Steichen, *ALP,* second page following plate twenty-eight.

42. Ibid., page following plate twenty-eight.

43. Ibid.
44. Ibid.
45. Alfred Stieglitz quoted in Dorothy Norman, *Alfred Stieglitz: An American Seer* (New York: Random House, 1973), 36.
46. Ibid.
47. Goals of publication committee as set forth in *Camera Notes*, vol. 1, no. 1 (July 1897): 3.
48. Walt Whitman, "As I Sit Writing Here," *Leaves of Grass*, 494.
49. See Sadakichi Hartmann, *Conversations with Walt Whitman* (New York: E. P. Coby, 1895).
50. Joseph T. Keiley, "The Philadelphia Salon," *Camera Notes*, vol. 2, no. 3 (January 1899): 112–132.
51. Gertrude Käsebier, "Studies in Photography," *The Photographic Times*, vol. 30, no. 6 (June 1898): 269–272.
52. Stieglitz, "Pictorial Photography," 528–537.
53. Sidney Allan [Sadakichi Hartmann], "A Visit to Steichen's Studio," *Camera Work*, vol. 1, no. 2 (April 1903): 25–29.
54. Steichen, "The American School," 22–24.
55. Allan, "A Visit to Steichen's Studio," 25–31. After this visit, Hartmann was so haunted by Steichen's print *Dawn Flowers* that he wrote a poem inspired by it and dedicated it to Maeterlinck. The poem, "Dawn, Flowers," was published in *Camera Work*, vol. 1, no. 2 (April 1903).

9. True Secessionists (1902–1903)

1. Sadakichi Hartmann, "The Photo-Secession Exhibition at the Carnegie Art Galleries, Pittsburgh, Pa.," in Harry W. Lawton and George Knox, eds., with the collaboration of Wistaria Hartmann Linton, *The Valiant Knights of Daguerre: Selected Critical Essays on Photography and Profile of Photographic Pioneers by Sadakichi Hartmann* (Berkeley: University of California Press, 1978), 107.
2. Beatrice Baxter Ruyl to Edward Steichen, March 11, 1956, ESA MoMA. Beatrice Baxter was one of the party of artists flocking around Gertrude Käsebier during the summer of 1901. A native of Colorado who studied art in Boston and Paris, Baxter became a successful illustrator of children's books. Gertrude Käsebier photographed Baxter at least twice, and *The Sketch*, depicting Baxter in silhouette sketching a beautiful landscape, is one of Käsebier's most widely reproduced images.
3. Sadakichi Hartmann, "A Plea for Straight Photography," *American Amateur Photographer*, March 1904, 101–109.
4. Edward Steichen, *ALP*, page following plate twenty-eight.
5. For detailed background on the evolution of events culminating in Stieglitz's creation of the Photo-Secession, see Richard Whelan, *Alfred Stieglitz: A Biography* (Boston: Little, Brown and Company, 1995); and William Innes Homer, *Alfred Stieglitz and the Photo-Secession* (Boston: Little, Brown and Company, 1983).
6. Edward Steichen, *ALP*, page following plate twenty-eight.
7. Hartmann, "A Plea for Straight Photography," 101–109; reprinted in *Camera Work*, no. 6 (April 1904): 25.
8. Alfred Stieglitz, "Valedictory," *Camera Notes*, vol. 6, no. 1 (July 1902): 3.

9. Ibid., 4.
10. Ibid.
11. Sue Davidson Lowe, *Stieglitz: A Memoir/Biography* (New York: Farrar Straus Giroux, 1983), 113.
12. Edward Steichen, *ALP*, page following plate twenty-eight.
13. Alfred Stieglitz quoted in Nathaniel Lyons, ed., *Photographers on Photography* (Englewood Cliffs, New Jersey: Prentice Hall, Inc., 1966), 121.
14. Sadakichi Hartmann, "The Photo-Secession Exhibition at the Carnegie Art Galleries, Pittsburgh, Pa.," 107.
15. Alfred Stieglitz quoted in Nancy Newhall, "Alfred Stieglitz: Notes for a Biography," in *From Adams to Stieglitz: Pioneers of Modern Photography* (New York: Aperture, 1989), 119. Note: As Newhall acknowledged, she said she interviewed Stieglitz without a tape recorder and without making notes during the interviews. On page 99, she said she "wrote down immediately afterward what had occurred and what, while alone or in congenial company, he had told me. So these notes are filtered through two memories, his and mine." Stieglitz was seventy-seven and seventy-eight at the time of these interviews. There are errors in his memory of events surrounding Steichen, or in Newhall's retroactive transcription of his words. For instance, there is an anecdote on page 120 about "Steichen's brother, Julius." Steichen had no brother, and only one sister, Lilian.
16. Norman, *Alfred Stieglitz*, 47.
17. Barbara Michaels, *Gertrude Käsebier: The Photographer and Her Photographs* (New York: Harry N. Abrams, Inc., 1992), 88. According to Mina Turner, Gertrude Käsebier's granddaughter, Steichen told her that he, Stieglitz, and Käsebier were traveling back into Manhattan from the Stieglitz family's country home. See "Material from Col. E. J. Steichen," Mina Turner's notes for a biography of Gertrude Käsebier, Gertrude Käsebier Papers, University of Delaware Library, Newark, Delaware. Nancy Newhall gives a slightly different account ("Alfred Stieglitz: Notes for a Biography," 119): The train goes from Newark rather than Long Island. Back at Käsebier's studio on Fifth Avenue, she does not speak to Steichen.
18. Michaels, *Gertrude Käsebier*, 88.
19. Alfred Stieglitz quoted in Newhall, "Alfred Stieglitz: Notes for a Biography," 119.
20. Edward Steichen to Alfred Stieglitz (Fall 1902), ASA Yale.
21. Ibid.
22. Ibid.
23. Edward Steichen, *ALP*, fourth page following plate twenty-eight.
24. Alfred Stieglitz quoted in Newhall, "Alfred Stieglitz: Notes for a Biography," 119.
25. Edward Steichen, *ALP*, fourth page following plate twenty-eight.
26. Steichen wrote in *ALP* that there were thirteen council members, but the actual list printed in *The Photo-Secession*, no. 1 (December 1902) gives the names of twelve such.
27. Edward Steichen, *ALP*, fourth page following plate twenty-eight.
28. *The Photo-Secession*, no. 1 (December 1902).
29. Alfred Stieglitz, "The Photo-Secession," in *The*

Bausch & Lomb Lens Souvenir (Rochester, New York: Bausch & Lomb Optical Company, 1903).

30. Alfred Stieglitz, "An Apology," *Camera Work,* no. 1 (January 1903).

31. Announcement for *Camera Work,* August 25, 1902.

32. Norman, *Alfred Stieglitz,* 46.

33. Ibid., 47.

34. For an excellent comprehensive study of the Photo-Secession, see William Innes Homer, *Alfred Stieglitz and the Photo-Secession* (Boston: Little, Brown and Company, 1983). See also Jonathan Green, ed., *Camera Work: A Critical Anthology* (New York: Aperture Inc., 1973).

35. Paul Rosenfeld, "The Boy in the Dark Room," in *America & Alfred Stieglitz,* Waldo Frank et al., eds. (New York: Literary Guild, 1934), 82.

36. William Innes Homer, *Alfred Stieglitz and the American Avant-Garde* (Boston: New York Graphic Society, 1977), 4.

37. Alfred Stieglitz quoted in Norman, *Alfred Stieglitz,* 16.

38. Edward Steichen, *ALP,* page following plate twenty-eight.

39. Emmeline Obermeyer Stieglitz to Alfred Stieglitz, August 25 (1914), ASA Yale.

40. Alfred Stieglitz quoted in Norman, *Alfred Stieglitz,* 15.

41. Norman, *Alfred Stieglitz,* 17.

42. Carl Sandburg, *Steichen the Photographer* (New York: Harcourt, Brace and Company, 1929), 30.

43. Ibid., 5.

44. Edward Steichen, *ALP,* second page following plate twenty-eight.

45. Carl Sandburg, *Steichen the Photographer,* 6–7; Edward Steichen, *ALP,* second page following plate twenty-eight. Steichen's photograph was used by Peruvian-American painter Carlos Bac-Flor as the basis for his painting of Morgan, which hangs in the Metropolitan Museum of Art, as does Alfred Stieglitz's gift of Steichen's original print of Morgan.

46. Carl Sandburg, *Steichen the Photographer,* 8.

47. Edward Steichen, "The American School," *The Photogram,* vol. 8 (January 1901): 4–9.

48. Carl Sandburg, *Steichen the Photographer,* 8.

49. Ibid.

50. John Steel Gordon, "The Magnitude of J. P. Morgan," *American Heritage,* July/August, 1989, 81. Morgan's mother and maternal grandfather also suffered from this disorder.

51. Edward Steichen, *ALP,* second and third pages following plate twenty-eight.

52. Ibid., third page following plate twenty-eight.

53. Ibid.

54. Edward Steichen, "Ye Fakers," *Camera Work,* vol. 1, no. 1 (January 1903): 48.

55. Edward Steichen to Lilian Steichen (no date), CSC UI.

56. Lilian Steichen to Carl Sandburg, February 29, 1908, CSC UI; Margaret Sandburg, ed., *The Poet and the Dream Girl: The Love Letters of Carl Sandburg & Lilian Steichen* (Urbana: University of Illinois Press, 1987), 20.

57. Philip Henderson, *William Morris: His Life, Work and Friends* (New York: McGraw-Hill Book Company, 1967), 262.

58. Lillian [*sic*] Steichen "Of Art in Relation to Life," *Camera Work,* vol. 1, no. 2 (April, 1903): 30.

59. "Colonial Club's Art Show," *New York Mail & Express,* April 3, 1903.

60. Ibid.

61. Ibid. The other painters who participated: George B. Luks, William Glackens, Ernest Lawson, Ed A. Kramer, M. Evergood Blashki, F. Ballard Williams, A. Groll, Carl Linden, George A. Traver, H. W. Tomlinson, Robert Henri, Paul Dougherty, Reynolds and Gifford Beal, Van D. Perrine, Jerome Myers, and Everett L. Warner.

62. Edward Steichen to Alfred Stieglitz, May 14, 1903, ASA Yale.

63. Charles H. Caffin, "Progress in Photography with Special Reference to the Work of Eduard J. Steichen," *The Century Magazine,* vol. 85, no. 4 (February 1908): 494.

64. Clara Smith, "An Ozark Childhood," unpublished manuscript, MSCC.

65. Agnes Ernst Meyer's 1909 diary, entry for April 9, Agnes Ernst Meyer Collection, Library of Congress, hereafter: AEMC LC.

66. Ibid.

67. Smith, "An Ozark Childhood."

68. Edward Steichen to Alfred Stieglitz (no date), ASA, Yale.

69. Helga Sandburg, *A Great and Glorious Romance: The Story of Carl Sandburg and Lilian Steichen* (New York: Harcourt Brace Jovanovich 1978), 82.

70. Edward Steichen to Clara Smith (September 1903), ESA MoMA.

71. Ibid.

72. Edward Steichen to Clara Smith (postmarked September 17, 1903), ESA MoMA.

73. Agnes Ernst Meyer's 1909 diary, entry for April 9, AEMC LC.

74. Alfred Stieglitz quoted in Newhall, "Alfred Stieglitz: Notes for a Biography," 121.

75. Edward Steichen to Clara Smith (postmarked September 17, 1903), ESA MoMA.

76. Edward Steichen to Alfred Stieglitz (October 1903), ASA Yale.

77. Wedding announcement, ESA MoMA.

78. Edward Steichen to Alfred Stieglitz (October 1903), ASA Yale.

79. Ibid.

80. Ibid.

81. Edward Steichen to Alfred Stieglitz, Monday, October 11, 1903, ASA Yale.

82. Lowe, *Stieglitz,* 185.

10. Working Out Salvation (1904–1905)

1. Alfred Stieglitz, "The Photo-Secession," in *The Bausch & Lomb Lens Souvenir* (Rochester, New York: Bausch & Lomb Optical Company, 1903). Stieglitz prepared this statement for a souvenir brochure that contained a reproduction of his photograph *The Street—Winter,* which had won the grand prize in the 1903 Bausch & Lomb photographic competition. In addition to a first prize for a portrait, Steichen received an honorable mention in the contest for "The Black Pool." This notice was given by Bausch & Lomb to outstanding photographs that did not conform to the rules and requirements of the competition but that were in some

cases of "greater pictorial merit than the pictures receiving the prizes" (Bausch & Lomb to Alfred Stieglitz, January 6, 1904, ASA Yale).

2. Sadakichi Hartmann, "The Photo-Secession Exhibition at the Carnegie Art Galleries, Pittsburgh, Pa.," *Camera Work,* no. 6 (April 1904): 47–50.

3. Alfred Stieglitz quoted in Nancy Newhall, "Alfred Stieglitz: Notes for a Biography," in *From Adams to Stieglitz: Pioneers of Modern Photography* (New York: Aperture, 1989), 121.

4. *Washington Post,* January 20, 1904.

5. Edward Steichen to Lilian "Paus'l," Mary, and John Peter Steichen (February 8, 1904), CSC UI.

6. Hartmann, "The Photo-Secession Exhibition," 47–50.

7. Alfred Stieglitz to Sadakichi Hartmann, quoted in Harry W. Lawton and George Knox, eds., with the collaboration of Wistaria Hartmann Linton, *The Valiant Knights of Daguerre: Selected Critical Essays on Photography and Profiles of Photographic Pioneers by Sadakichi Hartmann* (Berkeley: University of California Press, 1978), frontispiece.

8. Sadakichi Hartmann, "The Photo-Secession Exhibition," 47–50. In all, Hartmann had four articles in this issue; his frequent contributions help to account for his use of pen names such as Sidney Allan and Klingsor the Magician.

9. Sadakichi Hartmann, quoted in Lawton and Knox, eds., *The Valiant Knights of Daguerre,* frontispiece. This is an excerpt from Hartmann as Klingsor The Magician, "A Pilgrimage to the Secession Shrine at Pittsburgh," *Camera Work,* no. 6 (April 1904): 54–60.

10. Sadakichi Hartmann, "A Monologue," *Camera Work,* no. 6 (April 1904): 25.

11. Ibid.

12. Sadakichi Hartmann, "A Plea for Straight Photography," *American Amateur Photography,* March 1904, 101–109; reprinted in *The Valiant Knights of Daguerre,* 108–114.

13. Edward J. Steichen, "The American School," *The Photogram,* vol. 8 (January 1901), 2.

14. Joan Harrison, "Colour in the Gum-Bichromate Process," *History of Photography,* vol. 17, no. 4 (Winter 1993): 371. This article also provides a brief technical history of the gum-bichromate process.

15. Notation on original mount, "Experiment in Multiple Gum," collection of the Metropolitan Museum of Art. See Weston J. Naef, *The Collection of Alfred Stieglitz: Fifty Pioneers of Modern Photography* (New York: Metropolitan Museum of Art/Viking Press, 1978), 453. This is an excellent technical resource on the processes Steichen and other photographers used in the 580 photographs by fifty photographers that comprise Alfred Stieglitz's collection, given to the Metropolitan Museum of Art. Other sources on Steichen's technique include Dennis Longwell, *Steichen: The Master Prints 1895–1914: The Symbolist Period* (Boston: New York Graphic Society/Museum of Modern Art, 1978) and, of course, Steichen's own accounts in *A Life in Photography* and elsewhere.

16. Edward Steichen to Alfred Stieglitz (1904), ASA Yale, leaf 53; published in Longwell, *Steichen: The Master Prints,* 17. The archival reorganization of the Alfred Stieglitz papers at the Beinecke Library at Yale University, completed in 1996, has provided the most reliable, accurate dating yet of Steichen's letters—a major challenge given Steichen's failure to include dates in most of his correspondence. When dates can be determined through Yale archivist Sandra Markham's research and/or through my own chronological research, I have not cited the Yale leaf numbers for the letters. In a sequence such as the summer of 1904 letters, however, where exact days and/or months cannot be established in a series of letters, I have provided the leaf numbers so that other scholars may go to the source of each citation as needed.

17. Hartmann, "A Plea for Straight Photography," 108–114.

18. Alfred Stieglitz, editorial notes, *Camera Work,* no. 9 (January 1905): 55.

19. Sadakichi Hartmann to Alfred Stieglitz (August 1904), ASA Yale. After Hartmann sent the letter to Stieglitz, he sent another copy with handwritten corrections on September 2, 1904. At the end of the letter, Hartmann had typed, "No answer to this letter is expected."

20. Ibid.; see also Lawton and Knox, eds., *The Valiant Knights of Daguerre,* 20–25.

21. Edward Steichen to Alfred Stieglitz (1904), ASA Yale.

22. Edward Steichen to Lilian Steichen (postmarked February 9, 1904), CSC UI.

23. Lilian Steichen, unpublished manuscript (Chronology), MSC UI.

24. Edward Steichen to Alfred Stieglitz (summer 1904), ASA Yale.

25. Edward Steichen to Lilian Steichen (February 1904), CSC UI.

26. Sadakichi Hartmann to Alfred Stieglitz, December 11, 1902, ASA Yale.

27. See Naef, *The Collection of Alfred Stieglitz,* 453–455.

28. Robert Demachy and Alfred Maskell, "Photo Aquatint or the Gum Bichromate Process, a Practical Treatise on a New Process Especially Suitable for the Pictorial Worker," in Peter Bunnell, ed., *Non Silver Printing Processes: Four Selections 1886–1927* (New York: Arno Press, 1973), 13.

29. Robert Demachy to Alfred Stieglitz (no date), ASA Yale.

30. See also Arthur Carles's *Portrait of Mrs. C., 1911,* in Barbara A. Wolanin, *Arthur B. Carles: Painting with Color* (Philadelphia: Pennsylvania Academy of the Fine Arts, 1983), 45.

31. These two paintings have survived and have been exhibited in recent years; Steichen described *Lake George* in a letter to Stieglitz in the summer of 1904, indicating that he had worked diligently at the lake and was fairly pleased with the results (Edward Steichen to Alfred Stieglitz [1904], ASA Yale, leaf 282).

32. Edward Steichen to A. K. Boursault (May 1904), ASA Yale; Grace Mayer, "Biographical Outline," Edward Steichen, *ALP,* page following plate 249; Joan Harrison, "Colour in the Gum-Bichromate Process," 371. Weston Naef (*The Collection of Alfred Stieglitz,* 153–154) states that none of these photographs has survived.

33. Edward Steichen to Alfred Stieglitz (1904), ASA Yale, leaf 296.

34. Edward Steichen to Alfred Stieglitz (1904), ASA Yale, leaf 298.

35. See Sue Davidson Lowe, *Stieglitz: A Memoir/Biography* (New York: Farrar Straus Giroux, 1983), 122–123,

and Richard Whelan, *Alfred Stieglitz: A Biography* (Boston: Little Brown and Company, 1995), 200–201.

36. Emmeline Obermeyer Stieglitz to Alfred Stieglitz (1904), ASA Yale.

37. Edward Steichen to Alfred Stieglitz (1904), ASA Yale, leaf 39.

38. Ibid.

39. See The Chief [Sadakichi Hartmann], "The Salon Club and the First American Photographic Salon at New York," *American Amateur Photographer,* July 1904, 296–305; Edward Steichen to Alfred Stieglitz (1904), ASA Yale, leaf 282.

40. Edward Steichen to Alfred Stieglitz (1904), ASA Yale, leaf 40.

41. Stieglitz, "The Origin of the Photo-Secession and How It Became '291,' " Nathan Lyons, ed., *Photographers on Photography* (Englewood Cliffs, New Jersey: Prentice-Hall, Inc., 1966), 122.

42. Ibid.

43. Ibid., 122–123.

44. Alfred Stieglitz to Frank Eugene, August 8, 1904, ASA Yale.

45. Edward Steichen to Alfred Stieglitz (1904), ASA Yale, leaf 296.

46. A. K. Boursault to Alfred Stieglitz, July 29, 1904, ASA Yale.

47. Edward Steichen to Alfred Stieglitz (1904), ASA Yale, leaf 296; Edward Steichen to Emmeline Obermeyer Stieglitz (June 10, 1904), ASA Yale.

48. Emmeline Obermeyer Stieglitz to Alfred Stieglitz (July 1904), ASA Yale.

49. Edward Steichen to Alfred Stieglitz, July 7 (1904), ASA Yale.

50. Margaret Sandburg interview with PEN.

51. Edward Steichen to Alfred Stieglitz (1904), ASA Yale, leaf 50.

52. Ibid.

53. "State Normal School Board of Management Report for the Biennial Period Ending June 30, 1904," courtesy of Barnes County Historical Society, Valley City, North Dakota.

54. "History of Valley City," *Second Crossing of the Sheyenne* [Barnes County 75th Jubilee History] (Valley City, North Dakota: Barnes County Historical Society, 1976), 4. Valley City history was provided through the courtesy of the Barnes County Historical Society, and Kurt Meyer, academic librarian, Valley City State University.

55. *Quarterly Bulletin of the State Normal School, Valley City, North Dakota,* vol. 3, no. 2 (September 1903).

56. Edward Steichen to Alfred Stieglitz (1904), ASA Yale, leaf 50.

57. Ibid.

58. Ibid.

59. Ibid.

60. Ibid.

61. Edward Steichen to Alfred Stieglitz (1904), ASA Yale, leaf 56; Thomas H. Cummings to Edward Steichen, August 15, 1904, ASA Yale; Edward Steichen to Thomas H. Cummings, August 23, 1904, ASA Yale.

62. Thomas H. Cummings to Edward Steichen, August 15, 1904, ASA Yale.

63. Edward Steichen to Alfred Stieglitz (1904), ASA Yale, leaf 79.

64. Edward Steichen to Alfred Stieglitz (1904), ASA Yale, leaf 78.

65. Edward Steichen to Alfred Stieglitz (1904), ASA Yale, leaf 50.

66. A retroverted or tipped uterus leans backward rather than forward, a condition now known to affect about 20 percent of women, some from infancy and others after childbirth. Clara Steichen evidently had the condition before her pregnancy. Because retroversion can cause painful menstrual periods and painful intercourse, as well as infertility, it is tempting to speculate about how Clara's condition affected her marriage.

67. Edward Steichen to Alfred Stieglitz (1904), ASA Yale, leaf 60.

68. Edward Steichen to Alfred Stieglitz, September 6, 1904, ASA Yale.

69. Ibid.

70. Edward Steichen to Alfred Stieglitz, September 18, 1904, ASA Yale.

71. Edward Steichen to Alfred Stieglitz, September 6, 1904, ASA Yale.

72. Ibid.

73. Edward Steichen to Alfred Stieglitz, September 18, 1904, ASA Yale.

74. Ibid.

75. Ibid.

76. Curtis Bell to George H. Seeley, November 10, 1904; quoted in William Innes Homer, *Alfred Stieglitz and the Photo-Secession* (Boston: Little, Brown and Company, 1983), 116.

77. J. B. Kerfoot, "Black Art: A Lecture on Necromancy and the Photo-Secession," *Camera Work,* no. 8, (October 1904): 29–33.

78. Frederick H. Evans, "The Photographic Salon, London, 1904. As Seen through English Eyes," *Camera Work,* no. 9 (January 1905): 39.

79. *The Critic,* April 1905, 297.

80. Edward Steichen, *ALP,* second page following plate twenty-eight.

81. Charles FitzGerald, "Eduard Steichen: Painter and Photographer," *Camera Work,* no. 10 (April 1905): 42.

82. Charles H. Caffin, "Progress in Photography with Special Reference to the Work of Eduard J. Steichen," *The Century Magazine,* vol. 85, no. 4 (February 1908): 498.

83. The portrait, which was to be hung over the mantel in the ballroom of a new, much larger house the Conklins built on their Huntington property, was painted about 1911. See Anne Cohen DePietro, *The Paintings of Eduard Steichen* (Huntington, New York: Heckscher Museum, 1985), 30, 37.

84. A. C. R. Carter, *Photograms,* 1905, quoted in Grace Mayer unpublished biographical outline, ESA MoMA.

11. 291 (1905–1907)

1. Edward Steichen, *ALP,* page preceding plate twenty-nine.

2. Edward Steichen, "My Life in Photography," *The Saturday Review,* vol. 62, no. 13 (March 28, 1959): 14.

3. Nathan Lyons, ed., *Photographers on Photography* (Englewood, Cliffs, New Jersey: Prentice-Hall, Inc., 1966), 123.

4. Ibid.

5. Edward Steichen to René d'Harnoncourt, interview transcript 8, ESA, MoMA.

6. Ibid.

7. Lyons, ed., *Photographers on Photography,* 124.
8. For background on Josef Hoffmann's art and design, see Robert Waissenberger, ed., *Vienna 1890–1920* (New York: Rizzoli, 1984).
9. These and other details of the renovation were described in *Camera Work,* no. 14 (April 1906), 48.
10. Ibid.
11. Alfred Stieglitz, "Exhibition Notes: The Photo-Secession," *Camera Work,* no. 12 (October 1905): 59.
12. Clara Steichen, "291," *Camera Work,* no. 47 (dated July 1914, published January 1915): 20.
13. Charles H. Caffin, "Progress in Photography with Special Reference to the Work of Eduard J. Steichen," *The Century Magazine,* vol. 85, no. 4 (February 1908): 498.
14. Edward Steichen, *ALP,* page following plate forty-three.
15. Steichen quoted in Wayne Miller, "Wisdom Series Interview," National Broadcasting Company, televised January 30, 1954; transcribed in *Infinity,* December 1954–January 1955, 4.
16. Lilian Steichen to Carl Sandburg (April 26, 1908), CSC UI; Margaret Sandburg, ed., *The Poet and the Dream Girl: The Love Letters of Carl Sandburg & Lilian Steichen* (Urbana: University of Illinois Press, 1987), 137.
17. Minutes of the Committee on Exhibitions, Pennsylvania Academy of the Fine Arts, May 7, 1906, archives, Pennsylvania Academy of the Fine Arts, Philadelphia. Quoted by William Innes Homer, *Alfred Stieglitz and the Photo-Secession* (Boston: Little Brown and Company 1983), 122.
18. Other accounts suggest that Steichen and Clara departed for Paris in May of 1906, but his letters to Stieglitz in 1906 document that they spent the summer in Wisconsin and departed sometime in the fall.
19. Lilian Steichen quoted in "State Normal School Board of Management Report for the Period Ending June 30, 1905," courtesy Barnes County Historical Society, Valley City, North Dakota.
20. Reference letter from the State Normal School, Valley City, North Dakota, quoted in Helga Sandburg, *A Great and Glorious Romance: The Story of Carl Sandburg and Lilian Steichen* (New York: Harcourt Brace Jovanovich, 1978), 86.
21. Edward Steichen to Alfred Stieglitz (summer 1906), ASA Yale.
22. Margaret Sandburg, ed., *The Poet and the Dream Girl,* 48.
23. Edward Steichen to Alfred Stieglitz (summer 1906), ASA Yale.
24. Edward Steichen to Alfred Stieglitz (marked by Stieglitz "received June 14, 1906"), ASA Yale.
25. Edward Steichen to Alfred Stieglitz (summer 1906), ASA Yale.
26. Ibid.
27. Ibid.
28. Ibid.
29. Ibid.
30. Maurice Maeterlinck quoted by Steichen in a letter to Alfred Stieglitz (1906), ASA Yale.
31. Edward Steichen to Alfred Stieglitz (1906), ASA Yale.
32. Ibid.
33. Edward Steichen to Alfred Stieglitz (November 1906), ASA Yale.
34. Ibid.
35. Edward Steichen to Lilian Steichen (1906), CSC UI.
36. Edward Steichen to Alfred Stieglitz (December 1906), ASA Yale.
37. Ibid.
38. Ibid.
39. Edward Steichen to Lilian Steichen (1906), CSC UI
40. Lyons, ed. *Photographers on Photography,* 125.
41. Ibid.
42. Alfred Stieglitz to Heinrich Kühn, November 17, 1906, unpublished letter, Dorothy Norman collection; copy in ASA Yale.
43. Edward Steichen to Lilian Steichen (1906), CSC UI.
44. Charles H. Caffin, "Progress in Photography," 498.
45. Edward Steichen to Alfred Stieglitz (October 1906), ASA Yale.
46. Alvin Langdon Coburn to Alfred Stieglitz (September 1906), ASA Yale.
47. Edward Steichen to Alfred Stieglitz (October 1906), ASA Yale.
48. Ibid.
49. J. Craig Annan to Alfred Stieglitz, November 10, 1906, ASA Yale.
50. Edward Steichen to Alfred Stieglitz (October 1906), ASA Yale. For background on this Coburn photograph of Shaw, see Michael Holroyd, *Bernard Shaw: The Pursuit of Power* (New York: Random House, 1989), 182–183.
51. Edward Steichen to Alfred Stieglitz (October 1906), ASA Yale. This letter has been inadvertently misdated, as confirmed by the fact that in October of 1906, Alvin Langdon Coburn wrote a letter to Stieglitz describing his dinner with the Steichens in Paris. In addition, Steichen speculated in his letter about whether he would go to London for the Linked Ring Salon, which he eventually did, as confirmed in a letter from Steichen received by Stieglitz October 29, 1906, which contained an account of Steichen's visit to the salon. Consequently, I have dated this letter October 1906.
52. For an extensive account of the Rodin-Rilke relationship, see Ruth Butler, *Rodin: The Shape of Genius* (New Haven: Yale University Press, 1993).
53. Frederic V. Grunfeld, *Rodin: A Biography* (New York: Henry Holt and Company, 1987), 445.
54. Edward Steichen to Auguste Rodin (1903), Musée Rodin, Paris. In this letter, Steichen also shared with Rodin the news of his life in New York, describing his success with portrait photography. He thanked Rodin for his influence and encouragement, and he spoke of how he missed Paris, and his master.
55. Edward Steichen, *ALP,* page following plate forty-three.
56. Edward Steichen to Alfred Stieglitz (January 1907), ASA Yale.
57. Ibid.
58. Steichen, *ALP,* one page following plate forty-three.
59. Lyons, ed. *Photographers on Photography,* 125.
60. Ibid.

12. YOUNG AMERICANS IN PARIS (1907)

1. Edward Steichen, *ALP,* second page following plate forty-three.
2. Leo Stein to Mabel Weeks, September 19, 1902; Leo Stein, *Journey into the Self: Being the Letters, Papers and Journals of Leo Stein,* ed. Edmund Fuller (New York: Crown Publishers, 1950), 11.
3. Leo Stein to Mabel Weeks, September 19, 1902; Leo Stein, *Journey into the Self,* 10.
4. Leo Stein to Mabel Weeks, April 8, 1903; Leo Stein, *Journey into the Self,* 14.
5. Leo Stein to Mabel Weeks (no date); Leo Stein, *Journey into the Self,* 15.
6. The novel, *Q.E.D.,* was published in a limited edition in 1950, four years after Gertrude Stein died. When published, the novel was retitled *Things as They Are.*
7. Sarah Stein to Gertrude Stein, September 19, 1898, Gertrude Stein Collection, Yale, hereafter: GSC Yale.
8. Edward Steichen, *ALP,* second page following plate forty-three.
9. Leo Stein, *Appreciation: Painting, Poetry and Prose* (New York: Crown Publishers, 1947), 188.
10. Gertrude Stein, "Henri Matisse," *Camera Work,* Special Number (August 1912): 23.
11. Gertrude Stein, "And now—and so the time comes when I can tell the story of my life," *Vanity Fair,* September 1934, 35, 65.
12. Gertrude Stein, *The Autobiography of Alice B. Toklas* (New York: Vintage Books, 1990), 28.
13. Leo Stein, *Appreciation,* 188.
14. Leo Stein to Mabel Weeks (no date); Stein, *Journey into the Self,* 15.
15. Quoted in Alfred H. Barr, Jr., *Matisse: His Art and His Public* (New York: Museum of Modern Art, 1951), 55.
16. Quoted in Robert Hughes, *The Shock of the New* (New York: Alfred A. Knopf, 1991), 132.
17. Barr, *Matisse,* 56.
18. Leo Stein to Mabel Weeks, November 29, 1905, GSC Yale.
19. Gertrude Stein, *The Autobiography of Alice B. Toklas,* 9.
20. Mabel Weeks, foreword to Leo Stein, *Journey into the Self,* viii.
21. Gertrude Stein, *The Autobiography of Alice B. Toklas,* 35.
22. Leo Stein, *Appreciation,* 158–159.
23. Ibid.
24. Leo Stein, Matisse, and Picasso later disputed parts of Gertrude Stein's account of how the Stein family collected modern art. In a letter to Albert Barnes on October 20, 1934, not long after the publication of *The Autobiography of Alice B. Toklas,* Leo Stein called his sister's book "that farrago of rather clever anecdote, stupid brag and general bosh," adding that there was almost nothing in the book about the period before World War I with which he was not acquainted, and there was nothing that she had written that was true. Leo Stein wrote to Mabel Weeks on November 17, 1934: ". . . Barnes writes that both Matisse and Picasso say that Gertrude is an awful liar"; Leo Stein, *Journey into the Self,* 148 and 150.
25. Henri Matisse, "Testimony Against Gertrude Stein," *A Supplement, Pamphlet no. I, to Transition, no. 23, 1934–35* (The Hague: Service Press, 1935).
26. Edward Steichen to Alfred Stieglitz (1908), ASA Yale.
27. Edward Steichen to Alfred Stieglitz (1906), ASA Yale, leaf 197–leaf 200.
28. Edward Steichen to Alfred Stieglitz (1906), ASA Yale, leaf 198.
29. Edward Steichen to Alfred Stieglitz (1906), ASA Yale, leaf 197–leaf 200.
30. R. Child Bayley to Alfred Stieglitz (no date), ASA Yale.
31. Edward Steichen to Alfred Stieglitz (1906 or 1907), ASA Yale, leaf 228–236.
32. Ibid.
33. Sue Davidson Lowe, *Stieglitz: A Memoir/Biography* (New York: Farrar Straus Giroux, 1983), 145.
34. Edward Steichen to Alfred Stieglitz (1906), ASA Yale, leaf 198.
35. Ibid.
36. Gertrude Stein, *The Autobiography of Alice B. Toklas,* 120.
37. Ibid., 45.
38. Ibid., 46.
39. Gertrude Stein, "Pablo Picasso," *Camera Work,* Special Number (August 1912): 29. The word portraits of both Matisse and Picasso were later collected in Gertrude Stein, *Portraits and Prayers* (1934). These word portraits introduced Stein to the American audience and garnered much criticism and bemusement.
40. Leo Stein to Albert Barnes, December 29, 1920; Leo Stein, *Journey into the Self,* 84.
41. Leo Stein to Mabel Weeks (no date); Leo Stein, *Journey into the Self,* 142.
42. Leo Stein, "Last Notes," written a few days before his death on July 29, 1947, *Journey into the Self,* 298.
43. Leo Stein to Mabel Weeks, February 7, 1913; Leo Stein, *Journey into the Self,* 53.
44. Edward Steichen, *ALP,* second page following plate forty-three.
45. William Rubin, ed., *Pablo Picasso: A Retrospective* (New York: Museum of Modern Art/New York Graphic Society, 1980), 122.
46. Robert Demachy to Alfred Stieglitz, September 6, 1902, ASA Yale.
47. Robert Demachy to Alfred Stieglitz (no date), ASA Yale.
48. Edward Steichen to Edward Stieglitz (postmarked May 15, 1907), ASA Yale. As most of Steichen's Lake George paintings were done in oil, it can be conjectured that this was an oil painting. It apparently has not survived.
49. Ibid.
50. Edward Steichen to Alfred Stieglitz (1906), ASA Yale, leaf 198.
51. Edward Steichen to Alfred Stieglitz (1906), ASA Yale, leaf 206–leaf 210.
52. Ibid.
53. Ibid.
54. Ibid.
55. "Artist Aids Woman Wife Sues for Love," *New York Times,* March 3, 1921. In this article, Steichen recounted briefly the history of Clara's jealousy of his mother, which was first expressed soon after they were

married in 1903 and apparently was a perennial theme in Clara's discontent.

56. Francesca Calderone-Steichen interview with PEN; Mildred ["Mid"] Cain interview with PEN. "Mid" Cain and Clara and Edward Steichen's daughter Kate Rodina Steichen were schoolmates in the United States.

57. Ibid. Clara Steichen told Mid Cain this story, leaving the impression it happened early in these Paris years, although it is difficult to document when Gertrude Stein began working on the poem "Sacred Emily," which was not published until much later, and which contains the line "Rose is a rose is a rose...." James R. Mellow suggests that at least as early as 1912, Stein appears to have been working on "Sacred Emily." See James R. Mellow, *Charmed Circle: Gertrude Stein & Company* (New York: Praeger Publishers, 1974), 185. Unable to ascertain an exact moment in time, I have simply related Clara's story here in the context of the Paris years, 1906–1913.

58. Edward Steichen to Alfred Stieglitz (1906), ASA Yale.

59. Robert Demachy to Alfred Stieglitz (no date), ASA Yale.

60. Edward Steichen to Alfred Stieglitz (1907), ASA Yale.

61. Edward Steichen to Alfred Stieglitz (May 1907), ASA Yale.

62. Edward Steichen to Edward Stieglitz (postmarked May 15, 1907), ASA Yale.

63. Ibid.

64. Ibid.

65. Edward Steichen, *ALP*, page following plate forty-three.

66. There is a discrepancy between Steichen's narrative about these photographs (page following plate forty-three, *ALP*) and the dating of them (plates forty-five and forty-six, *ALP*).

67. Edward Steichen to Réne d'Harnoncourt, interview transcription, ESA MoMA.

68. Walt Whitman, "A Backward Glance O'er Travel'd Roads," *Leaves of Grass with Autobiography* (Philadelphia: David McKay, 1900), 548.

69. Lowe, *Stieglitz*, 133.

70. Alfred Stieglitz quoted in Dorothy Norman, *Alfred Stieglitz: An American Seer* (New York: Random House, 1973): 75.

71. Ibid., 76.

72. Ibid.

73. Ibid., 77. For a discussion of the irony of the fact that *The Steerage* shows people returning to Europe from the United States, not traveling to the United States, see Richard Whalen, *Alfred Stieglitz: A Biography* (Boston: Little, Brown and Company, 1995). For a thoughtful discussion of Stieglitz's "experimental mode" of narrative discourse, especially when recollecting and sharing his own history, see John Szarkowski, *Alfred Stieglitz at Lake George* (New York: Museum of Modern Art/Harry N. Abrams, Inc., 1995), 14–15.

74. Steichen quoted in Alfred Stieglitz, "The New Color Photography—A Bit of History," *Camera Work*, no. 20 (October 1907): 21.

75. Edward J. Steichen, "Color Photography," 13–14.

76. Stieglitz, "The New Color Photography," 21.

77. See Edward J. Steichen, "Color Photography," 13–23.

78. Stieglitz, "The New Color Photography," 20.

79. Edward Steichen, *ALP*, page following plate forty-three.

13. COLOR-MAD (1907–1908)

1. Alfred Stieglitz to R. Child Bayley, July 31, 1907; *Camera Work*, no. 2 (October 1907): 22.

2. Edward Steichen, *ALP*, page following plate forty-three.

3. Alfred Stieglitz, "The New Color Photography—A Bit of History," *Camera Work*, no. 20 (October 1907): 20.

4. J. Nilsen Laurvik, "The New Color-Photography," *The Century Magazine*, vol. 75, no. 3 (January 1908): 323–330.

5. Edward Steichen to Alfred Stieglitz (fall 1907), ASA Yale.

6. Ibid.

7. Edward J. Steichen, "Color Photography," *Camera Work*, no. 22 (April 1908): 13–23.

8. Edward Steichen to Alfred Stieglitz (July 11, 1907), ASA Yale.

9. Edward Steichen, *ALP*, page following plate forty-three.

10. Ibid. See also Edward Steichen to Alfred Stieglitz, July 11, 1907, ASA Yale.

11. Edward Steichen to Alfred Stieglitz, July 13, 1907, ASA Yale.

12. Ibid.

13. Ibid.

14. Ibid.

15. Ibid.

16. Ibid.

17. Ibid.

18. Stieglitz, "The New Color Photography," 23.

19. Alvin Langdon Coburn to Alfred Stieglitz, July 18, 1907, ASA Yale.

20. Stieglitz, "The New Color Photography," 23.

21. R. Child Bayley to Alfred Stieglitz, August 9, 1907, ASA Yale.

22. Edward Steichen, *ALP*, page following plate forty-three; Steichen's letters to Stieglitz, summer of 1907.

23. Stieglitz, "The New Color Photography," 22.

24. Dennis Longwell (*Steichen: The Master Prints 1895–1914: The Symbolist Period* [New York and Boston: New York Graphic Society/Museum of Modern Art, 1978], 174) offers this definition of the Lumière process: "The autochrome process was the first practical system of color photography... The process involved coating a glass plate with microscopic particles of starch that had been dyed in three primary colors. A panchromatic emulsion was applied over this color 'screen.' After exposure and reversal development, the image viewed through the color 'screen' was in full color. Small autochromes could be projected, just as one projects color slides today. Large autochromes were viewed by holding them up to the light, illuminating them from behind, or placing them in a special viewer that permitted light to pass through the glass plate onto a mirror, which reflected the image to the eye. The process was discontinued sometime in the 1930s."

In December 1907, Coburn began to collect photographs for a special *Studio* issue entitled *Colour Photography*. He eventually included samples of his own pictures, as well as photographs by Heinrich Kühn, George Bernard Shaw, Baron de Meyer, and Frank Eugene. Steichen declined to participate.

25. Edward Steichen to Alfred Stieglitz (fall 1907), ASA Yale, leaf 351.
26. See Alvin Langdon Coburn to Alfred Stieglitz, February 24, 1908, and April 12, 1908, ASA Yale, for instance.
27. Alvin Langdon Coburn to Alfred Stieglitz, April 12, 1908, ASA Yale.
28. Lilian Steichen to Carl Sandburg, February 15, 1908, CSC UI; Margaret Sandburg, ed., *The Poet and the Dream Girl: The Love Letters of Carl Sandburg & Lilian Steichen* (Urbana: University of Illinois Press, 1987), 10–12.
29. Many years later, Carl Sandburg wrote to Robert Hunter, "Steichen has lost his copy of your *Socialists at Work*, bemoaned to me that it was the only record he had of some of his photographs of that period" (Carl Sandburg to Robert Hunter [no date], CSC UI). Many of Steichen's prints in France were lost or irreparably damaged during World War I. Sandburg gave Steichen his copy of Hunter's book.
30. Edward Steichen to Alfred Stieglitz (1907), ASA Yale, leaf 309.
31. Clara Steichen to Alfred Stieglitz (summer 1907), ASA Yale. Note: There are six undated notes and letters from Clara Steichen to Alfred Stieglitz, apparently written in a series during the summer of 1907.
32. Ibid.
33. Ibid.
34. Ibid.
35. Ibid.
36. Emmeline Obermeyer Stieglitz to Alfred Stieglitz (August 1907), ASA Yale.
37. Clara Steichen to Alfred Stieglitz (summer 1907), ASA Yale.
38. Ibid.
39. This advice can be gleaned from Clara Steichen's letters to Alfred Stieglitz alluding to his responses to her.
40. Clara Steichen to Alfred Stieglitz (no date), ASA Yale.
41. Edward Steichen to Alfred Stieglitz (January 1908), ASA Yale.
42. Ibid.
43. Ibid.
44. Ibid.
45. Stieglitz, "The New Color Photography," 26.
46. Ibid.
47. Edward Steichen to Alfred Stieglitz (fall 1907), ASA Yale.
48. Ibid.
49. Steichen, "Color Photography," 22–23.
50. J. Nilsen Laurvik, "The New Color-Photography," *The Century Magazine*, vol. 75, no. 3 (January, 1908): 323–330.
51. Carl Sandburg, *Steichen the Photographer* (New York: Harcourt, Brace and Company, 1929), 31.
52. Stieglitz, "The New Color Photography," 24.
53. Edward Steichen to Alfred Stieglitz (1907), ASA Yale, leaf 316–leaf 317.
54. Edward Steichen to Alfred Stieglitz (1907), ASA Yale, leaf 255.
55. Edward Steichen to Alfred Stieglitz (1907), ASA Yale, leaf 345–leaf 346.
56. Ibid.
57. Ruth Butler (*Rodin: The Shape of Genuis* [New Haven: Yale University Press, 1993], 428) reports that of the more than seven thousand drawings in the Musée Rodin, more than 80 percent are of female nudes.
58. Auguste Rodin, *Art: Conversations with Paul Gsell*, Jacques de Caso and Patricia S. Sanders, trans. (Berkeley: University of California Press, 1984), 49.
59. Edward Steichen to Alfred Stieglitz (1907), ASA Yale, leaf 345–leaf 346.
60. Edward Steichen to Alfred Stieglitz (1907–1908), ASA Yale, leaf 350–leaf 352.
61. Edward Steichen to Alfred Stieglitz (1907), ASA Yale, leaf 316–leaf 317.
62. Edward Steichen to Alfred Stieglitz (1907), ASA Yale, leaf 316–leaf 317.
63. Edward Steichen to Alfred Stieglitz (1907), ASA Yale, leaf 255.
64. Edward Steichen to Alfred Stieglitz (1907), ASA Yale, leaf 345–leaf 346.
65. Edward Steichen to Alfred Stieglitz (January 1908), ASA Yale.
66. Steichen's letter survives in the Stieglitz Archive at the Beinecke Library at Yale University.
67. Edward Steichen to Alfred Stieglitz (December 1907), ASA Yale.
68. Edward Steichen to Alfred Stieglitz (January 1908), ASA Yale.
69. J. Nilsen Laurvik, "The Rodin Drawings at the Photo-Secession Galleries," *New York Times*; reprinted in *Camera Work*, no. 22 (April 1908): 35.
70. Arthur Symons, "Rodin," *Studies in Seven Arts*; reprinted in *Camera Work*, no. 22 (April 1908): 35.
71. Dorothy Norman, *Alfred Stieglitz: An American Seer* (New York: Random House, 1973), 73.
72. Georgia O'Keeffe, *Georgia O'Keeffe* (New York: Viking Press, 1976); this book is not paginated.
73. Norman, *Alfred Stieglitz*, 73.
74. O'Keeffe, *Georgia O'Keeffe*.
75. Marius de Zayas, "How, When, and Why Modern Art Came to New York," *Arts Magazine*, April 1980, 98.
76. Edward Steichen to Alfred Stieglitz (ca. late January 1908), ASA Yale.
77. Edward Steichen to Alfred Stieglitz, February 4, 1908, ASA Yale.
78. For background on Arthur B. Carles and views of his remarkable paintings, see Barbara A. Wolanin, *Arthur B. Carles: Painting with Color* (Philadelphia: Pennsylvania Academy of the Fine Arts, 1983).
79. Edward Steichen, *ALP*, third page following plate forty-three.
80. Gertrude Stein, *The Autobiography of Alice B. Toklas* (New York: Vintage Books, 1990), 11.
81. Ibid.
82. Edward Steichen, *ALP*, second page following plate forty-three.
83. Ibid., third page following plate forty-three.
84. Quoted in Elizabeth McCausland, *A. H. Maurer* (New York: A. A. Wyn, Inc., 1951), 54.
85. Edward Steichen, *ALP*, third page following plate forty-three; Sue Davidson Lowe, *Stieglitz: A Memoir/Biography* (New York: Farrar Straus Giroux, 1983), 444.
86. Edward Steichen, *ALP*, third page following plate forty-three.

14. THE INITIATOR (1908)

1. Marius de Zayas to Grace Mayer, May 31, 1960, ESA MoMA.

2. Edward Steichen to Alfred Stieglitz (winter 1907–1908), ASA Yale.
3. Ibid.
4. Edward Steichen, "My Life in Photography," *The Saturday Review,* March 28, 1959, 14.
5. Edward Steichen to Réne d'Harnoncourt, interview transcript, 7, ESA MoMA.
6. Edward Steichen to Alfred Stieglitz (no date), ASA Yale, leaf 295.
7. Edward Steichen to Alfred Stieglitz (spring 1908), ASA Yale.
8. Ibid.
9. Edward Steichen to Alfred Stieglitz (winter 1907–1908), ASA Yale.
10. Edward Steichen to Réne d'Harnoncourt, interview transcript, 8, ESA MoMA.
11. Ibid.
12. Ibid., 6.
13. "Eduard Steichen, Painter and Photographer," undated clipping (1908) from the *New York Globe,* Maternal Scrapbook, ESA MoMA.
14. Charles H. Caffin, "Progress in Photography with Special Reference to the Work of Eduard J. Steichen," *The Century Magazine,* vol. 85, no. 4 (February 1908): 483–498.
15. Agnes E. Meyer, *Out of These Roots* (Boston: Little, Brown and Company, 1953), 65.
16. Ibid., 67.
17. Ibid., 67–68.
18. Edward Steichen, *ALP,* third page following plate forty-three.
19. "The New School of the Camera," *New York Morning Sun,* April 26, 1908.
20. Lilian Steichen to Carl Sandburg, February 15, 1908, CSC UI; Margaret Sandburg, ed., *The Poet and the Dream Girl: The Love Letters of Carl Sandburg & Lilian Steichen* (Urbana: University of Illinois Press, 1987), 18.
21. Lilian Steichen to Carl Sandburg, March 15, 1908, CSC UI; Margaret Sandburg, ed., *The Poet and the Dream Girl,* 34. While Lilian spelled her brother's name Edward, he was still spelling it Eduard when he signed his work and his name in letters during that time.
22. Margaret Sandburg, ed., *The Poet and the Dream Girl,* 5–6.
23. Lilian Steichen to Carl Sandburg, March 18, 1908, CSC UI; Margaret Sandburg, ed., *The Poet and the Dream Girl,* 39.
24. Lilian Steichen to Carl Sandburg, February 29, 1908, CSC UI; Margaret Sandburg, ed., *The Poet and the Dream Girl,* 21.
25. Lilian Steichen to Carl Sandburg, March 7, 1908, CSC UI; Margaret Sandburg, ed., *The Poet and the Dream Girl,* 30.
26. Lilian Steichen to Carl Sandburg, March 7, 1908, CSC UI; Margaret Sandburg, ed., *The Poet and the Dream Girl,* 28–29.
27. Lilian Steichen to Carl Sandburg (April 6, 1908), Helga Sandburg Collection, hereafter: HSC. The first two pages of this fifty-page letter were destroyed in later years by Lilian Steichen Sandburg, in the presence of her daughter Margaret Sandburg, who convinced her mother not to destroy the rest of the letter, which is published in *The Poet and the Dream Girl,* 54–61. Fortunately, Helga Sandburg had earlier photocopied the entire letter, and she furnished a copy of the missing pages to me. After she and Sandburg had pledged to marry, Lilian Steichen wrote to Sandburg, "I am going to write to W. this evening—a short note—just *the fact.* It may keep him from taking a false step unwittingly. He has a right to know—so that he can act for himself in the *light of that* knowledge.

"It's an unpleasant job—but necessary—best for us all. So I do it with a glad heart. Not without Pity tho—be sure! And it's the Mother-heart's Pity in me that makes this the hard hard job it is—Enough—I'm braced for it. I'm glad—glad—glad—to do it. What an escape for him! As well as for others!"
28. See Margaret Sandburg, ed., *The Poet and the Dream Girl,* 54–61; Helga Sandburg, *A Great and Glorious Romance: The Story of Carl Sandburg and Lilian Steichen* (New York: Harcourt Brace Jovanovich, 1978); 87–88; Penelope Niven, *Carl Sandburg: A Biography* (New York: Charles Scribner's Sons, 1991), note 161; 730–731.
29. Lilian Steichen to Carl Sandburg (April 6, 1908), CSC UI; Margaret Sandburg, ed., *The Poet and the Dream Girl,* 58.
30. Lilian Steichen to Carl Sandburg, February 25, 1908, CSC UI; Margaret Sandburg, ed., *The Poet and the Dream Girl,* 18.
31. Lilian Steichen to Carl Sandburg, February 24, 1908, CSC UI; Margaret Sandburg, ed., *The Poet and the Dream Girl,* 15–16.
32. Carl Sandburg to Lilian Steichen, February 21, 1908, CSC UI; Margaret Sandburg, ed., *The Poet and the Dream Girl,* 13.
33. Lilian Steichen to Carl Sandburg, February 25, 1908, CSC UI; Margaret Sandburg, ed., *The Poet and the Dream Girl,* 18.
34. Lilian Steichen to Carl Sandburg, March 18, 1908, CSC UI; Margaret Sandburg, ed., *The Poet and the Dream Girl,* 39.
35. The letter is missing, according to Margaret Sandburg, but Lilian Steichen quotes it in her letter to Sandburg of March 16, cited in note 36.
36. Lilian Steichen to Carl Sandburg, March 16, 1908, CSC UI; Margaret Sandburg, ed., *The Poet and the Dream Girl,* 35.
37. Edward Steichen quoted by Lilian Steichen in a letter to Carl Sandburg, March 20, 1908, CSC UI; Margaret Sandburg, ed., *The Poet and the Dream Girl,* 41.
38. Lilian Steichen to Carl Sandburg, March 20, 1908, CSC UI; Margaret Sandburg, ed., *The Poet and the Dream Girl,* 41.
39. Edward Steichen, ed., *Sandburg: Photographers View Carl Sandburg* (New York: Harcourt, Brace & World, Inc., 1966), introduction, no pagination. Steichen misdates this event 1907.
40. Ibid.
41. Ibid.
42. Ibid.
43. Ibid.
44. Lilian Steichen to Carl Sandburg, April 15, 1908, CSC UI; Margaret Sandburg, ed., *The Poet and the Dream Girl,* 95.
45. Carl Sandburg to Lilian Steichen, April 27, 1908, CSC UI; Margaret Sandburg, ed., *The Poet and the Dream Girl,* 142.
46. Ibid.
47. Carl Sandburg to Lilian Steichen, May 9, 1908,

CSC UI; Margaret Sandburg, ed., *The Poet and the Dream Girl*, 193.

48. Lilian Steichen to Carl Sandburg, April 26, 1908, CSC UI; Margaret Sandburg, ed., *The Poet and the Dream Girl*, 137.

49. Carl Sandburg to Philip Green Wright, April 2, 1908, Clifton Waller Barrett Library, University of Virginia; *Carl Sandburg, Philip Green Wright, and the Asgard Press, 1900–1910* (Charlottesville: University Press of Virginia, 1975), 122. Sandburg mistakenly referred to a March *Century* article on Steichen, when it actually appeared in February.

50. Edward Steichen, *Sandburg*, introduction.

51. Exhibition announcement, April 1, 1908, ASA Yale.

52. J. Edgar Chamberlain et. al., "Henri Matisse at the Little Galleries," *Camera Work*, no. 23 (July 1908): 10.

53. Alfred H. Barr, Jr., *Matisse: His Art and His Public* (New York: Museum of Modern Art, 1951), 113.

54. Alfred Stieglitz, *Camera Work*, no. 23 (July 1908): 10.

55. J. Edgar Chamberlain, New York *Evening Mail;* quoted in "Henri Matisse at the Little Galleries," 10.

56. James Huneker, the New York *Sun;* quoted in "Henri Matisse at the Little Galleries," 11–12.

57. Alfred Stieglitz quoted in Dorothy Norman, *Alfred Stieglitz: An American Seer* (New York: Random House, 1973), 73.

58. Edward Steichen to Dimitrie Popescu, transcript of *Voice of America* interview, April 17, 1962, 8, ESA MoMA.

59. Carl Sandburg, *Steichen the Photographer* (New York: Harcourt, Brace and Company, 1929), 33–34.

60. Lilian Steichen to Carl Sandburg (April 12, 1908), CSC UI; Margaret Sandburg, ed., *The Poet and the Dream Girl*, 85.

61. *New York Times* (April 1908), news clipping, ESA, MoMA.

62. Edward J. Steichen, "Color Photography," *Camera Work*, no. 22 (April 1908): 13–24. This article is discussed in detail in Chapter 13.

63. *The Craftsman*, May 1908, 231–232.

64. Edward Steichen quoted in William Innes Homer, "Eduard Steichen as Painter and Photographer, 1897–1908," *The American Arts Journal*, no. 6 (November 1974): 45.

65. Lilian Steichen to Carl Sandburg (April 17, 1908), CSC UI; Margaret Sandburg, ed., *The Poet and the Dream Girl*, 100–103. Margaret Sandburg suggests in a note that Steichen's undated May letter came in response to this letter. Internal evidence suggests that the letter referred to herein is missing and that Steichen's undated May letter arrived later.

66. Edward Steichen to René d'Harnoncourt, interview transcript, 8, ESA MoMA.

67. Ibid.

68. Edward Steichen to Alfred Stieglitz (1908) ASA Yale, leaf 249.

69. Alvin Langdon Coburn to Alfred Stieglitz, May 28, 1908, ASA Yale.

70. Norman, *Alfred Stieglitz*, 78.

71. Ibid.

72. Edward Steichen to Alfred Stieglitz (1908), ASA Yale, leaf 249.

73. Lilian Steichen to Carl Sandburg (April 27, 1908),

CSC UI; Margaret Sandburg, ed., *The Poet and the Dream Girl*, 146.

74. Edward Steichen to Lilian Steichen (May 1908), CSC UI; this letter is published in full or in part in the following sources: Helga Sandburg, *A Great and Glorious Romance*, 133–134; Margaret Sandburg, ed., *The Poet and the Dream Girl*, 175–176; Niven, *Carl Sandburg*, 170.

75. Edward Steichen to Alfred Stieglitz (1908), ASA Yale, leaf 231.

76. Ibid.

77. Ibid.

78. Edward Steichen to Mary and John Peter Steichen (1908), CSC UI.

79. Ibid.

80. Kate Rodina Steichen owned the painting of her mother, heavy with child, in the garden at Voulangis; as related in Kate Rodina Steichen interview with PEN.

81. Edward Steichen to Mme. Auguste Rodin, May 27 (1908), Musée Rodin, Paris.

82. Edward Steichen to Mary Smith (May 1908), Kate Rodina Steichen Collection, hereafter: KRSC.

83. Lilian Steichen to Carl Sandburg, June 2 (1908), CSC UI; Margaret Sandburg, ed., *The Poet and the Dream Girl*, 229.

84. Edward Steichen to John Peter and Mary Steichen (1908), MSC.

85. Edward Steichen to Mary Smith (May 1908), KRSC. Details on naming Kate were given in Francesca Calderone-Steichen interview with PEN.

86. Edward Steichen to John Peter and Mary Steichen (1908), MSC.

15. VOULANGIS (1908–1909)

1. Edward Steichen quoted in Gilbert Millstein, " 'De Lawd' of Modern Photography," *New York Times Magazine*, March 22, 1959, 33.

2. Edward Steichen to Alfred Stieglitz (July 1908), ASA Yale.

3. Edward Steichen to René d'Harnoncourt, interview transcript, 6, ESA MoMA.

4. Edward Steichen, *ALP*, second and third pages following plate forty-three.

5. Edward Steichen to Alfred Stieglitz (summer 1908), ASA Yale, leaf 238.

6. Ibid.

7. Ibid.

8. Ibid.

9. Auguste Rodin quoted by Steichen to René d'Harnoncourt interview transcript, 5, ESA MoMA.

10. Kirk Varnedoe, "Rodin and Photography," in Albert E. Elsen, ed., *Rodin Rediscovered* (Washington: National Gallery of Art, 1982), 238.

11. Varnedoe, "Rodin and Photography." 208, n. 8. See also Albert E. Elsen, *In Rodin's Studio: A Photographic Record of Sculpture in the Making* (Ithaca, New York: Cornell University Press, 1980), 182–183.

12. Edward Steichen to René d'Harnoncourt, interview transcript, 5, ESA MoMA.

13. Edward Steichen, *ALP*, second page following plate forty-three. In this account, published in 1963, Steichen recalled that he worked for one night to photograph the *Balzac*. His letter to Stieglitz, written during that week in 1909, stipulates two nights. I rely here on the immediate account, not Steichen's later memory of it.

14. Edward Steichen, *ALP*, second page following

14. Edward Steichen, "Rodin's Balzac," *Art in America*, September–October 1969, 26.

15. Edward Steichen, *ALP*, second page following plate forty-three.

16. Ibid.

17. Edward Steichen to Alfred Stieglitz (1908), ASA Yale, leaf 334.

18. Edward Steichen to Alfred Stieglitz (1908), ASA Yale, leaf 135.

19. Edward Steichen, *ALP*, second page following plate forty-three.

20. Charles H. Caffin, "Prints by Eduard J. Steichen—of Rodin's 'Balzac,'" *Camera Work*, no. 28 (October 1909): 23–25.

21. Auguste Rodin quoted in George Besson, "Pictorial Photography: A Series of Interviews," *Camera Work*, no. 24 (October 1908): 14.

22. Edward Steichen, *ALP*, second page following plate forty-three.

23. Edward Steichen to Alfred Stieglitz (1908), ASA Yale, leaf 118.

24. Edward Steichen to Alfred Stieglitz (February 1909), ASA Yale.

25. Ibid.

26. Alfred Stieglitz quoted in Dorothy Norman, *Alfred Stieglitz: An American Seer* (New York: Random House, 1973), 97.

27. Ibid.

28. Ibid.

29. Ibid., 98–99.

30. Steichen wrote to Stieglitz that for the Dresden show, he was planning to work on prints of *Rodin—The Thinker* and his portraits of Maeterlinck, Duse, Watts, Strauss, Shaw, Craig, Morgan, Anatole France, and perhaps Roosevelt, Taft, and von Lenbach, as well as a new self-portrait. He also planned to include *In Memoriam, Round Mirror, Big Cloud, Chestnut Trees, Versailles, Flat Iron, Old Trinity, Colorado—Garden of the Gods*, two from the *Pool* series, and one from the *Balzac* series. Edward Steichen to Alfred Stieglitz (late 1908 or early 1909), ASA Yale.

31. Steichen had photographed Ellen Terry's husband, English artist George Frederick Watts, shortly before his death. Terry and Watts separated in 1865 and divorced in 1877. Terry began living with Gordon Craig's father, Edward W. Godwin, in 1868. Craig was born in 1872.

32. Agnes E. Meyer, *Out of These Roots* (Boston: Little, Brown and Company, 1953), 73.

33. Agnes Ernst Meyer's 1908–1909 diary, entry for October 25 1908, AEMC LC.

34. Agnes Ernst Meyer's 1909 diary, entry for March 1, AEMC LC.

35. Agnes Ernst Meyer's 1909 diary, entry for February 26, AEMC LC.

36. Agnes Ernst Meyer's 1909 diary, entry for March 5, AEMC LC.

37. Steichen wrote to Stieglitz about the visit of "the girl from the Sun," and about Meyer's purchase; he referred to him as Mr. Mayer. Edward Steichen to Alfred Stieglitz (1909), ASA Yale.

38. Agnes Ernst Meyer's 1909 diary, entry for March 5, AEMC LC.

39. Agnes Ernst Meyer's 1909 diary, entry for March 24, AEMC LC.

40. Agnes Ernst Meyer's 1909 diary, entry for March 10, AEMC LC.

41. Ibid.

42. Ibid.

43. Agnes Ernst Meyer's 1909 diary, entry for April 9, AEMC LC.

44. Agnes Ernst Meyer's 1909 diary, entry for March 4, AEMC LC.

45. Agnes Ernst Meyer's 1909 diary, entry for March 29, AEMC LC.

46. Agnes Ernst Meyer's 1909 diary, entry for March 3, AEMC LC.

47. Agnes Ernst Meyer's 1909 diary, entry for April 13, AEMC LC.

48. Agnes Ernst Meyer's 1909 diary, entry for March 11, AEMC LC.

49. Ibid.

50. Ibid.

51. Clara Smith Steichen to Mary Steichen Calderone (Thanksgiving Day) 1941, MSCC.

52. Agnes Ernst Meyer's 1909 diary, entry for April 9, AEMC LC.

53. Agnes Ernst Meyer's 1909 diary entry for April 12, AEMC LC.

54. Agnes Ernst Meyer's 1909 diary, entry ca. June 5, AEMC LC.

55. Ibid.

56. Agnes Ernst Meyer's 1909 diary, entry for June 12, AEMC LC.

57. Agnes Ernst Meyer's 1909 diary, entry for April 12, AEMC LC.

58. Agnes Ernst Meyer's 1909 diary, entry for April 13, AEMC LC.

59. Ibid.

60. Agnes Ernst Meyer's 1909 diary, entry for April 9, 1909, AEMC LC.

61. Agnes Ernst Meyer's 1909 diary, undated entry (June), AEMC LC. The 1908–1909 diary, written largely in the form of letters to "Babs" [Otto Merkel] and others, was deposited at the Library of Congress by Agnes Meyer and later withdrawn. A microfilmed copy of the original may be studied at the Library of Congress, but the original diary is no longer available there, although original diaries for other years are contained in the collection. Some of the pages of the 1909 diary appear out of sequence on the microfilm. The early June pages that might have explained the "scene with Steichen" are not included on the microfilm.

62. Agnes Ernst Meyer's 1909 diary, entry for August 9, AEMC LC.

63. Meyer, *Out of These Roots*, 79.

64. Edward Steichen to Alfred Stieglitz (June 1909), ASA Yale.

65. Mary Steichen to Mary Sandburg (spring 1909), MSC; Helga Sandburg, *A Great and Glorious Romance*, 170.

66. Lilian Steichen Sandburg to Esther Sandburg, (spring 1909), MSC; Helga Sandburg, *A Great and Glorious Romance*, 170–171.

67. Mary Steichen to Alfred Stieglitz, April 30, 1909, ASA Yale.

68. Edward Steichen to Alfred Stieglitz (April 1909), ASA Yale; Edward Steichen to Alfred Stieglitz (1909), ASA Yale, leaf 217.

69. Clara Steichen to Hedwig Stieglitz (summer 1909), ASA Yale.
70. Mary Steichen to Mary Sandburg (summer 1909), MSC; Helga Sandburg, *A Great and Glorious Romance,* 171.
71. Ibid.
72. Mary Steichen Calderone quoted in Don Gold, *Until the Singing Stops: A Celebration of Life and Old Age in America* (New York: Holt, Rinehart and Winston, 1971), 314–315.
73. Ibid.
74. Mary Steichen Calderone, M.D., "My Father," *Infinity,* December 1954–January 1955, 4.
75. Thomas C. Hunter, *Beginnings* (New York: Thomas Y. Crowell, 1978), 59.
76. Mary Steichen Calderone quoted in ibid.
77. Mary Steichen Calderone quoted in Gold, *Until the Singing Stops,* 315.
78. Gold, *Until The Singing Stops,* 319. During her distinguished career as head of the Sex Information and Education Council of the United States (SIECUS), Dr. Mary Steichen Calderone conducted a long study of human sexuality, particularly the effects of sexual repression in early childhood on later sexual behavior.
79. Mary Steichen Calderone quoted in Lynn Gilbert and Gaylen Moore, *Particular Passions: Talks with Women Who Have Shaped Our Times* (New York: Clarkson N. Potter, Publishers, 1982), 259–260.
80. Mary Steichen Calderone, "American's Biggest Problem?" *People,* January 21, 1980, 78.
81. Mary Steichen Calderone quoted in Gold, *Until the Singing Stops,* 315.
82. Alfred Stieglitz quoted in Norman, *Alfred Stieglitz,* 97–98.
83. Ibid., 110.
84. Ibid., 111.
85. Ibid.
86. Ibid.
87. Edward Steichen quoted by Stieglitz in Norman, *Alfred Stieglitz,* 111.
88. Alfred, Stieglitz quoted in Norman, ibid.
89. Edward Steichen to Alfred Stieglitz (summer 1909), ASA Yale, leaf 332.
90. Clara Steichen to Hedwig Stieglitz (summer 1909), ASA Yale.
91. Edward J. Steichen to Auguste Rodin (no date), Musée Rodin, Paris.
92. Edward Steichen to Alfred Stieglitz (summer 1909), ASA Yale, leaf 332; Clara Steichen to Hedwig Stieglitz (summer 1909), ASA Yale.
93. Clara Steichen to Hedwig Stieglitz (ca. June 1909), ASA Yale.
94. Mary Steichen Calderone, "Eduard Steichen as Painter: A Remembrance," *The Paintings of Eduard Steichen* (Huntington, New York: Heckscher Museum, 1985), 8.

16. THE GOSPEL OF NEW LIGHT (1909)

1. Sadakichi Hartmann, "Who Did It? A Mystery Play in Two Exposures Dedicated to the Photo-Secession: A Court-Martial in Cloudland," unpublished manuscript (ca. 1909–1910), ASA Yale.
2. Alvin Langdon Coburn to Alfred Stieglitz, July 31, 1909, ASA Yale.
3. Edward Steichen to Alfred Stieglitz (fall 1909), ASA Yale, leaf 245.
4. Hartmann, "Who Did It?" 1.
5. Ibid., 1–2.
6. Edward Steichen to Alfred Stieglitz (fall 1909), ASA Yale.
7. Clara Steichen to Hedwig Stieglitz, June 28 (1909), ASA Yale.
8. Clara Steichen to Hedwig Stieglitz (May 1909), ASA Yale.
9. Clara Steichen to Hedwig Stieglitz, June 28 (1909), ASA Yale.
10. Mary Steichen Calderone quoted in Don Gold, *Until the Singing Stops: A Celebration of Life and Old Age in America* (New York: Holt, Rinehart and Winston, 1971), 315.
11. Mary Steichen Calderone, "My Father," *Infinity,* December 1954–January 1955, 4.
12. Mary Steichen Calderone quoted in Gold, *Until the Singing Stops,* 315.
13. Lilian Steichen to Carl Sandburg (June 7, 1908), CSC UI; Margaret Sandburg, ed., *The Poet and the Dream Girl: The Love Letters of Carl Sandburg & Lilian Steichen* (Urbana: University of Illinois Press, 1987), 233. Steichen expressed similar ideas later in letters to Clara Steichen; this is evident in the undated series of letters from Clara Steichen to Alfred Stieglitz, in which Clara quotes at length from Steichen's letters.
14. Lilian Steichen to Carl Sandburg (June 7, 1908), CSC UI; Margaret Sandburg, ed., *The Poet and the Dream Girl,* 233.
15. Edward Steichen to Lilian Steichen, February 9, 1904, CSC UI; also quoted in Helga Sandburg, *A Great and Glorious Romance: The Story of Carl Sandburg and Lilian Steichen* (New York: Harcourt Brace Jovanovich, 1978), 85, and Penelope Niven, *Carl Sandburg: A Biography* (New York: Charles Scribner's Sons, 1991), 148.
16. Gertrude Stein, *The Autobiography of Alice B. Toklas* (New York: Vintage Books, 1990), 44.
17. Lady Kennet [Kathleen Bruce], *Self-Portrait of An Artist: From the Diaries and Memoirs of Lady Kennet* (London: John Murray, 1949), 61.
18. For background on Kathleen Bruce [Lady Scott, then Lady Kennet], see Louisa Young, *A Great Task of Happiness: The Life of Kathleen Scott* (London: Macmillan, 1993); *Scott's Last Expedition: Being the Journals of Captain R.F. Scott, C.V.O., R.N.* (London: Smith, Elder & Co., 1913); Peter Brent, *Captain Scott and the Antarctic Tragedy* (London: Weidenfeld and Nicolson, 1974); Roland Huntford, *Scott and Amundsen* (New York: G. P. Putnam's Sons, 1980). See also Francis Steegmuller, ed., *Your Isadora: The Love Story of Isadora Duncan & Gordon Craig* (New York: Random House, 1974).
19. Lady Kennet [Kathleen Bruce], *Self-Portrait of An Artist,* 67–68.
20. Ibid., 68.
21. Steichen to Alfred Stieglitz, [1907 or 1908], ASA Yale, page backing leaf 245.
22. Ibid.
23. Lady Kennet [Kathleen Bruce], *Self-Portrait of An Artist,* 68.
24. Ibid., 69.
25. Ibid.
26. Ibid.

27. "Artist Aids Woman Wife Sues for Love," *New York Times,* March 3, 1921.
28. Clara Smith Steichen to Mary Steichen Calderone (Thanksgiving Day), 1941, MSCC.
29. Clara Steichen to Hedwig Stieglitz (May 1909), ASA Yale.
30. Ibid.
31. Isadora Duncan, *My Life* (New York: Liveright, Inc., 1933), 90.
32. Ibid., 90–91.
33. Ibid., 91.
34. Edward Steichen, *ALP,* page following plate eighty-three.
35. "Artist Aids Woman Wife Sues for Love."
36. Clara Steichen to Mary Steichen Calderone (Thanksgiving Day), 1941, MSCC; Clara Steichen's letters to Alfred Stieglitz during 1916, ASA Yale.
37. American Psychiatric Association, *Diagnostic and Statistical Manual of Mental Disorders,* 3d. ed. (Washington, D.C.: The American Psychiatric Association, 1980), 309: criteria of paranoid personality disorder include questioning the loyalty of others; overconcern with hidden motives and special meanings; pathological jealousy; tendency to be easily slighted and quick to take offense; exaggeration of difficulties—that is, "making mountains out of molehills"; a tendency to be moralistic, grandiose, and extrapunitive. It is more in keeping with the histrionic personality disorder (313–314) to employ manipulative suicidal threats and gestures; to be prone to self-dramatizations, overreaction to minor events, and/or irrational, angry outbursts or tantrums; and to be dependent, helpless, and constantly seeking reassurance.
38. Clara Smith "An Ozark Childhood," unpublished manuscript, MSCC.
39. Steichen to Alfred Stieglitz (fall 1909), ASA Yale.
40. Auguste Rodin quoted in Albert Elsen, *Auguste Rodin: Readings on His Life and Work* (Englewood Cliffs, New Jersey: Prentice-Hall, Inc., 1965), 179.
41. Edward Steichen to Alfred Stieglitz, September 18, 1904, ASA Yale.
42. Steichen to Stieglitz (no date), ASA Yale.
43. Edward Steichen to Alfred Stieglitz (fall 1909), ASA Yale.
44. Ibid.
45. "Exhibition of Pictures by Eduard J. Steichen, January 17–29, 1910," Montross Gallery, 372 Fifth Avenue, New York.
46. Edward Steichen to Alfred Stieglitz (December 1909), ASA Yale.

17. DANTON (1910)

1. Joseph T. Keiley, "The Buffalo Exhibition," *Camera Work,* no. 33 (January 1911): 23–29.
2. Unsigned [Sadakichi Hartmann], "Unphotographic Paint: The Texture of Impressionism," *Camera Work,* no. 28 (October 1909): 20–23. For attribution of this article to Hartmann, see Harry W. Lawton and George Knox, *The Valiant Knights of Daguerre: Selected Critical Essays on Photography and Profiles of Photographic Pioneers by Sadakichi Hartmann* (Berkeley: University of California Press, 1978), 352.
3. Edward Steichen to René d'Harnoncourt, interview transcript, 6, ESA MoMA.
4. Edward Steichen, *ALP,* page following plate 164.

5. Elie Nadelman, "My Drawings," *Camera Work,* no. 32 (October 1910): 41.
6. Elizabeth Luther Cary, *New York Times;* quoted in "Criticisms of Steichen Exhibition," *Camera Work,* no. 30 (April 1910): 36–40.
7. Royal Cortissoz, *New York Tribune;* quoted in "Criticisms of Steichen Exhibition," *Camera Work,* no. 30 (April 1910): 36–40.
8. Later called *Across the Crest of the Great Divide,* this oil on canvas, dimensions 32 1/16 by 39 7/8 inches, survived because it was purchased in the United States. It belongs to the Regis Collection and was part of the exhibition entitled "The Paintings of Eduard Steichen," held June 29–August 18, 1985, at the Heckscher Museum in Huntington, New York.
9. Arthur Hoeber, *New York Globe;* quoted in "Criticisms of Steichen Exhibition," *Camera Work,* no. 30 (April 1910): 36.
10. James Huneker, New York *Sun,* January 23, 1910, 4.
11. The thirty-one paintings exhibited in 1910 were: *Across the Crest of the Great Divide; Nocturne of the Three Secrets; The Old Roadway—Valley of the Morin; Nocturne from Rodin's Garden—The Viaduct; The Rising Moon—Valley of the Morin; Across the Sound—Clouded Night; Nocturne at Château du Doux—Corrèze; Nocturne of the City of Paris—From Rodin's Studio; The Curtain of Rain—Valley of the Morin; Nocturne in the Pheasant Park—Château Cornon; Across the Valley of the Morin—Clouded Night; Across the Valley of the Morin—Fantastic Night; Across the Valley of the Morin—Autumn Morning; Across the Valley of the Morin—Summer Morning; Across the Valley of the Morin—Autumn Afternoon; Up the Valley of the Morin—Autumn Morning; Nocturne of the Valley of the Morin—Serbonne Mill; Still Life—Poppies; In Our Garden at Voulangis—White Phlox; In Our Garden at Voulangis—White Lilac; In Our Garden at Voulangis—Red Peonies; In Our Garden at Voulangis—Nasturtiums; In Our Garden at Voulangis—Baby Mary; Moonlight Dance—Voulangis; Montbarbin on the Hill from Voulangis; Spring Sunlight—Baby Mary; Apple Bloom; Lights Across the Sound; The Overhanging Branch—Bois du Boulogne; Autumnal Harmony—Valley of the Morin;* and *Opal Moonrise—Lake George.*
12. Gilbert Millstein, " 'De Lawd' of Modern Photography," *New York Times Magazine,* March 22, 1959, 34.
13. B. P. Stephenson, New York *Evening Post;* quoted in "Criticisms of Steichen Exhibition," *Camera Work,* no. 30 (April 1910): 36–40.
14. James B. Townsend, *American Art News;* quoted in "Criticisms of Steichen Exhibition," *Camera Work,* no. 30 (April 1910): 36–40.
15. Sadakichi Hartmann, quoted in *Camera Work,* no. 30 (April 1910): 36–40.
16. James Huneker, "Seen in the World of Art," New York *Sun,* April 24, 1910.
17. James Huneker, New York *Sun,* January 23, 1910.
18. Temple Scott [T. H. Isaacs], "Fifth Avenue and the Boulevard Saint-Michel," *The Forum,* vol. 44 (December 1910): 668–669. See also Scott, *The Silver Age and Other Dramatic Memories* (New York: Scott and Seltzer, 1919). Carl Sandburg was then campaigning for better wages for American working people, and he cited the going daily wage of $1.44 in "The Saloon Smashers," *Wilshire's Magazine,* May 1909.

19. Lilian Steichen Sandburg to Carl Sandburg (February 17, 1909), CSC UI.

20. Edward Steichen to Lilian Steichen Sandburg (April 1910), CSC UI; Helga Sandburg, *A Great and Glorious Romance: The Story of Carl Sandburg and Lilian Steichen* (New York: Harcourt Brace Jovanovich: 1978), 178.

21. Mary Steichen to Clara Sandburg, April 13, 1910, MSC.

22. Matthew Josephson, "Commander with a Camera—II," *The New Yorker,* June 10, 1944, 33.

23. Edward Steichen to Alfred Stieglitz (fall 1910), ASA Yale.

24. Thomas C. Hunter, *Beginnings* (New York: Thomas Y. Crowell, 1978), 59.

25. Mary Steichen quoted in Lynn Gilbert and Gaylen Moore, *Particular Passions: Talk with Women Who Have Shaped Our Times* (New York: Clarkson N. Potter, Inc./Publishers, 1982), 260.

26. Don Gold, *Until the Singing Stops: A Celebration of Life and Old Age in America* (New York: Holt Rhinehart and Winston, 1971), 316.

27. Mary Steichen Calderone quoted in Gilbert and Moore, *Particular Passions,* 260.

28. Mary Steichen Calderone, "Eduard Steichen as Painter: A Remembrance," *The Paintings of Eduard Steichen* (Huntington, New York: Heckscher Museum, 1985), 9.

29. Edward Steichen to Alfred Stieglitz, (fall 1910), ASA Yale.

30. Ibid.

31. F. Austin Lidbury, "Some Impressions of the Buffalo Exhibition," *American Photography,* vol. 4., no. 12 (December 1910): 675–677.

32. Alfred Stieglitz to Ernst Juhl, January 6, 1911, ASA, Yale.

33. Sadakichi Hartmann, "What Remains," *Camera Work,* no. 33 (January 1911), 30, reprinted in Lawton and Knox, eds., *The Valiant Knights of Daguerre,* 149.

34. Hartmann, "What Remains," 30–32; reprinted in Lawton and Knox, eds., *The Valiant Knights of Daguerre,* 151.

35. Sidney Allan [Sadakichi Hartmann], "Photography as Fine Art," New York *Evening Post,* November 9, 1910.

36. Joseph T. Keiley, "The Buffalo Exhibition," *Camera Work,* no. 33 (January 1911): 23–27.

37. Ibid., 27.

38. See Sue Davidson Lowe, *Stieglitz: A Memoir/Biography* (New York: Farrar, Straus Giroux, 1983), 187.

39. Edward Steichen, *ALP,* page preceding plate forty-four.

40. Temple Scott, "The Terrible Truthfulness of Mr. Shaw," *Camera Work,* no. 29 (January 1910): 17–20.

41. Scott [T. H. Isaacs], "Fifth Avenue and the Boulevard Saint-Michel," 668–669. See also Scott, *The Silver Age and Other Dramatic Memories.*

42. Edward Steichen to Alfred Stieglitz (no date), ASA Yale, leaf 144.

43. Edward Steichen to Alfred Stieglitz (fall 1910), ASA Yale.

44. Carl Sandburg, *Steichen the Photographer* (New York: Harcourt, Brace and Company, 1929), 34.

18. REAL FRIENDSHIP, REAL ART (1910–1912)

1. Photostat of inscription, "Memorabilia," ESA MoMA.

2. Edward Steichen to Alfred Stieglitz (fall 1910), ASA Yale, leaf 145.

3. Kitty Stieglitz to Alfred and Emmy Stieglitz, July 12, 1909, ASA Yale.

4. Edward Steichen to Alfred Stieglitz (no date), ASA Yale.

5. Edward Steichen to Alfred Stieglitz, (summer 1910), ASA Yale.

6. Edward Steichen to Alfred Stieglitz (fall 1910), ASA Yale.

7. Ibid.

8. Louis Vauxcelles quoted in William Rubin, ed., *Pablo Picasso: A Retrospective* (New York: Museum of Modern Art, 1980), 89. Louis Vauxcelles was also one of the first to use the word *Fauves.*

9. Leon Werth quoted in ibid., 121.

10. Edward Steichen to Alfred Stieglitz (fall 1910), ASA Yale.

11. Henri Matisse quoted in Alfred H. Barr, *Matisse: His Art and His Public* (New York: Museum of Modern Art, 1951), 561.

12. Edward Steichen to Alfred Stieglitz (1911), ASA Yale, leaf 347.

13. Ibid.

14. Ibid.

15. Ibid.

16. Miguel Utrillo, for instance, showed Picasso's pastels in Barcelona at the Sala Parés in 1901. There were Berthe Weill exhibitions in Paris in 1902 and in 1904, and an exhibition in 1910 at the Galerie Notre-Dames-des-Champs in Paris. There were several group exhibitions prior to 1911. For the chronology of Picasso's exhibitions, see Rubin, ed., *Pablo Picasso.* The exhibition at the Little Galleries of the Photo-Secession, however, marked the first major one-man show, and by far the largest, most comprehensive exhibition of Picasso's work up until that time.

17. Edward Steichen to Alfred Stieglitz (1911), ASA Yale, leaf 348.

18. Edward Steichen to Lilian Steichen Sandburg (no date), CSC UI.

19. Agnes E. Meyer, *Out of These Roots* (Boston: Little, Brown and Company, 1953), 10.

20. Eugene Meyer to Dean Alberts, interview transcript, 13, AEMC LC. Background on Eugene and Agnes Meyer is drawn from the Eugene Meyer Collection (hereafter: EMC LC) and the Agnes E. Meyer Collection (AEMC LC) at the Library of Congress.

21. All quotes regarding the incident concerning the Cézanne watercolors are from Dorothy Norman, *Alfred Stieglitz: An American Seer* (New York: Random House, 1973), 104–105.

22. Edward Steichen, *ALP,* third page following plate forty-three.

23. Edward Steichen to Alfred Stieglitz, telegram, January 24, 1911, ASA Yale.

24. Edward Steichen to Alfred Stieglitz (January 1911), ASA, Yale.

25. Carl Sandburg, *Steichen the Photographer* (New York: Harcourt, Brace and Company, 1929), 62.

26. Edward Steichen to Alfred Stieglitz (1912), ASA Yale.
27. Agnes Meyer to Alfred Stieglitz, February 22, 1911, ASA Yale.
28. Edward Steichen to Alfred Stieglitz (February 1911), ASA Yale.
29. Ibid.
30. Ibid.
31. Malcolm Arbuthnot to Alfred Stieglitz, June 6, 1910, ASA Yale.
32. Malcolm Arbuthnot to Alfred Stieglitz (no date, but after June 19, 1911), ASA Yale.
33. Malcolm Arbuthnot, "The London Secession," undated, ASA Yale.
34. Edward Steichen to Alfred Stieglitz (February 1911), ASA Yale.
35. Edward Steichen, *ALP,* third page following plate forty-three.
36. Alfred Stieglitz quoted in Norman, *Alfred Stieglitz,* 105–106.
37. Clive Bell, *Art* (London: Chatto and Windus, 1914), 207.
38. Edward Steichen, *ALP,* third page following plate forty-three.
39. Ibid.
40. Meyer, *Out of These Roots,* 102.
41. Edward Steichen, *ALP,* third page following plate forty-three.
42. Ibid., page preceding plate forty-four.
43. Arthur Hoeber, *New York Globe;* quoted in "The Exhibitions at '291,'" *Camera Work,* no. 36 (October 1911): 49.
44. Alfred Stieglitz quoted in Norman, *Alfred Stieglitz,* 108.
45. Ibid., 109.
46. Vogel would later work in partnership with Condé Nast on fashion journals in France, and Vogel's wife, Cosette, would edit Nast's French *Vogue.* Cosette Vogel was the sister of Jean de Brunhoff, who created the famous Babar stories for children.
47. Edward Steichen to Alfred Stieglitz (no date), ASA Yale, leaf 148.
48. "Will Paint New York for France as Typical of American Spirit," New York *Herald,* April 28, 1911.
49. Alfred Stieglitz to Sadakichi Hartmann, December 22, 1911, ASA Yale.
50. Alfred Stieglitz quoted in Norman, *Alfred Stieglitz,* 106.
51. Henri Matisse quoted by Alfred Stieglitz in Norman, *Alfred Stieglitz,* 106.
52. Alfred Stieglitz to Sadakichi Hartmann, December 22, 1911, ASA Yale.
53. Edward Steichen to Alfred Stieglitz (no date), ASA Yale, leaf 142.
54. Edward Steichen to Alfred Stieglitz (fall 1911), ASA Yale.
55. Alfred Stieglitz to Alvin Langdon Coburn, March 18, 1912, ASA Yale.
56. Elizabeth Luther Carey, "A Few Sculptures by Matisse," *New York Times,* March 31, 1912.
57. Alfred Stieglitz to R. Child Bayley, April 29, 1912, ASA Yale.
58. Ibid.
59. Meyer, *Out of These Roots,* 105.
60. Ibid.

61. Sue Davidson Lowe, *Stieglitz: A Memoir/Biography* (New York: Farrar Straus Giroux, 1983), 399. Lowe reports in a note that Clara Steichen named Rhoades as corespondent in their divorce action. I find reference only to Marion Beckett in later court records, and witnesses such as Arthur and Mercedes Carles, among others, thought even that was misdirected (Mercedes Carles to Arthur Carles, April 19, 1919; and August 13, 1919, Perry Ottenberg Collection, Archives of American Art, Smithsonian Institution, Washington, hereafter: AAA.) Richard Whelan (*Alfred Stieglitz: A Biography* [Boston: Little, Brown and Company, 1995], 339) also indicates that Steichen and Rhoades had a "brief romance," but I have been unable to locate a primary source to that effect.
62. Mary Steichen Calderone, "Eduard Steichen as Painter: A Remembrance," in *The Paintings of Eduard Steichen* (Huntington, New York: Heckscher Museum, 1985), 10.
63. Edward Steichen to Alfred Stieglitz (December 1913), ASA Yale.
64. Edward Steichen, "My Half-Century of Delphinium Breeding," *Delphinium,* no. 9 (1959), 8–21. See also Edward Steichen to Matthew Josephson (no date), Matthew Josephson Collection, Yale.
65. See Hugo de Vries, *Die Mutationstheorie* (1901–1903) and *Arten und Varietäten* (1906), for example. In 1900, de Vries and others discovered and promoted the work of Austrian botanist Gregor Johann Mendel (1822–1884), much of it done in Mendel's Augustinian monastery garden in Brunn.
66. Edward Steichen to Matthew Josephson (no date), Matthew Josephson Collection, Yale.
67. Mary Steichen Calderone, "Eduard Steichen as Painter," 10.
68. See Eduard Steichen, "The American School," *The Photogram,* vol. 8 (January 1901): 4–9.
69. Auguste Rodin quoted by Edward Steichen, in Sandburg, *Steichen the Photographer,* 62.
70. See John Malcolm Brinnin, *The Third Rose: Gertrude Stein and Her World* (New York: Addison-Wesley Publishing Company, Inc., 1987), 147. Brinnin points out that Stein's first word portrait was of Alice B. Toklas, soon followed by the portraits of Picasso and Matisse.
71. Gertrude Stein, "Matisse," *Camera Work,* special number (August 1912).
72. Gertrude Stein, "Picasso," *Camera Work,* special number (August 1912).
73. Carl Van Vechten, ed., *Selected Writings of Gertrude Stein* (New York: Vintage Books, 1990), 328.
74. Arthur Hoeber, "Art and Artists," *New York Globe,* August 13, 1912.
75. Edward Steichen to Alfred Stieglitz (December 1912), ASA Yale.
76. Edward Burns, ed., *Gertrude Stein on Picasso* (New York: Liveright, 1970), 23.
77. See Brinnin, *The Third Rose,* 142–150, for example, for a discussion of the Cubist and cinematic qualities of these essays. See also James R. Mellow, *Charmed Circle: Gertrude Stein & Company* (New York: Praeger Publishers, 1974), 188–189, for a discussion of Stein's "abstract word portraits," as well as the influence of Stein's word portraits on the "object portraits" and the "abstract-portrait mode" popular among the artists in the Stieglitz

group and in the Arensberg circle in New York in the years just before World War I.
78. Edward Steichen to Alfred Stieglitz (December 1912), ASA Yale.
79. Ibid.
80. Ibid.
81. Ibid.
82. Ibid.
83. Ibid.
84. Ibid.
85. Ibid.
86. Ibid.
87. Ibid.

19. THE WHIRLPOOL OF MODERN ART (1912–1913)

1. Leo Stein to Mabel Weeks, February 4, 1913; Leo Stein, *A Journey into the Self, Being the Letters, Papers and Journals of Leo Stein,* ed. Edmund Fuller (New York: Crown Publishers, 1950), 48.
2. Edward Steichen to Alfred Stieglitz (November 1913), ASA Yale.
3. Marius de Zayas to Alfred Stieglitz, December 20, 1910, ASA Yale.
4. Marius de Zayas to Alfred Stieglitz, April 21, 1911, ASA Yale.
5. Marius de Zayas, "The Sun Has Set," *Camera Work,* no. 39 (July 1912): 17.
6. Edward Steichen to Alfred Stieglitz (December 1912), ASA Yale.
7. "Dam true," ibid.; "indications of vitality" and "mechanical reflex ...," Marius de Zayas, "The Sun Has Set," 17.
8. Marius de Zayas, "The Sun Has Set," 19.
9. Ibid., 17.
10. Ibid., 18.
11. Ibid., 18.
12. Edward Steichen to Alfred Stieglitz (late March 1913), ASA Yale.
13. Edward Steichen to Alfred Stieglitz (1913), ASA Yale, leaf 169.
14. Ibid.
15. Ibid.
16. Edward Steichen to Alfred Stieglitz (1910), ASA Yale.
17. Edward Steichen to Alfred Stieglitz (December 1912), ASA Yale.
18. For a discussion of key events, see Ruth Butler, *Rodin: The Shape of Genius* (New Haven: Yale University Press, 1993), 472–476.
19. Kate Simpson to Auguste Rodin, October 16, 1912, Musée Rodin, Paris.
20. Auguste Rodin quoted in Paul Gsell, *Rodin on Art* (New York: Horizon Press, 1971), 161.
21. Edward Steichen to Alfred Stieglitz (March 1913), ASA Yale.
22. Edward Steichen to Alfred Stieglitz (December 1912), ASA Yale.
23. Ibid.
24. Stella Tillyard, "The End of Victorian Art: W. R. Sickert and the Defence of Illustrative Painting," in Brian Allen, ed., *Studies in British Art I: Towards a Modern Art World* (New Haven: Yale University Press, 1995), 189.
25. Sue Davidson Lowe, *Stieglitz: A Memoir/Biography* (New York: Farrar Straus and Giroux, 1983), 164.
26. Ibid., 163.
27. Alfred Stieglitz quoted (possibly by Charles Caffin, then art editor of the journal) in "The First Great 'Clinic to Revitalize Art,' " *New York American,* January 26, 1913.
28. Edward Steichen to Alfred Stieglitz (December 1913), ASA Yale.
29. Ibid.
30. Edward Steichen, *ALP,* second page following plate forty-three.
31. Edward Steichen to Alfred Stieglitz (March 1913), ASA Yale.
32. Edward Steichen to Alfred Stieglitz (late March 1913), ASA Yale.
33. Marsden Hartley to Alfred Stieglitz, November 20, 1912, ASA Yale.
34. Edward Steichen to Alfred Stieglitz (late March 1913), ASA Yale.
35. Ibid.
36. Ibid.
37. Ibid.
38. Ibid.
39. Ibid.
40. Ibid.
41. Edward Steichen, *ALP,* page preceding plate forty-four.
42. Edward Steichen to Alfred Stieglitz (late March 1913), ASA Yale.
43. Edward Steichen to Alfred Stieglitz (April 1913), ASA Yale.
44. This painting apparently was purchased by Agnes and Eugene Meyer, for as late as 1988, it was owned by their daughter Katharine Graham. See Ellen Dykes, ed., *The Paintings of Eduard J. Steichen* (Washington D.C.: Board of Governors of Federal Reserve System, 1988), 12, 19.
45. Mercedes Carles to Arthur B. Carles, April 4, 1914, Perry Ottenberg Collection, AAA. Records in ESA MoMA also document these identities.
46. Edward Steichen to Alfred Stieglitz (no date and no visible leaf number), ASA Yale.
47. Edward Steichen to Alfred Stieglitz (April 1913), ASA Yale.
48. Ibid.
49. Edward Steichen, *ALP,* second page following plate 164.
50. Edward Steichen to Alfred Stieglitz (April 1913), ASA Yale.
51. Although Steichen's memory later varied on when he first saw this Brancusi sculpture, one of a series Brancusi entitled *Maiastra* over the years, Steichen wrote to Alfred Stieglitz in April of 1913 about seeing it at the Salon des Indépendants, wanting to purchase it, and seeking out Brancusi. See Edward Steichen to Alfred Stieglitz (April 1913), ASA Yale. In a 1962 interview with Dimitrie Popescu (transcript of *Voice of America* interview, April 17, 1962, ESA MoMA), Steichen said that he first saw the figure at the Salon des Indépendants in 1913. In 1963, he wrote in *ALP* (two pages following plate 164) that he saw it in 1909 or 1910 at the Salon des Indépendants, and he indicated to others that the date was 1909. Brancusi's *Maiastra* is usually dated beginning in 1912. In any case, the important fact is that Steichen discovered the sculpture, loved it, and acquired it.

52. Edward Steichen, *ALP*, second page following plate 164.
53. Ibid.
54. Ibid.; Edward Steichen to Dimitrie Popescu, transcript of *Voice of America Interview*, 8–10.
55. Edward Steichen, *ALP*, third page following plate 164.
56. Ibid.
57. Edward Steichen to Dimitrie Popescu, transcript of *Voice of America* interview, 10; Edward Steichen, *ALP*, page preceding plate 164a.
58. Edward Steichen to Dimitrie Popescu, transcript of *Voice of America* interview, 10.
59. Edward Steichen, *ALP*, page preceding plate 164a. Mary's drawing remains among her papers.
60. Edward Steichen to Alfred Stieglitz (April 1913), ASA Yale.
61. Emmy Stieglitz to Alfred Stieglitz, September 9, 1913, ASA Yale.
62. Emmy Stieglitz to Alfred Stieglitz, September 19 (1913), ASA Yale.
63. Edward Steichen to Alfred Stieglitz (December 1913), ASA Yale.

20. Strategic Retreat (1913–1914)

1. Edward Steichen, *ALP*, page following plate sixty-two.
2. Alfred Stieglitz to Bausch & Lomb Optical Company, September 30, 1913, ASA Yale.
3. Edward Steichen to Alfred Stieglitz (December 1913), ASA Yale.
4. Marius de Zayas, "Photography and Artistic-Photography," *Camera Work*, no. 42/43 (April–July 1913): 14.
5. Alfred Stieglitz, "Our Plates," *Camera Work*, no. 42/43 (April–July 1913): 68.
6. Sadakichi Hartmann, "H. H. Pierce, A Traveling Photographer," in W. Lawton and George Knox, eds., *The Valiant Knights of Daguerre: Selected Critical Essays on Photography and Profiles of Photograph Pioneers by Sadakichi Hartmann* (Berkeley: University of California Press, 1978), 212.
7. Mary Steichen, "The Skylark," *Camera Work*, no. 42/43 (April–July 1913): 14.
8. Photostat of inscription, "Memorabilia," ESA MoMA.
9. Margaret Sandburg interview with PEN.
10. Edward Steichen to Alfred Stieglitz (April 1914), ASA Yale.
11. Agnes E. Meyer, *Charles Lang Freer and His Gallery* (Washington: Freer Gallery of Art, 1970), 13–14.
12. Agnes E. Meyer to Charles Freer (November 4, 1914), AEMC LC.
13. Agnes E. Meyer, *Charles Lang Freer and His Gallery*, 19.
14. Agnes E. Meyer, *Chinese Painting as Reflected in the Thought and Art of Li Lung-Mien 1070–1106* (New York: Duffield and Company, 1923).
15. Clara Steichen to Alfred Stieglitz (December 1916), ASA Yale.
16. Clara Steichen to Hedwig Stieglitz (1909), ASA Yale.
17. Mary Steichen Calderone, "My Father," *Infinity* (December 1954–January 1955): 14.
18. Ibid.
19. Edward Steichen to Alfred Stieglitz (April 1914), ASA Yale.
20. Mildred Aldrich, *A Hilltop on the Marne: Being Letters Written June 3–September 8, 1914* (Boston: Houghton Mifflin Company, 1915), 5.
21. Mildred Aldrich to Gertrude Stein and Alice B. Toklas, August 5, 1913, GSC Yale.
22. Aldrich, *A Hilltop on the Marne*, 16–17.
23. Kate Steichen quoted in Mary Vespa, "America's Biggest Problem?" *People*, January 21, 1980, 77.
24. Carl Sandburg, *Steichen the Photographer* (New York: Harcourt, Brace and Company, 1929), 35.
25. Ibid.
26. Katharine Rhoades to Alfred Stieglitz, October 9, 1914, ASA Yale.
27. Katharine Rhoades to Agnes Meyer (illegible and incomplete date [August 1914]), AEMC LC.
28. Alfred Stieglitz quoted in Nancy Newhall, "Notes for a Biography," in *From Adams to Stieglitz: Pioneers of Modern Photography* (New York: Aperture, 1989), 58.
29. Agnes E. Meyer, *Out of These Roots* (Boston: Little, Brown and Company, 1953), 104.
30. Agnes E. Meyer to Alfred Stieglitz, June 25, 1914, ASA Yale.
31. Ibid.
32. Ibid.
33. Emmy Stieglitz to Alfred Stieglitz, August 22 (1914), ASA Yale.
34. Agnes E. Meyer to Alfred Stieglitz, July 11, 1914, ASA Yale.
35. Alfred Stieglitz, "What is 291" [sic], *Camera Work*, no. 47 (July 1914): 3.
36. Gertrude Stein quoted in Mildred Aldrich to Gertrude Stein, July 28, 1914, GSC Yale; see also John Malcolm Brinnin, *The Third Rose: Gertrude Stein and Her World* (New York: Addison-Wesley Publishing Company, Inc., 1987), 209.
37. Meyer, *Out of These Roots*, 105.
38. Ibid., 106.
39. Edward Steichen, *ALP*, page following plate sixty-two.
40. Edward Steichen to Alfred Stieglitz, August 3, 1914, ASA Yale.
41. Ibid.
42. Ibid.
43. Ibid.
44. Ibid.
45. Aldrich, *A Hilltop on the Marne*, 54–55.
46. Clara Steichen's version of this event appears, for example, in the following letters to Alfred Stieglitz, ASA Yale: two long, undated letters written in February 1916; undated letter (March 27, 1916); May 8, 1916; undated letter (July 31, 1916); undated letter (August 8, 1916); letter written September 8 (1916); undated letter (September 18, 1916); undated letter (December 1916); undated letter (January 1, 1917); and letters written December 13, 1931; May 27, 1935; July 11, 1944. Stieglitz defended Steichen and Beckett in letters he wrote to Clara Steichen on March 1, 1916, and December 14, 1916.
47. Edward Steichen to Alfred Stieglitz, August 3, 1914, ASA Yale.
48. Edward Steichen to Eugene Meyer, August 6, 1914, EMC LC.
49. Aldrich, *A Hilltop on the Marne*, 5.

50. Edward Steichen to Eugene Meyer, August 6, 1914, EMC LC.
51. Ibid.
52. Ibid.
53. Mildred Aldrich to Gertrude Stein and Alice B. Toklas, August 14, 1914, GSC Yale.
54. Aldrich, *A Hilltop on the Marne*, 47–48.
55. Edward Steichen to Eugene Meyer, August 6, 1914, EMC LC.
56. Edward Steichen to Alfred Stieglitz (late summer 1914), ASA Yale.
57. Edward Steichen to Eugene Meyer, August 6, 1914, EMC LC.
58. Aldrich, *A Hilltop on the Marne*, 46.
59. Ibid.
60. Edward Steichen to Alfred Stieglitz (August 27, 1914), ASA Yale.
61. Ibid.
62. Edward Steichen, *ALP*, page following plate sixty-two.
63. Mildred Aldrich to Gertrude Stein, August 29, 1914, GSC Yale.
64. Meyer, *Out of These Roots*, 106.
65. Edward Steichen to Alfred Stieglitz, September 2, 1914, ASA Yale.
66. Ibid.
67. Edward Steichen to Matthew Josephson (no date), Matthew Josephson Collection, Yale.
68. Kate Steichen, "The Wonderful World and Life," unpublished poem, ASA Yale.
69. Katharine Rhoades to Alfred Stieglitz, October 9, 1914, ASA Yale.
70. Ibid.
71. Ibid.
72. Agnes Meyer to Charles Freer (October 1, 1914), AEMC LC.
73. Mildred Aldrich to Gertrude Stein and Alice B. Toklas, September 16 (1914), GSC Yale.
74. Mildred Aldrich to Alice B. Toklas, November 13, 1914, GSC Yale.
75. Edward Steichen to Matthew Josephson (no date), Matthew Josephson Collection, Yale.
76. Katharine Rhoades to Alfred Stieglitz, October 15, 1914, ASA Yale.
77. Alfred Stieglitz to Annie W. Brigman, September 28, 1914, ASA Yale.
78. Ibid.
79. Ibid.
80. Ibid.
81. Edward Steichen, *ALP*, page following plate sixty-two.
82. Alfred Stieglitz to Annie W. Brigman, September 28, 1914, ASA Yale.
83. Edward Steichen, *ALP*, page following plate sixty-two.
84. Ibid.
85. Ibid.
86. Ibid.

21. A Forum for Wisdom and Folly (1914–1915)

1. Eugene Meyer, "291," *Camera Work*, no. 47 (July 1914): 40.
2. Edward Steichen, *ALP*, page following plate sixty-two.
3. Ibid.
4. Edward Steichen, "291," *Camera Work*, no. 47 (July 1914): 65–66.
5. Emmy Stieglitz to Alfred Stieglitz, August 23, 1914, ASA Yale.
6. Ibid.
7. Emmy Stieglitz to Alfred Stieglitz, August 25, 1914, ASA Yale.
8. Mary Steichen Calderone quoted in Thomas C. Hunter, *Beginnings* (New York: Thomas Y. Crowell, 1978), 59.
9. Katharine Rhoades to Alfred Stieglitz, October 9, 1914, ASA Yale.
10. Paula Sandburg to Carl Sandburg (fall 1914, second letter in series), MSC.
11. Paula Sandburg to Carl Sandburg (fall 1914, third letter in series), MSC.
12. Margaret Sandburg interview with PEN.
13. Paula Sandburg quoted by Anthony Mancini, *New York Post Weekend Magazine*, January 13, 1968, 25.
14. Margaret Sandburg interview with PEN; Mancini, *New York Post Weekend Magazine*, 25.
15. Paula Sandburg to Carl Sandburg, n.d. (Fall 1914, fourth letter), MSC.
16. Katharine Rhoades to Alfred Stieglitz, October 29, 1914, ASA Yale.
17. Katharine Rhoades to Alfred Stieglitz, November 1, 1914, ASA Yale.
18. Katharine Rhoades to Alfred Stieglitz, November 26, 1914, ASA Yale.
19. Katharine Rhoades to Alfred Stieglitz, March 23–24, 1915, ASA Yale.
20. Katharine Rhoades to Alfred Stieglitz, April 5, 1915, ASA Yale.
21. Mildred Aldrich to Alice B. Toklas, September 10, 1914, GSC Yale.
22. Katharine Rhoades to Alfred Stieglitz, December 26, 1914, ASA Yale.
23. Mildred Aldrich to Kate Steichen, December 31, 1914, KRSC.
24. Ibid.
25. Mildred Aldrich to Alice B. Toklas, January 1, 1915, GSC Yale.
26. Edward Steichen, *ALP*, second page following plate 249.
27. Agnes E. Meyer to Charles Freer, January 28, 1915, AEMC LC.
28. Ibid.
29. Charles Freer to Agnes Meyer, February 15, 1915, AEMC LC.
30. Marion Beckett to Edward Steichen (ca. 1915), ASA Yale.
31. "Extreme Art Filling New York's Galleries," New York *Herald*, February 1, 1915. This article devotes a paragraph to Beckett and Rhoades, noting approvingly that they did not take "much liberty" with form, other than using "strident and striking color to the limit." The article also reviews separate shows elsewhere by Marsden Hartley and Max Weber, whom it calls "one of this country's pioneer art extremists."
32. Agnes E. Meyer to Charles Freer, January 28, 1914, AEMC LC.
33. Katharine Rhoades to Alfred Stieglitz, November 6, 1914, ASA Yale.
34. These letters are part of the ASA at Yale.

35. Alfred Stieglitz to Annie W. Brigman, February 15, 1915, ASA Yale.
36. Agnes E. Meyer to Charles Freer, March 4, 1915, AEMC LC.
37. Alfred Stieglitz quoted in Dorothy Norman, *Alfred Stieglitz: An American Seer* (New York: Random House, 1973), 125.
38. Agnes E. Meyer to Charles Freer, March 4, 1915, AEMC LC.
39. Charles Caffin, *New York American,* April 5, 1915.
40. Mildred Aldrich to Mary Steichen, March 4, 1915, KRSC.
41. Alfred Stieglitz to Annie Brigman, April 16, 1915, ASA Yale.
42. Clara Steichen to Alfred Stieglitz (February 1916), ASA Yale.
43. Ibid.
44. Ibid.
45. Kate Rodina Steichen, Wilton Library Oral History, Wilton, Connecticut, 3, KRSC.
46. Ibid., 2.
47. Ibid.
48. Edward Steichen, *ALP,* second page following plate sixty-two.
49. Ibid.
50. Alfred Stieglitz quoted in Norman, *Alfred Stieglitz,* 124.
51. Clara Steichen to Alfred Stieglitz, May 27, 1935, ASA Yale. In this letter, twenty years after the event, Clara reconstructed her impressions of that May of 1915.
52. Ibid.
53. Clara Steichen to Alfred Stieglitz (February 1916), ASA Yale.
54. Mary Steichen Calderone quoted in Don Gold, *Until the Singing Stops: A Celebration of Life and Old Age in America* (New York: Holt, Rinehart and Winston, 1971), 315.
55. Mildred Aldrich to Gertrude Stein, June 9, 1915, GSC, Yale.
56. Mildred Aldrich to Gertrude Stein, June 27, 1915, GSC Yale.
57. Emmy Stieglitz to Alfred Stieglitz (ca. 1915), ASA Yale.
58. Katharine Rhoades to Alfred Stieglitz, September 3 (1915), ASA Yale.
59. Clara Steichen to Alfred Stieglitz (September 18, 1916), ASA Yale.
60. Unsigned and undated news clipping, *New Orleans State,* KRSC.
61. Kate Steichen, "The Nearly Two Years War," ASA Yale.
62. Clara Steichen to Alfred Stieglitz (February 1916), ASA Yale.
63. Mildred Aldrich to Gertrude Stein and Alice B. Toklas, December 25, 1915, GSC Yale.
64. Clara Steichen to Alfred Stieglitz, May 27, 1935, ASA Yale.
65. Edward Steichen quoted in Clara Steichen to Alfred Stieglitz (February 1916), ASA Yale.
66. Clara Steichen to Alfred Stieglitz (no date), ASA Yale.
67. Clara Steichen to Alfred Stieglitz (February 1916), ASA Yale.

22. THE DEATH OF THE BLUE BIRD (1916)

1. Edward Steichen, *ALP,* page following plate 164.
2. American Psychiatric Association: *Diagnostic and Statistical Manual of Mental Disorders,* 3d ed. (Washington, D.C.: American Psychiatric Association, 1980), 195.
3. Ibid.
4. Ibid.
5. Ibid., 197.
6. Clara Steichen, "Peace," ASA Yale.
7. Alfred Stieglitz to Clara Steichen, April 17, 1916, ASA Yale.
8. Clara Steichen, "Friendship-/To M.A.," ASA Yale.
9. Clara Steichen to Alfred Stieglitz (February 1916), ASA Yale.
10. Ibid.
11. Ibid.
12. Ibid.
13. Ibid.
14. Emmy Stieglitz to Alfred Stieglitz, August 24, 1916, ASA Yale.
15. Alfred Stieglitz to Clara Steichen, March 1, 1916, ASA Yale.
16. Clara Steichen to Alfred Stieglitz, March 17 (1916), ASA Yale.
17. Alfred Stieglitz to Clara Steichen, April 17, 1916, ASA Yale.
18. Clara Steichen to Alfred Stieglitz, July 31 (1916), ASA Yale.
19. Mary Steichen Calderone quoted in Thomas C. Hunter, *Beginnings* (New York: Thomas Y. Crowell, 1978), 50. Account of Mary making house calls with Lee Stieglitz: Francesca Calderone-Steichen interview with PEN.
20. Mary Steichen Calderone quoted in Don Gold, *Until the Singing Stops: A Celebration of Life and Old Age in America* (New York: Holt, Rinehart and Winston, 1978), 313.
21. Mary Steichen Calderone, "My Father," *Infinity* (December 1954–January 1995): 14.
22. Mary Steichen Calderone quoted in Hunter, *Beginnings,* 57.
23. Clara Steichen to Alfred Stieglitz (February 1916), ASA Yale.
24. The franc was worth about nineteen cents in 1916.
25. Clara Steichen to Alfred Stieglitz (February 1916), ASA Yale.
26. Edward Steichen to Paula Sandburg (1916), CSC UI. This letter is quoted in part in Penelope Niven, *Carl Sandburg: A Biography* (New York: Charles Scribner's Sons, 1991), 272; and in Helga Sandburg, *A Great and Glorious Romance: The Story of Carl Sandburg and Lilian Steichen* (New York: Hartcourt Brace Jovanovich 1918), 214.
27. Ibid.
28. Katharine Rhoades to Alfred Stieglitz, May 30, 1916, ASA Yale.
29. Alfred Stieglitz to Katharine Rhoades, May 31, 1916, ASA Yale.
30. Edward Steichen to Alfred Stieglitz (September 10, 1916), ASA Yale.
31. Edward Steichen to Alfred Stieglitz (October 1916), ASA Yale.

32. Edward Steichen to Clara Steichen, January 17, 1917, ASA Yale.
33. Clara Steichen to Alfred Stieglitz (August 8, 1916), ASA Yale.
34. Clara Steichen to Alfred Stieglitz, July 31 (1916), ASA Yale.
35. Clara Steichen to Alfred Stieglitz (September 18, 1916), ASA Yale.
36. Ibid.
37. Clara Steichen, "A Tribute" (September 18, 1916), ASA Yale.
38. Ibid.
39. Ibid.
40. Ibid.
41. Clara Steichen to Rose Beuret, August 17 (1916), Musée Rodin, Paris.
42. Alfred Stieglitz to Clara Steichen, December 14, 1916, ASA Yale.
43. Ibid.
44. Clara Steichen, "Death of the Blue Bird," ASA Yale.
45. Alfred Stieglitz to Annie W. Brigman, May 17, 1916, ASA Yale.
46. See Sue Davidson Lowe's very interesting family perspective on the Stieglitz-Steichen friendship in *Stieglitz: A Memoir/Biography* (New York: Farrar Straus Giroux, 1983), 179–195.

23. THE ART OF READING LINES AND SHADOWS (1916–1918)

1. Carl Sandburg, *Steichen the Photographer* (New York: Harcourt, Brace and Company, 1929, 38.
2. Agnes Meyer to Alfred Stieglitz, August 16, 1915, ASA Yale.
3. Alfred Stieglitz quoted in Dorothy Norman, *Alfred Stieglitz: American Seer* (New York: Random House, 1973), 128–129.
4. Alfred Stieglitz to John Weichsel, November 8, 1915, John Weichsel Collection, AAA; Alfred Stieglitz to R. Child Bayley, November 1, 1916, ASA Yale.
5. Carl Sandburg, *Steichen the Photographer,* 36.
6. Alfred Stieglitz quoted in Dorothy Norman, *Alfred Stieglitz: An American Seer,* 130. Stieglitz used this phrase to others, including Annie Brigman and Anita Pollitzer.
7. Georgia O'Keeffe, *Georgia O'Keeffe: A Portrait by Alfred Stieglitz* (New York: The Metropolitan Museum of Art, 1978), n.p.
8. Ibid.
9. Alfred Stieglitz quoted in Dorothy Norman, *Alfred Stieglitz: An American Seer,* 130.
10. Ibid.
11. Steichen, *ALP,* second page following plate sixty-two.
12. Mary Kemp Steichen quoted in "Over the Top with Camera," undated and unidentified news clipping (only day and year visible: 24, 1917), KRSC.
13. Edward Steichen, *ALP,* second page following plate sixty-two.
14. Ibid.
15. Edward Steichen quoted in Mary Steichen Calderone, "Eduard Steichen as Painter: A Remembrance," in Alayne Shoenfeld, ed., *The Paintings of Eduard Steichen* (Huntington, New York: Heckscher Museum 1985), 10–11.
16. "Over the Top with Camera."
17. Carl Sandburg, dedication to *Smoke and Steel* (New York: Harcourt Brace and Company, 1920).
18. Col. C. McK. Saltzman, War Department Office Memorandum No. 83, August 2, 1917.
19. Edward Steichen, *ALP,* second page following plate sixty-two.
20. James Barnes, *From Then Till Now: Anecdotal Portraits and Transcript Pages from Memory's Tablets* (New York: D. Appleton-Century Company, 1934), 477.
21. Ibid., 476.
22. Ibid., 477.
23. Mary Kemp Steichen quoted in "Over the Top with Camera."
24. Barnes, *From Then Till Now,* 479.
25. "Lines ... camouflage" in Carl Sandburg, *Steichen the Photographer,* 38; "accurately ... scientifically" in Barnes, *From Then Till Now,* 479.
26. Barnes, *From Then Till Now,* 485.
27. Ibid.
28. Ibid.
29. Mary Kemp Steichen quoted in "Over the Top with Camera."
30. Barnes, *From Then Till Now,* 482.
31. Clara Steichen to Alfred Stieglitz (November 11, 1917), ASA Yale.
32. Ibid.
33. Clara Smith, "An Ozark Childhood," unpublished manuscript, MSCC.
34. Kate Steichen quoted in Susan Guerrero, "Kate Steichen, Skipper of the Pea Green Boat," *News-Times* [probably Wilton, Connecticut], September 5, 1980.
35. My understanding of the general context of the war was greatly facilitated by Barbara W. Tuchman's *The Guns of August* (New York: Macmillan, 1962). For a broad study of military photography, see Susan D. Moeller, *Shooting War: Photography and the American Experience of Combat* (New York: Basic Books, 1989).
36. Eduard Steichen to Alfred Stieglitz (January 8, 1918), ASA Yale.
37. Barnes, *From Then Till Now,* 484.
38. Ibid.
39. Steichen, *ALP,* third page following plate sixty-two.
40. This image may be seen in *Edward J. Steichen,* a television documentary by Claude Waringo, Luxembourg: Samsa Film Production, 1995.
41. Edward Steichen, *ALP,* third page following plate sixty-two.
42. Auguste Rodin, quoted in Albert E. Elsen, *Rodin* (New York: Museum of Modern Art, 1963), 113.
43. Edward Steichen, *ALP,* page preceding plate sixty-three.
44. Ibid., second page following plate sixty-two.
45. Ibid., third page following plate sixty-two.
46. Alfred Stieglitz to Annie W. Brigman (1917–1918), ASA Yale.
47. Alfred Stieglitz to Annie W. Brigman (late 1917 or early 1918), ASA Yale.
48. Barnes, *From Then Till Now,* 485.
49. Edward Steichen to Alfred Stieglitz (January 8, 1918), ASA Yale.
50. Mary Steichen Calderone, "My Father," *Infinity* (December 1954–January 1955): 16.

51. Edward Steichen to Alfred Stieglitz (January 8, 1918), ASA Yale.
52. Ibid.
53. Barnes, *From Then Till Now*, 485.
54. Ibid.
55. Ibid., 486.
56. Ibid., 489.
57. Ibid., 490.
58. Carl Sandburg, *Steichen the Photographer*, 38.
59. Edward Steichen to Maj. James Barnes, June 1 (1918), quoted in Barnes, *From Then Till Now*, 498.
60. Edward Steichen, *ALP*, third page following plate sixty-two.
61. Edward Steichen to Maj. James Barnes, June 1 (1918), quoted in Barnes, *From Then Till, Now*, 498.
62. Barnes, *From Then Till Now*, 498.
63. Carl Sandburg to Edward Steichen (1919 or 1920), CSC UI.
64. Barnes, *From Then Till Now*, 494–495.
65. Ibid., 495.
66. Major W. E. de B. Whittaker, "Aircraft in the War," in *Jane's Fighting Aircraft of World War I* (London: Studio Editions, 1992), 12.
67. Edward Steichen to Matthew Josephson (no date), Matthew Josephson Collection, Yale.
68. Edward Steichen, *ALP*, third page following plate sixty-two.
69. Ibid.
70. Edward Steichen to Oma and Opa Steichen, November 5 (1918), CSC UI.
71. Edward Steichen, *ALP*, fourth page following plate sixty-two.
72. Mildred Aldrich's sequels were *On the Edge of the War Zone* (1917); *The Peak of the Load* (1918); and *When Johnny Comes Marching Home* (1919).
73. Katharine Rhoades to Alfred Stieglitz, December 21, 1917, ASA Yale.
74. Katharine Rhoades to Alfred Stieglitz, February 21, 1918, ASA Yale.
75. Georgia O'Keeffe, *Georgia O'Keeffe*.
76. Mildred Aldrich to Gertrude Stein, May 27, 1918, GSC Yale.
77. Edward Steichen, *ALP*, fourth page following plate sixty-two.
78. Ibid.
79. Ibid.

24. ALIENATING THE AFFECTIONS (1919–1922)

1. "Answers Alienation Suit," *New York Times*, August 28, 1919.
2. Paula Sandburg to Carl Sandburg (February or March 1919), CSC UI; Helga Sandburg, *A Great and Glorious Romance: The Story of Carl Sandburg and Lilian Steichen* (New York: Harcourt Brace Jovanovich, 1978), 263.
3. Ibid.
4. Carl Sandburg to Leon Starmont, May 13, 1919, CSC UI; Herbert Mitgang, ed., *The Letters of Carl Sandburg* (New York: Harcourt, Brace & World, Inc., 1968), 160–161.
5. Kate Steichen to Mildred Aldrich, June 2 (1919), KRSC.
6. "Artist's Wife Sues for Loss of His Love," *New York Times*, July 5, 1919.
7. Ibid.
8. Ibid.
9. "Answers Alienation Suit," *New York Times*, August 28, 1919.
10. Edward Steichen to Alfred Stieglitz, August 21 (1919), ASA Yale.
11. Edward Steichen to Alfred Stieglitz (August 26, 1919), ASA Yale.
12. *New York Times*, November 9, 1920, and December 8, 1920. See also Helga Sandburg, *A Great and Glorious Romance*, 276–278.
13. Carl Sandburg to Edward Steichen, July 8 (1919), CSC UI; Mitgang, ed., *The Letters of Carl Sandburg*, 166–167.
14. Carl Sandburg, *Smoke and Steel* (Harcourt Brace and Company, 1920).
15. Edward Steichen to Carl Sandburg (no date), CSC UI.
16. Ibid.
17. Alfred Stieglitz to Sadakichi Hartmann, April 27, 1919, ASA Yale.
18. For a discussion of these portraits, and for the suggestion that Stieglitz was influenced by the erotic Rodin drawings that Steichen introduced him to at 291 and in Paris, see Benita Eisler, *O'Keeffe & Stieglitz: An American Romance* (New York: Doubleday, 1991), 183–193.
19. Alfred Stieglitz to Emmeline Stieglitz, February 17, 1919, ASA Yale.
20. Alfred Stieglitz to Kitty Stieglitz (February 1919), ASA Yale.
21. Kitty Stieglitz to Alfred Stieglitz, July 24, 1918, ASA Yale.
22. Edward Steichen to Alfred Stieglitz, August 21 (1919), ASA Yale.
23. Clara Steichen to Alfred Stieglitz, January 29, 1935, ASA Yale.
24. Carl Sandburg, *Steichen The Photographer* (New York: Harcourt, Brace and Company, 1929), 38.
25. Edward Steichen to Alfred Stieglitz (fall or winter 1919), ASA Yale.
26. Edward Steichen to Alfred Stieglitz (ca. winter 1919 or spring 1920), ASA Yale.
27. Ibid.
28. Ibid.
29. Ibid.
30. Ibid.
31. Edward Steichen to Alfred Stieglitz (ca. spring 1920), ASA Yale.
32. Ibid.
33. Edward Steichen, *ALP*, fourth page following plate sixty-two.
34. Edward Steichen to Robert Marks, no date, ASA Yale.
35. Carl Sandburg, *Steichen the Photographer*, 38–39.
36. Edward Steichen, *ALP*, fourth page following plate sixty-two.
37. Gilbert Millstein, "'De Lawd' of Modern Photography," *New York Times Magazine*, March 22, 1959, 34; Edward Steichen, *ALP*, fourth page following plate sixty-two.
38. Edward Steichen quoted in Millstein, "'De Lawd' of Modern Photography," 34.
39. Edward Steichen, *ALP*, page following plate eighty-three.
40. Isadora Duncan, *My Life* (New York: Liveright, Inc., 1933), 349.

41. Ibid.
42. Edward Steichen, *ALP,* page following plate eighty-three.
43. Ibid.
44. Ibid.
45. Duncan, *My Life,* 352–353.
46. Edward Steichen, *ALP,* page following plate eighty-three.
47. Ibid.
48. Ibid. Isadora Duncan gave the date of the trip as 1920, but in 1963, Steichen dated it 1921, and his dating is inaccurate. He probably drew the date from his dating of the prints of the photographs. Fredrika Blair, one of Isadora Duncan's biographers, also gives the date as 1920; see Fredrika Blair, *Isadora: Portrait of the Artist as a Woman* (New York: McGraw-Hill Book Company, 1986). For a detailed account of the trip, see Irma Duncan, *Duncan Dancer* (Middletown, Connecticut: Wesleyan University Press, 1965, 1966), 187–192. Irma Duncan wrote in her diary that she loaned Steichen her Brownie camera on August 30, 1920, so that he could take pictures (192).
49. Edward Steichen, *ALP,* page preceding plate eighty-four.
50. Mary Steichen Calderone quoted in Thomas C. Hunter, *Beginnings* (New York: Thomas Y. Crowell, 1978), 57.
51. "E. J. Steichen, Artist, Now Sues His Wife," *New York Times,* November 9, 1920.
52. Mildred Aldrich to Gertrude Stein, December 22, 1920, GSC Yale.
53. "Sues Husband's Friend," *New York Times,* December 8, 1920.
54. "Artist Aids Woman Wife Sues for Love," *New York Times,* March 3, 1921.
55. Clara Steichen to Alfred Stieglitz, May 27, 1935, ASA Yale.
56. "Artist Aids Woman Wife Sues for Love." This article bore sensational subheadings: "Edward Steichen Denies Affection in Defense of Miss Marian [*sic*] H. Beckett. Wife Jealous of Mother. After a Quarrel Both of Them Jumped into a Cistern, but the Water Was Shallow."
57. Mildred Aldrich to Gertrude Stein, March 21, 1921, GSC Yale.
58. Mildred Aldrich to Gertrude Stein and Alice B. Toklas, March 29, 1921, GSC Yale.
59. Edward Steichen to Alfred Stieglitz (1921), ASA Yale, leaf 302.
60. Ibid.
61. Ibid.
62. Ibid.
63. Edward Steichen to Paula Sandburg (fall 1921), CSC UI.
64. Kate Steichen to Mildred Aldrich, August 8, 1920, KRSC. Kate had written, "Next winter I am going to school—at the Model School of Hunter College...."
65. Edward Steichen to Alfred Stieglitz (1921), ASA Yale, leaf 302.
66. Mildred Aldrich to Gertrude Stein, January 24, 1922, GSC Yale.
67. Meaux Court of Writs and Judgments, July 27, 1922, Case 125, ESA MoMA.
68. Edward Steichen to Clara Smith (September 1903), ESA MOMA.
69. Meaux Court of Writs and Judgments, July 27, 1922, Case 125.
70. Edward Steichen to Clara Smith (September 1903), ESA MOMA.
71. Michael J. Joyce, Attorney-at-Law, to Clara Smith Steichen, August 7, 1922, ESA MOMA.
72. Margaret Sandburg interview with PEN.

25. A Sacrament of Fire (1922–1924)

1. Carl Sandburg, *Steichen the Photographer* (New York: Harcourt, Brace and Company, 1929), 44.
2. Carl Sandburg to Alice Corbin Henderson, September 12 (1920), CSC UI; Herbert Mitgang, ed., *The Letters of Carl Sandburg* (New York: Harcourt, Brace & World, 1968), 192.
3. Edward Steichen to Matthew Josephson (no date), Matthew Josephson Collection, Yale.
4. Edward Steichen, *ALP,* fourth page following plate sixty-two.
5. Ibid., fifth page following plate sixty-two.
6. Ibid., fourth page following plate sixty-two.
7. Ibid., fifth page following plate sixty-two.
8. Ibid.
9. Carl Sandburg, *Steichen the Photographer,* 43.
10. Edward Steichen, *ALP,* page preceding plate sixty-three.
11. Ibid.
12. Ibid., fifth page following plate sixty-two.
13. Ibid.
14. Ibid., page preceding plate sixty-three.
15. Ibid.
16. Edward Steichen to Paula Sandburg (ca. Christmas of 1923), CSC UI.
17. Carl Sandburg to Alice Corbin Henderson, September 12 (1920), CSC UI; Mitgang, *The Letters of Carl Sandburg,* 192.
18. Edward Steichen to Matthew Josephson (no date), Matthew Josephson Collection, Yale.
19. Edward Steichen to Paula Sandburg (no date), CSC UI.
20. Carl Sandburg, *Steichen the Photographer,* 43.
21. Edward Steichen, *ALP,* page preceding plate sixty-three.
22. Carl Sandburg, *Steichen the Photographer,* 44.
23. Edward Steichen, *ALP,* page preceding plate sixty-three.
24. Alfred Stieglitz to Arthur B. Carles, April 19, 1921, Perry Ottenberg Collection, AAA; Alfred Stieglitz to Arthur B. Carles (ca. 1921), Perry Ottenberg Collection, AAA.
25. Edward Steichen, *ALP,* page preceding plate sixty-three.
26. Helga Sandburg, *A Great and Glorious Romance: The Story of Carl Sandburg and Lilian Steichen* (New York: Harcourt, Brace Jovanovich 1978), 306.
27. Carl Sandburg, *The American Songbag* (New York: Harcourt, Brace and Company, 1927), 114–115; Margaret Sandburg interview with PEN.
28. Publicity notes, ESA MoMA.
29. Ibid.
30. Ibid.
31. Carl Sandburg, *Steichen the Photographer,* 42–43.
32. Ibid., 43.
33. Ibid., 42.

34. Ibid.
35. Ibid., 44.
36. Edward Steichen, *ALP,* page following plate ninety-five.
37. Edward Steichen to Carl Sandburg (no date), CSC UI. The painting may be seen in Steichen's archive at MoMA.
38. Frank Crowninshield, "Master American Portrait Photographers," *Vanity Fair,* January 1923, 54.
39. Edward Steichen to Alfred Stieglitz (no date), ASA Yale, leaf 314.
40. *Vanity Fair,* August 1917, 32.
41. *Vanity Fair,* January 1918, 48.
42. *Vanity Fair* masthead, quoted in Kennedy Fraser, ed., *On the Edge: Images from 100 Years of Vogue* (New York: Random House, Inc., 1992), 3.
43. Edward Steichen, *ALP,* page following plate ninety-four.
44. Ibid.; Lois Gordon and Alan Gordon, *Six Decades in American Life: 1920–1980* (New York: Atheneum, 1987), 2.
45. Helga Sandburg, "... *Where Love Begins*" (New York: Donald I. Fine, Inc., 1989), 36.
46. Carl Sandburg, *Steichen the Photographer,* 45.
47. Caroline Seebohm, *The Man Who Was Vogue: The Life and Times of Condé Nast* (New York: Viking Press, 1982), 282.
48. Edward Steichen to Agnes Ernst Meyer (April 6, 1923), EMC LC.
49. Child Bayley to Alfred Stieglitz, March 21, 1924, ASA Yale.
50. Edward Steichen, *ALP,* fourth page following plate sixty-two.
51. Carl Sandburg, *Steichen the Photographer,* 44.
52. Ibid.
53. Edward Steichen to Beaumont Newhall, July 14, 1958, ESA MoMA.
54. Ibid.
55. Edward Steichen, "My Life in Photography," *The Saturday Review,* March 28, 1959, 15–16.
56. Gilbert Millstein, " 'De Lawd' of Modern Photography," *New York Times Magazine,* March 22, 1959, 34.
57. Carl Sandburg, *Steichen the Photographer,* 45.
58. This incident is related in Aylesa Forsee, *Famous Photographers* (Philadelphia: Macrae Smith Company, 1968), 24. Forsee wrote that Steichen had checked the manuscript and supplied additional information.
59. Man Ray quoted in Paul Hill and Thomas Cooper, *Dialogue with Photography* (New York: Farrar Straus Giroux, 1979), 13.
60. Clara Steichen to Alfred Stieglitz, February 21, 1932, ASA Yale.
61. Edward Steichen, *ALP,* page following plate 164.
62. Dennis Longwell, *Steichen: The Master Prints 1895–1914: The Symbolist Period* (New York: Museum of Modern Art, 1978), 173.
63. "Raps Photography Today," *New York Times,* March 6, 1923.
64. Ibid.
65. Grace Mayer, curator of the Steichen Archive at MOMA, carefully researched this matter, investigating records in New York and New Jersey, including the New Jersey Bureau of Vital Statistics. Mary Steichen Calderone and members of Dana Steichen's family reported to Grace Mayer their belief that Steichen and Dana were married March 27, 1923. See "Wives" file, ESA MOMA.
66. Helga Sandburg, "... *Where Love Begins,*" 234.
67. Ibid., 36. Helga Sandburg interview with PEN; Margaret Sandburg interview with PEN; Francesca Calderone-Steichen interview with PEN.
68. Marion Beckett to Alfred Stieglitz, August 21, 1923, ASA Yale.
69. Marion Beckett to Alfred Stieglitz, October 11, 1924, ASA Yale.
70. Mrs. Carroll M. ["Mid"] Cain interview with PEN.
71. Clara Steichen to Alfred Stieglitz, July 9, 1924, ASA Yale.
72. Ibid.
73. Ibid.
74. Mary Steichen Calderone quoted in Lynn Gilbert and Gaylen Moore, *Particular Passions: Talks with Women Who Have Shaped Our Times* (New York: Clarkson N. Potter Publishers, Inc., 1982), 261. Francesca Calderone-Steichen interview with PEN.
75. Clara Steichen to Alfred Stieglitz, July 18, 1924, ASA Yale.
76. Clara Steichen to Alfred Stieglitz, July 9, 1924, ASA Yale.
77. Clara Steichen to Alfred Stieglitz, July 18, 1924, ASA Yale.
78. Clara Steichen to Alfred Stieglitz, June 7, 1924, ASA Yale.
79. Clara Steichen to Alfred Stieglitz, June 17, 1924, ASA Yale.

26. THE NEW PICTORIAL REVOLUTION (1924–1928)

1. Alexander Liberman, "Steichen's Eye: A Study of the Greatest Living Photographer," *Vogue,* August 1, 1959, 140.
2. Carl Sandburg, *Steichen the Photographer* (New York: Harcourt, Brace and Company, 1929), 46.
3. Alexander Liberman, "Steichen's Eye," 140.
4. Edward Steichen, *ALP,* second page following plate 164; "observation of ... seizing it," Pierre Mac Orlan, "La photographie et le fantastique social," *Les Annales,* November 1, 1928, 414. The author is grateful for the access granted to the Condé Nast Archives, including the *Vanity Fair* and *Vogue* archives and library at Condé Nast headquarters in New York City. The records and material therein provide much of the foundation for this chapter. A useful, much longer, detailed study could be written concentrating on Steichen's work for Condé Nast and its connections to the commercial, fashion, and photojournalistic photography of the period.
5. Carl Sandburg, *Steichen the Photographer,* 56.
6. Rosa Reilly, "Steichen—The Living Legend," *Popular Photography,* March, 1938, 12.
7. Margaret Case Harriman, "Steichen," *Vogue,* January 1, 1938, 92.
8. Ibid.
9. Edward Steichen, *ALP,* page following plate ninety-five.
10. Harriman, "Steichen," 94.
11. See Edward Steichen, *ALP,* page following plate 112; and Kennedy Fraser, ed., *On the Edge: Images from 100 Years of Vogue* (New York: Random House, 1992), 15–16 and passim for helpful background on *Vogue.*
12. Carl Sandburg, "Flesh and the Devil," Chicago

Daily News, February 18, 1927; reprinted in Dale Fetherling and Doug Fetherling, eds., *Carl Sandburg at the Movies; A Poet in the Silent Era 1920–1927* (Metuchen, New Jersey: Scarecrow Press, 1985), 176.

13. Edward Steichen, *ALP,* page following plate 112.

14. Carl Sandburg, "Chaplin's *The Gold Rush,*" Chicago *Daily News,* August 25, 1925; reprinted in Fetherling and Fetherling, eds., *Carl Sandburg at the Movies,* 136–137.

15. Edward Steichen, "A Fashion Photograph," *Vogue,* October 12, 1929, 99.

16. Edward Steichen quoted in Rosa Reilly, "Steichen," 12.

17. Robert Marks, undated, unpublished manuscript, 13, ASA Yale.

18. Samuel Eliot Morison, *The Oxford History of the American People,* vol. 3 (New York New American Library, 1972), 228.

19. Edward Steichen, *ALP,* page following plate ninety-five.

20. Ibid., page preceding plate ninety-six. This anecdote was also told to PEN by Lucy Kroll in one of many interviews on Sandburg and Steichen.

21. Caroline Seebohm, *The Man Who Was Vogue: The Life and Times of Condé Nast* (New York: Viking Press, 1982), 200–201.

22. Alexander Liberman quoted in Fraser, ed., *On the Edge,* 10; George Carroll Kaiser interview with PEN. Mrs. Kaiser went to New York from Texas at the age of seventeen accompanied by her mother and aunt, and found herself caught up in the "Condé Nast World," she said. She later married band leader Kay Kaiser.

23. M. F. Agha quoted in Caroline Seebohm, *The Man Who Was Vogue,* 233.

24. Edward Steichen, *ALP,* page following plate 156.

25. Carl Sandburg, *Steichen the Photographer,* 55.

26. Robert Marks, undated, unpublished manuscript, ASA Yale.

27. Edward Steichen to Eugene Meyer (1928), EMC LC. See also Minutes, J. Walter Thompson Archives, Duke University, Durham, North Carolina, January 31, 1928, for instance, and Steichen's contracts with J. Walter Thompson, December 1, 1924–November 30, 1931.

28. Carl Sandburg, *Steichen the Photographer,* 64, 68.

29. Ibid., 62, 63, 65.

30. Georgia O'Keeffe, *Georgia O'Keeffe: A Portrait by Alfred Stieglitz* (New York: Metropolitan Museum of Art, 1978), unpaginated.

31. Mrs. Carroll M. ["Mid"] Cain interview with PEN.

32. Ibid.

33. Ibid.

34. Ibid; "where Charlotte . . . the firelight," Kate Steichen, 1926 Album, KRSC.

35. Mary Steichen Calderone to Donelson F. Hoopes, April 17, 1967, MSCC.

36. Ibid.

37. Clara Smith Steichen to Alfred Stieglitz, January 15 (1935), ASA Yale.

38. Mildred Aldrich to Gertrude Stein, August 3, 1925, GSC Yale.

39. Mary Steichen Calderone quoted in Mary Vespa, "America's Biggest Problem," *People,* January 21, 1980, 78.

40. Mary Steichen Calderone quoted in Lynn Gilbert and Gaylen Moore, *Particular Passions: Talks with Women Who Have Shaped Our Times* (New York: Clarkson N. Potter Publishers, Inc. 1982), 261.

41. Mrs. Carroll M. ["Mid"] Cain interview with PEN.

42. Helga Sandburg, *Sweet Music: A Book of Family Reminiscence and Song* (New York: Dial Press, 1963), 32.

43. Mary Steichen Calderone interview with PEN; Helga Sandburg interview with PEN; Margaret Sandburg interview with PEN.

44. Helga Sandburg, *Sweet Music,* 32; Helga Sandburg, *A Great and Glorious Romance: The Story of Carl Sandburg and Lilian Steichen* (New York: Harcourt Brace Jovanovich, 1978), 305.

45. Mary Steichen Calderone, "My Father," *Infinity* (December 1954 to January 1955): 16.

46. Edward Steichen, *ALP,* page preceding plate ninety-six.

47. Carl Sandburg, *Steichen the Photographer,* 56.

48. Ibid., 63.

49. Ibid., 63–64.

50. Edward Steichen to Eugene Meyer (1926), EMC LC.

51. Edward Steichen to Carl Sandburg (1926), CSC UI.

52. Carl Sandburg, *Steichen the Photographer,* 67.

53. See Marielle Tabart, "Brancusi: L'Inventeur de la Sculpture Moderne." Collection de Couvertes Gallimard, *Séries et Variations,* no. 243, 72.

54. Ibid., 82–83.

55. Constantin Brancusi quoted by Edward Steichen to Dimitrie Popescu, transcript of *Voice of America* interview, April 17, 1962.

56. Steichen discussed the affair at length in *ALP,* as well as in interviews such as the one given to Dimitrie Popescu. For background, see also Marielle Tabart, "Brancusi; L'Inventeur de la Sculpture Moderne," and Aline B. Saarinen, "The Strange Story of Brancusi," *New York Times Magazine,* October 23, 1955. The particulars of the case are found in United States Treasury Department, Customs Court, Third Division, Protest Record No. 209109-G., "C. Brancusi vs. United States," New York, October 21, 1927–March 23, 1928; final decision rendered in favor of Brancusi, November 26, 1928.

57. Edward Steichen quoted by Linette Burton in the *Wilton* [Connecticut] *Bulletin,* December 5, 1962. It is interesting to speculate about whether there is any connection between Brancusi's egg forms and Steichen's *Triumph of the Egg.*

58. Helga Sandburg interview with PEN; Helga Sandburg, *". . . Where Love Begins"* (New York: Donald I. Fine, Inc., 1989), 49–50.

59. Helga Sandburg and Margaret Sandburg interviews with PEN; Helga Sandburg, *". . . Where Love Begins,"* 49–51.

60. Edward Steichen, *ALP,* page following plate 209.

61. Mary Steichen Calderone quoted in Lynn Gilbert and Gaylen Moore, *Particular Passions,* 255.

62. Mary Steichen Calderone quoted in Vespa, "America's Biggest Problem," 78.

63. Mary Steichen Calderone quoted in Thomas C. Hunter, *Beginnings* (New York: Thomas Y. Crowell, 1978), 62.

64. Ibid.

65. Mary Steichen Calderone quoted in Don Gold, *Until the Singing Stops: Life and Old Age in America* (New York: Holt, Rinehart and Winston, 1971), 318–319.

66. Edward Steichen to Eugene Meyer (1928), EMC LC.
67. Edward Steichen, "A Fashion Photograph," 99.

27. A NEW VISION (1929–1934)

1. Carl Sandburg, *Steichen the Photographer* (New York: Harcourt, Brace and Company, 1929), 57.
2. Carl Sandburg annotation, revised typescript, *Steichen the Photographer*, CSC UI.
3. Carl Sandburg, *Steichen the Photographer*, preface, n.p.
4. Ibid., 51–52.
5. Ibid., 52.
6. Ibid., 53.
7. Ibid., 53–54.
8. Ibid., 53–55.
9. Rosa Reilly, "Steichen—The Living Legend," *Popular Photography*, March 1938, 12.
10. Mike Gold, *The New Masses*, May 1930. Paul Strand, ostensibly the voice of Stieglitz, expanded the attack in "Steichen and Commercial Art," *The New Republic*, February 19, 1930.
11. Paul Rosenfeld, "Carl Sandburg and Photography," *The New Republic*, January 22, 1930, 251–252.
12. Carl Sandburg, *The People, Yes*, in *The Complete Poems of Carl Sandburg* (New York: Harcourt, Brace & World, 1950).
13. Clara Steichen to Alfred Stieglitz, May 3 (1928), ASA Yale.
14. Michael Joyce to Clara Steichen, June 22, 1928, ESA MoMA.
15. Clara Steichen to Alfred Stieglitz, May 27, 1935, ASA Yale.
16. Carl Sandburg, *Steichen the Photographer*, 65.
17. Mary Kemp Steichen, unpublished manuscript, MSC.
18. Mary Kemp "Oma" Steichen to Margaret Sandburg (no date), MCS.
19. Mary Kemp "Oma" Steichen to Margaret Sandburg (December 1932), MSC.
20. Edward Steichen to Paula Sandburg (May 24, 1933), CSC UI.
21. Edward Steichen to Mary and John Peter Steichen (May 24, 1933), CSC UI.
22. Carl Sandburg, *Steichen the Photographer*, 47–48.
23. Nicholas Haz, "Steichen," *Camera Craft*, January 1936, 8.
24. Edward Steichen to Alfred Stieglitz (October 7, 1932), ASA Yale. This date is written on the letter, but not in Steichen's handwriting. Georgia O'Keeffe apparently returned to Lake George alone on October 6. It can be conjectured, therefore, that either Steichen went to Lake George September 30, and someone misdated his letter to Stieglitz, or O'Keeffe, for whatever reason, did not see the Steichens during their visit.
25. See Benita Eisler, *O'Keeffe & Stieglitz: An American Romance* (New York: Doubleday, 1991), 370–372.
26. Alfred Stieglitz, "Letters to the Editor," *Art News*, April 1928.
27. Edward Steichen quoted in Lenore Cisney and John Reddy, "Steichen: Dissatisfied Genius," *The Saturday Review*, December 14, 1957, 28.
28. Alfred Stieglitz to Ansel Adams, October 20, 1933, ASA Yale.
29. Alfred Stieglitz to Ansel Adams, December 7, 1933, ASA Yale.
30. Alfred Stieglitz quoted in Dorothy Norman, *Alfred Stieglitz: An American Seer* (New York: Random House, 1973), 208.
31. Edward Steichen to Paula Sandburg (May 24, 1933), CSC UI.
32. Edward Steichen to Mary Kemp Steichen (May 24, 1933), CSC UI.
33. Dana Steichen to Mary Kemp Steichen (June 26, 1933), CSC UI.
34. Edward Steichen to Mary Kemp Steichen (no date), CSC UI.
35. Margaret Sandburg interview with PEN; Helga Sandburg interview with PEN.
36. Paula Sandburg to Edward and Dana Steichen (1933), CSC UI.
37. Helga Sandburg interview with PEN.
38. The account of Oma's death and funeral and Opa's decision comes from Helga Sandburg interviews with PEN and Margaret Sandburg interviews with PEN.
39. Edward Steichen quoted in Reilly, "Steichen—The Living Legend," Popular Photography, 89.
40. Kate Steichen to Edna Ferber, July 11, 1956, quoted in the *Wilton* [Connecticut] *Bulletin*, May 3, 1989.
41. Kate Rodina Steichen, Wilton Library Oral History, Wilton, Connecticut, 1983, 6, KRSC.
42. Margaret Sandburg interview with PEN; Francesca Calderone-Steichen interview with PEN; Carol Silverberg, *It Just Occurred to Me* (Wilton, Connecticut: private printing, 1981), 26.
43. Clara Steichen to Alfred Stieglitz (no date), ASA Yale.
44. Clara Steichen to Alfred Stieglitz, December 13, 1931, ASA Yale.
45. Ibid.
46. Clara Steichen to Alfred Stieglitz, February 21, 1932, ASA Yale.
47. Clara Steichen to Alfred Stieglitz, January 29, 1935, ASA Yale.
48. Haz, "Steichen," 6.
49. Sterling Patterson, "Fifty Thousand Children," *Better Homes & Gardens*, July 1938, 13.
50. Matthew Josephson, "Commander with a Camera—I," *The New Yorker*, June 3, 1944, 29.
51. Linda Roth, Henry Woolsey, and Ellen Baum, *Huckleberry Swamp and Adjacent Uplands, Redding Connecticut: An Ecological Survey of the Edward Steichen Memorial Wildlife Preserve* (Connecticut Audubon Society, 1979), 5.
52. Carl Sandburg quoted by Harry Golden in interview with PEN; Margaret Sandburg interview with PEN.
53. Carl Sandburg, *Steichen the Photographer*, 63; Margaret Sandburg interview with PEN.
54. Edward Steichen quoted in Josephson, "Commander with a Camera—I," 29.
55. Edward Steichen quoted in Reilly, "Steichen," 88–89.
56. Carl Sandburg, *Steichen the Photographer*, 62.
57. Edward Steichen to Matthew Josephson (no date), in preparation for Josephson's two-part article "Commander with a Camera" for *The New Yorker*, Matthew Josephson Collection, Yale.
58. Ibid.

59. Matthew Josephson, "Commander with a Camera—II," *The New Yorker,* June 10, 1944, 36–37.
60. Edward Steichen to Matthew Josephson (no date), Matthew Josephson Collection, Yale.
61. Edward Steichen to Mary and John Peter Steichen, June 26, 1933, CSC UI.
62. Edward Steichen to Matthew Josephson (no date), Matthew Josephson Collection, Yale.
63. Lucy Kroll interview with PEN; Margaret Sandburg interview with PEN; also quoted in Carl Sandburg, *Steichen the Photographer,* and in other published sources, such as Cisney and Reddy, "Steichen—Photography's Dissatisfied Genius."

28. VIOLATING EVERY RULE (1935–1939)

1. Edward Steichen quoted in Sterling Patterson, "Fifty Thousand Children," *Better Homes & Gardens,* July 1938, 13.
2. Edward Steichen, *ALP,* page preceding plate 157.
3. Ibid.
4. Ibid.
5. Matthew Josephson, "Commander with a Camera—I," *The New Yorker,* June 3, 1944, 30.
6. Ibid., 34.
7. Edna Chase quoted in Caroline Seebohm, *The Man Who Was Vogue: The Life and Times of Condé Nast* (New York: Viking Press, 1982), 217–218.
8. Edward Steichen, *ALP,* page following plate 209.
9. Carol Silverberg, *It Just Occurred to Me* (private printing, 1981), 9.
10. Clara Steichen to Alfred Stieglitz, January 15, 1935, ASA Yale.
11. Ibid.
12. Ibid.
13. Ibid.
14. Ibid.
15. Ibid.
16. Clara Steichen to Alfred Stieglitz, January 29, 1935, ASA Yale.
17. Mary Steichen Calderone quoted by Mary Vespa, "America's Biggest Problem?" *People,* January 21, 1980, 78.
18. Mary Steichen Calderone quoted in Don Gold, *When the Singing Stops: A Celebration of Life and Old Age in America* (New York: Holt Rinehart and Winston, 1971), 328.
19. Mary Steichen Calderone quoted in Thomas C. Hunter, *Beginnings* (New York: Thomas Y. Crowell, 1978), 57–58.
20. Edward Steichen quoted in Rosa Reilly, "Steichen—The Living Legend," *Popular Photography,* March 1938, 89.
21. Mary Steichen Calderone quoted in Hunter, *Beginnings,* 57–58.
22. Mary Steichen Calderone to Clara Steichen, November 13, 1941, MSCC.
23. Mary Steichen Calderone quoted in Hunter, *Beginnings,* 62.
24. Clara Steichen to Alfred Stieglitz, May 27, 1935, ASA Yale.
25. Clara Steichen to Mary Steichen [Calderone], October 26, 1939, MSCC.
26. Clara Steichen to Alfred Stieglitz, May 27, 1935, ASA Yale.
27. Sketch and text in MSCC.
28. Clara Steichen to Alfred Stieglitz, January 15, 1935, ASA Yale.
29. Ibid.
30. Tom Maloney quoted in Edward Steichen, ed., *U.S. Navy War Photographs: Pearl Harbor to Tokyo Bay* (New York: Bonanza Books, 1980 reprint), 9.
31. Patterson, "Fifty Thousand Children," 13.
32. Ibid.
33. Ibid.
34. Ibid.
35. Ibid.
36. Ibid.
37. "Bulliet's Artless Comment," Chicago *Daily News,* June 27, 1936.
38. J. W. Johnston, "Giant Growths of Delphinium Exhibited Here," New York *Herald Tribune,* June 25, 1936.
39. Carl Sandburg, "Experiments Toward a Poem on Delphiniums," unpublished manuscript, undated, CSC UI.
40. For a detailed study of the MoMA exhibition and its genesis, see Ronald J. Gedrim, "Edward Steichen's 1936 Exhibition of Delphinium Blooms: An Art of Flower Breeding," *History of Photography,* vol. 17, no. 4 (Winter 1993): 352–363. In terms of Steichen's motive in mounting the exhibit, Gedrim writes (361), "It is fair to say that Steichen mounted an exhibition that superseded the early concerns of modernism to challenge both the role of the museum and commonly held definitions of art. His philosophy of 'art for life's sake' opened museum doors to the art of flower breeding as one of a myriad of possible art forms."
41. Edward Steichen, notice in the advertising section, *Delphinium,* 1936.
42. Edward Steichen, "The F.S.A. Photographers," *U.S. Camera Annual* (New York: U.S. Camera Publishing Company, 1939), 43; Margaret Sandburg interview with PEN.
43. Gordon Parks, *Voices in the Mirror: An Autobiography* (New York: Doubleday, 1990), 75.
44. Ibid., 94.
45. Condé Nast's announcement of *Glamour,* February 1939, quoted in Seebohm, *The Man Who Was Vogue,* 332.
46. Carl Sandburg, *Steichen the Photographer* (New York: Harcourt, Brace and Company, 1929), 324.
47. Gilbert Millstein, " 'De Lawd' of Modern Photography," *New York Times Magazine,* March 22, 1959, 34.
48. Clare Boothe Brokaw, *Vanity Fair,* June 1932, quoted by D. J. Ebin, "Vanity Fair Magazine Photographer," *Infinity,* December 1954–January 1955, 7.
49. Edward Steichen, *ALP,* page following plate 209.
50. *Vogue,* January 1, 1938, 20c.
51. Ibid., 87.
52. Ibid, 77.
53. *Annual Advertising Awards Number of Advertising & Selling,* 1938, 40.
54. Margaret Case Harriman, "Steichen," *Vogue,* January 1, 1938, 37.
55. Reilly, "Steichen—The Living Legend," 11.
56. Ibid.
57. Carl Sandburg, *Steichen the Photographer,* 67.
58. Edward Steichen, "My Life in Photography," *The Saturday Review,* March 28, 1959, 17. Steichen is quoted

similarly by Millstein, " 'De Lawd' of Modern Photography," 34.

59. Reilly, "Steichen—The Living Legend," 11.
60. Carl Sandburg, *Steichen the Photographer,* 70.
61. Edward Steichen, *ALP,* page following plate 209.
62. Edward Steichen quoted in Reilly, "Steichen—The Living Legend," 12.
63. "Career, Camera, Corn," *Time,* January 10, 1938, 36.
64. Ibid.
65. *Life,* February 21, 1938. See pages 42–45. *Life* staff photographer Bernard Hoffman took the photographs of Sandburg.
66. Helga Sandburg, "... *Where Love Begins"* (New York: Donald I. Fine, Inc., 1989), 77.
67. Paula Sandburg to Edward and Dana Steichen, quoted in Helga Sandburg, "... *Where Love Begins,"* 74.
68. Carl Sandburg, untitled manuscript, CSC UI.
69. Edward Steichen, "The F.S.A. Photographers," 43.
70. Roy Stryker, "Documentary Photography," *Encyclopedia of Photography,* vol. 7 (New York: Greystone Press, 1963): 1180.
71. Edward Steichen, "The F.S.A. Photographers," 43–45.
72. Ibid., 44.
73. Ibid., 44.
74. Christopher Phillips, *Steichen at War* (New York: Portland House, 1987), 16.
75. Margaret Sandburg interview with PEN.
76. Edward Steichen, *ALP,* second page after plate 164.
77. Edward Steichen to Carl and Paula Sandburg, January 11, 1939, CSC UI.
78. "Modern Solution," *House & Garden,* February 1944, 24.
79. During the decade of the 1930s, Steichen was fascinated with all types of scientific photography, especially astronomical photography, ultraspeed photography, and photomicrography. Writing in the photographic monthly *Camera Craft* in 1936, Nicholas Haz reported on Steichen's tools and methods. His camera of choice was an eight-by-ten Eastman studio model, with a special built-in rising and falling shutter. Outside his studio, he worked with a Folmer eight-by-ten commercial camera and a Rolliflex. Outdoors, he used an Anco five-by-seven view camera. He kept a Bantam Kodak handy, recommending it as the best camera for the amateur interested in snapshots. It was a democratic tool, accessible, cheap, and easy to use. He preferred Nator and Protar lenses, in addition to Schneider Symmar lenses, in different focal lengths. He frequently used a tilting tripod head.

Long an expert in the applications of color photography, Steichen launched the 1930s affection for color with his 1931 direct-color photograph of Peggy Hopkins Joyce, and he produced the first color photograph for a *Vogue* cover in July 1932. His 1933 picture of Harriet Hoctor was the first indoor action snapshot in full color. He photographed the Radio City Music Hall corps de ballet in action in "high-speed color, at 1/1000 of a second shutter, synchronized to flash" (D. J. Ebin, "Vanity Fair Magazine Photographer," *Infinity,* December 1954–January 1955, 19). In 1936, he was working with the one-shot, three-color separation process, using eight-by-ten plates or films at high speed, with small lens stops and the necessary intense lighting.

He preferred semimatte surfaces for his prints. Asked to name the greatest advances in photographic techniques in the thirties, he listed the supersensitive panchromatic emulsion and the electric actinometer. He was also experimenting with infrared photography, and he admired Edgerton's and Germeshausen's stroboscopic photography. Over the years Steichen installed a highly efficient darkroom and laboratory at Umpawaug, and with the help of various technical assistants, including Rolf Petersen and Noel Deeks, he carried out his sophisticated experiments in photography.
80. Carl Sandburg, *Home Front Memo* (New York: Harcourt, Brace and Company, 1943), 307.
81. *House & Garden,* February 1944, cover.
82. Silverberg, *It Just Occurred to Me,* 27.
83. Edward Steichen to Carl and Paula Sandburg, January 11, 1939, CSC UI.

29. A REAL IMAGE OF WAR (1939–1943)

1. Edward Steichen, *ALP,* page following plate 222.
2. Clara Steichen to Alfred Stieglitz, October 23 (1939), ASA Yale.
3. Franklin Delano Roosevelt, Fireside Chat, September 3, 1939.
4. Edward Steichen, *ALP,* page following plate 222.
5. Eugene Meyer to Harold H. Anderson, January 22, 1937, EMC LC.
6. Edward Steichen to Eugene Meyer (1928), EMC LC.
7. Edward Steichen to Eugene Meyer (no date), EMC LC.
8. Eugene Meyer to Edward Steichen, October 10, 1940, EMC LC.
9. Eugene Meyer to Donald M. Nelson, October 26, 1940, EMC LC.
10. Carl Sandburg, *Home Front Memo* (New York: Harcourt, Brace and Company, 1943), 29. Sandburg gave November 6, 1940, as the date for his address.
11. Franklin Delano Roosevelt, Fireside Chat, December 29, 1940.
12. Edward Steichen, *ALP,* page following plate 222.
13. George Waters to Wayne Miller, December 10, 1980, WMC.
14. Alfred Stieglitz to Annie Brigman, February 15, 1940, ASA Yale.
15. Alfred Stieglitz to Edward Steichen, June 15, 1941, ASA Yale; ESA MoMA.
16. Ibid.
17. Beaumont Newhall, *Focus* (Boston: Bulfinch Press, 1993), 64.
18. Carl Sandburg, *Home Front Memo,* 311.
19. Edward Steichen, *ALP,* page following plate 222.
20. Carl Sandburg, *Home Front Memo,* 126.
21. Edward Steichen, *ALP,* page following plate 222.
22. Edward Steichen, ed., *U.S. Navy War Photographs: Pearl Harbor to Tokyo Bay* (New York: Bonanza Books, 1980), 10.
23. Helga Sandburg interview with PEN; see also Helga Sandburg, "... *Where Love Begins"* (New York: Donald I. Fine, Inc., 1989), 103.
24. George Waters to Wayne Miller, December 10, 1980, WMC. Waters was a photo officer in the Public Relations Department of the Secretary of the Navy's office, and later a photo officer for a navy reconnaissance

squadron. When he was assigned to Admiral Nimitz's Advance Headquarters staff on Guam, he worked with Steichen on at least one project.

25. George Waters to Wayne Miller, December 10, 1980, WMC.
26. Franklin Delano Roosevelt, Fireside Chat, December 9, 1941.
27. Carl Sandburg, *Home Front Memo,* 126.
28. Carl Sandburg, *Home Front Memo,* 308.
29. For more background, see Frederick R. Neely, "Wing Talk," *Collier's,* March 31, 1945.
30. Christopher Phillips, *Steichen at War* (New York: Portland House, 1987), 20.
31. Edward Steichen, *ALP,* page following plate 222.
32. Steichen gave the first names of these officers erroneously in some of his accounts; this is the correct name for Radford, and, as far as can be determined, for Doyle.
33. Phillips, *Steichen at War,* 22.
34. Helga Sandburg, "... *Where Love Begins,"* 103.
35. Carl Sandburg, *Home Front Memo,* 148.
36. Carl Sandburg, *Home Front Memo,* 306.
37. *The Bulletin of the Museum of Modern Art,* June 1942, 19.
38. Carl Sandburg, *Home Front Memo,* 308.
39. Herbert Bayer quoted in Paul Hill and Thomas Cooper, eds., *Dialogue with Photography* (New York: Farrar Straus Giroux, 1979), 125.
40. Ibid.
41. Carl Sandburg, *Home Front Memo,* 306.
42. Edward Steichen to Paula Sandburg (May 1942), CSC UI.
43. Carl Sandburg, *Home Front Memo,* 308–309.
44. Ibid., 309.
45. Ibid.
46. Edward Steichen to Paula Sandburg (May 1942), CSC UI.
47. For background on the exhibition, see Carl Sandburg, *Home Front Memo,* 306–310, and "Road to Victory: A Procession of Photographs of the Nation at War," *The Bulletin of the Museum of Modern Art,* June 1942, 5–6.
48. Steichen to Paula Sandburg (May 1942), CSC UI.
49. Christopher Phillips, *Steichen at War,* 19.
50. Henry McBride, New York *Sun,* May 22, 1942.
51. Edward Alden Jewell, *New York Times,* June 7, 1942.
52. Edward Steichen to Matthew Josephson (no date), Matthew Josephson Collection, Yale.
53. Nancy Newhall, "Alfred Stieglitz: Notes for a Biography," in *From Adams to Stieglitz: Pioneers of Modern Photography* (New York: Aperture, 1989), 99.
54. Ibid., 120.
55. Ibid.
56. Ibid.
57. Nancy Newhall to Alfred Stieglitz, Labor Day, 1942, ASA Yale.
58. Ibid.
59. Edward Steichen to Carl Sandburg, October 31, 1942, CSC UI.
60. Edward Steichen to Carl Sandburg (October 1942), CSC UI.
61. Paula Sandburg to John Peter Steichen, December 16, 1942, MSC.
62. Paula Sandburg to Edward Steichen, June 6, 1942, CSC UI.
63. Ibid.
64. John Peter Steichen to Carl and Paula Sandburg, September 10, 1939, MSC.
65. Edward Steichen to Carl Sandburg, October 31, 1942, CSC UI.
66. Dana Steichen to Paula Sandburg, December 30, 1942, MSC.
67. Ibid.
68. Ibid.
69. Edward Steichen to Wayne Miller, quoted in Victor Jorgensen, "Captain, USNR," *Infinity,* December 1954–January 1955, 9.
70. Edward Steichen, *ALP,* page following plate 222.
71. Wayne Miller quoted in Phillips, *Steichen at War,* 23.
72. Wayne Miller interview with PEN; see also Wayne Miller, "Steichen—My Friend," in *Steichen/109* (Milwaukee: University of Wisconsin—Milwaukee Art Museum, 1988), 15.
73. Jorgenson, "Captain, USNR," 9.
74. Wayne Miller, "Steichen—My Friend," 13.
75. Jorgenson, "Captain, USNR," 9.
76. Hill and Cooper, eds., *Dialogue with Photography,* 260.
77. Wayne Miller interview with PEN; Wayne Miller, unpublished manuscript, March 25, 1954, WMC.
78. Jorgenson, "Captain, USNR," 9.
79. For background on the Groton–New London expedition, see Catherine Tuggle, "Edward Steichen: War, History and Humanity," *History of Photography,* vol. 17, no. 4 (winter 1993): 364–368.
80. Jorgenson, "Captain, USNR," 9.
81. Ibid.
82. Edward Steichen to Carl and Paula Sandburg, November 10, 1943, CSC UI.
83. Ibid.
84. Ibid.
85. Jorgenson, "Captain, USNR," 9.
86. Ibid.
87. Jorgenson, "Captain, USNR," 20–21.
88. Margaret Sandburg interview with PEN.

30. THE UNIVERSAL LANGUAGE (1943–1946)

1. "Steichen's 'Family' Makes Him Proud Father," *Washington Post and Times Herald,* January 15, 1958.
2. Helga Sandburg, "... *Where Love Begins"* (New York: Donald I. Fine, 1989), 117.
3. Ibid.
4. Edward Steichen, *The Blue Ghost: A Photographic Log and Personal Narrative of the Aircraft Carrier USS Lexington in Combat Operations* (New York: Harcourt, Brace and Company, 1947), 125.
5. Carl Sandburg to Kenneth Dodson, June 6, 1947, CSC UI; Herbert Mitgang, ed., *The Letters of Carl Sandburg* (New York: Harcourt, Brace & World, Inc., 1968), 445.
6. Christopher Phillips, *Steichen at War* (New York: Portland House, 1987), 44.
7. Frederick R. Neely, "Wing Talk," *Collier's,* March 31, 1945, 74.
8. Ibid.
9. Edward Steichen to Paula Sandburg (no date), CSC UI.
10. Ibid.

11. Dana Steichen to Carl and Paula Sandburg, March 29, 1944, CSC UI.
12. Edward Steichen to Paula Sandburg (fall 1944), CSC UI.
13. Clara Steichen to Alfred Stieglitz, July 11, 1944, ASA Yale.
14. Ibid.
15. Mary Steichen to Clara Steichen, October 24 (no year date), MSCC.
16. Edward Steichen to Paula Sandburg (no date), CSC UI. Helga Sandburg interview with PEN.
17. John Peter Steichen to the Sandburgs, July 31, 1935, MSC.
18. Carl Sandburg, unpublished manuscript, December 9, 1944, CSC UI.
19. Carl Sandburg, unpublished notes, CSC UI.
20. Carl Sandburg, unpublished manuscript, December 9, 1944, CSC UI.
21. Edward Steichen to Eugene Meyer (no date), EMC LC.
22. Wayne Miller interview with PEN.
23. Steichen also encouraged the Sandburgs to consider Hawaii, predicting that modern air travel would soon make travel to and from the mainland quite convenient.
24. Helga Sandburg, ". . . Where Love Begins," 133.
25. Ibid., 134.
26. Ibid., 133.
27. Dana Steichen to Paula Sandburg (no date), CSC UI.
28. Tom Maloney quoted in Edward Steichen, ed., *U.S. Navy War Photographs: Pearl Harbor to Tokyo Bay* (New York: Bonanza Books), 11.
29. Wayne Miller interview with PEN. See also Phillips, *Steichen at War,* 43.
30. Edward Steichen, "My Life in Photography," *The Saturday Review,* March 28, 1959, 17.
31. Ibid.
32. In *Home Front Memo,* dedicated to Stephen Vincent Benét, Carl Sandburg wrote these words about Benét, reflecting his views about writing and art in general: "He illustrated the code and creed of those writers who seek to widen the areas of freedom for all men, knowing that men of ideas vanish first when freedom vanishes. He saw that a writer's silence on living issues can in itself constitute a propaganda of conduct leading to the deterioration or death of freedom. He wrote often hoping that men would act because of his words" (Carl Sandburg, *Home Front Memo* [New York: Harcourt, Brace and Company, 1943], dedication).
33. Carl Sandburg, *The People, Yes* (New York: Harcourt, Brace and Company, 1936), 55.
34. Susan D. Moeller, *Shooting War: Photography and the American Experience of Combat* (New York: Basic Books, Inc., 1989), 192.
35. George Bailey, "Photographer's America," *New York Times Magazine,* August 31, 1947, 39.
36. Margaret Sandburg interview with PEN. See also Phillips, *Steichen at War,* 53.
37. Dana Steichen to Paula Sandburg, January 1, 1946, CSC UI.
38. Matthew Josephson to Edward Steichen, January 25, 1944, Matthew Josephson Collection, Yale.
39. Carl Sandburg to Lloyd Lewis (December 1945), CSC UI; Mitgang, ed., *The Letters of Carl Sandburg,* 431.
40. Edward Steichen to Paula Sandburg (no date), CSC UI.
41. Edward Steichen, "My Life in Photography," 17.
42. Tom Maloney quoted in Edward Steichen, ed., *U.S. Navy War Photographs,* 10.
43. Maloney stated that it was Eugene Meyer's seventy-fifth birthday. Meyer was born October 31, 1875. Maloney must have meant the seventieth birthday, which would have been October 31, 1945. The seventy-fifth birthday, in 1950, postdates Steichen's appointment to the MoMA position.
44. Tom Maloney quoted in Edward Steichen, ed., *U.S. Navy War Photographs,* 10.
45. Edward Steichen, "My Life in Photography," 17.
46. Nancy Newhall quoted in Beaumont Newhall, *Focus: Memoirs of a Life in Photography* (Boston: Bulfinch Press, 1993), 128.
47. Beaumont Newhall, *Focus,* 128.
48. Ibid., 132.
49. Ibid., 148.
50. Ansel Adams quoted in Newhall, *Focus,* 148–149.
51. Newhall, *Focus,* 146.
52. Ibid., 147.
53. Ibid.
54. Ibid., 149.
55. See "Museum of Modern Art Photo Department," *U.S. Camera,* vol. 1, no. 14 (February 1941): 28, 82.
56. Ansel Adams to Alfred Stieglitz, March 2, 1941, ASA Yale.
57. Ansel Adams to Stephen Clark, April 19, 1946, quoted in Newhall, *Focus,* 150–152.
58. Ansel Adams to Alfred Stieglitz, March 15, 1946, ASA Yale.
59. Nancy Newhall to Edward Weston, June 1946; quoted in Newhall, *Focus,* 152.
60. Newhall, *Focus,* 152.
61. Ibid., 165.
62. Ibid.
63. Ibid.
64. Edward Steichen, "My Life in Photography," 18.
65. Edward Steichen, *ALP,* page following plate 225.
66. Dana Steichen to Paula Sandburg (March 1946), CSC UI.
67. Edward Steichen to Paula Sandburg (March 1946), CSC UI.
68. Alfred Stieglitz to Georgia O'Keeffe, June 3, 1946, ASA Yale; quoted in Anita Pollitzer, *A Woman on Paper: Georgia O'Keeffe* (New York: Simon & Schuster, 1988), 250.
69. Alfred Stieglitz to Georgia O'Keeffe, July 8, 1946, ASA Yale; quoted in Pollitzer, *A Woman on Paper,* 250.
70. Mary Steichen Calderone interview with PEN.
71. Edward Steichen, *ALP,* page preceding plate forty-four.
72. Paul Rosenfeld, "The Boy in the Dark Room," in Waldo Frank et al., eds., *America & Alfred Stieglitz* (New York: Literary Guild, 1934), 80.
73. Edward Steichen, "The Fighting Photo-Secession," *Vogue,* June 15, 1941, 22.
74. Sue Davidson Lowe, *Stieglitz: A Memoir/Biography* (New York: Farrar Straus Giroux, 1983), 194.
75. Ibid., 377.
76. Nancy Newhall quoted in Newhall, *Focus,* 162; Lowe, *Stieglitz,* 377.
77. Nancy Newhall quoted in Newhall, *Focus,* 162.

78. Penelope Niven, *Carl Sandburg: A Biography* (New York: Charles Scribner's Sons, 1992), 703, 804.
79. Anita Pollitzer, *A Woman on Paper,* 251.
80. Lowe, *Stieglitz,* 377.
81. Alfred Stieglitz quoted in Nancy Newhall, "Alfred Stieglitz: Notes for a Biography," in *From Adams to Stieglitz: Pioneers of Modern Photography* (New York: Aperture, 1989), 121. Because, as has been noted, there are inaccuracies in Nancy Newhall's notes on Stieglitz's comments about Steichen, I have quoted them judiciously.
82. Georgia O'Keeffe, *Georgia O'Keeffe: A Portrait by Alfred Stieglitz* (New York: Metropolitan Museum of Art, 1978), unpaginated.

31. "THE FAMILY OF MAN" (1947–1955)

1. Carl Sandburg's prologue, *The Family of Man* (New York: Museum of Modern Art/Maco Magazine Corporation, 1955), 3.
2. "A Portfolio of Photographs by Edward Steichen," *Life,* May 15, 1950, 117.
3. Edward Steichen to Wayne and Joan Miller (no date), WMC.
4. Nelson A. Rockefeller quoted in "Steichen Named to Museum Post," *U.S. Camera,* October 1947, 17, 50.
5. "Steichen Named to Museum Post," 50.
6. Ibid.
7. Ibid.
8. Ibid.
9. Edward Steichen, *ALP,* page following plate 225.
10. Edward Steichen, "My Life in Photography," *The Saturday Review,* March 28, 1959, 18.
11. Edward Steichen quoted in Wayne Miller, "Wisdom Series," NBC; reprinted in *Infinity,* December 1954–January 1955, 15.
12. Edward Steichen, *ALP,* second page following plate 225.
13. Beaumont Newhall, *Focus* (Boston: Bulfinch Press, 1993), 149.
14. Edward Steichen, *ALP,* third page following plate 225.
15. Steichen, "My Life in Photography," 18.
16. Edward Steichen quoted in Miller, "Wisdom Series"; reprinted in *Infinity,* December 1954–January 1955, 15.
17. Edward Steichen, *ALP,* third page following plate 225.
18. Ibid.
19. Ibid.
20. Ibid.
21. Ibid., second page following plate 225.
22. Edward Steichen to Helga Sandburg Golby and family (no date), HSC.
23. Wayne Miller, "Steichen—My Friend," in *Steichen/109* (Milwaukee: University of Wisconsin—Milwaukee Art Museum, 1988), 13.
24. Clara Steichen to Mary Steichen, October 26, 1939, MSCC.
25. Mary Steichen Calderone quoted in Lynn Gilbert and Gaylen Moore, *Particular Passions: Talks with Women Who Have Shaped Our Times* (New York: Clarkson N. Potter, Inc., Publishers, 1982), 260.
26. Clara Steichen to Alfred Stieglitz, July 11, 1944, ASA Yale.
27. Ibid.
28. Ibid.
29. Clara Steichen, "Peace," ASA Yale.
30. Wayne Miller interview with PEN.
31. Edward Steichen's introduction, *The Family of Man,* 4. Eric J. Sandeen, in his detailed study of "The Family of Man," suggests that the construction of the exhibit was foreshadowed in the section of Sandburg's *The People, Yes* containing the Lincoln phrase that prompted the title; see Eric J. Sandeen, *Picturing an Exhibition: The Family of Man and 1950s America* (Albuquerque: University of New Mexico Press, 1995), 43–44. Sandeen's useful book places the exhibition in the context of the times and the culture.
32. Edward Steichen's introduction, *The Family of Man,* 4–5.
33. Wayne Miller interview with PEN; Wayne Miller, "Steichen's Family of Man," 1994 typescript, WMC.
34. Steichen, notes, ESA MoMA.
35. Miller, "Steichen—My Friend," 15.
36. Edward Steichen quoted in Miller, "Wisdom Series"; reprinted in *Infinity,* December 1954–January 1955, 3; Wayne Miller, *Infinity,* 13.
37. Wayne Miller, annotations, "Wisdom Series" *Infinity,* December 1954–January 1955, 13.
38. Edward Steichen quoted in Miller, "Wisdom Series"; reprinted in *Infinity,* December 1954–January 1955, 3.
39. Miller, "Steichen's Family of Man."
40. Roger Angell, "Museum of Modern Art," unidentified magazine piece in KSC.
41. Miller, "Steichen—My Friend," 15.
42. Ibid.
43. Wayne Miller, notes, April 9, 1964, WMC.
44. Miller, "Steichen's Family of Man."
45. Wayne Miller, notes, April 9, 1964, WMC.
46. Ibid.
47. Ibid.
48. Miller, "Steichen's Family of Man."
49. Frank Stanton quoted in A. S. Sperber, *Murrow: His Life and Times* (New York: Freundlich Books), 456.
50. Edward Steichen, *ALP,* third page following plate 225.
51. Wayne Miller, notes, April 9, 1964, WMC.
52. Miller, "Steichen's Family of Man."
53. Joan Miller interview with PEN.
54. Wayne Miller, notes, April 9, 1964, WMC.
55. Miller, *Infinity,* December 1954–January 1955, 13.
56. Edward Steichen, *ALP,* third page following plate 225.
57. See Carl Sandburg, "The Unknown War," in *The Complete Poems of Carl Sandburg* (New York: Harcourt, Brace & World, 1950), 646–648.
58. Wayne Miller, *Infinity,* December 1954–January 1955, 13.
59. John Foster Dulles, testimony before the Senate Committee on Foreign Relations, January 15, 1953.
60. President Dwight D. Eisenhower, press conference, June 30, 1954.
61. Edward Steichen's introduction, *The Family of Man,* 4.
62. Edward Steichen, *ALP,* fourth page following plate 225.
63. Carl Sandburg to Edward and Dana Steichen (ca. December 1952), CSC UI; Herbert Mitgang, ed., *The*

Letters of Carl Sandburg (New York: Harcourt, Brace & World, Inc., 1968), 487–488.

64. Carl Sandburg's prologue, *The Family of Man*, 3.
65. Miller, "Steichen's Family of Man."
66. Ibid.
67. Ibid.
68. Steichen, *ALP,* fourth page following plate 225.
69. Wayne Miller interview with PEN.
70. Edward Steichen's introduction, *The Family of Man*, 4.
71. Ibid., 5.
72. Edward Steichen to the Wayne Millers, June 9, 1955, WMC.
73. Edward Steichen quoted in Miller, "Wisdom Series"; reprinted in *Infinity,* December 1954–January 1955, 15.
74. Edward Steichen, "The Family of Man," *Picturescope 3,* July 1955, 7.
75. Wayne Miller interview with PEN.
76. Sandeen, *Picturing an Exhibition,* 3.
77. "Steichen's 'Family' Makes Him Proud Father," *Washington Post and Times Herald,* January 15, 1958.
78. Edward Steichen quoted in James Nelson, ed., *Wisdom: Conversations with the Elder Wise Men of Our Day* (New York: W. W. Norton, 1958), 42–43.

32. THE LAST APPRENTICESHIP (1955–1959)

1. Edward Steichen, *A Life in Photography* (New York: Doubleday and Company, 1963), one page following plates 234–237.
2. Wayne Miller, *Infinity,* December 1954–January 1955, 13.
3. Dana Steichen to Eugene Meyer (Christmas 1954), EMC LC.
4. Ibid.
5. Wayne Miller, quoted by Eric J. Sandeen, *Picturing an Exhibition: The Family of Man and 1950s America* (Albuquerque: University of New Mexico Press, 1995), 50.
6. Wayne Miller interview with PEN. See also Sandeen, *Picturing an Exhibition,* 74–75.
7. Sandeen, *Picturing an Exhibition,* 75. See Sandeen, pp. 95–124, for a discussion of the international impact of the touring exhibition, and for the controversy over whether MoMA and the exhibition "entered willingly into the cultural warfare against the Russians."
8. "Steichen's 'Family' Makes Him Proud Father," *Washington Post and Times Herald,* January 15, 1958.
9. Miller, *Infinity,* December 1954–January 1955, 13.
10. Edward Steichen, *ALP,* fifth page following plate 225.
11. See "The Controversial Family of Man," *Aperture,* vol. 3 (1955).
12. Dorothy Norman quoted in ibid., 15–16.
13. Minor White quoted in Paul Hill and Thomas Cooper, *Dialogue with Photography* (New York: Farrar Straus Giroux, 1979), 357–358.
14. Ibid., 357.
15. Herbert Bayer quoted in Hill and Cooper, *Dialogue with Photography,* 127.
16. Hilton Kramer, "Exhibiting the Family of Man: 'The World's Most Talked About Photographs,'" *Commentary,* vol. 20 (October 1955): 365.
17. Ibid., 366–367.
18. Jacques Barzun, *The House of Intellect* (New York: Harper & Row, 1959), 28–30.
19. Carl Sandburg note to Harry Golden on the margin of page proofs for Golden's *Carl Sandburg* (New York: World Publishing Company, 1961), Harry Golden Collection, Charlotte-Mecklenburg Public Library, Charlotte, North Carolina.
20. André Maurois quoted in "Steichen's 'Family' Makes Him Proud Father."
21. Edward Steichen, *ALP,* page following plate 237.
22. Joan Miller interview with PEN.
23. Ibid.
24. Ibid.
25. Ibid.
26. Sandburgs to Steichens, March 2, 1950, CSC UI.
27. Dana Steichen to Sandburgs, March 2, 1950, CSC UI.
28. Dana Steichen to the Sandburgs (no date), CSC UI.
29. Paula Steichen, *My Connemara* (New York: Harcourt, Brace & World, Inc., 1979), 141–142.
30. Ibid., 143–144.
31. Edward Steichen, biographical notes for *Beethoven's Beloved,* ESA MoMA.
32. Helga Sandburg, "... *Where Love Begins"* (New York: Donald I. Fine, Inc., 1989), 233.
33. Wayne Miller interview with PEN.
34. Helga Sandburg, "... *Where Love Begins,"* 234.
35. Ibid., 234.
36. Carol Silverberg, *It Just Occurred to Me* (private printing, 1981), 26.
37. Helga Sandburg, "... *Where Love Begins,"* 233.
38. Wayne Miller interview with PEN.
39. Wayne Miller interview with PEN. See "Steichen Painting Rediscovered Just Before Hecksher Opening," *The Long-Islander* [Huntington, New York], July 11, 1985. Steichen gave the painting to the Millers, and Miller loaned the painting and the photograph to the Heckscher Museum for an exhibition entitled "The Paintings of Eduard Steichen" in 1985.
40. See Edward Steichen, "My Life in Photography," *The Saturday Review,* March 28, 1959, 18; and Gilbert Millstein, "'De Lawd' of Modern Photography," *New York Times Magazine* March 22, 1959, 36.
41. Edward Steichen, notes for book jacket, ESA MoMA.
42. Edward Steichen quoted in Richard Vesey, "Creative Lens Works in Semi-Doldrum State," *Wisconsin State Journal,* June 23, 1957, 5.
43. Helga Sandburg, "... *Where Love Begins,"* 233.
44. Ibid.
45. Edward Steichen to Agnes Meyer, December 6, 1967, AEMC LC. Steichen wrote that the fire in his laboratory—a separate building apart from the main house—happened about ten years earlier, destroying many of his negatives except, of course, for those stored in his house.
46. Edward Steichen quoted in Millstein, "'De Lawd' of Modern Photography," 38.
47. Ibid., 33.
48. Millstein, "'De Lawd' of Modern Photography," 33.
49. Alexander Liberman, "Steichen's Eye: A Study of the Greatest Living Photographer," *Vogue,* August 1, 1959, 142.

50. Edward Steichen quoted in Millstein, " 'De Lawd' of Modern Photography," 38.
51. Edward Steichen, "My Life in Photography," 18.
52. Lucy Kroll interview with PEN. Lucy Kroll helped to arrange this journey.
53. Kate Steichen to the Sandburgs, June 8, 1959, CSC UI.
54. Details on arrangements for this journey are drawn from a letter to Carl Sandburg from Martha G. Geesa, acting chief, American Specialists Branch, International Educational Exchange Service, Department of State document CU: IES/LSD/RWW, July 7, 1959, CSC UI.
55. Alexander Liberman, "Steichen's Eye," 142.
56. Dates are based on the official itinerary, "Department of State Transportation Information," and the accompanying letter and information from Martha G. Geesa to Carl Sandburg, Department of State document CU: IES/LSD/RWW, July 7, 1959, CSC UI.
57. Edward Steichen, *ALP*, third page following plate forty-three.
58. Mary Steichen Calderone to Agnes Meyer, September 19, 1958, MSCC.
59. Edward Steichen, *ALP*, third page following plate forty-three.
60. Gregory d'Alessio, *Old Troubadour: Carl Sandburg with His Guitar Friends* (New York: Walker and Company, 1987), 139.
61. Gregory d'Alessio interview with PEN.
62. Wayne Miller interview with PEN.
63. Helga Sandburg, "... *Where Love Begins,*" 246, 270.
64. Margaret Sandburg interview with PEN; Lucy Kroll interview with PEN.
65. Edward Steichen, *ALP*, fifth page following plate 225.
66. *Meet the Press* transcript, vol. 3, no. 31 (September 13, 1959): 3.
67. Lucy Kroll interview with PEN.
68. Edward Steichen, *ALP*, page preceding plate 226.
69. Ibid.
70. Silverberg, *It Just Occurred to Me,* 50.
71. *Meet the Press,* transcript, 4.
72. Edward Steichen, *ALP*, page preceding plate 226.
73. Ibid.
74. Helga Sandburg, "... *Where Love Begins,*" 249.
75. Carl Sandburg to Paula Sandburg (1959), MSC.
76. *Meet the Press,* transcript, 2.
77. Steichen would have been pleased to know that Goro Kuramochi, a fifteen-year-old Japanese student who saw "The Family of Man" in Tokyo in 1956, grew up to be an international broker of photography and exhibits, and he brought Steichen's exhibition to Japan in 1993, intact, no pictures held back. More than 36,000 people visited "The Family of Man" in Hiroshima in 1994. See " 'The Family of Man' à Tokyo et à Hiroshima," unidentified news clipping, June 3, 1994, WMC.
78. *Meet the Press* transcript, 4.
79. Clipping from *Afro-American* [Washington, D.C.], August 22, 1959, ESA MoMA.
80. *Meet the Press,* transcript, 4.
81. Ibid., 5.
82. Dana Steichen, *Beethoven's Beloved* (Garden City, New York: Doubleday & Company, 1959), 20.
83. Ibid., 500, 502, 506.
84. Ibid., 496.
85. Ibid.

33. ALL GIANTS BEING LONELY (1959–1973)

1. Carl Sandburg, "Topstone," in Margaret Sandburg, ed., *Breathing Tokens* (New York: Harcourt Brace Jovanovich, 1978), 162.
2. Margaret Sandburg, ed., *Breathing Tokens,* 177.
3. Carl Sandburg, journal note, no date, HSC. See Helga Sandburg, "... *Where Love Begins"* (New York: Donald I. Fine Inc., 1989), 252.
4. Carl Sandburg, "Accept Your Face with Serious Thanks," in Margaret Sandburg, ed., *Breathing Tokens,* 154.
5. Joanna Steichen, *Marrying Up: An American Dream & Reality: Why Some Make It Into the Inner Circle and Others Never Will* (New York: Rawson Associates, 1983), 229.
6. Carl Sandburg, journal note (no date), HSC. See Helga Sandburg, "... *Where Love Begins,"* 252.
7. Margaret Sandburg interview with PEN.
8. Helga Sandburg, "... *Where Love Begins,"* 264.
9. Edward Steichen to Francesca Calderone-Steichen, November 19, 1959, private collection.
10. Joanna Steichen, *Marrying Up,* 229; Mrs. Carroll M. ["Mid"] Cain Interview with PEN.
11. Helga Sandburg, "... *Where Love Begins,"* 264.
12. Mrs. Carroll M. ["Mid"] Cain interview with PEN.
13. Helga Sandburg, "... *Where Love Begins,"* 269.
14. Ibid., 270.
15. Ibid., 271.
16. Norman Corwin interview with PEN.
17. Helga Sandburg, "... *Where Love Begins,"* 278.
18. Margaret Sandburg interview with PEN.
19. Edward Steichen to the Sandburgs, August 5, 1960, CSC UI.
20. Carl Sandburg to Edward Steichen, December 7, 1960, CSC UI.
21. Carl Sandburg to Edward Steichen, May 25, 1961, CSC UI.
22. Guide to Records of the International Programs of the Museum of Modern Art, 1953–1991, MoMA Archives. The exhibition toured in Germany, Luxembourg, Austria, Switzerland, Italy, France, Yugoslavia, Greece, Israel, Greek and Turkish sections of Cyprus, Czechoslovakia, Hungary, Romania, and Poland.
23. Chronology, "Steichen the Photographer," broadside, the United States Information Service & the Royal Photographic Society of Great Britain, no date. The name of the study center was later changed to honor major donors to the museum.
24. For a brief summary, see "The Steichen Archive: For the Record," *The Saturday Review,* November 9, 1968.
25. Agnes Meyer to Edward Steichen, December 15, 1961, AMC LC.
26. Dimitri G. Popescue, transcript of *Voice of America* interview, April 17, 1962.
27. Carl Sandburg to Paula Sandburg, December 30, 1960, CSC UI; Herbert Mitgang, ed., *The Letters of Carl Sandburg* (New York: Harcourt, Brace & World, Inc., 1968), 532.
28. Ibid.

29. Carl Sandburg to Edward Steichen, May 25, 1961, CSC UI.
30. Edward Steichen, *ALP,* page following plate 237.
31. Ibid.
32. Ibid.
33. Ibid.
34. Ibid.
35. Ibid., page preceding plate 238.
36. Mary Steichen Calderone to Agnes Meyer, December 3, 1963, AEMC LC.
37. Ibid.
38. Frederick S. Beebe to Edward Steichen, January 29, 1964, AEMC LC.
39. Quote on book jacket of Edward Steichen's *ALP.*
40. Edward Steichen, *ALP,* page preceding plate one.
41. Popescue, *Voice of America* transcript.
42. Mary Steichen Calderone to Agnes Meyer, December 3, 1963, AEMC LC.
43. "Freedom Medal Citations," *New York Times,* December 7, 1963.
44. Dorothy McCardle, "Party Honors Artist Steichen," *Washington Post,* April 10, 1964.
45. Grace Mayer to Agnes Meyer, April 13, 1964, AEMC LC.
46. Edward Steichen, ed., *U.S. Navy War Photographs: Pearl Harbor to Tokyo Bay* (New York: Bonanza Books, 1980), 11.
47. Paul Strand quoted in Paul Hill and Thomas Cooper, *Dialogue with Photography* (New York: Farrar Straus Giroux, 1979), 5.
48. "The Family of Man," *Taboa,* May 1994.
49. Helga Sandburg, ". . . *Where Love Begins,"* 341.
50. Edward Steichen quoted in Alden Whitman, "Edward Steichen Is Dead at 93; Made Photography an Art Form," *New York Times,* March 26, 1973.
51. Helga Sandburg, ". . . *Where Love Begins,"* 351–352.
52. Ibid., 346.
53. Ibid., 356.
54. Edward Steichen, ed., *Sandburg: Photographers View Carl Sandburg* (New York: Harcourt, Brace & World, Inc., 1966), unpaginated.
55. Agnes Meyer to Joanna Taub Steichen, June 4, 1969; Agnes Meyer to Edward Steichen, June 4, 1969, and April 8, 1970, AEMC LC.
56. Dr. Frank Calderone, memo, June 3, 1969, MSCC.
57. Undated news clipping, Dr. Frank Calderone file, MSCC.
58. Mary Steichen Calderone to Stuart T. Hodes, March 30, 1971, MSCC.
59. Dr. Frank Calderone, memo, October 1, 1970, MSCC.
60. Mary Steichen Calderone, "Eduard Steichen as Painter: A Remembrance," in Alayne Shoenfeld, ed., *The Paintings of Eduard Steichen* (Huntington, New York: Heckscher Museum, 1985), 14–15.
61. "Light and Its Revealed Truths," *Washington Post,* November 11, 1971.
62. Ibid.
63. Elisabeth King to Mary Steichen Calderone, December 27, 1970, MSCC.
64. Dr. Frank Calderone, "Notes on a Meeting of Frank A. Calderone and Mary S. Calderone with Captain Steichen on Sunday, February 14, 1971," MSCC.

65. Dr. Frank Calderone, memo, February 8, 1971, MSCC.
66. Dr. Frank Calderone, notes, February 8, 1971, and February 11, 1971, MSCC.
67. Drs. Frank and Mary Calderone, memo, February 14, 1971, MSCC.
68. Joan D. Ensor, "Action Ends on Steichen Property," *Newtown Record,* March 12, 1971, ESA MoMA.
69. Elisabeth King to Mary Steichen Calderone, December 12, 1971, MSCC.
70. Joanna Steichen, *Marrying Up,* 8–9.
71. Ibid., 229.
72. Mary Steichen Calderone to Helga Sandburg Crile, November 3, 1972, MSCC.
73. Ibid.
74. Ibid.
75. Joanna Steichen to Joan and Wayne Miller, March 18, 1973, WMC.
76. Gilbert Millstein, " 'De Lawd' of Modern Photography," *New York Times Magazine,* March 22, 1959, 38.
77. Joanna Taub Steichen to the Steichen Family, March 18 (1973), MSCC.
78. Linda Roth, Henry Woolsey, and Ellen Baum, *Huckleberry Swamp and Adjacent Uplands, Redding, Connecticut* (Redding, Connecticut: Audubon Society, 1979), 7.
79. Carl Sandburg, "Experiments Toward a Poem on Delphiniums," unpublished manuscript, CSC UI.
80. Millstein, " 'De Lawd' of Modern Photography," 38.
81. Charles Sheeler quoted in "Light and Its Revealed Truths."
82. Remarks by Wayne Miller, Château de Clervaux, Luxembourg, June 3, 1994, typescript, WMC.
83. Carl Sandburg, *Steichen the Photographer* (New York: Harcourt, Brace and Company, 1929), 326–327.
84. Robert Hughes, "The Patriarch of the Family of Man," *Time,* April 9, 1973, 74.
85. Whitman, "Edward Steichen Is Dead at 93."
86. Helga Sandburg, ". . . *Where Love Begins,"* 356.
87. Helga Sandburg, ". . . *Where Love Begins,"* 357.
88. Carl Sandburg, "Experiments Toward a Poem on Delphiniums."
89. Mary Steichen Calderone quoted in Lynn Gilbert and Gaylen Moore, *Particular Passions: Talks with Women Who Have Shaped Our Times* (New York: Clarkson N. Potter, Inc., Publishers, 1982), 262.

Epilogue

1. Remarks delivered by Prime Minister and Minister of Cultural Affairs M. Jacques Santer on the occasion of the official inauguration of "The Family of Man" at the Château de Clervaux, June 3, 1994, Catalog of the Ministere des Affaires Culturelles and Centre national de l'audiovisuel, WMC.
2. Ibid.
3. Remarks by Wayne F. Miller, Château de Clervaux, Luxembourg, June 3, 1994, typescript, WMC.
4. *The Family of Man* (New York: Museum of Modern Art/Maco Magazine Corporation, 1955), 55.

Acknowledgments

THIS BOOK COULD NEVER HAVE BEEN written without the generosity of Francesca Calderone-Steichen and her husband, Joel Stahmer, keepers of the Steichen family legacy. They invited me into their home, allowing me access to their archives and their collection of photographs and paintings and sharing their memories and insights, thereby opening doors and windows to Steichen's world. I am immensely grateful. I owe enduring appreciation to Helga Sandburg for her counsel and insight, and for her rich collection of photographs of the Steichens and the Sandburgs. Without her encouragement and aid, I do not think I would have been able to finish this biography.

I thank my daughter, Jennifer Niven McJunkin, whose love and laughter sustain me, whose disciplined gifts as a writer inspire me, and whose astute and forthright criticisms improve my work.

Any book is a miracle, and my miracle has been made possible in part by the following persons and institutions. I am grateful to them for a variety of contributions, whether in the form of information, materials, research support, interviews, insights, encouragement, criticism, hospitality, or a combination thereof:

My agents, Barbara Hogenson and the late Lucy Kroll; Dr. Tim Redman of the University of Texas at Dallas, fellow biographer; Dr. Laura Dubus of Paris, who served as my eyes and ears in France; my intern and assistant, Robert Hamilton of Wake Forest University and Austin, Texas; my interns David Dritsas and Beth Young of Pennsylvania State University, under the direction of Dr. Shannon Duval; Pamela Allen; Louise Bailey; David Beckett; Dr. Scott Bennett, director of the Yale University Libraries, and Carol Bennett; Alice Birney of the Library of Congress; Nicholas Bragg, director of the Reynolda House Museum of American Art, Winston-Salem, North Carolina, and Nancy Bragg; Dr. John Broderick; Provost David Brown of Wake Forest University; Mid Cain; Maria Calderone; Philip Carson; Cynthia Cathcart, senior librarian, Condé Nast Publications, Inc.; Susan Mullally Clarke; Sophia Cody; Thomas Collins; Helga Mary Steichen Sandburg Crile; Azalee Davidson; Virginia Dodier of the Museum of Modern Art; Patricia Everett; Majie Failey; Patricia Fanning of the Norwood Historical Society; Hope and Evan Farber; Sarah Fieder; Coddy Granum; Maurice Greenbaum; Mary Anne Goley, Fine Arts Program director, the Federal Reserve System, Washington, D.C.; Lisa Hellman of Condé Nast Publications; Dr. George Hendrick of the University of Illinois; Dr. Robert Hobbs; Linda Joan Martin Hodes; Althea Huber of the Art Institute of Chicago; Michael Hurley; Linda and Al Hutchison; James Earl and Cecilia Hart Jones; Georgia Carroll Kaiser; Julia Ann Kelly; Judith Kessler; Joseph Kraemer; Melanie Kendall Kraemer; Jane Loewenstein Levy; Alexander Liberman; Dr. Anne McCauley of the University of Massachusetts; Deborah McKeon-Pogue, Special Collections Division, United States Military Academy; L. Rebecca Johnson Melvin of the University of Delaware Library Special Collections, Newark, Delaware; Kurt Meyer, Academic Librarian, Valley City State University, Valley City, North Dakota; Wayne and Joan Miller; John-Mark Mitchell; Dr. Perry Ottenberg; Mead Parce; Dr. Melinda Parsons of Memphis State University; Avril Peck of the Museum of Modern Art; Paula Steichen Polega; Father Keith Rhodes; Tristan Rhodes; Rona Roob of the Museum of Modern Art; Charles Scheips of Condé Nast Publications; Janet Mary Steichen Sandburg; Margaret Mary Steichen Sandburg; Dr. Christine Shea; Betsy

Acknowledgments

Wallin Sirot; David Solomon; Ariana Rodina Steichen Stahmer; Robert Stewart; Rob and Sara Martha Tyson; Florence and Franklin Wallin; Claude Waringo of Samsa Film, Luxembourg, and his colleagues; Warren Weber, Connie Backlund, Bill Berry, Bess Gibbs, Karen Gibbs, and the wonderful staff and volunteers at the Carl Sandburg Home NHS; Dr. Edwin Wilson of Wake Forest University; Emily Herring Wilson; and Isabel Zuber.

I am also grateful for the resources of the Z. Smith Reynolds Library at Wake Forest University, my indispensable library home. I send my enduring appreciation to Ralph Franklin, director, and Patricia Willis, curator of the Collection of American Literature, the Beinecke Rare Book and Manuscript Library, Yale University, that paradise for scholars because of the treasures and the people there. Sandra Markham, Stephen Jones, Lori Misura, William Hemmig, Tim Young, and Maureen D. Heher were particularly helpful in the research for this book.

I express loving gratitude to my wonderful family: Jennifer, of course, and my parents, Olin and Eleanor Marsh Hearon Niven; my sisters, Doris Niven Barron and Lynn Niven Duval Clark; my brother, William Olin Niven; my brother-in-law Phil Clark; my nieces and nephews, Lisa and Bob von Sprecken; Shannon Duval; Ashley and Scott Hurley; Derek Duval; Nathaniel and Learyn von Sprecken; and my cousins Patsy and Charles McGee. We have supported one another through losses, and through prolonged family illnesses and other challenges. As I have tried to write another life while living my own, they have encouraged me.

Appreciation and applause go to everyone at Clarkson Potter who joined in producing this book: Chip Gibson and Lauren Shakely, who believed it needed to be written; Annetta Hanna, who is that rare kind of editor, a true colleague, fully engaged in every line and nuance; Carol Edwards, who copyedited a huge manuscript, studded with notes, with insight and sensitivity as well as painstaking skill; Hilary Bass, Shanna Compton, Christian Red, and Rebecca Strong, who worked to make the book visible; Marysarah Quinn, Jane Treuhaft, Susan DeStaebler, and Lauren Monchik, who worked to make it beautiful; production editor Andrea Connolly Peabbles, production manager Joy Sikorski, proofreader Peter Grennen, and their colleagues, who worked wonders;

Acknowledgments

Nancy Wolff, who created the index, that reliable map to the worlds in this book; Random House senior counsel Steven Weissman and his associate G. E. Hollingsworth, who gave astute and thorough advice; and John Son, who provided invaluable help with countless details.

I could not have completed this work without the support of a year's fellowship from the National Endowment for the Humanities and a Visiting Fellowship at the Beinecke Rare Book and Manuscript Library at Yale University. I am indebted as well to the following institutions: the Carl Sandburg Collection, the University of Illinois, Urbana; the Museum of Modern Art in New York; the Archives of American Art, the Smithsonian Institution; the Freer Gallery of Oriental Art; the National Gallery of Art; the Metropolitan Museum of Art; the Houghton County Historical Society, Houghton, Michigan; the United States Military Academy at West Point; the Barnes County Historical Society, Valley City, North Dakota; the Arthur and Elizabeth Schlesinger Library on the History of Women in America; the Wisconsin State Historical Society, Madison, Wisconsin; the George Eastman House; the Art Institute of Chicago; the Musée Rodin, Paris; the University of Delaware Library; the Library of Congress; and the National Archives.

I pay memorial tribute to several people who graced my life, and whose work and interest enriched this book: my great-aunt, Helen Niven Gamble, and my aunt, Elinor Niven McLaughlin; Jennifer's grandmother and my friend Cleo Gunnells McJunkin; Carl Sandburg's son-in-law Dr. George "Barney" Crile; Steichen's assistant at the Museum of Modern art, Grace Mayer, who gave me a decade of instruction in Steichen matters; Sandburg trustee and my valued friend and adviser Judge Frank Parker; journalist, friend, and expert on the history of Hancock, Michigan, Tom Sieg; fellow biographer Ann Sperber; and Kate Rodina Steichen. Sadly, as this book was in its final stages, I lost two cherished mentors and friends, Lucy Kroll and Margaret Sandburg.

And finally, I send deep thanks to Dr. Mary Steichen Calderone, for courage and inspiration, and for reading to me aloud from *The Family of Man*.

Permissions

Grateful acknowledgment is made to the following for permission to reprint previously published material:

Harcourt Brace & Company for the following material:

Excerpts from *Breathing Tokens* by Carl Sandburg, copyright © 1978 by Maurice C. Greenbaum and Frank M. Parker, Trustees of the Sandburg Family Trust, and Harcourt Brace & Company, reprinted by permission of the publisher;

Excerpts from *Home Front Memo,* copyright © 1943 by Carl Sandburg and renewed 1971 by Lilian Steichen Sandburg, reprinted by permission of Harcourt Brace & Company;

Excerpts from *Sandburg: Photographers View Carl Sandburg,* copyright © 1966 by Edward J. Steichen and renewed 1994 by Joanna Steichen and Mary Calderone, reprinted by permission of Harcourt Brace & Company;

Excerpts from *Steichen the Photographer* by Carl Sandburg, copyright © 1929 by Harcourt Brace & Company and renewed 1957 by Carl Sandburg, reprinted by permission of the publisher;

Mildred Hayes Cain for excerpts from her interview;

PERMISSIONS

Francesca Calderone-Steichen for the papers of Clara Smith Steichen, Kate Rodina Steichen, Carol Silverberg, and Dr. Frank Calderone;

Maurice C. Greenbaum and Philip G. Carson, trustees for the Sandburg Family Trust, for excerpts from the unpublished writings of Carl Sandburg and Lilian Steichen Sandburg; and for excerpts from the letters of Lilian Steichen Sandburg and Carl Sandburg published in *The Poet and the Dream Girl: The Love Letters of Lilian Steichen & Carl Sandburg,* copyright © 1987 by the Board of Trustees of the University of Illinois Press;

Wayne and Joan Miller for excerpts from interviews, letters, speeches, and articles;

The Georgia O'Keeffe Foundation for quotations from the letters of Alfred Stieglitz, Emmeline Obermeyer Stieglitz, and Katherine "Kitty" Stieglitz Stearns;

Helga Sandburg for interviews, letters, journal pages, and excerpts from *Sweet Music,* copyright © 1963 by Helga Sandburg; *A Great and Glorious Romance,* copyright © 1978 by Helga Sandburg; and "... *Where Love Begins,*" copyright © 1989 by Helga Sandburg; for the letters and papers of John Peter and Mary Kemp Steichen;

Joel Stahmer, attorney-in-fact, for the writings of Dr. Mary Steichen Calderone;

The Yale Collection of American Literature, Beinecke Rare Book and Manuscript Library, Yale University and Dr. Patricia Willis, curator of American Literature, for excerpts from manuscripts by the following individuals: from the Alfred Stieglitz Archive (Ansel Adams), J. Craig Annan, Malcolm Arbuthnot, R. Child Bayley, Marion Beckett, A. K. Boursault, Charles Caffin, Alvin Langdon Coburn, Thomas H. Cummings, Fred Holland Day, Robert Demachy, Marius de Zayas, Sadakichi Hartmann, Gertrude Käsebier, Robert Marks, Agnes Meyer, Eugene Meyer, Nancy Newhall, Katharine Rhoades, Clara Steichen, Eduard Steichen, Kate Rodina Steichen, Mary Kemp Steichen, Alfred Stieglitz, Emmeline Obermeyer Stieglitz, Katherine "Kitty" Stieglitz Stearns; from the Gertrude Stein Collection, Mildred Aldrich, Leo Stein, Sarah Stein; and from the Matthew Josephson Collection, Matthew Josephson.

INDEX

Abbott, C. Yarnall, 195
Abbott, John "Dick," 632
Abel, Juan C., 157
Académie Julian, 88–91, 142
Adams, Ansel, 547, 586–87, 594, 595, 619–23, 656
Adams, Henry, 145
Adams, Phoebe Lou, 656
advertising photography, 516, 518, 526–27, 532–33, 536–37, 568–71
Agee, James, 584
Agha, Mehemed Fehmy, 517, 563
Albright Art Gallery, 335–38
Aldrich, Mildred, 389–90, 465, 524
  books by, 414, 415, 425, 464
  and Clara, 233, 390, 397, 399, 422, 433, 442, 482, 484–85, 487
  death of, 538
  Legion of Honor to, 560
  and war, 395, 397, 398–401, 403, 414–15, 425, 442
Alexander, John White, 127
Allan, Sidney, 98, 337; *see also* Hartmann, Sadakichi
Amateur Photographer, The (British), 87, 132
America and Alfred Stieglitz, 551–52, 627
American Amateur Photographer, 38, 73, 182
American Delphinium Society, 564
American Fine Art Company, 28, 33, 36–38, 41, 46, 51, 65, 182
American Institute of Architects, 635
American Place, An, 545, 547
Anderson, Marian, 685
Anderson, Sherwood, 551
Andersson, Clara, 666
Annan, J. Craig, 59, 218, 349
Aperture, 655
Arbuthnot, Malcolm, 349–50
Arensberg, Louise and Walter, 373
Arlen, Michael, 514
Armory Show (1913), 279, 321, 370–73, 375, 409
art:
  for art's sake, 518, 536–37, 567
  Ash Can School, 371, 373
  blank wall as beginning of, 640
  and censorship, 644
  as civilizing force, 542–43
  commercial uses of, 41, 70, 233, 518, 534–37, 560, 567
  Cubism, 326, 343–45, 348, 352, 361, 362, 365–67, 369, 381
  definitions of, 348, 529–30
  democratic, 144–47, 154, 170, 241–42, 270, 273, 366–67, 533, 536, 567, 574, 623, 631

Fauvism, 228, 269, 277, 278, 325, 344, 362, 374
future of, 437, 533
and Golden Section, 491, 495
Impressionism, 47–48, 65, 69–70, 80, 89, 116–17, 131, 132, 141, 142, 254, 262, 327
legal standard for, 529–30
lithography, 28, 33, 34, 41, 63, 141, 326–27
vs. mechanical media, 33–34, 75
modern, *see* modern art
and nature, *see* nature
philosophy of, 505
photography and, *see* photography; photography as art
Post-Impressionism, 117, 147, 370, 490
and reality, 43–44, 144, 147, 325, 373, 529, 615
Secessionist, 122
and society, 409, 437–38, 536, 542–43, 574–77
Steichen's work in, *see* painting by Steichen; photography by Steichen
subjectivity of, 33–34, 365–67, 437
Symbolism, 52–53, 69, 82, 96, 132, 142
vs. technology, 34, 40, 139, 241, 374
Art et Décoration, 352, 500
Ash Can School, 371, 373
Ashton, Ernest R., 38
Atget, Eugène, 632

Barnes, Maj. James, 449–53, 454–55, 457, 458–62, 499
Barr, Alfred, 618
Bartholomé, Paul Albert, 116, 170, 171
Barzun, Jacques, 656, 657
Bausch & Lomb, 171, 383–84
Baxter, Beatrice, 119, 155
Bayer, Herbert, 591, 634, 656
Bayley, Child, 232, 247–48, 349, 355, 501–2, 551
Beardsley, Aubrey, 97
Beaton, Cecil, 558
Bebel, August, 249
Beckett, Marion, 355–57, 404–5, 413
  as artist, 356, 363, 372, 391–92, 394, 416, 508
  children of, 508
  and Clara's jealousy, 410, 421, 428, 430–35, 442, 507–8
  and Clara's lawsuit, 470–71, 472, 482–85, 487
  as model, 359–60, 376–78, 382, 387, 389
  and war, 396, 402, 464–65
Bedding, Thomas, 101
Beethoven's Beloved (D. Steichen), 640, 657–58, 661, 662, 673–74
Bell, Clive, 350, 370
Bell, Curtis, 184, 190–92, 199–200, 205
Bellows, George, 493

Benito, Eduardo, 517
Benz, Karl, 28
Berenson, Bernard, 225, 227
Berger, Victor, 20, 53, 54, 272–73
Bergson, Henri-Louis, 361, 370
Besnard, Paul Albert, 89, 170
Besson, George, 292
Better Homes & Gardens, 565
Betz, Capt. Charles F., 449
Beuret, Rose, 108–10, 125, 255, 260, 368, 441, 455–56
Binford, Thomas, 611
Björncrantz, Carl, 42, 53, 65, 70, 76–80, 100, 105
Blanche, Jacques-Emile, 107
Bohrmann, Horst, 558
Boisbaudran, Horace Lecoq de, 256
Bonney, Thérèse, 621
Booth, Clare (Brokaw), 568
Borglum, Gutzon, 296
Borodin, Michael, 465
Boston Camera Club, 82–83, 85
Bourges, Fernand, 571
Bourke-White, Margaret, 584
Boursault, A. K., 192, 200
Brady, Mathew, 448, 614
Brancusi, Constantin, 325, 394, 476, 524, 685
  Bird in Space/L'Oiseau d'or, 379–82, 401, 528–30, 681
  exhibits of work by, 324, 373, 681
Brancusi v. the United States, 529–30
Braque, Georges, 225, 326, 343–44, 362, 365–66, 369, 373
Brigman, Annie W., 338, 349, 405, 417, 418
Brinley, D. Putnam, 264, 326
Bristol, Horace, 599–600
Brokaw, Clare Booth, 568
Bruce, Kathleen, 133, 313–16, 432, 482–83
Bruce, Patrick Henry, 262, 264, 372
Bruehl, Anton, 563, 571
Brussels, National Gallery of, 134–35, 143
Bullock, John, 160
Bullock, Wayne, 657
Bulloz, J. E., 290
Burbank, Luther, 357–58, 532

Caffin, Caroline, 193, 198
Caffin, Charles H., 193, 289, 327, 336, 446
  in *Camera Notes,* 150, 162
  in *Camera Work,* 169, 292
  as critic, 65, 86, 202, 216–17, 418
  Photography as Fine Art by, 44, 80–81
  on Steichen, 45, 86, 91, 130–31, 142, 147–48, 269
  on Stieglitz, 71
Cain, Mildred Hayes "Mid," 508–9, 522–23, 678
Calderone, Francesca, 562, 677

Calderone, Frank, 562, 608, 617, 667, 690–94
Calderone, Maria, 562, 677
Calderone, Mary Steichen, 691–97
  children of, 525, 531–32, 561–62
  early years of, *see* Steichen, Mary
  marriage of, 562
  as physician, 608, 636, 667
Caldwell, Erskine, 584
Callahan, Harry, 621
Camera Club of New York, 38, 40, 71, 83, 85, 139, 148, 149–50, 156, 157, 171
Camera Notes, 38–40, 48–49, 57, 63, 161
  reproduction quality of, 150, 162
  Steichen's work published in, 75, 106
  Steichen's work reviewed in, 59–60, 71, 128–29
  and Stieglitz, 38, 40, 73, 83, 85, 102, 106, 128–29, 141, 149–51, 156, 157
Camera Work, 100–101, 190, 200, 305, 325–26, 360–61, 365, 370
  contributors to (lists), 162, 169
  diminished fortunes of, 242, 268, 417
  first issue of, 143, 158–60, 161–62, 169
  and Photo-Secession, 143, 158, 161–63, 169, 180–82, 183–84, 207, 253, 268
  Steichen interviewed for, 152–54
  Steichen's assistance with, 143, 161–62, 199, 237, 294
  Steichen Supplement to, 212, 237, 383–85
  Steichen's work published in, 159–60, 169, 183–84, 212, 237, 248, 253–54, 280, 292, 338–39, 383–85
  Steichen's work reviewed in, 153–54, 169, 183–84, 212, 237, 248, 253–54, 292
  and 291 gallery, 207, 326, 394–95, 408, 417, 443
Campbell, Maj. C.D.M., 452, 461
Capa, Robert, 632
Carey, Elizabeth Luther, 327–28, 330, 355
Carles, Arthur B., 188, 261–64, 356, 382, 391–92, 471, 486, 493
  exhibits of work by, 352, 355, 372
  marriage of, 306
  as painter, 261–62, 288, 289, 352, 355, 358, 372, 495
  and Society of Younger American Painters, 264, 319, 326
  and war, 464
Carles, Mercedes de Cordoba, 377, 382, 389, 403–4, 483
  and Clara, 250, 439
  marriage of, 306
  as model, 188, 262
  at Voulangis, 355, 356, 486
Carl XII, king of Sweden, 671
Carrière, Eugene, 358
Carroll, Lewis, 632–33
Carter, A.C.R., 203

Casals, Pablo, 224, 225, 685, 686
Century Magazine, 254
Cézanne, Paul, 234, 361, 393
 exhibits of work of, 266–67, 324, 326–27, 343, 347–48, 350–51, 352, 370, 373
 influence of, 263, 325, 330, 354, 358, 377
 Steichen's fake of, 348, 350–51
 technique of, 230, 325, 344, 348
Chamberlain, J. Edgar, 277
Champs de Mars Salon, 106, 127–29, 132, 353
Chaplin, Charlie, 515
Chase, Edna, 558
Chase, William Merritt, 49, 70, 75, 138, 171, 199, 201
Cheruit, 519
Chicago:
 in 19th century, 5–6
 Columbian Exposition in, 25–27
 socialism in, 143–44
 world's fair (1933), 544
Chicago Photographic Salon, 64–65, 69–70
Cladel, Judith, 124, 455–46
Clark, Stephen, 618
Clothier, Florence, 532
Clurman, Harold, 551
Coburn, Alvin Langdon, 87, 118, 200, 230, 247, 355
 and color photography, 248, 249, 308
 and Day, 83, 99, 101, 180
 and exhibits, 101, 179–80, 218, 338, 349
 and mother, 83–84, 102, 217, 232
 photography by, 84, 99, 126, 181, 183, 187, 231–32, 249, 258, 267, 309, 338
Coburn, Fannie, 83–84, 102, 217, 232
Cocteau, Jean, 225
Columbian Exposition (1893), 25–27, 36
Compo-Photocolor, 648–49
Condé Nast Publications, 499–502, 511–20, 527, 533, 538, 558–59, 567–70
Conklin, Roland and Mary MacFadden, 203
Considine, Bob, 672
Copeland, Herbert, 82, 96
Cordoba, Mercedes de, *see* Carles, Mercedes de Cordoba
Cornell, Katharine, 514
Cornu, Paul, 352
Cortissoz, Royal, 328
Cottel, Charles, 269
Coudert, Claire, Duchesse de Choiseul, 125, 255–56, 362, 367–69, 499
Cox, Kenyon, 330
Craftsman, The, 280
Craig, Gordon:
 and Duncan, 294–95, 314, 317
 exhibits of work by, 319, 326
 influence of, 377
 portraits of, 295, 315, 317–18, 385
 as stage designer, 295

 and Steichen's influence, 289, 294, 295, 319, 321, 354
Crile, Helga Sandburg, *see* Sandburg, Helga; Thoman, Helga Sandburg
Crowninshield, Frank, 498, 500, 501
Cubism, 326, 343–45, 348, 352, 361, 362, 365–67, 369, 381
Cummings, Thomas, 196

Daguerre, Louis-Jacques Mandé, 33–34
daguerreotype, 31
Daimler, Gottlieb, 28
Daingerfield, Elliott, 330
d'Alessio, Gregory, 668
Dalou, Jules, 77
Danton, Georges-Jacques, 323
Darwin, Charles, 146, 370, 376
Davidson, Jo, 263, 264, 372
Davies, Arthur B., 371
Davison, George, 218, 248, 250, 253, 349
Dawson, Albert, 449–50
Day, Fred Holland, 94–99, 102–3, 118, 505
 and Coburn, 83, 99, 101, 180
 and exhibits, 56, 59, 84–86, 98, 99, 102, 130, 139, 180, 200, 349
 influence of, 38, 39, 40, 57, 74, 82–83, 84, 87, 97, 99, 155–56
 photography by, 38, 73–74, 81, 96, 99, 104, 200, 349
 and Photo-Secession, 160, 349
 portraits of, 96, 99, 115
 and Stieglitz, 73–74, 82–87, 97, 98, 102, 139, 155–56
Delehanty, Frances, 119
Demachy, Robert, 100–102, 235, 297
 and *Camera Notes,* 38, 63, 102
 influence of, 63, 130, 187–88
 and Linked Ring, 59
 and photography as art, 61, 86, 100–101
 photography by, 38, 103, 258, 355
de Meyer, Baron Adolf, 59, 230–31, 232, 308, 337, 349, 500, 513, 516
de Meyer, Olga, 230–31
Demuth, Charles, 551
de Rochemont, Louis, 610
Deskey, Donald, 544
Devens, Mary, 94, 181
de Vries, Hugo, 358
Dewey, John, 146
de Zayas, Marius, 327, 354, 364–67, 394, 417
 and exhibits, 261, 351, 365, 406, 445
 and modern art, 261, 351, 365–67, 369–70
 and Modern Gallery, 446
 on Steichen's work, 369–70, 384
d'Harnoncourt, René, 633, 680
Dove, Arthur G., 326, 327, 339, 355, 372, 545, 547, 551
Dow, Arthur Wesley, 150, 330

Doyle, Comdr. W. W., 589
Dreiser, Theodore, 146
Duchamp, Marcel, 225, 366, 373, 528
Duffy, Richard, 264
Duncan, Anna, 479, 480
Duncan, David Douglas, 633
Duncan, Isadora, 225, 294, 313–18, 334, 385, 432, 475, 479–81, 483–85, 528
Duncan, Raymond, 225, 313
Duncan, Thèrése, 480, 481
Duse, Eleonora, 166–67, 168, 236, 322
Dyer, William B., 160

Eastman, George, 31, 32, 145
Eickemeyer, Rudolf, Jr., 38, 59, 87
Eisler, Benita, 546
Elmendorf, Dwight L., 40
Emerson, Peter Henry, 26–27, 44, 138–39
Encke, Fedor, 165–66
Engelhard, George, 521
Englehard, Georgia, 544
Epstein, Jacob, 529
Ernst, Agnes, 172, 175, 270, 295–301, 311, 312; *see also* Meyer, Agnes Ernst
Eugene, Frank, 93–94, 102–3
 influence of, 107
 photography by, 81, 94, 139, 156, 182, 183, 248, 252, 253, 308, 338, 349, 355
 and Photo-Secession, 160, 161, 253, 309
Evans, Frederick H., 97, 104, 201, 217, 247
Evans, Walker, 575, 576, 584

"Family of Man, The":
 artistry of, 655–56
 catalog for, 649
 gala preview of, 649–50
 initial concept of, 144, 615, 633–35, 639
 installation of, 646
 organization of, 638–449
 as performance art, 635, 653, 654
 scope of, 635, 640–41, 650–51, 666–67
 success of, 650–51, 652–56, 657
 world tours of, 654–55, 666–72, 686, 687, 701–2
Farm Security Administration (FSA), 575–76, 584, 587, 683
fashion photography, 352–53, 500–502, 511–20, 533, 558–59, 568–69
Fauvism, 228, 269, 277, 278, 325, 344, 362, 374
Federation of Jewish Philanthropies, 557
Fellows, Lawrence, 297, 326
Fernande (Picasso's mistress), 225, 233
Fighting Lady, The, 606–7, 610–12
Fingal (dog), 530
FitzGerald, Charles, 201–2, 209
Ford, Henry, 28
Forrestal, James, 600, 611, 616
Foulois, Gen. B. D., 455

France, Anatole, 216, 322, 385
Frank, Robert, 635, 642
Frank, Waldo, 551
Frankfurter, Felix, 685
Fraser, William A., 38
Freer, Charles, 376, 386–87, 403, 404, 416, 417
Frick, Henry Clay, 237
Frost, David, 693
Frueh, Alfred J., 364
Fry, Roger, 225, 370
FSA (Farm Security Administration), 575–76, 584, 587, 683
Fuguet, Dallett, 150, 157, 160, 161, 169
Fuller, Loïe, 219–20

Gallagher, Barrett, 611
Garbo, Greta, 514–15, 699
Gates, Artemus, 588
Gauguin, Paul, 370, 373
Genthe, Arnold, 563
George Eastman House, 655
Gibran, Kahlil, 96
Glackens, William, 371
Glaezner, Eugene, 236–37, 240
Glaezner Gallery, 199, 201, 202, 216, 236, 279
Glover, Dana Desboro, *see* Steichen, Dana Glover
Gold, Mike, 537
Golden, Harry, 657, 689
Graham, Martha, 568
Graham, Phil, 667
Grand Central Station, exhibits in, 575–76
Great Depression, 537–38, 541–43, 546, 574, 575, 582, 683
Green, Ruzzie, 526
Greene, Belle, 168
Griffith, D. W., 621
Guesde, Jules, 249
Guilbert, Yvette, 118, 385, 519

Hale, Edward Everett, 171
Hambidge, Jay, 493
Hamilton, Lady, 248, 253
Hamilton, Sir Ian Standish Monteith, 248
Hancock, Michigan, 8–10, 11–12, 18
Harcourt, Alfred, 525
Hardman Piano Company, 532–33
Harriman, Margaret Case, 571
Harris, Eugene, 648
Harrison, Joan, 182
Hartley, Marsden, 233, 326, 327, 329, 339, 355, 356, 362, 370, 371, 374, 545, 551
Hartmann, Sadakichi:
 background of, 150–51
 and *Camera Work,* 152, 158, 169, 180–81, 182, 187, 196, 324–25
 as critic, 98, 130, 154, 180–81, 183–84, 191, 330, 337, 385

on photography as fine art, 151, 154, 155, 162, 178, 183, 337
and Photo-Secession, 157, 158, 162, 178, 192, 308–9, 327
on Steichen's work, 98, 130, 132, 152–54, 181–84, 385
and Stieglitz, 158, 180, 183–84, 320, 472
on straight photography, 98, 181, 183–84, 188
Hassam, Childe, 199, 330, 373
Haviland, Frank Burty, 344
Haviland, Paul, 281–82, 289, 302, 336, 339, 342, 351, 364, 370, 417, 446
Hayes, Mildred "Mid" (Cain), 508–9, 522–23, 678
Hearst, William Randolph, 500, 568
Henneberg, Hugo, 38, 337
Henri, Robert, 329
Herschel, Sir John, 34
Hiamovi, Chief, 647
Hill, David Octavius, 207
Hiller, Larry, 563
Hine, Lewis, 446
Hinton, A. Horsley, 38, 39, 61, 85, 127, 150, 162, 190, 218
Hitler, Adolf, 557, 598
Hoeber, Arthur, 328, 351, 361
Hoffman, Malvina, 356
Hoffmann, Josef, 206, 353
Homer, William Innes, 163
Horst, Horst P., 558
House & Garden, 579
Hughes, Robert, 699
Huneker, James, 129, 277–78, 328, 329, 330–31
Hunter, Robert, 249, 250, 276
Hyndman, Henry Mayers, 249

Impressionism, 47–48, 65, 69–70, 80, 89, 116–17, 131, 132, 141, 142, 254, 262, 327
Intimate Gallery, 545
Isaacs, T. H. (Scott), 340

Jacobs, Charles Fenno, 599, 615–16
James, Henry, 108–9
James, William, 146
James Kelway & Sons, 357
Jaurès, Jean-Joseph-Marie-Auguste, 215–16, 249
Jewell, Edward Alden, 593
John, Augustus, 372
Johnston, Frances B., 56
John XXIII, Pope, 686
Jorgensen, Victor, 598–603
Josephson, Matthew, 552, 617, 637
Juhl, Ernst, 69, 132, 137–38, 143, 337
Julian, Rodolphe, 88–89
J. Walter Thompson Advertising Agency, 516, 518, 519, 533, 534, 541, 542, 568–69

Kaiser, Georgia Carroll, 517
Käsebier, Gertrude, 118–20, 121, 122
and *Camera Notes,* 38, 57, 151
and *Camera Work,* 158–59, 160, 169, 190, 200
and exhibits, 56–57, 59, 85, 101, 139, 156, 218, 337
influence of, 38, 446
and Linked Ring, 59, 94–95, 161, 218
in New York, 148, 158–59
photography by, 80, 126, 139, 181, 183, 218, 231, 337, 338, 355
and Photo-Secession, 160, 161, 181, 309, 349
portraits of, 99, 119, 248
Käsebier, Hermine, 122
Keiley, Joseph T.:
and *Camera Notes,* 59–60, 71, 150, 151, 161
and *Camera Work,* 100–101, 161, 162
death of, 386
on photography as art, 64, 100–101, 151
photography by, 80, 85, 139, 156, 188
and Photo-Secession, 156, 160, 179, 195, 200, 210, 327, 337–38
on Steichen's work, 59–60, 71, 323, 337–38
and Stieglitz, 71, 156, 157, 337–38
Kelway, James & Sons, 357
Kemp, Marie, *see* Steichen, Marie Kemp
Kennedy, John F., 685, 686
Kennerly, Mitchell, 546
Kerfoot, J. B., 162, 169, 200
Kerlee, Charles, 599, 600, 603
Khrushchev, Nikita, 670
King, Elisabeth, 691, 693, 694–95
Kipling, Rudyard, 146
Klimt, Gustav, 353, 377
Knode, Katherine, 132, 142
Knoedler Gallery, 373, 415–16
Kodak:
and color photography, 246
competitions, 171
and early photography, 30–32, 36
exhibitions, 40–41
Kodachrome film, 571
Korean conflict, 633, 683
Kramer, Hilton, 656–57
Kroll, Lucy, 668
Kühn, Heinrich, 59, 215, 248, 294, 308, 337, 349
Kuhn, Walt, 371–72
Kurtz, Charles M., 336

La Farge, John, 199
La Follette, Robert, 280–81
Lange, Dorothea, 575, 576, 584, 592, 638
Lassalle, Ferdinand, 20
Lathrop, W. L., 330
Laurens, Jean-Paul, 89–90
Laurvik, J. Nilsen, 254, 260
Lawrence, Stephen, 327
LeBlanc, Georgette, 116

INDEX

Lecoq de Boisbaudran, Horace, 256
Lemoine, Victor, 357
Lenbach, Franz von, 123, 138, 170, 201
Levitt, Helen, 621
Liberman, Alexander, 512, 517, 568, 665, 666–67, 680
Life, 630, 635
A Life in Photography (Steichen), 102, 503, 684–85
Linked Ring, 26, 59, 86, 94–95, 127, 161, 195, 217–18, 258, 349
lithography, 28, 33, 36–38, 39, 41, 63, 141, 182, 326–27, 512
Little Galleries, *see* 291 gallery
London:
   Linked Ring in, *see* Linked Ring
   Royal Photographic Society, 26, 84–85, 86, 567, 681
   Secessionists in, 349–50
   Steichen in, 82–87, 95, 106
Long, Dwight, 599, 600, 603, 606, 610
Lorentz, Pare, 682
Lorenz, Richard, 20, 42, 43–44
Lowe, Sue Davidson, 158, 628
Lumière brothers, 243–44, 246, 253, 258
Lumière plates, 245–49, 253–54, 258, 308, 338, 358
Luxembourg:
   "Family of Man" in, 701–2
   Steichen family in, 1–2, 701
Lydig, Rita de Acosta, 201, 385
Lyon, Fred, 638

Macdonald-Wright, Stanton, 374
MacLaughlan, Donald Shaw, 264
MacLeish, Archibald, 584
Maco Magazine Corporation, 649
Maeterlinck, Maurice, 113, 116, 131–32, 159, 162, 169, 212
   L'Oiseau bleu by, 285–86, 295
   and Symbolism, 52–53, 82, 96
Maloney, Tom, 563, 599, 612, 614, 618–21, 624, 631
Manet, Édouard, 327, 347
Man Ray, 504, 558
Marin, John, 262, 263–64, 327, 417
   exhibits of work of, 264, 267, 293–94, 321, 326, 330, 364, 372, 373, 447, 545
   and Society of Younger American Painters, 264, 326
   and Steichen's influence, 267, 293, 321, 349, 384
   and Stieglitz, 294, 305, 521, 551
   at Voulangis, 288–89, 356, 358
Marks, Robert, 515
Martin, Linda, 531, 561, 608, 617, 637, 677
Martin, Mary Steichen, *see* Steichen, Mary
Martin, Nell, 525, 561–62

Martin, W. Lon, 525, 531, 561
Marx, Karl, 20, 146
Mason, Jerry, 649, 653
Matisse, Amélie, 229–30
Matisse, Henri, 89, 225–30, 307, 343–44, 347, 366, 385
   exhibits of work of, 277–79, 281, 326, 355, 362, 373, 381, 476
   influence of, 263, 268–69, 293–94, 325, 327–31, 344, 353–54, 358, 377
   and Steichen's influence, 257, 261, 265, 266–67, 268, 278–79, 319, 322, 324, 325, 358
   and Steins, 225–29, 233–35, 263, 360–61
Maurer, Alfred, 225, 233, 262–63, 264, 267, 293–94, 319, 326, 329, 330, 372
Maurois, André, 657
Mayer, Grace, 668, 680, 683, 686
McAlpin, David H., 586, 587
McBride, Henry, 225, 593
McCarthy, Joseph, 643–44
McCombe, Leonard, 632
McCormick, Ken, 661, 692
McKeon, James "Mac," 513–14
McKinley, William, 145–46
Meek, Samuel W., 588–89
Meet the Press, 672
Meserve, Frederick Hill, 577
Meyer, Agnes Ernst, 345–47, 667, 686
   as art patron, 339–40, 348, 393, 681
   early years of, *see* Ernst, Agnes
   and finances, 393–94, 415, 684, 690
   and Freer, 386–87, 404, 416, 417
   murals for home of, 347, 349, 352, 353, 355, 359–60, 363, 370, 376–78, 382, 393–94, 404, 415–16, 495
   and 291/*291,* 406, 416, 417, 445–46
   at Voulangis, 355, 356–57, 394
   and war, 395–96, 403, 464
Meyer, Elizabeth, 682
Meyer, Eugene, 296, 299, 345–47
   as art patron, 339–40, 347, 348–49
   death of, 667
   and finances, 393–94, 415, 569, 583
   marriage of, 301, 346
   and war, 393, 398–99, 400–401, 402–3, 464, 582–83
   and *Washington Post,* 582, 583, 667
Meyer, Eugene III "Bill," 690
Meyer, Florence, 347
Milaschewitsch, Serge and Helen, 690, 691
Miller, Joan, 638–39, 644, 648, 650, 658–59, 699
Miller, Wayne, 652, 661–62, 669
   and "Family of Man," 635, 638–46, 648–51, 654, 702
   and FDR's death, 615–16
   photographs by, 632, 640, 650, 699
   and Steichen's death, 697–98, 699

and war photography, 598, 599, 610, 614, 633, 639, 650
Millet, Jean-François, 237
Millstein, Gilbert, 665
Milwaukee:
  socialism in, 20, 53–54, 271–72, 332
  Steichens' move to, 16, 17–20, 54–55
Milwaukee Art Students' League, 42–44, 49, 58, 70, 142
Mitchell, Gen. Billy, 463, 503, 589, 598
modern art, 364–76
  as anti-photographic, 269
  Armory Show (1913) of, 279, 321, 370–73, 375, 409
  exhibits in U.S. of, 225–26, 235, 257, 264, 267, 277–79, 293, 350–51, 355; see also 291 gallery
  and financial reward, 307
  nature reconfigured in, 369
  post–World War I, 476
  Society of Younger American Painters, 264, 273, 319, 326, 329–30, 369, 372
  and Steichen's influence, 235, 257, 262–64, 265–67, 268–69, 277–79, 289, 293–95, 319, 320–22, 324, 326–27, 338, 343–45, 348, 355, 363, 368, 369, 371, 384, 687
  and Steins' salons, 225–29, 233–35, 262
  see also specific artists
Modern Gallery, 446
Moe, Henry, 618–19
Moeller, Susan D., 616
MoMA, see Museum of Modern Art
Monet, Claude, 47–48, 80, 89, 117, 372
Monroe, Harriet, 412
Montross Gallery, 322, 326, 327–28, 330, 331, 373
Morehouse, Marion, 19
Morgan, J. Pierpont, 165–68, 171, 258, 699
Morris, William, 82, 170
Morton, John Archer, 589
Mucha, Alphonse, 116, 138, 377
Mumford, Lewis, 551
Museum of Modern Art, 393–94, 543, 663
  Edward Steichen Photography Center in, 680
  and "Family of Man" exhibit, see "Family of Man, The"
  photography committee of, 566
  photography department of, 586–87, 618–25, 630–34, 639, 641, 665, 673, 680, 681, 682–83, 688
  "Power in the Pacific" exhibit in, 611, 620
  purpose of, 623
  "Road to Victory" exhibit in, 586, 587, 588, 590–92, 593–96, 620
  Steichen Archive in, 680
  Steichen's one-man show in, 564–66

"Steichen the Photographer" exhibit in, 678, 679, 680
Mydans, Carl, 575

Nadelman, Elie, 319, 321, 325–26
Nast, Clarisse, 248, 499, 519
Nast, Condé, 498–501, 507, 511, 515, 538, 558
Nast, Natica, 499
National Gallery of Brussels, 134–35, 143
nature:
  and color, 564
  and environmental concerns, 559
  geometrical forms in, 478
  harmony with, 113, 325–26, 370, 407, 490–93, 529, 553–54, 662, 664
  mastery of, 532
  reconfiguration of, 369
Nelson, Donald M., 583
Neokonkwo, Theophilus, 672
Newhall, Beaumont, 503, 575, 586, 587, 594, 619–23, 632, 655
Newhall, Nancy, 586, 594–96, 619–20, 622
New School of American Photography, 84–87, 95, 98, 99, 100, 101–2, 132, 138
New Yorker, 637
Nixon, Richard M., 670
Norman, Dorothy, 545–46, 551–52, 626, 628, 641, 646, 647–48, 655
Norman, Edward, 545
Norris, Frank, 146

Obermeyer, Joseph, 164, 204, 415, 419, 423, 472
O'Keeffe, Georgia, 476, 525
  exhibits of work of, 446–48, 457, 545
  health of, 545, 546, 563
  marriage of, 521
  mural designs of, 543–44, 545
  in New Mexico, 545, 585, 625–26
  portraits of, 465, 473, 629
  publication of work of, 551
  and Stieglitz, 164, 260–61, 417, 431, 446–48, 457, 465, 472–74, 482, 520–22, 544–47, 551, 563, 626, 628–29
  and 291/*291*, 260, 446, 448, 457
O'Keeffe, Ida, 521, 546
Oma, see Steichen, Marie Kemp
Opa, see Steichen, Jean-Pierre
Oppenheimer, Robert, 644
Orlan, Pierre Mac, 512–13
Otto (photographer), 116, 239–40
Outerbridge, Paul, 563

Pach, Walter, 371
Paddock, Charlotte Smith, 119–21, 174, 220–21, 259, 285, 430, 454, 510, 523–24
  and Clara's health, 431, 434, 439
  marriage of, 122, 172, 175

INDEX

Paddock, Willard "Billy," 119, 122, 171, 172, 174, 175, 188, 220–21, 259, 454, 510, 523–24
Paderewski, Ignacy, 63
Page, Homer, 632, 648, 665–66
painting by Steichen:
   abstract, 495
   control of materials in, 329, 359
   destruction of, 502–4
   and epiphany, 497
   in exhibits, 104–5, 106, 127, 129–32, 170–71, 199, 201–2, 240, 279–80, 322, 326–31, 372–373, 415–16
   income from, 45, 236–37, 280–81, 328, 340, 353, 475
   landscapes, 81, 130, 266
   Meyer murals, 347, 349, 352, 353, 355, 359–60, 363, 370, 376–78, 382, 393–94, 404, 415–16, 495
   portraits, 63, 104–5, 119, 130
   as self-taught, 28, 37, 39, 41–44, 46–47, 91, 116–17, 490–91
   use of color in, 81, 188, 202, 288, 344
   use of light in, 41–42, 98, 266, 279–80, 331, 344
   at Voulangis, 288–89, 309–10, 318, 331, 358, 490–91, 510
Paris:
   Académie Julian in, 88–91, 142
   exhibitions in, 99, 100, 101–2, 104–5, 106, 127–30
   modern art in, *see* modern art; *specific artists*
   Secessionists in, 264, 273
   Society of Younger American Painters in, 264, 273, 319, 326, 329–30, 369, 372
   Steichen in, 88–92, 93–110, 111–34, 209–10, 212–20, 223–44, 258–64, 266–67, 283, 298, 305, 321–22
   Steichen's first visit to, 65–66, 76–82
   Steins' salons in, 223–29, 233–35, 257, 262, 298, 305, 344–45
   World's Fair (1900), 76–79
Parks, Gordon, 567
Pavelle, Leo, 599
Péguy, Charles, 361–62
Pennell, Joseph, 140
Pennsylvania Academy of the Fine Arts, 49, 56, 210
Pershing, Gen. John "Black Jack," 455, 460, 475
Peterson, Christian A., 38
Philadelphia Photographic Salon, 48–49, 56–60, 71, 81, 94, 118, 156, 293
Phillips, Christopher, 589, 593, 606
Photo-Club de Paris, 101
Photographische Rundschau, Die, 132, 137–38
Photography, 247–48

photography:
   aerial (wartime), 448–53, 454–46, 457–64, 466, 505, 583
   as art, *see* photography as art
   cartes-de-viste, 31–32
   collectors of, 216–17
   color, 208, 243–44, 245–49, 252–55, 308
   commercial use of, 34, 37, 39, 115, 506, 567, 620
   and design, 532–33
   documentary, *see* photojournalism
   early years of, 26–27, 30–36
   for everyone, 30–35, 39, 140–41, 145–47, 151, 191, 270, 567
   fashion, 352–53, 500–502, 511–20, 533
   force of, 641
   for FSA, 575–76, 584, 587
   manipulation of, 94, 107, 182–84, 309, 337
   for mass communication, 512, 516, 542–43, 557–58, 615, 621, 623–24, 631–32, 634, 655, 688
   montage, 544
   as painting with light, 130, 131–32, 147
   political factions in, 85–87, 97, 102, 138–42, 155–56, 184, 190–92, 199–200, 217–18, 258, 336, 349
   portraits, 31–32, 114
   positive images in, 633–35, 640–41, 644–45
   protection of rights to, 196
   reality recorded by, 32, 33–34, 44, 241, 255, 506, 513, 533, 575, 615
   Smith lens in, 84, 362, 378
   as social commentary, *see* photojournalism
   soft-focus lens in, 104, 115, 506
   technology of, 33, 34, 36, 40, 73, 130–31, 183, 246, 254, 477–78, 491–93, 505–6, 512
   Time-Life files of, 642–43
photography as art, 114, 115, 145, 614–15
   in advertising and fashion, 518–19, 526–27, 532–33, 568–71
   in *Amateur Photographer,* 132
   and *Balzac* series, 292–93
   Caffin's book on, 44, 80–81
   and *Camera Notes,* 38–40, 75, 129
   and *Camera Work,* 161–63, 169
   color in, 245–46, 254–55
   critical reviews of, 61, 65, 128, 132, 203, 337–38; *see also specific critics*
   Demachy and, 61, 86, 100–101
   exhibits of, 64–65, 84, 101, 127–29, 335–38
   light in, 131–32, 254
   manipulation in, 182–84
   and modernism, 147
   and MoMA, *see* Museum of Modern Art
   vs. realism, 126, 254–55, 506
   secessionist movement in, 139–42, 158, 162, 178, 179–83, 191; *see also* Photo-Secession
   Stieglitz and, 26–27, 40, 49, 56, 71, 72–73,

106, 128–29, 138–42, 150, 151, 183, 191, 270, 323–25, 337, 585, 627
  uniqueness of, 92, 131–32
photography by Steichen:
  advertising, 516, 518, 526–27, 532–33, 536–37, 568–71
  After the Taking of Iwo Jima Island, 614
  artistry of, 47, 63, 86, 126, 153–54, 182–83, 324, 492–93, 526–27
  backgrounds in, 513–14, 552
  Balzac series, 290–93, 322, 324
  The Big Cloud, 195–96
  The Black Vase, 134–35
  The Brass Bowl, 188
  cameras used in, 29, 34, 378, 572, 682
  The Clinic, 541–42
  color, 189, 197, 208, 245–49, 252–55, 265–66, 269, 308, 326, 358, 505, 571
  commercial, 37, 45, 47, 50, 102, 148, 152, 201, 208–9, 254–55, 340, 511, 535–37, 570–71
  Cyclamen–Mrs. Philip Lydig, 201
  darkroom work of, 35–36, 37, 58, 63, 99, 123–24, 130–31, 168, 182–83, 187–88, 189, 265, 291, 505, 569
  in exhibits, 56–60, 64–65, 84, 101, 105, 127, 130–32, 134–35, 139, 156, 168, 195–96, 203, 236, 267, 269, 280, 322, 326, 349–50, 680
  Experiment in Multiple Gum, 183
  in "Family of Man," 650
  fashion, 352–53, 500–502, 511–20, 533, 558–59, 568–69
  fire destruction of, 664
  first camera for, 28–29, 31, 32–33, 34
  Heavy Roses, 394
  income from, 87–88, 107, 134, 149, 166, 171–72, 188, 201, 208–9, 216, 236–38, 258, 260, 269, 291, 337, 500–501, 519, 558, 694
  Keats, 64
  Lady in the Doorway, 58, 59–60, 66
  landscapes, 37, 80, 132
  Lotus, Mount Kisco, 439
  mission of, 688
  murals, 543–44, 583, 585, 592
  My Little Sister with the Rose-covered Hat, 46
  nudes, 115, 132, 153–54, 519
  photojournalism, 241–42, 512–15, 517, 541–43, 614, 618
  The Pool-Evening, 64, 65, 75, 125
  portraits, 37, 45, 50, 54, 57–58, 87–88, 96, 98–99, 106–8, 114–18, 122–28, 132, 138, 149, 153–54, 165–68, 170, 171, 177, 183–84, 187, 188, 201, 209, 236, 246–50, 253, 269, 276, 280–81, 295, 296–97, 317–18, 322, 385, 479–81, 496, 512–17, 536, 558–59, 567, 577–78, 699
  publication of, 132, 137–38, 159–60, 169–70, 183–84, 187, 196, 212, 248–50, 253–54, 269, 280–81, 292, 338–39, 383–85, 685, 699
  retirement from, 569–70, 572–73
  Rodin–Le Penseur, 123–24, 126, 128, 153, 154, 170, 201, 236, 269, 324
  The Rose, 104
  self-portraits, 57–58, 86–87, 125, 127, 138, 170, 498, 499–500
  as self-taught, 28–29, 33, 34–36, 37–38, 39, 40, 43, 44–45, 46–48, 59–61, 62–63, 69–70, 477–78, 490–91, 572–73, 623, 658, 664, 682
  spiral motif in, 478, 491, 492, 526–27
  use of light in, 58, 98, 99, 107, 115, 116, 290, 309, 512–13, 541, 552, 572, 573
  Vitality, 118
  in wartime, *see* World War I; World War II
  of women, 516–17, 569–71
photojournalism, 241–42, 512–15, 517, 541–43, 575–77, 583, 584–85, 614, 618, 627, 632; *see also* "Family of Man"; World War I; World War II
Photo-Secession, 155–63, 266
  birth of, 139–42, 157
  and *Camera Work,* 143, 158, 161–63, 169, 180–82, 183–84, 207, 253, 268
  critical attacks on, 308–9
  demise of, 242, 407
  exhibitions of, 156, 161, 179–82, 187, 195, 207–8, 210, 253, 335–38
  and Linked Ring, 217–18
  in London, 349–50
  mission of, 161, 178, 537
  and modern art, 278
  in Munich, 122, 140, 141
  organization of, 160–61, 178, 190–91
  in Paris, 264, 273
  and political factions, 190–92, 199–200, 232–33, 242
  Stieglitz as director of, 160–62, 232–33, 408, 585
  and 291 gallery, 205–8, 268, 278, 327, 407
  use of term, 158
Picabia, Francis, 225, 364, 372, 373, 381, 445–46
Picasso, Pablo, 307, 476, 686–87
  and Aldrich, 233
  and Cubism, 326, 343–45, 348, 352, 361, 362, 365–66, 369
  exhibits of work of, 289, 351–52, 372, 373
  and G. Stein, 225, 233–35, 345, 360–61, 395
  influence of, 257, 263, 324
  and Steichen's influence, 266–67, 289, 353–54, 687
  and Steins, 225, 227, 228, 233–35, 263
plant breeding, 617
  and Burbank, 357–58, 532
  at Umpawaug, 530–31, 539, 552–56, 564–67, 688

INDEX

plant breeding (cont.)
   at Voulangis, 287, 288, 333–34, 357–58, 376, 390–91
Plato, 648
Poiret, Paul, 352
Pollitzer, Anita, 447
Popescue, Dimitrie G., 681
Popular Photography, 571, 635
Post-Impressionism, 117, 147, 370, 490
Pownall, Adm. Charles A., 602
Pratt, Carolyn, 423
Pratt, George DuPont, 423
Pratt, Helen Sherman "Nell," 438, 470, 474, 482, 560

Radford, Arthur, 589, 598
Radio City Music Hall, murals, 544, 545
Redfield, Robert, 160
Redon, Odilon, 372
Reilly, Rosa, 571–72
Renoir, Pierre-Auguste, 326–27, 347, 372
Resor, Helen, 518, 534
Reyher, Ferd, 623
Rhoades, Katharine, 306, 355–57, 423, 438, 483, 508
   as artist, 363, 372, 391–92, 394, 416–17
   as model, 360, 376–77, 389
   and Stieglitz, 392, 404–5, 410, 412–13, 416–17, 431, 521, 626
   and war, 396, 411, 464
Rilke, Rainer Maria, 109, 113, 114, 219
Robinson, Mrs. Arthur, 63
Rockefeller, Nelson A., 586, 631, 634, 649, 654
Rodin, Auguste:
   Balzac, 48, 55, 77–79, 125, 126, 290–93
   and Brancusi, 379
   Burghers of Calais, 79, 89
   death of, 455–46
   drawings by, 255–57, 260, 278, 322, 342, 367–69, 559–60
   and Duncan, 316–17
   and Ernst, 296–97, 298–300
   exhibits of work by, 76–79, 89–90, 125, 255–57, 259–61, 266–67, 278–79, 281, 326, 342, 373
   friends of, 89, 107, 125, 298–99, 300
   Gates of Hell, 78, 79, 441
   health of, 441
   influence on Steichen of, 113–14, 131, 142, 155, 230, 257, 320, 325, 344, 359, 368, 456, 491
   Man with the Broken Nose, 112, 113
   nature as inspiration for, 113, 491, 529
   Le Penseur (The Thinker), 123, 125, 456
   Steichen's friendship with, 108–10, 111–17, 122, 362, 366, 368
   and Steichen's photography, 110, 112, 113–16, 122–26, 138, 260, 290–93

   and Stieglitz, 353
   tomb of, 671
   and 291 gallery, 219–20, 221–22, 255–57, 259–61, 278, 281, 319, 326, 342, 368
   Victor Hugo, 123–25
   wealth of, 307, 319
   and World War I, 440–41
ROLI (Redding Open Lands, Incorporated), 693–94
Roosevelt, Franklin D., 548, 575, 581, 582, 584, 587, 588, 592, 615–16
Roosevelt, Theodore, 145, 146, 280–81, 322
Roque, Jacqueline, 687
Rosa (friend), 103–4, 119, 121, 122, 418
Rosenfeld, Paul, 162, 537, 551, 627
Rothstein, Arthur, 575, 599
Rousseau, Henri, 225, 263, 339
Royal Photographic Society, 26, 84–85, 86, 567, 681
Rudolph, Paul, 646
Rugg, Harold, 551
Rummel, Walter, 479–81
Ruskin, John, 370
Russell, Morgan, 374

Salon de Maison des Artistes, 127
Salon des Beaux-Arts, 104–5, 127
Salon des Réfuses, 129
Sandburg, August, 666
Sandburg, Carl:
   autobiography of, 641
   awards to, 584, 671, 686
   at Connemara, 617–18
   death of, 688–89
   and "Family of Man," 641, 646–47, 649, 653, 656, 657, 666–67, 668, 670, 671–72
   and family visits, 274–77, 331–32, 468–69, 579–80
   grandchildren of, 549, 596
   health of, 679, 685
   influence on Steichen of, 113
   as journalist, 274, 332, 465, 468, 471–72, 493, 514, 538, 577, 587, 588, 590
   Lilian's friendship with, 271, 273–77, 279, 280
   on Mary Kemp Steichen (Oma), 17
   on Opa's death, 609–10
   as poet, 274, 275, 332, 388, 412, 437, 465, 472, 481, 493, 538, 542, 566, 574, 577, 615, 633, 645, 656, 668–69, 675, 676, 685, 689, 698, 700
   and socialism, 276–77, 331–32, 536
   on Steichen, 15–16, 278–79, 445, 449, 469, 512, 520, 527, 534–37, 572, 574, 590, 675–76, 699
   wedding of, 281
   as writer, 493–94, 525, 526, 527, 534–37, 574, 577, 584, 587, 592, 607, 612, 680, 681, 689

INDEX

Sandburg, Clara, 332
Sandburg, Helga, 465, 486, 507, 525, 526, 530, 553, 574, 596–97, 605, 660n; *see also* Thoman, Helga Sandburg
Sandburg, Janet, 465, 486, 525, 526, 613, 617, 696
Sandburg, Lilian Steichen (Paula):
  and brother's health, 677, 678
  and Carl's death, 689
  and Carl's work, 412
  and Connemara, 617–18, 696
  early years of, *see* Steichen, Lilian
  and family visits, 411–12, 449, 468, 579–80, 596–97, 612–13
  goats bred by, 553–54, 579, 609, 612, 617, 696
  grandchildren of, 549, 596
  health of, 681
  on love, 312
  and Opa's health, 596–97, 608–9
  and Paw Paw Patch, 530
  wedding of, 281, 282–83
Sandburg, Margaret, 388, 411, 485, 486, 525, 526, 613, 617, 675, 677, 696
Sandburg, Mary, 302
Sandburg, Paula, *see* Sandburg, Lilian Steichen; Thoman, Karlen Paula
Sandeen, Eric, 651, 653
Santer, J. Jacques, 701
Sargent, John Singer, 117
Saturday Review, The, 665–66
Schade, Robert, 42–43, 142
Schroeder, Marcel, 687
Schubart, Selma Stieglitz, 331
Scott, Robert Falcon, 314
Scott, Temple, 340
Secessionists, *see* Photo-Secession
Seebohm, Caroline, 516
Seeley, George, 349
Seidel, Emil, 332
Serkin, Rudolf, 685
Séverine, Caroline Rémy, 456
Shahn, Ben, 575
Shannon, Charles, 289
Shaw, George Bernard, 52, 113, 273, 504
  and *Camera Work,* 162
  portraits of, 218, 231, 246–47, 248, 253, 322, 385
  and socialism, 276
  and 291 gallery, 282
Sheeler, Charles, 527, 558, 563, 699
Siegfroid, Count of Ardennes, 1
Silks, George, 672
Silverberg, Carol, 550, 559, 579, 608, 661
Simon and Schuster, 649
Simpson, John Woodruff, 171, 198, 285
Simpson, Kate, 171, 198, 285, 438
Singer, Paris, 479
Sloan, John, 329
Small, Flora, 306
Smith, Charlotte, *see* Paddock, Charlotte Smith
Smith, Clara, *see* Steichen, Clara Smith
Smith, Frank Eugene, *see* Eugene, Frank
Smith, George Kidder, 634
Smith, Pamela Colman, 221–22
Smith, W. Eugene, 599
Snow, Carmel, 517
socialism:
  and art, 145–47, 241–42, 270, 366–67, 536
  in Chicago, 143–44
  in France, 215–16
  in Germany, 249–50
  and Lilian, 143–44, 170, 185, 241–42, 249, 271–72, 273
  in Milwaukee, 20, 53–54, 271–72, 332
  and Sandburg, 276–77, 331–32, 536
  and Shaw, 276
Socialists at Work (Hunter), 250
Société des Artistes Français, 127
Society of Younger American Painters, 264, 273, 319, 326, 329–30, 369, 372
Spivak, Lawrence E., 672
Stanton, Frank, 643
Stashin, Leo, 666
Stearns, Kitty Stieglitz, 520–21; *see also* Stieglitz, Katherine
Stearns, Milton Sprague, 520
Stearns, Milton Sprague Jr., 521
Steffen, Lincoln, 281
Stehli Silk Corporation, 526–27, 532
Steichen, Charlotte, *see* Steichen, Kate Rodina
Steichen, Clara Smith, 119–22, 172–77
  and Aldrich, 233, 390, 397, 399, 422, 433, 442, 482, 484–85, 487
  death of, 635
  and divorce, 487–89
  estrangements of, 133
  family background of, 120–21, 172–73, 430
  and family visits, 210, 420
  and father's death, 453–54
  and finances, 187, 252, 436–37, 439, 483, 488, 510, 522–23, 538–39, 559–60, 608
  grandchildren of, 561, 562–63
  health of, 197, 239–40, 250, 252, 285, 431, 434, 439, 559
  honeymoon of, 175–77
  jealousy of, 122, 230, 237–38, 250–52, 298, 311–19, 320, 382, 387–88, 410, 421, 426, 428–35, 442, 483–84, 507–8, 539
  and lawsuits, 470–71, 472, 474, 482–85, 486–87, 559
  as mother, 192–93, 198, 213, 238, 284–85, 304, 310, 311–12, 335, 508, 531, 550–51, 559–61, 635–36; *see also* Steichen, Kate Rodina; Steichen, Mary

Steichen, Clara Smith (*cont.*)
  in Paris, 209–10, 212–15, 223–26, 229, 233–34, 236–39, 242, 262
  physical appearance and personality of, 119–20, 172, 203, 319
  portraits of, 119–20, 121, 127–28, 284, 331
  post-divorce years of, 509–10, 522–24, 538–39, 559–61, 581, 608
  pregnancies of, 179, 184, 187, 189, 192, 252, 259, 283
  and Steichen's work, 172, 248, 251
  and 291 gallery, 206–7, 208, 281, 552
  unhappiness of, 173, 179, 238–39, 250–52, 267, 279, 283, 310–19, 333, 334–35, 338, 354, 359, 362–63, 397, 410, 411, 415, 418–19, 424–26, 522–24, 538–39, 550–51, 559, 608, 636–38
  at Voulangis, 288, 309–10, 474–75, 487
  wartime in Voulangis, 420–23, 424–26, 430, 436, 439–42, 454
  wedding of, 173, 174–76
  and World War I, 396–404, 414, 420, 422–23, 424, 440–42, 454, 465–66
Steichen, Dana Glover, 495–96, 527, 597, 617, 624–25
  acting career of, 496, 506–7, 659
  on Beethoven, 640, 657–58, 661, 662, 673–74
  and family visits, 507, 530, 618, 659
  illness and death of, 658–59, 660–63, 664, 673
  and Steichen's work, 591, 638, 639, 659
  and Umpawaug, 530–31, 552–53, 577, 578, 658
  wedding of, 507
Steichen, Eduard Jean (Edward John):
  American West visit of, 211, 266, 279, 322, 328
  articles written by, 87, 91–92, 115, 167
  autobiography of, 102, 503, 684–85
  awards to, 171, 187, 203, 475, 570, 593, 635, 663–64, 673, 680–81, 685–86
  birth of, 4
  and children's book, 494–95
  decline and death of, 696–98
  designs by, 532–33
  and divorce, 487–89
  early years of, 6, 8–10, 13–14, 17, 20–25, 27–29
  education of, 13–14, 15–16, 18, 20, 21–22, 28, 491–92
  as elder statesman of photography, 630–34, 665, 680–81, 699
  and family visits, 136–37, 173, 271, 274–77, 331–33, 425, 485, 525
  as father, 192, 303–4, 524–25; *see also* Steichen, Kate Rodina; Steichen, Mary
  finances of, 99, 118, 132, 143, 149, 184–87, 193, 195, 198, 201, 208–9, 216, 218–19, 236–40, 258–59, 267, 302, 319–20, 331, 385, 419, 428, 436–37, 439, 454, 485, 498, 500–501, 519, 539, 684, 690–94
  in France, *see* Paris; Voulangis
  and gardens, *see* plant breeding
  grandchildren of, 525, 531, 562, 677
  health of, 132, 134, 143, 197–98, 320, 394, 438, 527, 663, 665, 676–77, 678–79, 684, 686, 688, 690–93, 696
  and home life, 178–79, 184–85, 193, 198–99, 204, 213, 267, 310, 333, 354
  and lithography, *see* lithography
  marital problems of, 250–51, 259, 267, 279, 310–19, 338, 362–63, 386, 389, 397, 415, 418–19, 424–26, 428–35, 436–37, 444, 470–71, 474, 482–85
  media interviews of, 152, 169, 571–73, 665, 666–67, 672
  as mentor, 231–32, 567–68, 642
  mentors and influences on, 43, 47–49, 55, 57, 60–61, 66, 74–75, 87, 94, 97–99, 111–14, 117, 118–20, 125–26, 131, 142, 148–49, 155, 163–66, 196–97, 257, 320, 327–28, 377
  Mexican trip of, 572, 573–74
  and modern art, *see* modern art; *specific artists*
  names of, 21, 66, 469, 472
  nature as inspiration for, 113
  in New York, 141–50, 159–60, 170–72, 188–90, 200–203, 209, 267, 321, 345, 386–89
  as painter-photographer, 39, 41–42, 55, 74–75, 80–81, 86–87, 91–92, 95, 97–98, 106–7, 114–15, 125, 128–32, 142, 188–89, 201–2, 226, 235–38, 253–54, 265, 267, 292–93, 307, 309, 323–31, 341, 352–53, 383–84, 446, 495, 504–6; *see also* painting by Steichen; photography by Steichen
  personality of, 53, 118
  portraits of, 103, 171, 226, 416, 699
  postwar activities of, 475–77
  reputation of, 202, 558, 567–68, 571, 572, 652
  and Sandburg, *see* Sandburg, Carl
  and Stieglitz, *see* Stieglitz, Alfred
  and technology, 25–28
  tributes to, 699–700, 701, 702
  and 291, *see* 291 gallery
  as uncle, 525, 526, 613, 677, 678, 699
  wives of, *see* Steichen, Clara Smith; Steichen, Dana Glover; Steichen, Joanna Taub
  and women, 103–4, 133, 230, 297–98, 311–19, 391–92, 482–83
  work ethic of, 427–28
  and World War I, 448–53, 454–56, 457–64, 470
  and World War II, 588–92, 594, 597–604, 606–7, 611–12, 613–17, 650
Steichen, Elisabeth, 2–3

Steichen, Jean-Pierre (John Peter), 449
  anglicized name of, 15
  birth and early years of, 2–15
  death of, 609–10
  emigration of, 4–6, 666
  as father, 23, 55, 173–74, 275
  gardening by, 13, 17, 23, 174, 186, 194, 549, 609
  as grandfather (Opa), 193
  great-grandson of, 596
  health of, 11, 596–97, 608–9
  jobs of, 9–10, 11, 18, 22
  marriage of, 3; see also Steichen, Marie Kemp
  and son's work, 65, 179, 211–12
  and wife's death, 548–49
Steichen, Joanna Taub, 668–69, 676–80, 682, 695
  and finances, 692, 693, 694
  and Steichen's death, 697–98
  and Steichen's health, 676–77, 678, 690
  and Steichen's work, 678, 679, 680
  studies of, 690, 691, 693, 697
  wedding of, 677–78
Steichen, John Carl (Thoman), 608, 613, 660n
Steichen, Kate Rodina (daughter):
  birth of, 284–85
  childhood of, 288, 302–3, 311–12, 334–35, 389–90, 411–12, 414–15, 420, 421–23, 426, 431, 440, 453, 469, 470
  and Doubleday, 661, 673, 692
  education of, 334, 469, 486
  finances of, 684, 690, 692
  and music, 334, 411–12, 508–9, 522, 523, 549–50, 608, 636
  and Rodin drawing, 559–60
  and Silverberg, 550, 559, 608
  as teenager, 487, 489, 508–9, 522–25
  and World War I, 401–4, 414, 421–23, 426, 454
  and World War II, 616–17
Steichen, Lilian (Lily; Paula):
  birth of, 10
  and brother's work, 41, 51, 661
  childhood of, 13–14, 20–24
  education of, 13, 15, 16, 18, 24, 28, 46, 51–52, 55–56, 61–62, 66–68, 99, 105–6, 136–37, 143, 178
  and family visits, 210–11, 271, 275
  and finances, 185
  jobs of, 185, 186, 193, 194–95, 210, 216, 271
  and modernism, 146
  names for, 13, 21, 331
  personality and physical appearance of, 272–73
  and Sandburg, see Sandburg, Carl; Sandburg, Lilian Steichen
  and socialism, 143–44, 170, 185, 241–42, 249, 271–72, 273
  as teenager, 46, 51–52, 53–56
  as writer, 162, 169–70
Steichen, Marie Kemp (Mary):
  anglicized name of, 15
  and daughter's work, 170
  death of, 548–49, 610
  as dressmaker, 10–12
  emigration of, 6–8, 666
  and family visits, 275, 279, 302–7, 332–33, 342, 387, 425, 436, 449, 540
  financial support from, 29, 34, 35, 65–66, 99, 102, 132–33, 149, 152, 186
  as grandmother (Oma), 192–93, 194, 210, 306, 388, 436, 437, 485, 539
  health of, 184, 186, 216, 221, 302, 539–41, 548–49
  influence of, 54–55
  jobs of, 9–10
  marriage of, 3
  millinery shop of, 12, 18, 21, 22–23, 28, 45–46, 51, 62, 133, 149, 185
  as mother, 10, 22, 23–24, 173, 279, 387–88, 539–40, 547
  Sandburgs' help and support of, 280, 485–86, 539–41
  son's support of, 184–86, 193, 216, 237–38, 267, 282, 386, 539, 541
  and son's work, 39, 41, 45, 65–66, 105, 136, 137, 142, 170, 179, 269, 450
  strength of, 7–8, 11, 12, 17, 22, 549, 646
Steichen, Mary (daughter):
  birth of, 192–93
  and Calderone, see Calderone, Mary Steichen
  childhood of, 250, 252, 283, 285, 288, 302–4, 307, 311–12, 334–35, 357, 358, 380, 385, 389–90, 411–12, 414–15, 423–24, 435–36, 438–39, 636
  children of, 525, 531–32, 561–62
  divorce of, 531
  education of, 334, 469, 481, 486, 508, 524, 532, 561, 562
  and family breakup, 421–24, 435–36, 489
  and family visits, 210, 436, 617
  health of, 193, 197, 205, 213, 239–40, 250, 259, 306, 421, 422, 561
  as infant, 193, 197, 198, 203, 204, 205, 210, 212–13, 215, 230
  jobs of, 531–32
  marriages of, 525, 562
  as teenager, 453, 469–70, 481–82, 487, 508–10, 524
  and World War I, 401–4, 411
  as writer, 532
Steichen, Paula, see Steichen, Lilian; Thoman, Karlen Paula

767

Steichen at War, (Phillips), 606
Steichen the Photographer, 534–37, 572, 699
Stein, Allan, 224, 225
Stein, Gertrude, 223–29, 238–39, 263, 268, 369, 414, 436, 482
  and Aldrich, 560
  and *Camera Work,* 162, 360–62
  and Picasso, 225, 233–35, 345, 360–61, 395
  and Stieglitz, 305, 360–61, 551
Stein, Leo, 223–29, 234–35, 238–39, 268, 305, 360, 364, 395, 436
Stein, Michael, 223–29, 268, 305
Stein, Sarah, 224–29, 234–35, 238, 268, 305
Steinheimer, Charles, 611
Stephenson, B. P., 329–30
Stieglitz, Alfred:
  and An American Place, 545, 547
  and Armory Show, 372, 373
  and Bell, 191–92
  birth and background of, 71–73, 150, 163–66
  and *Camera Notes, see Camera Notes*
  and *Camera Work, see Camera Work*
  and Clara, 121, 175, 250–51, 410, 411, 426, 430–32, 434, 510, 563
  and color photography, 243–44, 247–49, 252–55, 308
  and commercial photography, 233, 501, 547, 573, 594, 623
  and Day, 73–74, 82–87, 97, 98, 102, 139, 155–56
  death of, 626, 628–29
  divorce of, 520, 521
  in Europe, 189–90, 199, 242–44, 268, 304–6, 342–43, 353–54, 626
  and exhibitions, 40–41, 56, 85, 129, 139–40, 156–57, 179–80, 187, 195, 210, 277, 293, 319, 327, 335–38, 355, 362, 364
  finances of, 164, 268, 472, 547
  health of, 157–58, 189–90, 243–44, 521, 585, 625–26
  and Intimate Gallery, 545
  and Linked Ring, 59
  and Marin, 294, 305, 521, 551
  marital problems of, 164, 251–52, 268, 381, 389, 392, 405, 410–11, 413, 434, 446, 465, 472–74, 520, 521
  as mentor, 148–49, 155, 163, 196–97, 199, 338, 341, 443, 594, 626, 641–42
  and MoMA, 619, 620
  and Norman, 545, 546, 551, 626, 628, 647
  and O'Keeffe, *see* O'Keeffe, Georgia
  and photography as art, 26–27, 40, 49, 56, 71, 72–73, 106, 128–29, 138–42, 150, 151, 183, 191, 270, 323–25, 337, 585, 627
  photography by, 38, 57, 64, 71, 80, 139, 148–49, 181, 183, 187, 242–43, 253, 255, 267, 309, 337, 349, 446, 465, 472–73, 632
  and Photo-Secession, *see* Photo-Secession
  portraits of, 248
  and Rhoades, 392, 404–5, 410, 412–13, 416–17, 431, 521, 626
  The Steerage, 242–43
  and Steichen lawsuits, 471, 472
  Steichen's first meeting with, 71, 74–75
  Steichen's friendship with, 204–8, 267–68, 339, 342–43, 385, 405, 409–10, 420–21, 443–44, 585–86, 626–29
  and Steichen's work, 75, 81, 98–99, 106, 128–29, 148, 280, 292, 320, 383–85
  and 291, *see* 291 gallery
  and *291* magazine, 417–18, 445
  and World War I, 405–6, 411, 420–21, 442–43, 627
Stieglitz, Edward, 163–64, 165, 193, 198, 204, 242, 302
Stieglitz, Emmeline Obermeyer "Emmy," 148, 164–65, 204, 423–24, 433–34
  in Europe, 189–90, 242, 304, 306, 342–43, 353, 381–82
  and husband's work, 164, 172, 215
  marital problems of, 164, 208, 251, 268, 410–11, 413, 465, 472–74, 520, 521
  money of, 164, 252, 381, 410, 472, 547
  portrait of, 248
Stieglitz, Hedwig Werner, 163, 193, 204, 302
Stieglitz, Katherine "Kitty," 164, 204, 423
  in Europe, 189, 242, 304, 306, 343, 353
  and family problems, 465, 473–74, 520–21
  illness and death of, 520–21
  portraits of, 171, 248
Stieglitz, Dr. Leopold "Lee":
  and Kitty's illness, 520
  Mary's home with, 421–22, 435, 443, 453, 469, 481–82, 509
  and Paddocks, 220–21
  as Steichens' physician, 164, 197–98, 204–5, 306
Stieglitz, Lizzie, 421, 423, 443, 453, 469, 482, 483, 509
Stirling, Edmund, 160
Strand, Paul, 446, 551, 687
Strand, Rebecca, 521
Strauss, John Francis, 150, 157, 160, 161
Strauss, Richard, 201, 322
Stryker, Roy, 567, 575, 587, 683
Stuck, Franz von, 127, 142, 149
Swope, John, 611
Symbolism, 52–53, 69, 82, 96, 132, 142
Symons, Arthur, 260
Szarkowski, John, 683

Taft, William Howard, 280–81, 322, 385
Talbot, William Henry Fox, 34
Taub, Joanna, 668–69, 676–80; *see also* Steichen, Joanna Taub
Taylor, Paul S., 584

technology:
  vs. art, 34, 40, 139, 241
  of photography, 33, 34, 36, 40, 73, 130–31, 183, 246, 254, 477–78, 491–93, 505–6, 512
  and science, 145–46, 254, 369–70, 374
  Steichen's early interest in, 25–28
  in U.S., 144–45
Terry, Ellen, 294
Terry, Hilda, 668
Thaulow, Frits, 106–8, 110, 138
Thoman, Helga Sandburg, 596–97, 608–9, 612–13, 617–18, 660*n*, 696; *see also* Sandburg, Helga
Thoman, Joe, 596, 617
Thoman, John Carl, 608, 613, 660*n*
Thoman, Karlen Paula, 608, 613, 660*n*
Thomas, Elizabeth, 53
Thompson, J. Walter, Advertising Agency, 516, 518, 519, 533, 534, 541, 542, 568–69
Thoreau, Henry David, 559
Time-Life photographic files, 642–43
tintype, 31–32
Titian, 97–98
Toklas, Alice B., 395, 414, 539
Toomer, Jean, 551
Toulouse-Lautrec, Henri de, 326, 347
Townsend, James B., 330
Troth, Henry, 56
Tugwell, Rexford G., 575
291 gallery, 205–8, 215, 375–76, 408–9, 443, 551–52
  and Cézanne, 347–48, 350–51
  closing of, 448, 457
  exhibits in, 207–8, 221–22, 252–53, 257, 259, 277–78, 281, 293–94, 322, 326–32, 345, 347–48, 350–52, 355, 360, 362, 372, 406–7, 416, 445–48, 457
  lease of, 268, 281–82, 417
  and Matisse, 225–26, 261, 265, 268, 277–79, 281, 319, 326, 355, 362
  and modern art, 235, 257, 267, 289, 293–94, 319, 320–21, 338, 343, 345, 347–48, 350–52, 354, 355, 362, 363, 364–65, 371, 384
  and O'Keeffe, 446–48, 457
  and Picasso, 235, 343, 345, 351–52
  and Rodin, 219–20, 221–22, 255–57, 259–61, 278, 281, 319, 326, 342, 368
  and Steichen, 207, 326, 394–95, 406–7, 408, 417, 443
291 magazine, 417–18, 445

Umpawaug Plant Breeding Farm, 538, 577–80, 617, 618, 640, 675
  plant breeding in, 530–31, 539, 552–56, 564–67, 688
  and ROLI, 693–94

  visitors to, 577, 579, 580
  and wildlife preserve, 698
U.S. Camera, 563–64, 576, 631, 635
USIA (United States Information Agency), 654, 666, 668
U.S. Navy Photographic Institute, 611–12
U.S. Navy War Photographs, 616

Vachon, John, 575
Van Dyke, Willard, 621
van Gogh, Vincent, 117, 370, 373
van Horn, Col. R. O., 460
Vanity Fair, 498–501, 506, 511–17, 568
Van Vechten, Carl, 360
Vauxcelles, Louis, 344
Victoria, queen of England, 101
Villa L'Oiseau bleu, *see* Voulangis
Vogel, Lucien, 352
Vogel, Professor, 72
Vogue, 498–502, 506, 512–19, 533, 558, 568, 570–71, 627–28, 665, 666–67
von Lenbach, Franz, 123, 138, 170, 201
von Stuck, Franz, 127, 142, 149
Voulangis, 283–86, 287–90, 301–4, 306–7, 333–35, 527–28
  Clara's wartime return to, 420–23, 424–26, 430, 435, 436, 439–42, 453, 454
  garden of, 284, 287–88, 307, 333–34, 357–60, 376, 378–79, 385–86, 390–91, 395, 412, 477, 554
  painting at, 288–89, 309–10, 318, 331, 358, 490–91, 510
  paintings destroyed in, 502–4
  postwar visits to, 474–75, 477, 486, 487, 524–25
  visitors to, 288–89, 301, 305, 306, 334, 355–60, 394
  and World War I, 396–97, 401, 402, 403, 405, 462–63, 467

Wagner, Alexander, 42
Walden Pond, 559
Walkowitz, Abraham, 364, 372
Warburg, J. C., 147
Washington Post, 582, 583, 667
Watson-Schütze, Eva, 160
Watts, George Frederick, 87–88, 98, 322
Watzek, Hans, 337
Weber, Max, 263, 264, 320, 326, 327, 329, 336, 339–41, 342, 350, 372
Weigle, Edwin F., 449–50
Wells, H. G., 162
Werth, Leon, 344
Wertin, Joseph, 9, 10, 11
Wertin, Mary Dorschey, 11
Weston, Brett, 621
Weston, Edward, 621
Wheeler, Monroe, 587, 649

Whistler, James Abbott McNeill, 47, 55, 86, 92, 97, 117, 141, 142, 293, 373, 386
White, Clarence:
  influence of, 57, 60–61, 64, 66, 70–71, 177, 337, 446
  and Linked Ring, 94, 217–18
  photography by, 57, 59, 80, 85, 86, 139, 156, 181, 183–84, 253, 267, 337–38, 349, 355
  and Photo-Secession, 160, 161, 183–84, 217–18, 309, 336
  portrait of, 177, 183–84, 248
White, E. B., 685
White, Jane, 177
White, Minor, 655–56
Whitman, Alden, 699
Whitman, Walt, 144, 145, 146, 151, 154, 241–42, 260, 273, 276
Whitnall, Charles B., 53–54
Whitney, Alice, 529
Wiesbaden Awards, 171
Wilder, Thornton, 685
Williams, William Carlos, 551
Willkie, Wendell, 584
Wilson, Edmund, 685
Wilson, Woodrow, 448
Wislocki, George, 532
Wolcott, Marion Post, 575
World of Carl Sandburg, The, 678, 679
World War I, 409, 427, 437–38, 470, 614
  aerial photography in, 448–53, 454–56, 457–64, 466, 505, 583
  Aldrich's books on, 414, 415, 425, 464
  armistice, 466–67
  Clara and Kate at Voulangis in, 420–23, 424–26, 430, 436, 439–42, 454
  early warnings of, 389, 393–94
  and *Lusitania,* 420
  onset of, 395–402
  and Stieglitz, 405–6, 411, 420–21, 442–43, 627
World War II:
  early warnings of, 557, 581–85
  escalation of, 584, 597
  films about, 606–7, 610–12
  Naval Aviation project in, 589, 597–604, 610, 611–12, 614, 616, 650
  Pearl Harbor in, 587–88, 592, 595
  and photo exhibits, 583, 587, 588, 590–92, 593–94, 607, 611
  Steichen and, 588–92, 594, 597–604, 606–7, 611–12, 613–17, 650
U.S. Navy War Photographs, 616
Wright, Bennett W., 601
Wright, Frank Lloyd, 621
Wright, Orville and Wilbur, 455
Wright, Philip Green, 276
Wyeth, Andrew, 685–86
Wyler, William, 610

Yeo, H. Vivian, 132
Yevtushenko, Yevgeny, 670

Zangwill, Israel, 118
Zeiss, Carl, 458, 572
Zola, Émile, 77
Zoler, Emil, 407

CPSIA information can be obtained
at www.ICGtesting.com
Printed in the USA
BVHW041128301120
594475BV00013B/1569